AN APPEAL

TO

ARTISTS

AND

AGENTS

Applications for inclusion in *Who's Who in Art* are always sympathetically considered. If you know of an artist who you think should be included an entry form will be sent on request. Ten lines are inserted free of charge and there is no obligation whatsoever to purchase a copy of the book. Any information that should be added to existing entries should be sent to the Editor immediately. *Who's Who in Art* is revised every two years.

WHO'S WHO IN ART

TWENTY-SIXTH EDITION

Biographies of leading Men and Women in the World of Art today—Artists, Designers, Craftsmen, Critics, Writers, Teachers and Curators, with an Appendix of Signatures

THE ART TRADE PRESS LTD
HAVANT HANTS

Distributed exclusively in the United States of America, its possessions, Canada and Mexico by The Gale Research Co., Book Tower, Detroit, Michigan 48226, U.S.A.

050539

©

THE ART TRADE PRESS LTD., 1994

9 BROCKHAMPTON ROAD, HAVANT, HANTS

First Published. *1927*

Sixth Edition (Reset) *1952*

Twenty-Sixth Edition *1994*

ISBN 0 900083 15 8

Printed in Great Britain by
Unwin Brothers Limited, Old Woking, Surrey

CONTENTS

PUBLISHER'S NOTES

IN COMPILING *Who's Who in Art* it is our aim to produce a comprehensive list of biographical details of living artists in Britain today.

Overseas artists are represented but we have decided not to add any new names, so that their numbers will gradually dwindle, until we are left with exclusively British artists.

Who's Who in Art embraces exponents of all forms of painting and drawing, graphic art and sculpture in their widest forms and in any mediums.

One of the criticisms always levied at "Who's Who"-type publications is that many famous names are excluded. The omission of well-known names is most regrettable, but we are limited to those artists who wish their names to appear.

If by any chance there are any artists of repute in Britain today who have never been approached by us, we can only apologize for the oversight and hope that if they should read these Publisher's Notes they will inform us of the omission so that they may appear in the next edition of *Who's Who in Art*, which will be published in 1996.

All the entries in the last edition have been submitted to the individuals concerned and any corrections or additions sent in by them have been incorporated in the *Twenty-Sixth Edition*. We have approached numerous additional artists, and many new names appear for the first time. We always welcome applicants and names of artists recommended by others.

Exactly the same procedure has been followed as in the compilation of former editions. We gratefully acknowledge the kind assistance of all who have contributed information, including the various societies, art galleries and numerous individuals who have helped us in this edition.

Production difficulties always frustrate the publisher's aim to ensure that a publication is absolutely up to date, and the readers' indulgence is asked if some of the latest dates and changes have evaded this issue. Unfortunately, several months must elapse between the closing dates for accepting revision of entries and final publication.

AIMS AND ACTIVITIES OF ACADEMIES, GROUPS, SOCIETIES, ETC.

Armed Forces Art Society

Annual Exhibition in the National Army Museum, usually in November. All who are currently serving or have ever served in any branch of the Royal Navy, the Army or the Royal Air Force (including auxiliary, territorial, volunteer and reserve units and the Women's branches of the services) and/or their spouses, are eligible to submit works for the exhibition.

Secretary: Lt. Col. C. D. A. Blessington, The Oast House, Peelings Manor, Hankham, nr. Pevensey, East Sussex BN24 5AP.

Bluecoat Studio Printmakers Group
(Etchings, wood engravings and all forms of relief print)

Established as an exhibitions title for the printmakers that Jim Fleming came in contact with whilst running the advanced etchers' group for the Bluecoat Gallery in Liverpool. Annual exhibitions are organised to promote the work of the group members. Their work has appeared in Editions Gallery, The Dorothy Almond Gallery, The Watergate Street Gallery and Dee Fine Arts. Mr. Fleming established the group to exploit the happy coincidence of people connected through their need for the old etching press housed at the Bluecoat, and to promote their mutual exploration or relief printmaking methods by regular exhibition and association.

Further information from: Jim Fleming, B.A.(Hon.), B.W.S., 45 Whitelands Meadow, Upton, Wirral, Merseyside L49 6PA.

British Society of Painters
(In Oils, Pastel and Acrylics) (1987)

Formed to promote the very best in works of art in these media. Society formed of Hon. Fellows, Fellows and Members, in a very short time has become a leading Society in the field with twelve Fellows and fifty members; promoting all that is best in traditional values, allowing artists in any media to compete unrestricted in open exhibition – showing their works alongside those of the Fellows and Members – with the opportunity of being selected for Membership. (Membership on merit – restricted by selection).

Major Prize "The Old Masters Award", presented annually. Also many other prestigious prizes. Exhibitions bi-annually, Spring and Autumn at the Kings Hall/Winter Gardens Complex, Ilkley, West Yorkshire – central geographical position, equi-distant from Scotland, the South, the West Country and the East Coast. Applications for exhibition to the Director.

Hon. Fellows: David Shepherd, O.B.E., F.R.S.A., Terence Cuneo, O.B.E., Rowland Hilder, P.P.R.I., R.S.M.A., O.B.E. *The First International Hon. Fellow:* The late Pietro Annigoni. *Secretary:* Margaret Simpson. *Director:* Leslie Simpson, F.R.S.A., Ralston House, 41 Lister St., Riverside Gdns., Ilkley, W. Yorkshire LS29 9ET.

The British Watercolour Society

Only the second major Art Society to leave London; formerly The Royal Watercolour Society Art Club, reverted its title to that of The British Watercolour Society (1911) which became defunct in 1961. The aims of The Society are to promote all that is best in the traditional values of watercolours, allowing watercolourists to compete in unrestricted open exhibition, showing their works alongside those of the Members and Associate Members – membership restricted by selection.

Several thousands of pounds in prizes annually – two Exhibitions per year, Summer and Christmas, at The Kings Hall/Winter Gardens Complex, Ilkley, West Yorkshire – central geographical position equi-distant from Scotland, the South, the West Country and the East Coast. Applications to The Director.

Hon. Members: Sir Robin Philipson, R.S., P.P.R.S.A., R.S.W., Rowland Hilder, P.P.R.I., R.S.M.A., O.B.E., Edith Hilder, W. J. L. Baillie, R.S.A., P.R.S.W., W. Heaton-Cooper, R.I. *President:* Kenneth Emsley, M.A. (Cantab), L.L.M., F.R.S.A. *Secretary:* Margaret Simpson. *Director:* Leslie Simpson, F.R.S.A., Ralston House, 41 Lister St., Riverside Gdns., Ilkley, W. Yorkshire LS29 9ET.

The Chartered Society of Designers

The Chartered Society of Designers is the professional body representing the interests of designers. Its function is to promote high standards of design, to foster professionalism and to emphasise designers' responsibility to Society, to the client and to each other.

Established in 1930 and granted its Royal Charter in 1976, it represents product, interior, fashion, textile and graphic designers, design educators and design managers.

The CSD provides a wide range of member benefits and services including events, training, seminars, a regular newsletter, a reference library, and information service, a wide range of specialist publications and professional services, and Design Review, its quarterly magazine.

The CSD is the British member of BEDA, Bureau of European Design Associations, and of the three international design organisations.

Director: Brian Lymbery. *Address:* 29 Bedford Square, London WC1B 3EG.

Chelsea Art Society

Exhibition held annually at the Chelsea Manor St. Gallery, London SW3.

President: Julian Barrow. *Vice-President:* David Griffin. *Hon. Secretary:* Edith M. Andrews. *Hon. Treasurer:* Ronald Webster. *Council:* Julian Barrow, Trevor Chamberlain, R.O.I., R.S.M.A., N.S., Dennis Gilbert, Alan Gourley, P.P.R.O.I., David Griffin, Gwen Mandley, Ronald Morgan, R.B.A., R.O.I., Ann Leyborne-Popham, Mary Remington, R.O.I., N.E.A.C., Bert Wright, R.S.M.A. *Address:* 101 Chesil Ct., Chelsea Manor St., London SW3 5QS.

European Group

When Britain officially became a part of Europe and joined the E.E.C. the European Group was formed. Its first major exhibition was held at The Mall Galleries, F.B.A. London, 1974. Since then the Group has staged major exhibitions in a different member country of the E.E.C. each year. Its intention is to exhibit the work of well known artists from member European countries together with work by guest artists. The aim of the European Group is to contribute towards friendship and understanding between European countries.

President: Charles White, D.F.A. (Lond.), F.R.S.A, S.G.A., F.F.P.S. *Co-ordinator:* Prof. Roger Dornseiffer, C.E.P. Luxembourg. *Secretary General:* Heinz Webeler, Zimmerplatzweg 6, 6551 Wonsheim, West Germany.

Federation of British Artists

The Federation of British Artists was incorporated on 13 Feb., 1961 with the following objects: (1) To provide adequate and modern facilities for art exhibitions, conferences, lectures, etc., at a reasonable cost to societies and individual artists. (2) By using the accommodation to the utmost extent, to reduce the costs to the art societies, thus enabling each society to retain its individual character and raise the standard of its exhibitions by being more selective. (3) To sponsor or help to sponsor exhibitions of work by younger or deserving painters, to enable them to become better known to the public. (4) To provide a central forum for the arts and to establish a representative body which would speak with authority. (5) To provide a central source of information on all contemporary art matters.

The Federation is a charity and incorporates the majority of London art societies, including the Royal Institute of Oil Painters, The Royal Institute of Painters in Watercolours, The Royal Society of British Artists, The Royal Society of Marine Artists, The Royal Society of Portrait Painters, The Hesketh Hubbard Art Society, The New English Art Club, The Pastel Society (incorporating The Pencil Society), The Society of Wildlife Artists.

The Singer and Friedlander and the Laing Group Awards for the Best Oil Painting and the Best Water-colours of the year are presented at Annual Exhibitions.

In addition, the Federation organises annually many exhibitions and important One Man Shows or group exhibitions.

No financial aid is given to the Federation which maintains itself upon the proceeds of its own activities.

Chairman of Governors: John Walton, R.P. *Address:* 17 Carlton House Terr., London SW1Y 5BD.

Free Painters and Sculptors (F.P.S.)

This FPS was founded in 1952 when painter members of the ICA formed an individual group devoted to the principle of a 'free association of painters for mutual assistance, without regard to style, with no theory held in common, but believing in vital experiment and friendship'. Initially known as the Free Painters Group, the name was changed in the mid-Sixties to the Free Painters and Sculptors to include sculptors who had become an integral part of the Group.

In 1972 the FPS opened the Loggia Gallery in Buckingham Gate where exhibitions of members' work, either in group or one-person shows, are held throughout the year. Group exhibitions are also held in galleries out of London.

Membership is £15 annually. Persons interested in the visual arts are welcomed and applications will be submitted to the Executive Committee. Full membership is awarded to practising artists whose work is of the required standard. Fellowship is awarded to Full members solely on the quality of their work.

The Free Painters and Sculptors is an Incorporated body and is registered as an Educational Charity.

Chairman: Robert de Quin. *Hon. Secretary:* Philip Worth. *Address:* 15 Buckingham Gate, London SW1E 6LB.

Glasgow Art Club

This Club was formed in 1867 to advance the cause of and stimulate interest in art in all its branches by means of exhibitions of works of art, life classes, the acquisition of publications on art, lectures on art subjects, and by such other means as the Council may decide from time to time. Consequently, the Club's membership comprises painters, sculptors and architects as Artist Members and ladies and gentlemen interested in art as Lay Members. To be admitted to Artist Membership, candidates must submit examples of their work for the approval of the Artist Members. Painters, sculptors and members pay on admission an entry fee of £5.

Secretary: Leslie J. McIntyre, C.A., Messrs. Wylie & Bisset, 135 Wellington St., Glasgow G2 2XE.

Hesketh Hubbard Art Society

Founded as RBA Art Club under the auspices of the Royal Society of British Artists. Members meet on Monday or Tuesday evenings to draw from the model throughout the year. New members admitted any Monday or Tuesday after a folio of work is inspected. No tuition unless specially requested. The Mall Galleries, The Mall, SW1.

President: Simon Whittle. *Chairman:* Colin McMillan. *Address:* 17 Carlton House Terr., London SW1Y 5BD.

The Hilliard Society of Miniaturists

Society founded in 1982. Membership of approximately 250 worldwide consisting of Patrons and Artists. Annual exhibition in May/June. Society dinner and lunch at that time. Seminars various parts of England. Two Newsletters a year. Full Exhibiting Artists entitled to use H.S. (H.S.F.—Founder member).

Enquiries: Mrs. S. M. Burton, Burwood House, 15 Union St., Wells, Somerset BA5 2PU.

The International Guild of Artists

Now exclusively restricted to 20 leading artists as Hon. Fellows and Fellows of the Society. Lesser activities have been suspended for 1992.

Principal: I.G.A., Ralston House, 41 Lister St., Riverside Gdns., Ilkley, W. Yorkshire LS29 9ET.

Ultimate aim of the Guild to promote the British Watercolour Society, Society of Miniaturists, British Society of Painters, Yorkshire Artists Exhibition. The four major National Societies annually on show at The Kings Hall/Winter Gardens Complex, Ilkley, West Yorkshire.

Ipswich Art Club

Founded in 1874, the Club today has approximately 150 Members and 50 Friends. The objects of the Club are to encourage a love of Art and an interest in its study and practice. An annual exhibition is held in the Summer, to which non members may submit up to two works, and a small Winter programme is arranged. The Members subscription is £6.00, the Friends subscription £3.00.

President: Bernard Reynolds, F.R.B.S. *Chairman:* David Thompson. *Hon. Treasurer:* Michael Cooke. *Hon. Secretary:* Richard Woollett, 94 Cliff Lane, Ipswich IP3 0PJ.

The National Acrylic Painters' Association

This Association, founded in 1985, is for all practising artists and painters, who wish to explore the potential of the acrylic medium. A person is elected into either full or associate membership. It is recognised that acrylic paint is but a medium amongst others, yet that as a painting substance it has a flexibility that renders it extremely versatile. Adrian Henri, the Liverpool painter and poet, was its first President. He is now a Patron, along with Brendan Neiland, R.A. and The Rt. Rev. David Sheppard. The present President is Alwyn Crawshaw, painter and author. The Vice-president is Dr. Sally A. Bulgin, painter, writer, and present Editor of The Artist Magazine.

Further information and details of membership obtainable from: National Acrylic Painters' Association, 134 Rake Lane, Wallasey, Wirral, Merseyside L45 1JW.

National Society of Painters, Sculptors and Printmakers

The National Society was formed in 1930 to escape rigid traditionalism by allowing Member Artists to exhibit a diversity of the best of creative art with full freedom of expression. The objects of the Society are to advance the awareness of the public by promoting, demonstrating or teaching painting, sculpture and printmaking and to hold an annual exhibition in London (and secondary exhibitions from time to time) of the work of artists of every creed and outlook representing all aspects under one roof without prejudice or favour to anyone.

Membership is in two categories: Members (N.S.) and Associate Members (A.M.N.S.). Members are elected on merit from among those Associates who have had at least two works selected for the annual exhibition for three years. Application information may be requested from the Hon. Secretary.

A Newsletter is sent to Members and Associates 3-4 times a year.

President: Denis C. Baxter, U.A., F.R.S.A. *Hon. Secretary:* Gwen Spencer. *Address:* 122 Copse Hill, Wimbledon, London SW20 0NL.

Nature in Art

NATURE IN ART, The International Centre for Wildlife Art, opened to the public in May 1988 and in June 1988 HRH Princess Alexandra attended a celebration of the opening. Nature in Art is an art museum, the first of its kind anywhere in the world. It is housed in a fine, early Georgian mansion set in its own grounds and is owned and managed by the Society for Wildlife Art of the Nations (SWAN), registered charity 1000553.

Nature in Art is readily accessible from M5 (J11) and the centre of Gloucester (both 10 minutes by car). The entrance is on A38 in Twigworth, one mile North of A40.

Wildlife art from all periods and parts of the world in any medium, including works by living artists, is included in the permanent collection. All aspects of nature are included (but domestic, farm and sporting animals etc. are excluded). All works exhibited are originals except where their size, origin etc. (eg. cave paintings) make this impossible. Temporary exhibitions are held regularly and the permanent collection on show is regularly changed.

Nature in Art was one of six museums "specially commended" in the National Heritage Museum of the Year Awards, 1989.

Handicapped people are specially welcome. Facilities include free car parking, meals and light refreshments all day, library and reference collection of slides and other information, childrens play area, shop, studios and nature garden with open air sculptures. Different artists are in residence nearly all the year and courses and demonstrations on a wide range of art techniques are arranged. An education centre is to be built soon.

Open Tuesday-Sunday and Bank Holidays 10am-5pm. Closed other Mondays, (except by special arrangement when the facilities of Wallsworth Hall can be privately hired), and on Dec. 24, 25 and 26. Full details are available from the Deputy Director.

Patron: H.R.H. Princess Alexandra. *President:* Lady Scott. *Hon. Director:* Dr. David H. Trapnell. *Address:* Wallsworth Hall, Sandhurst, Gloucester GL2 9PA.

New English Art Club

The New English Art Club was founded in 1886. Its origin was a wave of foreign influence in the person of a number of students who had worked in the Parisian schools. The New English Art Club came into existence as a protest against a false concept of tradition, and it stands today against an equally false rejection of tradition. The annual exhibition is held in the Mall Galleries, The Mall, SW1, when the work of non-members is considered for display, November/December.

Hon. Secretary: William Bowyer, R.A., R.W.S., R.P. *Hon. Treasurer:* Edward Pullée, C.B.E. *Keeper:* Charlotte Halliday, R.B.A. *Assistant Keeper:* Jacqueline Rizvi. *Address:* 17 Carlton House Terr., London SW1Y 5BD.

Newlyn Art Gallery

Newlyn Art Gallery presents an exciting and varied programme of contemporary art throughout the year. The gallery focuses on Exhibitions and Events of local, national and international importance. As well as quality exhibitions of painting and sculpture the gallery programmes work in more controversial forms, such as installation, site-specific work, time based and performance work. Events, lectures and video presentations are also an important part of the gallery's programme.

Director: Emily Ash. *Address:* Newlyn, Penzance, Cornwall TR18 5PZ.

Pastel Society

Founded 1898. Annual exhibition open to all artists who work in any 'dry' medium, i.e. pastel, pencil, charcoal, chalk, conté, sanguine, etc., at The Mall Galleries, The Mall, SW1, usually August/September.

President: John Blockley. *Vice President:* Thomas Coates. *Secretary:* Brian Gallagher. *Treasurer:* Moira Huntly. *Address:* 17 Carlton House Terr., London SW1Y 5BD.

Royal Academy of Arts

The Royal Academy was founded in 1768 under the patronage of George III. Sir Joshua Reynolds was the first President. It was to be a "Society for promoting the arts of design." Since that date it has fulfilled this role through promotion of the work of living artists with an unbroken series of Summer Exhibitions, held annually since 1769. It provides post-graduate training for 60 students in the Royal Academy Schools, which were established at the foundation. The Academy continues to administer trust funds for the benefit of artists and for the promotion of the visual arts, and has a distinguished Library. Loan exhibitions, of great international importance, date from the 1870's. The Royal Academy receives no direct Government subsidy. It is an independent, self-supporting institution, under the patronage of the Crown, and its activities are directed by its Members (Painters, Engravers, Sculptors and Architects) who serve in rotation on the Council. The President is elected annually.

The Royal Academy is supported by sponsorship, through the subscriptions of its Friends who number over 60,000, and of its Corporate Members, through an active fund-raising programme and through retail sales of art books and specially commissioned works and a fine art framing service.

President: Sir Philip Dowson. *Keeper:* Prof. Norman Adams. *Treasurer:* Sir Philip Powell, C.H., O.B.E. *Secretary:* Piers Rodgers. *Address:* Burlington House, Piccadilly, London W1V 0DS.

Royal Birmingham Society of Artists

The Royal Birmingham Society of Artists is a non-profit-making society, unique in the Midlands for possessing its own spacious exhibition galleries. Specially designed for art exhibitions and opening on to Birmingham's busiest central street, these galleries are well illuminated by day or night. Except when the Society's own functions are being held, the galleries are available for hire. Schedules for the two open Spring Exhibitions – oil and sculpture, water-colour and craft – may be obtained by including a stamped addressed 9 by 3 inch envelope in a letter to the Secretary during January. There is also a flourishing Friends of the R.B.S.A., for details apply Hon. Sec.

President: Ernest Horton. *Vice-Presidents:* Victor C. Kelly, Thomas Barker. *Hon. Treasurer:* Andrew Matheson. *Hon. Secretary:* James Davies. *Hon. Curator:* Marylane Barfield. *Address:* 69A New St., Birmingham, B2 4DU.

Royal Cambrian Academy of Art

The Royal Cambrian Academy of Art was founded in 1881, and was granted a Royal Charter in 1882. The headquarters have been established in Conwy since 1886. In 1993 the Academy moved to modern purpose-built galleries where exhibitions will be held throughout the year, the main one being the Annual Summer Exhibition of Paintings and Sculpture by Members. Non-members works may be submitted to these exhibitions and forms for the Annual Summer Exhibition may be obtained from the Secretary after March 1st of any year. The new modern galleries, with up-to-date lighting, heating and security, will enable the Academy to show exhibitions of historic interest from any National body.

President: Kyffin Williams, O.B.E., M.A., R.A. *Vice-President:* Keith Andrew. *Hon. Treasurer:* Edwin Forrest. *Hon. Secretary:* Mrs Audrey Hind. *Curator and Secretary:* Leonard H. S. Mercer. *Address:* Crown Lane, Conwy, Gwynedd LL32 8BH.

Royal Glasgow Institute of the Fine Arts

This Institute was founded in 1861, and has now over 1,500 Members. Its object is "to promote a taste for art generally, and more especially to encourage contemporary art; to further the diffusion of artistic and aesthetic knowledge, and to aid the study, advancement and development of art in its applications." Towards the attainment of this object, the Institute holds open annual exhibitions in the McLellan Galleries, Glasgow, and shows approximately 400 works in all mediums. The Membership fee is an initial payment of £35.00. Annual subscription £15.00.

President: Eric Hagman, C.A. *Secretary:* R. C. Liddle, C.A., 5 Oswald St., Glasgow G1 4QR.

Royal Hibernian Academy

The Academy was incorporated by Charter of King George IV in 1823 with the intention of encouraging the fine arts in Ireland by giving Irish artists the opportunity of exhibiting their works annually. It was reorganized under a new Charter in 1861 and enlarged to thirty Constituent Members, and up to the present time has consistently fulfilled its original aims.

In 1824 Francis Johnston, P.R.H.A., endowed the Academy with a house and exhibition gallery in Lower Abbey St. This was later enlarged by his widow, and again by Sir Thomas Jones, P.R.H.A., who erected a school for the study of the antique and living model, where many of the future artists received their training. The Academy House and Exhibition Galleries were destroyed by fire during the Easter Rising, 1916, and the Academy was without premises until 1939, when it acquired the house and garden of 15 Ely Place with the intention of erecting an exhibition hall when it had the funds to do so. In 1969 the late Mr. Matthew Gallagher undertook to build a new gallery for the Academy on the site. The building was well advanced at the time of his death four years later.

On Thomas Ryan becoming President in 1982 it was decided to attempt the completion of a building left derelict for over 12 years. The Academy attempted this on its own, but it was not until a committee of business interests was set up that funds were engendered and work resumed. The first Academy exhibition was held in the partially completed exhibition rooms in 1986. Since then completion of other phases of the operation has allowed the building to serve a variety of exhibition and display purposes. Though there is still work to be done to finish the building, the facilities available make it the finest exhibition amenity in Ireland and its rooms are used for R.H.A. exhibitions as well as local, national and international displays. Thomas Ryan retired as President in 1992 having seen the advancement of the Academy building from a concrete shell to a serviceable institution.

The Academy has encouraged and developed art in Ireland since its foundation. It has given the Irish artist his status; and the present position of Irish Art can be said to be the outcome of the encouragement it has afforded to Irish men and women of talent and the part it has taken in art affairs generally in the country. There is hardly an Irish artist of note living or dead who has not been a member of the Academy or who has not benefited in one way or another by its activities.

President: Carey Clarke. *Treasurer:* Arthur Gibney. *Secretary:* Brett McEntaggart. *Keeper:* John Coyle. *Address:* 15 Ely Place, Dublin 2.

Royal Institute of Oil Painters

Founded in 1883 as the Institute of Painters in Oil Colours. The annual exhibition, which is open to all artists, subject to selection, is held in the Mall Galleries, The Mall, SW1.

President: Brian Bennett. *Vice-President:* Julia Easterling, R.B.A. *Hon. Treasurer:* Harold Kopel, N.S. *Hon. Secretary:* Olwen Tarrant. *Address:* 17 Carlton House Terr., London SW1Y 5BD.

The Royal Institute of Painters in Water-colours

Formed in 1831 as the "New Society of Painters in Water-colours," a title which was afterwards changed to the "Institute of Painters in Water-colours." Shortly after the opening of the 1884 Exhibition the command of Queen Victoria was received that the Society should henceforth be called "The Royal Institute of Water-colours."

The honour of a diploma under the Royal Sign Manual was given to the members on August 29, 1884, by virtue of which they rank as *Esquires*.

Members are limited to 100. Annual Open Exhibition, March, at The Mall Galleries, The Mall, SW1.

President: Ronald Maddox, F.C.S.D., F.S.A.I. *Vice-President:* Peter Folkes, R.W.A. *Hon. Secretary:* Raymond Spurrier, A.R.W.A. *Exhibitions Secretary:* Richard Boden. *Address:* 17 Carlton House Terr., London SW1Y 5BD.

Royal Scottish Academy

The Academy is an independent body incorporated by Royal Charter for the furtherance of art and for educational purposes. Annual exhibitions of contemporary art: Mid-April to July; special Festival exhibitions: August to mid-September.

President: William J. L. Baillie, P.R.S.A., P.P.R.S.W., R.G.I., H.R.A., H.R.H.A., H.R.W.A., H.R.B.S., H.B.W.S., D.A.(Edin.). *Secretary:* Ian McKenzie Smith, O.B.E., D.A., R.S.A., P.R.S.W., F.R.S.A., F.S.S., F.M.A., F.S.A.Scot., LL.D. *Treasurer:* James Morris, R.S.A., D.A., A.R.I.B.A., F.R.I.A.S. *Librarian:* Peter Collins, R.S.A. *Administrative Secretary:* Dr. J. W. Robinson, B.Sc. *Address:* The Mound, Edinburgh EH2 2EL.

Royal Scottish Society of Painters in Water-colours

This Society was founded in 1878, and in 1888 Queen Victoria conferred on it the title "Royal." In its first Exhibition twenty-five artists showed their works; today there are 106 exhibiting Members. The object of the Society is to encourage and develop the art of painting in water-colours and the appreciation of this art, and toward the attainment of that object exhibitions of water-colour painting are held annually. While these are normally held in Edinburgh, they have on occasion been held in Glasgow, Aberdeen, Dundee and Perth. Candidates for Membership must be sponsored by Members of the Society, and must submit works for the consideration of the Members at an election meeting. The entrance fee is £30.00 and the annual subscription £45.00.

Secretary: Roger C. C. Frame, C.A. *Address:* 29 Waterloo St., Glasgow G2 6BZ.

Royal Society of British Artists

This Society was founded in 1823, incorporated by Royal Charter in 1847 and constituted a Royal Society in 1887. Membership is limited to 200. Associate Membership is by invitation. Annual exhibition held each year, when the work of non-members is admitted at The Mall Galleries, The Mall, SW1.

President: Vacant. *Vice-President:* Peter Peterson, R.B.A. *Hon. Secretary:* Ronald Morgan, R.O.I., R.B.A. *Hon. Treasurer:* Bert Carter. *Keeper:* Alfred Daniels. *Address:* 17 Carlton House Terr., London SW1Y 5BD.

Royal Society of British Sculptors

The Society of British Sculptors was founded in 1904 and by Royal Command in 1911 became The Royal Society of British Sculptors. Its primary aim is to promote and advance the art and practise of sculpture.

It provides a wide range of services to its members, to other professional sculptors and to those who seek to become professional practitioners of the art of sculpture.

The RBS disseminates technical, aesthetic, legal, national and international information which assists in the pursuit of excellence in the art of sculpture.

The RBS actively encourages the exchange of information of all kinds, by organising workshops, lectures, and seminars to stimulate interest not only amongst interested professionals of all disciplines, but also in the public at large.

The RBS channels enquiries for corporate, municipal and private commission, and uses all its best endeavours to seek a greater use of sculpture in public and private places, and for it to be included at the vital first stages of planning for any project.

The RBS has established a code of practice to protect the professional interests of sculptors and clients in all matters relating to the commissioning, servicing, maintenance and security of works of sculpture.

President: Philomena Davidson Davis, F.R.B.S., F.R.S.A. *Vice-President:* Philip Jackson, F.R.B.S. *Hon. Treasurer:* Maurice Blik, A.R.B.S. *Administrator:* Dr. Simon Hincks. *Address:* 108 Old Brompton Rd., S. Kensington, London SW7 3RA.

Royal Society of Marine Artists

Founded 1939, following a major exhibition entitled "Sea Power" under the patronage of King George V and opened by Winston Churchill. First exhibition was not until 1946 owing to the war. Initially known as The Society of Marine Artists, the right to use the title "Royal" was granted by H.M. The Queen in 1966.

Membership in two categories: Artist Members and Lay Members who are not necessarily painters but wish to further marine painting. The latter are admitted for a subscription of £15.00 p.a. and are given many advantages i.e. invitation to annual party, Private Views, prizes of pictures and first choice of pictures for sale. Open exhibition annually at The Mall Galleries, The Mall, SW1 Oct./Nov.

President: Terence Storey. *Vice-President:* Mark Myers, R.S.M.A. *Hon. Secretary:* David Curtis, R.O.I. *Hon. Treasurer:* Geoff Hunt. *Address:* 17 Carlton House Terr., London SW1Y 5BD.

Royal Society of Miniature Painters, Sculptors and Gravers

This Society was founded in 1895 and its aim is to promote the fine art of miniature painting or any allied craft. The annual exhibition will usually be held in November (handing-in day in September) at the Westminster Gallery, Westminster Central Hall, Storey's Gate, London SW1H 9NU.

The Golden Bowl award was established in 1985 and is one of the highest accolades for miniature art in the world. Non-members may submit work.

Membership is by selection after establishing a consistently high standard of work. (A.R.M.S. - Associate Member, R.M.S. - Full Member).

WHO'S WHO IN ART

President: Suzanne Lucas, F.L.S. *Hon. Treasurer:* Alastair MacDonald. *Hon. Secretary:* Pauline Gyles.

For further information contact the *Executive Secretary:* Mrs. S. M. Burton, Burwood House, Union St., Wells, Somerset BA5 2PU.

Royal Society of Painter-Printmakers

The Royal Society of Painter-Printmakers was founded in 1880. The Society was granted a Royal Charter in 1911. Eminent Past-Presidents have been Sir F. Seymour Haden, Sir Frank Short, Malcolm Osborne and Robert Austin. All the well-known printmakers have exhibited with the Society, whose exhibitions cater for all forms of printmaking. The spring exhibition is open to non-members only, who may submit work for the consideration of a selection committee. An election of Associates is held annually in June.

An important associated body is the Print Collectors' Club, which is open to those interested in etching and engraving. Members receive a presentation print annually.

President: Joseph Winkelman, R.W.A. *Secretary:* Michael Spender. *Address:* Bankside Gallery, 48 Hopton St., Blackfriars, London SE1 9JH.

Royal Society of Portrait Painters

This Society was founded in 1891 and has for its object the promotion of the fine art of portrait painting. The annual exhibition is held during April/May in The Mall Galleries, The Mall, SW1 and non members may submit work in any medium, except miniatures or sculpture, to the Selection Committee.

President: George J. D. Bruce. *Vice-President:* Richard Foster. *Hon. Treasurer:* Carlos Sancha. *Hon. Secretary:* Jeff Stultiens. *Address:* 17 Carlton House Terr., London SW1Y 5BD.

Royal Ulster Academy of Arts

President: Rowel B. Friers, M.B.E., M.A., P.R.U.A. *Secretary:* Harry Reid, 23 Ranfurly Ave., Bangor, Co. Down BT20 3SJ. *Hon. Treasurer:* Evelyn Dwyer. All communications to *Secretary.*

Royal Water-Colour Society

The Royal Water-Colour Society, which is next in seniority to the Royal Academy, was founded in 1804. It has numbered amongst its distinguished Members John Varley, Peter de Wint, David Cox, John Sell Cotman, Samuel Prout, Samuel Palmer, Ambrose McEvoy and D. Y. Cameron to mention but a few. Two exhibitions are held annually – in the spring and autumn. These exhibitions are confined to the works of Members. An annual exhibition open to all water-colour painters working in Britain is held in the summer. There is an annual election of Associates.

The Old Water-Colour Society's Club for connoisseurs and those interested in water-colour painting is run in conjunction with the main Society. Members receive a privately printed volume on water-colour painting and painters annually.

President: Leslie Worth. *Secretary:* Michael Spender. *Address:* Bankside Gallery, 48 Hopton St., Blackfriars, London SE1 9JH.

Royal West of England Academy

The Academy was founded in 1844. Election to Associateship (A.R.W.A.) and full Membership (R.W.A.) is by postal ballot. The Academy is an independent, self-supporting institution, founded to assist professional artists, sculptors and architects, through exhibitions and other activities. The prinicipal exhibitions are organised on behalf of its Members, but because of its excellent galleries, exhibitions from other sources are accepted, subject to their standards and the approval of the R.W.A. Council. An open exhibition is held every autumn; information may be obtained from the Secretary.

President: Leonard Manasseh, O.B.E., R.A., P.R.W.A., F.R.I.B.A., A.A.Dip., F.C.S.D. *Academy Secretary:* Jean McKinney. *Address:* Queen's Rd., Clifton, Bristol BS8 1PX.

St. Ives Society of Artists

Annual Exhibition of new works by Members, open March–November and Christmas.

President: Lord St. Levan. *Secretary and Curator:* Ingrid Lang. *Address:* Old Mariners Church, Norway Sq., St. Ives, Cornwall TR26 1NA.

Scottish Artists' Benevolent Association

This Association was formed in 1889, and gives assistance to distressed deserving artists, their widows and dependants. Each year it disburses over £10,000. Membership is open to anyone and the fees payable are £5.25 (Life).

Secretary: R. C. Liddle, C.A. *Address:* Second Floor, 5 Oswald St., Glasgow G1 4QR.

Society for Wildlife Art of the Nation (SWAN)
(See: Nature in Art)

Established as a Registered Charity (No. 1000553) in 1982, SWAN owns and manages Nature in Art, The International Centre for Wildlife Art. This centre has been created in which to exhibit, study and teach fine, decorative and applied wildlife art in all media from all national origins and all historical periods depicting any living (or previously living) wild thing. The facilities of Nature in Art are described under that title.

Members of SWAN receive a regular Newsletter, *Nature in Art,* free admission to all regular activities of the Society, use of the library etc. Gallery membership for commercial and institutional galleries is available. Further details from the Membership Secretary, SWAN.

Patron: H.R.H. Princess Alexandra. *President:* Lady Scott. *Chairman:* Dr. David H. Trapnell. *Address:* Wallsworth Hall, Sandhurst, Gloucester GL2 9PA.

Society of Botanical Artists

The Society of Botanical Artists is an International Society, founded in 1985. Holds an open exhibition in the Westminster Gallery, Westminster Central Hall, Storey's Gate, London SW1H 9NU each year March/April with other exhibitions of members work. Combines art and science and strives to enhance botanical art by proper promotion. Newsletter and Social meetings for members.

Founder President: Suzanne Lucas, F.L.S. *Hon. Treasurer:* Pamela Davis. *Hon. Secretary:* Christine Hart-Davies. Enquiries to *Executive Secretary:* Mrs. S. M. Burton, Burwood House, Union St., Wells, Somerset BA5 2PU.

Society of Designer-Craftsmen

The Society of Designer-Craftsmen founded, in 1888 as the Arts and Crafts Exhibition Society by William Morris and Walter Crane, exists to uphold and strengthen the professional standards and status of the Designer-Craftsman in Great Britain, and to bring the best work of fine craftsmanship before the public through major comprehensive exhibitions and more specialised displays. It represents the interest of the largest group of independent professional craftsmen in Britain and its main concern is that of organizing exhibitions and assisting in the promotion of members' work. Licentiateship of the Society (L.S.D.-C.) is awarded to students on assessment at the end of their training; those achieving Distinction are eligible to submit work for the annual Distinction Licentiates Exhibition, at which the Marlow and assessors' awards are made.

Applications for Membership (M.S.D.-C.) supported by examples of work are usually considered on a Saturday of March, September and December by a Sub-Committee of the Society. Fellowship of the Society is awarded by the unanimous vote of the Council. Subscriptions: Fellows, £40; Members, £35; Licentiates, £20; and Associates, £15.

Hon. Secretary: Richard O'Donogue. *Address:* 24 Rivington St., London EC2A 3DU.

Society of Graphic Fine Art

(formerly Society of Graphic Artists)

Inaugurated in 1919. This is a professional Society whose members show a high quality of draughtsmanship in their work. An annual open exhibition includes drawings, pencil or pen and wash, pastels, water-colours with linear content and all the forms of printmaking.

President: Lorna B. Kell, F.S.B.A., F.R.S.A. *Vice-President:* Leo Gibbons-Smith, P.U.A. *Hon. Treasurer:* Michael J. Taylor, Dip.Arch., R.I.B.A., M.S.A.I. *Secretary:* Sharon Curtis. *Address:* 9 Newburgh St., London W1V 1LH.

Society of Miniaturists

(Founded London, May 1895)

The oldest Miniature Society in existence and the first major Society to leave London – its main aim is to promote the traditional, ancient and precise art of miniature painting that goes back many centuries. The Society holds two Exhibitions per year, Summer and Christmas, at The Kings Hall/Winter Gardens, Ilkley, West Yorkshire – a central geographical position equi-distant from the South, Scotland, West Country and the East Coast.

A major prize is presented at each Exhibition for the best miniature. Non-members can exhibit alongside Members work – applications to the Director.

President: Kenneth Emsley, M.A. (Cantab), L.L.M., F.R.S.A. *Secretary:* Margaret Simpson. *Director:* Leslie Simpson, F.R.S.A., Ralston House, 41 Lister St., Riverside Gdns., Ilkley, W. Yorkshire LS29 9ET.

Society of Scottish Artists

The Society, founded in 1891, has a professional membership drawn mainly from all over Scotland, and divided into painting, sculpture, architecture and applied art sections, and Associate membership: artists under the age of twenty-five.

There is also an ordinary membership. The Annual Exhibition is normally held in the Royal Scottish Academy Galleries, Edinburgh, in September to November each year. Non-members may submit works which are subject to selection and hanging under exactly the same conditions as Members' works. For particulars of membership and exhibitions, write to the Secretary. For submitting for the Exhibition and applying for professional membership, write before the middle of August in each year.

Secretary: Mrs. Anne Wishart. *Address:* 69 Promenade, Portobello, Edinburgh EH15 2DX.

Society of Wildlife Artists

Founded in 1964 to foster contact and co-ordinate activities among the many wildlife artists resident in this country and to improve both the standard and recognition of their work. The Society is supported by a number of Lay Members interested in the Society's work but not necessarily artists themselves. An annual exhibition is held in The Mall Galleries, The Mall, SW1 during June/July and this is open to non-members who may submit work.

President: Robert Gillmor. *Hon. Vice-Presidents:* Roger Tory Peterson and Keith Shackleton. *Hon. Secretary:* Simon Turvey. *Address:* 17 Carlton House Terr, London SW1Y 5BD.

Society of Women Artists

This Society was founded in 1855 for the encouragement of women painters and sculptors, etc. Annual Exhibitions February/March at the Westminster Gallery, Westminster Central Hall, Storey's Gate, London SW1H 9NU. Open to all women artists.

Patron: Princess Michael of Kent. *President:* Barbara Tate, R.M.S., A.S.A.F.(HC), F.S.B.A., F.R.S.A. *Vice-Presidents:* Joan Hadfield, Muriel Owen, U.A., N.D.D., A.T.D., F.R.S.A., Joyce Wyatt, R.M.S., Hon. U.A., A.S.A.F.(HC). *Hon. Treasurer:* Susan Millis, A.S.E.A. *Hon. Secretary:* Joyce Rogerson, R.M.S. *Executive Secretary:* M. Fuller, 29c Osterley Ave., Osterley, Middx. TW7 4QF.

The Society of Wood Engravers

Founded in 1920 by Gibbings, Gill, Hagreen, Raverat et al., and revived, after a brief lapse, in 1984, the Society promotes the practice and appreciation of wood engraving and related relief printmaking arts through an annual, open, touring exhibition, occasional publications and a regular newsletter. It is an international contact organisation for those interested in the subject. Subscription (£15 p.a.) is open to all, artists, collectors or enthusiasts. Membership is by election.

Chairman: Ian Stephens, R.E. *Hon. Treasurer:* Simon Brett, R.E. *Secretary:* Hilary Paynter, R.E., P.O. Box 355, Richmond, Surrey TW10 6LE.

United Society of Artists

Founded in 1921, the aim of this Society is to exhibit work of a professional quality in all media in venues in Central London and throughout Britain. Non-members' work is included when possible.

Election of new members is based on a portfolio of work. "News and Views" is a newsletter produced several times a year by Leo Gibbons Smith.

President: Leo Gibbons Smith, S.G.A. *Vice-President:* Constance Nash, N.D.D., A.T.D. *Hon. Treasurer:* Arthur Cotterell. *Chief Executive and Hon. Secretary:* Michael Palmer, U.A., V.R.D., M.A., R.N.R. (Retd.), Manager's Flat, Addison Court, Addison Rd., Guildford, Surrey.

Yorkshire Artists Exhibition

Now recognised as the largest event of its kind in Great Britain, with between 1,000 and 1,500 paintings by over 200 artists on show, bi-annually. Exhibitions Spring and Autumn at The Kings Hall/Winter Gardens Complex, Ilkley, West Yorkshire.

The Exhibitions attract leading artists from all over Britain and abroad. Established over ten years, it is well supported by the art-buying public and commercial galleries, etc.

Application for entry to: The Director.

Hon. Patron: David Shepherd, F.R.S.A., O.B.E. *Director:* Leslie Simpson, F.R.S.A., Ralston House, 41 Lister St., Riverside Gdns., Ilkley, W. Yorkshire LS29 9ET.

WHO'S WHO IN ART

A

AARONS, Andrew, N.D.D. (1958), Postgrad.Dip. Printmaking (1991); painter/printmaker in oil and etching, art historian, teacher; senior lecturer, Anglia University, Cambridge; *b* London, 1 Feb., 1939; *m* Paula; one *s*, one *d*. *Educ.:* Camberwell School of Art, Junior Dept. (1951-54); *studied art* at Camberwell School of Art (1954-58). *Exhib.:* solo shows in Europe, Canada and U.S.A. *Work in permanent collections:* Berlin Museum; C.B.C. Toronto; York University, Toronto; Barclays Bank; Bank of Mexico. *Publications:* Two Nations in a New Land; A History of Canadian Painting. *Address:* 16 Huntingdon Rd., Cambridge CB3 0HH. *Signs work:* "AARONS" normally followed by year.

ABBASSY, Samira, B.A. (Hons.) (1987); painter in oil on paper, canvas and board, gouache on paper; *b* Ahwaz, Iran, 29 May, 1965; *m* Guy Buckles. *Educ.:* Hillview School for Girls, Tonbridge; West Kent College of F.E.; *studied art* at Maidstone College of Art and Design, Canterbury College of Art. *Exhib.:* Mercury Gallery, East West Gallery London. *Work in permanent collection:* South East Arts. *Publications:* book jackets: Landscape Painted with Tea by Milorid Pavich, The Ice Factory by Russell Lucas. *Address:* c/o Mercury Gallery, 26 Cork St., London W1X 1HB. *Club:* Rye Soc. of Artists. *Signs work:* "Samira Abbassy."

ABDULLAH, Raden Basoeki, R.A.; artist in oil, known as "The Art Ambassador of Painting from Indonesia"; *b* Solo, Java, 27 Jan., 1915; *m* Nataya Nareerat; one *d*. *Educ.:* Royal Academy of Fine Arts, The Hague. *Exhib.:* Europe, Asia, U.S.A. Won 1st prize painting contest on The Coronation of Princess Juliana as Royal Dutch Queen of the Netherlands. *Address:* Jalan senopati Sisingamangaraja 46, Jakarta Selatan, Indonesia.

ABEL SMITH, Pamela; artist in charcoal and oil; *b* London, 20 June, 1923; *d* of Reginald H.M. Abel Smith (decd.). *Educ.:* privately and at Southover Manor School, Lewes; *studied art* at Camden Art Centre, 1970-74 (Sargy Mann, David Clark), Josh Partridge, Sue Dunkley, Oliver Bevan. *Exhib.:* Chelsea Library, F.P.S., Loggia Gallery, Chelsea Art Soc., Hampstead Artists Council Open. *Address:* 4 Harley Gdns., London SW10 9SW. *Signs work:* "P.A.S."

ABELL, Roy, R.B.S.A., A.R.C.A. (Silver Medal, Painting, First Class Hons. 1957); oils, water-colour, etching; Head of School of Painting, Birmingham College of Art; Course Director B.A. Fine Art, Birmingham Polytechnic (retd.); *b* Birmingham, 21 Jan., 1931; *s* of Alfred Abell, engineer and Muriel; *m* Mary Patricia; two *s*, one *d*. *Educ.:* Waverley Grammar School, Birmingham (Jack Davis); *studied art* at Birmingham College of Art (1947-52, Harold Smith,

Fleetwood-Walker); Royal College of Art (1954-57, Carel Weight, Ruskin Spear, John Minton). *Exhib.:* Young Contemporaries, R.A., John Moores; one-man exhbns.: National Museum of Wales, Ikon, Oriel (Cardiff), Thackeray (London), Tegfryn (Menai), Birmingham Centenary Artist 1989. *Work in permanent collections:* National Museum of Wales, A.C.G.B., Art Galleries of Birmingham, Bradford, Lichfield, Walsall, University of Wales, Birmingham Polytechnic. *Address:* 204 Birmingham Rd., Sutton Coldfield, Birmingham B72 1DD. *Signs work:* "Roy Abell."

ABLETT, Dorothy, F.S.D-C. (1958), A.T.D., V.P., E. Sussex Guild of Weavers, Spinners and Dyers; designer-craftsman in weaving, spinning and dyeing in cotton, wool, silk, linen, fleece, vegetable and chemical dyes; *b* Egypt, 1 July, 1918; *d* of Norman Lloyd Ablett, B.Sc., M.I.M.E., Whit. Ex. Order of the Nile. *Educ.:* Wimbledon High School, G.P.D.S.T.; *studied art* at Kingston, Central and Chelsea Art Schools under Graham Sutherland in book production. Wartime art/craft teaching: Bedford Modern School, Bishop Otter College (evacuated from Chichester – Bromley), art lecturer, Lowther College, N. Wales, Beaumont Secondary Modern School St. Albans, Redbourn Adult Educ. in Art, Tutor, Assist.-County Art Organiser, Herts.; Ethel Mairet, R.D.I. workshop in textiles. *Exhib.:* one-man shows, Grange (2), Rottingdean and Worthing A.G., Building Centre-Design Centre, London, Gardner Centre, Univ. of Sussex, Commonwealth Inst., B.C.C., R.S.A., London, Winchester, Lincoln, Chichester (3) and Coventry (4), Cathedrals (hangings). Register of Craftspeople (Crafts Council). *Work in permanent collections:* V. & A., Stoke-on-Trent Educ. Com., Contemp Crafts. *Publications:* articles in quarterly Journal of Weavers, Newsletter of S.D-C. and of E. Sussex Guild of Weavers, Spinners and Dyers, and of "Craftsman" of Guild of Sussex Craftsmen. *Address:* The Chimes, 50 Saltdean Vale, Saltdean, Brighton BN2 8HA. *Clubs:* Contemporary Applied Art, S.D-C., B.C.C., E. Sussex Guild of Weavers, Spinners and Dyers, Guild of Sussex Craftsmen. *Signs work:* "Dorothy Ablett."

ABRAHAMS, Ivor, R.A., Sir Winston Churchill Fellow (1989); sculptor in bronze; *b* Lancs., 10 Jan., 1935; *m* Evelyne; two *s* (one decd.). *Educ.:* Wigan Grammar School; *studied art* at St. Martin's School of Art (Frank Martin, Anthony Caro), Camberwell School of Art (Prof. Karel Vogel). *Exhib.:* Kölnischer Kunstverein, Cologne (1973), Ikon Gallery, B'ham (1976), Yorkshire Sculpture Park, Wakefield (1984). *Work in public collections:* A.C.G.B.; Bibliotheque National, Paris; British Council; Denver Museum, Colorado; Metropolitan Museum, N.Y.; V. & A.; Wilhelm Lembruck Museum, Duisburg; Boymans Museum, Rotterdam, etc. *Publications:* E.A. Poe (1975), Oxford Gardens Sketchbook (1976). *Address:* 67 Bathurst Gdns., London NW10 5JH. *Clubs:* Chelsea Arts, Colony. *Signs work:* "Ivor Abrahams."

ABRAHAMS, Ruth, N.D.D. (Painting) (1955), Cert. R.A.S. (1959), Leverhulme award; painter in oil and water-colour on canvas and paper; part-time lecturer, Loughborough College of Art; *b* London, 11 Mar., 1931; *d* of S.B. Abrahams, importer; *m* formerly to David Willetts; one *s*. *Educ.:* Dagenham Grammar School, Essex; *studied art* at St. Martin's School of Art (1951-55, Frederick Gore, Bateson Mason), R.A. Schools (1955-59, Peter Greenham, R.A.). *Exhib.:* Young Contemporaries, London Group, John Moores, R.A., Middlesbrough Drawing Biennale (1980); work selected for Sunday Times water-colour competition (1990). *Work in permanent collections:* Durham University, J. Walter Thompson. *Address:* Pear Tree Cottage, 1 Allington Rd., Sedgebrook, nr. Grantham, Lincs. *Signs work:* "R.A." or "Ruth Abrahams."

ACHESON, Joseph, B.A. Lond., Dip. F.A., Lond., M.S.I.A.D.; artist in oil, gouache, line; Tutor, Universities of London, Surrey and the Open University; Capt., R.A. (1942-46); *b* Marylebone, London, 30 Dec., 1918; *s* of Capt. Joseph Acheson, M.C.; *m* Eileen Veronica Adie; two *d. Educ.:* U.S.A.; Canada; England; *studied art* at Slade School and Courtauld Institute, London (1946-65), and subs. France, Italy, Greece, U.S.A. *Exhib.:* R.A., R.P.S., Arts Council, private galleries. *Official purchases:* Min. of Works, Army, Football Assoc. and public bodies, and for leading publishers and industrial concerns (1958-92). *Address:* Littleworth Cross Lodge, Seale, nr. Farnham, Surrey. *Signs work:* "Joseph Acheson."

ACKROYD, Jane V.M., B.A. (Hons.), M.A., R.C.A. (Sculpture); sculptor in mild steel; *b* London, 25 Feb., 1957; *d* of John Ackroyd, M.A.; *m* David Annesley. *Educ.:* Godolphin and Latymer School, London; *studied art* at St. Martin's School of Art (1975-79, Adrian de Montford, David Annesley, Anthony Caro); R.C.A. (1980-83, Philip King, Bryan Kneale). *Exhib.:* International Garden Festival Liverpool (1984), Serpentine Gallery (1984), Anti-Thesis Angela Flowers Gallery (1986), R.A. Summer Exhbn. (1988, 1989); one-man shows Anderson O'Day (1988). *Work in permanent collections:* A.C.G.B., Contemporary Arts Soc., Leics. Educ. Authority, London Docklands Development Corp. *Address:* c/o Anderson O'Day Gallery, 255 Portobello Rd., London W11 1LR. *Signs work:* "Jane Ackroyd."

ACKROYD, Norman, A.R.A.; painter/etcher; *b* Leeds, 26 Mar., 1938; *s* of Albert Ackroyd, master butcher. *Educ.:* Cockburn High School, Leeds; *studied art* at R.C.A. (1961-64). *Exhib.:* extensively in Europe and U.S.A. *Work in permanent collections:* Tate Gallery, V. & A., Museum of Modern Art, N.Y., National Galleries of Scotland, Canada, S. Africa, Norway, The Rijksmuseum and Stedelijk Amsterdam, The Albertina Vienna, Musee d'Art Historie Geneva, British Council, Leeds, Manchester, Sheffield, Hull, Glasgow, Aberdeen, Norwich, Preston, Bradford, Newcastle, and other city A.G's. *Publications:* Thirty minute film on etching for B.B.C., writing for Studio International. *Address:* 1 Morocco St., London SE1 3HB. *Signs work:* see appendix.

ADAIR: see PAVEY, Don.

ADAIR, Hilary, N.D.D. (1963), A.T.C. (1965), R.E. (1991); painter/ printmaker in water-colour, acrylic, oil, etching, silkscreen; *b* Sussex, 29 May, 1943; *m* Julian Marshall; two *s. Educ.:* Chichester High School for Girls; *studied art* at Brighton College of Art (1960-61; 1964-66, J. Dickson), St. Martin's School of Art (1961-63, F. Gore, A. Reynolds). *Exhib.:* British Council, R.A., Sue Rankin Gallery, Jill Yakag Gallery Athens, R.W.A., Concourse Gallery, The Barbican. *Work in permanent collections:* Arts Council, Gray's Library, Eastbourne, Lancs., Oldham, Stoke-on-Trent. *Address:* Halse Cottage, Winsford, nr. Minehead, Som. TA24 7JE. *Signs work:* "Hilary Adair" on prints, "Adair" on paintings.

ADAM-TESSIER, Maxime; sculptor; *b* Rouen, France, 2 June, 1920. *Work in permanent collections:* museums of Modern Art, Paris, São Paulo, Le Havre and Rouen. Steel Relief, Metro Station, La Defense. *Address:* 3 rue Schoelcher, 75014 Paris, 14. *Signs work:* see appendix.

ADAMS, Anna: see BUTT, Anna Theresa.

ADAMS, Hervey, R.B.A. (1932); art master, Berkhamsted School, 1937-40, Tonbridge School, 1940-63 (Lecturer on Painting); landscape painter in oils and water-colour; *b* 15 Feb., 1903; *s* of C. E. Adams, company director; *m* Iris

Gabrielle Bruce. *Educ.*: Charterhouse, and *studied art* with Bernard Adams, 1928-30. *Exhib.*: R.A., R.B.A., Leicester Galleries. *Publications:* The Student's Approach to Landscape Painting (Pitman), Art and Everyman (Batsford), 18-19th Century Painting in Europe (Medici), The Adventure of Looking (Bell). *Address:* Pummel, Houndscroft, nr. Stroud, Glos. *Signs work:* "Hervey Adams."

ADAMS (Dorothea Christina) Margaret, A.R.M.S. (1990), R.M.S. (1992), H.S. (1989); Suzanne Lucas award H.S. (1989), Hon. Men. R.M.S. Gold Bowl award (1991); portrait miniature painter in water-colour on ivorine; *b* Haslemere, 17 Feb., 1918; *m* Stanley V. Adams, O.B.E. (decd.); four *s*, two *d*. *Educ.*: St. Mary's School, Colchester, The Grove School, Hindhead; *studied art* at Farnham School of Art, Bloomsbury Trade School. *Exhib.*: R.M.S., H.S. *Address:* The Old Chapel, The Mead, Ilchester, Yeovil, Som. BA22 8NZ. *Signs work:* "Margaret Adams" and see appendix.

ADAMS, Marina, A.L.I. (1968); landscape architect in private practice: drawings in ink, water-colour, gouache, crayon; *b* Athens, 27 Aug., 1940; *d* of Nicholas Haidopoulos and Maria Stavropoulou; *m* (1964) Robert John Adams; one *s*, one *d; m* dissolved (1980). *Educ.*: Pierce College, Athens; Dip. L.A. Reading University (1959-62). *Exhib.*: R.A. Summer Exhbn. (1987, 1988, 1989, 1990, 1992, 1993). *Address:* 3 Pembroke Studios, Pembroke Gdns., London W8 6HX. *Signs work:* "Marina Adams."

ADAMS, Norman, A.R.C.A., R.A.; painter; Prof. of Painting and Keeper, Royal Academy, London; Prof. of Fine Art, Newcastle University (1981-86); *b* London, 9 Feb., 1927; *s* of A. Adams; *m* Anna Butt; two *s*; *studied art* at Harrow Art School, and R.C.A. *Exhib.*: R.A., Tate Gallery, City Art Galleries of Bradford, Leeds, York; also Rome, Paris, Brussels, Pittsburgh. *Official purchases:* C.A.S., Arts Council, National Gallery, N.Z., Tate Gallery, most provincial galleries, various education committees. Murals in public buildings. Décor for Sadler's Wells and Covent Garden. *Work repro.*: magazines, etc. *Addresses:* Butts, Horton-in-Ribblesdale, Settle, Yorks. BD24 0HD; Royal Academy of Arts, Piccadilly, London W1V 0DS. *Signs work:* "Norman Adams," "N.A."

ADAMSON, Edward James, F.R.S.A.; psychotherapist, author, artist; Curator, Adamson Collection of Psychopathological Art; Founder, Adamson Foundation for Creative Therapy, Canada; Founder, British Assoc. Art Therapy; Council mem., Société International de Psychopathologie de l'Expression, Paris; International Consultant and lecturer. *Exhib.*: Art Gallery of Ontario, Albright-Knox A.G., N.Y., Commonwealth Inst., London. *Publications:* Art as Healing (Coventure); winner of Alan Lane Literary Award for the best book on Mental Health in 1984: Art for Mental Health (Tavistock). Work featured widely in films, radio, press, television. *Addresses:* (Home and private practice): The Studio, 16 Hollywood Rd., Chelsea, London SW10 9HY; (Gallery and Art Psychotherapy workshops): The Gallery, Ashton, nr. Peterborough. *Signs work:* "Adamson."

ADAMSON, George Worsley, R.E., M.C.S.D.; illustration, humour, design; *b* N.Y.C., 7 Feb., 1913; *s* of George William Adamson, engineer; *m* Peggy Diamond; two *s*. *Studied* Wigan and Liverpool City Schools of Art. *Exhib.*: W.A.G.; R.A.; Arts Council Exhbn.; American Inst. of Graphic Arts: covering Punch; British humour, Paris, Los Angeles; illustrations to Ted Hughes Poems Word Perfect/Ginn. *Work in permanent collections:* V. & A., B.M., Imperial War Museum, Air Ministry Coll., Ulster Museum, Exeter Museum. *Work* *repro.:* British Airports Authority magazine, Nursing Times, Letters of Denis Thatcher, Faber Book of Nursery Verse, Finding 1-10, Alphabet, Rome Done Lightly. *Address:* 46 Bridge Rd., Countess Weir, Exeter, Devon.

ADDISON, Michael John, B.A.(Hons.) (1979), M.A.(1980); Fulbright Scholar (1981-82); lecturer in printmaking, artist; lecturer, Maidstone College of Art, and Portsmouth Polytechnic; *b* York, 1957; *s* of I.N. Addison; *m* Jane L. Brigstock. *Educ.:* Huntington School, York, and Bishop Holgate's School, York; *studied art* at York School of Art (1975-76), Manchester Polytechnic (1976-79), Chelsea School of Art (1979-80), California College of Arts (1981-82). *Exhib.:* London and U.K., Spain, U.S.A. *Work in permanent collections:* Wigan Metropolitan Council, K.C.C., Manchester Educ. Com., S.T.C. Pk., Mattell Corp., Sericol Ltd. *Address:* 3 Victoria St., Maidstone, Kent ME16 8HY. *Signs work:* "Michael Addison."

AERON, Idris: see WILLIAMS, Idris Elgina.

AIERS, Pauline Victoria; painter and printer in oil, pastel, charcoal, monoprint, collagraph; *b* Inverness, 1926; *m* David Aiers (decd.); one *s*, one *d.* *Educ.:* West Heath School, Sevenoaks; *studied art* at Warsaw Beaux Arts (1947-48), Ju I. Hsiung, Philippines (1959-62), Morley College (1984-85), with Oliver Bevan, London (1984-89). *Exhib.:* solo shows: Lionel Wendt Gallery, Colombo, Gallery 47 and Wine Gallery, London, National Museum of Fine Arts, Malta; two person: Hyde Park Gallery, London, Riverside Gallery, Richmond; others, Singapore Art Soc., Spirit of London, Royal Festival Hall, Camden Annual, Southwark Cathedral, Gallery 10, Flying Colours Gallery, International Arts Fair, Islington, Art for Sale. *Work in permanent collection:* National Museum of Fine Arts, Malta. *Address:* 20 Littleworth Rd., Esher, Surrey KT10 9PD. *Signs work:* "P.A."

AINLEY, John Anthony; Headmaster of St. Philip's Special School, Chessington; *b* Sheffield, 1931; *m*; two children. M.Sc., Diploma in the Visual Arts; Diploma in Child Development. Secretary of Leatherhead Art Club. *Address:* Brideside, Yarm Ct. Rd., Leatherhead, Surrey.

AINSCOW, George Frederick, Associé Mem. Société des Artistes Français; Paris Salon gold and silver medallist (1980, 1981); textile designer, artist in water-colour and oil; *b* Manchester, 10 Feb., 1913; *s* of the late George Ainscow, manufacturer and designer; *m* (1) Margaret Shackleton (decd.); (2) Marjorie Standring; one *s*, one *d.* *Educ.:* Derby St. School, Rochdale; *studied art* at Rochdale College of Art (1929-33, G.Wheeler, Principal). *Exhib.:* R.A., R.I., R.B.A., N.E.A.C., Preston A.G., R.W.S. Open; one man shows, Rochdale A.G., Mall Galleries, Salford A.G., Oldham A.G. *Work in permanent collection:* R.A.F. Museum, Hendon. *Address:* 4 Saxonholme Rd., Castleton, Rochdale, Lancs. OL11 2YA. *Signs work:* "G.F. Ainscow."

AIVALIOTIS, Sharon Firth, R.E., B.A.(Hons.) (1979), Postgrad. Dip. (Printmaking) (1980); artist/printmaker in mezzotint, all intaglio processes and graphite; part-time lecturer, St. Martin's School of Art and Design; *b* Trinidad, 12 Apr., 1951; *m* Stak Aivaliotis. *Studied art* at St. Martin's School of Art (1975-79, Albert Herbert), Slade School of Fine Art (1979-80, Bartolomeo Dos Santos). *Exhib.:* solo shows: Jill George Fine Art London since 1985; many mixed shows nationally and internationally. *Work in permanent collections:* V. & A., Library of Congress Washington D.C., Whitworth Gallery Manchester, Ferens A.G. Hull. *Publication:* The Mezzotint: History and Technique by Carol

Wax (Thames and Hudson). *Address:* 22 Brownlow Mews, London WC1N 2LA. *Signs work:* "Sharon Firth Aivaliotis" or "S. Aivaliotis."

ALEXANDER, Elsie W. M., A.M.N.S. (1977); artist in oil on canvas; retired company director; *b* Ware, Herts., 13 Feb., 1912; *d* of George Albert Barker, farmer; *m* Herbert John Alexander, Ph.D.; one *d. Educ.:* Grammar School, Ware; *studied art:* pastel and abstract painting at Montclair State College, N.J. (1958); graphic art with Hyman J. Warsager; also pupil of the late Victor Askew, R.O.I., F.I.A.L. (1972-73). *Exhib.:* City of London (awarded vellum and freedom, Worshipful Co. of Painters and Stainers, freedom, City of London), Leicester, Chelsea, Cornwall, Norfolk; one-man show, Mill Hill (1971). First prize winner of She comp. (Chelsea, 1968). *Address:* 20 Parkside Drive, Edgware, Middx. *Clubs:* Buckingham Art Soc., Wine Trade Art Soc. *Signs work:* "ALEXANDER."

ALEXANDER, Eugenie, N.D.D., A.T.D.; artist in fabric, collage and water-colour; *b* Wallasey, 2 Sept., 1919; *m* Bernard Carter; one *s. Educ.:* Froebel, St. Anne's College; *studied art* at Chelsea School of Art; Goldsmiths' College of Art. *Exhib.:* solo shows, Arthur Jeffress, William Ware, Museum of Garden History, etc.; mixed, V. & A., Redfern, Portal. *Work in permanent collections:* National Museum of Wales, Derby Museum, American Embassy (London), V. & A. *Publications:* Art for Young People, Fabric Pictures, Museums and how to use them. *Work repro.:* Observer Colour supplement, House and Garden, Homes and Gardens, Ideal Home, etc. Work shown on television (B.B.C. & I.T.V.). *Address:* 56 King George St., London SE10 8QD. *Signs work:* "Alex."

ALEXANDER, Hazel; sculptor in bronze and cold cast bronze; *b* Newcastle-on-Tyne, 1 Feb., 1912; *d* of Charles Zuckerman, Co. Director; *m* John Alexander; one *s*, three d. *Educ.:* Smarts College; *studied art* at Luton Art School (1936), Camden Inst. (1970, Joan Armitage), and Fred Kormis. *Exhib.:* Mall Gallery, Ben Uri Gallery, Bristol Cathedral (Amnesty), St. Paul's Cathedral, Festival Hall. *Work in permanent collections:* Cambridge University Library, All England Lawn Tennis Club (Members Lounge), Museum of Israel Defence Forces, King Solomon Hotel, Elat, Wimbledon Museum, Wolfson-Poznansky Home, London, Ben Uri Gallery; private collections in England, France, Italy, Germany, U.S.A., Israel. *Address:* 34 West Heath Rd., Hampstead, London NW3 7UR. *Signs work:* "Hazel Alexander."

ALEXANDER, Naomi, N.D.D. (1959), R.O.I. (1982), S.F.G.A. (1985); asst. mem. British Picture Restorers Assoc.; Publicity Officer, R.O.I.; Organiser, Middle Eastern Art tours; old master conservator copiest; Cornelissen prize, Stanley Grimm prize; *b* 1938. *Studied art* at Hornsey College of Art (1954-59, J. Titchell, Alfred Daniels), Central School of Art (1961-63) post graduate. *Exhib.:* R.A., Spink, Mercury Gallery, N.E.A.C., R.B.A., R.O.I., R.P., S.F.G.A., Fosse and Hallam Galleries, municipal galleries in Britain, Young Contemporaries, C.P.S., Munchick and Franks, Mall Galleries, Llewellyn Alexander Gallery, Compton Gallery, Century Gallery, Sheila Harrison Gallery; one-man shows Ben Uri Gallery, Kacyzyski Gallery, Seen Gallery. *Work in permanent collections:* V. & A.; Japanese Broadcasting Assoc.; Salomon Bros. Bank, Tokyo; Morgan Grenfell Bank, N.Y.; Christies, Tel-Aviv; The Yeungling Collection, Arizona; Merryfield Gallery; Oscar Woollens; Sir Richard Storey; Katharine, Viscountess Macmillan; Daniel Macmillan; 2nd Royal Tank Regt. *Publications:* The Arts Review, Royal Academy Illustrated, Graves Encyclopedia of R.A. Exhbns., The Observer, Artist and Illustrator, Homes and Gardens, House and Garden, Women Draw 84, The Bread-givers by Yezierska, This is London, What's on in

London, Antique Collector, Tableaux, Mail on Sunday, Women's Press, Hampstead and Highgate Express. *Address:* 6 Bishops Ave., Hampstead, London N2 0AN. *Signs work:* "Naomi Alexander."

ALEXANDRI, Sara; Dip. of Royal Academy of Fine Arts in Painting (Florence, Italy); art teacher; landscape, flower and figure painter in oil and watercolour; etcher; *b* Kherson, Russia, 22 Oct., 1913; *d* of Schneior Alexandri, teacher; *m* Michael Perkins; one *s*. *Educ.:* High School, Palestine, and privately in Italy and Switzerland; *studied art* at Royal Inst. d'Arte, Florence, and Royal Academy of Fine Arts, Florence (1936-40, 1946-47). *Exhib.:* R.A., R.B.A., W.I.A.C., R.W.A., Paris Salon, foreign and main provincial galleries. *Address:* 28 Gensing Rd., St. Leonards-on-Sea, Sussex. *Signs work:* "S. ALEXANDRI" or "S. Alexandri."

ALFORD, John, R.B.A., N.E.A.C.; painter in oil and water-colour; Director of Art, Shrewsbury School (retd. 1989); *b* Tunbridge Wells, 14 Oct., 1929; *s* of Arthur William Alford; *m* Jean; one *s*, two *d*. *Educ.:* Reading School; *studied art* at Camberwell School of Art (1949-53, Gilbert Spencer, Richard Eurich, Bernard Dunstan). *Exhib.:* R.A., R.W.E.A., R.B.A., R.S.M.A., N.E.A.C.; numerous one-man shows in England, S. Africa, France, Canada. *Official purchases:* Reading A.G., Shropshire C.C. *Work in public and private collections:* at home and abroad, including many commissions from the Royal Navy and Royal Canadian Navy. *Address:* 47 Porthill Rd., Shrewsbury, Shropshire SY3 8RN. *Signs work:* "John Alford."

ALLAN, Rosemary; painter and draughtsman; *b* Bromley, Kent, Oct., 1911; *d* of H. P. Allan; *m* Allan Gwynne-Jones, C.B.E., D.S.O., R.A., painter; one *d*. *Educ.:* Kinnaird Park School; *studied art* at Slade School. *Exhib.:* R.A., R.W.A., London Group, Wildenstein's, Redfern Gallery; one-man shows, Upper Grosvenor Gallery, Bath, Swindon. *Official purchases:* Contemp. Arts Soc., Nuffield Trust, War Artists, National Trust, H.R.H. the Prince of Wales. *Address:* Eastleach, Cirencester, Glos. GL7 3NQ. *Signs work:* "R. Allan."

ALLCOCK, Annette; painter in oil and gouache, greeting card designer, illustrator; *b* Bromley, Kent, 28 Nov., 1923; *d* of John William Rookledge; *m* James Allcock; one *s*, one *d*. *Educ.:* various private schools; *studied art* at West of England College of Art (Stanley Spencer). *Exhib.:* R.A., R.W.A., Bath Contemporary Arts Fair. *Work in permanent collection:* Japan. *Work repro.:* illustrating childrens books. *Address:* 22 South St., Corsham, Wilts. SN13 9HB. *Signs work:* "Annette Allcock."

ALLINSON, Sonya Madeleine, M.F.P.S. (1989); artist in oil, acrylic, gouache, collage, pen and wash; *b* London; *d* of Bertrand P. Allinson, M.R.C.S., L.R.C.P. *Studied art* at St. Martin's School of Art (Fine Art 5 year course); Landscape scholarship from R.A.; R.A. Schools (3 year post-grad. course). *Exhib.:* one-man shows: Federation of British Artists, Cirencester Workshops, Everyman, Cheltenham; mixed: R.A., Leicester Galleries, R.W.A., R.B.A., New English, Tooth's, Heal's, Brighton, Fosse, Manor House, Delahaye, Loggia, Bloomsbury Anderson Galleries, Waterman Fine Art. *Work in private collections:* Britain, France, Holland, Israel, U.S.A., S. America. *Address:* 13 Cleevemont, Evesham Rd., Cheltenham GL52 3JT. *Clubs:* Cheltenham Group, F.P.S. *Signs work:* "Allinson" or "S.M. Allinson."

ALLSOPP, Bruce, B.Arch. 1st Class Hons. (1933), Dip. C.D. (1935), A.R.I.B.A. (1935), A.M.T.P.I. (1938), F.R.I.B.A. (1955), F.S.A. (1968); author, painter and designer; Chairman of Oriel Press, Ltd. (1962-87); Chairman of the

Society of Architectural Historians (1960); Master of the Art Workers Guild (1970); Chairman of the Independent Publishers Guild (1971); *b* Oxford, 4 July, 1912; *s* of Henry Allsopp; *m* Florence Cyrilla Woodroffe, A.R.C.A.; two *s*. *Educ.*: Manchester Grammar School; *studied art* at Liverpool University. *Address:* 3 Batt House Rd., Stocksfield, Northumberland NE43 7QZ. *Club:* Athenaeum. *Signs work:* "Bruce Allsopp" or "B.A.," the "A" lower than the "B."

ALSOP, Roger Fleetwood, S.G.F.A. (1991); painter in water-colour, crayon, oil; *b* Skipton, 1946; *s* of Alan Alsop, accountant. *Educ.:* Queen's Boys' Sec. Mod., Wisbech; *studied art* at Cambridge School of Art (1966-72). *Exhib.:* Amalgam Gallery, Barnes, Roy Miles Gallery, Heifer Gallery, Islington, Old Fire Engine House, Ely. *Address:* 4 St. John's Villas, London N19 3EG. *Signs work:* "Roger Alsop."

ALSOP, Will, A.A.dip. (1973), S.A.D.G. (1973), William Van Allen Medal (1972), Bernard Webb Rome Scholarship (1973); architect, artist, lecturer in photography, video; partner, Will Alsop & John Lyall, Architects (1980); tutor, St. Martin's School of Art (Sculpture Dept.); *b* Northampton, 12 Dec., 1947; *s* of Francis John Alsop; *m* Sheila Bean. *Educ.:* Eaglehurst College, Northampton; *studied art* at Northampton School of Art (1967) under Malcom Pollard. *Exhib.:* 'Client show', Riverside Studios (1979), Fruit Market Gallery, Edinburgh (1976), R.C.A. (1975), Padua, Italy (1975), 5 Young Architects, Art Net (1974). *Publications:* Bit Book of Visions (1973). *Address:* 72 Pembroke Rd., London W8. *Club:* London Architecture. *Signs work:* "Will Alsop."

AMBRUS, Victor Gyozo Laszio, A.R.C.A. (1960), R.E. (1973), F.R.S.A. (1978); Library Assoc., Kate Greenaway Gold Medal (1966 and 1975); book illustrator, graphic designer; visiting lecturer, Graphic Design; *b* Budapest, 19 Aug., 1935; *s* of Gyozo Ambrus, Dipl. Eng. of Chemistry; *m* Glenys Rosemary, A.R.C.A., two *s*. *Educ.:* St. Imre Grammar School, Budapest; *studied art* at Hungarian Academy of Fine Art, Budapest; R.C.A., London. *Exhib.:* R.A., R.E., Biennale: Bratislava; Bologna, Italy, Belgium, Japan, Belgrade, New York. *Work in permanent collections:* University of Southern Mississippi, U.S.A.; Library of Congress, U.S.A.; O.U.P., London. *Publications:* The Royal Navy, British Army, Royal Air Force, Merchant Navy, Three Poor Tailors, Brave Soldier Janos, The Little Cockerell, The Sultan's Bath, Hot Water for Boris, Country Wedding, Mishka, Horses in Battle, Under the Double Eagle, O.U.P.: Dracula (1980), Dracula's Bedtime Storybook (1982), and Blackbeard (1983) author and illustrator. *Address:* 52 Crooksbury Rd., Farnham, Surrey. *Signs work:* "V.G. Ambrus."

AMERY, Shenda, A.R.B.S. (1984); sculptor in bronze; Council mem. R.B.S.; *b* England, 1937; *d* of William Charles Garrett; *m* Sheikh Nezam Khazal; two *s*. *Educ.:* Municipal College, Southend-on-Sea (H.N.C. chemistry). *Exhib.:* R.A., Paris Salon, Mall Galleries, Locus Gallery, Osbourne Studio Gallery, Orangery, Holland Pk., Tehran Gallery, Iran, Kessel Long Gallery, Scottsdale, Ariz. *Portrait bust commissions:* Rt. Hon. John Major M.P., Prime Minister, H.H. Queen Noor of Jordan, Rt. Hon. Margaret Thatcher, The Earl of Bessborough, Sir Francis Dashwood, President Roh Tae Woo of S. Korea, Sir John Richards, Mayor Herb Drinkwater. *Address:* 25A Edith Grove, London SW10 0LB. *Club:* Arts. *Signs work:* "Shenda Amery."

ANDERSON, Douglas Hardinge, R.P.; portrait painter and wildlife artist in oils; *b* 8 Aug., 1934; *studied art* under Pietro Annigoni in Florence. *Exhib.:* R.P.,

R.A. Paintings in private collections worldwide. *Address:* 56036 Palaia, (Pisa), Italy. *Club:* Turf. *Signs work:* "Douglas Anderson."

ANDERSON, James, B.A.; East of England art show Under-30 award (1993); printmaker, painter, writer, teacher; *b* Cambridge, 3 Mar., 1965. *Educ.:* Worcester College, Oxford; *studied art* at Central School of Art and Design. *Exhib.:* mixed and solo shows in Oxford, Bristol, London, Svendborg Denmark, Lvov Ukraine. *Work in permanent collection:* Museum of History of Religion, Lvov, Ukraine. *Address:* 18c Digby Cres., London N4 2HR. *Signs work:* "J.W. ANDERSON."

ANDERSON, Margaret Denise, A.R.M.S., H.S., M.M.A.S., S.M.; portrait painter of miniatures in water-colour and pastels; *b* Newport, Gwent, 29 Dec., 1926; *d* of Herbert Charles Giddings, A.I.M.C.E.; *m* Michael Anderson (decd.); two *s. Educ.:* privately; *studied art* at Newport Polytechnic (1944). *Exhib.:* R.A., P.S., R.M.S. *Work in permanent collection:* Gurney Dixon Centre, Lymington. *Address:* 314 Everton Rd., Everton, nr. Lymington, Hants. SO41 0JX. *Signs work:* "Margaret Anderson."

ANDERTON, Eileen, A.R.M.S., S.M., H.S., F.R.S.A.; Gold Medal (1981) Accademia Italia delle Arti e del Lavoro, Gold plaque (1986) Premio d'Italia Targa Djoro; freelance artist in body-colour, water-colour, mixed media; *b* Bradford, Yorks., 26 April, 1924; *d* of Sam Anderton, schoolmaster (art), M.R.S.T. *Educ.:* Bradford Girls' Grammar School; *studied art* at Bradford Art School (1939-44) under John Greenwood and Vincent Lines. *Exhib.:* Cartwright Hall, Bradford, Wakefield, Halifax, S.W.A., Royal Water-colour Soc. Gallery; one-man show at Bradford Library Gallery. *Work in permanent collections:* Bradford University. *Address:* 4 Braybrook Ct., Keighley Rd., Bradford BD8 7BH. *Club:* Bradford Arts. *Signs work:* "E. Anderton."

ANDREW, Keith, R.C.A. (1981); artist, painter/printmaker in water-colour, tempera, etching; elected V.P. Royal Cambrian Academy (1993); *b* London, 26 Jan., 1947; *s* of John Albert Andrew, shopkeeper; *m* Rosemary; two *s. Educ.:* Picardy Secondary, Erith, Kent; *studied art* at Ravensbourne College of Art and Design (1963-67, Mike Tyzack, John Sturgess). *Exhib.:* R.A. Summer Exhbn. (1981), Mostyn A.G., Llandudno, Oriel Cardiff (1982), Bangor A.G. (1982), Aberystwyth Arts Centre (1982), Williamson A.G., Birkenhead (1982), National Eisteddfod Swansea (1982) and Anglesey (1983), Oriel Mold (1983), Tegfryn Gallery, Anglesey (1983); group exhbn. 'Through Artists Eyes'. *Work in permanent collection:* National Library of Wales, Contempory Art Soc. for Wales, University of Wales, Amoco, Ocean Transport, British Gypsum, Milk Marketing Board. *Address:* Gwyndy Bach, Llandrygarn, Tynlon P.O., Holyhead, Anglesey LL65 3AJ, Wales. *Signs work:* "Keith Andrew."

ANDREWS, Marcia; painter in oils; *b* London; *d* of Walter James Tricker; *m* Edward Andrews; one *s*, one *d. Educ.:* St. Andrews; New City, London. *Exhib.:* London, Mexico City and Paris. *Work in permanent collections:* University of Surrey; Medway Council Library Loan Service; private collections at home and abroad. New project: Aspects of Mexico by a British Artist. *Address:* 40 Robin Hood La., Walderslade, Chatham, Kent ME5 9LD. *Signs work:* "M. ANDREWS," "M. Andrews" or "M.A."

ANDREWS, Mrs. Pauline Ann; graphic artist and designer in Bournemouth; *b* Bournemouth, 4 Mar., 1968; *d* of Graham Teasdill, museum and art gallery curator; *m* Jonathan Lawrence Andrews. *Educ.:* Stourfield and Beaufort Schools, Bournemouth. Work includes book illustration, leaflet, poster, card and badge design and production in addition to normal commercial work. Also undertakes drawings and sketches as Fine art. *Address:* 99 Carbery Ave., Southbourne, Bournemouth BH6 3LP.

ANGADI, Patricia, artist in oil; *b* Hampstead, 23 Sept., 1914; *m* Ayana Angadi, Indian author and lecturer; three *s*, one *d*. *Educ.:* Prior's Field, Godalming; *studied art* at Heatherleys (1933-37). *Exhib.:* R.P., W.I.A.C., S.W.A., R.B.A., R.O.I., Goupil Galleries, Paris Salon, N.E.A.C., Utd. Artists, Camden Arts Centre. *Official purchases:* Portraits of James Maxton, M.P., by Glasgow People's Gallery, C. E. M. Joad by Birkbeck College, Baron Reuter by Reuter's Press Museum, Aachen. *Publications:* novels: The Governess, The Done Thing, The Highly Flavoured Ladies, Sins of the Mothers, Playing for Real, Turning the Turtle (Gollancz). *Address:* 32A Belsize Park, London NW3 4DX. *Signs work:* "Angadi" in red.

ANGEL, Marie, A.R.C.A. (1948); calligrapher, illustrator; *b* 1923; *d* of Cyril Angel. *Educ.:* Coloma Convent, Croydon School of Art (1940-45), R.C.A. Design School (1945-48). *Exhib.:* R.A., S.S.I., and widely in U.S.A.; one-man shows: San Francisco (1967), Casa del Libro (1975). *Work in permanent collections:* Harvard College Library, Hunt Botanical Library, Casa del Libro, San Francisco Library and V. & A. *Publications:* A Bestiary, A New Bestiary, Two Poems by Emily Dickinson, An Animated Alphabet (Harvard), Fables de la Fontaine (Neugebauer Press); illustrated: The Tale of The Faithful Dove, The Tale of Tuppenny by Beatrix Potter (Warne), Bird, Beast and Flower (Chatto & Windus), Catscript, Cherub Cat, Angel Tiger (Pelham); author: The Art of Calligraphy (Hale), Painting for Calligraphy (Pelham). *Address:* Silver Ley, 33 Oakley Rd., Warlingham, Surrey CR3 9BE. *Signs work:* "Marie Angel," "Angel" or "M.A."

ANNAND, David; sculptor in clay, bronze resin, bronze, mixed media; *b* Insch, Aberdeenshire, 30 Jan., 1948; *s* of J.S. Annand, bank manager (decd.); *m* Jean; one *s*, one *d*. *Educ.:* Perth Academy; *studied art* at Duncan of Jordanstone College of Art, Dundee (Scott Sutherlands). *Exhib.:* Royal Scottish Academy, Open Eye, Edinburgh, etc. *Work in permanent collections:* throughout the world, including Edinburgh, Dundee, Perth, Canberra, Wisconsin, etc. *Commissions:* "Deer Leap" Dundee Technology Pk.; "Man Feeding Seagulls" Glasgow Gdn. Festival; "Grey Heron" Edinburgh Botanic Gdns., etc. *Awards:* Royal Scottish Academy: Latimer (1976), Benno Schotz (1978), Ireland Alloys (1982); Sir Otto Beit medal, R.B.A. (1987). *Address:* Pigscrave Cottage, The Wynd, Kilmany Cupar, Fife KY15 4PU. *Signs work:* "David A. Annand," a tiny frog on a lily leaf.

ANSCHLEE: see SCHLEE, Anne H.

ANSELMO (Anselmo Francesconi); painter in oil, acrylic on canvas, drawing and etching, sculptor in clay for bronze; *b* Lugo (Ravenna), Italy, 29 July, 1921; *s* of Cesare Francesconi; *m* Margherita Francesconi. *Educ.:* Lugo; *studied art* at Liceo Artistico, Ravenna; School of Fine Art, Bologna; Brera, Milan. *Exhib.:* one-man shows: Catherine Viviano, N.Y., Engelberths, Geneva, Galleria d'Eendt, Amsterdam, Musée d'Art et d'Histoire, Geneva, Fine Art Faculty, University of Teheran, Iran, Galleria Toninelli, Milan, Galleria Giulia, Rome, Bedford House Gallery, London, stained glass windows and murals for two churches - Canton de Friburg, Switzerland, Mussavi Art Center, N.Y., Fante di Spade, Milano, Museum of Bagnacavallo, Museum of Bulle, Switzerland, Palazzo Trisi - Lugo, Palazzo Corradini, Ravenna, etc. *Work in permanent collections:* Musée d'Art et d'Histoire, Geneva; Musée Cantonale de Lausanne; Cabinet delle Stampe,

Castello Sforzesco, Milan; Museum of Fine Art, N.Y.; Museum of Fine Art, Buffalo. *Address:* 8B Berkeley Gdns., London W8 4AP. *Signs work:* "Anselmo."

ANTHONY, John, F.R.S.A., F.A.F.A.S.; portrait painter in oil; Founder Mem. and Life Hon. Pres., John Anthony (Fine Art) Soc.; *b* Glasgow, 1 May, 1918; *m* Lillian; one *s*, one *d*. *Educ.:* Bellahouston Academy, Glasgow; *studied art* at Glasgow School of Art. *Exhib.:* one-man shows: Mall Galleries. *Work in permanent collection:* Russell-Cotes Gallery and Museum. *Publications:* "War Humour" (illustrated); "John Anthony's People" (Art). Known as the Royal Portrait Painter, now in semi-retirement. *Address:* 2 Colebrook Grange, 58A Christchurch Rd., Bournemouth BH1 3PF. *Signs work:* "John Anthony."

APPELBEE, Leonard, A.R.C.A. (1938); artist in oils, wood-engraver, lithographer and writer of verse; *b* London, 13 Nov., 1914; *s* of John Alexander Appelbee; *m* Frances Macdonald, painter; one *d*. *Studied art* at Goldsmiths' College (1931-35, Clive Gardner), R.C.A. (1935-38, Barnett Freedman). *Exhib.:* Wildenstein (1947), Leicester Galleries (1948, 1951, 1955, 1962), Fine Art Soc. (1968), Plymouth City A.G. (1977), R.A., Scottish Academy, Welsh Academy, Salon 1970 (silver medal). *Work in permanent collections:* Tate Gallery; National Galleries of N.S.W. and Victoria, Australia; Aberdeen, Carlisle, Southport, Preston, Reading, Newport, Coventry galleries; Arts Counci; M. of S.; M. of W.; Contemporary Art Soc., British Council, etc. *Publication:* published, designed and illustrated, book of verse 'That Voice' (1980). At present, painting landscape, portrait, etc. *Address:* Rosemount, Toll Rd., Kincardine-on-Forth, Fife FK10 4QZ. *Signs work:* "LEONARD APPELBEE", from 1971 "APPELBEE."

AP **RHYS PRYCE, Vivien Mary,** F.R.B.S.; sculptor in modelling clay and wax for bronze; *b* Woking, 1 Nov., 1937; *d* of Brig. M. H. AP Rhys Pryce. *Educ.:* Claremont School, Esher, Surrey; *studied art* at City and Guilds of London Art School. *Exhib.:* R.A., R.W.A., Jonathan Poole Gallery, London, and various provincial galleries. *Work in permanent collection:* National Gallery of N. Zealand, Wellington. *Address:* 15 North St., Calne, Wilts. SN11 0HQ. *Signs work:* Impress of signet ring (Lion's head).

ARCHAMBAULT, Louis, sculptor, B.A. (1936), D.E.B.A. (1939), R.A.I.C. Allied Arts Medal (1958), O.C. (1968), R.C.A. (1968), C.C.A. Diplôme d'honneur (1982); *b* Montreal, 4 Apr., 1915; *s* of A.S. Archambault, K.C.; *m* Mariette Provost; four children. Teaching career: Musée des Beaux-Arts, Montreal; Ecole des Beaux-Arts, Montreal; University of British Columbia, Vancouver; Université du Québec, Montreal; Concordia University, Montreal. *Exhib.:* group: Festivals Britain (1951), 10th and 11th Milan (1954-57), XXVIIIth Venice (1956), Brussels Universal (1958), Pittsburgh International (1958), Montreal Expo 67, 300 Years of Canadian Art, National Gallery, Ottawa (1967), etc.; one-man, Canada, France, England. *Work in permanent collections:* National Gallery, Ottawa; Musée du Québec, Quebec City; Musée d'art contemporain and Musée des Beaux Arts, Montreal; Art Gallery of Ontario, Toronto; Winnipeg A.G., Winnipeg; Museo Internazionale della Ceramica, Faenza, Italy; Sun Life building, Quebec City; Place des Arts, Montreal; Malton Airport, Toronto; Scarborough College, Toronto; Macdonald Block, Queen's Park, Toronto; Federal Food and Drug building, Longueuil, Quebec; Canadian Imperial Bank of Commerce, Montreal; Canada Council Art Bank, Ottawa; Justice Court building, Quebec City, etc. *Outstanding commissions:* Canadian Pavilion, Brussells (1958), Canadian Pavilion, Expo 67, Montreal, etc. *Address:* 278 Sanford Ave., St. Lambert, Quebec, Canada J4P 2X6. *Signs work:* "Louis Archambault."

11

ARCHER, Cyril James, R.I.; self taught artist in water-colour; retd. company director; *b* London, 7 Aug., 1928; *s* of Walter James Archer; *m* Betty; two *s*. *Educ.:* West Ham Municipal College. *Exhib.:* numerous galleries in London, south of England, also one-man shows. *Work in private collections:* England, U.S.A., Canada, Middle and Far East, Japan. *Address:* 4 Willowbrook Way, Hassocks, W. Sussex BN6 8QD. *Club:* Sussex Water-colour Soc. *Signs work:* "ARCHER."

ARCHER, Frank Joseph, R.W.S. (1976), R.E. (1960), A.R.C.A. (1937), Rome Scholar (1938); painter in oil, water-colour, tempera, etching; Retd.-Head, School of Fine Art, Kingston College of Art/Polytechnic; *b* Walthamstow, 1912; *s* of Joseph Archer; one *s*, one *d*. *Educ.:* Eastbourne Grammar School; *studied art* at Eastbourne School of Art, Brighton College of Art, R.C.A., British School at Rome. *Exhib.:* R.A., R.W.S., R.E., London and provincial galleries. *Work in permanent collections:* Whitworth, Manchester, Rochdale, Graves, Eastbourne. *Address:* Flat 1 Stonydown, 8 Milnthorpe Rd., Eastbourne, E. Sussex. *Signs work:* "Frank Archer."

ARCHER, Patricia Margaret Alice, Slade Dip., A.T.D.; medical artist in various media; Head of Dept. of Medical Illustration, Guy's Hospital Medical School (1964-83); *b* London. *Educ.:* Convent Collegiate School, Sacred Heart of Mary; *studied art* at Ruskin School of Drawing, Slade School of Fine Art (1944-47). *Exhib.:* Medical Artists' Assoc., London (1952, 1964, 1970, 1989, 1993); one-man shows, London Hospital (1955), Medical Picture Show, Science Museum (1978). *Work repro.:* illustrated books on medicine and surgery. *Address:* Rangemore, Park Ave., Caterham, Surrey CR3 6AH. *Clubs:* Fellow, Medical Artists' Assoc., Hon. Sec. (1964-68), Chairman (1984-86) and (1990-93), Vice-Chairman (1993-1995), Archivist (1986-); Founder Associate, Inst. of Medical Illustrators (1969); Mem. F.P.S. *Signs work:* "ARCHER."

ARDIZZONE, Charlotte, N.E.A.C., N.D.D., R.W.A., Byam Shaw Dip. (1st); artist in oil; *b* London, 24 Oct., 1943; *d* of David Ardizzone, solicitor. *Educ.:* Rye St. Antony School, Oxford; *studied art* at Byam Shaw Art School under Maurice de Sausmarez. *Exhib.:* one-man shows: Blond Fine Art, Bohun Gallery, Curwen Gallery, Drian Gallery, Sally Hunter Fine Art. *Work in permanent collections:* National Gallery, Australia, National Gallery, Warsaw, Dublin University, Nuffield Foundation. *Address:* The Old School, Whinburgh, Norfolk NR19 1RR. *Clubs:* N.E.A.C., R.W.A. *Signs work:* "Charlotte Ardizzone."

ARGAN, Giulio Carlo, C.I.A.M.; late professor of History of Art, University of Rome; Mayor of Rome (1976); senator of the Italian Republic; *b* Turin, 17 May, 1909. *Educ.:* University of Turin. *Publications:* about ancient and modern art, Roman and Gothic architecture in Italy (1936-37), Borromini (1952), Brunelleschi (1955), Angelico (1955), Botticelli (1957), Modern Art and Architecture (W. Gropius, 1951), Marcel Breuer (1957), H. Moore (1948), Studi e Note (1955), Salvezza e caduta nell'arte moderna (1964), L'Europa delle capitali (1964), Progetto e destino (1965), The Renaissance City (1969), Storia dell'arte italiana (1968-70), Dal Bramante al Canova (1969), L'arte moderna 1770-1970 (1971). *Address:* via Filippo Casini 16,00153, Roma, Italy. *Signs work:* "Giulio Carlo Argan."

ARKLESS, Lesley Graham, B.A. Hons.; painter/illustrator in oil, gouache, water-colour; *b* Northumberland, 30 Jan., 1956; *d* of Norman G. Arkless; *m* John M. Butterworth; one *s*. *Educ.:* Church High School for Girls, Newcastle-upon-Tyne; *studied art* at West Surrey College of Art and Design (1974-78). *Exhib.:* Ash Barn Gallery, Petersfield, St. Edmund's Art Centre, Salisbury,

12

National Museum of Wales, 'Pictures for Schools', Astoria Theatre, London, Le Havre Municipal Gallery, Sanderson's Gallery, London. *Publications:* author and illustrator: 'What Stanley Knew' (Andersen Press, London). *Address:* 2 Nun's Walk, Winchester, Hants. *Signs work:* "LESLEY ARKLESS."

ARLOTT, Norman Arthur, S.WL.A.; freelance wildlife illustrator in watercolour, author; *b* 15 Nov., 1947; *s* of R.W.A. Arlott; *m* Marie Ellen; one *s*, two *d. Educ.:* Stoneham Boys School. *Exhib.:* Annual S.WL.A., London, widely in U.K., also U.S.A. *Publications:* over fifty, including Norman Arlott's Bird Paintings, and many commonwealth stamp issues, i.e. Bahamas, Jamaica, British Virgin Islands. *Address:* Hill House, School Rd., Tilney St. Lawrence, Norfolk PE34 4RB. *Signs work:* "Norman Arlott."

ARMFIELD, Diana M. (Mrs. Bernard Dunstan), R.A. (1991), R.C.A. (Wales) (1992), M.C.S.D., N.E.A.C., R.W.A., R.W.S.; painter, textile and wallpaper designer; taught at Central School; Artist in Residence, Jackson Hole, U.S.A. (1989); *b* Ringwood, Hants, 1920; *d* of Harold Armfield; *m* Bernard Dunstan, R.A.; three *s. Educ.:* Bedales, Slade School, Central School. *Exhib.:* Festival of Britain; one-man shows, Browse and Darby, National Eisteddfod Wales, etc. *Work in permanent collections:* V. & A., R.W.A., Govt. picture collection, Contemporary Art Soc. for Wales, National Trust, Reuters, Yale Centre for British Art, Farringdon Trust, B.M., H.R.H. Prince of Wales, Lancaster City Gallery. *Work repro.:* David & Charles, Collins, Watson-Guptill, Quarto, Studio Vista, Phaidon, Mitchell Beazeley publications, series consultant to latter. Artist in Residence, Perth (1985). *Address:* 10 High Park Rd., Kew, Surrey. *Signs work:* "D.M.A."

ARMITAGE, Joshua Charles; freelance artist in black and white and colour; *b* Hoylake, Cheshire, 26 Sept., 1913; *s* of Joshua Armitage; *m* Catherine Mary Buckle; two *d. Studied* at Liverpool School of Art (1929-36). *Work in permanent collection:* twelve water-colour drawings for the United Oxford and Cambridge University Club. *Work repro.:* Punch, The Countryman, etc. *Publications:* 100th Open Championship at Royal Birkdale and illustrations for many books for adults and for children. Many water-colour drawings with golf as the subject. Long association with Penguin Books editions of P.G. Wodehouse. *Address:* 34 Avondale Rd., Hoylake, Cheshire. *Club:* Royal Liverpool Golf. *Signs work:* "Ionicus."

ARMITAGE, Kenneth, C.B.E. (1969); sculptor; *b* 18 July, 1916, *Exhib.:* works shown in North and South America, France, Italy, Germany, Austria, Yugoslavia, Malta, Cyprus, Gibraltar, Israel, Lebanon, Ethiopia, Spain, Portugal, Australia, New Zealand, Sarawak, Sebah, Malaysia, Singapore, Bermuda, Jamaica, Trinidad, Cuba, Argentina, Peru, Venezuela, Chile, Brazil, Japan, Finland, Norway, Sweden, Denmark, Poland. Works in major public collections throughout the world. *Address:* 22A Avonmore Rd., London W14 8RR.

ARMOUR, Mary, A.R.S.A. (1941), R.S.W. (1956), R.S.A. (1958), R.G.I. (1977), LL.D. (Glasgow) 1982; Hon. Pres.: Glasgow School of Art (1982), Royal Glasgow Inst. (1983); Hon. Fellowship: Paisley University (1989), Glasgow School of Art (1993); artist in oil, water-colour; *b* Blantyre, Lanarkshire, 27 Mar., 1902; *d* of William Steel, iron-dresser; *m* William Armour. *Educ.:* Low Blantyre Public School; Hamilton Academy; *studied art* at Glasgow School of Art under D. Forrester Wilson, R.S.A., Maurice Grieffenhagen, R.A. (1920-25). *Exhib.:* R.A., R.S.A., S.S.A., Royal Glasgow Institute. *Work in permanent collections:* Glasgow Municipal Gallery, Greenock A.G., Victoria (Australia), Paisley A.G., Aberdeen A.G., Perth A.G., Edinburgh A.G. *Work repro.:* The

Studio. *Address:* 2 Gateside, Kilbarchan, Renfrewshire PA10 2LY. *Signs work:* "Mary Armour."

ARMSTRONG, Arthur Charlton; artist in oil, water-colour, etchings, etc.; *b* Carrickfergus, Co. Antrim, 12 Jan., 1924; *studied art:* self-taught. *Work in permanent collections:* Arts Council, (N. of Ireland); Arts Council (Irish Republic); Belfast Museum and Art Gallery; Waterford Art Gallery; Cork Museum; many Irish public and private collections, also in England, U.S.A., Spain, France, Canada. *Address:* 28 Chelmsford Ave., Ranelagh, Dublin 6, Ireland. *Clubs:* Arts Club, Dublin and Belfast. *Signs work:* "Armstrong."

ARN or ARNEAL: see NEAL, Arthur Richard.

ARNETT, Joe Anna; painter in oil; *b* Texas; *d* of John Gary Arnett; *m* James D. Asher. *Educ.:* Baylor University and University of Texas; *studied art* at Art Students' League, N.Y. (1979-83), University of Texas (1970-72). *Exhib.:* Salmagundi Club, National Audubon Soc., American Artist Professional League, Artists of America, Denver (1988, 1989), Katherine Lorillard Woolfe Art Club, Catto Gallery, London (1987), O'Brien Art Emporium, Scottsdale, A.Z. *Address:* P.O. Box 8022, Santa Fe, New Mexico 87504-8022, U.S.A. *Signs work:* "J.A. Arnett."

ARNOLD, Gordon C., A.R.Cam.A.; artist in water-colour; *b* Sheffield, 30 Mar., 1910. *Studied art:* Liverpool School of Art (Will Penn, R.O.I., R.P., R.C.A., G. Wedgwood, R.E.). *Exhib.:* Birkenhead A.G., Warrington A.G., Bootle A.G., Wrexham Library, Weaver Gallery, Weaverham, Pratts Hotel, Bristol, etc. *Work in permanent collections:* Williamson A.G., Birkenhead, Warrington A.G., Liverpool Corp. Library, etc. *Address:* 58 Fairfield Terr., Newton Abbot, Devon TQ12 2LH. *Signs work:* "Gordon Arnold."

ARNOLD, Phyllis Anne, R.M.S. (1988), A.R.M.S. (1983), S.M. (1976), U.S.W.A. (1982), P.U.S.W.A. (1988-91), P.U.S.M. (1987), U.W.S. (1984), H.S. (1985); miniaturist, artist in water-colour, ink and gouache; Hunting Group finalist (1980, 1981, 1983), R.M.S. Memorial Gold Bowl (1988); *b* Belfast, 1938; *d* of David McDowell, engineer; *m* Michael J. Arnold, C.Eng.; two *s. Educ.:* Victoria College, Wallace High School; *studied art:* self taught, entered Commercial Art Dept. Short Bros & Harland (1956-58). *Exhib.:* S.M., R.M.S., R.A., U.S.W.A., H.S., U.W.S., R.U.A. *Work in permanent collection:* Ulster Museum, Belfast. *Address:* Phyllis Arnold Studio, Deepwell House, Lowry Hill, Bangor, Co. Down, N. Ireland. *Signs work:* "P.A. ARNOLD" or "P.A.A." for miniatures, see appendix.

ARNUP, Sally, A.R.C.A. (1954); sculptor in bronze; *b* London, 15 July, 1930; *d* of L. Baynton-Williams; *m* Mick Arnup, A.R.C.A.; two *s*, two *d. Studies art* at Kingston School of Art (1943-50, H. Parker), Camberwell School of Art (1951, Dr. Vogel), Royal College of Art (1952-55, John Skeaping). *Exhib.:* Tryon Gallery (1973, 1976, 1981), U.S.A. (1977, 1980, 1986, 1987), Drobak Norway (1976), Wexford Festival (1974, 1978, 1982, 1986), York Festival (1969, 1976, 1978, 1980, 1984, 1988, 1992), Florence (1983), Edinburgh Festival (1988), Stamford Art Centre (1987, 1990). *Work in permanent collections:* H.M. The Queen, Burton Agnes. *Address:* Studio Holtby, York YO1 3UA. *Club:* R.B.S. *Signs work:* "ARNUP."

ARRIDGE, Margaret Irene Chadwick, N.S. (1988), F.S.B.A. (1988), A.R.M.S.; artist in water-colour, pastel, oil, private teacher; *b* Salisbury, Wilts., 13 Feb., 1921; *d* of Herbert Chadwick Arridge, A.C.A.; *m* I.M.C. Farquharson, M.A., F.I.A.; one *s. Educ.:* Croydon High School; *studied art* at Chelsea School of Art

(Bernard Adams, Violet Butler, miniaturist). *Exhib.:* R.A., Paris Salon, Mall Galleries; one-man shows Johannesburg. *Address:* 5 Dudley Rd., Parkwood, Johannesburg 2193, S.A. *Signs work:* "M. Arridge."

ARTHUR, Harry H. Gascoign, F.L.A. (1948), F.R.S.A. (1949), F.I.M. (1974), Mem. Museums Assoc. (1949); lecturer, writer and broadcaster on the arts; W.E.A. lecturer on art, architecture and art history; Director of Libraries, Museums and Arts, Wirral (1974-80); formerly held libraries and arts posts at Bath, Bristol and Blackpool; Librarian and Curator, Buxton (1949-50), Director of Libraries and Arts, Wigan (1950-68), Borough Librarian and Director, Williamson A.G. and Museum, Birkenhead (1968-74); *b* Bristol, 30 June, 1920; *s* of H. J. M. Arthur of Liverpool; *m* Kathleen Joan Fuge; one *s*, one *d*. *Educ.:* Bristol Cathedral School; *studied art* at West of England College of Art. *Publications:* History of Haigh Hall; Guide to the Williamson A.G. and Museum; Guide to the Wirral Maritime Museum; Lee Tapestry Room. *Address:* 20 Christchurch Rd., Oxton, Birkenhead L43 5SF.

ASCHAN, Marit Guinness; enamellist and painter; President, Artist Enamellers since foundation 1968; *d* of H. S. H. Guinness; formerly *m* to C. W. Aschan; one *s*, one *d*. *Exhib.:* R.A., Leicester Galleries, Lincoln Center, N.Y., Worshipful Company of Goldsmiths, etc.; one-man shows, Beaux Arts, International Faculty of Arts, The Leicester Galleries, Roy Miles, Saga Gallery, London; The Minories, Colchester; Lilienfeld Gallery and Van Diemen-Lilienfeld Galleries, Bodley Gallery, N.Y.; Waldhorn Company Inc., New Orleans; Galerie J. Kraus, Paris; Inter Art Gallery, Caracas, Venezuela; Oslo Kunstforening, Galleri Galtung, Oslo; etc. *Work in permanent collections:* V. & A., central enamel of Louis Osman Cross, Exeter Cathedral; Worshipful Company of Goldsmiths, London; Oppé Coll., Brooklyn Museum; New York University Art Coll.; Fordham University Art Coll.; Yale University A.G.; Nelson Gallery and Atkins Museum, Kansas; North Carolina State Museum of Art, Raleigh; Rochester A.G., N.Y.; University of Kansas Museum of Art, New Orleans Museum of Art; Parrish Art Museum, Southampton, N.Y.; Weatherspoon A.G., University of North Carolina; Finch College A.G.; The Housatonic Museum, Bridgeport, Connecticut; The Snite Museum of Notre Dame University; The Ian Woodner Family Collection, N.Y.; The Royal Norwegian Embassy, London; Kunstindustrimuseet, Hans Rasmus Astrup Coll. Oslo, etc. *Addresses:* (residence) 25 Chelsea Park Gdns., London SW3; (studio) Moravian Close, 381 King's Rd., London SW10. *Club:* Chelsea Arts.

ASHBY, Derek Joseph, D.A. (Edin.); artist in oil painting and steel and aluminium; lecturer in drawing and painting, Gray's School of Art, Aberdeen; *b* 24 June, 1926; *s* of Oswald Roy Ashby; *m* Mairi Catriona; one *s*, one *d*. *Educ.:* Oldham High School; *studied art* at Edinburgh College of Art (1948-51) under Gillies, Henderson, Blyth; R.A. Schools (1953-55) under Rushbury. *Exhib.:* R.S.A., Aberdeen Artists, S.S.A. *Work in permanent collection:* Scottish Arts Council. *Address:* Old Invery, Auchattie, Banchory, Kincardineshire. *Clubs:* A.A.S., S.S.A. *Signs work:* "Derek Ashby."

ASHE, Faith: see WINTER, Faith.

ASHER, James; artist in water-colour, oil, lithograph; *b* Butler, Missouri, 14 Apr., 1944; *s* of Glenn William Asher; *m* Joe Anna Arnett; one *s*, one *d*. *Educ.:* Central Missouri University; *studied art* at The Art Center College of Design, Los Angeles, Calif. *Exhib.:* Catto Gallery, London, O'Brien's Art Emporium, Scottsdale, AZ. *Address:* P.O. Box 8022, Santa Fe, New Mexico 87504-8022, U.S.A. *Signs work:* "James Asher."

ASHMORE, Lady, Patricia, P.S. (1953); landscape and portrait painter in pastel, oil and water-colour; *b* Horsham, 13 July, 1929; *d* of Admiral Sir Henry Buller; *m* Vice Admiral Sir Peter Ashmore; one *s*, three *d*. *Educ.:* North Foreland Lodge; *studied art* at Chelsea Polytechnic (portrait painting with Sonia Mervyn). *Exhib.:* Pastel Exhbn. (annually), Women Artists. *Address:* Netherdowns, Sundridge, Sevenoaks, Kent. *Signs work:* "Patricia Ashmore."

ASHTON-BOSTOCK, David A., F.I.A.L. (1960), N.D. (1950), intermed. (1949); artist in oil and interior decorator; member of I.D.D.A. Ltd.; *b* London, 17 Feb., 1930; *s* of Cdr. J. Bostock, D.S.C., R.N. (retd.) (additional surname Ashton assumed by deed poll); *m* Victoria Rosamond White (divorced); one *d*. *Educ.:* Wellington College; *studied art* at Maidstone College of Art (1947-50) under A. G. Cary and W. Eade, Byam Shaw School of Art (1953-54) under P. E. Philips. *Exhib.:* United Artists, Nat. Soc., R.B.A., N.E.A.C., R.O.I., Paris Salon, Summer Salon, Chelsea Artists, City of London Artists, Ridley Art Club, Hambledon Galleries (Blandford). *Work repro.:* La Revue Moderne, Queen, Country Life, Times, Sunday Express, Christmas cards, posters. *Addresses:* Danes Bottom Place, Wormshill, nr. Sittingbourne, Kent ME9 0TS; 28 Sutherland St., London SW1V 4LA. *Signs work:* "Ashtock."

ASSCHER, Sofy, Gold Medal, Academy of Art, Parma (1980); painter of portraits, flowers and miniatures; *b* 29 Sept., 1901; *d* of the late Benjamin Asscher; *m* Ronald J. Horton. *Educ.:* Amsterdam; *studied art* in Amsterdam, Chelsea Polytechnic and privately in London. *Exhib.:* R.A., Bond St. Galleries and abroad. *Work in private collections:* Preparatory School, Alcester, Warwicks; Town Hall, Bourne, Lincs (1980); paintings, U.K., U.S.A., and Far East. *Work repro.:* home and abroad. *Address:* 11 Bainbridge Cl., Heathfield Rd., Seaford, Sussex. *Club:* New Century. *Signs work:* "S. Asscher," "Sofy Asscher," and flower painting after 1958 see appendix.

ATKIN, Ann; *b* Lindfield, Sussex, 1937; graduate of Brighton College of Art and Royal Academy Schools. Organic abstract paintings of rhythms and energy flows between centres. *Exhib.:* Young Contemporaries, R.A. Summer Exhbn.; solo show: Beaford Centre. *Official purchases:* Dartington Hall Trust (Oct. 1992). Paintings discussed on 'Hayes on Saturday' Radio 2 (May 1993), and shown on GMTV (May 1993). Mem. Abstract Artists Organisation. *Address:* Warren Cottage, Abbots Bickington, N. Devon EX22 7LQ. *Signs work:* see appendix.

ATKIN, Peter, U.A. (1968); artist in water-colour; *b* Wallasey, 16 Aug., 1926; *s* of Stanley Atkin; *m* Joyce Wood; one *s*, one *d*. *Educ.:* Stamford School, Lincolnshire; no formal art training, instruction from the late Wilfred R. Wood of Barnack, nr. Stamford. *Exhib.:* R.B.A., R.I., U.A., Britain in Water-colour, N.S.; one-man shows, York Galleries and Municipal Gallery, Northampton, Savage Fine Art, Northampton. *Address:* 1 High St., Collingtree, Northampton NN4 0NE. *Signs work:* "PETER ATKIN."

ATKIN, Ron, F.R.S.A.; painter in water-colour and oil; *b* Leics., 3 Feb., 1938. *Studied art* at Loughborough College of Art (1954-57), R.A. Schools (1957-61). *Exhib.:* regularly at R.A.; mixed shows: Roland, Browse and Delbanco. *Work in permanent collections:* Lincoln College Oxford, Dartington Trust, Devon C.C. Schools Museum Service, Alexander Theatre, B'ham, Plymouth City Museum and A.G. *Address:* Warren Cottage, Abbots Bickington, Devon EX22 7LQ. *Signs work:* "Atkin" or "Ron Atkin."

ATKINSON, Anthony, A.R.C.A. (1954); painter in oil; Dean, Colchester Inst.; Moderator B/TEC; *b* 20 July, 1929; *s* of Claude Atkinson; *m* Joan Dawson; one *s*, one *step-d. Educ.:* Wimbledon College; *studied art* at Royal College of Art. *Exhib.:* R.A., Leicester Galleries; one-man: Minories, Colchester, Leighton House, London, Gainsborough's House, Sudbury, Mercury Theatre, Colchester, British Council, Kuwait, Phoenix, Lavenham, Coach-House Gallery, Guernsey, Phoenix, Highgate, Hayletts, Colchester. *Work in collections:* Essex Museum; Ernst & Young; Essex C.C, Colchester Hospital, etc. *Work repro.:* Shell, London Transport, G.P.O. *Address:* Coach House, Great Horkesley, Colchester, Essex. *Signs work:* "ATKINSON."

ATKINSON, Eric Newton, N.E.A.C., R.C.A.; painter in oils and collage; Nat. Dipl. (1st hons., painting), R.A. Drawing Medal, Silver Medal for Painting; Dean, Faculty of Arts, Fanshawe College, London, Canada; *b* W. Hartlepool, 23 July, 1928; *s* of James Atkinson; *m* Muriel H. Ross; one *s*, one *d. Educ.:* Dyke House, W. Hartlepool; *studied art* at W. Hartlepool College of Art and R.A. Schools. *Exhib.:* Redfern Gallery, Tate Gallery, Austin Hayes, York, Leeds Univ., Wakefield and Middlesbrough city galleries, Zwemmer Gallery, Corcoran Gallery, Rothman Gallery, Kingpitcher Gallery, Capponi Gallery, Pollock Gallery, Mendal Gallery, Carnegie Mellon. *Work in permanent collections:* Contemporary Art Soc., M. of W., Leeds, Leicester, Wakefield, Hereford and Kendal A.G., Leeds City A.G. Collection, McIntosh Gallery U.W.O., etc. *Address:* 69 Paddock Green Cres., London N6J-3P6, Ontario, Canada. *Signs work:* "Eric Atkinson."

ATKINSON, Ted, D.F.A. (Lond., 1952), R.E. (1988), F.R.B.S., F.R.S.A. (1957), Slade Prize Winner (1952); sculptor; Head of Sculpture School, Coventry Polytechnic (1968-83); *b* Liverpool, 21 Mar., 1929; *s* of Edward Atkinson, musician. *Educ.:* Oulton School, Liverpool; *studied art* at Liverpool College of Art, Slade School (under Butler, Moore), Slade Post-graduate Scholar (1952-53). *Work in permanent collections:* Arts Council, London, Dallas Art Museum, Kunst Academie, Dresden, Manchester Art Gallery, Museum of Modern Art, N.Y., Seattle Art Museum, etc.; public sculptures in Coventry, Dusseldorf, Hamburg, Univ. Birmingham. One of six sculptors chosen to represent Britain at Expo 88 Brisbane. *Address:* 4 De Vere Pl., Wivenhoe, Essex CO7 9AX.

ATTREE, Jake (Jonathan), Dip.A.D. (Painting) (1972), R.A. Schools Post-Grad. Cert. (1977); Landseer prize, Creswick prize, David Murray Scholarship; painter; *b* York, 13 Oct., 1950; *s* of Noel and Mary Attree; *m* Lindsay Knight. *Educ.:* Danesmead, York; *studied art* at York College of Art (1966-68), Liverpool College of Art (1969-72), R.A. Schools (1974-77). *Exhib.:* regular solo and group shows include R.A. Summer Exhbn. (1975, 1985), Serpentine Summer (1982), General Huis Maastricht, Kunstlerhaus Dortmund (1992), Leeds City A.G. (1993). *Work in permanent collections:* Leeds City Council, City of Dortmund, Sheffield University, Nuffield Trust. *Publication:* illustrated At This Time and The Purblind Man, poetry by John Holmes. *Address:* 33 Titus St., Saltaire, Shipley BD18 4LU. *Signs work:* usually unsigned, unless requested, then "J. Attree."

AUERBACH, Frank Helmut; painter; *b* Berlin, 29 Apr., 1931. *Educ.:* privately; St. Martin's School of Art; R.C.A. *Exhib.:* one-man shows: Beaux-Arts Gallery (1956, 1959, 1961, 1962, 1963); Marlborough Fine Art (1965, 1967, 1971, 1974, 1983, 1987); Marlborough-Gerson, N.Y. (1969, 1982); retrospective, Hayward Gallery (1978), Venice Biennale (1986) (joint winner Golden Lion), Hamburg (1986), Essen, Madrid (1987), many others. *Work in permanent collections:*

Metropolitan Museum, N.Y.; Museum of Modern Art N.Y.; Los Angeles County Museum; National Gallery of Australia; B.M.; Tate Gallery, London; and many other museums; British Council; Arts Council; Contemporary Art Society, etc. *Address:* c/o Marlborough Fine Art Ltd., 6 Albemarle St., London W1X 4BY.

AULD, John Leslie M., D.A. Belfast, A.R.C.A., N.R.D., F.I.A.L.; art teacher, designer-craftsman in goldsmiths' work; head, Art Dept., Municipal Tech. College, Londonderry (1940-46); Senior Lecturer, Glasgow School of Art (retd. 1979); *b* Belfast, 21 Jan., 1914; *s* of Joseph Auld; *m* Doreen M. W. Auld (*née* Sproul). *Educ.:* Methodist College, Belfast; *studied art* at Belfast Coll. of Art (1931-35); Royal Coll. of Art (1935-39). *Exhib.:* London, Brussels, Paris, New York, Stockholm, Arts Council, etc. *Work in permanent collections:* Goldsmiths' Company, London; New York City Corpn.; University of Glasgow. *Publication:* Your Jewellery. *Address:* Braehead Rd., Thorntonhall, Glasgow. *Signs work:* "J. L. AULD," but see appendix.

AVATI, Mario; Prix de la Critique, Paris (1957), Gold Medal First International Prints Exhbn., Florence (1966), Prix du Lion's Club (1972), Grand Prix des Arts de la Ville de Paris (1981); painter/printmaker in mezzotint; *b* Monaco, 27 May, 1921; *m* Helen. *Educ.:* College de Grasse, France; *studied art* at Ecole des Arts Decoratifs, Nice, Ecole des Beaux Arts, Paris. *Exhib.:* one-man shows worldwide. *Work in permanent collections:* museums in Europe, America, Asia, Oceania. *Publication:* 12 'Livres de Luxe' illustrated with original prints. *Address:* 12 Cite Vaneau, Paris, France F75007. *Clubs:* Soc. Les Peintres-Graveurs Paris, La Jeune Gravure Contemporaine Paris, R.E. *Signs work:* "AVATI."

AYERS, Eric, A.R.C.A., M.S.I.A.; designer; *b* 12 Aug., 1921; *s* of Vivian Ayers; *m* Duffy Rothenstein (*née* Fitzgerald). *Educ.:* Balgowan Grammar School; *studied art* at Beckenham School of Art, R.C.A. *Exhib.:* Design in Business Printing Exhibition, Festival of Britain (Dome of Discovery); Milwaukee Library, Wisconsin (U.S.A.); C. of I.D. "100 Good Catalogues." *Work in permanent collections:* Museum of Modern Art, N.Y., B.M. Dept. of Prints and Books, V. & A. Dept. of Prints and Books. *Work repro.:* Graphis, Graphis Annual, Visiting Fellow, Fine Art Dept., University of Newcastle. *Address:* 4 Regent Sq., London WC1H 8HZ. *Signs work:* "ERIC AYERS."

AYNSCOMB-HARRIS, Martin John, N.D.D. (1958), A.T.D. (1959); artist in oil and gouache, sculptor; teacher, Daniel Defoe's Secondary School (1959-60), Hundred of Hoo County Secondary School (1960-61), Nuneaton School of Art (1961-63); *b* Farnham, Surrey, 20 Aug., 1937; *s* of Dennis Aynscomb-Harris; banker; *m* Susan; two *d. Educ.:* St. Lawrence College, Ramsgate; *studied art* at Folkestone and Dover School of Art (1953-55); Medway College of Art (1955-56); Wimbledon College of Art (1956-58); Hornsey College of Art (1958-59). *Exhib.:* one-man shows, London: Woodstock Gallery, Weitzmann Gallery, Mansard Gallery, Heals Gallery, Liberty's, Ogilvy & Mather, Seen Gallery, Nicholas Martine Gallery; Kar Gallery of Fine Art, Toronto, British Week Exhbn. Calif., The Forum, Soho, N.Y.; mixed shows: Grafton Gallery, London; Phoenix Gallery, Lavenham; John Neville Gallery, Canterbury; Francis Iles Gallery, Rochester; De Ligney Gallery, Fort Lauderdale; Gallerie Colbert, Montreal; Gallerie Forlane, Paris; Hilton Gallery, London; Broadway Gallery, Broadway; Canaletto Gallery, London; Nicholas Treadwell Gallery, London; and in Germany, Italy and Holland. *Work in permanent collections:* London: National Bank of Detroit, Marks & Spencer Ltd., General Reinsurance Ltd., CNA Reinsurance of London Ltd., Holbourn Aeros, Cado Furniture, G Plan

18

Furniture, Gatx Shipping, Metropolitan Water Board, Rank Leisure Hotels, British Airways, Chase Manhattan Bank; Oxfordshire Educ. Com. *Work repro.:* for Solomon & Whitehead, Frost & Reed, Royle Publications, Henry Ling & Son. *Address:* 24 Marine Parade, Sheerness, Kent. *Signs work:* see appendix.

AYRES, Gillian, O.B.E., A.R.A.; painter; taught at Bath Academy, St. Martin's; Head of Painting, Winchester School of Art since 1978; *b* Barnes, London, 3 Feb., 1930; two children. *Educ.:* St. Paul's Girls' School; *studied art* at Camberwell School of Art. *Exhib.:* group shows: Musée d'Art Moderne; Bienale de Paris, Paris (1959); Situation, London (1960-61); one-man shows, Gallery One (1956), Kasmin Gallery (1965-66, 1969), Hayward Gallery (1972), Kasmin/Knoedler (1979), Knoedler London (1979, 1982, 1985, 1987), Knoedler New York (1985), R.A. British Art (1987), London, and Stuttgart, Germany. Awarded Japan International Art Promotion Association Award (1963). *Work in permanent collections:* Tate Gallery, Museum of Modern Art, N.Y. *Address:* Tall Trees, Gooseham, nr. Bude, Cornwall. *Signs work:* "Gillian Ayres."

AYRTON, Millicent, M.B.E. (1946), R.Cam.A. (1948); painter in oil and water-colour, teacher; Past Chairman and Founder, Deeside Art Group; *b* Hoylake, Ches., 23 Nov., 1913; *m* Bertram Ayrton (decd.); one *s. Educ.:* The Westlands, Acton Reynold, Salop.; *studied art* at Liverpool Art College (1930-35, Will C. Penn, R.O.I.). *Exhib.:* R.A., Liverpool Academy, Royal West Academy, R.Cam.A. *Work in permanent collections:* Liverpool University, Birkenhead Williamson Gallery, Stafford University. *Publications:* A Northern School by Peter Davies, Liverpool Seen by Peter Davies. *Address:* The Anchorage, Townfield Rd., West Kirby, Merseyside L48 7EY. *Signs work:* "M.E. AYRTON."

B

BACK, Ken, Cert. R.A.S. (1967), N.D.D. (1964); painter in oil and ink; part-time school lecturer; *b* Guildford, 2 Apr., 1944; *m* Corinne Jones, artist; one *s,* one *d. Educ.:* Astor School, Dover; *studied art* at Dover, Folkestone and Canterbury Colleges of Art (1959-64), R.A. Schools (1964-67, Peter Greenham, Charles Mahoney). *Exhib.:* R.A., Piccadilly Gallery, Park Walk Gallery, Chappel Galleries, Colchester, etc. *Work in private and public collections:* Europe and U.S.A. *Address:* White Cottage, The Moor, Dickleburgh, nr. Diss, Norfolk IP21 4NT. *Signs work:* "K.W. BACK" or "K.B."

BACKHOUSE, David John, R.W.A., F.R.B.S.; sculptor in bronze; *b* Corsham, Wilts., 5 May, 1941; *s* of J. H. Backhouse; *m* Sarah Barber; one *s,* two *d. Educ.:* Lord Weymouth School, Warminster; *studied art* at West of England College of Art. *Work in collections:* R.W.A., British Steel Corp., Royal Opera House, Covent Garden, Morgan Crucible Co., Mercantile and General Reinsurance Co., Haslemere Estates, Telford Dev. Corp., City of Bristol, Tesco plc, J. Sainsbury plc., Standard Life, and private collections throughout Europe and in U.S.A. *Addresses:* The Old Post Office, Lullington, Frome, Som.; *studio:* Lullington Studio, Lullington, Frome, Som. BA11 2PW. *Signs work:* "Backhouse," and see appendix.

BACZKOWSKA, Pamela; sculptor in cast bronze and aluminium, cement, carved wood and stone; *b* Bradford, Yorks., 8 Jan., 1938; *d* of Maurice Lacy

Wright; *m* Henry Baczkowski, painter; one *d. Educ.*: Bradford Girls' Grammar School, Hubbard College of Scientology, E. Grinstead; *studied art* at Regional College of Art, Bradford (pottery under Bruce Adams). *Exhib.*: Centrum Gallery, Bern; mixed shows: Woodstock Gallery, London, Sackville Gallery, E. Grinstead. *Work in permanent collections:* mainly private in Switzerland. *Address:* Rozel, Coombe Hill, E. Grinstead, Sussex. Member of F.P.S., Greenpeace, C.N.D. *Signs work:* circle within a square and see appendix.

BAFFONI, Pier Luigi, N.S. (1975), R.O.I. (1979); artist in oil, water-colour and pastel; *b* Turin, Italy, 11 Aug., 1932; *s* of Pierpaolo Baffoni, accountant; *m* Mary Bainbridge. *Educ.*: College of the Missioni Consolata, Turin; *studied art* at College of Art, Turin (1954-58) under Luigi Guglielmino and privately from Alessandro Pomi of Venice. *Exhib.*: one-man shows, Italy, Hertford, Cambridge, Bedford, Hitchin; mixed shows, Biennale di Castelfranco Veneto, Bologna, Mall Galleries, London. *Work in permanent collection:* Montebelluna Town Hall, Bedfordshire Educ. Art Loan Service. *Address:* 140 Station Rd., Lower Stondon, Beds. *Signs work:* "P. L. Baffoni."

BAGHJIAN, Manouk; artist in water-colour, pastel, oil; *b* Nicosia, Cyprus, 1 Jan., 1929; *m;* one *s,* one *d. Educ.*: Armenian High School, Cyprus; *studied art* at Richmond A.E.C. *Exhib.*: Gulbenkian Hall Kensington, Clarendon Gallery Holland Pk., Chiswick Library, Pinacoteca Tossa de Mar, R.S.M.A. Mall Galleries (1989, 1990, 1991), B.B.C. Bush House, Hogarth Club W4. *Work in permanent collection:* 8 Turnham Green Terr., London W4. *Address:* 213 Popes La., London W5 4NH. *Club:* Ealing Art. *Signs work:* "Manouk."

BAILEY, Julian, B.F.A. Oxon. (1985), R.A.Dip. (M.A.) (1988); artist in oil and pastel; *b* Cheshire, 8 Apr., 1963; *m* Sophie Cullen, ceramist. *Educ.*: Malvern College; *studied art* at Ruskin School of Art (1982-85), R.A. Schools (1985-88, Jane Dowling, Norman Blamey, R.A.). *Exhib.*: R.A., New Grafton Gallery, New Academy Gallery. *Work in permanent collections:* National Trust (F.F.A.), New College, Oxford. *Address:* 16 Pembridge Mews, London W11 3EQ. *Signs work:* "J.B." or "JULIAN BAILEY."

BAILEY, Terence Robert, N.D.D. (1958), A.T.D. (1962), R.B.S.A. (1991); painter in oil; Senior lecturer, Northumberland C.H.E. (1962-79); *b* Wolverhampton, 21 Dec., 1937; *m* Kate (Valerie Ann Browning); three *s. Educ.*: Wolverhampton Technical High School; *studied art* at Wolverhampton College of Art (1954-58), Bournemouth College of Art (1962). *Exhib.*: Northern Painters (1966), Northern Art Exhbn. (1978), prize winner R.B.S.A. Open (1986), R.P., R.O.I., regularly at R.B.S.A.; several one-man shows. Winner in Alexon "Women on Canvas" portrait competition (1990). *Work in permanent collections:* Northumberland C.C., Northern Arts, National Library of Wales, R.B.S.A.; many private collections. *Address:* Dovey Studio, Aberdyfi, Gwynedd LL35 0LW. *Signs work:* "Terry Bailey."

BAILLIE, William James Laidlaw, P.R.S.A., P.P.R.S.W., R.G.I., H.R.A., H.R.W.A., H.B.W.S., D.A.Edin. (1950); painter in oil and water-colour; President, Royal Scottish Academy; *b* Edinburgh, 1923; *s* of James L. Baillie; *m* Helen Baillie; one *s,* two *d. Educ.*: Dunfermline High School, Fife; *studied art* at Edinburgh College of Art (1941-42; (War Service 1942-46) 1946-50, Gillies, Maxwell, Rosoman, Philipson, MacTaggart), Diploma 1950. *Exhib.*: one-man shows: Edinburgh, Harrogate, Newcastle, Salisbury, London, etc. *Work in permanent collections:* Aberdeen, Edinburgh, Glasgow, Kansas, U.S.A. etc. *Address:* 6A Esslemont Rd., Edinburgh EH16 5PX. *Clubs:* Scottish Arts and New Club. *Signs work:* "W.J.L. Baillie."

BAIN, Julia Mary, M.F.P.S. (1985), Mem. Chelsea Art Soc. (1984); Woodrow Award (1986); sculptor in terracotta, wax and bronze; *b* London, 22 June, 1930; *d* of Guy Warrack, conductor and composer; *m* David Bain, F.R.C.S.; three *s,* one *d. Educ.:* The Legat School of Russian Ballet; *studied art* at I.L.E.A. Chelsea/Westminster (1978-81), Sir John Cass College (1981-83). *Exhibs.:* F.B.A. (1983-89), R.B.A., S.W.A., N.S., F.P.S. Trends, Art of Living S.P.S., Chelsea Art Soc.; one-man shows, Windsor Festival (1981, 1986, 1989), Century Gallery, Datchet (1990), The Deanery, Windsor Castle (1993). Work in private collections. *Address:* The Studio, Hadleigh House, Sheet St., Windsor, Berks. SL4 1BN. *Signs work:* "Julia Bain."

BAIN, Peter; painter in oil; *b* London, 15 December, 1927; *m* Jennifer; four *s. Studied art* at Bath Academy of Art. *Address:* Tiled Cottage, Old Bosham, Sussex PO18 8LS. *Signs work:* "Bain."

BAINES, Richard John Manwaring, M.A., R.O.I., R.D.S., N.D.D., A.T.D.; painter, writer, lecturer, critic and broadcaster (radio & TV); Senior lecturer London Inst., London College of Fashion; *b* Hastings, 1940; *s* of John Manwaring Baines, B.Sc., F.S.A., F.M.A.; divorced; two *s,* one *d. Educ.:* Eastbourne College; *studied art* at Regent St. Polytechnic, Goldsmiths' College, Birmingham Polytechnic. Past-president, East Sussex Arts Club. *Exhib.:* R.O.I., R.B.A., N.S., London and provinces; one-man shows Hastings (1968, 1987). *Work in permanent collections:* County Borough of Hastings, The Manx Museum, The London Inst. Royal Arms and mural restorations, All Saints Church, Hastings. *Address:* 138 St. Helens Rd., Hastings TN34 2EJ. *Signs work:* see appendix.

BAINES, Valerie, A.R.M.S. (1985), F.S.B.A. (1988), F.L.S. (1991); botanical artist, miniature painter and natural history illustrator in water-colour and oil; *b* Romford, 1935; *m* Brian Norman; one *s. Educ.:* Roxeth Mead School, Harrow on the Hill; Royal College of Music; *studied art* at Harrow Art School. *Exhib.:* R.A., R.M.S., S.B.A., R.H.S. Westminster Galleries, Mall Galleries, Alpine Gallery, Medici Gallery, Llewellyn Alexander Gallery, International Botanical Art, Carnegie Mellon University Pittsburgh. *Work in permanent collections:* Carnegie Mellon University Botanical Library Pittsburgh, Port Lympne Kent. *Publications:* The Naturalist's Garden by John Feltwell (Ebury Press, 1987), Botanical Diary (St. Michael, 1989), The Story of Silk by J.F. Allen Sutton (1990), The Big Book (Collins, 1991), Meadows by J.F. Allen Sutton (1992), Glorious Butterflies (B.B.C., 1993). *Address:* Shreives Oak, 16 Medway Rd., Gillingham, Kent ME7 1NH. *Signs work:* "V.B."

BAIRSTOW, Elizabeth Ann, F.S.B.A., S.W.A.; professional artist in water-colour, gallery owner; *b* White River, S.Africa, 11 Apr., 1938; *g-d* of Sir Edward Bairstow of York Minster; *m* Dr. D.G. Gourley; three *s. Educ.:* New Hall, Chelmsford. *Exhib.:* Dorset County Museum (1984), Tate Gallery (1983), Mall Galleries, Westminster Gallery. *Work in permanent collection:* The Bairstow Gallery, Cerne Abbas. *Publication:* illustrated, Piddle Valley Book of Country Life. *Address:* The Bairstow Gallery, Cerne Abbas, Dorset DT2 7JG. *Signs work:* "Elizabeth Bairstow" or "E.A.B."

BAKER, Christopher William, B.A.Hons. (Fine Art, 1978), P.G.C.E. (1981), R.B.A. (1981); etcher, oil on canvas, dramatic landscape paintings; Tutor, West Dean College; *b* Essex, 27 May, 1956. *Educ.:* Kingham Hill School, Oxon.; *studied art* at West Surrey College of Art and Design (1974-75, M. Fairclough), Glos. College of Art and Design (1975-78, D. L. Carpanini), Exeter University. *Exhib.:* R.W.A., R.B.A., Mall Galleries, Phoenix Gallery, Highgate, Burstow Gallery, Brighton College, Wyckeham Gallery, Stockbridge. *Work in permanent* *collections:* Coventry Adult Educ., Oundle School, Eartham House. *Work repro.:* The Artist, Quattro Publications. *Address:* 110 Fitzallan Rd., Arundel, W. Sussex. *Signs work:* "Christopher Baker."

BAKER, Hilary Jayne, B.A.Hons. Fine Art (1984); artist, drawings in charcoal, etchings and oil paintings, principal subjects — the figure and reportage portraiture; *b* Cheltenham, 1 Mar., 1962; *d* of C. E. Baker, company director. *Educ.:* Cheltenham Grammar School; *studied art* at Sheffield Art College (1981-84), Cheltenham Art College (1980-81). *Exhib.:* one-man shows: Ogle Gallery, Cheltenham (1986), Brewery Court Gallery, Cirencester (1985), Iris Ryman Gallery, Marbella (1990). *Work in permanent collections:* portrait, Gen. Sir John Hackett, in N.P.G.; many private collections in Europe, U.S.A., Australia. *Address:* Harford House, Naunton, Cheltenham, Glos. GL54 3AG. *Signs work:* see appendix.

BALDWIN, Arthur Mervyn, N.D.D. (1955), Rome Scholarship, Sculpture, 1960; sculptor in metals and synthetics; self employed artist and restorer; 1978, retired defeated by lack of public appreciation — now restores antique watches — for which service people happily pay; *b* Immingham, Lincs., 1 Feb. 1934; *s* of William Henry Baldwin; *m* Patrica Mary; two *s. Educ.:* Humberstone Foundation School, Old Clee, Lincs.; *studied art* at Grimsby School of Art, Leicester College of Art. *Work in permanent collections:* National Museum of Wales, Arts Council (Wales); Städtischen Kunstammlungen, Ludwigshafen. *Address:* 18 The Walk, Cardiff. *Signs work:* sculpture unsigned; drawings etc. signed "MERVYN BALDWIN."

BALDWIN, Gordon, N.D.D. (1952), Central Dip. (1953); ceramist; teacher, Central School of Art and Design, and Eton College; *b* Lincoln, 1932; *s* of the late Lewis Nelson; *m* Nancy Chandler; one *s,* two *d. Educ.:* Lincoln School; *studied art* at Lincoln School of Art (1949-51, Toni Bartl), Central School of Art and Design (1951-53, Dora Billington). *Work in permanent collections:* V. & A.; Southampton A.G.; Crafts Council; Leicester Educ. Authority; Usher Gallery, Lincoln; Abbots Hall, Keswick; Paisley A.G.; Boymans van Beuningen, Rotterdam; Bellrive Museum, Zurich; Penn. State University, U.S.A.; Gateshead A.G.; Swindon A.G.; Museum of Art, Melbourne; Museum of Art, Perth; Knukke-Heiste, Keramion, W. Germany; Octagon Centre, Idah., U.S.A. *Address:* 1 Willowbrook, Eton, Windsor, Berks.

BALDWIN, Martyn John, Dip.A.D.; painter in oil; *b* Edgware, 18 May, 1959. *Educ.:* Downer Grammar School; *studied art* at Harrow School of Art (1979-83). *Exhib.:* R.A. *Address:* 64 Hibbert Rd., Harrow Weald, Middx. HA3 7JS. *Club:* Wembley Arts Soc. (President). *Signs work:* "M. Baldwin" or "BALDWIN."

BALDWIN, Nancy; painter in acrylic; *b* Sunderland, 3 Mar., 1935; *d* of Hayden Thomas Chandler; *m* Gordon Baldwin; one *s,* two *d. Educ.:* St. Joseph's Convent, Lincoln; *studied art* at Lincoln School of Art (1949-52, Toni Bartl), Central School of Art and Design (1952-54, Dora Billington). *Exhib.:* Reading Gallery, Thames Gallery, Windsor, The Gallery, Eton College, Cross Keys Gallery, Beaconsfield, Salix, Windsor, Oxford Gallery, City Museum and Gallery, Stoke-on-Trent, Midland Group, Nottingham, Ikon, Birmingham, Holsworthy, London, Carmel College Gallery, Bohun Gallery, Henley, Ellingham Mill, Bungay; prize winner Midland View (1980). *Work in permanent collections:* Ashmolean Museum, Oxford and private collections in U.K., Italy, Switzerland, Belgium. *Address:* 1 Willowbrook, Eton, Windsor, Berks.

BALFOUR, Maria, Associated Mem. Paris Salon, M.F.P.S., F.R.S.A.; Medal Winner, Internationale Academie de Lutece, Paris (1977); painter in oil; *b* London, 27 June, 1934; *d* of late Morogh Bernard, interior decorator; *m* Lord Balfour of Inchrye; one *d. Educ.:* America and British Isles; *studied art* privately. *Exhib.:* Loggia Gallery (1975, 1980, 1985), Paris Salon, Galerie Internationale, N.Y., Chelsea Art Soc., F.P.S., A.N.S., Kensington & Chelsea Artists; R.I. Galleries, Medici Galleries, Lloyds Bank (Pall Mall) in aid of Mental Health Foundation (1990). *Commission:* crest for Bridal Kneeler to celebrate 250th year of founding of Guy's Hospital (1976). *Work in permanent collections:* New Zealand, S. Africa, Belgium, Holland, U.S.A., British Isles, Israel and Italy. *Address:* 10 Limerston St., London SW10 0HH. *Signs work:* initials "MB" joined, see appendix.

BALL, Gerald, R.C.A. (1979); painter in water-colour and tempera; *b* Ashton-under-Lyne, 24 May, 1948; *s* of Robert Ball, musician; *m* Ann. *Educ.:* Hartshead Comprehensive; *studied art* at Ashton-under-Lyne C.F.E. *Exhib.:* R.W.S., Richard Hagen, Ltd., R.I., Manchester Academy, Agnews, Tegfryn Gallery, Bourne Gallery, Lion and Lamb Gallery, N.Y. Hilton. *Work in permanent collection:* Coleg Harlech. *Address:* Lane End Cottage, Golderfield, Pudleston, Leominster, Herefordshire HR6 0RG. *Signs work:* "GERRY BALL."

BALL, Robert, A.R.C.A. (1942), R.E. (1943), R.B.S.A. (1943), F.R.S.A. (1950), R.B.A. (1979), A.R.W.A. (1988); British Inst. Scholarship for Engraving (1937); teacher of painting, drawing and anatomy, Birmingham College of Art (1942); Princ. Stroud School of Arts and Crafts (Jan., 1953); teacher of painting, Glos. College of Art (1959-81); artist in oil, water-colour, drawing, etching, line-engraving, mezzotint, aquatint, and wood-engraving; *b* Birmingham, 11 July, 1918; *s* of John William Ball, silversmith; *m* Barbara Minchin; one *s*, two *d. Studied art* at Birmingham Junior School of Art (1930-33), Birmingham College of Art (1933-40); R.C.A. (1940-42). *Exhib.:* R.A., R.W.A., R.E., R.B.S.A., R.B.A. *Work in permanent collections:* V. & A., Ashmolean, Gloucester, Cheltenham and Birmingham Museums. *Publications:* illustrated Cotswold Ballads by Mansell. *Address:* Beth-shan, Kingsmead, Painswick, Glos. GL6 6US. *Signs work:* "Robert Ball."

BALMER, Barbara, A.R.S.A. (1973), R.S.W. (1966), R.G.I. (1988); painter in oil and water-colour; *b* B'ham, 23 Sept., 1929; *m* George Mackie, R.D.I., R.S.W.; two *d. Educ.:* Solihull High School for Girls; *studied art* at Coventry School of Art; Edinburgh College of Art. *Exhib.:* one-man shows: Demarco Gallery, Edinburgh (1965-70), Scottish Gallery, Edinburgh (1975, 1980, 1985, 1988), Posterngate Gallery, Hull (1983), Stirling Gallery (1976), Usher Gallery, Lincoln (1984). *Work in permanent collections:* Glasgow City A.G., Edinburgh City Art Centre, Aberdeen A.G., Perth A.G., S.N.P.G., S.A.C. *Address:* 32 Broad St., Stamford, Lincs. PE9 1JP. *Signs work:* "Barbara Balmer."

BALMER, Derek Rigby, R.W.A.; painter in oil and acrylic; *b* Bristol, 28 Dec., 1934; *s* of Geoffrey Johnson Balmer; *m* Elizabeth Mary Rose; one *s*, one *d. Educ.:* St. Gabriel's Convent, Waterloo House, Sefton Pk.; *studied art* at West of England College of Art (Dennis Darch, Derek Crowe, Paul Feiler). *Exhib.:* Arnolfini (four), New Art Centre, Leicester Gallery, R.W.A. *Address:* Mulberry House, 12 Avon Grove, Sneyd Pk., Bristol 9. *Signs work:* "Balmer" or "Derek Balmer."

BANEY, Ralph R., F.R.B.S. (1984), M.F.A. (1973), Ph.D. (1980), A.T.C. (1962), Who's Who in American Art (1973); Professor of Art; sculptor in wood, bronze, ceramic, fibreglass; *b* Trinidad, 22 Sept., 1929; *m* Vera; one *s. Educ.:*

Naparima College, Trinidad; *studied art* at Brighton College of Art (1957-62, A.J.J. Ayres), University of Maryland, U.S.A. (1971-76, Ken Campbell). *Exhib.:* Washington County Museum, O.A.S. Gallery, Washington D.C.; Sculpture House, N.Y.C.; Georgetown University. *Work in permanent collections:* H.M. The Queen; Washington County Museum of Fine Arts, Hagerstown, Md.; Central Bank, Trinidad. *Address:* 5203 Talbot's Landing, Ellicott City, Md. 21043, U.S.A. *Clubs:* R.B.S., Sculptors Guild Inc. N.Y., Washington Sculptors Group. *Signs work:* "R. BANEY."

BANKS, Brian; painter in acrylic, oil, mixed media; *b* London, 21 Oct., 1939; *s* of William John Ralph; *m* Christine, divorced 1974; two *s*, one *d. Educ.:* Sir Walter St. John's Grammar School, London; *studied art* at St. Martin's (1956-57), Peter de Francia, Edward Middleditch, James Dring; privately with John Flavin, A.R.C.A. (1958). *Exhib.:* one-man shows: Colin Jellicoe Gallery, Manchester; Ansdell Gallery, London; Zaydler Gallery, London; Fermoy Art Gallery, King's Lynn; Conway Hall, London; Leigh Gallery, London, (1984, 1985), Trinity Arts Centre, Tunbridge Wells. Represented by Leigh Gallery, Bloomsbury, London. *Work in private collections:* Britain, Australia, France, U.S.A., Denmark. *Address:* 8 Ravenet Ct., Battersea Pk. Rd., London SW11 5HE. *Signs work:* "BANKS" (year).

BANKS, Nancy, U.A., M.F.P.S.; sculptor in bronze, direct plaster, terracotta; *b* St. Helens, 12 Feb., 1923; *d* of the late W.J. Yates; *m* John Banks, M.Eng., F.Eng.; two *s. Educ.:* Nutgrove, Rainhill, Lancs.: *studied art* at Sir John Cass College of Art (Clive Duncan). *Exhib.:* Mall Galleries, R.B.A., U.A., N.S., R.M.S., S.W.A., S.P.S., Barbican, Bloomsbury, Guildhall, Alpine, Weighouse galleries, I.E.E., Blackheath, Usher, Lincs., Worthing Museum and A.G., M.A.S.-F. *Work in permanent collections:* U.K., U.S.A., Japan, Spain. *Address:* B.1. Marine Gate, Marine Drive, Brighton, E. Sussex BN2 5TQ. *Club:* L.L.L.C. *Signs work:* "N. BANKS" or "Nancy Banks."

BANNISTER, Geoffrey Ernest John; served Royal Navy Minesweepers (1942-46); E.V.T. instructor in Commercial Art (Royal Navy, 1945-46); artist/designer, figure, scraper-board, water-colour; *b* Birmingham, 15 Jan., 1924; *s* of Henry J. Bannister; *m* Beryl Parr Robinson, 1949 (deceased, 1966); one *s*, one *d.*; remarried, 1967, Susan Jennefer Peters; two *s. Educ.:* St. Philip's Grammar School. Proprietor, Minster Print & Packaging. Commissions for portraits, animals, landscapes in oils. *Address:* Crossways, 811 Sutton Rd., Aldridge, Walsall, W. Midlands WS9 0QJ. *Clubs:* Birmingham Publicity Assoc., Great Barr Golf, Catenian Assoc. *Signs work:* "Geoff Bannister."

BARANOWSKA, Janina; artist in oil; *b* Poland, 28 Oct., 1925; *d* of Josef Zbaraszewski, officer in Polish Army; *m* Maksymilian Baranowski; one *s. Educ.:* In Poland, Middle East and Scotland; *studied art* at Borough Polytechnic under Prof. Bomberg (1947-50), School of Art at the Polish University of Stefan Batory in London (1951-54). *Exhib.:* One-man shows: Drian Gallery (1958, 1978, 1982), Grabowski Gallery (1960, 1962, 1965, 1971, 1973, 1975), Raymond Duncan Galleries (1960, 1966), Alwin Gallery (1969), Grand Prix Rencontre Lyon, France (1970), Det Lille Galleri, Norway (1978), State Galleries in Krakow and Poznan, Poland (1965), Royal Festival Hall, London (1978), Dixon Gallery — University of London (1985), Bloomsbury Gallery (1988), Woburn Fine Arts Gallery (1990), Polish Cultural Inst. (1993). Mixed exhib.: Royal Academy, Burlington Gallery, Cassel Gallery, R.B.A. Galleries, New Vision Centre, Walker's Galleries, Whitechapel Art Gallery, Edinburgh. *Publication:* Editor of Contemporary Polish Artists in G.B. (1983). *Clubs:* W.I.A.C., Group

49, International Institute of Art and Letters, International Assoc. of Art – U.K. National Committee, Assoc. of Polish Artists in Gt. Britain (Chairman), N.S.P.S. (Mem.). *Address:* 20 Strathmore Rd., London SW19 8DB. *Signs work:* "Baranowska."

BARBARIGO, Ida, M.A.; artist in oil and etching; *b* Venice, 1925; *d* of Guido Cadorin, painter, Professore Accademia Belle Arti, Venice. *Educ.:* Marco Polo H.S., Venice; *studied art* at Accademia Belle Arti, Venice. *Exhib.:* one-man shows at Musee d'Art Moderne de la Ville de Paris (1972), Fond. Querini-Stampalia, Venice (1975), Galerie de France, Paris (1976, 1980), Venice Biennale (1978), München Bayerische Staatsgemäldesammlungen (Cat. Jean Clair, 1982), Museo di Vicenza, Italy, Museo d'Arte Moderna of Llubljana, Zagreb, Rijeka, Yugoslavia, Wolfsbourg, Germany, Handschin Gallery, Basle. *Work in permanent collections:* Grosvenor Gallery, London, Kunsthalle, Nürnberg, Bergamini Gallery, Milan, Paul Facchetti Gallery, Paris. *Work repro.:* XX Siecle, Paris, Quandrum, Brussels, Art International, Lugano, Le Arti, Milan, Kunstwerk, Baden-Baden, and newspapers. *Publications:* I Cadorin (Marchiori); monograph: Chairs and Voyeurs (De Sölier ed. Alfieri). *Addresses:* 21 Rue du Bac, Paris, VII, and Carmini 2534, Venice. *Signs work:* "BARBARIGO."

BARBER, Raymond, A.C.F.I., A.M.II.M., City and Guilds, London Inst. (1943), E.M.E.U. (1937), S.S.I.A. (1945); Course Tutor at Footwear Dept Wellingborough Technical College; Footwear Section Head (retd.); *b* 30 Sept., 1921. *Educ.:* Kettering Rd. Inst., Northampton, College of Technology, Northampton, Leicester College of Technology. *Exhib.:* Walsall, London, in conjunction with "Leather, Footwear and Allied Industries" Export Corp., Ltd.; Quality Footwear Exhib., Seymour Hall, London. *Address:* 10 Wantage Cl., Moulton, Northampton. *Clubs:* N.C.T.S.A., N.G.C., N.S.M.E. *Signs work:* "Renny."

BARCLAY, Sir Colville, Bart., M.A.; painter in oil and water-colour; *b* London, 7 May, 1913; *s* of Sir Colville Barclay, K.C.M.G.; *m* Rosamond Elliott; three *s. Educ.:* Eton and Oxford; *studied art* at Ruskin School, Oxford. *Exhib.:* R.B.A., R.A., London Group, Brighton and Bradford A.G. *Official purchases:* L.C.C. Schools, Arts Council, Bradford City Art Gallery. *Address:* Pitshill, nr. Petworth, Sussex. *Club:* The Naval. *Signs work:* "Barclay."

BARKER, Clive, sculptor in bronze and chrome; *b* Luton, Beds., 29 Aug., 1940; *s* of F. Barker; *m* Rose Bruen; two *s. Educ.:* Beech Hill Secondary Modern; *studied art* at Luton College of Technology and Art (1957-59) under Clifford Barry, A.R.C.A. *Exhib.:* Robert Fraser Gallery, Hanover Gallery, Musee d'Art Moderne, Museum of Modern Art, N.Y., Palais des Beaux-Arts, Palazzo Strozzi, etc. *Work in public collections:* Arts Council of Gt. Britain, British Council, V. & A., Tate Gallery, etc. *Work repro.:* Pop Art Re-defined (Thames & Hudson), Image as Language (Penguin), Pop Art (Studio Vista), Art in Britain 1969-70 (Dent), Objekt Kunst (Dumont). *Address:* 6 The Clocktower, Heath St., Hampstead, London NW3. *Signs work:* "Clive Barker."

BARKLAM, Harold, A.R.C.A. (1936); artist in oil, water-colour; art lecturer, Derby College of Art; art teacher, Lowestoft School of Art (1946-50); *b* Tipton, Staffs., 14 Jan., 1912; *s* of George R. Barklam; *m* Marjorie Hale; one *d. Educ.:* Ryland Memorial School of Art, W. Bromwich, R.C.A. and College of Art, Birmingham. *Exhib.:* Birmingham A.G., Derby A.G., Norwich Castle, Nottingham Castle. *Work repro.:* oil paintings of Dunster Castle, Hardwicke Hall, Serlby Hall, Berkeley Castle, Blithfield Hall, Ingestre Hall; mural paintings entitled "Children's Games" painted for Lady Bagot of Blithfield Hall. *Address:* 9 Eastwood Drive, Littleover, Derby. *Signs work:* "H. BARKLAM."

BARNARD, Roger, B.F.A. (1974); artist, participatory set-ups some include video; painting, drawing, photography, holography, writing; *b* London, 4 Nov., 1951; *s* of E.C. Barnard; *m* (1) Suzan Swale (divorced); one *d*; *Educ.:* Chichester High School for Boys; *studied art* at West Sussex College of Design (1970-71), North Staffs. Polytechnic (1971-74). *Exhib.:* one-man shows, Tate Gallery, Air, Scottish Arts Council Gallery, Third Eye Centre, South Bank London, Truro, etc.; mixed shows, Tate, Serpentine, Hayward, Air, Holborn Underground Comp., Whitechapel, Arts Council of G.B. touring exhbn., Coventry, Chichester, Third Eye Centre, Osaka Triennale '90' (Painting), '91' (Print) Japan, etc. *Works* in Royal Inst. of Cornwall County Coll., Contemporary Art Centre Osaka, Japan; private collections in U.K., U.S.A., France, Germany; U.C.H. London. *Address:* 151 Archway Rd., London N6 5BL. *Signs work:* paintings since 1970 unsigned, drawings dated, some signed "R. Barnard."

BARNARD, Thomas Henslow, A.T.D. (1938), A.R.W.A. (1961), R.W.A. (1972); artist in oil, wood-engraving; art teacher, 1938-59; Army officer (1917-37 and 1939-45); *b* 25 Aug., 1898; *s* of Henslow Barnard, civil engineer; *m* Ruth Anderson; one *s*, one *d*. *Educ.:* Malvern College; R.M.C., Sandhurst; *studied art* at W. of England College of Art, Bristol, under D. E. Milner. *Exhib.:* R.A., N.E.A.C., R.W.A. *Work in permanent collections:* Germany, America and Canada, Municipal Galleries of Gloucester and Cheltenham, Hinckley U.D.C., M. of W., and private collection R.W.A. *Address:* Giffards, Church Rd., Leckhampton, Cheltenham, Glos. *Club:* Cheltenham Group of Artists. *Signs work:* "T. H. Barnard."

BARNDT, Helen Grace, artist in sepia ink, oil, tempera. *Commissioned by:* Dr. J. Trenton Tully for the Metaphysical Research Society of Denver, Colorado (1968-92) for series of religious oil paintings, ceiling murals and interior designs. *Work in private collections:* Dr. J. Trenton Tully, Ronald M. Tully, Victor Hansen Gallery. *Address:* 1001 E. 7th Ave., Denver, Colorado. *Signs work:* "H. G. Barndt."

BARNES, Ann Margaret, B.Ed.(Hons.) (1973), M.F.P.S. (1974), A.M.N.S. (1978); artist in airbrush on botanical themes, head teacher; *b* London, 1951; *d* of William Barnes, water-colour artist. *Educ.:* Wimbledon County School for Girls; Stockwell College of Education, Bromley. *Exhib.:* F.P.S., N.S., Soc. of Botanical Artists; one-man shows: London, Chiswick, Leatherhead, Henley, Croydon, Morden. *Address:* 16 Mount Pleasant, Ewell, Epsom, Surrey KT17 1XE. *Signs work:* "A. Barnes."

BARNES-MELLISH, Glynis Lily, B.A.Hons. Fine Art (1975), Advanced Combined Fine Art Dip. (1983); artist and illustrator in water-colour; *b* Bromley, Kent, 10 June, 1953; *d* of Alan John Mellish; one *d*. *Educ.:* The William School, Letchworth; *studied art* at St. Albans School of Art (1971-72, 1981-83), W. Surrey College of Art and Design (1972-75). *Exhib.:* R.I. (1988, 1989, 1990, 1991, 1992, 1993), S.W.A. (1989, 1990, 1991, 1993), P.S. (1989, 1990). *Work repro.:* The Artist, Hodder & Stoughton, Penguin Books. *Address:* 16 Lytton Ave., Letchworth, Herts. SG6 3HT. *Clubs:* S.W.A., Cambridge Drawing Soc. *Signs work:* "Mellish."

BARNS-GRAHAM, Wilhelmina, D.A. (Edin.), D. Litt. (Dr.) University of St. Andrews (1992); painter in oil, acrylic, gouache; Founder Mem. Penwith Soc. of Artists (1949); *b* St. Andrews, Fife, 8 June, 1912. *Exhib.:* one-man shows,

London, Edinburgh, Oxford, St. Ives Cornwall, Leeds, Cumbria, Orkney, Germany, St. Andrews, Wakefield, Penzance, Perth, Kendal, Glasgow, Exeter, Truro, Dundee. *Work in permanent collections:* Arts Council; S.A.C.; British Council; B.M.; V. & A.; Contemporary Art Soc.; Scottish National Gallery; Government Coll.; Tate Gallery; D.O.E.; Edinburgh City Coll.; New South Wales A.G., Sydney, Australia; Universities of Michigan U.S.A., Aberdeen, Cambridge, Edinburgh, Manchester, Oxford; Museums of Glasgow, Ayr, Dundee, Hove, Kirkcaldy, Leeds, Plymouth, Portsmouth, Sheffield; Educ. authorities of Cornwall, Herts., Leeds, W. Riding. *Addresses:* 1 Barnaloft, St. Ives, Cornwall TR26 1NJ.; Balmungo, St. Andrews, Fife KY16 8LW. *Signs work:* W. Barns-Graham."

BARRATT, Mary H., B.A. (1969); painter in oil; part time art lecturer; *b* Annesley Woodhouse, Notts., 27 Mar., 1948; *d* of A.H. Fryer, head teacher; *m* Michael Ian Barratt. *Studied art* at Loughborough College of Art and Design (1966-69, Philip Thompson, Colin Saxton). *Exhib.:* 359 Gallery, Nottingham, Crucible Theatre, Sheffield, Rufford Country Pk., Ollerton, Merlin Gallery, Sheffield, Pierrepont Gallery Thoresby Park, Newark. *Address:* 7 Craigston Rd., Carlton-in-Lindrick, Worksop, Notts. S81 9NG. *Signs work:* "M. Barratt."

BARRETT, Franklin Allen, chartered accountant (retd.); mem. English Ceramic Circle; Chairman Church Stretton and S. Shropshire Arts Festival (1979-81); *b* Edgbaston, Birmingham, 4 Apr., 1906; *s* of Frank Bernard Barrett, B.Sc.; *m* Winifred Mary Webb; one *s. Educ.:* King Edward's Grammar School, Five Ways, Birmingham. *Publications:* Caughley and Coalport Porcelain (F. Lewis); Worcester Porcelain (Faber and Faber); Lund's Bristol & Worcester Porcelain (Faber and Faber); papers in English Ceramic Circle Transactions; co-author (with A. L. Thorpe), Derby Porcelain (Faber and Faber); contributor to English Porcelain, 1745-1850 (Ernest Benn), Joint Editor (with A. L. Thorpe), Pinxton China Factory, Exley (Cook-Steel, Derby), revised edition 'Honey Old English Porcelain' (Faber and Faber, 1977). *Address:* Mallards Keep, Alison Rd., Church Stretton, Salop. SY6 7AT.

BARRETT, Roderic, artist in oil; visiting lecturer, Central School of Art and Design (1947-68); invited to P.E.A., Exeter, U.S.A. (1957-58); tutor, Royal Academy Schools (1968—); *m* Lorna Blackmore; two *s*, one *d. Educ.:* St. Christopher's School, Letchworth; *studied art* at the Central (1936-40). *Exhib.:* One-man shows: London (1954, 1956, 1964, 1966, 1970, 1976, 1978, 1980), Cambridge (1947, 1963, 1966), Exeter, N.H., U.S.A. (1957), Boston, U.S.A. (1958), Oxford Gallery (1971, 1975, 1981), The Minories Colchester (1962, 1974, 1984), Chilham (1969, 1972), Harlow (1974, 1984), University of Essex (1966), University of Southampton (1975), University of Warwick (1975), Norwich Museum (1974), Ipswich (1987), Phoenix Gallery (1988), Chappel (1993), London Group, Wildensteins, Beaux Arts, Manchester, Cardiff, Aldeburgh, Bath Festival, Bristol City Art Gallery, Brussels, Zürich, Nice, Holland, Boston Arts Festival, U.S.A. Princetown U.S.A., Worcester Museum, U.S.A., Chicago, U.S.A., New York, etc. *Work in permanent collections:* V. & A., Lamont Gallery, U.S.A., University of Essex, University of Southampton, Essex Museum, Southend A.G., Christchurch Mansion, Ipswich; in private collections in France, England, Belgium, Italy, Eire, U.S.A. *Address:* Rooks End, Church Lane, Stanway, Colchester, Essex CO3 5LR. *Signs work:* "R.B."

BARRIE, Mardi, M.A., D.A. (1953), R.S.W. (1969); painter in oil, acrylic/water medium; *b* Kirkcaldy, Fife, 25 Apr., 1931; *d* of Jenny and David Gatherum. *Educ.:* Kirkcaldy High School; *studied art* at Edinburgh University and

Edinburgh College of Art (Prof. D. Talbot Rice, W.G. Gillies). *Exhib.:* regularly in group and solo exhbns. since 1963; principal private galleries include Scottish Gallery, Edinburgh, Macaulay Gallery, Stenton, Thackeray Gallery, London, Bruton Gallery, Somerset. *Work in private and public collections:* U.K. and abroad, including H.R.H. Duke of Edinburgh, R.S.A., S.A.C., Glasgow A.G., Scottish National Gallery of Modern Art. *Address:* Studio 5, 33 Melville St., Edinburgh EH3 7JF. *Signs work:* "Mardi."

BARTLETT, Charles, P.P.R.W.S., R.E., A.R.C.A.; artist in oil and water-colour, printmaker; *b* Grimsby, 23 Sept., 1921; *s* of Charles Henry Bartlett; *m* Olwen Jones; one *s*. *Educ.:* Eastbourne Grammar School; *studied art* at Eastbourne School of Art, R.C.A. *Exhib.:* two one-man shows in London. *Work in permanent collections:* V. & A. Museum, National Gallery of S. Australia, Arts Council of Great Britain, numerous public and private collections in Britain and abroad. *Address:* St. Andrew's, Fingringhoe, nr. Colchester, Essex CO5 7BG. *Signs work:* "Charles Bartlett."

BARTLETT, June Rosalyn, U.A. (1976); artist in oil and pencil; *b* Barnet, 30 June, 1947; *d* of H. R. W. Bartlett, saddler. *Educ.:* Holywell School for Girls, Folkestone, *Exhib.:* U.A., R.O.I.; one-man shows, Abu Dhabi, U.A.E., Dubai, U.A.E.(6), Caithness, Scotland (3). *Work in permanent collection:* Fleet Air Arm Museum, Yeovilton, Som. (portrait of Earl Mountbatten of Burma). *Address:* 60 Barnsbury St., London N1. *Club:* Toynbee Art. *Signs work:* "J.R. Bartlett."

BARTLETT, Paul Thomas, R.B.A. (1981), R.A. Schools P.G. Cert. (1980), B.A.Hons. Fine Art (Falmouth 1976), B'ham Poly.: F.E.T.C. (1987), P.G. Dip. hist. art/design (1990). *Prizes:* Turner Gold Medal, Landseer Life Painting, Sir James Walker; scholarships: David Murray, Elizabeth Greenshield; painter/printmaker/lecturer; *b* B'ham, 7 July, 1955; *s* of H.T. Bartlett, designer. *Exhib.:* (major Prizes): Stowells Trophy, Royal Overseas League, Spirit of London, Mid Art, Mid 25, Hunting Group, R.B.A., R.B.S.A., Alexon Women on Canvas; other exhbns.: R.A., V. & A., N.P.G., I.C.A. *Work repro.:* Alan Hutchison, Quarto, Dorling Kindersley. *Address:* 144 Wheelers Lane, Kings Heath, B'ham. B13 0SG. *Signs work:* "Paul Bartlett" or " P.T.B."

BARTOLO, Maria; painter in mixed media, including wax and varnish; *b* Cardiff, 7 Dec., 1967; *d* of N.A. Bartolo. *Educ.:* Oaklands R.C. Comprehensive; *studied art* at City and Guilds of London Art School (Roger de Grey). *Exhib.:* The Discerning Eye, Mall Galleries, Christie's, Sotheby's, R.A. Summer Show, Barbican. *Work in permanent collections:* Art Council, De Beers. *Work repro.:* R.A. magazine, C.V. magazine, Evening Standard Newspaper (four edns.). Winner of Evening Standard prize. *Address:* 23A Milner Sq., London N1.

BARTOLOME, Jaime, painter: 1958 Press Assoc., Barcelona, 1st Prix; 1970 Grand Prix New York, Nice (France), 2nd Prix; 1971 Grand Prix Paques, Nice, 2nd Prix; *b* Santander, Spain, 4 Apr., 1927. *Educ.:* Barcelona. *Exhib.:* Individual show in Barcelona, 1958-62-64-65 and 1969, Bilbao, 1966. Madrid, Palma, Mallorca, 1967; group shows in Barcelona, Madrid, Alicante, München, Italy, Sweden, Hong Kong, France. *Work in permanent collections:* Museum of Modern Art, Barcelona. *Address:* Studio, Diputación, 321, Barcelona, Spain. *Clubs:* Circulo Artistico "Saint Lluc," Instituto Estudios Hispanicos, Barcelona. *Signs work:* "Bartolomé."

BARTON, Patricia: see MYNOTT, Patricia.

BASIA: see WATSON-GANDY, Basia.

BASKO, Maurice P. Duviella, Dip. Salon Automne, France; Prize, Figuratif Chateau of Senaud, France; painter in oil and water-colour, art researcher; *b* Biarritz, 30 Sept., 1921; *s* of J.L. Duviella, contractor and art dealer. *Educ.:* Jules Ferry College, Biarritz; *studied art* at Academy Frochot, Paris. *Exhib.:* Museum of Modern Art, Paris, Salon Automne, Salon Bosio, Grand Prix, Pont Aven, Salon Art Libre, Paris, Salon Versailles, France, Paris Gallery, N.Y., Galerie Colise, Paris, Fontainebleu Gallery, N.Y.; one-man shows: Paris, N.Y., Lyon, Mallorca, Vichy, etc. *Work in permanent collections:* Guggenheim Museum, N.Y., Albertina Museum, Vienna, Museum of Modern Art, Miami, Public Library, N.Y.; and more than 400 works in private collections. *Address:* Résidence Arverna/Bloc C, 26 Ave. Lahouze, 64202 Biarritz, France. *Signs work:* "BASKO" and sometimes "Duviella."

BATCHELOR, Bernard Philip, R.W.S.; painter in water-colour and oil; *b* Teddington, May, 1924. *Trained* at St. Martin's School of Art (R. Kirkland Jamieson) and City and Guilds (A. R. Middleton Todd, R.A.); Company of Fanmakers Design Award (1950); David Murray Scholarship (1952). *Exhib.:* R.A., R.W.S. *Official purchases:* M.O.W. (1953), Richmond Parish Charity Lands (perm. records) 1976, Basildon Arts Trust, and various private collections. *Address:* 31 The Avenue, St. Margaret's-on-Thames, Middx. TW1 1QU. *Signs work:* "B. P. Batchelor" or "Bernard Batchelor" or "B.P.B."

BATEMAN, Robert McLellan, O.C., R.C.A., D.Litt., D.Sc., Ll.D., D.F.A.; artist in oil and acrylic; *b* Toronto, 24 May, 1930; *s* of J.W. Bateman, electrical engineer; *m* Birgit Freybe Bateman. *Studied art* at University of Toronto (1950-54, Carl Schaeffer). *Exhib.:* major one-man shows in museums throughout Canada and U.S.A. incl. Smithsonian Institution, Washington D.C. (1987) and the Joslyn Fine Arts Museum, Nebraska (1986); Tryon Gallery, London (1975, 1977, 1979, 1985); Le Conseil International de la Chasse et de la Conservation de Gibier, Monoco-extensive tour of Europe (1982). *Work in permanent collections:* the late Princess Grace of Monaco, H.R.H. Prince Philip, H.R.H. Prince Charles, H.R.H. Prince Bernhard, Hamilton Art Museum, Canada, Leigh Yawkey Woodson Art Museum, U.S.A. etc. *Commissions:* numerous. *Publications:* numerous articles, three major books and three films on Robert Bateman. *Address:* Box 115, Fulford Harbour, B.C. Canada V0S 1C0. *Clubs:* Life membership in numerous clubs and conservation organizations. *Signs work:* "Robert Bateman."

BATES, Joan Elliott, D.F.A. (Lond. 1952); painter, draughtsman and printmaker in oil, water-colour, gouache, drawing materials, etching and lithography; *b* Sheffield, 22 Jan., 1930; *d* of John Elliott, solicitor; *m* John F. Bates; three *s*. *Educ.:* Harrogate College; *studied art* at Sheffield College of Art (1947-49), Slade School of Fine Art (1949-52, Prof. William Coldstream). *Exhib.:* R.A. Summer Shows, N.E.A.C., R.O.I., R.W.S., R.I., R.B.A., R.W.A., R.E., The Hunting Award and in numerous galleries in London and the provinces. *Work repro.:* Quarto Publications. *Awards:* Laing Painting Competition 3rd prize (1981) 2nd prize (1984), Cornelissen award (1986). *Official purchases:* paintings in hospitals, The House of Commons. *Address:* 17 Marlow Mill, Mill Rd., Marlow, Bucks. SL7 1QD. *Signs work:* "J. Elliott" or "J.E."

BATES, Patricia Jane, B.Ed. (Lond.) (1976), M.F.P.S. (1980); artist in oil, oil collage, graphics, teacher; *b* Surbiton, 8 Jan., 1927; *d* of George Percival Simon (decd.); *m* Martin Colin Bates; one *s*, one *d*. *Educ.:* Priors Field, Godalming; *studied art* at Bartlett School of Architecture (1944-46), Epsom School of Art (1947-48), Byam Shaw (1952-53). *Exhib.:* one-man shows: Loggia

Gallery, London, Cranleigh Art Centre; mixed shows: Trends, N.S., Guildford, Westcott Gallery, Art Attack, Wallingford. *Work in private collections:* England and many other countries. *Address:* Brackenhurst, Wonham Way, Gomshall, Guildford, Surrey GU5 9NZ. *Signs work:* "PAT BATES" (sometimes "SIMON").

BATTERBURY, Reg., R.W.A., A.T.D., N.D.D.; painter (all mediums) and graphic designer; former Head Art Dept., Bristol Comprehensive School; Lecturer, Further Education, in Painting and Print Design; *b* London, 25 Apr., 1913. *Trained:* West Ham Municipal College of Art, St. Martin's College of Art, London, West of England College of Art. *Exhib.:* R.A. and West of England societies. *Work in permanent collections:* Private, including Longleat House, and American Museum, Bath. *Address:* 80 Dundridge La., Bristol BS5 8SJ. *Club:* Bristol Savages. *Signs work:* "Reg Batterbury, A.T.D., R.W.A."

BATTERSHILL, Norman James, R.B.A. (1973), R.O.I. (1976), P.S. (1976), F.S.I.A.D. (1968); R.O.I. Stanley Grimm award (1989); landscape painter in oil, pastel, acrylic and water-colour, author, tutor; *b* London, 23 Apr., 1922; *s* of Leslie Battershill, scenic artist; two *s,* three *d. Exhib.:* R.A., R.B.A., R.O.I., N.E.A.C., P.S., etc., numerous one man shows etc. *Work in permanent collections:* Ciba Geigy, Beechams, Post Office, etc. *Publications:* Light on the Landscape, Draw Trees, Drawing and Painting Skies, Draw Landscape, Draw Seascapes (Pitman Publishing), Working with Oils, Painting Flowers in Oils, Painting Landscapes in Oils, Drawing for Pleasure, Teach Yourself to Draw (Search Press Ltd., London; and Pentalic Corp. U.S.A.), Painting and Drawing Water (A. & C. Black Ltd., 1984), Learn to Paint Trees (Collins, 1990), Painting Gardens (Batsford 1994). *Address:* The Old School House, Woolland, Blandford Forum, Dorset. *Signs work:* "Norman Battershill."

BAWTREE, John Andrew, D.Arch (Kingston, 1977), A.R.B.A. (1982), R.B.A. (1984); Greenshield Foundation Award (1978, 1980); painter in oil on canvas; *b* Cheam, Surrey, 1 Nov., 1952; *s* of Harold Maurice Bawtree. *Educ.:* Bradfield College, Berks. (1966-70); *studied* at Kingston Polytechnic School of Architecture (1970-73, 1975-77). *Exhib.:* R.A., R.B.A., Richmond Gallery, London W1; one-man: Caius College, Cambridge, Christ Church, Oxford, Deben Gallery, Woodbridge, Aldeburgh Cinema Gallery, Falcon House, Boxford, Piers Feetham Gallery, London, Melitensia Gallery, Malta. *Work in permanent collection:* Greenshield Foundation, Montreal. *Address:* Pine View, Peasenhall, Suffolk IP17 2HZ. *Club:* Chelsea Arts. *Signs work:* "John Bawtree."

BAXANDALL, David, C.B.E. (1959), B.A.; director, National Galleries of Scotland (1952-70); asst. keeper (1928-39) and keeper (1939-41), Dept. of Art, National Museum of Wales; director of Manchester City Art Galleries (1945-52); *b* London, 11 Oct., 1905; *s* of David Baxandall, deceased; *m* Isobel Thomas; one *s,* two (twin) *d. Educ.:* King's College School, Wimbledon; University of London, King's College. *Publications:* Ben Nicholson, 1962; gallery handbooks and catalogues, numerous articles and broadcast talks. *Address:* 24 Guardian Ct., Ferrers St., Hereford HR1 2LP.

BAXTER, Denis Charles Trevor, F.R.S.A., U.A. (1986), Mem. Printmakers Council (1981), N.S. (1987), President, N.S. (1989); teacher, lecturer, artist in oil and etching; *b* Southsea, 1 Mar., 1936. *Educ.:* Ryde School, I.o.W.; *studied art:* Bournemouth and Poole College of Art (1964-65); Stockwell College, Bromley, Kent (1965-68). *Exhib.:* R.A., R.W.A., R.E., N.E.A.C., P.S., N.S., U.A. *Work in private collections:* Canada, France, Germany, Japan, Switzerland,

U.K., U.S.A. *Address:* 20 Church Rd., Southbourne, Bournemouth, Dorset BH6 4AT. *Club:* Chelsea Arts. *Signs work:* "Denis Baxter" or "D.B."

BAYLY, Clifford John, R.W.S. (1981), N.D.D. (1950); painter in oils, acrylic, water-colour, illustrator, lecturer, writer; *b* London, 1927; *s* of Paul Bayly; *m* Jean Oddell; two *s*, one *d. Studied art* at St. Martin's and Camberwell Schools of Art (Sir William Coldstream, Prof. Sir Lawrence Gowing). *Exhib.:* R.A., R.W.S., various galleries in U.K., also Sydney, Melbourne and Adelaide, Australia. *Work in permanent collections:* State Bank of S. Australia, Westpac Bank, T.V. South, Tricentrol, London. *Publications:* children's educational books, books on painting and drawing techniques. *Address:* The Stables, Oaks Farm, High St., Staplehurst, Tonbridge, Kent TN12 0BH. *Signs work:* "CLIFFORD BAYLY."

BAYNES, Pauline Diana, M.S.I.A.; designer and illustrator; *b* 1922; *studied art* at Farnham School of Art and Slade. *Books illustrated* include: A Treasury of French Tales, Farmer Giles of Ham and Tom Bombadil (Allen and Unwin), Arabian Nights and Fairy Tales of the British Isles (Blackie), seven Narnia Books by C. S. Lewis (Bles and Bodley Head), Sister Clare, Miracle Plays, St. George and the Dragon (Houghton Mifflin, U.S.A.), Dictionary of Chivalry (Longmans), Kate Greenaway Medal (1968), Companion to World Mythology (Kestrel Books, 1979). *Address:* Rock Barn Cottage, Dockenfield, nr. Farnham, Surrey GU10 4HH. *Signs work:* "PAULINE BAYNES"—occasionally with a small bird—see appendix.

BAYS, Jill, S.W.A. (1988), B.A. (Open)(1985); artist in water-colour and oil, teacher; *b* Ambala, India, 24 Nov., 1931; *d* of W.C. Burton, R.A.F. (decd.); *m* Bernard Bays; two *d. Educ.:* Sir William Perkins', Chertsey; *studied art* at Guildford School of Art (1947-51). *Exhib.:* R.I., S.WL.A., S.W.A., numerous shared exhbns. with husband and others. *Publication:* The Watercolourist's Garden (David and Charles, 1993). *Address:* Bayswater, Hamm Ct., Weybridge, Surrey KT13 8YB. *Signs work:* "Jill Bays."

BAZAINE, Jean; painter; *b* Paris, 1904. *Educ.:* L. ès L. *Work in permanent collections:* most important museums in Europe and America. *Awards:* Prix National des Arts (1964). Executed stained-glass windows for the church of Assy (1946), Saint Séverin, Paris (1966), Cathedrale St. Die (1986); ceramic mural and windows at Audincourt (1951-54); ceramic mural at U.N.E.S.C.O. (1960); Maison de l'O.R.T.F., Paris (1963), Se'nat, Paris (1986), Subway 'Cluny' (1987). *Exhib.:* Galerie Carré and Maeght, Paris, Retr. exhbn., Berne (1958), Eindhoven (1959), Hanover, Zürich, Oslo (1963), Paris (1965), Athènes, London, Edinburgh (1977), Oslo (1983), Maeght's Foundation (1987); repr. Biennele de Venice, São Paulo and Carnegie (member of the jury, 1952). *Publications:* Notes sur la peinture d'aujourd'hui (ed. Seuil, Paris, 1948), Exercise de la peinture (ed. Seuil, 1973). *Address:* 36 r. P. Brossolette 92140 Clamart.

BEAUVAIS, Walter John; artist in oil and water-colour; *b* Datchet, Bucks., 14 Mar., 1942; *s* of Arnold Beauvais (decd.), President, London Sketch Club; *g-s* of Charles Henri Beauvais (decd.), artist and lithographer; *m* Anne Veronica; one *s*, one *d. Educ.:* Staines Grammar School; *studied art* under Arnold Beauvais in his London, Paris and Rome studios. *Exhib.:* regular annual exhbns. both national and international. *Work in permanent collections:* two royal and many international. *Address:* Englefield Green, Surrey. *Club:* Chelsea Arts. *Gallery affiliation:* John Campbell Gallery, 164 Walton St., London SW3 2JL. *Signs work:* see appendix.

BECK, Stuart, R.S.M.A. (1980); artist in water-colour and oil; former technical illustrator and graphic designer; *b* London, 18 June, 1903; *s* of the late Capt. E. D. Beck, master mariner; *m* Jane Gwendoline (decd.); one *s*, one *d*. *Educ.:* Kings School, Rochester; *studied art:* at Rochester School of Art (1919-21). *Exhib.:* R.S.M.A., R.B.A., S.G.A., etc. Abroad: R.S.M.A. (Vancouver 1982), Paris (1984), New Zealand (1984), R.S.M.A. (Mystic Seaport, U.S.A. 1987), Dusseldorf (1987). *Work in permanent collections:* National Maritime Museum, Greenwich, R.N.L.I. Museum, Poole. *Publications:* How to Draw Fishing Craft; How to Draw Pleasure Craft; Ships, Boats and Craft; The Ship, how she Works. *Address:* 22 Parish Ct., Emsworth Rd., Lymington, Hants. SO41 9BS. *Signs work:* "STUART BECK."

BECKER, Haidee; draughtsman, painter in oil; *b* Los Angeles, Calif., 13 Jan., 1950; *d* of John Becker, writer; *m* David Kenedy; one *s*, one *d*. *Educ.:* French Lycée; *studied art* with Uli Nimptsch, R.A., Elizabeth Keys, Adrian Ryan. *Exhib.:* R.P., H.A.C., R.A., Ben Uri, Roland, Browse & Delbanco, New Grafton, C.D. Soar & Son, Odette Gilbert Gallery, Timothy Tuv Galerie, Atlanta, Georgia; managed by Odette Gilbert Gallery, 5 Cork St., London W1. *Work in permanent collection:* N.P.G. *Address:* 46 Glebe Pl., London SW3 5JE. *Signs work:* "Becker."

BEDDINGTON, Roy; landscape painter (especially water-colour); illustrator; *b* 16 June, 1910; *s* of Reginald Beddington, C.B.E.; *m* Diana Dobson. *Educ.:* Rugby; Corpus Christi College, Oxford; *studied art* at Slade School (Prof. Schwabe) and Florence. *Exhib.:* R.A., New English Art Club, Brighton, Huddersfield, Eastbourne, Ackermann's, R.W.S., Walker Galleries. *Work repro.:* illustrations to numerous books, etc., and contributions to Country Life, Field, etc. *Publications:* The Adventures of Thomas Trout (Methuen), To be a Fisherman (Geoffrey Bles), The Pigeon and the Boy (Geoffrey Bles), Pindar—a dog to remember (Michael Joseph, 1975). *Poetry:* A Countryman's Verse. *Address:* Home Farm, Chute Cadley, nr. Andover, Hants. SP11 9EB. *Clubs:* F.R.S.A., Arts Club. *Signs work:* "Roy Beddington."

BEECROFT, Glynis: see OWEN, Glynis.

BEESON, Jane; Arnolfini Open Competition prize winner, 1963; painter in P.V.A., oil and enamel; *b* Weybridge, Surrey, 10 Apr., 1930; *d* of Sir Noel Bowater, Bt.; *m* Christopher Beeson; three *s*, one *d*. *Studied art* at Kingston School of Art, Surrey (1949-51); Beaux Arts, Paris (1951-52), under Brianchon; Slade, London (1953). *Exhib.:* John Moore's (1961); London exhib., Rowan Gallery and New Art Centre; Arnolfini, Bristol. *Work in permanent collections:* "Mauve and Yellow" bought by Director, Ferens Art Gallery, Hull. *Address:* Ford Farm, Manaton, S. Devon. *Signs works:* "J. Beeson."

BEESTON, Enid, A.S.A.F. (1975); landscape and portrait painter in oil and water-colour; Mem. Womens Inst. National Art Com.; *b* 3 Jan., 1918; *d* of Rev. J.R. Edwards; *m* Charles E. Beeston; one *s*, one *d*. *Educ.:* London; *studied art* at Kathleen Browne School of Painting, Avenue Studios, Chelsea (Kathleen Browne, Marian Kratochwil). *Exhib.:* Paris Salon, R.O.I., National Society, Hesketh Hubbard Art Soc., Chenil Galleries, Chelsea, Croydon Art Soc., Nicosia, Cyprus, Canterbury Art Soc., Guildhall, London; one-man show, Mall Galleries. *Address:* Marley Brooks, Preston, Canterbury, Kent. *Signs work:* "Enid Beeston."

BEILBY, Pauline Margaret, N.D.D. (1950); portrait and equestrian sculptor in clay, textile designer, freelance; *b* Bramcote, Notts., 21 June, 1927; *d* of Percy Goold Beilby; *m* Keith David Barnes, lace manufacturer; two *s*. *Educ.:*

Nottingham Girls' High School; *studied art* at Nottingham College of Arts and Crafts under A. H. Rodway, A.R.C.A., F.R.S.A., principal. *Address:* Burleigh House, 15 Albemarle Rd., Woodthorpe, Notts. NG5 4FE. *Signs work:* see appendix.

BELL, Stanley Fraser, D.A. (Mural Design) Glasgow (1970); artist in mixed media reliefs and painted murals; Lecturer, Glasgow School of Art; *b* Glasgow, 12 Jan., 1928; *s* of the late John Armour Bell; *m* Catherine MacDonald; one *s*. *Studied art* at Glasgow School of Art (1966-70). *Exhib.:* Scottish Young Contemporaries (1969, 1970, 1971), The Clyde Group, Edinburgh (1971), John Player Bienalle 2 Touring Exhbn. (1971), 'With Murals in Mind' Acheson House, Edinburgh (1974), Glasgow League of Artists Group shows 'Un Certain Art Anglais' Paris, Brussels (1979). *Work in permanent collections:* large scale exterior murals in Glasgow. *Address:* 419 North Woodside Rd., Glasgow G20 6NN. *Club:* Glasgow Art. *Signs work:* "Stan Bell."

BELLANY, John, D.A. (Edin.), M.A. (Fine Arts), A.R.C.A., A.R.A., Hon. R.S.A.; artist in oil, water-colour, etching; *b* Port Seton, Scotland, 18 June, 1942; *s* of Richard Bellany; *m* Helen; two *s*, one *d*. *Educ.:* Preston Lodge, Prestonpans, Scotland; *studied art* at Edinburgh College of Art (1960-65), R.C.A. (1965-68). *Exhib.:* one-man shows in major galleries and museums throughout the world. *Work in permanent collections:* National Galleries of Scotland, N.P.G., Tate Gallery, V. & A., etc. *Publication:* John Bellany — Retrospective (Scottish National Gallery of Modern Art). *Address:* 59 North Side, Clapham Common, London SW4 9SA. *Signs work:* "John Bellany."

BELSEY, Hugh Graham, B.A. (1976), M.Litt. (1981); museum curator; Curator, Gainsborough's House; *b* Hemel Hempstead, 15 May, 1954; *s* of Graham Miles Belsey, F.M.I.C.E. *Educ.:* University of Manchester and The Barber Inst. of Fine Arts, Birmingham. *Publications:* articles for art periodicals and exhbn. catalogues. *Address:* Gainsborough's House, 46 Gainsborough St., Sudbury, Suffolk CO10 6EU.

BELSKY, Franta, A.R.C.A., F.R.B.S., P.P.S.P.S.; *b* Brno, 1921; *m* Margaret C. Owen (d. 1989). *Studied sculpture* at Prague Academy, R.C.A. (Hons. Dip.). *Work in permanent collections:* The Queen, Queen Mother, Universities, N.P.G., Europe and U.S.A., c. councils, ind. and pte. companies, e.g., "Joy-ride," Stevenage; "Triga," Tattersalls, Knightsbridge; "Lesson," Bethnal Green; "Astronomer Herschel," Slough; "Oracle," Temple Way, Bristol, "Totem," Arndale Centre, Manchester; Admiral Cunningham, Trafalgar Square; Mountbatten Memorial, Horse Guards Parade; Winston Churchill statue, Fulton, Missouri; Winston Churchill sculpture, Prague; Harry S. Truman, Pres. Library, Independence; Lord Cottesloe, National Theatre; fountains: Shell Centre, London; "Leap," Jamestown Harbour, London Dockland. *Address:* 4 The Green, Sutton Courtenay, Oxford OX14 4AE.

BELTON, Leslie Frederick, D.F.C. (1945), A.T.D. (1934), F.R.S.A. (1958); artist in pastel, water-colour, conte, teacher, cabinet maker; *b* Birmingham, 1912; *s* of E. J. G. Belton; *m* Helen G. Rodgers; one *s*, one *d*. *Educ.:* King Edward VI's School, Birmingham; *studied art* at College of Art, Birmingham (1929-34). *Exhib.:* R.A., R.B.A., P.S., N.S., Birmingham, Rye, Winchester, Southampton, Basingstoke, Swindon, Marlborough, Reading, Isle of Wight. *Work in permanent collections:* Reading A.G., Swindon A.G., R.A.F. College, Cranwell. *Address:* 132 Westwood Rd., Tilehurst, Reading, Berks. RG3 6LL. *Club:* Basingstoke Art. *Signs work:* "Leslie F. Belton" (on furniture, a belt carved or inlaid).

BELTRAN, Felix, B.A., B.Sc.; American Inst. of Graphic Arts, N.Y. (1961), Internationale Buchkunst Ausstellung, Leipzig (1971), Bienale Uzite Grafiky, Brno (1972), International Print Biennale, Listowel (1980); painter, printmaker, illustrator; Titular Prof. Universidad Autónoma Metropolitana, México; *b* Havana, 23 June, 1938; *s* of Joaquín Beltrán, industrial designer; *m* Lassie Sobera; one *d. Educ.:* Colegio Cubano Arturo Montori, Havana; *studied art* at School of Visual Arts, N.Y., American Art School, N.Y. *Exhib.:* Rousski Gallery, Sofia; Galerie Manes, Praha; Sala Ocre, Caracas; Galería Elisava, Barcelona. *Work in permanent collections:* Museo de Arte Contemporaneo, Panamá; Brooklyn Museum, N.Y.; Museo de Bellas Artes, Caracas; Muzeum Sztuki, Lodz; National Museum, Stockholm; Museum Narodowe, Warsaw. *Publications:* Desde el Diseño (Havana, 1970), Artes Plásticas (Havana, 1982). *Address:* Apartado M-10733, México 06000 DF, México. *Clubs:* World Print Council, San Francisco, Print Club, Philadelphia, L'Accademia d'Europa, Parma, Assoc. Internationale des Arts Plastiques, Paris. *Signs work:* see appendix.

BENENSON, Leslie Charlotte, R.E. (1978), N.D.D. (1962), S.S.I. (1964), S.E.A. (1979); sculptor, painter, engraver and calligrapher in resin casting, ceramic sculpture, wood, water-colour, wood engraving, calligraphy on vellum; *b* London, 13 Jan., 1941; *d* of Marcel Benenson, L.S.C. (Antwerp University). *Educ.:* La Sagesse Convent High School, London; *studied art* at Regent St. Polytechnic (1958-63) under Geoffrey H. Deeley, A.R.C.A., James Osborne, R.E.; privately (calligraphy) with Anthony Wood, F.R.S.A. (1963-64). *Exhib.:* one-man shows: John Gage Gallery, Eastbourne (1975), Michelham Priory (1971, 1976), Rye A.G. (1971); group shows: R.A. (1966, 1967, 1969-72), R.E. (from 1968); V. & A. (1971, 1979), Linz, Austria (1980), Sint-Niklaas, Antwerp, Belgium (1981), Biała Podlaska, Poland (1981). *Work in permanent collection:* Towner Gallery, Eastbourne, Ashmolean, Oxford, Hereford Museum, International Exlibriscentrum, Sint-Niklaas. *Publication:* illustrated, Coursing (The Standfast Press, 1976). *Address:* Roselands, 138 Barnhorn Rd., Little Common, Bexhill, E. Sussex. *Signs work:* see appendix.

BENHAM, Clive Graham, R.B.S.A., City and Guilds (1951); teacher/artist in wood (wood carving, sculpture and cabinet making); Retd. Head of Dept. Careers Education; V.P.R.B.S.A. (1984-87); *b* Melbourne, Australia, 23 Sept., 1929; *s* of Leonard H. Benham; *m* Doreen Hazel; two *s. Studied art* at Moseley Rd. School of Art, B'ham College of Arts and Crafts (A. Gregory), Aston Technical College (now B'ham Polytechnic). *Exhib.:* joint shows, lectures and demonstrations in Wales and the Midlands. *Address:* 53 Spiceland Rd., Northfield, Birmingham B31 1NL. *Club:* Chairman and organiser 'Winter Salon' Group of Artists. *Signs work:* "C. Graham Benham."

BENJAMIN, Anthony; artist in sculpture, painting and print-making; *b* 29 Mar., 1931. *Studied art* at F. Leger Studio, Paris (1951), Atelier 17 (1957). *Work in permanent collections:* Museum of Modern Art, N.Y.; Tate Gallery, London; V. & A., London; Museum of Modern Art, Japan; Museum of Modern Art, Poland; Museum of Modern Art, Yugoslavia; Albright-Knox Gallery, U.S.A.; J. Hershon Museum of Contemporary Art, U.S.A., etc. *Publication:* Empty Swings (Two Printers Press, 1965). *Dealers:* Gimpel Fils, London, Graffiti, London, Mira Godard, Toronto. *Publishers:* Christies Contemporary Art, London. *Address:* Lowes Farm, Kelling, Holt, Norfolk NR25 7EB. *Signs work:* see appendix.

BENNETT, Brian Theodore Norton, M.A. Oxon. (1954), R.O.I. (1973), P.R.O.I. (1987), N.S. (1985), Hon. U.A. (1985); landscape painter in oil;

Director of Art, Berkhamsted School; *b* Olney, Bucks., 1927; *s* of Horace T. Bennett; *m* Margrit Elizabeth Brenner. *Educ.:* Magdalen College School, Oxford and Magdalen College, Oxford; *studied art* at Ruskin School of Art, Oxford (1950) part-time; Regent St. Polytechnic (1956) evening classes. *Exhib.:* R.A., R.B.A., R.O.I., R.S.M.A., etc. *Publications:* Choir Stalls of Chester Cathedral (1965), Oil Painting with a Knife (1993). *Address:* 18 Upper Ashlyns Rd., Berkhamsted, Herts. HP4 3BW. *Signs work:* "Brian Bennett" or "B.T.N.B."

BENNETT, June, N.D.D., A.T.D.; painter/jeweller in silver and gold; *b* Grange over Sands; *d* of E. B. Steer; *m* Michael Bennett; two *s. Educ.:* Ulverston G.S.; *studied art* at Lancaster and Leicester Colleges of Art. *Exhib.:* Goldsmiths Hall, Midland Group Gallery, Nottingham, Park Square Gallery, Leeds, Mignon Gallery, Bath, Ashgate Gallery, Farnham; one-man shows, Castlegate House Gallery, Cockermouth (1988, 1989, 1991). *Work in permanent collections:* Jewellery: Abbot Hall Gallery, Kendal, Shipley A.G.; Paintings: Carlisle Museum and A.G., Copeland C.C. Painting full time from 1987. *Address:* The Hollies, Port Carlisle, Cumbria. CA5 5BU. *Signs work:* "June Bennett," "J.B." and Sheffield Assay Office hallmark.

BENNETT, Michael, N.D.D., A.T.D.: painter in oils; *b* Windermere, 1934; *s* of T. W. Bennett; *m* June Steer; two *s. Educ.:* Windermere Grammar School; *studied art* at Lancaster and Leicester Colleges of Art. *Exhib.:* one-man shows: Park Square Gallery, Leeds, Mignon Gallery, Bath, Bluecoat Gallery, Liverpool, Ashgate Gallery, Farnham, Abbot Hall, Kendal, A.I.A. Gallery, London; Leeds, Birmingham, Hull and Lancaster Universities, Castlegate Gallery, Cockermouth. *Work in permanent collections:* Abbot Hall Gallery, Wakefield City A.G., Lincolnshire Arts Assoc., John Player Collection, Leeds Educ. Authority, Kettle's Yard, Univ. of Cambridge and Northern Arts Assoc. *Address:* The Hollies, Port Carlisle, Carlisle, Cumbria. CA5 5BU. *Signs work:* "Bennett" and date.

BENNETT, Terence, N.D.D., F.R.S.A., Yorkshire Television Fine Art Fellowship (1973-74); painter in oil on canvas, teacher; Head of Fine Art, Thomas Rotherham College, Rotherham; *b* Doncaster, 7 Nov., 1935. *Studied art* at Doncaster School of Art (Eric Platt, T.A. Anderson). *Exhib.:* R.A., R.O.I., N.E.A.C., Drian Gallery, Travelling exhbn. Yorkshire, Lincolnshire, N.S., British Painting, Mall Galleries. *Work in permanent collections:* Nuffield Foundation, Bank of England, Yorkshire Television, Yorkshire Arts Assoc., Leeds Educ. Authority, Halifax Bldg. Soc., Sheffield University, Cambridge University, Doncaster Borough Council, I.C.I. Ltd . *Address:* Rambler Cottage, 43 Main St., Sprotbrough, Doncaster, S. Yorks. DN5 7RH. *Signs work:* "Terence Bennett."

BENNETT, William, R.M.S.; freelance artist of miniature portraits, still life and marine paintings in water-colour and oil; Council mem. R.M.S.; *b* London, 21 June, 1917; *s* of Cecil Percy Bennett, merchant; *m* Isabel Weaver; one *s*, one *d. Educ.:* Heritage School; *studied art* at Sir John Cass College, London. *Exhib.:* R.A., F.B.A. Gallery. *Work in permanent collections:* H.M. The Queen Elizabeth II Collection, Balmoral Galleries, Geelong, Australia, Manyung Gallery, Mt. Eliza, Victoria, Australia. *Addresses:* 2 Crossingfield Drive, Exmouth, Devon EX8 3LP; and Route d'Hennebont, St. Yves 56310 Bubry, Morbihan, France. *Signs work:* monogram of initials — see appendix and "Wm. Bennett."

BENNEY, Prof. Adrian Gerald Sallis, R.D.I. (1971), Hon. M.A. (Leics., 1963), Des. R.C.A. (1954); goldsmith and silversmith; Visiting Professor of Silversmithing and Jewellery at Royal College of Art (1974-83); *b* Hull, 21 Apr., 1930; *s* of Ernest Alfred Sallis Benney, A.R.C.A.; *m* Janet Edwards; three *s*, one *d. Educ.:* Brighton Grammar School; *studied art* at Brighton College of Art (1946-50); Royal College of Art (1951-54) under Prof. Robert Gooden, R.D.I. Royal Warrants of Appointment to H.M. The Queen (1974), Queen Elizabeth, The Queen Mother (1975), H.R.H. The Duke of Edinburgh (1975) and H.R.H. The Prince of Wales (1980). *Address:* Beenham House, Beenham, nr. Reading, Berks. RG7 5LJ. *Signs work:* "Gerald Benney."

BENSON, Rosemary, A.R.E. (1993); artist in engraving, water-colour and oil; *b* Malawi, 1948; *m* Mark Burgess, author and illustrator. *Educ.:* Livingstone High School, Zambia; Cambridge High School for Girls; *studied art* at Cambridge College of Arts and Technology (1965-67), Michaelis School of Fine Art, University of Cape Town (1973-75), Slade School of Fine Art (1977-79). *Exhib.:* R.A., R.E., R.W.S. *Address:* 137 Ivydale Rd., London SE15 3DX.

BENSUSAN-BUTT, John Gordon; landscape painter in water-colour; *b* Colchester, 6 June, 1911; *s* of Geoffrey Crawford Bensusan-Butt, F.C.A. *Educ.:* Gresham's School, Holt; Magdalen College, Oxford; *studied art* as pupil of Lucien Pissarro (1935-39), and at R.C.A., etching (1935), Central School of Art and Crafts, lithography (1939). *Exhib.:* R.A., N.E.A.C., R.B.A., Leicester Galleries, Redfern, etc. One-man shows at French Gallery (1937), Kensington A.G. (1949), Leicester Galleries (1957), Minories, Colchester (1962, 1964, 1975), Ashmolean (Eldon Gallery) Oxford (1986). *Publications:* On Naturalness in Art (1981), Thomas Gainsborough in his Twenties (1993). *Address:* 31B Lexden Rd., Colchester CO3 3PX. *Signs work:* see appendix.

BENT, Medora Heather, F.I.A.L.; painter in oil, water-colour; from 1965 has taken up pottery; *b* North Kilworth, family home and chief influence, Connemara; *m* Roger Bent; one *s. Educ.:* The Laurels, Rugby, and Upper Chine, I.O.W.; *studied art* at Slade School (1930-33), Diploma under Professor Schwabe; Central School of Arts and Crafts: stained glass, pottery and modelling; worked in Ireland, France, Hungary, Sark and Belgium. *Exhib.:* N.E.A.C., London Group, S.G.A., S.W.A., Nat. Soc. *Publication:* Paintings of Historical Houses of Purbeck (1958). *Address:* 10 East St., Wareham, Dorset. *Signs work:* "M. H. Bent."

BENTON, Graham, N.D.D. (1964), A.R.B.S.A. (1986); abstract painter/illustrator in oil, gouache, collage, charcoal, pastel; part-time art tutor; Chairman, Walsall Arts Council; Sec. Walsall Soc. of Artists; Council, R.B.S.A.; Associate mem. Penwith Soc. of Arts; Mem. N.S.E.A.D.; *b* Birmingham, 24 Oct., 1934; *s* of Sidney Benton. *Studied art* at Walsall School of Art (1952-56, George Willott, Angus Macauley), Wolverhampton College of Art (1962-64, John Finnie, Bernard Brett). *Exhib.:* Stafford A.G., Lichfield A.G., Walsall A.G., Letchworth A.G., 273 Gallery, London, Keele University, Salthouse Gallery, St. Ives, Penlee House, Penzance, R.B.S.A. *Address:* 17 Clarendon St., Bloxwich, Walsall, W. Midlands. *Signs work:* "(Graham) Benton" - see appendix.

BERESFORD-WILLIAMS, Mary E., B.A.Hons. Fine Art, Reading (1953 Class 1); Cert. Educ. (1954); painter, printmaker and photographer; mem. Newlyn Society of Artists; mem. Devon Guild of Craftsmen; *b* London, 30 Apr., 1931; *d* of F. N. Elliott; *m* David Beresford-Williams; one *s. Educ.:* Watford Grammar School; *studied painting* at Reading University under Prof. J. A. Betts. Since 1970 made many screen prints, sold in limited editions. South-West Arts Major Award (1978). Photographer in Residence, Television South-West (1986-87). 1988 book: A Portrait of TSW. Paintings and prints in public and private collections. *Address:* 11 Langdon Lane, Galmpton, nr. Brixham, S. Devon. *Signs work:* "M. Beresford-Williams" or "MBW."

BERG, Adrian, R.A.; Gold medal, Florence Biennale (1973), major prize, Tolly Cobbold (1981), third prize, John Moores (1982); painter; *b* London, 1929. *Educ.:* Charterhouse; Caius College, Cambridge (M.A.); Trinity College, Dublin (H.Dip.Ed.); *studied art* at St. Martin's (1955-56), Chelsea (1956-58), R.C.A. (1958-61). *Exhib.:* 5, Tooth's (1964-75); 3, Waddington Galleries (1978-83), Waddington Galleries, Montreal, Toronto (1979), Rochdale A.G. (1980), 5, Piccadilly Gallery (1985-93), Serpentine Gallery, Walker A.G. (1986), Barbican Touring Exhbn. (1993-94). *Work in permanent collections:* Arts Council, British Council, B.M., European Parliament, Govt. Picture Coll., Hiroshima City Museum of Contemporary Art, Tate Gallery, Tokyo Metropolitan Art Museum. *Address:* c/o Piccadilly Gallery, 16 Cork St., London W1X 1PF. *Signs work:* "Adrian Berg."

BERGMANN, Catherine; artist in water-colour, gouache, pastel; *b* London, 11 Dec., 1952; *d* of Jack Fedor Bergmann, LL.B., solicitor. *Educ.:* Streatham Hill and Clapham High School, G.P.D.S.T.; *studied art* at Kingston Polytechnic (fashion design, 1974-76); designed clothes for own label (1976-82). *Exhib.:* International House, St. Katherine's Dock, London; one-man shows: The Wine Gallery, Fulham, Hallam Gallery, Ebury Galleries (various shows), Wykeham Gallery, Barnes, Chelsea Art Soc., Felpham Gallery, Sussex. *Address:* Vine Cottage, Leech La., Headley, Surrey KT18 6PJ. *Signs work:* "C. Bergmann."

BERLIN, Sven; sculptor in stone, painter and writer; *b* 14 Sept., 1911; *s* of Karl Berlin, Swedish; mother English; two *s*, one *d*. *Educ.:* St. Winifred's, Kenley; *studied art* at Redruth, Cornwall, under A. C. Hambly. *Exhib.:* Lefevre, Tooth's, London, Houston, Texas, New York, etc, *Work in permanent collections:* Tate Gallery, V. & A., B.M., Musee de la Bataille de Normandie (1944), Nat. Library of Scotland, Musee d'Art, Ovar, Portugal, Imperial War Museum, I.S.R., Fawley, Poole Technical College, Lord Weymouth, Longleat. *Publications:* Alfred Wallis; Primitive (Nicholson & Watson, 1948), I Am Lazarus (Dent, 1961), Dark Monarch (Dent, 1962), Jonah's Dream (Dent, 1964), Dromengro (Collins, 1971), Pride of the Peacock (Collins, 1972), Amergin (David and Charles, 1978), Coat of Many Colours (Redcliffe Press, 1993). *Address:* Old Keeper's Cottage, Gaunts, Wimborne, Dorset BH21 4JS. *Signs work:* see appendix.

BERNARD, Paul, A.T.D.C.; painter/designer in oil and acrylic, lecturer; *b* London, 20 June, 1929; *s* of George Patterson Rose, hairdresser; *m* Carole Bright; one *d*. *Educ.:* Lyon Park/Alperton Senior; *studied art* at Ealing School of Art (1943-46, Miss Palmer, Miss Owen, Miss Ockenden). *Exhib.:* twenty-two one-man shows including Avgarde, Manchester (1960), Belgrade Theatre, Coventry (1960), St. Martin's Gallery, London (1963-66), Compendium, London (1970), Brangwyn Gallery, London (1975), Collective Design, Kingston (1975), Ramair, Reigate (1982), British Academy of Film and Television Arts, London (1985), Ginnel Gallery, Manchester (1988), La Galerie, Moraira, Spain (1990-91), Centre Gallery, Bletchingley (1989-91-92), Guildhall Gallery, Winchester (1992). *Address:* 37 Fengates Rd., Redhill, Surrey RH1 6AQ. *Club:* B.A.F.T.A. *Signs work:* "Paul" or "Paul Bernard."

BERRISFORD, Peter, N.D.D., A.T.D., F.R.S.A. (1986); painter (oils, watercolours), lecturer, (Arts Council, National Trust, National Association of Decorative and Fine Art Societies, etc.). Since 1970, Guest Lecturer for Swans (Hellenic) Italian Tours; *b* Northampton, 11 Feb., 1932; *s* of Ernest Berrisford;

m Jacqueline; one *s*. *Studied art* at Northampton, Chelsea, Bournemouth Art Colleges (Travelling Scholarship 1953). *Exhib.:* Bear Lane, Wildensteins, Piccadilly Gallery, Trafford Gallery, London, R.B.A., R.A., John Moore's, regularly at Melitensia Gallery, Malta. *Work in permanent collections;* Hertfordshire, Hull, Surrey, Leicester, Sheffield, Northampton, Wales University, East Sussex C.C. Lithographs: New York Book of Month Club, Curwen Studios. Paintings for B.B.C.'s 'The Clothes in the Wardrobe' and 'The House of Eliott' (filmed 1992 and 1993). *Address:* 73 Woodgate Rd., Eastbourne BN22 8PD. *Signs work:* oils "Berrisford," water-colours "Peter Berrisford."

BERRY, June, D.F.A.Lond. (1948), R.E. (1986), R.W.S. (1993), N.E.A.C. (1990), A.R.W.A. (1993); artist in etching and water-colour; *b* Melbourne, Derbyshire; *d* of Edwin Reeve; *m* John Berry; one *s*, two *d*. *Educ.:* Boston Lincs.; *studied art* at Slade School of Fine Art (1941-42, 1946-49). *Exhib.:* R.A., R.E., R.W.S., and in Germany and U.S.A. *Work in permanent collections:* Graphotek, Berlin, National Museum of Wales, Kettering A.G., Oldham A.G. *Publication:* Limited Edn. Livre d'Artiste 'Passing Days' (1984). *Address:* 45 Chancery La., Beckenham, Kent BR3 2NR. *Signs work:* "June Berry."

BERRY-HART, David James, M.A.; painter and sculptor; *b* Trinidad, 1940; *s* of Ralph and Alice Berry-Hart. *Studied art* at St. Martin's School of Art (1959-1961), City of Birmingham Polytechnic (1981-83). *Exhib.:* one-man shows: A.I.A. Gallery, London (1969), Herbert A.G. Coventry (1970), Camden Arts Centre (1975), University of Warwick (1977), Imperial College (1979); Royal National College for the Blind (1979); Cannon Hill Park (1979); Whitefriars Coventry (1988), mid-Warwickshire College Gallery (1990), Worcester City A.G. (1991); group: Spectrum Central (1971), Art in Steel (1972), Gawthorpe Festival (1974), On the Town sculpture (1987); as member of "The Firm". exhib. Hampshire (Touring) (1983-4), Carlisle A.G. (1984), Liverpool University (1985), Williamson A.G. (1986), Beecroft A.G. (1987), Chelmsford A.G. (1987). *Work repro.:* Midlands Arts Magazine, Spectrum Central Catalogue. *Awards:* Arts Council (1975), West Midlands Arts Association (1978). *Address:* 13 Tennant St., Nuneaton, Warwickshire CV11 4NT. *Signs work:* D.J.B-H.

BERTHOLD: see DUNNE, Berthold.

BEST, Ronald O'Neal; Artist in Residence, Essendine Art Centre, London; artist in oil, teacher; *b* London, 25 May, 1957. *Educ.:* Sladebrook High School, London; *studied art* at Byam Shaw School of Art; Croydon College of Art; R.C.A. London; Asst. to Winston Branch, painter. *Exhib.:* R.O.I., N.E.A.C., P.S., S.G.A., Salon des National, Paris, Lynn Stern Young Artists, London, Eva Jekel Gallery, Twentieth Century British Art Fair, R.C.A. London, 1492-1992 Un Nouveau Regard sur les Caraibes, Paris, Art House, Amsterdam, President Portobello Group, Pall Mall Deposit Gallery, the Portobello Group. *Work in permanent collection:* R.C.A., Croydon College, Grange Museum, London. *Address:* 51 Exton Cres., Stonebridge, London NW10 8DA. *Clubs:* H.H.A.S., B.A.R. *Signs work:* "Ronald Best."

BETHEL, David, C.B.E., LL.D.(Leic.), D.Litt. (Lough), A.R.W.A., F.R.S.A., N.D.D., A.T.D., F.S.A.E., F.C.S.D.; graphic and typographic designer; Director, Leicester Polytechnic (1973-87); Chairman, CNAA Committee for Art and Design (1974-80); mem. Design Council (1980-88); Chairman, Design Council Educ. Advisory Com. (1981-88); Hong Kong University and Polytechnic Grants Com. (1982-92); Chairman, Provisional Council for Academic Awards, Hong Kong (1986-89); Chairman, Hong Kong Council for Academic Accreditation

(1990-92); Chairman, Education and Training Committee, Chartered Society of Designers (1987-90); *b* Bath, 7 Dec., 1923, *s* of Wm. Geo. Bethell; *m* Margaret; one *s*, one *d*. *Educ.:* King Edward's School, Bath; *studied art* at Gloucester College of Art (1946-48), West of England College of Art (1948-51). *Work in permanent collections:* Gloucester and Stafford Art Galleries, R.W.A., and private collections in U.S.A. and Israel. *Address:* 48 Holmfield Rd., Stoneygate, Leicester LE2 1SA. *Signs work:* "David Bethel."

BETHEL, Marion Ross; illuminator and letterer in water-colour, gold leaf, ink, parchment in illuminated books; *b* Wiesbaden, Germany, 19 Mar., 1929; *d* of Herbert H. Bethel, D.D.S. (U.S.A.). *Educ.:* P.N.E.U. correspondence course; *studied art* with Gladys Best, R.W.A., and Daisy Alcock, A.R.C.A., F.R.S.A. *Exhib.:* Salon de Soc. des Artistes Français. *Work repro.:* in Revue Moderne. *Address:* 17 Strand, Topsham, Devon. *Signs work:* "M.R.B." or "Marion Ross Bethel."

BEVAN, Daniel Vaughan Gwillim, R.I.; artist in water-colour; *b* Cardiff, 8 June, 1921; *s* of Daniel Thomas Bevan; *m* Betty Eileen, divorced; two *d*. *Educ.:* Willesden and Hendon Technical Colleges. *Address:* Bryn Glas, Garndolbenmaen, Gwynedd, LL51 9UX. *Signs work:* "Vaughan Bevan."

BEVAN, Oliver, A.R.C.A. (1964); painter in oil, pastel, monoprint; *b* Peterborough, 28 Mar., 1941; *s* of David Bevan, painter, photographer, garden designer. *Educ.:* Eton; *studied art* at R.C.A. (Carel Weight, Colin Hayes, Leonard Rosoman). *Exhib.:* Angela Flowers Gallery (1981), Odette Gilbert Gallery (1984), Gallery 10 (1991), "City/Two Views" with Ron Bowen, Barbican (1986); exhib. in and curated "The Subjective City" touring exhbn. (1990-91), Witnesses and Dreamers. *Work in permanent collections:* Contemporary Art Soc., Museum of London, Cleveland Gallery, Unilever, Sainsbury, Guildhall A.G. *Publications:* articles for art magazines and catalogues. *Address:* 130 Percy Rd., London W12 9QL. *Signs work:* signed on back "Oliver Bevan" – elongated vertical in "B"; works on paper initialled "O.B." plus two digit date, e.g. "OB'87."

BEVAN, Tony, Dip.A.D. (1974), H.D.F.A. (1976); painter in acrylic and oil; *b* Bradford, 1951; *partner* Glenys Johnson; one *d*. *Studied art* at Bradford College of Art (1968-71), Goldsmiths' College (1971-74), Slade School of Fine Art (1974-1976). *Exhib.:* I.C.A. London touring Britain (1980-87), Haus der Kunst Munich (1989), Kunsthalle Kiel (1988), Whitechapel A.G. (1993). *Work in permanent collections:* Staats Galerie Moderner Kunst Munich, Kunsthalle Kiel, Metropolitan Museum of Art N.Y., Yale University, B.M., Theo Wormland Foundation Munich, British Council, Arts Council. *Address:* Studio 2, Acme Studios, 165 Childers St., London SE8 5JR. *Signs work:* "Bevan."

BEVIS, Michael John Vaughan, Cert Ed., A.I.E., A.R.P.S., F.R.S.A., M.F.P.S., M.CollP., D.F.A. (Painting); Head of Art and Design Dept., St. Peter's High School, Burnham-on-Crouch; artist in oil, photographer; *b* London, 11 Oct., 1948; *s* of the late Albert John Bevis, actor stage manager; *m* Marie Janice Gair; two *d*. *Educ.:* Clarks College (1960-65); *studied art* at Hornsey College of Art (Foundation, 1966-67), Walthamforest Technical College and School of Art (1967-70), Barking N.E.L.P. (1970-72), London University Inst. of Educ. (Associateship, 1980-81). *Exhib.:* one-man: Loggia Gallery, London (1980); group: Mall Gallery, London. *Publications:* associateship report 'Some Art activities in Prison'. *Address:* 2 Bergen Ct., Maldon, Essex CM9 6UH. *Signs work:* "M.J.V. BEVIS."

BICAT, Andre, O.B.E.; painter, sculptor, printmaker, ceramist; tutor, R.C.A.; *b* 1909. *Work in permanent collections:* B.M., V. & A., Arts Council, Ministry of the Environment, British Steel, South London A.G., Greenwich Library, National Gallery of Wales, City of Portsmouth, City of Leeds, Nottingham College, West of England College of Art, Reading, Oxford University, Dublin University, National Gallery, S. Australia, Toledo Museum, Ohio, Brooklyn Museum, Oregon, Dallas Museum, Cleveland Museum. *Exhib.:* one-man shows: London, Leicester Galleries (1949, 1958, 1959, 1960, 1961, 1966, 1968, 1970); Grafton Gallery (1984); Bruton Gallery (1983); Milan (1972); Paris, Galerie de l'Institut (1962); Dublin (1963); Reading (1964-66); Newcastle (1966); Oxford (1969, 1973); Swansea (1974); Henley (1976, 1978, 1979, 1981, 1982, 1984). *Address:* 233 Putney Bridge Rd., London SW15 2PU. *Signs work:* see appendix.

BICKNELL, John, B.A.(Hons.) (1980), H.Dip.F.A.(Lond.) (1983), Slade prize (1983), Boise Scholarship (1983), Greater London Arts award (1986), John Moores prize (1987), Henry Moore Fellow, Leeds Polytechnic (1989-90); painter; *b* Surrey, 1958; *s* of Peter Bicknell; *m* Christina Dorees. *Educ.:* Ottershaw School; *studied art* at W.S.C.A.D. (1975-77), N.E. London Polytechnic (1977-80), Slade School of Fine Art (1981-83). *Exhib.:* numerous group shows, including John Moores, Whitechapel Open, Christie's, New Contemporaries, R.C.A., Contemporary Art Soc., London Contemporary Art Fair, Miro Foundation, Barcelona, Monjuic, Girona; one-man shows: Pomeroy Purdy Gallery, London. *Work in permanent collections:* Slade, Boise Scholarship, Leics. C.C., Nat. West, Reed International. *Addresses:* 44 Chertsey Rd., Chobham, Surrey GU24 8PJ; 19 Tindu St., Kipseli 11257, Athens. *Signs work:* "John Bicknell."

BIDDULPH, Elizabeth Mary, R.O.I. (1952), Hon. senior mem. R.O.I. (1982), N.D.D. (1947), Hon.Cert.R.D.S. (1942); painter chiefly in oils, portraits, landscapes, still-life, flowers; *b* Port Elizabeth, S.A., 17 June, 1927; *d* of the late A. D. S. Dunn, Comdr. R.N.; *m* Nicholas Osborne John Biddulph; one *s. Educ.:* Hamilton House School, Tunbridge Wells; *studied art* at Wimbledon School of Art (1944-47) under Gerald Cooper, A.R.C.A., Slade School of Fine Art (1949-51). *Exhib.:* yearly at R.O.I.; one-man shows, Hornsey Library (1971), Barclays Bank, Egham (1977), Egham Library (1985), murals in shop, Virginia Water (1984). *Publication:* articles for Leisure Painter Magazine (1980-81, 1987). Repainted and designed ceiling panels for writer Ralph Dutton's home 1961-62 (original ones destroyed by fire). Judging panel, John Laing Painting Competition (1988). *Address:* 74 Clarence St., Egham, Surrey. *Signs work:* "E. Biddulph."

BILL, John Gordon, R.W.A. (1978); artist in oil, abstract and landscape painter and teacher; *b* London, 6 Nov., 1915; *s* of Lieut.-Col. James G. Bill; *m* Coral Nerelle, R.W.A., portrait painter. *Educ.:* Radley College; *studied art* at Byam Shaw School, under Charles Mahoney, A.R.A., and Bernard Dunstan, R.A. *Exhib.:* R.A., R.P., R.B.A., N.E.A.C., R.W.A., and Cheltenham Group; one-man shows: Oxford, Cheltenham and Cotswolds. *Work in permanent collections:* Cheltenham Art Gallery, Royal West of England Academy. *Address:* Rosemary House, The Green, Northleach, Glos. *Signs work:* see appendix.

BILL, Max, M. of B.S.A., S.W.B., Hon. F.A.I.A., Berlin Art Academy, Flamish Academy, French Architects Academy; architect, painter, sculptor, writer; Director Hochschule für Gestaltung, Ulm, Germany (1951-1956); professor for Environmental Design, Hochschule für bildende Künste, Hamburg, Germany (1967-1974); architect, Cultural Section, Swiss National Exhibition (1964); Grand Prix Biennale São Paulo (1951), Grand Prix Triennale di Milan

(1936 and 1951), Zürich Art Prize (1968), Dr. Ing. h.c. (1980); *b* Winterthur, Switzerland, 22 Dec., 1908. *Studied at:* "Bauhaus" Dessau. *Work repro.:* Monographs by Margit Staber (1963 English and 1971 g.e.f.), Hüttinger (1989 German, 1978 English). *Address:* Rebhusstr. 50, 8126, Zumikon, Switzerland. *Signs work:* see appendix.

BILLIN, Edward S.; artist in water-colour, wood engraving; *b* Sheffield, 19 June, 1911; *s* of H. M. Billin; *m* Dorothy Mount; one *d. Educ.:* Western Rd. Secondary School, Sheffield; *studied art* at Sheffield College of Art under Eric Jones, R.S., A.R.C.A., in engraving, Noel Spencer, A.R.C.A., in design. *Exhib.:* Soc. of Wood Engravers, R.A., R.I., R.B.A., Britain in Water-colour, B.W.S. Soc., Art Institute of Chicago, On tour with Arts Council and Art Exhbns. Bureau. *Work in permanent collections:* Graves A.G., Sheffield, Derby Educ. Com. *Work repro.:* The Studio (1951), Woman's Journal, Coronation Issue. *Publications:* Drawing on scraper board (Pitman). *Address:* West View, West La., Holdworth, Sheffield S6 6SN.

BILLINGS, Kathleen Wyatt, R.I., S.M.; *b* Christchurch, N.Z.; *m* F. J. W. Billings; one *s*, one *d. Studied* at Canterbury College School of Art (1928-31). *Exhib.:* R.I., S.M., N.Z. Academy of Fine Arts, N.Z. Craft Council invited artists exhbn. N.Z. Academy (1978); abstract collages with Group 60 (1967); one-man show, Osborne Galleries, Auckland (1973), 'Hand-made Paper Plus' Canterbury Art Soc. (1986). *Work repro.:* La Revue Moderne, Craft New Zealand (1981), Handmade Paper Today (1983). *Publication:* folio of prints entitled Flowers of the South Pacific. Spent 1964-66 in Cook Islands; painted flowers there, sixteen of which were printed for Cook Islands' first definitive issue of stamps. Commissioned to design set of flower paintings to form first definitive issue of stamps for Niue (1969). At present engaged on imaginative collages, and making hand-made paper. *Address:* 15A Desmond St., Christchurch, N.Z. *Signs work:* "Kay W. Billings."

BINNS, David, N.D.D. (1956), S.WL.A. (1968); R.S.P.B. Fine Art Award (1990 and 1992); freelance artist in water-colour, lino, scraperboard; teacher SP courses; with wife runs own Brent Gallery; *b* Sutton-in-Craven, 30 Sept., 1935; *s* of Dan Binns, teacher and artist; *m* Molly; one *s*, two *d. Educ.:* Ermysted's Grammar School, Skipton; *studied art* at Skipton Art School (Dan Binns, J. C. Midgley), Leeds College of Art and Pulée. *Exhib.:* S.WL.A., R.I., H.C. Dickens, Bloxham, Oxfordshire, Manor House, Ilkley, Aquarious Gallery, Harrogate, Leigh Yawkey Woodson Museum, Wisconsin, U.S.A. *Work repro.:* Dalesman, childrens animal books, circular jigsaws, print by Soloman & Whitehead, Medici cards, Yorkshire Journal. *Address:* Holmestead, Boundary Ave., Sutton-in-Craven, Keighley, Yorks. BD20 8BL. *Clubs:* S.WL.A., B.W.S., Y.W.S., F.I.G.A. *Signs work:* "David Binns."

BINNS, Lorna, A.R.C.A. (1938), R.W.S. (1977); painter in water-colour; *b* Sheffield, 23 Oct., 1914; *d* of Harold John Harrison; *m* John Dawson Binns (decd.); two *d. Educ.:* Abbeydale Girls' Grammar School, Sheffield; *studied art* at Sheffield College of Art (1930-35) under Maurice Wheatley, R.C.A. (1935-39) under Prof. Tristram. *Exhib.:* R.A., F.B.A. Gallery, The Guildhall, R.W.S. Gallery. *Address:* 7 Egmont Ave., Surbiton, Surrey KT6 7AU. *Signs work:* "Lorna Binns."

BIRCH, David William; painter/printmaker in water-colour and wood engraving; *b* 28 Jan., 1945; *s* of Eric Birch, engineer/designer. *Educ.:* Wellesbourne School, Birmingham; *studied art:* mentors: water-colour – Kay Kinsman, wood engraving – William T. Rawlinson. *Exhib.:* R.A., R.I., R.W.S.,

41

R.E., S.W.E., R.W.A.; one-man shows: Birmingham and Midland Inst., John Noott Gallery, Broadway, Ombersley Gallery, Worcester, twice yearly at his studio, Confederation Life, Bristol. *Work in permanent collections:* University of Bristol, Confederation Life Insurance Co. *Publication:* illustrated, Spinning Wheels at Snowshill Manor (National Trust). *Address:* Croftsbrook, Blind La., Chipping Campden, Glos. GL55 6ED. *Signs work:* "David W. Birch."

BIRD, Henry, A.R.C.A. (1933), Art Workers Guild, Peterborough Diocesan Advisory Com., Civil List for Services to Art; figure draughtsman, mural decorator; *b* Northampton, 1909; *s* of William Bird; *m* Freda Jackson (decd.), actress; one *s. Educ.:* Northampton; *studied art* at Northampton and R.C.A. *Exhib.:* many exhbns. in public and private galleries. *Work in permanent collections:* University & Nat. Library, Wales; Carlisle; Brighton; Northampton; Theatre Museum, Covent Gdn., Drottningholm Theatre Museum, Sweden. Mural paintings in Conference Centre, Ecton, Northants.; Earls Barton Church; University Commonwealth Studies, London; Royal Theatre, Northampton; Ashcroft-Fairfield, Croydon; Drottningholm Theatre Museum, Sweden. Total decorative schemes, St. Crispin Hospital Chapel, Northants.; Daventry Hospital Chapel; Denton Church, Northants; Charwelton Village Chapel, Northants. *Address:* Hardingstone House, Northants. *Signs work:* "H. Bird."

BIRNE, Max Sidney, F.F.P.S.; landscape and abstract painter in water-colour and gouache; *b* London, 12 Jan., 1927; *m* Rosemarie Kesselman; one *s. Studied art* at City Literary Inst., London; Harrow School of Art. *Exhib.:* one-man shows: Burgh House, Hampstead, Lauderdale House Highgate, Mandel's Gallery Goodmayes, Margaret Fisher Gallery London, Tricycle Theatre London; group shows: Loggia Gallery, Chenil Gallery, Alpine Gallery, Mall Galleries, Barbican Arts Centre, Bloomsbury Gallery, Usher Museum Lincoln, Brighton Polytechnic A.G. Work in private collections. *Address:* 82 Preston Rd., Wembley, Middx. HA9 8LA. *Signs work:* "BIRNE."

BIRO, Val (B. S.); freelance illustrator, painter, author; assistant production manager, Sylvan Press (1945-46), production manager and art director, C. & J. Temple (1946-48), John Lehmann, Ltd. (1948-53); *b* Budapest, Hungary, 6 Oct., 1921; *s* of Dr. B. Biro, solicitor; *m* (1) Vivien Woolley; one *d*; (2) Marie-Louise Ellaway; one *step-s*, one *step-d. Educ.:* School of the Cistercian Monks, Budapest; *studied art* at Central School of Arts and Crafts, London. *Publications:* Author of the Gumdrop Series; Hungarian Folk Tales, Rub-a-Dub-Dub and other books for children; illustrated some 300 books. *Work in permanent collections:* V. & A. Museum. *Address:* Bridge Cottage, Brook Ave., Bosham, W. Sussex PO18 8LQ. *Signs work:* "Biro" or "Val Biro."

BISHOP, Edward, R.B.A. (1950), N.E.A.C. (1960); artist in oil, pastel, lithography, pencil, and graphic designer; *b* 11 Nov., 1902; *s* of Jacob Bishop and Eliza Harriet Metcalfe; *m* Celeste Radloff. *Educ.:* Elementary School; *studied art* at Central School of Arts and Crafts under A. S. Hartrick, F. W. Jackson, A.R.A., Bernard Meninsky, Noël Rooke (1920-26). *Exhib.:* R.A., Leicester Galleries, Wildenstein Gallery, N.E.A.C., R.B.A., Arts Council, etc. *Work in permanent collections:* National Gallery, Sydney, Australia, Nottingham Art Gallery and private collections. *Work repro.:* various newspapers and magazines. *Address:* 6 East Heath Rd., Hampstead, London NW3 1BN. *Club:* Past President, Chelsea Arts. *Signs work:* see appendix.

BISHOP, William Henry; self taught artist in water-colour and oil of seascapes and landscapes; *b* Liss, Hants., 21 June, 1942; *s* of Henry Bernard Bishop; *m* Helen Dunkerley; three *s. Educ.:* King's School, Canterbury. *Exhib.:* R.S.M.A.,

Armed Forces, Southampton Maritime Year; one-man show: Royal Exchange Gallery, London (1991). *Work in private collections:* U.S.A., Australia, New Zealand, Oman, Singapore, Hong Kong, Falkland Islands, U.K., Gibraltar, Germany. *Work commissioned:* R.N. Museum, Portsmouth, and Mary Rose Museum, Portsmouth. *Address:* West Mill, Mill Lane, Langstone, Havant, Hants. *Signs work:* "W. H. Bishop."

BIZON, Edna, S.W.A. (1987); artist in oil; *b* 13 Aug., 1929; *m* Ken Bizon. *Educ.:* Honor Oak School; *studied art* at St.Martin's School of Art (1943-44), Camberwell School of Art (1944-46, Lawrence Gowing, John Minton). *Exhib.:* R.A.; one-man shows: Thorndike, Leatherhead (1970, 1977), Augustine, Holt (1973), Munich, W.Germany (1982), O'Nians King St.Galleries (1987), Look of Helmsley (1988), King St. Galleries (1990), Llewellyn Alexander (1991). *Address:* Drove End, West St., North Creake, Norfolk NR21 9LQ. *Signs work:* "Edna Bizon."

BLACK, Ian, Art Teaching Diploma, Bristol University (1956), R.W.A. (1978); art teacher and artist in oil, acrylic, pen and ink; Head of Art, Bristol Cathedral School; Hon. Sec. R.W.A.; *b* Bury St. Edmunds, 31 May, 1929; *s* of Frederick Black, chemist; *m* Judith Rhiannon. *Educ.:* Culford School, Bury St. Edmunds; *studied art* at Southampton College of Art (1949), Bath Academy of Art (1952-56) under William Scott, Martin Froy, Jack Smith, Terry Frost, Peter Lanyon. *Exhib.:* five one-man shows, R.W.A., R.A., travelling exhibs. *Work in permanent collections:* R.W.A., Walsall Educ. Centre, Bath University, N.Z. Government, St. Catherine's College, Oxford, Wadham College, Oxford, Oxford Corp., Clifton High School, Redland School, Dorset House, Oxford. *Address:* Blakes Farm, Englishcombe, Bath BA2 9DT. *Signs work:* "IB" or "Ian Black."

BLACK, John Frederick, N.D.D. (1964), D.L.C.A. (Hons. 1964), A.T.C. (Distinction 1965), M.A. (Manc. 1979); senior lecturer, (Art and Design), Bedford C.H.E., and freelance designer (textiles); artist in oil, water-colour and screen printing; *b* Appleby Magna, Leics., 2 June, 1943; *s* of the late John Frederick Black; marriage dissolved; one *s*, one *d. Educ.:* Loughborough College School; *studied art* at Loughborough College of Art (1960-64, Edward Sharp, Malcolm Baum); Brighton College of Art (1965, Ronald Horton); Manchester Polytechnic (1978-79, Peter Perritt). *Exhib.:* England, Holland, U.S.A., Germany. Work in permanent and private collections. Director of "The Gallery", 108 Midland Rd., Wellingborough, Northants. *Address:* "The Gallery", 108-112 Midland Rd, Wellingborough, Northants. *Signs work:* "John F. Black."

BLACKBURN, Mavis, N.D.D. (Painting), A.T.D. (1948), R.C.A. (1952), B.A. (1979); artist in oil, polymer and gouache; *b* Wallasey, Ches., 29 Oct., 1923; *d* of Ernest Hubert Blackburn. *Educ.:* Upton Hall Convent School; *studied art* at Liverpool College of Art (1942-48, Alfred Wiffen, R.C.A., Will C. Penn, R.O.I., R.S.P. R.C.A., Martin Bell, A.R.C.A.). *Exhib.:* Royal Cambrian Academy, Wirral Soc. of Art, Deeside Art Group, Atkinson Gallery, Southport, Glasgow Inst. of Fine Arts, R.B.A., R.A., etc.; one-man shows, Liverpool, R.C.A., Williamson Gallery, Birkenhead. *Work in permanent collections:* Williamson A.G., Birkenhead, Senate House, Liverpool University. *Address:* The Bend, Village Rd., West Kirby, Wirral, Merseyside L48 7EL. *Signs work:* "Mavis Blackburn."

BLACKLOCK, George, Dip.A.D. (1974), M.F.A. (1976); painter in oil and wax on canvas; Senior lecturer in painting, Wimbledon School of Art; *b* Durham, 11 Apr., 1952; one *s. Studied art* at Stourbridge College of Art (1971-74, Barrie Cook), Reading University (1974-76, Terry Frost). *Work in permanent collection:*

A.C.G.B. *Address:* 11-31 Oarsmen Rd., London N1. *Signs work:* "George Blacklock."

BLACKMORE, Clive David; painter; *b* Kingston-on-Thames, 1940. *Studied art* at Twickenham and Kingston Schools of Art. *Exhib.:* Exibits regularly in the west country and New Academy, London. *Address:* Eastcliff Farm, Rinsey, Ashton, Helston, Cornwall TR13 9TS. *Signs work:* "Clive Blackmore."

BLACKWOOD, Simon Anthony James, Dip.Ad. (1970); artist in oil; *b* Chelmsford, 17 May, 1948; *s* of H.J. Blackwood, policeman; *m* Laura C.M. Blackwood; one *d. Educ.:* Gilberd School, Colchester; *studied art* at Colchester School of Art, Coventry School of Art (Anthony Atkinson, Don Foster). *Exhib.:* Art and Mysticism (1975) I.C.A. London; one-man shows: Dundas Gallery 'Bus Stop' Series (1985), Netherbon Arts Centre 'Aquatic Light' Series (1986), Anthony Mould Ltd. London (1989), Michael Parkin Fine Art (1991), William Hardie Gallery Glasgow (1992), Brian Sinfield Gallery Burford (1992). *Address:* Breyberry Ltd., Kingham House, Kingham, Oxon. OX7 6YA. *Signs work:* "S.A.J.B." or "S.B."

BLAKE, Frederick Donald, R.I., R.S.M.A.; artist in oil, water-colour, pen and ink; *b* 7 June, 1908; *s* of F. H. Blake. *Educ.:* Camberwell School of Arts and Crafts; Goldsmiths' College; Brixton School of Building. *Exhib.:* R.A., R.O.I., R.I., R.B.A. *Work repro.:* newspaper maps, war illustrations, railway posters, advertising drawings. *Address:* Flat 2, Hereford House, Lauriston Rd., London SW19 4TJ. *Clubs:* London Sketch, Chelsea Arts. *Signs work:* "F. Donald Blake."

BLAKE, Jane, R.M.S (1987), M.A.A. (1987); portrait painter, speciality: miniatures on ivory and vellum; sculptor, stained glass artist, writer, lecturer; *b* N.C., 1933; three *s. Educ.:* Central Wesleyan College, S.C.; *studied art* privately (1947-85). *Exhib.:* international miniature shows R.M.S. England, Ireland, Canada, Florida, N.J., D.C., Tampa Museum (1989). *Work in private collections:* Governor's Mansions, Florida and S.C., U.S.A. hospitals and state bldgs. *Address:* 11148 Freedom Way, Seminole, Florida 34642, U.S.A. *Signs miniatures:* "Jane Blake, R.M.S., M.A.A."

BLAKE, Marie Dora, N.D.D. (1958), A.T.C. (1959), S.W.A. (1987); artist in oil and water-colour; tutor and organiser, Lyme Regis Painting Holidays; *b* London, 12 Mar., 1938; *d* of Eric Blake; *m* Charles Calcutt Smith; two *s*, one *d. Educ.:* Richmond and E.Sheen Grammar School; *studied art* at Kingston-on-Thames School of Art (1954-58), London University Inst. of Educ. (1959). *Exhib.:* N.E.A.C., R.O.I., R.S.M.A., S.W.A. *Publication:* regular contributor to Leisure Painter magazine. *Address:* Long Close, Clappentail La., Lyme Regis, Dorset. *Signs work:* "Marie Blake."

BLAKE, Naomi, F.R.B.S.; sculptor in bronze; *b* Czechoslovakia, 1924; one *s*, one *d. Studied art* at Hornsey School of Art (1955-60). *Exhib.:* Salon de Paris, R.B.S., City of Leicester Museum, R.A. International Art Fair, St. Paul's Cathedral, Barbican London, Exhbn. Gallery Swansea University. *Work in permanent collections:* Leicester Arts Council, North London Collegiate, Oxford Synagogue, Waterlow Park Highgate, Fitzroy Sq. London, Bristol Cathedral, Hebrew University Jerusalem, Leo Baeck College London, Tel Aviv University Israel, Yarnton Manor Oxford, Norwich Cathedral, Duai Abbey Reading, St. Botolph's Church Aldgate, St. Anthony's College, Oxford. *Publications:* contributor, Anthologies, Each in his Prison, The Bridge is Love, London Statues,

The A.A. Book of London, Open Air Sculpture in Britain. *Address:* 41 Woodside Ave., London N10 3HY. *Signs work:* "N.B."

BLAKE, Quentin, O.B.E., R.D.I., M.A., F.C.S.D.; illustrator and teacher; Head of Dept. of Illustration, Royal College of Art (1978-85), Visiting Professor (1988-); *b* Sidcup, Kent, 16 Dec., 1932. *Educ.:* Downing College, Cambridge; *studied art:* part-time, Chelsea School of Art. *Exhib.:* one-man shows, Workshop Gallery, Illustrators A.G.; retrospective of illustration work, National Theatre (1983). *Publications:* illustrated over one hundred children's books, also books for adults; Mr. Magnolia (Kate Greenaway medal 1981). *Address:* 30 Bramham Gdns., London SW5. *Signs work:* "Quentin Blake."

BLAKELEY, John, L.S.I.A.D. (1965), A.R.B.S. (1979), S.P.S. (1979), C. & G. (Illustration 1965), C. & G. Dip. (Sculpture, 1969), Travel Scholarship (Sculpture, 1968); sculpture in clay and stone; lecturer, Sir John Cass College; *b* Blackpool, 19 Jan., 1946; *s* of Harry Blakeley; *m* Carole Crane; two *s. Educ.:* St. George's; *studied art* at Blackpool (1962-65), St. Martin's (1965-66), Kennington (1966-70), Athens (1968), Accademy Carrara (1968). *Exhib.:* Preston A.G., Guildhall, Royal Exchange, Waterperry House, Gordon Hayward Gallery, Digswell House, Heatherley's, Hertford Corn Exchange, Gulbenkian Museum, Mall Galleries. *Address:* 6 Ingles, Welwyn Garden City, Herts. *Signs work:* "BLAKELEY."

BLAKER, Michael, R.E. (1975), R.W.A. (1987); painter, etcher, writer; *b* Hove, 19 Jan., 1928; *s* of John Blaker; *m* Catriona McTurk. *Educ.:* Brighton Grammar School, Heversham School; *studied art* at Brighton College of Art. *Exhib.:* R.A., R.E., R.W.A., R.P., etc. *Work in permanent collections:* Tate Gallery, V. & A., S. London A.G. *Work purchased:* Barclays Bank, Lloyds of London, Bank of Vienna, Ocean Transport, Bolton Steamship Co., etc. *Publications:* The Autobiography of a Painter-Etcher (1986); M.B. Etchings (1985); M.B. Paintings (1986); editor, Printmakers Journal. *Address:* Prospect Lodge, 122 Grange Rd., Ramsgate, Kent CT11 9PT. *Signs work:* see appendix.

BLAMEY, Norman Charles, R.O.I. (1952), A.R.A. (1970), R.A. (1975); painter in oil; *b* London, 16 Dec., 1914; *s* of Charles Henry Blamey; *m* Margaret Kelly; one *s. Educ.:* Holloway School, London; *studied art* at The Polytechnic School of Art, Regent St. (1931-37). *Exhib.:* R.A., R.H.A., R.O.I., R.B.A., N.E.A.C. and provincial galleries. Work in permanent and private collections. *Address:* 39 Lyncroft Gdns., London NW6.

BLASZKOWSKI, Martin, Bronze Medal, Brussels (1958), Grand Prize, Buenos Aires (1960), First Prize, Competition: "Homage to Peace" of the City of Buenos Aires (1986); painter in oil, sculptor in wood; lecturer at Tulane University, New Orleans, U.S.A. (1976); *b* Berlin, 1920 (Argentine citizenship since 1958). *Exhib.:* Brussels, Biennale Venecia, Argentine, Chile, Tate Gallery, London, Bienale de São Paulo, Brazil. *Work repro.:* Leonardo, 2.223 (1969) Oxford, Sculpture International 2.26 (1968) Oxford, Sculpture International 3.28 (1970) London, Sculpture of this Century, Editions du Griffon, Neuchatel, Switzerland (1959), Dictionnaire de la Sculpture Moderne, Fernand Hazan, Paris (1970). *Address:* Santa Fé 3786-11-A, Buenos Aires, Argentine. *Signs work:* "BLASZKO."

BLESKY, Wiltold John; sculptor in stainless steel, resin, ceremic, mixed media; painter in oil and acrylic paints: *b* Poland, 26 July, 1934 (U.S.A. Nationality); *m;* two *s,* two *d. Educ.:* Poland; U.S.A.; U.K. *Exhib.:* Le Salon, Paris, Marjorie Parr Galleries, London Hilton Galleries, Loggia Gallery, Mall Galleries, Round

House Gallery, New Metropole, Folkstone, Slater Gallery, Canterbury, Birmingham U. open-air exhbn. and other London and provincial galleries and open-air exhbns. *Address:* 13 Marlow Copse, Walderslade, Kent ME5 9DP. *Clubs:* F.P.S., The Artists' League of Great Britain, I.C.A., Association Internationale des Arts Plastiques-UNESCO. *Signs work:* "W. John Blesky."

BLIK, Maurice, A.T.C. (1968), F.R.B.S. (1992); sculptor in bronze; *b* Amsterdam, 21 Apr., 1939; *s* of Barend Blik; one *s,* one *d. Educ.:* Downer Grammar School; *studied art* at Hornsey College of Art (1956-60), University of London (1968-69). *Exhib.:* Mall Galleries, Ben-Uri Gallery, R.A., Alwin Gallery, Art for Offices Gallery, Cavalier Galleries (U.S.A.). Work in private and public collections. *Address:* 501 Bunyan Ct., Barbican, London EC2Y 8DH. *Signs work:* see appendix.

BLISS, Ian Reynolds, N.D.D. (1954), A.T.D. (1955), R.I. (1992); artist in water-colour and wood engraving; social worker; *b.* Derby, 2 Apr., 1930; *m* Jill Michelle Cheney; one *s,* three *d. Educ.:* Repton; *studied art* at Leicester (1950-55). *Exhib.:* R.A., R.I., Piccadilly Gallery, Nevill Gallery Canterbury. *Address:* 8 Beaudesert, Leighton Buzzard LU7 8HZ. *Signs work:* "IAN BLISS."

BLOCH, Gunther, F.R.A.I.; 1st prize winner of first National Crafts Competition (1948); art master of L.C.C. schools since 1948; sculptor in wood, stone, clay and ivory; *b* Dt. Krone, Germany, 24 Aug., 1916; *s* of Mendelsohn Bloch; *m;* one *s. Educ.:* German Colleges; Leeds College of Art (John Frank Kavanagh); Regent St. Polytechnic; and in Germany under Gerhard Priedigkeit. *Exhib.:* Berkeley Galleries, Cooling Galleries, Ben Uri Galleries, Leeds Art Gallery, Britain Can Make It. *Work in private collections:* Denmark, France, Australia, New Zealand. *Address:* 88 Camden Mews, London NW1 9BX. *Signs work:* "Gunther Bloch" or "G. Bloch."

BLOCKLEY, Gwilym John, R.I., P.S.; artist; conducts private painting schools, lectures, demonstrations; *b* Knighton, Radnorshire, 1921; *s* of Thos. Blockley: *m* Margaret Blockley; two *d. Exhib.:* R.A., Mall Galleries, and many provincial galleries. *Publications:* The Challenge of Water-colour (Pitman); Learn to paint with Pastels (Collins); John Blockley Water-colour Course (Pitman Correspondence College); contributor to art magazines. *Addresses:* Ashfield, Donnington, Moreton-in-Marsh, Glos. GL56 0XX; and John Blockley Gallery, Church St., Stow-on the-Wold, Glos. *Signs work:* "G. John Blockley."

BLOXHAM, Judith Anne, B.Ed.Hons. (1985); artist; *b* Workington, Cumbria, 28 Jan., 1961; *d* of Donald Bone; *m* David Gerald Bloxham; one *s,* one *d. Educ.:* Whitehaven Grammar School; *studied art* at Cumbria College of Art and Design, Carlisle, St. Martin's College, Lancaster. *Exhib.:* R.S.M.A. 4th International Miniatures Exhbn., Toronto, Fitz Park Museum, Keswick, St. Martin's, Lancaster, Cumberland Pencil Museum, Keswick, Wild ties V. & A., Whale tail Nairobi. Work in private collections. Mural commissions in Carlisle City. *Address:* 3 Boston Ave., Carlisle, Cumbria CA2 4DR. *Signs work:* "J.A.B." or "J.A. Bloxham."

BOCKING, Helen; Harrow Dip. in Illustration (1976); artist in water-colour of wildlife, country sports, animal and equestrian portraits; *b* Gillingham, 4 June, 1954. *Educ.:* Fort Pitt School, Kent; *studied art* at Goldsmiths' College (1972), Harrow School of Art (1973-76, Sam Marshall, Brian Liddel). *Exhib.:* S.WL.A., R.S.P.B., B.F.S.S., Game Conservancy; various one-man shows. *Work in permanent collections:* S. London A.G., and many private collections. *Address:*

30 Town Dam Lane, Donington, nr. Spalding, Lincs. PE11 4TP. *Signs work:* "H. Bocking."

BODEN, Leonard, R.P., F.R.S.A.; portrait painter; *b* Greenock, Scotland, 1911; *s* of John Boden; *m* Margaret Tulloch; one *d. Educ.:* Sedbergh; *studied art* at School of Art, Glasgow; Heatherley School of Art, London. *Exhib.:* R.P., R.S.A. *Official portraits:* Her Majesty Queen Elizabeth II, H.R.H. The Prince Philip, Duke of Edinburgh, K.G., K.T., G.B.E., His Holiness Pope Pius XII, Field-Marshal Lord Milne, G.C.B., G.C.M.G., D.S.O. *Work repro.:* The Connoisseur; The Artist: many periodicals in this country and abroad; and as Fine Art Prints. *Address:* 36 Arden Rd., London N3 3AN. *Clubs:* Savage, Chelsea Arts. *Signs work:* "LEONARD BODEN."

BODEN, Margaret, P.S., S.W.A., U.A., F.R.S.A.; portrait painter; *b* Ecclesmachen, Scotland; *d* of A. P. S. Tulloch, M.A., B.D.; *m* Leonard Boden; one *d. Educ.:* Dowanhill; *studied art* at School of Art, Glasgow; Heatherley School of Art, London. *Exhib.:* R.P., R.O.I., Royal Inst. of Fine Arts, Glasgow; National Soc.; Summer Salon; Royal B'ham Soc. of Artists; City of Bradford A.G., etc. Honourable Mention, Paris Salon. *Work repro.:* The Times, The Artist, many magazines and periodicals, etc. *Address:* 36 Arden Rd., London N3 3AN. *Signs work:* "MARGARET BODEN."

BOGART, Bram; 1970 Notionnalité Belge; painter; *b* Delft, Holland 12 July, 1921; *s* of Abraham van den Boogaart; *m* Abelina Sjoukje-Vos; one *s,* two *d. Studied art:* self-taught. *Work in permanent collections:* Gallery Gimpel Fils, London; Gallerie Rive Gauche, Paris; Galerie Internationale d'Art Contemporain, Paris; Gallerie Bleue, Stockholm; Galleria Senior, Roma; Galerie Françoise Mayer, Galerie Collection d'Art Amsterdam, Fondation Veranneman Kriushoutem, Galerie Cogeim Bruxelles. *Address:* Rue du Poinçon 37, 1000 Bruxelles.

BOHUSZ-SZYSZKO, Marian; Degree (h.c.) Polish University abroad, Art and teaching Dip., Poland; Alfred Jurzykowski Foundation prize, N.Y.; Academic prize, Catholic University of Lublin; artist in oil, oil pastel, and ink drawings; Principal (retd.), Polish School of Art, London; *b* Wilno, Poland, 15 Feb., 1901. *Studied art* at Fine Arts Faculty, Wilno, Academy of Fine Art, Cracow, and Academy of Fine Art, Warsaw. *Exhib.:* eighteen one-man shows Poland (1934-39), Grabowski and Drian galleries (1959-73). *Work in permanent collections:* Poland: Warsaw, Gdansk, Wroclaw, Cracow, Lublin; St. Christopher's Hospice, London. *Publications:* Paris and London by Tymon Terlecki; Marian Bohusz-Szyszko (Drian Gallery). *Address:* 50 Lawrie Park Gdns., Sydenham, London SE26. *Signs work:* see appendix.

BOLAN, Sean Edward, G.R.A.; artist in ink and water-colour of landscapes, architecture and historical transport subjects; *b* Rowlands Castle, Hants., 25 May, 1948; *s* of Edward Bolan, Ex. C.Q.M.S., Grenadier Guards; *m* Margaret Janina; two *d. Educ.:* Warblington Secondary Modern School, Havant, Hants.; *studied art* at Portsmouth College of Art (1965-68). *Work in permanent collections:* private, municipal and Science Museum, S. Kensington. Plays cornet, leader 'The Charleston Chasers'. *Address:* Smallthorns Cottage, Springhill, Moreton in Marsh, Glos. GL56 9TQ. *Signs work:* "Sean Bolan."

BOLTON, Richard Marston; artist in water-colour; *b* Aberdeen, 28 June, 1950; *m* Margaret; two *s. Studied art* at Shrewsbury School of Art. *Exhib.:* Linda Blackstone Gallery, Pinner. *Work in permanent collection:* St. Ives Museum. *Publications:* written and illustrated: Weathered Textures in Water-colour, and Weathered Textures, Workshop (Watson & Guptil). *Address:*

Granville House, 27 London Rd., St. Ives, Huntingdon, Cambs. PE17 4ES. *Signs work:* "R.M. Bolton."

BONADA, Cinzia, A.R.B.A.; painter in oil and pencil; *b* Jersey, C.I., 22 Apr., 1938; *m* Johnny Bonada; one *s*, two *d. Educ.:* Jersey Ladies College; *studied art* at Richmond Adult College (1975-79, Charles Fowler) and with Peter Garrard (1982-87). *Exhib.:* R.A., R.B.A., R.P., N.E.A.C., etc. *Work in permanent collections:* Drapers' Hall, A.W.G. *Address:* 9 Alexandra Rd., E. Twickenham, Middx. TW1 2HE. *Signs work:* "Cinzia."

BOND, Jane, R.P., N.E.A.C., D.F.A. (1981), Postgrad. D.F.A. (1984); painter in oil, charcoal, pencil, formerly theatre and T.V. designer; *b* Umtali, Zimbabwe, 1 Apr., 1939. *Educ.:* Holy Trinity Convent, Bickley; Kinnaird Park School, Bromley; *studied art* at St. Martin's School of Art (1954-56), City and Guilds (1978-81, Roger de Grey), R.A. Schools (1981-84, Peter Greenham). *Exhib.:* R.A.., N.E.A.C., R.P., Hayward Gallery, etc. *Address:* 8 Ceylon Rd., London W14 0PY. *Signs work:* see appendix.

BOND, Marj, D.A. (Glas.), S.S.W.A. (1974), R.S.W. (1989), S.S.A. (1989); artist in oil, acrylic, etching; Vice-Pres., Scottish Artist Artist Craftsmen; *b* Paisley, Scotland, 23 May, 1939; *d* of Hubert McKechnie, organist and ships draughtsman; *m* James Agray, architect; one *s*, two *d. Educ.:* Paisley Grammar School; *studied art* at Glasgow School of Art (1956-60, David Donaldson, Mary Armour, Benno Schotz). *Exhib.:* many one-man shows, R.S.A., S.S.A., R.S.W., Scottish Soc. of Woman Artists now Scottish Artist Artist Craftsmen, R.S.I. *Work in permanent collections:* Arts in Fife, Edinburgh University. *Address:* Eden Cottage, Old Town, Gateside, Fife KY14 5SL. *Signs work:* "Marj."

BONE, Charles, P.P.R.I., A.R.C.A., F.R.S.A., Hon F.C.A. (Canada); F.B.I. Award for Design; painter and designer; former Governor, Federation of British Artists (Mall Galleries); Past President, Royal Institute of Painters in Watercolour; artist in water-colour, oil, variety of mediums including ceramic for murals; *b* Farnham, Surrey, 15 Sept., 1926; *m* Sheila Mitchell, P.S.P.S., F.R.B.S., A.R.C.A., sculptor; two *s. Studied art* at Farnham School of Art; Royal College of Art. *Exhib.:* 33 one-man. *Work in permanent collections:* many mural paintings in public buildings and water-colours and oils in private collections. Awarded Hunting Group prize of £5000 for a British water-colour (1984). *Publication:* author, Charles Bone's Waverley, Foreword by H.R.H. Prince of Wales. *Address:* Winters Farm, Puttenham, nr. Guildford, Surrey. *Signs work:* "BONE."

BONE, Ronald, Dip.A.D. (1972), M.A. (R.C.A.) (1976); painter and designer in acrylic and water-colour; *b* Consett, Co. Durham, 22 June, 1950; *s* of George Bone; *m*; one *s*, one *d. Educ.:* Consett Grammar School; *studied art* at Bath Academy of Art (1968-72), R.C.A. (1973-76). *Exhib.:* R.A., R.W.E.A., C.C.A. Galleries, Linfield Galleries, John Noott, Broadway, Llewellyn Alexander. *Work in private collections:* U.K., Europe and America. *Work repro.:* illustrations in various books from London publishing houses. Many T.V. programmes. *Address:* Manor Farm Cottage, Pump La., Bathford, Bath, Avon BA1 7RT. *Signs work:* "BONE."

BOOTH, Rosa-Maria, A.R.M.S., H.S.F., M.P.S.G., Dip. Fashion (1970); painter and miniaturist in oil, acrylic, water-colour; *b* Olot, Spain, 9 Nov., 1947; *m* Peter Booth. *Educ.:* Sagrado Corazón de Maria, Olot; Inst. Marti, Barcelona; *studied art* privately and in Paris under Madeleine Scali; L'Escola Olotina, Spain (Emilio Parejo, J.M. Agusti); Thurrock Technical College (M. Martin).

Exhib.: R.A., R.M.S., Mall Galleries, Barbican, Westminster Gallery, Llewellyn Alexander, N. Ireland, Spain, France, Sweden, Canada, U.S.A. Work in private collections. *Awards:* 16 including 1st place I.M.A.S. Florida (drawing and pastel 1982; abstract 1984, 1988), Best in Mixed Media—Allegheny I.A.E. W. Virginia (1985). *Societies:* Founder mem. H.S., M.P.S.G., M.M.A.S., M.A.S.-F., G.M.A.S., M.A.S.-N.J. *Address:* 36 Windsor Ave., Grays, Essex RM16 2UB. *Signs work:* "ROSMAR."

BORCHARDT, Karolina, M.F.P.S., A.P.A., Mem. International Professional Artist (UNESCO); *b* Minsk, Lit, 26 July, 1913; *d* of Julian Iwaszkiewicz, civil servant official; *m* Karol; one *d. Educ.:* Krakow, Poland. Now a British subject and lives in London. First Polish woman air pilot. *Studied art* at University of Stephen Batory in London. Diploma di Merito at Universita Delle Arti, Italy. *Exhib.:* one-man shows, English Painters Art Group, London, Gallerie Internationale, New York, Richmond Gallery and Barrett Gallery, London; group shows, Barbican A.G., Bloomsbury Galleries, Mall Gallery, Weighouse Gallery, London, Salon des Nations, Paris, London Cassel Gallery, Loggia Gallery, New Vision Gallery, Centaur Gallery, and POSK Gallery, Germany Gallery P.R.O. Stuttgart, and many others. *Publication:* Karolina Borchardt, Introduction by Pierre Rouve, V.P. of World Art Critics Assoc. *Work in private collections:* U.S.A., Poland, England, Spain and France. *Address:* 4 Somerset House, Somerset Rd., Wimbledon, London SW19. *Club:* F.P.S. *Signs work:* "K. Borchardt."

BORKOWSKI, Elizabeth Irena, Dip.A.D., Prix de Rome, Feodora Gleichen award (1971) Sculpture; sculptor/painter in clay, bronze, water-colour, charcoal, pencil, art teacher; *b* Redhill, 7 May, 1949. *Educ.:* Ursuline High School, Brentwood: *studied art* at Camberwell School of Art and Crafts, British School at Rome (Brian Taylor, Paul de Moncheaux). *Exhib.:* R.A. Summer Show (1973), Palazzo Barberini National Museum of Rome (1973), Chelsea School of Art Rome Scholars (1986), Chelsea Harbour (1993). *Address:* 3 High Trees Rd., Reigate, Surrey RH2 7EH. *Signs work:* "Lissa Borkowski."

BORRIE: see HOPE HENDERSON, Eleanor.

BOSTOCK, James Edward, R.E. (1961), A.R.C.A. (Lond.) 1939; illustrator, wood engraver, painter; formerly Academic Development Officer, Bristol Polytechnic; mem. Soc. Wood Engravers, East Kent Art Society; *b* Hanley, Staffs, 11 June, 1917; *m*; three *s. Educ.:* Borden Grammar School, Sittingbourne, Kent; *studied art* at Medway School of Art, Rochester (1933-36), Royal College of Art (1936-39). *Exhib.:* R.A., R.B.A., N.E.A.C., Crafts Centre of Great Britain, V. & A. Museum, many provincial galleries, travelling exhbns. to Poland, Czechoslovakia, S. Africa, New Zealand and the Far East. *Work in permanent collections:* V. & A. Museum, British Museum, Wakefield Collection, Hunt Botanical Library, Pittsburgh, U.S.A., Hereford Museum. *Publications:* Roman Lettering for Students (Studio), 1959; wood engravings for Poems of Edward Thomas published by Folio Soc. (1988); articles in The Studio, The Artist, Guardian, Staffordshire Sentinel, Times Ed. Supp. *Address:* White Lodge, 80 Lindenthorpe Rd., Broadstairs, Kent CT10 1DB.

BOSWELL, William Aubrey, R.C.A., F.R.S.A.; artist; Principal Design Officer, County Planning Clwyd (Rtd.); *b* Nottingham, 30 May, 1926; *s* of W. E. Boswell, F.T.I.; *m* Jessie; one *s*, two *d. Studied art* at Nottingham College of Arts and Crafts (1942). *Exhib.:* Annual Summer Exhbns., Royal Cambrian Academy of Art. *Work repro.:* writer and illustrator of town trails: Denbigh,

Corwen, Llangollen, Carrog, Wrexham, etc. *Address:* 24 Hilltop View Rd., Borras Park, Wrexham, Clwyd LL12 7SF. *Signs work:* "William A. Boswell."

BOSZIN, Endre; founded, Taurus Artists (1961), London; painter in oil and water-colour, sculptor in bronze; President, Sculptors Society of Canada (1971-73), (1979-83); *b* Hungary, 1923; *s* of Julius Boszin, merchant; *m* Charlotte de Sarlay; one *s*, one *d*. *Studied art* at Budapest, R.C.A. *Exhib.:* London Group; Festival of Visual Art at Harrogate, Edinburgh Festival; Grabovsky, Crane Kalman, Chiltern, Woodstock; Piccadilly Galleries, London, Gallery Raymond Creuze, Paris; International Medal Exhbns.: Madrid, Cologne, Helsinki, Prague; Sculpture Biennale: Dante Centre, Ravenna; Palace of Art, Budapest. *Work in permanent collections:* Budapest, National Museum of Hungarian Art, Ujpest, City Collection, B.M., Pennsylvania Univ. *Address:* 39 Gilgorm Rd., Toronto, Canada. *Club:* Sculptors Soc. of Canada.

BOTHWELL, Dorr; painter, printmaker and teacher in oil, gouache, and serigraphic printing; Mendocino Art Centre; *b* San Francisco, 3 May, 1902; *d* of John Stuart Bothwell. *Educ.:* Russ High School, San Diego; Univ of Oregon; *studied art* at Calif. School of Fine Arts and Rudolph Schaeffer School of Design, San Francisco. *Work in permanent collections:* Metropolitan Museum, Museum of Modern Art and Brooklyn Museum, N.Y.; Achenbach Foundation of Graphic Art, San Francisco; Bibliotheque Nationale, Paris; V. & A.; Fogg Museum, Cambridge, Mass.; Whitney Museum, N.Y.; San Francisco Museum of Art. *Address:* 925 N. Plaza Dr., Sp. 93 Apache Jct., Az. 85220, U.S.A. *Signs work:* "Bothwell."

BOTT, Dennis Adrian Roxby, Dip.A.D. (1972), Cert.Ed. (1973), A.R.W.S. (1981), R.W.S. (1983), A.W.G. (1989); painter in water-colour and oil; *b* Chingford, 29 Apr., 1948; *s* of Frederick William Roxby Bott. *Educ.:* Forest School, nr. Snaresbrook, London E17; *studied art* at Colchester School of Art (1967-69), Norwich School of Art (1969-72). *Exhib.:* one-man shows, Ogle Gallery, Eastbourne, Gallery 33, Billingshurst, The Grange, Rottingdean, Ogle Gallery, Cheltenham, Bourne Gallery, Reigate, Worthing Museum and A.G., Canon Gallery, Chichester. *Work in permanent collections:* National Trust, Towner A.G., Eastbourne, Hove Museum, Brighton Museum. *Address:* Maplewood, Cherry Tree Rd., Milford, Surrey GU8 5AX. *Signs work:* "Roxby Bott."

BOTTOMLEY, Eric, G.R.A. (1985); artist/illustrator in oil and gouache; *b* Oldham, 14 July, 1948; *s* of Clifford Bottomley; *m* Jeanette. *Educ.:* N. Chadderton Secondary Modern; *studied art* at Oldham School of Art and Crafts. *Exhib.:* Omell Gallery, Shell House Gallery, Ledbury. *Work in permanent collections:* National Museum of Wales (Industrial and Maritime Museum). *Publications:* illustrated three books, Limited Edn. prints, calendars, greetings cards, magazines and posters. *Address:* The Old Coach House, Much Marcle, Ledbury, Herefordshire HR8 2NL. *Signs work:* "Eric Bottomley."

BOULTON, Janet; painter in water-colour; *b* Wiltshire, 14 Sept., 1936; *d* of E.F. Boulton, farmer; *m* Keith Baines, poet and translator; one *d*. *Studied art* at Swindon and Camberwell Schools of Art (1953-58). *Exhib.:* widely in mixed shows including Belfast Arts Council Open, Chichester National, London Group, R.A. Summer Exhbn., etc; one-man shows: Mercury Gallery (1988, 1991). *Work in permanent collections:* Southern Arts, Radcliffe Infirmary, John Radcliffe Hospital, I.O.W. Area Health Authority, National Gallery, Ottawa. *Publication:* edited and translated, Paul Nash Letters to Mercia Oakley 1909-1918 (Fleece Press, 1991). *Address:* 64 Spring Rd., Abingdon OX14 1AN.

BOURDON SMITH, Diana, R.W.A. (1990); painter in oil; *b* 16 Dec., 1933. *Studied art* at Kingston Art School. *Exhib.:* R.A., N.E.A.C., R.W.A. *Work in permanent collection:* Royal West of England Academy. *Address:* 19 Crescent La., Bath, Avon BA1 2PX. *Signs work:* "D.M.B.S."

BOURGUIGNON, Doris (née Blair), A.R.C.A.; painter in acrylic, oil, water-colour and gouache. *Studied art* at College of Art, Belfast; R.C.A., London; Wallace Harrison, N.Y.; Fernand Leger, Paris; Andre Lhote, Paris. *Exhib.:* one-man and group shows: Belfast, Galerie l'Angle Aigu, Brussels; Museum and A.G., Belfast. *Work in permanent collection:* Museum and A.G., Belfast. *Publication:* illustrated Various Verses by John O'The North. *Address:* 8A Gunter Grove, London SW10 0UJ. *Signs work:* "Doris Bourguignon."

BOURNE, D. Peter, D.A. (Glasgow), R.S.W. (1982); painter in oil, gouache, water-colour; *b* Madras, India, 1 Nov., 1931; *s* of D.J. Bourne, B.A., M.I.C.E.; *m* Marjorie; two *s. Educ.:* Glasgow; *studied art* at Glasgow School of Art (1950-54, David Donaldson). *Exhib.:* R.S.A. Edinburgh, R.G.I. Glasgow, R.S.W. Edinburgh. *Work in permanent collections:* City Art (Edinburgh), Pictures for Schools (Edinburgh). *Address:* Tressour Wood, Weem, Aberfeldy, Perthshire PH15 2LD. *Signs work:* "Bourne."

BOURNE, Jean Susan, B.A.Hons. (1971), Dip.Mus.Stud. (1972), A.M.A. (1974), F.M.A. (1992); Museum curator; Curator, Towneley Hall Art Gallery and Museum, Burnley; President, North West Federation of Museums and Art Galleries (1993-94); *b* Rochdale, 23 Feb., 1950; *d* of Bernard Bourne. *Educ.:* Queen Margaret's School, Escrick, Lancaster University, Manchester University. *Publications:* museum guides, exhbn. catalogues, articles on oak furniture. *Address:* 94 Higham Hall Rd., Higham, Lancs.

BOWEN, Denis, A.R.C.A. (1949), Mem. A.I.C.A.; painter; directed The New Vision Centre (1956-66); Premio Internationale Europa Arte (1964) Silver Star with Antonioni Pasolini; visiting Associate Prof., University of Victoria, B.C., Canada (1969-71); *b* Kimberley, 5 Apr., 1921. *Studied* at King James I Grammar School, Almondbury; Huddersfield School of Art (1938-40); Royal College of Art (1946-49). *Exhib.:* First Retrospective Bede 1300 Festival, Bede Gallery, Jarrow (1973); '50 years on', Second Retrospective Exhbn., Huddersfield A.G. (1989) and Ljubljana Municipal A.G., Slovenia (1992). Exhib. The Sixties Art Scene London, Barbican A.G. London, and internationally. Lecture tour Australia (1993). *Publications:* illustrated, A Concise History of English Painting by William Gaunt (Thomas & Hudson, 1964), Dream of Icarus by Kenneth Coutts-Smith (Hutchinson, 1969), Etching and Engraving by John Brunsdon (Batsford, 1969), Art since 1945 by Herbert Read, Les Peintres Célèbres III Angleterre et Irlande, Alan Bowness (Mazenod, Paris 1964), L'Art Abstrait, Maeght Vols. 3.4. Michel Seuphor/Michel Ragon; critical writings in Art International Lugano, Vie des Arts, Art and Artists, D'Ars Milano, Arts Canada Toronto, R.S.A. Journal and Arts Review, London. Founder mem., Celtic Vision, co-ordinating Ireland, Wales, Scotland, Cornwall, Brittany and Galicia. Mem., Celtic League. *Address:* 4A Seymour Pl., London W1H 5WF.

BOWEN, Thomas Alfred Edwin, F.R.S.A., M.S.I.A., fore-edge book painter; medal designer in gold and platinum (Canterbury Tales); government artist; art director (publicity); engineering draughtsman; industrial designer; lithographer, photo-lithographer; violin-maker; *b* Clapham, London, 2 Feb., 1909; *s* of Thomas Edward Bowen; *m* Mary Dorothy Brooker; two *s. Educ.:* St. John's Bowyer School; *studied art, colour printing and lithography* at London School of Printing, Bolt Court School of Photo-Engraving, Clapham School of Art. *Exhib.:*

R.W.S., London, Coventry and Bristol, Olympia. *Work in permanent collections:* Poznan Museum, Poland, and New York (illuminated MSS.), over 100 fore-edge paintings in Canada—America. *Address:* 9 Crescent Grove, Southside, Clapham Common, London SW4. *Signs work:* "BOWEN" (underlined, with year below line), and see appendix.

BOWETT, Druie; artist in oils, and mixed media; *b* Ripon, Yorks., 1924; *d* of S. A. W. Glover; *m* John Bowett, M.R.C.V.S.; three *s. Educ.:* Queen Margaret's School, Harrogate College of Art. *Exhib.:* one-man shows include Austin Hayes, York (1958, 1961), Wakefield (1964), Sheffield University (1965), Abbot Hall (1966), Midland Group (1961, 1963, 1969), Florence (1970), 359 Gallery (1975), Lincoln sponsored T.S.B. (1978), Worksop Notts C.C. (1980), Rotherham (1980), Drian Gallery (1982), Rufford (1987); group shows include I.P.G., W.I.A.A., R.A., R.S.A., Crane Kalman (1989), etc. *Work in public and private collections* include H.R.H. The Duke of Edinburgh, D. & C.C.'s of Bassetlaw, Rochdale, Nottinghamshire, Leicestershire, Sussex, Wakefield, Kendal, John Players Ltd., Boots plc, Tetley Brewery and other companies. *Publications:* author, Painter's Poetry (Ryton Books, 1989). *Work repro.:* Arts Review (1982), B.B.C. Television. *Address:* Wilton Lodge, Blyth, Worksop, Notts. S81 8EH. *Club:* Lansdowne. *Signs work:* "Bowett."

BOWLES, John Gilbey, A.R.C.A. (1952), A.R.E. (1952); artist in oil, watercolour, printmaker; retd. lecturer, Ruskin School of Drawing, Oxford; and City of London Polytechnic; *b* Matlock, 1929. *Educ.:* Crayord School for Boys, Kent; *studied art* at Gravesend School of Art; R.C.A. *Exhib.:* R.A., R.P.; one-man shows: London, Salford, Eastbourne. *Work in permanent collections:* R.C.A., Eccles Museum, Birkenhead Museum; private collections, England and abroad. *Address:* Sandown, Spott La., Small Hythe, Tenterden, Kent. *Signs work:* "John G. Bowles."

BOWNESS, Sir Alan, C.B.E., M.A.; art historian; Director, Henry Moore Foundation, formerly Director of the Tate Gallery, and Professor of History of Art and Deputy Director, Courtauld Inst. of Art, University of London; *b* London, 11 Jan., 1928; *s* of George Bowness; *m* Sarah Hepworth Nicholson; one *s,* one *d. Educ.:* University College School, Downing College, Cambridge; and Courtauld Inst. of Art. *Publications:* William Scott: Paintings (Lund Humphries, 1964); Modern Sculpture (Studio Vista, 1965); Henry Moore: Complete Sculpture 1949-1986 (Five vols. Lund Humphries, 1965-1988); Alan Davie (Lund Humphries, 1968); Gauguin (Phaidon, 1971); Complete Sculpture of Barbara Hepworth 1960-69 (Lund Humphries, 1971); Modern European Art (Thames & Hudson, 1972); Ivon Hitchens (Lund Humphries, 1973); The Conditions of Success (Thames & Hudson, 1989). *Address:* 91 Castelnau, London SW13 9EL.

BOWYER, Francis David, B.A. Hons. (1974), R.W.S. (1991); artist in watercolour and oil; part time teacher; *b* London, 20 May, 1952; *s* of William Bowyer, R.A., R.W.S., N.E.A.C., R.P.; *m* Glynis Porter; one *s,* one *d. Educ.:* St. Mark's School, London SW6; *studied art* at St. Martin's School of Art (1971-75, Ken Roberts, Ken Bale), Hammersmith School of Art (1976-77, Ruskin Spear). *Exhib.:* R.A. Summer Exhbn., N.E.A.C., R.W.S. *Work in permanent collection:* Bankside Gallery. *Address:* 12 Gainsborough Rd., Chiswick, London W4 1NJ. *Signs work:* "Francis Bowyer."

BOWYER, Jason Richard, M.A., N.E.A.C.; Greenshield Foundation (1983), Daler-Rowney award R.A. Summer Exhbn. (1986), William Townesend scholarship (1987); British Council visit, Bulgaria (1991); painter in oil and pastel, draughtsman; part-time lecturer, University of Westminster; Founder, New English School of Drawing (1993); *b* Chiswick, London, 4 Mar., 1957; *s* of William Bowyer, R.A. *Educ.:* Chiswick School; *studied art* at Camberwell School of Art (1975-79), R.A. Schools (1979-82). *Exhib.:* R.A. (1980-85, 1992-93); one-man show New Grafton (1991). *Publication:* Starting Drawing (Bloomsbury Press, 1988). *Address:* 35 Clifden Rd., Brentford, Middx. TW8 0PB. *Club:* Arts, Dover St. *Signs work:* "J.R. Bowyer."

BOWYER, William, R.A. (1981), R.W.S., N.E.A.C., R.P.; artist in oil paint, water-colour; Head of Fine Art, Maidstone College of Art (1970-81); Hon. sec. N.E.A.C.; *b* Leek, Staffs., 25 May, 1926; *s* of Arthur Bowyer; *m* Vera Mary; two *s*, one *d*. *Educ.:* Burslem School of Art; *studied art* at R.C.A. (Carel Weight, Ruskin Spear). *Exhib.:* R.A., N.E.A.C., R.W.S., many galleries London and provinces. *Work in permanent collections:* R.A., R.W.S., N.P.G., Sheffield City A.G., City of Stoke-on-Trent, many provincial, and private collections home and abroad. *Address:* 12 Cleveland Ave., Chiswick, London W4. *Club:* Dover St. Arts. *Signs work:* "William Bowyer."

BOYD, Arthur Merric Bloomfield; painter in oil, graphics, ceramic; *b* Murrumbeena, Australia, 1920; *s* of William Merric Boyd; *m*; one *s*, two *d*. *Educ.:* State School, Murrumbeena, Victoria, Australia; *studied art* with parents. *Work in permanent collections:* Australian National collections, V. & A., B.M. *Publications:* Monograph by Franz Phillipp (1967), illustrated St. Francis by T. S. R. Boase, Lysistrata (1970), Nebucadnezzar, intro. T. S. R. Boase (Thames & Hudson), Arthur Boyd Drawings (Secker & Warburg, 1973), The Artist and the River (Bay Books 1982), The Art of Arthur Boyd by Ursula Hoff (Andre Deutsch). *Address:* c/o Fischer Fine Art, 30 King St., London SW1.

BOYD, G., A.T.D. (1951), B.A. Hons. Fine Art; Scheme Leader, University of Hertfordshire; *b* Bristol, 1928; *s* of Herbert Leslie Boyd; *m* Pauline Lilian; one *s*, one *d*. *Educ.:* Watford Grammar School; *studied art* at Watford School of Art and London University. *Exhib.:* include London Group, R.A., John Moores, Belfast 68, Shapes in Spaces, Cleveland Drawing International, Triangle Artists, N.Y., London and Barcelona; one-man shows: A.I.A. (1962, 1967), Molton Gallery (1963), Oxford Gallery (1969, 1971, 1982), Herts. College of Art and Design (1980, 1988), Spacex 1983, Sandra Higgins Fine Arts (1991). *Public collections:* Walker Gallery, Trinity College, Oxford, City of Barcelona. *Address:* Blackapple, 54 Scatterdells Lane, Chipperfield, Herts. WD4 9EX. *Signs work:* "Graham Boyd" or "G. BOYD."

BOYD, James Davidson, O.B.E., D.A. (Glas.), F.M.A., F.S.A.Scot., F.R.S.A., M.I.L.G.A.; director Dundee Art Galleries and Museums (1949-82); curator on staff of Glasgow Art Galleries and Museums under Dr. T. J. Honeyman (1946-49); artist in oil and water-colour; enamellist; *b* Glasgow, 10 Aug., 1917; *m* Elizabeth A. Ogilvie, D.A. (Glas.). *Educ.:* Falkirk High and Technical Schools; *studied art* at Glasgow School of Art (1936-40). *Publications:* articles on art and history in various publications. *Address:* 16 Strips of Craigie Rd., Dundee DD4 7PZ.

BOYD, John G., R.P., R.G.I.; part-time lecturer and painter; *b* Stonehaven, Kincardineshire, 7 Apr., 1940; two *s*. *Educ.:* Mackie Academy, Stonehaven; *studied art* at Gray's School of Art, Aberdeen (1958-62) under R. H. Blyth; Hospitalfield College of Art (summer 1961) under James Cumming. *Exhib.:* Graeme Mundy Fine Art (1991), Open Eye Gallery (1989), Henderson Gallery, Edinburgh (1978, 1980), Present Gallery, Lanark (1975), Armstrong Gallery, Glasgow (1970), New 57 Gallery, Edinburgh (1967), R.S.A., R.G.I., R.P.,

Glasgow Art Club. *Address:* 26 Cleveden Rd., Glasgow G12 0PX. *Club:* Glasgow Art. *Signs work:* "Boyd."

BOYDEN, John, B.A.(Lond.), Dip.A.G.M.S.(Manc.), A.M.A.; sculptor in wood and stone; Curator, Hove Museum of Art, Sussex (1973-86); *b* Tunbridge Wells, 1942; *s* of G. J. Boyden, M.A., H.M.I.; *m* Christine Portsmouth; two *s*. *Studied art* at Ruskin School of Drawing. *Publications:* illustrations for The Farthing Press, Museum catalogues. *Address:* 3 Rosslyn Rd., Shoreham-by-Sea, W. Sussex BN43 6WL.

BOYES, Judy Virginia, S.W.A. (1984), B.W.S. (1985); self taught landscape painter in water-colour; *b* Alton, Hants., 1 July, 1943; *d* of S.D. Potter, art teacher; *m* John Boyes; two *d*. *Educ.:* Eggars Grammar School, Alton. *Exhib.:* R.I., Mall Galleries, S.W.A., Westminster Gallery; one-man shows: Liverpool University, Atkinson A.G., Southport, Guildford House A.G., Forest Gallery, Guildford. *Publications:* front cover of Artist Magazine, features and articles on water-colour technique in Artist. *Address:* Town Foot, Troutbeck, nr. Windermere, Cumbria LA23 1LB. *Signs work:* "Judy Boyes."

BOYLE, Alicia; painter; *b* Bangkok; childhood in Ireland and London; *studied art* at Byam Shaw School of Drawing and Painting under F. Ernest Jackson. *Exhib.:* Leger and Leicester Galleries, Arts Council of Northern Ireland, Dublin Galleries etc. Retrospective Exhbn. Crawford Gallery, Cork (1988), Royal Hospital, Kilmainham, Dublin (1989). *Work in permanent collections:* Arts Council of N. Ireland; Ulster Museum; Irish Arts Council; Nottingham Castle Art Gallery; Herbert Art Gallery, Coventry; Abbot Hall Art Gallery, Kendal; Northampton Art Gallery; North West Art Trust, N.I.; Crawford Gallery, Cork; Education committees and private collections in Great Britain, Republic of Ireland, U.S.A., Sweden, etc. *Work repro.:* Apollo, Studio, Arts Review. *Address:* 17 Grosvenor House, Pakenham Rd., Monkstown, Co. Dublin. *Signs work:* "BOYLE" and "AB."

BRABANT, Rosemary, M.F.P.S. (1970); artist in oil, impressionist-abstract; *d* of Cecil Grave; *m* William Brabant; one *d*. *Educ.:* Presentation Convent, Windsor; *studied art* at Melbourne National Gallery; Hammersmith College of Art (Ruskin Spear), Atelier, Florence, Italy. *Exhib.:* London: Woodstock Gallery, New Vision Centre, Loggia Gallery, International Arts Centre, The Place, Cockpit Theatre; Brighton: Vincitore Gallery; Italy: New Medusa Gallery, La Spezia; Palazzo dei Priori, Volterra; Group shows: National, F.P.S. (Trends), Chelsea, Kensington, Paddington, Westminster, Royal Overseas League, Sussex & Kent Artists, Ridley Art Soc. *Work in private collections:* worldwide. *Address:* 36 Arundel Gdns., London W11. *Clubs:* W.I.A.C., I.C.A., F.P.S. *Signs work:* "R. Brabant."

BRADLEY, Frank, R.C.A., R.I.B.A.; architect, painter and theatrical designer; *b* Manchester, May, 1903; *s* of Frank Bradley; *m* Constance Mary Davey, M.A. *Studied art* at College of Art, Manchester, Manchester Academy of Fine Arts, Newlyn School of Painting. *Exhib.:* Utd. Soc. of Artists, V. & A., City Art Gallery, Manchester, Lancashire Artists, Cheshire Artists, R.Cam.A., Paris Salon etc., and in Norway, Germany and the U.S.A.; one-man show Salford Art Gallery (1958). Mem. Royal Cambrian Academy. *Work repro.:* La Revue Moderne and other journals. *Address:* Spring Cottage, Maynestone Rd., Chinley, Derbyshire. *Signs work:* see appendix.

BRADSHAW, Peter; freelance artist in oils and gouache; *b* London, 23 Oct., 1931; *s* of Billing A. Bradshaw, telephonist; *m* Barbara Cameron; one *d*. *Educ.:*

Kingsthorpe Grove, Bective; *studied art* at Northampton School of Art (1945-47) under F. Courtney, E. Goodson. *Exhib.:* United Artists, R.O.I., Northampton Town and County and local exhbns. *Work repro.:* Railway Art. *Address:* 4 Bective Rd., Northampton NN2 7TD. *Club:* Northampton Town and County. *Signs work:* "P. Bradshaw" (cat and robin featured in work).

BRADSHAW, Raymond Henry, A.T.D.; draughtsman, portrait and figure artist in oil, crayon and ink; formerly Head of Art Dept. and Housemaster, Bancroft's School; vice-president, Hesketh Hubbard Art Soc. (Federation of British Artists); *b* 9 Jan., 1918; *s* of Herbert Edward Bradshaw; *m* Marjorie Bayliss; two *d. Educ.:* Bancroft's School; *studied art* at West Ham School of Art (1935-36); Westminster School of Art (1936-38) under Mark Gertler, Bernard Meninsky, Mervyn Peake and Adrian Hill; Hornsey School of Art (1938-39). *Exhib.:* R.B.A., R.A., R.P., etc. Work in private ownership in England, France, Switzerland, Sweden, America and Australia. *Publication:* illustrated, Introducing Local Studies (Dent.) *Address:* Little Monkwood Lodge, Baldwins Hill, Loughton, Essex IG10 1SF. *Signs work:* "Raymond H. Bradshaw."

BRAMMER, Leonard Griffiths, A.R.C.A. (Painting) 1929, Travelling Scholar (Engraving) R.C.A. (1930), R.E. (1956); painter and etcher; Supervisor of Art, Stoke-on-Trent Educ. Authority (1951-1969); *b* Burslem, Stoke-on-Trent, 1906; *s* of Frederick William Brammer, designer and builder of pottery ovens and kilns; *m* Florence Barnett; one *d. Studied art* at Burslem School of Art (1923-26, Gordon M. Forsyth); R.C.A. (1926-1930, Sir William Rothenstein, Malcolm Osborne, Robert Austin, Job Nixon, E. Constable Alston, Gwyn-Jones). *Exhib.:* R.A., R.P.E. *Work in permanent collections:* Tate Gallery, B.M., V. & A., Ashmolean, Oxford, Wedgwood Museum, Stoke-on-Trent A.G., Carlisle A.G., University of Keele, British Council, Gladstone Pottery Museum; and private collections. *Address:* "Swn-y-Wylan", Morfa Bychan, Porthmadog, Gwynedd. *Signs work:* "L. G. Brammer."

BRAND, Margaret, M.M.A.A. (1969), A.I.M.B.I. (1968); medical artist, landscape and surrealist painter in oil, water-colour and mixed media; *b* London, 1938. *Educ.:* Stella Maris Convent, Bideford; *studied art* at Reigate and Redhill School of Art (1957-60); Post-grad. course in medical illustration, Guy's Hospital Medical School (1960-61). Deputy Head of Dept. of Medical Illustration, Guy's Hospital (1962-69). Royal Commission 1974. *Exhib.:* R.A., R.M.S., London and provincial societies and galleries. *Work repro.:* illustrations in numerous medical and scientific books and journals. *Address:* 31 Taunton Ave., Caterham, Surrey CR3 5EB. *Signs work:* "M. Brand" or "M.B."

BRANDEBOURG, Margaret (previously listed as M. E. Winter); part-time teacher in adult educ. for I.L.E.A.; *b* Surbiton, Surrey, 28 Apr., 1926; *d* of Eric Brandebourg, solicitor; *m* Deryck Winter. *Educ.:* Tiffin Girls' School; *studied art* at Kingston Art School and R.A. Schools. Since 1976 has worked in textiles. *Exhib.:* British Crafts Centre, Seven Dials Gallery, etc. *Commissioned work* in Portsmouth Museum. *Publication:* book on Seminole Patchwork (Batsford, 1987). Lectures and demonstrates on this subject. *Address:* 3 Cedars Rd., Hampton Wick KT1 4BG. *Club:* Quilter's Guild (founder mem.).

BRANNAN, Noel Rowston, A.T.D. (1952); painter; *b* Tynemouth, 25 Dec., 1921; *s* of the late Edward Eaton Brannan, artist; *m* Mavis Annie (*née* Leitch); one *s,* one *d. Educ.:* Humberstone Foundation School, Clee, Lincs.; *studied art* at School of Art, Lincoln (1947-51), College of Art, Leicester (1951-52). *Exhib.:* one-man: Willoughby Gallery, Corby Glen, Lincs. (1985); R.A., R.B.A., New English, A.I.A., etc. *Work in permanent collections:* Usher A.G., Lincoln, Fison's

Fertilizer Works, water-colour (1948), Wolvey, gouache (1960), Riversley A.G. Nuneaton, Street Scene, oil (1973), Industrial Landscapes, gouache. *Address:* Athelstan, Hinckley Rd., Burbage, Leics. LE10 2AG. *Signs work:* "Noel Brannan."

BRANNAN, Peter Arthur, R.B.A. (1960), N.D.D., painting (1951); artist in oil, water-colour, etc.; *b* Cleethorpes, 13 Dec., 1926; *s* of the late Edward E. Brannan, artist. *Educ.:* Humberston Foundation School, School of Art, Grimsby, and Leicester College of Art. *Exhib.:* R.A., R.B.A., N.E.A.C., etc.; one-man shows, Trafford Gallery, London (six), Usher Gallery, Lincoln (1978). *Work in permanent collections:* Usher Art Gallery, Lincoln, G.L.C., Manchester College of Art, Grundy Gallery, Blackpool, Notts. and Kesteven Ed. Committees. *Address:* Manor Cottage, Welbourn, Lincoln LN5 0NW. *Clubs:* R.B.A., Lincolnshire Artists' Soc. *Signs work:* "PETER BRANNAN."

BRANSBURY, Allan Harry, F.R.B.S., F.I.T.D., M.I.Mgt., N.D.D., A.T.C. (Lond.); artist, designer, educationalist; *b* Jersey, 1942; *s* of H. G. Bransbury. *Educ.:* Victoria College; *studied* at West of England College of Art, Bristol, and the University of London Inst. of Educ., followed by study-travel in Canada and U.S.A.; *m*; two *s. Commissioned work* in Jersey and England. Artist in Residence, University of Sussex (1976). Principal of the London Borough of Bromley Centre for Arts and Crafts (1977-80). Resident in Scotland since 1980. *Address:* Burnside, Kilmuir, North Kessock, Inverness IV1 1XG. *Signs work:* see appendix.

BRAYER, Yves; painter; Member of Académie des Beaux-Arts, Paris; Officer Légion d'Honneur; Director, Marmottan Museum, Paris; *s* of General Victor Brayer. Born at Versailles, France, on 18 Nov., 1907, he showed a great individuality from the start of his career and is now one of the best-known French painters of his generation. He studied art in Montparnasse academies, then in the National School of Arts. In 1927, he was deeply impressed by a first trip to Spain, but the Prix de Rome, which he won in 1930, led him to make a prolonged stay in Italy. He also visited Greece, Constantinople and Morocco. Attracted by the quality of the light, he likes working in Provence and in Camargue (since 1945), and it marks a new stage in his development. He has designed sets and costumes for the operas of Paris, Amsterdam and Monte Carlo, and designed tapestries for Gobelins and Aubusson. He illustrated luxury editions, including texts from Henry de Montherlant, André Gide, Ernest Hemingway and Paul Claudel. The Paris Museum of Art Moderne, many museums in France and foreign countries and many collectors have bought his works. *Address:* 22 rue Monsieur le Prince, Paris, 6°. *Signs work:* "Yves Brayer."

BRAZDA, Jan; abstract painter, stained glass artist and stage designer, working in oils, tempera, stained glass, mosaic, church textiles, fresco, stage décor and costumes *inter alia* Covent Garden, Lyric Opera, Chicago, Staatsoper, Munich; *b* Rome, 4 Dec., 1917; *s* of Oki Brazda. *Studied art* at Academy of Fine Arts, Prague, 1st Prize, Triennale, Milan and Biennale, Venice. *Work in permanent collections:* National Museum, Prins Eugen Gallery (Stockholm), Art Museums of Gothenburg, Malmö, Röhsska Konstslöjd Museum, Archive Museum at Lund University. *Work repro.:* Svenska Konsntnärer, Allhems, Armitage Stained Glass. Member of National Organisation of Swedish Artists (K.R.O). *Address:* Rindögatan 44, Stockholm, S115 58, Sweden.

BRAZIER, Connie, S.W.A. (1980); artist in water-colour, and engraved glass; Glass Engraving Tutor (retd.), Sutton College of Liberal Arts; *b* Croydon; *d* of

Arthur Philip Guerrier, solicitor; *m* Desmond Brazier; two *s. Educ.:* Stamford High School for Girls, Lincs.; *studied art* at Croydon School of Art (Reginald Marlow, Frederick Hinchliffe, Michael Cadman). *Exhib.:* Europa Gallery, Sutton (1977, 1979, 1981, 1983, 1984), Whitehall, Cheam (1986), Fairfield Halls (shared) (1987), Civic Centre A.G., Tunbridge Wells (1987), Playhouse, Epsom (1991), R.I., R.M.S., S.B.A. *Address:* Pensilva, 10 Heights Cl., Banstead, Surrey SM7 1DR. *Club:* Reigate Soc. of Artists. *Signs work:* see appendix.

BRECKMAN, Barbara Rosamund; City and Guilds Fine Arts Dip. (1971); portrait, figure (nude) artist in oil, pen and ink, gouache, etching and aquatint; *b* London, 19 Mar., 1947. *Studied art* at City and Guilds of London Art School. *Exhib.:* City of London Festival at Royal Exchange (1969,1970), Arthouse Gallery, Jerusalem (1972), Chelsea (March 1990), Staircase Gallery, Kew (1990), Drey Gallery, Chelsea (1991). *Address:* 106 Kings Ct., King St., London W6 0RW. *Club:* Kew Studios. *Signs work:* "Barbara Breckman" or "B. BRECKMAN."

BREEZE, George, M.A., F.R.S.A., F.M.A.; museum curator; Chief Art Gallery and Museums Officer, Cheltenham Borough Council; *b* Wilmslow, Ches., 12 Mar., 1947; *s* of George Breeze, M.A.; *m* Rachel M. Breeze; two *s. Educ.:* University of Manchester (B.A.), Barber Inst. of Fine Arts, University of B'ham (M.A.). *Publications:* Edith Payne (1978); Joseph Southall (1980); Arthur and Georgie Gaskin (1981) (co-author); Margaret Gere (1984) (co-author). *Address:* c/o Cheltenham Art Gallery and Museums, Clarence St., Cheltenham, Glos. GL50 3JT.

BRENNAND, Catherine, B.Ed. Art and Design, R.I.; artist in water-colour, water-colour with wax resist, line and wash; Market Analyst, Construction Industry; *b* Woking, 11 Oct., 1961; *m* Mark Brennand. *Educ.:* Dover Grammar School; *studied art* at Bishop Otter College, Chichester (1980-83, Geoff Lowe, Malcolm Norman, Alan Saunders). *Exhib.:* Linda Blackstone Gallery Pinner, Stafford A.G., David Curzon Gallery Thames Ditton. *Address:* Studio Fifteen, The Wheatlands, Perton, S. Staffs. WV6 7XP. *Club:* Wolverhampton Art Soc. *Signs work:* "Brennand."

BRENT, Isabelle; painter/illustrator in water-colour and gold leaf; painter of commissioned portraits of animals throughout the world; *b* Caversham, 17 Mar., 1961; *d* of Norman Edmund Brent. *Studied art* at Loughborough College of Art and Design; further studies in France and Italy; research studies in the Dept. of Decorative Arts, Leicester Museum. *Exhib.;* R.A., London and provincial galleries. Work in private collections throughout the world. *Publications:* written and illustrated: The Christmas Story, Cameo Cats, The Well-travelled Cat, A Cat for all Seasons, Noah's Ark. *Address:* 5 Bouverie Ct., Whissendine, nr. Oakham, Rutland LE15 7HA. *Signs work:* see appendix.

BRENT, Ralph Richard Angus; land and seascape painter in oil and water-colour; *b* 5 Oct., 1903; *studied art* St. Martin's, London, under Bertram Nicholls, P.R.B.A. *Exhib.:* R.A., R.B.A., Fine Art Soc., Newlyn Soc. of Artists, Bladon Art Gallery, Hurstbourne Tarrant. *Invited exhib.:* Southport, Blackpool, Bolton, Bradford, Exeter, Devon Art Soc., Torquay, Auckland Soc. and Christchurch, N.Z., Beaulieu Gallery, Southampton Art Soc., Bournemouth Art Soc., Southampton Civic Art Gallery, etc. *Addresses:* c/o Lloyds Bank Ltd., Fordingbridge, Hants.; Marchwood, Hyde, Fordingbridge, Hants. SP6 2QL; Chapel House Gallery, Dummer, Basingstoke. *Signs work:* see appendix.

BRETT, Simon, S.W.E., A.R.E. (1986); wood engraver; Chairman, S.W.E. (1986-92); *b* Windsor, 27 May, 1943; *s* of Antony Brett, hospital administrator; *m* Juliet Wood; one *d. Educ.:* Ampleforth College; *studied art* at St. Martin's School of Art (1960-64, as a painter; learned engraving from Clifford Webb). *Exhib.:* S.W.E., R.E., R.A., and occasional one-man shows. *Publications:* for own Paulinus Press (Francis Williams Award 1982 for 'The Animals of Saint Gregory'); Readers Digest Bible (1990), 'Clarissa', 'Jane Eyre' (Folio Soc. 1991); edited 'Engravers' (1987 and 1992); 'Confessions of St. Augustine' (1993); 'Wood Engraving' (1993). *Address:* 12 Blowhorn St., Marlborough, Wilts. SN8 1BT. *Signs work:* "Simon Brett."

BRETTINGHAM, Walter David, N.D.D. (1953), A.T.D. (1954); painter in oil; *b* London, 1924; *s* of John Robert Brettingham. *Educ.:* Marley School and Royal Navy; *studied art* at Sir John Cass College, London (1948-51), St. Martin's School of Art (1951-53), Bournemouth College of Art (1953-54). *Exhib.:* one-man shows, Berystede Hotel, Ascot (1972), 3 Households Gallery, Chalfont (1973), Upper St. Gallery, Richmond (1974), Century Gallery, Henley (1979), Guildford House, Guildford (1981), Holkham Gallery, Norfolk (1982), Bloomsbury Gallery, London (1984). *Work in permanent collections:* Deanery, Westminster Abbey, London University Educ. Inst. *Publications:* colour supplements, 'Pictorial Education' (1963-69); 'De Brethenham and Brettingham' (1971). *Address:* 25 Cabrera Ave., Virginia Water, Surrey GU25 4EZ. *Signs work:* "Brettingham."

BREWSTER, Martyn Robert, B.F.A. (1974), Post. Grad. Dip. in Printmaking (1975), A.T.C. (1978); Eastern Arts award (1977), British Council travel grant (1991); painter in oil and acrylic, drawings, printmaking — mainly silkscreen, etchings; *b* Oxford, 24 Jan., 1952; *s* of Robert Brewster; *m* Hilary Carter; one *d. Educ.:* Watford Boys' Grammar School; *studied art* at Herts. College of Art (1970-71), Brighton Polytechnic (1971-75, Dennis Creffield), Brighton Polytechnic Art Teachers' Centre (1977-78). *Exhib.:* one-man shows: Peterborough City Museum and A.G. (1983), Winchester Gallery, Hants. (1986), Warwick Arts Trust, London (1986), Woodland A.G., London (1987), Bede Gallery, Jarrow (1988), Thumb Gallery, London (1988, 1989, 1990). *Work in permanent collections:* Warwick Arts Trust, Winchester School of Art, St Thomas' Hospital, Bede Gallery, Cable and Wireless, Cambridge Inst. of Educ., Epping Forest District Museum, Open University, Unilever, I.B.M. *Address:* 15 West Rd., Boscombe, Bournemouth, Dorset BM5 2AN. *Signs work:* "Brewster" either on front or back of work with date.

BRIDGE, Muriel Elisabeth Emily (Mrs. Millie Taylor), N.D.D.; artist in water-colour and oils; art critic at local art societies; part-time lecturer, Chichester College of Technology; part-time teacher, Littlemead Grammar School; *b* Rome, 1934; *m* John R. Taylor; one *s*, two *d. Studied art:* (graphic design) at St. Martin's School of Art under Mr. Rowe and John Minton; recently studied under Peter Folkes to obtain Cert. of Advanced Painting. *Exhib.:* Mall Gallieries, Chenil Galleries, London, Hiscock Gallery, Southsea, Havant Art Centre, and Bishops Kitchen, Chichester (1986) with Emsworth Group. *Address:* 22 Victoria Rd., Chichester, W. Sussex. *Signs work:* "M. Bridge."

BRIDGEMAN, John, A.R.C.A. (1949), F.R.B.S. (1960); sculptor; *b* Felixstowe, Suffolk; *m* Irene Dancyger, journalist; one *s*, one *d. Studied* at Colchester School of Art; Royal College of Art. Exhibited widely. *Work in permanent collections:* sculptures at St. Helen's, Birmingham, Queen Elizabeth Hospital, Dudley Road Hospital, Keighley, Coventry Cathedral; 8ft. bronze group, St. Bartholomew's,

Barking Rd., London; Mother and Child (Relief), West Bromwich; public gardens, Coventry, private gardens, private collections; font, Hillmorton Church, Rugby etc. *Address:* 27 Hyde Pl., Leamington, Warwickshire CV32 5BT. *Signs work:* see appendix.

BRIDGWATER, Barbara Helen, A.T.D. (1941), A.I.I.D. (1948); on staff of Malvern School of Art (1941-48), Greenmore College (1950-56); senior lecturer at City of Birmingham College of Education (1956-75); Birmingham Polytechnic Centre for Education (1975-77); works in oils, textiles and photography; *b* 2 Dec., 1919; *d* of Harold G. Brunt; *m* Alan Bridgwater, A.R.B.S. (decd.); one *d; studied art* at Birmingham College of Art (1936-41). *Exhib.:* R.A., N.E.A.C., R.S.A., R.B.A., etc. *Address:* Conghurst Oast, Hawkhurst, Kent. *Signs work:* "Barbara H. Bridgwater" or "BHB."

BRIERTON, Irene Annette, S.W.A. (1988); painter of wildlife in water-colour; *b* Belper, 10 Dec., 1948; *d* of William Gibson, M.B.I.M.; *m* Robert Brierton; one *s*, one *d. Educ.:* Burnham Grammar School, Bucks. *Exhib.:* R.I. (1985-88), S.WL.A. (1985), S.W.A., Llewellyn Alexander (Fine Paintings) Ltd., London, Duffield Art Galleries, Duffield, Derbyshire. *Work repro.:* paintings by W.W.F. as cards. *Address:* 17 St. Michael's Cl., Crich, Derbyshire DE4 5DN. *Signs work:* "Irene Brierton."

BRIGHT, Madge, A.R.O.I. (1990); winner, R.O.I. award Cornellissen prize; self taught artist in oil and mixed media; *b* S. Africa, 15 Feb., 1939; *m* P.S. Johnson; three *s. Educ.:* Chaplin Gwelo, Rhodesia. *Exhib.:* R.O.I. Mall Galleries, S.B.A., Britain's Painters, Hertford-Century Gallery Henley-on-Thames, Iwano Gallery Osaka Japan, Noor Gallery Bahrein, Look Out Gallery Plettenberg Bay S. Africa, Llewellyn Alexander Fine Art. *Work in permanent collection:* National Gallery Zimbabwe. *Address:* 1 Great Ash, Lubbock Rd., Chislehurst, Kent BR7 5JZ. *Clubs:* S.B.A., Hertford Art Soc., Five Women Artists Plus. *Signs work:* "Madge Bright."

BRIGSTOCK, Jane Lena, B.A. Hons. (Painting) (1979), M.A. (Printmaking) (1980), British Institution Fund Printmakers award (1981); guest artist, California College of Art and Crafts (1981-82); painter in pastel, water-colour, printmaker; lecturer, Nene College, Northampton; Maidstone School of Art; Chelsea School of Art; *b* 28 Mar., 1957; *d* of Michael John Brigstock; *m* Michael John Addison. *Educ.:* Wellingborough County High School for Girls; *studied art* at Maidstone School of Art, and Chelsea School of Art. *Exhib.:* R.A., Cleveland Drawing Bienale, Royal Overseas League, Drew Gallery, Canterbury. *Work in permanent collection:* Northampton C.C. *Address:* 56 Fallowfield, Wellingborough, Northants. *Signs work:* "J.L. Brigstock."

BRINDLEY, Donald, A.R.C.A. Sculpture (1951), F.R.B.S. (1973); sculptor in clay, bronze, ceramics of portraiture, equestrian subjects; Consultant to Josiah Wedgwood & Sons, Royal Worcester Porcelain Co., and continental and American businessses; *b* Penkhull, Stoke-on-Trent, 22 Feb., 1928; *s* of Albert Brindley, pottery manager; one *s*, one *d. Educ.:* Junior Art Dept. Burslem College of Art; *studied art* at R.C.A. (1948-51, Profs. Frank Dobson and John Skeaping, R.A.). *Work in permanent collections:* H.M. The Queen, the late Lord Mountbatten. *Address:* Fernlea, Leek Rd., Stockton Brook, Staffordshire Moorlands ST9 9NH. *Signs work:* "D. BRINDLEY" and see appendix.

BRINE, John Nicholas, R.B.A., A.R.C.A. (1949); artist in oils and acrylic; Curator and Master of Painting and Drawing, Royal Academy Schools (Sept. 1955-Dec. 1960); Head of School of Fine Art, Ravensbourne College of Art and

Design, Chislehurst; *b* 25 June, 1920; *s* of George Edward Brine; *m* Janet Pace, Cert. R.A.S. (1964); two *d. Studied art* at Clapham School of Art (1935-1939), R.C.A. (1946-49). *Address:* 1 Herne Cottages, Walshes Rd., Crowborough, E. Sussex TN6 3RA. *Signs work:* "BRINE."

BRISCOE, Michael J., B.A. (Hons.); artist in oil and acrylic on canvas; *b* Colwyn Bay, 11 May, 1960; *s* of T.J. Briscoe; one *s*, one *d. Educ.:* Eirias High School; *studied art* at Wrexham College of Art (1978-79, David Cooper), Sheffield City Polytechnic (1979-82, Brian Peacock, Terry Lee). *Exhib.:* Sheffield National (1980), Stowells Trophy (prize winner), Wales '83 Travelling Exhbn., R.A. Summer Exhbn. (1983-85), Through Artists Eyes Mostyn A.G., Paris Salon des Nations (1984); mixed shows, Piccadilly Gallery (1984-85). Produces illustrations for advertising since 1988. *Address:* 81 Coed Coch Rd., Colwyn Bay, Clwyd LL29 9UW. *Signs work:* "Mike Briscoe."

BROAD, Ronald Arthur; freelance artist in oil and water-colour specialising in winter landscape and line drawing; *b* Crookham, Berks., 2 Sept., 1930; *s* of A.B. Broad, farmer and landowner. *Educ.:* Newbury Grammar School, St. Aidan's College (C. of E.), Birkenhead; *studied art:* tutored by George Bissill. *Exhib.:* regularly at R.A. *Address:* Belmont, Orchard Rd., S. Wonston, Winchester, Hants. SO21 3EX. *Club:* Hockley Golf. *Signs work:* "Ronald A. Broad."

BROADFIELD, Aubrey Alfred (Alan), M.A. (1934); librarian and author; art teacher at Alleyn's School, Dulwich (1936-37), librarian (1938-1975); *b* Doncaster, 1910; *s* of Rev. A. L. Broadfield; *m* Robina Margaret Hedley. *Educ.:* Manchester Grammar School; New College, Oxford; Birmingham University; *studied art* at Loughborough College, Slade School under Randolph Schwabe (1935-36), Courtauld Inst. *Author of:* Philosophy of Classification (1946), Philosophy of Librarianship (1949), Leicester as it was (1972); contributions to T.L.S., World Review, National and English Review, Bookseller, Leicester Archaeological Soc., Library Review. *Address:* 99 Station Rd., Glenfield, Leics. LE3 8GS. *Signs work:* "AB."

BROADFIELD, Robina Margaret; artist in oil, water-colour, tempera; mem. of Council, Leicester Soc. of Artists (1954); *b* Hebburn-on-Tyne; *d* of Francis Hedley; *m* A. Broadfield, M.A. (Oxon.), historian and author. *Educ.:* Grammar School, Jarrow; High School of Commerce, Toronto; *studied art:* mainly self-taught. *Exhib.:* Wiesbaden, Leicester, Nottingham Castle, Galleria Europa Arte, Ancona, Italy, Annuale Italiana D'Arte Grafica, Mostra Internazionale (1968) (Medaglia e Diploma d'Onore), Bienalle delle Regioni (1968-69), Mostra Confronto Internazionale (Medaglia e Diploma di Menzione Onorevole). *Address:* 99 Station Rd., Glenfield, Leics. LE3 8GS. *Signs work:* "R.M.B."

BROCKWAY, Michael Gordon, N.E.A.C.; artist in oil and water-colour; *b* 11 Apr., 1919; *m* Margaret, *d* of Sir William Harris, K.C.V.O., D.Mus.; two *s. Educ.:* Stowe and Peterhouse, Cambridge; *studied art* at Farnham School of Art (1946-50), Cheltenham School of Art (1950), and Ruskin School of Drawing, Oxford (1951-54). *Exhib.:* R.A., R.I., R.B.A., N.E.A.C. *Publication:* Charles Knight, R.W.S., R.O.I., 1952. *Address:* 1 Swan Lane Cl., Burford OX18 4SP. *Signs work:* "MICHAEL BROCKWAY."

BRODERICK, Laurence John, A.R.B.S., N.D.D. (1965); sculptor in figurative art — bronze and stone, well known for otter carvings and portrait heads; *b* Bristol, 18 June, 1935; *s* of John Leonard Broderick; *m* Ingrid; three *s. Educ.:* St. Nichol's, Clifton, Bristol; Bembridge School, I.O.W.; *studied art* at Regent St. Polytechnic (1952-57, Ray Millard, Geoffrey Deeley), Hammersmith School of Art (1964-65, Sidney Harpley, Keith Godwin). *Exhib.:* Century Galleries, Henley-on-Thames; Park St. Gallery, Bristol; Belgrave Gallery, London; Gallery 1667, Halifax, Canada; City of London Festival; Rue Paradis, Monte Carlo, Monaco; Manor Gallery, Royston; Printmakers Gallery, Inverness; Malcolm Innes Gallery, Edinburgh; Phoenix Gallery, Lavenham; Chester Arts Festival; Warrington Museum A.G.; since 1980 annual sculpture exhbn. Isle of Skye; mixed shows: Keats House, Hampstead; C.P.S., London; R.W.E.A., Bristol; R.A., London; R.B.A., London; Art London '91; Broxbourne Festival. *Work in permanent collections:* Crucifix, Christchurch, Hants.; Madonna of the Magnificat, Priory, Dunstable, Beds.; St. George, Haberdashers' Aske's School, Elstree, Herts.; Elation, Mother and Child, The Otter, Cherrybank Gdns., Perth (Bell's); Teko — The Swimming Otter, The Otter Trust, Earsham, Suffolk; Leaping Salmon, Chester Business Park; Head of Philippe Chatrier (Pres. ITF), Queen's Club, London and Roland Gaross, Paris; Turtle, Prudential, London. *Publications:* Life of Purcell (Chatto & Windus), Uncle Matts Mountain (Macmillan), Village life through the Ages (Evans), Soapstone Carving (Alec Tiranti). *Address:*Thane Studios, 10 Vicarage Rd., Waresley, Sandy, Beds. SG19 3DA. *Signs work:* "Laurence Broderick."

BRODY, Frederick J., A.V.C.M. (1931), A.R.C.A. (1937), M.S.I.A. (1946), F.I.A.L. (1952), F.R.S.A. (1960); lecturer in art, interior designer, silversmith, cabinet-maker, painter in tempera; *b* Sheffield, 31 May, 1914; *s* of Solomon Brody, master cabinet manufacturer; *studied art* at Sheffield College of Art (1929-34); R.C.A. (1934-37) under Prof. Tristram, Sir William Rothenstein, John Nash, Bawden, Ravilious, Spencer, Barnett Freedman. *Exhib.:* London, provinces, International Exhbn. (Paris, 1937), B.I.F. exhbns., Britain Can Make It exhbn. Festival of Britain (1951) and U.S.A. *Work repro.:* silverware at Sheffield and London, furniture in own furniture factory. *Address:* 15 Cherry Tree Drive, Sheffield S11 9AE. *Signs work:* see appendix.

BRONDUM-NIELSEN, Birgitte, R.I., S.S.W.A.; Diplome d'Honneur, Vichy (1964); artist in water-colours; illustrator; *b* Copenhagen, 1917; *d* of Dr. E. Bocher; *m* H. Brondum-Nielsen. *Educ.:* Copenhagen; *studied art* at College of Arts and Crafts, Copenhagen. *Exhib.:* group shows: R.A., R.S.A., S.S.A., R.S.W., Pitlochry Festival Theatre, Charlottenborg (Copenhagen), Salon International de Vichy, Brighton Art Gallery, Royal Glasgow Institute of Fine Arts; one-man shows: Bristol, Stirling, Edinburgh (four), Roskilde (Denmark), Edinburgh Festival, Copenhagen. *Work in permanent collection:* Glasgow Art Gallery, the private collection of H.R.H. The Duke of Edinburgh. *Work repro.:* illustrations for songbooks for children (Danish), De Smaa Synger; Fairytales from many Lands; Switzerland, etc. *Address:* Killichonan, Rannoch Station, Perthshire, Scotland. *Signs work:* "BITTE B-N."

BROOK, Peter, R.B.A.; painter in oil; *b* Holmfirth, Yorks., 6 Dec., 1927; *s* of Hildred Brook; *m* Margaret Thornsby; two *d. Studied art* at Goldsmiths' College, London University. Works in many public and private collections in this country, Switzerland, U.S.A., South Africa and Australia. *Painted:* West Riding; Pennine Landscapes; Oxford Almanak, 1974; Cornwall, 1974; Hannah Hauxwell (40 pictures) 1979-81; Scotland 1981-88; Bowland 1987-88; Sheepfarms 1988; Jim Cropper (One Man and His Dog winner) 15 paintings 1989-90. *Publication:* 'Peter Brook—The Pennine Landscape Painter' (Ryburn Pub. Co., Halifax) The Life and Work, with 106 paintings in colour, hardback and softback. *Address:* 119 Woodhouse La., Brighouse, W. Yorks. HD6 3TP. *Signs work:* "PETER BROOK."

BROOKE, Anne Isabella, A.T.D.; landscape painter and former art teacher; *b* nr. Huddersfield, 1916. *Studied art* at The Byam Shaw, Chelsea and Huddersfield Schools of Art and London University Institute of Educ. *Exhib.:* R.A., R. Scottish A., N.E.A.C., Paris Salon, R.B.A., R. Cambrian A., R.O.I., W.I.A.C., R.I. Salon, United Artists, National Soc. and many provincial exhbns. *Official purchases:* Harrogate A.G., Wakefield A.G., Keighley A.G., The Beecroft A.G., Southend-on-Sea, the former Herts., Lincs., Bristol and Northumberland Educ. Coms. *Address:* 3 Oak Terr., Harrogate HG2 0EN. *Signs work:* "A. Brooke."

BROOKE, Geoffrey Arthur George, D.S.C., R.N. (retd.); oil painter; *b* Bath, 25 Apr., 1920; *s* of Capt. J. Brooke, D.S.C., R.N. (retd.). *Educ.:* R.N. College, Dartmouth; *studied art* under Miss Sonia Mervyn, 28 Roland Gdns., SW7 (1949-50). *Exhib.:* Army Art Soc. exhbns. *Address:* Beech House, Balcombe, Sussex RH17 6PS. *Signs work:* "G.A.G.B."

BROOKES, Malcolm John, A.T.D. (1964), R.B.S.A. (1974), A.R.Cam.A. (1990); teacher, painter in gouache and oil; Head of Art, Craft and Design, Stourport-on-Severn High School; *b* Birmingham, 11 July, 1943; *s* of William Brookes, telephone engineer; *m* Norma Turner; one *s*, one *d. Educ.:* Moseley School of Art; *studied art* at Birmingham College of Art and Crafts (1959-64, Gilbert Mason). *Exhib.:* R.B.S.A., Worcester A.G., Lichfield, Malvern, Stoke-on-Trent A.G., Dudley A.G., Icon Gallery, Birmingham, Royal West of England Academy, Mall Galleries, Royal Cambrian Academy. *Address:* 3 Clive Rd., Bromsgrove, Worcs. B60 2AY. *Clubs:* R.B.S.A., R.Cam.A., Malvern Festival Artists. *Signs work:* "M.J. Brookes."

BROTHERSTON, Daphne, F.S.B.A.; artist specializing in flower drawing with water-colour tint, and botanical painting; *b* 19 Apr., 1920; *d* of Eric A. Price, solicitor; *m* Peter Brotherston, engineer; one *s*, one *d. Educ.:* Sutton High School, G.P.D.S.T.; *studied art* at Epsom A.E.C. *Exhib.:* S.B.A. Westminster Hall, S.G.F.A. Knapp Gallery; three-man shows: Fairfield Halls, Hampton Court International Flower Show. *Work repro.:* wedding cards/Christmas cards (C.C.A. Stationery Ltd.). *Address:* 8 Bushby Ave., Rustington, W. Sussex BN16 2BZ. *Club:* S.B.A. *Signs work:* "Daphne Brotherston."

BROUGHTON, Aya, N.S., M.F.P.S., W.I.A.C., S.W.A.; artist in water-colour and oil, mural painter; Associate, Société des Artistes Français; Paris Salon silver medal (1972); Lecturer for the Embassy of Japan; *b* Kyoto, Japan; *d* of Dr. T. Kumagai (M.D.); *m* B. L. Broughton, M.A. (Oxon). *Educ.:* Kyoto Furitsu Daiichi High School and the College, Kyoto, Japan; *studied art* at Newton Abbot School of Art and Dartington Adult Centre. *Exhib.:* R.A. (1958), W.I.A.C., N.S., R.B.A., R.I., R.O.I., London Group, Paris Salon, United Soc., R.W.S. Exhbn. Flower Painting, Festival of Women, Wembley, London Exhbn. of Living British Women Artists, Flower Painters of the World (1971). *Work collected privately* in U.K., Japan, Switzerland, America, New Zealand. *Work repro.:* La Revue Moderne, Western Morning News, Herald Express and Torquay Times, TV BBC 1 Peninsula. *Publications:* Article on Buddhism and Japanese Art (The Mahabodhi Journal). *Address:* Greylands, 14 Cleveland Rd., Torquay, Devon. *Signs work:* "AYA"; see appendix.

BROUGHTON, Neville, M.B., Ch.B.Liverpool (1943), D.C.H., R.C.S. (1953); retd. medical practitioner; self taught painter in acrylic, water-colour and oil since 1970; *b* Lincoln, 11 Sept., 1919; *m* Dorothy Mary Cunliffe; two *d. Educ.:* Baines Grammar School, University of Liverpool. *Exhib.:* R.A., Chenil Galleries London, Graves Gallery Sheffield, Usher Gallery Lincoln, Stockport Gallery, galleries in U.S.A. *Address:* Long Acre, Laneham Rd., Rampton, Retford, Notts.

DN22 0JX. *Club:* Lincolnshire and S. Humberside Artists' Soc. *Signs work:* "N. Broughton" or "Neville Broughton."

BROWN, Deborah; sculptor in glass fibre, papier mache and bronze; *b* Belfast, 1927. *Studied art* in Belfast, Dublin, Paris. *Exhib.:* one-man shows and major group exhbns. in Ireland, Gt. Britain, France, Germany, Scandinavia, U.S.A. *Work in private and public collections* in Ireland, Gt. Britain and U.S.A. *Commissions:* 1965, by Ferranti Ltd., panels for their building at Hollinwood, Manchester; 1989 and 1991, major commissions in bronze. *Prizes:* 1970 First Prize Carroll Open Award, Irish Exhibition of Living Art, Dublin; 1970 Prize Open Painting Arts Council of N. Ireland; 1980 Sculpture Prize Eva Limerick. Included in ROSC Dublin 1984. *Address:* 115 Marlborough Pk. Sth., Belfast BT9 6HW.

BROWN, Doris, S.W.A. (1987); freelance landscape artist in water-colour and ink, tutor and lecturer; *b* Newcastle under Lyme, Staffs., 17 Apr., 1933; *d* of Cecil Brown. *Educ.:* Burslem College of Art, Stoke-on-Trent; *studied art* at Burslem and Stoke Schools of Art and privately under Reginald G. Haggar, R.I., F.R.C.A. *Exhib.:* R.I., B.W.S., S.W.A., and numerous one-man shows. *Work in permanent collections:* Hanley Museum, Stoke-on-Trent and Newcastle Fine A.G., University of Keele; paintings in private collections in England, America, Italy, S. Africa. *Address:* 86 Dunbrobin St., Longton, Stoke-on-Trent, Staffs. ST3 4LL. *Clubs:* President and tutor to: Newcastle Water-colour Soc., Blythe Bridge Water-colour Soc., Oulton Water-colour Soc. *Signs work:* "Doris Brown."

BROWN, John Robert, A.R.B.S.; sculptor in bronze and stone; Head of Art, Hampstead Garden Suburb Inst.; *b* London, 7 July, 1931; *s* of Robert Brown; *m* Pauline Brown; one *s*, one *d*. *Educ.:* Queen Elizabeth's, Barnet; *studied art* at Hornsey School of Art, Hampstead Garden Suburb Inst. (Howard Bate, R.A.). *Address:* The Bow House, 35 Wood St., Barnet EN5 4BE. *Signs work:* "J.R. Brown."

BROWN, Julian Seymour, A.T.D., N.D.D.; painter and graphic designer in water-colour, acrylic and oil; *b* Swansea, 3 July, 1934; *g-s* of Seymour Brown, A.T.C.; *m* Gillian Thomas; two *s*, two *d*. *Educ.:* Swansea Grammar School; *studied art* at Swansea College of Art (1950-55, Howard Martin), University College of Wales (1955-56). *Exhib.:* one-man shows: W.W.A.A. Gallery, Henry Thomas Gallery, Trapp Art Centre (1989, 1990, 1991); work exhib. throughout the Principality. *Official purchases:* Dyfed C.C. *Address:* Penyrallt, Alltycnap, Johnstown, Carmarthen, Dyfed SA31 3QY. *Signs work:* "Julian Brown."

BROWN, Lucy, M.A.(Hons.) Fine Art (1991); tutor; artist in mixed media installations; *b* Herts., 4 Aug., 1967. *Educ.:* Haberdashers' Aske's School for Girls, Elstree; *studied art* at Edinburgh University and Edinburgh College of Art (1986-91). *Exhib.:* S.S.A., group and solo shows in Scotland. *Work in permanent collections:* Edinburgh City Arts Centre, Glasgow Museums and Galleries. *Address:* 48 Montrose Terr., Edinburgh EH7 5DL. *Signs work:* "Lucy Brown" or not at all.

BROWN, Mary Rachel: see MARAIS.

BROWN, Neil Dallas, D.A. (Drawing and Painting, 1958); major prizewinner, Arts Council of N. Ireland Open Painting Exhibition (1970); painter in oil; lecturer in painting studios, Glasgow School of Art; *b* Elgin, 10 Aug., 1938; *s* of Robert Duncan Brown; *m*; two *d*. *Educ.:* Bell Baxter High School, Cupar, Fife; *studied art* at Dundee College of Art (1954-59, Alberto Morrocco), Royal

Academy Schools (1960-61, Peter Greenham). *Work in permanent collections:* Scottish Arts Council, Dundee City Museum, Skopje Museum, Yugoslavia, Nottingham City Art Gallery, Scunthorpe Education Committee, Hertfordshire County Council, Schools Collection, Walker Art Gallery, Liverpool, Kingsway Technical College, Dundee. *Address:* 55 Abbeywall Rd., Pittenweem, Fife KY10 2NE. *Signs work:* see appendix.

BROWN, Philip, A.M.G.P., former V.P.S.I.A.C., former V.P.S.C.A.; painter in water-colour and acrylic, stained glass artist, author, tutor; *b* London, 4 Nov., 1925; *s* of Leslie Norman Brown, M.A.; *m* Gounil Hallin; five *d. Educ.:* St. Paul's School, London; *studied art* at Slade School of Fine Art, Ateliers d'Art Sacre, Paris. *Exhib.:* one-man shows: London, Brighton, Oxford, Paris, Provence, Carmargue, Madrid, Malaga, Alicante, Sweden. *Work in permanent collections:* stained glass in St. John's Cathedral, Umtata, S.A., and many churches in England. *Publications:* How You can learn to Draw and Paint; Still-life and Plant Drawing; Working Outside (all Icon Press), numerous articles in Spain. *Address:* 71 Northbourne Rd., Eastbourne, E. Sussex. *Signs work:* "Philip Brown."

BROWN, Ralph, R.A. (1972), F.R.B.S., (1992); sculptor in bronze, draughtsman; *b* Leeds, 24 Apr., 1928; *s* of W.W. Brown; *m* (1) Margaret Elizabeth; (2) Caroline Ann Clifton; two *s*, one *d. Educ.:* Leeds Grammar School; *studied art* at Leeds College of Art, R.C.A. and in Paris, Italy and Greece. *Exhib.:* frequent one man and group exhbns. in this country and abroad, since 1954. *Work in permanent collections:* Tate Gallery, Rijksmuseum Kroller-Muller, Arts Council, Gallery of N.S.W., Sydney, Stuyvesant Foundation, S.A., Contemporary Art Soc., Leeds City A.G., and many other provincial and foreign museums. *Address:* The Old House, Frampton-on-Severn, Glos. GL2 7DY. *Signs work:* see appendix.

BROWN, William McClure; artist in painting, printmaking and sculpture; *b* Sunnyside, Toronto, Canada, 11 Dec., 1953. *Exhib.:* ubiquitous. *Work in permanent collections:* National Maritime Museum Greenwich, Plymouth City Museum, Peel Heritage Gallery Ontario, etc. *Publications:* written and illustrated: Contemporary Printmaking in Wales, Someone Stole a Bloater, Five Schools: Image and Word, etc. *Address:* (studio) 31 Newcastle Hill, Bridgend, Mid Glamorgan CF31 4EY. *Signs work:* "Wm. Brown."

BROWNE, Clive Richard; landscape painter in oil; *b* Keelby, 27 July, 1901; *s* of Canon Neville Lord Browne; *m* Edna Mary Garrard; one *s*, one *d. Educ.:* St. James' Secondary School, Grimsby; St. John's College, York; *studied art* at Grimsby Art School and under H. Rollett, R.B.A. *Exhib.:* R.A., R.Scot.A., R.H.A., R.Cam.A., R.W.A., R.B.A., R.O.I., N.S., British Empire Soc. Arts, W.A.G., Men of the Trees, Paris Salon, and provinces. *Work in permanent collections:* Usher Art Gallery, Lincoln. *Work repro.:* in Salon, Illustrated. *Address:* Beech House, Scotland Lane, Horsforth, Leeds. *Clubs:* N. Lincs. Art Soc., Lincs. Art Soc. *Signs work:* see appendix.

BROWNE, Gilbert Mitchell Ellis, B.A. (graphic design), M.A. (autographics); freelance artist/printmaker in etching, aquatint, mezzotint and engraving; currently working from own studio in London; *b* Girvan, Ayrshire, 13 July, 1954; *s* of Richard J.E. Browne; *m* Leylä Browne. *Educ.:* Girvan Academy, Scotland; *studied art* at Leeds Polytechnic (1973-76, Norman Webster), Chelsea School of Art (1976-77, Dick Hart). *Exhib.:* R.A. Summer Exhbn., Art Deko Gallery and British Consulate, Istanbul, International Biennale Ljubljana, Graffiti

Gallery, London, Worcester Mass. U.S.A., Christies Contemporary Art, London. *Address:* 40A St. Stephen's Gdns., London W2. *Signs work:* "G. Browne."

BROWSE, Lillian; founder partner of Roland, Browse & Delbanco, 19 Cork St. W1; editor and writer of books on art; Hon. Fellow, Courtauld Inst. of Art (1986); former ballet critic, Spectator; organized wartime loan exhbns. at National Gallery, London (1940-45); also exhbns. for C.E.M.A. and British Inst. of Adult Education. *Publications:* Augustus John Drawings (Faber & Faber, 1941); Sickert (Faber & Faber, 1943); Degas Dancers (Faber & Faber 1949); general editor of Ariel Books on the Arts, published for the Shenval Press by Faber & Faber; William Nicholson (Rupert Hart-Davis, 1955); Sickert (Rupert Hart-Davis, May 1960); Forain—the Painter (Elek, 1978); contributed articles to Apollo and Burlington Magazines; Sunday Times and Country Life. *Address:* 19 Cork St., London W1.

BRUCE, George J. D., elected R.P. (1959), Hon. Sec. (1970-84), Vice President (1985-90), President (1991-); portrait painter and painter of landscapes, still life, flowers etc. in oil; *b* London, 28 Mar., 1930. *Educ.:* Westminster; *studied art* at Byam Shaw School of Drawing and Painting (Brian D. L. Thomas, O.B.E., Patrick Phillips, R.P., Peter Greenham, R.A.). *Club:* Athenæum. *Address:* 6 Pembroke Walk, Kensington, London W8. *Signs work:* see appendix.

BRUCE, Matt, D.A. (Edin.), R.I.; teacher of painting and crafts, artist in all media, teacher at Victoria College, Jersey, Varndean School for Boys, Brighton, and Brighton College of Art evening classes (now retd.); *b* London, 17 Nov., 1915; *s* of M. W. Bruce, C.P.A.; *m* M. F. Bruce; one *s. Educ.:* Dollar Academy, Scotland; *studied art* at Edinburgh College of Art (1932-39) under W. Gillies and J. Maxwell. *Exhib.:* R.A., R.I., R.B.A., Brighton. *Address:* The Coach House, Old London Rd., Brighton BN1 8XQ. *Signs work:* "Matt Bruce."

BRUNSKILL, Ann, Assoc. of Royal Society of Painter Etchers (1969); painter and printmaker; *b* London, 5 July, 1923; *d* of Hugh George Edmund Durnford, M.C.; *m* John Brunskill; three *s*, one *d. Educ.:* Langford Grove School; *studied art* at Central School of Arts and Crafts, Chelsea College of Art. *Work in permanent collections:* V. & A., Bibliothèque Nationale, University College, Oxford, South London Collection of Original Prints, Lib. of Congress, Washington, U.S.A., J. Lessing Rosenwald Alverthorpe Coll., U.S.A., Universities of Princeton, Yale, U.S.A., National Library of Australia, Canberra. *Address:* Star & Garter Cottage, Egerton, Ashford, Kent. *Signs work:* "Ann Brunskill" and "AB" with date on paintings.

BRYAN, Peter Bernard, M.A.; painter in water-colour and acrylics; *b* Birmingham, 26 May, 1928; *s* of E.E. Bryan (decd.); *m* Elisabeth Brodie. *Educ.:* King Edward VI School, Birmingham; Selwyn College, Cambridge. *Exhib.:* R.I., H.H., S.G.A., East Anglian Artists (1987,1988), etc. *Work in permanent collection:* Aegon Insurance Co. (U.K.) Ltd. *Address:* 28 Drury St., Metheringham, Lincoln LN4 3EZ. *Signs work:* "P.B. Bryan."

BRYANT, Dena; artist in oils, scraper-board, water-colour; gallery owner and restorer; *b* Gloucester, 19 Mar., 1930; three *s. Educ.:* Red Maid's School, Westbury-on-Trym, Bristol; *studied art* at Royal West of England Academy of Art. *Exhib.:* St. Albans Gallery (1975), St. Albans Museum (1970), Paris, Salon de Nations (Jan. 1983), R.H.S. International Exhbn. (Mall Galleries, 1984), St. Albans Gallery (1987), Paris (1987), Galerie Salammbo, Paris (1988), St. Albans Abbey (1991), etc. *Work in permanent collections:* St. Albans Gallery,

South Africa, Canada, America. *Address:* Luton Hoo Station House, New Mill End, East Hyde, Luton, Beds. LU1 3TR. *Signs work:* "D.B.", "Dena" or a snail.

BUCHANAN, Elspeth, D.A. (Edin.); painter in oil; mem. of Council of S.S.W.A. (1956-59), S.S.A.; *b* Bridge of Weir, 29 Nov., 1915; *d* of John Buchanan. *Educ.:* St. George's School for Girls, Murrayfield, Edinburgh; *studied art* at Edinburgh College of Art (1933-38) under Wellington. *Exhib.:* R.A., R.Scot.A., S.S.A., S.S.W.A., G.I., N.E.A.C.; first one-man show, Great King St. Gallery. *Publication:* illustrated Land Air Ocean (Duckworth). *Address:* Viewpoint Residential Club, 7 Inverleith Terr., Edinburgh. *Club:* Soroptomist, Edinburgh. *Signs work:* "Elspeth Buchanan."

BUCKMASTER, Ann Devereaux, M.S.I.A. (1951-80); freelance artist in pen; *b* London, 27 Mar., 1924; *d* of Arthur D. Buckmaster; *m* Anthony Gilbert. *Educ.:* Bromley High School; *studied art* at Beckenham School of Art, Bromley College of Art. Illustration and fashion drawing for magazines and advertising. *Address:* Kimbell House, Charlbury, Oxon.

BUDD, Kenneth George, A.R.C.A. (1950); mural designer; *b* London, 16 Oct., 1925; *s* of Henry Walter Budd; *m* June Casburn (1956); two *s*, one *d*. Studied art at Beckenham School of Art (1941-44) and R.C.A. (1947-50). *Murals* include Kettering Boys' School; Derby College of Technology; Birmingham Inner Ring Road, Colmore Circus, Horse Fair; Priory Ringway (bas-relief); St. Chad's Circus, G.W.R. and Kennedy Memorial; Manzoni Gardens, Medieval Fair; Brighton, Church of Good Shepherd (windows); Swindon, Newport St. Offices; Newport, Gwent, M.R. and C.C., Chartists, Shop windows and Pleasure Steamer mosaics, bronze lion, Civic Centre marble Coat-of-Arms, Concrete finishes; Guys Hospital Foyer, Coat-of-Arms; Westerham Medical Centre; Oman, Chamber of Commerce Ruwi; Telford, Nab Wall and Donnington Giotto mosaic; Crosskeys Gwent, Valley Life in 1920's (three mosaics) and concrete finishes; Abertillery Gwent, Local Life 1890-1910 (eight mosaics); Gravesend, Ancient Arms mosaic; Pontypool: 'Japanning' bas relief concrete and mosaic. Mem. A.W.G. *Address:* Caragana, Trotts La., Westerham, Kent TN16 1SD. *Signs work:* see appendix.

BUDD, Rachel, R.C.A., B.F.A. (Hons.), M.F.A. (Hons.); painter in oil on canvas; part-time lecturer, Cheltenham College of Art and Design, and Central St. Martin's School of Art; *b* Norwich, 6 Mar., 1960; *d* of David John Budd. *Studied art* at University of Newcastle upon Tyne (1978-82, Prof. Rowntree), R.C.A. (1983-86, Peter de Francia). *Exhib.:* one-man shows: Purdy Hicks (1991), '3 Ways' British Council travelling show, Hungary, Poland, Czechoslovakia (1990), Athena Art Awards (1987), London Group (1987), Lloyds Bldg. Art for the City (1987), R.A. Summer Exhbn. (1987), Contemporary Arts Soc. Market, Covent Gdn. (1987). *Work in permanent collections:* County Nat.West. London, I.B.M., Contemporary Art Soc., Lloyds of London, Arthur Anderson Collection, I.C.I. *Address:* 67-71 Columbia Rd., London E2 7RG. *Signs work:* see appendix.

BUFFET, Bernard; *b* Paris, 10 July, 1928. Ecole des Beaux-Arts de Paris (1943); Prix de la Critique (1948); Chevalier de la Légion d'Honneur (1971). Elected at Académie des Beaux-Arts (1974). Has his own private Museum in Japan. The paintings of his chapel in Château l'Arc permanently shown in the Vatican. *Main exhibits in Paris:* La Passion, Horreur de la guerre, le Cirque, Jeanne d'Arc, les Oiseaux, la Corrida, l'Enfer de Dante, la Révolution Française. *Main publications:* Bernard Buffet by Pierre Bergé (1958), by Maurice Druon (1964), by Yann le Pichon (1986). *Address:* c/o Maurice Garnier, 6 avenue Matignon, Paris, 8.

BUHLER, Michael Robert, A.R.C.A.; artist in oil and acrylic; *b* London, 13 June, 1940; *s* of Robert Buhler, R.A.; one *s*. one *d. Educ.:* Bryanston School; *studied art* at Royal College of Art (1960-63, Carel Weight, Roger de Grey, Ruskin Spear, Colin Hayes). *Exhib.:* Galeria Boitata, Porto Alegre, Brazil, Museo do Estado da Bahia, Brazil, Eastern Arts Assoc. *Work in permanent collections:* Liverpool University, Carlisle City A.G., B.M., Arts Council, R.A., D.O.E. *Publication:* Tin Toys 1945-1975 (Bergstrom and Boyle). *Address:* 6 Cavell St., London E1 2HP. *Club:* Chelsea Arts. *Signs work:* "Michael Buhler."

BULGIN, Sally, B.A.(Hons.), M.A., Ph.D. (History of Art); painter in acrylic; Editor, The Artist magazine; Vice-Pres., National Assoc. of Acrylic Painters; *b* Ashford, Kent, 8 Nov., 1957; *d* of Ernest Arthur Bulgin. *Educ.:* Highworth School for Girls, Ashford; *studied art* at Reading University (1977-81, Martin Froy, Terry Frost), Courtauld Inst., London (1981-91). *Exhib.:* R.A. Dip Galleries, N.A.P.A. Annual, Clare College, Cambridge. Work in private collections. *Address:* 25B Somerset Rd., Ashford, Kent TN24 8EJ. *Signs work:* "Sally Bulgin."

BULLEN, Maud, F.P.S.; artist in water-colour; *b* Dorking, 14 Feb., 1906; *d* of George Batts; *m* Stanley Bullen; one *s. Educ.:* St. Paul's, Dorking; *studied art* at Rentwood Occupational Therapy Centre, Fetcham, Leatherhead under Ursula Hulme. *Exhib.:* one-man shows: Loggia Gallery, Liberty's; group shows: Dickins & Jones, Post Offices (London), Mall Galleries, Folkestone Art Centre, Da Carlo Restaurant, Best of British Naive Artists at Lyric, Hammersmith and others. Had work in permanent collection: Liberty's, London. *Address:* 30 Hart Rd., Dorking, Surrey. *Clubs:* F.P.S., Conquest (The Society for Art for the Physically Handicapped). *Signs work:* "M. Bullen."

BULLOCK, Hazel, M.F.P.S. (1970); painter in oil and acrylic. *Studied art* at Sir John Cass School of Art (1962) under R. V. Pitchforth, Percy Horton, David Graham. *Exhib.:* R.B.A., F.P.S., H.A.C., Browse and Darby, Whitechapel; one-man shows, Loggia Gallery (1973), Judd St. Gallery (1985), Phoenix Gallery, Highgate (1989), Phoenix Gallery, Lavenham (1989). Private collections in England and Spain. *Address:* 32 Devonshire Pl., London W1. *Club:* Arts. *Signs work:* "H. Bullock."

BULLOCK, Jean, S.P.S. (1964); sculptor in clay cast in foundry bronze and polyester resins, occasionally wood and stone, printmaker; *b* Bristol, 27 Apr., 1923; *d* of Walter Scott; *m* John Bullock, artist. *Educ.:* Bishopshalt, Haberdasher Askes, George Watsons Ladies College, Edinburgh; *studied art* at Watford School of Art (Guido Belmonte), Camberwell School of Art (Dr. Karl Vogel). *Exhib.:* R.A., S.P.S., Singapore Art Soc., Art Exhbns. Bureau Travelling Exhbns., Phillip Francis Gallery, Sheffield, etc. *Work in permanent collections:* M. of D., Central Institute, NW1, South Norwood School, Tulse Hill; stained glass window, St. Giles, Lockton. *Address:* Fern Cottage, Lockton, Pickering, N.Yorks. *Signs work:* "JEAN BULLOCK."

BUMPHREY, Nigel; schoolmaster, gold and silversmith, and furniture maker; Diocesan adviser to Diocese of Norwich for Church Plate; *b* Norwich, 22 Feb., 1928; *s* of Herbert Bumphrey. *Educ.:* The City of Norwich School and Loughborough College; *studied art* at Central School of Arts and Crafts and Norwich Art School. *Exhib.:* Norfolk Contemporary Crafts Soc., and others. Works mainly on commissions. *Address:* 28G Jessopp Rd., Norwich. *Signs work:* see appendix.

BUNTING, John Joseph, F.R.B.S. (1972), A.R.C.A. (1954); sculptor in wood, stone and bronze; *b* 3 Aug., 1927. *Educ.;* Ampleforth College, Oriel College, Oxford; *studied art* at St. Martin's School of Art (1949-51); R.C.A. (1951-54). *Exhib.:* One-man shows at Paris (1965), Billingham (1972). *Work in permanent collections:* Churches: St. Michael and All Angels (Oxford), War Memorial Chapel (Hambledon), St. Aidan's Church (Oswaldkirk); schools: St. Wilfrid's (Featherstone), St. Thomas à Becket (Wakefield), St. Bernard's (Rotherham). *Work repro.:* Monthly Report (1958-60), illustrations to Partage de Midi Paul Claudel (1963), Stages of the Cross (1972), John Bunting, sculptor (Paris, 1966). *Address:* Nunnington, York YO6 5UP.

BURDEN, Daniel, A.R.C.A. (1955), R.W.A.; painter in oil, pastel, chalks, lino, collage; *b* Paris, 20 Jan., 1928; *s* of William Burden; *m* Sallie Turner; two *d. Educ.:* Kilburn Grammar School, London; *studied art* at Willesden Art School (1949-52, Ivor Fox, James Neal, Francis Gower), R.C.A. (1952-55, John Minton, Rodrigo Moynihan, Ruskin Spear, Colin Hayes). *Exhib.:* R.A., R.W.A., A.I.A., R.B.A., Drian Gallery, Mignon Gallery, David Durrant Gallery, London Group, N.E.A.C., Salon des Independants Bordeaux. *Work in permanent collections:* Leicester University, Southend Museum, Walsall Educ. Development Centre, Avon Art and Design Loan Service, R.W.A. Collection. *Address:* Atelier Moulin A Vent, 47800 Moustier, Miramont de Guyenne, Lot et Garonne, France. *Club:* R.W.A. *Signs work:* "Burden."

BURDETT-SOMERS, Wilhelmina Maria, A.R.M.S. (1983), H.S.F. (1983), M.A.S.-F. (1980), M.A.S.-N.J. (1985), M.A.S.-W. (1983), Mem. Min. Art of America (1990); Grumbacher Art award Gold Medal (1986); artist in miniature oil painting on copper, larger painting on canvas and board; *b* The Hague, Netherlands, 23 July, 1923; *m* John Richard Burdett. *Educ.:* Convent School, The Hague; *studied art* at Netherlands Royal Academie of Art. *Exhib.:* all socs. annually to date, solo show: Queen's Gate, London (1981); R.A. Summer Show (1984). *Address:* 18 Hunter Pl., Louth, Lincs. LN11 9LG. *Signs work:* "W. Burdett-Somers, A.R.M.S., M.A.A."

BURGESS, Peter, B.A.Hons., P.G.Cert. R.A.S.; painter of figure compositions, landscapes and still-life in oil; *b* St. Albans, 16 June, 1952; *s* of Douglas Burgess. *Studied art* at Watford School of Art (1970-71, Michael Werner), Wolverhampton Polytechnic (1971-72, Norman Rowe), Wimbledon School of Art (1972-74, Ernest Edwards), R.A. Schools (1974-77, Peter Greenham). *Exhib.:* one-man shows: Nottingham Castle Museum (1982), Thackeray Gallery (1986, 1988, 1990, 1992); mixed shows: R.A., Nottingham Castle Museum, Derby City A.G., etc. *Work in permanent collections:* Contemporary Art Soc., Nottingham City Council, Leics. Educ. Authority, S. Derbyshire Health Authority, S. Nottingham College, Adam and Co.; private collections in Britain, U.S.A. and Europe. *Address:* 43 Lees Hill St., Nottingham NG2 4JW. *Signs work:* "Peter Burgess" on reverse of painting, and "BURGESS" on front of painting.

BURKE, Peter; sculptor using reclaimed materials; Lecturer, Trowbridge College; *b* London, 29 Feb., 1944; *m* Wendy; two *d. Educ.:* Bristol Technical School and Rolls Royce Bristol; *studied art* at Bristol Polytechnic (1972). *Exhib.:* one-man shows: Festival Gallery, and Cleveland Bridge Gallery Bath, New Art Centre London (1992); mixed shows: London, Chicago, New Mexico, Berlin, Basel, Miami, Madrid. *Work in permanent collection:* Contemporary Art Soc. *Address:* 9 Woolley Green, Bradford on Avon, Wilts. BA15 1TZ. *Signs work:* "P. Burke." or not at all.

BURLEIGH, Veronica; Slade Scholarship (1927); portrait and landscape painter in oils and water-colour; *b* Hove, 17 Apr., 1909; *d* of C. H. H. Burleigh, R.O.I. and Averil Burleigh A.R.W.S. *Educ.:* Hoove Lea, Hove; *studied art* at Brighton School of Art (1926-27), Scholarship to Slade School (1927-30). *Exhib.:* 31 one-man shows in England, Rhodesia and Zambia. *Work in permanent collection:* Worthing. *Address:* 2 Corner Cottages, Blackstone, Henfield, Sussex. *Clubs:* S.W.A., Sussex Water-colour Soc., Sussex Painters. *Signs work:* "Veronica Burleigh."

BURMAN, Chila Kumari, B.F.A.(Hons.) (1980), M.F.A. (1982); mixed media artist, printmaker, photographer; *b* Liverpool, 17 Jan., 1957; *s* of Bachan Singh Burman, ice cream vendor. *Studied art* at Southport College of Art, Leeds Polytechnic, and Slade School of Fine Art (Phil Redmond, Barto dos Santos, Stanley Jones). *Exhib.:* widely in Britain, recently in Canada. Work in private collections. *Publications:* contributed to Framing Feminism, and Visibly Female. *Address:* 20 Woodview Cl., Hermitage Rd., London N4 1DG. *Signs work:* "C.K. Burman."

BURN, Hilary, B.Sc.Hons. (Zoology) (1967), S.WL.A. (1983); freelance wildlife artist/illustrator in gouache, specialising in birds; *b* Macclesfield, Ches., 8 Apr., 1946; *d* of Colin Barber, engineering draughtsman. *Educ.:* Macclesfield High School, and University of Leeds. *Exhib.:* S.WL.A. Annual, regularly with R.S.P.B., Wildfowl Trust, Wildlife A. G., Lavenham, Suffolk, etc. *Publications:* illustrated, R.S.P.B. Book of British Birds (1982); Wildfowl: An Identification Guide to the Ducks, Geese and Swans of the World (1987); Crows and Jays: An Identification Guide (1993). *Address:* Huish Cleeve Cottage, Huish Champflower, Taunton, Som. TA4 2HA. *Club:* S.WL.A. *Signs work:* "Hilary Burn."

BURNAND, Robert Alan Lewis, A.R.E. (Jan., 1968), A.T.D. (July, 1949); artist in glass/wood-engraving and water-colour; lecturer at Bridgwater Tertiary College; *b* Malacca, Malaya, 19 Feb., 1929; *s* of John Robert Burnard, A.I.S.P., F.I.R.I.; *m* Wendy June; one *s*, two *d*. *Educ.:* Slough Grammar School for Boys; *studied art* at College of Art, High Wycombe, College of Art, Harrow, Middx., College of Art, Brighton (Morgan Rendle, Frederick Herrick). *Publications:* She (Rider Haggard), Longmans, Green; Let's Look It Up (school textbook), Chatto & Windus. *Address:* 6 Parkfield Cl., N. Petherton, Bridgwater, Som. TA6 6QY. *Signs work:* "R. Burnand."

BURNS, William, R.I.B.A., F.S.A.I., F.R.S.A.; artist in oil; *b* Sheffield, 1923; *m* Betty. *Studied art* at Sheffield Art School and architecture at Sheffield University. *Work in permanent collection:* John Campbell Gallery London. *Publication:* assisted with illustrating The Official War Diaries 1942-45. *Address:* 29 Newfield Cres., Dore, Sheffield S17 3GE. *Club:* Hesketh Hubbard Art Soc. *Signs work:* "William Burns."

BURNS McKEON, Katherine Balfour Kinnear, D.A.(Edin.) 1950; Hong Kong Urban Council painting prize (1979), 1st prize (Painting) R.S.A., W.R.N.S. Art Competition (1945); artist in oil on canvas, muralist in mosaic, fresco; *b* Edinburgh, 10 Oct., 1925; *d* of Joseph William Burns; *m* Leonard J. McKeon; two *s*, one *d*. *Educ.:* Trinity Academy, Edinburgh; *studied art* at Edinburgh College of Art (1946-50, William Gillies, Leonard Rosoman). *Exhib.:* Arts Council, S.S.A., Edinburgh, East Africa, Aden, Fiji, Hong Kong, Perth, Australia; murals: Hong Kong and Shanghai Bank, Paris; mosaic murals: Q. E. Stadium, Mosque and Social Centre, Hong Kong (1980-83). 1st Prize, St. Raphael International Exhbn. (1990). *Address:* Hameau de Sauve Clare, Flayosc 83780, France. *Signs work:* "Kitty Burns."

BURR, Victor; artist in oil; *b* Wandsworth, 5 July, 1908; *s* of James Burr; *m* Elizabeth Tidy. *Educ.:* Honeywell Rd. School, Battersea; *studied art* at West Sussex School of Painting and Drawing under R. O. Dunlop, R.A. *Exhib.:* R.A., R.O.I., R.P., N.E.A.C., Brighton Art Gallery, etc. *Address:* 38 East Park, Crawley, Sussex. *Signs work:* "Victor Burr."

BURROUGH, Helen Mary (Mrs.), R.W.A.; artist in oil, water-colour, sepia and wash; *b* Ceylon, 17 Feb., 1917; *d* of Axel J. Austin Dickson; *m* T. H. B. Burrough; two *s. Educ.:* St. George's Ascot; *studied art* at Miss McMuns Studio, Park Walk, Chelsea (1937), Prof. Otte Skölds' Ateljé, Stockholm (1938-39). *Address:* The Old House, Frenchay, nr. Bristol BS16 1ND. *Club:* Royal Commonwealth Society. *Signs work:* "Helen."

BURROUGH, Thomas Hedley Bruce, T.D., R.W.A., F.R.I.B.A.; chartered architect, artist in drawing and water-colour; Special Lecturer (Architecture), University of Bristol; Ex-Pres. Bristol Society of Architects; *b* Newport, Mon., 30 Apr., 1910; *m* Helen Mary Dickson, R.W.A.; two *s. Educ.:* Clifton College; *studied art* at R.W.A. School of Architecture (1928-32) (G. D. Gordon-Hake). *Work in permanent collections:* R.W.A., Bristol City Art Gallery, Red Lodge. *Publications:* An Approach to Planning (Pitman), South German Baroque (Tiranti), Bristol Buildings (Studio Vista); contributor to The Banister Fletcher History of Architecture, XVIII Edition (Athlone) and Who's Who in Architecture (Weidenfeld and Nicholson). *Address:* The Old House, Frenchay, nr. Bristol BS16 1ND. *Clubs:* Royal Empire Soc., Bristol Savages. *Signs work:* see appendix.

BURROWS, Geoffrey Norman; painter in oil and water-colour; *b* St. Faiths, Norfolk, 16 May, 1934; *s* of the late Alfred Norman Burrows, automobile engineer. *Educ.:* The Paston Grammar School, N. Walsham, Norfolk. *Exhib.:* R.A., R.B.A., R.O.I., R.M.S.A., N.E.A.C., R.I., Paris Salon, various mixed exhbns. at home and on the continent. *Work in permanent collections:* Atkinson A.G., Southport, Norfolk C.C., Norwich Union Insurance Co. *Address:* 84 Crostwick La., Spixworth, Norwich NR10 3AF. *Club:* Norfolk and Norwich Art Circle. *Signs work:* "Geoffrey Burrows."

BURTON, Andrew Gerard Crossley, M.F.A.; 1st prize, McGrigor Donald Sculpture Prize (1990); tutor/sculptor in clay, metal, rubber, stone; *b* 22 May, 1961; *s* of Neil Burton, M.A. *Educ.:* Sevenoaks School; *studied art* at University of Newcastle-upon-Tyne (Derwent Wise, Norman Adams). *Exhib.:* R.A., Laing Gallery, Hatton Gallery, Middlesbrough Gallery, etc. *Work in permanent collections:* Newcastle University, Northern Arts Educ. Authority, Leicester Educ. Authority. *Address:* 65 Sidney Grove, Fenham, Newcastle-upon-Tyne NE4 5PD. *Signs work:* "Andrew Burton."

BURTONSHAW, Keith, B.W.S., U.A., N.S.: artist, teacher and demonstrator in water-colour; *b* Beckenham, 25 Sept., 1930. *Educ.:* Beckenham and Penge County School; *studied art* at Beckenham School of Art. *Exhib.:* R.I., R.S.M.A. *Address:* 150 Beckenham Rd., Beckenham, Kent BR3 4RJ. *Societies and Clubs:* London Sketch Club, Armed Forces Art Soc., Croydon Art Soc., Cantium Group of Artists, West Wickham Arts Assoc., Lewisham Soc. of Art. *Signs work:* "Keith Burtonshaw."

BUSBY, George Cecil, M.S.I.A.D. (1970), R.B.S.A. (1971), S.G.A. (1979), F.R.S.A. (1970), G.R.A. (1987); painter and illustrator in water-colour, gouache, ink, acrylic; *b* Birmingham, 2 Feb., 1926; *s* of George Albert Busby (decd.); *m* Dora Snape; three *s*, one *d. Educ.:* Montpelier College, Brighton; *studied art* at

Birmingham College of Art (part time). *Exhib.:* R.I., S.G.A., R.B.S.A., Edwin Pollard Gallery, Beckstone's Gallery, Cumbria, Tegfryn Gallery, Anglesey, and several Midland galleries. *Work in permanent collections:* Warwick Castle, National Library of Wales; illustrations commissioned by: Courage Breweries, Abbey National Bldg. Soc., Amoco Oil Co., British Waterways, British Gas. *Work repro.:* Illustrator of city scenes for Christmas cards. *Address:* 377 Lugtrout La., Solihull, W. Midlands B91 2TN. *Signs work:* "George Busby."

BUSBY, John P., A.R.S.A., R.S.W., S.WL.A.; lecturer, Edinburgh College of Art (1956-88); *b* Bradford, 2 Feb., 1928; *s* of Eric Busby, M.B.E.; *m* Joan; one *s*, two *d. Educ.:* Ilkley Grammar School; *studied art* at Leeds Art College (1948-52), Edinburgh Art College (1952-54); Post Grad. (1954-55), major travel scholarship (1955-56). *Work in permanent collections:* S.A.C., Flemmings Bank, Bradford, Glasgow and Wakefield A.G's., Yorks Arts Assoc.; many private collections including H.R.H. The Duke of Edinburgh. *Publications:* The Living Birds of Eric Ennion (Gollancz), Drawing Birds (R.S.P.B.), Birds in Mallorca (Christopher Helm), many illustrated books. *Address:* Easter Haining, Ormiston Hall, E. Lothian EH35 5NJ. *Signs work:* "John Busby."

BUSHE, Frederick; sculptor; *b* Coatbridge, Scotland, 1931; *studied* at Glasgow School of Art (1949-53), University of Birmingham (1966-67). Elected R.S.A. (1986); Scottish Arts Council Awards (1971, 1973) and S.A.C. Major Bursary (1977-78). Established Scottish Sculpture Workshop (1980) and Scottish Sculpture Open Exhbn. (1981). *Address:* Scottish Sculpture Workshop, 1 Main St., Lumsden, Aberdeenshire AB54 4JN.

BUSHELL, Dorothy, R.M.S., S.W.A., Mundy Sovereign award (1983); miniature portrait painter in water-colour; *b* Halifax, Yorks., 3 Feb., 1922; *d* of Donald Clifton; *m* Philip Bushell; two *s*, one *d. Studied art* at Halifax School of Art. *Exhib.:* R.A. (1974, 1983, 1984), S.W.A. (1986, 1987), Mall Galleries, Westminster Gallery, R.M.S. (1982-87). *Work in private collections:* Comte et Comtesse de Martigny, Soc. of Apothecaries, London, The Royal Anglian Regiment. *Address:* 90 Fairdene Rd., Coulsdon, Surrey CR3 1RF. *Signs work:* "D. Bushell, 90"

BUTCHER, Sue, U.E.I. Cert. A.D. (1979); artist in acrylic and plant fibres; *m* Edward Butcher; two *s. Educ.:* Penarth Grammar School; *studied art* at Hereford College of Art (1977-80). *Exhib.:* regular exhibitor R.A. and West of England, winner, Sainsbury's National Touring Exhib. (1982-83), Japan (1987, 1993), S.W.A. (1987), various mixed and one-man shows. B.B.C. and I.T.V. television programmes (1990), radio broadcasts to U.S.A. and Canada. *Work in permanent collections:* Tayor Gallery, London, Hereford City A.G., Hereford Council Offices. *Address:* Litley Orchard, Gorsty La., Hereford HR1 1UN. *Signs work:* "S. Butcher."

BUTLER, Alice Caroline, R.M.S. (1960); miniaturist in water-colour and pen and ink; *m* Maurice H. Bizley; one *d.* Educ.: private and State schools; *studied art* at St. Albans School of Art. *Exhib.:* St. Ives Society of Artists, Royal Society of Miniature Painters, Sculptors and Gravers. *Publications:* author and illustrator of The Slate Figures of Cornwall; illustrated Friendly Retreat (M. H. Bizley), Cornish Windmills (H. L. Douch, B.A.). *Address:* St. Annes, Tywarnhayle Rd., Perranporth, Cwll TR6 0DX. *Signs work:* see appendix.

BUTLER, Anthony, R.C.A. (Cambrian, 1960), A.T.D. (1950); schoolmaster; artist in oil and gouache; head of art, Birkenhead School (retd.); *b* Liverpool, 1927; *s* of George Butler; *m* Jean; two *s*, one *d. Educ.:* Liverpool Institute;

studied art at Liverpool School of Art (1944-45, 1948-50) under Martin Bell, Alfred Wiffin, Alan Tankard. *Exhib.:* R.A., New Burlington, Agnews, Northern Young Contemporaries. *Work in permanent collections:* Walker Art Gallery, Liverpool; Whitworth Art Gallery, Manchester; Williamson Art Gallery, Birkenhead; and various county educational collections; ceramic decoration commissioned by Dudley C.C. for new shopping precinct. *Address:* Otthon, Llannefydd Rd., Henllan, nr. Denbigh, Clwyd LL16 5BD. *Signs work:* "BUTLER."

BUTLER, Auriol, F.R.S.A., Fellow, International Institute of Art, Associate, Société des Artistes Français; Gold and Silver medallist, Academia Internazionale, Rome; Life Fellow of the Royal Society of Arts; Gold medal and diploma from the Academia Italia (1981); artist in oil, pastel, water-colour; *b* Pitney, Somerset; *d* of Alexander Biddle, B.A.; *m* Richard Butler. *Studied art* at Byam Shaw School, London, under Ernest Jackson, and at Slade School, pastel with Mlle. Landau in Paris. *Exhib.:* Pastel Soc., London, R.B.A., S.W.A., Kenn Group, London Group, Paris Salon, United Society, etc. *Work repro.:* La Revue Moderne. *Address:* Glebe Studio, Cornwood, Ivybridge, Devon. *Signs work:* "A. Butler." or "Auriol."

BUTLER, George, R.W.S., R.B.A., N.E.A.C.; painter in oil and water-colour; *b* Sheffield, 17 Oct., 1904; *m* Kcenia; one *s*, one *d. Educ.:* King Edward VII School, Sheffield; *studied art* at Sheffield College of Art (1922-23), Central School of Arts and Crafts (1923-26). *Work in permanent collections:* Graves Art Gallery, Mappin Art Gallery. *Address:* Riversdale, Bakewell, Derbyshire DE4 1DU. *Club:* Arts. *Signs work:* "George Butler."

BUTLER, James, R.A. (1972), R.W.A. (1980), F.R.B.S. (1981); sculptor in bronze and stone; *b* Deptford, 25 July, 1931; *s* of Walter Arthur Butler; *m* Angela Berry; five *d. Educ.:* Maidstone Grammar School; *studied art* at Maidstone School of Art (1948-50); St. Martin's School of Art (1950-52). *Major commissions:* portrait statue of President Kenyatta of Kenya, Nairobi; monument to Freedom Fighters of Zambia, Lusaka, Zambia; Sculpture of The Burton Cooper, Burton-upon-Trent; memorial statue of Richard III, Castle Gardens, Leicester; statue of Field Marshal Earl Alexander of Tunis, Wellington Barracks, London; Dolphin fountain, Dolphin Sq., London; statue of A. John Wilkes, New Fetter La., London; bronze sculpture of the Leicester Seamstress, Hotel St., Leicester. *Address:* Valley Farm, Radway, Warwicks. CV35 0UJ. *Club:* Arts. *Signs work:* surname and year.

BUTLER, Richard Gerald Ernest; painter, graphic designer; *b* Essex, 31 Dec., 1921; *s* of Major Gerald Butler, A.P.T.C.; *m* Mary Driscoll; three children. *Studied art* at Salisbury School of Art. *Exhib.:* R.A., Arts Council Touring Exhbns., etc., one-man shows: Walker Galleries. *Work repro.:* book illustration (Macmillan Educ.), mural designs (Fitzroy Robinson & Partners). *Address:* 32 Denne Rd., Horsham, Sussex. *Signs work:* "Richard Butler."

BUTLER, Vincent; sculptor, figurative, bronzes; mem. Royal Scottish Academy, Royal Glasgow Inst.; *b* Manchester, 1933. *Exhib.:* numerous one-man shows in various parts of the country, Work in private collections in Britain, U.S.A., Germany, Italy, Israel, etc. *Address:* 17 Dean Park Cres., Edinburgh EH4 1PH. *Signs work:* see appendix.

BUTT, Anna Theresa (until 1985 Anna Adams); N.D.D. Painting (1945), N.D.D. Sculpture (1950); artist in water-colour, terracotta; *b* Richmond, Surrey, 9 Mar., 1926; *d* of George Butt, writer; *m* Norman Adams; two *s. Educ.:* St.

Michael's Modern School, Eastcote; *studied art* at Harrow School of Art (1939-46), Hornsey College of Art (1948-50). *Exhib.:* widely in north of England as Anna Adams; R.A. Summer Show (1986, 1987, 1988, 1989, 1990, 1991). *Work in permanent collections:* terracottas in Abbot Hall, Kendal, W. Yorks. Educ. Com., Moorside Mills Museum, Rochdale Museum. *Publications:* several collections of poems under name of Adams. *Address:* Butts Hill, Horton in Ribblesdale, Settle, N. Yorks. BD24 0HD. *Signs work:* "Anna Butt" and see appendix.

BUTTERFIELD, Sarah Harriet Anne, B.Soc.Sci. Architecture Edin. (1975) 'Magna cum Laude', Cert. Fine Art Ruskin School of Fine Art, Oxford (1978), Distinction; qualified as architect 1983; artist; *b* London, 28 Aug., 1953. *Exhib.:* Judd St. Gallery, London (1987), Agnew's Young Contemporaries (1988), Richmond Gallery, Cork St. (1990), Roy Miles Gallery (1991); one-man show: Cadogan Contemporary (1991). *Work in permanent collections:* British Airways: Terminal 4 Departure Lounge; David Lloyd Slazenger Racquet Club; Trusthouse Forte Hotels in Yorkshire and Exeter; Wimbledon Lawn Tennis Museum; 'Davies', Gt. Newport St., London; State St. Bank, London. *Awards:* Egerton Coghill Landscape prize (1977), Winsor and Newton award, Hunting Group Competition finalist, commendation Spectator Magazine Three Cities Competition. *Address:* 21 Ashchurch Grove, London W12 9BT.

BUTTERWORTH, John Malcolm, M.A.(Ed.), F.R.S.A., N.D.D., A.T.D.; artist in oils, water-colour, etching, silkscreen and lithography; Fine Art Courses Leader (P/T) Design Division, Southampton I.H.E.; *b* Lancs., 16 July, 1945; *s* of Jonathan and Annie (Tilling) Butterworth; *m* Lesley G. Arkless, B.A.Hons.; two *s*, one *d*. *Educ.:* Rochdale Technical School for Boys; *studied art* at Rochdale College of Art (1961-63), Newport College of Art (1965-66), Cardiff College of Art (1965-66), David Murray Scholarship (R.A.) 1965. *Exhib.:* Wills Lane Gallery, St. Ives, University of Surrey, Southampton Civic A.G. (one-man shows), Pictures for Schools Exhbn., National Museum of Wales, Cardiff, Midsommergarten Gallery, Stockholm, Cleveland, Drawing Biennale, International Print Biennale, Monaco. *Work in permanent collections:* Bristol Educ. Authority, Kent Educ. Authority, Surrey University. *Address:* 2 Nuns Walk, Winchester, Hants. SO23 7EE. *Signs work:* normal signature for prints, "J.M.B." monogram for paintings.

BUXTON, Jennifer, H.R.M.S. (retd.), Hon. Sec. R.M.S. (1980-87), Hilliard Soc.; portrait, animal and landscape painter in water-colour, silverpoint, pastel, oil, gouache; *b* Hornsey, 12 Apr., 1937; *d* of N. Pearson, company director; *m* Captain Vic (R.N.); two *s*. *Educ.:* Northfield School, Watford; *studied art* at Frobisher School of Animal Painting (1948-53, Marguerite Frobisher), Byam Shaw School of Art (1954-57, Dunstan, Phillips, Mahoney). *Exhib.:* Watford, Manchester, Bath, Wells, Paris Salon, Kendal, Ulverston, Ilkley, Toronto, annually R.M.S. London. First winner of R.M.S. Gold Memorial Bowl Award for best miniature (1985). *Address:* Windy Ash, Ulverston, Cumbria LA12 7PB. *Signs work:* "jb" or "J. Buxton."

BUYERS, Donald Morison, D.A.(Aberdeen), R.S.W.; artist in oil and water-colour; lecturer retired; *b* Aberdeen, 1930; *s* of James Buyers, chief engineer; *m* Margaret; one *s*, one *d*. *Educ.:* Aberdeen Grammar School; *studied art* at Gray's School of Art, Aberdeen, (1948-52). *Exhib.:* Arts Council, Young Scottish Contemporaries, Contemporary Art in Scotland, Painting 70, Edinburgh Open 100, Glasgow Group, etc. *Work in permanent collections:* Arts Council, I.B.M., Aberdeen A.G., Universities of Colorado, U.S.A., Boston, U.S.A. and Aberdeen,

Dunbartonshire Educ. Trust, Schools Pictures Leeds and Midlothian, Robert Flemming, London, H.R.H. The Duke of Edinburgh, etc. *Address:* 96 Gray St., Aberdeen AB1 6JU. *Signs work:* "Buyers."

C

CADENHEAD, William Collie Milne, D.A., cert.R.A.S., Bronze Medal R.A. Schools (1957), David Murray Landscape Scholarship (1957), elected prof. member S.S.A. (1969); painter in oil and water-colour; lecturer in drawing and painting, Duncan of Jordanstone College of Art, Dundee; *b* Aberdeen, 8 Oct., 1934; *s* of A. L. Cadenhead, L.D.S., R.C.S. Edin.; *m. Educ.:* Aberdeen Grammar School; Forfar Academy; *studied art* at Dundee College of Art (1951-55); travelled Europe (1956); Hospitalfield Art College, Arbroath; R.A. Schools, London (1957-61). *Exhib.:* R.S.A., S.S.A., R.S.W., Savage Gallery, Compass Gallery, Royal Overseas League, Edinburgh Festival (1968), etc., one-man shows, The Scottish Gallery (1981, 1983), Woodstock Gallery. *Work in permanent collections:* H.M. Queen Elizabeth, The Queen Mother, Scottish Arts Council, (Stations of the Cross), St. Fergus, Forfar: Meffan Institute, Forfar; Steel Company of Wales, Dundee A.G., and private collections in U.K. and U.S.A. *Address:* The Rowans, Muir of Lownie, Forfar, Angus DD8 2LJ. *Signs work:* "Cadenhead."

CADMAN, Michael Lawrence, R.I. (1970), A.R.C.A.; painter in water-colour, acrylic, oil and pastel; Instructor Epsom School of Art (1945-68); *b* Epsom, 1920; *m* Anne Phyllis Burden. *Educ.:* Glyn Grammar School; *studied art* at Wimbledon School of Art (1937-41), R.C.A. (1941-44, Gilbert Spencer). *Exhib.:* R.A., R.W.S., R.B.A., R.O.I., eight one-man shows. *Work in permanent collection:* Croxton and Garry (Protexulate Ltd., Esher). *Publications:* Orange Cap - Red Cap (Paul Hamlyn, 1968); four fine art prints (Cornish Harbours and Hedgerow themes, 1981). B.B.C. TV (1947,1964). *Address:* Melrose Studio, 43 Hound St., Sherborne, Dorset DT9 3AB. *Societies:* R.I., St. Ives Soc. of Artists. *Signs work:* "Michael Cadman."

CAINE, Osmund, B.A.(Hons.), M.D.C.S., A.S.M.G.P., M.S.I.A.; teacher, painter in oil, water-colour, illustrator, lithographer, artist in stained glass and mosaic; Principal Lecturer, Graphic Design, Twickenham College of Technology (1962); *b* Manchester. *Studied art* at Birmingham College of Art (1930-37) and in Italy (1938). *Exhib.:* R.A., N.E.A.C., R.B.A., R.B.S.A., V. & A., Craft Centre, Lambeth Palace, Guildhall, and Walker, Adams, Piccadilly Galleries, Leicester, Whitworth Gallery, R.I.B.A., Southwell-Brown Gallery, Richmond, Hampton-Hill & Ashbarn Gallery, Petersfield, and Garden Gallery, Kew, London; one-man exhbns.: Walker's Gallery; Richmond Hill Gallery (1961); Foyles A.G. (1966); Canaletto Gallery (1966, 1969); Open Studio, Kingston-on-Thames (1980); Old Bell Gallery, Chepstow (1981); Century Display Gallery, Surbiton (1982); Southwell-Brown Gallery, Richmond (1984); Garden Gallery, Kew; Merlin Theatre, Frome (1985); Duncan Campbell Fine Art, London (1986); Galerie Salammbo, Paris (1987); Questra Gallery, Kingston-on-Thames. *Official purchases:* Ministry of Transport; Nottingham Castle A.G.; University of London; Dorset House, London; Borough of Richmond-on-Thames; Borough of Kingston-on-Thames; Melbourne A.G.; Erdington Abbey, B'ham; V. & A.;

B'ham A.G. *Stained glass:* St. Gabriel's Church, Cricklewood, London (N. Aisle window); St. Paul's Church, Kingston (Porch window); St. Augustine's Church, Edgbaston, B'ham (Lady Chapel); St. Cuthbert's Church, Copnor, Portsmouth (E. window); St. Luke's Church, Wadestown, N.Z. (S. Aisle window); St. Keyne's Church, St. Keyne, Liskeard (N. Aisle window); All Saint's Church, Stechford, B'ham (S. Aisle window); All Saint's Church, Four Oaks, B'ham (N. & four S. Aisle windows); Private Chapel, Chile, S. America (E. window); Mortuary Chapel, Erdington Infirmary, B'ham (E. window); Old Church, Smethwick (S. Aisle windows); Fourteen Stations of the Cross, St. Mary's, Hong Kong; Private House, N. Wales (Memorial window); Private House, Knowle, B'ham (Geometric window). *Publications:* The Studio, The Artist, L'Art Moderne, Careers in Art, The School Leaver, etc. Films: The Glastonbury Giants (in conjunction with Mary Caine), (1966); The Ruskin Country (1966). *Address:* 25 Kingston Hill, Kingston-on-Thames. *Signs work:* see appendix.

CAINS, F. Blanche, S.W.A., A.T.D. (1927); artist in water-colour, mixed media, fabric collage, embroidery; art teacher, Head of Dept. Grammar School (mixed); *b* Bristol, 1905; *d* of William Charles Cains, craftsman. *Educ.:* St. George Grammar School, Bristol; *studied art* at West of England College of Art (1922-27) Princ. R. E. J. Bush, R.E. *Exhib.:* R.A., R.I., R.W.A., S.W.A., various other galleries in London, Brighton, Bristol, etc. *Address:* 99 Summerhill Rd., St. George, Bristol BS5 8JT. *Signs work:* "F.B. Cains."

CAINS, Gerald Albert, N.D.D. (Painting S.L. 1953), A.T.D. (1957), A.R.W.A. (1971), elected R.W.A. (1978), A.D.A.E. (University of Wales, 1975); painter in oil and water-colour; *b* Stubbington, Hants., 11 May, 1932; *s* of Albert George Cains; *m* Ruth Lillian Blackburn; one *s*, one *d*. *Educ.:* Gosport County Grammar School; *studied art* at Southern College of Art, Portsmouth (1949-53). *Work in permanent collections:* Lancashire Museum Service, R.W.A., Walsall Museum Service, Wessex Longleat House. *Address:* 1 Broadway Cottages, Broadway Lane, Clandown, nr. Bath, Avon. *Clubs:* R.W.E.A., Bath Soc. of Artists. *Signs work:* "G. A. CAINS."

CALDICOTT, Glenys Rita, C. & G. (1982), A.R.M.S. (1990), S.W.A. (1991), S.M. (1991); Margaret Ryder award, R.M.S. (1989), Dartington Rose Bowl, S.M. (1991), Llewellyn Alexander award, R.M.S. (1992); miniaturist, specialising in animal portraits in gouache on card and vellum; *b* Nottingham, 20 Aug., 1941; *d* of Wallace C. Collington, scenic artist (decd.); *m* Harvey C. Caldicott; one *s*. *Educ.:* Mablethorpe, Highfield College, Grimsby; *studied art* at Grimsby School of Art (1958-60, Peter Todd), Bourneville College of Art (1979-82, Alex Jackson). *Exhib.:* R.M.S., S.W.A., S.M. Work in private collections. *Address:* Rose Cottage, 16 Flaxley Rd., Stechford, B'ham B33 9AS. *Signs work:* "G.R. Caldicott."

CALLMAN, Jutta Gabrielle: see SAUNDERS, Jutta Gabrielle.

CALVOCORESSI, Richard, B.A., M.A.; Keeper, Scottish National Gallery of Modern Art, Edinburgh (since 1987); research asst., Scottish National Gallery of Modern Art (1977-79); research asst., Modern Collection, Tate Gallery (1979-82), asst. keeper (1982-87); *b* 1951; *m* Francesca Temple Roberts; one *s*, two *d*. *Educ.:* Magdalen College, Oxford; Courtauld Inst. of Art, University of London. *Publications:* author, Magritte (1979, 1984, 1990); exhbn. catalogues: Tinguely (1982), Reg Butler (1983), Cross Currents in Swiss Art (1985), Oskar Kokoschka 1886-1980 (1986), and catalogue essays on Miró, Penck, Baselitz, Lüpertz, von Motesiczky, Gormley, Picabia, etc.; various articles and reviews. *Address:* Scottish National Gallery of Modern Art, Belford Rd., Edinburgh 4.

CAMBRON, Ghislaine; Officier de l'Ordre de Léopold II (1990); artist, painter, ceramist; Directrice de L'Académie des Beaux-Arts de Molenbeek Saint-Jean (Brussels); Academie de Molenbeek, Brussels; Grand Prix de Belgique (1954), Grand Prix de Decoration (1955), Grand Prix de Belgique (1956), Prix de l'État Belge (1942), Distinction-Prix Europe Peinture (1962); *b* St. Amand-les-Eaux, 6 July, 1923; *m* Mariee. *Studied art* at Académie de Bruxelles. *Work in permanent collections:* Musée Art Moderne, Brussels, Centre Culturel, Uccle, Musée de Molenbeek, Timbres-Poste du Congo (Serie Masques). *Address:* Dréve Angevine, Domaine de la Motte, Bousval 1470, Brabant, Belgique. *Signs work:* "Cambron, Ghislaine."

CAMERON, Gordon Stewart, R.S.A. (1971); painter in oil; senior lecturer, School of Drawing and Painting, Duncan of Jordanstone College of Art, Dundee (retd. 1981); *b* Aberdeen, 27 Apr., 1916; *s* of John Roderick Cameron; *m* Ellen Malcolm, R.S.A. *Educ.:* Robert Gordon's College, Aberdeen; *studied art* at Gray's School of Art, Aberdeen (1935-40) (Dr. D. M. Sutherland, R.S.A., Robert Sivell, R.S.A.). *Work in permanent collections:* Aberdeen Art Gallery, Perth Art Gallery, Royal Scottish Academy, Dundee Art Gallery. *Publication:* illustrations for Lockhart's Anatomy of the Human Body. *Address:* 7 Auburn Terr., Invergowrie, Perthshire DD2 5AB. *Signs work:* "G. S. CAMERON."

CAMERON, Ronald, N.D.D. (1951); sculptor in bronze, terracotta, pewter and silver; *b* London, 8 Oct., 1930; *m* Dorothy; two *d. Educ.:* Wilson's Grammar School; *studied art* at Camberwell School of Art (1947-51). *Exhib.:* bronzes at Art Scene Gallery, London; also galleries in Europe and N. America. *Address:* 9 Morecambe St., London SE17 1DX. *Signs work:* "R. Cameron."

CAMP, Ann, A.R.C.A. (1946), F.S.S.I.; freelance calligrapher and lettering designer; lecturer at Digby Stuart College, Roehampton Institute; retd. from teaching (1990); *b* London, 1924; *d* of Leonie Camp and Instructor/Capt. John Camp, R.N. *Studied* at Hampstead Garden Suburb Inst. and R.C.A. *Work in permanent collections:* loan collections of V. & A., L.C.C. and National Museum of Wales; Book 4, R.A.F. Book of Remembrance in St. Clement Dane's Church; lettering on stamps, murals, etc. *Publication:* Pen Lettering (first published 1958 by Dryad Press; republished by A. & C. Black, 1984). *Address:* 115 Bridge La., London NW11 9JT. *Club:* Soc. of Scribes and Illuminators. *Signs work:* "Ann Camp."

CAMP, Jeffery, R.A. (1984); artist; lecturer, Slade School. *Educ.:* Edinburgh College of Art, D.A. (Edin.). *Exhib.:* one-man, Galerie de Seine (1958), Beaux Arts Gallery (1959, 1961, 1963), New art Centre (1968), Serpentine Gallery (1973), S. London A.G. (retrospective, 1973), Bradford City A.G. (1979), Browse and Darby (1984), Nigel Greenwood Gallery (1986, 1990); retrospective, Royal Albert Memorial Museum, Exeter, Royal Academy of Arts, London, Manchester City A.G., Laing A.G., Newcastle (1988-89); group shows: Hayward Annuals (1974, 1982, 1985), British Council Touring Exhbns. to China and Edinburgh (1982) and to India (1985), Chantrey Bicentenary, Tate Gallery (1981), Narrative Painting I.C.A., London Arts Council Touring, The Hard Won Image Tate Gallery (1984); Twining Gallery, N.Y. (selected by William Feaver 1985), Peter Moores Liverpool Exhbn. (selected by William Feaver 1986); Athena Art Awards, Barbican Centre, London (1987), Land: Sea: Air, Herbert Read Gallery, Canterbury and tour (1987), 'The Self Portrait' Artsite Gallery, Bath and tour (1987). *Publication:* Draw (1981). *Address:* 27 Stirling Rd., London SW9 9EF. *Signs work:* see appendix.

CAMPBELL, Alexander Buchanan, P.P.R.I.A.S. (1979), A.R.S.A. (1972), B.Arch. (1937), F.R.I.B.A. (1955); architect; *b* Findochty, 14 June, 1914; *s* of Hugh Campbell, master mariner; *m* Sheila Smith; one *s*, one *d*. *Studied architecture* at Glasgow School of Architecture (Strathclyde University) (1930-37) under Prof. T. Harold Hughes, Dr. J. A. Coia. *Address:* 19 Lochan Ave., Kirn, Dunoon, Argyll PL23 8HT. *Club:* Glasgow Art. *Signs work:* "A. Buchanan Campbell."

CAMPBELL, Joan Betty, R.M.S. (1980), S.W.A. (1975); artist in water-colour, oil and acrylic; teacher of miniature painting, private tuition; *b* London, 4 May, 1923; *d* of Joseph Longhurst; *m* Archie Campbell; one *d*. *Educ.:* Loughton County High School for Girls, Essex; *studied art* at Ilford Evening Institute (mostly self-taught). *Exhib.:* Westminster Galleries, Llewellyn Alexander Gallery, M.A.S.-F., Paris Salon (1973, 1974), Bilan l'Art Contemporain of Paris (1978). *Publication:* Art Editor, Hillingdon Writer. *Address:* 3 Fineshade Cl., Barton Seagrave, Northants NN15 6SL. *Signs work:* miniatures "J.B.C." or "JC" entwined; larger works "Joan Campbell."

CAMPBELL, Raymond; self taught artist in oil and acrylic, known for still life subjects; *b* Morden, Surrey, 2 Apr., 1956. *Educ.:* Garth High, Morden. *Exhib.:* R.A., etc. *Work in permanent collections:* England, Germany, Austria, Australia. *Work repro.:* limited edn. prints. *Address:* 63 Courtnay Rd., Woking, Surrey GU21 5HG. *Signs work:* "Raymond Campbell."

CAMPBELL-QUINE, Nina; Jane Plotz scholarship; water-colour, mixed media, gouache, oil; enamellist, designer, jewellery; costume, theatre sets and decor, furniture and interior architecture; mem. Artist Enamellists U.K.; *Book design and graphics:* Stage Door Cookbook, I'll make me a World, etc., and my biography Nina Observed; *b* Pretoria, Transvaal, 17 July, 1911; *d* of Alexander John Arbuckle, M.I.Mech.E/M.I.M.E.; *m* William Campbell-Quine. *Educ.:* by private tutors; *studied art* at School of Art, Johannesburg (1926-28) under Prof. Winter-Moore and Prof. Armstrong. *Work in permanent collections:* Anton Rupert and Schlesinger Collection, William Humphreys Gallery, Pietersburg Civic A.G., Wits University A.G., Johannesburg Municipal Archives. *Address:* 79 Third Rd., Hyde Pk., Sandton, 2196, Tvl. *Signs work:* "Nina."

CANNELL, Edward Ashton, R.S.M.A., B.W.S., N.D.D., A.T.D.; painter and illustrator; *b* Isle of Man, 12 Sept., 1927. *Educ.:* King William's College; *studied art* Isle of Man School of Art, Liverpool College of Art. *Exhib.:* R.A., R.I., R.B.A., R.S.M.A., Paris Salon (Silver Medal 1973, Gold Medal 1975), Bankside Gallery, Davy's of London Award (1983), Royal Exchange A.G., Francis Iles Gallery, Oliver Swann Gallery, Bourne Gallery, Clairmonte Galleries, Linda Blackstone Gallery. *Work in private collections:* U.S.A., Canada, South Africa, Japan, Saudi Arabia and most European countries. *Publications:* freelance work for various publications, Foyle's, Cassells, Bass International, British Petroleum. *Address:* Studio House, 52 Dyne Rd., London NW6 7DS. *Clubs:* London Sketch, Wapping Group. *Signs work:* "Ashton Cannell."

CANNEY, Michael Richard Ladd, A.T.D., N.D.D.; Principal Lecturer in Painting, Bristol Polytechnic; Curator, Newlyn Art Gallery (1956-64); Director, Fore Street Gallery, St. Ives, and Porthleven Art Gallery; Visiting lecturer, University of California, Santa Barbara; Director, University Art Gallery (1965-66); *b* Falmouth, 16 July, 1923. *Studied art* at Goldsmiths' School of Art (1947-51); Redruth, Penzance and St. Ives (1939-42). *Exhib.:* Waddington Galleries, Piccadilly Gallery, A.I.A., Royal West of England Academy, London Group, Ostend, Chicago, Santa Barbara, Plymouth City A.G. Exeter, Newlyn and St.

Ives, Arnolfini, Bristol, Bath Festival. *Address:* 2 Swancombe, Clapton-in-Gordano, Bristol BS20 9RR.

CANNING, Neil, A.R.B.A. (1983); artist in mixed media and oils; *b* Enstone, Oxon., 28 Apr., 1960; *s* of Gerald Canning. *Educ.:* Spendlove School, Charlbury, and Chipping Norton School; *studied art* privately with Betty Bowman (1979-82). *Exhib.:* R.A. (1981, 1982, 1984), John Player Portrait award N.P.G. (R.B.A.). *Work in permanent collections:* I.C.I., and paintings in hospitals. *Publication:* illustrated Skylighters (Methuen). *Address:* The Post Office House, Ffarmers, Llanwrda, Dyfed SA19 8LQ. *Club:* Oxford Art Soc. *Signs work:* "N. Canning."

CANTER, Jean Mary, S.G.F.A. (1977); painter in gouache, water-colour and scraperboard; lecturer; tutor, Mid-Surrey Adult Inst.; Council mem. S.G.F.A.; *b* Epsom, 18 Mar., 1943; *d* of Henry Canter (Major). *Educ.:* Convent of the Sacred Heart, Epsom; *studied art* at Epsom School of Art (1956-61); Wimbledon School of Art (1961-63). *Exhib.:* S.G.F.A., U.A., R.W.S., S.B.A., R.I., R.S.M.A., P.S., etc.; Frisk Prize winner S.G.F.A. (1983, 1985), Rexel Prize winner S.G.F.A. (1984), Daler-Rowney Prizewinner S.G.F.A. (1990). *Work in permanent collection:* Museum Collection, Ewell. *Work repro.:* Encyclopedia of Water-colours, and others for Quarto, cards, music covers, etc. *Address:* 7 Cox Lane, Ewell, Epsom, Surrey KT19 9LR. *Club:* S.G.F.A. *Signs work:* "JEAN CANTER."

CAPRARA, Julia Rosemary, N.D.D., A.T.C. Lond. (1961), M.S.D-C., mem. 62 Group (1970); designer in embroidery, textile artist; *b* London, 27 Feb., 1939; *d* of John I. L. Jenkins: *m* Alex. Caprara; one *s. Educ.:* Perse School for Girls, Cambridge; Henrietta Barnett School, Hampstead; *studied art* at Hornsey College of Art (1955-61). *Exhib.:* one-man show of Embroidery at Commonwealth Institute A.G.; 62 Group shows: Guildford House, National Museum of Wales, Congress House, Foyle's A.G. Australia, U.S.A., Japan. *Work in permanent collections:* National Museum of Wales, Cardiff, Holocaust Museum, Israel; private collections. *Address:* 20 Crown St., Harrow-on-the-Hill, Middx. *Signs work:* "Julia Caprara."

CARLETON, Elyn, R.A.A. (1984), R.A.S. (1986), M.F.P.S. (1988); teacher/writer, lecturer, creative artist (all mediums); founder, Creator's Group (1980), Innovators (1988); Council and Publicity Officer, Ridley Art Soc. (1987-89); *b* Palmyra, W.A.; *d* of Alexander Armund Oders of Estonia, and Constance Wakeman; *m* Laurence Edward Carleton; one *s*, two *d. Educ.:* Australia; *studied art* privately with Wesley Penberthy, Melbourne (1968-69); Victoria University, Wellington, N.Z. (Paul Olds, 1970-74); Dr. Desiderius Orban, O.B.E., Sydney (1975-79). *Exhib.:* R.A. Wellington, N.Z. (1973), (In Mind) Eight Wellington Artists (1974), Victoria University (1973), galleries in N.Z., Sydney, Melbourne, Tasmania; U.K.: Mall Galleries, R.O.I., H.A.C., C.P.S., R.A.S., U.A., F.P.S., C.W.A.C., Bloomsbury, Intaglio Crafts (Creative Images 1987), Richmond Antiquary (Two Hemispheres 1988), Chertsey Hall (Australian Paintings 1988-89), Bourne Hall (1989), Queensland House (1990), Loggia (1991). *Work in permanent collections:* B.H.P. H.Q. Sydney, N.C.R. World H.Q. Dayton, Ohio, Queensland House, London; private collections in U.K., Netherlands, Switzerland, U.S.A., Singapore, N.Z., Australia. *Publications:* articles written: Creative Images, Creative Art, Art Today, Art Appreciation, Constructive Criticism, Developed Unique Creative Art Teaching Method (1980). *Address:* 3 Glenwood House, Callow Hill, Virginia Water, Surrey GU25 4LW. *Clubs:* B-A.S., Foxhills, Portsea, Tura Beach, Pambula. *Signs work:* "Elyn Carleton."

CARNIE, Andrew, B.A. (1982), R.C.A. (1986); painter/sculptor in mixed medium; *b* 8 Jan., 1957; *m* Judith Mary Wallas; one *s. Educ.:* Lakes School, Windermere; *studied art* at Goldsmiths' School of Art, Royal College of Art. *Exhib.:* many mixed person shows and one-man shows at Girray Gallery London, Winchester Gallery, Bracknell Gallery, Plymouth Art Centre. *Work in permanent collections:* Unilever London, Chase Manhattan Bank London, Coopers and Lybrand London, Kaempher Corp., Washington, U.S.A. *Address:* 5 Powell Rd., London E5 8DJ. *Signs work:* "ANDREW CARNIE" or not at all.

CARO, Sir Anthony, Kt. (1987), C.B.E., D.Litt.; Hon. Degree, Yale University (1989), awarded: Nobutaka Shikamai Memorial Prize, Tokyo (1990), Praemium Imperiale by Japan Art Assoc.; sculptor; part-time teacher of sculpture, St. Martin's School of Art (1953-79); Trustee, Tate Gallery (1982-); initiated with Robert Loder Triangle Summer Workshop, Pine Plains, N.Y. (1982); *b* London, 8 Mar., 1924; *s* of Alfred Caro; *m* Sheila Girling; two *s. Educ.:* Charterhouse School and Christ's College, Cambridge; *studied art* at Regent St. Polytechnic and R.A. Schools. *Exhib.:* numerous one-man shows world-wide including Galleria del Naviglio, Milan (1956), Andre Emmerich Gallery, N.Y. (1964, 1966, 1968, 1970, 1972-74, 1977-79, 1982, 1984, 1986, 1988, 1989, 1991), Washington Gallery of Modern Art (1965), Kasmin Gallery, London (1965, 1967, 1971, 1972), Mirvish Gallery, Toronto (1966, 1971, 1974), Kroller-Muller Museum, Holland (1967), Richard Gray Gallery, Chicago (1976, 1978, 1986, 1989), Knoedler Gallery, London (1978, 1982-84, 1986, 1989, 1991), Tate Gallery (1991), etc.; retrospective 1975: Museum of Modern Art, N.Y., Walker Art Center, Minneapolis, Museum of Fine Arts, Houston; 1976: Museum of Fine Arts, Boston; 1977: Tel Aviv Museum — retrospective of Table Pieces; exhbn. organised by British Council travels to N.Z. and Australia; 1992: Trajan Markets, Rome. *Commission:* The Ledge Piece, National Gallery of Art, East Wing Building opened June, 1978, Washington D.C. Presented with the keys to New York City by Mayor Beame, March, 1976. *Address:* 111 Frognal, Hampstead, London NW3.

CARPANINI, Prof. David Lawrence, Dip.A.D., M.A. (R.C.A.), A.T.C., R.B.A., R.C.A., R.W.A., R.E., N.E.A.C.; painter, printmaker; British Inst. Awards Committee Sch. Engraving (1969); *b* Abergwynfi, Glam., 1946; *s* of Lorenzo Carpanini; *m* Jane Allen; one *s. Educ.:* Glan Afan Grammar School, Port Talbot; *studied art* at Gloucestershire College of Art (1964-68), Royal College of Art (1968-71), University of Reading (1971-72). *Exhib.:* R.A., R.B.A., R.W.A., R.E., N.E.A.C., Bankside Gallery, New Academy Gallery, Agnews, Piccadilly Gallery, Tegfryn, Albany, Mostyn, Fosse and Brandler Galleries, Welsh Arts Council, etc. *Work in permanent collections:* National Library and National Museum of Wales, Contemporary Art Society for Wales, Newport A.G., Glynn Vivian A.G., Dept. Environment, R.W.A., N.C.B., A.S.T.M.S., Glam., Glos., Clwyd., Avon, Yorks. Educ. Authorities, and private collections in U.K., U.S.A., Canada, Europe Australia, etc. Television Films: C4 (1984), H.T.V. (1987). *Publications:* regular contributor to art periodicals. *Address:* Fernlea, 145 Rugby Rd., Milverton, Leamington Spa, Warwickshire CV32 6DJ. *Signs work:* "David L. Carpanini."

CARPANINI, Jane, Dip.A.D., A.T.C., R.B.A., R.W.A., R.W.S., R.C.A.; artist in water-colour and pencil; *b* Luton, 1949; *d* of Derrick Stanley Allen; *m* David L. Carpanini; one *s. Educ.:* Bedford High School; *studied art:* at Luton College of Art (1967-68), Brighton Polytechnic (1968-71), University of Reading (1971-72). *Exhib.:* R.A., R.W.A., R.B.A., R.W.S., Bankside Gallery, Tegfryn, New

Academy Gallery, Fosse and Brandler Galleries, Welsh Arts Council, Mostyn, Albany, etc. Winner of Hunting Group prize Watercolour of the Year (1983). *Work in permanent collections:* National Library and National Museum of Wales, Burnley Building Soc., etc., and private collections in U.K., U.S.A., Europe. *Publications:* regular contributor to art periodicals, reproductions; cards, prints, calendars, catalogues, etc. *Address:* Fernlea, 145 Rugby Rd., Milverton, Leamington Spa, Warwickshire CV32 6DJ. *Signs work:* "Jane Carpanini."

CARRICK, Desmond, R.H.A.; artist in sculpture, oil, water-colour and tempera, lithography, stained glass and ceramics; secretary, Royal Hibernian Academy of Arts (1971-1982 resigned); *b* Dublin, 18 Dec., 1928; *s* of Henry Carrick. *Educ.:* Synge St. School; *studied art* at Dublin National College of Art. *Exhib.:* R.H.A., Oireachtas, Waterford, Dublin Painters, Water-colour Soc. of Ireland, Living Art, Irish Contemporary Painters organized by the Cultural Relations Com. of Ireland, English and Canadian Contemporary Painters; one-man shows: Dublin (15) 1953-1992, England (1) 1989. *Commissions:* Murals in Guinness Visitors' Waiting Room (Dublin). *Address:* "Studio," Woodtown, Rathfarnham, Co. Dublin 16. *Signs work:* see appendix.

CARRUTHERS, Derek William, Prof., (Emeritus), B.A., A.R.B.S.; artist in various media, mainly oil painting; *b* Penrith, Cumbria, 1935; *s* of William Edward Carruthers; *m* Eileen; one *s*, one *d. Educ.:* Royal Grammar School, Lancaster; *studied art* at Durham University, King's College (now Newcastle University) (Victor Pasmore, Richard Hamilton, Lawrence Gowing). *Exhib.:* John Moores Liverpool, 'Structure' Bradford Arts Festival, Midland View. *Work in permanent collections:* Northern Arts, Leics. Educ. Authority, Bradford A.G., Abbot Hall Gallery Kendal, Leicester University, etc. *Publication:* Artisan (1979), Haunting Monuments (1985), Recent Paintings (1985-88). *Address:* The School House, Harston, nr. Grantham NG32 1PS. *Signs work:* "CARRUTHERS."

CARTER, Albert Henry, B.Ed.(Hons., 1977), R.B.A. (1983); artist in water-colour, acrylic, etc.; Hon. Treasurer, R.B.A.; former Director of Art, Oundle School; *b* Trowbridge, Wilts., 22 Feb., 1928; *s* of Edward Guy Carter; *m* Eunice Enfield; one *s*, three *d. Educ.:* Trowbridge Boys' High School; *studied art:* at St. Paul's College, Cheltenham (1973-77, Harold W. Sayer, A.,R.C.A.). *Exhib.:* R.B.A., R.W.S., R.W.A., and provincial galleries. *Work in permanent collections:* American Embassy, and private collections. *Address:* Haydn Studio, 27 South Rd., Oundle, nr. Peterborough PE8 4BU. *Signs work:* "A. H. Carter."

CARTER, Bernard Thomas, Hon.R.E. (1975), N.D.D. (1950), A.T.D. (1951); artist in oil; former keeper in charge of Pictures and Conservation, National Maritime Museum, Greenwich (retd. 1977); *b* London, 6 Apr., 1920; *m* Eugenie Alexander, artist; one *s. Educ.:* Haberdasher Aske's; *studied art* at Goldsmiths' College of Art. *Exhib.:* one-man shows, Arthur Jeffress (1955), Portal Gallery (twelve); mixed, R.A., Arts Council, British Council, galleries in Europe and U.S.A. *Publication:* Art for Young People (with Eugenie Alexander). Work shown on television (BBC and ITV). *Address:* 56 King George St., Greenwich, London SE10 8QD. *Signs work:* "Carter."

CARTER, Joan Patricia, R.M.S. (1986), S.W.A. (1985); Gold medallist Paris Salon (1974), finalist Hunting Group prizes (1980), Hon. men. Gold Bowl R.M.S.; freelance portrait painter, book illuminator, illustrator and calligrapher in water-colour, pastel, acrylic and silverpoint; writer; *b* Vancouver, B.C., Canada, 11 Mar., 1923; *d* of Major G.F.B. Willcox, R.A. (India), soldier and artist; *m* Alan Henry Carter; two *s. Educ.:* Lord Selkerk School, Vancouver,

Canada; C.F.E., Longbridge Rd., Ilford; Havering C.F.E., Hornchurch; *studied art*: 'A' level art and Art History (Mr. L. Lipman). *Exhib.*: Schweinfurt, Germany, Paris Salon, R.A., numerous one-man shows etc., M.A.S.-F. *Work in permanent collection:* miniature portrait (1½" x 1") of Mrs. S. Lucas on gold bowl, R.M.S. (1985). *Publications:* Uncle Bill and Aunt Ethel, Allergy Cooking (Ian Henry Pub.), Solo Cooking on a Shoe String (Ian Henry Pub.), Illuminated Calligraphy (Search Press), Illuminated Alphabet (Search Press), numerous Remembrance books – thirteen in England, one Normandy, France, one Tristan da Cunha, various talks and broadcasts, and articles; art work for book cover (Fowler Wright). *Address:* Hobbema House, King St., Neatishead, Norwich, Norfolk NR12 8BW. *Signs work:* art books: "Patricia Carter"; other books: "J.P. Carter"; and see appendix.

CARTER, Kenneth, N.D.D. (Sculpture), A.T.D. (1955), F.R.B.S. (1970); sculptor in bronze and synthetic resins; *b* Hull, 16 June, 1928; *s* of Walter Carter; *m* Brenda Hubbard; two *s*, two *d*. *Educ.*: Kingston High School, Hull; *studied art* at Hull and Leicester Colleges of Art (1944-46, 1948-50, 1954-55). *Exhib.*: Woodstock Gallery, London; various mixed exhbns. London and provinces. *Work in permanent collections:* Exeter Cathedral Chapter House: 15 life-size niches; Ferens A.G., Hull. *Address:* Figgins Gallery, Church Rd., Lympstone, Devon EX8 5JT. *Signs work:* "K. Carter."

CARTER, Mary; painter in oil, egg tempera, gouache, water-colour; *b* Hartsdale, N.Y., 12 Apr., 1931; *m* Peter Gould, decd.; one *s*. *Studied art* at Art Students League of N.Y. (1951-55, Reginald Marsh, R.B. Hale). *Exhib.*: Audubon Artists Annual N.Y. (1954, 1972), National Academy Design, N.Y. (1955, 1972), Hartford Athaneum, Conn. (1955), National Competition, Springfield Art Museum, Missouri (1966), Annual Drawings and Sculpture Show, Del Mar College, Corpus Christi, Tex. (1967), Hudson Guild Invitationals, N.Y. (1975-present). *Address:* 253 W. 16 St. New York, N.Y. 10011.

CARTER, Mary Elizabeth, M.A., A.R.C.A.; painter in oil of miniatures, portraits, rural and domestic scenes; *b* London, 1947; *d* of H.E. Carter; *m* J. B. Hiscock, painter; two *s*, one *d*. *Educ.*: Ursuline Convent, Wimbledon; *studied art* at Kingston School of Art, Royal College of Art (Carel Weight, Roger de Grey). *Exhib.*: Zaydler Gallery, Patricia Wells Gallery, R.W.A., Linfield Galleries, Bradford-on-Avon, Miniaturist for New Grafton Gallery, R.A. Summer Exhbn. since 1968. *Work in permanent collections:* Southend-on-Sea Library, R.A., Camden Council. *Publication:* The Dog Who Knew Too Much. *Address:* 2 Hodges Cottages, Hemyock, Cullompton, Devon EX15 3RW. *Signs work:* "Mary E. Carter."

CARUANA, Gabriel; sculptor, painter, ceramist; *b* Malta, 7 Apr., 1929; *s* of Anthony; *m* 1980 Mary Rose Buttigieg; two *d*. Artistically active since 1953. *Exhib.*: one-man shows: Malta, England, Italy, Switzerland, Germany; participated in International Exhbn. of Ceramic Art (Faenza). *Work in permanent collections:* Museum of Fine Arts, Valletta, Malta; Whitworth A.G., Manchester; City of Manchester A.G.; Museum of Ceramics, Faenza, Italy; Albert Einstein (1879-1955) International Academy Foundation, Delaware, U.S.A., also several private collections. Artist of the Year, Malta (1985-86); 1988, town of Faenza hosts one-man show to honour 25 Years of Artistic Activity within the City. Founder and Hon. Director, Culture and Crafts Centre, The Old Mill, B'kara, Malta. *Addresses:* Dr. Zammit St., Balzan, Malta, and 30 Carmel St., B'kara, Malta. *Studio:* 37, Balzan Valley, Balzan, Malta; c/o

Scultore Bianco Donato, Via Kafka 5, 00143, Roma, Italia. *Signs work:* "Gabriel Caruana."

CARVER, Margaret, A.R.M.S. (1986); artist in oil, pastel, water-colour, pencil; Chairperson, Gt.Yarmouth Soc. of Artists; *b* Caister-on-Sea, 10 Sept., 1941; *m* Richard Carver; two *s. Educ.:* Caister High School; Gt. Yarmouth C.F.E.; *studied art:* evening classes and part-time courses. *Exhib.:* Westminster Galleries with S.W.A. and R.M.S., Norwich, Gt. Yarmouth. *Work in permanent collection:* Gt. Yarmouth and District. *Address:* 3 Orchard Cl., Caister-on-Sea, Gt. Yarmouth, Norfolk NR30 5FDS. *Signs work:* "M. CARVER."

CARY, Caroline Anne M., F.P.S.; painter in acrylic and water-colour; *b* 28 July, 1940; *m* Lucius Cary; one *s*, three *d* (one decd.). *Studied art* at Camberwell and Chelsea under Lawrence Gowing. *Exhib.:* London: Loggia Gallery, Langton Gallery, Clarges Gallery, Jonathon Poole Gallery, Clark Fine Art, Lord Leighton's Studio, Leighton House, Sue Rankin Gallery, Bruton St. Gallery (1993); Watatu Gallery, Nairobi; Century Gallery Henley; Galerie Souham, Paris; Austin Desmond Fine Art and William Desmond Fine Art, Huxham, Devon; solo show 2 Gallery, N.Y. (1993). *Work in private collections:* R. Agnew, C. Lloyd-Jones. *Address:* The Studio, 14 Gunter Grove, London SW10. *Signs work:* "C.A.C."

CASSELDINE, Nigel, A.R.W.A. (1985), R.W.A. (1991), Brandler Painting prize (1988); artist/painter in oil on gesso/drawing; Council mem. R.W.A. (1990-93); *b* Havering, Essex, 1947; *m* Jenny Partridge; one *s*, one *d. Educ.:* N. Romford Comprehensive School; *studied art* at Camberwell and Sir John Cass Schools of Art (1966-68, part-time); studio assistant to F.V. Magrath (1969-72). *Exhib.:* R.A., R.W.A., Bath Festival, Edinburgh Festival, Medici Gallery, Gloucester A.G. and Museum, etc. *Work in permanent collections:* R.W.A., Cheltenham and Gloucester. *Publications:* 20th Century Painters and Sculptors by F. Spalding; Light by L. Willis. *Address:* Mount Cottage, St. Marys, Chalford, nr. Stroud, Gloucs. GL6 8PU. *Signs work* "CASSELDINE" in red.

CASSON, Sir Hugh Maxwell, C.H., K.C.V.O., M.A., P.P.R.A., R.D.I., F.R.I.B.A., F.S.I.A.; Hon. Dr. R.C.A. (1975); architect; President, Royal Academy (1976-1985); director of architecture, Festival of Britain (1951); Prof. Environmental Design, R.C.A. (1953-75); *b* London, 23 May, 1910; *s* of Randal Casson, I.C.S.; *m* Margaret Macdonald, A.R.I.B.A.; three *d. Educ.:* Eastbourne College; St. John's College, Cambridge; *studied architecture* at Cambridge, British School at Athens, Bartlett School, University College, London. Regular contributor as author and illustrator to lay and technical press: Albert Medal R.S.A. (1984): Italian Order of Merit (1980). *Publications:* Homes by the Million, Victorian Architecture, New Sights of London, Nanny Says, Diary, Hugh Casson's London, Hugh Casson's Oxford, Hugh Casson's Cambridge, Japan Observed, The Tower of London. *London Address:* 6 Hereford Mans., Hereford Rd., London W2 5BA.

CASSON, Simon John, A.R.E. (1992), R.A.S.(M.A.) (1994), Central Printmaking Dip. (1990), B.A.(Hons.) Fine Art (1988); painter in oil, printmaker in etching; *b* York, 17 May, 1965. *Educ.:* Rose Avenue School, Zambia, Lime House School, Cumbria, Penistone Grammar School, Sheffield; *studied art* at Barnsley College of Art (1985), Exeter College of Art and Design (1985-87), Central St. Martin's (1988-90, Norman Ackroyd), Royal Academy of Arts (1991-94, Prof. Norman Adams). *Exhib.:* numerous group shows. *Work in permanent collection:* R.E. (Dip. Coll.). *Publication:* Printmakers Journal (1993).

Address: c/o J. Casson, West Swilletts Cottage, Seaborough, nr Beaminster, Dorset DT8 3QZ. *Signs work:* "S. Casson" with date.

CASTLE, Roger Bernard, U.A. (1988); landscape marine artist in oil; council mem. U.A.; *b* Dartford, 30 Apr., 1945; *m* Brenda; two *s,* one *d. Educ.:* Dartford; *studied art* under the late William Walden, R.B.A. *Exhib.:* R.A., R.O.I., N.E.A.C., R.B.A., U.A.; gallery artist at Century Gallery Henley, Roger Freen Fine A.G. Kent, Blackheath Gallery, F. Illes, Rochester. *Work in permanent collection:* K.C.C. Ashford. *Addresses:* 26 Harper Rd., Ashford, Kent; studio: Hales Pl., High Halden, Kent. *Signs work:* "R.B. CASTLE."

CATCHPOLE, Heather O., R.M.S.; National Dip. in commercial and Applied Art (1962); portrait artist in water-colour on ivorine, pastel; *b* Winnipeg, Canada, 26 Aug., 1942; *d* of Kenneth Siddons Osler, M.A.; *m* Brian E. Catchpole, L.D.S. *Educ.:* Durban Girls' High School; *studied art* at Natal School of Arts and Craft. *Exhib.:* R.M.S., R.A., Hilliard Soc. *Address:* Heelers, Fitzhead, Taunton, Som. TA4 3JW. *Signs work:* "Heather O. Catchpole," miniatures: the letter O with H inside with the year underneath it.

CATTRELL, Annie Katherine, B.A.(Hons.) Fine Art (1984), M.A. Fine Art (1985); artist in glass, paper and mixed media; lecturer, Sculpture Dept., Cheltenham School of Art; *b* 15 Feb., 1962. *Studied art* at Glasgow School of Art (1980-84, Sam Ainsley), University of Ulster (1984-85, Alistair MacLennan). *Exhib.:* Collins Gallery Strathclyde University (1989), 369 Gallery 'Artist's Choice' (1990), Artist in Residence, Chessel Gallery (1991), Paperworks, Seagate Gallery (1992). *Work in permanent collections:* S.A.C., MacManus A.G. and Museum Dundee, Glasgow Museums and A.G's., City Art Centre Edinburgh. *Publications:* reviews, Edinburgh Medicine vol.65, Alba (1991) Mar./Apr., etc. *Address:* 10A Greenhill Park, Churchill, Edinburgh EH10 4DW. *Clubs:* S.S.A. (Council mem.), Collective Gallery, Edinburgh. *Signs work:* "Annie Cattrell."

CAULKIN, Martin, R.I. (1983), R.B.S.A. (1983); artist in water-colour and ink; *b* B'ham, 12 Feb., 1945; *s* of Howard Caulkin; *g-s* of F.E.H. Caulkin, Hon. R.B.S.A.; *m* Anne Cherry, S.W.A.; one *d. Educ.:* Great Barr Comprehensive; *studied art* at B'ham College of Art (1962-65, Glyn Griffiths). *Exhib.:* R.W.S., R.B.S.A., R.I., R.A. Summer Show, Singer and Friedlander water-colour exhbn., Shell House Gallery, Ledbury, Ombersley Galleries, Worcs., Montpellier Gallery, Cheltenham, Manor House Gallery, Chipping Norton, Bill Toop Gallery, Salisbury. *Address:* September Cottage, Naunton, Upton upon Severn, Worcester WR8 0PY. *Club:* Easel, B'ham. *Signs work:* "Martin Caulkin."

CAVANAGH, John; couturier (retd. Sept. 1974); *b* Belmullet, 28 Sept., 1914; *s* of Cyril Cavanagh. *Educ.:* St. Paul's School; *trained* with Molyneux and Balmain in Paris. *Exhib.:* Munich, 1954 (Gold Medal); designed Wedding Dress for H.R.H. Duchess of Kent (June, 1961); designed Wedding Dress for H.R.H. Princess Alexandra (April, 1963). *Work in permanent collections:* V. & A., Museum of Costume, Bath. *Address:* 10 Birchlands Ave., London SW12 8ND. *Signs work:* "JOHN CAVANAGH."

CECIL, Roger; artist in oil and oil pastel; David Murray Award (1966); *b* Abertillery, 18 July, 1942. *Studied art* at Newport College of Art. *Exhib.:* Howard Roberts Gallery, Cardiff (1966), R.A. Summer Exhbn. (1987, 1989); one-man shows, New Academy Gallery, London (1988, 1989), Cleveland Drawing Biennale (1989). *Publication:* B.B.C. documentary The Gentle Rebel. *Address:* c/o The New Academy Gallery, 34 Windmill St., London W1P 1HH. *Signs work:* "Roger Cecil."

CERCI, Sharon L., F.M.A.S., A.R.M.S. (1983); scrimshander scribing on ivory with ink, lecturer; heraldic artist and designer; *b* Providence, R.I., U.S.A., 4 July, 1942; *d* of the late Gordon L. Keith; two *s*, one *d. Educ.:* Brockton High School; *studied art* at B.H.P. Art School (1963). *Exhib.:* I.F.M.A.S., R.M.S., International Circle of Miniature Artists, Spencer Gallery, Dunedin Fine Art Center. *Address:* 1358 N. Lotus Drive, Dunedin, Florida, U.S.A. *Signs work:* S within a C, "S.Cerci," "Sharon Cerci," "Cerci."

CHADWICK, Lynn, C.B.E.; 1st Prize, Venice Biennale (1956); sculptor, chiefly in iron and bronze; *b* London, 24 Nov., 1914; *s* of V. R. Chadwick, J.P.; *m* Eva Reiner; two *s*, two *d. Educ.:* Merchant Taylors. *Exhib.:* Stedelijk Museum (Amsterdam, 1957), Palais des Beaux Arts, Bruxelles (1957), Arts Council of G.B. (London, 1957). *Work in permanent collections:* Tate, Museum of Modern Art (N.Y.), Allbright Art Gallery (Buffalo), The Kroller-Müler Museum (Otterlo). *Work repro.:* Contemporary British Art (Herbert Read), Sir Herbert Read, Lynn Chadwick (Bodensee Verlag, Amriswill, Swiss), Pelican, Lynn Chadwick (Dr. J. P. Hodin, Zwemmer), Lynn Chadwick (Alan Bowness, Methuen), Dennis Farr and Eva Chadwick, Lynn Chadwick (O.U.P.). *Address:* Lypiatt Pk., Stroud Glos. GL6 7LL.

CHAMBERLAIN, Trevor, R.O.I. (1972), R.S.M.A. (1970), N.S. (1968); Bourlet Prize Winner at 1980 R.O.I. Exhbn.; marine, town and landscape painter in oil and water-colour; *b* Hertford, 13 Dec., 1933; *s* of Frederick Joseph Chamberlain; *m* Elaine Waterfield; one *s. Educ.:* Ware Central School. *Work in permanent collections:* Guildhall Art Gallery, London, Government House, N. Ireland, National Maritime Museum, Greenwich, Hertford Museum. *Work repro.:* The Connoisseur, Studio International, Dictionary of Sea Painters, 20th Century Marine Painting, Water-colour Impressionists; Co-author of 'Oil-Painting, — Pure and Simple', 'Oils'. *Address:* Braeside, Goldings La., Waterford, Hertford, Herts. SG14 2PT. *Signs work:* "T. Chamberlain."

CHAMBERS, Basil, M.I.P.A.; artist in water-colour; advertising designer; illustrator; graphic designer; *b* 14 Aug., 1920. *Studied art* at Chelsea School of Commercial Art, Hornsey College of Art, Beckenham School of Art. *Address:* Summerford Farm Studio, Fairwarp, Uckfield, Sussex. *Signs work:* "B. H. A. Chambers."

CHAMBERS, Stephen Lyon, B.A.Hons., M.A., Rome Scholarship; painter in oil on canvas; *b* London, 20 July, 1960; *m* Denise de Coruova; two *s. Educ.:* Holland Park Comprehensive; *studied art* at Winchester School of Art (1978-79), St. Martin's School of Art (1979-82), Chelsea School of Art (1982-83). *Exhib.:* widely in Europe, U.S.A. and U.K. Represented by Flowers East, London. *Publications:* Strange Smoke by John Gillett; Paintings 1988-89 by Gerard Wilson; Felonies and Errors by Isabella Oulton. *Address:* 129 Offord Rd., London N1 1PH. *Signs work:* paintings on canvas only signed on reverse.

CHANDLER, Cynthia Ann; landscape and coastal scene painter in water-colour and oil and portrait painter in oil, pastel and water-colour; *b* Isleworth, Middx., 1 Jan., 1937; *d* of Thomas Joseph Wilfred Elliott; *m* Frank Chandler; two *s*, one *d. Educ.:* Hampton High School; *studied art* at Twickenham School of Art (Mr. Duffy, Mr. Kane, Miss Palby). *Exhib.:* U.A., P.S., and several Midland exhbns. *Work in permanent collection:* Nuneaton Art Gallery (3). *Address:* 36 Dunsmore Ave., Rugby, Warwickshire CV22 5HD. *Societies:* President, Rugby and District Art Soc., Coventry and Warwickshire Soc. of Artists, Banbury and District Art Soc. *Signs work:* "Cynthia Chandler," "CYN-THIA CHANDLER."

CHANDLER, Eileen, S.W.A.; international portrait painter, landscape and flower in water-colour, pastel and pencil; *b* London, 10 June, 1904; *m* Roland M. Chandler, illustrator; one *d. Educ.:* Elmshurst, E. Finchley; *studied art* at Hornsey School of Art; R.A. Schools. *Exhib.:* R.A., R.I., R.B.A., R.W.S., R.P., P.S., etc.; one-man shows: Walker Gallery (1951), Clarges Gallery (1986), Guy Morrison (1988), Henry Brett Gallery, Stow-on-the-Wold (1990), also own gallery Los Angeles (1950). *Publications:* written and illustrated: Too Bright and Too Early; Poems for Parents (1990). *Address:* 17 Ashlone Rd., London SW15 1LS. *Signs work:* "EILEEN CHANDLER"; pre-1930 "EILEEN HARRIS."

CHANEY, Judith Hilary Desforges, B.Soc.Sc., M.Soc.Sc.; Director of Quality Control, The London Inst.; *b* 31 May, 1944. *Educ.:* Nottingham High School for Girls, G.P.D.S.T., University of Birmingham. Taught at University of Leicester, University of Hong Kong, Sunderland Polytechnic. Registrar, Art and Design, C.N.A.A. (1985-91). *Address:* c/o The London Inst., Davies St., London W1.

CHANG, Chien-Ying B.A. (1935); artist in water-colour; mem. of R.I., R.W.A. and Soc. of Woman Artists; *b* 27 June, 1915; *d* of Peh-Sung Chang; *m* Cheng-Wu Fei, artist. *Educ.:* National Central University, China, and Slade School of Fine Art. *Exhib.:* R.A., R.I., R.B.A.; one-man shows at Leicester Gallery (1951, 1955, 1960). *Work in permanent collections:* London University; St. John's College, Oxford; R.W.A., Bristol; Grave's Gallery, Sheffield; Derby Art Gallery. *Work repro.:* Studio, Art News and Review, Future, Picture Post, La Revue Moderne, Kunst, etc. *Address:* 52 Dollis Pk., London N3. *Signs work:* see appendix.

CHANNING, Leslie Thomas, A.R.I.B.A. (1941), U.A. (1973), A.N.S.P.S. (1975); artist in water-colour; architect (retd.); *b* Weymouth, 24 Apr., 1916; *s* of Richard Channing, engineer; *m* (1st) Florence Helen (decd.); (2nd) Audrey Joan; one *s*, one *d. Educ.:* The Wandsworth School and Regent St. Polytechnic Evening Inst. School of Architecture (1934-39). *Exhib.:* R.I., U.A., N.S.P.S., Thames Valley Arts Club. *Address:* 6 Spinnaker Ct., Becketts Pl., Hampton Wick KT1 4EW. *Clubs:* U.A., N.S.P.S., Thames Valley Arts. *Signs work:* "L. T. Channing."

CHAO, Shao-an, M.B.E. (1980); Prof. in Art (Canton University, 1948); painter in ink and water-colour; *b* Canton, China, 6 Mar., 1905. Studied painting at 15 under Kao Chi-feng, a key figure in the early development of 'Lingnan Painting'. Awarded International Art Gold Medal by the Belgium Centenary Independence World Fair, Brussels and founded 'Lingnan School of Art' in Canton (1930); moved to Hong Kong in 1948 and re-established 'Lingnan School of Art' there. To date, he has students in many parts of the world. *Exhib.:* repeated one-man shows in major cities in China: Nanking, Shanghai, Canton, Chungking, etc. (1929-48); one man shows, in major universities and art museums and galleries in U.S.A., England, Japan, France, W. Germany, Switzerland, Italy, Canada, Australia, New Zealand, Singapore and Malaysia (1951-78); Urban Council Hong Kong Museum of Art (1979), National Museum of History, Taiwan (1980). *Lectures:* at a number of universities including University of Leeds, U.K. (1954), Harvard University and Berkeley University, U.S.A. (1960). *Work in permanent collections:* Boston Museum of Fine Art, Washington County Museum, Nanyang University Museum, Singapore, Hong Kong Museum of Art and National Museum of History, Taiwan, Museum für Kunsthandwerk, Übersee-Museum, Romer-Museum, Museum der Stadt Ettlingen, W. Germany (1989). *Publications:* Charming Cicadas Collection (1 vol.), Shao-an's Paintings (1 vol.), Recent Paintings by Prof. Chao Shao-an (3 vols.), Collection of Shao-an's Paintings (20 vols.), The Art of Chao Shao-an (1 vol.), The Paintings of Chao Shao-an (1 vol.). Conferred the honorary degree of Doctor of Letters by University of Hong Kong (1994) in recognition of services to the Arts. *Address:* 295A Prince Edward Rd., (2nd Floor), Kowloon, Hongkong. *Signs work:* "CHAO Shao-An" and see appendix.

CHAPLIN, Michael James, N.D.D., F.R.E.; printmaker, water-colourist; Vice-Pres. Royal Soc. of Printer-Printmakers; *b* St. Neots, 19 Sept., 1943; *m* Gay Lloyd; one *s*, one *d. Educ.:* St. Albans Boys' Grammar School; *studied art* at Watford College of Art (1961-64), Brighton College of Art (1966-67), postgraduate. *Exhib.:* R.E. Annual, R.W.S. Open (Prizewinner 1989), R.A. Summer Shows. *Work in permanent collections:* Kent, Sussex, Essex County Councils, S.E. Arts; public and private collections worldwide, Royal Collections. *Publication:* included in Encyclopedia of Water-colour Techniques. *Address:* Suffield, Orchard Drive, Weavering, Maidstone, Kent ME14 5JG. *Signs work:* "Michael Chaplin, R.E."

CHAPMAN, John Lewis; artist in water-colour, gouache, oil; *b* Blackburn, 11 Sept., 1946. *Studied art* at Blackburn Art College (James Dolby). *Exhib.:* R.A. Summer Exhbn., Patersons, London, Lewis Textile, Blackburn, Haworth A.G., Accrington, Jersey, Birmingham, Warrington, Newcastle. *Work in permanent collections:* Blackburn A.G. *Address:* 25 Silverwell St., Bolton BL1 1PP. *Signs work:* "J.L. CHAPMAN."

CHAPMAN, June Dianne; awarded, Diploma di Merito University of the Arts, Accademia Italia, Salsomaggiore, Italy (1982); painter in oil; *b* Ruislip, 12 June, 1939. *Educ.:* St. Joan of Arc's Convent School, Rickmansworth; *studied art* at Camberwell School of Art (1955-56). *Exhib.:* R.A., R.B.A., R.O.I., U.A., Blackheath Gallery, Edwin Pollard Gallery, Foyles A.G. *Address:* 13 King William Walk, Greenwich, London SE10 9JH. *Signs work:* "J. Chapman" or "June Chapman."

CHAPMAN, Max; painter, critic; *b* Dulwich, 24 Feb., 1911; *s* of Joshua Chapman, M.A. *Educ.:* Dulwich College; *studied art* at Byam Shaw Art School and by travelling scholarship in Italy. *Exhib.:* one-man shows, Storran, Leger, Gallery One, New Vision Centre, Molton, Leicester Galleries, Camden Arts Centre, Middlesbrough A.G. Retro. '81, Drian; shared exhbns.: Paris, Zürich, Grabowski Gallery, London Forum, Bristol; group shows, R.A., Glasgow, London Group, Bradford A.G., Towner, Bladon, Commonwealth Biennial, etc. *Work repro.:* Quadrum, Apollo, Arts Review, Times, Architects' Journal, Connoisseur. *Address:* c/o Camden Arts Centre, London NW3 6DE. *Signs work:* "Chapman."

CHARLES, Agnes E.; designer and maker of stained-glass windows for ecclesiastical and secular buildings under name of St. Crispin's Glass; also glass mosaics, sculpture with mosaics; landscape and portrait painter in oil; *d* of the late A. P. Charles. *Educ.:* Kensington High School; *studied art* at R.A. schools. *Exhib.:* R.A., Leicester Gallery, Leger Gallery, Heals, Foyles, Alpine Gallery, provinces, *Permanent exhbns.:* in records of Council for Places of Worship, 83 London Wall, EC2; in Craftsman's Index of Crafts Council of Great Britain Ltd., 47 Victoria St., SW1. *Address:* 28 St. Albans Rd., Codicote, Herts. SG4 8UT. *Signs work:* "A. Charles."

CHARLESTON, Robert Jesse, M.A., F.S.A., F.S.G.T.; keeper at V. & A. (1963-1976); *b* 3 Apr., 1916; *s* of S. J. Charleston, M.A.; *m*; one *s*, one *d. Educ.:* Berkhamsted School, Herts.; New College, Oxford. *Publications:* Roman Pottery

(1955); (ed.) English Porcelain, 1745-1850 (1965); (ed.) World Ceramics (1968); The James A. de Rothschild Collection at Waddesdon Manor; (with J. G. Ayers) Meissen and Oriental Porcelain (1971); (with D. M. Archer and M. Marcheix) Glass and Enamels (1977); Islamic Pottery (1979); Masterpieces of Glass (1980); English Glass (1984); etc. *Address:* Whittington Ct., Whittington, Cheltenham, Glos. GL54 4HF.

CHASE, Michael; Barcham Green Co. award (1985); painter in water-colour; *b* London, 1 Aug., 1915; *s* of William A. Chase, painter and designer; *m* (1) Rowena Witham; (2) Valerie Thornton, etcher and printmaker; one *d. Educ.:* Newbury; *studied art* at Hornsey, Central, Chelsea Schools of Art (evening classes). *Exhib.:* R.A. Summer Exhbn., Oxford Gallery, Bruton Gallery, New Ashgate, Open Exhbn. Contemporary British Water-colours, Bankside Gallery; 1990-92: Clare Hall Cambridge, Redfern Gallery London, Printworks Colchester, John Russell Gallery Ipswich, Chappell Galleries Essex. *Work in permanent collections:* D.O.E., Bolton, Sheffield, Leicester, Portsmouth, Plymouth Museum and A.G., Ptarmigan Trust, I.C.I., Surrey C.C., Arthur Young International, B.A.S.F.,The Minories, Colchester, and Lancs., Durham, Norfolk, Suffolk, W. Yorks. Educ. Coms., Ipswich Museum and A.G. *Publications:* paintings published as posters by Art Group Ltd., rep. Dictionary of British Art (Vol. VI) by G. Spalding, cover design, Illustrated London News (Autumn, 1989). *Address:* Lower Common Farmhouse, Chelsworth, Ipswich, Suffolk. *Agent:* Chlöe Bennett, 47 The Grove, Henley Rd., Ipswich. *Signs work:* "Michael Chase."

CHATTEN, Geoffrey, A.R.B.A. (1988); self taught painter of E. Anglian life and landscape, figures and marine subjects in oil; *b* Gorleston, Norfolk, 20 Sept., 1938. *Exhib.:* R.A., R.B.A., R.O.I., Southwell Brown Gallery, Richmond, Surrey, John Noott Gallery, Broadway, Fosse Gallery, Fosse on the Wold, Waterman Gallery, London, Dassin Gallery, Los Angeles, Gt. Yarmouth Galleries. *Work in permanent collections:* Maritime Trust, many private collections throughout Britain and overseas. *Publication:* Lydia Eva (Maritime Trust). *Address:* 82 Suffield Rd., Gorleston, Norfolk NR31 7AL. *Signs work:* "Chatten."

CHATTERTON, George Edward, F.I.A.L.; Accademia Italia Gold Medal (1979), Prize of Italy Distinction (1980); artist, cartoonist and photographer; *b* Kidderminster, 15 July, 1911; *s* of Benjamin Chatterton; *m* Iris Betty Wilce; two *s. Educ.:* Toronto; *studied art* at Kidderminster School of Art; *photography* at School of Photography, Farnborough. *Work repro.:* since 1932 in leading London and Dundee illustrated journals, including London Opinion, Daily Mirror, Daily Sketch, Weekly News, etc. R.A.F. Artist/Photographer (1938-50). Cartoon creations include "Chad" of "Wot, No-?" fame (1938), "Sheriff Shucks" (1948), "Leo CV" mascot of Lions Clubs, G.B. (1969), etc. *Address:* Canal Cottage, Ryeford, Stonehouse, Glos. *Signs work:* see appendix.

CHATZIDAKIS, Manolis; Hon. Director of the Benaki Museum, Athens (since 1941); hon. director of Byzantine Museum (since 1960); mem. Academy of Athens; Hon. Vice-President of the Association Intern. D. Etudes Byzantines and President of the Christian Archaeol. Soc. (Athens), and of the Greek Com. of the A.I.E.B:, *b* Candia, Crete, 1909; *s* of Gerasimos A. Chatzidakis; *m* Eugenie Chatzidakis, ex-assist. curator in the Benaki Museum; one *s*, one *d. Educ.:* Athens; *studied history of art:* Athens, Paris and Berlin. *Publications:* on Islamic, Byzantine, Post-Byzantine and Modern Greek Art and art criticism. Specialised in the study of icons. *Address:* 32, Odos Dimokritou, Athens.

CHAUVIN, Enid; Board of Educ. art dip. (1934), elected M.A.I.A. (1948), Hon. S.G.A. (1969); artist in oils, lithography and water-colour; art teacher;

awarded Medal and Diploma of Merit, Annuale Italiana d'Arte Grafica (1968), Medal and Honourable Mention, Biennale degli Regioni, Ancona (1968); Diplome Palme d'Or des Beaux Arts (1969); Grand Prix de Bastia (1976); Mention International (1977); Fondation Michel Ange; Mention Speciale "Arts Inter" (Avignon) 1978; elected Conseiller Culturel of International Arts Guild (1969); Diplome d'Honneur I.A.G. (1984); Hon. Vice-President L'Internazionale de Centro Studi e Scambi Internazionali (1972); *b* Blackheath, 21 June, 1910; *d* of Laurence Chauvin; *m* Victor Patrick Law; one *s. Educ.:* Blackheath High School; *studied art* at Blackheath School of Art and Goldsmiths' College. *Exhib.:* R.A., R.B.A., R.O.I., A.I.A., United Artists, S.W.A., R.P., N.S., Senefelder Group, Redfern, Kensington, Mercury, Piccadilly, Curwen, and Furneau Galleries, Ganymed Editions, Exhbn. Grand Prix International de la Corse Porto Vecchio (1993); one-man exhbn. Heal's Gallery, Maison de la Culture, Ajaccio (1971, 1976, 1978, 1981), Bastia (1972, 1975, 1976), Calvi (1972, 1973, 1974), Ile Rousse (1978, 1979, 1980, 1986), Geneva (1980), Monaco (1985), Marseille (1986), in artist's studio Santa Reparata-di-Balagna (1987-1993). *Work purchased* by Southampton Education Authority and Maison de la Culture. *Work repro.:* Circus Horses in Children's Oxford Ency., biography and reproduction in La Femme dans L'Art Contemporain (1972), Dix Ans d'Arts Graphiques et Plastiques (1970-80), Artistes et Modeles (1982) and Repertorium Artis (1984). *Address:* Place de L'Ormeau, Santa Reparata-di-Balagna, 20220 Ile-Rousse, Corsica. *Signs work:* see appendix.

CHEESE, Bernard, R.E. (1988), A.R.C.A. (1950); printmaker in lithography and water-colour; *b* London, 1925; *s* of Gordon William Cheese, taxi driver; one *s*, three *d. Educ.:* Beckenham Grammar School; *studied art* at Beckenham School of Art (Wolf Kassemoff), R.C.A. (Edwin Ladell). *Exhib.:* Bankside Gallery, Zwemmer Gallery (1965), R.A., John Russell Gallery, Ipswich, St. John's Gallery, Bury St. Edmunds. *Work in permanent collections:* Library of Congress, Washington, Cincinnati Museum, N.Y. Public Library, Leeds Library, V. & A. (Print Room). *Publications:* illustrated many music books for A. & C. Black. *Address:* 2 High St., Nayland, Colchester CO6 4JE. *Signs work:* "Bernard Cheese."

CHEN, Chi; painter-artist; *b* Wusih, China, 2 May, 1912. *Studied art* in China; 1940-46 art instructor St. John's University. *Exhib.:* first one-man show Shanghai (1940). In 1947 invited to come to U.S.A.; one-man shows at universities, museums, galleries in New York, Boston, Philadelphia, Washington, D.C., Chicago, New Orleans, Houston, Dallas, Fort Worth, San Antonio, Denver, Seattle, San Francisco, Los Angeles, San Diego, etc. Recipient numerous gold medals: 1955 A.W.S. Spl. $1000 Award for Water-colour of the Year, 1960 Nat. Inst. Arts and Letters $1500 Grant, 1961 Nat. Academy Samuel Finley Breese Morse Medal, 1969 Nat. Academy Saltus Gold Medal of Merit, 1976 A.W.S. Bicentennial Gold Medal and many others. *Publications:* Aquarelles de Chen Chi (Shanghai 1942), A Portfolio of Chen Chi Paintings, Limited Edition (Switzerland 1965), Sketchbooks of Chen Chi (New York 1969), China from Sketchbooks of Chen Chi (New York 1974), Chen Chi Watercolours, Drawings, Sketches (New York 1980), Chen Chi Watercolour (Shanghai, The People's Republic of China 1981), Heaven and Water, Chen Chi (New York 1983), Heart & Chance (New York 1993). *Addresses:* 23 Washington Sq. North, New York, N.Y. 10011; Studio: 15 Gramercy Park, New York, N.Y. 10003, U.S.A. *Clubs:* Nat. Academy of Design, American Watercolour Society, Nat. Arts Club, Century Club, Dutch Treat Club and others. *Signs work:* "Chen Chi."

CHERRY, Anne, M.A. (R.C.A.) (1973), S.W.A. (1987), A.R.B.S.A. (1990); artist in water-colour; *b* Isle of Sheppey, 16 Oct., 1948; *d* of George William Cherry, M.A., M.Sc.(Oxon); *m* Martin Caulkin, R.I., R.B.S.A.; one *d. Educ.:* John Willmott Grammar School; *studied art* at Sutton Art College (1967-68), B'ham College of Art (1968-71), R.C.A. (1971-73, Joanne Brogden, Zandra Rhodes). *Exhib.:* R.B.S.A. Galleries, R.W.S., R.I., Shell House Gallery, Ledbury, Ombersley Galleries, Worcs., Montpellier Gallery, Cheltenham, Manor House Gallery, Chipping Norton. *Address:* September Cottage, Naunton, Upton upon Severn, Worcester WR8 0PY. *Signs work:* "Anne Cherry."

CHESSER, Sheila; prize-winner, Festival of the Church and the Arts, Nottingham; painter in acrylic; *b* Cheshire, 21 Feb., 1915; *d* of John Blayney-Jones; *m* Dr. Eustace Chesser. *Educ.:* Howells School, Denbigh; *studied art:* no formal art training. *Exhib.:* Leicester Gallery, Redfern Gallery, Whitechapel Gallery, W.I.A.C., Art Council, Northern Ireland, Municipal Gallery, Modern Art, Dublin, Bradford City Art Gallery, Royal Scottish Academy; one-man shows: Midland Group Gallery, Nottingham, Thames Gallery, Eton, Greenwich Theatre Gallery. *Work in permanent collection:* Leicester University. *Publication:* Through a Glass. *Address:* 17 Wimpole St., London W1M 7AD. *Clubs:* W.I.A.C., H.A.C., F.P.S. *Signs work:* see appendix.

CHEVINS, Hugh Terry, M.S.I.A.; artist, oil, gouache, pen and ink, commercial and book illustrator, landscape, mural painter, portrait painter; R.A. Bronze Medal (1953), Paris Salon Medaille d'Argent (1955, 1956); *b* Retford, 2 July, 1931; *s* of K. C. Chevins. *Educ.:* Gunnersbury Grammar School; *studied art:* Twickenham School of Art, Paris, R.A. Schools. *Exhib.:* R.A., R.B.A., United Artists, Glasgow Academy, Paris, Piccadilly Gallery, Brighton Art Gallery, Bournemouth. *Work in permanent collections:* Rijksmuseum, Amsterdam, Science Museum, London. *Work repro.:* Imperial Chemical Industries, Reed Paper Group, Shell, John Laing, John Mowlem. *Address:* 2 Gaston Way, Shepperton, Middx. TW17 8EX. *Signs work:* "HUGH CHEVINS."

CHILD, Heather, M.B.E.; painter in pen and ink, water-colour, calligrapher; chairman, Federation of British Crafts Societies (1973-76). *Educ.:* St. Swithun's School, Winchester; *studied art* at Chelsea College of Art (exhbn. to R.C.A.). *Work in permanent collections:* V. & A., Harvard University Library, Boston Public Library, U.S.A. *Publications:* Decorative Maps (Studio Ltd., 1956), The Armorial Bearings of the Guilds of London (Warne, 1960), Calligraphy Today (Studio Vista Books, 1963), Heraldic Design (G. Bell & Sons, 1969), Formal Penmanship (Lund Humphries, 1971), Christian Symbols (G. Bell & Sons, 1971). *Address:* 70 Heath Rd., Petersfield, Hants. GU31 4EJ. *Clubs:* Soc. of Designer-Craftsmen, Soc. of Scribes and Illuminators, Art Workers' Guild.

CHILTON, Elizabeth; Ruskin Cert. Fine Art and Design (1965-68); artist in oil, some etching and sculpture; *b* Darlington, 1 Mar., 1945; *d* of E. R. Chilton, F.R.I.B.A., M.T.P.I.; *m* R. G. Denning; two *s. Educ.:* Headington School for Girls, Oxford: *studied art* at Ruskin School, Oxford University, University of Illinois, U.S.A., Mem. of the Italian Academy. *Exhib.:* R.A., Paris Salon, Oxford University Colleges, N.E.A.C., R.O.I. *Address:* Purlin House, Toot Baldon, Oxford. *Signs work:* "Chilton."

CHILTON-STRONG, Valarie; portrait and landscape painter in oils; *b* Northumberland, 27 Jan., 1921; *m;* three *s. Studied art* at Stafford College of Art (1952-54). *Work in permanent collections:* portraits in military establishments including two life-size portraits hanging in Victory College, The Royal Military Academy, Sandhurst; private collections in Australia, Canada, U.S.A.,

Switzerland, Singapore, U.K. *Address:* Russell Cottage, Miserden, nr. Stroud, Glos. GL6 7JA. *Signs work:* paintings "Valarie Chilton."

CHRISTIE, Talbot Patterson Wescott; Dip.A.D. (Lond.) (1969), Byam Shaw Dip. A.D. (1969), R.A. Cert. A.D. (1973), Byam Shaw drawing prize; artist in acrylic and oil; *b* Montreal, Canada, 22 Aug., 1946; *s* of Archibald Mowatt Christie; *m* Foller Earnshan; one *s*, one *d*. Educ.: Canada, Libya, Switzerland, France; *studied art* at Byam Shaw School of Art (1966-70, Maurice de Sausmarez); R.A. Schools (1970-73). *Exhib.:* Fine Art and Market Print Gallery, Exeter, Market Place Gallery, Colyton, Heim Gallery, London, Museum of Wales, Cardiff, Grand Palais, Paris. *Address:* 57 Bainton Rd., Oxford OX2 7AG. *Signs work:* "T.P. Christie."

CHRISTOPHER, Ann, R.A., F.R.B.S., R.W.A., B.A.; sculptor in bronze; *b* Watford, Herts., 4 Dec., 1947; *d* of Wm. Christopher; *m* K. Cook. *Educ.:* Watford Girls' Grammar School; *studied art* at Harrow School of Art (1965-66), West of England College of Art (1966-69) under Ralph Brown, R.A., and Robert Clatworthy, R.A. *Work in permanent collection:* Bristol City A.G., Contemporary Arts Soc., Chantrey Collection, London, Glynn Vivian A.G. *Address:* The Stable Block, Hay St., Marshfield, nr Chippenham SN14 8PF. *Signs work:* "AC."

CHUGG, Brian J., N.D.D., A.T.D. (1951); painter in oil, etc., author; lecturer, North Devon College (1953-79); *b* Braunton, Devon, 3 Nov., 1926; *s* of John Chugg, F.R.G.S.; *m* Mary Bryan Cooper. *Educ.:* Challoners School; *architectural training* under B.W. Oliver F.R.I.B.A. (1944-46); *studied art* at Bideford Art School (1946-49), Camberwell Art School under M. Bloch and K. Vogel (1949-50). *Exhib.:* Westward Ho! Art Soc., one-man exhbns., Barnstaple (1953, 1958). *Publications:* author, Devon a Thematic Study; Victorian and Edwardian Devon from Old Photographs, etc. *Address:* Sharlands House, Braunton, Devon EX33 1AY. *Signs work:* "BRIAN CHUGG" (plus date).

CHUHAN, Jagjit (Ms.), D.F.A.(Lond.) (1977); artist in oil on canvas; part-time lecturer, Liverpool Polytechnic; *b* India, 10 Jan., 1955. *Studied art* at Slade School of Fine Art (1973-77). *Exhib.:* one-man shows: Ikon Gallery, B'ham (1987), Commonwealth Inst., London (1987), Horizon Gallery, London (1987); mixed shows: Barbican Centre, London (1988), Horizon Gallery, London (1990), Tate Gallery, Liverpool (1990-91), Ente Mostra Nezionale Di Pittura, Marsala, Sicily (1991), Arnolfini, Bristol (1991). *Work in permanent collections:* Oldham A.G., Leics. Schools Coll., Horizon Gallery, London (Indian Arts Council in the U.K.), Arthur Anderson & Co. *Address:* 233 Manley Rd., Chorlton, Manchester M21 1RB.

CINZIA: see BONADA, Cinzia.

CIPRIANI-BOND, Douglas (exhibits: Doug Cipriani), A.R.D.S., L.S.I.A.D., F.F.P.S; painter in oil and acrylic, designer and design consultant own practice in London; U.K. National Art Comm. for UNESCO (International Association of Art); *b* London, 12 June, 1928; *s* of Lt. D. G. Cipriani-Bond. *Educ.:* Collegiate and St. Martha's College, Feltham; *studied art:* Twickenham College of Art (1942-46) under F. Coulson-Davies. Also private tuition under E. Manning (1944-46). *Exhib.:* one-man shows: Sussex University; Worthing Museum and A.G.; group shows: 'Invasion Artistique' exchange exhbns—France/Britain; Pittsburgh, U.S.A.; New Burlington; U.A.; Loggia Gallery; International Arts Centre; Cambridge, Surrey, Southampton and London Universities; 'Today's Art' Brighton A.G.; 'Modern Art', Victoria A.G. (Bath Festival); transferred to

Bristol City A.G.; Towner Gallery; 'Painting South East 1975' (touring art colleges and galleries). *Work in permanent collections:* Feltham Council and private collections in Canada, Holland and Britain. *Publications:* Designs and illustrations for BBC Publications 'Time & Tune', Radio Times, etc., and for BBC in conjunction with Sadler's Wells Ballet. Artist to United States Third Air Force (1958-59). Designed Thanksgiving display Coventry Cathedral (1978). *Biography and work repro.:* Studio Vista, Graphis International (Zurich), Who's Who in Western Europe, Dic. of International Biography, Men of Achievement, British Contemporary Art (1993). *Address:* Delroy House, 14 Melville Rd., Hove, Sussex. *Clubs:* R.D.S., I.A.A., S.I.A.D., F.P.S., Forum Soc. *Signs work:* "Cipriani."

CLAESSEN, George; artist in oil and graphic media; *b* Colombo, Ceylon, 5 May, 1909; *s* of Granville Claessen. *Educ.:* St. Joseph's College, Colombo; *studied art:* self-taught. *Exhib.:* R.B.A., London, Kensington Gallery, London, Utd. Soc. of Artists, London, Imperial Inst., London, Hampstead Arts Council, Petit Palais (Paris), S.G.A., A.I.A., New Vision Gallery (London), Venice Bienale (1956), hon. mention (plaque) V Biennial, São Paulo, Brazil (1959). *Work in permanent collection:* Lionel Wendt Coll., Ceylon. *Publication:* Book of drawings (1946), Poems of a Painter (Mitre Press, London, 1967), Poems about Nothing (Arthur H. Stockwell Ltd., Devon, 1981). *Address:* 5 Spencer Rise, London NW5 1AR. *Signs work:* "Claessen" and "G.C."

CLARK, Bruce Michael, M.A., D.A.E., Cert. Ed.; painter in oil; part-time lecturer; *b* Bedfont, 17 July, 1937; *s* of William Clark, artist in water-colour; *m* Jill Clark; two *s. Educ.:* Strodes School; *studied art* at Bath Academy of Art, Corsham (1958-60) under Howard Hodgkin, Gwyther Irwin, William Crozier. *Exhib.:* one-man shows: Chiltern Gallery, Compendium Galleries, Birmingham, Worcester City A.G., Graphics Gallery, University of Kent, One Off Gallery, Dover; group shows: Walker's Gallery, Woodstock Gallery, Kootenay Gallery, Canada, Assembly House, Norwich, Festival de Provence, France, Minotaur Gallery, Toronto, Calgary Arts Council, Royal Academy. *Address:* Mingladon, Manns Hill, Bossingham, Canterbury, Kent CT4 6ED. *Signs work:* "Clark."

CLARK, Jean Manson, R.W.S. (1972), hon. mem. N.E.A.C. (1981); artist in water-colour and oil; *b* Sidcup, Kent, 6 Aug., 1902; *d* of Daniel William Wymer, engineer; *m* Cosmo Clark, R.A. (decd.); one *d. Educ.:* Merton Court School, Sidcup; *studied art* at Sidcup School of Art, R.A. Schools. *Exhib.:* R.A.; retrospective exhbn. Bankside Gallery (June 1983) including work by the late Cosmo Clark. *Murals* in Hadfield Hall, Cutlers' Hall, Sheffield (1954), Bankers' Clearing House, Carpenters' Hall, London. *Ceiling painting* in Woodford Green United Free Church; *three murals* for Corpus Christi Church, Weston-super-Mare, (1967); *Water-colours and oils* in private collections. *Address:* Church Lane Cottage, Shottisham, Woodbridge, Suffolk IP12 3HH. *Signs work:* "Jean Clark."

CLARK, John M'Kenzie, D.A. (Dundee, 1950); N.D.D. (Painting) St. Martin's (1956); artist in oil, water-colour, ink; winner of Punch scholarship; *b* Dundee, 29 Nov., 1928; *s* of James Clark, commercial artist. *Educ.:* Harris Academy, Dundee; *studied art* at Dundee College of Art (1945-50), Norwich Art College (1950-51), Hospitalfield Art School (1953), St. Martin's Art School (1955-56). *Exhib.:* R.A., R.S.A., R.S.W., S.S.A., R.G.I., United Soc. of Artists, one-man shows at Dundee, Edinburgh (1960). Mem. Royal Glasgow Institute of Fine Art. *Official purchase:* City of Dundee Permanent Collection (1961). *Work repro:* in

Glad Mag. *Address:* 2 Birchwood Pl., Dundee. *Signs work:* "J. M'KENZIE CLARK."

CLARK, Kenneth Inman Carr, M.B.E. (1990), D.F.A. (Lond. 1948); artist in ceramics; partner with Ann Clark, Kenneth Clark Pottery, Lewes; *b* 31 July, 1922; *s* of Aubrey Clark; *m* Ann Clark; one *s*, one *d*. *Educ.:* Nelson College, N.Z.; *studied art* at Slade School of Fine Art (1945-48) painting, Central School of Art and Design (1949) under Dora Billington, ceramics, and G. Friend, engraving. *Exhib.:* one-man shows, Piccadilly Gallery, Zwemmer Gallery, and many group shows in England. *Work in permanent collections:* Wellington, N.Z., Auckland, N.Z., Japan. *Publications:* Practical Pottery and Ceramics, Throwing for Beginners, The Potters Manual. *Address:* Merton House, Vicarage Way, Ringmer, Lewes, E. Sussex BN8 5LA, The Potters Manual. *Signs work:* see appendix.

CLARK, Norman Alexander, R.W.S.; Royal Academy Schools Gold Medallist and Edward Stott Scholar in Historical Painting (1931), Armitage Bronze Medallist in Pictorial Design (1931), Landseer prize-winner in Mural Decoration (1932), Leverhulme Scholar (1935); painter in oil and water-colour; *b* Ilford, Essex, 17 Feb., 1913; *s* of Hugh Alexander Clark (decd.); *m* Constance Josephine Barnard; one *d*. *Educ.:* Bancroft's School, Woodford; *studied art* at Central School, London (1929), R.A. Schools (1930-35). *Exhib.:* R.A., R.W.S. *Work in permanent collections:* Harris Museum and Art Gallery, Preston, Lancs., Imperial War Museum, and in private collections. *Address:* Mountfield, Brighton Rd., Hurstpierpoint, Sussex. *Signs work:* "Norman Clark."

CLARK, Peter Christian; Oxford University Certificate of Fine Art; professional painter; *b* Bradford, Yorks., 19 Apr., 1950; *s* of T. H. Clark, A.C.P., A.R.D.S., F.R.S.A. *Educ.:* Clifton House School, Harrogate, H.M.S. Conway, Anglesey, N. Wales; *studied art* at Ruskin School of Drawing and Fine Art under Richard Naish, M.A. *Address:* 40 Delancey St., London NW1. *Signs work:* "Peter Clark" and "Christian Clark."

CLARK, Thomas Humphrey, A.C.P., A.R.D.S., F.R.S.A.; artist in black and white, water-colour; *b* Manchester, 30 Jan., 1921; *s* of Edwin George Clark; *m* Betty Whitley Clark; two *s*. *Educ.:* Leeds Grammar School; *studied art* at Bradford Regional College of Art under Frank Lyle, A.T.D., Fred C. Jones, A.T.D., R.B.A. *Address:* Woodland Rise, Beemire, Windermere, Cumbria. *Signs work:* "T. H. Clark."

CLARKE, Edward, B.F.A. Hons. (1982), R.A. Postgraduate Dip. (1988); portrait artist painting in oils and drawings in charcoal; *b* Hartlepool, 16 Feb., 1962; *s* of Edward Clarke, painter and decorator. *Educ.:* Manor Comprehensive School, Hartlepool; *studied art* at Hartlepool College of Art (1980-81), Sheffield Polytechnic (1982-85), R.A. Schools (1985-88). *Exhib.:* R.A. Summer Show (1986-87), R.A. Dip. Gallery, Manchester Academy of Art. *Address:* 304 Catcote Rd., Hartlepool, Cleveland. *Signs work:* "Edward Clarke."

CLARKE, Geoffrey, R.A., A.R.C.A.; artist and sculptor; *b* 28 Nov., 1924; *s* of John Moulding Clarke and Janet Petts; *m* 1947, Ethelwynne Tyrer; two *s*. *Educ.:* Royal College of Art (Hons.). *Work in permanent collections:* (stained glass) Coventry and Lincoln Cathedrals, Taunton, Ipswich, Crownhill Plymouth; (sculpture) Coventry and Chichester Cathedrals; Cambridge (Churchill, Homerton, Newnham), Exeter, Liverpool, Newcastle, Manchester and Lancaster Universities; Bedford, Chichester and Winchester Colleges. *Other Principal Work:* Castrol House, Thorn Electric, Newcastle Civic Centre, Nottingham

Playhouse, Culham Atomic Energy, Guard's Chapel, Birdcage Walk, Aldershot Landscape, St. Paul Minnesota. *Address:* Stowe Hill, Hartest, Bury St. Edmunds, Suffolk.

CLARKE, Hilda Margery; artist in oils and other media; Director of 'The First Gallery'; *b* Manchester, 10 June, 1926; *d* of Frank Thompson; *m* Geoffrey Clarke; two *s. Educ.:* Eccles Secondary School; *studied art* privately in Manchester (Master: L. S. Lowry) and Hamburg; Southampton College of Art (1960-65); Ruskin School Print Workshop, Oxford (1975); B.A. Southampton. *Exhib.:* Tibb Lane, Manchester; London Galleries: Camden Town, F.P.S., Buckingham Gate; Southampton City A.G., Hiscock Gallery, Southsea, New Ashgate, Farnham; one-man shows, Hamwic, Southampton, Westgate Gallery, Winchester, Southampton University. *Address:* The First Gallery, 1 Burnham Chase, Bitterne, Southampton. *Signs work:* "H.M. Clarke."

CLARKE, Pat, N.S., M.F.P.S., Surrey Dip. (1969); artist in water-colour, oil, pastel and textiles, printmaker; Adult Education teacher, and teacher of the mentally handicapped (1970-80); *b* Banstead; *d* of Samuel Clarke; *m* Peter Elliott. *Educ.:* Reigate County School, Surrey and Hull University; *studied art* at Reigate Art School (1966-69). *Exhib.:* Mall Galleries, Loggia Gallery and other galleries; 30 one-woman shows, through Wales and England. Since January 1984, joint owner with husband of art gallery, Oriel y Odraig, Blaenau Ffestiniog, N. Wales. *Address:* 2 Diffwys Sq., Blaenau Ffestiniog, Gwynedd LL41 4TR. *Clubs:* N.S., F.P.S. *Signs work:* "Pat Clarke."

CLARKE, Peter John; painter in water-colour, etcher; *b* 6 Dec., 1927; *s* of Bertie Clarke. *Educ.:* Northampton; *studied art* at Northampton School of Art under Henry Bird, Peter Atkin. *Exhib.:* U.A., R.I. *Address:* 5 Harvey Lane, Moulton, Northampton NN3 1RB. *Signs work:* "P.J. Clarke" and year.

CLARKE, Richard Cambridge, B.A.(Hons.) (Open Univ.); water-colour artist; *b* Ilford, Essex, 1909; *m* 1939 Titia Faber (decd.); one *d; m* 1955 Ursula Davies (decd.); *m* 1987 Josephine Cox. *Educ.:* Bishop's Stortford College (1921-26), Regent St. Polytechnic (part-time: 1937-38). *Exhib.:* regularly at R.I. (1951-67). *Publications:* various books illustrated for Longman, Heinemann, etc. *Address:* Saffron Cottage, 107 Ashdon Rd., Saffron Walden, Essex CB10 2AJ. *Signs work:* "Richard C. Clarke."

CLARYSSE, Maggy, Dip. Brussels Academy of Art (1956); painter in oil, water-colour, pastels, silk-screen printing; *b* Brussels, 21 Oct., 1937; *m;* one *s. Educ.:* Convent Sacre Coeur, Brussels; *studied art* at Brussels Academy of Art. *Exhib.:* numerous exhbns. in U.K., France, Belgium. *Work in permanent collections:* Bourne Gallery Reigate; private collections in U.S.A., Japan, Australia, S. America. *Publication:* The Graphic Artist (1980). *Address:* 13 The Elms, Vine Rd., London SW13 0NF. *Signs work:* "Maggy Clarysse."

CLATWORTHY, Robert, R.A. (1973); sculptor; mem. Fine Art Panel of National Council for Diplomas in Art and Design (1961-71); head of Fine Art, Central School of Art and Design (1970-75); *b* 1 Jan., 1928. *Studied art* at West of England College of Art, Chelsea School of Art, The Slade. *Exhib.:* Hanover Gallery (1954, 1956), Waddington Galls. (1965), Holland Park Open Air Sculpture (1957), Battersea Park Open Air Sculpture (1960, 1963), Tate Gallery British Sculpture in the Sixties (1965), Basil Jacobs Gallery (1972), British Sculpture '72, Burlington House, Diploma Galleries R.A. (1977), Photographer's Gallery (1981). *Official purchases:* Monumental Horse and Rider installed at 1 Finsbury Ave., EC2. (1984); portrait of Dame Elisabeth Frink purchased by

N.P.G. (1985). *Work in permanent collections:* Arts Council, Contemporary Art Society, Tate Gallery, V. & A., G.L.C. *Address:* 1A Park St., London SE1.

CLAUGHTON, Richard Bentley, F.R.B.S.; sculptor; *b* London, 1917; *m*; one *s. Educ.:* Woodford House School, Kent; *studied art* at Slade School (1946-49). Public commissions in London and provinces; Australia; Nigeria. *Work in private collections* in Britain; Canada; Iraq and U.S.A. *Exhib.:* in galleries and open-air exhbns. in London and provinces; Holland and Lisbon. Director of Sculpture Studies, Slade School, University College, London until 1982. *Address:* Telham Lodge, Telham Lane, Battle, E. Sussex TN33 0SN.

CLEMENT SMITH, Winifred May; final diplomas in art subjects; artist in oil, water-colour and pastel; V.P. of Tunbridge Wells Art Club; *b* Tunbridge Wells, 26 Nov., 1904; *m* Clement Smith, architect. *Educ.:* Tunbridge Wells; *studied art:* Regent St. Polytechnic, London. *Exhib.:* S.W.A., R.I., R.O.I., R.P.S., and P.S., and provincial galleries. *Address:* 14 Queens Rd., Tunbridge Wells.

CLEMENTS, Keith, N.D.D., A.T.D., D.A.E., Ph.D.; painter, illustrator; designer, author, lecturer; *b* Brighton, 9 May, 1931; *s* of Cecil Clements; *m* Jackie Sinclair; one *s*, one *d. Educ.:* Varndean Grammar School, Brighton; *studied art* at Brighton College of Art (1947-53), Birmingham School of Art Education (1964-65). *Exhib.:* Alwin Gallery, Bloomsbury Workshop, R.A., R.E., Young Contemporaries, Arts Council tours. *Publication:* Henry Lamb: The Artist and his Friends (1985). *Address:* 29 Meeching Rd., Newhaven, E. Sussex BN9 9RL. *Signs work:* "Keith Clements."

CLEMENTS, Raymon John, F.I.A.L. (1957), A.T.D. (1951), N.D.D., painting (1950); painter and potter; Director, Creative Studies, Rowley Regis College, Warley, W. Midlands (1974-82) retd.; visiting specialist, Leamington School of Art (1951-52); lecturer Birmingham College of Technology; Housemaster, Rowley Grammar (1956-74); *b* Dudley, Worcs, 19 July, 1927; *s* of John Alfred Clements, A.M.I.Mech.E., engineer; *m* Hazel Tite; one *s. Educ.:* Dudley Grammar School; *studied art* at Birmingham College of Arts and Crafts under Harold Smith, Bernard Fleetwood-Walker, R.A., etc. *Exhib.:* Birmingham, Glasgow, S. America, Europe (touring exhbn.). *Address:* Roseland Cottage, The Avenue, Penn, Wolverhampton WV4 5HW. *Signs work:* "Clements."

CLIFTON, David James, A.R.C.A., M.A.; professor fine art; exhbn. artist, painter in water-colour and oil, various media; *b* Derby, 10 July, 1938; *s* of S. J. Clifton. *Educ.:* at private and public schools; sometime placed Truro's (Eton); *studied art* at Bournville School of Art (Ruskin Hall), Birmingham College of Art (1956-58), Royal College of Art (1958-61). *Work repro.:* Contemporary Situation; New Wave Writing; Poetry; Serious Matters; Existential Surreal Metaphysical Metaphor Ethic Image and Criterion. *Address:* Flat 12A, 63 Fountain Rd., Edgbaston, Birmingham B17 8NP. *Signs work:* "D. J. Clifton." Ref: no third party agent.

CLOUGH, Carolyn Stafford: see STAFFORD, C. Carolyn.

CLOUGH, Pauline Susan, P.S. (1982); artist in pastel, acrylic and oil; Council mem. Pastel Soc.; *b* 16 Oct., 1943; *d* of Lesley J. Bird and Millie F. Bird; *m* Peter Clough; one *s*, one *d. Educ.:* Sharmans Cross High School; *studied art* at Bournville School of Art, Birmingham (Phyllis Devey). *Exhib.:* R.A., R.I., P.S., S.W.A., R.B.S.A. and many provincial galleries. *Work in permanent collection:* Worthing Museum. *Address:* Sundown, 103 Allington Rd., Newick, Lewes, E. Sussex BN8 4NH. *Signs work:* "P.S. Clough" and "Clough."

CLUTTERBUCK, Jan; painter in water-colours; teacher of painting, Cassio College, Watford; Chairman, Women's International Art Club (1973-76); *b* Newton, Mass., 16 July, 1919; *d* of Sier Diefendorf, Greenwich, Conn.; *m* Jeremy R. H. Clutterbuck; one *s*, one *d. Educ.:* Greenbrier College, West Virginia; *studied art:* self-taught; studied printmaking at Harrow School of Art. *Exhib.:* R.A., N.S., American Embassy. *Work in permanent collections:* Gloucester Education Committee, Coventry Education Committee. *Address:* Penthands House, Sarratt, Herts. *Club:* W.I.A.C. *Signs work:* "Jan Clutterbuck."

CLYNE, Henry Horne, D.A.(Edin.); sculptor; Principal Lecturer i/c Sculpture Dept. (retd.); *b* Caithness, Scotland, 5 Mar., 1930; *s* of W. A. Scott Clyne; *m* Elaine Dunnett; one *s. Educ.:* Edinburgh College of Art (1948-54); Harkness Fellow, U.S.A. (1959-61); IWCAT Tokoname, Japan (1986). *Exhib.:* generally group shows and major Festivals (1954-66), and several one-man shows. *Work in collections:* University of Stirling (S.A.C.); University of East Anglia and Sainsbury Collection; and many private collections in U.K., U.S.A., Europe and Japan. 1990 started "Sheepshapes", ceramic sheep individually hand-made. *Address:* Sunnymede, Horsebridge Rd., Kings Somborne, Stockbridge, Hants. SO20 6PT. *Signs work:* "Henry H. Clyne" and see appendix.

CLYNE, Thora, M.A.Hons. in Fine Art (1960); Special Prize (S.S.W.A., 1984); Anne Redpath Award (S.S.W.A., 1979); Andrew Grant postgrad. Scholarship and Travel Fellowship (1960-61); artist in oil, water-colour, pastel, pen and ink; *b* Wick, Caithness, 10 Nov., 1937; *m* G. Clemson, composer. *Educ.:* Edinburgh University; Edinburgh College of Art (1955-61). *Exhib.:* one-man show: Solitude, Torrance Gallery, Edinburgh (1991); Lybster Gallery, Caithness (1993); group shows, Cornelia Sontag, Paris (1985), Kettle's Yard, Cambridge (1988); Morrison Portrait Exhbn., Royal Scottish Academy (1991), R.S.W. (1993), St. Andrews Fine Art, St. Andrews (1992, 1993); Laing Coll. Competition (1991). *Work in permanent collections:* Edinburgh Corporation Schools, Ross & Cromarty Educ. Authority, First Scottish-American Trust Co., Ltd., Gillies Bequest, Royal Scottish Academy. *Address:* Tillywhally Cottage, Milnathort, Kinross-shire KY13 7RN. *Signs work:* "Thora Clyne."

COATE, Peter, A.T.D., R.W.A., Chelsea Dip. (1950); painter in oil, water-colour, and teacher; Director, Mendip Painting Centre; *b* Nailsea, Som., 9 Mar., 1926; *s* of Redvers Coate, cidermaker; *m* Margaret Bickerton (died 1978); one *s*, one *d; m* Pamela Somerville 1980. *Educ.:* Sherborne; *studied art* at Chelsea under Robert Medley. *Exhib.:* London Group, R.A., S.WL.A., R.W.A., R.O.I., many exhbns. in the west country, specialising in landscape, churches and other buildings in Somerset. *Work in permanent collections:* R.W.A., Hertfordshire and Cumberland County Councils, Nuffield Foundation. *Address:* Manor House, Stone Allerton, nr. Wedmore, Som. *Signs work:* "Peter Coate."

COATES, Betty, S.W.A.; painter in water-colour and oil; *b* Wales, 5 Dec., 1917; *d* of T. Vaughan Milligan, A.R.C.A.; *m* Harold Coates, R.M.S.; one *d. Educ.:* Hereford High School; *studied art* at Hereford College of Art (T. Vaughan Milligan, A.R.C.A.). *Exhib.:* R.A., R.B.A., R.I., R.O.I., R.P., S.W.A., R.W.A., and private galleries. *Work in permanent collections:* Hereford City A.G., Hereford Medical Centre; private collections in U.K. and abroad. *Address:* The Coach House, Clyro, Hereford HR3 5SE. *Signs work:* "Betty Coates" or "BC" monogram.

COATES, Thomas J., P.R.B.A., N.E.A.C., R.W.S., R.P.; awarded De Lazlo Medal, 1st and 3rd prizes in Sunday Times Water-colour Exhbns. (1988, 1989); painter of landscapes, townscapes and portraits in oil and water-colour; *b* 1941.

Studied art at Bournville and Birmingham Colleges of Art (1956-61), R.A. Schools (1961-64). *Exhib.:* R.A., R.B.A., and many one-man shows including New Grafton Gallery. *Address:* Bladon Studio, Hurstbourne Tarrant, Hants. SP11 0AH.

COBB, David, P.P.R.S.M.A., R.O.I.; *m* Jean Main, Associate Fellow, Guild of Glass Engravers. *Address:* Woodis, Setley, Brockenhurst, Hants. SO42 7UH. *Signs work:* "DAVID COBB."

COCHRAN, Margi, C.L.W.A.C. (1976), A.R.M.S. (1987), M.A.A. (1989); artist in oil, pastel and opaque water-colour; *b* Philadelphia, Pa., 30 Aug., 1925; *m* Arthur Oschwald, Jr.; one *s*, one *d*. *Studied art* at Philadelphia Museum School of Art (1945-47), Montclair Art Museum (1974-79, Tom Vincent), Somerset Art Assoc. (Adolph Konrad, art teacher – private groups 1973-83). *Exhib.:* 15 solo shows; many mixed shows; many juried shows N.Y.C. since 1960's. *Work in permanent collection:* M.A.S.-F. *Address:* Box 483, Bernardsville, New Jersey 07924-0483, U.S.A. *Clubs:* C.L.W.A.C., A.R.M.S., M.A.A., M.A.S.-F., M.P.S.G.S. (Washington D.C.), G.M.A.S. *Signs work:* see appendix.

COCKER, Doug., D.A., A.R.S.A.; sculptor; *b* Alyth, Perthshire, 1945; *m* Elizabeth; two *s*, one *d*. *Educ.:* Blairgowrie High School; *studied art* at Duncan of Jordanstone, Dundee (1963-68). *Exhib.:* R.S.A., Yorkshire Sculpture Pk., The British Art Show, Air Gallery London, Serpentine Gallery London, Fruitmarket Gallery, Edinburgh, Third Eye Centre, Glasgow. *Work in permanent collections:* Arts Council, Scottish Arts Council, Contemporary Art Soc., Kelvingrove A.G., Glasgow, Peterborough A.G., Greenshields Foundation, Montreal, Leicester University, Hunterian A.G., Glasgow, Essex C.C., Staffs. C.C., M.M.A. Sarajevo. *Address:* Craigveigh, Gordon Cres., Aboyne, Aberdeenshire AB34 5HJ. *Signs work:* "DOUG COCKER."

COCKRILL, Maurice; artist in oil on canvas; *b* England, 1936; *m* Helen Cockrill; three *s*. *Studied art* at Wrexham School of Art (1960-64). *Exhib.:* one-man shows: Edward Totah Gallery (1984, 1985), Kunstmuseum, Düsseldorf (1985), Bernard Jacobson Gallery (1987, 1988, 1990). *Work in permanent collections:* A.C.G.B., Walker A.G., Unilever, Kunstmuseum. *Address:* c/o Bernard Jacobson Gallery, 14A Clifford St., London W1. *Signs work:* full signature on back.

CODNER, Stephen Milton; painter in oil, pastel, portrait, landscape, still life, etcher; *b* Clevedon, Som., 1952; *s* of John Codner, R.W.A.; *g-s* of Maurice Codner, R.P., R.O.I.; *m* Carolyn Hamilton; three *d*. *Educ.:* Bryanston School Dorset, Camberwell School of Art and Crafts, City and Guilds Art School. *Exhib.:* R.A., R.P., R.W.A. *Address:* 23 Maplestead Rd., London SW2 3LY. *Signs work:* "S. M. CODNER" or "STEPHEN CODNER."

COE, Miriam, B.F.A., graduate studies in M.F.A., L.S.U., Ph.D.(Hon.), Louisiana area representative for The American Soc. of Artists Inc.; artist, author, lexicographer, inventor. *Studied art* at Liverpool City School of Art, School of Chinese Brushwork, N.Y.C., Columbia University, N.Y.C., and Louisiana State University; studied with Prof. Wang Chi Yuan, former President of The College of Fine Art, Shanghai, China, and other teachers. *Exhib.:* one-man and collection shows in New York and Louisiana. Awarded numerous prizes and trophies. Reported in American Art Digest (Art News, 1938). *Publications:* Haiku, Ancient/Modern, East/West; Poems for the Young; Poets, Poems, Portraits, Paintings; Chinese Culture, Ancient/Modern, East/West; in preparation: Art Theory, Criticism, Philosophy and Sociology; also other non-fiction

MSS. *Listed in:* Who's Who in Art and Antiques, Marquis Who's Who in the South and South-west, International Scholars Directory, American Library Assoc. Directory, American Sociological Assoc. Directory, L.I.U. and L.S.U. Alumni Directories. *Address:* P.O. Box 18184 University Station, Baton Rouge, Louisiana 70893, U.S.A. *Clubs:* Louisiana Art and Artists Guild, Assoc. Louisiana Art and Artists, Louisiana Water-color Soc., American Soc. of Artists Inc.

COHEN, Bernard, Slade Dip.; professional artist in painting and printmaking; Slade Professor and University of London Chair in Fine Art; Director of Slade School, U.C.L.; *b* London, 28 July, 1933; *s* of Victor Cohen; *m* Jean; one *s*, one *d.* *Studied art* at Slade School of Fine Art (1951-54, Sir William Coldstream). *Exhib.:* Gimpel Fils (1958, 1960), Hayward Gallery (1972 touring), Waddington Galleries (1972, 1974, 1977, 1979, 1981, 1990), Tate Gallery (1976) and major group exhbns. worldwide. *Work in permanent collections:* Arts Council, M.O.M.A. (N.Y.), Tate Gallery, V. & A., etc. *Address:* 80 Camberwell Grove, London SE5. *Signs work:* "Bernard Cohen" on works on paper only.

COHEN, Mary; artist in oil, pen and wash, water-colour; *b* London, 21 Nov., 1910; *d* of the late Ernest M. Joseph, C.B.E., F.R.I.B.A., architect; *m* Cdr. Kenneth Cohen, C.B., C.M.G., R.N.; one *s*, one *d.* *Studied art:* Florence, Slade under Prof. Tonks and Prof. Schwabe (1928-31), and Euston Road School. *Exhib.:* Leicester Galleries Mixed Exhbns., R.A., R.B.A., N.E.A.C., London Group, Roland, Browse and Delbanco, New Grafton Gallery. *Work in permanent collections:* National Trust, Whitworth, A.G. and private collections in Gt. Britain, France and U.S.A. *Address:* 33 Bloomfield Terr., London SW1. *Signs work:* "Mary S. C."

COLE, Sibylle (née Duijts), R.B.S.A., F.R.S.A., L.F.A.C.; artist in oil, water-colour, etching, jewellery in silver and gold; *b* Amsterdam; *m* Boris N. Cole; two *s*, one *d.* *Studied art* at Birmingham College of Art (B. Fleetwood-Walker, R.A.). *Exhib.:* R.A., and many art galleries; six solo shows. *Publication:* monograph on F.W. Elwell, R.A. *Address:* 6 Wedgewood Grove, Roundhay, Leeds LS8 1EG. *Signs work:* "Sibylle Cole (Duijts)."

COLEBORN, Deanne, A.R.C.A., R.E.; painter/etcher; *b* Worcs., 30 Dec., 1931; *m* Keith; six *d.* *Studied art* at R.C.A. *Exhib.:* R.A., R.E. *Address:* Downe Hall Farm, Downe, Kent. *Signs work:*"DEANNE."

COLEBORN, Keith, A.R.C.A., A.T.D., F.R.S.A.; until July 1976 principal, Ravensbourne College of Art and Crafts; regional art principal, N.W. Kent; principal, Bromley College of Art (1946-62); principal, Stourbridge School of Art (1937-40); principal, Wallasey School of Art (1940-46); *b* Portsmouth. *Address:* Downe Hall Farm, Downe, Kent.

COLEMAN, Alan, F.R.B.S. (1961), R.B.A. (1952), A.R.C.A. (1st Class, 1951); sculptor; *b* Croydon, Surrey, 1920; *m* Joan Bradley, M.B., C.H.B., M.R.C.Psych.; three *s*, one *d.* *Studied art* at Goldsmiths' College School of Art, R.C.A. *Address:* Derrysbourne, Wonersh, Guildford, Surrey GU5 0QZ.

COLEMAN, Brian; painter in water-colour; Art Director/Graphic Designer, advertising; *b* Cheam, Surrey, 3 Sept., 1935; *m* Joan Coleman. *Educ.:* Stoneleigh Secondary Modern. *Exhib.:* Edwin Pollard Gallery, Wimbledon. *Address:* 2 Sheraton Drive, West Hill, Epsom, Surrey KT19 8JL. *Signs work:* "Brian Coleman."

COLLES, Dorothy Margaret Tyas; Mem. Pastel Soc.; portrait painter in pastel and oil, drawings in pencil and chalk; *b* Cairo; *d* of William Morris Colles.

Educ.: Parsons Mead, Ashtead; *studied art* at Epsom Art School; Westminster Art School; St. Martin's School of Art. *Exhib.:* P.S., R.P., R.A. Work in private collections. *Publications:* Portraying Children; Christian Symbols Ancient and Modern with Heather Child. *Address:* 70 Heath Rd., Petersfield, Hants. GU31 4EJ. *Signs work:* "COLLES."

COLLET, Ruth Isabelle; artist in water-colour, mixed media, oil, linocut; *b* Royston, Herts., 15 June, 1909; *d* of Redcliffe Salaman, F.R.S.; *m*; three *d*. *Educ.:* Bedales School, Petersfield, Hants.; *studied art* at The Slade School of Fine Art (Prof. Henry Tonks, Wilson Steer), and later with Kathleen Brown and Marion Kratochurl. *Exhib.:* one-man shows: Goupil Gallery, Gainsborough House, Suffolk, Ben Uri (2), English Speaking Gallery, Oxford, Annexe Gallery, Wimbledon, George Large Gallery, Redbourn, Sue Rankin Gallery, London; also many mixed exhbns. at Mall Gallery. *Work in permanent collections:* Israel and Ben Uri, London. *Address:* 13 Roy Rd., Northwood, Middx. HA6 1EQ. *Signs work:* "Ruth Collet."

COLLETT, Paula, B.A.(Hons.); public/community artist in textile/soft sculpture; workshop leader; *b* Wakefield, 16 July, 1969. *Educ.:* Woodkirk High; *studied art* at Chelsea School of Art and Design (1989-92, Roger Hoare). *Exhib.:* tree art: Oakwell Hall. *Work in permanent collections:* Montague St. Clinic London, Pinderfields Hospital. *Address:* 11 Boldgrove St., Earlsheaton, Dewsbury, W. Yorks. WF12 8NA. *Signs work:* "P. Collett."

COLLINGBOURNE, Stephen; painter and sculptor; prize winner, R.S.A., and John Moores; teaches at Edinburgh College of Art; *b* Dartington, 15 Aug., 1943. *Studied art* at Dartington College of Art (1960-61); Bath Academy, Corsham (1961-64). *Exhib.* British Council, Malaya; Chapter, and Oriel, Cardiff; Camden Arts Centre, Zella 9, Fisher Gallery and Serpentine, London; Kettles Yard, Cambridge; MacRobert Arts Centre, Stirling University; Third Eye Centre, Glasgow; City Art Centre, Edinburgh. *Work in collections:* Leicester A.G., Scottish and Welsh Arts Councils, Devon, Leicestershire and Hertford Educ. Authorities, City Art Centre, Edinburgh. *Public commissions:* Welsh Arts Council, and Leicester University. *Address:* Tofts, Netherurd, West Linton, Peeblesshire.

COLLINGS, David, Dip. (1969), A.T.D. (1972); artist in oil on board, canvas; teacher of mentally handicapped; *b* London, 1949; *s* of Arthur Robert Collings. *Studied art* at Redruth School of Art (1965-69), Berks. College of Education (1969-72). *Exhib.:* widely in S.W. England, Brittany and Ireland. *Work in permanent collection:* Contemporary Art Soc. *Address:* 3 Lyn Terr., Newlyn, Penzance, Cornwall. *Club:* Newlyn Soc. of Artists. *Signs work:* "David Collings."

COLLINS, Michael, Inter.Dip.A.C., N.D.D., A.T.D., S.G.F.A., F.S.A.I., F.R.S.A.; mixed media draughtsman/painter; schoolmaster; Head of Art Dept., Emanuel School, London; *b* New Malden, Surrey, 13 Mar., 1936; *s* of William Ralph and Annie Joan Myra Collins. *Educ.* King's College School, Wimbledon; *studied art* under E. M. Scales; and at Wimbledon School of Art (1962-65), Swansea College of Art (1965-66). *Exhib.:* S.G.F.A., S.A.I. *Address:* 53 Lauderdale Drive, Petersham, Richmond, Surrey TW10 7BS. *Signs work:* see appendix.

COLLINS, Peter Gerald, A.R.C.A. (1950); artist in oil, water-colour, pen and ink; *b* London, 11 June, 1923; *s* of Wilkie Collins, engineer; *m* Georgette Andreassi 1943. *Educ.:* Willesden; *studied art* at Willesden School of Art, Hornsey School of Art, Royal College of Art. *Exhib.:* by appointment in own studio. *Address:* 7 Stanley Studios, Park Walk, Chelsea, London SW10 0AE. *Club:* Chelsea Arts. *Signs work:* "Peter Collins."

CONNER, Angela; American Institute of Architects (Hons.) award, S.E.A. award; sculptor/painter in stone, bronze, water, light, wind; *b* London; *d* of Judge Cyril Conner; *m* John Bulmer; one *d. Studied art:* self taught; apprentice to Dame Barbara Hepworth. *Exhib.:* solo shows: Lincoln Center, N.Y., Browse & Darby; mixed shows: Gimpel Fils Gallery, N.Y., Tryon Gallery, Lincoln Center, N.Y., R.A. Summer Show, V. & A., Carnegie Museum of Modern Art, etc. *Work in permanent collections:* Arts Council G.B., National Portrait Gallery, Jewish Museum, N.Y., Eton College, Chatsworth, House of Commons, etc. *Private collections* include Paul Mellon, Dr. Roy Strong, Lucien Freud, Lord Goodman, Crown Prince of Saudi Arabia, Princess Firyal of Jordan, etc. *Winner:* competitions for Economist Plaza, St. James's London; Aston University; de Gaulle, Carlton Gardens London. *Address:* George and Dragon Hall, Mary Pl., London W11 4PL. *Signs work:* see appendix.

CONNON, William John, D.A. (1959), post-Dip. (1960); painter in oil, draughtsman, teacher; lecturer in drawing and painting at Grays School of Art, Aberdeen; *b* Turriff, 11 Dec., 1929; *s* of Albert Connon; *m* Margaret R. Mair; one *s*, one *d. Educ.:* Turriff Academy; *studied art* at Grays School of Art under R. Henderson Blyth, R.S.A., Ian Fleming, R.S.A. *Exhib.:* R.S.A., S.S.A., A.A.S. *Work in permanent collections:* Aberdeen A.G., Scottish Arts Council, City of Edinburgh Art Centre. *Address:* 8 Fonthill Rd., Aberdeen AB1 2UB. *Signs work:* "wjconnon."

CONSTABLE, Richard Golding; artist in gouache; mem. Bath Soc. of Artists; *b* Lewes, 8 June, 1932; *s* of Lt. Col. John Constable, R.A.; *m* Valerie Zelle; two *s*, four *d. Educ.:* Marlborough College, Millfield School, Cambridge University. *Exhib.:* London, Ipswich, Bath, Norwich, Lincoln, Woodbridge, Halesworth, Hereford, Spanish Biennale, Versailles, Singapore, W. Germany, Eire, Glasgow, New York, Cincinnati, Dubai, Al Ain, Abu Dhabi, Muscat. *Address:* Courtfield, Norton sub Hamdon, Stoke sub Hamdon, Somerset TA14 6SG. *Signs work:* "R. Constable."

CONTRACTOR, Dorab Dadiba, N.S.; sculptor, artist, jeweller, designer; *b* Bombay, 13 Feb., 1929 into a Parsee Zoroastrian parents (naturalised British citizen). *Studied art* at Sir J.J. School of Art, Bombay, and obtained Government of India Dip. in Modelling and Sculpture (1957). Won special awards for wood sculptures, Bombay State (1958-59). Employed by the Government of India in Archaeological Dept. to restore the famous rockcut sculptures of Ellora, Ajanta and Elephanta Caves. Sculpture in wood, marble, stone, clay, plaster, school chalkstick, avocado stone, mango stone, toegua nut, betelnut and nutmeg. Also excels in pencil, pastel, pen and ink, water-colour and scraperboard. Part-time instructor for creative art, sculpting in wood and stone, and modelling at several Adult Educ. Centres and technical colleges in the U.K. *Awards:* 'Premier Award' for the most outstanding work in miniature sculpture in school chalkstick, London (1969); 'Dennis Price Challenge Trophy' for the best wood sculpture, London (1970-78); silver medal for wood sculptures, London (1985-86). *Exhib.:* group: Guggenheim Gallery, London (1970); joint: Central Library, Romford (1972), Euro Arts and Crafts, B'ham (1976), Mall Gallery, London (1978-81), Le Salon des Nations a Paris (1983); one-man shows: India House, London (1972), Woodstock Gallery, London (1975), Queen's Theatre, Hornchurch (1977), Central Library, Romford (1982), Kenneth More Theatre, Ilford (1988). His works are very widely appreciated and regarded as collectors pieces for their uniqueness. They are in private collections of art connoisseurs throughout the world, and in public libraries, schools, hospitals and Town Hall, Romford. *Work in permanent collections:* H.R.H. Prince Philip, Duke of Edinburgh (Windsor Castle), H.M. The Queen (Buckingham Palace), H.M. The Queen Mother (Clarence House), the late Dame Barbara Hepworth (St. Ives, Cornwall), the late Henry Moore (in his collection). *Address:* 10 Elizabeth House, Elvet Ave., Gidea Park, Essex RM2 6JU. *Signs work:* "DORAB" or "D.C."

CONWAY, Frances, A.R.W.A.; painter in oil, conté, water-colour, collage; *b* Bristol; *m*; two *s*, two *d*. *Studied art* at West of England College of Art, Bristol, under George Sweet, Robert Hurdle, Francis Hoyland, William Townsend. *Exhib.:* England and France. *Address:* 37 Cornwallis Cres., Clifton, Bristol. *Club:* R.W.A.

CONWAY, Jennifer Anne, R.M.S. (1979), S.M. (1981), Dip.B.C.P.E. (1957); painter and miniaturist in water-colour and oils; *b* Brecon, Oct., 1935; *d* of Ernest Brookes; *m* John F. Conway; one *s*, one *d*. *Educ.:* Brecon Girls' Grammar School; Bedford College of Physical Education (1954-57). *Exhib.:* R.A., Paris Salon, R.M.S., S.W.A., Mall Galleries, Westminster Gallery, Bankside Gallery, Woburn Abbey, Miniature Art Soc. Florida, Soc. of Miniature Painters, S and G, Washington, U.S.A.; one man shows: Brecknock Museum (1980, 1989), Lion House Gallery (1988), Hay Festival, Brobury Gallery (1991). *Work in private collection:* Marchioness of Tavistock. *Publications:* illustrated book 'A Pocketful of Posies'. *Work repro.:* Welsh Crafts. *Address:* Copper Beech, Maescelyn, Brecon, Powys, Wales LD3 7NL. *Signs work:* "J. Conway" and see appendix.

COOK, Christian Manuel, N.D.D. (1965); artist in acrylic, gouache, pastel, charcoal, collage; lecturer in painting and drawing (Westminster Adult Educ. Inst.); *b* Grossenheim, Germany, 26 June, 1942; one *s*. *Educ.:* Kent College, Canterbury; *studied art* at Camberwell School of Art (Robert Medley, Frank Auerbach, Frank Bowling, Patrick Proctor, Charles Howard). *Exhib.:* Kingsgate Gallery, Hornsey Library (New Gallery), H.A.C. (Camden Arts Centre), City Literary Inst., Loggia Gallery. *Work in permanent collection:* Westminster City Council. *Address:* 17 Formosa St., Maida Vale, London W9 2JS. *Club:* F.P.S. *Signs work:* "Christian Cook" or "C. Cook."

COOK, David Albert; wildlife artist in various media; paper sculptor; lecturer; has given workshops in Britain, America, Canada, Japan; *b* Rochester, 18 Mar., 1940; *s* of Albert Victor Cook, R.N. (decd.); *m* (1) Pauline Jean Head (decd.); two *d*; (2) Anne Page. *Studied art* at Medway College of Art and Regent St. Polytechnic. *Exhib.:* S.WL.A., R.S.M.A. (Mall Galleries), and many one-man shows. Art Advisor to Historical Link Flanders-Kent; initiator and sponsor of the British Birds, Bird Illustrator of the Year P.J.C. Award for Individual Merit. *Work* in numerous civic, corporate, educational and private collections. *Publications:* greetings cards, prints, articles, techniques guides, instructional videos. *Address:* 182 Hebden Ave., Keld Pk., Carlisle, Cumbria CA2 6TW. *Signs work:* see appendix.

COOK, Ian David, R.I., R.S.W. (1978); Post. Dip. Drawing and Painting (Glasgow 1973), Cargill Scholarship (1974); artist in gouache, oils, water-colour, teacher; *b* Paisley, 2 Mar., 1950; *s* of the late William Cook, shipyard manager; *m* Elaine; one *s*. *Educ.:* Camphill High School, Paisley; *studied art* at Glasgow (1969-72, D. Ferguson, D. Donaldson). *Exhib.:* R.G.I. since 1975, R.S.W. since 1978, Gallery 22 Dublin, Aitken and Dott (1980, 1981), Scottish Contemporary (1980), Herald Art Comp. (1981); one-man shows: Henderson's Gallery, Edinburgh (1981), Kelly Gallery, Glasgow (1979, 1981), Scottish Gallery

(1984,1986): Scottish Arts Council award to Central Africa (1984). *Address:* Upper Flat, 3 Falside Rd., Paisley PA2 6JZ. *Signs work:* "I.D. Cook."

COOK, Jennifer Martin, N.D.D., A.T.D.; painter; *b* Preston, Lancs., 1942; *d* of Jane and Albert J. Heathcote. *Educ.:* Casterton School; *studied art* at Harris College, Preston (1960-65); Leicester College of Art (1965-66). *Exhib.:* R.A. (1975, 1976, 1981, 1982, 1983); one-man shows: Mercury Gallery, London (1976, 1978), Leics. Museum and A.G. (1982); group shows: Yew Tree Gallery, Derbys., Oxford Gallery, Gallery on the Green, Lexington, Mass., U.S.A. *Work in public collections:* Middlesbrough, Leic., Oxfordshire. *Work repro.:* greeting cards for Aries Design and Medici Soc. *Address:* 17 Brookhouse Ave, Leicester LE2 0JE. *Signs work:* "Jenny Cook."

COOK, Richard, Dip.A.D. (Painting), M.A.(R.C.A.) Painting; artist; *b* Cheltenham, 31 Oct., 1947; *s* of Richard Leonard Cook; *m* Michelle; one *s*. *Educ.:* Salesian College, Oxford; *studied art* at St. Martin's School of Art (1966-70), R.C.A. (1970-73). *Exhib.:* House Gallery, London (1981), Hayward Gallery, London (1976, 1980), Artists Market, London (1976-80), Serpentine Gallery, London (1987), Odette Gilbert Gallery, London (1989, 1991). *Work in permanent collections:* B.M., Arts Council, Manchester City A.G. *Address:* 13 North Corner, Newlyn, Penzance, Cornwall TR18 5JG. *Signs work:* "Richard Cook."

COOK, Richard Peter, R.B.A., Dip.A.D. Maidstone (1971), Post Grad. Royal Academy Schools (1975), A.T.C. (1977), R.B.A. (1978), E.T. Greenshield Travelling Scholarship (1972), Richard Ford Spanish Scholarship (1981); landscape and portrait painter in oil, water-colour, gouache; *b* Grimsby, 27 Feb., 1949; *s* of R. P. Cook and M. A. Cook; *m* Christine Jones-McGuinness; two *d*. *Educ.:* Grimsby College of Art, Maidstone College of Art (1968-71), Royal Academy Schools (1972-75). *Exhib.:* one-man show, R.A. Schools (1980); R.B.A. (1977-); R.A. Summer Shows (1975-81, 1983, 1993); Art in Action (1988-93); N.E.A.C.; Royal Portrait Soc.; N.P.G. in 1984 John Player Award Show; Singer & Friedlander Water-colour Exhbns. and commercial galleries. *Work in private collections:* in U.K. and overseas. *Address:* 17 Windlesham Gdns., Brighton BN1 3AJ. *Signs work:* "Richard P. Cook."

COOKE, Jean, R.A., N.D.D., R.B.A.; painter; lecturer, Royal College (1965-74); *b* London, 18 Feb., 1927; *d* of A. O. Cooke; *m* John Bratby; three *s*, one *d*. *Educ.:* Blackheath High School; *studied art* at Central School of Arts and Crafts, Goldsmiths' College of Arts, Camberwell School of Art, City and Guilds, Royal College. *Exhib.:* one-man show: Farnham (1962, 1964, 1973), Establishment (1963), Leicester Gallery (1964), Bear Lane, Bladon Gallery (1966), Phoenix (1970), New Grafton (1971); mixed show: R.A., Zwemmer, London Group, R.B.A., Arts Council, Young Contemporaries, Royal College of Art, Upper Grosvenor, Arundel, Furneaux (1968), Agnew (1974). *Work in permanent collections:* R.A., R.C.A., Tate. *Address:* 7 Hardy Rd., Blackheath, London SE3. *Signs work:* "Jean E. Cooke."

COOKE, Stanley; artist in oil and water-colour; *b* Mansfield, Notts., 11 Jan., 1913; *s* of John Cooke; *m* Anne M. Clayton (decd.); one *s*. *Educ.:* King Edward School, Mansfield; *studied art* at Mansfield School of Art (1924-32) and The Press Art School. *Exhib.:* R.A., R.I., R.O.I., Britain in Water-colours exhbns., provinces; one-man shows at Drian Galleries, London and Mansfield Art Gallery. *Work in permanent collection:* Quarry at Mansfield, Mansfield Art Gallery. *Work repro.:* in Apollo, Arts Review and greeting cards. *Address:* Broadlands, Grasmere Cl., Guildford GU1 2TG. *Signs work:* see appendix.

COOKSON, Dawn, R.B.S.A. (1974); artist of portraiture, still-life, flower and landscape paintings in oil, tempera, pastel and water-colour; V.P. Birmingham Water-colour Soc.; *b* B'ham, 11 June, 1925. *Educ.:* Westonbirt School, Glos.; *studied art* at Birmingham College of Art (1943-48, B. Fleetwood-Walker, R.A.), Accademia di Perugia, Italy (1954-56), Nerina Simi Studio, Florence (1955-58), and under Pietro Annigoni, Florence (1958-68). *Exhib.:* R.P., P.S., R.B.S.A., B'ham Water-colour Soc., Fosseway Glos. bi-annually; one-man shows: Lygon Arms and Dormy House, Broadway, Worcs. (1972-82-85), Guildhouse, Stanton, Glos. (1976-79), Reade's Gallery, Aldeburgh, Suffolk (1977). *Work in private collections:* throughout G.B., Europe and Overseas. *Address:* Quiet Place, Lifford Gdns., Broadway, Worcs. WR12 7DA. *Signs work:* "Dawn Cookson."

COOKSON, Delan, F.S.D-C., Gold Medal (Vallauris, 1974), Churchill Fellow (1966); Senior Lecturer in ceramics at Buckinghamshire College of Higher Education; *b* Torquay, 13 Sept., 1937; *s* of W. R. Cookson; *m* Judith; two *s.* *Educ.:* Bournemouth School; *studied art* at Bournemouth College of Art, Central School of Arts and Crafts. *Exhib.:* Oxford Gallery, British Crafts Centre, Craftsman Potters Assoc., Design Centre, Midland Group Gallery, Whitworth Art Gallery; one-man shows: Salix, Windsor, Bohun Gallery, Henley and Galerie an Cross, St. Martin, Cologne. *Work repro.:* Ceramic Review, Studio Porcelain and Studio Ceramics by Peter Lane. *Address:* Lissadell, St. Buryan, Penzance, Cornwall TR19 6HP. *Clubs:* International Academy of Ceramics, C.A.C. Index Member.

COOLIDGE, John, A.B. (Harvard University, 1935), Ph.D. (New York University, 1948); director, Fogg Art Museum (1948-68); Prof. of Fine Arts, Harvard University (1955-85); *b* Cambridge, Mass., 16 Dec., 1913; *s* of Julian Lowell Coolidge, Prof. of Maths., Harvard University; *m* Mary Welch Coolidge; one *d. Educ.:* Groton School, Harvard and New York Universities. *Publication:* Mill and Mansion (Columbia University Press, 1943); Patrons and Architects (University of Texas Press, 1990). *Address:* Fogg Art Museum, Quincy St. and Broadway, Cambridge, Mass.

COOPER, Constance Mary, S.W.A., F.R.S.A.; painter in oil; *b* Shoreham, Kent, 2 Nov., 1905; *d* of A.E. Robertson; *m* D.G. Cooper; one *d. Educ.:* privately; *studied art* at Croydon College of Art. *Exhib.:* Mall Galleries, various London and provincial galleries, Australia, America. *Address:* 35 Shirley Pk. Rd., Croydon CR0 7EW. *Signs work:* "Constance Cooper."

COOPER, Eileen; artist in oil and works on paper; *b* Glossop, 1953; *m* M. Southward; two *s. Studied art* at Goldsmiths' College and R.C.A. (1971-77). *Exhib.:* numerous solo and group shows. *Work in permanent collections:* Arts Council, various museums. *Address:* c/o Benjamin Rhodes Gallery, 4 New Burlington Pl., London W1X 1SB. *Signs work:* "Eileen Cooper" on reverse.

COOPER, Emmanuel; potter stoneware and porcelain, writer and broadcaster; Asst. Senior Lecturer (ceramics), Middlesex University; *b* Derbyshire, 12 Dec., 1938. *Educ.:* Tupton Hall Grammar School, Derbyshire. *Exhib.:* British Crafts Centre, London, many other one-man and mixed exhbns. here and abroad. *Work in permanent collection:* V. & A. *Publications:* A Handbook of Pottery, A History of Pottery (Longman); Taking up Pottery (Arthur Barker); New Ceramics (with E. Lewenstein); Pottery (Macdonalds); A Potters Book of Glaze Recipes (1979); A History of World Pottery (Batsford, 1980); co-editor with Eileen Lewenstein of Ceramic Review. Contributes art criticism to Time Out, Tribune, etc. *Address:* 38 Chalcot Rd., London NW1 8LP. *Signs work:* see appendix.

COOPER, Josephine Mary, S.M. (1974), R.M.S. (1983), U.A. (1975), S.W.A.(1988); Silver Medallist, Paris Salon (1974), Prix Rowland (1977); artist in oil and water-colour, also drypoint engravings and monotypes; *b* Brighton, 8 Aug., 1932; *d* of Everard Frisby; *m* Tom Cooper; one *s*, one *d*. *Studied art* at St. Albans School of Art under Kathleen Pargiter; Mid-Herts. College of Further Education under Kenneth Haw; Hertfordshire College of Art and Design under Peter Jacques; Will Raymont, privately. *Exhib.:* R.M.S., U.A., S.M., R.I., R.S.M.A., R.B.A., Laing, S.G.A., Britain in Water-colour, Bilan de l'Art Paris and Quebec, Liberty of London, Medici Gallery, R.A. Summer Exhbn. (1980-85); one-man shows throughout mid-Herts area, also Liberty of London. *Publication:* included in 20th Century Marine Paintings. *Address:* 27 Parkfields, Welwyn Garden City, Herts. AL8 6EE. *Clubs:* Welwyn Garden City Art, Hertford Art Soc. *Signs work:* "Jo Cooper" and "JMC" (miniatures dated).

COOPER, Julian, B.A.(Hons.) Fine Art; painter in oil, water-colour, pastel; *b* Grasmere, 10 June, 1947; *s* of William Heaton Cooper, landscape painter; *m* Linda. *Educ.:* Heversham Grammar School; *studied art* at Lancaster Art College (1963-64), Goldsmiths' College (1964-69), Boise Travelling Scholarship (1969-70). *Exhib.:* London Group, Serpentine Gallery, J.P.L. Fine Art, Paton Gallery, V. & A., Laing A.G., University of Durham. *Work in permanent collections:* A.C.G.B., Laing A.G., Bolton A.G., Lancaster University, Northern Arts, I.L.E.A., Abbot Hall A.G., Reuters, Unilever, Pentagram, Davy Offshore Modules, Ferguson Industrial Holdings. *Work repro.:* book cover for Fleur Adcock's Under Loughrigg. *Address:* 100 Lake Rd., Ambleside, Cumbria LA22 0DB. *Signs work:* "Julian Cooper."

COOPER, Paul Anthony, N.D.D. (1951), F.R.B.S.; sculptor in all traditional and modern materials including precious metals and stones; *b* Wool, Dorset, 23 May, 1923; *s* of John Thomas Cooper; *m* Audrey Beryl Carnaby, A.R.C.A.; one *d*. *Studied art* at Poole College of Art (1939-41), Goldsmiths' College, London (1948-51), Lincoln College (1958). *Exhib.:* R.A., Covent Garden London, Scone Palace Perth, R.I.B.A. *Work in permanent collections:* Oxford City Educ. Authority, Lincoln Educ. Authority, and places open to the public at Bond St., Westminster, City of London, Thorpe Tilney, Lincoln and Denton, Grantham; private collections in this country and in Holland, Israel, U.S.S.R.; ecclesiastical work in churches in England, Westminster Abbey, Wales and the Falkland Islands. *Address:* Quarr Hill Cottage, Wool, Dorset. *Signs work:* "Paul Cooper."

COOPER, William Alwin, R.W.A.(1973); Sherborne School (1952-83), Lecturer, Bristol University Extra Mural Dept. (1983-); artist in oil and collage; *b* Merthyr Tydfil, 2 June, 1923; *s* of L. H. Cooper, M.B.E.; *m* Dorothy Tustain, G.R.S.M.; one *s*, two *d*. *Educ.:* Westminster School, Corpus Christi College, Cambridge. *Exhib.:* one-man shows: Drian Gallery (1971), Albany Gallery, Cardiff (1972), Hambledon Gallery, Blandford, Pentagon Gallery, Stoke on Trent (1977), St. John's, Smith Sq. (1986), Rona Gallery, R.W.A.(1988); group shows include: R.A., N.E.A.C., UNESCO, New York; Westward TV Open (Prizewinner), Wessex Artists. *Work in permanent collections:* Royal West of England Academy, Bryanston School, Staffordshire Educ. Com., Welsh Development Corporation, Sherborne School and various public and private collections. *Publication:* illustration in History of Corpus Christi College, Cambridge. *Address:* Elizabeth House, Long St., Sherborne, Dorset DT9 3BZ. *Signs work:* "Cooper."

COOPER, William Heaton, R.I.; landscape painter; elected R.I., 1953; *b* Coniston, 1903; *m* Ophelia Gordon Bell, sculptor; two *s*, two *d*. *Educ.:* Kelsick

School, Ambleside; *studied art* under father, A. Heaton Cooper, and at R.A. Schools (1922-25). *Exhib.:* R.A., R.I., R.B.A., etc., three London exhbns. and several in other cities. *Work in permanent collections:* Alpine Club, Bolton A.G., Abbott Hall Gallery, Kendal, and Lancaster University. *Work repro.:* wrote and illustrated Hills of Lakeland (1938, 1947, 1985), Lakeland Portraits (1954, 1958), The Tarns of Lakeland (1960, 1970, 1983), The Lakes (1966, 1970), Mountain Painter (1984, 1985). Illustrated Lakeland Prose and 10 climbing guides; publishes colour prints. *Address:* Studio, Grasmere, Cumbria LA22 9SX. *Clubs:* Fell and Rock Climbing (Hon. Mem.), Lake Artists Society (Hon Life Mem.). *Signs work:* "W. Heaton Cooper."

COOTE, Michael Arnold; painter in oils, water-colour, acrylic, oil and soft pastel, charcoal, pencil; Company Director – Lithographers; Freeman of the City of London (1977); *b* London, 1939; *m* Anita Davies; two *s*, one *d. Studied art:* mainly self-taught; Sir John Cass (sculpture and life class). *Exhib.:* P.S., R.O.I., Mall Galleries, Alpine Gallery, many provincial galleries including John Noott Gallery. *Work in permanent collections:* London, Bath, America, Germany, Italy. *Address:* 1 Tadlows Cl., Upminster, Essex RM14 2BD. *Signs work:* see appendix.

COPELAND, Lawrence Gill, Cranbrook Medal, U.S. State Dept. Purchase Award, Y.S.C. First Prize, National Merit Award, Craftsmen, U.S.A.; designer in metal; prof., Art Dept., City College of City University of New York (retd.); *b* Pittsburgh, Pa., U.S.A., 12 Apr., 1922; *s* of Lloyd D. Copeland, college professor; *m* Mary Cuteri; two *s*, one *d. Educ.:* Ohio State Univ., Cranbrook Academy of Art, Univ. of Stockholm, Univ. of Paris; *studied art* at Stockholm (1947-48, Baron Erik Fleming), Paris (1948-49, Emeric Gomery). *Work in private collection:* National Gallery, Washington, D.C. *Address:* 5 Peach Tree La., Warwick, N.Y. 10990, U.S.A.

COPNALL, John; painter in acrylics and oils; *b* Slinfold, Sussex, 16 Feb., 1928; *s* of Bainbridge Copnall, sculptor. *Studied art* at R.A. Schools (1950-55). *Exhib.:* one-man shows: Piccadilly Gallery, Bear Lane Gallery (Oxford), Stone Gallery (Newcastle), I.C.A. (London), Ikon (Birmingham), Sala Vayreda (Barcelona), Wolfgang Gurlitt (Munich), Boisserée (Cologne), Universa-haus (Nüremberg), Institut für Auslandsbeziehungen (Stuttgart), Aberdeen Museum, Demarco (Edinburgh), Galeri Mörner (Stockholm), Oxford Gallery, Oxford, Windsor Art Centre, Austin/Desmond (London); mixed shows: John Moores of Liverpool, R.A., Art Spectrum, London, Wildenstein, Hayward 72, Whitechapel Open. *Work in permanent collections:* Bristol and York Universities, A.C.G.B., Aberdeen Museum, Ateneum Museum, Helsinki, Sara Hildred Museum, Tampere, Finland. *Work repro.:* Studio International, Artist, Arts Review. *Address:* 9 Fawe St. Studios, London E14. *Signs work:* "john copnall" or "copnall."

COPPINGER, Sioban, B.A.Hons. (1977), A.R.B.S. (1991); sculptor in bronze, concrete and re-constituted stone; *b* 20 May, 1955. *Educ.:* New Hall School, Boreham, Essex; *studied art* at Bath Academy of Art (1975-77). *Exhib.:* 1993: The Bronze Bird, Gallery Pangolin, Glos.; R.B.S. Gallery, Chelsea Harbour Sculpture '93, London; 1st Royal West of England Academy Open Sculpture Exhbn. Bristol. *Work in public places:* Man and Sheep on a Park Bench, Rufford Country Park, Nottingham; The Gardener and the Truant Lion (Chelsea Flower Show 1986); Stoke Mandeville Station, Bucks.; Sundial (Gateshead Garden Festival 1990); Templecombe Station, Somerset; The Birmingham Man,

Chamberlain Sq., Birmingham. *Address:* Riverside Works, West Mills, Newbury, Berks. RG14 5HY. *Signs work:* "S. Coppinger."

CORBETT, Peter George, B.A. Hons. (1974); artist in oil on canvas, pencil; *b* Rossett, N. Wales, 13 Apr., 1952; *s* of John Hotchkins Corbett, G.P. *Educ.:* Liverpool College; *studied art* at Liverpool College of Art and Design (1970-71, Maurice Cockrill), Manchester Regional College of Art and Design (1971-74, Brendan Neiland, Keith Godwin). *Exhib.:* Centre Gallery (1979), Acorn Gallery, Liverpool (1985, 1988), Major Merseyside Artists, Liverpool (1988), Marie Curie Art (Open), Albert Dock, Liverpool (1988), Surreal Objects Exhbn. Tate Gallery, Liverpool (1989), Merkmal Gallery "Alternative 17" Liverpool (1991); one-man shows: Southport Arts Centre (1980), Liverpool Playhouse (1982), Pilgrim Gallery, Liverpool (1984), Royal Institution, Liverpool (1986), Church Gallery, London (1988), Anglican Cathedral (1988); Senate House Gallery, Liverpool University (1993); two-man shows: Liverpool University (1983, 1990), Acorn Gallery, Liverpool (1985), Royal Liver Bldg., Pier Head, Liverpool (1991). *Work in private collections:* Liverpool, London, Manchester, America and Australia. Founder Mem. Chair, Merseyside Visual Arts Festival (1989-90). *Address:* Flat 4, 7 Gambier Terr., Hope St., Liverpool 1. *Signs work:* see appendix.

CORNELL, David, F.R.S.A. (1970), F.R.B.S. (1971), V.P.S.P.S. (1977); sculptor in bronze; *b* Enfield, 18 Sept., 1935; *s* of Henry Arthur Cornell; *m* Geraldine; four *s*. *Educ.:* Essendene; *studied art* at Central School of Art, London and Harrow School of Art (1952-62, Friend, Fryer and Philip Turner) Engraving and Sculpture; Academy of Fine Art, University of Pennsylvania (1968-70, Robert Beverley Hale) Anatomy. *Exhib.:* London: R.A., Mall Galleries, Guildhall, R.B.S. Hall Place, Pavlova Soc., Park Walk Galleries, Plazzotta Studio, Edith Grove Gallery, Harrods; Iberian Bronze Gallery, London and Dublin, Newmarket Gallery, Newmarket, Royal Fine Art, Tunbridge Wells, Armstrong-Davis Gallery, Arundel, Scone Palace Scotland, English Gallery, Beverly Hills, U.S.A. *Work in permanent collection:* Wellcome Foundation, London. *Address:* Highview, 10 Nevill Pk., Tunbridge Wells, Kent. *Signs work:* "David Cornell."

CORNWELL, Arthur Bruce, S.G.F.A.dip.(1947); illustrator in gouache, oil, water-colour, indian ink; *b* Vancouver, B.C., 11 Feb., 1920; *s* of Arthur Redfern Cornwell; *m* Peggy Brenda Huggins; one *s*. *Educ.:* Palms Public School, and Page Military Academy, California; *studied art* at Art Centre School, Los Angeles, Regent St. Polytechnic, London, Heatherly's, London, Academy Julien, Paris. *Exhib.:* R.A., N.E.A.C., S.M.A., S.G.F.A., Sunderland Gallery, Bolton Gallery. *Work in permanent collection:* Diploma Gallery, R.A. *Official purchase:* Stott Bequest, R.A., The Coaster. *Work repro.:* Yachting Monthly, Macmillan teach-visuals. *Publications:* The Ship's Crew. *Address:* Westways, 132 Eastcote Rd., Ruislip, Middx. HA4 8DU. *Signs work:* see appendix.

CORSELLIS, Jane, R.B.A., N.E.A.C., A.R.W.A., A.R.W.S.; artist in oil, water-colour, etching, lithography; *b* Oxford, 1940. *Studied art* at Byam Shaw School of Art (Maurice de Sausmarez, Bernard Dunstan, R.A., Peter Greenham, R.A.). *Exhib.:* R.A., R.B.A., N.E.A.C., R.W.A, R.W.S.; one-man shows: Hong Kong, Ottawa, Kuala Lumpur, Upstairs Gallery, R.A. London (1985, 1986), New Academy Gallery, London (1988, 1990). *Work in collections:* in Canada, U.S.A., Italy, France, Malaysia, Singapore and U.K. *Publications:* Painting Figures in Light (Phaidon and Watson Guptil, N.Y.). *Address:* 8 Horbury Mews, London W11 3NL. *Signs work:* "Corsellis."

COSMAN, Milein, Slade Diploma Fine Art; painter, graphic artist; *b* Gotha; *d* of Hugo Cosmann; *m* Hans Keller. *Educ.:* Düsseldorf; International School, Geneva; *studied art* at Slade School. *Exhib.:* one man shows: Berkeley Galleries, Matthiesen, Molton Gallery, City of London Festival, Camden Arts Centre, Aldeburgh Festival, Stadtmuseum, Düsseldorf. *Books:* Musical Sketchbook (Bruno Cassirer, Faber & Faber, 1957), Stravinsky at Rehearsal (Dobson, 1962), Strawinsky Dirigiert (Ullstein, 1962), Stravinsky Seen and Heard (Toccata Press, 1982). *Book illustrations:* Penguin Music Magazine, A Composer's Eleven (Cardus, Cape, 1975), etc. *Work in numerous private and public collections.:* e.g. N.P.G., R.C.M., V. & A., British Academy, Cardiff University; *and repro.:* Radio Times and other national and foreign press, art and musical magazines. Series of Educational Programmes on Drawing for ITV. *Address:* 3 Frognal Gdns., Hampstead, London NW3.

COTTERELL, Arthur George, B.A., U.A. (1979); artist in oil or alkyd; *b* London, 8 Aug., 1917; *s* of Henry George Cotterell; *m* Iris Esme; one *s*, one *d*. *Educ.:* Bermondsey Central School; *studied art* at Regent St. Polytechnic (1937), Hereford, Leicester, Hamburg. *Exhib.:* R.O.I., Armed Forces, City of London, U.A.; one-man shows, Fairfield Hall, Woodlands, Blackheath, Bromley, Sidcup and Chislehurst Libraries. *Work in permanent collection:* Whitbreads. *Address:* 87 Allington Rd., Orpington, Kent BR6 8AZ. *Clubs:* Orpington Sketch, London Sketch. Mem. United Artists, Cantium Group, S.E. London Art Group. *Signs work:* "A. Cotterell" or "Arthur Cotterell."

COTTINGHAM, Grenville George, R.S.M.A.(1988), R.B.A.(1989); painter/printmaker in oil, water-colour, acrylic, lithography; Senior lecturer, Sir John Cass Faculty of Arts; *b* Exeter, 16 Apr., 1943; *s* of George Edward Cottingham, A.R.I.C.S.; *m* Lucy June. *Educ.:* Exeter School; *studied art* at Exeter College of Art (1960-63), Liverpool College of Art (1963-64). *Exhib.:* R.A, R.S.M.A., R.B.A., R.I., Bonhams; one-man shows, Woodlands A.G. (1982), Quay Arts Centre, I.O.W. (1988), Royal Parade Gallery, SE3 (1988), Gallery Seven, SE10 (1987-88), Hallam Gallery, SW14 (1989). *Work in permanent collections:* P. & O., Marine Soc., 2nd Batt. Royal Fusiliers, R.N. Reserve (London Division), Royal Artillery, Woolwich, London Mutual Insurance, Securities Investment Board. *Publications:* Seafarers' Sketchbook (Bartholomew Press), You Can Paint. *Address:* 83 Kidbrooke Grove, London SE3 0LQ. *Club:* Wapping Group of Artists. *Signs work:* "Grenville Cottingham."

COTTON, Alan, N.D.D., A.T.D.(B'ham), F.R.S.A., M.Ed.; painter in oil, water-colour and pastel; works on art films for television; Director, Devon and Exeter Art Centre, Executive Com., Devon Arts Forum, Arts Advisory Com., University of Exeter; *b* Redditch, 8 Oct., 1937; *m* Patricia Esme; two *s*, two *d*. *Educ.:* Redditch County High School; *studied art* at Redditch School of Art, Bournville College of Art, B'ham College of Art, Universities of B'ham and Exeter (Research Fellow). *Exhib.:* over 40 one-man shows in U.K., Canada, France and the U.S.A. including Hammer Galleries N.Y. (1993). *Work in permanent collections:* City of Exeter A.G., City of Plymouth A.G., West Country Television, Royal Marines, Lympstone, Universities of Southampton and Exeter, etc. *Represented by:* David Messum Galleries since 1983. *Publication:* Learning and Teaching through Art and Crafts (Batsford). *Address:* Brockhill Studio, Colaton Raleigh, nr. Sidmouth, Devon EX10 0LH. *Clubs:* Dover St. Arts, University of Exeter Staff Club. *Signs work:* "Alan Cotton."

COULOURIS, Mary Louise, A.R.E. (1973); Dip. A.D. (London) (1961); Post Grad. Scholarship, Slade School (1962); French Government Scholarship (1963);

Churchill Fellowship in U.S.A. and Mexico (1993); Mem. Printmakers Council; artist and printmaker; *b* New York, 17 July, 1939; *d* of George Alexander Coulouris, actor; *m* Gordon Wallace; one *s*, one *d*. *Educ.:* Parliament Hill School; *studied art* at Slade School, London University (1958-62) under Antony Gross; Ecole des Beaux Arts, Paris (1963-64); Atelier 17, Paris (1963-64) under William Hayter. *Exhib.:* R.A. (1966, 1971, 1972, 1973); one-man shows: London, Oxford, Paris, Aberdeen, Glasgow, Athens. Mural commission British Rail (1985). Print commission British Healthcare Arts (1993). Artists Exchange: Athens for Glasgow Year of Culture (1990). *Work in permanent collections:* Bibliotheque Nationale, Paris, New York Public Library, Nuffield Trust, Trinity College, Oxford, Bank of Scotland, Edinburgh District Council. *Address:* 5 Strawberry Bank, Linlithgow, West Lothian. *Signs work:* "Mary Louise Coulouris."

COULSON, Nancy Diana, F.P.S., S.C.A.; sculptor in stone, alabaster marble, designs animals, portrait heads in terrcotta, clay for bronze, collages; *b* Kenilworth, 6 Mar., 1926; *d* of J.P.M. Hibbert, M.C.; *m* Robert Coulson; two *s*, one *d*. *Educ.:* Leamington High School; *studied art* at Leamington Spa, Chelsea Art School (1946-48), Chelmsford (Ivor Livi). *Exhib.:* R.A., F.P.S., S.C.A., Vaughan College Leicester, Bury St. Edmunds, Aldeburgh, Chelmsford. *Work in permanent collections:* Guy Harlings, Chelmsford; Mansion House, London; Churchill College, Cambridge; *private collections:* Lord St. John of Fawsley, Abe Lerner, N.Y., Prof. Richard Gregory, Peter Rippon, and others. *Address:* Medlars, Mounthill Ave., Chelmsford CM2 6DB. *Club:* F.P.S. *Signs work:* "N.C." incised in capitals.

COUSENS, Ruth Margaret, F.S.A.I.; Medaille d'Or, Paris Salon (Tricentenaire 1973) T.C., Women of the Year Luncheon; artist in water-colour; art teacher of history, architecture and painting: St. George's Ramsgate, Maidstone Technical High, Sittingbourne Girls' Grammar, pupils of Wilmington Grammar Schools; Founder-Project Director, Castle Trust Arts Centre, Ramsgate; *b* London, 1930; *d* of Abbot Winstanley Upcher (Burke's Landed Gentry), Pioneer Missionary to Arabia, and Ruth Wingate, niece of Sir George Pirie, late Pres. Scottish R.A.; *m* Stanley G. Cousens; one *s*. *Educ.:* St. George's Ramsgate, and Clarendon Malvern; *studied art* at Rolle College, Exeter (1948-50, E.T. Arnold). *Exhib.:* Paris Salon, R.A., R.I., R.I.B.A., etc.; one-man shows, 'Regency Ramsgate', Townley House, Ramsgate (1973), Royal Museum, Canterbury (1978), Geneva (1985), Westend, London (1986); by invitation: 'La Femme Creatrice d'Art', Monte Carlo (1976) (Brit. rep.), 'British Artists', Paris (1979), Expo Quebec, Canada (1980). *Work in permanent collections:* Thanet Council, Ramsgate Charter Trustees; private: Sir Robert Bellinger, Rt. Hon. Edward Heath, M.P. *Work repro.:* book jackets, retail postcards; booklet 'Regency Ramsgate'. *Address:* 17 Spencer Sq., Ramsgate, Kent. *Signs work:* "R.M. COUSENS."

COUTU, Jack, A.R.E., A.R.C.A.; printmaker and sculptor; etching and engraving on copper, miniature carving in boxwood and ivory; *b* Farnham, Surrey, 1924; *s* of Herbert Coutu. *Educ.:* Farnham Grammar School; *studied art* at Farnham School of Art (1947-51), R.C.A. (1951-54). *Work in permanent collections:* King Gustave of Sweden, Museum of Fine Art, Boston, Mass., Bradford City Art Gallery, V. & A., Arts Council of Great Britain. *Address:* Bramblings, 22 Quennells Hill, Wrecclesham, Farnham, Surrey GU10 4NE. *Signs work:* "Coutu" and see appendix.

COUVE DE MURVILLE-DESENNE, Lucie-Renée; portrait, flower, landscape and marine painter, oil; *b* Majunga, Madagascar, 15 Apr., 1920; *d* of J. L. E.

Couve de Murville, artist and engineer; *m* F. H. Desenne; one *s*, one *d*. *Educ.:* Paris; *studied art* in Paris as private pupil of E. Ruff. *Exhib.:* Wakefield, Bradford, London, R.W.A.; one-man show: R.W.A. (1975). *Main works:* Official portrait of the Rt. Rev. Joseph Rudderham, Bishop of Clifton, in Clifton Cathedral; The Radiant Virgin, Church of St. Mary-of-the-Sea, St. Agnes, Cornwall. *Address:* 56 Worrall Rd., Clifton, Bristol BS8 2TX. *Club:* Hon. Pres. Bristol French Circle. Chevalier de l'Ordre National du Mérite, Chevalier de l'Ordre des Palmes Academiques. *Signs work:* see appendix.

COVENTRY, Frederick Halford; mural painter, stained glass, mosaic, engraving; *b* New Zealand, 19 Jan., 1905; *s* of Harry Coventry; *m*; one *s*, one *d*. *Educ.:* Dannevirke High School, Wellington Technical College, Elam School of Art, Auckland, Julian Ashton Art School, Sydney, and Grosvenor School of Art, London. *Exhib.:* R.A.; XXI Gallery, London; N.Z. Hse., London; C.O.I.D.; Imperial Inst., London; Macquarie Gallery, Sydney; Society of Artists, Sydney; N.Z. Academy. *Official purchases:* B.M.; Imperial War Museum; Campion Hall, Oxford; Plymouth Guildhall; Methodist Church, Plymouth; Harrow District Masonic Council; C.O.I., St. Alphage Hse., Barbican; Art Gallery of N.S.W.; Australian National Gallery, Canberra; N.Z. Govt.; Town Hall, Wellington, N.Z.; Queensland Govt.; Newcastle Region A.G. *Address:* 49 Brunswick Gdns., London W8 4AW. *Club:* Chelsea Arts. *Signs work:* "F. H. Coventry"

COWAN, Ralph Wolfe, A.P.S., A.A.A., A.S.A., P.I.; Royal Portrait Painter to: Sultan of Brunei (1984—), Monaco (1956, 1981), Morocco (1983), Malacanang Palace, Philippines (1982, 1983); portrait painter in oil; *b* Phoebus, Va., 16 Dec., 1931; *s* of Joseph Carl Cowan; *m* Judith Page; two *s*. *Studied art* at Art Students League (1949-50, Bouché and Frank Reilly). *Work in permanent collections:* Royal Palace Brunei, Palace Monaco, Royal Palace Morocco, Malacanang Palace Philippines, Carter Presidential Center, Atlanta, Reagan Private Coll., Los Angeles, Graceland Coll., Memphis, Portsmouth Museum, Portsmouth Va. *Work repro.:* seven Johnny Mathis album covers.; first book "A Personal Vision" collector plate of His Holiness Pope John Paul II; greeting card line featuring Elvis Presley. *Address:* 243 29th St. West Palm Beach, Fl.33407 U.S.A. *Signs work:* "Ralph Wolfe Cowan."

COX, Michael, Cert.Ed. (1973), Holbrook Award (1985); painter/etcher in water-colour, acrylic, oil, coloured pencil, copperplate etching; teacher; *b* Nottingham, 23 Aug., 1949; *s* of Thomas Cox; *m* Joanna Cox; one *s*. *Educ.:* Bilborough Grammar School, Nottingham; *studied art* at Trent Polytechnic (1970-73, Rosemary Hebden). *Exhib.:* The Gallery, Wirksworth, Derbys. (1986), John Noott Gallery, Broadway. *Work in permanent collection:* Nottinghamshire C.C. *Address:* 45 Mornington Cres., Nuthall, Nottingham NG16 1QQ. *Signs work:* "Michael Cox."

COX, Stephen B., B.A.Hons., British Council Research Scholar, P.G.C.E. (Merit); artist, interior designer, teacher; director, 'Club Anglia' international summer school; taught art: Wellington College, Reading Grammar, Langley College; arts organiser, Hexagon Reading; founder, Regional Secretary Artists Union; production manager independent British films (1977-80); promoter pop groups/artists; fashion model photographer; sponsor, Manpower Services Commission YTS; *s* of the late Bernard Cox. *Educ.:* Grange and Kingwood Grammar Schools; *studied art:* Reading University; *researched:* Bucharest Fine Arts University. *Exhib.:* now average four one-man shows and group shows annually U.K. and Europe. *Public and private commissions:* painting/sculpture England. *Work in private/public collections:* U.K., Europe, U.S.A. *Events:*

produced/performed (as Nevetz) Germany, France, U.K., Romania. *Work repro.:* many catalogues, radio, TV interviews U.K. and Europe. Council mem./ Head of Westminster lobby: Design and Artists Copyright Soc. *Addresses:* 60 Elmhurst Rd., Reading RG1 5HY; (studio) Chalkpit Farm, Englefield, Berks. *Signs work:* "STEPHEN" and see appendix.

COX, Sir Trenchard, C.B.E., D.Litt, M.A., F.S.A., F.M.A., Chevalier de la Légion d'Honneur; formerly director, V. & A. Museum, London; *b* 31 July, 1905; *s* of the late William Pallet Cox; *m* Mary Desirée Anderson (*d.* 1973). *Educ.:* Eton and King's College, Cambridge. *Publications:* The National Gallery, a Room-to-Room Guide (1930); Jehan Foucquet, Native of Tours (1931); part editor of Catalogue to Exhbn. of French Art at Burlington Hse. (1932); The Renaissance in Europe (1933); A General Guide to the Wallace Collection (1933); A Short Illustrated History of the Wallace Collection and its Founders (1936); David Cox (1948); Peter Bruegel (1951); Pictures: a Handbook for Curators (1956). *Address:* 33 Queen's Gate Gdns., London SW7. *Club:* Athenæum.

COXON, Raymond James, A.R.C.A.; painter, lithographer and writer; officially commissioned war artist; mem., London Group; *b* Hanley (Stoke-on-Trent), 18 Aug., 1896; *m* Edna Ginesi. *Educ.:* Leek High School, R.C.A. *Exhib.:* London, Leicester Galleries, International Exhbn. Brussels, Pittsburgh, New York, Tokyo. *Official purchases:* B.M., V. & A., Tate, Chantrey Bequest, Courtauld Inst., Imperial War Museum, National Gallery of Wales, Univ. of South Tennessee, Columbia Museum, S. Carolina, and principal provincial public galleries. *Publications:* Art (Pitman, 1932); Critic for World of Art Illustrated (1938). *Address:* Rowfant Mill Studio, Old Hollow, Pound Hill, Crawley, W. Sussex RH10 4TB. *Signs work:* "R. COXON."

CRABBE, Richard Markham, A.R.C.A. (1951), F.R.S.A.; painter; principal lecturer, Portsmouth Polytechnic Dept. of Fine Art (retd.); *b* Horley, Surrey, 1927; *s* of Sydney Crabbe; *m* Peggy Crabbe; three children. *Studied art* at Croydon School of Art and Royal College of Art. *Work in permanent collections:* Portsmouth Museum, Wigan Educ. Com. Koenig Braures, Duisburg, Germany, Southern Arts Assoc., S.W. Handelsbanken, Artothek, Düsseldorf, Germany, Hampshire C.C. *Address:* 22 Andover Rd., Southsea PO4 9QG. *Signs work:* "R. Crabbe."

CRAIG-MARTIN, Michael, B.A. (1963), M.F.A. (1966); artist; Trustee, Tate Gallery; *b* 28 Aug., 1941; one *d. Studied art* at Yale University (1961-63, 1964-66). *Address:* c/o Waddington Galleries, 11 Cork St., London W1X 1PD. *Signs work:* "Michael Craig-Martin."

CRAIGMILE, Heather, U.A.; Mem. Chelsea Art Soc.; artist in oil and crayon; *b* Birkenhead, 13 Sept., 1925; *d* of Major H.W.C. Craigmile, M.A.Cantab. *Educ.:* Downe House, Cold Ash, Newbury, Berks; *studied art* privately under Arnold Mason, R.A., Harold Workman, R.B.A., R.C.A., also at Chester Art School. *Exhib.:* R.B.A., R.C.A., U.A., Chelsea Art Soc., one man show every two or three years at Beddgelert in Snowdonia. *Address:* Bron Dyffryn, Llanbedr, Conwy, Gwynedd, N. Wales. *Signs work:* "Heather Craigmile".

CRAMP, Jonathan David, A.T.D., R.W.S.; painter; Head of Art Dept., Fishguard C.S. School (1954-1981); *b* Ninfield, Sussex, 29 Jan., 1930; *s* of David Cramp; *m* Elizabeth (painter); one *d. Educ.:* Huish Grammar School, Taunton, Bexhill Grammar School; *studied art* at Hastings School of Art (1946-51) (Vincent Lines). *Work in permanent collections:* Welsh Arts Council,

Contemporary Art Society for Wales, Pembrokeshire County Museum, Schools Service, National Museum of Wales, Dept. for the Environment, Shell Oil (U.K.) Ltd., National Grid Co., Cartrefle and Caerleon Colleges of Education, various education authorities. *Address:* Heatherdene, Windy-Hall, Fishguard, Pembs. SA65 9DU. *Signs work:* see appendix.

CRAMPTON, Seán, M.C. (1943), G.M. (1944), T.D. (1948), P.R.B.S. (1966-71), Master, A.W.G. (1978); sculptor; Professeur de sculpture, Anglo-French Art Centre (1946-50); Chairman of College Council, Camberwell School of Art (1988-90); Governor, London Institute (1989-90); Civic Trust Award (1984); R.B.S. Silver Medal (1965), R.B.S. Bronze Medal (1985), Civic Trust Award (1983); *b* Manchester, 15 Mar., 1918; *s* of Joshua Crampton, L.R.I.B.A.; *m*; five children. *Studied art* at Vittoria Junior School of Art, and Central School of Art, Birmingham; Paris. *Exhib.:* R.A., R.S.A., R.I. and R.I.B.A. Galleries, S.P.S.; 15 one-man shows in West End, etc. *Work in permanent collections:* Sculpture in many churches throughout England and Scotland, and private collections. *Address:* Rookery Farm House, Calne, Wilts. SN11 0LH. *Clubs:* Chelsea Arts, Athenæum. *Signs work:* "Seán Crampton" or "SC" within circle.

CRAWFORD, Alistair, D.A. (1966), A.T.C. (1968), M.C.S.D. (1973-1986), M.S.T.D. (1977), Fellow, Printmakers Council (1978), Churchill Fellow (1982), F.R.P.S. (1991); painter, printmaker, photographer, art historian; Professor of Graphic Art, Head of the School of Art, University of Wales, Aberystwyth; *b* Fraserburgh, 1945; *s* of John Gardiner Crawford; *m* Joan Martin. *Studied art* at Glasgow School of Art (1962-66). *Exhib.:* 30 one-man, over 100 group shows throughout Britain and U.S.A. Work in permanent collections throughout Britain and U.S.A. Various awards including Welsh Arts Council, British Council, British Academy, Gold Medal Fine Art, Royal National Eisteddfod of Wales (1985), Kraszna Krausz Award (1992). *Publications* include John Thomas 1838-1905 photographer (Wales); Mario Giacomelli (Paris); Elio Ciol, Italia Black and White (Milan); Carlo Bevilacqua (Wales); Elio Ciol Assisi (Milan, Paris, Munich). Numerous articles in U.K. and abroad. *Address:* Brynawel, Comins Coch, Dyfed SY23 3BD. *Signs work:* "Crawford."

CRAWFORD, John Gardiner, D.A. (1963), Post Dip. (1964), R.S.W. (1974), A.R.B.A. (1982), R.B.A. (1983), R.I. (1984); painter in oil, water-colour, acrylic, egg tempera; *b* Fraserburgh, 16 Aug., 1941; *s* of John Gardiner Crawford, fisherman; *m* Elspeth Younger; one *s*, one *d*. *Educ.:* Fraserburgh Academy; *studied art* at Gray's School of Art, Aberdeen (1959-63, post graduate year 1963-64), Hospitalfield College of Art, Arbroath. *Awards:* Gray's School of Art, First Prize for Painting (1962); Governor's Award for Painting, Hospitalfield College of Art (1963); Royal Scottish Academy, Bursary Award (1964); First Prize, Scottish Arts Council Open Exhbn. (1969); Scottish Arts Council, Bursary Award (1981); Hunting Award, First Prize for Water-colour (1982); R.I. Bronze Medal (1983); Hunting Award, Second Prize for Oil (1984). *Exhib.:* Internationally. *Work in permanent collections:* Worldwide. *Address:* 34 Strachan St., Arbroath, Angus DD11 1UA, Scotland. *Signs work:* "CRAWFORD" in capital letters.

CRAWSHAW, Alwyn, S.E.A., B.W.S., P.N.A.P.A., F.R.S.A. (1978); artist in acrylic, water-colour and oil; director (partner), Russell Artists Merchandising Ltd., Kingston-upon-Thames, Surrey (1957-80); Lecturer and demonstrator on acrylic, oil and watercolour painting for Daler-Rowney & Co., Ltd. Bracknell Berks; President, National Acrylic Painters Assoc.; elected Top Ten Art Video Teachers in America (1991); Founder/President, Soc. of Amateur Artists (1992);

b Mirfield, Yorks., 20 Sept., 1934; *s* of Fred Crawshaw; *m* June Crawshaw; one *s*, two *d*. *Educ.*: Hastings Grammar School for Boys; *studied art* at Hastings School of Art (1949-1951) under Vincent Lines. *Exhib.*: R.B.A.; one-man shows: Harrods, St. Paul's Gallery, London, Marina Gallery, Weybridge, Barclay A.G., Chester, Guildford Galleries, Guildford, Mensing Gallery, Germany; joint exhbn. with June Crawshaw, St. Helier Gallery, Jersey, C.I. (1992). *Work sold* in galleries in Europe, Australia and Canada. *Publications:* Pub. by Harper Collins: Alwyn Crawshaw's Oil Painting Course (1992), A Brush with Art (1991), Alwyn Crawshaw Paints Oils (1992), Alwyn Crawshaw Paints on Holiday (1992), Alwyn Crawshaw's Acrylic Painting Course (1993), Alwyn Crawshaw's Watercolour Painting Course (1991); Painting with Acrylic Colours (Daler-Rowney & Co., Ltd.) now in German, Italian and Finnish; Learn to paint with Acrylic Colours (Collins); Learn to paint with Watercolours (Collins); Learn to paint landscapes (Collins); Learn to paint boats and harbours (Collins); Learn to Sketch (Collins); Learn to Paint Still Life (Collins); Learn to Paint Outdoors in Watercolour (Collins); Learn to Paint in Oils for the Beginner (Collins); The Artist at Work—Alwyn Crawshaw (Collins); Sketching with Alwyn Crawshaw (Collins); The Half-Hour Painter (Collins). Guest on BBC Radio, BBC T.V., Independent Radio, discussing painting techniques; guest on the 'Gay Byrne Radio Show' R.T.E. Ireland (Mar. 1991), T.S.W. television series 'A Brush with Art' by Alwyn Crawshaw, 12 half hour programmes, 'Crawshaw Paints in Oils', 8 half hour programmes; all TV series screened network by Channel 4, and screened by P.B.S. America from April 1993: 'Crawshaw Paints on Holiday', 6 half hour programmes (1992), 'Crawshaw's Watercolour Studio' 8 half hour programmes (1993). *Address:* The Crawshaw Gallery, 3 Priory Rd., Dawlish, Devon EX7 9JF. *Signs work:* "ALWYN CRAWSHAW."

CRAWSHAW, Donna, S.W.A., S.E.A.; animals and landscape painter in acrylic and water-colour; *b* Woking, Surrey, 1960; *d* of Alwyn Crawshaw; *m* Andrew G.L. Goolding (Fine Art Dealer). *Studied art* at West Surrey College of Art and Design. *Exhib.*: Omell Galleries Windsor, London, Ascot, Harrods London, John Magee Belfast, Forest Gallery Guildford, Godalming Galleries, Gallery at Trapp, Dyfed, Mall Galleries and Westminster Hall (various). *Published by* Country Fine Arts and Solomon & Whitebread – Fine Art Prints; Royal Worcester Porcelain by Bradford Exchange; greetings cards by various. *Address:* Rhiwe Farm, Llanddeusant, Llangadog, Dyfed SA19 9SS. *Signs work:* "Donna Crawshaw."

CRAWSHAW, June, B.W.S. (1987), S.W.A. (1988); artist in water-colour, oil, potter in ceramics, porcelain; Director, Teaching Art Ltd., Newark, Notts.; *b* Woking, Surrey, 20 June, 1936; *d* of Ernest Bridgman, mechanical engineer; *m* Alwyn Crawshaw; one *s*, two *d*. *Educ.*: Kingfield Secondary School, Woking; *studied art:* painting under Alwyn Crawshaw, S.E.A., B.W.S., F.R.S.A. (1970-87); ceramics at Danefield College, Woking (1975-80, June Duckworth). *Exhib.*: joint exhbns. with Alwyn Crawshaw, Donna Crawshaw, S.W.A., Godalming Galleries (1985), Yorkshire Artists (1987), Sidmouth Visual Arts Festival (1981-87), B.W.S. (1987), joint exhbn. with Alwyn Crawshaw Harrods (1986), S.W.A. Annual Exhbn., B.W.S. Annual Exhbn., joint exhbn. with Alwyn Crawshaw at The Patricia Wells Gallery, Bristol (1989), and St. Helier Gallery, Jersey, C.I. (1992). Teaches with Alwyn Crawshaw on painting courses every year since 1982. Featured in TV series 'Crawshaw Paints on Holiday' Channel 4 (1992) and P.B.S. America (1993); also in book of this TV series. *Address:* The Crawshaw Gallery, 3 Priory Rd., Dawlish, Devon EX7 9JF. *Signs work:* "June Crawshaw" (paintings), and see appendix.

CRAXTON, John; artist in oil, tempera, conté crayon; *b* London, 3 Oct., 1922; *s* of Harold Craxton, O.B.E., pianist, composer, teacher. *Educ.:* various private schools; *studied art* at Goldsmiths' College and Academie Julian. *Exhib.:* Leicester Galleries, London Gallery, Galerie Gasser, Zürich, British Council, Athens, Retrospective, Whitechapel (1967). *Work in permanent collections:* Tate Gallery, City Art Gallery, Bristol, Manchester and Birmingham A.G., Melbourne A.G., British Council, Arts Council, Victoria and Albert Museum, Ministry of Works, British Museum. *Work repro.:* John Craxton, by Geoffrey Grigson, Horizon (1948), The Poet's Eye (1944: 16 lithographs), sets and costumes for Royal Ballet, Daphnis et Chlöe (1951), Apollo (1966). *Address:* Moschon 1, Hania, Crete. *Signs work:* "Craxton."

CREBER, Frank, B.F.A. (1981), M.F.A. (1987); artist in oil on canvas, watercolour, pen and ink; *b* Amersham, Bucks., 12 Jan., 1959; *m* Marguerite; two *s*. *Studied art* at Newcastle University (Roy Kitchen), Chelsea School of Art (Ian Stephenson). *Exhib.:* Sue Williams, Portobello Rd. (1988, 1989, 1991), Barclays Bank Young Painters £10,000 competition, Henry Moore Gallery, R.C.A. London (awarded joint winner 1987), Paton Gallery, London (1990), Artist of the Day, Flowers East, London (1989). *Work in permanent collections:* Unilever, Arthur Andersen & Co., Art for Hospitals, Leics. Schools Coll., Stanhope Construction Ltd. *Address:* 43 Jennings Rd., E. Dulwich, London SE22 9JU. *Signs work:* see appendix.

CREE, Alexander, D.A.(Edin.) 1950; painter in oil, pastel and watercolour; *b* 24 Feb., 1929; *s* of John Cree. *Educ.:* Dunfermline High School; *studied art* at Edinburgh College of Art (1946-52), Post Graduate Scholarship (1950), Travelling Scholarship (1951). *Exhib.:* Scottish Lyceum Club (1957), Demarco Gallery (1968, 1976), Loomshop Gallery (1969), Shed 50 (1974), Macaulay Gallery (1990), Solstice Gallery (1991), Westgate Gallery (1991), Ewan Mundy Gallery, Broughton Gallery, Open Eye Gallery, Kingfisher Gallery. *Work in permanent collections:* Scottish Arts Council, Nuffield Foundation. *Address:* Braeheads, E. Linton, E. Lothian EH40 3DH, Scotland. *Signs work:* "A. Cree."

CREFFIELD, Dennis; *b* London, 29 Jan., 1931. *Educ.:* Colfes Grammar School; *studied art* at Borough Polytechnic with David Bomberg (1948-51), Slade School (1957-61); Gregory Fellow in Painting at the University of Leeds (1964-67). *Exhib.:* many mixed and one-man exhbns. *Public collections* include, Tate Gallery, Contemporary Art Soc., National Trust Foundation for Art, House of Commons, Arts Council of Gt. Britain, Eastern Arts, Leeds City A.G., Dept. of the Environment. *Address:* 45 Marine Parade, Brighton. *Signs work:* "Dennis Creffield."

CREME, Benjamin; artist in oil; *b* Glasgow, 1922; *s* of Maurice Charles Creme; *m* Phyllis Power; two *s*, one *d*. *Educ.:* Queens Park, Glasgow; *studied art* with Jankel Adler. *Exhib.:* A.I.A., London Group, Carnegie International (1952), Whitechapel (1954), Arts Council (1974), I.C.A. (1979); one-man shows: Gallery Apollinaire (1952), St. George's Gallery (1955), Bryant M. Hale Gallery (1964), Dartington New Gallery (1977), Themes and Variations Gallery (1985), England & Co. (1988); group shows: South Molton Gallery, Gimpel Fils, Redfern, Roland Browse and Delbanco, Leger Gallery, Reid and LeFevre. *Work in permanent collections:* Pembroke College, Oxford, V. & A., B.M. *Publications:* Cage Without Grievance (W.S. Graham, Parton Press, 1942). *Address:* 59 Dartmouth Pk Rd., London NW5 1SL. *Signs work:* "Creme."

CRESWELL, Alexander Charles Justin; artist in water-colour, author; tutor, Prince of Wales Inst. of Architecture; *b* Helsinki, 14 Feb., 1957; *m* Mary Curtis

Green. *Educ.:* Winchester College; *studied art* at Byam Shaw School of Art (1976), W. Surrey College (1976-78). *Exhib.:* Spink & Son, Richmond Gallery, Cadogan Gallery, New Academy, also Europe and S. Africa. *Work in permanent collections:* Palace of Westminster, The Royal Collection. *Publication:* The Silent Houses of Britain (1991). *Address:* Copse Hill, Ewhurst, Surrey GU6 7NN. *Clubs:* Arts, Architecture, A.W.G. *Signs work:* "Alexander Creswell."

CREW, Rowan Alexander, A.R.B.A. (1987), R.B.A. (1988); self taught artist in water-colour, acrylic and oil; *b* Woodchurch, Kent, 31 Dec., 1952; *s* of Alfred Crew, teacher; *m* Shirley Bean; two *d. Educ.:* Homewood Secondary Modern. *Exhib.:* R.I., R.B.A. *Work in permanent collections:* K.C.C., and private collections. *Address:* 42 Brattle, Woodchurch, Ashford, Kent TN26 3SW. *Signs work:* "Rowan Crew."

CRISFIELD CHAPMAN, June, D.A. (Glasgow) (1955); wood engraver, portrait painter, illustrator (specializing in literary themes and subjects) in wood engraving, oil and gouache; *b* Kent, 4 June, 1934; *m* William Woodside Chapman; two *s. Educ.:* Kilmarnock Academy; *studied art* at Glasgow School of Art (1951-55, W. Bone, Lennox Paterson). *Exhib.:* solo shows: Royal National Theatre London, International Shakespeare Globe Centre London, Edinburgh College of Art, Royal Scottish Academy of Music and Drama Glasgow, Glasgow City A.G. Kelvingrove, etc.; group shows: Edinburgh International Festival, Royal Scottish Academy, Royal Society of Painter Printers' Open, Chaucer/Caxton, Westminster Abbey, etc. *Work in permanent collections:* engravings in Glasgow and Edinburgh City Collections, paintings in theatres including 'Tribute to Scottish Theatre' in Glasgow. *Publications:* engravings in Folio Book Society's Shakespeare (1988), 'The Countryman' regular series, etc. *Address:* 23 Smythe Rd., Billericay, Essex CM11 1SE. *Signs work:* "CRISFIELD/CRISFIELD CHAPMAN."

CROCKER, Barbara; painter and illustrator in oil, water-colour, lithography; *b* London, 4 Feb., 1910; *d* of George Ashcombe Crocker; *m* Eric Whelpton. *Educ.:* Putney High School; *studied art* at the Slade School (1927-30), France and Italy. *Exhib.:* one-man shows in London, Sussex, Kent and Suffolk; also New York. *Work in permanent collections:* South Africa House, and private collections in England, Australia, Hong Kong, U.S.A., Germany and Italy. *Work repro.:* illustrations for L'Air de Londres, by Jean Queval (Paris), Collins Pocket Guide Series, wall decorations for London offices. *Publications:* Barbara Whelpton, The Florentine Portrait (trans. from Jean Alazard), French Tapestry (trans. from Jean Lurçat), Myths and Legends Series (trans. from French, Burke), Unknown Ireland (Johnson), Unknown Austria, 3 vols. (Johnson), Art Appreciation Made Simple (W. H. Allen). *Address:* West Watch, Traders' Passage, Rye, E. Sussex TN31 7EX. *Club:* Arts. *Signs work:* "B. Crocker" or "BARBARA CROCKER."

CROFT, Ivor John, C.B.E., M.A. (Oxon. and Lond.); painter and former civil servant; *b* 6 Jan., 1923; *s* of Oswald Croft. *Educ.:* Westminster School; Christ Church, Oxford; Institute of Education, University of London; London School of Economics and Political Science. *Exhib.:* group shows: Piccadilly Gallery (1958); John Whibley Gallery (1963); Camden Arts Centre (Survey of Abstract Painters, 1967); Bear Lane Gallery, Oxford (1968); John Player Open Exhbn. (1968, 1969); Covent Garden Gallery (Critical Discoveries, 1973); Arts in Mann Gallery (1992); Newport, Isle of Wight, Art Gallery (Islands Apart, 1993); Lorient, Brittany (Festival Interceltique, 1993); one-man shows: Gardner Centre for the Arts, University of Sussex (1970); University of Warwick (1971). *Work repro.:*

Art and Artists, postcard. *Address:* 30 Stanley Rd., Peel, I.O.M. *Club:* Reform. *Signs work:* "John Croft" on back.

CRONYN, Hugh Verschoyle, G.M., F.R.S.A.; artist in oil, water-colour, lithography, mural painter, director of art, A.A. School of Architecture (1946-49); painting instructor, Colchester School of Art (1949-75); Lt.-Cdr. R.N.V.R. (1939-45); *b* Vancouver, B.C., Canada; *s* of V. F. Cronyn; *m* Jean Harris, M.A.; two *d. Educ.:* Ridley College; *studied art* at Ontario College of Art; Art Students' League, New York; American School of Fine Arts, Fontainebleau; various Paris academies. *One-man exhbns.:* London, Colchester, Lavenham, Montreal, Toronto, Victoria. *Work in permanent collections:* England, Sweden, Canada, U.S.A. and France. *Address:* Studio 3, St. Peter's Wharf, Hammersmith Terr., London W6 9UD.

CROOK, P. J., R.W.A. (1993); painter; *b* Cheltenham, 28 June, 1945; *d* of Jack Hagland; *m* Richard Parker Crook, painter; one *s*, one *d. Studied art* at Gloucestershire College of Art (1960-65). *Exhib.:* solo shows: Portal Gallery, London (1980, 1983, 1984, 1986, 1988, 1992), Cheltenham A.G. and Museum (1986), 112 Greene Street, N.Y. (1989), Galerie Alain Blondel, Paris (1991, 1993); group shows: R.A. (1978-83, 1985, 1987, 1988, 1990, 1991), R.W.A. (1978-94), First prize (1984), Royal Bath and West Open, First prize (1978), World of Newspapers, Sotheby's, R.A., Prizewinner (1982), Tolly Cobbold/Eastern Arts (1985), Athena International Art Awards (1985, 1987), John Player Portrait Awards exhbn. (1986), Small Pictures, Salisbury, Prizewinner (1986), Leicestershire Collection for Schools and Colleges, exhbn. and purchase (1987-94) Artist in Residence (1992), Picturing People, British Figurative Art since 1945, British Council touring exhbn. (1989/90), Denim, Brighton A.G. and Museum, tour (1990), Art and Dance, Leicester A.G. and Museum (1990), Cheltenham Group, First prize (1990), Friends of Carel Weight, C.B.E., R.A., Arts Club, London (1991), Laing touring exhbn. (1991), Hunting/Observer (1992), South West Open, Specially commended (1992), Singer & Friedlander/Sunday Times (1992), The Discerning Eye, Marina Vaizey (1992), Contemporary Icons, Royal Albert Memorial Museum, Exeter (1992), The Gift of Life, Prizewinner (1993), Dept. of Transport exhbn., Purchase prize (1993). *Work in permanent collections:* Imperial War Museum; Dept. of Transport; Cheltenham A.G. and Museum; Allied Lyons plc; Ralli Inst. and Museum, Geneva and Ceaseria; University of Pennsylvania; London Business School; Cheltenham Racecourse. *Publication:* P.J. Crook (Editions Ramsay, Paris, 1993). *Address:* The Old Police Station, 39 Priory La., Bishop's Cleeve, Cheltenham GL52 4JL. *Signs work:* "P.J. Crook."

CROSBIE, William, B.A. (1935), R.S.A. (1975), R.G.I. (1980); painter in oil, water-colour, pastel; *b* Hankow, Hupeh, China; *s* of A.S. Crosbie, marine engineer; *m* Anne Roger; two *d. Educ.:* Glasgow Academy; *studied art* at Glasgow School of Art (1930-36); Ecole de la Grand Chaumière; Studio of Fernand Leger (1936-39, Aristide Malol). *Exhib.:* Sydney State Gallery, Wellington State Gallery (approx. every two years since 1945). *Work in permanent collections:* Kelvingrove Gallery Glasgow, Aberdeen, Bradford Gallery. *Publications;* Childrens readers, poetry books. *Address:* Rushes House, 10 Winchester Rd., Petersfield, Hants. GU32 3BY. *Clubs:* R.N.C.Y.C., Glasgow Art. *Signs work:* "Crosbie" followed by year in roman numerals.

CROSBY, Theo, R.A., R.I.B.A., F.C.S.D.; architect, author and sculptor; partner, Pentagram Design Partnership; Prof. of Architecture and Interior Design, Royal College of Art (1990-93); *b* Mafeking, S. Africa, 3 Apr., 1925; *s* of Nicholas John Crosby; *m* (1) Anne Buchanan; (divorced); one *d;* (2) Polly Hope. *Educ.:* University of Witwatersrand, Johannesburg; *studied art* at various London art schools. Sculptures in Hyde Park, London (1985), Plaza Centre, Rotterdam (1992). *Publications:* Architecture: City Sense (1965); The Necessary Monument (1970); How to play the Environment Game (1973); Let's Build a Monument (1987). *Address:* Tower 3, Whitehall Ct., London SW1.

CROSS, Roy, R.S.M.A. (1977), S.A.A. (1952); historical marine and aviation painter in gouache and oils; *b* London 1924; *m* Rita May; one *s.* *Exhib.:* Malcolm Henderson Gallery, St. James's, (1973); one-man shows: Börjessons Gallery, Gothenborg, Sweden, (1975 and 1977); Marine Arts Gallery, Salem, Massachusetts (1976 and 1989). *Recent publications* eleven limited edition prints of marine pictures signed and numbered by the artist (1977-1989) published in Sweden (2), U.S.A. (7) and Britain (2), plus art prints by Franklin Mint, Rosenstiel's, plates by Hamilton Collection, etc. *Address:* Squirrels, Hither Chantlers, Langton Green, Tunbridge Wells, Kent TN3 0BJ. *Signs work:* "Roy Cross ©" and usually dated.

CROSS, Tom, N.D.D.(1953), Dip.(Lond.)(1956); painter in oil and gouache; Principal, Falmouth School of Art (1976-87); mem. London Group; Chairman, Penwith Soc. of Artists (1982-84); *b* Manchester, 1931; *s* of Frederick Cross; *m* Patricia; one *s.* *Studied art* at The Slade School, Abbey Minor Scholarship, Rome, French Govt. Scholarship. *Exhib.:* one-man shows, Penwith Galleries, Montpelier Studio, Charleston, S.C. *Work in permanent collections:* Welsh Arts Council, Contemporary Art Soc. for Wales, Leicester and Glamorgan Educ. Authorities. *Publication:* Painting the Warmth of the Sun, St. Ives Artists 1939-75 (Alison Hodge and Lutterworth). *Address:* Dinyan, Port Navas, Constantine, Cornwall. *Club:* Chelsea Arts. *Signs work:* "Tom Cross."

CROSSLEY, Bob; painter, printmaker; *b* Northwich, 1912; *s* of Edwin; *m* Marjorie; one *s*, two *d.* *Educ.:* Heybrook School, Rochdale. *Exhib.:* 9 one-man shows: Crane Gallery, Manchester (1959), Reid Gallery, London (1960, 1964), Gallery Bique, Madrid (1965), Reid Gallery, Guildford (1966), Curwen Gallery, London (1972), Singers Fridden Division, Stevenage (1972), John Player & Sons, Nottingham (1972), Bristol Arts Centre (1980), Penwith Galleries, St.Ives (1987). *Work in permanent collections:* Contemporary Art Society, Rochdale A.G., Durban, A.G., S.A., Winnipeg A.G., College of Advanced Education, Port Elizabeth, S.A., Hereford A.G., Open University, Sommerfield College. *Address:* Studio Annexe, Porthgwidden, St. Ives, Cornwall TR26 1PL. *Signs work:* "Crossley."

CROSSLEY, Gordon, N.S. (1983), M.Inst.M.; painter in oil; Senior lecturer in Art and Design, Barking College of Technology; *b* Surrey, 6 Dec., 1929; *s* of Fred Eric Crossley; *m* Jo Glosby; one *s*, three *d.* *Educ.:* Rutlish School, Merton; *studied art* at Wimbledon School of Art. *Exhib.:* R.A., R.B.A., N.E.A.C., P.S., N.S., Madden Gallery; one-man shows, Phoenix Gallery (1984), Gainsborough Gallery, Beecroft Gallery. *Work in permanent collection:* Essex Museum. *Address:* The Sanctuary, Sheering, nr. Bishop's Stortford, Herts. CM22 7LN. *Signs work:* see appendix.

CROW, Barbara Joan (née Walmsley), R.C.A.; wood engraver and illustrator; teacher; *b* Liverpool, 1942; two *d.* *Educ.:* Merchant Taylors' School for Girls, Liverpool; *studied art* at Slade School (1959-62, Sir William Coldstream), Bristol Polytechnic (1982-84) postgraduate printmaking. *Exhib.:* R.W.A., R.C.A., S.W. Arts 'Artists in Schools', Arnolfini (1983), S.W.E. *Address:* Manor

Lodge, Llangattock-vibon-Avel, Monmouth, Gwent. *Clubs:* A.A.D.W., Assoc. of Illustrators. *Signs work:* "Barbara Crow."

CROW, Kathleen Mary, R.O.I. (1988), N.S. (1983); painter in oil and water-colour; *b* Oxton, Notts., 4 June, 1920; *d* of Levi Hopkin, company director; *m* John Richard Crow; one *s*, one *d*. *Educ.:* Ackworth; Basel, Switzerland; *studied art* at Nottingham Polytechnic (1964-76 part-time, Ronald Thursby), Leicester (1976-82 part-time, Leslie Goodwin). *Exhib.:* R.A. Summer Exhbns., R.W.A., R.O.I., R.I., N.S., Nottingham, Rufford, Leicester, Oakham. *Address:* 2 Blind La., Oxton, Southwell, Notts. NG25 0SS. *Club:* Nottingham Soc. of Artists. *Signs work:* see appendix.

CROWE, Barbara, R.I., S.W.A., S.B.A.; painter in water-colour and oil, teacher, demonstrator; *b* Wirrall, Ches.; *d* of Benjamin Jones, master printer; *m* Ronald Crowe; four *d*. *Studied art* at Bolt Court, Croydon, but mostly self-taught. *Exhib.:* R.I., S.W.A., Mall Galleries. *Publications:* contributor to Artist and Leisure Painter. *Address:* Dormers, Hammerfield, Abinger Hammer, nr. Dorking, Surrey. *Clubs:* Dorking, Guildford and Sussex Art Soc. *Signs work:* "Barbara Crowe."

CROWE, Maida, F.F.P.S.; sculptor in wood and stone; *b* Axminster, 1915; *d* of Stafford Heal, engineer; *m* Jim Crowe. *Educ.:* privately; *studied art* at City and Guilds of London (1957-62). *Exhib.:* R.B.A., F.P.S., A.I.R., Barbican, Surrey, Birmingham, Southampton and London Universities, etc.; open air, Berkeley Sq., and Brixton; one-man shows, Loggia Gallery, Cockpit Gallery, I.A.C., Bridport and Southwark Cathedral. *Address:* 906 Keyes House, Dolphin Sq., London SW1. *Clubs:* F.P.S., Westminster Arts Soc., N.F.T. *Signs work:* "MAIDA."

CROWE, Victoria Elizabeth, N.D.D. (1965), M.A. (R.C.A.) (1968), R.S.W. (1983), A.R.S.A. (1987); artist in oil and water-colour; part-time lecturer, Edinburgh College of Art; *b* 1945. *Studied art* at Kingston College of Art (1961-65), R.C.A. (1965-68). *Exhib.:* R.A., R.S.A.; one-man shows, Scottish Gallery, Edinburgh (1970, 1974, 1977, 1982), Thackeray, London (1983, 1985, 1987, 1989, 1991, 1994), Mercury Gallery, Edinburgh (1986). *Work in permanent collections:* R.A., R.C.A., Scottish National Gallery of Modern Art, Scottish Arts Council, N.P.G. London, Scottish N.P.G., I.L.E.A., Edinburgh Educ. Authority. *Address:* The Bank House, Main St., W. Linton, Peeblesshire. *Signs work:* "Victoria Crowe."

CROWTHER, Hugh Melvill; artist in oil, pastel; *b* Newby, nr. Scarborough, Yorks., 25 June, 1914; *s* of Guy Fenwick Crowther, civil engineer; *m* Margaret Steele Wainey. *Educ.:* St. John's, Tutshill, Chepstow; *studied art* at Newport Technical College, Gwent. *Exhib.:* Royal Glasgow Institute of Fine Arts, Cardiff, Newport, Monmouth, Hereford, Gloucester, London. *Work in permanent collection:* Newport Museum, Gwent. *Work repro.:* Chepstow Castle, Village Smithy, Naturalist's Collection, all in La Revue Moderne. *Address:* Meadow End, Tidenham, Chepstow, Gwent. *Clubs:* West Gloucestershire Art Soc., Wye Valley Art Soc., Gloucestershire Soc. of Artists. *Signs work:* see appendix.

CROWTHER, Stephen, A.R.C.A., R.B.A. (1958); artist in oil, charcoal, conté, pastel; *b* Sheffield, 23 Aug., 1922; *s* of Henry Crowther; *m* Sheila Maria Higgins; two *s*, one *d*. *Educ.:* De la Salle College, Sheffield; *studied art* at Sheffield College of Art; Royal Scholarship to Royal College of Art (1941); war service (1941-46); R.C.A. (1946-49). *Exhib.:* R.A., R.B.A., R.P., and many provincial galleries; one-man shows: Gray A.G., Hartlepool; Billingham A.G.; Zaydler

Gallery, London; Green Dragon Yard A.G., Stockton; Abbot Hall A.G., Kendal; Middlesbrough A.G. *Work in permanent collections:* Gray A.G., Derbyshire and Hartlepool Education Committees, Abbot Hall A.G., Kendal, Hartlepool, South Tees, Cleveland and Bradford General Hospitals. *Work repro.:* in The Complete Portrait Painting Course including front cover; and Perspective for Artists, both by Angela Gair (Mitchell Beazley, 1990); The Oil Painter's Question and Answer Book by Hazel Harrison (Quarto Publishing, plc), and many other books published by Studio Vista, Harper Collins, Quarto, etc. *Address:* 5 The Cliff, Seaton Carew, Hartlepool, Cleveland TS25 1AB. *Signs work:* see appendix.

CRYAN, Clare, A.T.C., D.A.; artist specializing in water-colour; Tutor-in-Charge, The Blue Door Studio; *b* Dublin, 1935. *Educ.:* Dominican Convent, Sion Hill; *studied art* at National College of Art, Dublin; Ulster College of Art, Belfast and with Kenneth Webb in The Irish School of Landscape Painting. *Exhib.:* R.H.A., R.U.A., N.S., Salon d'Automne, Festival International Paris, Osaka, Brussels, Luxembourg, Hong Kong. *Work in permanent collections:* Killiney Castle, Dublin, H.M. Queen Beatrix of the Netherlands. *Address:* The Blue Door Studio, 16 Prince of Wales Terr., Dublin 4. *Club:* European Inst. of Water-colours. *Signs work:* "Clare Cryan."

CRYER, Ian David; painter in oils; *b* Bristol, 1959; *m* Wendy Patricia. *Educ.:* Ridings High School, Bristol; *studied art:* part-time Bristol Polytechnic (1978-82); and in Kensington under Leonard Boden, R.P. (1978-81). *Exhib.:* Bristol Art Centre (1976), P. Wells Gallery (1983), Linfield Galleries (1984, 1985), R.A., R.B.A., R.W.A., N.E.A.C., Hunting Group finalist (1990), Discerning Eye (1991), Cooling Gallery (1992). *Work in permanent collections:* many private collections including Price Waterhouse and Longleat House. *Address:* 93 Bath Rd., Willsbridge, Bristol BS15 6ED. *Signs work:* "Ian Cryer."

CUBA, Ivan; D.Litt.; professor extraordinary of art, proclaimed for distinguished service, Dictionary of International Biography, Vol. V (1968); elected The Temple of Arts, U.S.A. (1970); elected Fellow, Academy Leonardo da Vinci and Poet Laureate Award (1979); President, Temple of Art Academy, N.Z.; developed educational composite painting, segment painting and aluminium engravure, discovered colour-balancing by mathematics and weight changes in matter; decorations include 11 diplomas, three sets of other letters and two gold medals, eight other. *Studied* at University of Auckland, N.Z. *Exhib.:* U.K., U.S.A., N.Z. Author of books. *Address:* P.O. Box 5199, Wellesley St., Auckland, N.Z.

CULL, Peter George, M.B.E. (1991), O.St.J. (1991), Hon. F.I.M.I. (1984), F.M.A.A. (1969); medical artist in water-colour, graphite and colour pencil; Prof. of Medical Art, London University; Director, Education and Medical Illustration Services, St. Bartholomew's Hospital, London; *b* Feltham, 25 Nov., 1927; *s* of George Edward Cull; *m* Bettine Murray; two *s,* one *d. Educ.:* Twickenham School of Art and Guy's Hospital, London. *Exhib.:* works exhib. and published widely in the realms of medicine; public exposure through television and press. *Address:* 326 Ben Jonson House, Barbican, London EC2Y 8DL. *Club:* Players Theatre. *Signs work:* "PETER CULL."

CULLINAN, Edward, C.B.E., R.A.; architect, artist; *b* London, 17 July, 1931. *Studied architecture* at Architectural Assoc., Cambridge and Berkeley, Calif. Has taught and lectured in Canada, U.S.A., Australia, N.Z., Norway, Malta, Japan, Eire, etc. and many places in England, Wales and Scotland. Founder and principal architect, Edward Cullinan Architects, authors of many modern bldgs.

and receivers of many awards. *Address:* The Wharf, Baldwin Terr., London N1 7RU. *Signs work:* "E.C." or "Edward Cullinan Architects."

CUMMINGS, Albert Arratoon Runciman, U.A. (1973), F.S.A. (Scot.)(1973); painter in tempera, oil and water-colour, book illustrator, picture restorer; *b* Edinburgh, 20 Aug., 1936; *m* Marjorie Laidlow; one *s*, one *d*. *Educ.:* Edinburgh; *studied art:* apprentice stage designer under William Grason, Edward Bowers, Charles Napier, Robert Jardine. *Exhib.:* U.A., Scottish Gallery. *Work in permanent collections:* Leeds Educ. authorities, Edinburgh Hospital Board. *Address:* 4 School Rd., Aberlady, E. Lothian. *Signs work:* "A. Runciman, pinx."

CUNEO, Terence Tenison, O.B.E., R.G.I., P.S.E.A.; *b* 1 Nov., 1907; *s* of Cyrus Cuneo; *m* Catherine Mayfield Monro; two *d*. *Educ.:* Sutton Valence School; *studied art* at Chelsea and Slade; mem. War Artists Advisory Com. *Exhib.:* R.A., R.P., R.O.I.; one-man shows: R.W.S. Galleries (1941-58), Sladmore Gallery (1971-73), Mall Gallery (1986). *Official purchases:* Coronation of Queen Elizabeth II in Westminster Abbey; *portraits:* H.M. Queen as Col.-in-Chief, Grenadier Guards, on Imperial, Royal Academy (1963), The Ceremony of the Garter (June, 1964), Prime Minister Edward Heath (1971), Field Marshal Montgomery (1972), the Queen, opening New Stock Exchange (1973), the Queen as Patron of Kennel Club (1974), Duke of Beaufort as Master of the Horse (1976), King Hussein (1980), Falklands, Scots Guards, 'D' Day Landing (1984); 1st stamp issue, 150th anniversary G.W.R. (1985). *Publications:* autobiography, The Mouse and His Master (1977); The Railway Painting of Terence Cuneo (1984); Terence Cuneo, Railway Painter of the Century (1990). Freedom of City of London (1993). *Address:* 201 Ember Lane, East Molesey, Surrey. *Signs work:* see appendix.

CURMANO, Billy, M.S. (1977), B.F.A. (1973); mixed media artist; *b* U.S.A., 1949. *Educ.:* Art Students League, N.Y.C.; University of Wisconsin; former director, Broadway Galleries. *Exhib.:* one-man shows: Minneapolis, Milwaukee, La Crosse, Winona, St. Joseph; group shows: Vienna Graphikbiennale, Austria (1977), International Miniprint, Ourense, Spain (1992-93), Franklin Furnace, N.Y.C. (1987), Small Works, N.Y.C. (1986), Public Works, N.Y.C. (1984), Metronom, Barcelona, Spain (1981), Chautauqua National, N.Y. (1980), Art in the Mail, N.Z. (1976), #18, N.Y.C. (1972), Paula Insel Annual, N.Y.C. (1972), Tyler National, Texas (1972), Graphics U.S.A., Chicago (1971). *Address:* Route #1, Rushford, Mn. 55971, U.S.A. *Signs work:* "Billy Curmano."

CURTIS, Anthony Ewart, Dip.A.E.(Lond.), R.W.A., M.F.P.S.; experimental and landscape artist; *b* Wakefield, 7 July, 1928; *s* of G. E. and G. L. Curtis née Provis (both decd.); *m* Joyce Isabel Yates; three *s*, one *d*. Served R.N. (1946-48). *Educ.:* Kingswood Grammar School, Loughborough (1948-50); Post-grad. Diploma, London (1974-76); *studied art* at Bath Academy, Corsham (1950-51, Peter Potworowski, William Scott, Ken Armitage, Peter Lanyon, Bryan Wynter). *Exhib.:* (1951-): Redfern, Zwemmers, Daily Express Young Painters, London Group, R.W.A. (1950 to date), Arts Council Modern Stained Glass (1960-61), R.I. (1983), R.W.S. (1984), 'Migraine Images' at St. Martins-in-the-Fields (1993). One-man shows include Bear Lane, Oxford (1959), Reading (1961), Cookham (1964); ceramic sculpture: Scopas, Henley (1975), Century, Henley (1980), Recent and Retrospective Work, Bloomsbury Gallery, University of London (1987), Retrospective show 'Recollections', Wooburn Festival (1992). Five-month working visit to Australia (1988-89); working visits to Oregon, U.S.A. (1990-93). *Work in public collections:* R.W.A., Bristol Educ. Com., sand-blasted screen, St.Andrew's, High Wycombe. *Work repro.:* Young Artists of Promise (1957). *Address:* Oak Tree House, 143 Heath End, Flackwell Heath, High Wycombe, Bucks. HP10 9ES. *Signs work:* "Anthony Curtis," or see appendix (on small works).

CURTIS, David Jan Gardiner, R.O.I. (1988), R.S.M.A. (1983); artist in oil and water-colour, designer; *b* Doncaster, 15 June, 1948; *s* of Arthur Gardiner Curtis, writer. *Educ.:* Doncaster Grammar School. *Exhib.:* R.A., R.S.M.A., R.I., R.W.S., R.B.A., N.E.A.C. Singer Friedlander/Sunday Times water-colour competition 1st prizewinner (1992). *Publication:* author, A Light Touch—The Landscape in Oils, and film of the same title. *Address:* The Cottage, Slaynes La., Misson, Doncaster, S. Yorks. DN10 6DY. *Clubs:* R.O.I., R.S.M.A. *Signs work:* "D.J. Curtis."

CURTIS, Joyce, Dip.A.E.(Lond.); artist and book illustrator in gouache, oil, pencil; Organiser (S.Bucks.), Bucks. Art Week Visual Images Group; *b* Sulhamstead, 5 Aug., 1934; *d* of H.J. Yates; *m* Anthony Curtis; three *s*, one *d*. *Educ.:* Faringdon Grammar School; Post-grad. Dip., London (1985-86); *studied art:* Bath Academy of Art, Corsham (1952-54, Potworowski, Litz Pisk, Frost, Meadows, Armitage, Ellis). *Exhib.:* solo shows, Dixon Gallery, University of London (1986), Corsham (1990), High Wycombe Museum (1993); three joint exhbns. with husband; mixed shows including R.W.A. *Publications:* illustrated children's fiction: Satis textbooks. *Address:* Oak Tree House, 143 Heath End Rd., Flackwell Heath, High Wycombe, Bucks. HP10 9ES. *Signs work:* "Joyce Curtis."

CZERWINKE, Tadeusz., N.D.D. (1957), A.T.C. (1973), S.P.S. (1976), D.A.E. (1981); sculptor, carver, modeller and potter in stone, wood, perspex, bronze and terracotta; Head of Arts and Crafts Dept., Shoeburyness Comprehensive School; *b* Poland, 19 May, 1936; *s* of Sylvester Czerwinke, industrial thermal design engineer; *m* Ewa; one *s*, one *d*. *Educ.:* St. Peter's Winchester; *studied art* at Winchester School of Arts and Crafts (1957, Norman Pierce, F.R.B.S.). *Exhib.:* regularly at S.P.S., Mall Galleries, Federation of British Artists, A.P.A. in G.B., Salon des Nations, Paris; one-man portrait sculpture exhbn. Posk Gallery (1987) and at the Polish Hearth, London. *Work in permanent collections:* Church of Czestochowa, Huddersfield; Kosciuszko Museum, Rappersville, Switzerland; St. Peter's Hinkley, Leics.; Les Laurents, Dordogne, France; St. Catherine's Dock, London; Our Lady of Lourdes Convent, Kent; Town Hall, Monte Cassino, Italy; Parish Church, Devonia Rd., London; St. Sebastian & John the Baptist, Preston; Andrzej Bobola Church, London; Memorial, Eaton Pl., London; General Sikorski Museum, London; Memorial, Marshal J. Pilsudzki Inst., London; Posk (Centre of Polish Culture, London); Dom Narodowca, London; S. Michalowski, Shute House, nr. Honiton; sculptures and portraits in private collections in U.K. and overseas. *Address:* 20 Whitehouse Way, Southgate, London N14 7LT. *Signs work:* "Tad. Czerwinke."

CZIMBALMOS, Magdolna Paal, S.I. Museum, N.Y., Gold Med. (1958, 1960, 1962, 1963, 1966); personal letter from President J. F. Kennedy for portrait of Jacqueline Kennedy (1961); Italian Culture Award, N.Y. (1967); Szinyei Merse Gold Med., N.Y. (1971); several Silver Med. and Hon. Men.; artist in oil; *b* Esztergom, Hungary; *m* Kalman Sz. Czimbalmos; one *d*. *Studied art* under Prof. A. Bayor pr. Art Sch. Esztergom, Hung., Radatz pr. Art Sch. Germ. *Exhib.:* Paris, Germany, Monaco, Canada, U.S.A., Budapest (1982), Esztergom, Hungary (1985); several one-man and group shows. *Work in permanent collections:* S.I. Museum, N.Y., International Inst., Detroit, Carnegie International Cent., N.Y., Bergstrom Art Cent., Ill., City Museum, Esztergom and Budapest, Hungary. *Address:* 31 Bayview Pl., Ward Hill, Staten Island, New York, 10304. *Clubs:* S.I. Museum, N.Y., World Fed. of Hung. Artists, International Soc. of Fine Artists, U.S.A. *Signs work:* "Magdolna Paal Czimbalmos" and see appendix.

CZIMBALMOS, Szabo Kalman, Hung. Roy. Acad. Pr. (1933), S.I. Museum, N.Y., Pr. Gold Med. (1950, 1956, 1962, 1963, 1967), St. Stephen Gold Medal, N.Y. (1971), several Silver Med. and Hon. Men.; M.F.A., painter-educator, Dir. Czimbalmos Pvt. Art Sch., N.Y.; owner, Czimbalmos Fine Art Studio, S.I., N.Y.; artist in oil, water-colour, tempera; *b* Esztergom, Hungary, 1914; *s* of Janos Czimbalmos; *m* Magdolna Paal Bohatka; one *d. Studied art* at Royal Academy of Fine Art, Budapest (1936) under Prof. J. Harahghy, E. Domanowsky; postgrad. Vienna, Munich, Paris, Rome. *Exhib.:* Munchen, Paris, Monaco, Canada, U.S.A., Budapest (1982), Esztergom, Hungary (1985); several one-man and group shows. *Work in permanent collections:* S.I. Museum, N.Y., S.I. Com. Coll. N.Y., Bergstrom Art Center, Ill., City Museum, Esztergom, Hung., etc.; murals in churches, convents and private inst., U.S.A. *Address:* 31 Bayview Pl., Ward Hill, Staten Island, New York, 10304. *Clubs:* Bavaryan Fine Art Soc., S.I. Museum, N.Y., World Fed. of Hung. Artists, International Soc. of Fine Artists, U.S.A. *Signs work:* "K. Sz. Czimbalmos" and see appendix.

D

DADY, William St. Alban Rae, N.D.D., A.T.C. (1961), S.P.S. (1979); painter and sculptor; Director of Art, Stowe, Buckingham; *b* Delhi, India, 5 Feb., 1938; *s* of Cyril St. A. R. Dady; *m* Elizabeth D. Tabor; three *s*, three *d. Educ.:* Abingdon School, Berks.; *studied art* at University of London Goldsmiths' College School of Art (1956-61, John Mansbridge, Ivor Roberts Jones, Ken Martin, Harold Parker, Sam Rabin, Clifford Frith). *Exhib.:* R.A., F.B.A., *Address:* Rutland House, Chandos Rd., Buckingham, Bucks. *Signs work:* "W.St.A.R. Dady" or "DADY".

D'AGUILAR, Michael, gold, silver and bronze medals, Royal Drawing Soc., Armitage and silver medal, R.A. (1949); artist in oil and lithograph; *b* London, 11 May, 1924. *Educ.:* privately in Spain, Italy and France; *studied art* at R.A. Schools under Henry Rushbury, R.A., Fleetwood-Walker, A.R.A., William Dring, R.A. (1948-53). *Exhib.:* R.A., R.B.A., N.E.A.C., Irving Galleries, Gimpel Fils, Leicester Galleries, Young Contemporaries; one-man shows, Gimpel Fils, Irving Galleries, New Grafton Gallery. *Work repro:* Artist, Studio, La Revue Moderne des Arts. *Publications:* articles in Diario de Tarragona, La Revue Moderne, The Artist, Studio. *Address:* Studio 4, Chelsea Farm House, Milmans St., London SW10. *Signs work:* "M. D'Aguilar."

D'AGUILAR, Paul; artist in oil, water-colour; 1st prize for drawing at R.A. schools (1949); gold, silver and bronze medals, R.D.S.; *b* London, 9 Sept., 1927. *Educ.:* privately in Spain, Italy and France; *studied art:* R.A. schools (1948-53) and with Prof. Barblain (Siena). *Exhib.:* R.A., Redfern, Young Contemporaries, Leicester Galleries, Daily Express Young Artists, R.B.A., N.E.A.C., Sindicato de Iniciativa (Spain), Irving Gallery (1952), Temple Gallery (1960), New Grafton, Canaletto (1971), Southwell Brown Gallery (1974), Langton Gallery (1973, 1976). *Work in permanent collection:* Lord Rothermere. *Work repro.:*

Artist, Studio, Collins Magazine, La Revue Moderne, Drawing Nudes (Studio Vista). *Address:* 11 Sheen Gate Gdns., London SW14. *Signs work:* "P. D'Aguilar."

DAINES, Deirdre; R.A. Silver medal, bronze medal and Greenshields Award, R.A. Cert., Eric Kennington prize for drawing, Winsor and Newton prize; painter in oil drawing and pastel, mainly figure paintings; teacher, London Sketch Club; *b* Ware, 2 May, 1950. *Educ.:* Tottenham High Grammar School; *studied art* at R.A. Schools (1970-73, Peter Greenham). *Exhib.:* New Grafton, R.A. Summer Exhbn., R.P., Agnew's, Watermans; one-man shows, Thomas Agnew (1988), Cole Art (1982). *Address:* 34A Eardley Cres., London SW5 9JZ. *Clubs:* N.E.A.C., Dover St. Art. *Signs work:* "Daines."

DAKEYNE, Gabriel; Associé Société des Artistes Français; Hon. Mem. Paris Salon (1972); *b* Marske-by-the-sea, Yorkshire, 23 Feb., 1916; *d* of Cecil R. B. Dakeyne, Clerk in Holy Orders; *m* Wing-Cdr. Jack Brain, Retd.; two *d. Educ.:* home; *studied art* at Swindon School of Art, Press Art School. *Address:* Sadlers Cottage, Sadlers End, Sindlesham, Wokingham RG11 5AL. *Signs work:* see appendix.

DALBY, Claire, R.W.S., R.E.; artist in water-colour drawing, wood-engraving and botanical illustration; *b* St. Andrews, 1944; *d* of Charles Longbotham, R.W.S.; *m* D. H. Dalby, Ph.D. *Studied art* at City and Guilds of London Art School (1964-67). *Exhib.:* R.A., R.W.S., R.E.; one-man shows: Consort Gallery, Imperial College, London (1981, 1988), Shetland Museum, Lerwick (1988, 1991). *Publications:* "Claire Dalby's Picture Book" (J.L. Carr, Kettering 1989); designed and illustrated two wallcharts "Lichens and Air Pollution" and "Lichens on Rocky Seashores" (British Museum (Nat. Hist., 1981, 1987). *Address:* 132 Gordon Rd., Camberley, Surrey GU15 2JQ. *Signs work:* see appendix.

DALE, Tom, R.M.S. (1982); Mem. Hilliard Soc.; artist in water-colour and gouache; Art Master, Selwood School, Frome; *b* Greenock, Renfrewshire, 23 June, 1935; *s* of Alexander Dale; *m* Myra Thomson; two *d. Educ.:* Greenock High School; *studied art* at Glasgow School of Art (1953-57), Dip. in Design and Decorative Art (1957). *Exhib.:* Contemporary Art Fair, Nevill Gallery, Pump Rooms Bath, Burwood Gallery Wells, Colyton Devon. *Address:* Little Paddock, W. Horrington, nr. Wells, Som. *Signs work:* "Dale."

DALE, William Scott Abell, M.A. (Toronto, 1946), Ph.D. (Harvard, 1955); Prof. Emeritus; Professor of Art History, University of Western Ontario (1967-87); Deputy Director, National Gallery of Canada (1961-67); director, Vancouver Art Gallery (1959-61); curator, Art Gallery of Toronto (1957-59); research curator, Nat. Gallery of Canada (1951-57); mem. College Art Assoc. of America, Medieval Academy of America, R.S.A.; research fellow, Dumbarton Oaks, Washington (1956-57); *b* Toronto, 18 Sept., 1921; *s* of Prof. Ernest A. Dale, M.A. (Oxon); *m* Jane Gordon Laidlaw; three *s. Educ.:* University of Toronto Schools; Trinity College, Toronto; Harvard University. *Address:* 1517 Gloucester Rd., London, Ont., N6G 2S5, Canada.

DAMINATO, Vanda; Accademico Accademia Arti Incisione, Pisa; Mem. Galerie Internationale, N.Y.; M.D. Fine Art, Milano; Dumont-Landis Fine Art, N.J.; La Permanente, Milano; painter in oil, constructions, collages, prints, image inventor for industrial Groups like: "Sirti - Pirelli", "Goglio Luigi"; *b* Mezzolombardo, 1951; *d* of Giovanni Daminato, officer. *Exhib.:* Palazzo Grassi, Venezia; Galerie Internationale, N.Y.; Wallace Gallery, Miami; Museo Leonardo da Vinci, Milano; Palazzo Gran Guardia, Verona; Villa Olmo, Como; Museo

D'Annunzio, Pescara; Museo d'Arte Moderna, Malta. Creator of Maristel - Sirti - Pirelli's image "Telecom" exhbn. Geneve (1991). *Address:* Corso XXII Marzo 28, 20135 Milano, Italy. *Signs work:* "DAMINATO."

DANIELS, Alfred, R.W.S., R.B.A., A.R.C.A.; painter in oil, alkyd and acrylic; *b* London, 1924; *s* of Samuel Daniels; *m* Margot Hamilton Hill. *Educ.:* George Greens School; *studied art* at Woolwich Polytechnic, R.C.A. *Exhib.:* R.A., Belgrave Gall. *Work in permanent collections:* Tate Gallery, G.L.C., Cambridgeshire Educ. Com., Leicester Educ. Com., Sheffield A.G., Leeds University, Bezalel Museum, Israel. *Official purchases:* Hammersmith Town Hall, British Rail, O.U.P. *Publications:* Drawing and Painting (1961), Drawing Made Simple (1963), Enjoying Acrylics (1975), Painting with Acrylics (1988). *Work repro.:* Studio International, The Artist, Art and Artists, R.A. Illustrated, Arts Review. *Address:* 24 Esmond Rd., London W4. *Signs work:* "Alfred Daniels."

DANIELS, Harvey; artist in all paints and inks; *b* London, 17 June, 1936; *s* of Charles S. Daniels, artist designer; *m* Judy Stapleton; two *d*. *Studied art:* Willesden School of Art; Slade School of Fine Art (Ceri Richards). *Exhib.:* London, U.S.A., Scandinavia. *Work in permanent collections:* Museum of Modern Art, N.Y., V. & A., Towner A.G., Metropolitan Museum, N.Y., Bergens Kunstforening, Norway. *Publications:* article for catalogue of Peacock Printmakers, 'The Day Book: 378 British Artists', edited by Andrew Jones, exhbn. by Harvey Daniels. *Address:* 70 Southdown Ave., Brighton BN1 6EH. *Signs work:* "H. Daniels."

DANNATT, George, F.R.I.C.S.; painter and constructivist; music critic; *b* Blackheath, 1915; *s* of George Herbert Dannatt; *m* Ann Doncaster. *Educ.:* Colfe's School and College of Estate Management; self-taught as a painter. *Exhib.:* one-man shows: Newlyn-Orion, retrospective (1960-81); Galerie Schreiner, Basel, Switzerland (1981); Galerie Artica, Cuxhaven, Germany (1984, 1990); Michael Parkin, London (1988); New Ashgate, Farnham (1992); Dorset County Museum (1993); mixed shows: Newlyn-Orion and Penwith Galleries, Cornwall; Gordon Hepworth, Exeter; Parkin, Redfern, Austin-Desmond Galleries, London; Galerie Artica, Germany. Mem. Newlyn Society of Artists; Hon. Mem. Critics' Circle (Music Section). *Established* The George Dannatt Charitable Trust (1986). *Publications:* "One Way of Seeing", an anthology in English and German with reproductions of his work in painting and photography. Introductions to several catalogues of the sculpture of Denis Mitchell. Music criticism for the News Chronicle (1945-56), Penguin Music Magazine (1946-49). On the life and work of Arthur Bliss (Novello complete catalogue, 1982) and the D.N.B. entry upon this composer, 1971-80 Edn. Concert and record-sleeve programme notes. *Address:* East Hatch, Tisbury, Wilts. SP3 6PH. *Clubs:* Lansdowne, Savage, Garrick.

DANVERS, Joan, I.A.A.; painter in oils, potter, calligrapher; *b* Diss, Norfolk, 4 Feb., 1919; *d* of Frank W. Gotobed; *m*; one *s*. *Educ.:* Diss Grammar School; Norfolk and Norwich Hospital, S.R.N. (1940); *studied art* at Chelmsford School of Art under Clifford Smith; Belstead House, Ipswich under Cavendish Morton, R.O.I., R.I.; calligraphy at Wensom Lodge under Mr. Webster, and at Belstead House with Gerald Mynott. Silver Palette award (1966) International Amateur Art Exhbn. *Address:* Little Haven, Cromer Rd., W. Runton, Cromer, Norfolk. *Clubs:* Writtle Art Group (until 1976), Norfolk and Norwich Art Circle. *Signs work:* "Joan Danvers" and see appendix.

d'ARBELOFF, Natalie; painter, printmaker, book-artist; *b* Paris, 7 Aug., 1929; *d* of Alexandre d'Arbeloff, Prince (Russian). *Educ.:* Marymount School, N.Y.; *studied art* at Art Students' League, N.Y., Central School of Art, London. *Exhib.:* numerous group shows; solo shows include: Museum Fine Arts, Colorado Springs, Camden Arts Centre, V. & A., Rijksmuseum, Meermano-West-reenianum, The Hague. *Work in permanent collections:* V. & A., Manchester Polytechnic Library, Leeds City A.G., Library of Congress, Washington D.C., N.Y. Public Library, Harvard, Princeton, Newberry Library, Humanities Research Center, Austin, National Library, Australia, etc. *Publications:* Creating in Collage (Studio Vista), An Artist's Workbook (Studio Vista), Designing with Natural Forms (Batsford), Livres d'Artiste (own NdA Press). *Address:* 6 Cliff Villas, London NW1 9AL. *Signs work:* see appendix.

DARBISHIRE, Stephen John, B.Ed. (1971), R.B.A. (1983); painter in oil, water-colour, pastel; Governor, Brewer Arts Centre, Kendal; *b* Greenodd, Cumbria, 9 Dec., 1940; *s* of Dr. Stephen Bright Darbishire; *m* Kerry Delius; two *d. Educ.:* Ulverston Grammar School, Cumbria; *studied art* at Byam Shaw School of Art (1958-59). *Exhib.:* R.A., R.B.A., R.P., R.I.O., N.E.A.C. *Address:* Agnes Gill, Whinfell, Kendal, Cumbria LA8 9EJ. *Signs work:* "Stephen J. Darbishire."

DARBY, Philip; self taught artist in oil; *b* Birmingham, 14 June, 1938; *s* of Wilfred Darby; *m* Susan; two *s. Exhib.:* Newlyn Orion, Penwith Soc., Galerie Artica, Cuxhaven, Germany, R.W.E.A. *Work in permanent collection:* Open University. *Address:* Prospect House, Trevegean, St. Just, Penzance, Cornwall TR19 7NX. *Signs work:* "Phil Darby."

DARTON WATKINS, Christopher, M.A.(Oxon.) (1951); painter in oil, wax, collage and mixed media; *b* Alverstoke, Hants., 1928; *s* of Ricard Watkins, sculptor; *m* Torun; one *s. Educ.:* Ampleforth College; *studied art:* privately with Francis Marshall-Malagola; part time at Ruskin School of Art (1949-51). *Exhib.:* Bear Lane Gallery, Oxford, Arnolfini Gallery, Bristol, Gallery Aix, Stockholm, Seifert-Binder Gallery, Munich, Alwin Gallery, Indar Pasricha Fine Art, Anthony Dawson Fine Art, Edwin Pollard Gallery. *Work in permanent collections:* Linacre and Hertford colleges, Oxford, Liverpool University, Royal Hospital, Chelsea, S.N.E.E., Lisbon, Soc. of Apothecaries, Stockholm, Svenska Handels Bank, Stockholm, Charterhouse Bank, London. *Address:* 7 Parkstead Rd., London SW15 5HW. *Club:* Chelsea Arts. *Signs work:* "Darton Watkins."

DARWIN, Thomas Gerard, F.R.B.S. (1976), B.Ed. (1976); sculptor in resins and metal powders; *b* Standish, Lancs., 10 June, 1928; *s* of Thomas Darwin, coal miner; *m* Marie Agnes (decd.); three *s*, two *d. Educ.:* St. Peter's College, Freshfield; *studied art:* St. Mary's College, Strawberry Hill (1951-53, L. de C. Bucher, K.S.S., A.R.C.A.), Wigan School of Art (1955-57, Woffenden). *Exhib.:* one-man show: Rural and Industries Bank, Perth, W.A.; numerous joint shows. *Work in permanent collections:* Monument (Warrior and Maiden) Manzini, Swaziland; several religious works in churches and schools in England and Australia, busts in private collections and public places in Swaziland and Australia. *Address:* Ezulwini, 34 Croyden Rd., Roleystone, W.A. 6111. *Signs work:* "G. Darwin."

DAS, Jatin; artist in oil on canvas, pen and ink on paper and graphics; was Mem. General Council, LKA–National Academy of Art; *b* Orissa, India, 2 Dec., 1941; *s* of Gopinath Das; *m* (divorced); one *s*, one *d. Studied art* at Sir J. J. School of Arts, Bombay. *Exhib.:* Paris Biennale (1971), Venice Biennale (1978), Commonwealth Institute, Triennale, India 2nd., 3rd., 4th., London (1978),

Birmingham City Museum (1975), Kassel (1975), and many exhbns. in India. *Work in permanent collections:* National Gallery of Modern Art, New Delhi, Dalhem Museum, Berlin, Lalit Kala Academy, New Delhi, Smithsonian Inst., Washington, Grey Foundation, U.S.A. *Publication:* Book of Poems (1972). *Addresses:* C.12 Nizamuddin East, New Delhi 13, India; Studio: 134 Asian Games Village, Siri Fort, New Delhi-49. *Signs work:* see appendix.

DAVIDSON, Anne, D.A. (1959), A.R.B.S. (1988); sculptor in bronze, resin bronze, fibreglass; *b* Glasgow, 3 Feb., 1937; *d* of William W. Ross; *m* James G. Davidson; one *s*, three *d. Educ.:* Convent of the Sacred Heart, Aberdeen; *studied art:* Gray's School of Art (1955-59, Leo Clegg). *Exhib.:* Aberdeen Artists Soc., Institut Français, London, Posk Gallery, London, Coventry Cathedral, Dundee A.G., etc. *Work in permanent collections:* St. Mary's Cathedral, Aberdeen, St. Mary's, Inverness, and other churches; public works in Edinburgh and Aberdeen; portraits etc. in private collections. *Address:* 15 Redmoss Pk., Aberdeen AB1 4JF. *Signs work:* "Anne Davidson."

DAVIDSON DAVIS, Philomena, R.A.S.Dip., P.R.B.S., F.R.S.A.; sculptor in bronze; *b* Westminster, 1949; *d* of Thomas Davidson, violinist; *m* Michael Davis, sculptor/founder; two *d. Educ.:* Convent of Jesus and Mary, Willesden; *studied sculpture* at City and Guilds, London (1967-70, James Butler, R.A.), R.A. Schools (1970-73, Willi Soukop, R.A.). *Exhib.:* R.A. Summer Show, R.W.A. Bristol, sculpture at Margam, Chelsea Harbour Sculpture 93. April 1990 elected first woman President Royal Society of British Sculptors. *Public work:* life-size bronzes Queens Ct., Milton Keynes Shopping Centre; Lady Henry Somerset Memorial, Victoria Embankment Gdns., London. *Address:* The Mike, Davis Bronze Foundry, St James St., New Bradwell, Milton Keynes, Bucks. *Club:* Arts. *Signs work:* see appendix.

DAVIDSON-HOUSTON, Aubrey Claud; portrait artist in oil, pencil; *b* Dublin, 2 Feb., 1906; *s* of Lt.-Col. W. B. Davidson-Houston, C.M.G.; *m*; one *d. Educ.:* St. Ronan's School, W. Worthing; St. Edward's School, Oxford; Royal Military College, Sandhurst; *studied art* at St. Martin's School; Slade School. *Exhib.:* R.S.A., R.C.A., R.P., R.B.A., R.O.I., N.S., United Artists, Paris Salon. *Work repro.:* Sketch, Woman's Journal, etc. *Address:* Hillview, West End Lane, Esher, Surrey KT10 8LA. *Club:* Buck's. *Signs work:* see appendix.

DAVIES, Gordon Lionel, A.R.C.A.; artist; *b* 14 Apr., 1926; *s* of William Colin Davies. *Educ.:* Sevenoaks School; *studied art* at Camberwell School of Art (1949-50), R.C.A. (1950-53). *Exhib.:* R.A. Summer Exhbns. (1953-91); oneman shows: Wye College, Kent (1964, 1967), King St.Galleries (1973, 1975, 1977, 1979, 1983, 1985). *Work in permanent collections:* mural decorations at Wolfson College, Cambridge, Wye College, Kent, Braxted Park, Essex, Clerical and Medical Assurance Bldg., Bristol. *Publications:* botanical illustrations for House and Garden magazine (1949-70); Working with Acrylics (Search Press). *Address:* South View, Hastingleigh, Ashford, Kent TN25 5HU. *Signs work:* "Gordon Davies."

DAVIES, Iris Mary, F.S.B.A. (1986), S.W.A. (1987), B.Sc. (1949), Cambs. Cert. in Teaching (1950); artist in water-colour; retd. from teaching (1979); *b* Shotley, Ipswich, 4 Oct., 1919; *d* of Frederick William Wheeler (decd.); *m* David Maldwyn Davies, B.Sc.; one *d. Educ.:* University College of Wales, Aberystwyth, Cambridge University; *studied art* at Cambridge University and privately. *Exhib.:* R.I. (1982-89), S.B.A. (1986-93), S.W.A. (1987-93). *Address:* High Trees, Minstead, Lyndhurst, Hants. SO43 7FX. *Signs work:* "Mary Davies."

DAVIES, Ivor, N.D.D. (1956), A.T.D. (1957), Ph.D. (Edin.) (1975), R.C.A. (1993); artist/painter in oil, tempera, water-colour, gouache, crayon; *b* Wales, 9 Nov., 1935. *Studied art* at Cardiff (1952-56) and Swansea (1956-57) Colleges of Art, Lausanne University, Edinburgh University. *Exhib.:* over 20 one-man shows worldwide since 1963, also Multi-media Destruction in Art 1960's. *Work in permanent collections:* Deal Coll. Dallas, A.C.G.B., W.A.C., National Museum of Wales, etc. *Publications:* articles on Modern Art History, others in Welsh language journals; illustrations: Spirit (1971), Rubaiyat (1981), Science and Art (1981). *Address:* 99 Windsor Rd., Penarth CF6 1JF. *Signs work:* "Ivor Davies."

DAVIES, Raymond Edgar Monsen, M.Pharm., F.R. Pharm.S.; artist in water-colour; lately Senior asst. editor (Science), The Pharmaceutical Journal; Liveryman, Society of Apothecaries of London; Freeman of the City of London; *b* Bridgend, Glam., 30 Dec., 1924; *s* of Caleb William Davies, master draper; *m* Avril Duff; two *s. Educ.:* Llandovery College and University of Wales. *Exhib.:* R.A. (1982, 1985, 1986), R.I., R.B.A., R.M.S., N.S., etc. and locally in Surrey. *Publication:* contributor to Leisure Painter. *Address:* Rowan Ley, 47 Amberley Drive, Woodham, Weybridge, Surrey KT15 3SN. *Club:* Savage. *Signs work:* "Raymond E.M. Davies," miniatures "R.E.M.D."

DAVIS, Derek Maynard, F.C.P.A.; Artist in Residence, University of Sussex (1967); potter; Mem. International Academy of Ceramics, Mem. Contemporary Applied Arts, Craft Potters Assoc.; *b* London, 1926; *s* of James A. Davis, craftsman; *m* Ruth; one *s. Educ.:* Emanuel School, Wandsworth; *studied painting* at Central School of Arts and Crafts, London, under Keith Vaughan, Robert Buhler. *Exhib.:* Istanbul, Munich, Toronto, Zurich, Tokyo, Paris, Primavera (London and Cambridge). *Work in permanent collections:* Paisley Museum, V. & A., Portsmouth Museum, Prinsenhof, Holland, Southampton Museum, Keramion, Frechen, Germany, University of Sussex, Bradford Museum, Garth Clark Collection, U.S.A. *Address:* Duff House, Maltravers St., Arundel, Sussex BN18 9AP.

DAVIS, James, L.I.F.A.; Freeman the Worshipful Company Painter-Stainers (1972); Freeman of the City of London (1973); sculptor, carver and restorer in stone, marble; *b* London, 16 July, 1926; *s* of James E. Davis, engineer; *m* Joan Davis; one *s*, one *d. Educ.:* Eastbrook Boys School, Dagenham, Essex; *studied art* at Sir John Cass School of Art (1949-53) under Bainbridge Copnal. *Exhib.:* Guildhall; Leighton House, Royal Exchange, Mall Galleries. *Work in permanent collections:* Painters Hall, Chelsea and Kensington Town Hall, Community Centre, Shoeburyness, Barclay International, Gracechurch St., St. Nicholas Church, Elm Park, Essex, St. Nicholas Church, Canewdon, Essex, Hyde Park Corner, London W1. *Address:* Studio Workshop, 39A West Rd., Shoeburyness, Essex, SS3 9DR. *Signs work:* "J. Davis."

DAVIS, John Warren, M.C., A.T.D.; sculptor in wood, stone and metal; *b* Christchurch, 24 Feb., 1919; *s* of Capt. J. Warren Davis, M.C.; *m* Evelyn Ann; three *s*, one *d. Educ.:* Bedford School; *studied art* at Westminster School of Art (1937-39), under Bernard Meninsky and Mark Gertler; Brighton College of Art (1948-52), under James Woodford, R.A. *Work in permanent collections:* Cardiff, Leeds, Southampton, New York, Arts Council, Contemporary Art Soc., London and Houston, Texas. *Address:* Northfields Farm, Eastergate, Chichester, Sussex PO20 6RX.

DAVIS, Kate, B.A. (1982), H.Dip. (1986), M.A. (Status) Oxon. (1992), Stanley Picker Fellow (1986-87), Whitechapel Young Artist of Year (1988); sculptor/lecturer in a wide range including mirror, paper, photography, drawing; Tutor of

Fine Art, Ruskin School of Drawing, Oxford; *b* Chesham, Bucks., 23 Feb., 1960; *m* A. Ruethi; one *d. Educ.*: Loreto College, St. Albans; *studied art* at Herts. College of Art and Design (1978-79), Falmouth School of Art (1979-82), Slade School of Fine Art (1983-85). *Exhib.*: Whitechapel A.G., and numerous group shows. Work in private collections. *Address*: c/o Anderson O'Day Gallery, 255 Portobello Rd., London W11 1LR. *Signs work:* "K.A. DAVIS," "KAD" or not at all.

DAVIS, Robin; self-taught painter in oil; *b* Bournemouth, 28 Feb., 1925; one *s,* one *d. Educ.*: St. Catherine's College, Oxford; Birkbeck College, London. *Exhib.*: one-man shows: Woodstock Gallery, London (1960), New Vision Centre, London (1964), Aston University, B'ham (1965), Horizon Gallery, London (1988). *Address:* Chy-an-Gwel, Britons Hill, Penzance, Cornwall TR18 3AF. *Signs work:* "Robin Davis."

DAWSON, Edward, B.A. (1964); artist in oil; *b* Northumberland, 1941; *m* Gillian Furlong, B.A. *Educ.*: Dukes Grammar School, Alnwick; *studied art* at King's College, Durham University (1960-64, Victor Pasmore). *Exhib.*: one-man shows, Furneaux Gallery (1973-74), Edwin Pollard Gallery (1985, 1987, 1989, 1991). *Address:* New Barn House, Buckhorn Weston, Dorset. *Club:* N.E.A.C. *Signs work:* "Dawson."

DAWSON, Gladys, A.R.C.A. (1943), R.C.A. (1946), F.R.S.A. (1952), S.W.A. (1953), V.P.S.W.A. (1976), P.S.W.A. (1982-85), P.P.S.W.A. (1985-); artist in water-colour, oil, black and white; *b* Castleton, Rochdale; *d* of Ernest Jacques Dawson; *m* Ronald G. Woodruff, Mines and Geology Dept., Nairobi, Kenya. *Educ.*: private schools; Heatherley's (1936-39). *Exhib.*: R.C.A., R.I., R.W.A., S.W.A., Lancashire Artists, Preston, Walker Art Gallery. Liverpool, etc.; one-man shows, N. Wales, Trinidad, Epsom, etc. *Work in permanent collections:* Birkenhead A.G., Shire Hall, Archives Dept., Anglesey. *Work repro.:* Illustrations in books and magazines. *Address:* 10 Courtlands Cres., Banstead, Surrey SM7 2PJ. *Signs work:* "G. Dawson" (G and D linked together, horizontal stroke of G into top of D).

DAWSON, Patricia Vaughan; printmaker, sculptor and writer; *b* Liverpool, 23 Jan., 1925; *d* of Theodore James Wright, army officer; *m* James N. Dawson; one *s,* two *d. Educ.*: Croham Hurst School; *studied art* at Croydon School of Art (1941-45) under Reginald Marlow and Ruskin Spear. *Exhib.*: Bear Lane Gallery. *Work in permanent collections:* B.M., Bibliothèque Nationale. *Publication:* The Artist Looks at Life (a series of books and slide strips published by Visual Publications introducing art to children). *Address:* 99 Corve St., Ludlow, Salop.

DAWSON, Peter, R.I., B.Ed.; painter in water-colour, oil; teacher; Adviser for Art and Design, Hertfordshire; *b* Leeds, 19 Mar., 1947; *s* of William Henry Dawson, painter and policeman, and Mary Elizabeth Dawson; *m* (1) Andrea Dixon, (2) Sarah Harrison. *Educ.*: Roundhay School, Leeds; *studied art* at Bingley College of Educ. (1967-71). *Exhib.*: R.I., Yorkshire Artists, Hitchin Museum, Luton A.G., October Gallery, San Francisco, Federation of Canadian Artists Gallery, Vancouver, Fry Art Museum, Seattle. *Work in permanent collections:* Herts. Educ. Authority, Luton A.G. *Publication:* Co-author, Albania – A Guide and Illustrated Journal. *Address:* Rosemary Cottage, Little Hadham, Ware, Herts. SG11 2BP. *Signs work:* "P. Dawson" or "Peter Dawson."

DAY, D.P.A., Prof., A.G.P.P. (1979), S.G.A. (1986); artist in oil and water-colour. *Exhib.*: Mall Galleries and S.G.A. *Address:* 20 The Avenue, Bedford Pk., Chiswick, London W4 1HY. *Signs work:* "Daphne Day."

DAY, Lucienne, R.D.I., A.R.C.A. (1940), F.C.S.D.; textile designer; Royal Designer for Industry (1962); *b* Coulsdon, Surrey, 1917 *d* of Felix Conradi; *m*

Robin Day; one *d. Educ.:* Convent of Notre Dame di Sion, Worthing; *studied art:* Croydon School of Art (1934-37), R.C.A. (1937-40). *Exhib.:* London, Manchester, Zürich, Amsterdam, Milan, Dublin, Oslo, Bergen, Stavanger, Washington, Toronto, Bulawayo, New York, Tokyo, Kyoto, Gothenberg. *Work in permanent collections:* V. & A., museums of Cranbrook, Michigan, Museum of Industrial Design Trondheim, Norway, Röhsska Konstslöjd Musuem, Gothenburg, Sweden, Musee des Arts Decoratifs, Montreal, and Art Inst. of Chicago. *Address:* 49 Cheyne Walk, Chelsea, London SW3 5LP. *Signs silk mosaic tapestries:* "L."

DAY, Robin, O.B.E., A.R.C.A., F.C.S.D., R.D.I.; designer; *b* High Wycombe, Bucks., 1915; *studied art* at High Wycombe School of Art and R.C.A. *Exhib.:* Museum of Modern Art, New York, I.C.A., Triennale, Milan (1951), Copenhagen, Oslo, Stavanger, Bergen, Zürich, Canada. *Work in permanent collections:* Museum of Modern Art, New York, Trondheim Industrial Art Museum, V. & A. *Work repro.:* many architectural and design publications here and abroad. *Address:* 49 Cheyne Walk, Chelsea, London SW3 5LP.

DAYKIN, Michael, M.A. (R.C.A.); artist, curator; *b* Yorkshire, 1947. *Studied art* at Watford School of Art (1970-71), St. Martin's School of Art (1971-74), R.C.A. (1974-77). *Exhib.:* City University Gallery, Cleveland College of Art Gallery, XO Gallery, The Figure of Eight Gallery. *Work in collections:* Northern Arts, Brown and Wood, Benchmark Holdings (commission), Quaglino's (commission). *Address:* 9 Lowder House, Wapping Lane, London E1 9RJ. *Signs work:* "Daykin."

DEAKIN, Liz (née Boatswain), S.W.A.; artist in water-colour, gouache and acrylics of landscapes, flower painting, interiors, silk painting and murals; *b* Dorchester, 1929; marriage dissolved; two children. *Trained* at Poole School of Art, and with Edward Wessen. Runs painting courses and gives demonstrations to societies. Works in many private collections throughout the world, including the Royal Family. *Publications:* "Deakin's Dorset"; designs hotel brochures. *Address:* 3 Hunters Mead, Motcombe, Shaftesbury SP7 9QG. *Signs work:* "Liz Deakin."

DEAKINS, Cyril Edward, A.R.E. (1948), A.T.D. (1947); painter in tempera and water-colour, wood-engraver; *b* Bearwood, nr. Birmingham, 5 Oct., 1916; *s* of Charles H. Deakins; *m*; one *s*, one *d. Educ.:* Christ's College, Finchley; *studied art* under J. C. Moody, Norman Janes, at Hornsey School of Art. *Exhib.:* R.A., N.E.A.C., R.E., R.B.A., R.I. *Official purchase:* Print Collectors' Club, presentation print, 1948.Third prize, Ellingham Mill E. Anglian Artists Exhbn. (1977), Beecroft A. G., Westcliff (1986). *Work repro.:* four postage stamp designs for Govt. of Bermuda, 1953, book and magazine illustrations; articles on water-colour, Leisure Painter since 1977. *Address:* 1 Mill Lane, Dunmow, Essex CM6 1BG. *Signs work:* "C.D." or "Cyril Deakins."

DEAKINS, Sylvia, A.T.D. (1946), S.G.F.A. (1986), C.D.S. (1987); painter and illustrator in oil, gouache, pastel, ink, collage; Pres. Cambridge Drawing Soc. (1994); *b* Eccleshill, W. Yorks., 18 Oct., 1924; *d* of A.N. Leeming; *m* C.E. Deakins; one *s*, one *d. Educ.:* Hendon County Grammar; *studied art* at Hornsey College of Art (1941-46, Douglas Percy Bliss, Russell Reeve, Francis Winter). *Exhib.:* R.A., R.B.A., N.E.A.C., and numerous galleries in E. Anglia. *Publications:* illustrated many for O.U.P. Longmans, Ward Lock, including A Beginner's Bible (1958), and Listening to Children Talking (1976). *Address:* 1 Mill La., Gt. Dunmow, Essex CM6 1BG. *Signs work:* "Sylvia Deakins."

DEAKINS, Thomas William (Tom), B.A. (Hons.) (1980), A.T.C. (1982), Charles Spence Memorial prize (1977); painter in oil, acrylic, body colour, drawing media; *b* Barnet, 8 Dec., 1957; *m* Ann Logan. *Educ.:* Newport Grammar School, Essex; *studied art* at University of Newcastle upon Tyne (1976-80, Kenneth Rowntree, Derwent Wise). *Exhib.:* R.A. Summer Shows since 1983, R.S.A., R.G.I., R.O.I. Annual Shows, Medici Gallery (1989), William Hardy Glasgow (1991). *Work in permanent collections:* Hatton Gallery, University of Newcastle, Epping Forest District Museum, Beecroft A.G. Westcliff on Sea. *Address:* Clock House Cottage, 79A The Causeway, Gt. Dunmow, Essex CM6 2AB. *Signs work:* "T. Deakins" or "T.D."

DEAN, Beryl, M.B.E. (1975), A.R.C.A. (1937), F.S.D-C. (1970); freelance designer, author, lecturer, embroiderer; *b* Bromley, 1911; *d* of Herbert Charles Dean; *m* W. M. Phillips; two stepsons. *Educ.:* Bromley High School, G.P.D.S.T.; *studied art* at Bromley School of Art (1932), Royal School of Needlework (1929), Royal College of Art (1935). *Exhib.:* solo shows, Ecclesiastical Embroidery: St. Paul's Cathedral, etc., and abroad. *Work in permanent collections:* V. & A., Collection of the Embroiderers Guild, London, etc. *Publications:* Ecclesiastical Embroidery, Ideas for Church Embroidery, Church Needlework, Creative appliqué, Embroidery in Religion and Ceremonial, Church Embroidery, Designing Stitched Textiles for the Church. *Address:* 59 Thornhill Sq., London N1 1BE.

DEAN, Dorothy, S.W.A., A.M.N.S.; artist in gouache, oil, pastel; *b* 14 May 1920; *d* of A.J. Dean (decd.); *m* K.W. Howard; one *s*. *Educ.:* Bromley County School, Kent; *studied art* at Goldsmiths' School of Art (1936-39), Eastbourne Art School, Guildford (part-time post war). *Exhib.:* R.I., R.O.I., R.B.A., R.P.S., P.S., numerous solo and shared exhbns. in S. England. *Address:* Ashley Cottage, Bentworth, Alton, Hants. GU34 5RH. *Signs work:* "Dorothy Dean" and "D. Dean."

DEAN, John H. W., R.M.S., S.M., F.R.S.A.; Fellow British Soc. of Painters; self taught artist in oil of large river landscapes, miniatures on ivory in oil; *b* Grassington, N. Yorks., 25 Mar., 1930; *s* of Newland Walton Dean, master butcher. *Educ.:* Grassington C. of E. School. *Exhib.:* R.M.S., U.A., S.M., Yorkshire Artists, International Art Fair, Olympia, Salon des Nation, Paris. *Work purchased* by Shell Oil International, A.E. Auto Parts, John Ward Textiles, Lord Harewood, The Earl of Burlington, etc.; and in most countries of the world. Limited Edition prints by Delta Prints, Guernsey. *Address:* Norwood, 13 Southwood La., Grassington, Skipton, N. Yorks. BD23 5NA. *Signs work:* "John Dean, R.M.S." in black on oils, "J. Dean" in black on miniatures.

DEAN, Ronald Herbert, R.S.M.A. (1970), F.C.I.I. (1965); self-taught painter in water-colour and oil; Insurance broker; *b* Farnborough, Hants., 1929; *s* of Herbert Dean, B.E.M.; *m* Audrey Grace Payne; two *d*. *Educ.:* Farnborough Grammar School. *Exhib.:* R.S.M.A., R.I., R.B.A., Biarritz, Salem Or., U.S.A., National Maritime Museum. *Address:* 8 Glebelands, Bidborough, Tunbridge Wells, Kent. *Club:* Tonbridge Art Group. *Signs work:* "RONALD DEAN" printed.

DEANE, Frederick, R.P. (1972); painter in oil, gouache, pastel; *b* Manchester, 1924; *m* Audrey Craig; two *s*, one *d*. *Studied art* at Manchester College of Art (1940-43), R.A. Schools (1946-51, Philip Connard). Served with Para Regt. 1st Airborne Div. (1943-45). Visiting tutor: Manchester College of Art (1952-60), City of London Polytechnic (1970-82). *Exhib.:* R.A., R.P. *Work in permanent collections:* Chatsworth; Oxford, Cambridge, Manchester, Rhodes, McGill and

Kent Universities; Manchester City A.G. *Address:* Penrallt Goch, Llan Ffestiniog, Gwynedd LL41 4NS. *Club:* Chelsea Arts. *Signs work:* "Deane."

DEANE, Jasper, Cert.F.A. (Oxon.) (1971), Dip.F.A. (1974), M.A. (1978); artist in water-colour and oil; *b* Ches., 15 July, 1952. *Educ.:* Bryanston School, Blandford; *studied art* at Ruskin School of Drawing (1969-71), Ealing School of Art (1972-74), R.C.A. (1975-78). *Exhib.:* Ruskin R8 Show, Oxford Graduate Centre (1970), Folio Soc. (1976, 1977, 1978), Valentine Show, Illustrators Gallery (1977), The Animal in Art, R.C.A. (1977), Spirit of London, Royal Festival Hall (1978), 'Well Travelled', Gardiner Centre, University of Sussex (1987), 'Maginot Line' drawings for an opera, Riverside Studios (1988), 'Breakthrough' 25 years of illustration at the R.C.A. (1988); one-man shows: Cale Art (1985), Stephen Bartley Gallery (1986, 1987), Friends of the Arts, London (1990), 'Artistes 93 avec Stop à la Destruction du Monde', Paris (1993). *Publications:* A Duck Flies Up (Ealing, 1974), Cornish Travel Sketches (R.C.A., 1978), The Pillow Book of Siesho-Nagon (Folio Soc., 1979), Ink Flamingoes (1981), Renditions Magazine (University of Hong Kong, 1982), Field Magazine, Sporting Horse. *Address:* 7B Coverdale Rd., London W12 8JJ. *Club:* Old Students Assoc. R.C.A. *Signs work:* "J.D." or "Jasper Deane."

de BURGH, Lydia, R.U.A., U.W.S., U.W.A., Dip.Mem. Chelsea Art Soc. (1958-65); portrait and landscape painter in oil and water-colour; lecturer; *b* London, 3 July, 1923; *d* of Capt. Charles de Burgh, D.S.O., R.N. *Educ.:* privately; *studied art* under Sonya Mervyn, R. P. (1948-51), Byam Shaw School of Art (1952), Edward Wesson, R.I. *Exhib.:* London, N. Ireland Office (1955), Boston, Vose Gallery (1957), R.P., R.B.A., R.G.I., R.U.A., Royal Birmingham, Wildlife Artists, etc. *Work in permanent collections:* (personal sittings) of H.M. The Queen and the Royal Family; numerous works in public and private collections. *Publication:* autobiography, "Lydia's Story" (1991). *Address:* Coolattin Lodge, Seaforde, Downpatrick, Co. Down, N. Ireland BT30 8PD. *Signs work:* "L. de Burgh, R.U.A."

de FRANCIA, Peter; painter in oil, author; Principal, DFA, School of Art, Goldsmiths College, University of London; Professor, School of Painting, R.C.A. London (1972-87); *b* Beaulieu, Alpes Maritimes, France, 25 Jan., 1921; *s* of Fernand de Francia. *Studied art:* Academy of Brussels, Slade School. *Work in permanent collections:* Museum of Modern Art, N.Y., Arts Council of Gt. Britain, Tate Gallery, V. & A., National Gallery of Modern Art, Prague, B. M., Imperial War Museum; private collections in U.K., and U.S.A. *Publications:* Fernand Léger (Cassells, 1968-69); Fernand Léger (Yale University Press, London, Sept. 1983); "Untitled" 49 drawings (Brondums Forlag, Copenhagen 1989). *Address:* 44 Surrey Sq., London SE17 2JX. *Signs work:* see appendix.

de FRESNES, the Baron (Robert); *b* Conroy-Robertson, Capt. Royal Artillery, assumed by deed poll 1944 surname of de Fresnes in lieu of patronymic upon succeeding French title; artist in oil on canvas., water-colour and gouache in abstractions, flowers, still life, portraits, thoroughbred race horses: favourite works, a Pieta and a Crucifixion; artist and designer of Interiors (now consultant), personal mem. of Interior Decorators and Designers Assoc., London; *b* Scotland, 6 July, 1908; *s* of James Conroy-Robertson, designer engineer; *m* Lady Fiona, 4th *d* of the late 12th Countess of Loudoun; four *s*, one *d*. *Educ.:* privately; *studied art* at Glasgow School of Art (1930, Sir William Hutchison, R.S.A., Hugh Adam Crawford, R.S.A., worked with the late Sir Stanley Spencer, R.A., Augustus John, R.A.), D.A. in Art and Architecture. Post-graduate studies in London, Paris, Milan and Perugia. Contemporary of Colquhoun and McBride;

studied painting of thoroughbreds with Sir Alfred Munnings, R.A. *Work in private collections:* France, Belgium, U.S.A. and Brazil. *Address:* Cessnock Castle, Galston, nr. Kilmarnock KA4 8LJ, Scotland. *Club:* Ayr County. *Signs work:* "de FRESNES."

DE GOEDE, Julien Maximilien; painter in mixed media; *b* Rotterdam, Holland, 20 May, 1937; *s* of Maximilien Julien de Goede, builder. *Educ.:* High School, Nijmegen; *studied art* at Academie voor Beeldende Kunsten en Kunstnijverheid, Arnhem (1953-55), Eindhoven School of Art (1955-56), Julian Ashton School of Art, Sydney (1957-58). *Exhib.:* Three one-man shows, Canberra, four one-man shows, Grabowski, London, two House, London, one Riverside Studios, London. *Work in permanent collections:* Australian National University, Leicestershire Educ. Com., Contemporary Art Society, Eastern Arts Assoc., Laing A.G., Newcastle upon Tyne, Museum Sztuki, Lodz, Poland, Arts Council of Gt. Britain, Bedfordshire Educ. Service, City Art Gallery, Bristol, Deutsche Bank, Unilever, Jhonson & Jhonson. *Address:* 71 Stepney Green, London E1. *Signs work:* "Jules de Goede."

de GOYA (Gerendassy), Gyorgy, H.F., Prof., F.R.S.A. (1979), D.Phil. (1939), M.des B.A. (1940), D.P.A. (1948); artist in oil, aesthetician, author, lecturer; *b* Budapest, 29 Aug., 1915; *s* of Laszlo, M.D.; *m* I.D. Sebestyen; one *s*, two *d*. *Educ.:* Budapest University of Economy and Science; *studied art* at Budapest Fine Arts Academy, Sorbonne, l'Ecole des Beaux Arts, Academie Julian; Lectured: Budapest Academy, Reading, Hampstead, Courtauld Inst., Oxford College of Arts; Masters: (Gabor, Egry, Csok, Derain, Kupka, Jonvier, M. Weiss, P. Guilbot-Trepas). *Exhib.:* Budapest, Frankfurt, Milan, Oxford, London, Watford, Windsor, St. Albans, Peterborough, Hemel Hempstead, Vienna, Paris, Amsterdam, Brussels, Southampton, Baden Baden, Bonn, Vancouver, Geneva. *Publications:* Les Miniaturists de la Renaissance Française; Egyptian Murals; Danube, Volga. *Address:* 33 Beech Drive, Berkhamsted, Herts. HP4 2HG. *Clubs:* F.P.S., I.C.A., Unesco-A.I.A.P., R.S.A., F.I.B.A. *Signs work:* "de Goya."

de GREY, Sir Roger, K.C.V.O. (1991), P.P.R.A., P.R.A. (1984), R.A. (1969), Hon. A.R.C.A. (1959); Principal, City and Guilds of London Art School since 1973; *b* 18 Apr., 1918; *s* of Nigel de Grey, C.M.G., O.B.E.; *m* Flavia Hatt (née Irwin); two *s*, one *d*. *Educ.:* Eton College; *studied art* at Chelsea School of Art. War Service 1939-45: Royal West Kent Yeomanry (1939-42), R.A.C. (1942-45) (U.S. Bronze Star 1945). Lecturer, Dept. of Fine Art, King's College, Newcastle upon Tyne (1947-51), Master of Painting, King's College (1951-53), Senior Tutor, later Reader in Painting, R.C.A. (1953-73), Treasurer, R.A. (1976). *Work in permanent collections:* Arts Council; Contemporary Arts Soc.; Chantrey Bequest; Queensland Gallery, Brisbane; Manchester, Carlisle, Bradford and other provincial galleries. *Addresses:* City and Guilds of London Art School, 124 Kennington Park Rd., London SW11 4DJ; 5 Camer St., Meopham, Kent.

DE LA FOUGÈRE, Lucette, R.B.A., R.O.I., N.S.; painter in oil, water-colour, gouache, and sculptor in ceramics; *b* London. *Educ.:* both in Touraine, France, and London; *studied art* under Leopold Pascal and Krome Barratt, P.P.R.O.I., R.B.A. *Work in permanent collections:* The National Museum of Wales, Cardiff. *Exhib.:* R.A., Royal Society of British Artists, Royal Institute of Oil Painters, National Soc. of Painters, Printers and Engravers; one-man show: Mall Galleries; works permanently on tour in Great Britain and U.S.A. *Address:* The Studio, 20 Lower Common South, Putney, London SW15. *Club:* Chelsea Arts. *Signs work:* "FOUGÈRE."

DELHANTY, Denys, A.T.D. (1949), R.W.A. (1963); artist in collage, oil, water-colour, gouache; past Hon. Sec. and council mem. R.W.A.; Head of Art, Cheltenham Ladies College (1951-1964), Senior Lecturer, Rolle College, Exmouth and Gloucester (1964-1981); *b* Cardiff, 13 Oct., 1925; *m* Kate Ormrod; three *s*, one *d. Educ.:* St. Illtyd's College, Cardiff; *studied art* at Cardiff College of Art (1942-44, 1949-51, Ceri Richards). *Exhib.:* R.W.A., etc. *Work in permanent collections:* R.W.A., Welsh Arts Council, Cheltenham A.G. *Address:* Combe House, Sheepscombe, Stroud, Glos. GL6 7RG. *Signs work:* "Denys Delhanty."

DELHANTY, Kate Elizabeth, D.F.A. (Slade); artist in oil; artist mem. R.W.A.; taught art at Cheltenham Ladies College (1953-1960); *b* London, 8 Nov., 1928; *d* of Frank Ormrod, artist/lecturer; *m* Denys Delhanty; three *s*, one *d. Educ.:* Downe House, Newbury, Berks.; *studied art* at Reading University, Slade School of Fine Art (1950-53, Prof. Coldstream). *Exhib.:* R.A., Bristol (R.W.A.), Cheltenham A.G., Bristol Guild, etc. *Work in permanent collections:* R.W.A., Cheltenham A.G. *Address:* Combe House, Sheepscombe, Stroud, Glos. GL6 7RG. *Signs work:* "Kate Delhanty."

de MAJO, Willy M., M.B.E., F.C.S.D., Hon. F.S.T.D., Hon. B.N.O., Hon. S.R.F. (S.A.F.F.T.), Hon. C.B.G., Hon. G.D.A.; graphic and industrial designer; founder Pres., I.C.O.G.R.A.D.A.; co-ordinating designer, Festival of Britain, N.I. (1951); consultant designer to: Charles Letts & Co., John Millar & Sons, Cronmatch Ltd., Ti-Well Ltd., *b* Vienna, 25 July, 1917; *s* of Maks de Majo; *m* Veronica Mary Booker; three *d. Educ.:* Commercial Academy, Vienna; auto-didact. *Exhib.:* Vienna, Belgrade, Paris, London, Belfast, Brussels, Zagreb, Brno, Bulawayo, U.S.A., Japan and Canada. Recipient of 1969 S.I.A.D. Design Medal for outstanding services to international design. *Address:* 99 Archel Rd., London W14 9QL. *Signs work:* "W. M. de MAJO," or "de MAJO."

DEMARCO, Richard, O.B.E., l'Ordre des Arts et Lettres de France, Cavaliere de la Reppublica d'Italia, Gold Order of Merit Republic of Poland, Hon. F.R.I.A.S., Hon.D.F.A. (A.C.A.), R.S.W., S.S.A.; water-colourist/printmaker in water-colour, gouache, pen and ink, screen printing, etching; Prof. of European Cultural Studies, Kingston University; Artistic Director, Demarco European Art Foundation; *b* Edinburgh, 9 July, 1930; *m* Anne Muckle. *Educ.:* Holy Cross Academy, Edinburgh; *studied art* at Edinburgh College of Art (1949-54, Sir William Gillies, Leonard Rosoman). *Exhib.:* over sixty one-man shows including Third Eye Centre, Aberdeen Artspace, Editions Alecto Gallery. *Work in permanent collections:* S.N.G.M.A., Dundee City A.G., V. & A., Aberdeen A.G., Hunterian Museum Glasgow, S.A.C., Edinburgh City A.G., Citibank, Chemical Bank, Bank of Scotland, Royal Bank of Scotland, Clydesdale Bank, H.R.H. Prince Philip, H.R.H. Prince Charles. *Publication:* The Road to Meikle Seggie—The Artist as Explorer. *Addresses:* (home) 23A Lennox St., Edinburgh EH4 1PY; (office) Kingston University, Millenium House, 21 Eden St., Kingston-on-Thames, Surrey. *Club:* Scottish Arts. *Signs work:* "Richard Demarco."

DEMEL, Richard, Ph.D. (1981), Art Diploma (1948), F.I.L.Incorp. Linguist, F.R.S.A.; retd. art master, writer; lecturer: Univ. of Padova; stained glass artist (transparent mosaic method inventor), painter, engraver; *b* Ustron, Poland, 21 Dec., 1921; *s* of Joseph (artist) and Anna (née Bieta); *m* Anna Parisi; one *s*, one *d. Educ.:* Andrychow and Biala-Bielsko; *studied art* at Accad. d. Belle Arti (1945-47), Rome, Polish Accad. Art Centre, Rome, London (1945-49); London University Slade School (1949); LCC Central School of Art (1949-51) B.A. Lang, Venice University; M.A. Lang, Polish University, London; asst. to J.

131

Nuttgens (St. Etheldreda's Church windows); asst. lecturer to Prof. M. Bohusz-Szyszko. *Exhib.:* 22 one-man and 110 collective; ITV film (1961), BBC TV on pupils' work (with Miró 1962); Polish TV Documentary (1992); designed and exec; H.C. Comu. S.Leonards O.S. (4); Rome (1); 3 mosaic windows: Cathedral, Padua; Duomo Cittadella (4); Codevigo Church (2) Italy. *Biography and work repro.:* in 60 art encyclopaedias and art publications. *Address:* Via S. Domenico 21-35030 Tencarola, Padova, Italy. *Signs work:* see appendix.

de MEO, P. (Pamela Synge); artist in oil and water-colour; *b* London, 2 Sept., 1920; *d* of Dr. Boris Vinyk; *m* Major Brian Synge; three *s*. *Educ.:* Cheltenham Ladies' College; *studied art* at St. Martin's College of Art, Chelsea School of Art, Heatherleys (1953). *Exhib.:* R.A. (1988), Paris Salon, R.B.A. Galleries, Chelsea Artists, Bankside Gallery (G.B., U.S.S.R. Assoc., 1985), Mall Galleries, Bowmore Gallery, Halkin St., W1 (1989); one-man show: Tradescant Trust Museum (1988). *Address:* 4 Pembroke Cl., Grosvenor Cres., London SW1X 7ET. *Clubs:* Dover St. Arts, Chelsea Arts. *Signs work:* "P. de Meo."

de MERIC, Rosalie, F.F.P.S., B.A. (Fine Art) Norwich; painter; *b* 1916; *d* of V. E. de Meric; *m* Thomas Blackburn, 1945; one *d*. *Exhib.:* E. Anglia and London (England & Co. Needham St., W11, and Art for Offices, Dock St., E1.). *Address:* Lavender Cottage, Westleton, Saxmundham, Suffolk IP17 3AG. *Signs work:* "de Meric."

DENAHY, John Albert, N.E.A.C. (1980); painter in oil, water-colour and pastel; *b* London, 1922; *s* of Joseph Francis Denahy; *m* Judith Eveline Partington; two *d*. *Educ.:* St. Joseph's, Deptford; *studied art* at Eltham Art Centre. *Exhib.:* R.A., N.E.A.C., R.B.A., R.W.E., W.H. Pattersons (N.E.A.C.); one-man show Anna-Mei Chadwick Gallery (1989, 1991, 1993); mixed exhbns.: Moya Bucknall Fine Art, Woodlands A.G., Greenwich Theatre, Tudor Barn, Eltham. Prize winner N.E.A.C. Centenary Exhbn. (1986), Daler Rowney 1st prize R.B.A. (1987), prize winner Ass. Artistique de la Banque de France (1986). *Work in permanent collections:* B.P. International, Bank of England Services Ltd., I.B.M. *Publications:* Leisure Artist magazine. *Address:* 37 Middleton Ave., Sidcup, Kent DA14 6JJ. *Club:* Arts. *Signs work:* "J.D." or "J. Denahy."

DENISON, David; surrealist artist in acrylic and oil; tutor, Prison Staff College, Wakefield; *b* Wakefield, 21 May, 1939; *s* of Ernest Denison; *m* Linda; one *s*, two *d*. *Educ.:* Snapethorpe Secondary Modern School, Wakefield; *studied art* at Doncaster College of Art (1972). *Exhib.:* Wakefield, Skipton, London, Keighley, Bradford, Camden Arts Centre; one-man shows: Manor House Public A.G., Ilkley (1970, 1977), Goole Museum and A.G. (1971), Wakefield Museum and A.G. (1972, 1974), Leeds City Gallery (1973), Doncaster A.G. (1973), Arthur Koestler Exhbn. London (1977), Bradford Cartwright Hall (1980), Angela Flowers Gallery, Arts Council of Gt. Britain. *Work in permanent collections:* Brighton Museum and A.G., Sir Roland Penrose Collection. *Publication:* illustrated The Battle of Wilderness Wood by R. Adams. *Address:* 58 Station Rd., Burley in Wharfedale, W. Yorks. *Signs work:* "D. Denison."

DENLEY-HILL, William George, A.R.C.A. (1929); artist in water-colour and oil; H.M. Inspector Art Schools (1949-72); Principal, Newton Abbott School of Art (1939-45), Bournville School of Art (1945-49); *b* London, 27 June, 1906; *m* G.M. Denley-Hill, A.R.C.A.; two *s*. *Studied art* at R.C.A. (1926-29, Sir William Rothenstein). *Exhib.:* Manor House Fine Arts, Cardiff, York City A.G. *Work in permanent collections:* B'ham City A.G., Newport A.G. *Publication:* illustrated numerous children's books for Blackwell of Oxford. *Address:* 19 Lower St., Merriott, nr. Crewkerne, Somerset TA16 5NL. *Signs work:* "W.G.D. Hill."

DENNIS, Jeffrey, B.A. (1980); artist in oil; *b* 15 July, 1958. *Educ.:* Colchester Royal Grammar School; *studied art* at Slade School of Fine Art (1976-80). *Exhib.:* 14 solo and many mixed shows in U.K., U.S.A. and Europe since 1979. *Work in permanent collections:* Tate Gallery, Arts Council, British Council, Stedelijk Museum Amsterdam. *Address:* 63A Napier Rd., London N17 6YG. *Signs work:* "DENNIS" or not at all.

DENTON, Kenneth Raymond, R.S.M.A., F.C.S.D., F.R.S.A., I.S.M.P.; landscape and marine artist in oil; *b* Chatham, 20 Aug., 1932; *s* of Stanley Charles Denton; *m* Margaret Denton; three *s. Educ.:* Troy Town School, Rochester; *studied art* at Rochester School of Art and Technical School, Medway College of Art for decorative design and painting, landscape painting with David Mead. *Exhib.:* York, Rochester, London, Eastbourne, Thames Ditton, Stratford-on-Avon, Norwich, Los Angeles, Mystic, Vancouver, San Francisco, Pennsylvania, Tunbridge Wells; thirty one-man shows, R.O.I., R.B.A., etc. *Work repro.:* Medici Soc., Royles, Artists Britain, Yachting Monthly, Yachting World, Connoisseur, Guild Prints. *Address:* Priory Farm Lodge, Sporle, Kings Lynn, Norfolk PE32 2DS. *Clubs:* R.S.M.A., Rotary. *Signs work:* "Kenneth Denton."

de QUIN, Robert, N.D.D. (1950); abstract and figurative sculptor mainly working in welded metals; retd. head of design faculty; *b* Namur, Belgium, 6 July, 1927; *s* of Col. Urbain de Quin; two *d. Educ.:* in Belgium and England; *studied art* at Hornsey School of Art (1945-50). *Exhib.:* numerous group exhbns. in Britain and abroad, including Mall Galleries (1972), Old Bakehouse, Sevenoaks (1973); represented at B.P. OIL Sculpture exhbn. South Bank, London (1990), and at Dolphin Square Sculpture, London (1993). *Work in permanent collections:* Britain, Belgium, S. Africa, U.S.A.; several commissioned works. *Address:* 95 Fortis Green, London N2 9HU. *Clubs:* Chairman, F.P.S. and Loggia Gallery, London. *Signs work:* "Robert de Quin."

DERRY, Pamela Mary, N.S.; artist in oil; *b* Welwyn Garden City, 13 Apr., 1932; *d* of Oscar Arthur Derry; *m*; two *s*, two *d. Educ.:* Bedford High School. *Exhib.:* Mermaid Theatre, London, New Ashgate Gallery, Farnham, Century Gallery, Henley, Bladon Gallery, Andover, Fortescue Swann Gallery, London. *Work in permanent collections:* Chelmsford Council, Russell Coates Museum and Gallery, Bournemouth *Work repro.:* Leisure Painter. *Address:* Whitemoor Farm, Whitemoor, Holt, Wimborne, Dorset BH21 7DA. *Club:* N.S. *Signs work:* "Pamela Derry."

de SAULLES, Mary, A.R.I.B.A., (1948), A.A.dip (1947), F.C.S.D. (1959), F.R.S.A. (1981); architect and designer, interior, exhbn., display; deputy to chief officer of specialized design section, L.C.C. Architects' Dept. (1950-52); partnership with John Lunn, F.S.I.A. (1951-55); Industrial Designer, B.E.A. (1959); private practice (1960), interiors, exhbns., housing, etc.; *b* Westcliff-on-Sea, 1925. *Studied* architecture at the Architectural Assoc. School of Architecture. *Publication:* The Book of Shrewsbury (Barracuda Books Ltd.). Work repro.: Designers in Britain, Nos. 4 and 5, Architectural Review. *Address:* Watergate House, St Mary's Water Lane, Shrewsbury SY1 2BX. *Club:* Architectural Assoc. *Signs work:* "Mary de Saulles."

DESMET, Anne, M.A.(Oxon.) (1986), R.E. (1991), Dip. (Advanced Printmaking) (1988), Rome Scholar in Printmaking (1989-90); artist in wood engraving and collage; *b* Liverpool, 14 June, 1964. *Educ.:* Sacred Heart High School, Liverpool; *studied art* at Ruskin School of Art (1983-86), Central School of Art (1987-88). *Exhib.:* group shows: U.K., Italy, Malta, U.S.A., R.A., Bradford Print Biennale, Discerning Eye; solo shows: Duncan Campbell

Contemporary Art, Royal Overseas League. *Work in permanent collection:* Ashmolean Museum. *Work repro.:* Engravers Two (Silent Books), The Times, O.U.P. *Address:* c/o Duncan Campbell Contemporary Art, 15 Thackeray St., London W8 5ET. *Signs work:* "ANNE DESMET" or "A.J.D."

DE VASCONCELLOS, Josefina, M.B.E., F.R.B.S., Hon. D.Litt.; sculptor in stone, bronze, wood, perspex, lead; *b* Molesey-on-Thames; *d* of Hippolyto De Vasconcellos; *m* Delmar Banner. *Educ.:* Bournemouth High School; *studied art* at Regent St. Polytechnic; Florence; Paris. *Exhib.:* R.A., Salon. *Work in permanent collections:* National Gallery, Rio de Janeiro; Glasgow A.G.; Southampton A.G.; Sheffield A.G.; Gloucester Cathedral; Liverpool Cathedral; National Memorial to the Battle of Britain, Aldershot; Mary and Child, St. Paul's Cathedral. *Address:* Old Wash House Studio, Ambleside, Cumbria. *Club:* Royal Overseas. *Signs work:* see appendix.

DEVLIN, George, R.S.W. (1964); painter in oil, water-colour, etching and ceramics; *b* Glasgow, 8 Sept., 1937; *s* of George Devlin. *Studied art* at Glasgow School of Art (1955-60). *Exhib.:* many one-man shows; Belfast Open 100, 2nd British Biennale of Drawing, Contemporary Scottish Painting (Arts Council), etc. *Work in permanent collections:* H.M. The Queen, Scottish National Gallery of Modern Art, Arts Council, Aberdeen A.G., Essex County Council, Leicester and Strathclyde Universities, Edinburgh City Collection, Argyle County Council. *Publications:* illustrations for Scotsman and Maclellan Publishers. Designed set and costumes for new ballet by Walter Gore (1973) and presented by Scottish Ballet. *Address:* 6 Falcon Terr. Lane, Glasgow G20 0AG. *Signs work:* "Devlin."

DEWSBURY, Gerald, B.A.; landscape, architecture and natural history painter in oil and water-colour; *b* Dartford, 11 Jan., 1957; *s* of John Russell Dewsbury, engineer; *m* Kim Rolling; one *s*, one *d*. *Educ.:* King Edward VI Grammar School, Retford; *studied art* at Falmouth School of Art (1977-80). *Exhib.:* R.A., John Noott Gallery, Broadway, Theatr Clwyd, Mold, Theatr Ardudwy, Harlech, Oriel Mostyn, Llandudno, Oriel-y-Ddraig, Blaenau Ffestiniog, St. David's Hall, Cardiff, Alderley Gallery, Alderley Edge, Oriel Ceri Richards, Swansea. *Work in permanent collections:* Stowells of Chelsea, and private collections. *Address:* Tyn-Y-Ffridd, Llangwm, nr. Corwen, Clwyd LL21 0RW. *Signs work:* "Gerald Dewsbury" or "G.D."

DEXTER, James Henry; designer; *b* 23 July, 1912; *s* of James Badby Dexter; *m* Marjorie Ellen Gurr. *Educ.:* Leicester College of Art. *Exhib.:* N.E.A.C., R.A., London Group, various provincial galleries. *Official purchases:* Corporation of Leicester. *Address:* 52 Scraptoft Lane, Leicester LE5 1HU. *Signs work:* "James Dexter."

DIAMOND, Peter Michael, M.A. (1967), F.M.A. (1980), F.R.S.A. (1990); Director, Birmingham Museums and Art Gallery; *b* Calcutta, 5 Aug., 1942; *s* of Peter Diamond, B.A.; *m* Anne; one *s*, one *d*. *Educ.:* Bristol Grammar School; Queens' College, Cambridge. *Publications:* several exhbn. catalogues and articles. *Address:* City Museum and Art Gallery, Chamberlain Sq., B'ham B3 3DH.

DICKENS, Alison Margaret; company director; painter in oil; *b* London, 1917; *d* of J.D. Jamieson, senior civil servant, Home Office; *m* G.E.J. Dickens (decd.); one *s*, one *d*. *Educ.:* Haberdasher Aske's Girls' School; *studied art* at Ealing Art School (Kenneth Procter). *Exhib.:* R.A., N.S., R.P., S.W.A.; numerous one-man shows at own studio, E. Horsley, and Thorndike Theatre, Leatherhead. *Work in permanent collection:* Japan. *Publication:* dust cover for Foyles. *Address:* Norrels

Lodge North, Norrels Drive, E. Horsley, Surrey KT24 5DL. *Signs works:* "Alison M. Dickens" and see appendix.

DICKER, Molly, S.W.A.; Fellow, Printmakers Council, award, Salons de Nations, Paris; painter/printmaker in oil, oil pastel, pencil, etching materials, etc.; retd. teacher; *b* Kent, 1924; *m* Basil H. Dicker; one *s*, one *d*. *Educ.:* Gads Hill Place; *studied art* at Medway College of Art (Dip.), Southampton College of Art. *Exhib.:* R.A., R.B.A., R.O.I., U.S., Federation of British Artists, S.W.A., Wessex Artists, private galleries, three solo shows, other mixed exhbns. Work in private collections. *Address:* Garston House, East Meon, Petersfield, Hants. *Signs work:* "Molly Dicker."

DICKERSON, John, M.F.A., (1968), Dr.R.C.A. (1974); artist and lecturer in painting, ceramics, mixed media sculpture, drawing; subject leader for studio art, Richmond College, London; *b* Swaffham, Norfolk, 11 Oct., 1939; *s* of F.E. Dickerson, businessman. *Educ.:* Hammond's School, Swaffham; *studied art* at Goldsmiths' College, Art Students' League, N.Y., Pratt Inst., N.Y. (1966-68), R.C.A. (1971-74). *Work in exhbns. and collections:* Japan, U.S.A., U.K., Taiwan, Malaysia, Sweden, Australia, Yugoslavia, Hong Kong, Spain. *Publications:* author: Raku Handbook; Pottery Making – A Complete Guide; Aspects of Raku Ware; Pottery. *Address:* 47 Creffield Rd., London W5 3RR. *Signs work:* some ceramics and sculpture carry "JD" monogram; works on paper "John Dickerson."

DICKSON, Evangeline Mary Lambart, B.W.S.; artist in water-colour and other media; *b* 31 Aug., 1922; *d* of Hugh A.L. Sladen; *m* John Wanless Dickson, F.R.C.S.; one *s*, two *d*. *Educ.:* Stover, Newton Abbot; *studied art* under Anna Airy, R.I., R.O.I., R.E. *Exhib.:* solo shows: E. Anglia, London, Ipswich B.C. Museums and Galleries, Salisbury and S. Wiltshire Museum, English Heritage (Framlingham Castle); group shows include Cambridge, Hertfordshire, Yorkshire, Scotland, R.W.S. Open and R.I. exhbns. (London), Ipswich B.C. Museums and Galleries, Gainsborough's House, Sudbury, Suffolk. *Work in permanent collections:* Sheffield City A.G's (Picture lending scheme), Ipswich B.C. Museums and Galleries. *Work repro.:* illustrations "In Search of Heathland", Lee Chadwick (Dobson Books Ltd.) and for Collins publishers. *Address:* Stow House, Westerfield, Ipswich, Suffolk IP6 9AJ. *Societies:* B.W.S., Yorks., Ipswich Art Soc., Eight Plus One Group. *Signs work:* "E.M. Dickson" and see appendix.

DICKSON, James Marshall, D.A. (Edin., 1964), R.S.W. (1972); artist in ink, gouache, P.V.A.; Head of Art, Lochgelly Centre.; *b* Kirkcaldy, 31 July, 1942; *s* of James Dickson, driver. *Educ.:* Beath High School; *studied art* at Edinburgh College of Art (1960-64, Stuart Barrie). *Exhib.:* R.S.W. (Edin.), R.G.I. (Glasgow), Kirkcaldy A.G., Perth A.G., Loomshop Gallery. *Work in permanent collections:* Banff County, Angus County, Aberdeen, Tayside, Leeds Educ. *Address:* 44 Main St., Lochgelly, Fife. *Signs work:* "James Marshall Dickson, R.S.W."

DICKSON, Jennifer, R.A., R.E., L.L.D. (1988); printmaker and photographer; *b* Piet Retief, S. Africa, 17 Sept., 1936. *Studied art* at Goldsmiths' College School of Art (University of London, 1954-59) and Atelier 17, Paris, under S. W. Hayter. *Work in permanent collections:* V. & A.; National Gallery of Canada; Hermitage, Leningrad; Cleveland Art Institute, etc. *Published* 28 major suites of original prints. *Address:* 20 Osborne St., Ottawa, Ontario K1S 4Z9, Canada.

DIGGLE, Philip; painter in oil on canvas; *b* 30 Dec., 1956; *s* of Dedalus Diggle, B.A., M.A., Ph.D. *Educ.:* Ancoats Manchester Grammar; Trinity College, Oxford. *Exhib.:* Bede Gallery, Jarrow, Warwick Arts Trust (1985), Angela Flowers Gallery (1986, 1987), Art Now, London (1986, 1987, 1988), Festival of the 10th Summer, Manchester (1986), Barcelona Workshop (1988), Flowers East (1989, 1991); one-man shows: Rochdale A.G. (1985), Angela Flowers Gallery (1985), Warwick Arts Trust (1985), Some Bizarre Gallery (1988, 1989), Barbizon Gallery, Glasgow (1989, 1990, 1991), Barcelona Workshop (1989), Flowers East (1991); Granda/LWT (1988), B.B.C. Playbus (1990). *Work in permanent collections:* Chase Manhattan Bank, N.Y., Rockefeller Center. *Address:* 498 Archway Rd., London N6 4NA.

DI GIROLAMO, Megan Ann, M.A. Ceramics (1987), A.T.C. (Lond.) (1963), N.D.D. Pottery (Main) Terracotta (A.D.D.) (1962); ceramist in ceramics, stoneware and raku; lecturer; *b* New Delhi, 13 Jan., 1942; *d* of Robert Surdivall; *m* Romeo di Girolamo; two *d. Educ.:* Aylesbury Grammar School; *studied art* at High Wycombe College F.E.; Hornsey School of Art; S. Glamorgan Inst. of Higher Educ. *Exhib.:* Grosvenor Sq., London (1985), The Mall, London (1987), Brighton Polytechnic (1987), N.C.A. Dublin (1987). Work in private collections. *Publications:* illustrated, The Crab and its Relatives, Animal Weapons, Animal Defenses. *Address:* Bridge Bend, Nash Lee Rd., Wendover, Bucks. *Signs work:* see appendix.

DI GIROLAMO, Romeo, R.B.A., N.D.D.; artist in oil; Bcks Architectural Competition (1953, 1954); Bucks Art Scholarship (1954-59); Granada Theatre National Painting Prize (1957); David Murray Travelling Scholarship awarded by R.A. (1959); formerly Head of Art Depts., Gt. Marlow Secondary, Slough Grammar for Boys, The Radcliffe Comprehensive; at present Head of Painting Dept., Amersham College of Further Education and School of Art (formerly High Wycombe School of Art); mem. of the Academic Board and Governor of the College; *b* Civitella Casanova, Italy, 1939; *s* of Paolo Emilio di Girolamo; *m* Megan, A.T.C. *Educ.:* Quainton and Waddesdon secondary schools; *studied art* at High Wycombe School of Art (1954-59). *Exhib.:* R.A., R.B.A., Art Bureau Travelling exhbns. and many one-man shows. *Work in permanent collections:* private collections in many countries. *Address:* Bridge Bend, Nash Lee Rd., Wendover, Bucks. *Signs work:* "Romeo di Girolamo."

DINKEL KEET, Emmy Gerarda Mary, A.R.C.A. (1933), R.W.A. (1987); artist in water-colour brush drawings; former teacher of art and crafts, Sherborne School for Girls; Principal Asst., Malvern College of Art; and part-time in schools in Scotland; *b* 5 Sept., 1908; *m* E. Michael Dinkel, R.W.S., R.W.A., F.S.G.E., A.R.C.A.; two *s,* two *s-d. Studied art* at Southend College of Art (1927-30), R.C.A. (1930-33, Sir William Rothenstein, Prof. Tristram, Prof. Osborne, Robert Austin, Edward Johnston, Eric Ravilious); studied peasant art and design in Hungary. *Exhib.:* R.A., R.W.A., R.S.A., Laing A.G., Brighton A.G., many provincial art galleries. *Publication:* "Dream Children", collected works of Emmy Dinkel-Keet, recently published. *Address:* N⁰1 The Mead, Cirencester, Glos. GL7 2BB.

DINN, Catherine Margaret, B.A. (1979), M.A. (1980), Dip, Art Gallery and Museum Studies (1981); Curator, Falmouth Art Gallery, since 1981; freelance writer and lecturer; *b* Norfolk, 4 Sept., 1957; *d* of Dr. and Mrs. A.J. Dinn; *m* Michael E. Richards. *Educ.:* Walthamstow Hall, Sevenoaks; *studied* History of Art and English, University of Nottingham (1976-79), Courtauld Inst. of Art (1979-80), University of Manchester (1980-81). *Publication:* Co-author (with

David Wainwright) of biography of Henry Scott Tuke, R.A. (Sarema Press, 1989; reprinted 1991). *Address:* Boscolla, Florence Pl., Falmouth, Cornwall.

DI STEFANO, Arturo, M.A. Fine Art (1981); painter in oil on linen, woodcuts, etchings; *b* England, 25 Feb., 1955; *m* Jan Di Stefano. *Studied art* at Goldsmiths' College, University of London (1974-77, Jon Thompson), R.C.A. (1978-81, Peter de Francia). *Exhib.:* Kettle's Yard, Cambridge (1988), Serpentine Galler (1989), John Hansard Gallery (1989); one-man shows, Oxford O4 Gallery, Pomeroy Gallery, London (1987), Woodlands Gallery (1987), Fasolino Gallery, Turin (1987), Pomeroy Purdy Gallery, London (1989). *Work in permanent collections:* Unilever, Arthur Andersen. *Publication:* The School of London: A Resurgence in Contemporary Painting (Alistair Hicks, Phaidon 1989). *Address:* 92 Fairfoot Rd., Bow, London E3 4EH. *Signs work:* "A. Di Stefano."

DOBSON, Mary: see THORNBERY, Mary.

DOCHERTY, Michael, D.A. (Edin.) (1968), Post-Grad. Dip. (1969), A.R.S.A. (1984); artist in oil/acrylic on canvas/wood, ink/graphite on paper/card; lecturer, Edinburgh College of Art; *b* Alloa, 28 Dec., 1947; *s* of George Docherty; *m* Odette Dominique Vitse; one *s*, one *d. Educ.:* St. Modan's High School, Stirling; *studied art* at Edinburgh College of Art (1964-68, 1968-69). *Exhib.:* Richard Demarco Gallery, New 57 Gallery, Fruitmarket Gallery, French Inst., National Gallery of Modern Art, Freemantle Art Centre, Western Australia, Canabias, France, R.S.A., R.S.W., Air, London, Fine Art Soc. *Work in permanent collections:* Contemporary Art Soc., Scottish National Gallery of Modern Art, Scottish Arts Council, Edinburgh College of Art. *Address:* 20 Howard Pl., Edinburgh EH3 5JY. *Signs work:* "Michael Docherty" on reverse.

DODD, Alan, Cert. R.A.S. (1966); painter, interior designer, muralist; *b* Kennington, Ashford, Kent, 23 Nov., 1942. *Studied art* at Maidstone College of Art, Royal Academy Schools. *Exhib.:* R.A. Bicentenary Exhibition (1968); one-man shows: New Grafton Gallery (July, 1969, Nov., 1970, Oct. 1972), 'Four English Painters' Galleria Estudio Cid, Madrid (Nov., 1970). *Work in permanent collections:* V. & A., Sir John Soane's Museum; also in private collections in England, U.S.A., Australia, Spain, Portugal. *Addresses:* 295 Caledonian Rd., London N1 1EG; High Hall, Weston, Beccles, Suffolk NR34 8TF. *Signs work:* "Dodd" with date.

DODDS, Andrew, F.C.S.D., N.D.D.; freelance illustrator and painter; Principal Lecturer, Suffolk College, School of Art and Design (retd. 1991); *b* Gullane, Scotland, 5 May, 1927. *Studied art* at Colchester School of Art (1942-45), L.C.C. Central School of Arts and Crafts (1947-50). *Exhib.:* R.A.; one-man exhib.: Drawn from London, Mermaid Theatre (1961), Minories, Colchester (1968). *Work repro.:* Designers in Britain, Radio Times and other national publications. Has illustrated 30 books including 'East Anglia Drawn' (1987). *Address:* The Round House, Lower Raydon, Ipswich, Suffolk IP7 5QN. *Signs work:* "Andrew Dodds."

DODDS, James, Shipwright (1976), B.A. (1980), M.A. (1984); artist in oil and linocut; *b* Brightlingsea, 3 May, 1957. *Studied art* at Colchester School of Art (1976-77), Chelsea School of Art (1977-80), R.C.A. (1981-84). *Exhib.:* Sue Rankin Gallery (1992), Aldeburgh Festival (1984, 1990), Bircham Gallery, Norfolk (1988, 1989, 1992), Printworks, Colchester (1989, 1990, 1992), Chappel Galleries, Colchester (1989, 1990). *Work in permanent collections:* Britten-Pears Library, Ipswich and Horniman Museums. *Publications:* Peter Grimes, The

Wanderer, The Shipwright Trade. *Address:* Barnacle House, 20 St. John's Rd., Wivenhoe, Colchester, Essex CO7 9DR. *Signs work:* "James Dodds" or "J.D."

DONALD, George M., D.A. (1967), A.T.C. (1969), M.Ed. (1980), R.S.A. (1993), R.S.W. (1976); artist in printmaking, papermaking; lecturer in drawing and painting, Edinburgh College of Art; *b* Ootacamund, S. India, 12 Sept., 1943; one *s,* one *d. Educ.:* Aberdeen Academy; *studied art* at Edinburgh College of Art and Hornsey College of Art; Edinburgh University. *Work in permanent collections:* V. & A., R.S.A., S.A.C., Aberdeen A.G., S.N.G.M.A., Hunterian Museum; and in public and private collections in U.K., U.S.A., Europe, Far East. *Address:* Bankhead, By Duns, Berwickshire TD11 3QJ. *Signs work:* "George Donald."

DONNE, Leonard David, N.D.D., A.T.D. (1951); artist in oil, water-colour and etching; Head of Art, Cheshunt School; *b* Leicester, 19 June, 1926; *s* of W. D. B. Donne, local government officer; *m* Elizabeth Donne; one *s,* two *d. Educ.:* Wyggeston School, Leicester; *studied art* at Leicester College of Art under D. P. Carrington. *Exhib.:* one-man shows: Gordon Maynard Gallery (1974), Loggia Gallery (1973), Countesthorpe College (1976), Hitchin Museum (1977), Loggia Gallery (1984), Birmingham University (1992), and various provincial and London galleries. *Address:* 15 Church St., Leintwardine, Herefordshire SY7 0LD. *Club:* F.P.S. *Signs work:* "D.D."

DOREY, Russell Peter, B.A. Hons. (Painting), Post.Grad.Dip. R.A. Schools; artist in oil on canvas, pencil drawing; *b* Chelmsford, Essex, 26 Mar., 1961. *Educ.:* Felsted School, Essex; *studied art* at Maidstone College of Art (1979-82, John Titchell, A.R.A.), R.A. School (1983-86, Norman Blamey, R.A.). *Exhib.:* R.A. Summer Exhbns. (1985-86), Agnews Young Contemporaries (1988). *Address:* 29 Norland Sq., Holland Pk., London W11 4PU. *Signs works:* "Russell Dorey."

DORMENT, Richard, B.A. (1968), M.A. (1969), M. Phil. (1975), Ph.D. (1975); art critic, Daily Telegraph; *b* U.S.A., 15 Nov., 1946; *m* Harriet Waugh; one *s,* one *d* (by a previous marriage). *Studied art* at Princeton University (1964-68), Columbia University (1969-75). *Publications:* Alfred Gilbert (1985); Alfred Gilbert, Sculptor and Goldsmith (exhbn. catalogue, R.A. London, 1986); British Painting in the Philadelphia Museum of Art, From the Seventeenth through the Nineteenth Century (1986). *Address:* 181 Marsh Wall, London E14 9SR.

DOUBLEDAY, John; sculptor; *b* Langford, Essex, 1947; *s* of G. V. Doubleday, farmer; *m* Isobel J. C. Durie. *Educ.:* Stowe; *studied art* at Goldsmiths' College (1965-68). *Exhib.:* one-man shows in London, New York, Amsterdam, Cologne. *Public works:* include Mary and Child Christ (1980) Rochester Cathedral; Charlie Chaplin (1981) Leicester Square; Caduceus (1981) Harvard Medical Centre, Boston, U.S.A; Isambard Kingdom Brunel (1982) Bristol and Paddington; The Beatles (1984) Liverpool; Commando Memorial C.T.C.R.M. (1986); Sherlock Holmes (1991) Switzerland; Graham Gooch (1992) Chelmsford. *Work in public collections* include Ashmolean Museum, B.M., V. & A., and Tate. *Address:* Lodge Cottage, Great Totham, Maldon, Essex CM9 8BX.

DOUGLAS, Jon, F.R.B.S., F.R.S.A.; sculptor in foundered bronze and resin bonded bronze, decorative art designer; *b* London, 7 Mar., 1911; *m* Doris Helen; two *s,* one *d. Educ.:* University College School, Frognal, Hampstead; Bethany College, Goudhurst, Kent; *studied art* at Institute Quinche, Lausanne (1928-31). *Exhib.:* Mall Galleries, Camden Art Centre, R.B.S. Work in permanent collections worldwide. *Address:* 47 Finchley La., Hendon, London NW4 1BY. *Signs work:* "Jon Douglas."

DOUGLAS, Marguerite France, C.I.A.L.; farmer; artist in oil and water-colour; *b* 12 July, 1918; *d* of Edouard Dommen, Swiss engineer; *m* John Haig Douglas; one *s*, three *d. Educ.:* Cheltenham Ladies' College; *studied art* at Derby, Lausanne (1935) and R.A. Schools under Russell and Monnington (1936-39). *Exhib.:* S.S.A., R.S.W., Ancona. *Work repro.:* illustrated three books of James Hogg's poetry. *Address:* Craigsford, Earlston, Berwickshire TD4 6DJ. *Club:* Reynolds. *Signs work:* "M.F.D."

DOUGLAS, Phoebe Lawson, R.M.S. (1972); portrait miniature painter in water-colour on ivory, oil on canvas, artist enameller on copper; former Head of Art Dept. Bethany School, Goudhurst, Kent; *b* Chiswick, 27 Dec., 1906; *d* of the late Lawson Wood, artist; *m* Keith Sholto Douglas (decd.). *Educ.:* privately; *studied art* at Eastbourne College of Art under Reeve-Fowkes and R. Senior. *Exhib.:* R.M.S., R.I., R.B.A., R.A., Christchurch Centenary Exhbn. N.Z., local galleries, Tunbridge Wells and Canterbury. *Work in permanent collections:* Lawson Wood in his Studio, Sunderland A.G. *Address:* Curfew Cottage, Curtisden Green, Goudhurst, Kent. *Signs work:* "Phoebe Sholto Douglas" or "PSD".

DOWLING, Jane, B.A. (Oxon.) Hons. (1946), M.A. (Oxon.) (1977); painter in oil, water-colour, egg tempera; etcher and wood engraver; tutor, R.A. Schools, class at Ruskin School, Oxford, Mem. A.W.G., *b* London, 6 Dec., 1925; *d* of Geoffrey Barrow Dowling, M.D., F.R.C.P.; *m* Peter Greenham, artist; one *s*, one *d. Educ.:* St. Anne's College, Oxford; *studied art* at Slade and Ruskin, Oxford (Randolph Schwabe, Albert Rutherston); Byam Shaw School (Peter Greenham, Charles Mahoney, Bernard Dunstan, Brian Thomas, Patrick Phillips); Central School (Gert Hermes). *Exhib.:* New Grafton Gallery, R.A. Summer Exhbn. since 1954; many mixed exhbns., Travelling Arts Council exhbn. with Peter Greenham (1984), 'The Glass of Vision' at Chichester Cathedral, 'The Long Perspective' Agnews (1987), 'A Personal Choice' Kings Lynn (1988). *Work in permanent collections:* Farringdon Trust Buscot House, Southampton City A.G., John Radcliffe Hospital, Oxford. *Address:* The Old Dairy, Charlton-on-Otmoor, nr. Islip, Oxon. OX5 2UG. *Club:* Oxford Union. *Signs work:* "J.D." and see appendix.

DOWLING, Tom; artist in oil; *b* Dublin, 23 June, 1924; *s* of G.B. Dowling, M.D., F.R.C.P., Consultant Dermatologist. *Educ.:* Royal Naval College, Dartmouth; *studied art* at City & Guilds of London Art School (1963-67, Gilbert Spencer, Rodney Burn, Bernard Dunstan). *Exhib.:* R.A., R.B.A., N.E.A.C., R.O.I., R.P., R.E., Richard Allen Gallery, New Grafton Gallery, Pictures for Schools exhbn. *Address:* 31 Slipper Rd., Emsworth, Hants. PO10 8BS. *Club:* Emsworth Sailing. *Signs work:* "TOM DOWLING" or "T.B.D." (on small paintings).

DOWNIE, Kate, D.A., Post Dip.F.A.; artist/lecturer in acrylic, collage, printmaking, photography; part-time tutor, Fine Art Dept., Edinburgh College of Art; *b* N. Carolina, U.S.A., 7 June, 1958; *m* Peter Clerke; one *d. Educ.:* Ellon Academy, Aberdeenshire; *studied art* at Gray's School of Art, Aberdeen (1975-80, Alexander Fraser, Francis Walker). *Exhib.:* Collins Gallery, Glasgow (1991), Talbot-Rice Gallery, University of Edinburgh (1992), Amsterdam, Brussels, Utrecht, Cardiff, Aberdeen. *Work in permanent collections:* Aberdeen A.G., Aberdeen University, Edinburgh University, Kelvingrove A.G., Peoples Palace Glasgow, Allied Breweries, Cleveland A.G., S.A.C., B.B.C. Scotland. *Address:*

12 Iona St., Edinburgh EH6 8SF. *Club:* Scottish Arts, Edinburgh. *Signs work:* "Kate Downie."

DOWSON, Sir Philip Manning, C.B.E., P.R.A., R.A., M.A., A.A.Dip., R.I.B.A., F.C.S.D., Hon. F.A.I.A., Hon. F.R.C.A.; architect; Founder architectural partner, Arup Associates, and a seniopartner, Ove Arup Partnership; *b* Johannesburg, 16 Aug., 1924; *s* of Robert Dowson; *m* Sarah; one *s*, two *d*. *Educ.:* Gresham's School, University College, Oxford University (1942-43), Clare College, Cambridge University (1947-50); *studied art* at Architectural Assoc. (1950-53, Arthur Korn, Ernesto Rogers, Edwardo Catalano). *Exhib.:* Arup Associates: R.A. Summer Exhbns., R.I.B.A. Anthology of British Architecture (1981), Venice Biennale (1982), R.I.B.A. Architecture Now (1983), R.I.B.A. The Art of the Architect (1984). *Address:* 2 Dean St., London W1V 6QB. *Club:* Garrick. *Signs work:* "Philip Dowson."

DOYLE, John, R.W.S.; artist in water-colour and aquatint; *b* London, 15 Feb., 1928; *s* of Eric Doyle; *m* Elizabeth; two *s*, two *d*. *Educ.:* Sherborne School. *Exhib.:* Canterbury Cathedral (1973, 1976), R.A., R.W.S., Spinks (1981, 1983, 1990), Catto Gallery, Hampstead (1989), numerous local exhbns. *Work in permanent collection:* The Vatican. *Publications:* An Artist's Journey down the Thames (Pairllion Books, 1989). *Address:* Church Farm, Warehorne, Ashford, Kent TN26 2LP. *Signs work:* "J.D." on small works, "John Doyle" on large works either pencil or water-colour.

DRAGER, Bertha; artist in water-colour and oil; teacher of art, Washington Junior High School, Honolulu (1930-33); fashion: Okla. City University (1940), Cornell Extension, N.Y. (1962); *b* Moorefield, W.Va., U.S.A., 29 Dec., 1905; *d* of Guy Ours; *m* John C. Drager. *Educ.:* B.F.A. University, Okla. (1930), Art Students' League, N.Y. (1940), Traphagen School of Fashion, N.Y. (1941), Kokoschka's School, Salzburg (1960). *Exhib.:* National, Manila, Philippines, Okla. Museum of Art, Crespi A.G., N.Y.C. (1960), Art's Place II Okla. City A.G. *Work in permanent collection:* University of Okla. Museum of Art. *Publications:* author and illustrator, Hat Tactics (and film 'Hat Tactics'). *Address:* 3116 Hackberry Rd., Oklahoma City, Okla. 73120, U.S.A. *Signs work:* "BRETT DRAGER."

DRAGER, Brett: see DRAGER, Bertha.

DREISER, Peter; glass designer and engraver; copper-wheel technique; Founder Mem. and Fellow, Guild of Glass Engravers, Fellow, Soc. of Designer Craftsmen, Vice President, Royal Miniature Soc.; teacher of glass engraving at Morley College, London; *b* Cologne, 11 June, 1936. *Studied art* at School for Art Glass, Rheinbach, Bonn (1951-54, Prof. A. Dorn, Prof. O. Pietsch, Prof. O. Lippert). *Work in permanent collections:* City of Portsmouth Museum, Northampton Museum, V. & A., Corning Museum of Glass, Fitzwilliam Museum Cambridge, Ulster Museum Belfast. *Work repro.:* Engraving and Decorating Glass by Barbara Norman; Modern Glass by R. Stennett-Wilson; International Modern Glass by Geoffrey Beard; Glass Engraving: Lettering and Design by David Peace; co-author of The Techniques of Glass Engraving. *Address:* 18 Rowland Ave., Kenton, Harrow, Middx. HA3 9AF. *Signs work:* "P. Dreiser".

DREW, Joanna Marie, C.B.E. (1985), Officier, l'Ordre des Arts et Lettres, 1988 (Chevalier, 1979); Director, Hayward and Regional Exhbns., South Bank Centre, (1987-92); *b* Naini Tal, India, 28 Sept., 1929; *d* of Brig. Francis Greville Drew, C.B.E. *Educ.:* Dartington Hall; Edinburgh University (M.A.Hons. Fine

Art); Edinburgh College of Art (D.A.). Arts Council of G.B. 1952-88: Asst. Director of Exhbns. (1970), Director of Exhbns. (1975), Director of Art (1978-86), Mem. Council, R.C.A. (1979-82). *Address:* Lloyds Bank, Wallingford, Oxon.

DRING, Lilian M., A.R.C.A. (1929); F. Soc. Designer-craftsmen; designer-embroiderer, specialist in hand-machine stitched applique; *b* Surbiton, 15 Mar., 1908; *d* of G. R. Welch; *m* James Dring (divorced 1946); one *s. Studied art* at Kingston School of Art under A. J. Collister (1922-26), R.C.A. under Profs. Tristram and Reco Capey (1926-29). Retro-exhbn. (July 1987), Kingston Heritage Centre 60 years work — early graphics, needlework, water-colours Courtesy Kingston on Thames Polytechnic (graphics) for student of original school of Art, 1922-26; 2nd Retro-exhbn. (Aug. 1989), Orleans Gallery Riverside, Twickenham; (B.B.C.) "Kaleidoscope" (3/5/91); R.E. "Patchwork of Century" 40th Anniv.: Royal Festival Hall. *Official purchases:* Modern Church Embroidery (Council for Care of Churches), includes sets of vestments for Gloucester Cathedral, cope for Kew Church, etc. Specializes in fabric house-portraits (including Hovingham Hall, etc.), two works, Royal Scottish Museum Edinburgh, one, Dundee College of Art. *Work in permanent collections:* V. & A., Royal Festival Hall, National Film Inst., London Transport Museum, National Trust. *Recent work:* Needlework "Tribute" to the late Lord Reilly. *Address:* 6 Devoncroft Gdns., Twickenham, Middx. *Signs work:* see appendix.

DRLJACHA, Zorica, A.R.B.S.; awarded First Prize British Institute in Sculpture (1961), anatomy drawing competition (1962). Landseer Scholarship, first prize and silver medal (1963), Catherine Adeline Sparkes prize; sculptress in bronze, aluminium, resin, ciment fondu; *b* Yugoslavia, 14 July, 1942; *d* of Rajna and Ilija Drljacha, detective sergeant; *m* Mladen; two *d. Educ.:* Grammar school (Yugoslavia), Luton College of Technology; *studied art* at Goldsmiths' College under H. W. Parker, F.R.B.S., R. Jones, R.A.; R.A. Schools under C. Mahoney, R.A., Sir Arnold Machin, O.B.E., R.A., Sir Henry Rushbury, K.C.V.O., C.B.E. *Exhib.:* R.A. summer exhbns., R.B.S., Alwyn, Chelsea, Forty Hall, Portrait Society, open-air Holland Park, Davies St., Ealing, Chiswick, etc. *Commissions:* figures for "Battle of Trafalgar" at Madame Tussauds (1966), Expo '67 (Canada). *Work in permanent collections:* England, U.S.A., Yugoslavia, Germany, Italy, France. *Address:* 152 Sutton Ct. Rd., Chiswick, London W4 3HT.

DRUMMOND, V. H.; artist and author of children's books; water-colour painter; *b* London, 1911; *d* of D. R. Drummond; *m* A. C. Swetenham. *Studied art* at St. Martin's (1930). *Exhib.:* Oliver Swann Gallery. *Publications:* Library Association's award (1957) best illustrated children's book, Mrs. Easter and the Storks, Mr. Finch's Pet Shop, Mrs. Easter and the Golden Bounder, Lady Talavera, Tidgies Innings, Little Laura, Mrs. Easter's Parasol (Faber), The Flying Postman, I'll Never be Asked Again (Debrett, 1979). Drawings for B.B.C. animated film Little Laura. *Address:* 24 Norfolk Rd., St. John's Wood, London NW8. *Signs work:* "V. H. Drummond."

DRURY, Christopher, Dip.A.D. (1970); sculptor, land artist in objects and materials from nature, photography; *b* Colombo, Ceylon, 1948; two *d. Educ.:* Canford School; *studied art* at Camberwell School of Art (1966-70, Paul de Moncheaux, Brian Taylor). *Exhib.:* one-man shows: London, Los Angeles, Leeds, Dublin, Edinburgh; mixed shows: Europe and America. *Work in permanent collections:* C.A.S., Leeds City A.G., Towner A.G. Eastbourne, Cheltenham A.G. *Publications:* The Unpainted Landscape, Medicine Wheel, Shelters and

Baskets, Amanita Muscaria, Stones and Bundles. *Address:* 18 Eastport La., Lewes, E. Sussex BN7 1TL. *Signs work:* "Chris Drury."

DUBERY, Fred, A.R.C.A.; painter in oil, illustrator; Prof. of Perspective, Royal Academy; *b* Croydon, 12 May, 1926; *m* Joanne Brogden. *Educ.:* Whitgift School, Croydon; *studied art* at Croydon School of Art, and R.C.A. *Exhib.:* Leicester Gallery, Rowland, Browse and Delbanco. R.A., N.E.A.C., New Grafton Gallery, Trafford Gallery, Markswood Gallery, Patterson Fine Arts, Waterman Fine Art. *Publications:* Drawing Systems, Dubery and Willats (Studio Vista); Perspective and other Drawing Systems, Dubery and Willats (Herbert Press). *Address:* Buxhall Lodge, Gt. Finborough, Stowmarket, Suffolk IP14 3AU. *Club:* N.E.A.C. *Signs work:* "Fred Dubery."

DUCHIN, Edgar, M.A. (Oxon.), B.A. (O.U.); artist in oil and gouache; consultant solicitor; founder chairman, Solicitors Art Group; *b* 3 Sept., 1909; *s* of Dr. Charles Duschinsky, historian; *m* Betty Margaret Bates; two *s*, two *d*. *Educ.:* St. Paul's School; Brasenose College, Oxford. *Exhib.:* Margaret Fisher Gallery, Hesketh Hubbard Art Soc. (prize winner). *Work in private collections:* Prof. Dr. Paul Hodin, Dr. M. Altmann, Mr Nigel Wray, Mrs Alice Schwab. *Address:* 16 West Heath Drive, London NW11 7QH. *Club:* Savile. *Signs work:* "Edgar Duchin."

DUCKETT, Ernest John, P.S. (1951); portrait and landscape painter in oil, pastel and water-colour; *b* Much Wenlock, Shropshire; *s* of E. L. Duckett; *m* A. P. J. Wyse. *Educ.:* Much Wenlock and Birmingham; *studied art:* Shrewsbury Art School under M. S. A. Daynes and at Stoke-on-Trent. *Exhib.:* R.A., Paris Salon, R.P., R.O.I., R.B.A., N.S., and provincial galleries. *Address:* The Orchard, London Rd., Southborough, Tunbridge Wells, Kent TN4 0RJ. *Clubs:* Imperial Arts League, Chelsea Arts. *Signs work:* "E. John Duckett."

DUCKWORTH, Barbara, F.M.A.A., A.I.M.B.I., S.R.N.; medical artist, artist in water-colour, conté, black and white, oil and pastel; *b* Wallasey, Ches., 31 Oct., 1913; *d* of William Duckworth, solicitor. *Educ.:* Sandford Private School, Blundellsands; *studied art:* Liverpool College of Art (1934-38). *Exhib.:* Walker Art Gallery, Liverpool; Liver Sketching Club; medical work at B.M.A. House, London, and Med. Institution, Liverpool. *Work in permanent collection:* Fundus and eye paintings, St. Paul's Eye Hospital, Liverpool. *Work repro.:* many illustrations in medical journals; medical text-books. *Address:* 131 Milner Rd., Heswall, Wirral, Ches. L60 5RX. *Signs work:* "Barbara Duckworth."

DUDLEY NEILL, Anna, D.F.A. (Lond., 1957), R.I. (1980); artist in water-colour and oil; *b* Merton, London, 26 July, 1935; *d* of Arthur Leonard Dudley, flooring specialist; *m* Michael A. Neill; two *s*. *Educ.:* Tolworth Secondary School; *studied art* at Winchester School of Art (1950-54), Slade School of Fine Art (1954-57). *Exhib.:* Deist, Belgium (1977, 1979), R.I., R.B.A., etc. *Addresses:* 15 Putney Heath La., London SW15; 4 Cossack Lane House, Lower Brook St., Winchester, Hants SW15 3JG. *Club:* R.I. *Signs work:* "Anna Dudley."

DUFFY, Stephen James; artist, potter, printmaker in linocuts, screen-print, lithography, water-colour, ceramics; *b* Winchelsea Beach, E. Sussex, 5 Feb., 1962; *s* of James Duffy. *Educ.:* Rye Comprehensive. *Exhib.:* Rye Soc. of Artists, Fremantle Print Biennial, W.A., Farnham Maltings Gallery, Modern Print Gallery, Wirksworth, Ormond Rd. Printmakers, Grundy A.G., Blackpool, Rye A.G. Easton Rooms, U.A., various mixed exhbns. *Publications:* Rye Nature Reserve, Irish Folk Tales (to be published). *Address:* 88 New Winchelsea Rd.,

Rye, E. Sussex TN31 7TA. *Clubs:* Printmakers Council, U.A., Rye Fishheads. *Signs work:* see appendix.

DUFFY, Terry, B.A.Hons.; painter in oil on canvas/paper; Chair: British Art and Design Assoc. (1986-91), Mem.: Arts Board North West (1991), Dean, Art and Design, Liverpool (1986-91); *b* Liverpool, 25 Mar., 1948; *m* Angela; one *s*, one *d. Studied art* at Liverpool Art College (1972-75). *Exhib.:* Contemporary Arts Soc. (1991), Francis Graham Dixon Gallery, London (1991), numerous exhbns. in England, W. Germany and N.Y. Work in many private and corporate collections. *Address:* 136 Grove Rd., Wallasey, Merseyside L45 0JF. *Signs work:* see appendix.

DUFORT, Antony, M.A. (1975), Dip.A.D. (1974) Chelsea School of Art; painter, sculptor, draughtsman, printmaker, and portrait painter; *b* Belfast, 12 June, 1948; *s* of Timothy Nesbitt-Dufort, M.A.; *g-s* of Doris Travis (Dorothea de Halpert) painter, pupil of Sickert. *Educ.:* Ampleforth College, New College Oxford; *studied art* at Central School of Art (1971, Norman Ackroyd), Winchester School of Art (1971, John Bellany), Chelsea School of Art (1972-74, Norman Blaney, painting; 1974-75, Dick Hart, printmaking). *Exhib.:* R.A., N.E.A.C., R.W.S., R.O.I., R.B.A., R.P., Maas Gallery, Milne and Moller, 20th Century British Art Fair, World of Water-colours, Art 91 (Olympia), Gallery Seiho, Tokyo, Leaving portraits from Eton College, Dulwich Picture Gallery (1991), Dept. of Transport (1992), St. James's Art Group (1993); one-man shows: St. Catherine's College, Oxford (1971), Arts Theatre, London (1981), Leighton House Museum (1988), Maas Gallery (1990), Artbank Gallery, Glasgow (1993), Knöll Gallery, Basel (1994). *Work in permanent collections:* Eton College, Brooks' Club, Hard Rock Cafe, Los Angeles, M.V.E.E. Chobham, Oriel College, Oxford. *Publications:* wrote and illustrated: Ballet Steps, Practice to Performance (Clarkson N. Potter, N.Y. 1985; Kingswood Press/Methuen 1991) — selected by N.Y. Public Library as 'one of the best books for young adults' (1986, 1991); paper back edition, Hodder & Stoughton (1993). *Address:* 126 Branksome Rd., London SW2 5JA. *Signs work:* "Antony Dufort" or "Dufort."

DUFTY, Arthur Richard, C.B.E. (1971), A.R.I.B.A. (1935), F.S.A. (1946); Sec. (1962-73) to Royal Commn. on Historical Monuments (England) and (1964) National Monuments Record; Master of the Armouries, H.M. Tower of London (1963-77); Pres. of Soc. of Antiquaries (1978-81); Chairman, Corpus Vitrearum Medii Aevi (1970-84); Standing Com. on Conservation of West Front of Wells Cathedral (1974-85); Farnham (Buildings Preservation) Trust (1968–); received Times Conservation Award (1986); Vice-Chairman, Cathedrals Advisory Commission (1981-89); Chairman of Governors of Farnham Art School (1953-64); Hon. Mem. A.W.G. (1977); *b* 23 June, 1911; *m* (1) Kate Brazley Ainsworth (d. 1991); one *s*, two *d;* (2) Jean Wells (*née* Hughes). *Educ.:* Rugby, Liverpool School of Architecture. Recipient of London Conservation Award (1984). *Work repro.:* Drawings in Commission Inventories, etc. *Publications:* on architecture, W. Morris and Kelmscott, etc. *Address:* Church Cottage, Kelmscott, nr. Lechlade, Glos. GL7 3HE. *Clubs:* Athenæum, Arts, Naval. *Signs work:* see appendix.

DUNBAR, Lennox, A.R.S.A. (1990); artist in drawing, painting and printmaking (etching); Lecturer in Charge of Printmaking, Grays School of Art, Aberdeen since 1993; *b* Aberdeen, 17 May, 1952; *s* of Lennox Dunbar; *m* Jan Storie; two *s*, one *d. Educ.:* Aberdeen Grammar School; *studied art* at Grays School of Art, Aberdeen (1969-74). *Exhib.:* New Scottish Prints (1983, N.Y.

and touring U.S.A.), Bradford Print Biennale (1984), Cleveland Drawing Biennale (1989), Intergrafik, Berlin (1990), and many group exhbns. national and international. *Work in permanent collections:* Aberdeen, Paisley, Middlesbrough A.Gs., Portland Museum, Oregon, U.S.A., B.B.C., Mobil Oil, Royal Scottish Academy, Contemporary Art Soc., etc. *Address:* West Denmore, Auchnagatt, Ellon, Grampian AB41 8TP. *Signs work:* "Dunbar" or "L.R. Dunbar."

DUNCAN, Clive Leigh, F.R.B.S. (1983), R.B.A. (1984), N.D.D. (1966); sculptor; Principal lecturer and Head of Sculpture, London Guildhall University, Sir John Cass Faculty of Arts, Design & Manufacture; President, Thomas Heatherly Educational Trust; *b* London, 1944; *s* of the late John Charles Duncan; *m* Janet McQueen, painter; one *s*, one *d. Educ.:* John Colet School, Wendover; *studied art* at High Wycombe College of Art (1961-64), Camberwell School of Art (1964-66 under Sidney Sheppard), City and Guilds School of Art (1966-68 under James Butler, R.A.). *Exhib.:* R.A., R.B.A., Guildhall, London, G.I., Nicholas Treadwell, Portland Sculpture Pk., Playhouse Gallery, Harlow. *Address:* Holme Cottage, Shiplake, Henley on Thames, Oxon. RG9 3JS. *Signs work:* "DUNCAN."

DUNCAN, Terence Edward; picture framer and artist in oil and water-colour; mem. Guild of Master Craftsmen (1980); *b* Herts., 17 Aug., 1947. *Educ.:* Manland Secondary Modern, Harpenden; *studied art* at St. Albans School of Art; Harpenden Art Centre. *Exhib.:* St. Albans Gallery (1971), Amateur Artists' Exhbn., London (1967), Batchwood Hall, St. Albans. *Publication:* article, Hertfordshire Countryside; woodwork projects Guild of Mastercraftsmen; Traditional Woodworking Tools (Eddington Press, 1989). Lecturing on woodwork, Oaklands College, Harpenden (1993). *Address:* Luton Hoo Station House, New Mill End, E. Hyde, Luton, Beds. LU1 3TR. *Signs work:* "Terry" with date.

DUNHAM, Peter Browning, Dip., architecture, London (1933), Donaldson medallist (1933), F.R.I.B.A.; architect and painter in oil and water-colour; *b* Luton, 9 Oct., 1911; *s* of F. W. Dunham; *m* Constance Young; one *s*, one *d. Educ.:* Malvern College; *studied art* at Bartlett School of Architecture. *Exhib.:* R.A. (oils, water-colour and architecture). *Principal architectural works:* Luton and Dunstable Hospital; schools in Hertfordshire and Bedfordshire; Housing. Winner of several awards in open architectural competitions, housing medals and Civic Trust awards. *Work repro.:* illustrated in technical press. *Address:* 5 Wherry Quayside, Coltishall, Norwich NR12 7AQ. *Signs work:* "PETER DUNHAM."

DUNHAM, Susan; Curator, Doll Museum of Oregon, Mem. U.F.D.C., Mem. O.D.A.C.A.; artist, designer and doll maker in porcelain buisque; Owner, Dunham Arts, designer of artist original dolls; *b* Portland, Oregon, 6 Aug., 1943; *d* of Alan Bowmen Cathey; *m* Jack Dunham, Jr., D.M.D.; two *s. Educ.:* Grants Pass, Oregon High School; *studied art* at University of Oregon (1983-85, Paul Buckner). *Exhib.:* U.F.D.C. National Doll Convention (1983), Convention of Dolls, Victoria, Australia (1985). *Work in permanent collections:* Ruth Doll Museum, China; Favel Museum, Klamath Falls, Oregon; Doll Castle Museum, N.J.; Jimmy Carter Library Collection, Ga.; Yokohama Doll Museum, Japan. *Address:* 36429 Row River Rd., Cottage Grove, Oregon 97424. *Clubs:* Eugene Doll, O.D.A.C.A. *Signs work:* "SUSAN Dunham" hand printed.

DUNLOP, Alison M., B.A.(Hons.) (1980), R.S.W. (1990); Greenshield Foundation award (1982, 1986); painter in water-colour, oil, graphite; *b* Chatham, Ontario, Canada, 24 Mar., 1958; *d* of M.E. Dunlop (decd.); *m* R.F.

Hood. *Studied art* at University of Western Ontario, London (1976-78), L'Ecole des Beaux-Arts, Besançon, France (1978-79), University of Guelph, Canada (1979-80), Edinburgh College of Art (1982-83). *Exhib.:* Canadian Soc. of Painters in Water-colours, Gallerie Rochon, Toronto, R.S.W., S.S.A. S.S.W.A., Scottish Gallery, Thackeray Gallery, Kingfisher Gallery, Bruton Gallery. *Work in private collections:* Canada, U.S.A., G.B. *Address:* Croft Cottage, Crichton, By Pathhead, Midlothian EH37 5UZ. *Signs work:* "DUNLOP" and year.

DUNLOP, Jim; artist in oil, water-colour, pen and ink, damask designer; *b* 15 Oct., 1929; *s* of Samuel Dunlop. *Educ.:* Brownlee School, Lisburn; *studied art* privately with Sidney Smith at his studio in Belfast. *Exhib.:* Ulster, Australia, Germany. *Work in permanent collections:* Ulster Bank Head Office, Zoltan Frankl, and various military collections in Gt. Britain and Germany. *Commissioned work:* limited editions, signed prints of N. Ireland street scenes (Shelden Fine Art); Ulster Bank: water-colours of their premises of architectural merit in the Republic of Ireland and Northern Ireland. *Address:* 20 Ashgrove Pk., Belfast 14. *Signs work:* see appendix.

DUNN, Alfred, A.R.C.A. (1961); artist; Senior Tutor, Royal College of Art; *b* Wombwell, Yorks, 4 Oct., 1937; *s* of George Simeon Dunn; one *s,* one *d.* *Educ.:* Wath-upon-Dearne Grammar School; *studied art* at Royal College of Art (1959-61). *Exhib.:* Galerie Buchhandlung Claus Lincke, Dusseldorf (1976), Monika Beck Gallery, Hamburg (1976, 1993), Redfern Gallery, London (1965, 1966, 1969, 1971, 1975, 1978, 1983), L'Umo del Arte, Milan (1971), Atlantis Gallery (1982). *Work in permanent collections:* Manchester City A.G., Cadillac Co., Houston, General Hardware Manufacturing Co., New York, Monika Beck Gallery, Germany, L'Umo del Arte, Milan, Yorkshire Sculpture Park, V. & A., Arts Council, London. *Address:* Little Moss Farm, Trawden, nr. Colne, Lancs. BB8 8PR. *Signs work:* "Alf Dunn."

DUNN, Anne; painter, all mediums; *b* London, 4 Sept., 1929; *d* of Sir James Dunn, Bt.; *m* (1) Michael Wishart, 1950; one *s*; *m* (2) Rodrigo Moynihan, 1960; one *s. Studied art* at Chelsea, Academie Julian, Paris. *Exhib.:* one-man shows, Leicester Galleries (8); Redfern Gallery, London; Fischbach Gallery, N.Y.(8); Philadelphia; Ville de Paris (2); Gallery 78, Federicton, Canada (2); many group shows world-wide, R.A. (1978-88). *Work in permanent collections:* Arts Council, M. of W., Carlisle City A. G., Columbus Gallery of Fine Arts, U.S., Beaverbrook A.G., N.B., Financial Times Inc. G.B., Commerce Bankshares, Kansas City, Mo., Amerada Hess Corp. N.Y., Xerox Corp. N.Y., Chemical Bank N.Y., Bank of Nova Scotia, Canada, New Brunswick Provincial Art Bank, Canada, The Art Centre, University of New Brunswick, Canada. *Publication:* Editor, Art and Literature (1964-68). *Address:* Domaine de St. Esteve, Lambesc, B.D.R. 13410, France. *Club:* W.I.A.C. *Signs work:* "Anne Dunn."

DUNN, Philip, Dip.A.D. (Fine Art) (1968), A.T.C. (1969); painter/printmaker in acrylic, oil, gouache, screenprinting; Mem. Fiveways Artists' Open House since 1990; *b* London, 26 May, 1945; *m* Carole-Anne White. *Educ.:* Chiswick Grammar School, London; *studied art* at Twickenham College of Technology (1964), Hornsey College of Art (1964-68), Brighton College of Art (1968-69). *Exhib.:* many including London, N.Y., Brighton, Bath, Cheltenham, also twenty solo exhbns. since 1968. Exhib. exclusively through Window Gallery, Brighton since 1982. *Work in permanent collection:* Brighton Centre. *Address:* c/o Window Gallery, 3 Dukes La., Brighton, E. Sussex BN1 1BG. *Club:* Brighton Arts. *Signs work:* "Philip Dunn."

DUNNE, Berthold; Mem. Water-colour Soc. of Ireland (1951); artist in water-colour; *b* Dublin, 21 Sept., 1924; *s* of Michael D. Dunne; *m* Barbara Kelly; two *d. Educ.:* Christian Brothers Schools, Synge Street; *studied art* at National College of Art, Dublin, under John Keating, P.R.H.A., and Maurice MacGonigal, R.H.A. (1946-51). *Exhib.:* R.H.A., Oireachtas Art Exhbn., Water-colour Soc. of Ireland. *Work in permanent collections:* Self-portrait in the National Self-Portrait Collection; nine paintings in Water-colour Soc. of Ireland Coll.; University of Limerick. *Address:* Goa, Shrewsbury Rd., Shankill, Co. Dublin, Ireland. *Signs work:* "Berthold," see appendix.

DUNSTAN, Bernard, R.A. (1968), N.E.A.C., R.W.A. (past president, 1980-84); painter; Trustee, R.A.; *b* 19 Jan., 1920; *s* of the late Dr. A. E. Dunstan; *m* Diana Armfield; three *s. Educ.:* St. Paul's School; *studied art* at Byam Shaw School (Ernest Jackson), Slade School of Fine Art. *Exhib.:* R.A., etc., one-man exhbns. at Agnew's, etc. *Work in permanent collections:* Bristol, Rochdale, Coventry, National Gallery of New Zealand, London Museum, National Portrait Gallery, etc. *Official purchases:* Contemporary Art Soc., Arts Council. *Publications:* Painting Methods of the Impressionists, The Paintings of Bernard Dunstan (1993), ed. Ruskin's Elements of Drawing. *Address:* 10 High Pk. Rd., Kew, Surrey TW9 4BH *Club:* Arts. *Signs work:* "B.D."

DURANTY, Charles Henry; artist in water-colour; *b* Romford, Essex, Feb., 1918; *s* of W. H. Duranty, M.C. (decd.); *m* Vivian Marguerite. *Educ.:* St. Lawrence College, Ramsgate Kent. *Exhib.:* Leicester Galleries, Roland, Browse & Delbanco, New Grafton, Mercury, Heal's, Zwemmers, Medici, Thackeray Gallery, London; outside London: Ashgate, Farnham, Rye Art Gallery, Sussex, Brighton Art Gallery, Sussex, Guildford House and Reid's Gallery, Guildford, Westgate Gallery, Winchester, Phoenix Gallery, Lavenham, Blakesley Gallery, Northamptonshire; abroad: Johannesburg, S.A., Galerie Racines, Brussels. *Publications:* Audition (poetry). *Address:* Blue Horses, Levylsdene, Merrow, Guildford, Surrey GU1 2RT. *Signs work:* "Charles Duranty."

DURBIN, Leslie, C.B.E. (1976), L.V.O. (1943), Hon. LL.D. (Cambridge) 1963; silversmith; liveryman of Worshipful Company of Goldsmiths (1943); *b* Fulham, London, 21 Feb., 1913; *m* Phyllis Ginger, R.W.S.; one *s*, one *d.* Apprenticeship and journeyman with late Omar Ramsden (1929-1938). *Official purchases (commissions):* Altar plate for Guildford Cathedral (1938); principal part in making Stalingrad Sword to Prof. R.M. Gleadowe's design (1943); R.A.F. (1941-1945); Regional variants of £ coin design (1983); Coventry Cathedral; Smithsonian Institution, Washington D.C.; St. George's Chapel, Windsor. *Address:* 298 Kew Rd., Richmond, Surrey TW9 3DU.

DURRANT, Roy Turner, N.D.D. (1952), F.R.S.A. (1953), F.F.P.S., N.E.A.C. (1985); painter; *b* Lavenham, Suffolk, 4 Oct., 1925; *s* of Francis Henry Durrant and Edna May, *née* Turner; *m* Jean, *née* Lyell; four *s. Educ.:* Camberwell School of Art (1948-52); served in Suffolk Regt. (1944-47). *Exhib.:* R.A., Artists of Fame and Promise (Leicester Galleries), London Group, N.E.A.C., etc.; about thirty one-man exhbns. in London and provinces including: Beaux Arts Gallery (1950), Artists' International Assoc. Gallery (1953, 1957, 1969), Roland, Browse and Delbanco (1954), Grabowski Gallery (1959), Loggia Gallery (1973, 1975, 1981, 1984), Galerie of M.A. Lausanne (1988), Belgrave Gallery, London (retrospective) 1991. *Work in permanent collections:* Impingdon Village College, Cambs.; Sirrell Collection, C.W.A.C.; City Museum and A.G., Gloucester; Leeds University; Linton Village College, Cambs.; Leicester Educ. Dept., Grammar School, Ashby-de-la-Zouch; Tate Gallery, London; Museum and A.G., Luton;

Graves A.G., Sheffield; Dept. of Biochemistry, Cambridge University; British Rail (Sealink); Usher Gallery, Lincoln; Imperial War Museum, London; Bury St. Edmunds Town Council; City of Bradford A.G.; Southampton A.G.; Carlisle A.G.; Kettles Yard Collection, Cambridge University; Holywell Manor, Oxford; Bertrand Russell Foundation, Nottingham; Castle Museum, Norwich; University of Adelaide, Australia; Western Australia A.G., Perth; University of Mass., Amherst, U.S.A.; Beecroft A.G., Westcliff-on-Sea, Essex; G.M.A., Rio de Janeiro; Worthing A.G.; Museum of Art, Hove; R.A.F. Museum, Hendon; 8th Air Force Museum, Barkside, Louisiana, U.S.A. Work in many private collections. *Publication:* A Rag Book of Love, poems (Scorpion Press, 1960). *Address:* 38 Hurst Pk. Ave., Cambridge CB4 2AE. *Signs work:* see appendix.

DUVAL, Dorothy Zinaida; mem. U.A. (1962), F.B.A. (1963-78); gold medal, Accademia Italia (1980); silver medal, Paris Salon (1959), art merit, Stock Exchange Art Soc., (1969, 1973, 1981, 1986); oil painter, teacher of art; *b* Ipplepen, Newton Abbot, Devon, 26 Sept., 1917; *d* of Frederick William Hecht (decd.), mem. London Stock Exchange. *Educ.:* Bedford Park High School; *studied art* at Slade School. *Exhib.:* R.A., R.P., N.E.A.C., R.B.A., R.O.I., R.Scot.A., U.A., R.S.M.A. (1987, 1990), Paris Salon, Galerie Vallombreuse, Biarritz (1976) awarded Dip. of Merit (1986); one-man shows: Saffron Gallery, Saffron Waldon, Broadstairs Library (1978), Margate Library (1979). *Official purchases:* Grenadier Guards, H.Q., (Harry Nicholls, V.C.). *Address:* 166 Percy Ave., Kingsgate, Broadstairs, Kent CT10 3LF. *Signs work:* "D. Z. Duval."

DYKE, John C. A.; National Trust illustrator. Former Lundy resident and editor and illustrator of the island magazine The Illustrated Lundy News (quarterly) and designer of the Island's local stamps; *b* Rossett, E. Denbighshire, 16 May, 1923; *m* Beatrice Joan Leach; one *s*, one *d*. *Educ.:* Holly Bank, Chester; *studied art* at Chester School of Art, principal, A. J. Mayson, A.R.C.A.; awards, Westminster Gold Medal and Randolph Caldecott Memorial Prize for book illustration (1937-41). *Address:* Bohetheric, St. Dominick, via Saltash, Cornwall PL12 6SZ. *Signs work:* see appendix.

DYNEVOR, Lucy (née Rothenstein); painter and formally conservator of works of art; *b* Sheffield, 1934; *m* Lord Dynevor; (divorced); one *s*, three *d*. *Studied art* at Ruskin School of Fine Art in Oxford and conservation of art with Dr. Helmuth Ruhemann. *Exhib.:* one-man shows: University College of Swansea, New Grafton Gallery, London (1991). *Address:* 4 Magnolia Wharf, Strand-on-the-Green, London W4 3NY. *Club:* Chelsea Arts. *Signs work:* "L.D." or "Lucy Dynevor."

DYRENFORTH, Noel; artist in batik; *b* London, 17 June, 1936; one *s*. *Educ.:* St. Clement Danes, London; C.A.C. Bursary (1977); Craftsmen-in-residence Arts Victoria '78, Toorak State College; study/travel in U.S.A., Indonesia, India, China. *Exhib.:* one-man shows: 1965-90: Cambridge, London, Coventry, Bradford, Loughborough, Oxford, Nottingham, L.A., Lincoln, Hull, Halifax, Melbourne (Australia), Bremen and Cologne (Germany), Banbury, Tokyo (Japan), Indonesia, Guizhou University, China (1990). *Work in public collections:* V. & A., and six others. *Publication:* Batik with Noel Dyrenforth by J. Houston (Orbis Publications, London); The Technique of Batik by Noel Dyrenforth (Batsford Publishing Co. 1988). *Address:* 11 Shepherds Hill, Highgate, London N6.

DYSON, Douglas Kerr, A.R.C.A. (1949); painter and draughtsman; lecturer (retd.), Department of Visual Studies, Faculty of Art and Design, Manchester Polytechnic; *b* Halifax, 11 Dec., 1918; *s* of Coningsby Dyson; *m* Sylvia Varley;

one *s. Educ.:* Royds Hall Grammar School, Huddersfield; *studied art* at Huddersfield School of Art (1935-39), R.C.A. under Gilbert Spencer and Rodrigo Moynihan (1946-49). *Exhib.:* R.A., Manchester Academy. *Work in permanent collections:* The Manchester Education Committee, The Manchester City Art Gallery; Co-operative Insurance Society; private collections. *Address:* 32 Broomfield La., Hale, Cheshire WA15 9AU. *Signs work:* "Dyson."

E

EAMES, Angela, B.A.Hons., H.D.F.A., M.A.(Computing in Art and Design); artist/lecturer in drawing/electronic media; *b* Malmesbury, Wilts., 28 May, 1951; *m* Bill Watson. *Educ.:* Woking County Grammar School; *studied art* at Bath Academy of Art (1971-74, Michael Kidner), Slade School of Art (1974-76, Tess Jaray, Noel Forster), Middlesex University (1991-92, John Lansdown). *Exhib.:* widely, including London, Berlin, Linz, Bratislava and the U.S.A. *Lectures:* Associate Senior Lecturer in Computer Aided Studies, University of Wolverhampton. Work commissioned and in private collections. *Address:* 15 Chapter Rd., Kennington, London SE17 3ES. *Signs work:* "A. Eames."

EARDLEY, Enid Mary, S.W.A., Hon. Paris Salon (1976); portrait painter in oil and water-colour; *d* of Matthew Wharton Ford; *m* Edward Derek Eardley; one *s. Educ.:* Northwood College; *studied art* at Central School (1939) and under Steven Spurrier and Stanley Grimm (1964). *Exhib.:* one-man shows, Cooling Galleries (1968), Marlow Gallery (1970), Alpine Gallery (1981), R.P., R.O.I., N.S. *Address:* Stable Cottage, Old Amersham, Bucks. *Signs work:* "E. EARDLEY."

EARLE, Donald Maurice, A.T.D., D.A.E., M.Phil., Ph.D., F.R.S.A.; artist; taught art in variety of secondary schools (1951-88); *b* Melksham, Wilts., 15 Aug., 1928; *m* Jennifer Mary Isaac. *Educ.:* Trowbridge (Wilts.) Boys' High School; *studied art* at W. of England College of Art, Bristol (1944-47, 1949-51). *Exhib.:* N.E.A.C., R.W.S., R.W.A., R.B.S.A. and one-man shows in public galleries. *Address:* 50 Maltese Rd., Chelmsford, Essex CM1 2PA. *Signs work:* "D. M. Earle."

EASTON, Arthur Frederick, Surrey Dip. (1964), R.O.I. (1979), N.S. (1980); Dip. of Merit for Painting, University of Arts, Italy (1982); Pres. Reigate Soc. of Artists; artist in oil and water-colour, art teacher; *b* Horley, Surrey, 9 Feb., 1939; *s* of Frederick William Easton; *m* Carolle; three *d. Studied art* at Reigate School of Art and Design (1961-64). *Exhib.:* R.A., R.O.I., R.B.A., N.S., R.P., N.E.A.C.; fifteen one-man shows; ten shared shows; twenty-six mixed shows. Prize winner Upper St. Gallery (1973), Hunting Art Prize exhbn. (1990), International Arts Fair, Olympia (1991). *Work repro.:* The Artist, Leisure Painter; posters, Ikea of Sweden; greetings cards, Les Editions Arts et Images du Monde. *Work in public collection:* Museum of British Labour. *Address:* 4 Winfield Grove, Newdigate, Surrey RH5 5AZ. *Club:* Reigate Soc. of Artists. *Signs work:* "A. Easton."

EASTON, David William, R.I. (1985), N.D.D. (1956), B.Ed.(1976); painter in water-colour, pastel, oil, gouache; *b* Leicester, 29 Aug., 1935; *s* of John Donald Easton; *m* Shirley; two *s,* one *d. Educ.:* Wyggeston School, Leicester; *studied art* at Leicester College of Art (1952-56). *Exhib.:* R.A., P.S., R.I., and many galleries throughout the U.K. *Publication:* Watercolour Flowers (Batsford, 1993). *Address:* 9 Evington La., Leicester LE5 5PQ. *Signs work:* "David Easton."

EASTON, Frances; 1st Class Dip. (Florence, 1960); painter of landscapes, nudes and still life in oil; *b* Kenya; *d* of Brig. G.L. Easton, M.C. (decd.); *m* Keith Stainton; three *s-s,* three *s-d. Educ.:* Wycombe Abbey; *studied art* at Accademia di Belle Arti, Florence (1957-60, Prof. Giovanni Colacicchi). *Exhib.:* one-man shows: London, Paris, Rome, most F.B.A. socs., Paris Salon (1977), Laing Competition (1986), Venice — Treviso (award). *Work in private collections:* U.K., France, Canada. *Commissions:* Kennedy Inst., London (Founder's portrait); Suffolk/W. Germany 'Twinning' landscape of Gainsborough's birthplace. *Address:* 5 Chelsea Studios, 410 Fulham Rd., London SW6. *Clubs:* Hesketh Hubbard Art, Hurlingham, The Arts. *Signs work:* "Frances Easton (Stainton)."

EASTON, Shirley, S.W.A. (1988-92), N.D.D. (1956), A.T.D. (1957); painter in water-colour and acrylic, painting tutor; *b* Leicester, 28 Apr., 1935; *d* of Herbert A. Swift; *m* David Easton, R.I.; two *s,* one *d. Educ.:* Gateway Girls' School, Leicester; *studied art* at Leicester College of Art (1952-57, D.P. Carrington). *Exhib.:* R.A. (1986), R.I. (1985-93), S.W.A. (1988, 1990, 1991). *Work in permanent collection:* Leicester University. *Address:* 9 Evington La., Leicester LE5 5PQ. *Signs work:* "Shirley Easton."

EASTON, Timothy; Heatherley's Scholarship, London (1966), Elizabeth Greenshields Memorial Award, Montreal (1973); painter in oil on canvas, sculptor in bronze; *b* 26 Aug., 1943; *s* of Dendy Bryan Easton, M.I.Hort., D.H.R.U.; *m* Christine Darling; two *d. Educ.:* Cranleigh, Mowdon and Christ College; *studied art* at Kingston School of Art (1960-64), Heatherley School of Art (1966-67). *Exhib.:* Chicago, Kansas, Los Angeles, Washington, New York and various Art Expos in America between 1968 and 1987; London and provinces from 1970 onwards; Germany, Luxembourg and Jersey 1984-1987. *Work in permanent collection:* Hereford City A.G. *Publications:* John Hedgecoe's Nude Photography (Ebury Press, 1984). *Address:* Bedfield Hall, Bedfield, Woodbridge, Suffolk. *Signs work:* "Timothy Easton" or "Easton."

EASTOP, Geoffrey Frank, N.D.D. (1951), A.T.D. (1952), F.S.D-C. (1979), lecturer, potter; *b* London, 16 Jan., 1921; *s* of Charles Alfred Eastop; *m* Patricia Haynes; three *s,* one *d. Educ.:* St. Olave's Grammar School; *studied art* at Goldsmiths' College (1949-52); Academie Ranson, Paris (1952-53). *Exhib.:* "Studio Ceramics Today" V. & A., London (1983), Stuttgart (1982), Cologne (1983). Retrospective "Ten Years" University College, Cardiff (1985), Centenary S.D-C. (1988), "Celebration of Ceramics", Rufford, Notts. (1988), International Ceramics, Holland (1990), Contemporary Ceramics, London (1991) (solo); Touring retrospective: Portsmouth City Museum, Newbury Museum, Holburne Museum, Bath (1992-93). *Work in permanent collections:* V. & A., National Museum of Wales, Fitzwilliam Museum, Cambridge, Southampton Museum A.G., Reading Museum, B'ham City Museum, Portsmouth City Museum. *Publication:* 'The Hollow Vessel' (1980). *Address:* The Pottery, Ecchinswell, Newbury, Berks. RG15 8TT. *Clubs:* Craftsmen Potters' Assoc. of Gt. Britain, S.D-C. *Signs work:* see appendix.

EAVES, John, A.T.C. (1952); *b* Bristol, 10 Nov., 1929; *m* Cecily Edith; two *s,* two *d. Educ.:* Bembridge School, Bembridge, I.O.W.; *studied art* at Bath Academy of Art, James Tower (ceramics), William Scott (painting) (1949-52). *Work in permanent collections:* Arts Council of G.B.; City A.G., Bristol; Royal

West of England Academy; South West Arts; Victoria A.G., Bath; University of Bath; Prediger, Schwäbisch Gmünd, W.G. *Work repro.:* in Henry Cliffe's Lithography (Studio Vista, 1965). Awarded Winston Churchill Travelling Fellowship to U.S.A. (1966), Print and Water-colour Prizes, Westward T.V. Open Competition (1973, 1975), Leverhulme Emeritus Fellowship (1986) to study painter Emil Nolde. *Address:* 2 Belgrave Pl., Bath, Avon BA1 5JL. *Signs work:* "Eaves '94."

ECCLESTON, Harry Norman, O.B.E., P.P.R.E. (1975-89), Hon. R.B.S.A. (1989), R.W.A. (1991), P.R.E. (1975), R.W.S. (1975), R.E. (1961), A.R.E. (1948), A.R.C.A. (1950), A.T.D. (1947), A.R.W.S. (1964); engraver in all processes; artist in oil and water-colour; artist designer at the Bank of England Printing Works (1958-83); *b* Bilston, Staffs., 21 Jan., 1923; *s* of Harry Norman Eccleston; *m*; two *d. Educ.:* Wednesbury County Commercial College: *studied art* at Birmingham College of Art (1939-42) and R.C.A. (1947-51). *Exhib.:* R.A., R.E., R.W.S., etc. *Address:* 110 Priory Rd., Harold Hill, Romford, Essex RM3 9AL. *Club:* Arts. *Signs work:* "H. N. Eccleston."

EDEN, Max Nigel Byron, N.D.D. (1950), A.T.D. (1951); painter in oil, acrylic, water-colour; *b* St. Helens, Lancs., 12 Nov., 1923; *s* of Isaac Eden; *m* Valerie Currie; one *s,* one *d. Educ.:* Cowley School, St. Helens (1928-41), Borough Rd. College, London (1942-43, 1947-48), R.A.F. (1943-47); *studied art* at Liverpool College of Art (1948-51, Martin Bell), Ecole des Beaux Arts de Paris (1951-52, Prof. Souverbie), Copenhagen Academy of Art (1954-55, Prof. Scharff). *Exhib.:* from 1952 in France, Denmark, England, U.S.A., Canada and Spain. Recent, "Orsini" London (1991), "Academy" Liverpool (1993), Gallery "Arabal", Callosa, Spain. *Address:* 36 Ash St., Southport, Merseyside PR8 6JE. *Signs work:* "Eden."

EDGAR, Jennie M., N.D.D. (1962), A.R.M.S. (1989), S.W.A. (1991); painter in gouache, acrylic, pen and ink, lecturer in painting; *b* 10 Dec., 1940; *d* of John Patrick Colin Brett, engineer (decd.); *m* David Bowes Edgar, M.D.; one *s. Educ.:* Prep. School; *studied art* at Gt. Yarmouth College of Art, and Norwich College of Art (1957-62, Paul Millichip, Joan Charnley). *Exhib.:* R.M.S. Westminster Gallery, S.W.A., S.B.A., Mall Galleries, R.B.S.A., and many one-man shows. *Work in permanent collections:* U.S.A., N.Z., Holland, U.K. *Publication:* Evolution of the Paisley Design. *Address:* Pendower House, 150 Norton Rd., Stourbridge, W. Midlands DY8 2TA. *Signs work:* "Jennie Edgar."

EDGERTON, Charmian, B.A. (Hons.) (Graphic Design), S.B.A., S.W.A.; painter in pastel; *b* 16 Sept., 1944; *m* Nick Edgerton, psychologist; one *d. Educ.:* Hillcourt School, Dublin; *studied art* at Zurich Kunstgeverbe Schule (1961), Dublin (1962, K. McGonigal), Stoke-on-Trent Polytechnic (1967, graphic design/illustration). *Exhib.:* Medici (1991), Airesford Gallery (1993), Gallery Artist of John Thompson Gallery and Airesford Gallery, Aldburgh and Albemarle St., assorted Opens. *Publication:* Pastel Painting, and Flowers and Plants Ed. Jenny Rodwell (Cassell, 1993). Regular contributor to Leisure Painter magazine, and demonstrator for Rowney's Pastels. *Address:* 13 Camden Row, London SE3 0QA. *Signs work:* "Charmian."

EDWARDS, Alan C.L., B.A. (Hons.) (1982), P.G.C.E. (1983), A.T.D. (1983), M.Ed. (1990); painter/teacher; Executive Com. N.A.P.A.; *b* 1947; *m* Carmel Wood; two *s,* two *d. Studied art* at Laird School of Art (1965-67), Liverpool Polytechnic (1979-83), Liverpool University (1986-90). *Exhib.:* Five Artists, Unity Theatre, Liverpool (1981), School of Architecture, Liverpool (1982), Stowells Trophy, R.A. Galleries London (1982), Artists of Wirral, Williamson

A.G., Birkenhead (1984), Merseyside Artists 3, Touring Exhbn. (1986-87), N.A.P.A. Annual Exhbn. (1988-93). *Work in private collections:* England and N.Z. *Publication:* Visual Resource Packs for Teachers. *Address:* 6 Berwyn Boulevard, Bebington, Wirral, Merseyside L63 5LR. *Signs work:* "Alan Edwards."

EDWARDS, Benjamin Ralph; C. & G. Dip. (1972), R.A.S. Cert. (1977), A.T.C. P/G Goldsmiths' College (1978); painter/etcher in black and white etching, drawing, charcoal and pencil, lecturer; painting tutor P/T City and Guilds Art School, London; *b* London, 11 Dec., 1950; *s* of Eric Fredrick Edwards; *m* Ylva; one *s. Educ.:* St. Christopher School, Letchworth, Herts; *studied art:* pre college with Capt. P.J. Norton, D.S.O., R.N.; City and Guilds Art School (1968-72, Eric Morby), Atelier 17, Paris (1972-73, S.W. Hayter), R.A. Schools (1973-77, Roderick Barret). *Exhib.:* R.A. Summer Exhbn. (1977 onwards), Kanagawa Prints, Okohama, Japan (1982-84), R.E. (1969-75). *Work in permanent collections:* V. & A., Wellesley College Library, Mass., Newberry Library, Chicago, Bridwell Library, Dallas, Texas. *Publications:* illustrated, The Four Seasons at Parkgate Cottages (Parkgate Press), A Fox under my Bed (Macmillan). *Address:* The Parkgate Press, 7 Argyle Rd., N. Finchley, London N12 7NU. *Signs work:* see appendix.

EDWARDS, Carl J.; liveryman, Worshipful Company of Glaziers; Studio, Apothecaries Hall, Black Friars Lane, EC4; governor, Harrow Technical College and School of Art (1949-51); *b* London, 1914; *m* Kathleen Margaret; two *d. Studied art* at Polytechnic School of Architecture, Central School of Arts and Crafts, Harrow School of Art. *Exhib.:* V. & A., Empress Hall. *Work in position:* Liverpool Cathedral, Cairo Cathedral, House of Lords and Temple Church, Mossley Hill, Liverpool, Portsmouth Cathedral, Lambeth Palace Chapel, R.A.F. Church, St. Clement Danes, St. David's Cathedral. *Work repro.:* Studio. *Address:* The Glasshouse, 11 Lettice St., London SW6 4EH. *Signs work:* "C.E." (usually).

EDWARDS, Iorwerth Eiddon Stephen, C.M.G., C.B.E., Litt.D., F.B.A.; Keeper, Dept. of Egyptian Antiquities, B.M. (1955-74); Vice-President of Egypt Exploration Soc. (1962-88); Visiting Prof. in Egyptology, Brown Univ., Providence, R.I., U.S.A. (1953-54); Corresponding Member of the French Academy; *b* London, 21 July, 1909; *s* of Edward Edwards, M.A.; *m* Elizabeth Lisle; one *s* (decd.), one *d. Educ.:* Merchant Taylors' School and Gonville and Caius College, Cambridge. Pioneered and chose objects for Tutankhamun Exhibition in London (1972). *Publications:* The Pyramids of Egypt, Hieratic Papyri in the B.M., Fourth Series, Treasures of Tutankhamun, joint editor of the Cambridge Ancient History (3rd edition). *Address:* Dragon House, Deddington, OX15 0TT. *Club:* Athenæum.

EDWARDS, John Colin, R.P., Cert. R.A. Schools; portrait, sporting and wildlife painter in oil, pencil, chalk, etc.; *b* Kidderminster, 23 Aug., 1940; *s* of William Edwards; *m* Patricia Rose, B.A.Hons.; two *d. Studied art:* Pietro Annigoni in Florence; R.A. Schools; E.T. Greenshields Foundation award, Canada (1970, 1972); Silver and Bronze Medallist R.A. Schools; W.W.F. award (1986). *Exhib.:* R.P., R.A., S.WL.A., F.B.A. Malcolm Innes, Chesterville Gallery. *Work in permanent collections and commissions:* H.M. The Queen; Baroness Thatcher, O.M.; Royal Collection, Windsor; H.M. The Queen Adjutant General's Corps; Royal College of Radiologists; The Law Society; Carpenters Company; Cambridge, Oxford, Birmingham (Aston), Leicester universities; Hertford C.C.; N.P.G.; O.U.P.; Sultan of Oman; Helen Mirren; Vintner's Co.; Earl of Inchcape; M. Mates, M.P.; Earl of Halifax; W.D. & H.O. Wills; Rhodes

Trust, etc. *Publications:* Collins Publishers: Paper House, etc. *Address:* Chesterville Gallery and Studio, Chester Rd. North, Kidderminster, Worcs. DY10 1TP. *Signs work:* "John Edwards" and "Edwards."

EDWARDS, Sylvia, B.A.; artist in water-colour, acrylic, pastel; *b* Boston, Mass.; *d* of Junius Griffiths Edwards, music impressario (decd.), and Sylvia E. Mailloux (decd.); *m* Sadredin Golestaneh; one *s*, two *d*. *Educ.:* Boston public schools; *studied art* at College of Art, Boston, Mass. (1956-60, Prof. Lawrence Kupferman), Boston Museum of Fine Arts. *Exhib.:* Cape Museum of Fine Arts, Cape Cod, Mass. (1987), Coach House Gallery, Guernsey, C.I. (1986), Christopher Hull Gallery, London (1985), Hamiltons, London (1980, 1982), Morehead Planetarium, University of N.Carolina (1982), Parkman House, Boston (1982), Belgrave Gallery, London (1978), C.E.R.N., Geneva (1977), C.H. Gallery, Rolle, Vaud, Switzerland (1976). *Work in permanent collections:* Tate Gallery Foundation, London; National Museum for Women in the Arts, Washington D.C.; Massachusetts General Hospital, Boston; Alexandria Museum of Fine Arts, Egypt; Alexandrian Governorate. *Publications:* The Nucleus, narrative book of drawings; work widely published by U.N.I.C.E.F. and Bancrest Worldwide Ltd.; numerous international one woman and group exhibitions gallery handbooks and catalogues; articles and television talks (video) – 'Sylvia Edwards Talks with Mel Gooding'. *Address:* 14 Cadogan Sq., London SW1. *Signs work:* "Sylvia Edwards."

EGONU, Uzo, F.R.S.A.; painter, graphic artist, illustrator and designer; *b* Onitsha, Nigeria, 1931; *s* of Chukuma Egonu; *m* Hiltrud Streicher. *Educ.:* Holy Trinity School, Onitsha, Sacred Heart College, Calabar; *studied art* at Camberwell School of Arts and Crafts, London (1949-52). *Exhib.:* consistently in one-man, mixed and group exhbns. in Europe, Africa, America, Korea, Japan, Iraq. *Prizes:* First Prize B.B.C. Morning Show International Competition (1970); Bronze Medal, Les arts en Europe (1971), Brussels; Cup of the City of Caserta, ITALIA 2000, Naples (1972); Second Prize, University of California, Los Angeles (1972); Second Prize, UNESCO, Paris, Poster Competition (1976). Purchase prize, Graphic Biennale, Ljubljana, Yugoslavia (1979); Hon. Mention, Third World Biennial of Graphic Art, London and Baghdad (1980); Hon. Counsellor (for life), International Assoc. of Art (Unesco), Paris (1983); Medal, International Graphic Biennale, Cracow (1984). Public and private collections. Fellow, Printmakers Council, London. *Address:* 32 Coniston Gdns., South Kenton, Wembley, Middx. HA9 8SD.

EICHLER, Richard W., Professor, holder of "Schiller-Preis" (1969); art writer and critic; *b* Liebenau, Bohemia, 8 Aug., 1921; *s* of Richard H. Eichler, printer; *m* Elisabeth Eichler (*née* Mojr); one *s*, six *d*. *Educ.:* Gymnasium at Reichenberg; *studied art* at Vienna, Munich (history of art). *Publications:* Könner-Künstler-Scharlatane (Munich, 1960; 7th ed., 1970), Künstler und Werke (Munich, 1962; 3rd ed., 1968), Der gesteuerte Kunstverfall (Munich, 1965; 3rd ed., 1968), Die tätowierte Muse (Velbert, 1965), Viel Gunst für schlechte Kunst (Munich, 1968; 2nd ed., 1969), Verhexte Muttersprache (1974), Wiederkehr des Schönen (Tübingen, 1984; 2nd ed. 1985), and many papers. *Address:* Steinkirchner Strasse 16, D-81475 München, Bundesrepublik Deutschland.

EISELIN, Louise, A.I.A.L.; artist-painter; *b* Zürich, 2 Mar., 1903. *Individual shows:* Internat. Inst. of Arts and Letters, Lindau; Galérie Ror Volmar, Paris; Fondazione Europa, Milano. *Group shows:* Helmhaus, Zürich; Annuale Italiana d'Arte Grafica, Mostra Internazionale, Ancona (Medal of Honour); Biennale delle Regioni e Mostra Confronto Internazionale, Ancona (Medal of Honour);

Grand Prix Internat. de Peinture, Antibes/Juan-les-Pins (Diploma); Bertrand Russell Centenary Int. Art Exhib., Nottingham, England. *Work repro.:* La Revue Moderne, Paris (1968), Guida all'Arte Europea (1969). *Member:* Swiss Painters, Sculptors and Architects Society; Internat. Inst. of Arts and Letters. *Address:* Kappelergasse 13, 8001 Zürich, Switzerland.

EISELIN, Rolf; Architect SIA dipl.EPFZ, reg. arch. State of Illinois, U.S.A. and Switzerland; *b* Zürich, 6 Nov., 1925. Architect with Skidmore, Owings & Merrill, Chicago (in team for U.S. Air Force Academy design), and other firms in New York, Boston, Paris. *Exhib.:* individual show, prints: San Francisco Museum of Modern Art; group shows: architecture: Univ. Zürich; sculpture: Oakland Art Museum; painting: Univ. California; prints: U.S. National Museum, Washington; photography: Musée d'histoire naturelle, Fribourg; Honour Medal, Nat. Exhbn., Jersey City Museum; hon.mention, Photography USA 88, 89. *Work in collections:* San Francisco Museum of Modern Art, Graphik-Sammlung ETH Zürich. *Address:* Rés. La Côte 60, 1110 Morges, Switzerland.

ELDRIDGE, Harold Percy, A.R.C.A. (1950), artist in oil, mural painter; *b* London, 8 June, 1923; *s* of Horace Frank Eldridge; *m* Sheila May Smith; one *s*, two *d.* Studied art at Camberwell School of Arts and Crafts and R.C.A. *Exhib.:* R.A., R.B.A., London Group. Murals at European Patisserie (S. Kensington), Mortlake Primary School (Surrey). *Work repro.:* in The Sketch. Also illustrations, scale models and historical reconstructions for Schools Television Programmes. Taught art at school in Coventry, but now retired. Now makes harpsichords and restores early pianos. *Address:* 42 Beechwood Ave., Coventry.

ELIAS, Harold, B.F.A., M.F.A., Ph.D.(honoris causa); teacher at various colleges (1952-80); *b* 3 Mar., 1920; *m* two children; served with U.S. Air Force (1941-45). *Exhib.:* over 90 juried regional and national exhbns. including "American Art Today", Metropolitan Museum of Art; Pennsylvania Academy of Fine Arts; Detroit Inst. of Art; Chicago Art Inst.; Creative Gallery, N.Y.; Denver Art Museum, etc.; over 200 one-man shows throughout the United States; American Federation of Arts and the Smithsonian Inst. Travelling shows; International Sculpture Competition, Brussels. *Work in permanent collections:* University of Idaho, Illinois State Museum, University of Illinois, Massillon Museum, Massillon, Ohio; private collections in the East, Midwest, South and Western states. *Address:* 2612 High Oak Drive, Arlington, Texas 760012-3544 U.S.A.

ELLIOTT, J.: see BATES, Joan.

ELLIOTT, Walter Albert, F.B.I.S., L.F.I.B.A., S.G.F.A., P.S., U.A.; artist in pastel, oil, water-colour, acrylic; mem. Academy of Italy, Pres. Ilfracombe Art Soc., mem. International Assoc. of Art; *b* Wembley, 24 Oct., 1936; *s* of Albert Elliott; *m* Beryl Jean; one *s*, one *d. Educ.:* Pinner Grammar School; de Havilland Aero College; *studied art* at Hammersmith Polytechnic, Harrow College of Art. *Exhib.:* annually: P.S., S.G.F.A., U.A. (Mall Galleries), Pilton Arts Exhbn., Ilfracombe Art Soc.; Burton Gallery, Bideford (1976), Salon de Paris (1984), Torbay Guild of Artists. *Permanent exhbn.* of artwork at the Elliott Gallery, Hillsview, Braunton, N. Devon. EX34 9NZ. *Work in permanent collections:* 'The Ascent of Man' (N. Devon Atheneaum 1970-81); Europe, Geneva, Canada, Australia, U.S.A. *Publications:* articles, Spaceflight, British Interplanetary Soc. *Address:* Sollake Studio, Warfield Villas, Ilfracombe, N. Devon EX34 9NZ. *Signs work:* "Walter A. Elliott."

ELLIS, Christine Elizabeth, A.D.B. (1960), S.G.F.A. (1989); landscape and portrait artist and illustrator in water-colour, pencil, ink, acrylic; *b* London, 10 Sept., 1939; *m* J. Ellis, M.Sc., D.I.C.; one *s*, one *d. Educ.:* Sacred Heart High School; *studied art* at Maria Assumpta College, Kensington (1957-59), Theatre Arts at Rose Bruford College, Kent (1959-60), part-time at Regent St. Polytechnic, Richmond and Putney Schools of Art. *Exhib.:* S.G.F.A. (1989), Fraser Carver Gallery (1989-90), A.O.I. (1990). *Work in permanent collections:* All England Club, Wimbledon, David & Co., Equitable Life. *Publications:* B.B.C. short stories for children broadcast (1979-82). *Address:* North Cottage, 6B High St., Hampton on Thames, Middx. TW12 2SJ. *Signs work:* "C.E. Ellis."

ELLIS, E.N., R.E. (1987), S.W.E. (1984); wood engraver; *b* Sydney, Australia, 14 May, 1946; *m* P.J.N. Ellis. *Educ.:* Manly Girls, Sydney; *studied art:* John Ogburn, and National Art School, Sydney. *Exhib.:* R.A., R.E., Duncan Campbell (1988, 1990, 1993), Southern Arts touring (1991-92). *Work in permanent collections:* V. & A., University Library of California, Australian National Library Canberra, Ashmolean Museum Oxford, Fitzwilliam Museum Cambridge. *Publications:* The Maxims of the Duc de la Rochefourcauld (1986); Garden Prigs (1987); Mulga Scrub (1990); illustrations in: Women Engravers (Virago 1988); Relief Printmaking (Dorling Kindersly 1988); A Guide to Making Decorated Pattern Papers (Andre Deutsch 1989). *Address:* c/o Duncan Campbell, Thackeray St., London W8 5ET. *Club:* Chelsea Arts. *Signs work:* "E.N. Ellis."

ELLIS, Harold; draughtsman and artist in oil, water-colour, line; *b* Baildon, 10 Apr., 1917; *s* of Frederick Ellis, rating officer; *m* Margaret Lovatt; one *s*, one *d. Educ.:* Bradford Grammar School: *studied art* as apprentice in commercial art studio, Messrs. Field, Sons & Co., Lidget Green, Bradford (1933-39). *Exhib.:* Bradford City A.G. *Work repro.:* cartoons, general anonymous commercial work. *Address:* 5 Whitelands Cres., Baildon, Shipley, Yorks. BD17 6NN. *Signs work:* "H. Ellis" or "ELLIS."

ELLIS, John Colin, U.A. (1988), M.B.I.A.T. (1971), M.I.P.D. (1973); artist/architectural illustrator in water-colour, oil, acrylic; artist working mainly on architectural subjects, plus land and town scapes developing into abstract art; designer/illustrator within retail commercial and residential sectors; *b* Fleetwood, Lancs., 1945; *m* Penny; one *s*, one *d. Educ.:* Bailey Secondary, Fleetwood; *studied art* at Blackpool School of Art (1961-67). *Exhib.:* one-man shows: N.Wales, Stamford, Peterborough, London. *Work repro.:* housing sale illustration and brochure design. *Address:* The Gallery, Braceborough, Stamford, Lincs. *Club:* U.A. *Signs work:*"John C. Ellis."

ELLIS, Noel, A.R.C.A. (1948); painter and printmaker; *b* Plymouth, 25 Dec., 1917; *s* of George Ellis; *m* Linda Zinger. *Educ.:* Sutton High School, Plymouth; *studied art* at Plymouth School of Art, R.C.A. *Exhib.:* R.A., R.O.I., R.B.A., N.E.A.C., London Group, Grundy A.G., Blackpool, Plymouth A.G., Works in public and private collections. *Address:* 95 Bennerley Rd., Battersea, London SW11 6DT. *Signs work:* "Noel Ellis" (cursive script).

ELLIS, Robert, A.R.C.A., R.B.A., F.R.S.A., M.N.Z.S.I.D., M.F.I.M.; University professor, Auckland University, N.Z.: *b* Northampton, 2 Apr., 1929; *s* of Frederick Ellis; *m* Elizabeth; two *d. Educ.:* Kingsthorpe C. of E. School, Northampton; *studied art* at Northampton School of Art (1943-47), R.C.A. (1949-52). *Exhib.:* 50 one-man shows in N.Z., Australia and U.S.A.; group shows in Australia, Canada, Malaysia, India, Japan, England, U.S.A. *Work in permanent collections:* all major N.Z. public collections, National Gallery of S.

Australia, British Foreign Office, N.Z. Arts Council, etc. *Address:* 23 Berne Pl., Auckland 10, N.Z. *Signs work:* "Robert Ellis."

ELLIS, William John, F.R.S.A.; artist in oil, water-colour, crayon; author/ artist; *b* Rhyl, 21 Sept., 1944; *s* of John Ellis; *m* Gaynor Ellis; one *s*, one *d*. *Educ.:* Glyndwr Secondary Modern, Rhyl; *studied art* at Glyndwr Secondary and later under Robert Evans Hughes. *Exhib.:* Rhyl Town Hall and Holywell Library. *Publications:* author of Seaside Entertainments 100 Years of Nostalgia; Rhyl in old Picture Postcards. *Address:* 2A Carlisle Ave., Rhyl, Clwyd LL18 3DU. *Clubs:* Clwydian Art Society, Clwyd Assoc. for the Visual Arts, Prestatyn 57 Group, Flint and Deeside Art Society. Mem. of Rhyl Liberty Players, Abergele Players British Music Hall Soc., Manchester Music Hall Soc., Derbys. and Notts. Music Hall Soc. *Signs work:* "B. Ellis."

ELMORE, Pat, A.R.B.A. (1981); sculptress in stone and wood, also portraits and ceramics; *b* Rugby, 10 Sept., 1937. *Exhib.:* solo shows, Bampton Arts Centre, Bedford Central Library, Swindon Links Library, Wantage Museum, The Stable Gallery at Green College Oxford; group shows: R.B.A., Mall Galleries, R.W.A., Cheltenham Art Soc., Syon Lodge London, Salammbo Galerie Paris, Gloucester Museum. *Work in permanent collections:* Thamesdown Arts, Abingdon Town Council, The Church Army Exeter, Magdalen College Oxford. Permanent sculpture garden and gallery, and ongoing sculpture tuition at Nutford Lodge. *Address:* Nutford Lodge, Longcot, nr. Faringdon, Oxon. SN7 7TL.

ELSTEIN, Cecile; N.W. Arts Bursary Award (1983), Sericol colour prize, 9th British International Print Biennale, Bradford (1986); *b* 8 Feb., 1938; *d* of Michael Hoberman; *m* Max Elstein; one *s*, one *d*. *Educ.:* Cape Town, S. Africa; Michaelis School of Art (part time), studied ceramics and influenced by Catherine Yarrow, London (1965-69), sculpture and printmaking at West Surrey College of Art and Design (1975-76). *Exhib.:* U.K. and abroad, Clare Hall, Cambridge (1988), Whitworth A.G., Manchester (1991). *Work in private and permanent collections:* include Tuft's Collection of Fine Prints; Carbofrio, Brazil; Suffolk C.C.; Mini Print Cadaghes, Spain; Sericol Print Collection; Clare Hall, Cambridge; Whitworth A.G., Manchester. *Address:* 25 Spath Rd., Didsbury, Manchester M20 8QT. *Clubs:* M.A.F.A., M.P.C., F.I.B.A., F.P.S. *Signs work:* see appendix.

ELWES, Helen, B.F.A. (Oxon), Post-Grad.Dip. R.A. Schools; painter in oil and tempera; *b* London, 5 Apr., 1958; *d* of Nicholas Elwes, inventor. *Studied art* at West Surrey College of Art and Design (1976-77), Ruskin School of Drawing and Fine Art, Oxford (1979-82), R.A. Schools (1983-86, Peter Greenham, R.A.). *Exhib.:* R.A., R.P., N.E.A.C., Agnews, New Grafton Gallery; one-man shows: Oxford Arts Centre (1982). Awards: Landseer Scholarship (1984), Richard Ford Award (1986). Commissions include: The Archbishop of Liverpool—Rev. Derek Worlock (1989), and work for: The National Trust, and Sir Brinsley Ford (1988). *Work repro:* 'Art School' (Macmillan). *Address:* 24 Cheyne Row, London SW3 5HL. *Signs work:* "H.E." joined.

ELWYN, John, A.R.C.A., R.I., A.R.Cam.A., (Hon); artist in oil, acrylic and water-colour; lecturer, Portsmouth College of Art (1948-53); lecturer, Winchester School of Art (1953-77); *b* Newcastle Emlyn, Dyfed, 20 Nov., 1916; *m* Gillian Butterworth, pianist. *Educ.:* Llandyssul Grammar School; *studied art* at Carmarthen Art School (1935-38), West of England College of Art, Bristol (1937-38), Royal College Art (1938-40, 1946-47). *Official purchases:* Welsh Arts Council; Southampton University; Cardiff University; Ministry of Public

Buildings, Whitehall; Aberystwyth University; Pembroke College, Cambridge; Steel Company of Wales; Glynn-Vivian Gallery, Swansea; National Library of Wales; Gregynog Collection; Contemporary Art Soc. for Wales; Newport Art Gallery; Leeds University; North Wales Assoc. of Arts; Nuffield Foundation; Exeter University; and 15 other education authorities; National Eisteddfod Gold Medal (1956). Commissioned work for Shell, G.P.O., Radio Times, Glaxo Laboratories, Midland Bank Ltd., etc. *Address:* 5 Compton Rd., Winchester SO23 9SL. *Signs work:* "JOHN ELWYN."

EMERY, Edwina, A.R.B.S. (1984); Freeman of Worshipful Company of Goldsmiths (1986); sculptor and designer in chalk, oil and acrylic; retained exclusively by Garrard, the Crown Jewellers, animalier, portrait and design since 1982; *b* Huntingdonshire, 10 May, 1942; divorced; two *s*, two *d*. *Educ.:* Grammar School and privately. *Exhib.:* permanently at Garrard, Regent St., Oscar and Peter Johnson Gallery. Work collected by Royalty and Heads of State worldwide, also private collectors. *Commissions:* include prestigious confidential commissions, also racing, polo, portraits Lester Piggott and Willie Shoemaker, many for industry and commerce. *Publication:* Commercial Art in Youth. *Address:* Little Manor, Ibberton, Dorset DT11 0EN. *Club:* The Farmers, Whitehall Court. *Signs work:* see appendix.

EMMERICH, Anita Jane (née MOSSIE POLLOCK), R.M.S. (1993), H.S.F. (1982), S.M. (1985-91), S.Lm. (1990-93), A.S.M.A.(Q) (1993), G.M.A.S. (1993); self taught miniature painter specializing in portrait silhouettes in oil, ink and oil, on vellum or old ivory; contemporary art consultant, Diocese of Rochester, Kent; *b* London, 3 Feb., 1938; *m* W. M. Ernst; two *s. Educ.:* Sydenham High School for Girls (G.P.D.S.T.); *studied art* at Goldsmiths' College, London. *Exhib.:* England, N. Ireland, France, U.S.A., Australia. *Work in permanent collections:* Llewellyn Alexander Gallery, London, R.M.S. *Address:* Wychling Over, Pilgrims Way, Westwell, nr. Ashford, Kent TN25 4NQ. *Signs work:* see appendix.

EMMS, John Victor, A.T.D. (1948); artist in oil, water-colour and art teacher; art teacher, Raine's Foundation Grammar School, E1, Woolwich Polytechnic Secondary Art School; *b* Borden, nr. Aldershot, 13 Feb., 1912; *s* of John Emms, Army (ranks); *m*; one *d. Studied art* at Woolwich Polytechnic Art School under A. Buckley, L. S. M. Prince (1930-34), Hornsey School of Art under A. S. H. Mills, F. Mitchell (1946-48), Goldsmiths' College School of Art (1948-49). *Exhib.:* R.A., Surrey, South Coast and London galleries. *Address:* 23 Poplar Rd., Leatherhead, Surrey KT22 8SF. *Signs work:* "John V. Emms."

EMSLEY, Kenneth, M.A. (Cantab.), LL.M. (Newcastle), F.R.Hist.S., F.R.S.A.; artist in water-colour, pen and ink, author, retd. lecturer; President, Soc. of Miniaturists, President, British Water-colour Soc.; former chairman, Bradford Arts Club; *b* Shipley, 7 Dec., 1921; *s* of C.B. Emsley, chief designer, motor manufacturers; *m* Nancy Audrey Slee, B.Sc., Dip. Ed. *Educ.:* Loughborough College, St. John's College, Cambridge; *studied art* at various schools under Edward Wesson, Arnold Dransfield. *Exhib.:* Mall and Bankside galleries, London, Florida, U.S.A., Cartwright Hall, Bradford, Town Hall Ilkley, Town Hall Skipton, Cliff Castle, Keighley, etc. *Publications:* Northumbria, Tyneside, Tyne and Tweed, etc. *Address:* 34 Nab Wood Drive, Shipley, W. Yorks. BD18 4EL. *Club:* Leeds Fine Art. *Signs work:* "K.E." or "K. EMSLEY."

ENGLAND, Frederick John, N.D.D., A.T.C. (Lond.), I.A.G., M.F.P.S., Norwegian Scholarship (1960), Medaille d'Argent, Paris Salon (Gold Medal, 1975), Diploma d'Honneur, International Arts Guild, Monte Carlo; painter in oil, lithograph, etching, water-colour; ex-lecturer in painting and design at Leek School of Art; Pres. Soc. of Staffordshire Artists; director, England's Gallery, Cross St. Mill, Cross St., Leek; *b* Fulham, London, 5 Mar., 1939; *s* of Frederick Thomas England; *m* Sheelagh Jane. *Educ.:* Deacons School; *studied art* at Brighton College of Art and Crafts (1956) under Sallis Bonney, R.O.I., R.W.S., Charles Knight, R.O.I., R.W.S., R.T. Cowen, Principal; Hardanger Folkschule, Norway (1960) under Oddmund J. Aarhus; London University (1961) under Ronald Horton. *Exhib.:* Paris Salon, Arts Council of N. Ireland, R.B.A., R.I. Summer and Winter Salon, R.B.S.A., Manchester Academy, Bradford Open Exhibition, Trends Free Painters and Sculptors, R.W.A., S.I.A. (travelling shows included). Open Exhibition Stafford, Society of Staffordshire Artists; one-man shows: Galerie Helian, Montreux, England's Gallery, Burlington Gallery, Buxton Schaffer Gallery, Market Drayton, Galerie für Zeitgenössische Kunst, Hamburg, Galerie Bernheim-Jeune, Paris, I.A.G. Monte Carlo, Zilina, Czechoslovakia, Octagon Gallery, Bolton, University of Keele. *Work in permanent collections:* Nicholson Institute, Goritz Coll., Fenning Coll., Geneva, City of Stoke-on-Trent Art Gallery. *Reviewed work* in La Revue Moderne, Les Journal des Jeunes, Boomerang (Paris Salon Edition of One Hundred Young European painters), Dictionnaire des Artists, Repertorium Artis, Dictionnaire International d'Art Contemporain. *Address:* England's Gallery, Cross St.Mill, Cross St., Leek ST13 6JU., Staffs. *Signs work:* "England."

EVANS, Bernard, N.D.D. (1954), A.T.D. (1955); artist in oil, water-colour, pastel; Tutor/Director, Mounts Bay Art Centre, Newlyn, Penzance; Com. Mem., Newlyn Soc. of Artists; *b* Liverpool, 6 July, 1929; *s* of G. F. Evans; *m* Audrey M. Evans; three *s*, two *d*. *Educ.:* St. Francis Xavier's Grammar School, Liverpool; *studied art* at Liverpool College of Art, Camberwell School of Arts and Crafts (Martin Bloch, Richard Eurich, R.A.). *Exhib.:* Darlington Nottingham, Lincoln, Newlyn, Penzance. *Address:* Trevatha, Faugan La., Newlyn, Penzance, Cornwall TR18 5DJ. *Signs work:* "Bernard Evans" or "B. Evans" or "B.E.".

EVANS, Brenda Jean, B.A.Hons. (1976), R.A.S. (1979), S.W.A. (1986); artist in water-colour; *b* Birmingham, 6 June, 1954; *d* of Alfred John Evans. *Educ.:* Aldridge Grammar School; *studied art* at Sutton Coldfield School of Art, Loughborough College of Art, R.A. Schools. *Exhib.:* R.A. Summer Shows, Highgate Gallery, Tenterden, S.W.A., Grape Lane Gallery, York, Edinburgh, New Grafton Gallery, Business Art Galleries. *Work in private collections:* H.R.H. Princess Michael of Kent, Mr. and Mrs. Ronnie Corbett. *Address:* 61A Beulah Rd., Walthamstow, London E17 9LD. *Signs work:* "Brenda Evans."

EVANS, David Pugh, A.R.C.A. (1965), R.S.W. (1975), R.S.A. (1989); artist/ lecturer in oil and acrylic; lecturer, Edinburgh College of Art; Mem. of Council, Royal Scottish Academy; *b* Abercarn, Gwent; *s* of John David Charles Evans, lorry driver. *Educ.:* Newbridge Grammar School, Gwent; *studied art* at Newport College of Art (1959-62, Thomas Rathmell), R.C.A. (1962-65, Prof. Carel Weight). *Exhib.:* Fruit Market Gallery, Edinburgh, University of York, Mercury Gallery, London. *Work in permanent collections:* Carlisle A.G., S.A.C., Hunterian Museum, Glasgow, Glasgow A.G., Royal Scottish Academy, R.A., City A.G., Edinburgh. *Address:* 17 Inverleith Gdns., Edinburgh EH3 5PS. *Signs work:* "D.P. Evans."

EVANS, Eurgain, N.D.D. (1958), R.A. Schools Cert. (1961); lecturer, artist in oil and water-colour; lecturer, Faculty of Art and Design, W. Glamorgan Inst. of Higher Educ., Swansea; *b* Betws y Coed, Gwynedd, 28 Mar., 1936; *d* of Tom Wern. *Educ.:* Llanrwst Grammar School; *studied art* at Wrexham College of

Art; R.A. Schools. *Exhib.:* Pritchard Jones Hall, Bangor University Wales, London Welsh Assoc. Young Contemporaries, R.A., F.P.S., etc. *Work in permanent collections:* National Museum of Wales, Aberystwyth, and many private collections. *Address:* 8 Coed Mor, Derwen Fawr, Swansea SA2 8BQ, S. Wales. *Signs work:* "Eurgain."

EVANS, Garth; sculptor and draughtsman; *b* Cheadle, Ches., 23 Nov., 1934; *s* of Cyril John Evans. *Studied* at Regional College of Art, Manchester, and Slade School. *Work in permanent collections:* Metropolitan Museum, N.Y.; Museum of Modern Art, N.Y.; Tate Gallery; V. & A.; Power Gallery of Contemporary Art, Sydney; Manchester City A.G.; Portsmouth City A.G.; Bristol City A.G.; Contemporary Arts Soc. of G.B. *Represented* by Mayor Rowan Gallery, 31A Bruton Pl., London W1X 7AB. Lives and works in both London and New York. *Address:* 106 North 6th St., Brooklyn, N.Y.11211.

EVANS, Margaret Fleming, D.A., A.T.C., U.A.; portrait painter in oils and pastels, art tutor; teacher in adult education in Kent; *b* Glasgow, 9 Apr., 1952; *d* of Thomas Carswell; *m* Malcolm William Evans; one *s*, one *d. Educ.:* Whitehill Senior Secondary School, Glasgow; *studied art* at Glasgow School of Art (1970-74, Dr. David Donaldson, R.P., A. Goudie, R.P., L. Morocco, J. Robertson, A.R.S.A.). *Exhib.:* London and S.E. England. *Address:* Larasset, High Halden, Ashford, Kent. TN26 3TY. *Signs work:* see appendix.

EVANS, Marlene Elizabeth, S.W.A. (1990), A.B.W.S. (1987), A.Y.A. (1989); artist of botanical studies and landscapes in water-colour, ink, mixed media; *b* Barking, Essex, 17 Feb., 1937; *d* of J.B. Stringer, taxi business proprietor (decd.); *m* Lyn Evans (decd.). *Educ.:* Racecommon Rd. School, Barnsley; *studied art* at Barnsley School of Art (textile design, L.H.H. Glover, A.R.C.A., A.T.D., R. Skinner, A.T.D.). *Exhib.:* one-man shows: Cawthorne S.Y. (1990), Ossett, W. Yorks. (1991), annually S.W.A. and B.W.S., also various mixed exhbns. *Address:* 14 Spencer St., Barnsley, S. Yorks. S70 1QX. *Club:* Barnsley and District Art Soc. *Signs work:* "M.E. Evans."

EVANS, Nicholas, R.C.A. (1981); Welsh Arts Council award; self-taught artist in oil on board and canvas, and water-colour, sculptor and lecturer; *b* Aberdare, S.Wales; *s* of David Nicholas Evans, coal-miner; *m* Annie Maud Lambert; two *s*, one *d. Educ.:* Junior and Secondary schools. *Exhib.:* R.A.; R.C.A.; National Eisteddfodau; N.E.A.C.; Oriel, Cardiff; Browse & Darby; Herbert, Coventry; National Gallery, Bulgaria; Rechlingshausen, Germany; Turner Gallery, Penarth; Bury St. Edmunds; Swansea University; Glynn Vivian, Swansea; York University; Barbican; Chapter Arts; Doncaster A.G. (purchased by Contemporary Art Soc., Tate); MacRoberts Arts Centre; Hayward Gallery; Bede, Jarrow; R.W.A. *Work in permanent collections:* National Museum of Wales, Arts Council of G.B., Welsh Arts Council, Sir Richard Hyde-Parker, Duke of Devonshire, Dept. of Environment, Contemporary Art Soc., National Library of Wales, Aberystwyth, West Wales Assoc. for Arts, New York, California, Alberta. *Publication:* Symphonies in Black (Y Lolfa, Wales, 1987). *Address:* Shalom, 16 College St., Abernant, Aberdare, Mid. Glam. CF44 0RN. *Signs work:* "NICK EVANS."

EVANS, Ray, R.I., F.S.A.I.; painter, writer and illustrator in water-colour; *b* 1920; *s* of Evan Price Evans; one *s*, one *d. Studied art* at Manchester College of Art (1946-48), Heatherleys under Iain Macnab. *Work in permanent collections:* Gulbenkian Foundation; Nat. Library of Wales; Winchester Guildhall Gallery and many private collections in Europe, Britain, U.S.A. and Canada. *Publications:* Many books written and illustrated for John Murray, Consumers Assoc., Harper

Collins and Batsford 'How to be a Successful Illustrator' (1993). Prints and calendars for Royles, I.O.D., B.P., Whitbreads, Co-op, Abbey National, Allan & Bertram etc. Agents, F.B.A. also designs greetings cards and specialises in architectural subjects. Entry in new 20th Century Painters and Sculptors, pub. by Antique Collectors Club. *Address:* New House, Eversglade, Devizes Rd., Salisbury, Wilts. SP2 7LU. *Signs work:* see appendix.

EVE, Esmé Frances, A.R.C.A.; book illustrator, commercial designer. *Studied art* at Croydon College of Art, R.C.A. *Publishers* include Blackie, Nelson, Warne, Hamlyn, Lutterworth, Oxford University Press, Odhams, Longmans, Macdonald, Chatto, Boyd and Oliver, Reader's Digest, Book Tokens, etc. Educational and encyclopaedic work, greetings cards for Medici, Oxfam and other charities. *Address:* Southernwood, Meads Rd., Seaford, E. Sussex BN25 1SY. *Signs work:* "eve."

EVETTS, Leonard Charles, M.A., M.Sc., A.R.C.A.; stained glass artist, letterer, water-colour painter; Master of Design, Department of Fine Art, University of Newcastle upon Tyne (retd.); *b* 12 Jan., 1909; *s* of C. H. Evetts, lettering craftsman; *m* (1) Joan C. M. Macdonald; (2) Phyl Dobson. *Educ.:* Royal College of Art (Prof. E. W. Tristram, Edward Johnston, 1930-33), student demonstrator under Edward Johnston. *Exhib.:* R.A. *Publications:* Roman Lettering (Pitman, 1938); numerous articles on English stained glass and Roman inscriptions in periodicals and archæological journals. *Address:* The Stead, Woolsington Bridge, Newcastle upon Tyne NE13 8BL. *Club:* Pen and Palette. *Signs work:* "L. C. Evetts" or "Leonard Evetts."

EYTON, Anthony, R.A. (1986), R.W.S., R.W.A., Mem. London Group, N.E.A.C., N.D.D., Abbey Major Scholarship in Painting (1950); prize winner, John Moore's Exhbn. (1972), awarded Grocer's Co. Fellowship (1973), 1st prize, Second British International Drawing Biennale, Middlesbrough (1975), Charles Wollaston Award, R.A. (1981), British Painting 1952-77, R.A. (1977); artist in oil, teaches at Royal Academy Schools; *b* Teddington, 17 May, 1923; *s* of Capt. John Eyton, I.C.S., author. *Educ.:* Twyford School (1932-37), Canford School (1937-41); *studied art:* Reading University (1941); Camberwell School of Arts and Crafts (1947-50). *Exhib.:* London Group, R.A.; one-man shows: Browse and Darby (1981, 1985, 1987, 1990, 1993); Retrospective: South London A.G. (1980). *Official purchases:* Arts Council, Tate Gallery, Imperial War Museum, Govt. Picture Collection, Plymouth A.G. *Address:* 166 Brixton Rd., London SW9 6AU.

F

FABER, Rodney George, S.G.F.A.; self taught artist in water-colour and pen and ink drawing; *b* Liverpool, 8 June, 1935; *s* of Leslie Faber; *m* Asne Wainer. *Educ.:* Hasmonean Grammar School. *Exhib.:* S.G.F.A. Annual exhbns. and mixed exhbns. in various galleries in London and the Home Counties. Commission and other works in numerous private collections both in U.K. and abroad. *Address:* Studio: 37 Darwin Ct., Gloucester Ave., London NW1 7BG. *Signs work:* "FABER."

FAILES, Colin Michael, City & Guilds Dip. (Sculpture) (1972), Beckworth travel scholarship to Egypt (1972), Postgrad. (Sculpture) Cert. R.A. Schools,

Silver medal (Sculpture) (1975), bronze medal (Sculpture) (1976); mural artist and sculptor in acrylic, wax modelling; *b* Farnborough, Kent, 2 Oct., 1948. *Educ.:* Arle School, Cheltenham; *studied art* at City & Guilds of London Art School (1969-72, James Butler, R.A.), R.A. Schools (1973-76, Willi Soukop, R.A.). Exhib.: R.A. Summer Exhbns. (1976, 1980, 1987, 1988). *Work in private collections:* London, Monaco, Luxembourg. *Address:* 6 Elfindale Rd., London SE24 9NW. *Signs work:* "COLIN FAILES" or "C.M. Failes."

FAIRCLOUGH, Bernard Peake, A.T.D., D.A., Manc., F.R.S.A., Head of School of Art, Darlington, until 1975; artist in oil, gouache, acrylic; *b* Glossop, Derbyshire, 5 Dec., 1915; *s* of Leonard Fairclough; *m* Patricia Mary Poulton; one *s*, one *d. Educ.:* Glossop Grammar School; *studied art* at Manchester School of Art, principal, R. C. Dawson, A.R.C.A., painting, L. R. Baxter. *Exhib.:* Manchester, Salford, Birmingham, Derby municipal galleries, Whitechapel A.G., private galleries in London, Arts Council Travelling exhbn., R.S.A. *Official purchases:* Manchester Educ. Com. Schools Collection. *Address:* Newholme, Newbiggin, Barnard Castle DL12 0TY. *Signs work:* "Fairclough."

FAIRCLOUGH, Michael, R.E. (1964), Rome Scholar in Engraving (1964-66); painter and printmaker; lecturer, Belfast College of Art (1962-64); West Surrey College of Art (1967-79); *b* Blackburn, 16 Sept., 1940; *s* of W. Fairclough; *m* Mary Malenoir; two *d. Studied art* at Kingston School of Art (1957-61); British School at Rome, (1964-67); Atelier 17, Paris (1967). *Exhib.:* one-man shows Bohun Gallery, Henley-on-Thames (1981), Gallery Deux-tetes, Toronto (1981). *Work in permanent collections:* V. & A., Ashmolean, Usher Gallery, Bowes Museum, Oldham, Royal Albert Museum, Museum Boymans Van Beunegen, Rotterdam, New York Public Library, etc. *Commissions:* mural, Farnham Post Office (1970), Print Collectors Club, London (1974), Christies Contemporary Art (1978-81), National Trust Collection (1979-81, 1983), Post Office 'National Trust' special commemorative issue of five stamps (1981). *Address:* Tilford Green Cottages, Tilford, Farnham, Surrey GU10 2BU. *Signs work:* "Michael Fairclough."

FAIRCLOUGH, Wilfred, A.R.C.A. (1934), R.E., A.R.W.S. (1961), R.W.S. (1967); Rome Scholar (engraving, 1934), R.E. 1946; artist engraver; Principal, Kingston College of Art (1962-72); *b* 13 June, 1907; *m*; one *s*, one *d. Educ.:* All Saints, Blackburn; Royal College of Art (1931-34); British School at Rome, Italy (1934-37). *Exhib.:* R.A., R.E., R.S.A., Bradford, Brighton, Chicago, Los Angeles, Copenhagen, Stockholm, Madrid. *Official purchases:* Contemporary Art Soc. *Work repro.:* Fine Prints of the Year, Recording Britain, Londoner's England, The Etchings of Wilfred Fairclough by Ian Lowe (Scolar Press). *Publications:* paintings, etchings, engravings. *Address:* 12 Manorgate Rd., Kingston-upon-Thames KT2 7AL. *Signs work:* "W. Fairclough."

FAIRFAX-LUCY, Edmund, N.E.A.C.; painter of interiors, still-life and landscapes in oil; *b* 1945. *Studied art* at City & Guilds of London Art School, and R.A. Schools (1967-70) winning David Murray Travelling Scholarship (1966, 1967, 1969). *Exhib.:* R.A. since 1967, New Grafton Gallery since 1971. *Work in permanent collection:* Brinsley Ford. *Address:* Charlecote Park, Warwick.

FAIRGRIEVE, James Hanratty, D.A. (Edin.), R.S.W., A.R.S.A.; Gillies award, R.S.W. (1987); full time lecturer, painter in acrylic; *b* Prestonpans, E. Lothian, 17 June, 1944; *s* of Andrew D. G. Fairgrieve, ex-miner; *m* Margaret Fairgrieve; two *s*, one *d. Educ.:* Preston Lodge Senior Secondary School; *studied art* at Edinburgh College of Art. *Exhib.:* Hawarth A.G. (1974), Triad Arts

Centre (1974), Scottish Gallery (1974), Scottish Arts Club (1973), New 57 Gallery (1969, 1971); one-man shows: Edinburgh University (1975), Scottish Gallery (1978), Mercury Gallery, London (1980, 1982, 1987), Macauley Gallery (1983), Mercury Gallery, Edinburgh (1984), Stichell Gallery (1990). *Work in permanent collections:* Edinburgh Corp., Scottish Arts Council, National Bank of Chicago, Milngavie A.G., H.R.H. The Duke of Edinburgh, Argyll Schools, R.C.P., Perth A.G., Lord Moray, Leeds Schools. *Address:* Burnbrae., Gordon, Berwickshire, Scotland. *Signs work:* "James H. Fairgrieve."

FAIRMAN, Sheila, R.M.S., S.W.A., F.S.B.A., H.S.F.; awarded R.M.S. Gold Bowl (1989), Hunting Group art prize, runner up (1982); painter in oil and water-colour and miniaturist; *b* Benfleet, Essex, 18 Aug., 1924; *d* of Harry Kingston Newman; *m* Bernard Fairman, F.A.P.S.A.: one *s. Studied art* at Southend-on-Sea College of Art (1938-41). *Exhib.:* R.A., R.M.S., R.S.M.A., R.P., R.I., R.O.I., S.W.A., S.B.A. *Work in permanent collection:* Beecroft A.G., Southend-on-Sea. *Address:* 39 Burnham Rd., Leigh-on-Sea, Essex SS9 2JT. *Signs work:* "SHEILA FAIRMAN" or "S.F."

FAIRS, Tom, N.D.D. (1950), A.R.C.A. (1953); painter in oil paint, oil pastel, stained glass designer; Senior lecturer, Theatre Dept. Central School of Art and Design (retd.); *b* London, 3 Oct., 1925; *m* Elisabeth Russell Taylor, author/academic. *Studied art* at Hornsey School of Art (1948-50), R.C.A. (1950-54). *Exhib.:* Arts Council Travelling Exhbns., Beaford Centre, Dartington Hall, Covent Garden Gallery, Roland, Browse & Delbanco, Hambledon Gallery, Illustrators Art, Rooksmoor Gallery, Leeds Playhouse, Stables Folkestone, The Thackeray Gallery, Ombersley Gallery, R.A. Summer Exhbns. *Commissions:* stained glass in Britain and Bahrain. *Address:* 21 Steeles Rd., London NW3 4SH. *Signs work:* "FAIRS."

FAIRWEATHER, Dorothy; painter/etcher; *b* 4 Aug., 1915; *d* of Benjamin Stewart, F.A.I.; *m*; one *s. Educ.:* privately; *studied art* at Folkestone School of Art (1930-34), Liverpool School of Art (1942-44). *Exhib.:* leading London galleries including R.A., Barbican, Paris (1983-84), Germany (1989).*Work in permanent collections:* Britain and abroad. President Soroptimist Club of Sevenoaks (1973-74, 1984-85). *Address:* Lanterns, 4 Cade La., Sevenoaks, Kent TN13 1QX.

FAKHOURY, Bushra, B.A., M.A., Ph.D. (Lond.); sculptor in bronze, stone; *b* Beirut, 1 Apr., 1942; *d* of Bachir Fakhoury, chemist; two *s. Educ.:* St. Paul's, Wimbledon School of Art and Emanuel; *studied art* at Beirut University College, American University of Beirut, University of London. *Exhib.:* Bloomsbury Galleries (1986), Mall Galleries (1986), Jablonski Gallery (1987), Ashdown Gallery (1988), Kufa Gallery (1989). *Publication:* Art Education in Lebanon. *Address:* 57 Madrid Rd., Barnes, London SW13 9PQ. *Signs work:* see appendix.

FALLA, Kathleen M., F.F.P.S (1985); painter in water-colour and pastel, relief printmaker and sculptor in wood; *b* Guernsey, C.I., 25 Jan., 1924; *d* of John Hocart Falla (decd.); *m* Kenneth R. Masters; one *s,* one *d. Educ.:* Ladies College, Guernsey; *studied art* at Guildford School of Art and Morley College, London. *Exhib.:* solo shows: Lauragais, France; shared shows: Loggia Gallery, Farnham Maltings; group shows: Barbican, West of England Academy, Brighton Polytechnic Gallery, Bloomsbury Galleries, University of Surrey, etc. *Address:* Old Barn Cottage Church La., Witley, Surrey GU8 5PW. *Signs work:* "Kit Falla."

FALLSHAW, Keith George, N.S. (1979); artist in oil, pastel and pencil, graphic designer, sculptor in clay, plaster, Perspex, wood, brass, and bronze; former council mem. N.S.; M.D. of Creative Media Communications Ltd., design and advert. consultants; *b* London, 17 Nov., 1946; *s* of George James Fallshaw. *Educ.:* Broxhill School, Romford and privately; *studied art* privately with Leonared Boden, F.R.S.A.; *studied graphic design* at the London College of Printing (Leonard Cusdens and Don Smith); *studied sculpture* privately with Edmund Holmes. *Exhib.:* Mall Galleries, N.S., U.A., Deben Gallery; various London and U.K. *Address:* Bay Tree Cottage, No. 1 Crown Terr., Bishop's Stortford, Herts. CM23 2DP. *Signs work:* "Fallshaw" or in sculpture "KF."

FARLEY, James Osmer, A.R.B.S. (1990), A.N.S.S. (1985); portrait and architectural sculptor in clay, wax, direct metal, steels, bronze, copper; *b* Cleveland, Ohio, 10 Apr., 1935; *s* of Wayne B. Farley, mechanical process engineer (decd.); *m* Gillian Lewin; one *d.* *Studied art* at Pennsylvania Academy of Fine Art (1952-56, Walker Hancock, Harry Rosin, Andrew Wyeth), Chicago Art Inst. (1957-59, Edvard Chaisang). *Exhib.:* Art and the Corporate Image (1981). *Work in permanent collections:* Arizona: Bell Center, Sun City; City Hall, Glendale; Centennial Hall, Mesa; St. Luke's Hospital, Phoenix; Hanna Boys Center, Sonoma, Calif. *Addresses:* 150 Scott Ellis Gdns., St. John's Wood, London NW8 9HG; 4718 E. Portland, Phoenix, AZ. 85008, U.S.A. *Club:* F. & A. Masonic Lodge. *Signs work:* "James Farley."

FARQUHARSON, Andrew Charles; artist in water-colour; *b* Johannesburg, S. Africa, 14 Dec., 1959; *s* of Margaret Irene Chadwick Arridge, N.S., F.S.B.A., A.R.M.S. *Educ.:* St. John's College, Johannesburg; *studied art* under his mother. *Exhib.:* group show Johannesburg. *Lectured:* University of Wales, Anglo Spanish Soc., Inst. of Spain. *Address:* 80B Naylor Rd., Peckham, London SE15. *Signs work:* "A.C. Farquharson."

FARR, Dennis Larry Ashwell, C.B.E., M.A., Hon.D.Litt., F.R.S.A., F.M.A.; Director, Courtauld Institute Galleries (1980-93); Director, Birmingham Museums and Art Gallery (1969-80); Senior Lecturer in Fine Art and Deputy Keeper, University of Glasgow (1967-69); Curator, Paul Mellon Collection, Washington, D.C. (1964-66); Asst. Keeper, Tate Gallery, London (1954-64); *b* Luton, 3 Apr., 1929; *s* of Arthur Farr; *m* Diana Pullein-Thompson, writer; one *s*, one *d.* *Educ.:* Luton Grammar School; *studied art* at Courtauld Inst. of Art, University of London (1947-50). *Publications:* William Etty (1958), Catalogue of the Modern British Paintings, Drawings and Sculpture in the Tate Gallery (with M. Chamot and M. Butlin, 1964-65), English Art 1870-1940 (1978), Lynn Chadwick, Sculptor (with Eva Chadwick, 1990), etc. *Address:* 35 Esmond Rd., London W4 1JG.

FARRELL, Alan Richard, A.R.M.S. (1984); painter in water-colour and oil, dealer in antiques and paintings, chartered electrical engineer (M.I.E.E.); *b* London, 17 May, 1932; *m*; two *d.* *Studied art* at S.E. Essex Technical College and School of Art (1953-56). *Exhib.:* R.M.S., R.I., R.S.M.A., R.B.A., U.A., Chelsea Art Soc., International Boat Show, Britain in Water-colours, Laing Exhbn., Armed Forces Art Soc. *Address:* The White House, Whitesmith, nr. Lewes, E. Sussex BN8 6JD. *Signs work:* "ALAN FARRELL" printed bottom right or left-hand corner; paintings dated on reverse; and see appendix.

FARRELL, Anthony, N.D.D. (1965), R.A.Dip. (1968); artist in oil, etching; *b* Epsom, 28 Mar., 1945; *s* of William Farrell; *m* Sarah; one *s*, two *d.* *Educ.:* Belfairs High School; *studied art* at Camberwell School of Art (1963-65), R.A. Schools (1965-68). *Exhib.:* R.A. Common Room, Minories, Colchester, R.A.

Summer Exhbns., Serpentine Gallery, Christchurch Mansions, Ipswich. *Work in permanent collections:* A.C.G.B., The Minories, Colchester, Epping Forest Museum, Manchester City A.G., Beecroft A.G., Westcliff-on-Sea, Borough of St. Edmundsbury and Suffolk C.C., Essex Health Authority, Ipswich Borough Council. *Address:* 6 Avenue Rd., Leigh-on-Sea, Essex SS9 1AX. *Signs work:* "Anthony Farrell."

FARRELL, Don, R.I. (1984), R.B.A. (1985), F.C.A.; bronze medal R.I. (1984); Daler Rowney award R.B.A. Exhbn. (1992); painter in water-colour; *b* Vancouver, B.C., 3 Oct., 1942; *m* Margaret; two *s. Exhib.:* annually at R.I. (1984-91), R.B.A. (1983-91). *Work in permanent collection:* H.R.H. The Prince of Wales; private and corporate collections: Britain, Canada, U.S.A. and France. *Address:* 6461 McKenzie Drive, Delta, B.C., Canada V4E 1N8. *Signs work:* "Don Farrell."

FASTNEDGE, Ralph William, D.F.C., B.A.; formerly curator, The Lady Lever Art Gallery, Port Sunlight, Merseyside; *b* London, 16 Apr., 1913. *Educ.:* University College School; Worcester College, Oxford; Courtauld Inst. of Art. *Publications:* English Furniture Styles (1500-1830), Penguin Books, 1955; Sheraton Furniture, Faber; Shearer Furniture Designs, Tiranti; Regency Furniture (revision), Country Life. *Address:* Glannant, Llanfechain, Powys.

FAULDS, James Alexander, D.A.; artist in water-colour and oil; art teacher; founder mem., Group 81, Glasgow; *b* Glasgow, 15 Jan., 1949; *s* of Alexander Faulds. *Educ.:* Knightswood Secondary School; *studied art* at Dundee College of Art (1968-72). *Exhib.:* Dundee under 30's, R.S.A., S.S.A., Colquhoun Memorial, Group 81, Glasgow, Eden Court Gallery, Contemporary British Water-colours, Festival Theatre, Pitlochry, R.S.W., John Laing, London, Nürnberg, Germany. *Address:* 3 Camphill Ave., Glasgow G41 3AV. *Club:* Glasgow Art. *Signs work:* see appendix.

FAULKNER, Amanda, B.F.A.(Hons.) (1982), M.F.A. (Printmaking) (1983); artist in charcoal and pastel on paper, acrylic on canvas, lithography and etching; Principal lecturer in Printmaking, Chelsea School of Art; *b* Poole, 5 Dec., 1953; *d* of Richard Faulkner, B.Sc. *Educ.:* St. Anthony's, Leweston, Dorset, and Canford School, Dorset; *studied art* at Bournemouth College of Art (1978-79), Ravensbourne College of Art and Design (1979-82), Chelsea School of Art (1982-83). *Exhib.:* regularly at Angela Flowers Gallery and Flowers East since 1983; and in U.K. and internationally. *Work in permanent collections:* including A.C.G.B., Unilever plc, V. & A., Contemporary Art Soc., Whitworth A.G., Silkeborg Kunstmuseum, Denmark. *Address:* 131 Listria Pk., London N16 5SP. *Club:* Chelsea Arts. *Signs work:* "Amanda Faulkner."

FAULKNER, Robert Trevor, A.R.C.A. (1955), F.R.B.S.; figurative sculptures in bronze, terracotta, ciment-fondu and direct metal; specialist in polychrome metal wild-life subjects; *m;* one *d. Educ.:* Penistone Grammar School; *studied art* at Sheffield School of Art (1946-50); R.C.A. (1952-55). *Exhib.:* Moorland, Alwin (London). *Work in permanent collections:* Ulster Museum, Derbys., Oxford, Lancs., and Sheffield Educ. Authorities. *Publication:* Manual of Direct Metal Sculpture (Thames & Hudson, 1978). *Address:* 4 Birchitt Cl., Bradway, Sheffield S17 4QJ. *Signs work:* "TREVOR FAULKNER" or "T.F."

FAUR, Aurel-Sebastian; 1st prize for portrait sculpture (1939) School of Beaux Arts, Bucharest; painter on porcelain in water-colour and oil, portrait sculptor in clay (bronze casted), alabaster; *s* of Philippe Faur, businessman; *m* Yvonne-Constance. *Educ.:* School of Beaux Arts, Bucharest; *studied art* at

School of Beaux Arts, Bucharest (1934-37), School of Ceramics, Sèvres, France. Worked at Manufacture Nationale de Sèvres (Iser, Despiaux, Maillol). *Exhib.:* Paris: Salon d'Automne, Salon des Indépendants, Salon des Tuileries, Grandes Galeries d'Art Contemporain; Bruxelles: Musée de Peinture Moderne, Wauxhall. *Work in permanent collections:* Simu and Dona State Museums, Bucharest. *Address:* 91–41 71st. Road, Forest Hills, New York, N.Y.11375. *Signs work:* "Sebastian Faur" see appendix.

FAUSSET, Shelley, Dip. F.A. (Lond.), (1954); sculptor in stone, metal, wood and resin; formerly taught at Central School of Art and Design, London; *b* Newbury, Berks, 5 Apr., 1920; *s* of H. I'A. Fausset, author; *m* Ann; one *s*, five *d. Educ.:* Friends' School, Saffron Walden; *studied art* at Chelsea School of Art (1948-52), Slade School, University College (1952-54). *Work in permanent collections:* Arts Council of Wales and numerous private collections; Herts and Derbyshire Education Committees, Harlow Art Trust, etc. Represented by Mercury Gallery and 'Art for Offices', London. *Address:* 21 Royal Oak La., Pirton, Hitchin, Herts. SG5 3QT. *Signs work:* "Shelley Fausset" or "S.F."

FAUST, Pat; artist in oil, water-colour, pastel, theatrical designs, murals; *b* Lancs.; *d* of the late William Faust. *Educ.:* Culcheth Hall, Ches.; *studied art* at Manchester Regional College of Art; Crescent Theatre, Birmingham. *Exhib.:* R.G.I., Manchester Academy, Birmingham A.G., Sewerby Hall, Bridlington, Scarborough A.G. and Town Hall, Ferens A.G., Hull, Beverley, Cartwright Hall, Bradford, Pannett, Whitby, R.A., R.B.A., S.W.A., R.Cam.A., U.A.S., Leeds City A.G., Paris Salon, Gallery Vallombreuse Biarritz, Brye A.G., Glaisdale, City Gallery, Darlington, Francis Phillips Gallery, Sheffield, Northern Academy of Art, Harrogate A.G., Guildhall, York, Yorkshire Artist Biennal; one-man shows: Marshalls, Scarborough, Hull University. *Work in permanent collections:* Scarborough A.G., Scarborough Town Hall, Menston Hospital and private collections. *Official purchase:* painting of Scarborough A.G. (hung R.A.) by Scarborough Corp. *Address:* Sea-Point, Upper Flat Cliffs, nr. Filey. *Clubs:* Leeds Fine Art, Scarborough Arts Soc. *Signs work:* "Pat Faust."

FAWSSETT, Ann: see ATKIN, Ann.

FEASEY, Judith Mary, Cert. R.A.S. (1976), A.T.C. (1977); painter/etcher in oil on canvas, water-colour, etching; Head of Art and Design, Brixton College; *b* Southgate, 3 Sept., 1945; *d* of Cyril Feasey, mechanical engineer. *Educ.:* St. Maurs Convent, Weybridge, Surrey; *studied art* at Guildford School of Art (1965-69), R.A. Schools (1973-76) Turner gold medal for landscape painting. *Exhib.:* R.A., G.L.C. Spirit of London; four-man show, Alfred East Gallery, Kettering, Mall Galleries, London, etc. *Address:* 90 Webster Rd., London SE16 4DF. *Signs work:* "J. Feasey" or "J.M.F."

FEDDEN, Mary, R.A.; Slade Diploma of Fine Arts; teacher of painting at Royal Coll. of Art (1958-64); Yehudi Menuhin School (1965-70); President, Royal West of England Academy (1983-88); *b* Bristol, 14 Aug., 1915; *d* of Vincent Fedden; *m* Julian Trevelyan (decd.). *Educ.:* Badminton School, Bristol. *Exhib.:* Tate Gallery, Leicester Gallery, Heals Gallery, Gimpel Fils, R.W.E.A., London Group, Edinburgh, Dublin, Brighton; solo shows: Christopher Hull, Redfern Gallery (6), New Grafton Gallery (6), Hamet Gallery (3), Beaux Arts Gallery (3). *Work in permanent collections:* H.M. The Queen, Prince Hassan of Jordan, Bristol, Hull, Carlisle, Edinburgh, Melbourne. *Official purchases:* murals, Charing Cross Hospital, Contemporary Arts Soc., Yorkshire C.C., Leicestershire C.C., Hertfordshire C.C., Min. of Works, Orient Line, Bristol Educ. Com.,

Barnet Hospital. *Address:* Durham Wharf, Hammersmith Terr., London W6 9TS. *Signs work:* "Fedden."

FEENY, Patrick A., F.M.G.P.; ecclesiastical artist and watercolourist; *b* Harrow, Middx., 30 Nov., 1910. *Educ.:* Stonyhurst College. *Address:* Enstone Cottage, High St., Feckenham, Worcs. B96 6HS. *Signs work:* see appendix.

FEI, Cheng-Wu; painter; Prof. (1941-46), College of Fine Art, National Central University, China; *b* China, 30 Dec., 1914; *s* of Mai-Chu Fei, poet, prof. of Chinese literature; *m* Chien-Ying Chang, artist. *Educ.:* National Central University, China (1930-34), Slade School of Fine Art (1947-50). *Exhib.:* R.A., R.I., R.W.A., R.W.S., N.E.A.C.; one-man shows at Leicester Galleries. *Work in permanent collections:* Royal West of England Academy, Universities' China Committee, Grave's Gallery, Sheffield, Derby A.G., etc. *Work repro.:* Studio, Art News & Review, La Revue Moderne, Kunst, etc. *Publication:* Brush Drawing in the Chinese Manner (Studio). *Address:* 52 Dollis Pk., London N3. *Signs work:* see appendix.

FEILER, Paul; painter; *b* 30 Apr., 1918; *s* of Prof. E. Feiler, M.D.; *m* Catharine Armitage; three *s*, two *d*. *Educ.:* Canford School, Dorset; *studied art* at Slade School of Fine Art. *Exhib.:* one-man shows since 1953. Redfern Gallery, London, Grosvenor Gallery, Warwick Arts Trust, London, U.S.A. *Public collections:* Tate Gallery, Arts Council, British Council, Liverpool, Manchester, Warwick, London, Oxford, Cambridge, Newcastle Universities; galleries in England, U.S.A., France, Austria, Canada and New Zealand. *Address:* Kerris, nr. Penzance, Cornwall.

FELL, Michael Anthony, F.S.D.-C.; painter/printmaker in oil, etching, lithography; Head of Foundation Studies, City & Guilds of London Art School; *b* London, 31 Jan., 1939; *m* Maureen; two *s*. *Educ.:* St. George's, Weybridge; *studied art* at St. Martin's School of Art, City & Guilds of London Art School. *Exhib.:* Jordan Gallery (1972-84), Halesworth Gallery (1972-85), Mall Galleries, Clementi House Gallery (1991), Gallery Renata, Chicago, Belanthi Gallery, N.Y., Chappel Galleries (1993), numerous R.A. Summer Exhbns. *Work in permanent collections:* B.M.; Arts Council; Victoria National Gallery and University of Melbourne, Australia; Churchill Library, Massachusetts. *Addresses:* The Music House, Bridge St., Bungay, Suffolk NR35 1HD; Barrere, Vic Fezensac, 32190 France. *Signs work:* "Michael Fell."

FELLOWS, Elaine Helen, B.A.(Hons.) (1981), H.S. (1987), S.W.A. (1988), R.M.S. (1992), U.S.M. (1990); professional painter of portraits and still life in miniature in water-colour on vellum or ivorine; *b* Walsall, 27 Nov., 1959. *Studied art* at Walsall College of Art (1977), Wolverhampton Polytechnic (1978-81). *Exhib.:* R.M.S. (Hon. mention 1989), S.W.A., Hilliard Soc. (Bell award 1990), Ulster Soc. of Miniaturists (Madam MacCarthy Mór memorial award 1991), Montellimar, France, Llewellyn Alexander Gallery, Medici Galleries, Limpsfield Water-colours, Riverside Gallery, Jane Marler Gallery. *Work in private collections:* G.B., U.S.A., France, Germany. *Publication:* contributor to The Magic of Miniatures. *Address:* Ridgebourn, 1/84 Church Rd., Netherton, W. Midlands DY2 0JJ. *Signs work:* see appendix.

FEREDAY, Joseph, R.E.; Diploma in Fine Art, Slade School; *b* Dudley, 9 Feb., 1917; *studied art* at Wolverhampton and Birmingham College of Art, Slade School (1946-48). *Work in permanent collections:* Portsmouth A.G., Southampton University, De Witt Gallery, Holland, Michigan, Plymouth A.G., Bilston A.G., St. Mary's College, Twickenham, Portsmouth Corp., Seely Library,

Ryde, I.O.W., British Embassy, Helsinki, Galerie Alphonse Marré, Chartres; one-man shows: Woodstock Gallery, London, Hiscock Gallery, Portsmouth, Galerie de Vallombreuse Biarritz, Southampton University, Vectis Gallery, Bembridge. *Address:* Yarborough House, New Rd., Brading, I.O.W. PO36 0AG.

FERGUSON, Malcolm Alastair Percy, R.W.A., D.F.A.(Lond., 1950); religious landscape and portrait painter; visiting teacher; *b* Blackwater, Hants., 19 Dec., 1913; *s* of Capt. P. F. H. Ferguson; *m* R.J.M. Holdsworth; one *s*, one *d*. *Educ.:* Durham School, R.M.A., Sandhurst, (invalided shortly after); *studied art* at Portsmouth and Croydon Schools of Art (1935-38), Slade School (1939, 1948-51). *Exhib.:* R.A., N.E.A.C., R.P., R.W.A., Paris Salon, Nat. Gall. of Wales, Bradford City A.G., etc.; one-man shows: London, provinces and abroad. *Official purchases:* Plymouth City A.G., R.W.A. Permanent Coll. Sponsored by Anglo American and De Beers, to design and carry out 'True Fresco' (1982, 1985), domed apse, St. Cuthbert's, Transkei. 1985-89 also designed and executed four altar panels and 30 ft. choir balustrade in egg tempera in St. Augustine's Church, Penhalonga, Zimbabwe; similar work completed on 10 ft. triptych in U.K., the High Altar in St. Mark's, the 13c. Lord Mayor's Chapel, Bristol (1990-92). *Work repro.:* various magazines. *Address:* 7 Mill St., North Petherton, Som. TA6 6LX. *Signs work:* "Malcolm A.P. Ferguson."

FERGUSON, Mary, M.F.P.S.; painter in oil, charcoal, pen and wash; *b* 6 May, 1919; *m* E.A. Ferguson; two *s*. *Educ.:* Friends School, Ackworth; *studied art* at The Gallery Schools, Melbourne, Australia (1953-55, Charles Bush), Reigate School of Art (1957-60, Denis Lucas, Walter Woodington). *Exhib.:* one-man shows: London including Loggia Gallery, F.P.S.; mixed shows: London and provincial galleries. *Work in private collections:* U.K. and Australia. *Address:* Bayhorne Lodge, 164 Balcombe Rd., Horley, Surrey RH6 9DS. *Clubs:* F.P.S., Reigate Soc. of Artists. *Signs work:* "Ferguson" or "MF" joined.

FERRIAN, Marie; sculptor in wood, terracotta, stone; *b* Hummelstown, Pa., 1 Jan., 1927; *d* of Harry Reigle; *m* George Ferrian; one *s*. *Educ.:* S.T.H.S.; *studied art* at Corcoran School of Art (painting: 1945-47, Eugene Weisz; sculpture: 1963-65, Heinz Warneke). *Exhib.:* St. Camillus, Women's National Bank, Firenze House, Corcoran Gallery, Art Barn (2). *Work in permanent collection:* National Museum of Women in the Arts. *Publications:* three children's books; featured in American Craftsmen (1975). *Address:* 4230 Silverwood La., Beth, M.D. 20816, U.S.A. *Signs work:* "M.F."

FERRY, David Dawson, B.A. (Hons.) (1979), H.D.F.A. (Lond.) (1981); printmaker/painter etching, lithography, oil and acrylic; lecturer, Camberwell/Canterbury Art Schools; 1993, appointed Head of Printmaking, Winchester School of Art; *b* Blackpool, 5 Feb., 1957; *s* of Brian Ferry. *Studied art* at Blackpool College Tech. (1975-76), Camberwell School of Arts and Crafts (1976-79, Mario Dubsky, Agathe Sorell), Slade School of Fine Art (1979-81, Stanley Jones). *Exhib.:* Contemporary Printmaking Air Gallery, R.A., S. London A.G., Ferens A.G., Hull, Offenbach, W. Germany, Paris 'Trace' Biennale; one-man shows, first and second International Contemporary Art Fairs at Barbican A.G., London Olympia, 5 Contemporary Printmakers, National Museum of Wales British Tour, The Star Chamber, Herbert Read Gallery, Canterbury, Kent University, Drew Gallery Canterbury, Boundry Gallery, London, Fachhochschule, Düsseldorf, Germany. *Work in permanent collections:* Grundy A.G., Blackpool, University College and St.Thomas Hospital, London, Maidstone A.G., Nuclear Electric. *Publication:* author, Painting Without a Brush (1991).

Address: 17 Monastery St., Canterbury, Kent CT1 1NJ. *Signs work:* "D.D. Ferry" or "D.D.F."

FESTING, Andrew Thomas, R.P. (1992); portrait painter in oil; *b* Chalford, 30 Nov., 1941; *m* Virginia Fyffx; one *d. Educ.:* Ampleforth College. *Exhib.:* R.P. *Work in permanent collections:* National Gallery Dublin, Royal Coll. *Address:* 3 Hillsleigh Rd., London W8. *Signs work:* "A.T. Festing."

FIDLER, Frank John, F.F.P.S. (1985); self taught artist in oil, water-colour, pastel, ceramic; *b* London, 1910; *s* of George Thomas Fidler, rose grower; *m* Ida Beatrice Elizabeth (decd.). *Exhib.:* British Artists in Moscow, F.P.S., 'Towards the Future', Paris, Drian Galleries, Ben Uri A.G., Letchworth A.G., Harlow A.G.; one-man shows: Drian Galleries (1958, 1959, 1961, 1963, 1969), Lundsbjerg A.G., Denmark (1961). *Work in permanent collections:* Gdansk National Museum, Leicester Educ. Authority, Art Gallery of N.S.W., ceramic murals in public bldgs. in Herts.; many private collections. *Address:* 130 High St., Barkway, Royston, Herts. *Signs work:* "Frank Fidler."

FIELD, Peter L., A.T.D., F.R.S.A.; artist, teacher and lecturer; Head of Faculty of Art and Design, City of Birmingham Polytechnic (retd. 1982); *b* Winson, Glos., 7 Feb., 1920; *s* of W. W. Field; *m* Cynthia G. Barry; two *d. Educ.:* Rendcomb College; *studied art* at Cheltenham School of Art (1937-39) under A. Seaton-White, Goldsmiths' College School of Art (1946-49) under Clive Gardner. *Exhib.:* London and provincial exhbns. *Work in permanent collections:* Swindon Art Gallery. *Official purchases:* Swindon Corporation. *Address:* 264 Mary Vale Rd., Bournville, Birmingham B30 1PJ. *Signs work:* "Peter L. Field."

FIENNES-FOSTER: see OTLEY, Barbara Kathleen.

FINCH, Michael, B.A.(Hons.) (1980), M.A.(R.C.A.) (1986); painter in mixed media; Senior tutor, Parsons School of Art, Paris; *b* London, 6 July, 1957; *s* of Reginald Finch; *m* Bridget Strevens. *Studied art* at Ravensbourne College of Art (1976-80, Brian Fielding), R.C.A. (1982-86, Peter de Francia). *Exhib.:* one-man shows: City Museum, Peterborough (1983), Groucho Club (1987, 1988), Pomeroy Purdy (1990, 1992). *Work in permanent collections:* Unilever, T.I. Group Coll. *Publication:* Sodium Nights (1990). *Address:* 59 rue de Meaux, 60300 Senlis, France. *Club:* Groucho. *Signs work:* see appendix.

FINCH, Patricia, F.R.B.S., S.W.A., C.P.S., F.S.N.A.D., F.R.S.A., A.W.G. (1992); sculptor; *b* London, 1921; *d* of W.M. Feldman, M.D., F.R.C.P.; two *d.* Mem. Royal Academy of Dancing. Silver medal for sculpture, International Grollo d'Oro (1976), Silver cups (1981, 1983). *Exhib.:* London, New York, Geneva, Glasgow, Venice, Malta, Le Touquet; mixed annual exhbns.: London, Mall Galleries, Westminster Galleries, R.A. Summer exhbn. (1979), FIDEM XIII British Museum. Demonstrator, Tate Gallery Sculpture Course (1983). *Work in permanent collections:* B.M. Coins and Medal Dept., Bank of England Museum: portrait busts of the Governor, Rt. Hon. Robin Leigh-Pemberton and Lord O'Brien, Royal Academy of Music, Musée Quentovic, Le Touquet, Museum of Fine Arts, Malta, Town Hall, Rhodes. *Work in private collections* in U.K., various European countries; also Canada, U.S.A., S. America, Japan, Australia. Over 100 portrait commissions carried out. Mem. Contemporary Portrait Soc. Tutor, Hulton Studio for Visually Handicapped (1986-90). Demonstrator, Design Centre, Islington (1990). Finalist in L.D.D.C. competitions (1988, 1989). Life-size figurative bronze for Golders Hill Park unveiled July 1991. *Address:* 851 Finchley Rd., London NW11 8LY. *Signs work:* "P. Finch."

FINCH, William Robert, F.I.A.L. (1953), free-lance journalist; artist various media, etcher; lecturer art country life; late head art dept. Beal Grammar School, Ilford; Chigwell School, Essex; founder-tutor, Over 40's Art Groups; lecturer Extra Mural Dept., Cambridge and London Universities; *b* Lowestoft, 6 Apr., 1905; *s* of William Henry Austin Finch, master mariner; *m* Peggy Doreen Hill; two *s. Educ.:* Lowestoft Grammar School, College St. Mark and St. John, Chelsea; *studied art:* self taught. *Exhib.:* R.A., East End Academy, Reading Art Guild, Assembly Rooms, Norwich, Southwold and Ilford, etc.; one-man show, Starston Gallery, Norfolk. *Work in collections:* Bury St. Edmund's Cathedral; Mrs. Lewis L. Douglas, New York; R. Hone, Esq.; Chigwell School, private Germany, France, Canada, Australia, U.S.A., Italy, etc. *Official purchases:* Ilford Libraries, Boy Scouts' Assoc., Westminster Bank, "Snowdrift" Lubricants. *Work repro.:* East Anglian Magazine, Review Assoc. Agriculture, Essex Countryside, Y.H.A. publications, etc. *Publications:* author/illustrator: Journeying into Essex, In and Around Folkestone, Introducing Essex to America, Country Buildings, 100 years of Snowdrift Lubricants, The Sea in My Blood. *Address:* Waveney Cottage, Weybread, Diss, Norfolk IP21 5UA. *Signs work:* "Finch."

FINDLAY, Sheila Anne Macfarlane, R.W.S., D.A.(Edin.), Post-Grad.(1950), Travelling Scholar (1951); artist and illustrator in water-colour and oil; *b* Auchlishie, Kirriemuir; *d* of William R. Findlay, farmer; *m* Alfred Hackney, A.R.W.S., A.R.E., D.A.(Edin.); two *d. Educ.:* Webster's Seminary; *studied art* at Edinburgh College of Art (1945-51) under John Maxwell, Sir William MacTaggart, Leonard Rosoman. *Work in permanent collections:* private collections. *Publications:* children's books illustrated for Faber & Faber, Adprint, Harrap, Odhams, Medici Soc. *Address:* Barnside, Lodge La., Cobham, nr. Gravesend, Kent DA12 3BS. *Signs work:* "Sheila Findlay."

FINEGOLD, Stephen M.; artist in oil, acrylic, pastel, collage, print; Artistic Director, F.C.A. Gallery; *b* London, 17 June, 1959; *m* Josephine; one *s. Educ.:* Beal Grammar School, Ilford; *studied art* at Bradford College, Croydon O.C.A. (1988). *Work in permanent collections:* F.C.A. Gallery, U.K., Spain, France, Australia. *Address:* Chantry House, Warley Town Lane, Warley, Halifax, W. Yorks. HX2 7SA. *Signs work:* "Finegold."

FINER, Stephen; artist in oil on canvas; *b* London, 1949. *Studied art* at Ravensbourne College of Art (1966-70). *Exhib.:* one-man shows: Four Vine Lane, London (1981, 1982, 1985), Anthony Reynolds Gallery (1986, 1988), Berkeley Sq. Gallery (1989), Bernard Jacobson Gallery (1992), Woodlands A.G. (1994); mixed shows: British Art 1940-1980, from the Arts Council Coll., Hayward Gallery (1980), Collazione Ingleze 2, Venice Biennale (1984), The Portrait Now, N.P.G. (1993), etc. *Work in permanent collections:* A.C.G.B., British Council, Contemporary Arts Soc., Southport A.G. *Address:* c/o Bernard Jacobson Gallery, 14A Clifford St., London W1. *Signs work:* "S.A. Finer" on reverse.

FINLAY, Ian, C.B.E., M.A. (Hons.), H.R.S.A., F.R.S.A.; Liveryman, Worshipful Company of Goldsmiths, London; Professor of Antiquities to Royal Scottish Academy; formerly Director, Royal Scottish Museum and Secy. Royal Fine Art Commission, Scotland; *b* Auckland, N.Z.; *s* of W. R. Finlay, artist; *m* Mary Scott Pringle; two *s*, one *d. Educ.:* Edinburgh Academy, University of Edinburgh. *Publications:* Scotland (O.U.P.), Art in Scotland (O.U.P.), Scottish Crafts (Harrap), History of Scottish Gold and Silver Work (Chatto), The Lothians (Collins), The Highlands (Batsford), The Lowlands (Batsford), Celtic

Art (Faber), Priceless Heritage: the Future of Museums (Faber), Columba (Gollancz). *Address:* Currie Riggs, Balerno, Midlothian EH14 5AG.

FIRTH, Sir Raymond William, M.A. (N.Z.), Ph.D.(Lond.), F.B.A., Emeritus Prof. of Anthropology, University of London; field research in Solomon Islands, 1928-29, 1952, 1966; Malaya, 1939-40, 1963; *b* Auckland, N.Z., 25 Mar., 1901; *m* Rosemary Upcott; one *s. Educ.:* Auckland University College, London School of Economics. *Publications:* Art and Life in New Guinea (Studio), 1938; The Social Framework of Primitive Art (ch. in Elements of Social Organization), (Watts, 1951), Tikopia Woodworking Ornament, (Man 40, 27), Tikopia Art and Society in Primitive Art and Society (ed. A. Forge) O.U.P. (1972), Art and Anthropology in Anthropology Art and Aesthetics (ed. J. Coote & A. Shelton) Clarendon (1992). *Address:* 33 Southwood Ave., London N6 5SA.

FISHER, Don Mulready, M.S.I.A., M.F.P.S.; portrait and landscape painter in oil and gouache; TV film and theatre designer; writer; *b* Finchley, 27 Apr., 1923; *s* of Capt. Henry Cecil Fisher, M.C., playwright, and Louisa Mary Maddock; *m* Lyliane Guelfand; one *s*, one *d. Educ.:* Golders Hill School and Ravensfield College; *studied art* at Hampstead Garden Suburb Institute, Art Class (1940-41); St. Martin's School of Art under Ruskin Spear, R.A. (1943-46). *Exhib.:* London Group, R.O.I., R.B.A., N.E.A.C., N.S., Berkeley Galleries, New Burlington Galleries, Piccadilly Gallery, Salon des Nations, Paris (1984), Trends (1984), Barbican Centre, Paris Salon (1985-87); one-man shows, Dowmunt Gallery (1980), Cork St. Fine Arts Gallery (1983). *Work in private collections:* Britain, France, Sweden, Spain, Canada, U.S.A., Australia, Italy, Belgium. *Work repro.:* Designers in Britain Nos. 6 & 7. *Address:* 26 Rue Monsieur le Prince, 75006 Paris. *Club:* Chelsea Arts. *Signs work:* see appendix.

FISHER, Isabelle Diane Mulready; Diplomée Beaux Arts, Paris; stained glass artist; *b* Hampstead, 10 Dec., 1954; *d* of Donald G. Mulready Fisher, g-g-g-s of William Mulready, R.A. and Lyliane Guelfand of Paris; one *s. Educ.:* Lycee Français de Londres; *studied art* at Sir John Cass College (1973-74), Wimbledon School of Art (1974-77), Beaux Arts, Paris (1978-82, Allain, Master of stained glass). *Exhib.:* U.F.P.S. Luxembourg Museum, Paris (1981), Chartres Stained Glass Museum (1982), Sacred Art, le Salon des Nations (1984), Homage to Joan Miro Exhbn., Barcelona (1985). *Commissions:* window, 'Noah after the flood' l'Eglise de Ligny le-Ribaut, Loiret, France (1981); four windows, Hotel le Kern, Val d'Isere; six memorial windows for the St. Martin's Chapel (Benedictine Monastery) Monte Cassino, Italy (1989-91). *Addresses:* Rue de la Halle, Martel, Lot, 46.600 France; and 26 Rue Monsieur le Prince, 75006, France.

FISHER, Myrta, D.F.A.(Lond.) Slade School (1937-40); awarded Henriques Scholarship (1938); student of the British School at Athens (1954-55); *b* Wimbledon, 28 Aug., 1917; *d* of Harold and Gladys Fisher. *Exhib.:* widely in London and Sussex, also Suffolk. Work in many private collections, also purchased by American Express and the Towner A.G., Eastbourne. Exhib. with the Eastbourne Group. Works in acrylic. *Address:* Pennyhaven, Norton Rd., Newhaven, E.Sussex. BN9 0BP. *Signs work:* "M.F."

FISHWICK, Clifford, A.T.D. (1947); painter, Principal, Exeter College of Art (1958-1984); *b* nr. Accrington, 21 June, 1923; *s* of Norman Fishwick, draper; *m* Patricia Fishwick; two *s*, two *d. Educ.:* Chester Grammar School; *studied art* at Liverpool College of Art. *Exhib.:* (one-man) St. George's Gallery (1957), Dartington Hall, Exeter University, Plymouth Museum, Exeter Museum, Essex University, Greenwich Theatre, Woodstock Museum, Austin-Desmond Fine Art (1989-90); (mixed) Newlyn, Penwith Soc., John Moores, Bradford A. G., various private galleries. *Official purchases:* Bradford, Exeter and Plymouth Museums, B.M., Christchurch, Oxford, Exeter University, Devon C.C., Christchurch (N. Z.) A. G., Rolle College. *Publications:* places, poems and illustrations. *Address:* Salisbury House, Monmouth St., Topsham, Devon EX3 0AJ. *Signs work:* "Clifford Fishwick."

FITZROY, Cornelia, B.A.(Hons.); painter in oil, acrylic, pastel; *b* London, 11 Sept., 1962; *m* Michael; one *s,* one *d. Educ.:* Priors Field, Godalming; *studied art* at Byam Shaw School of Art (1980-81), Chelsea School of Art (1981-84). *Exhib.:* A.O.I. (1984), Osbourne Studio Galleries, John Russell Gallery, Ipswich. *Address:* Hackney Cottage, Fressingfield, Eye, Suffolk IP21 5SG. *Signs work:* "Cornelia FitzRoy."

FLANDERS, Dennis, R.W.S., R.B.A, Hon. Freeman, Painter-Stainers' Co., water-colours and black and whites; *b* 2 July, 1915; *m* Dalma Darnley Taylor; one *s,* one *d. Educ.:* Merchant Taylor's School. *Exhib.:* R.A.; one-man shows in London galleries (1947, 1951, 1953, 1955, 1964, 1967, 1984, 1986, 1990), and in provincial galleries, Bedford, Edinburgh, Southport, Worthing. *Work in permanent collections:* Guildhall, National War Collection, Fitzwilliam Museum, Cambridge, Wolverhampton, Bury, Southport, National Library of Wales. *Work repro.:* Famous Streets in Sunday Times (1952-53); special artist to the Illustrated London News (1956-64); The Great Livery Companies of The City of London (1974), portfolios of Drawings; Dennis Flanders' Britannia, being collection of 214 drawings (half in colour) of Britain, best of 3,000 works done over period of forty years (Oriel Press, 1984), facsimile prints of Oxford Colleges. *Address:* 51 Gt. Ormond St., London WC1N 3HZ. *Club:* Art Workers' Guild (Master, 1975). *Signs work:* see appendix.

FLEMING, Ian, R.S.W. (1946), A.R.S.A. (1947), R.S.A. (1965); painter in oils and water-colour, etcher; senior lecturer, Glasgow School of Art (1931-47), Warden, Patrick Allan Fraser Art College, Arbroath, Angus, (1948-54); head of Gray's School of Art, Aberdeen (since 1954); *b* Glasgow, 19 Nov., 1906; *s* of John Fleming; *m* Catherine Weetch, D.A.; one *s,* two *d. Educ.:* Glasgow School of Art and Paris. *Exhib.:* R.A., R.S.A., Royal Glasgow Institute of Fine Art, Soc. Scottish Artists, Walker Art Gallery, etc. *Official purchases:* Belfast, Liverpool, Bradford, Glasgow and other municipal galleries; Thorburn Ross Memorial Fund, R.S.A. *Address:* 15 Fonthill Rd., Aberdeen. *Club:* Glasgow Art. *Signs work:* "Fleming."

FLEMING, James Hugh, B.A.Hons. (1987); printmaker, painter, illustrator, lecturer, poet; *b* Barrow in Furness; *s* of James Arthur Fleming; *m* Norma; one *s,* one *d. Studied art* at Open University, Liverpool Polytechnic. *Exhib.:* Acorn Gallery, Bluecoat Gallery, Hanover Gallery, Davey Gallery, Williamson A.G., Dee Fine Arts, Marie Curie Foundation, Merseyside Artists Touring Exhbn., Heffers, Oriel Mostyn, Cadaques Mini Print, Intaglio Mini Print, Manchester Academy, Humberside Printmaking Exhbn. Theatre Clwyd, Ruthin Craft Centre, Broekman A.G. *Address:* 46 Whitelands Meadow, Upton, Wirral L49 6PA. *Clubs:* N.A.P.A., Wirral Soc. of Arts, A.B.W.S., Bluecoat Studio Print-makers' Group. *Signs work:* "Jim" and see appendix.

FLETCHER, Alistair Richard, B.A.Hons. (1985), A.R.E. (1985), British Inst. award (1983), Commendation Stowells Trophy (1984), Garton and Cook award (1985); teacher, artist in etching, drawing and water-colour; *b* Gosforth, Northumberland, 25 Jan., 1963; *s* of Gordon Richard Fletcher, B.A.Hons.; *m* E.M. Fletcher; one *s,* two *d. Educ.:* Henry Smith School, Hartlepool; *studied art* at Cleveland College of Art and Design (1981-82), Kingston Polytechnic (1982-

85), Bretton Hall (1986-87). *Exhib.:* R.E., Coach House Gallery, Guernsey, Darlington A.G. *Address:* Wyndham School, Egremont, Cumbria. *Club:* R.E. *Signs work:* "Alistair R. Fletcher."

FLETCHER-WATSON, James, R.I. (1952), R.B.A. (1957); painter in water-colour; *b* Coulsdon, Surrey, 25 July, 1913. *Educ.:* Eastbourne College; *studied art* at R.A. School of Architecture (silver medal for design, 1936). *Exhib.:* R.A., R.I., R.B.A., Paris Salon, Stockholm, Windrush Gallery (annually). *Work repro.:* British Railways carriage posters; written instruction book on watercolour painting (Batsford, 1982, second book 1985, third book 1988, fourth book 1993), third video painting instruction (1993). *Address:* Windrush House, Windrush, nr. Burford, Oxford. *Signs work:* "J. Fletcher-Watson."

FLOWER, Rosina, M.F.P.S.; painter; *b* London; one *s*, one *d*. *Educ.:* London and Headley; *studied art:* 1971-75: P.D. Dennis Syrett, Bassetsbury Manor (Tom Coates), Burleighfield House (Anne Bruce). *Exhib.:* R.A., R.B.A., R.O.I., P.S., Britains Painters, Boathouse Gallery Weybridge, Galerie Hautefeuille Paris, Bloomsbury Gallery London, Medici Gallery London; solo shows: Loggia Gallery London, Henley Management College Berks. Work in hospitals and private collections. *Work repro.:* greetings cards. *Address:* 132 Roberts Ride, Hazlemere, Bucks. *Clubs:* Cookham Painters, F.P.S., F.B.A. *Signs work:* "Flower," "R. Flower" or "Rosie."

FLYNN, Mary Theresa, R.S.W. (1969), D.A. (1951); landscape, figurative and still life freelance artist in water-colour, acrylic and oil; former principal teacher of art, John Paul Academy, Glasgow; *b* Selkirk, 30 Nov., 1923; *d* of James Flynn (decd.). *Educ.:* Galashiels Academy; *studied art* at Edinburgh College of Art (1946-51, Sir Robin Philipson, P.P.R.S.A., R.A., R.S.W., Leonard Rosomon, O.B.E., R.A., R.S.W., Derek Clarke, A.R.S.A., R.S.W., J. Kingsley Cook). *Exhib.:* R.S.W., R.S.A., R.G.I., S.S.W.A., S.A.A.C.; one-man shows: B.B.C. Club, Blythswood Gallery, R.S. Acad. of Music and Drama, Galashiels Scott Bi-centenary show, Gallery Paton, E.S.U. Gallery; numerous shared exhbns. *Work in permanent collections:* Lillie A.G., S.A.C., Leeds Museum Service. *Address:* 6 Rosebery Cres., Edinburgh EH12 5JP. *Signs work:* "Theresa Flynn."

FOLKES, Peter Leonard, A.T.D., R.W.A., V.P.R.I., Hon. F.C.A.; painter in oil, water-colour and acrylic; Demonstrator for Winsor and Newton; Tutor, Artscape Painting Holidays; *b* Beaminster, 3 Nov., 1923; *s* of Leonard Folkes; *m* Muriel Giddings; two *s*. *Educ.:* Sexey's School Bruton; *studied art* at West of England College of Art, Bristol (1940-42 and 1947-50). *Exhib.:* R.A., R.W.A., R.I.; one-man shows: Crespi Gallery, New York (1965), University of Southampton (1965, 1973), Barzansky Gallery, New York (1967), Alwin Gallery, London (1970), Gainsboroughs' House Gallery, Sudbury (1977), R.W.A. Galleries, Bristol (1986). *Official purchases;* Arts Council of Great Britain, R.W.A. *Address:* 61 Ethelburt Ave., Swaythling, Southampton SO2 3DF. *Signs work:* "Folkes."

FOLLAND, Ronald Norman; self-taught artist in oil, acrylic and water-colour; *b* Portsmouth, 5 Dec., 1932; *s* of Norman Sidney Folland; two *s*. *Educ.:* Cowplain Boys' School, Hants. *Exhib.:* one-man shows, Frost and Reed (Bristol, Worthing, London), To-Day Southern TV., Nationwide B.B.C. TV., Harrogate, Birmingham. St. Helier, Jersey, Bournemouth, etc. *Work in permanent collections:* U.S.A., Canada, Australia, New Zealand, France, Ireland, Russia, Scandinavia, Germany and Israel. Rated in Top Ten Artists Poll yearly since 1965. *Address:* Eland

House, 19 The Avenue, Ickenham, Uxbridge, Middx UB10 8NR. *Club:* Fine Art Trade Guild. *Signs work:* see appendix.

FOOT, Victorine Anne, D.A.; artist in oil, mural painting; Directorate of Camouflage (1941-45); *b* Kent, 1 May, 1920; *d* of Major Hammond-Foot, R.E.; *m* Eric Schilsky, R.A., R.S.A. (decd.); one *d,* Clare. *Educ.:* Oakdene School; *studied art* at Central School of Arts and Crafts, Chelsea School of Art, Edinburgh College of Art. *Exhib.:* R.A., R.S.A., S.S.A., N.E.A.C., London Group, etc., exhbn. at Institut Français, Edinburgh (1949), Scottish Gallery, Edinburgh (1969, 1979, 1984), LYC Gallery (1981). *Work in permanent collections:* Arts Council (Scottish Committee), War Artists' Advisory Commn. (1943), Scottish National Portrait Gallery. *Address:* The Studio, 16A Meadow Pl., Edinburgh EH9 1JR. *Signs work:* "Victorine Foot," "V.F."

FORBES, Donald, D.A. Glas. (1974); painter in oil, restorer; Paintings Restorer at National Galleries of Scotland, Edinburgh; *b* Glasgow, 31 Aug., 1952; *s* of Donald Forbes. *Educ.:* Bellahouston Academy; *studied art* at Glasgow School of Art (1970-74, David Donaldson, R.S.A., R.P., LL.D.). *Exhib.:* R.G.I., R.S.A.; one-man, John D. Kelly Gallery, Lillie A.G., Milngavie. *Address:* 19 Wardlaw St., Edinburgh EH11. *Club:* Glasgow Art. *Signs work:* "FORBES" (printed in a dark colour).

FORD, Jenifer, V.P.N.S., F.R.S.A., Cert. Fine Art (University of Cape Town) (1953); portrait, landscape and still-life painter; *b* Cape Town, 25 June, 1934; *d* of Richard Dekenah; *m* His Hon. Judge Peter Ford; one *d. Educ.:* Rustenburg School, Cape Town; *studied art* at Michaelis Art School and under Bernard Adams, R.P. *Exhib.:* R.P., R.O.I., N.S., C.P.S., Arts Exhbn. Bureau, Painting South East (1975), Haus der Kunst, Munich (1988-89), Kunst in Giesing (1985-90), European Patent Office, Munich (1980-89), S.W.A.; solo shows in England and Germany. *Official purchases:* European Patent Office, Bayern Versicherung, Munich, Patents Appeal Court, Stockholm. *Address:* 59 Lancaster Ave., Hadley Wood, Barnet EN4 0ER. *Signs work:* "Jenifer Ford."

FORD, Michael, free-lance artist in oils, water-colour, black and white; *b* 28 July, 1920; *s* of Major E. M. Ford, M.C. *Educ.:* privately; London University; Goldsmiths' College Art School (Clive Gardiner, 1937-40). *Exhib.:* R.A., R.P., N.E.A.C., R.B.A., United Soc., P.S., Paris Salon, Russell Cotes Gallery, Towner Art Gallery, also touring exhbns. on loan, etc. *Official purchases:* Three oil paintings by M. of I. (War Artists' Exhbn.). *Works repro.:* Two paintings bought by M. of I.; portraits commissioned by magazines and newspapers. *Address:* Studio Cottage, Winsor Rd., Winsor, Southampton SO4 2HP. *Signs work:* "Michael Ford."

FORD, Olga Gemes, M.S.I.A. graduated in arch. (Techn. University, Berlin); lecturer, The City of Leicester Polytechnic and School of Architecture; traveller and freelance photographer, works for distinguished art publishers here and abroad (Photographic Illustrations); *d* of L. Gemes; *m* Oliver E. Ford, B.Sc. (London), Ph.D. (Zürich), F.R.I.C. (decd.). *Educ.:* Realschule, Vienna; *studied architecture* at Vienna, Dresden, Berlin, Paris; under Prof. Poelzig. *Exhib.:* Britain Can Make It, Cotton Board, Manchester. *Work repro.:* in Architectural Review, L'Architecture d'Aujourd'hui, La Construction Moderne, Design, 46 Designers in Britain 2 and 4, Decoration, etc. *Address:* 12 Highgate Spinney, Crescent Rd., London N8 8AR. *Signs work:* "OLGA GEMES FORD" or "OLGA FORD."

FORTNUM, Peggy; book illustrator and designer; *b* Harrow-on-the Hill, 23 Dec., 1919; *d* of Comdr. Arthur John Fortnum; *m* Ralph Nuttall-Smith, painter and sculptor. *Educ.:* St. Margaret's, Harrow; Central School of Arts and Crafts. *Work repro.:* textile designs, magazines, illustrations for eighty books, which include The Happy Prince and Other Stories (Oscar Wilde), The Reluctant Dragon (Kenneth Grahame), A Bear Called Paddington, 12 Books (Michael Bond), Thursday's Child (Noel Streatfield), Robin (Catherine Storr), Little Pete Stories (Leila Berg), A Few Fair Days (Jane Gardam), Running Wild (Autobiography) (Chatto & Windus); drawings for television: Playschool, Jackanory. *Address:* 10 Hall Barn, West Mersea, Essex CO5 8QD. *Signs work:* "PEGGY FORTNUM" or "P.F."

FORWARD, Hubert W.F., N.D.D. (1951), A.T.D. (1952); artist in oil, watercolour, lithography, ceramics, calligraphy; art master, lecturer in ceramics; Head of Art, Hewett School, Norwich; Lecturer i/c Ceramics, Norwich School of Art (1953-82); *b* Tottenham, 1927; *s* of H.E. Forward, signwriter; *m* Beryl Woodward; two *s. Educ.:* Tottenham Grammar School; *studied art* at Hornsey College of Art (1945-52, Alun Braund, Russell Reeve, Henry Holzer, F. J. Mitchell, F. J. Winter, A.S.H. Mills). *Exhib.:* East Anglian Artists, R.I. (1969), British Artists, Los Angeles (1961). *Work in permanent collections:* Guildhall, City of London (calligraphy), University of East Anglia (lithographs) and many private collections, Dr. V. Jewson, Rev. W. Feast, Dr. Stokes-Whittaker. *Work repro.:* by Studio Publications and New York Times. *Address:* 12 Mill Hill Rd., Norwich, Norfolk. *Clubs:* S.G.F.A., Norwich Twenty Group. *Signs work:* "H. FORWARD" and see appendix.

FOSTER, Judith, N.D.D., A.R.C.A.: painter/printmaker in oil, water-colour, pastel, etching; *b* 19 Oct., 1937; *m* Richard Pinkney; two *s. Educ.:* Bath High School G.P.D.S.T.; *studied art* at Ipswich School of Art (1955-59, Philip Fortin, Colin Moss), R.C.A. (1959-62, Carel Weight, Ruskin Spear, Ceri Richards). *Exhib.:* R.A., R.C.A.; one-man shows: Ipswich, Bath, Peterborough, Edinburgh, Northampton. *Work in permanent collection:* local authority collections. *Address:* 10 The Street, Bramford, Ipswich, Suffolk IP8 4EA. *Signs work:* "J. Foster" or occasionally initials on small works.

FOSTER, Sir Norman Robert, A.R.A., R.D.I. Dip.Arch. (Manc.), M.Arch. (Yale), R.I.B.A., F.C.S.D., Hon. F.A.I.A., Hon. B.D.A.; architect; Director, Foster Associates Ltd.; *b* Reddish, 1 June, 1935; *s* of Robert Foster; *m* Wendy Ann Cheesman (d. 1989); four *s. Educ.:* Burnage Grammar School, Manchester; *studied architecture* at Manchester University School of Architecture and Dept. of Town and Country Planning, Yale University School of Architecture. *Exhib.:* R.A., London, Paris, Bilbao, Barcelona, Seville, Tokyo, Florence, Nimes, Sainsbury Centre for Visual Arts, Manchester, Milan, New York. *Work in permanent collection:* Museum of Modern Art, N.Y. *Publications:* The Works of Foster Associates (1979); Norman Foster: Buildings and Projects Vols. 1, 2 & 3 (1990); plus numerous books and articles. *Address:* Foster Associates Ltd., Riverside Three, 22 Hester Rd., London SW11 4AN. *Signs work:* see appendix.

FOSTER, Richard Francis, R.P.; Lord Mayor's award for London Views (1972); painter in oil; *b* London, 6 June, 1945; *s* of William Foster, M.A.; *m* Sally Kay-Shuttleworth; one *s*, two *d. Educ.:* Harrow and Trinity College, Oxford; *studied art:* Signorina Simi, Florence (1963-66), City and Guilds, London (1967-70). *Exhib.:* R.A., R.P.; one-man shows, Jocelyn Feilding Gallery (1974), Spink & Son (1978, 1982, 1984, 1991). *Address:* 5A Clareville Grove, London SW7 5AW. *Clubs:* A.W.G., Chelsea Arts. *Signs work:* "Richard Foster."

FOUNTAIN, Desmond Hale, F.R.B.S. (1986), Dip.A.D. (Exeter) (1969), A.T.D./Cert.Ed. (Bristol) (1970); sculptor, mainly female nudes and life-size children, in bronze editions of nine; *b* Bermuda, 29 Dec., 1946; *s* of D.O.T. Fountain, accountant; *m* Miranda M.C. Hay; one *s*, one *d*. *Educ.:* Normanton College, Buxton, Derbys.; *studied art* at Stoke-on-Trent College of Art, pre-Dip. (1964-66, Dennis Westwood), Exeter College of Art (1966-69, Kenneth Carter). *Exhib.:* one-man shows: Alwin Gallery (1980, 1983), Coach House Gallery, Guernsey (1983), Sally le Gallais, Jersey (1983), Windjammer Gallery, Bermuda (1984-90), Renaissance Gallery, Conn., U.S.A. (1986), Cavalier Galleries, Conn., U.S.A. (1988), The Sculpture Gallery (1989-91). *Work in permanent collections:* Leaders Magazine's Desmond Fountain Sculpture Pk., Bath, N.Y.; I.T.T., N.Y.; City Museum, Stoke-on-Trent; Lantana Cottage Colony, Bermuda; Bank of Bermuda, Bermuda. Founded The Bermuda Fine Art Trust (1982), vehicle for Bermuda's National Gallery, radio and television U.K., U.S.A. and Bermuda. *Address:* P.O. Box FL317, Flatts FLBX, Bermuda. *Club:* Royal Bermuda Yacht. Signs work: "Desmond Fountain" or "Fountain."

FOWKES, David Reeve, B.A.; *b* Eastbourne, 15 Dec., 1919; *s* of A. F. Reeve Fowkes; *m* Lorna Fowkes; one *s*, one *d*. *Educ.:* Eastbourne Grammar School; Reading University (1938-40, 1946-48). *Exhib.:* Scottish Gallery Edinburgh (1973, 1976, 1980), Aberdeen University (1974, 1983), Peter Potter, Haddington (1979), Manor House, Ilkley (1984), Stonegate Gallery, York (1984, 1985, 1988, 1990, 1993), Towner, Eastbourne (1985), Abbot Hall, Kendal (1989), Charlotte Lampard, London (1989). *Collections:* H.M. The Queen, Aberdeen A.G., Angus County, Towner A.G., Eastbourne, N. of Scot. College of Agriculture, Rowett Inst., Rowntree, Scottish Arts Council. *Publication:* A Gunner's Journal (1990). *Address:* 75 Bishopthorpe Rd., York YO2 1NX. *Signs work:* "FOWKES."

FOWLE, LeClerc, R.O.I., R.W.A., F.R.S.A., Paris Salon gold and silver medallist; 1st prize Laing Comp. (1979); painter in oil, pen and pencil, and pastel; *b* Haslar, Hants.; *d* of Gerald Sichel, F.R.C.S., etc.; *m* Brigadier J. LeC. Fowle, C.B., C.I.E. (decd.). *Studied art* privately and at Slade School of Fine Art. *Exhib.:* Extensively 'One Painter Exhbns.' Bond St., London, R.A., R.O.I., R.W.A., R.S.A., Leicester Galleries (Fame and Promise), N.E.A.C., R.B.A., and many galleries in London and all over England. *Work in permanent collections:* America, Australia, Portugal, Switzerland, England. *Address:* 23 Casson House, Kramer Mews, London SW5 9JG. *Clubs:* Cavalry and Guards, Chelsea Arts. *Signs work:* "LeClerc Fowle."

FOWLER, Ronald George Francis, S.G.F.A. (1982); Mem. of Council (1985); printmaker in etching, aquatint, drypoint and wood engraving; *b* London, 15 Apr., 1916; *s* of the late George Edward Fowler; *m* Elizabeth Jean Stewart; one *s*, two *d*. *Educ.:* Strand School, London, and Birkbeck College, University of London; *studied art* at Glasgow School of Art, Warrington School of Art, and Chester C.F.E. *Exhib.:* R.S.B.A., N.S.P.S., S.G.F.A., Mall Prints and numerous one-man shows in N.W. England. *Work in permanent collection:* Buxton Museum and A.G., Derbyshire. *Address:* Yew Tree Cottage, Lower Whitley, Ches. WA4 4JD. *Signs work:* "FOWLER."

FRAME, Roger Campbell Crosbie, C.A. (1973); Secretary of: R.S.W.; Chartered Accountant; *b* Glasgow, 7 June, 1949. *Educ.:* Glasgow Academy. *Address:* 29 Waterloo St., Glasgow G2 6BZ. *Club:* Glasgow Art.

FRANCESCONI, Anselmo: see ANSELMO (Anselmo Francesconi).

FRANCIS, Henry Sayles; formerly curator of painting, prints and drawings at the Cleveland Museum of Art, Cleveland, Ohio (1931-67); curator of prints, Cleveland (1927-29), retired, Apr., 1967; *b* Boston, Mass., 4 Mar., 1902; *s* of George Tappan Francis; *m* Frances Meriam Burrage; one *s. Educ.:* St. Paul's School, Concord, New Hampshire; Harvard University, A.B. (1924); *studied art* at the Fogg Art Museum, Harvard University. *Publications:* articles in the Bulletin, Cleveland Museum of Art, Gazette des Beaux-Arts, Print Collectors Quarterly, The Art Quarterly, Bulletin of the Medical Library Assoc. *Address:* Wentworth Rd., Walpole, New Hampshire 03608. *Signs work:* "Henry S. Francis."

FRANCYN (Dehn Fuller), F.F.P.S., W.I.A.C., N.S.; painter in oils and gouache; *b* Portsmouth; *d* of Walter Henry Fuller, lecturer; *m* Curt Dehn; one *s*, one *d. Educ.:* at home. *Exhib.:* one-man shows: Paris, The Hague, Utrecht, Sydney, London; group shows: Free Painters and Sculptors, W.I.A.C., Hampstead Artists, N.S., etc. *Work in private collections:* Holland, Germany, U.S.A., Australia. *Publications:* Poems, Man's Moment (U.S.A.), portfolio of folk-songs, collection of poems. *Address:* 6 Elsworthy Ct., Elsworthy Rd., London NW3. *Clubs:* I.C.A., Hampstead Artist. *Signs work:* see appendix.

FRANKENTHALER, Helen; First Prize, Paris Biennale (1959); painter in oils, acrylic, on unsized cotton-duck; *b* New York, 12 Dec., 1928; *d* of Alfred Frankenthaler, Supreme Court Justice. *Educ.:* Bennington College, Vermont, U.S.A. (B.A.). *Exhib.:* retrospective: Museum of Modern Art, N.Y. (1989), Guggenheim Museum, N.Y. (1985), Sterling and Francine Clark Art Inst. (print retrospective), Williamstown, Ma. (1980), United States Information Agency Travelling Exhbn.; Japan, Australia, Philippines, Singapore, Korea, Hong Kong, Mexico, Brazil, Venezuela, Colombia (1978), Corcoran Gallery of Art, Washington, D.C. (1975), Whitney Museum of American Art, N.Y. (1969). *Work in permanent collections:* New York City: Solomon R. Guggenheim Museum, Museum of Modern Art, Whitney Museum, Met. Museum of Art; Washington D.C.: National Gallery of Art, Corcoran Gallery of Art, Smithsonian Institution—Hirshhorn Museum and Sculpture Garden; Albright-Knox A.G., Buffalo; Art Institute, Chicago; Cleveland Museum of Art; San Francisco Museum of Art. *Address:* 173 East 94th St., New York 10128. *Signs work:* see appendix.

FRANKLAND, Eric Trevor, N.D.D. (1956), Cert. R.A.S. (1958), F.R.S.A. (1960), A.R.E. (1992), Leverhulme Fund award (1959), Landseer Scholarship (1956-57), R.A. Silver Medal for Drawing (1957); painter and printmaker in oil, water-colour and print-making media; *b* Middlesbrough, 7 July, 1931; *m* Dorothy Southern, artist. *Educ.:* Middlesbrough Technical School and Constantine College; *studied art* at Laird School of Art, Birkenhead; R.A. Schools. *Exhib.:* R.A., R.E., R.W.S., R.B.A., London Group, etc. Work in municipal art galleries. *Address:* 13 Spencer Rd., London SW18 2SP. *Signs work:* "Trevor Frankland" on prints, "FRANKLAND" on other works, sometimes "T.F."

FRANKLIN, Ellen, F.P.S.; Mem. Ben Uri Gallery; painter in oil; *b* Berlin, 18 Aug., 1919. *Studied art:* Reiman School of Art, Berlin (1936-38), Morley College, London. *Exhib.:* Gladstone Pk. Gables Gallery (1980), Loggia Gallery (1985, 1991), Trends (1987, 1989), Ben Uri (1988, 1992), Cardiff (1988), Morley Gallery (1991, 1993). Work in private collections. *Address:* 44 Beechcroft Gdns., Wembley, Middx. HA9 8EP. *Signs work:* "E. Franklin."

FRANKLIN, Kim Hunsdon Eastwood, B.F.A. (1977), S.WL.A.; painter in water-colour, tempera, oil; *b* Natal, 26 July, 1955; *s* of Deryk Eastwood Franklin, architect; *m* Marianne; one *s. Educ.:* Hilton College; *studied art* at University of Capetown Michaelis School of Fine Art (Peggy Delport, Stanley Pinker). *Exhib.:* Belgium, Botswana, Gt. Britain, Holland, Spain. *Work in permanent collection:* National Gallery of Botswana. *Publications:* Ferguson-Lees, I., Burton, P., Franklin, K., Mead, D., Birds of Prey — An Identification Guide to Raptors of the World (Christopher Helm, Ltd., 1992). *Address:* 17 York Rd., Teddington, Middx. TW11 8SL. *Club:* S.WL.A. *Signs work:* "K.H.E. Franklin."

FRASER, Donald Hamilton, R.A.; painter; *b* London, 30 July, 1929; *m* Judith Wentworth-Sheilds, 1954; one *d. Studied art:* St. Martin's School of Art, London (1949-52) and in Paris (French Gov. Scholarship). Tutor, Royal College of Art (1958-84); Hon. Fellow R.C.A. (1984); Hon. Curator, Royal Academy (1992); Vice-Pres. Artist's General Benevolent Inst.; mem. since 1986 of Royal Fine Art Commission. Over 60 individual exhbns. in Europe, N. America and Japan. Work in public collections throughout the world. *Address:* c/o Royal Academy of Arts, London W1V 0DS. *Signs work:* see appendix.

FRASER, Elizabeth Bertha, Mem. Society of Portrait Sculptors; sculptor in wax, plaster, bronze, painter in oil; *b* Teddington, London, 1914; *d* of Arthur Marks, F.I.C., A.R.S.M., A.R.C.Sc., A.M.I.Mech.E.; *m* Lindley Maughton Fraser. *Studied art* at Birmingham School of Art, Central School of Art, London, Westminster School of Art, London, under Schilsky, Edinburgh College of Art under Schilsky. *Exhib.:* R.A.; one-man shows, London and Edinburgh, Tour of Britain Sculptors Society, Society of Portrait Sculptors Yearly Exhbn., Edinburgh Younger Academy. *Address:* The Studio, 7 Ridgway Gdns., London SW19. *Signs work:* "Liz Frazer," "Elizabeth Scott-Fraser" or "Elizabeth Fraser."

FREDRICK, Waveney, R.B.S.A. (1978), P.S. (1983); Feeney award, Birmingham (1977), Herring award, Pastel Soc. (1983), Pastel Soc. of Canada award (1989); painter in pastel, gouache, water-colour, oil; *b* Luton, 1921; *d* of W.R. Payne; *m* J.A. Fredrick; one *s. Educ.:* King Edward VI School, Birmingham; *studied art* at East Anglian School of Painting (Sir Cedric Morris, Arthur Lett Haines). *Exhib.:* P.S., R.B.S.A., Walsall A.G., Oxford, Keele and Birmingham universities, Gallery of Modern Art, Washington D.C. *Work in permanent collection:* Herbert A.G., Coventry. *Address:* 4 Dinmore Ave., Birmingham B31 2BG. *Signs work:* "Waveney Fredrick."

FREEMAN, Lily, F.B.S., B.A. Hons. (1978); painter in oil and water-colour; lecturer on Modern Art, University of 3rd Age; *b* Vienna, 7 Feb., 1920; *d* of Hans Fischer; widow; one *d. Educ.:* Realgymnasium, Vienna; *studied art* at Vienna, Arthur Segal School, Hampstead (A. Segal, Marianne Segal). *Exhib.:* N.Y. Expo (1985), Barbican (1982), Orangery, Holland Pk. (1979, 1981-85), Alicante, Spain (1983), Loggia Gallery (1978, 1982, 1984), Cockpit Theatre, Odeon Marble Arch, Hampstead Town Hall, New Art Theatre, Alpine Club, Hampstead Art Centre, Ben Uri Gallery, Royal Overseas League, Guildhall, London, Tradescant Trust, Leighton House, Burgh House. *Work in permanent collection:* Dr. Lansky, Vienna. *Address:* 65 Dunstan Rd., London NW11 8AE.

FREER, Roy, N.D.D., A.T.D., R.O.I., R.I.; artist in oil, pastel and water-colour; art course tutor and organiser, demonstrator, lectures on appreciation of painting and drawing; mem. Pastel Soc. *Studied art* at Bournville School of Art, Birmingham College of Art. *Exhib.* P.S., N.E.A.C., R.P., R.I., R.A. Summer Exhbn. *Address:* 184 Maple Rd., Penge, London SE20 8JB. *Signs work:* "ROY FREER" dated.

FREETH, Peter, Dip. Fine Art, A.R.A. (1990), R.A. (1992), R.E. (1991); printmaker in etching, aquatint, water-colour, teacher; Tutor of Etching, R.A. Schools, London; *b* B'ham, 15 Apr., 1938; *s* of A.W. Freeth; *m* Mariolina; two *s. Educ.:* K.E.G.S. Aston, B'ham; *studied art* at Slade School of Fine Art (1956-60, Antony Gross, William Coldstream). *Exhib.:* R.A., R.E., Christopher Mendez, London SW1. *Work in permanent collections:* V. & A., B.M., Arts Council, Fitzwilliam Cambs., Metropolitan Museum, N.Y., National Gallery, Washington. *Address:* 83 Muswell Hill Rd., London N10 3HT. *Signs work:* "P. Freeth."

FRENKIEL, Stanislaw, R.W.A.; painter and writer on art; Emeritus Reader, University of London; Head of Dept. of Art and Design, Institute of Education (1973-83); Mem. London Group; *b* Cracow, 14 Sept., 1918; *s* of Dr. A. Frenkiel; *m* Anna; one *s*, one *d. Educ.:* Cracow Grammar School; *studied art* at Cracow Academy of Fine Arts, Académie des Beaux Arts, Beirut, Sir John Cass College and the Courtauld Institute, London. *Exhib.:* one-man shows: American University, Beirut (1947); Sheffield (1954); Grabowski Gallery, London (1960-1973); Cracow (1965); Poznan (1965); Galerie Tamara Pfeiffer, Brussels (1973, 1978, 1980); Warsaw, Zacheta; retrospective 1981 touring Lodz, Cracow, Torun and Katowice; Drian Gallery, London (1981); retrospective Bloomsbury Gallery, University of London (1983, 1987); R.W.A., Bristol (1985); Polish Cultural Inst. London (1990); Cracow Art Palace (1992); Vilnius (1993); mixed shows: London, Munich, Hamburg, Wroclaw, Cracow, Lyons, London Group (since 1977), Sacred Art, Stuttgart (1983), Lincoln Centre N.Y. (1985), Congress of Polish Culture, London (1985). *Work in permanent collections:* London, Geneva, Bristol, Paris, Brussels, N.Y. and Cleveland; Hampstead Hospital Memorial Collection, London; Polish Cultural Foundation, London; R.W.E. Academy, Bristol; University of London; National Museums: Warsaw, Cracow, Poznan and Lodz; Penn State University, U.S.A. *Publications:* articles and essays on art; "Beirut Drawings 1944-1947" (1986); B.B.C. broadcaster. *Address:* Cedry, 6 Clement Rd., London SW19 7RJ. *Signs work:* see appendix.

FREUNDLICH, Grace Ruth; Travelling Fellowship, Scottish Arts Council (1979), Fellowship, Provincetown Workshop (1976); artist in acrylic, ink, oil, graphite; instructor; exhbn. com., Provincetown Art Assoc.; *b* New York, 6 May, 1939. *Educ.:* University of Wisconsin (1964); *studied art* at Hunter College Graduate School (Bob Swain), Provincetown Workshop (Leo Manso, Victor Candell). *Exhib.:* Foundry Gallery, Washington, D.C. (1981), Demarco Gallery, Edinburgh (1980), Provincetown Workshop (1976), Provincetown Art Assoc. (1986, 1987, 1989); one-man show, Roosevelt House, N.Y. (1975). *Work in permanent collections:* University of Wisconsin, Hunter College, Histadrut, Israel. *Address:* Box 90, Truro, Mass. 02666, U.S.A. *Clubs:* College Art Assoc., Women in the Arts, Westside Artists, Foundation for the Community of the Artists, Women's Museum, Washington, D.C. *Signs work:* "G.F." or "G. Freundlich."

FRIEDEBERGER, Klaus; painter; *b* Berlin, 1922; *m* Julie. *Educ.:* Quakerschool Eerde, Holland; *studied art:* E. Sydney Tech. College. *Exhib.:* one-man shows: Belfast (1963); London (1963, 1986, 1990, Retrospective 1992); group shows since 1944. Europe Prize, Ostende 1964 (Gold Medal). *Official purchases:* Mosman Art Prize 1949, National Gallery of Australia. *Work in private collections:* Australia, England, Europe, U.S.A. *Work repro.:* Arts Review, Art and Australia, Twenty Five Years Annely Juda Fine Art/Juda Rowan Gallery,

Surrealism (Canberra 1993), etc. *Address:* 16 Coleraine Rd., London SE3 7PQ. *Signs work:* "Friedeberger."

FRIERS, Rowel Boyd, M.B.E., Hon. M.A. Open University, R.U.A., U.W.S.; oil painter and cartoonist (Belfast Telegraph, Irish Times), stage designer, illustrator (TV. Graphics, B.B.C. & U.T.V.); President, Royal Ulster Academy (1993); *b* Belfast, 13 Apr., 1920; *s* of William Friers; *m* Evelyn Maude Yvonne Henderson; two *s,* one *d. Educ.:* Belfast; *studied art* at Belfast College of Art. *Exhib.:* London, R.H.A., Royal Ulster Academy; many one-man shows, included in National Self Portrait Gallery (Limerick, Ireland), Kneafsey Gallery (1985). *Work in permanent collections:* Haverty Trust for Irish National Collection, Belfast Art Gallery. *Official purchases:* C.E.M.A. (N.I.) and Haverty Trust. *Work repro.:* in Dublin Opinion, Punch, London Opinion, Radio Times, Belfast Telegraph, Lines of Laughter, This is My Best Humour. *Publications:* Wholly Friers and Mainly Spanish, Riotous Living, Pig in the Parlour, Book of Friers and The Revolting Irish, On The Borderline. Cartoonist for Irish Times and now drawing for Ulster News Letter. *Address:* Millbank House, Victoria Rd., Holywood, Co. Down BT18 9BD. *Signs work:* see appendix.

FRÖHLICH-WIENER, Irene; sculptress in bronze, stone, wood and fibreglass; *b* Luzern, Switzerland, 26 Aug., 1947; *d* of Sigmund Wiener; *m* Josef Fröhlich; two *d. Educ.:* Kantons-Schule, Luzern (Matura), Institut Maïeutique (Art-therapy); *studied art* at Centre de la gravure Contemporaine, Geneva (1969), Marylebone Inst. (1973-74, carving under E. Mehmet), H.G.S. Inst. (John Brown), Sir John Cass School of Art (Clive Duncan). *Exhib.:* R.B.A., Royal Festival Hall, Camden Art Centre, Woodstock Gallery, Smee Gallery, Norfolk, Ben Uri Gallery, Mall Galleries, Old Bull Art Centre, Draycott Gallery, Blenheim Gallery, Cecilia Coleman Gallery, October Gallery. *Work in permanent collections:* The Silver Gallery, Bury St. Edmunds, Helmut Stern Collection, Michigan. *Address:* 53 Oakleigh Ave., London N20 9JE. *Signs work:* "Irene."

FROST, Anthony, D.F.A. (1973); artist in acrylic paint on canvas; *b* Redruth, Cornwall, 4 May, 1951; *s* of Terry Frost, artist; *m* Linda Macleod; two *s. Educ.:* North Oxon. Technical College and School of Art, Banbury; *studied art* at Cardiff College of Art (1970-73, Eric Malthouse, Terry Setch, Alan Wood). *Exhib.:* Four Young Artists, Penwith Gallery, St. Ives; John Moores, Liverpool; Public Hanging, St. Ives; Dangerous Diamonds, Hull; Anthony Frost—on Colour, Newlyn Gallery; "Whiff of Magic" new paintings, Wolf at the Door Gallery, Penzance. *Work in permanent collections:* Littlewoods Organisation, Liverpool, Nuffield Trust, Contemporary Arts Soc., Cornwall C.C. *Address:* Rosemergy Cottage, Morvah, Pendeen, Penzance TR20 8YX. *Club:* Subbuteo Football. *Signs work:* "Anthony Frost."

FROY, Martin, D.F.A. (1951); Emeritus Professor of Fine Art, Reading University; *b* London, 9 Feb., 1926. *Studied* at Slade School; Gregory Fellow in Painting, Leeds University (1951-54); Trustee, National Gallery (1972-79), Tate Gallery (1975-79); Fellow U.C.L. (1978). *Commissions:* Artist Consultant for Arts Council to City Architect, Coventry (1953-58); mosaic decoration, Belgrade Theatre (1957-58); two murals in Concert Hall, Morley College (1958-59). *Work in public collections:* Tate Gallery, Museum of Modern Art, N.Y., Chicago Art Institute, Arts Council, Contemporary Art Society, Royal West of England Academy, Leeds University, Art Galleries of Bristol, Carlisle, Leeds, Reading, Southampton, Wakefield. *Address:* University of Reading, RG1 5AQ.

FRUHMANN, Johann; painter; *b* Weissenstein a.d. Drau Kärnten, Austria, 22 Apr., 1928; *m* Christa Hauer. *Studied art* at Kunstgewerbeschule Graz with

Prof. Silberbauer and Wickenburg (1943-48), Akademie der bildenden Künste Wien with Prof. Andersen and Prof. Gütersloh (1948-50). *Work in permanent collections:* Graphische Sammlung Albertina, Wien, Neue Galerie, Graz, Sammlung der Stadt Wien, Bundesminsterium für Unterricht, Art Museum, Cincinnati, Museum des 20. Jhd., Wien (1965), Österr. Sraatspreis for Painting. *Address:* 1A 3552 Schloss Lengenfeld, Lengenfeld dei Krems, Austria. *Signs work:* "JOH. FRUH." on back of painting.

FRY, Arthur Malcolm, M.B.E., Hon. Rtd. R.W.S., Hon. Mem. American Watercolor Soc.; late director R.W.S. and R.E.; *b* 20 May, 1909; *s* of C. S. Fry; *m;* one *s*, one *d. Educ.:* Latymer Upper School; Bournemouth School of Art (Geoffrey Baker, Leslie Ward, R.E.). *Exhib.:* principal London galleries; one man shows, Bavaria, London, Bournemouth, Salisbury, Swindon. *Official purchase:* water-colour Bournemouth Corp. *Work in private collections:* U.S.A., Canada, Denmark, Australia. *Address:* 24 Goddington Chase, Orpington, Kent BR6 9EA. *Club:* Athenaeum. *Signs work:* "Malcolm Fry."

FRY, Minne, B.A. (1953); painter and printmaker in oil, water-colour, etching; *b* Johannesburg, 20 Dec., 1933; *d* of J.S. Zidel, M.R.C.S., L.R.C.P.; *m* Lionel Fry; one *s*, two *d. Educ.:* University of the Witwatersrand; *studied art* at Central School of Art (1955, Cecil Collins, Mervyn Peake). *Exhib.:* New Vision Centre (1958), Camden Galleries (1989). *Work in permanent collection:* C.A.S. *Address:* 16 Caroline Pl., London W2. *Signs work:* "Minne Fry."

FRYER, Katherine Mary, A.T.D. (1932); Princess of Wales Scholarship for wood engraving (1932), Hoffmann Wood (Leeds) gold medal for painting (1968); artist in oil and water-colour; 1937-47 taught at Bath School (later Academy) of Art Corsham; lecturer in School of Painting, B'ham College of Art (retd.); *b* Roundhay, Leeds, 26 Aug., 1910; *d* of John E. Fryer. *Educ.:* Roundhay High School, Leeds; *studied art* at Leeds College of Art (1926-32, E. Owen Jennings). *Exhib.:* R.A., R.B.S.A., etc. *Work in permanent collections:* R.A., B'ham Register Office, etc. *Address:* 47 Moor Pool Ave., Harborne, Birmingham B17 9HL. *Signs work:* "K.M. Fryer."

FULLER, Martin, S. E.; artist in oil, water-colour; *b* Leamington Spa, 9 Feb., 1943; *s* of Sidney Fuller. *Exhib.:* one-man shows, Arnolfini Gallery, Bristol (1968, 1971), Midlands A.G., Birmingham (1968), Centaur Gallery, Bath Festival (1969), Bristol City A.G. (1970), Bear Lane Gallery, Oxford (1971, 1973), Camden Arts Centre, London (1971), Festival Gallery, Bath, (1973), Grabowski Gallery, London (1973), Thumb Gallery, London (1976, 1979), Oxford Gallery, Oxford (1983), R.Z.A. Gallery, Dusseldorf (1983), Austin-Desmond Fine Art (1985, 1989), On the Wall Gallery, Belfast (1987), Hendriks Gallery, Dublin (1987), Spengler Gallery, Paris (1989). *Work in permanent collections:* Bristol City A.G. and Museum, Trinity College, Oxford, Unilever. *Address:* 58 Fentiman Rd., London SW8 1LF. *Club:* Chelsea Arts. *Signs work:* "Martin Fuller" or "MARTIN FULLER."

FULLER, Peter Frederic, R.A.I. (1976), A.A.H. (1976), F.P.S. (1991); Whatman prize; painter in water-colour; art historian; *b* Ramsgate, 10 Apr., 1929; *s* of Frederic Fuller, R.A.F.; *m* Rosemary Blaker; one *d. Educ.:* John Hezlett School; *studied art* at Maidstone College of Art. *Exhib.:* R.A., R.B.A., R.P.S., R.W.S. (Open), R.I., N.E.A.C., F.P.S., R.S.M.A., K.C.C. 'Kent Artists', Britain in Water-colours, Towner A.G., E. Stacey-Marks Gallery Eastbourne, Arts Centre Folkestone, Arune Arts Centre Arundel, Roger Green Fine Art High Halden, Bakehouse Gallery Sevenoaks, Cloisters Gallery Canterbury, etc.

Address: 31 Sandling La., Penenden Heath, Maidstone, Kent ME14 2HS. *Clubs:* Maidstone Art, Maidstone Archaeological Group. *Signs work:* "Peter Fuller."

FULLER, Violet; F.F.P.S.; artist in water-colour, oil, pastel; *b* Tottenham, 26 July, 1920; *d* of Charles Fuller. *Studied art* at Hornsey School of Art (1937-40) under Russell Reeve, R.B.A., A.R.E.; Stroud School of Art (1942-44) under Gwilym E. Jones, A.R.C.A. *Exhib:* Paris, R.A., R.I., R.B.A., N.E.A.C., W.I.A.C., Whitechapel A.G. (1967), 9 painters of East London, Bath Festival (1967), Brighton Festival (1988, 1989, 1991, 1993); one-man shows: Woodstock Gallery (1958, 1959, 1961, 1963, 1967, 1970), Old Bakehouse Gallery, Sevenoaks (1968, 1970), Hornsey Library (1968, 1973), New Gallery, Hornsey (1975), Forty Hall, Enfield (1974, 1984), Bruce Castle, Tottenham (1980), Loggia Gallery (1983, 1986, 1991). *Official purchases:* London Borough of Haringey, London Borough of Enfield. *Address:* 1 Helena Rd., Woodingdean, Brighton, Sussex BN2 6BS. *Signs work:* "VIOLET FULLER."

FURLONG, Gillian, B.F.A. (1970), David Murray (Landscape) prizewinner (1967); artist in oil; *b* Kingston upon Thames, 1 May, 1948; *d* of P.B.H. Furlong, D.F.C., A.R.I.C.S.; *m* Edward Dawson; one *s*, three *d*. *Educ.:* Hull High School; Sutton High School; *studied art* at Epsom School of Art (1965-67), Camberwell School of Art and Crafts (1967-70, Anthony Eyton, R.A., Ben Levene, R.A., Richard Lee). *Exhib.:* R.A. Summer Exhbns. (1969, 1972-74, 1978-85, 1987-89), Church St. Gallery, Stow-on-the-Wold (1979, 1986, 1987), Linfield Gallery, Bradford-on-Avon (1983, 1985), Edwin Pollard Gallery (1983, 1986, 1989), John Noott 20th Century (1991). *Address:* New Barn House, Buckhorn Weston, Gillingham, Dorset SP8 5HG. *Signs work:* "G. Furlong" or "G.F."

FURNIVAL, John P., A.R.C.A.; artist in pen and ink and mixed media; lecturer, Bath Academy of Art; editor, Openings Press; *b* London, 29 May, 1933; *m* Astrid Furnival; two *s*, one *d*. *Studied art* at Wimbledon College of Art; Royal College of Art. *Exhib.:* Biennale des Jeunes, Paris; one-man show: Thumb Gallery, London; retrospective: Laing Gallery, Newcastle, Arnolfini, Bristol, plus various international exhbns. of visual and concrete poetry. *Work in permanent collections:* Arts Council of Gt. Britain, Arnolfini Trust, Munich Pinakothek. *Publications:* The Bang Book (Jargon Press), The Lucidities (Turret Books). *Address:* Rooksmoor House, Woodchester, Glos. GL5 5NB. *Club:* Dorothy's Umbrellas Dining Society (DUDS). *Signs work:* "John Furnival."

G

GABRIEL, Caroline S., F.R.S.A.; sculptress in stone and clay casts in bronze, etc; sculptor tutor to I.L.E.A. Evening Class; Lecturer in Art, Avery Hill College of Educ.; *d* of Leon J. H. Gabriel, mining engineer. *Educ.:* North London Collegiate School; *studied art* at Camberwell College of Art; Slade School of Fine Art, University of London. *Exhib.:* R.A., N.E.A.C., W.E.A.C., R.B.A., Society of Portrait Sculptors, R.W.A., Royal Glasgow Inst. Fine Arts, Royal Scottish Academy, Edinburgh, etc. *Publications:* text books for schools and colleges. *Addresses:* 5 Windmill Cl., Ashington, Sussex RH20 3LG; Brighton Art Museum and A.G.

GAGE, Anthea Dominique Juliet, S.S.A., R.S.W.; art teacher, artist in gouache and water-colour; full time teacher, Royal High School, Edinburgh; *b* Edinburgh, 21 Mar., 1956; *d* of Edward A. Gage, S.S.A., R.S.W. *Educ.:* John Watsons School, Stevenson's College of Educ.; *studied art* at Edinburgh College of Art (Dip. 1974-78, Post. Dip. 1978-79, David Michie, George Donald). *Exhib.:* annually at S.S.A., R.S.W.; various mixed exhbns. *Address:* 16/8 Craighous Gdns., Edinburgh EH10 5TX. *Signs work:* "Anthea D.J. Gage."

GAGE, Edward Arthur, R.S.W. (1963), D.A.(Edin.) (1950), Past President S.S.A.; painter in oil and water-colour, illustrator, journalist, broadcaster; art master, Fettes College (1952-68); Senior Lecturer, Napier College; art critic, The Scotsman; *b* Gullane, East Lothian, 28 Mar., 1925; *s* of Thomas Arthur Gage; *m* Valerie Alexandra; one *s*, two *d. Educ.:* Royal High School of Edinburgh; *studied art* at Edinburgh College of Art (1941-42, 1947-52) under Sir W. G. Gillies. *Work in permanent collections:* Scottish Arts Council, Glasgow Art Gallery, Edinburgh City Collection, Universities of Aberdeen and Edinburgh, Argyll County Council. *Publications:* The Eye in the Wind (Scottish Painting since 1945) Collins, 1978. *Work repro.:* Radio Times and B.B.C. Publications, and illustrations in books published by Bodley Head, Dents, Cassell, Michael Joseph, Longmans. *Address:* 6 Hillview, Edinburgh, 4. *Signs work:* "Edward Gage."

GALE, Raymond David George, N.D.D. (1958), A.T.C. (Lond.1959); printmaker, teacher; *b* Hanwell, London 25 June, 1937; *s* of A. E. Gale. *Studied art* at Ealing School of Art (1953-58), Hornsey College of Art (1958-59). *Address:* 283 Hounslow Rd., Hanworth, Middx. *Club:* S.G.A. *Signs work:* "Ray Gale."

GALE, Richard John, Dip. A.D. (1968), M.A. (R.C.A., 1973); artist in oil; *b* Bristol, 8 Feb., 1946; *s* of C. L. Gale; *m* Francis Joan. *Educ.:* Weston-super-Mare Grammar School; *studied art* at Kingston upon Thames School of Art (1965-68), R.C.A. (1970-73). *Address:* 5 Hillside Rd., Clevedon, Avon. *Signs work:* "R. Gale."

GALLAGHER, Brian; artist in water-colour, pastel and pencil; Frank Herring Award; secretary, Pastel Soc.; Exhbn. Sec., Pastel Soc.; *b* Chester, 31 May, 1935; *s* of Frederick Alexander Gallagher, musician; *m* Rosemary June Webb; one *s. Studied art* privately under Herbert Green. *Exhib.:* P.S., S.WL.A., Porthill Gallery London, and many provincial galleries. *Work repro.:* contributor to art magazines. *Address:* 99 Gilmore Cres., Ashford, Middx. TW15 2DD. *Club:* London Sketch. *Signs work:* "Brian Gallagher."

GALVANI, Patrick; painter in water-colour and oil, journalist, author; *b* Bures, Suffolk, 11 Sept., 1922; *s* of Dino Galvani, actor and broadcaster; *m* Madeleine; one *s. Educ.:* University College School; *studied art* at U.C.S. and self-taught. *Exhib.:* Debenham, Framlingham, and various in Suffolk. *Address:* 5 Gracechurch St., Debenham, Suffolk IP14 6RA. *Club:* Ipswich Art. *Signs work:* "PATRICK GALVANI."

GAMBLE, Tom, R.W.S.; painter in oil and water-colour; Mem. A.W.G.; senior lecturer, Art and Design, Loughborough College of Art (1952-84); Freeman of City of London and of the Worshipful Company of Painter/Stainers; *b* Norton-on-Tees, 6 Feb., 1924; *s* of Thomas Gamble, engineer; *m*; one *s. Studied art* at Constantine College, Middlesbrough. *Exhib.:* R.A., R.W.S., Bankside Gallery London, Royal Festival Hall, Mall Galleries, Brian Sinfield, Milne & Moller, Leicester A.G., Middlesbrough A.G., Exposicion International de Aquarda Barcelona, American and Canadian Water-colour Socs., and various provincial galleries. *Work in permanent collections:* Lloyds of London, University of Loughborough, Notts. C.C., Leics. C.C., Crathorne Collection; private collections in Europe, U.S.A., Canada. *Address:* 10 Blythe Green, East Perry, Huntingdon, Cambs. *Club:* Arts. *Signs work:* "Tom Gamble."

GAMES, Abram, O.B.E., R.D.I., Hon. Fellow R.C.A. (1992); graphic designer, War Office poster designer (1941-46); *b* 29 July, 1914; *s* of Joseph Games; *m*; one *s*, two *d*. *Exhib.:* One-man shows London, Stockholm, Brussels, Jerusalem, Tel Aviv, New York, Chicago, Rio de Janeiro. Represented Gt. Britain in poster exhibition at Museum of Modern Art, N.Y.; first prizes, British Trade Fair Poster Competitions, Helsinki, 1958, Lisbon, 1959, New York, 1960, Stockholm, 1962, Barcelona, 1964. Designed stamps for G.B. and Israel; First Prize, International Tourist Stamps (1976); Festival of Britain, B.B.C. television and the Queen's Award to Industry Emblems. Society of Industrial Artists Design Medal (1960), Royal Society of Arts Silver Medal (1962), D. & A.D. President's Award (1991). *Address:* 41 The Vale, London NW11 8SE. *Signs work:* "A. Games."

GAMLEN, Mary, A.T.D. (Lond. 1936); Hon. U.A.; sculptor in wood and terracotta, painter in oil and water-colour; *b* London, 1913; *d* of Hugh Gamlen, Freeman of City of London and Liveryman of the Company of Goldsmiths; *m* Alan Somerville Young; one *s*, two *d*. Student at Hornsey School of Art; on staff there (1937-1945). *Exhib.:* R.A., R.B.A., N.E.A.C., R.W.S., Edinburgh R.A., Fermoy Gallery, Kings Lynn, Premises, Norwich, Mall Galleries. *Work in permanent collections:* Museum of the Royal Marines (Lying-in-State of Sir Winston Churchill), Belize Cathedral (reredos), Norfolk (village signs), Holt Church (carving of St. Andrew), Thorpe Market Church (restoration work). *Address:* Ham House Pottery, Southrepps, Norwich, Norfolk NR11 8AH. *Signs work:* "GAMLEN" or "Mary Gamlen" and see appendix.

GANLY, Rosaleen Brigid, H.R.H.A. (1983); artist in oil, water-colour, eggtempera, pastels, pen and ink, etc.; *b* Dublin, 29 Jan., 1909; *d* of Dermod OBrien, P.R.H.A., H.R.A., etc.; *m* Andrew Ganly; one *s*, one *d*. *Studied art* at Dublin School of Art under Sean Keating, Patrick Tuohy, Oswald Reeves, Oliver Sheppard and George Atkinson, and at R.H.A. School under D. OBrien, Sean O'Sullivan, Richard Orpen, etc. *Exhib.:* R.H.A. (yearly since 1928), Waterford, Limerick, Galway, Cork, Berlin, America, Canada, Dublin Municipal Gallery of Modern Art, Royal Dublin Soc., Waterford, Blackrock (All Souls Church), mural in church, Ennis, Co. Clare; one-man show, Lincoln Gallery, Dublin (1980); two-man shows with B. M. Flegg, Wexford and Dunlaoghaire; retrospective exhbn. Gorry's Gallery, Dublin (1987). *Official purchases:* Haverty Trust. *Work repro.:* numerous book illustrations and dust jackets. *Address:* 6A Laurel Hill, Upper Glenageary Rd., Dunlaoghaire, Co. Dublin. *Signs work:* Early work, up to 1936, signed two capital B's within a circle or "Brigid OBrien"; all works, from 1936 signed "RBG."

GARDINER, Vanessa, B.A. (Hons.) (1982); painter in acrylic, collage on canvas; *b* Oxford, 7 Apr., 1960. *Studied art* at Oxford Polytechnic (1978-79), Central School of Art and Design (1979-82, David Haughton). *Exhib.:* solo shows: Duncan Campbell Contemporary Art (1991, 1992). *Address:* Lilac Cottage, Fernhill, Charmouth, Dorset DT6 6BX. *Signs work:* "Vanessa Gardiner."

GARDNER, Annette; painter in oil; Principal and Teacher, Wood Tutorial College NW3.; Founder and Director, New End Gallery NW3.; *b* 11 June, 1920;

m C. J. Wood, M.A., (decd.1972); one *s*, one *d* (B.A. Fine Arts, A.T.C.). *Studied art* at Twickenham Art School (1952-54); Hampstead Garden Suburb Institute (1954-56) under Mr. Gower; St. Martin's (1960-63) under David Tindle; principal teacher Walter Nessler. *Exhib.:* Numerous group shows and travelling exhbns.; finalist, Woman's Journal Painting of the Year (1961). *Work in private collections:* Australia, England, U.S.A., Israel, Hungary. *Address:* The Studio, 18 Canons Drive, Edgware, Middx. HA8 7QS. *Clubs:* F.P.S., Ben Uri, H.A.C., B.A.A.T. *Signs work:* "A. Gardner."

GARDNER, Derek George Montague, V.R.D., R.S.M.A., Commander R.N.V.R.; Hon. vice-president for life R.S.M.A.; marine artist in oil and water-colour; Rudolph Schaefer award at International Exhbn. of Marine Art, Mystic, U.S.A. (1984); *b* Gerrards Cross, Bucks, 13 Feb., 1914; *s* of Alfred Charles Gardner, F.R.S.E.; *m* Mary neé Dalton; one *s*, one *d*. *Educ.:* Monkton Combe Junior School and Oundle School. *Exhib.:* R.S.M.A., United Artists, R.I., Bermuda, IPG; one-man shows, Polak Gallery, London (1972, 1975, 1979, 1982, 1987, 1990). *Work in permanent collections:* National Maritime Museum, Greenwich; Bermuda Maritime Museum; R.N. College, Dartmouth. Mentioned in Despatches, H.M.S. Broke (1942). *Address:* High Thatch, Corfe Mullen, Wimborne, Dorset BH21 3HJ. *Club:* Naval Club. *Signs work:* "Derek G. M. over Gardner."

GARDNER, Peter Colville Horridge, R.O.I. (1977), A.T.D. (1951), F.R.S.A. (1969); artist in oil; *b* London, 25 Oct., 1921; *s* of Ronald E. Gardner; *m* Irene. *Educ.:* St. Matthias C. of E. School, London SW5; *studied art* at Hammersmith School of Art (1935-38, 1946-50), London University Inst. of Educ. (1950-51). *Exhib.:* R.A., R.B.A., R.O.I., N.E.A.C. *Work in permanent collections:* Nuffield Foundation, York University. *Address:* 11 Pixmead Gdns., Shaftesbury, Dorset SP7 8BZ. *Signs work:* "Peter Gardner."

GARFIT, William, R.B.A.; I.L.E.A. Dip with hon., Byam Shaw School Cert. with Distinction, R.A.S. Cert.; artist in oils, specialising in River Landscapes and pen and wash illustration work; *b* Cambridge, 9 Oct., 1944; *m* Georgina Joseph; one *s*, two *d*. *Educ.:* Bradfield College; *studied art* at Cambridge School of Art (1963), Byam Shaw (1964-67), R.A. Schools (1967-70). *Exhib.:* one-man shows, Waterhouse Gallery (1970, 1972, 1974), Mall Galleries (1976), Stacey Marks, Eastbourne (1978), Tryon and Moorland Gallery, London (1981, 1983, 1985, 1988, 1991). *Publications:* illustrated, Dudley worst dog in the World, Amateur Keeper, Your Shoot, The Woods Belong to Me, The Fox and the Orchid, Prue's Country Kitchen, Cley Marsh and its Birds, The Game Shot, How the Heron got Long Legs. *Address:* The Old Rectory, Harlton, Cambridge CB3 7ES. *Signs work:* "William Garfit."

GARIN Ortiz de Taranco, Felipe Maria, Doctor of Philosophy in Literature and Lawyer, Presidente de la Real de Bellas Artes de San Carlos (Valencia), and director of review Archivo de Arte Valenciano, Correspondiente de la Academia de la Historia and de la de Bellas Artes de San Fernando (Madrid); de la Academia de Cultura Valenciana; *b* Valencia, Spain, 14 Feb., 1908; *s* of Dr. Felipe N. Garin; *m* Da. Maria Angeles Llombart Rodriguez; two *s*. *Educ.:* Universidad, Valencia, Zaragoza and Madrid; *studied art* at Valencia. *Publications:* Yañez de la Almedina (1953; 2nd Edn. Ciudad Real, 1978), Catalogo del Museo de Bellas Artes de Valencia (1955), Valencia Monumental (Madrid, 1959), El Museo de Valencia (Madrid, 1964), Vinculaciones universales del gotico valenciano, Valencia, (1969), Historia del arte de Valencia (1978), Inventario Artistico de Valencia y su Provincia (Madrid, 1983), Catalogo

Monumental de la Ciudad de Valencia (Valencia 1983), Catalogo Monumental de la Provincia de Valencia, (Valencia, 1986), etc. *Address:* Valencia 46001. Calle Reloj Viejo, 9.

GARLICK, Kenneth John, M.A., Ph.D., F.M.A., F.S.A.; art historian; Keeper of Western Art, The Ashmolean Museum, Oxford (1968-84); *b* Glastonbury, 1 Oct., 1916; *s* of David Ernest Garlick. *Educ.:* Elmhurst Grammar School, Street, Balliol College, Oxford, Courtauld Institute of Art, University of London. *Publications:* Sir Thomas Lawrence: a Catalogue (Walpole Society, Vol. XXXIX, 1964); Sir Thomas Lawrence (Phaidon, 1989). *Address:* 39 Hawkswell Hse., Hawkswell Gdns., Oxford. *Club:* Reform.

GARMAN, Evelyn Daphne, N.S. (1980), S.W.A. (1985); sculptor in clay, wax, bronze, resin bronze; *b* Beaconsfield, 6 Apr., 1913; *d* of W. G. Wingate Morris, solicitor; *m* R. C. Garman, artist; three *d*. *Educ.:* Convent of the Holy Child Jesus, Sussex; *studied art* at London studio of A. Acheson, A.R.A. privately (1933-38). *Exhib.:* S.W.A., N.S., S.P.S., Winchester, Andover, and two private shows with husband. *Work in permanent collection:* Heads of Founders in Winsor and Newton Museum, Wealdstone, Harrow. *Address:* Ashburnham, 8 Charnwood Cl., Cheltenham, Glos. GL53 0HL. *Clubs:* Cheltenham and Cotswold. *Signs work:* "E.D.G." or "D. GARMAN."

GARRARD, Peter John, P.P.R.B.A., R.P., N.E.A.C., R.W.A.; painter in oil; *b* 4 Jan., 1929; *s* of Col. W. V. Garrard, M.B.E., T.D.; *m* Patricia Marmoy; one *s*, two *d*. *Educ.:* Magdalen College School, Brackley; *studied art:* Byam Shaw School of Drawing and Painting. *Work in permanent collections:* in public and private collections in England, America, Australia, Canada, Germany, etc. *Address:* 340 Westbourne Park Rd., London W11 1EQ. *Signs work:* "P.J.G."

GAULT, Kate, Dip. (Byam Shaw) (1974), Dip. Dance and Choreography (1977); painter in oil on canvas, pastel; *b* Midhurst, 12 Apr., 1954; *d* of David Hamilton Gault; *m*; two *s*. *Educ.:* Dartington Hall School; *studied art* at Byam Shaw School of Art (1971-74, Diana Armfield); London School of Contemporary Dance (1974-77). *Exhib.:* solo shows: Christopher Hull Gallery, Sue Rankin Gallery (1993); three mixed exhbns. Piccadilly Gallery. *Address:* Telegraph House, North Marden, nr. Chichester, Sussex PO18 9JX. *Signs work:* "Kate Gault."

GAY, Barbara, A.R.W.A. (1958); artist potter in glazed, coloured stoneware, also painter in oils; *b* Bristol, 20 June, 1921; *d* of Henry Valentine Gay, B.Sc., F.R.G.S., Schoolmaster. *Educ.:* privately; *studied art* at West of England College of Art (1936-46), Principal, Donald Milner, O.B.E., M.A., A.R.C.A. (Lond.), R.W.A., modelling master, Roy Smith, R.W.A., and Monkton Combe Pottery with Rachel Warner (1949). *Work in permanent collections:* Cast, stone statue of St. George (1940) (War Memorial), statue of Madonna (1945), both in St. George, Brandon Hill, Bristol; painting War v. Healing (1945) in Medical Library, Pentagon, Washington, D.C.; also many sets of stoneware figures of Canterbury Pilgrims in private colls. in the U.S.A. *Address:* 12 Miles Rd., Clifton, Bristol BS8 2JN. *Clubs:* R.W.E.A., Clifton Arts, Portfolio Soc. *Signs work:* Paintings, "Barbara Gay," pottery, see appendix.

GEAR, William, D.A. (Edin.); Head of Dept. of Fine Art, Birmingham Polytechnic (retd. 1975); Member, Fine Art Board, C.N.A.A.; Curator, Towner Art Gallery, Eastbourne (1958-64); R. Signals (1940-45); M.F.A. & A., Germany (1946-47); *b* Methil, Fife, 2 Aug., 1915; *m* Charlotte Chertok; two *s*. *Studied art* at Edinburgh (1932-37), Academie Fernand Leger, Paris (1937).

Worked in Paris (1947-50). *Exhib.:* numerous one-man and group exhbns. in U.K. and abroad. *Work in permanent collections:* include B.M., Tate Gallery, V. & A., Arts Council, Scottish Arts Council, Arts Council of N. Ireland, British Council; Scottish Nat. Gallery of Modern Art, Nat. Gallery of Canada, Nat. Gallery of N.S.W., and at Aberdeen, Birmingham, Brighton, Buffalo, N.Y., Cambridge, Dundee, Eastbourne, Glasgow, Liege, Lima, Manchester, Nelson, N.Z., Newcastle, New York, Oxford, Southampton, Tel Aviv, Toronto, Toledo, Caracas, Chichester, Cincinnati, Fort Lauderdale, Kirkcaldy, Strathclyde, Stromness, Canberra, Edinburgh, etc. *Prizes and Awards:* Festival of Britain (1951), David Cargill Award (1967), Lorne Fellowship (1975). *Address:* 46 George Rd., Birmingham B15 1PL. *Signs work:* see appendix.

GEARY, Robert John, S.G.A. (1969), F.C.S.D. (1980), F.R.S.A. (1981); graphic artist and illustrator in ink and water-colour; Graphics Officer, Geological Museum S. Kensington (1971-85); *b* London, 15 Jan., 1931; *s* of the late Robert and Ada Florence Geary; *m* Hazel Mair Plant; one *d.* *Studied art* at Hammersmith School of Arts and Crafts (1945-48) under Wm. Washington, D.V. Playfair and Ernest Fedarb. *Exhib.:* S.G.A. *Work repro.:* several childrens books, Radio Times, The Folio Soc., humorous illustrations for Punch and commemorative stamp designs for Guernsey Post Office (1987). *Address:* 70 Felton Lea, Sidcup, Kent DA14 6BA.

GEDDES, Stewart John, B.A. (Hons.) Fine Art (1983); landscape painter in oil, tutor; *b* Aylesford, Kent, 4 Mar., 1961; *s* of Brian Malcolm Geddes. *Educ.:* Maidstone School for Boys; *studied art* at Canterbury College of Art (1979-80, Eric Hurran), Bristol Polytechnic (1980-83, Alf Stockham). *Exhib.:* R.A., R.W.A., Rooksmoor Gallery, Bath, Waterman Gallery, Cadogen Contemporary, London. *Address:* 33 Hampton Pk., Redland, Bristol BS6 6LG. *Signs work:* "S.J. Geddes" on back of work.

GEE, Arthur, S.WL.A. (1969), A.B.W.S. (1988), N.A.P.A. (1993); painter/ printmaker including wildlife and landscape; Cert. of Merit, University of Art, Salsomaggiore, Italy (1982); Purchase prizewinner (1990), Mini-print International, Barcelona; Finalist, Laing Competition (1991), Manchester/ London; Daler Rowney cryla award, N.A.P.A. Exhbn. B'ham (1993); *b* Latchford, Warrington, 10 Jan., 1934; *s* of the late George Arthur Gee; *m* Margaret Ray Robinson; one *s*, one *d.* *Educ.:* Penketh and Sankey Sec. School, Warrington; *studied art* at St. Helen's College of Art and Design (1983-84). *Exhib.:* throughout U.K. and abroad. *Address:* 31 Karen Cl., Burtonwood, Warrington, Ches. WA5 4LL. *Signs work:* "Arthur Gee."

GELDART, William; artist/illustrator in pencil, pen and ink, scraperboard, pen and wash, gouache; *b* Marple, Ches., 21 Mar., 1936; *s* of William Edmund Geldart; *m* Anne Mary; one *s*, one *d.* *Educ.:* Hyde Grammar School; *studied art* at Regional College, Manchester (1956-57). *Exhib.:* R.A., Manchester Fine Arts, various others. *Work in permanent collections:* Hallé Orchestra, Manchester International Airport, Ciba Geigy, I.C.I., Rolls Royce, C.J.S., I.C.L., Reynolds Chains, Manchester Grammar School, Chetham School of Music. *Publications:* written and illustrated: Geldart's Cheshire (The Whitethorn Press); illustrated: Fox at Drummer's Darkness (Joyce Stranger/Dents), Kym (Joyce Stranger/ Michael Joseph), Ghostly Laughter (Barbara Reson/Beaver), Un Petit Soldat (Jack London/Editions Gallimard), La Forêt des Verts Lutins (Philippa Pearce/ Editions Gallimard), Kes (Barry Hines/Editions Gallimard), Kit (Jane Gardam/ Julia Macrae books), etc. *Address:* Geldart Gallery, Chelford Rd., Henbury, nr. Macclesfield, Ches. SK11 9PG.

GELLER, William Jasper, F.R.S.A.; artist in pen and ink, gouache, egg tempera; designer; Past Pres., Soc. of Graphic Artists; *b* London, 21 Dec., 1930; *s* of Henry Geller, master butcher; *m* Olive; two *d. Educ.:* Loughton School; *studied art* at City of London, Apprentice in Art, Central School, Regent Polytechnic (1947-52). *Exhib.:* R.S.M.A. Annual show, S.G.A. Annual show, F.B.A. Touring Exhbn. *Work in permanent collection:* Port of London Authority and private collections. *Publication:* 20th Century British Marine Painting. *Address:* 17 Silver St., Maldon, Essex CM9 7QE. *Clubs:* Maldon Art Soc., Stone Sailing. *Signs work:* "William Geller."

GENEVER, Margaret; artist in oil; *b* London; *d* of Charles T. Genever, architect and contractor. *Educ.:* privately and Southend-on-Sea Grammar School; *studied art* at St. Martin's School of Art, London (1945-55) under Otwell McCannell, Herbert Holt; Hammersmith School of Art under Carel Weight, R.A., and Ruskin Spear, R.A.; Central School of Art, London (lithography). *Exhib.:* R.A., A.I.A., F.P.S., various London and provincial galleries; solo show, Loggia Gallery. *Work repro.:* La Revue Moderne des Arts et de La Vie. *Address:* Chilton Cottage, 1 Chesham Rd., Guildford, Surrey GU1 3LS. *Signs work:* "Margaret Genever."

GENTLEMAN, David, R.D.I. (1972); artist and designer in water-colour, lithography, etc.; *b* London, 11 Mar., 1930; *s* of Tom Gentleman; *m* Susan Gentleman; one *s*, three *d. Educ.:* Hertford Grammar School; *studied art* at St. Albans School of Art (1947-48), R.C.A. (1950-53, Edward Bawden, John Nash). *Exhib.:* eight exhbns. at Mercury Gallery, London (1970-91). *Work in permanent collections:* B.M., Tate Gallery, National Maritime Museum. *Publications:* David Gentleman's Britain, — London, — Coastline, — Paris; and many illustrated. *Address:* 25 Gloucester Cres., London NW1 7DL. *Signs work:* "David Gentleman."

GEORGE, Grace Courtenay, University of Oxford Secondary Teachers Art Cert.; artist in water-colour and lino and wood block; Head of Art Department, The Grammar School, Chipping Sodbury, Bristol (1939-69); art mistress, Hereward School, March, Cambs. (1934-38); exchange teacher, South High School, Lima, Ohio, U.S.A. (1948); Mem. National Society of Art Education; *b* Bristol, 9 Sept., 1909; *d* of the late Frank Courtenay George, bookseller. *Educ.:* Hillside House School and Duncan House School, Clifton, Bristol; *studied art* at W. of England College of Art, Bristol, principal, R. E. J. Bush. *Address:* Middle Thatched Cottage, Lower St., West Harnham, Salisbury, Wilts. SP2 8EY. *Signs work:* "G. C. George."

GEORGE, Patrick; artist; *b* Manchester, 1923; *m* 1st 1955 June Griffith (*m* dissolved 1980); four *d; m* 2nd 1981 Susan Ward. Taught, Slade School, University College London (1949-88); Prof. of Fine Art (1983); Slade Prof. (1985-88). *Exhib.:* retrospective, Serpentive Gallery (1980). *Work in permanent collections:* Arts Council, Tate Gallery, etc. *Address:* 33 Moreton Terr., London SW1 2NS. *Dealer:* Browse and Darby.

GEORGIOU, Elpida, B.A.Hons. (1986), M.A. (1990); artist in oil on canvas; *b* London, 23 Sept., 1958; *d* of Lucas Georgiou (decd.). *Educ.:* St. Marylebone School for Girls; *studied art* at St. Martin's School of Art (1983-86), R.A. Schools (1987-90). *Exhib.:* R.O.I. at Lloyd's, Royal Overseas League (prizewinner), 'New Generation' Bonham's, R.A. Summer Show (1991) (prizewinner, Guinness award), R.A. Premium Show (Winsor and Newton award), Berlin Academy of Art; one-man shows: Christopher Hull Gallery, Lynne Sterne Gallery, 'The Leicestershire Collection', Leicester, 'East End Open

Studios', Acme Studios, London. *Work in permanent collections:* Unilever plc, Guinness Collection. *Address:* 65 Ellesmere Rd., Chiswick, London W4 3EA. *Signs work:* "Elpida Georgiou."

GIARDELLI, Arthur, M.B.E., M.A. (Oxon); Chairman, 56 Group Wales; painter in mixed media (wood, brass, burlap, oil, etc.) for wall panels, water-colour, and lecturer; *b* London, 11 Apr., 1911; *s* of Vincent Giardelli; *m*; one *s*, one *d. Educ.:* Alleyn's School, Dulwich, Hertford College, Oxford; *studied art* at Ruskin School of Art, Oxford. *Exhib.:* Amsterdam, Paris, Chicago, Washington, Bologna, Bratislava, London, New York. *Work in permanent collections:* Arts Council of Great Britain, Welsh Arts Council, National Museum of Wales, National Library of Wales, Museum of Modern Art, Dublin, National Gallery Slovakia, National Gallery Prague, Musée des Beaux Arts, Nantes, Estorick Collection, Grosvenor Gallery, London, Tate Gallery. *Publication:* The Delight of Painting (University College, Swansea). *Work repro.:* art magazines. *Address:* Golden Plover, Warren, Pembroke SA71 5HR. *Signs work:* see appendix.

GIBB, Avril V.: see WATSON STEWART, (Lady) Avril Veronica.

GIBBONS, John, B.A. Hons. (Sculpture); Head of Sculpture, Winchester School of Art; *b* Ireland, 1949. *Educ.:* Ireland; *studied art* at St. Martin's School of Art (1972-75, David Anneley, William Tucker). *Exhib.:* one-man shows: International Arts Centre, London (1975), Project Gallery, Dublin (1979), Nicola Jacobs Gallery, London (1981), Triangle Center, N.Y.C. (1984), Serpentine Gallery (1986), John Hansard Gallery, Southampton University (1986), Galerie Wentzel, Köln (1987), Madeleine Carter Fine Art, Boston, Mass. (1988), Flowers East (1990, 1992). *Work in permanent collections:* A.C.G.B., Syracuse University, N.Y., Edmonton A.G., Alberta, Gulbenkian Foundation, Comino Foundation, Museum of Contemporary Art, Barcelona, Tate Gallery; private collections: U.K., U.S.A., Germany, Ireland, Canada. *Publications:* Gonzalez: A Legacy; Introduction to catalogue, South Bank Centre, Whitechapel. *Address:* 14 Almond Rd., London SE16 3LR. *Signs work:* "J.G." welded on.

GIBBONS-SMITH, Leo Illesley, P.U.A.; Past Mem. of Executive Council, Federation of British Artists, Pres. Herts. Visual Arts Forum, Vice-Pres. Soc. of Graphic Fine Arts, Pres. United Society of Artists; painter in water-colour, pastel, acrylic, landscape, portrait, works of the imagination, Art Director in publishing and advertising, illustrator, typographer; latterly art editorial, Radio Times; *b* Cobham, Surrey; *s* of Cecil Arthur Smith, engineer, and Ethel Illesley Smith; *m* Constance Hilda; one *d. Educ.:* Kingston Grammar School; *studied art* at Hornsey College of Art (1945-49). *Exhib.:* Mall Galleries, R.B.A., R.I., R.P., P.S., N.E.A.C.; several one-man shows. *Work in permanent collection:* Ealing Educ. Com.*Address:* 207 Sunnybank Rd., Potters Bar, Herts. EN6 2NH. *Signs work:* "Leo Gibbons-Smith" or "L.I.G.S."

GIBBS, Timothy Francis, M.A. (Oxon.), 1947), C.F.A. (Oxon 1948); painter in oils, acrylic and water-colour; deputy Ruskin master (1974-79), Ruskin School of Drawing; *b* Epping, Essex, 21 Aug., 1923; *s* of G. Y. Gibbs; *m* Bridget Fry; one *s*, two *d. Educ.:* Trinity College, Oxford; Ruskin School (1947-48). *Exhib.:* one-man shows: Piccadilly Gallery (1955), Leicester Galleries (1962, 1963, 1966, 1969), Ashmolean Museum (1981), Rockefeller Art Collection, New York (1986), Clarendon Gallery (1987, 1990), Cadogan Contemporary (1993). *Work in permanent collections:* Government Art Collection, Atkinson A.G., Southport, Financial Times, Royal College of Music, Royal Borough of Kensington and Chelsea, Nottingham, Hertfordshire Educ. Authority, mural Barclays Bank,

Guildford. *Address:* 131 Elgin Cres., London W11 2JH. *Signs work:* "T. F. Gibbs."

GIBSON, Jean; awarded minor travelling scholarship to Italy; sculptor in hardboard, fibreglass, resin, herculite; *b* Staffs., 17 Dec., 1935; *d* of Harvey Gibson, L.R.A.M.; *m* Anthony Whishaw; two *d. Educ.:* Abbots, Bromley; *studied art* at Royal College of Art. *Exhib.:* Leicester Gallery, London (1968, 1969), Oxford Gallery (1974), Metropole A.G. and Centre, Folkestone (1973), Nicola Jacobs Gallery, London (1981). *Work in permanent collections:* U.S.A., London, Israel, private collections. *Address:* 7A Albert Pl., Victoria Rd., London W8. *Signs work:* "J. Gibson."

GIFFARD, Colin Carmichael, M.A. Cantab., Dip.Arch. London (A.R.I.B.A. 1947-57), R.W.A.; R.I.B.A. Schools Drawing Prize (1932), Rome finalist (Arch.) 1939; painter in oil, acrylic; lecturer, Bath Academy of Art, Sydney Place (1951-68); *b* London, 1915. *Educ.:* Charterhouse, Clare College, Cambridge; University College, London; *studied painting* at Bath Academy of Art (1948-51). *Exhib.:* R.A., R.W.A., London Group, Bristol City A.G., Salon des Nations, Paris; one-man shows, Woodstock Gallery, London (3). *Commissions:* murals in schools for Herts., Wigan Educ. Coms. *Purchases:* R.W.A., Newton Park Coll., Bath, Bristol, Walsall Educ. Coms. *Address:* Little Mead, Freshford, Bath BA3 6DH.

GIFFORD, Denis: strip cartoonist, author, editor, cartoon historian, lecturer, collector; *b* 26 Dec., 1927; *s* of William Gifford, printer; *m* Angela Kalagias (divorced); one *d. Educ.:* Dulwich College. *Exhib.:* "Aaargh" (I.C.A.), International Comic Festival (Lucca), S.S.I., B.D. 86 (Sierre). *Publications:* British Comic Catalogue (Mansell), Happy Days — 100 Years of Comics (Jupiter), Victorian Comics (Allen & Unwin), Discovering Comics (Shire), Stap Me the British Newspaper Strip (Shire), Stewpot's Fun Book (ITV), Morecambe and Wise Comicbook (Carousel), Eric and Ernie's TV Funbook (ITV), Two Ronnies Comicbook (Carousel), Comics of World War One, Penny Comics of the Thirties, Great Cartoon Stars (Jupiter), Best of Eagle (Joseph), Quick On The Draw (ITV), British Comics Price Guide (Ace), International Book of Comics (Dean), Complete Catalogue of British Comics (Webb & Bower), British Animated Films (McFarland), Encyclopedia of Comic Characters (Longman). *Address:* 80 Silverdale, Sydenham, London SE26. *Clubs:* Assoc. of Comics Enthusiasts (founder), Soc. of Strip Illustration (founder-mem.), Cartoonists.

GILBERT, Christopher G., M.A., F.M.A., F.S.A.; Director, Leeds City Art Galleries; Hon. Curator, Chippendale Soc.; Chairman, Furniture History Soc.; *b* Lancaster, 1936; *s* of Dr. F.L. Gilbert; *m* Mary Catriona; two *d. Educ.:* St. George's School, Harpenden; Keele University; University of Durham. *Publications:* Thomas Chippendale (1978), Catalogue of the Leeds Furniture Collection (1978), English Vernacular Furniture (1991); numerous exhbn. catalogues and articles on historic furniture. *Address:* Temple Newsam House, Leeds LS15 0AE.

GILBERT, Dennis, N.E.A.C., N.S.; portrait and landscape painter; formerly senior lecturer, Chelsea School of Art; *b* London, 7 Jan., 1922; *s* of Gordon S. Gilbert; three *s*, one *d. Educ.:* Weston-super-Mare; *studied art* at St. Martin's School of Art (1946-51). *Exhib.:* R.A., Paris Salon, R.P., R.B.A., N.E.A.C., C.P.S., Roland, Browse & Delbanco, Leicester Galleries, Redfern, O'Hana and Zwemmer Galleries, etc.; one-man shows: F.B.A. Gallery (1968), Langton Gallery (1982), Gill Drey Gallery (1989). *Address:* Top Studio, 11 Edith Gr., Chelsea, London SW10 0JZ. *Clubs:* Arts, Chelsea Arts. *Signs work:* "Dennis Gilbert."

GILBERT, George, R.S.W. (1973), D.A. (Glasgow) 1961, Post. Dip. (1962); artist in water-colour, acrylic, pen and wash; *b* Glasgow, 12 Sept., 1939; *s* of Samuel Gilbert, railwayman; *m* Lesley; three *s*. *Educ.:* Glasgow; *studied art* at Glasgow School of Art (1957-61): Guthrie Book Prize (portraiture). *Exhib.:* one-man shows: Kelly Gallery, Glasgow (1967), Byre Theatre, St. Andrews (1979), Loomshop Gallery, Lower Largo (1981, 1988, 1990), Torrance Gallery, Edinburgh (1991); several joint shows in Glasgow and Edinburgh; regular exhibitor at R.S.A., R.S.W., etc., also Commonwealth Arts Festival, Bath Art Fair, Cleveland International Drawing. *Work in permanent collections:* Nuffield Foundation, Fife Regional Council; many private home and abroad. *Address:* 44 Marketgate South, Crail, Fife KY10 3TL. *Signs work:* "George Gilbert."

GILBERT, Stephen, Diploma, Slade School (1935); sculptor and painter; *b* Fife, Scotland, 1910; *s* of Capt. F. G. W. Gilbert, R.N.; *m* Jocelyn Chewett; one *s*, one *d*. *Educ.:* University College School, University College, London. *Exhib.:* Galerie Nova Spectra, The Hague (1984), Galerie 1900-2000, Paris (1987), Art Fair, Bâle (1987), Galerie Jean-Paul Villain, Paris (1987). *Work in permanent collections:* Tate Gallery, Stedelijk Museum, Arts Council, British Council, Leicester Museum, Leicester University, Sheffield Museum, Norwich Museum, Alborg Museum, British Steel Corp., G.L.C. *Address:* 7 Impasse du Rouet, Paris, 14e. *Signs work:* "Stephen Gilbert."

GILDEA, Paul Rudolph, B.A. Hons. Fine Art; artist in oil on canvas; part time tutor, Fulham and Chelsea A.E.I.; *b* London, 3 Jan., 1956; *s* of John Robert Denis Gildea, B.A. Hons. *Educ.:* Dulwich College; *studied art* at Camberwell School of Arts and Crafts (1975-76), Middlesex Polytechnic (1976-79). *Exhib.:* Serpentine Summer Show (1982), Whitechapel Open (1987), Riverside Open (1987), R.A. Summer Show (1987). *Address:* 41 Ballater Rd., Brixton, London SW2 5QS. *Signs work:* "Gildea."

GILES, A. Frank Lynton, Médaille d'Argent, Paris Salon (1948), A.R.W.A. (1970), R.W.A. (1978); artist in oil, acrylic, water-colour, pastel and graphics, etc.; Sunday Times water-colour competition (1990); *b* London; *s* of Henry Edward Giles; three *s*. *Studied art* at Goldsmiths', St. Martin's. *Exhib.:* R.A., and most other societies including R.S.A., R.H.A., Eastbourne, Bradford, R.P., R.B.A., R.I., R.W.S., N.E.A.C., Alresford Gallery Arundel, Bertrand Russell Centenary, Arts Council. *Work in permanent collections:* Sheffield, Bristol, Worthing, Canada and private collections. *Address:* 19 Browning Rd., Worthing, W. Sussex BN11 4NS. *Signs work:* "FRANK LYNTON GILES" or "Lynton Giles."

GILES, Peter Donovan, N.D.D. (Special level Illustration) 1959, A.T.C. (Lond.) 1960, F.R.G.S.; painter, illustrator and sculptor; counter tenor; teaches part-time, Manwood Grammar School, Sandwich; *b* Perivale, Middx., 15 Feb., 1939; *s* of Donovan Eric Giles and Evelyn Mary Sherlock; *m* Elizabeth Ann Broom; one *s*, one *d*. *Educ.:* Castlehill College, Ealing; *studied art* at Ealing School of Art (1954-59), Hornsey College of Art (1959-60). *Exhib.:* All Hallows on the Wall, EC2; provincial one-man shows; lecture tours, U.S.A. and Canada (1973, 1975, 1978). *Work in permanent collections:* Lichfield City A.G., War Memorial Ely Cathedral. *Publications:* novels, non-fiction, cartoon collection, board games. *Address:* Filmer House, Bridge, Canterbury, Kent. *Signs work:* "Peter Giles."

GILES, Phyllis Margaret, M.A. (Cantab., 1928), Founder Fellow of Lucy Cavendish College, Cambridge, University of London School of Librarianship Diploma (1930); Librarian of Fitzwilliam Museum, Cambridge (1947-74); Asst.

University of London Library (1933-43); Asst. Librarian, Min. of Town and Country Planning (1943-47); *b* London, 20 Jan., 1907; *d* of Charles Giles, parliamentary journalist. *Educ.*: Clapham High School and Girton College, Cambs. *Address*: 25 Mill Ct., Wells on Sea, Norfolk NR23 1HF. *Club*: Cambridge Drawing Society.

GILL, Stanley Herbert, A.R.C.A., A.T.D.; art teacher (retd.), painter in oil, water-colour, lithographer; painting instructor, York and Dewsbury Schools of Art (1936-41); Head of Dept., School of Fine Art and Graphic Design, Salisbury College of Art (1947-72); *b* Leeds, 21 May, 1912; *s* of Fred Gill, lithographer; *m* Lavinia P. Leader; one *s. Educ.*: City of Leeds School; *studied art* at Leeds College of Art (1928-31), R.C.A. (1931-35) under Gilbert Spencer, Sir William Rothenstein. *Exhib.*: R.A., British Art Centre, Leeds, Yorkshire Artists, Bradford, York, Wakefield, Preston, Brighton, Southampton, Salisbury, Bethnal Green Museum of Childhood. *Address*: 1 Hadrian's Cl., Salisbury SP2 9NN. *Signs work*: "S. H. Gill."

GILLESPIE, Michael Norman, A.R.B.S.; sculptor in bronze; *s* of Reginald Gillespie; *m* Lesley Todd; two *s*, one *d. Educ.*: St. Paul's School; *studied art* at Hammersmith College of Art (1952-56). *Exhib.*: nineteen plus mixed shows. *Publication*: Studio Bronze Casting (Batsford, 1969). *Address*: 53 Cottenham Rd., Histon, Cambridge CB4 4ES. *Signs work*: "M.N. Gillespie."

GILLEY, Leonard Christopher; free-lance artist in oil and water-colour; *b* Camberwell, 28 May, 1915; *s* of Christopher George Gilley, engineer; *m* Eleanor Betty Shadbolt. *Educ.*: Strand School, Tulse Hill; *studied art* at Camberwell School of Art. *Work repro.*: in magazines, Press, posters, etc., for national advertisers at home and overseas, also art galleries and private collections. *Address*: Springfield House, Trellech, Monmouth, Gwent NP5 4PF. *Signs work*: see appendix.

GILLISON TODD, Margaret, M.C.S.P., Dip.Ed.Lond., Dip.P.E. Bedford; painter and illustrator; Keeper of Display, Grosvenor Museum, Chester (1966-77); *b* Warwick, 1916; *d* of Douglas Gillison; *m* Hugh Michael Todd. *Educ.*: Howell's School, Denbigh. *Exhib.*: R.Cam.A., N. Wales Group, S. Wales Group, S.E.A. Pictures for Schools, National Eisteddfod, Royal Horticultural Soc. (Silver Gilt and Silver Medals), Alpine Garden Soc. (Gold Medal), etc. *Work repro.*: medical and botanical publications, etc. *Publications*: A Histology of the Body Tissues, illustrated (E. & S. Livingston, Edinburgh); Louise Rayner (Grosvenor Museum, Chester). *Address*: Pen-y-Llwyn, Llanarmon-yn-lâl, Mold, Clwyd. *Signs work*: "MARGARET GILLISON," "MARGARET GILLISON TODD," or initials.

GILLMOR, Robert, N.D.D. (1958), A.T.D. (1959); freelance illustrator, designer, painter in water-colour, black and white, lino-cut prints; Director Art and Craft, Leighton Park School (1959-65); President, S.WL.A.(1984-94), President, Reading Guild of Artists (1969-84); *b* Reading, 6 July, 1936; *s* of Gerald Gillmor; *m* Susan Norman, painter; one *s*, one *d. Educ.*: Leighton Pk. School, Reading; *studied art* at School of Fine Art, Reading University (1954-59, Prof. J.A. Betts, William McCance, Frank Ormrod, Hugh Finney). *Exhib.*: S.WL.A. *Work in permanent collections*: Ulster Museum and A.G., Belfast, Reading Museum and A.G. *Publications*: 100 books illustrated. *Address*: 58 Northcourt Ave., Reading, Berks. RG2 7HQ. *Signs work*: "R.G." or "Robert Gillmor."

GILMORE, Sidney; sculptor in steel, wood, stone and glassfibre; *b* London, 3 June, 1923, *Educ.:* Willesden Grammar School; *studied art* at Willesden College of Technology. *Exhib.:* R.A., F.P.S., Chicago British Fortnight, U.S.A., Bradford A.G., Heals, London, City of Westminster, etc. *Address:* 111 Sudbury Ave., N. Wembley, Middx. HA0 3AW. *Club:* F.P.S. *Signs work:* "Sidney Gilmore."

GILMOUR, Albert Edward; artist in oil, pen and ink; sec., Gateshead Art Club (1950-51); retd. B.R. train driver; *b* W. Hartlepool, 31 May, 1923; *s* of A. E. Gilmour; *m* Elaine Bolton; one *s*, one *d*. *Educ.:* Heworth and Felling Elementary Schools; *studied art:* courses at Gateshead Technical College, King's College, Newcastle. *Exhib.:* Federation of Northern Arts Socs. Exhbns., Artists of the Northern Counties Exhbns., Artists of Durham Exhbn., Gateshead Art Club Exhbns. *Work repro.:* Locomotive Express, British Railways Magazine, N.E. Region. *Address:* 11 Limewood Grove, Woodlands Pk., North Gosforth, Newcastle upon Tyne NE13 6PU. *Clubs:* Park Rd., and West End Group, Newcastle; Gateshead Art. *Signs work:* "GILMOUR."

GILMOUR, Pat, B.A.(Hons.), Hon.R.E.; Visiting Prof., History of Graphic Art, E. London University; Founding Curator of Prints, Tate Gallery (1974-77) and Australian National Gallery, Canberra (1982-89); *b* Woodford, Essex, 19 Mar., 1932; *m* Alexander Gilmour; two *d. Educ.:* Glasgow Art School, Sidney Webb College, London University. *Publications:* author: Modern Prints (1970); Tate: Henry Moore, Graphics in the Making (1975), Artists at Curwen (1977); A.C.G.B.: The Mechanised Image (1978); B.B.C.: Artists in Print (1981); A.N.G.: Ken Tyler Master Printer (1985) and Lasting Impressions: Lithography as Art (ed.) (1988); Hayward Gallery: Shiko Munakata (1991); Japan, Yokohama Museum: Innovation in Collaborative Printmaking (1992). *Address:* 25 Christchurch Sq., London E9 7HU.

GINESI, Edna, A.R.C.A.; figure draughtsman and painter in oil; Mem. London Group, Mem. Chiswick Group; *b* Leeds, 15 Feb., 1902; *m* Raymond Coxon. *Educ.:* privately; *studied art* at Leeds College of Art, R.C.A. *Exhib.:* London and provinces, Canada and U.S.A. *Work in permanent collections:* Tate Gallery (2); Nat. Gallery of Wales, Leeds, Wakefield, Bradford and Manchester City Art Galleries. *Address:* Rowfant Mill Studio, Old Hollow, Pound Hill, Crawley, W. Sussex RH10 4TB. *Signs work:* "E. Ginesi" or "E. GINESI."

GINGER, Phyllis Ethel, R.W.S. (1958); free-lance illustrator and water-colour artist; *b* London, 19 Oct., 1907; *d* of Arthur James Ginger, civil servant; *m* Leslie Durbin; one *s*, one *d. Educ.:* Tiffin's Girls' School, Kingston-on-Thames; *studied art* at Richmond School of Art (1932-35), Central School of Arts and Crafts (1937-39) (John Farleigh, William Robins, Clark Hutton). *Work in permanent collections:* water-colours, Pilgrim Trust Recording Britain Scheme; drawings and lithographs in Washington State Library, Victoria and Albert Museum, London Museum, South London Art Gallery. *Publications:* Alexander the Circus Pony (Puffin Book); London and The Virgin of Aldermanbury, by Mrs. Robert Henrey. *Address:* 298 Kew Rd., Kew, Richmond, Surrey. *Signs work:* "Phyllis Ginger."

GLANVILLE, Christopher, R.W.A.; David Murray Landscape Scholarship (1968, 1970); landscape painter in oil on canvas, oil on panel; *b* London, 10 Aug., 1948; *s* of Roy Glanville, R.B.A., R.S.M.A, marine artist and illustrator; *m* Zelda Glanville, potter; one *s. Educ.:* St. Clement Danes Grammar School, London; *studied art* at Heatherly School of Art (1965), Byam Shaw School of Art (1967-70, B. Dunstan, M. de Sausmarez), R.A. Schools (1970-73, P. Greenham). *Exhib.:* R.A., R.W.A., Bruton Gallery, Kaplan Gallery, Woburn

Abbey, Sandford Gallery, National Museum of Wales. *Work in permanent collections:* R.W.E.A., Richmond Museum. *Address:* 8 Mill St., Kingston-upon-Thames, Surrey KT1 2RF. *Signs work:* "GLANVILLE."

GLASS, Margaret, Mem. Pastel Soc., Associate Société des Artistes Français, Société des Pastellistes de France, F.R.S.A.; landscape and marine artist; *b* Chesham, Bucks., 1950. *Address:* Grange Barn, Wickham Market, Suffolk IP13 0SB. *Signs work:* "M.R.G."

GLAZEBROOK, Christina Fay, S.G.F.A. (1987); artist in pastel, water-colour; teacher of art for Herts. C.C., and Watford Borough Council; *b* Watford, 1 Apr., 1934; *d* of George Cornish (decd.); *m* Charles Michael Glazebrook; two *s*. *Educ.:* Watford Technical College; *studied art* at Cassio College, Watford (1976) and St. Alban's College of Art (1981). *Exhib.:* P.S. (1980-81), Liberty's (1982), S.G.A. (1985, 1987), Herts. in the Making (1986-87), and many one-man shows. *Address:* 11 Monkshood Cl., Highcliffe, Christchurch, Dorset BH23 4TS. *Signs work:* "Fay Glazebrook."

GOAMAN, Michael & Sylvia; banknote and stamp designers; *b* East Grinstead, 14 Feb., 1921; *s* of John F. Goaman; *m* Sylvia Priestley; *b* London, 30 Apr., 1924; *d* of J. B. Priestley; three *d*. *Studied art* (Michael) at Reading University (1938-39); (Sylvia) at Slade (1940-41); (Michael and Sylvia) at London Central School of Arts and Crafts (1946-48). *Work repro.:* U.K. and widely overseas. *Exhib.:* similarly. *Address:* 91 Park Rd., Chiswick, London W4 3ER. *Signs work:* see appendix.

GOBLE, Anthony Barton, painter in oil; Director, Oriel Llanover, National Eisteddfod prize winner (1974); Artist in Residence, Llanover Hall, Cardiff (1979); W.A.C. grants/burseries, including award to visit artists/galleries, U.S.S.R. (1982); Oppenheim/John Downes award (1984); Church in Wales/W. A. C. mosaic commission (1985); national chairman, A.A.D.W. (1985); president, Artists Benevolent Soc. (1986-87); St. Saviours, Cardiff High Altar reredos painting commission (1988); *b* Oct., 1943; *s* of H. Barton Goble; *m* Janice Anne Morgan; two *s*, two *d*. *Educ.:* St. Mary's College, Rhos-on-Sea, Wrexham School of Art. *Exhib.:* including London Group, R.A., Camden Arts Centre, N.P.G., Salford A.G., National Museum of Wales, Galerie der Stadt, Stuttgart, Cardiff University, Westminster Cathedral, Dublin, Waterford, Wexford, Cork, Glasgow, Isle of Lewis. *Work in permanent collections:* W.A.C., University College, N. Wales, N. Wales Assoc. of the Arts, Church in Wales, Leeds Museum. *Address:* 25 Glynrhondda, Cardiff CF2 4AN. *Clubs:* A.A.D.W., R.Cam.A., The Welsh Group, Penwith Soc. of Arts. *Signs work:* "Goble."

GOELL, Abby, B.A., M.F.A.; painter in oil, acrylic, collage, lithograph, assemblage; Senior Mem., American Soc. of Appraisers; *b* U.S.A. *Educ.:* Syracuse University; Columbia University (M.F.A. 1965); Art Students' League, N.Y. (Life Mem.). *Exhib.:* Childe Hassam Purchase Exhbn. N.Y.C. (1977), American Academy and Inst. of Arts and Letters (1977), U.S. Dept. of State, Havana Cuba (1979-82). *Work in permanent collections:* Museum of Modern Art, N.Y., Yale University A.G., Grafisches Kabinet, Munich, Chase Manhatten Bank, N.Y., Atlantic-Richfield Oil Co., Sloane-Kettering Memorial Center, N.Y., New York Public Library Print Collection, Neuberger Museum, Purchase N.Y. Founder and Publisher of Arcadia Press, N. Y. *Address:* 37 Washington Square W, New York, N.Y. 10011, U.S.A. *Club:* Coffee House, N.Y. *Signs work:* "Goell" and date.

GOLDBACHER, Fiona C.; water colourist, sculptress in marble and wood; *b* London, 1935; *d* of Donald Robertson; *m* Zodolfo Goldbacher; one *s*, one *d*. *Educ.:* Iona College, N.Z.; *studied art* under Ruth Liezman. *Exhib.:* Bow House, Barnet (1990), Blackheath Gallery (1990), Medici Gallery (1991); solo show: Stable Gallery (1991). *Work in permanent collections:* Medici Gallery, Stable Gallery, John Noott, Broadway, Turtle, Cheltenham, Long Island, N.Y. *Addresses:* 14 Edmunds Walk, London N2 0HU; 43 via Borgo, Strettoia (Lucca), Tuscany. *Signs work:* "Fiona C. Goldbacher."

GOLPHIN, Janet (Miss), A.R.W.S. (1992), R.O.I. (1990); artist in oil, gouache, water-colour; *b* Pontefract, 7 Nov., 1950; one *s*. *Address:* 25 Carleton Crest, Pontefract, W. Yorks. WF8 2QP. *Club:* Leeds Fine Art. *Signs work:* "Janet Golphin."

GOMBRICH, Sir Ernst Hans, O.M.(1988), Kt. (1972), C.B.E. (1966), Ph.D. (Vienna, 1933), F.B.A. (1960), F.S.A. (1961), Hon. degrees: Belfast (1963), Leeds, St. Andrews (1965), Oxford (1969), Cambridge (1970), Manchester (1974), Chicago (1975), Harvard (1976), London (1976), Philadelphia (1977), Essex (1977), Brandeis (1981), R.C.A. (1984), New York U.N. (1986), Emory (1991); Director, Warburg Institute and Prof., History of the Classical Tradition in the University of London 1959-76; *b* Vienna, 30 Mar., 1909; *s* of Karl Gombrich, lawyer; *m* Ilse Heller; one *s*. *Educ.:* Theresianum and University, Vienna. *Publications:* Caricature (with E. Kris, 1940); The Story of Art (1950); Art and Illusion (1959); Meditations on a Hobby Horse (1963); Norm and Form (1966); Aby Warburg (1970), Symbolic Images (1972); The Heritage of Apelles (1976); The Sense of Order (1979); Ideals and Idols (1979); The Image and The Eye (1982); Tributes (1984); New Light on Old Masters (1986); Reflections on the History of Art (ed. R. Woodfield, 1987); articles in learned journals. *Address:* 19 Briardale Gdns., London NW3 7PN.

GOODALL, John Strickland, R.I., R.B.A.; draughtsman, artist in water-colour, pen and ink; *b* Heacham, 7 June, 1908; *s* of Joseph Strickland Goodall, M.B., M.R.C.P., F.R.C.S., F.R.S., M.S.A.; *m* Margaret Nicol; one *d*. *Educ.:* Harrow School: *studied art* under Sir Arthur Cope, R.A. (1923), J. Watson Nicol, Harold Speed (1924), R.A. Schools (1925-29). *Exhib.:* R.A., R.I., R.B.A., Walker Galleries. *Work repro.:* in own books and exhbn. pictures. *Address:* Lawn Cottage, Tisbury, Wilts. *Signs work:* "J. S. Goodall."

GOODCHILD, Francis Philip, A.R.C.A. (1926), F.S.A.E. (1946), Royal Exhibitioner (1923); Princ., Tiverton School of Art (1934-47), Princ., Newton Abbot College of Art (1947-64); artist in water-colour; *b* Leyton, 12 Mar., 1904; *s* of Thomas Abraham Goodchild, of London; *m* Emily Grace Muton; one *d*. *Studied art* at High Wycombe School of Art under W. J. Stamps, A.R.C.A. (1919-23) and at R.C.A. under Sir William Rothenstein, Profs. Tristram and Bell (1923-26). *Exhib.:* R.W.A., Devon Art Soc.; R.C.A. Old Students Arts Council of Gt. Britain Touring Collection and privately. *Address:* Spindlewood, Churston Cl., Galmpton, Brixham, S. Devon TQ5 0LP. *Signs work:* "FRANCIS, PHILIP, GOODCHILD."

GOODE, Mervyn; landscape painter known for his oil paintings of the English countryside; *b* 1948. *Educ.:* Gloucestershire College of Art. *Exhib.:* has exhib. widely through the U.K. and also in the U.S.A.; one-man exhbns.: Highton Gallery, EC4 (1970), Alpine Gallery, W1 (1970, 1971), King St. Galleries, SW1 (1974), Furneaux Gallery, SW19 (1975), Southwell Brown Gallery (1976, 1984), Fraser Carver Gallery (1977), Reid Gallery (1978, 1981, 1983, 1985, 1987, 1989, 1991, 1993), Windsor and Eton Fine Arts (1978, 1980), Century Gallery

(1982, 1984, 1985), David Messum (1982, 1993), Medici Gallery, W1 (1983, 1985, 1990), H.C. Dickins, W1 (1987, 1989), Arun Art Centre (1987), Bennet Galleries, U.S.A. (1988), Bourne Gallery (1992); mixed exhbns.: Medici Gallery, W1; H.C. Dickins, W1; Mall Galleries (R.O.I.); Royal Academy Business Art Galleries, W1; Southampton A.G.; Bruton Gallery, Somerset; Southwell Brown Gallery, Richmond; Edwin Pollard Gallery, SW19; Bourne Gallery, Reigate; David Curzon Gallery, Thames Ditton; Century Galleries — Hartley Wintney and Henley-on-Thames; Nevill Gallery, Canterbury; Omell Galleries — Windsor and Beaconsfield; Kingsmead Gallery, Bookham; Wykeham Gallery, Stockbridge; Peter Hedley Gallery, Wareham; River Gallery, Arundel; H.C. Dickins, Bloxham; David Messum., Beaconsfield; Burlington Paintings, W1; John Noott, Broadway, Worcs. *Work repro.:* by the Medici Soc., Kingsmead Publications, Bucentaur Gallery and Southwell Brown Gallery; in numerous periodicals and books; on I.T.V. and B.B.C. TV, etc. *Address:* The Stone House, Hawkley Hurst, Hampshire. *Signs work:* "Mervyn Goode."

GOODWIN, Leslie Albert, R.W.A., F.R.S.A.; artist in oil, water-colour, pastel, book illustrator; Chairman, Leicester Soc. Artists; *b* Leicester, 13 June, 1929; *s* of Joseph Henry Goodwin; *m* Elizabeth Whelband. *Studied art* at Leicester College of Art (1949-55). *Exhib.:* R.A., R.W.A., R.I., P.S.; six one-man shows, Vaughan College, Leicester University; mixed shows, Leicester A.G. Work in various public collections. *Official purchases:* English Electric—Nuclear Power Division; Bristol Old Vic Co.; Leicester Royal Infirmary; N.H.S. Founder 'Asterisk' Soc. of Artists; broadcaster/art critic for B.B.C. *Work repro.:* The Artist. *Address:* The Studio, 28 Lubbesthorpe Rd., Leicester. *Signs work:* see appendix.

GOOSEN, Frederik Johannes, V.B.K.H'sum (1981), R.S.M.A. (1990), E.K.C. (1992), K.V. Gooi & Vechtstreek (1993); artist in oil and water-colour; *b* Hilversum, 13 Dec., 1943; *m* M.R. Bekenkamp; two *s. Exhib.:* one-man shows: Netherlands: Wassenaar, s'-Hertogenbosch, Enschede, Alkmaar, Nieuwkoop; Bale, Geneva, New York, Washington D.C., Mystic and Westport U.S.A., London, Edinburgh, Mönchengladbach. *Work in permanent collections:* Mystic Seaport Museum, C.T., and several public bldgs. in Holland. *Address:* Waterschapslaan 14, Blaricum, Netherlands. *Signs work:* "F.J. Goosen."

GORALSKI, Waldemar Maria; sculptor in silver and amber, jewellery designer, architect; *b* Lwow, 2 Jan., 1942; *s* of Olgierd Goralski, M.Sc., engineer; *m* Agnieszka, M.Sc. *Educ. and studied art:* Faculty of Architecture and Dept. of Sculpture and Painting, Gdansk Polytechnic (1962-68). Artistic acknowledgement, Fachhochschule Köln, Dept. of Art and Design (1981). *Work in permanent collections and exhbns.:* Arts Gallery Centre, University of London; Polish Culture Inst., London; Sac Freres, London; Museum Zamkowe, Malbork; Galerie Walinska, Arnhem; Galerie Konstrast, Nijmegen; Kunst-Treff Galerie, Worpswede; Old Warsaw Galleries, Alexandria, Virginia; Aleksander Galleries, St. Petersburg, Florida; Amber Gallery, Skodsberg, Copenhagen. *Address:* Einigkeitstr. 34, D-45133 Essen. *Signs work:* "W. Goralski" or "W.G."

GORDON-LEE, Michael, A.L.I. (1977), P.S. (1984); landscape architect and garden designer, painter in pastel, pencil, oil, water-colour, sculptor in wood; Environmental Action Manager, Cheshire C.C., Pastel Soc.; *b* Harrow, 1943; one *s,* one *d. Educ.:* Whitehawk Boys School, Hammersmith College of Art and Building. *Exhib.:* Manchester Academy, Pastel Soc. (Mall Galleries), R.W.A., Theatre Clwyd, Mold, Cheshire Artists, Finalist Look North TV painting competition (1984), Merseyside Artists. Work in private collections. *Address:* 2

Orchard Cottages, Eaton Rd., Tarporley, Cheshire CW6 0BP. *Clubs:* P.S., Grosvenor Art Soc. *Signs work:* "GORDON-LEE."

GOULD, Cecil Hilton Monk, Keeper and Deputy Director, National Gallery (1973-78), (Assistant Keeper, 1946); *b* London, 24 May, 1918; *s* of the late Lt.-Com. R. T. Gould, R.N. *Educ.:* Westminster School. *Publications:* An Introduction to Italian Renaissance Painting (1957), The Sixteenth-century Venetian School (1959), The Sixteenth-century Italian Schools (excluding the Venetian) (1962), Trophy of Conquest (1965), Leonardo (1975), The Paintings of Correggio (1976), Bernini in France (1981), National Gallery catalogues, articles in the main art journals in England and abroad. *Address:* Jubilee House, Thorncombe, Dorset. *Club:* Reform.

GOURDIE, Thomas, M.B.E., D.A.(Edin.); Soc. of Scribes and Illuminators; calligrapher and handwriting consultant; *b* Cowdenbeath, 18 May, 1913; *s* of Thomas Gourdie; *m* Lilias Taylor; one *s*, two *d*. *Studied art* at Edinburgh College of Art. *Official purchases:* Imperial War Museum; Kirkaldy A.G. *Publications:* Puffin Book of Handwriting (Penguin Books); Handwriting For Today, Improve Your Handwriting and Calligraphy for the Beginner (A. & C. Black); Handwriting Made Easy (Taplinger, U.S.A.); Mastering Calligraphy (Pitman, Australia); Mastering Calligraphy (Search Press); The Simple Modern Hand (Blackie and Son); The Sonnets of Shakespeare (Cassell). *Address:* 3 Douglas St., Kirkcaldy, Scotland.

GOW, Neil; sculptor in wood; *b* Greenford, Middx., 22 Mar., 1940; *s* of Herbert Nelson Gow (decd.); *m* Jean Evans; one *s*, one *d*. *Educ.:* Fitzgeorge, Malden, Kingston Technical College. *Exhib.:* R.W.A., S.W.A., Amnesty International Sculptures (Bristol and London), Henry Brett Gallery, 5D Gallery, Kennys Galway, etc. *Address:* Brownshill Cottage, Brownshill, Stroud, Glos. GL6 8AG. *Clubs:* Glos. Soc. of Artists, Marlborough Artists. *Signs work:* see appendix.

GRAHAM, David, R.P., A.R.C.A.; painter in oil; Senior Lecturer, Sir John Cass School of Art; *b* Hammersmith, 20 May, 1926; *s* of Philip Graham. *Educ.:* Latymer Foundation School; *studied art* at Hammersmith School of Art, St. Martin's School of Art, and Royal College of Art. *Exhib.:* R.A., R.P., Arts Council, Leicester Galleries, Browse and Darby, Damkar Burton, Ontario, Brighton A. G. Herbert A.G., and Museum, Coventry (retrospective, 1987), etc. *Work in permanent collections:* Guildhall A.G., I.L.E.A., Coca Cola Ltd., London Museum, Contemporary Art Soc., I.B.M., Belgrave House Art Coll., and private collections. *Address:* 77 Horniman Drive, Forest Hill, London SE23. *Signs work:* "David Graham."

GRAHAM, Halina (Lady Graham), B.A., M.A., B.Ed.; curator, Cecil Higgins Art Gallery, Bedford, since 1971; *d* of Wiktor Grubert, diplomat (decd.); *m* Sir James Graham, Bt. Responsible for building of new wing (opened 1976), setting up of Victorian Mansion (1978 and 1984) and major purchases at dispersal of Handley-Read collection (1972), and subsequently. *Publications:* Cecil Higgins, Collector Extraordinary; Guide to the Cecil Higgins Art Gallery (with husband), articles in Burlington Magazine, Apollo, Arts Review, Antique Collector, reviews and broadcast talks. *Addresses:* Cecil Higgins Art Gallery, Castle Cl., Bedford MK40 3NY; Norton Conyers, nr. Ripon, N. Yorks. AG4 5EH.

GRANGER-TAYLOR, Nicolas; artist in oil; *b* London, 18 June, 1963. *Educ.:* Latymer Upper School, Hammersmith; *studied art* at Kingston Polytechnic (1981-82), Bristol Polytechnic (1982-85), R.A. Schools (1987-90). *Exhib.:* Royal

Festival Hall (1986, 1987, 1988), N.P.G. (1987, 1990), R.A. Summer Exhbn. (1987, 1989, 1992), Cadogan Contemporary (1989, 1990); one-man shows Cadogan Contemporary (1988), Waterman Fine Art (1991, 1993). *Address:* c/o Waterman Fine Art Ltd., 74A Jermyn St., London SW1Y 6NP. *Signs work:* "N. Granger-Taylor" or "N.G.T."

GRANT, Alistair, F.R.C.A., R.B.A., R.S.A.; painter/printmaker in oil, etching, lithography and silkscreen; retd. as Professor Emeritus from R.C.A.; *b* London, 3 June 1925; *s* of Duncan Grant, chemist; one *d. Educ.:*Froebel; *studied art* at B'ham School of Art (1941-43), R.C.A. (1947-51). *Exhib.:* numerous shows throughout the world including Redfern, Zwemmer and Oxford Galleries, Berkeley Sq. Gallery (1989), Austin Desmond, London (1989), Scottish Gallery, London (1990), Eva Jekel Gallery, London (1991), Le Touquet Museum, France (1991). *Work in permanent collections:* England, Scotland, U.S.A., Canada, Israel, Egypt, Australia, Sweden, and H.R.H. The King of Sweden. *Address:* 13 Redcliffe Gdns., London SW10 9BG. *Clubs:* Chelsea Arts, Arts Club. *Signs work:* "Alistair Grant" or "A.Grant."

GRANT, Ian MacDonald, D.A. (Glasgow, 1926), A.R.C.A. (1929), F.R.S.A.; oil and water-colour painter, pastel artist; art historian; *b* 6 Sept., 1904; *s* of H. M. Grant; *m* Margaret Gumuchian; one *d. Educ.:* privately; Glasgow School of Art (1922-26); Colorossi, etc., Paris (1927); R.C.A. (1927-30). *Exhib.:* one-man shows, Manchester, Salford, Winnipeg. *Official purchases:* Derby, Eccles, Manchester, Salford, Southport, Stockport Art Galleries, Rutherston Collection; Royal College of General Practitioners. *Address:* Barrachnie, Aldersgreen Ave., High Lane, Stockport, Ches. SK6 8EB. *Club:* Lancs. and Ches. Car. *Signs work:* "IAN GRANT" (date below).

GRANT, Keith Frederick, A.R.C.A.; landscape and portrait painter; Artist in Residence, The Roehampton Inst., London; *b* Liverpool, 10 Aug., 1930; *m* Gisele Djouadi; one *s*, one *d. Work in permanent collections:* Mural/mosaics, Charing Cross Hospital, London (1979), Gateshead Metro Station (1981/83), Beaverbrook Foundation, Peter Stuyvesant Coll., Arts Council of G.B., Contemporary Art Soc., V. & A., Fitzwilliam Museum, Cambridge, Manchester City A.G., National Gallery of N.Z. and other public and private collections at home and abroad. *Agents:* Bruton Gallery, Crane Kalman Gallery. *Address:* Dept. of Art, R.I., Froebel Institute, Grove House, Roehampton Lane, London SW15 5PJ. *Signs work:* "Keith Grant" or "K. F. Grant."

GRANT, Marianne, N.S. (1977), F.R.S.A. (1975); painter in oil; *b* St. Gallen, Switzerland, 1931; *m*; one *s*, one *d. Educ.:* High School, Zürich; *studied art* at Art Colleges in Zürich and Geneva. *Exhib.:* one-man shows B. H. Corner Gallery, Cooling Gallery, Century Galleries, Henley-on-Thames, East London Gallery, El Greco Gallery, Royal Northern College of Music, Debenhams of Romford. *Work in permanent collections:* Ernst Waespe (Zürich), Standard Telephone and Cables Ltd., Arts Centre Hornchurch. *Work repro.:* Fine Art Prints for 'Prints for Pleasure' and Peinture. *Address:* Erlenwiesenstrasse 18, 8152 Glattbrugg (Zürich), Switzerland. *Clubs:* N.S., Essex Art. *Signs work:* "Marianne Grant."

GRAVETT, Guy Patrick; photographer and painter; *b* Wye, Kent, 2 Nov., 1919. *Educ.:* Lewes County Grammar School; *studied art* at Brighton College of Art (1937-39) under Sallis Benney, Laurence Preston and Walter Bayes. *Exhib.:* various. *Address:* Hope Lodge, 41 Hassocks Rd., Hurstpierpoint, Sussex BN6 9QL. *Club:* Royal Ocean Racing. *Signs work:* "Gravett" or "Guy Gravett" followed by year.

GRAY, Elizabeth, L.R.A.M.; self taught painter in watercolour; *b* Scarborough, Yorks, 1928; *d* of John W. Gray; *m* Dr. David Trapnell; two *s. Educ.:* Queen Margaret's School, Yorks. *Exhib.:* one-man shows, Tryon Gallery, London; Sportsmans Edge Gallery, N.Y.; Old Amersham, Bourton-on-the-Water, etc. *Work in permanent collections:* Nature in Art, The International Centre for Wildlife Art, (U.K.); The Bank of England; Leigh Yawkey Woodson Art Museum, Wausau, Wisconsin, U.S.A. *Publications:* The Wild and the Tame by H. Beamish (1957). *Address:* Dumbles Cottage, Awre, Newnham GL14 1EP. *Signs work:* "Elizabeth Gray."

GRAY, Jane Campbell, A.R.C.A., F.M.G.P.; stained glass artist; Liveryman, Worshipful Company of Glaziers (1983); *b* Lincoln, 1931; *d* of Archibald Denison Ross, M.A.; *m* Kiril Gray; two *d. Studied art* at Kingston School of Art (1948-52); Royal College of Art (1952-55) under Lawrence Lee and assisted him with Coventry Cathedral nave windows (1955-58). Examples of own work: Uxbridge – St. Margaret's, Crown windows; Civic Centre entrance screen and Alphabet of Flowers in Marriage Room; Hillingdon Hospital Chapel (26 panels); St. Peter's, Martindale, Cumbria (15 windows); Pitminster, Somerset (East window, 1989); Shrewsbury Abbey (1992); Apothecaries' Hall; Glaziers Hall, London Bridge. Over 100 lights in 50 churches; coats-of-arms, domestic windows. *Address:* Ferry Cottage, Shrawardine, Shrewsbury SY4 1AJ. *Signs work:* "Jane Gray," and see appendix.

GRAY, Milner Connorton, C.B.E., R.D.I., F.C.S.D., A.G.I., Hon. Dr. R.C.A.; designer; founder partner, Design Research Unit; Master, Faculty of Royal Designers for Industry (1955-57); Pres., Soc. Industrial Artists and Designers (1943-49 and 1968); Master, Art Workers Guild (1963); mem. Royal Mint Advisory Committee (1956-86); Vice-Pres. Artists' General Benevolent Inst.; *b* 1899; *s* of A. Campbell Gray; *m. Studied painting and design* at London University; Goldsmiths' College. *Publications:* The Practice of Design, Lund Humphries Ltd. (jointly with others); Package Design, Studio Ltd.; Lettering for Architects and Designers, jointly with Ronald Armstrong, Batsford Ltd. *Address:* Felix Hall, Kelvedon, Essex CO5 9DG. *Club:* Arts.

GRAY, Nicolete; art historian and designer of lettering; *b* Stevenage, 1911; *d* of Laurence Binyon; *m* Basil Gray; two *s*, three *d.* (one *d* decd.). *Educ.:* St. Paul's Girls' School, Lady Margaret Hall, Oxford, British School at Rome. *Publications:* XIX century ornamented Typefaces (1938), revised expanded 2nd edition 1976; Rossetti, Dante and Ourselves, 1947; The Paleography of Latin Inscriptions in Italy, 700-1000 A.D., 1948; Jacob's Ladder, a Bible Picture Book from English MSS. (1949); Lettering on Buildings (1960); Lettering as Drawing (1969); The Painted Inscriptions of David Jones (1981); A History of Lettering (1986). The Paintings of David Jones (1989). *Work:* wall-relief in the Shakespeare Centre, Stratford; inlaid and mosaic lettering in Westminster Cathedral. *Address:* Dawber's House, Long Wittenham, Abingdon, Oxon.

GRAY, Stuart Ian; lithographer, painter in water-colour; water-colour officer, N.S.; *b* 19 Apr., 1925; *s* of Alfred Stephen Gray. *Educ.:* Streatham Grammar School. *Exhib.:* R.S.M.A., R.I., Mall Galleries, Guildhall. *Work repro.:* British Marine Painting by Denys Brook-Hart. *Address:* 29 Yarborough Rd., E. Cowes, I.O.W. PO32 6SH. *Signs work:* "Stuart Gray."

GREAVES, Derrick, A.R.C.A. (1952): painter and printmaker; *b* Sheffield, 5 June, 1927; *s* of Harry Greaves, steel worker; *m* Mary Margaret; two *s*, one *d. Studied art* at R.C.A. (Carel Weight, John Minton) and in Italy. *Exhib.:* Contemporary Art Soc., Venice Biennale, Pushkin Museum Moscow, John

Moores, Carnegie International Pittsburgh, R.A., Mall Galleries; one-man shows: Beaux Arts (1953), Zwemmer, Inst. of Contemporary Arts, Bear Lane Oxford, Belfast and Dublin, Whitechapel Gallery, Cranfield Inst. of Technology; annually at Monika Kinley, City Gallery Milton Keynes. *Work in permanent collections:* A.C.G.B.; Bank of Ireland, Dublin; N.Y. Public Library; Leeds, Reading, Sheffield, Southampton and Walker A.Gs.; Wesleyan University, Chicago, etc. *Publications:* folios and books: Also (with Roy Fisher) 1971; Songs of Bilitis (1977); Sanscrit Love Poems (1987). *Address:* The School, Weston Longville, nr. Norwich, Norfolk. *Signs work:* "Derrick Greaves."

GREAVES, Jack, A.R.C.A., R.W.A., Rome Scholar; sculptor in bronze, painter in pastel, oil; Visiting Prof. O.S.U.; *b* Leeds, 24 Sept., 1928; *s* of Joseph Greaves; *m* Mildred Place; four *s. Studied art:* Leeds College of Art, R.C.A. *Exhib.:* Zwemmer, R.A., O.S.U. Gallery, Bruton Gallery, Vorpal, N.Y. and Francisco, Gallery 200, Columbus, Ohio. *Work in permanent collections:* Naiad Fountain, Capital Sq., Columbus, Ohio; The Guardian, Police Memorial Gdn., Toledo; Christ Teaching, Cols., Ohio; Family Planning Bldg., Tucson, Arizona; Coventry A.G.; Bristol A.G.; Arts Council; R.W.A.; National Revenue Corp., U.S.A.; Columbus Museum, State Saving, U.S.A.; Sirak Collection, U.S.A. *Addresses:* Cherry Tree Cottage, Hovingham, York; The School House, 6143 St. Rt. 42, Mt. Gilead, Ohio, U.S.A. *Signs work:* "Greaves."

GREEN, Alan, A.R.C.A.; painter; *b* London, 22 Dec., 1932; *s* of F. J. Green, F.R.I.C.; *m* June Green; two *d. Studied art* at Royal College of Art (1955-58). *Agent:* Annely Juda Fine Art London. *Exhib.:* Documenta VI Kassel (1977), 'British Art Now' Guggenheim Museum, N.Y. (1979), 'British Contemporary Art' Japan (1982). *Work in public collections:* includes Arts Council of Gt. Britain; British Council; Guggenheim Museum, N.Y.; McCrory Corp., N.Y.; Tate Gallery, London; Kunstmuseum Hannover; National Museum of Art, Osaka, Japan; Power Gallery, Sydney, Australia; Kunsthalle Bielefeld; Musee d'Ixelles, Brussels. *Address:* c/o Annely Juda Fine Art, 23 Dering St., London W1R 9AA.

GREEN, Anthony, R.A. (1977), Dip.F.A. Slade (1960), Harkness Fellow (1967-69); painter in oil; *b* London, 30 Sept., 1939; *m* Mary Cozens-Walker; two *d. Educ.:* Highgate School, N.6.; *studied art* at the Slade School of Fine Art. *Exhib.:* over fifty one-man shows worldwide since 1962. *Work in permanent collections:* Tate Gallery, Arts Council, museums and art galleries in U.S.A., Japan, Brazil, etc. *Address:* 17 Lissenden Mans., London NW5 1PP. *Signs work:* "Anthony Green," "A. Green," "Anthony," "A.G." or not at all.

GREEN, David John, R.O.I., N.S.; landscape painter in water-colour and oil; *b* London, 23 Feb., 1935; *m* Eileen Ann; two *s. Educ.:* Goldington Rd. Secondary Modern, Bedford. *Exhib.:* R.I., R.B.A., R.O.I.; one-man shows: London, Cambridge, Bedford. *Work in permanent collections:* Luton Museum, Boston English Gallery. *Address:* The Wilden Gallery, Wilden, Beds. MK44 2QH. *Signs work:* "DAVID GREEN."

GREEN, Richard, Dip.A.D. (1968), M.A. (1970), F.R.S.A. (1988); Curator, York City Art Gallery (since 1977); previously Keeper of Fine Art, Laing Art Gallery, Newcastle upon Tyne (1971-77); *b* 12 Oct., 1946; *s* of George William Green. *Educ.:* Palmer's School, Grays; *studied art* at S.W. Essex Technical College and School of Art; Bath Academy of Art; Goldsmiths' College School of Art (1964-68); *studied history of art* at University of London, Courtauld Inst. of Art (1968-70). *Publications:* numerous exhbn. catalogues, articles and reviews. *Address:* c/o York City Art Gallery, Exhibition Sq., York YO1 2EW.

GREENBURY, Judith Pamela, R.W.A. (1979); painter in oil, water-colour; *b* Bristol, 17 Feb., 1924; *d* of Bernard Spielman; *m* C. L. Greenbury, M.D., three *s. Educ.*: Badminton School, Westbury-on-Trym, Bristol; *studied art* at West of England College of Art (1943-46) under George Sweet, Slade School (1946-47) under Prof. Schwabe. *Exhib.*: R.A., R.W.A., R.S.P.P., N.E.A.C., Bear Lane Gallery, Oxford, Mall Galleries, London. *Work in permanent collection:* R.W.E.A. *Address:* Clarence House, 11 New St., Henley-on-Thames, Oxon. RG9 2BP. *Signs work:* "J.G."

GREENHALF, Bette, B.Sc. (Econ.) Hons. Lond.; Advanced Printmaking Central St. Martin's; contemporary artist, writer, trade unionist; *b* London, 28 Dec., 1932; *d* of Archie and Maud Harmer; *m* Tom Greenhalf (decd.). *Educ.*: Camden Inst. and Central/St. Martin's, London. *Publication:* British Contemporary Art (1993). Interested in making art including artist's books to reflect the contemporary world and pursuing cultural studies. *Address:* 91 Greenhill, Hampstead High St., London NW3 5TY. *Signs work:* "Bette Greenhalf."

GREENHALF, Robert Ralph, R.B.A. (1982), S.WL.A. (1981), Dip. A.D.(Graphics)(1971); artist in etching and water-colour; *b* Haywards Heath, 28 June, 1950; *s* of Robert Henry Taylor Greenhalf; *m* Sally Grace; one *s. Educ.*: Haywards Heath Secondary Modern School; *studied art* at Eastbourne School of Art (1966-68), Maidstone College of Art (1968-71). *Exhib.* R.A., R.B.A., S.WL.A., many mixed exhbns. and one-man shows London, England and Wales, Switzerland, Holland and U.S.A. *Work in permanent collections:* South East Arts, Hastings Museum. *Publication:* chapter with illustrations in Twentieth Century Wildlife Artists by Nicholas Hammond (Croom Helm, 1986). *Address:* Romney House, Saltbarn La., Playden, Rye, E. Sussex TN31 7PH. *Signs work:* "Robert R. Greenhalf."

GREENMAN, Edwin, A.R.C.A., R.P., F.R.S.A.; artist in oils; head of dept., drawing, painting and design, Guildford School of Art; head of Sir John Cass School of Art, London; elected to Royal Society of Portrait Painters (1968), Hon. sec. (1984-85), Hon. treasurer (1985-89); *b* Beckenham, Kent; *s* of Edwin Greenman; *m* Freda Johns; one *s. Studied art* at Beckenham School of Art (1926-29) under Henry Carr, R.A.; R.C.A. (1929-33) under Rothenstein, Spencer, Tristram and Malcolm Osbourne. *Exhib.*: engravings at World's Fair, New York (1938), and at Prague; paintings at R.A. Portrait Commissions include Windsor Herald, Moderator of Church of Scotland, Lord Northbrook, Dame Sheila Quinn, Sir Lynton White. *Work in permanent collections:* V. & A. *Official purchases:* Contemporary Art Fund; Travelling Art Exhbns., Bureau Collections. *Address:* 7 Southfields Cl., Donnington, Chichester, W. Sussex PO19 2SD. *Club:* Chelsea Arts. *Signs work:* "Greenman."

GREENSMITH, John Hiram, N.D.D. (1955), A.T.D. (1956), A.R.W.S. (1976), N.E.A.C. (1978), R.W.S. (1983), A.R.Cam.A. (1986); painter in water-colour; former Head of Fine Art, All Saints School, Sheffield; *b* Sheffield, 22 Apr., 1932; *s* of John Herbert Greensmith, clerk; one *s*, one *d. Educ.*: De la Salle College, Sheffield; *studied art* at Sheffield College of Art. *Exhib.*: R.A., R.W.S., R.B.A., R.C.A., N.E.A.C., M.A.F.A. *Address:* 77 Whirlowdale Cres., Sheffield S7 2ND, Yorks. *Signs work:* "John Greensmith."

GREENWOOD, Eileen Constance, A.R.C.A. (Design) 1935-38 F.B.I. award, Pedagogic Dip. (1939); artist, printmaker: etching/aquatint, draughtswoman: mixed media; Lecturer/Founder Principal, Sittingbourne College of Educ. (retd.); *b* Middx., 26 May, 1915; *d* of Harold Messenger, A.C.I.I.; *m* Ernest

Greenwood, A.R.C.A., P.P.R.W.S.; one *d. Educ.*: Camden School for Girls, Frances Mary Buss Foundation; *studied art* at R.C.A., Courtauld Inst., Goldsmiths' College. *Exhib.*: R.A., Bankside, many London and provincial galleries; four solo shows. *Work in public and private collections:* G.B., France, Germany, Japan, America, Australia. *Address:* Well House Studio, Brushings Farm House, Broad St., nr. Hollingbourne, Kent ME17 1RB. *Signs work:* "Eileen Greenwood" (all prints with 'cat' logo in margin).

GREENWOOD, Ernest, P.P.R.W.S. (1976), A.R.C.A. (1931-35), F.R.S.A.; artist in oil and water-colour; Inspector of Art Educ. for K.E.C.; guest lecturer for W.F. & R.K. Swan (Hellenic) Ltd.; since 1977 on "Art Appreciation", "The Art and Architecture of Roman and Romanesque France"; *b* Welling, Kent, 12 Feb., 1913; *m* Eileen C. Greenwood; one *d. Educ.*: Gravesend Grammar School. *Exhib.*: R.A., N.E.A.C., R.I., R.B.A., etc.; lectures and exhbns. given annually since 1985 in U.S.A. Exhbns. with wife at Tubac Arts Centre, Arizona, by invitation of the Director; one-man show at Bankside Gallery, London (Sept., 1991). *Work in permanent collections:* Preston, Southend, Tate Gallery, Middlesbrough A.G., Lannards Gallery Billingshurst, Wenlock Fine Art; private collections, U.S.A., Municipal Galleries of Brighton, Hastings, Hull. *Address:* Brushings Farm House, Broad St., nr. Hollingbourne, Kent ME17 1RB. *Signs work:* "Ernest Greenwood."

GREENWOOD, Maurice Arthur, A.R.Cam.A. (1988); artist in water-colour and oil; art tutor; part-time lecturer, Llandrillo Technical College: Extra Mural Dept., University College, N. Wales since 1982; *b* Rochdale, 12 Dec., 1930; *s* of Frank Greenwood; *m* Joan; two *s. Studied art:* part-time Rochdale Art School (1946-48, Peter Burgess Shorrock). *Exhib.*: R.Cam.A., and many open and one-man shows. *Work in permanent collections:* Gwynedd Library Services; private collections in U.S.A., British Columbia, Australia, U.K. *Address:* Woodlands, 12 Shaftesbury Ave., Penrhyn Bay, Llandudno, Gwynedd LL30 3EH. *Signs work:* "Maurice A. Greenwood, A.R.Cam.A."

GREENWOOD, Philip John, N.D.D. (1965), A.T.C. (1966), R.E. (1982); printmaker in etching and painter; Council Mem. Royal Soc. of Painter, Etchers and Engravers; *b* Dolgellau, N. Wales, 20 Nov., 1943; *s* of John Edward James Greenwood, R.A.F.; *m* Valery Ratcliff (decd.); four *s. Educ.*: Dolgellau Grammar School; *studied art* at Harrow College of Art (1961-65), Hornsey Teachers Training College (1965-66). *Exhib.*: R.A., R.E., Tate Gallery, R.G.I., 'Printmaking in Britain', Sydney; British Council Gallery, Athens; British Printmakers, Melbourne; Galerie Tendenz, Germany; J. One Fine Arts, Tokyo; Galerie Deux Tetes, Canada; 'Overseas Printmakers', Auckland, N.Z., Galerie Beumont, Brussels. *Work in permanent collections:* Tate Gallery, Arts Council, British Council, Derby Museum, Greenwich Museum, Oldham A.G., Graves A.G., Warwick Museum and A.G., Lincoln A.G. and Museum, etc. *Address:* 30 Leigh Hill Rd., Cobham, Surrey KT11 2HX. *Signs work:* "Greenwood."

GREENWOOD, Sydney, A.T.D., R.W.A., F.R.S.A.; work in lithography, etching, water-colour, oil; formerly Lecturer in Painting, Manchester College of Art, later Head of Fine Art and Design, and Vice Principal, Southampton College of Art; *b* Stalybridge, Ches., 11 Jan., 1913. *Studied art* under C. Hanney, later at Goldsmiths' College, London University and Croydon School of Art, and in France. *Exhib.*: R.A., W. of England Academy, Mall Galleries. Represented in private and public collections in U.S.A. etc. *Address:* Cross Oaks, Sway. *Signs work:* "Sydney Greenwood."

GREIG, Donald, R.S.M.A. (1967), Gold Medal Paris Salon (1967); painter in water-colour and oil, printmaker; *b* London, 1916; *s* of James Greig, Scottish water colourist; *m* Rita Greig, R.W.A., R.O.I., N.E.A.C.; one *s. Studied art* at Southend College of Art (Charles Taylor, R.W.S). *Exhib.:* R.A., R.W.A., R.B.A., N.E.A.C., R.I., R.S.M.A., and various one-man shows. *Work in permanent collections:* National Maritime Museum, Greenwich, Municipal Gallery, Scunthorpe. *Address:* Tor Brook Studio, Woodleigh, Kingsbridge, S. Devon TQ7 4DF. *Signs work:* "DONALD GREIG."

GREIG, Rita, R.W.A. (1983), R.O.I. (1974), N.E.A.C. (1974), Silver Medal Paris Salon (1974); painter principally in oil, also water-colour and pastel, printmaker; *b* Norwich; *d* of Harry David Wimblett; *m* Donald Greig, R.S.M.A.; one *s. Educ.:* Selhurst Grammar School, Ware Grammar School; *studied art* privately. *Exhib.:* R.A., R.W.A., R.O.I., N.E.A.C., R.B.A., various one-man shows in Britain and abroad, also shared shows with husband, Donald Greig. *Work in permanent collections:* Royal West of England Academy, Chase Manhattan Bank Collection, Bishop Otter College. *Address:* Tor Brook Studio, Woodleigh, Kingsbridge, S. Devon TQ7 4DF. *Signs work:* "R.G."

GRESTY, Kenneth H., F.R.S.A. (1971), F.I.A.L. (1966), A.T.D. (1951), D.A., Manc. (1950), N.D.D., painting (1950); Head of Faculty, North Bolton Sixth Form College; Mem. Manchester Academy (1954); *b* Manchester, 17 May, 1928; *s* of Harry Gresty; *m* Marjorie Ingred Smith; four *s. Educ.:* Sale Grammar School; *studied art* at Manchester Regional College of Art under H. Williamson, R.W.A. (1944-46, 1948-51). *Exhib.:* R.A., Manchester Academy of Fine Arts. *Official purchase;* Rutherston Collection. *Work repro.:* in Cheshire Life, Lancashire Life, and local press. *Address:* 5 Ivy Terr., Borth-Y-Gest, Porthmadog, Gwynedd LL49 9TS. *Signs work:* "K. H. Gresty."

GRIBBIN, Lancelot Benedict, A.T.D. (1949); B.A. (Hons.) Hist. of Art (1953); painter in oil, photographer; lecturer, Victoria and Albert Museum; former principal lecturer, London College of Printing; visiting lecturer, Messrs. Sotheby's Educational Studies; *b* Gateshead-on-Tyne, 7 Nov., 1927; *s* of L. B. Gribbin (senior), pharmacist; *m* Joanna Mary Satchell; two *s,* two *d. Educ.:* Dartford Grammar School; *studied art* at Sidcup School of Art under Ruskin Spear, A.R.A., Robin Guthrie, William Clause. *Exhib.:* R.A., N.E.A.C., London Group, National Soc.; one-man shows, Artists' House, Manette St., etc. *Address:* 8 Mile House La., St. Albans, Herts. AL1 1TB. *Signs work:* "L. B. GRIBBIN" (written with brush).

GRIERSON, Janet (Deaconess), B.A. Hons. (Lond.) (1934), M.A. Lambeth (1982); painter in oil and water-colour; *b* Dublin, 10 Apr., 1913. *Educ.:* Westfield College (1931-34), King's College, University of London (1934-36); *studied art* (part time) at N. Worcs. College (1978-82), Malvern Hills College (1984-89). *Exhib.:* galleries in Malvern, including one-man shows. *Address:* Flat 8 Parkview, Abbey Rd., Malvern, Worcs. WR14 3HG. *Signs work:* "Janet Grierson."

GRIFFIN, Alison Mary, B.A. Art and Design (1974); landscape artist and designer in water-colour and acrylic; *b* Sutton Coldfield, 23 May, 1953; *d* of Charles Green (decd.); *m* Charles Griffin; one *s,* one *d. Educ.:* Bolomere High School for Girls, Sutton Coldfield; *studied art* at Sutton College of Art (1969-71, H. Muskett), Bath Academy of Art (1971-74, M.Flinn). *Exhib.:* Francis Iles Gallery, Rochester, Sloman and Pettit Gallery, Maidstone, Mall Galleries, London. Work in private collections. *Address:* 2 Mays Cottages, St. Helen's La., E.Farleigh, Maidstone, Kent ME15 0LA. *Signs work:* "Alison Griffin."

GRIFFIN, David Brian; graphic designer painter in oil and water-colour, subject matter mainly nautical; Council mem. Chelsea Art Soc. (1974-85), Vice-Pres. (1991); *b* Brighton, 15 Feb., 1927; *m* Kathleen Martin; one *s*, one *d. Educ.:* Central School, Catford and Sayers Croft, Ewhurst; *studied art* at Camberwell, Northampton and St. Martin's Schools of Art (1940-43, Roland Vivian Pitchforth, R.A., R.W.S.). *Exhib.:* R.S.M.A., Armed Forces, Omell Galleries, Piccadilly. *Work in private collections:* Europe, U.S.A., and Far East. Listed in "20th Century British Marine Painting". *Commissions* include Eagle Star and British Petroleum. Served R.A.S.C. (maritime) and R.N.V.R. *Address:* 19 Ross Rd., Wallington, Surrey SM6 8QN. *Clubs:* Wapping Group of Artists, Chelsea Art Soc. *Signs work:* "David Griffin."

GRIFFITH, David Lloyd, A.R.Cam.A. (1988); artist in oil, alkyd, acrylic, gouache; local government officer; Tutor, life-drawing evening class at Conwy, sponsored by University of N. Wales; *b* Colwyn Bay, 30 Mar., 1956; *s* of Roy Lloyd Griffith. *Educ.:* Ysgol Emrys Ap Iwan, Abergele, Clwyd; *studied art* at N.E. Wales Inst. (1975-76, N.D. Mackinson, R. Hore), Open College of the Arts (1989-93 E. Williams, H. Bowcott, N. Griffiths). *Exhib.:* Theatr Clwyd (1980). *Address:* 39 Nant Yr Efail, Glan Conwy, Colwyn Bay. *Signs work:* "D.L.G."

GRIFFITHS, David, D.F.A. (Slade); portrait painter in oils; *b* Liverpool, 1939; *s* of Robert Frederick Griffiths, banker. *Educ.:* Pwllheli Grammar School (1951-57); *studied art* at Slade School of Fine Art (1957-61, Sir William Coldstream). *Exhib.:* Royal National Eisteddfod. *Work in permanent collections:* City Hall, Cardiff; Museum and A.G., Newport; Croydon Town Hall; House of Lords; Eton College; R.C.S.; National Library of Wales; University of Wales, Cardiff, Swansea and Aberystwyth; Llandovery College; Trinity College; Assoc. of Anaesthetists; Speaker's House, Westminster; H.T.V. Television; Waverley School; Liverpool University; Assoc. of Chartered Surveyors; University of Indianapolis; several public and private collections throughout the country. *Address:* Westville House, 49 Westville Rd., Cardiff CF2 5DF. *Signs work:* "David Griffiths."

GRIFFITHS, Tom; painter, designer and illuminator on vellum; Senior lecturer, Norwich School of Art (1942-49); chairman, Norfolk and Norwich Art Circle (1957, 1958, 1978), President (1983—). *Educ.:* City of Norwich School; *studied art* at Norwich School of Art, Heatherleys' and The Grosvenor (London). *Exhib.:* R.A., R.O.I., N.S., and provincial art galleries; one-man shows of townscapes (Norwich). *Official purchases:* many illuminated vellums include Loyal Address (Norwich); Freedom Scrolls for H.M. Queen Elizabeth the Queen Mother, Sir John Barbirolli (King's Lynn); the Royal Air Force and Regimental presentations and the County War Memorial Book of Remembrance, Norwich Cathedral. *Address:* 15 Essex St., Norwich. *Signs work:* "Tom Griffiths."

GRIGSBY, John Higham, N.D.D., A.T.D., A.R.E. (1973), R.E. (1978); *b* Staffs., 18 Dec., 1940. *Studied art* at Stoke and Leicester Colleges of Art. *Exhib.:* Young Contemporaries, R.A., N.E.A.C., R.W.A., R.W.S. Galleries, Mall Galleries, F.B.A. Touring Exhbns., Woburn Abbey, Glasgow Institute, London Group, Buenos Aires Print Biennale; Exhbn. of etchings at Market Print Gallery, Exeter, Phoenix Gallery, Henley and Bedford School. *Work in permanent collections:* City Gallery, Milton Keynes; Reading Museum; Whitgift Foundation; Graves Gallery, Sheffield; Open University; National Museum of Wales; Williamson Gallery, Birkenhead; Portland State University (U.S.A.); Camden and Greenwich Councils; Hertfordshire, mid-Glamorgan and Sheffield

Education Authorities; Exeter University; Bedford School; Fylde Arts Assoc; Imperial College. *Commissions:* Two murals for Trust Houses (1962); Limited edition etching for Unistrut U.K. (1978) and the P.C.C. (1982). *Address:* 152A Mackenzie Rd., Beckenham BR3 4SD. *Signs work:* "John Grigsby."

GRIMSHAW, Gladys, A.R.C.A. (1934); potter; awarded Medaille de Bronze, Paris Salon (1963); visiting lecturer, Oxford School of Art; lecturer for Wedgwood's; *b* Nelson; *d* of Harry Elliott, master printer; *m* Reginald Grimshaw, A.R.C.A., A.T.D.; two *s. Educ.:* Nelson Grammar School; *studied art* at Liverpool School of Art under George Marples (1928-31), R.C.A. (1931-34), Sir William Rothenstein and Staite Murray. *Exhib.:* R.A., R.B.A., Paris Salon, G.I., W.I.A.C. Awarded Mention d'Honneur, Paris (1957); religious sculpture exhbn., Edinburgh and Oxford and Cambridge *Address:* The Old Rectory, Noke, Oxford. *Signs work:* "G. Grimshaw."

GRIMSHAW, Reginald, A.R.C.A., A.T.D., F.R.S.A.; former head, Oxford School of Art; asst. teacher, Cheltenham School of Art (1934-35); Maidstone School of Art (1935-40); artist in oil and water-colour; *b* Farsley, Yorks., 27 Sept., 1910; *s* of Harry Grimshaw; *m* Gladys Grimshaw, A.R.C.A.; two *s. Educ.:* Pudsey Grammar School; *studied art* at Pudsey School of Art (1927-30), Leeds College of Art (1930-31), R.C.A. (1931-34) under Sir William Rothenstein and Prof. Tristram. *Exhib.:* R.A., R.B.A., A.I.A. *Address:* The Old Rectory, Noke, Oxford. *Signs work:* "R. Grimshaw."

GROARKE, Michael, M.A., M.C.S.D., chartered designer; B.E.D.A. Cert. (Registered European designer); wallpaper/textile/ceramics designer, painter in water-colour and oil; *b* Manchester, Oct., 1943; *s* of Thomas Groarke, stage director; *m* Prudence J. Hyde; two *s. Educ.:* Manchester High School of Art; *studied art* at Calico Printers Assoc. Design School, Manchester Polytechnic Faculty of Art and Design, Rochdale College of Art. *Exhib.:* R.A., R.W.S., R.I., R.Cam.A.; design work/exhib. Britain, Europe and America. *Address:* Fourways, 2 Grosvenor Rd., Marple, Stockport SK6 6PR. *Signs work:* "M.G." or "Michael Groarke."

GROSSMAN, Vera, S.W.A. (1987), U.A. (1986); sculptor for portrait and ethnic characters in clay, artist in oil on canvas; *b* London; one *s. Educ.:* Reading Bluecoat School; *studied art:* no formal training; private tuition for: portrait painting (1976-82, Leonard Boden, R.P.; 1983-85, Joyce Wyatt, R.M.S., P.S., U.A.); sculpture (1979-84, Alan Sly, R.A., A.R.B.S.). *Exhib.:* Mall Galleries, Westminster Central Hall, Ben Uri Gallery, Alpine Gallery, Chelsea Manor St. Gallery, "Smiths" Covent Gdn. *Address:* 16 Bedford Rd., Chiswick, London W4 1JH. *Signs work:* "Vera Grossman."

GROSVENOR, Stella Athalie (Mrs.), R.B.S., Slade Dip. Fine Art (1937); sculptor in bronze, resin, stone, wood, painter in oil; *b* Beaconsfield; *d* of Sidney Henderson; *m* Hugh N. W. Grosvenor, A.R.I.B.A. *Educ.:* St. Margaret's School, Hampstead; *studied art* at Slade School under Prof. Schwabe and Prof. Gerrard. *Exhib.:* group shows, Society Portrait Sculptors, Hampstead Artists Council, R.A., Travers Gallery, Erica Bourne Gallery; one-man show, Foyles, London (1968). *Publications:* Art Editor, National Trade Press; Illustrated, Caxton Publishing Co. *Address:* 35 Flask Walk, London NW3. *Clubs:* Hampstead Artists Council, R.B.S. *Signs work:* "A. Grosvenor."

GROVES, John Michael, R.S.M.A. (1977), N.D.D. (Illustration, 1957); artist in pastel, oil, pen and ink; *b* Lewisham, London, 9 Mar., 1937. *Educ.:* Kilmorie Secondary School, London; *studied art* at Camberwell School of Arts and Crafts

(1953-57). *Exhib.:* R.S.M.A., Guildhall, London. *Address:* 114 Further Green Rd., Catford, London SE6 1JQ. *Signs work:* "JOHN M. GROVES."

GRUBB, Gerald, M.F.P.S.(1986); painter in oil, pastel, acrylic; *b* Dublin, 10 Sept., 1912; *s* of H.T. Hunt Grubb and Maud, née Stack; *m* Sheilah, née Pain (divorced); two *s*. *Educ.:* St. Stephen's Green School, Dublin; *studied drawing* at Metropolitan College and Royal Hibernian Academy Life Class (George Atkinson, Dermot O'Brien); Academie des Beaux Arts, Brussels, Central School of Art, London, Ealing, Anglo French Art Centre and other life classes. *Exhib.:* F.P.S. (inc. "Trends"), C.W.A.C., A.S.P., H.A.C., R.A. Work in private collections. *Address:* 7 Staveley, Varndell St., London NW1 3RL. *Signs work:* "G" followed by last two digits of year completed.

GRUFFYDD, Pegi, B.A. (Hons.) (1982), A.R.C.A. (1985), Dip.R.A. (1986); painter/printmaker in oil, water-colour, etching, lithography; *b* Pwllheli, N. Wales, 28 Apr., 1960; *d* of Morris Griffiths. *Educ.:* Ysgol Glan-y-Môr, Pwllheli; *studied art* at Manchester Polytechnic (1978-79), Wolverhampton Polytechnic (1979-82), R.A. Schools (1983-86). *Exhib.:* R.A. Summer Exhbn. (1984-85), Royal National Eisteddfod of Wales (1980-88), Young Artists Forum, Cardiff University, Wales '83, the Welsh Group Touring Exhbn., Midwales Open, Aberystwyth, North Wales Open, Llandudno; one-man show, Theatre Gwynedd, Bangor; group show, Oriel, Bangor. *Gallery:* Oriel Glyn-y-Weddw, Llanbedrog. *Address:* Llymgwyn Farm, Chwilog, Pwllheli, Gwynedd LL53 6HJ. *Signs work:* "Pegi Gruffydd" or "P.G."

GRÜNEWALD, Eleanor Mavis (née Wilson), N.D.D. (Painting), A.T.D. (Leeds); artist in oil, acryl, aquarelle; teaches art at Kronberg Art School, Germany; *b* Stockton-on-Tees, 2 Mar., 1931; *d* of Harold Wilson; *m* Karl-Heinz Grünewald; three children. *Educ.:* Richard Hind School, Stockton; *studied art* at Middlesbrough School of Art, Leeds College of Art. *Exhib.:* Frankfurt, Wiesbaden, Marburg, Paris, Le Salon, Grand Palais des Champs-Elysees, China: Peking, Shanghai; Egypt: Cairo, Alexandria, with the Frankfurt Union of Professional Artists. *Official purchases:* Cities of Frankfurt, Wiesbaden, Marburg, Middlesbrough Town Council. *Address:* Fahrgasse 21, 6000 Frankfurt/Main. *Club:* Berufsverband Bildender Künstler. *Signs work:* "Mavis Wilson-Grünewald."

GUEST, Alan Sexty; artist in oil; teacher, private tutor, lecturer, autodidact; teacher, Coventry City Council; *b* 11 Dec., 1920; *s* of Robert Sexty Guest, B.A., accountant; *m* Kathleen Guest; two *s*, five *d*. *Educ.:* Woodlands, nr. Doncaster. *Exhib.:* Nuneaton A.G., Coventry, Chalk Farm; two paintings selected by BBC Search for an Artist; TV appearances. *Commission:* by owner of L'escargot, now hanging in the Curragh. *Address:* 19 Sharp Cl., Holbrooks, Coventry. *Club:* Unicorn. *Signs work:* "A. Guest."

GUEVARA José; painter, playwright; creator of the technique today known as "oil by combustion of the pigment"; *b* Puebla de Guzmán (Huelva), Spain, 12 Mar., 1928. *Educ.:* Instituto de Segunda Enseñanza "La Rábida" de Huelva, Escuela Superior de Comercio de Sevilla; *studied art* at Academic Provincial de Bellas Artes (1940-41-42, Prof. Pedro Gómez and Enrique Garcia Orta), Atelier Guillermo Rodriguez (1955-56-57), Atelier Prof. Armando Balloni (1955-56-57-58); Armando Balloni has been only one teacher. Travelled through five continents and taken part in many international competitions such as the XXXI Bienal de Venecia, VII Bienal de São Paulo, II Bienal de Paris, VI Bienal de Alexandria, and I Bienal de Arte Español de Paris; 100 one-man shows and participated in 500 collective exhibitions. *Work in permanent collections:* Museo

Español de Arte Contemporaneo, Madrid; Museo Provincial de Huelva, Huelva; Museum of Modern Art of Australia, Melbourne; Gadsden Museum of Fine Art, Gadsden, Alabama; Memphis State, Memphis, Tenns.; National Museum, Baghdad; National A.G., Baghdad; Ministry of Culture and Guidance, Baghdad; Museo de Arte Moderno de Buenos Aires, Buenos Aires; Museo de Arte Moderno, Montevideo; Galleria Comunale d'Arte Moderna, Jesi; Museo d'Arte Contemporánea, Sassoferrato; Museo d'Arte Contemporánea, Marsala; Museo del Alto Aragón, Huesca; Instituto Panameño de Arte, Panama; Universidad L. de Huesca; Clun La Rábida, Sevilla; Círculo de la Amistad, Córdoba; Caja de Ahorros de Murcia, Murcia; Caja de Ahorros de Huelva, Huelva; Caja de Ahorros de Zamora, Zamora; Fondation Taylor, Paris; Museo Ambiente Villa Lauri, Pollenza, Italy; Pinacoteca Comunale de Pollenza, Italy; Museo Internazionale dell'Etichetta, Comune di Cupramontana, Italy; Museo Internazionale dell'Imagine Postale, Belvedere Ostrense, Italy. *Published dramas:* The Telephones, After the Escalade, The Vindication of Judas, etc. First to produce in Spain The Last Tape by Samuel Beckett. *Address:* Claudio Coello, 52, Madrid 1, Spain. *Signs work:* see appendix.

GUISE, Christopher John, M.A., A.R.M.S.; marine painter in oil on wood panels, miniaturist in oil on ivorine; formerly on staff, Hurstpierpoint College; *b* Darjeeling, India, 19 June, 1928; *m* Phyllis Gibson; one *s*, one *d. Educ.:* Charterhouse and Brasenose College, Oxford. *Exhib.:* R.M.S. since 1983, Brighton, Washington, N.Y., Boston, Maritime and Sailing Centres. *Address:* Carys, West Furlong La., Hurstpierpoint, W. Sussex BN6 9RH. *Signs work:* "C.J. GUISE."

GUMUCHIAN, Margaret, D.A. (Manc.), A.T.D., F.R.S.A.; artist in oil, gouache and lithography; *b* Manchester, 8 June, 1927; *d* of Leon Gumuchian; *m* Ian MacDonald Grant; one *d. Studied art* at the Regional College of Art, Manchester. *Exhib.:* R.A., R.B.A., M.A.F.A., S.M.P. regional galleries, Paris, and Biarritz. *Official purchases:* School Loans Collection, Salford; Salford Art Gallery, Rutherston Loans Collection, Manchester City A.G. and various private collections, Arctophile. *Address:* Barrachnie, Aldersgreen Ave., High Lane, Stockport, Cheshire SK6 8EB. *Signs work:* "Mgt. Gumuchian."

GUNN, James Thomson, F.I.A.L., A.I.P.D., D.A., R.I.Dipl; artist in oil, watercolour, gouache, mixed media and designer; Letter of Commendation from H.M. The Queen (R.A.F. 1957); Diploma of Merit conferred by University delle Arti (1982); Highland Society of London award, R.S.A. (1985): *b* Gorebridge, 9 Apr., 1932; *s* of late George J. T. Gunn, B.Sc., A.AM.I.E.E.; *m* Mary Lang (née Linton); one *d. Educ.:* Dalkeith High School; *studied art* at Edinburgh College of Art (1956), Diploma (Travelling Scholar). *Exhib.:* R.S.A., R.S.W., R.I., S.S.A., R.G.I., City Art Centre (1983). *Work in permanent collections:* Royal Collection, Argyll Educ. Com.; represented in private collections. *Address:* 3 Park Cres., Easthouses, Dalkeith, Midlothian, Scotland. *Clubs:* I.A.L., I.P.D. *Signs work:* see appendix.

GUNSTON, Irene, B.A.(Hons.) (1982); sculptor in clay, bronze, plaster; *b* Aberkenfig, S. Wales, 19 Aug., 1960. *Studied art* at Cardiff College of Art (1978-79), Canterbury College of Art (1979-82). *Work in permanent collection:* B.M. Coins and Medals Dept. *Publication:* 1/50,000: poems by Elizabeth James (Vennell Press, 1992). *Address:* 86 Barchester St., London E14 6BE. *Signs work:* sculptures usually unsigned; drawings and prints "I.G." or "I. Gunston."

GUTHRIE, Jane Gordon, A.R.C.A. (1950); painter in oil and water-colour, specializing in portraits; *b* Farningham, Kent, 1 May, 1927; *d* of Alexander

Gordon Guthrie (decd.); *m* Sir John M. R. Best-Shaw, Bart; two *s*, one *d*. *Educ.:* St. Andrews, Fife; *studied art* at Sidcup Art School, Goldsmiths' College of Art and R.C.A. *Exhib.:* R.A., N.E.A.C., Young Contemporaries, R.P., Pastel Soc.; solo shows, Upper Street Gallery (1971), Staplehurst (1980), Maidstone (1984, 1987), Lullingstone (1993). *Address:* The Stone House, Boxley, Maidstone, Kent ME14 3DJ. *Signs work:* "Jane G. Guthrie" or "J.G.G."

GWYNNE-JONES, Emily, A.R.C.A. (1970); Mem. Contemporary Portrait Soc.; painter in oil and water-colour; *b* 7 July, 1948; *d* of Allan Gwynne-Jones, D.S.O., C.B.E., R.A., painter; and Rosemary E. Allan, painter; *m* M. Frank Beanland, painter; one *s*, two *d*. *Studied art* at R.A. Schools, R.C.A. (1966-70), N.E. London Polytechnic (textiles), Central School (etching) (1977-78). *Exhib.:* R.A. (1966-90), Mayor Gallery, New Grafton Gallery, Pigeon Hole Gallery, Brotherton Gallery, Discerning Eye, Mall Galleries (1991-92), N.E.A.C.; one-man show, Michael Parkin (1977). John Player Award N.P.G. (1987-88). *Work in permanent collections:* R.A., Nuffield Trust, National Trust, Eton College, paintings for hospitals, B.S.I. *Publication:* illustrated, Pavane for a Dead Infanta by Hugh Ross Williamson. *Address:* Metfield Lane Farm, Fressingfield, Eye, Suffolk IP21 5SD. *Signs work:* "E.G.J." or "E. Gwynne-Jones."

GYLES, Pauline Yvonne, A.R.M.S. (1981), R.M.S. (1985), F.S.B.A. (1986); self taught miniature painter in water-colour; Hon. Sec., Royal Miniature Soc.; *b* Bournemouth, 31 Aug., 1931; *d* of E. Stoddart Fox, F.R.I.C.S., F.A.I.; *m* Brian Gyles. *Educ.:* private schools England and Switzerland. *Exhib.:* Medici, Liberty's, Llewellyn Alexander, London, Linda Blackstone, Pinner, Peter Hedley, Wareham, S.B.A., R.M.S. *Work in permanent collection:* Russel Cotes A.G. and Museum, Bournemouth, Soc. of Apothecaries. *Address:* Balcombe Cottage, 11 Wilderton Rd., Branksome Pk., Poole, Dorset BH13 6ED. *Signs work:* "Pauline Gyles."

H

HABGOOD, Yvonne Veronica, M.F.P.S. (1981); painter in oil and alkyd on canvas, pastel on paper; *b* Lincoln, 2 Oct., 1954; *d* of Windell Oliver Walcott, R.A.F. and Civil Service retd.; *m* Richard Lee Habgood. *Educ.:* St. John's School, Episkopi, Cyprus. *Exhib.:* Mall Galleries, F.P.S., Loggia Gallery, N.S.P.S. (1982), Manchester Academy, Commonwealth Inst.; one-man shows: Bagazzo Gallery Marlborough, Loggia Gallery, etc. *Work in permanent collections:* Bath Rd. Gallery, Old Town, Swindon and numerous private collections including Jamaica and Canada. *Address:* 15 Priors Hill, Wroughton, Swindon, Wilts. SN4 0RT. *Signs works:* "'Habgood."

HACCURIA, Maurice; painter and sculptor; distinctions and mentions: Jeune Peinture Belge (1958), Prix Talens (1959), Prix de la Critique (1962), Prix Olivetti (1961), Prix Europe (1962); Fellow of Institut International des arts et des lettres (Kreuzlingen). Teacher; *b* Goyer, 13 Jan., 1919. Autodidact. *Exhib.:* (1951-65) Antwerp, Brussels, Rotterdam, Brugge, Ljubljana, Grenchen, Lausanne, Venice, Trieste, Vienna, Lille, Frankfurt-am-Main, Köln, Skopje, Ostend, Knokke. *Work in permanent collections:* Royal Library (Brussels), Belgian Government, Middelheim (Antwerp), Musée d'art contemporain de

Skopje, Art Gallery Ado (Bonheiden); public and private collections in Belgium, Rotterdam, Suisse, New York. *Address:* Stwg. op Gelrode 88, Rotselaar, Belgium. *Signs work:* see appendix.

HACKETT, Frank, B.A., A.M.A.; Curator, Luton Museum and Art Gallery, Wardown Park, Luton, Beds.

HACKNEY, Alfred, R.W.S., A.R.E. (1951), D.A., Edin. (1950); artist in etching, engraving, pen and water-colour; senior lecturer, Medway College of Art, Rochester; free-lance illustrator and designer; *b* Yorks., 18 May, 1926; *s* of John Thomas Hackney. *Educ.:* Burslem School of Art, Stoke-on-Trent; *studied art* at Edinburgh College of Art and travelling scholarship to France and Italy. *Exhib.:* R.A., London Group, Soc. of Staffordshire Artists, S.E.A., R.E., R.S.A., S.S.A. *Work in permanent collection:* R.A., and numerous public and private collections. *Address:* Barnside, Lodge La., Cobham, nr. Gravesend, Kent DA12 3BS. *Signs work:* "Alfred Hackney."

HACKNEY, Arthur, V.P.R.W.S. (1973-76), R.E., A.R.C.A.; etcher; painter in oil and water-colour; Head of Dept., West Surrey College of Art and Design (retd. 1985); Mem. Fine Art Board, Council for National Academy Awards (1975-78); *b* Stainforth, Yorks., 13 Mar., 1925; *s* of John Thomas Hackney. *Educ.:* Stoke-on-Trent; *studied art* at Burslem School of Art and R.C.A. (travelling scholarship). *Exhib.:* R.A., R.E., R.W.S. *Work in permanent collections:* V. & A. Museum; Bradford City A.G.; Nottingham Castle A.G.; Keighley A.G.; Wakefield City A.G.; Graves A.G. (Sheffield); Wellington A.G. (N.Z.); Stoke-on-Trent A.G. *Work repro.:* in 20th Century Painters and Sculptors. *Address:* Woodhatches, Spoil La., Tongham, Surrey GU10 1BP. *Signs work:* see appendix.

HADDOCK, Aldridge, M.B.B.S. (1953), D.Obst.R.C.O.G. (1955), M.R.C.G.P.; medical practitioner; self taught painter in oil and mixed media; *b* Durham, 21 May, 1931; *s* of the late Christopher Haddock, musician; one *d*. *Educ.:* Durham University. *Exhib.:* 26 one-man shows, Ferens, Hull, Westgate, Newcastle, Drian, London, Municipal, Doncaster, Graves, Sheffield, University of Leeds, Loggia, London, Heathrow Hotel, London, Woodstock, London, Scunthorpe Museum, Avanti Galleries, N.Y., Central Library, Grimsby, Anderson-Marsh, St. Petersburg, Edward Mayor Gallery, Sheffield, Century Galleries, Henley-on-Thames, Usher Gallery, Lincoln. *Work in permanent collections:* Ferens A.G., Hull, Laing, Newcastle, Municipal Museum, Doncaster, Drian Gallery, London, Nicholas Martine Gallery, London; private collections: Sydney, Los Angeles, New York, Vancouver, Paris, Gothenburg, Bergen. *Work repro.:* Underwater World Journal. *Address:* The Gables, 26 Abbey Pk. Rd., Grimsby, Lincolnshire. *Clubs:* F.P.S., Lincolnshire Artists Soc. *Signs work:* "ALDRIDGE HADDOCK."

HADDON, Joyce Critchley, N.E.A.C., R.B.A.; genre painter of portraits in oil and water-colour; *b* Cambridge, 15 Aug., 1913; *d* of Prof. J. Stanley Gardiner, F.R.S.; one *s*, two *d*. *Educ.:* Perse High School, Cambridge; *studied art* at R.A. Schools. *Exhib.:* R.A., N.E.A.C., R.B.A.; one-man show at Blackheath Gallery and others. *Address:* 46 High St., Sutton Courtenay, Abingdon, Oxon.

HAENGGI, Fernand Francis; art dealer and consultant; founder-director, Gallery 101, Johannesburg (1961-72), director/owner, Gallery 21, Johannesburg (1972-1993) and Gallery 21, London (1974-76), created The Haenggi Foundation Inc. (1978); *b* Dijon, France, 28 Jan., 1934 (Swiss nationality); *s* of Heinrich Walter; *m* Caroline Nicholson; one *s*, two *d*. *Educ.:* Basel and St. Gallen, Switzerland. *Publications:* Armando Baldinelli (1974), Lucas Sithole (1979),

Zoltan Borbereki (1981). *Address:* Postfach 203, CH-3803 Beatenberg, Switzerland.

HAFFKIN, Arthur; former Director, Rotunda Gallery, Hampstead. *Educ.:* Grocers, City University London; *studied art* at St. Martin's School of Art under Kenneth Martin, Ruskin Spear; Central School of Art. *Address:* The Penthouse, 116-118 Finchley Rd., London NW3 5HT.

HAGUE, Jonathan, N.D.D., A.T.D., Netherland State Scholarship; *b* Llandudno, 18 Nov., 1938, *Studied art* at Liverpool College of Art (1957-63), Royal Academy of Fine Art, The Hague (1964-66). *Exhib.:* one-man shows: The Germeente Museum, The Hague; The Royal Institute Gallery, Piccadilly; sponsored John Lennon. *Address:* 2 Regent St., Leamington Spa, Warwicks. *Signs work:* "HAGUE."

HAIDER, Ghulam: see YUNUS.

HAIG, George Douglas (The Earl Haig), Associate Royal Scottish Academy; painter in oil and water-colour; *b* London, 15 Mar., 1918; *s* of F.M. Earl Haig. *Educ.:* Stowe and Christ Church, Oxford; *studied art* at Camberwell School of Art (1945-47) under Victor Pasmore, other members of Euston Rd. School and privately with Paul Maze. *Exhib.:* Redfern Gallery. The Scottish Gallery and elsewhere; paintings in collections of Arts Council and Scottish National Gallery of Modern Art. *Address:* Bemersyde, Melrose. *Signs work:* "Haig."

HAINARD, Robert; Doctorat es sciences honoris causa de l'Université de Genève; Prix Ed. M. Sandoz d'art animalier de l'Academie Grammont, Paris; wildlife artist in colour woodcuts, stone, bronze and wood sculptures, field observer and nature conservationist; *b* 11 Sept., 1906; *s* of Philippe Hainard, professor of painting; *m* Germaine; one *s*, one *d*. *Educ.:* Ecole des Arts Industriels, Ecole des Beaux Arts, Genève. *Exhib.:* numerous every year in Switzerland and abroad. *Work in permanent collection:* Musée d'Art et d'Histoire, Genève. *Publications:* author, Et la nature ? (1943), Les Mammifères Sauvages d'Europe (1948-49, 1961-62, 1971-72, 1986-87), Défense de l'Image (1967), Expansion et Nature (1972), Le Monde sauvage de Robert Hainard (1988), etc., illustrator of more than fifty books. *Address:* 51 chemin de Saule, CH 1233 Bernex-Genève, Switzerland. *Signs work:* "ROBERT HAINARD."

HAINAULT, June; essentist painter/printer; *d* of Henry Lane Eno, U.S.A.; *m* H.J. Mundy (decd.); two *s*. *Studied art* at Regent St. Polytechnic; Heatherley School of Art. *Exhib.:* one-man: Cork St. Gallery, London (1994), Fitzroy Gallery, London (1980), Carnival '75, University of Manchester (1975), Loggia Gallery (1972, 1975), Upper St. Gallery, Islington (1972, 1975), Cockpit Theatre (1970), Old Bakehouse, Sevenoaks (1970), New Town Gallery, Uckfield (1969, 1976), Lightning Mark, Rye (1967), Il Traghetto Gallery, Venice (1966), St. Martin's Gallery, London (1965), Hanover Galleries, Liverpool (1986). *Addresses:* The Oast House, Five Ashes, nr. Mayfield, Sussex TN20 6NL; and Kinkwall, Walls, Shetland ZE2 9PD. *Club:* F.P.S. Eastbourne Group. *Signs work:* "Hainault."

HAINSWORTH, George; Slade Dip., Gulbenkian scholar (Rome); artist in oil paint, variety of sculptural media: stone, bronze, etc.; senior lecturer; *b* Leeds, 15 Dec., 1937; *m* Lucy M. Rogers; one *s*, one *d*. *Educ.:* Leeds; *studied art* at Leeds College of Art (1955-60, Harry Thubron), Slade School of Fine Art (1960-62, William Coldstream), British School at Rome (1962-63). *Exhib.:* one-man shows: Serpentine Gallery, Ikon Gallery, B'ham, Spacex Gallery, Exeter, Sue Rankin Gallery; two-man (with Lucy): Cartwright Hall, Bradford, York

University, Bradford University, Leeds Polytechnic, Dean Clough, Halifax. *Work in permanent collections:* Leeds University, Hammond Suddard, Baring Investors. *Address:* Otter House, Hunsingore, nr. Wetherby, W. Yorks. LS22 5HY. *Clubs:* M.M. Arts Group, London, Yorkshire Sculptors Group. *Signs work:* "G. Hainsworth."

HALE, Elsie, H.S., Paris Salon (Gold medal, 1978), Le Diploma de Societaire Bilan de Contemporain (Paris), Marie-Louise Jules Richard prize (Paris Salon, 1978); painter in oil on canvas, water-colour, (specialising in miniatures on ivorine); *b* Worcester, 5 May, 1913; *d* of Walter Williams; *m* Arthur James Hale, A.I.A.C.; one *d. Educ.:* St. George's School, Worcester; *studied art* at Worcester College of Art (G. Williams). *Exhib.:* Paris Salon (1978, 1979, 1980), Town Hall Paris (1978), R.A. (1980-86), London, Brighton and Yorkshire Galleries. *Work in permanent and private collections:* U.K., America, Australia, Canada, New Zealand, Norway. *Address:* Wren Cottage, 47 Sarum Cl., Salisbury, Wilts. SP2 7LE. *Signs work:* "Elsie Hale."

HALE, Helen Margaret; painter and sculptor; *b* Harpenden, 18 Apr., 1936; *d* of Robert Hale; *m* Horne Shepherd. *Educ.:* St. George's School, Harpenden; *studied art* at St. Martin's School of Art and Sir John Cass School of Art. *Exhib.:* group shows: London, Edinburgh, Paris. *Address:* Atheldene, Loxwood Rd., Rudgwick, Horsham, W. Sussex RH12 3DW. *Clubs:* Royal Institute of Oil Painters, Free Painters and Sculptors, National Society of Painters, Sculptors and Printmakers, The Society of Women Artists. *Signs work:* "HALE."

HALES, Gordon Hereward, R.S.M.A. (1981), A.R.B.A., F.R.S.A., M.Cam.; painter in water-colour, pastel and oil; *b* Matlock, Derbys., 24 Feb., 1916; *s* of Joseph Hales and Gertrude Annie Hales (née Graves); *m* Margaret Lily Adams; two *d. Educ.:* Avenue Road School and The Gateway School, Leicester; *studied art* at Leicester College of Art, Northampton School of Art. *Exhib.:* R.I., R.O.I., P.S. *Address:* 11 Rosecroft Drive, Watford, Herts. *Clubs:* Wapping Group of Artists, London Muster of Artists (founder), The Artists Soc., and Langham Sketching Club, Armed Forces Art Soc. *Signs work:* "GORDON HALES."

HALL, Christopher Compton, R.B.A. (1988), D.F.A. (1954); painter in oil; *b* Slaugham, Sussex, 25 Dec., 1930; *s* of Donald John Hall; *m* Maria Galassi; three *s. Educ.:* Bedales School; *studied art* at Slade School of Fine Art (1950-54). *Exhib.:* Portal Gallery, New Grafton Gallery, R.A., Waterman Fine Art, Lynne Stern Assoc. *Work in permanent collections:* London Museum, National Library of Wales, Reading A.G., Arts Council, O.U.P. *Address:* Catherine Villa, Station Rd., Newbury, Berks. *Signs work:* "C.C. Hall."

HALL, Margaret MacLeod, A.T.D. (1944), S.G.A. (1952), A.M.A. (Indian Art) (1966); illustrator in pen and ink, water-colour, wood engraving, author and lecturer; panel lecturer, V. & A.; *b* Hampstead, London, 1 Jan., 1922; *d* of Richard Hall. *Studied art* at Harrow School of Art (1938-43), Hornsey College of Art (1943-44). *Work in permanent collections:* The Hall, W. Bridgford, Notts., Castle Museum, Nottingham. *Publications:* with John Irwin: Indian Painted and Printed Fabrics (Ahmedabad, 1971), Indian Embroideries (Ahmedabad, 1973); illustrations, The Sanchi Torso, V. & A. Year Book (1973); and in periodicals; chapters, 'Indian Textiles'; 'Indian Tribal Textiles', 5,000 years of Textiles, British Museum Press (1993); now completing work with John Irwin. *Address:* 174 Portland Rd., London W11 4LU. *Signs work:* "Margaret Hall" or "Margaret M. Hall."

HALL, Nigel John, M.Art R.C.A.; sculptor; *b* Bristol, 30 Aug., 1943; *s* of H.J. Hall. *Educ.:* Bristol Grammar School; *studied art* at West of England College of Art (1960-64), Royal College of Art (1964-67), Harkness Fellowship (1967-69). *Exhib.:* one-man shows, Galerie Givaudan, Paris; Wilder Gallery, Los Angeles; Galerie Neuendorf, Hamburg and Cologne; Serpentine Gallery, London; Juda Rowan Gallery, London; Nishimura Gallery, Tokyo; Elkon Gallery, N.Y., Galerie Maeght, Paris. *Work in permanent collections:* Tate Gallery, V. & A., Arts Council of Great Britain, National Galerie, Berlin; Dallas Museum of Fine Art, Tokyo Metropolitan Museum, Chicago Art Institute, Kunsthaus, Zurich, Museum of Modern Art, N.Y. *Address:* 11 Kensington Pk. Gdns., London W11 3HD. *Signs work:* "NIGEL HALL."

HALL, Pauline Sophie, B.Sc. (1938); artist in woodcut, wood engraving, linocut; ex-mem. S.WL.A.; *b* Birmingham, 23 June, 1918; *d* of Dr. E. W. Assinder; *m* Prof. K. R. L. Hall (decd.). *Educ.:* Birmingham University, Oxford University; *studied art* at Michaelis School of Art, Cape Town (1955-60). *Exhib.:* R.E., S.WL.A. (Mall Galleries), local exhbns. in aid of conservation; one-man shows, Cape Town (1973), The Shakespeare Centre, Stratford-on-Avon (1984). *Work in permanent collection:* "SWAN", Wallsworth Hall, Glos. *Address:* Park View Flat, Church Rd., Snitterfield, Warwickshire CV37 0LE. *Signs work:* "Pauline S. Hall."

HALLETT, Roger Michael, D.F.A. (Slade) 1957; painter in oil, water-colour, tempera, sculptor; Director, Hallett's Panorama, and Bath Panorama Ltd.; *b* Bristol, 1 June, 1929; *s* of Edwin Arnold Hallett; *m* Sylvia Craig; one *s*, two *d*. *Educ.:* Bristol Cathedral School; *studied art* at Slade School of Fine Art (1954-57). *Exhib.:* London, Paris, Edinburgh, Sydney, Melbourne, Newcastle, Bristol. *Work in permanent collection:* Hallett's Panorama of Bath, Britain's largest oil painting (200 ft. x 20 ft.) hung in a circle, on permanent display at the Thames Barrier Visitors Centre. *Address:* The Old Vicarage, Watery Lane, Twerton, Bath, Avon. BA2 1RL. *Club:* London Sketch. *Signs work:* "Roger Hallett."

HALLIDAY, Charlotte Mary Irvine, R.W.S. (1976), N.E.A.C. (1961); topographical artist; Keeper, New English Art Club since 1989; *b* Kensington, 5 Sept., 1935; *d* of Edward Halliday, C.B.E., P.P.R.P., P.P.R.B.A., A.R.C.A. *Educ.:* Wester Elchies, Francis Holland; *studied art* at R.A. Schools (1953-58). *Exhib.:* R.W.S., R.B.A., N.E.A.C., etc. *Publications:* Illustrations for Dictionary of Edwardian Architecture by A. Stuart Gray (1985) and co-author, with him, of "Fanlights", a visual architectural history (1990). *Address:* 36A Abercorn Pl., London NW8 9XP. *Signs work:* "Charlotte Halliday" or "CMIH."

HALLIDAY, Irene, D.A. (1952), R.S.W. (1955); artist in gouache; *b* Kingsmuir, Angus, Scotland, 26 Sept., 1931; *d* of Andrew Halliday, School master. *Educ.:* Arbroath High School; *studied art* at Dundee College of Art (1948-53, Alberto Morrocco, R.S.A., R.S.W.). *Exhib.:* 35 one-man shows, Arbroath, Dundee, Edinburgh, Manchester, Salford, New York State. *Work in permanent collections:* art galleries of Arbroath, Bolton, Dundee, Glasgow, Greenock, Salford; education authorities of Dundee, Dunbartonshire, Edinburgh, Fife, Manchester, Wigan; Granada TV., British National Oil Co., Shell Centre, London, Manchester Ship Canal Co. *Address:* 46 Highfield Dene Rd., Didsbury, Manchester M20 8ST. *Signs work:* "Halliday."

HALLIDAY, Thomas Symington, M.B.E., F.R.S.A., F.I.A.L.; European Banner of Arts (1984); World Culture Award (1984); Italian Oscar (1985); gold medal, Accademia Italia; Gold Medal, International Parliament, U.S.A.; Contemporary Art Soc., Milan; awarded Gold Medal, Artist of the Year (1988);

"Stag" sculpture, official presentation to H.M. The Queen; drawings "H.M.S. Duke of York" and "Valiant" purchased by H.R.H. Duke of Edinburgh; Founder Mem. Guild of Aviation Artists: *b* Thornhill, Dumfriesshire, 1902; *studied art* at Glasgow. *Exhib.:* R.A., Paris Salon, R.S.A., G.I., R.S.W., S.S.A., N.E.A.C., R.S.M.A. Work in many public collections. *Work repro.:* in Studio, Scots Magazine, Life and Work, Wood. *Publications:* Scottish Sculpture. *Address:* 9 Hill Cres., Wormit, Newport-on-Tay DD6 8PQ. *Signs work:* "T. S. HALLIDAY."

HAMBLING, Maggi; Boise Travel award, N.Y. (1969), Arts Council award (1977), Artist in Residence, National Gallery (1980-81); artist in oil on canvas, water-colour; *b* Suffolk, 1945. *Studied art* at Camberwell School of Art (1964-67), Slade School of Fine Art (1967-69); studied with Lett Haines and Cedric Morris (1960). *Exhib.:* solo shows: National Gallery (1981), Serpentine Gallery (1987), Arnolfini Gallery, Bristol (1988), Bernard Jacobson Gallery (1990), Yale Center for British Art (1991). *Work in permanent collections:* Tate Gallery, Whitworth A.G., A.C.G.B., National Gallery. *Address:* c/o Bernard Jacobson Gallery, 14A Clifford St., London W1. *Signs work:* surname on back.

HAMILTON, Thomas Gottfried Louis, B.A.Hons.(Arch.), R.I.B.A. (1956); architect, artist in pen, pencil and water-colour; *b* Berlin, 29 Mar., 1930; *s* of Louis Hamilton (decd.); *m* Georgina Vera Craig; one *s*, one *d*. *Educ.:* King's School, Canterbury; U.C.L.; *studied architecture* at Bartlett School of Architecture (1949-55), Prof. A.E. Richardson). *Address:* 55 Addison Ave., London W11 4QU. *Club:* Arts. *Signs work:* "Thomas Hamilton."

HAMMOND, Hermione, Rome Scholar (Painting, 1938); *studied art* at Chelsea Polytechnic, R.A. Schools (Dip.). *Exhib.:* one-man exhbns.: Bishopsgate Institute (1956); Colnaghi's (1957); Arthur Jeffress (1961); All Hallows, London Wall (1965); New Grafton (1970); Great King St. Gallery, Edinburgh (1972); Six Portfolios, Chelsea (1973); Hartnoll & Eyre Studies of Iran & Cyprus (1978). *Work in permanent collections:* ceiling decoration, University of London, Guildhall collection, Museum of London, Fondation Custodia, Institut Néerlandais, Paris, Fitzwilliam Museum, Hunterian A.G., Glasgow. *Work repro.:* Oxford Almanack, Arts Review, R.I.B.A. Journal, Country Life. *Address:* 2 Hans Studio, 43A Glebe Pl., London SW3. *Signs work:* "Hermione Hammond."

HAMPTON, F. Michael; wildlife artist in water-colour, scraper-board and acrylic; S.WL.A.-W.W.F.N. Fine Art award (1988); *b* Croydon, 29 May, 1937; *s* of Francis Wilkie; *m* Julie. *Studied art* at Croydon Art School. *Exhib.:* R.S.P.B., Sandy, Arnhem Gallery, Croydon, Blackheath Gallery SE3, The Wildlife Gallery, Lavenham, Lion and Lamb Gallery, Farnham, Surrey, Medici Gallery, London, Port Lympne Zoo Park, Hythe, Kent, Ringstead Gallery, Hunstanton. *Work repro.:* three jackets of 'British Birds', two jackets of R.S.P.B. 'Birds', (1980-1983), Calendar for Sussex Fine Arts, S.WL.A. Calendars (1987,1988), S.WL.A.-R.S.P.B. Calendar (1990, 1991, 1992), B.B.C. Wildlife Magazine (Aug. 1992). *Address:* 6 Pinewood Cl., Shirley, Surrey CR0 5EX. *Clubs:* S.WL.A., Croydon Art. *Signs work:* "M" and "H" with grebe's head, see appendix.

HANCERI, Dennis John, R.S.M.A. (1970); graphic designer, water-colour and gouache; *b* London, 7 June, 1928; *m* Jill; one *s,* one *d. Studied art* at St. Martin's School of Art. *Exhib.:* one-man show, Denver, Colorado, U.S.A., Centaur Gallery, Dallas, Texas, Southport, Connecticut, U.S.A.; also shows at Mystic Seaport, Connecticut. *Address:* 97 Horncastle Rd., London SE12. *Club:* Wapping Group of Artists. *Signs work:* "Dennis John Hanceri."

HANKEY, Christopher Alers, O.B.E., M.A., B.Sc.; painter in oil; Mem. Armed Forces Art Soc.; retd. Civil Servant; *b* Oxted, Surrey, 27 Apr., 1911; *s* of The Rt. Hon. Lord Hankey, G.C.B., G.C.M.G.; *m* (1) Prudence Brodribb; one *d*; (2) Helen Cassavetti; one *s. Educ.:* Rugby School, New College, Oxford, University College, London. *Exhib.:* R.A., R.B.A., R.O.I., National Soc., R.A. Artists in Japan, Anna-Mei Chadwick Gallery (Parsons Green), Nevill Gallery, Canterbury. *Address:* New Cottage, French St., nr. Westerham, Kent TN16 1PW. *Club:* Ebury Court. *Signs work:* "Hankey" or "Christopher Hankey."

HANLEY, Liam Powys; self-taught painter in oil on canvas, water-colour, pen and ink; *b* S. Kensington, 4 Apr., 1933; *s* of James Hanley, novelist; *m* Hilary Hanley; one *s,* one *d. Educ.:* Wrekin College, Salop. *Exhib.:* Stone Gallery, Newcastle, Mermaid Theatre, Thackeray Gallery, London, R.A., Abbot Hall A.G., Kendal, Phoenix Gallery, Lavenham, Suffolk, Bronwen White, New Orleans, U.S.A. *Publication:* The Face of Winter by James Hanley. *Address:* 21 Woodsome Rd., London NW5. *Signs work:* "Hanley."

HANLY, Daithi Patrick, B.Arch., F.R.I.A.I., F.R.I.B.A., F.R.T.P.I.; architect, planner, landscaper, sculptor in stone; former Dublin City Architect; *b* Cavan, 11 Mar., 1917; *s* of Joseph Hanly, F.R.C.Sc.I.; *m* Joan Kennedy; one *s,* one *d. Educ.:* National University, College of Art, Dublin. *Exhib.:* R.H.A., Oireachtas. Won competition Garden of Remembrance, Dublin (1966). Architect to Royal Dublin Society for Simmonscourt Pavilion large exhibition complex, seaside garden village in Blainroe, Wicklow with golf clubhouse, on 550 acres. Designed Basilica at Knock for 7,500 pilgrims with Brennan Associates. Advisory consultant architect, National College of Art and Design. *Address:* San Elmo, Vico Rd., Dalkey, Dublin, Ireland. *Signs work:* "D. P. Hanly" or "D.P.H."

HANSCOMB, Brian, A.R.E. (1991); self taught artist in copperplate, engraving, drawing and pastel; *b* Croxley Green, Herts., 23 Sept., 1944; *m* Jane Wilkins, née Hunt; two *d. Educ.:* Rickmansworth Grammar School. *Exhib.:* R.A., R.W.A., R.E., N.E.A.C., Clarges Gallery; one-man shows: England and Germany. *Work in permanent collections:* D.O.E., V. & A., National Art Library, Royal Cornwall Museum and A.G. *Publications:* On the Morning of Christ's Nativity (Folio Soc., 1987), Sun, Sea and Earth (Whittington Press, 1989), Cornwall – An Interior Vision (Whittington Press, 1992). *Address:* Tor View, Limehead, St. Breward, Bodmin, Cornwall PL30 4LU. *Signs work:* "B. Hanscomb" or "B.H."

HARDAKER, Charles, A.R.C.A. (1958), N.E.A.C. (1969), R.B.A. (1984); painter in oil, pastel, charcoal of still life, allegorical and symbolic subjects, also landscape and portraits; tutor in painting and drawing; *b* Oxford, 1 May, 1934; *s* of Charles Hardaker, businessman. *Educ.:* Wellesbourne School, B'ham; *studied art* at B'ham College of Arts and Crafts (1949-53), R.C.A. (1955-58). *Exhib.:* R.A., N.E.A.C., R.B.A., R.P., five one-man shows, San Francisco (2), London (3). *Work in permanent collections:* Tate Gallery (Chantrey Bequest), Guildhall of London, G.L.C., National Library of Wales, Northumbria Water, B.P. *Address:* Studio 1, St. Oswald's Studios, Sedlescombe Rd., Fulham, London SW6 1RH. *Signs work:* "Hardaker."

HARDEN, Gerald A. C., A.R.C.A., Cadet Forces medal (1951); artist in pencil, pen and ink, water-colour, oil, calligraphy and painted and enriched lettering, engraving; art master, Cambridgeshire High School, Cambridge (1938-71); art master, Grammar School, Maidstone (1932-38); *b* Charlton Kings, nr. Cheltenham, 2 Feb., 1909; *s* of Arthur Graty Harden; *m* Edith Eva Lampard; one *s,* two *d. Educ.:* Pate's Grammar School, Cheltenham; *studied art* at

Cheltenham School of Arts and Crafts, R.C.A. *Exhib.:* Cheltenham, Maidstone, Folkestone, Rochester, London, Cambridge, R.A. and Tate Gallery (pictures for schools exhbn.). *Address:* 22 Hartington Grove, Cambridge CB1 4UE. *Clubs:* Cambridge and County Bowling, County Badge. *Signs work:* see appendix.

HARDIE, Gwen, Richard Ford award, R.A. (1982), Hons. Degree (1983), Daad Scholarship, W. Berlin (1984), Edward 7th British-German Foundation, W. Berlin (1986); painter in oil, sculptor in cement, plaster; *b* Newport, Scotland, 7 Jan., 1962. *Educ.:* Inverurie Acadamy; *studied art* at Edinburgh College of Art (1979-84, John Houston), H.D.K., W. Berlin (1984-85, Baselitz). *Exhib.:* solo shows: Fruitmarket Gallery, Edinburgh (1987), Fischer Fine Art, London (1989), S.N.G.M.A. (1990); group shows: Vienna (1986), American tour (1989-92), Frankfurt (1993). *Work in permanent collections:* S.N.G.M.A., Metropolitan Museum N.Y., Gulbenkian Museum Lisbon, Arts Council, etc. *Address:* c/o Annely Juda Fine Art, 23 Dering St., London W1R 9AA. *Signs work:* "G. HARDIE" or "G.H."

HARDING, Jane Mary, S.W.A. (1982); artist in line and water-colour; *b* London; *d* of Edwin Harvey, civil servant; *m* David Harding. *Educ.:* Haberdashers' Aske's Girls' School; *studied art* at Lytham St. Annes School of Art (1940-41). *Exhib.:* S.W.A. annually, Britain in Water-colour, Ealing Art Group. *Work in public collection:* London Borough of Ealing Central Library. *Publications:* editorial illustrations for Amalgamated Press, Odhams, Franey's London Diary, Grolier Press, Sunday Times, Ward Gallery. *Address:* Melvin House, Hartington Rd., Ealing, London W13 8QL. *Club:* Ealing Arts. *Signs work:* "Jane Harding."

HARDY, Irma, S.W.A.; portrait painter in pencil, pastel, oil, and ballet sketches; *b* Budapest, 30 Nov., 1912; *m* Channell Hardy; one *s*. *Educ.:* Maria Theresa College, Baccalaureate; *studied art* at Royal Academy of Arts, Budapest (1931-36) under B. Karlovszky. *Exhib.:* Budapest, Hungary regularly between 1937-44, R.P., S.W.A., P.S.; one-man shows, Cooling Galleries, R.I. Gallery, Wright Hepburn Gallery. *Work in permanent collections:* H.M. Queen Elizabeth II, H.M.S. Excellent, Portsmouth, the Hon. Mr. Justice Cusack, Gray's Inn. *Address:* 77 Cornwall Gdns., London SW7 4AZ. *Signs work:* "Irma Hardy."

HARDY HENRION, Daphne; sculptor in clay for terracotta or bronze; *b* 20 Oct., 1917; *d* of Clive Hardy, D.S.O.; *m* F.H.K. Henrion; two *s*, one *d*. *Educ.:* The Hague, Holland; *studied art* at R.A. Schools (1934-38). *Exhib.:* Beaux Arts Gallery (1946), A.I.A. Gallery (1966), Old Fire Engine House, Ely (1975, 1979), Bury St. Edmunds (1981). *Work in permanent collection:* bust of Arthur Koestler at N.P.G. *Address:* 13 Owlstone Rd., Cambridge CB3 9JH. *Signs work:* "Daphne Hardy Henrion," "Daphne Henrion," "D.H." or "D.H.H."

HARGAN, Joseph R., D.A. (1974), P.P.A.I. (1989); Stirling Smith award (1978), Cargill award (1980), Torrance award (1982), Meyer Oppenheim prize R.S.A. (1985), Hunting Group prizewinner, London (1988), Paisley Art Inst. award (1993); Founder Mem. and Chairman of Group 81; elected Pres. P.A.I. (1989); *b* Glasgow, 23 Jan., 1952; *s* of Patrick Joseph Hargan, postman and Elizabeth Scott; *m* Anne Louise Clarke. *Studied art* at Glasgow School of Art (1970-74, Danny Ferguson, Drummond Bone, David Donaldson). *Exhib.:* R.S.A., R.G.I., R.S.W., Art Club, Group 81, R.A., P.A.I., B.W.S. (1983), S.S.A., etc. *Address:* 40 Oakshaw St., Paisley PA1 2DR. *Club:* Glasgow Art. *Signs work:* "Hargan."

HARLE, Dennis F.; artist in oil and gouache, naturalist; nature reserve warden; *b* Sandwich, 26 May, 1920; *s* of the late F. W. Harle, saddler; *m* Heather Harle;

three *d* from first marriage. *Educ.:* Sandwich; studied art at Ramsgate and Canterbury Schools of Art (Evening classes). *Exhib.:* Reading Museum and A.G., S.WL.A.; one-man shows, Deal (1978), Maidstone (1963), Sandwich (1960). *Address:* The Studio, Strand St., Sandwich, Kent. *Club:* S.WL.A. (founder mem.). *Signs work:* "Dennis F. Harle" or "D".

HARPLEY, Sydney Charles, A.R.C.A. (1956), F.R.B.S. (1963), A.R.A. (1974), R.A. (1981); sculptor in bronze; *b* Fulham, London, 19 Apr., 1927; *s* of Sydney Frederick Harpley; marriage dissolved; two *s*, one *d*. *Studied art* at Hammersmith College of Art (1950-53), R.C.A. (1953-56). *Exhib.:* R.A. (1954-81), etc. *Work in permanent collections:* S.A. National Gallery, N.Z. National Gallery. *Addresses:* London Gallery: Chris Beetles, Ryder St., London SW1; Home and Studio: Belline House, Piltown, Co. Kilkenny, Ireland. *Signs work:* "Harpley."

HARRIGAN, Claire, B.A. Hons. (1986), R.S.W. (1992); painter in water-colour, acrylic, gouache and pastel; *b* Kilmarnock, 8 Nov., 1964. *Educ.:* Sacred Heart Academy, Girvan; *studied art* at Glasgow School of Art (1982-86, Barbara Rae). *Exhib.:* solo shows: Christopher Hull Gallery, London; Gatehouse Gallery, Glasgow; Open Eye Gallery, Edinburgh; Macaulay Gallery, Stenton. *Address:* 53 King St., Crosshill, By Maybole, Ayrshire KA19 7RE. *Signs work:* "Claire Harrigan."

HARRIS, Alfred, A.R.C.A., F.R.S.A.; painter in acrylic and oil, printmaker in mixed media; Chairman (retd.), Dept of Art and Design, University of London Inst. of Educ.: Mem. London Group; *b* London, 21 July, 1930; *s* of Morris Harris; *m* Carmel; one *s*, two *d*. *Studied art* at Willesden School of Art (1952), R.C.A. (1955). *Exhib.:* Beaux Arts Gallery, New Vision Art Centre, Leeds City A.G., Grosvenor Gallery, Tate Gallery,Whitechapel A.G.; one-man shows, Drian Gallery, Ben Uri Gallery, Södertälje Museum, Sweden, Uppsala Arts Festival, Limetragarten, Sweden, Falum Museum, Orebro Museum, Dalarnas Museum, Sweden. *Address:* 25 Stanhope Rd., Highgate, London N6 5AW. *Signs work:* "A. Harris" and see appendix.

HARRIS, Geoffrey, A.R.C.A. (1954); sculptor; Senior lecturer, Ravensbourne College of Art and Design (1960-86); Assistant to Leon Underwood (1954), Assistant to Henry Moore, O.M., C.H. (1957-60); *b* Nottingham, 1928; *m* Gillian Farr, M.S.I.A., textile designer; two *s*. *Educ.:* Leeds Modern School; *studied art* at Leeds College of Art (1948-51), Royal College of Art (1951-54). *Exhib.:* one-man shows: Leicester Galleries, London (1964), Queen Square Gallery, Leeds (1964). *Work in private collections* in Britain, Europe, U.S.A. *Public commissions:* Baildon Primary School, Yorkshire, L.C.C. Maitland Park Housing Scheme, St. Pancras, Eurolink Industrial Centre, Sittingbourne, Kent. *Address:* 5 Queen's Rd., Faversham, Kent ME13 8RJ. *Signs work:* "Harris."

HARRIS, Josephine, R.W.S., R.B.A., N.E.A.C.; artist in water-colour, drawing and engraved glass; *d* of P. A. Harris. *Educ.:* privately; *studied art* at Plymouth College of Art (1948-52) under William Mann, A.R.C.A. *Official purchases:* Plymouth A.G., Graves A.G., Sheffield, South London A.G., I.L.E.A., K.C.C. *Address:* 37 Melville Rd., Barnes, London SW13. *Signs work:* "Josephine Harris" or "J.H."

HARRIS, Lyndon Goodwin, R.I., R.S.W., R.W.A., Dip. Fine Art (Lond.), A.T.D., Courtauld Certificate, Leverhulme, Pilkington, and Slade Scholar; Slade Anatomy Prizeman, Gold Medal Paris Salon (painting, 1956), Hon. Men. (painting, 1948) and Hon. Men. (etching, 1949); artist in oil, water-colour, stained glass; etcher; *b* Halesowen, Worcs., 25 July, 1928; *s* of the late S. E. Harris, A.C.I.S. *Educ.:* Halesowen Grammar School; *studied art* at Birmingham College of Art, L.C.C. Central School of Art and Crafts, Courtauld Inst., Slade School (Profs. Randolph Schwabe and Sir William Coldstream) and University of London Institute of Education. *Exhib.:* Paris Salon, R.A. (first exhib. at age of 13), R.S.A., R.I., N.E.A.C., R.B.A., R.S.W., R.G.I., R.W.A., Britain in Water-colour, Birmingham, Bradford, Wolverhampton, Bournemouth, Blackpool, Southport and other principal provincial galleries. *Work in permanent collections:* University College, London; Min. of Works; Birmingham and Midland Inst.; City of Worcester; stained-glass window, Gorsty Hill Methodist Church, Halesowen. *Work repro.:* Masters of Water-colour and Their Techniques (The Artist), Young Artists of Promise, Souvenir Handbook of Halesowen, Birmingham Post, etc. *Address:* c/o Lloyds Bank, 23 Hagley St., Halesowen, W. Midlands B63 3AY. *Signs work:* "Lyndon G. Harris."

HARRIS, Phyllis, S.W.A., N.D.D., S.G.F.A.; artist in water-colour and pen, lithography, linocut, school teacher; *b* London, 3 Aug., 1925; *m* David Harris; one *s*, one *d*. *Educ.:* Brondesbury High School, London and Abbey School, Reading; *studied art* at Reading University School of Art, Brighton and Camberwell, Harrow School of Art (lithography). *Exhib.:* S.W.A., Brent and Harrow. *Address:* 55 Slough Lane, Kingsbury, London NW9 8YB. *Clubs:* S.W.A., Wembley Art Soc., Harrow Art Soc., S.G.F.A. *Signs work:* "Phyl Harris."

HARRISON, Christopher David, B.A. (Hons.), A.T.C.; artist in water-colour; Director, Bircham Art Gallery; *b* Gt. Yarmouth, 21 Oct., 1953; *m* Deborah Margaret; two *s*. *Educ.:* Bromley Grammar School, Kent, Boston Grammar School, Lincs.; *studied art* at Jacob Kramer College of Art, Leeds (1973-74), Reading University (1974-78), London University Inst. of Educ. (1978-79). *Exhib.:* R.B.A., R.A., R.I., R.W.S.; many mixed exhbns. throughout England; regular one-man shows Norfolk. *Address:* 49 Church La., Bircham, King's Lynn, Norfolk PE31 6QW. *Signs work:* "Christopher Harrison."

HARRISON, Claude, R.P., A.R.C.A.; artist in oil, oil and tempera, pen and wash, etc.; primarily a painter of conversation pieces and imaginative landscapes; *b* Leyland, Lancs., 31 Mar., 1922; *s* of Harold Harrison, engineer; *m* Audrey Johnson, painter; one *s*. *Educ.:* Hutton Grammar School, Lancs; *studied art* at Preston (1938-40), Liverpool (1940-41), R.C.A.(1947-49). *Exhib.:* R.A., R.P., R.S.A., R.B.A., etc. *Official purchases:* Harris A.G., Preston, Abbott Hall, Kendal, Lancaster City Museum, Bournemouth A.G., etc. *Publications:* The Portrait Painters' Handbook (Studio Vista, 1968); Book of Tobit (1970). *Address:* Barrow Wife, Cartmel Fell, Grange over Sands, LA11 6NZ, Cumbria. *Signs work:* "CLAUDE HARRISON."

HARRISON, Eric, A.R.C.A., M.S.I.A., A.T.I.; textile designer, woven and printed fabrics; designer for Henry Nathan & Co. Ltd. (1949-55), Floral Furnishing Fabrics Ltd. (1955-56), T. F. Firth & Sons Ltd. (1956-58). Lecturer in Textile Design and Colour, Inst. of Technology, Bradford, Yorks (1958-66), University of Bradford (Oct. 1966-70), senior lecturer (1970-85); *b* Oswaldtwistle, Lancs., 5 Nov., 1919; *s* of John H. Harrison, cotton industry. *Educ.:* Accrington Grammar School; *studied art* at Accrington School of Arts and Crafts (1935-39), R.C.A. (1946-49). *Address:* 3 Temple Rhydding Drive, Baildon, Shipley, West Yorkshire BD17 5PX.

HARRISON, Margot; artist in water-colour, oil; *b* 2 Jan., 1915; *m* George Francis Harrison, M.B.E.; two *d*. *Educ.:* Queen Anne's, Caversham; *studied art* privately under Prescoe Holeman (1938), and Kingsley Sutton, F.R.S.A. (1965); Farnham School of Art, part-time (1966-69, John Wilkinson, A.R.C.A.). *Exhib.:* Paris Salon (1972, 1973); one-man shows: Alpine Gallery (1975), Bradshaw Room F.B.A. (1978), Mall Galleries (1974), Bradshaw Room F.B.A. (1982), R.O.I., Britain in Watercolours, R.B.A. *Work in permanent collections:* B.P. (1974), National Trust (1980). *Address:* Stoney Cottage, The Bury, Odiham, Hants. RG25 1LY. *Signs work:* "Margot Harrison."

HARRISON, Marguerite Hazel, National Froebel Foundation Diploma in Art; artist in oil, pen and wash, and pastels; *b* Llandudno, N. Wales, 7 Oct., 1927; *d* of Judge R. O. Roberts, d 1929; *m* Michael Harrison; three *s*, two *d*. *Educ.:* Royal Masonic School, Rickmansworth, Herts.; *studied art:* mainly self-taught; tuition for a period under Kenneth A. Jameson. *Exhib.:* R.A., R.Cam.A., Wallasey Soc. of Arts. *Address:* 2 The Courtyard, Poulton Hall, Bebington, Merseyside L63 9LN. *Signs work:* "Marguerite Harrison" and see appendix.

HARRISON, Stephanie Miriam, N.D.D., F.S.B.A., R.M.S.; painter, book illustrator, graphic designer; *b* Kings Lynn, 10 Dec., 1939; *d* of Cyril Gurr; *m* John Harrison. *Educ. and studied art* at Medway College of Art, Rochester (1955-60). *Exhib.:* Westminster Gallery, Mall Galleries, Linda Blackstone Gallery and galleries throughout the U.K.; several one-man shows. *Work in permanent collections:* Science Museum, B.M. (Natural History), and private collections. *Publications:* Wild Flowers of Britain, Marine Life, Handbook of British Mammals, Private Life of a Country House, greetings cards, stationery. *Address:* 1 Leydens Ct., Stick Hill, Edenbridge, Kent TN8 5NH. *Signs work:* "Stephanie Harrison," "S. Harrison" or "S.M.H."

HART, John; painter; *b* Manchester, 1921; *s* of Harold Hart; *m* Gwendoline Prichard; three *d*. *Educ.:* Merchant Taylors' School, Crosby; *studied art* at Liverpool College of Art and in Paris. *Exhib.:* Redfern, Beaux Arts, Zwemmers, Leicester Galls., I.C.A., Whitechapel, Molton, Hamilton, Marjorie Parr, Annely Juda, London Group, Art Spectrum London, Galleria Torbandena Trieste, John Moores, Bear Lane, Oxford, Camden Arts Centre, London, Hogue Gallery Tulsa, U.S.A., Lyon, France, etc. *Official purchases:* Nottingham, Leicester, Birmingham, Liverpool, Granada TV, Universities of Liverpool, Manchester, York and Tulsa; mural at Daresbury Nuclear Physics Laboratory. *Address:* Le Cognassier, 26570 Montbrun-les-Bains; and 7 Ave de la Viguerie, 13260 Cassis, France.

HART-DAVIES, Christine Ann, B.A. (Hons. 1970), R.M.S. (1985), F.S.B.A. (Hon. Sec.) (1985), R.H.S. Gold medal (1984, 1986, 1988), S.W.A.; botanical artist and illustrator in water-colour; *b* Shrewsbury, 1947; *d* of Ernest Underwood, B.Sc., F.C.I.S., D.P.A., F.R.S.A. and Evelyn Underwood, H.S. *Studied art* at Reading University (1966-70, Rita Donagh, Terry Frost), typography under Michael Twyman. *Exhib.:* Poole Arts Centre, Medici Gallery, London, Spring Hill Gallery and Young Masters Gallery, Brisbane, Australia, R.H.S. *Publication:* illustrated: A Year in a Victorian Garden. *Address:* 31 Shaftesbury Rd., Poole, Dorset BH15 2LT. *Signs work:* "CHRISTINE HART-DAVIES," "CHD" (miniatures).

HARTAL, Paul, Ph.D.; artist and theorist, originator of Lyrical Conceptualism (1975); founder of the Centre for Art, Science and Technology; *b* Hungary, 1936. *Exhib.:* Musée du Luxembourg, Paris (1978), Véhicule, Montreal (1980), Montreux Centre, University of Lausanne (1983), Seoul International Fine Art Centre (1987), OURS, Montreux (1990), Ward-Nasse Gallery, N.Y. (1992), Milan Art Centre, Italy (1993). *Work repro.:* Encyclopedia of Living Artists;

Olympic Catalogue, Seoul; UNICEF Italia; Artists/USA, Phil. *Publications:* Black and White (1984), The Brush and the Compass (1988); articles: Leonardo, Pulsar, Contemporary Philosophy. *Address:* Box 1012, St. Laurent, Quebec H4L 4W3, Canada. *Signs work:* "Hartal."

HARTILL, Brenda, R.E., Dip.F.A. Hons. (1964); artist/printmaker in etching, collagraph, oil (previously theatre design); *b* London, 27 Feb., 1943; *m* Harold Moores; one *s*, one *d. Educ.:* Kings School, Ottery St. Mary; Kelston High, Auckland, N.Z.; *studied art* at Elam School Fine Art, N.Z.; Central School of Art (theatre design, Ralph Koltai). *Exhib.:* R.A. Summer Show, R.E. Bankside Gallery, over 50 galleries worldwide; solo shows: New Academy Gallery and galleries in Australia, N.Z., U.S.A. *Address:* 11 Honley Rd., London SE6 2HZ. *Club:* R.E. *Signs work:* "Brenda Hartill."

HARVEY, Jake, D.A. (1972), R.S.A. (1989); sculptor in welded steel, cast aluminium, bronze carved stone; lecturer, Edinburgh College of Art; *b* Yetholm, Kelso, Roxburghshire, 3 June, 1948. *Educ.:* Kelso High School; *studied sculpture* at Edinburgh College of Art (1966-72) postgraduate (1971-72), Travelling Scholarship to Greece (1971-72). *Exhib.:* R.S.A., S.S.A., Talbot Rice A.G., City Art Centre, Edinburgh, Third Eye Gallery, Glasgow, Camden Arts Centre, Leinster Gallery, London, Brazil. *Major commissions:* Dunn and Wilson, Grangemouth; Hugh MacDiarmid Memorial, Langholm; Charles Mackintosh Sculpture, Glasgow; Compaq Computers Commission, Glasgow; Newcraighall Mining Commission, Edinburgh. *Work in public collections:* Scottish Arts Council, Edinburgh Museums and Galleries, Borders Educ. Authority, University of Edinburgh, Contemporary Art Soc. *Address:* Maxton Cross, Maxton, St. Boswells, Roxburghshire. *Signs work:* "Jake Harvey" and see appendix.

HARVEY, Michael Anthony, N.D.D. (1957), F.R.S.A. (1972), Linton prize (1973); artist in oil, pastel; journalist and art critic; Council mem. S.G.A., Reigate Soc. of Artists, life mem. I.A.A. (Unesco); *b* Kew; *s* of E.C. Harvey, solicitor; divorced; one *s. Educ.:* Bryanston; trained at Epsom (1948-50) and Wimbledon School of Art (1955-57). *Exhib.:* Whibley, Rutland, Fine Arts, Qantas Galleries W1.; fourteen one-man shows, six dual shows. *Work in collections:* Johns Hopkins University, Camden Council, E. Sussex Council. *Work repro.:* B.B.C. TV, The Times, Standard, Artist. *Address:* 15 Waterloo Sq., Bognor Regis, W. Sussex PO21 1TE. *Club:* Royal Society of Arts, London. *Signs work:* "Michael" or "Michael A. Harvey."

HARVEY, Pat: see YALLUP, Pat.

HARVEY, Susan, B.A. (Hons.) (1982), M.A. (1987); artist in water-colour, tempera, tapestry; lecturer, Scottish College of Textiles; *b* Greenock, Scotland, 20 Jan., 1960. *Educ.:* Greenock Academy; *studied art* at Glasgow School of Art (1978-82), R.C.A. (1985-87, Mary Farmer). *Exhib.:* mixed exhbns. and two-person show, Collective Gallery, Edinburgh. *Address:* 10 Balmoral Pl., Edinburgh EH3 5JA. *Signs work:* "Susan Harvey."

HAUGHTON, Wilfred James, President and Founder, Ulster Watercolour Soc. (1977), F.R.S.A. (1960), A.R.U.A. (1951), R.U.A. (1956), vice-president, R.U.A. (1956), president R.U.A.(1964-70), mem. W.C.S.I.; artist in oil, water-colour and pastel; past managing director, Frazer & Haughton Ltd.; *b* Hillmount, 14 Dec., 1921; *s* of J. Wilfred Haughton, C.B.E. and Mafe Haughton, C.B.E., M.A.; *m* Priscilla Elizabeth McLaughlin; three *s*, one *d. Educ.:* Terra Nova School, Birkdale, Southport, Lancs.; Worksop College, Notts.; *studied art:* self-taught. *Exhib.:* R.H.A., R.U.A., Royal Scottish Water-Colour Soc., R.I.,

W.C.S.I. *Official purchases:* oil painting by C.E.M.A., oil painting by Thomas Haverty Trust (Dublin). *Publication:* Author of "Brush Aside" and "Purely Watercolour". *Address:* 17 Dromona La., Cullybackey, Ballymena, Co. Antrim, N. Ireland BT42 1NT. *Signs work:* see appendix.

HAWDON, Paul Douglas, B.A. (Hons.) (1982), Dip. R.A. Schools, R.E.; painter/printmaker in oil, gouache, etching; *b* Manchester, 13 Oct., 1953; *s* Joseph Douglas Hawdon; *m* Helena Earl. *Educ.:* Hyde County Grammar School; *studied art* at St. Martin's School of Art (1978-82), R.A. Schools (1982-85), Rome Scholar, British School (1988-89). *Exhib.:* R.E., London Group, Twelve Contemporary Figurative Artists, R.A., Christie's Print prize (1985, 1990), 11th International Print Biennale, Bradford, Metropolitan Museum of Fine Art, N.Y. *Address:* 118 Salisbury Rd., Moseley, Birmingham B13 8JZ. *Signs work:* "Paul Hawdon" or "P.D.H."

HAWES, Meredith William, A.R.C.A., R.W.S., F.R.S.A., A.S.I.A.; artist in water-colour, oil, gouache; College of Art Principal (retd.); tutor (P.T.), Exeter University (Extra-mural Dept.); *b* Thornton Heath, Surrey, 17 Apr., 1905; *s* of Walter Osborne; *m* Margaret Charlotte; one *s*, six *d*. *Educ.:* Selhurst Grammar School, Croydon; *studied art* at Croydon School of Art (1922-24), R.C.A. (1924-28). *Exhib.:* R.A., R.W.S., N.E.A.C., Paris, U.S.A. and many provincial galleries. *Publications:* illustrations for John Murray, Jonathan Cape, V. & A. Museum, O.U.P. *Address:* Emslake House, 2 Anderton Villas, Millbrook, Torpoint, Cornwall PL10 1DR. *Signs work:* "M.W. HAWES."

HAWKEN, Anthony Wellington John, A.R.B.S. (1979), Cert. R.A.S. Sculpture (1971); sculptor in plastics and stone, etcher; *b* Erith, Kent, 4 July, 1948; *s* of Ronald Hawken, F.C.A., F.I.C.A.; *m* Deirdre Bew; two *s*. *Educ.:* Northumberland Heath Secondary Modern School; *studied art* at Medway College of Art (1965-68, John Cobbett), R.A. Schools (1968-71, Willi Soukop). *Exhib.:* Hammersmith Summer Exhbn., R.B.S., Chichester, Stratford upon Avon; one-man show, Blackheath Gallery. *Address:* 1 Chevening Rd., Greenwich, London SE10 0LB. *Signs work:* "A. Hawken."

HAWKINS, Barbara; potter in stoneware ceramics; *b* Yorks., 18 Oct., 1952; *m* Michael Hawkins; two *d*. *Studied art* at Cornwall and Bristol. *Exhib.:* solo shows: Open Eye Edinburgh, J.K. Hill London, Simon Drew Dartmouth, Rooksmoor Gallery Bath, etc. *Address:* The Pottery, Rooksmoor Mills, Bath Rd., Stroud, Glos. GL5 5ND. *Clubs:* Ceramic Potters Assoc., S. Wales Potters.

HAWKINS, Michael; potter in stoneware ceramics; *b* Epping, 2 Aug., 1950; *m* Barbara; two *d*. *Studied art* at Cornwall and Bristol. *Exhib.:* one-man shows: Open Eye Edinburgh, J.K. Hill London, Simon Drew Dartmouth, Rooksmoor Gallery Bath, etc. *Address:* The Pottery, Rooksmoor Mills, Bath Rd., Stroud, Glos. GL5 5ND. *Clubs:* Ceramic Potters Assoc., S. Wales Potters.

HAWKINS, Philip Dennis, G.R.A.; artist in oil, pencil; *b* B'ham, 26 Sept., 1947; *s* of Dennis Walter Arthur Hawkins; *m* Catherine; one *s*, one *d*. *Educ.:* Lordswood Boys' Technical School, B'ham; *studied art* at B'ham College of Art (1964-68). *Exhib.:* N.R.M. York, Science Museum, B'ham, Festival Hall London, regularly with G.R.A. *Work in permanent collections:* B'ham Post and Mail Ltd., Bristol United Press, B.B.C. *Publications:* Fine art prints, work featured in calendars, "Footplate" (Eversheds Ltd.), "Railfreight" (British Rail), greetings cards, magazines, books, etc. Co-director, Quicksilver Publishing. *Address:* 112 Chaffcombe Rd., Sheldon, Birmingham B26 3YD. *Club:* Chairman, Guild of Railway Artists. *Signs work:* "Philip D. Hawkins."

HAWTHORN, Raymond Humphrey Millis, A.T.D. (1940), A.R.E. (1960), R.E. (1975); invited to membership, S.W.E. (1985); lecturer, Wirral College of Art and Design and Adult Studies (1976-78); Laird School of Art and Crafts, Birkenhead (1947-76); Medway School of Art and Crafts, Rochester (1946-47); wood engraver; *b* Poole, Dorset, 18 Mar., 1917; *s* of the late Wilfrid Charles Hawthorn; *m* Beryl Hine Moore; two *d. Educ.:* Bablake School, Coventry; *studied art:* Coventry School of Art (1935-39); Hornsey School of Art and Crafts, London (1939-40). *Exhib.:* R.E., A.I.A., Soc. of Wood Engravers, Society of American Illustrators Gallery, N.Y.; one-man: Birkenhead (1980). *Work in permanent collections:* Atkinson Art Gallery, Southport, Williamson Art Gallery, Birkenhead. *Publications:* book illustrations for Folio Society, S.C.M. Press. *Address:* 97 Wirral Gdns., Bebington, Wirral L63 3BG. *Signs work:* "Raymond H. M. Hawthorn," and see appendix.

HAY, Ian, N.D.D. (1960), A.R.C.A. (Painting 1963); awarded the Andrew J. Lloyd prize for landscape painting; artist in pastel, water-colour, etching, art lecturer; Senior Lecturer in drawing, Colchester School of Art; *b* Harwich, 25 Jan., 1940; *s* of the late John Hay; *m* Teresa Sliska; two *s. Educ.:* Harwich School; *studied art* at Colchester School of Art (1955-60, Hugh Cronyn), R.C.A. (1960-63, Ruskin Spear). *Exhib.:* Craftsman Gallery and Minories, Colchester, Sandford Gallery, London, Phoenix Gallery, Lavenham, Wivenhoe Arts Centre. *Work in permanent collections:* Doncaster City A.G., The Guildhall A.G., Graves A.G., Sheffield. *Address:* 32 Tall Trees, Mile End, Colchester, Essex CO4 5DV. *Club:* Colchester Art Soc. *Signs work:* "Ian Hay."

HAYES, Colin Graham, R.A., M.A.(Oxon), Hon.A.R.C.A., Hon. F.R.C.A.; painter in oil and water-colour; reader, Royal College of Art (1949-84); *b* London, 17 Nov., 1919; *s* of Gerald Hayes; *m* (1) Jean Westbrook Law (d. 1988); three *d;* (2) Marjorie L. M. Christensen. *Educ.:* Westminster School; Christ Church, Oxford; *studied art* at Bath School of Art; Ruskin School of Drawing. *Exhib.:* Marlborough, Agnews, Search, New Grafton. *Work in permanent collections:* Arts Council, British Council, Carlisle A.G. and others. *Publications:* Stanley Spencer, Renoir, Rembrandt, A Grammar of Drawing. *Address:* 26 Cleveland Ave., London W4. *Signs work:* "Hayes."

HAYNES, Alexandra, B.A.; artist in oil and water-colour; *b* 17 Mar., 1966. *Educ.:* New Hall, Boreham, Chelmsford, Essex; *studied art* at Shrewsbury Foundation Course, Cheltenham Art College (Michael Hollands, Leslie Prothero). *Exhib.:* Mail on Sunday, Dover St. (1988), Contemporary Fine Art Gallery, Eton; one-man shows: Soloman Gallery, London (1988), Mistral Gallery, London (1989, 1990, 1991), Flying Colours Gallery, Edinburgh (1990), Bruton Street Gallery (1992). *Publication:* A Life with Food, Peter Langan by Brian Sewell. *Address:* Edgcote, Banbury, Oxon. OX17 1AG. *Signs work:* "A. Haynes."

HAYNES, Kirkham Karolyn, S.W.A. (1986); landscape artist in water-colour, pastel, pencil; *b* B'ham, 8 Jan., 1946; *d* of J. Kirkham; *m* Geoffrey Haynes; two *s. Educ.:* Manor High School; *studied art:* self taught with some help and advice from Thomas Jenkins, a Fellow of the Norwich School of Art. *Exhib.:* numerous mixed exhbns. including Mall Galleries, Westminster Gallery, Wolverhampton, plus several joint shows. *Work in permanent collections:* British Telecom House, Wolverhampton, Featherstone Hall Farm, Wolverhampton. *Publications:* illustrated several phone book covers for British Telecom. *Address:* Oaklands, 56 Oaken Pk., Codsall, nr. Wolverhampton WV8 2BW. *Club:* Wolverhampton Soc. of Artists. *Signs work:* "K.K. Haynes."

219

HAYWARD-HARRIS, Martin John; artist and sculptor of wildlife subjects in oil, water-colour, etchings, bronze; *b* Reading, 28 Oct., 1959; *s* of John Stanley Harris. *Educ.:* Maiden Erlegh Comprehensive; *studied art* at Berks. College of Art and Design (1978-84). *Exhib.:* S.WL.A., B.T.O., R.S.P.B., W.T.N.C.; one man show: Phyllis Court Club, Henley-on-Thames (1990, 1993), East African Wildlife Soc. *Work in permanent collections:* Natural History Museum London, Zoologisk Museum, Copenhagen. *Work repro.:* etchings published by H.C. Dickins, auctioned at Sotheby's; Birding World. *Address:* 47 Clarendon Rd., Earley, Reading, Berks. RG6 1PB. *Signs work:* "Martin Hayward-Harris."

HAZELWOOD, David; painter and collagist; *b* Ipswich, 20 Feb., 1932; *m* Pauline Woodard; two *d. Exhib.:* R.A. and R.B.A.; and internationally: New York Expo (1986), Chicago (1985, 1986, 1987, 1988, 1989, 1990), Tokio (1986), Basle (1985, 1986, 1987, 1988, 1989, 1990, 1991), Cologne (1985, 1986, 1987, 1988, 1991, 1992), Madrid (1987), Frankfurt (1989, 1990, 1991). *Official purchases:* Birmingham City A.G., Beecroft A.G. Southend, Camden Arts Centre, Chelmsford and Essex Museum, Dept. of Environment, Graves A.G. Sheffield, Herts. C.C., Manchester Educ. Com., Portsmouth City Museum, St. Thomas' Hospital London, V. & A., Bolton A.G., Oldham A.G., Worcester A.G. *Address:* 83 Arundel Way, Ipswich IP3 8QG. *Signs work:* "Hazelwood."

HAZZARD, Charles Walker, B.A. (Hons.) Fine Art (1987), Fellowship, Sir Henry Doulton School of Sculpture (1988-90), Postgrad. H.Dip. Sculpture (1991), A.R.B.S. Dip. (1992); sculptor in resin, plaster and bronze; *b* B'ham, 5 Feb., 1964. *Studied art* at Cheltenham University (1984-87, Roger Luxton), Sir Henry Doulton School of Sculpture (1988-90, Colin Melbourne), City and Guilds of London (1990-91, Alan Sly). *Exhib.:* Manchester Academy (1992), Cheltenham Soc. of Artists (1992), London Group Barbican (1992), R.A. Summer Show (1993); one-man show: London (1993). *Address:* c/o South Bank Office Services, Ransome's Dock, 35-37 Parkgate Rd., London SW11 4NP. *Club:* Arts. *Signs work:* "C.W.H." or not at all.

HEALER, George, A.R.B.S. (1974); sculptor in clay, plaster, wood, cast aluminium, brass and bronze; *b* 25 Sept., 1936; *s* of John Healer; *m* Brenda Maureen Healer; one *s*, two *d. Educ.:* Bullion Lane School; *studied art* at Sunderland College of Art (1952-56) under Harry Thubron, A.R.C.A., and Robert Jewell, A.R.C.A. *Exhib:* R.A., R.G.I., Commonwealth Institute, Woolgate House, London, D.L.I. Durham City, Gulbenkian Gallery, Newcastle-upon-Tyne. *Work in permanent collection:* life-size figures of John and Josiphe Bowes, Bowes Museum, Barnard Castle, Co. Durham. *Publication:* article, Aluminium for Schools for the British Aluminium Federation. *Address:* 12 Melville St., Chester-le-Street, Co. Durham. *Signs work:* "HEALER" hammered into metal with flat chisel.

HEALER, Reuben John, H.N.D. (1984); graphic designer/illustrator; *b* Gateshead, 17 Dec., 1963; *s* of George Healer, A.R.B.S., N.D.D. *Educ.:* Hermitage Comprehensive; *studied graphic design* at New College, Durham (N.D.A.D. 1980-82); Cumbria College of Art and Design (H.N.D. 1982-84). Graphic designer for: Newcastle Architecture Workshop (1984-85), Pendower Hall, E.D.C. (1985-88), By Design, Seaham, Co. Durham (1988). *Address:* 21 Bede Terr., Chester-le-Street, Co. Durham.

HEAT, Ann Olivia; artist in oil; *b* Esher, Surrey, 30 July, 1945; *d* of Edward Charles Telling; *m* Trevor Harvey Heat. *Educ.:* Waynfleet, Surrey; *studied art* at The Kathleen Browne School under Kathleen Browne and her Polish husband Marian Kratochwil. *Exhib.:* R.A.., R.B.A., R.P., R.O.I., N.E.A.C. *Address:*

Slough Farm, Telegraph La., Claygate, Surrey KT10 0DT. *Club:* A.R.B.A. *Signs work:* "A.H."

HECHLE, Ann, F.S.S.I.; calligrapher in vellum, water-colour, gold leaf; *b* 31 Dec., 1939; *d* of James Hechle, stockbroker. *Studied art* at Central School of Art and Crafts (1957-60, Irene Wellington). *Exhib.:* 'Lavenders Blue' Paperpoint (1988), other group exhbns. *Work in permanent collections:* Minnesota Manuscript Initiative, U.S.A., V. & A., Crafts Study Centre, Bath. *Publication:* co-author: More than Fine Writing (Life and work of Irene Wellington). Film: In the Making (B.B.C. 1979). *Address:* The Old School, Buckland Dinham, Frome, Somerset BA11 2QR.

HEINDEL, Robert; self taught artist; Director, The Obsession of Dance Co; *b* Toledo, Ohio, 1 Oct., 1938; *s* of Robert Heindel; *m* Rosalie; three *s. Educ.:* St. Angus Grade School, Central Catholic High School. *Exhib.:* Atlanta, Georgia; American Artists Gallery; Kansas City A.G.; Dallas, Texas — The Vineyard Gallery; San Francisco Gallery One; Royal Festival Hall, London; New London Theatre; Hotel de Paris, Monte Carlo. *Work in permanent collections:* Smithsonian Inst., Washington D.C.; Caltex Corp., Dallas; Chrysler Corp., Detroit; Columbia Pictures, Los Angeles; Ford Motor Co., Detroit; Goodyear Rubber Co., Akron; The Grace Co., N.Y.; The Ladd Co., Los Angeles; Manufacturers Hanover Bank, N.Y.; Phillips Petroleum, Dallas; Quasar Oil Corp., N.Y.; Readers' Digest Inc., N.Y.; Time Inc., N.Y.; United Artists, Los Angeles; United Energy Resources Corp., Houston; Coca Cola; Champion Paper. *Publications:* illus. The Complete Phantom of the Opera (Pavilion Books); J. Steinbeck — The Grapes of Wrath; All the Kings Men. *Address:* 140 Banks Rd., Easton, Connecticut 06612, U.S.A. *Club:* Mortons, London. *Signs work:* "R. Heindel."

HEINDORFF, Michael, M.A. (1977), Fellow, R.C.A. (1988); painter in oil, water-colour, pencil, print; senior tutor, R.C.A.; *b* Braunschweig, Germany, 26 June, 1949; *s* of Hans Heindorff; *m* Monica Buferd; one *s*, one *d. Educ.:* Wilhelm Gymnasium, Braunschweig; *studied art* at Braunschweig University (1970-75, Hubertus von Pilgrim, Alfred Winter-Rust), R.C.A. (1975-77, Peter de Francia, Philip Rawson). *Exhib.:* Bernard Jacobson Gallery, London, New York, Los Angeles since 1978, R.A. (1988-89), and others internationally. *Work in permanent collections:* Herzog Anton Ulrich Museum, A.C.G.B., British Council, Imperial War Museum, Museum of Modern Art, N.Y. *Address:* 2 Shrubland Rd., London E8 4NN. *Club:* Chelsea Arts. *Signs work:* "M. HEINDORFF."

HEINE, Harry, R.S.MA., F.C.A., C.S.M.A., N.W.S.; self taught artist in water-colour; *b* Edmonton, Alberta, Canada, 24 July, 1928; *s* of Bernard Heine; *m* Teresa; one *s*, two *d. Exhib.:.* R.I., R.S.MA., F.C.A., Mystic International (U.S.A.), Northwest Marine exhbn. (U.S.A.), and one-man shows in Canada and U.S.A. *Work in permanent collections:* U.S.A.: Washington State Arts Commission, Mystic Seaport Museum, Conn.; Canada: Legislative Bldgs., Victoria, Mendel Gallery, Saskatoon, Maritime Museum, Victoria, Government House, Victoria, Alberta Art Foundation; England: Capt. Cook Museum, Middlesbrough, National Maritime Museum, Greenwich. *Publication:* Pacific Salmon (Govt. of Canada, Dept. of Fisheries and Oceans). *Address:* 7059 Brentwood Dr., Brentwood Bay, B.C. VO5 1AO, Canada. *Signs work:* "HEINE."

HELD, Julie, B.A. (Hons.) (1981), R.A. Schools Postgrad. Dip. (1985); painter in oil on canvas; visiting teacher, Kingsway College, Barnet College, University of Wolverhampton; *b* 25 Mar., 1958. *Educ.:* J.F.S. Comprehensive School; *studied art* at Camberwell School of Art (1977-81, Philip Mathews),

R.A. Schools (1982-85, Peter Greenham). *Exhib.:* Piccadilly Gallery, Boundary Gallery, R.A., Waterman Gallery, Festival Hall, Hayward Gallery, Royal Overseas League, 5th International Cleveland Drawing Biennial. *Work in permanent collections:* Limerick, Keele University, Nuffield College, Oxford University, Ben Uri Art Soc., Museum of the Negev, Israel. *Address:* 73 Weston Park, London N8 9TA. *Signs work:* "J. HELD" or "J.H." on small works.

HELLEBERG, Berndt; sculptor; *b* Stockholm, 17 Dec., 1920; *s* of Sigurd Helleberg, inspector of assurance; *m* Margareta Kinberg. *Educ.:* High School, Härnösand; *studied art* at Stockholm (1945-48), Konstfackskolan, Stockholm (1947-49), France (1950-52). Prize, The Unknown Political Prisoner, London (1953), first prize winner, competition of modern medals (Stockholm 1955), first prize winner 20,000 Sw. crowns, competition of underground station decoration (Stockholm 1960). *Exhib.:* Tate Gallery, London, Stockholm, Paris, U.S.A., etc. *Official purchases:* The underground station, Hornstull, Stockholm; Cathedral Window, Baptist Church, Stockholm; several playground sculptures in Sweden; several sculptures in Stockholm and Sweden; Sculpture 9m high in Riyadh, Saudi Arabia (1981). *Address:* Saturnusu 7, 18400 Akersberga, Sweden. *Signs work:* "Berndt Helleberg."

HEMMANT, Lynette, N.D.D. (1958); landscape and still-life painter in oil, mixed media and black and white drawing; *b* London, 20 Sept., 1938; *m* Jüri Gabriel, literary agent. *Studied art* at St. Martin's School of Art (1954-58, Roger Nicholson, Bernard Cheese, Vivian Pitchforth). *Exhib.:* R.E.., and various solo and mixed shows in London, Home Counties, Italy and Australia since 1984. *Work repro.:* Heineman Group, Hamish Hamilton, Random House, O.U.P. *Address:* 35 Camberwell Grove, London SE5 8JA. *Signs work:* "HEMMANT."

HEMPTON, Paul Andrew Keates, M.A., R.C.A.; artist in oil paint, watercolour, and etching; assoc. lecturer, University of Wolverhampton; Fellow in Fine Art, University of Nottingham (1971-73); *b* Wakefield, Yorks., 3 Oct., 1946; *s* of Revd. Canon G. B. Hempton, B.A.; *m* Margaret Helena; one *s*, two *d*. *Educ.:* King's School, Chester; *studied art* at Goldsmiths' College School of Art (1964-68), R.C.A. (1968-71) under Prof. Carel Weight. *Work in permanent collections:* Whitworth A.G., V. & A., British Council, C.A.S., Bury A.G., University of Nottingham, Nottingham Castle A.G., Leicester Educ. Authority, Wakefield A.G., Newport A.G., Arts Council of Gt. Britain, Arnolfini Trust, South West Arts. *Address:* 9 West End, Minchinhampton, Stroud, Glos. GL6 9JA. *Signs work:* "P.H."

HEMSLEY, George Philip, R.A. Schools cert. (1958), N.D.D. (1954), British Institution award (1958), R.A. Silver medal, Landseer Scholarship, Leverhulme Scholarship, David Murray studentships; painter in oil and water-colour; teacher and lecturer; *b* Stocksbridge, Yorks, 9 Dec., 1933; *s* of Joseph Norman Hemsley, A.M.I.Prod.E. *Educ.:* Surbiton Grammar School; *studied art* at Kingston School of Art, R.A. Schools (Henry Rushbury, Peter Greenham). *Exhib.:* R.A., R.B.A, N.E.A.C., R.P., Redfern, Guildhall. *Work in permanent collections:* Guildhall, London Boroughs of Camden, Hackney, Kingston-upon-Thames, Dept. of Educ. and Science, Leicester Educ. Authority. Work loaned to Inst. of Practitioners in Advertising.. *Work repro.:* T.E.S. *Address:* 18 Ellis Farm Cl., Mayford, Woking, Surrey GU22 9QN. *Club:* Ridley Art Soc. *Signs work:* "Philip Hemsley."

HEMSOLL, Eileen Mary, A.T.D. (1946), R.B.S.A. (1978); artist in enamel on earthenware, oil, oil pastels, water-colour; retd. art teacher; *b* West Bromwich, 4 Feb., 1924; *d* of Harold Cashmore, M.D. of John Cashmore Ltd.; *m* Eric Hemsoll; one *s*, one *d*. *Educ.:* Queen Mary's, Walsall; *studied art* at B'ham

College of Art (1941-46, Eggison, Fleetwood Walker). *Exhib.:* R.A., R.A. Travelling Exhbn., Local Artists, B'ham A.G., Artists for Art, R.B.S.A. Paint the City (1989); one-man shows: Worcester College (1978), Flint Gallery, Walsall (1984), Summer Show Sally Hunters, Belgrave Sq. (1986). *Address:* 18 Mead Rise, Edgbaston, Birmingham B15 3SD. *Signs work:* "Eileen Hemsoll."

HENRI, Adrian, Hons. B.A. Fine Art (1955), Hon. D. Litt. (1990); artist and author; President, Liverpool Academy of Arts (1972-81); *b* Birkenhead, 1932; *s* of Arthur Maurice Henri. *Studied art* at Dept. of Fine Art, King's College, Newcastle. *Exhib.:* one-man shows: Touring Retrospective (1986); Wolverhampton City A.G. (1976), Williamson A.G. (1975), Art Net, London (1975), I.C.A. (1968); other shows: John Moores Liverpool (1962, 1966, 1968, 1974, 1978, 1980, 1989), John Moores £2,000 Prize (1972), murals, Royal Liverpool Hospital (1980 and 1983). *Work in permanent collections:* Walker A.G., Williamson A.G., and A.C.G.B. Collection. *Publications:* a number of books of poetry. *Address:* 21 Mount St., Liverpool 1. *Club:* Chelsea Arts. *Signs work:* "Adrian Henri."

HENRY, Bruce Charles Reid, B.D. (Lond.) (1943), S.WL.A. (1982); painter in water-colour, pastel, oil, retd. school teacher; *b* nr. Kandy, Sri Lanka, 22 July, 1918; *s* of the late G.M.R. Henry, naturalist artist; *m* Joyce M. Henry; one *s*, one *d. Educ.:* Colchester Royal Grammar School, Tettenhall College, Staffs. *Exhib.:* Mall Galleries (annually), S.WL.A., Budleigh Salterton, Newport, I.O.W., Sladmore Gallery, London. *Publication:* Author/illustrator, Highlight the Wild — The Art of the Reid Henrys (Palaquin Publishing, 1985). *Address:* 90 Broomfield Ave., Worthing, W. Sussex BN14 7SB. *Signs work:* "Bruce Henry."

HENSHALL, John, F.I.A.L. (1959), F.R.S.A. (1959, resigned 1976); artist in water-colour and oil, tutor and lecturer, calligrapher; *b* Stockport, 26 Oct., 1913; *s* of John Henshall; *m* Margaret Winifred Passmore; one *s*, one *d. Educ.:* St. Thomas' School, Stockport; *studied art* at Stockport College (M. James). *Exhib.:* R.I., Bradford, Huddersfield, Stockport, N. Wales, Soc. of Church Craftsmen and Red Rose Guild; one-man shows, Wakefield, Wigan and various in N. Wales. *Work in permanent collections:* Stockport A.G., Wigan A.G., Leigh, Manchester Museum. *Address:* 34 Adswood Lane East, Cale Green, Stockport SK2 6RG. *Signs work:* "john henshall" in script form with lower case initials, oils signed "HENSHALL" in caps.

HENTALL, Maurice, F.R.S.A. (1951), S.B.A. (1987); retd. 22 years Managing Director of London Studios; part-time Art Tutor, painter in water-colour, acrylic, oil; several years Easter tutorial at Pendley Manor; *b* Hornsey; *m* Nora Nelson. *Studied art* at Hornsey College of Art. R.A.F.V.R. from 1940, injured March 1942. Whilst convalescent official War Publication artist: encouraged by R. Stanton, Sir Alfred Munnings, Sir James Gunn. *Exhib.:* R.A., Mall Galleries, Westminster Central Hall – portraits, wildlife, botanical, including miniatures. *Commission:* motif Golden Jubilee of Sperry Gyroscope Co. (unveiled by Earl Mountbatten of Burma 1963). *Publications:* Royal Manor of Hanworth; repros. Gordon Fraser, Medici, etc. *Address:* 42 The Broadway, Gustard Wood, Wheathamstead, Herts. AL4 8LP. *Signs work:* "MAURICE HENTALL."

HENTHORNE, Yvonne, R.B.A. (1978), N.D.D. (Painting 1965), A.T.C. (1966), F.R.S.A. (1967), Italian Government Bursary (1969), Brazilian Government Scholarship (1971), W. German Research Grant (1974-75); painter in acrylic, oil on canvas; Head of Visual Arts, Havering Technical College, London; *b* Wetherby, Yorks., 1942; *d* of Leslie Henthorne; *m* Gary Crossley, writer. *Educ.:* Grey Coat Hospital, Westminster; *studied art* at London University Goldsmith's College of Art (1961-66, Patrick Millard, Albert Irwin, Andrew Forge). *Exhib.:* open, Young Contemporaries, Tate, Birmingham Festival, Midland Group Gallery, Sheffield Open National, S.W.A., R.B.A.; one-man shows, Ikon Gallery, Birmingham; Belgrade, Coventry; Abbotsholme Arts Soc.; Laing Gallery, Newcastle-on-Tyne. *Work in private collections:* U.K., Europe, U.S.A. *Address:* 11 Annandale Rd., Greenwich, London SE10 0DD. *Signs work:* "Yvonne Henthorne."

HENTY-CREER, Deirdre, F.R.S.A.; Utd. Artists Council (1947-1955); F.C.I.A.D. (1945); Artists of Chelsea (1961); Com. Chelsea Art Soc.; Com. Armed Forces Art Soc.; artist in oil; *b* Sydney, Australia; *d* of Capt. Reginald Creer, R.N., and Eulalie Henty. *Educ.:* privately. *Exhib.:* R.A., R.O.I., R.B.A., N.E.A.C., N.S., U.A., Towner A.G., Eastbourne, Russell-Cotes Gallery, Bournemouth, Williamson A.G., Birkenhead, Municipal Galleries of Blackpool, Bolton, Bedford, Worthing, Wolverhampton, Worcester, Rotherham, Darlington, Submarine Museum, Gosport, H.M.S. Victory Museum, Portsmouth, etc. One-man shows, Fine Art Soc., Frost & Reed, Cooling Galleries, Bond St., Upper Grosvenor Gallery, Harrods, Palais Marie Cristine, Nice XIV Olympiad Sport in Art at V. & A., Qantas Gallery, R.N. College, Greenwich. *Work repro.:* The Artist, Cover of Studio, Medici Soc., T.A.V.R. Mag., Royal Sussex Regt. Mag., Poster for Municipality of Monaco, The Sphere, Stanton Corp., N.Y., Chrysons of California, U.S.A., Gruehen of Innsbruck. Portraits include: H.R.H. Prince Michael of Kent; Governor-Gen. of Australia, Sir John Kerr; Mayor of Kensington, Sir Malby Crofton, Bt.; Prime Minister of Malta, Dr. Borg Olivier; First Sea Lord and Admiral of the Fleet, Sir Henry Leach, etc. *Work in permanent collections:* H.R.H. the Prince of Wales, Lord Rank, Lord Rootes, Ronald Vestey, Esq, Museum of Cape Town and Oxford Museum. *Address:* 5 St. Georges Ct., Gloucester Rd., London SW7.

HEPPLE, Norman, R.A. (1961), A.R.A. (1954), R.P. (1948), N.E.A.C. (1950); *b* 1908; *m* Jillian Pratt; one *s*, one *d*. *Educ.:* Colfe's Grammar School, Blackheath; Goldsmiths' College; R.A. Schools. *Address:* 10 Sheen Common Drive, Richmond, Surrey TW10 5BN. *Signs work:* "Norman Hepple."

HEPWORTH, Elizabeth Barbara; painter in oil, water-colour, pastel; retd. teacher, until recently took summer school at Pendley Manor, Tring; *b* Walton on Thames, Surrey, 1904; *d* of Cecil Hepworth, pioneer of kinematography. *Educ.:* Maybury House School, Woking, Convent of St. Mawr, Weybridge; *studied art* at Camberwell School of Art (William Coldstream, Victor Pasmore, Claude Rogers). *Exhib.:* R.A., N.E.A.C., Leicester Gallery, and various one-man shows. *Address:* 21B Regents Park Rd., London NW1 7TL. *Signs work:* "E.B.H."

HERBERT, Albert, A.R.C.A.; painter of mainly religious subjects in oil and etching; ex Princ. lecturer, St. Martin's School of Art; *b* London, 10 Sept., 1925; *m* Jacqueline; three *d*. *Studied art* at R.C.A. (1949-53), British School at Rome (1953-54). *Exhib.:* R.A., Poetry Soc., University of California, Westminster, Norwich and Winchester Cathedrals, Castlefield Gallery, England and Co., Lancaster University, etc. *Work in permanent collections:* Contemporary Art Soc., Coventry Training College, Methodist Educ. Com., Shell, Stoke-on-Trent A.G., Glamorgan, Herts., Notts. and Somerset C.C's. *Address:* 4 Clifton Terr., Cliftonville, Dorking RH4 2JU. *Signs work:* "Albert Herbert."

HERBERT, Barry; artist/printmaker, drawings and prints; Head of Fine Art Dept., University of Leeds (1985-92); *b* York, 19 Mar., 1937; *m*; one *s*, one *d*.

Educ.: Archbishop Holgate's School, York; *studied art* at James Graham College. *Exhib.:* 34 one-man shows include: Serpentine Gallery, London (1971); Mappin Gallery, Sheffield (1972), Galerie Brechbühl, Switzerland (1972, 1976, 1979, 1982, 1984), Galerie Steinmetz, Bonn (1979, 1984), Karl-Marx-Universität, Leipzig, (1980), Gilbert Parr Gallery, London (1982). *Publications.:* 30 editions of prints published in Germany, Switzerland and England; "Barry Herbert – Künstler-Grafiker" 20pp. illustr. (1979). *Address:* 43 Weetwood Lane, Leeds LS16 5NW. *Signs work:* "Barry Herbert."

HERIZ-SMITH, Bridget, B.F.A. (Hons.), S.G.A. (1985); award with commendation, History of Art (1977); sculptor in cast, cement and bronze, and ink drawings, etchings; administrator, Clock House Studios (1979-86); *b* Hamburg, 13 Dec., 1949; *d* of Patrick Heriz-Smith, glass engraver, and Audrey Pilkington, painter. *Educ.:* Framlingham Mills Grammar School; *studied art* at Goldsmiths' College, Ravensbourne College (1974-77, Eric Peskett). *Exhib.:* Sculpture in Anglia (1978, 1981, 1989), R.A. Summer Show (1988, 1992), Young Blood Group (1990, 1991, 1992, 1993). *Address:* 1 Allums Yd., Low Rd., Badingham, Suffolk IP13 8JS. *Signs work:* "B.Heriz."

HERMAN, Josef, O.B.E. (1981); Gold medal for services to art in Wales; painter in oil, water-colour, drawing; *b* Warsaw, 3 Jan., 1911; *s* of David Herman, cobbler; *m* Eleanore; one *s*, one *d*. *Educ.:* Warsaw; *studied art* at Warsaw School of Art and Decoration. *Exhib.:* Glasgow (1942), Edinburgh (1942), London (1943), Roland, Browse & Delbanco (1946-), British Council, Arts Council, retrospective Whitechapel A.G. (1956), Camden Arts Centre (1980). *Work in permanent collections:* Arts Council, British Council, B.M., National Museum Cardiff, Contemporary Art Soc., National Museum Bezalel, Jerusalem, Tate, V. & A., National Galleries of: Johannesburg, Melbourne, Ottawa, Wellington, etc. *Publications:* Ystradgynlais, a Welsh mining village; Related Twilights; Notes from a Welsh Diary. *Address:* 120 Edith Rd., London W14 9AP. *Signs work:* all works signed on the back – see appendix.

HERON, Patrick; painter; *b* Leeds, 1920. *Exhib.:* one-man shows: Waddington Galleries, Bertha Schaefer Gallery (N.Y.), Galerie Lienhard (Zürich), São Paulo Bienal (1953 and 1965), Edinburgh, Oslo, Dublin, Rio de Janeiro, B. Aires, Santiago, Lima, Caracas, Waddington Fine Art, Montreal, Sydney, Melbourne, Toronto, etc. *Work in permanent collections:* Tate Gallery; Gulbenkian Foundation; N.P.G.; Contemporary Art Society; V. & A.; B.M.; Arts Council; British Council; Stuyvesant Foundation; Wakefield; Manchester; Cardiff; Aberdeen; Belfast; Eastbourne; Exeter Univ.; Plymouth; Univ. of Warwick; Univ. of Stirling; Bedford; Oxford; Oldham; Leeds; Montreal; Toronto; Vancouver; Toledo, Ohio; Smith College, Mass.; Brooklyn; Albright-Knox, Buffalo; Univ. of Michigan, Ann Arbor; Nat. Gall. of W. Australia, Perth; Boymans Museum, Rotterdam; Power Collection, Sydney, etc. *Addresses:* Eagles Nest, Zennor, St. Ives, Cornwall, and 12 Editha Mans., Edith Grove, London SW10.

HERON, Susanna, B.A. (Hons.) (1971); sculptor in stone, photographer; senior lecturer, Middlesex University; *b* England, 22 Sept., 1949. *Educ.:* Penzance Girls' Grammar School; *studied art* at Central School of Art and Design (1968-71). *Exhib.:* solo shows since 1985 include Whitechapel A.G., Camden Arts Centre, Newlyn A.G. *Work in permanent collections:* Stedelijk Museum, Arts Council, V. & A., C.A.S., etc., museums in Europe and Australia. *Publication:* photographs and text: Shima: Island and Garden (Abson, 1992). *Address:* 39 Norman Gr., London E3 5EG. *Signs work:* see appendix.

HERRIOT, Alan B.; artist/sculptor in cold cast GRP, painting in oil, acrylic and water-colour; Proprietor, Endeavour Art Studios, Edinburgh; *b* 20 Feb., 1952. *Studied art* at Duncan of Jordanstone, Dundee (1969-74, Scott Sutherland, James Morrison). *Exhib.:* Aros Centre Skye, Whisky Heritage Centre Edinburgh, Inverary Court House. *Work in public collection:* Miner's Monument, Newton Grange. *Publications:* The Foundling; Christmas is Coming; Travellers Tales; Broonies, Silkies and Fairies; Quest for a Kelpie. *Address:* Endeavour Art Studios, 75 Trafalgar La., Leith, Edinburgh EH6 4DQ. *Signs work:* "Alan B. Herriot" and see appendix.

HESELTINE, John Robert, B. of E. Drawing (1941), B. of E. Pictorial Design T.D. (1941); artist in oil and water-colour; *b* Ilford, Essex, 14 Sept., 1923; *m* Pam Masco; one *s*, one *d* (previous marriage). *Educ.:* Mayfield; *studied art* at S.E. Essex College of Art (Francis Taylor, A.R.C.A., Allen Wellings, A.R.C.A.). *Exhib.:* V. & A., R.W.S., R.P.S., Bourne Gallery, David Messum London, Priory Gallery Cheltenham, Thompson Gallery London, U.S.A. and Scandinavia. *Work in permanent collections:* Dartmouth Naval College, Fleet Air Arm, Yeovilton. *Publications:* illustrated 1949-88: Odhams Press, Fleetway, I.P.C., U.S.A. and Europe. *Address:* Keepers, Norwood La., Graffham, W. Sussex GU28 0QQ. *Club:* Wentworth. *Signs work:* "John R. Heseltine."

HEWISON, William, N.D.D., painting (1949), A.T.D. (1950), M.S.I.A. (1954); illustrator in ink; line and line and wash, and colour; Art Editor, Punch (1960-1984); *b* South Shields, 15 May, 1925; *s* of Ralph Hewison; *m* Elsie Hammond; one *s*, one *d*. *Educ.:* South Shields High School; London University; *studied art* at South Shields Art School (1941-43), Regent St. Polytechnic Art School (1947-49). *Exhib.:* Three one-man shows, National Theatre; drawings permanently in V. & A. and B.M. *Work repro.:* illustrations and cartoons; Press advertisements, Punch; book jackets; books, Types Behind the Print, Mindfire, The Cartoon Connection, How to Draw and Sell Cartoons. *Address:* 5 Southdown Drive, London SW20 8EZ. *Signs work:* "Hewison" or "H."

HEYWORTH, James Charles; L.D.A.D. distinction University of London (1982); illustrator/painter in gouache, water-colour, pen and ink, airbrush; *b* London, 28 Feb., 1956; *s* of James Heyworth. *Educ.:* Wandsworth School; *studied art* at Putney School of Art (1975), Byam Shaw School of Drawing and Painting (1976, D. Nixon), Goldsmiths' College (1979-82, Bernard Cheese). *Exhib.:* Battersea Arts Centre, Ripley Arts; one-man Bury Metro Arts Assoc. Work in private collections. *Address:* 99 Sutton Common Rd., Sutton, Surrey SM1 3HP. *Club:* Assoc. of Illustrators. *Signs work:* "James Heyworth."

HICKLING, Edward Albert; artist in oil and water-colour; retired; *b* Nottingham, 2 May, 1913; *s* of A. Hickling. *Educ.:* Nottingham; *studied art* at Nottingham College of Art (1927-39) under A. Spooner, R.B.A. *Exhib.:* R.A., R.B.A., R.I., R.O.I., R.P., R.S.M.A. *Work in permanent collection:* City of Derby Museums and A.G. *Address:* 25 Wilsthorpe Rd., Breaston, Derbys. DE72 3EA. *Club:* Nottingham Soc. of Artists. *Signs work:* "E. A. Hickling."

HICKS, Anne, R.W.A., Slade Dip.; artist in oil and gouache of portraits, murals, costume design, environmental design; Adult Education Avon and Visiting Lecturer, University Architects Dept., Bristol (1976-84); *b* London; *d* of J. R. G. Hayward, C.Eng, F.I.E.E.; *m* Jerry Hicks; one *s*, one *d*. *Educ.:* Hampstead and Minehead; *studied art* at Slade School under Profs. Schwabe and Coldstream. *Exhib.:* R.W.A., British Women Painters Musée de l'Art Moderne, Paris (1967); two-man shows with husband: Bristol, Cardiff, Dorchester, etc. (1954-90). *Work in private collections* in England, France, America, New

Zealand. *Address:* Goldrush, Gt. George St., Bristol BS1 5QT. *Work unsigned* unless requested.

HICKS, Jerry, A.T.D., R.W.A., Slade Dip., Judo 6th Dan; painter including portraits, murals; environmentalist; *b* London, 12 June, 1927; *s* of Algernon Hicks, actor; *m* Anne Hayward, painter; one *s*, one *d. Educ.:* Actors' Orphanage, Rishworth, Sandhurst; *studied art* at Slade under Coldstream, Freud and with Stanley Bird and Walter Bayes. *Exhib.:* R.A., R.W.A., R.B.A., two-man shows with wife: Bristol, Cardiff, Dorchester, etc. (1954-90). Winner of Bristol 600 Competition (1973), Queen's Jubilee Award (British Achievement), Olympic Painting prize (1984). *Work in collections* in Britain, U.S.A., Canada, St. Lucia, Germany, Italy, France, Australia, Japan. *Address:* Goldrush, Gt. George St., Bristol BS1 5QT. *Signs work:* "Hicks."

HICKS, Philip, Dip.R.A.S.; painter in oil, acrylic and water-colour; Hon. Treas., A.G.B.I.; *b* England, 1928; *s* of Brig. P. H. W. Hicks, C.B.E., D.S.O., M.C.; *m* Jill; one *s*, one *d. Educ.:* Winchester College; *studied art* at Chelsea School of Art and R.A. Schools. *Exhib.:* one-man shows, Marjorie Parr, Robert Self, Hoya, New Art Centre Galleries, Gallery 10, London, Oxford Gallery, V.E.C.U. Antwerp, Engström Galleri, Stockholm; retrospective, Battersea Arts Centre, London, Bohun Gallery, Henley, 1977 British Council award. *Work in permanent collections:* Tate Gallery, V. & A., Contemporary Art Soc., Imperial War Museum, Nuffield Foundation, R.C.M., De Beers, Mirror Group, Wates Ltd., Nat. West. Bank, B.P., APV Holdings, Chandris Shipping. *Address:* Radcot House, Buckland Rd., Bampton, Oxon. OX18 2AA. *Clubs:* Chelsea Arts and Arts Club. *Signs work:* "Philip Hicks" (often on reverse) or "HICKS."

HIGSON, John, M.F.P.S.; self taught sculptor in wood and ceramic, painter in water-colour and pastel; *b* 30 Oct., 1936; *s* of Albert Edward Higson. *Educ.:* Malden West County Secondary. *Exhib.:* one-man shows: Bourne Hall, Ewell, Russell Studio, Wimbledon, Malden Centre, New Malden. *Address:* 22 Croxton, Burritt Rd., Kingston upon Thames, Surrey KT1 3HS.

HILDER, Rowland, O.B.E. (1986), P.P.R.I., R.S.M.A.; painter; *b* 28 June, 1905. *Work repro.:* illustrated: Moby Dick (Cape), Treasure Island (Oxford Press), Precious Bane (Cape), The Bible for Today (O.U.P.), The Shell Guide to Flowers of the Countryside (Phoenix House) (with Edith Hilder). *Publications:* Starting with Watercolour (Herbert Press, 1988); Biography: Rowland Hilder painter of the English Landscape (Antique Collectors Club); Painting Landscapes in Water-colour (Collins, 1983); Rowland Hilder's England and Rowland Hilder's Country (Herbert Press); Rowland Hilder's Sketching Country (Herbert Press, 1991). *Address:* 7 Kidbrooke Grove, Blackheath, London SE3 0PG.

HILL, Anthony; artist, plastician and theorist: works in industrial materials; awarded Leverhulme Fellowship, Hon. Research Fellow, Dept. Mathematics, University College, London (1971-73); currently visiting research associate (Maths. Dept. UCL); *b* London, 23 Apr., 1930; *s* of Adrian Hill, R.B.A. *Educ.:* Bryanston; *studied art* at St. Martin's (1947-49), Central School (1949-51). *Exhib.:* Kasmin Gallery (1966, 1969, 1980); retrospective exhbn. Hayward Gallery (1983). *Publications:* edited Data Directions in Art Theory and Aesthetics (Faber, 1986). *Articles and work repro.:* in English, Continental and American publications since 1950. *Address:* 24 Charlotte St., London W1. *Signs work:* "Anthony Hill." and see appendix. Since 1975 has made works signed "Rem Doxford", and "Redo."

HILL, Derek; painter in oil and stage designer; director of Art, British School at Rome (1953-55 and 1957-59); organiser of Degas Exhbn. at Edinburgh Festival and Tate Gallery; *b* Southampton, 6 Dec., 1916; *s* of A. J. L. Hill. *Educ.:* Marlborough College; *studied art* at Munich, Vienna, Paris, and theatre design in Russia, China and Japan. *Exhib.:* Marlborough Gallery, London (1978), Leicester Galleries, Whitechapel Gallery (1961). *Work in permanent collections:* Tate Gallery, Belfast Art Gallery, Dublin Municipal Gallery, Arts Council, National Gallery of Canada. *Publication:* co-author, Islamic Architecture—Its Decoration (Faber & Faber, 1964); co-author, Islamic Architecture in N. Africa (1976). *Address:* St. Colomb's, Churchill (Letterkenny), Co. Donegal, Ireland. *Signs work:* "D.H." in a circle when picture is signed.

HILL, Francis, Cert. Criminology (1959); self taught painter in oil; retd. police chief inspector; formerly Head of Security, National Gallery and N.P.G.; *b* Barnsley, 11 Sept., 1917; *m* Barbara Heward; two *s,* two *d. Educ.:* Leeds University. *Exhib.:* R.A. (1982, 1984, 1992, 1993), National Gallery (staff). Work in private collections. *Publications:* chapter with illustration: A World of Their Own (Pelham); Royal Academy Exhibitors 1971-1989. *Address:* Three Roses, 38 Brockswood La., Welwyn Garden City, Herts. AL8 7BG. *Clubs:* Welwyn Garden City Golf, Music. *Signs work:* "Francis Hill."

HILL, Ronald James, U.A., S.G.F.A., F.S.A.I.; freelance artist in oil, water-colour, pen and ink; tutor; *b* London, 19 Oct., 1933; *s* of James George Hill; *m* Betty Bunn. *Educ.:* Willesden Technical College; *studied art* at Heatherley's School of Art (1958-65, Jack Merriot, Patrick Larkin, Harry Riley). *Exhib.:* Paris Salon (1966-69), R.B.A., U.A.; one man shows, Brent, Wantage. *Address:* Orpheus Studio, Pound Cottage, Kingston Lisle, Wantage, Oxon. *Signs work:* "RONN."

HILL, Sonia Geraldine; painter in oil; *b* 26 Sept., 1939. *Educ.:* Dorchester Abbey School, Oxon.; *studied art* at Maidenhead Art College, Berks.; Zambia (pupil with Andrew Hayward). *Exhib.:* R.A. (1993). *Address:* 6A Warfield Rd., Hampton, Middx. TW12 2AY. *Signs work:* "S.G. Hill."

HILLHOUSE, David, B.A. (1969), A.T.D. (1971), R.C.A. (1979), A.M.A. (1982); artist in water-colour and egg tempera; Principal Museum Officer, Wirral Museum Services, Birkenhead; *b* Irby, Wirral, 19 June, 1945; *s* of Harry Hillhouse; *m* Paula Lane; two *s. Educ.:* Birkenhead Institute; *studied art* at Laird School of Art (1964-66), Liverpool College of Art (1966-69). *Exhib.:* Merseyside, Wales and Bristol. Work in private collections. *Address:* 49 Cortsway, Greasby, Wirral L49 2NA. *Clubs:* R.Cam.A., Wirral Soc. of Arts, Museums Assoc., Deeside Art Group. *Signs work:* "David Hillhouse."

HILLS, Peter Faber, N.D.D., R.A.Cert., F.R.B.S., Past Secretary of the 65 Group (Public School Art Masters); Churchill Fellow in Sculpture (1972); sculptor in clay, stone, wood; schoolmaster; Director of Art, Tonbridge School (1963-79), retd. from Tonbridge School (1988); Examiner Oxford and Cambridge Joint Board (A Level); N.A.D.F.A.S. Lecturer; *b* Bearsted, Kent, 4 Dec., 1925; *m* Ann-Mary Ewart (née Macdonald); two *s,* one *d. Educ.:* Tonbridge School; *studied art* at Bromley College of Art (1948-50), R.A. Schools (1950-55); assistant to Maurice Lambert, R.A. (1955-60), and worked for Sir Henry Rushbury, R.A., Sir Albert Richardson, P.R.A. *Work in permanent collections:* Lord Leighton Museum, Kensington, Skinner's Library, Tonbridge School. *Address:* 33 Yardley Park Rd., Tonbridge, Kent. *Signs work:* "HILLS."

HINCHCLIFFE, Michael; artist in water-colour, designer; *b* London, 25 Apr., 1937; *s* of Tom Hinchcliffe; *m* Gillian; two *d*. *Educ.:* St. Marylebone Grammar School; *studied art* at St. Martin's School of Art. *Exhib.:* R.I., U.A., Edwin Pollard Gallery, and many one-man shows. *Work in permanent collection:* Weybridge Museum. *Address:* 37 The Furrows, Walton on Thames, Surrey KT12 3JG. *Signs work:* see appendix.

HINKS, Thomas, N.D.D. (1951), F.R.S.A. (1981); lecturer-demonstrator, artist in water-colour, oil, acrylic; demonstrator, Daler Rowney; visiting lecturer at res. colleges and art societies; *b* Newcastle, 26 Apr., 1930; *s* of Thomas Hinks; *m* Vera; one *s*, one *d*. *Educ.:* Newcastle School of Art, Stoke-on-Trent College of Art; *studied art* under Arthur Berry. *Exhib.:* 15 one-man shows in Midlands. *Work in permanent collections:* Stoke-on-Trent City A.G., Newcastle Museum and A.G., Keele University, W.E.A. Centre; paintings in America, Canada, Spain, Greece, France, Norway, and many private U.K. collections. *Publications:* author of New Methods and Techniques in Art - for schools. *Address:* Fairways, High St., Caverswall, Stoke-on-Trent, Staffs. ST11 9EF. *Clubs:* Chairman, Unit Ten Art Soc., N.A.P.A., Soc. of Staffs Artists. *Signs work:* "Tom Hinks."

HINWOOD, Kay, P.S., U.A.; painter in oil, pastel, etc.; *b* Bromley, 26 Nov., 1920; *d* of the late Robert Wylie, M.C., banker; *m* (1) the late George Hinwood, (2) the late Douglas Zeidler; one *s*, one *d*. *Educ.:* Stratford House School, Bickley; *studied art:* first Paris, with Edouard MacAvoy, later privately with Sonia Mervyn; City and Guilds Art School, London; Kathleen Browne Studios, Chelsea under Marian Kratochwil and Kathleen Browne. *Exhib.:* R.P., R.B.A., R.O.I., P.S., U.A., S.W.A., Mall Galleries. *Work in private collections:* England, U.S.A., Canada, France, Spain, Australia, Holland. *Address:* 27 Edward Rd., Bromley, Kent BR1 3NG. *Club:* Chelsea Arts. *Signs work:* "K. Hinwood."

HIPKISS, Percy Randolph, R.B.S.A. (1971); freelance artist in oil, water-colour and pastel; jewellery designer; past-president, Birmingham Water-colour Soc.; President, Dudley Society of Artists; *b* Blackheath, Birmingham, 8 Aug., 1912; *s* of William Hipkiss, woodworker; *m* Dorothy Alice Boraston; one *s*, one *d*. *Educ.:* at Blackheath. *Work in permanent collections:* Dudley A.G., and in private collections throughout U.K., America, Australia, Belgium. *Address:* 18 Lewis Rd., Oldbury, Warley, W.Mid B68 0PW. *Signs work:* "Hipkiss."

HIRST, Barry Elliot, N.D.D. Painting (1956), Dip.F.A. (1958), F.R.S.A. (1989); painter in water-colour; Emeritus Prof. of Fine Art, University of Sunderland; *b* Padstow, Cornwall, 11 June, 1934; *m* Sheila Mary; one *s*, two *d*. *Educ.:* Alleyns School, Dulwich; *studied art* at Camberwell School of Art (1950-52, 1954-56), Slade School (1956-58, Keith Vaughan, Claude Rogers). *Exhib.:* over twelve one-man shows, London, Sydney, N.Y., Glasgow, Edinburgh, Newcastle upon Tyne, Riga. *Work in permanent collections:* Contemporary Arts Soc., British Council, Sunday Times, Croydon Educ. Com., Northern Arts Assoc., Tyne & Wear Museums, University of Sunderland, Darlington Memorial Hospital, Olinda Museum Brazil, Derby Museum and A.G., H.R.H. Duchess of Kent, Latvian National Museum Riga, Latvian Academy of Art Riga, R.A.C., Sunderland and Portsmouth Newspapers, Sao Paulo Museum Brazil, B.P. *Publications:* 'From a Painting by Masaccio' with C. Day-Lewis, 'The Way of It' with R.S. Thomas, 'Waiting for the Barbarians' with Roy Fuller, 'An Ill-Governed Coast' with Roy Fuller, 'Kisses' with Alistair Eliot. *Address:* c/o Mercury Gallery, 26 Cork St., London W1X 1HB. *Club:* Sunderland Assoc. Football. *Signs work:* "BARRY HIRST" or "B.E. HIRST."

HIRST, Derek, A.R.C.A.; artist; *b* Doncaster, 11 Apr., 1930. *Studied art* at Doncaster School of Art (1946-48), R.C.A. (1948-51). *Exhib.:* Drian Galleries (1961), Tooth's Gallery (1962-63), Stone Galleries, Newcastle upon Tyne (1962), University of Sussex (1966), Towner A.G. (1966), Angela Flowers Gallery (1970, 1972, 1975, 1979, 1984, 1987, 1989), Victorian Centre for the Arts, Melbourne, Australia (1980), Pallant House Gallery, Chichester (1987, 1991), Flowers East (1991), Flowers East at London Fields (1993). *Work in permanent collections:* Tate Gallery, V. & A., National Gallery of Canada, A.C.G.B., Contemporary Art Soc., D.O.E., Fundaçao dos Museus Regionaise de Bahia, Brazil, Bank of Ireland, Dublin, Universities of Sussex and Southampton, Art Inst. of Detroit, Brooklyn Museum, N.Y., Arizona State University, Phoenix Art Museum, etc. *Address:* 3 The Terrace, Mill La., Sidlesham, Chichester, W. Sussex PO20 7NA. *Signs work:* "Derek Hirst."

HITCHCOCK, Harold Raymond, F.R.S.A. (1972); Hon. Col. of State of Louisiana U.S.A. (1974); artist in water-colour and oil; *b* London, 23 May, 1914; *s* of Thomas R. Hitchcock; *m* Rose Hitchcock; two *s*, one *d*. *Studied art* at Working Mens College, Camden Town (1935-36) under Percy Horton, Barnett Freedman. *Exhib.:* one-man shows: Hanson Gallery, New Orleans (1990), M.K. Vance Gallery, Chicago (1992), Campbell & Franks (Fine Art) Ltd. (1975), Pilkington Glass Museum (1973), Hilton Gallery (1970), Upper Grosvenor Gallery (1969), Woburn Abbey (1967), Walker Gallery (1956); retrospective shows: R.I. Galleries (1967), Philadelphia Art Alliance, U.S.A. (1982); touring exhbn. in U.S.A.: New Orleans, Huntsville, Atlanta City, Daytona Beach, Corpus Christi and Winston Salem (opened by the Duke of Bedford, 1972); R.S.A., London (1984), Gallery 106, Perrysberg, Ohio (1984), Clossons Gallery, Cincinnati (1985), Christopher Wood Gallery, London (1986). *Work in permanent collections:* V. & A., Rowntree Memorial Trust, Lidice Memorial Museum, Czechoslovakia, Museum of Fine Art, N. Carolina, University of Louisiana, Hannema-de Stuers Foundation, Nijenhuis Castle, Netherlands, New Orleans Museum of Fine Art. *Publications:* Harold Hitchcock — A Romantic Symbol in Surrealism (1982) by Dr. Ian Williamson. *Address:* Meadow View, Ugborough, Ivybridge, Devon. *Signs work:* see appendix.

HITCHCOCK, Malcolm John, R.W.A.; painter in oil or oil over egg tempera of railway subjects, also nudes in mixed media; *b* Salisbury, 17 Apr., 1929; *m* Zaidee Lindsay, author. *Educ.:* Andover Boys' School; *studied art* at Andover School of Art. *Exhib.:* one-man shows, London and provinces; R.A., R.W.A., Paris Salon, Brussels and Dusseldorf. *Work in permanent collections:* Reading Museum and A.G., Bristol R.W.A. *Work repro.:* series of articles in The Artist. *Address:* Quint, Rectory Rd., Padworth Common, Reading, Berks. RG7 4JD. *Signs work:* "M.J. HITCHCOCK" and date.

HITCHENS, John; painter on canvas, also works in variety of three-dimensional materials; *b* Sussex, 1940; *s* of Ivon Hitchens, painter; *g-s* of Alfred Hitchens, painter; *m;* two *s* (one a sculptor). Educ.: Bedales School; *studied art* at Bath Academy of Art. Regular London exhbns. since 1964. Work in public and permanent collections U.K. and abroad. 1979: 52' mural, "A Landscape Symphony". *Address:* The Old School, Byworth, Petworth, Sussex GU28 0HN. *Signs work:* "John Hitchens."

HO, Dr. Kok-Hoe, D.Sc. (Hon.), P.B.M., M.S.I.A., F.R.A.I.A., F.R.I.B.A., A.P.A.M., A.R.A.S., A.R.P.S.; awarded St. Andrew's Gold (1935) and Bronze (1937); 2nd Inter-School Art gold medal (1939); architect; artist in oil and water-colour painting, pen and pencil drawing; art-photographer; president-director, Ho Kwong-Yew & Sons, Architects, Singapore; Chairman, Singapore Art Soc. (1953-70); *b* Singapore, 14 July, 1922. *Educ.:* St. Andrew's School, Singapore; graduated N.S.W. College of Architecture, Sydney. *Exhib.:* Sydney (1948-49); Singapore (1954-62); Kuala Lumpur (1960-62), etc. Photo salons: London (1957); La Coruna (1958); Hongkong (1958), etc. Architectural Work: National Museum, Kuala Lumpur, etc. *Publications:* Travel Sketches and Paintings, etc. *Clubs:* Royal Art Soc.; Royal Institute of Australian Architects; R.I.B.A.; Royal Photographic Soc. of Great Britain; Singapore Art Soc. *Address:* 9 Camden Park, Singapore 1129. *Signs work:* "Ho Kok-Hoe."

HOARE, Diana C., B.A. Hons.; lettering designer, calligrapher, letter carver, carving on stone and slate, calligraphy; *b* London, 10 Feb., 1956; *d* of Reginald Hoare, picture restorer; *m* William Taunton; one *s*, two *d*. *Educ.:* Godolphin and Latymer; University of Kent, Canterbury; *studied art:* privately with Vernon Shearer, Ievan Rees, Heather Child, Sam Somerville. *Exhib.:* solo exhbns. in Dorset, London and B'ham. *Work in permanent collection:* two MS. books at University of Austin, Texas. *Publications:* Advanced Calligraphy Techniques (Cassells), Everybodys Wine Guide (Quarto). *Address:* Upper House Farm, Dilwyn, Hereford HR4 8JJ. *Signs work:* see appendix.

HOBART, John, B.Sc. (Lond.), R.C.A.; self taught artist in oil and watercolour; past Vice-Pres. Royal Cambrian Academy; Fellow, University College of N. Wales, Bangor; *b* London, 27 May, 1922; *s* of Percy John Hobart; one *s*, two *d*. *Educ.:* University College, London. *Exhib.:* one-man, Theatre Gwynedd; group shows, Plas Mawr, Conway, Tegfryn Gallery, Cambrian Academy, R.I., N.Wales Group, Newlyn, Penwith. *Work in permanent collections:* University College of N.Wales, Bangor; private collections in U.S.A., Canada, Australia, G.B., Holland, Germany. *Address:* Buswisnan, Ludgvan, Penzance, Cornwall TR20 8BN. *Signs work:* "J. Hobart."

HOBSON, Anthony Francis, Ph.D., N.D.D., A.T.D., F.R.S.A., F.S.E.A.D., Hon.F.H.S.; painter, art historian; Hon. Research Fellow, Coventry University; *b* Leicester, 28 Feb., 1920; *s* of Francis John Hobson; *m* June Lea; one *s*, one *d*. *Educ.:* Wyggeston School, University of Leicester; *studied art* at Leicester College of Art (1936-38, 1946-51). *Exhib.:* R.A., R.S.A., R.P., R.B.A., R.O.I., R.S.M.A., R.B.S.A., P.S., Aviation Artists, etc.; one-man shows: Leamington Spa (1971, 1975, 1980, 1985, 1986). *Work in permanent collections:* Imperial War Museum; R.A.F. Museum; Leamington Spa A.G. *Publications:* J. W. Waterhouse, R.A. (Studio Vista, 1980; Phaidon, 1989, 1992). *Address:* Pear Tree Cottage, Ilmington, Warwickshire CV36 4LG. *Club:* Past President, Coventry and Warwickshire Soc. of Artists. *Signs work:* "Anthony Hobson."

HOCKIN, Julie, A.R.M.S. (1990), H.S. (1984); self taught professional artist in water-colour, graphite and coloured pencils specialising in wildlife and botanical subjects, also cats; Creative Director, Hockin and Roberts Ltd., St. Austell; Council mem. Hilliard Soc.; *b* St. Austell, 3 Feb., 1937; one *d*. *Educ.:* St. Austell Grammar School. *Exhib.:* National Trust Cotehele, Marwell Zoological Pk. Winchester. *Address:* Cedar Lodge, Trevarth, Mevagissey, St. Austell, Cornwall PL26 6RX. *Signs work:* "Julie Hockin" or "JH" joined.

HODGES, Cyril Walter, Hon. D.Litt. (Sussex) 1979; author, mural painter, illustrator, stage designer; *b* Beckenham, 1909; *m* Greta Becker; two *s*. *Educ.:* Dulwich College; *studied art* at Goldsmiths' College. *Work repro.:* advertisements, books, magazine illustrations in England and U.S.A. Special subjects: costume and period illustrations, theatre, Shakespeare. Designer of Mermaid Theatre (1951), Lloyd's 1951 Exhbn., executed mural painting for United Kingdom

231

Provident Inst. (1957). *Publications:* Columbus Sails, The Globe Restored, The Namesake, Shakespeare's Theatre, The Overland Launch, Shakespeare's Second Globe, Playhouse Tales. Awarded Kate Greenaway Medal for Illustration (1964). *Address:* 36 Southover High St., Lewes, Sussex BN7 1HX. *Signs work:* "C. Walter Hodges."

HODGES, Gillian Mary, S.W.A. (1987); portrait painter in oil, pastel and water-colour; tutor for Adult Educ., Hants. and Surrey; *b* Twickenham, Middx., 6 July, 1933; *d* of Harry Leslie Snook; *m* Peter Steer Hodges; two *s. Educ.:* St. Catherine's Covent, Twickenham; *studied art* at Salisbury School of Art and Heatherley School of Art (part time). *Exhib.:* S.W.A., various societies in S. and S.W. of England, Northern Ireland. *Address:* 23 Coniston Drive, Folly Hill, Farnham, Surrey GU9 0DB. *Signs work:* "G. M. Hodges."

HODGKINS, Barbara; sculptor in marble, bronze; *b* U.S.A. *Educ.:* Wellesley College, Columbia University, U.S.A.; *studied art* at Chelsea School of Art, London. *Sculpture in corporate collections:* Prudential, Bank of China, Bank of Denmark, B.P., Reynolds, Hewlett-Packer, Foote, Cone, Belding, MCL (Art and Work award 1987) and in private European, Asian and American collections. Mem. Royal Soc. of British Sculptors. *Addresses:* 5 Hurlingham Ct., Ranelagh Gdns., London SW6 3SH; C.P.200, Pietrasanta (Lucca) 55045, Italy.

HODGKINSON, Wilfred Philip, A.T.D.; artist, craftsman and author; Princ., Truro School of Art (1935-39); Princ., Bilston School of Art (1939-46); Curator, Bilston Art Gallery (1939-46); retd. Principal Art Lecturer; *b* 30 Apr., 1912; *m. Educ.:* King Charles I School, Kidderminster; Kidderminster School of Art; Birmingham College of Art. *Work repro.:* by Austin Motors Ltd. (Milestones of Progress). *Publications:* The Eloquent Silence, The Kingdom is a Garden (English Universities Press); frequent contributor to The Artist. *Address:* 90 Stanmore La., Winchester. *Signs work:* "W. P. Hodgkinson," or, on cartoons, "W.P.H."

HODGSON, Carole, H.D.F.A. (1964); sculptor in cement, bronze, wax, ceramics, lead; Senior lecturer, Kingston University; *b* London, 1940. *Studied art* at Wimbledon School of Art (1957-62), Slade School of Fine Art (1962-64). *Exhib.:* Angela Flowers Gallery, Flowers East, A.C.G.B., W.A.C., Wustum Museum, U.S.A., Whitefriars Museum, Coventry, New Ashgate, Farnham, Llanelli Festival, Christie's Fine Arts. *Work in permanent collections:* Welsh Contemporary Arts Soc., A.C.G.B., W.A.C., British Council, D.O.E., Contemporary Arts Soc., Unilever House, Universities of Wales, London, Wisconsin U.S.A., British Medal Soc. *Address:* c/o Flowers East, 199-205 Richmond Rd., London E8 3NJ. *Signs work:* "Carole Hodgson."

HODGSON, Kenneth Jonah, B.A., G.O.E. Dip. S.W. C.Q.S.W.; artist in acrylic, oil and water-colour; *b* Liverpool, 2 Aug., 1936; *s* of Jonah Hodgson; two *d. Educ.:* Liverpool, Herts, Oak Hill College, London, The Open University, N.E.W.I. Wrexham Cymru. *Exhib.:* R.Cam.A., Williamson A.G.,various Liverpool and Chester galleries; collective exhbns. in Newcastle-Staffs, Ludlow, Crosby and R.B.S.A. Gallery B'ham; individual exhbns. on Merseyside and Wirral. Daylight Group – a Tate Liverpool/Metropolitan Borough of Wirral S.S.D. Arts Project, Art Forum – M.B.W. – S.S.D. (1993). Paintings in private and public collections in U.K. and other countries. Sec., Wirral Soc. of Arts (1983-87); Exec com. mem., Merseyside Arts (1985-87); Steering com. sec., Merseyside Contemporary Artists (1988-89); Founder, National Acrylic Painters' Assoc. *Address:* N.A.P.A., 134 Rake La., Wallasey, Merseyside L45 1JW. *Signs work:* "Kenneth J. Hodgson."

HODIN, Josef Paul, L.L.D. (Prague), Ph.D. (Hon., Uppsala), D.S.M., 1st Class, Czech; Commander order of merit, Italian; St. Olav Medal, Norwegian; Grand Cross, order of merit, Austrian; Grand Cross, order of merit, German; Silver Cross of Merit, Vienna; Prof. Art History h.c.(Vienna); author, art historian, critic; press attaché to the Norwegian Govt. (1944-45); director of Studies, I.C.A. (1949-54); co-editor of Quandrum, Brussels; mem. executive comm. British Society of Aesthetics; hon. mem. Editorial Council J.A.A.C., Cleveland; awarded intern. 1st prize for art criticism, 1954 (Biennale, Venice); *b* Prague, 17 Aug., 1905; *s* of Edouard D. Hodin; *m* Doris Pamela Simms; one *s,* one *d. Educ.:* Realschule, Realgymnasium, and Charles University, Prague; *studied art:* Dresden, Berlin, Paris, Stockholm, and Courtauld Inst. of Art, London University. *Publications:* numerous. *Address:* 12 Eton Ave., London NW3 3FH.

HODSON, John; painter in oil, sculptor in stone and bronze; *b* Oxford, 19 Aug., 1945; *s* of Frank George Hodson, toolmaker. *Educ.:* Cardinal Hinsley School, London. *Exhib:* one-man show London (1973), Paris Salon, Salon des Independants and other international exhbns. *Work repro.:* Modern Art Revue, Courtauld Inst. of Art, London. *Address:* 40 Clement Cl., London NW6. *Signs work:* "Hodson."

HOFER, Paul, Dr.-phil. (1938), Privatdocent Univ. Bern (1948), ao. Prof. (1956); Prof. of Ecole polytechnique, Univ. Lausanne (1961); Prof. Eidg. Techn. Hochschule, Zürich (1964, o. Prof., 1967-80); historian of Art; *b* Bern, 8 Aug., 1909; *s* of Friedrich Hofer; *m* Gertrud Wild, Dr.-phil. *Educ.:* Bern, Elementary School and Gymnasium; *studied art* history at Univ. of Bern under Prof. Artur Weese and H. R. Hahnloser, Univ. of Munich under Prof. Wilhelm Pinder. *Publications:* Die Italienische Landschaft im 16. Th. (1946), Die Kunstdenkmäler des Kantons Bern, Vol. I, Basle (1952), Vol. II, Basle (1959), Vol. III, Basle (1947), Vol. V, Basle (1969); Die Wehrbauten Berns (1953), Flugbild der Schweizer Stadt (with Prof. Hans Boesch, Univ. of Zürich, 1963), Palladios Erstling (1968), Fundplätze, Bauplätze (1970), Die Frühzeit von Aarberg (1973), Die Stadtanlage von Thun im 12 und 13 Jahr hundert (1981), Die Burg Nydegg in Bern (1991), Spätbarock in Bern (1992). *Address:* Villettegässchen 32b, Muri near Bern.

HOFFER, Francis Peter Bernard, Dip.Arch., F.C.S.D., F.F.B.; architect/ designer, painter; hon. sec., Society of Mural Painters (1948-51); *b* Berlin, 1924; *s* of Dr. W. Hoffer; *m* Maria Pilar Perez Vales; three children. *Educ.:* Bunce Court School, Kent; *studied art* St. Martin's School of Art, London, and Cambridge. *Exhib.:* R.B.A., Leicester Gallery, Arts Council, Amsterdam, Milan. *Work in permanent collections:* U.S. Theatre Library, Washington and private collections. *Work repro.:* Das Kunstwerk, Gebrauchsgraphik, Designers in Britain, Studio, Domus, Architectural Review, Architectur und Wohnen, Abitare. *Address:* 16 Downshire Hill, London NW3. *Signs work:* "F. P. Hoffer."

HOFFMANN, Edith, Ph.D., Munich, 1934; art historian and critic; editorial asst. Burlington Magazine (1938-46); asst. editor of the Burlington Magazine (1946-50); Lecturer, Hebrew University of Jerusalem (1960-61); art editor of the Encyclopaedia Hebraica (Jerusalem, 1953-65); *d* of Camill Hoffmann, author; *m* Dr. E. Yapou; one *d. Educ.:* in Berlin, Vienna, Munich. *Publications:* Kokoschka: Life and Work (1947); Chagall: Water-colours (1947); contributions to the Burlington Magazine, Apollo, Art News (New York), Phoebus (Basle), Studio, Manchester Guardian, Listener, New Statesman, Twentieth Century, Neue Zürcher Zeitung, etc. *Address:* Alfasi St. 27, 92 302 Jerusalem, Israel.

HOFLEHNER, Rudolf; skulpturen and painter; Professor an der Akademie der bildenden Künste, Stuttgart; skulpturen in Eisen, massiv; *b* Linz, 8 Aug., 1916; *s* of Johann Hoflehner; *m* Luise Schaffer. *Studied art* at Akademie der bild. Künste, Vienna. *Addresses:* Italien, Val d'Elsa, Podere Pantaneto, Provincia Siena.; Ottensteinstrasse 62, 2344 Maria Enzersdorf-Südstadt, Österreich. *Signs work:* see appendix.

HOGAN, Prof. Eileen, M.A. (R.C.A.), R.W.S.; painter; Dean, Camberwell College of Arts; *b* London, 1 Mar., 1946; *m* Ken Ersser. *Educ.:* Streatham Hill and Clapham High School; *studied art* at Camberwell School of Art and Crafts (1964-67), British School of Archaeology at Athens, Royal College of Art (1971-74, Carel Weight). *Exhib.:* regularly at the Fine Art Soc., numerous one-man shows in Europe and America. *Work in permanent collections:* V. & A., Imperial War Museum, R.A., and overseas museums and galleries. *Publications:* 'A Selection of Poems' by C. P. Cavafy, numerous private press publications. *Address:* 31 Pretoria Rd., London SW16 6RR. *Clubs:* Chelsea Arts, Double Crown. *Signs work:* "Eileen Hogan."

HOGARTH, Arthur Paul, O.B.E., R.A., Dr. R.C.A., R.D.I.; illustrator, printmaker and draughtsman; senior tutor, Royal College of Art (1964-71), visiting lecturer (1971-85), *b* Kendal, Cumbria, 4 Oct., 1917; *s* of Arthur Hogarth. *Studied art at* Manchester School of Art and St Martin's School of Art, London. *Exhib.:* regularly at Francis Kyle Gallery, London. *Official purchases:* Library of Congress, Washington D.C., Boston Public Library (U.S.), Fitzwilliam Museum, Cambridge, Imperial War Museum, V. & A., B.M. *Works in permanent collections* include: city art galleries of Bradford, Bury, Blackburn, Carlisle, Kendal, Manchester, Newcastle-on-Tyne. *Publications* include: Creative Pencil Drawing (1964), Drawing Architecture (1973), Arthur Boyd Houghton (1981), Artist as Reporter (revised enlarged edn., 1986); illustrator of Brendan Behan's Island and Brendan Behan's New York (with Brendan Behan); Majorca Observed (with Robert Graves); Russian Journey (with Alaric Jacob); America Observed (with Stephen Spender); Graham Greene Country (with Graham Greene); The Mediterranean Shore (with Lawrence Durrell). *Address:* c/o Tessa Sayle, 11 Jubilee Pl., London SW3 3TE. *Signs work:* "Paul Hogarth" or "P.H."

HOLCH, Eric Sanford; artist in oil, printmaker of limited edition serigraphs; *b* Andover, Mass., 17 Sept., 1948; *s* of Carl E. Holch and Rita S. Holch, sculptress; *m* Elspeth R. Holch; one *s*, one *d. Educ.:* Trinity-Pawling School; *studied art* at Hobart College (1969-70), mostly self taught in serigraphy. *Exhib.:* one-man shows: Gallery 39, Osaka, Japan (1990), Martha Lincoln Gallery, Florida (1987), The Little Gallery, Nantucket (1986), D. Christian James Gallery, N.J. (1985), Portfolio Gallery, C.T. (1982-87), *Work in permanent collections:* Champion International, Chesebrough-Ponds, E. F. Hutton, First National Bank of Boston, Merrill Lynch, Societé General. *Address:* 49 Gerrish La., New Canaan, C.T. 06840, U.S.A. *Signs work:* "Eric Holch."

HOLISTER, Frederick Darnton, M.A. (Cantab.) (1957), M.Arch. Harvard (1953), A.R.I.B.A., Wheelwright Fellowship, Harvard (1952); Fellow, Clare College, Cambridge; Director of Studies in Architecture, Clare College, Cambridge; University Lecturer, Department of Land Economy, Cambridge University; architect in private practice; Consultant Architect to Clare College, Cambridge, Consultant Architect to University of Buckingham; *b* Coventry, 14 Aug., 1927; *s* of F. D. Holister, M.I.Mech.E.; *m* Patricia Ogilvy Reid (marriage dissolved); two *s*, two *d. Educ.:* Bablake School; *studied art* at Birmingham School of Architecture under A. Douglas Jones (1944-46, 1948-51), Harvard

University under Prof. Walter Gropius (1951-53). *Address:* Clare College, Cambridge CB2 1TL.

HOLLAND, Claerwen Belinda, N.D.D. (1964); David Murray landscape studentship (1963); artist in ink, water-colour, pastel and oils; *b* Cwmdauddwr, 4 Mar., 1942; *d* of Sir Jim Sothern Holland, Bt. *Educ.:* Miss Lambert's School, Queens Gdns., London; *studied art* at Byam Shaw School of Art (1960-64, Maurice de Sausmarez). *Exhib.:* R.A., N.E.A.C., Bath Contemporary Art Fair (1991); one-man shows: Sue Rankin Gallery (1990, 1992), Countryworks Gallery, Montgomeryshire (1990, 1992). *Work in permanent collection:* The Library, University College, Cardiff. *Publication:* illustrations to A Year and a Day by J.L.G. Holland (Hodder and Stoughton). *Address:* Dderw, Cwmdauddwr, Rhayader, Powys LD6 5EY. *Signs work:* "C.B. Holland."

HOLLAND, Harry; artist in oil on canvas, printmaking; *b* Glasgow, 11 Apr., 1941; *m* Maureen; two *d. Educ.:* Rutlish School, Merton; *studied art* at St. Martin's School of Art (1964-69). *Exhib.:* extensively in Britain, France, Belgium, U.S.A.; one-man shows: Jill George Gallery (1990, 1992, 1994); retrospective travelling Britain Nov. 1991–Jan. 1993. *Work in permanent collections:* Newport Museum and A.G., National Museum of Wales, Tate Gallery Print Coll. *Publication:* Painter in Reality (1991). *Address:* c/o Jill George Gallery, 38 Lexington St., London W1R 3HR. *Club:* Chelsea Arts. *Signs work:* "Harry Holland."

HOLLAWAY, Antony Lynn, A.T.D. (1953), A.R.C.A. (1956), F.R.S.A., F.C.S.D.; stained glass designer; *b* Kinson, Dorset, 1928. *Educ.:* Poole Grammar School; *studied art:* Bournemouth College of Art, and R.C.A., London. *Exhib.:* Whitechapel Gallery, John Moores Liverpool and in U.S.A. *Work in permanent collections* include collection of Baroness Alix de Rothschild Paris, and others. *Work repro.:* Architectural Press and elsewhere. Major new work designing and making new stained glass for Manchester Cathedral. *Address:* Home Farm House, Bottesford Rd., Allington, nr. Grantham, Lincs. NG32 2DH. *Signs work:* "Hollaway."

HOLLEDGE, Bryan Raymond, A.R.C.A., F.R.S.A., M.I.P.R., A.F.B.A.; part-time lecturer, Hammersmith School of Art (1949); part-time teacher, St. Hubert's Special School, Brook Green; lecturer, London School of Printing and Graphic Arts; part-time teacher, Chelsea School of Art; graphic designer, Metal Box (1955); Head of Graphics, Swiss Co. Sulzer Bros. (1958); freelance corporate design/mural, Chelsea Arts Club (1950); *b* Ealing, Middx., 1919; *s* of Raymond John Holledge, interior designer and decorator; *m* Maria Haid; two *d. Educ.:* Ealing College; *studied art* at Ealing College of Art (1937-40); H.M.F. 1940-46; Royal College of Art (1946-49). *Exhib.:* painting in National Gallery Exhbn. for Young Artists, Whitechapel Gallery (1953), Arts Council U.K. tour, Mural painting, Shipping Co. and Theatres joint exhbn., London (1984); one-man show, London (1955) in assoc. with Atomic Energy Soc. Exhib. regularly at London galleries for painting/etching/wood engraving. A Companion of Western Europe Dip. *Address:* 5 The Green, Feltham, Middx. *Signs work:* "Bryan R. Holledge."

HOLLICK, Kenneth Russell, F.C.S.D.; designer; mem. of the Designers and Art Directors Assoc. of London; *b* Essex, 5 Jan., 1923. *Studied art and design* at Central School of Arts and Crafts. *Work repro.:* trade marks, symbols, logotypes, corporate identity programmes, vehicle livery, booklets, packaging, exhibition stands, display panels, industrial photography. Designs shown in books on graphic design published in Japan, Italy, Switzerland and Britain. *Address:* 4 Knighton House, 102 Manor Way, Blackheath, London SE3 9AN.

HOLLOWAY, Edgar, R.E., R.B.A.; painter, etcher; *b* 6 May, 1914; *m* (1) Daisy Hawkins; three *s,* one *d*; (2) Jennifer Boxall. *Exhib.:* one-man shows, London (1931, 1934, 1979, 1993), Brighton and Oxford (1980), Doncaster (1982), Edinburgh (1986), Abergavenny (1989), U.S.A. (1972, 1973, 1974, 1975); retrospective Ashmolean (1991-92). *Official purchases:* B.M., V. & A., Ashmolean, Fitzwilliam, New York Public Library, Birmingham City A.G., Scottish Gallery of Modern Art, Scottish National Portrait Gallery, National Museum of Wales, National Library of Wales, University College of Wales, Oxford and Cambridge colleges. *Work repro.:* Dictionary of 20th Century British Art (1991), British Printmakers, 1855-1955. *Address:* Woodbarton, Ditchling Common, Sussex BN6 8TP.

HOLT, Gwynneth, F.R.B.S.; sculptor in wood, ivory, bronze, terra-cotta; *b* Wednesbury, Staffs., 18 Jan., 1909; *d* of Benjamin Holt. *Educ.:* St. Anne's Convent, Birmingham; Wolverhampton School of Art. *Exhib.:* R.A., R.S.A., R.B.S.A., S.P.S. *Work in permanent collections:* Newport (Mon.) Art Gallery, Aberdeen Art Gallery, Wolverhampton Art Gallery, Hopkins Center, Hanover, N.H., U.S.A., Leamington Art Gallery; many churches in Essex, East Mission Stepney, London, Balsham Church, Cambridge; Eynsham Parish Church, Buxhall Church, and St. Felix School, Southwold, Suffolk. *Address:* Cobden, Queen St., Eynsham, Oxford OX8 1HH. *Signs work:* "GWYNNETH HOLT."

HOLTAM, Brenda, R.W.S., B.F.A.Hons. (1983), R.A. Schools Postgraduate Dip. (1986); painter in oil, gouache, water-colour; *b* Whiteway, Glos., 2 Oct., 1960. *Educ.:* Stroud Girls' High School; *studied art* at Glos. College of Art and Design (1979, T. Murphy), Falmouth School of Art (1980-83, F. Hewlett), R.A. Schools (1983-86, Peter Greenham, C.B.E., R.A.). *Exhib.:* Newlyn Orion Gallery (1981), R.A. Summer Exhbn. (1985-88), R.W.S. Members Exhbn. Bankside (1987-93), N.E.A.C. Annual Exhbn. (1987-92), 20th Century British Art Fair (1988, 1989). Elected Associate of Royal Soc. of Painters in Water-colour (1987), elected to full membership (1992). Figurative painter of landscapes, still life, interiors and portraits. *Address:* 29 Hayter Rd., London SW2 5AR. *Signs work:* "Brenda Holtam" or "Holtam."

HOMER, Sidney Frederick, A.R.B.S.A. (1969), R.B.S.A. (1975); painter in water-colour and oil; graphic artist/illustrator (retd.); *b* 15 Feb., 1912; *s* of F. W. Homer; *m* Ethel May; one *s*. *Studied art* at Advertising Art Studio, Birmingham College of Art (B. Fleetwood-Walker, R.A., Gilbert Mason). *Exhib.:* R.B.S.A., B'ham Water-colour Soc., B'ham Art Circle, Ombersley Gallery, Helious Pictures, R.S.P.W.C. (Open Exhbn.), R.I., Laing, Sunday Times/Singer Friedlander, etc. *Work in permanent collection:* Dudley A. G. *Address:* 94 Bakers La., Sutton Coldfield, W. Midlands B74 2BA. *Signs work:* "HOMER."

HOMES, Ronald Thomas John, D.F.C., F.C.S.D.; artist/industrial designer; winner of R.S.A. industrial design bursaries (1948-49); Central School of Arts and Crafts Dip for Industrial Design; *b* London, 3 Oct., 1922; *s* of Arthur Leopold Homes; *m* Ione Winifred Amelia; two *d*. *Educ.:* Willesden Technical College; *studied art* at Central School of Arts and Crafts. *Address:* 69 Linden Pk., Shaftesbury, Dorset SP7 8RN. *Signs work:* see appendix.

HOMESHAW, Arthur Howard, R.W.A., A.T.D.; artist in water-colour, pastel, colour prints; *b* 27 Nov., 1933; *m* Wendy Bennetto; two *s*. *Educ.:* Chipping

Sodbury Grammar School; *studied art* at West of England College of Art (1951-54, 1956-57). *Exhib.:* R.A., R.W.A., R.E.; one-man show, Patricia Wells Gallery (1981). *Work in permanent collections:* R.W.A., Bristol Educ. Com., Devon County Hall, Stoke-on-Trent Educ. Com., Exeter University, Exeter Arts Centre. *Address:* Arwen, Alexandra Rd., Crediton, Devon EX17 2DH. *Signs work:* "HOMESHAW."

HONE, David, P.P.R.H.A., Hon. R.A., H.R.S.A.; portrait and landscape painter in oil; *b* Dublin, 1928; *s* of Joseph M. Hone, biographer; *m* Rosemary D'Arcy; two *s*, one *d*. *Educ.:* St. Columba's College; Univ. College, Dublin; *studied art* at National College of Art, Dublin (1947-50), under J. Keating and M. MacGonical. *Work in permanent collections:* Portrait Collection, National Gallery, Dublin, Cork Municipal Gallery. *Address:* 25 Lr. Baggot St., Dublin, 2. *Signs work:* "D. Hone."

HOODLESS, Harry Taylor, A.R.C.A. (1936), A.T.D. (1933); painter in oil, tempera and water-colour, etcher; Princ., Laird School of Art, Birkenhead (1946-76); *b* 29 June, 1913; *s* of William Hoodless; *m* Hilda Lilian Grimes; three *s*. *Educ.:* Leeds Central High School; Leeds College of Art (D.S. Andrews, A.R.C.A., S.G.A., 1929-33); R.C.A. (P.H. Jowett, A.R.C.A., E.W. Tristram, A.R.C.A., 1933-36). *Exhib.:* R.A. and provinces. *Official purchases:* W.A.G., Liverpool, Williamson Art Gallery, Birkenhead, Liverpool University. *Address:* Craigroy, Village Rd., West Kirby, Wirral, Merseyside. *Signs work:* "HOODLESS" (on oil and tempera) and "Hoodless" (water-colours and etchings).

HOOKE, Robert Lowe, Jr.; sculptor of figures, wild animals and birds in bronze; gallery owner; investment banker; Managing Director: Art Scene Ltd.; R. Hooke and Partners Ltd.; Research Vision Ltd.; *b* Canton, Ohio, 12 Sept., 1942; *s* of Robert Hooke, industry executive. *Educ.:* Bowdoin College, Brunswick, Maine (B.A.); Columbia University, N.Y. (M.B.A.); *studied art* at N.Y. School of Visual Arts (1973-75, Herbert Kallem). *Exhib.:* one-man shows: London, Geneva, Basel, Sydney, Johannesburg, Capetown; group shows: Paris, Zurich, Amsterdam, San Francisco. *Work in permanent collections:* Compton Acres, Poole; Oppenheimer Collection, S. Africa. *Address:* 61 Holland Pk., London W11. *Signs work:* see appendix.

HOOPER, George; Rome Scholarship in Mural Painting (1935), R.A. Gold Medal and Travelling Scholarship (1933); artist in oil and water-colour; lecturer at Brighton College of Art; *b* Gorakhpur, India, 1910; *s* of A.P. Hooper; *m* Joyce Gayford. *Studied art* at Slade School (1931-32), R.A. Schools (1932-35), Rome Scholarship (1935-38). *Exhib.:* R.A., N.E.A.C., Leicester Galleries, Wildenstein's Gallery, Odette Gilbert Gallery, Sally Hunter Gallery, Hooper Gallery, St. John's Wood. *Official purchases:* Contemporary Art Soc., Recording Britain Pilgrim Trust Grant, V. & A., Towner A.G., Eastbourne, Brighton A.G., Ferens A.G., Hull, Hertford College, Oxford, Reading University. *Publications:* articles in The Artist. *Address:* 10 Regent Cres., Redhill RH1 1JN. *Signs work:* see appendix.

HOPE HENDERSON, Eleanora, D.A., S.S.A., Post Grad. Scholarship, Guthrie Award (1940); artist in oil; *b* Edinburgh, 1917; *d* of Major David A. Spence, farmer and land agent; *m* David Hope Henderson; two *s*. *Educ.:* St. George's, Edinburgh; *studied art* at Edinburgh College of Art under Sir William Gillies, Sir W. Mac'Taggart, Westwater, Maxwell. *Exhib.:* S.S.A., R.S.A., R.A., R.P., Dumfries Art Soc., McGill Duncan Gallery and Harbour Gallery, Kircudbrightshire; one-man shows: Chelsea A.G., Kirkcudbright A.G.; Woodstock and Pittenweem A.G's. Work in private collections. *Address:* Achie, New Galloway, Kircudbrightshire. *Signs work:* "E. Hope Henderson", before marriage "BORRIE."

HOPKINS, Clyde David F., B.F.A.(Hons.) (1969); painter in oil on linen, wood, canvas; lecturer; Head of Painting, Chelsea College of Art; *b* Sussex, 26 Sept., 1946; *s* of Paul Hopkins, teacher and cricketer; *m* Marilyn Hallam. *Educ.:* Barrow-in-Furness, Cumbria; *studied art* at University of Reading (Claude Rogers, Terry Frost). *Exhib.:* Serpentine Gallery, Hayward Gallery, Ikon Gallery, Francis Graham-Dixon Gallery, Joan Prats Gallery, N.Y.C., etc. *Work in permanent collections:* A.C.G.B., etc. *Address:* 55 Marischal Rd., London SE13 5LE. *Club:* G.A.S.A. *Signs work:* "Clyde Hopkins."

HOPKINS, Peter; painter, teacher, writer; Dean of Men, Emeritus, New York-Phoenix School of Design; Lecturer, Art Students League of New York; grantee, American Academy and National Institute of Arts and Letters (1950); Correspondent, Christian Science Monitor; *b* New York, 1911; *s* of Charles R. Hopkins; *m* Gertrude L. Beach. *Educ.:* Art Students League of New York. *Work in permanent collection:* Museum of City of New York. *Works reproduced:* The American Heritage History of the 1920s and 1930s; The USA, a History in Art; The Complete Book of Painting Techniques. *Address:* 36 Horatio St., New York, N.Y. 10014, U.S.A.

HORE, Richard Peter Paul, A.R.C.A. (Painting 1959, Mural Painting, Silver Medal 1960), N.D.D. (Illustration 1955), F.R.S.A. (1964), R.C.A. (Cambrian 1978); painter in gouache and mixed media; Lecturer, Wrexham College of Art; *b* Clacton-on-Sea, 1935; *m* Janice Hart; one *s*, one *d*. *Educ.:* Colebaynes High School, Clacton; *studied art* at Colchester School of Art (1951-55, John O'Conner), R.C.A. (1956-60, Carel Weight, Ruskin Spear, Leonard Rosoman). *Exhib.:* R.A.; Minories, Colchester; Welsh Arts Council; W.A.G., Liverpool; Mostyn, Llandudno; Artist in an Industrial Landscape, N. Wales Arts. *Work in permanent collections:* R.C.A., Cheshire and Clwyd C.C., National Maritime Museum, Dept. of the Environment, various private collections. *Address:* 65 Parkgate Rd., Chester, Ches. *Signs work:* "RICHARD HORE."

HORNBY, Anna, N.E.A.C. (1971); Mem. A.W.G. (1967); painter in oil, tempera and water-colour, calligrapher; *b* 6 Apr., 1914. *Educ.:* Weston Birt School, Glos.; *studied art* in Florence with Aubrey Waterfield (1934), and at Byam Shaw School (1934-40, F. Ernest Jackson, A.R.A.). *Exhib.:* R.A., R.B.A., N.E.A.C., R.P., R.W.A., etc. Founder mem., first Hon. Sec. of the Society for Italic Handwriting (1952). *Address:* Rose Cottage, Upper Slaughter, Cheltenham, Glos. GL54 2JQ. *Signs work:* "A.H."

HORNE, Cleeve, R.C.A., O.S.A., S.S.C.; pres. Ontario Soc. of Artists (1949-51); painter, sculptor and artist consultant; *b* Jamaica, B.W.I., 9 Jan., 1912; *s* of A. C. W. Horne; *m* Jean Horne (sculptor); three *s*. *Educ.:* England and Canada; *studied art:* sculpture under D. Dick of England (1928); painting at Ontario College of Art, Toronto (1930); R.A.I.C. Allied Arts Medal for 1963; Europe in 1936. *Exhib.:* Canada, U.S.A. and England. *Work in permanent collections:* portraits of leading Canadians; memorials and architectural sculpture. *Address:* 181 Balmoral Ave., Toronto, Canada M4V 1J8. *Clubs:* Art and Letters (Pres. 1956-57), York Club. *Signs work:* "Cleeve Horne."

HOROVITZ, Isabel, B.A.(Hons.) (1978), Dip.Cons. (1982); paintings conservator; freelance conservator and consultant to Royal Academy of Arts; *b* London, 1957; *m* Jonathan Blake; three *s*, one *d*. *Educ.:* St. Paul's Girls' School;

studied art at University of London (History of Art), Courtauld Inst. of Art (Conservation of Easel Paintings). *Exhib.:* Conservator for R.A. Loans Exhbns. *Publications:* contributions to various catalogues and conservation literature. *Address:* The Painting Conservation Studio, Belgravia Workshops, Marlborough Rd., London N19 4NP.

HORSBRUGH, Patrick B., A.A. (Hons.) Dipl., F.A.I.A., A.C.I.P., A.P.A., F.R.G.S., F.R.S.A., F.B.I.S.; Hon. Mem. A.S.L.A.; Hon. Mem. A.I.I.D.; architect; town planner and artist in ink, water-colour, gouache, etc.; Visiting Prof. of Architecture, Universities of Nebraska and Texas; organized Texas Conference on Our Environmental Crisis (1966) and International Conference, Cities in Context; Cultural, Ethical and Natural (1968); Chairman of the Board, Environic Foundation International Inc; V.P., Channel Tunnel Assoc.; Co-chairman, Earthday (International); Prof. Emeritus of Architecture, Former Director of Graduate Programme in Environic Design, University of Notre Dame; *b* Belfast, 21 June, 1920. *Educ.:* Canford and A.A., School of Architecture, Dept. of Civic Design, University of London. *Address:* 916 St. Vincent St., South Bend, Indiana 46617, U.S.A. *Signs work:* "Patrick Horsbrugh."

HORSNELL, Walter Cecil; Academician of Italy (1981) Gold Medallist; Premio d'Italia award Cremona (1986); painter in oil, pastel and watercolour of landscapes, figures and portraits; designer of art film production presentation; Photographic Reconnaissance R.A.F. (1941); Official Technical Illustrator Min. of Aircraft Production (1942-47); *b* Ware, Herts, 18 Dec., 1911; *s* of John Horsnell; *m* Kathleen Chappel (neé Leslie); two *s*, two *d. Educ.:* Musley Secondary School, Ware; *studied art* at St. Martin's and Bolt Court Schools of Art. *Exhib.:* R.A., R.B.A., National Portrait Gallery (1944), Municipal Galleries of Blackpool, Bradford, Brighton, Harrogate, Keighley, Leeds, Wakefield, Yorkshire Arts Association (1974), Rural Preservation Association, Edinburgh, Liverpool (1977), and other provincial galleries; one-man shows, Harrogate Festival of Arts 1970 and in various galleries. *Work in permanent collections:* Grundy Gallery Blackpool (oil) and private collections in Australia, British Isles, (including Lambeth Palace, London and Canterbury Palace, Kent), Canada, Chile, Denmark, France, Germany, Holland, India, Italy, Kenya, New Zealand, Norway, United States of America, South Africa, Spain, Switzerland, Yugoslavia. *Official purchases:* Blackpool Corporation, Coal Board, Milk Marketing Board, Football Association, West Riding of Yorkshire Educ. Cttee. (Misterton School), Scargill House C. of E. Council (presentation: Archbishop of York), National Westminster Bank, Barclays Bank, Midland Bank, Risparmio Bank Italy, Alliance Building Society, Wakefield Hospital Cttee., North-Eastern Electricity Board, Nidderdale R.D.C., Parents-Teachers Association (Bilton Grange School), British Poliomyelitis Fellowship, Harrogate General Hospital, Mary Fisher Home, Harrogate College (3 works). *Works include:* "Bishopthorpe, Palace of the Archbishop of York" (Dr. D. Coggan) (1970); "Wharfedale Landscape" (Sir Michael Blundell K.B.E.) (1971); "Autumn on the River Ouse" (Archbishop of Canterbury) (1976); "Low Bridge, Knaresborough" (Lord Mills) (1981); "Trees, Lambeth Palace" (Lady Jean Coggan) (1980); "Wensleydale" (Coun. Brenda Towler, Harrogate Mayor) (1985); "The River Ure, West Tanfield" (Winchester Cathedral Endowment) (1991-1993). *Work repro.:* in Ambassador Magazine, Ford Times, R.A.F. Supply Magazine, Evening Post, Yorkshire Post, First Prize Poster Design Min. of Defence 1975, publications for John Waddington, Gratton (Bradford), Sampietro Italy, technical publications for H.M. Government, Dizionario Internazionale Degli Artisti Contemporanei, Knaresborough Post, Royle Print, Who's Who in the World (Marquis, New Jersey 07974 U.S.A.,

1993-1994). *Address:* Studio, 89 Knox Ave., Harrogate, North Yorkshire HG1 3JF. *Signs work:* "Walter Horsnell", see appendix.

HORTON, Antony Brian; landscape painter in oil and gouache; *b* Birmingham, 21 Aug., 1933; *s* of E. Victor Horton, M.C., J.P.; *m* Sheila Horton; three *d.* *Educ.:* Shrewsbury School and Exeter College, Oxford; *studied art* at Cheltenham College of Art (R.S. Dent). *Exhib.:* R.A., David Messum Gallery, and local exhbns. *Address:* The Old Rectory, Taplow, Bucks. SL6 0ET. *Club:* M.C.C. *Signs work:* "A. B. Horton" or "Brian Horton."

HORTON, Ernest Charles, R.B.S.A. (1988); artist in oil, pastel, water-colour; Curator, Royal Birmingham Soc. of Artists; *b* 8 Jan., 1935; *s* of Ernest William Horton, printers compositor; *m* Maureen; one *s*, one *d.* *Studied art* at Moseley Rd. School of Art (C.H. Adams, E. Mason), Margaret St. College of Art, B'ham (R. Ball). *Exhib.:* R.B.S.A., P.S., R.W.A., also Germany, France, Italy, New York, Hong Kong. *Work in permanent collection:* R.B.S.A. *Address:* 29 Redacre Rd., Sutton Coldfield, W. Midlands B73 5EE. *Clubs:* B'ham Art Circle (Past Pres.), Sutton Coldfield Soc. of Art (Past Pres.), B'ham Water-colour Soc., B'ham Easel, R.B.S.A. *Signs work:* "E.C. Horton."

HORWITZ, Angela Joan, N.S. (1982), R.A.S. (1983); sculptress in stone, bronze, painter in oil and pastel; steward, A.G.B.I. (1985-86); *b* London, 14 Oct., 1934; *d* of the late M. Carson; two *s*, one *d.* *Educ.:* Colet Court Girls' School, Rosemead Wales, Lycée Français de Londres; *studied art* at Marylebone Inst. (1978), Sir John Cass College (1983). *Exhib.:* Grand Palais, Paris (1985, 1986), R.B.A., N.S., S.W.A. (Mall Galleries), Civic Centre, Southend, S.E.F.A.S., Guildhall, Ridley Soc., City of Westminster Arts Council, Alpine Gallery, Smiths Gallery Covent Gdn., Wintershall Gallery, nr. Guildford, The Orangery, Holland Pk. W8, Hyde Park Gallery (Winchester Cathedral, 1993). *Work in permanent collection:* Sculpture in stone for Winchester Cathedral. *Address:* 6 Wellington House, Aylmer Drive, Stanmore, Middx. HA7 3ES. *Signs work:* "A.H." or "Angela Horwitz."

HOSKINS, Stephen, M.A. (1981), A.R.E. (1989), B.A. (Hons.) (1977); printmaker in silkscreen, lithography and drawing; *b* Eastleigh, Hants., 31 Aug., 1955; *m* Barbara Munns; one *s.* *Educ.:* Barton Peverk Grammar School; *studied art* at W. Surrey College of Art and Design (1974-77), R.C.A. (1978-81). *Exhib.:* R.A., R.E., mixed exhbns. worldwide. *Work in permanent collection:* V. &. A. *Publication:* 5[3] A pop-up book. *Address:* 62 Monk Rd., Bishopston, Bristol BS7 8NE. *Signs work:* "S. Hoskins."

HOUSE, Ceri Charles; artist in oil; gilding restorer; *b* London, 20 Mar., 1963; *partner* Amanda Wainwright; one *d.* *Educ.:* St. Christopher School, Herts.; *studied art* with father, Gordon House. *Exhib.:* R.A. Summer Shows (1992, 1993). Numerous private commissions. *Publication:* R.A. Illustrated catalogue (1993). *Address:* 109 Highbury New Park, London N5 2HG. *Signs work:* see appendix.

HOUSTON, Ian, A.R.C.M., President, East Anglian Group of Marine Artists, Associate, French Soc. of Artists, F.R.S.A.; Silver medal, Paris Salon, Gold medal, F.N.C.F.; artist in oil and water-colour; *b* Gravesend, Kent, 24 Sept., 1934; *s* of Angus Houston; *m* Angela Adams; one *s*, one *d.* *Educ.:* St. Lawrence College, R.C.M., London. *Exhib.:* over 30 one-man shows U.K., U.S.A., Australia. Official artist to "Young Endeavour"; limited edition prints, 15 signed by Premiers Thatcher and Hawke, sold to raise funds for project. *Work in* *collections:* U.K. and abroad. *Address:* c/o Polak Gallery, 21 King St., London SW1. *Signs work:* "Ian Houston."

HOWARD, Ian, M.A. (Hons.), A.R.S.A.; artist in acrylic, oil, mixed media, printmaking; Head of Painting, Duncan of Jordanstone College of Art, Dundee; Director, Alba Magazine; *b* Aberdeen, 1952; *s* of H.G.Howard; *m* Ruth D'Arcy; two *d. Educ.:* Aberdeen Grammar School; *studied art* at Edinburgh University, Edinburgh College of Art (1970-76). *Exib.:* numerous one-man and group exhbns. *Work in permanent collections:* S.A.C., A.C.G.B., Aberdeen A.G., Dundee A.G., Hunterian A.G., City Art Centre Edinburgh, Contemporary Art Soc., Warwick University Art Centre. *Publication:* Ian Howard, Painting, Prints and Related Works (Third Eye Centre Glasgow/Peacock Printmakers, Aberdeen). *Address:* 66 Camphill Rd., Broughty Ferry, Dundee DD5 2LX. *Signs work:* "I.H." or "Ian Howard."

HOWARD, James Campbell, S.G.A.; artist in oil and water-colour; *b* London, 26 Oct., 1906; *s* of James Wilson Howard; *m* Frances Maud Howard; two *s. Studied art:* self-taught. *Exhib.:* R.A., R.I. *Address:* 95 Dale Ave., Hassocks, W. Sussex. *Club:* Langham Sketch. *Signs work:* "J. C. HOWARD" (followed by date).

HOWARD, Ken, R.A. (1992), Hon. R.B.S.A. (1991), R.W.S. (1983), R.W.A. (1981), R.O.I. (1965), N.E.A.C. (1961); *b* London, 26 Dec., 1932; *s* of Frank Howard. *Educ.:* Kilburn Grammar School; *studied art* at Hornsey College of Art (1949-53), Royal College of Art (1955-58). *Exhib.:* New Grafton Gallery (1971, 74, 76, 78, 81, 83, 86, 88, 90, 93), Oscar Peter Johnson Ltd. (1987, 88, 89, 90, 91, 92, 93). Appointed Official Artist Northern Ireland Imperial War Museum (1973-78). *Address:* 8 South Bolton Gdns., London SW5 6DH. *Signs work:* "Ken Howard."

HOWARD-JONES, Ray, Fine Art Dip. University of London, Slade Scholar; 1st class Hons. History of Art; painter, poet, mosaics; *b* Lambourne, Berks., 30 May, 1903; *d* of Capt. Hubert Stanley-Howard-Jones, R.A.V.C., M.R.C.V.S. *Educ.:* London Garden School; *studied art* at Slade School, University of London (1921) under Henry Tonks, Wilson Steer, Elliot-Smith (anatomy), Tancred Borenius (History of Art); Postgraduate School of Painting, Arbroath. *Work in permanent collections:* National Museum of Wales, National Museum of S. Australia, Glynn Vivian Gallery Swansea, Contemporary Art Society, Museum and Gallery Glasgow, Imperial War Museum, Arts Council for Wales, M. of W., City Art Galleries of Aberdeen, Glasgow, Burton-on-Trent, large mosaic— exterior Thomson House Cardiff and Grange Church Edinburgh. *Publication:* Heart of The Rock Poems 1973-92 (Rocket Press, 1993). *Work repro.:* various contributions to The Anglo-Welsh Review. *Addresses:* Studio House, 29 Ashchurch Park Villas, London W12; St. Martin's Haven, Marloes, W. Wales. Agents: Rocket Contemporary Art, Blewbury, Didcot, Oxon. *Signs work:* "Ray."

HOWARTH, Constance M., B. of E. intermed. (1946), N.D.D. (1947); winner, Vogue Cotton Design Competition 1960 designer hand painted dresses; *b* Rochdale, Lancs., 14 May, 1927; *d* of Edward Howarth, civil servant. *Educ.:* Merchant Taylors' School for Girls, Crosby; Bolton School; *studied art* at Manchester Regional College of Art. *Exhib.:* Rayon Design Centre, London. *Work in permanent collections:* V. & A. New works: mixed media abstract mirror windows, wall scenics and ornamental flower trees. *Address:* 17 Upper Wimpole St., London W1 7TB. *Signs work:* "Constance Howarth" and "Constanza."

HOWELLS, Patricia Frances, A.T.D. (1954), N.D.D. (1953); artist in oil and water-colour, teacher; Head of Art, St. John's-on-the-Hill; *b* London, 27 July, 1929. *Educ.:* P.N.E.U. Hazlemere, Brecon Grammar School; *studied art* at Cardiff College of Art, London Central St. Martin's College of Art. *Exhib.:* annually for S.B.A., S.W.A. Mall Galleries, Guernsey Coach House Gallery, University of Leicester, W.A.C., Museum of Wales, Gallery 20 Brighton, etc. *Address:* 5 Mount Pleasant, Chepstow, Gwent NP6 5PS. *Club:* S.B.A. *Signs work:* "PAT" with date of year.

HOWORTH, Nancy: landscape artist in oil; *b* 25 Mar., 1912; *d* of H. P. Peacock, M.A.; *m* John H. E. Howorth. *Educ.:* Eastbourne; *studied art* at Eastbourne School of Art (1930-32); and under Jon Peaty of Sussex (1963-66). *Exhib.:* one-man shows: Ditchling Gallery, Sackville Gallery, E. Grinstead; group shows: S.W.A., F.P.S., R.B.A.; Sussex galleries: Rye, Burwash, Ditchling, Seaford, Uckfield, etc. *Address:* Cornwells Cottage, N. Chailey, Sussex. *Clubs:* Assoc. of Sussex Artists, Attic, Ditchling, Adventurer's, Sussex.

HOWSON, Peter; painter in oil; *b* London, 27 Mar., 1958; *s* of Tom William Howson; *m* Terry; one *d. Educ.:* Prestwick Academy; *studied art* at Glasgow School of Art (1975-77 and 1979-81, Alexander Moffat). *Work in permanent collections:* Tate Gallery, V. & A., Metropolitan Museum of Modern Art, N.Y., M.O.M.A., N.Y., Oslo Museum of Modern Art, Glasgow Art Galleries. *Address:* c/o Flowers East, 199-205 Richmond Rd., London E8 3NY. *Signs work:* "Howson."

HOYLAND, John; artist; *b* Sheffield, 12 Oct., 1934; divorced; one *s. Studied art* at Sheffield College of Art (1951-56, Eric Jones), R.A. Schools (1956-60). *Exhib.:* numerous exhbns. including one-man: Marlborough New London Gallery, Whitechapel A.G., Waddington Galleries, Robert Elkon Gallery N.Y., Nicholas Wilder Gallery, Los Angeles, Andre Emmerich Gallery, N.Y., Austin Desmond Fine Art, London, also in Canada, Germany, Italy, Portugal, Australia, Sweden; two-man shows: Brazil, London, U.S.A.; group shows: R.A. Summer Exhbns., R.B.A. Gallery, John Moores, Liverpool, Ulster Museum, Belfast, Edinburgh Open, Chichester Natural Art, Barbican A.G., Francis Graham-Dixon Gallery, R.C.A., McLellan Galleries, Glasgow, etc. Television and radio broadcasts. *Publication:* John Hoyland (1990). *Address:* 41 Charterhouse Sq., London EC1M 6EA. *Signs work:* see appendix.

HUBBARD, Deirdre, B.A. (Summa cum Laude) (1957), A.R.B.S. (1981); Sohier prize (1957), Wapping Arts Trust 'Art and Work' (1987); sculptor in bronze; *b* N.Y.C., 1935; *d* of R.L. Hubbard, sculptor; *m* Dr. John L. Wilson; three *s,* one *d. Educ.:* Radcliffe College, Harvard University (1953-57); *studied art:* painting with Andreas Feininger (1954-55), Chelsea Art School (1957-61, sculpture with Willi Soukop and Bernard Meadows). *Exhib.:* R.A., R.B.S., R.W.A., Essex University, Bristol Cathedral, Camden Arts Centre, National Museum of Wales, Bloomsbury Gallery, Barbican Centre, etc. *Work in permanent collections:* Royal Free Hospital, Inst. of Educ. London University, Towner A.G., Usher Gallery, Lincoln. *Address:* 101 Woodsford Sq., London W14 8DT. *Signs work:* "D.H."

HUCKVALE, Iris, R.M.S., S.W.A., S.B.A., S.M.; miniaturist in oil on ivorine, wood, card; *b* Northampton, 27 Sept., 1930; *d* of Herbert Leeding; *m* John Huckvale, O.B.E.; one *s,* one *d. Educ.:* Northampton Grammar School for Girls; *studied art* at Nottinghamshire Evening Inst., but mainly self taught. *Exhib.:* R.A., R.M.S., S.W.A., S.B.A., S.WL.A., Medici, S.M., M.A.S.-F., M.A.S.-N.J.; one-man show, Coach House Gallery, Guernsey. *Work repro.:* Medici greetings cards. *Address:* 4 Heath Green, Heath and Reach, Leighton Buzzard, Beds. LU7 0AB. *Signs work:* see appendix.

HUDSON, Eleanor Erlund, R.W.S. (1949), R.E. (1946), A.R.C.A. (1937); graphic artist, portraitist, figure subjects, water-colourist; costume designer, artistic advisor to Brooking Ballet School, Marylebone; *b* S. Devon; *d* of Harold Hudson and Helen Ingeborg Olsen. *Educ.:* Wentworth Hall, Surrey; *studied art* at R.C.A. (School of Engraving) under Professors Malcolm Osborne, R.A., R. S. Austin, R.A., Drawing Prize, 1936, Continuation Schol. (4th year) 1938, Travelling Schol. 1939. *Exhib.:* R.A. and international. *Work in permanent collections:* Boston Pub. Library, Fogg Museum, U.S.A., Imperial War Museum, London. *Official purchases:* War Artist's Advisory Comm. *Address:* 6 Hammersmith Terr., London W6. *Signs work:* "ERLUND HUDSON."

HUDSON, Thomas Roger Jackson; Teachers' Cert. (1951), Teachers' Dip. (1961), M.Coll.H. (1962), Mem. A.W.G.; self employed furniture maker and designer; *b* Bicester, Oxon., 24 July, 1929; *s* of Frederick Thomas John Hudson; *m* Ragnhild Ann Schanche; one *s*, two *d*. *Educ.:* Bicester Grammar School; *studied art* at Oxford School of Art (1947), Shoreditch College (1949-51), Camberwell School of Art (1961), Goldsmiths' College (1962). *Publication:* Wheelstocks and Ploughshares (Tabb House, 1988). *Address:* The Barn, 117 High St., Odell, Bedford MK43 7AS. *Signs work:* carved into all major works (cow), see appendix.

HUGGLER, Max Melchior; Dr. Phil., Director of Museum of Fine Art, Berne; Director Kunsthalle Berne (1931); Director Kunstmuseum Berne (1944 until Mar., 1965); e.o. Prof. (since 1946) Univ. Berne; Mem. Federal Art Commission (1945-50); *b* Berne, 12 Oct., 1903. *Educ.:* Gym. Berne, Paris, Berlin. *Publications:* Schweizer Malerei im 19, Jahrhundert; Raoul Dufy; Paul Klee, die Malerei als Blick in den Kosmos, Huber Frauenfeld (1969), with 4 coloured and 34 black-and-white plates and 27 reproductions in the text. Catalogues of exhbns. Kunsthalle Berne and Berne Museum of Fine Art. *Address:* Sent CH (Switzerland).

HUGHES, Jim, D.A. (1954), S.G.A. (1972), A.T.C. (1955), T.G.C. (1956); artist/designer/calligrapher; teacher of art and design, Adult Educ. Dept., University of Glasgow; *b* Glasgow, 1934; *s* of Janet Orr, craftswoman. *Educ.:* Ayr Academy; *studied art* at Glasgow School of Art (1950-54); Jordanhill College (1954-56) under Sam Black, D.A., R.S.W. *Work in permanent collection:* Glasgow Art Gallery, other work in private collections throughout the world. *Publications:* Graphic Design for S.S.A.E. and Ayr Adult Educ. Booklets. Work featured in B.B.C. TV series "The Quest"(1989). *Address:* 32 Macadam Pl., Ayr KA8 0BZ. *Signs work:* initials on work, name on back, see appendix.

HUGHES, Kevin Michael, B.Sc. (1969), A.L.A. (1971); artist in water-colour, oil and pastel; *b* Colwyn Bay, 4 Sept., 1947; *m* Teresa Vonesch; one *s*, one *d*. *Educ.:* Reading University, Polytechnic of N. London; *studied art* at Balham and Clapham A.E.I. (1977-78, Caroline Clough). *Exhib.:* R.W.S., R.W.A.; one-man shows: many since 1980 including four at Rooksmoor Gallery Bath. *Address:* Edge Hill, Helscott Rd., Marhamchurch, Bude, Cornwall EX23 0JE. *Signs work:* "Kevin Hughes."

HUGHES, Malcolm, A.R.C.A., D.A. (Manc.); artist (painter) and lecturer; Hon. Fellow, University College, London, Emeritus Reader in Fine Art, University of London, Hon. Research Fellow, Slade School of Fine Art; *b* Manchester, 1920. *Studied art* at Regional College of Art, Manchester, Royal

College of Art, London. *Work in permanent collections:* Tate Gallery, Arts Council of Great Britain, Contemporary Arts Society, Walker Art Gallery, Liverpool, Ashmolean Museum, Oxford, etc. Works and lives in London. *Address:* c/o The Slade School of Fine Art, Gower St., WC1E 6BT. *Signs work:* name written on the back of each work.

HUGHES, Robert, H.S. (1986), R.M.S. (1989), S.M. (1991); artist in oil and gouache; *b* London, 5 Nov., 1934. *Exhib.:* R.M.S., H.S., S.M. *Publication:* Magic of Miniatures compiled by Jo Clay. *Address:* Easton Barns, Easton Royal, Pewsey, Wilts. SN9 5LY. *Signs work:* "Robert Hughes" or "R. HUGHES."

HULBERT, Thelma; painter; *b* Bath, 1913; *d* of Richard John Hulbert. *Studied art* at Bath School of Art. *Exhib.:* one-man shows, Cambridge, Leicester Gallery, Whitechapel Retrospective, Bath, Bristol, Cardiff City museums, Arts Council Tour, four London galleries; group shows, English Eye, Marlborough Gerson, N.Y., Whitechapel, Redfern, Bath. *Work in permanent collections:* City museums: Bath, Bristol, Preston, Arts Council, Contemporary Art Soc., Kansas, Sydney National Gallery, Queensland National Gallery, Embassy in Tehran, Derbyshire Educ. Com.; private collections in Zürich, Geneva, Italy, Israel, Brazil, Cape Town, England. Film: television, Thelma Hulbert; interviews BBC. *Address:* 2 Kelfield Gdns., London W10. *Signs work:* "Thelma Hulbert."

HULME, Ursula, M.B.E., N.R.D., F.P.S., B.A.A.T.; artist in oil, water-colour, pastel, felt pen and collage; textile designer; art therapist for the physically handicapped; Founder of 'Conquest' The Society for Art for the Physically Handicapped (1979); *b* Cottbus, 5 Mar., 1917; *d* of Dr. Karl Neumann; *m* Ernest Hulme. *Educ.:* Berlin; *studied art* at Reimann School, Berlin under Maria May. *Exhib.:* one-man shows: Woodstock Gallery, London (3), Talent Store, London (1990); group shows: F.P.S., Mall Galleries, Loggia Gallery, Nimes, France, Leatherhead Theatre, Richmond Art Group, etc. *Publication:* entries in London Diary in book form from 1970-72. ABC book, and two videos on Conquest Teaching Methods produced 1988; book, Guide for Group Leaders. *Address:* 3 Beverley Cl., E. Ewell, Epsom, Surrey KT17 3HB. *Signs work:* "Ursula Hulme."

HUMPHREYS, David, B.A. (Dunelm); Thomas Penman Scholar and State Scholar at Durham University (1958-62); painter and constructor; *b* London, 27 Oct., 1937; *s* of J. H. Ll. Humphreys. *Educ.:* Battersea Grammar School and King's College, Durham University (Dept. of Fine Art). *Work in permanent collections:* Arts Council, Leicester, Newcastle, London Universities, Ministry of Works, Bishop Otter College, Ashridge College, Nuffield Foundation, I.C.I., J. Sainsbury, Shell, American Express Bank (London and N.Y.), P. & O., Financial Times, H.M. the Queen Mother, their Royal Highnesses, the Prince and Princess of Wales. *Address:* Maudlin Hill House, Sopers La., Steyning, W. Sussex BN44 3PU.

HUMPHREYS, John Howard, R.O.I.(1977, resigned 1992); artist in oil; Press Officer, R.O.I. (1978-81); Winner of Stanley Grimm Prize (1981); *b* Bethlehem, S. Africa, 20 Oct., 1929; *s* of H.H. Humphreys; *m* Mary Mack; one *s*, one *d*. *Educ.:* King Edward VII School, Johannesburg; *studied art* at Heatherley's Art School (Iain Macnab), and privately under Stanley Grimm (1953-57). *Exhib.:* R.A., R.O.I., R.B.A., R.I., R.S.M.A., S.WL.A., Paris Salon, etc.; also in the U.S.A. and Japan. *Address:* 94 Kings Ave., Greenford, Middx. UB6 9DD. *Signs work:* "J. Humphreys."

HUNDERTWASSER (Friedrich Stowasser); *b* Vienna, 15 Dec., 1928; Matura (1948). *Exhib.:* (1952-81): Vienna, Paris, Tokyo, Hanover, Bern, Amsterdam, Stockholm, London, Geneva, Berlin, U.S.A., N.Z., Australia, Luxembourg, Marseille, Cairo, Tel Aviv, Warsaw, Reykjavik, Copenhagen, Dakar, Yokohama, Hong Kong, Cape Town, Pretoria, Rio de Janeiro, Brasilia, Sao Paulo, Caracas, Mexico City, Montreal, Toronto, Brussels, Budapest, Madrid, Rome, Milan, Oslo, Cologne, Graz, Helsinki, Bucharest. *Cassette of graphic works:* Look at it on a rainy day (1972); first Japanese colour woodcut portfolio Nana Hiaku Mizu (1973); Midori No Namida portfolio (1975). *Publications:* Verlag Galerie Welz, Salzburg (1965), Buchheim Verlag, Feldafing (1965), Bruckmann Verlag, Munich (1972). *Address:* P.O. Box 28, A-1182 Vienna, Austria. *Signs work:* see appendix.

HUNDLEBY, A. R.; designer-packaging and graphics, artist in water-colour; *b* 1923; *m* Marion Smallshaw, A.T.D.; *studied art* at Lincoln and Leicester. *Addresses:* 35 Kelross Rd., London N5 2QS; Hill House, Binham, Norfolk NR21 0DW. *Signs work:* "HUNDLEBY."

HUNT, Geoffrey William, R.S.M.A. (1989); marine artist and illustrator in oil, acrylic, water-colour; *b* Twickenham, 11 Mar., 1948; *s* of Eric William Hunt; *m* Vivienne Anne Hobbs; two *s*. *Educ.:* Hampton Grammar School; *studied art* at Kingston School of Art (1966-67), Epsom School of Art (1967-70). *Exhib.:* R.S.M.A. since 1977, Oliver Swann Gallery, SW3, Solent Gallery, Lymington, Llewellyn Alexander Gallery, John Stobart Gallery, U.S.A. (1985), Mystic Maritime Gallery, U.S.A. (1989). *Work in permanent collections:* Royal Naval Museum, Portsmouth, R.N. Submarine Museum, Gosport, H.M.S. Neptune, Faslane. *Publications:* illustrated many book covers including complete series of Patrick O'Brian's Jack Aubrey novels. *Address:* 191 South Park Rd., Wimbledon, London SW19 8RX. *Club:* Cruising Assoc. *Signs work:* "Geoff Hunt."

HUNTER, Alexis, Dip.F.A. Hons. (Painting) (1970), Teaching Dip. (1971); painter in oil on canvas (used photography and xerox 1976-81); lecturer; *b* Auckland, N.Z., 4 Nov., 1948; *d* of Jack Carlye Hunter, industrial chemist; *m* Baxter Mitchell, I.B.M.S. *Educ.:* Auckland Girls Grammar; *studied art* at Elam School of Fine Arts, Auckland (1965-69, Colin McCahon). *Exhib.:* over 100 exhbns. including Hayward, Serpentine, Musee d'Art Moderne, Paris, Auckland City A.G., etc. *Work in permanent collections:* Imperial War Museum, Scottish National Gallery of Modern Art, Zurich Museum, Auckland City A.G., Museum of N.Z., etc. *Address:* 13 Hiller Ho.46, Camden Sq., London NW1 9XA. *Signs work:* "Alexis Hunter."

HUNTLEY, Dennis, N.D.D. (1951), A.T.C. (1952), F.R.B.S. (1970); sculptor in bronze, plastics, stone, wood; educationalist; Head of Sir John Cass School of Art; Governor, City of London Polytechnic; *b* Weybridge, Surrey, 6 Dec., 1929; *s* of William Lanchbury Huntley, management executive; *m* Gillian Huntley; one *s*, two *d*. *Educ.:* Wallington Grammar School for Boys; *studied art* at Wimbledon School of Art (1947-51), Gerald Cooper (principal), London University Senior House (1951-52). *Exhib.:* several galleries. *Works permanently displayed:* 6 major works (4 stone, 2 wood) Guildford Cathedral, 7ft. metal fig. for L.C.C. Patronage of the Arts Scheme at Henry Thornton School, Clapham, life-sized wood fig. of Anne Boleyn, London Borough of Sutton, awarded Sir Otto Beit medal in open competition for best work, 1967, in United Kingdom and Commonwealth. *Publications:* book reviews for L.C.C. and Studio Vista and various articles for Education. *Address:* The Studio, 30 Hawthorn Rd., Sutton,

Surrey. *Clubs:* Arts, Chelsea Arts. *Signs work:* "D. W. Huntley" on prints and drawings, "D. HUNTLEY" on sculptured work.

HURDLE, Robert Henry; painter; senior lecturer until 1981, Faculty of Fine Art, Bristol Polytechnic; *b* London, 1918; *s* of Arthur E. Hurdle and Flora Bensted; two *s*, one *d.* Studied art at Richmond School of Art (1935-37), Camberwell School of Arts and Crafts (1946-48) under Coldstream. *Exhib.:* one-man shows, University College of Swansea (1973); Albany Gallery, Cardiff (1974); New Ashgate Gallery, Farnham (1977); City A.G., Bristol (1977); Pao Sui Loong Galleries, Hong Kong Arts Centre (1978); King St. Gallery, Bristol (1982); Farnham Maltings (1983); Pelter/Sands Gallery (1988); Cleveland Bridge Gallery, Bath (1989). *Work in permanent collections:* University College, Swansea; R.W.E.A.; Bristol Corporation; Bath University; Hong Kong Arts Centre; Wessex Collection, Longleat and various private collections. *Address:* 14 Oxford St., Kingsdown, Bristol BS2 8HH. Signs or seals work on front or back.

HURN, J. Bruce, A.T.D. (1946), F.R.S.A. (1966), P.P.R.B.S.A. (President 1973); painter/designer in oils, acrylic, gouache; former teacher, examiner and H.M.I. (Art), mem. advisory com. N.E.C.A.; *b* Spalding, 18 May, 1926; *s* of H.D.T. Hurn; *m* June Barbara; one *s*, three *d. Educ.:* King Edward's, Camp Hill, B'ham; *studied art* at Birmingham College of Art (1942-46). *Exhib.:* Universities: B'ham, Aston, Keele, Oxford, Leicester, Kent; group shows: municipal art galleries, R.B.S.A., R.A. *Work in permanent collections:* private, colleges, universities, schools, industrial collections in U.K., private collections in U.S.A., Europe, Australia. *Publication:* Practical Biology (Dodds and Hurn). *Address:* Sandy Ridge, 64 Lubbock Rd., Chislehurst, Kent. BR7 5JX. *Signs work:* see appendix.

HURN, Peter Henry Charles; figurative, landscape and figure artist in oils and mixed media; *b* Bristol, 1942; *s* of Henry Charles Hurn. *Educ.:* Patchway Secondary Modern, U.K.; Perth Technical College, W.A.; Perth Boys School, W.A.; *studied art* at Perth Faculty of Arts (commercial and poster art); St. Martin's School of Art, London; Camden Technical Inst., University of London (Sir Peter Murray). Lived and exhib. in Australia, farmed for eight years, painted for four years. Exhib. Perth St, George's Terrace Arts – club formed by artists from Faculty of Arts. Influenced by work of Albert Tucker and James Montgomery. Returned to U.K. – travelled to France, Belgium, Holland, Germany, Italy. *Exhib.:* France, Italy, Switzerland, etc.; mixed shows: R.A. Summer Show, John Moores Liverpool, Corn Exchange City of London, etc. *Address:* 189c Haverstock Hill, Hampstead, London NW3. *Signs work:* "HURN" or "P.H." within a circle.

HURST, Stephanie; Dip. in illustration (1974), R.A. Dip. of advanced studies – B.A. equivalent (1984); painter in oil on board with gesso ground; *b* Wimborne, Dorset, 3 July, 1952; *d* of James Hurst, Chartered architect (retd.). *Educ.:* Convent of the Sacred Heart, Weymouth; *studied art* at Bournemouth and Poole College of Art (1970-71), Hornsey College of Art (1971-74), Byam Shaw School of Painting and Drawing (1976-77), R.A. Schools (1981-84). *Exhib.:* R.A., Royal Festival Hall, Spirit of London Competition (awarded prize), South Bank Show, Camden Arts Centre – Druce Competition (awarded prize), Bath Contemporary Arts Fair, Elgin Fine Art, Bath, Jonathan Poole Gallery, London. *Address:* 3 King's Ave., Muswell Hill, London N10 1PA. *Signs work:* "S. Hurst" on back of painting.

HUSON, Cedric Nigel, Dip.A.D. (1973), R.A. Schools Post. Grad. Cert. (1978); painter; *b* Salop, 1 June, 1951; *s* of Eric Huson; *m* Kitta Potgieter.

Educ.: Marlborough Grammar School, Wilts.; *studied art* at Salisbury School of Art (1967-68), Swindon School of Art (1968-69), Winchester School of Art (1970-73), R.A. Schools (1975-78). *Exhib.:* group shows, Piccadilly Gallery (1987-93), R.A. Summer Exhbn. (1988-93), Hunting Group (1988, 1989), Leicestershire (1989), Cleveland Bridge Gallery, Bath (1990), The London Group Open (1990, 1992), The Discerning Eye (1992). *Address:* 11B Camberwell Green, London SE5 7AF. *Signs work:* "Cedric Huson."

HUSSEY, John Denis, F.R.B.S., R.W.A.; sculptor of assemblages; principal lecturer, Director of Studies, Fine Art Dept., Bristol Polytechnic (retd. 1983); *b* Slough, 26 Apr., 1928; *s* of F. W. and Louisa Hussey; *m* Katherine Hiller; two *s. Educ.:* Slough Grammar School; *studied art* at Goldsmiths' College (1946-49); research Diploma in Fine Art/Sculpture at Bristol Polytechnic (1969-70). *Exhib.:* R.A., R.W.A. *Work in permanent collections:* Tallboys, R.W.A. *Address:* Sanderling, 21 Colne View, Point Clear, St. Osyth, Essex CO16 8LA. *Signs work:* "J. Hussey."

HUSTON, John I.; History's Most Significant Artist . . . in oil, egg tempera, pastels, sculptures, landscapes, figures, abstracts, upon canvas, wood, masonite; writer; scientist; *b* Saltillo, Penna., U.S.A., 22 Jan., 1915; *s* of Harry E. Huston, merchant. *Educ.:* Juniata College and University Special Studies; completely self-trained in art via Commercial Art, Industrial Art, Cinema Art, Fine Art. Work in private collection. *Publication:* The Art of Life as permanent. *Address:* 1215 Jackson Tower, Harrisburg, Pa. 17102. *Club:* International Directory of Arts. *Signs work:* see appendix.

HUTCHESON, Tom, D.A. (1949) R.G.I.; artist in mixed media; principal art lecturer; *b* Uddingston, Lanarkshire, 13 Nov., 1924; *m* Mary McKay. *Educ.:* Motherwell; *studied art* at Glasgow School of Art (1941-49) under Hugh Adam Crawford, R.S.A., David Donaldson, R.S.A. *Exhib.:* R.S.A., G.I., R.S.W., Moores; three one-man shows. *Work in permanent collections:* H.M. the Queen, H.R.H. Prince Philip, Arts Council, Liverpool and Glasgow Universities, Scottish Educ. Authorities. *Address:* 73 Woodend Dr., Glasgow G13. *Club:* Art, Glasgow. *Signs work:* "Tom Hutcheson."

HUTCHISON, Sidney Charles, C.V.O., F.S.A., F.M.A., F.A.A.H., F.R.S.A., London Univ. Dip. in Hist. of Art, Lt.-Cdr. (S), R.N.V.R.; Antiquary and Hon. Archivist, R.A. of Arts; on administrative staff of R.A. from 1929 (Librarian 1949-68, Secretary 1968-82); Chantrey Bequest Trustee; President, Southgate Soc. of Arts. Lecturer for Univ. of London Extension Courses (1957-67); *b* London, 26 Mar., 1912. *Educ.:* Holloway School, London. *Publications:* The Homes of the Royal Academy (1956), The History of the Royal Academy, 1768-1968 (1968) and updated edition 1768-1986 (1986). *Address:* 60 Belmont Cl., Mount Pleasant, Cockfosters, Herts. EN4 9LT. *Clubs:* Athenaeum, Arts.

HUXLEY, Paul, R.A., Cert.R.A.S. (1960), Harkness Fellow (1965-67); painter in acrylic, oil, printmaking; Professor of Painting, Royal College of Art; *b* London, 12 May, 1938; *m* Susie Allen; two *s. Studied art* at Harrow School of Art (1951-56, Edward Middleditch), R.A. Schools (1956-60, Peter Greenham). *Exhib.:* over sixteen one-man shows and numerous group shows worldwide. *Work in permanent collections:* Tate Gallery, V. & A., plus various museums in the U.K., Europe, U.S.A. and Australia. *Publication:* Exhibition Road – Painters at the Royal College of Art. *Address:* c/o Royal College of Art, Kensington Gore, London SW7 2EU. *Club:* Chelsea Arts. *Signs work:* "Paul Huxley" in bottom margin of prints and small works on paper, verso on larger works on canvas.

HUYGHE, René, de l'Académie Française, Grand Officier Legion d'Honneur etc.; Hon. Prof. College de France (Psychologie des Arts Plastiques); Director, Museum Jacquemart-Andre; International Praemium Erasmianum, La Haye (1966); Conservateur en chef hon. Musée Louvre (1930-50); anc. President du Conseil des Musées; *b* Arras, 3 May, 1906; *s* of Louis Huyghe; *m* Lydie Bouthet; two *d. Educ.:* Sorbonne and École du Louvre. *Publications:* Dialogue avec le Visible (1955), L'Art et l'Ame (1960), L'Art et le Monde Moderne (2 vol. 1970-71), Formes et Forces (1971), Ceque je crois (1976), La Nuit appelle l'Aurore, avec Ikeda (1980), Les Signes du temps et l'Art moderne (1985), Delacroix (1990), Psychologie de l'Art (1991), etc. *Address:* 3 rue Corneille, Paris, 75006.

HYATT, Derek James, A.R.C.A.; painter/writer; *b* Ilkley, Wharfedale, Yorkshire, 1931. *Educ.:* Ilkley Grammar School; *studied art:* Leeds College of Art (1948-52), Royal College of Art (1954-58). Edited ARK (1958). *Exhib.:* London one-man shows include Austin Desmond/Gillian Jason Gallery (1987, 1989). Waddington Galleries (1974, 1977), New Art Centre (1960, 1961, 1963, 1966); group shows include John Moores, Cincinnati Bienniale, Arts Council Travelling Exhbns., and two Critics Choice exhbns. *Work in permanent collections:* Museum of Modern Art, New York, Contemporary Art Soc., Carlisle, Hull, Bradford, Sheffield and Bootle Art Galleries and Nuffield Foundation. *Addresses:* Rectory Farm House, Collingham, Wetherby, Yorks; Studio: Bishopdale, N. Yorks.

HYMAN, Timothy, Slade Dip. (1967); painter in oil, pastel and drawing, writer, lecturer; *b* Hove, 17 Apr., 1946; *m* Judith Ravenscroft. *Educ.:* Charterhouse; *studied art* at Slade School of Fine Art (1963-67). *Exhib.:* Blond Fine Art (1981, 1983, 1985), Lincoln Portraits touring (1984-85), Austin Desmond London (1990), Manchester Castlefield (1993), Gallery Chemould Bombay (1994). *Work in permanent collections:* Arts Council, B.M., Contemporary Art Soc., Bristol City A.G., Sheffield City A.G., Usher A.G. Lincoln, Westfield College (University of London). *Address:* 62 Myddelton Sq., London EC1R 1XX. *Signs work:* "Timothy Hyman," "T.H." or "HYMAN."

I

I'ANSON, Charles, F.R.B.S. (1967), F.R.S.A. (1956), R.B.S.A. (1966), M.Sc. (1980), O.L.J. (1981); sculptor in steel; *b* Birmingham, 1924. *Studied art* at Birmingham College of Art. *Exhib.:* F.P.S., London Group, Commonwealth Inst., New Vision and Alwyn Galleries, London; "Sculpture 1971", York, etc. *Work in permanent collections:* Cardiff Civic Centre, Midlands Art Centre, Bristol and Leeds Universities, Trinity and All Saint's College, Leeds; Birmingham, Bradford and Wakefield A.G.'s, R.D.C., Walmley, Bristol, Minard Castle, Inveraray, Argyll; R.A. Gamecock Barracks, Nuneaton; Dore School, Sheffield; Windmill Hill School, Stourport; St. Paul's Church, Doncaster; St. Winefrid's Church, Wibsey, Bradford, etc. *Address:* Baystones, Parish Ghyll La., Ilkley, W. Yorks. LS29 9QP. *Signs work:* "I'ANSON."

IBBETT, Vera, R.M.S. (1990), Grenfell Silver medal – botanical illus. (1970), F.S.S.I. (1970); painter and illustrator in oil, water-colour, pastel; *b* Kingswood, Surrey, 30 May, 1929; *m* Raymon Strank. *Educ.:* Banstead Central School; *studied art* at City and Guilds of London Art School (1955-63, Innes Fripp,

John Nash, R.A.), Reigate School of Art (1968-70). *Exhib.*: R.A., R.M.S., S.W.A., R.H.S. *Work in permanent collection*: R.A.F. Chapel of Remembrance, Biggin Hill. *Publications*: Flowers in Heraldry (Alcuin Soc. Vancouver B.C., 1977), La Revue Moderne (1960), European Illustrators (1974-75). *Address*: 89 Chipstead La., Lower Kingswood, Tadworth, Surrey KT20 6RD. *Signs work*: "Vera Ibbett."

INCHBALD, Michael, F.C.S.D.; Architectural and Interior Designer; *studied*: A.A.; twice married; two children. *Work includes* 1st Class Lounge "Queen's Room" and Library on Q.E.2, and other Liners, Ballroom, all banquet areas and suites at Berkeley Hotel, Post House, Heathrow, Claridges' Penthouse, Savoy's River Room and Lincoln Room, Crown Commissioner's H.Q., Carlton House Terr., Banks of America and Trust Hanover, Player's and Plessey's H.Q. Offices, Justerini and Brooks, Boardroom etc. for Imperial Group, Law Society's Lady's Annexe, Dunhill's, Jermyn Street and Worldwide; Residential: Duke of St. Albans, Duc de la Rochefoucauld, Earls of Dartmouth and St. Aldwyn, Countess of Lonsdale, etc. *Address*: 10 Milner St., London SW3 2PU.

IND, John William Charles, F.R.S.A.; painter in oil, water-colour, sculptor in wood, designer, illustrator; *b* London, 1927; *s* of William Ind, engineer; *m* Greta Bambridge-Butler; two *s. Educ.*: London and Cambridge; *studied art* in London and Oslo. *Exhib.*: Royal Exchange, Madden Gallery, Barle Gallery, Harrods Gallery; one-man shows: Halford House, Newton Gallery, Kensington Ct. Gdns. *Work in permanent collections*: Harris Bank, Barclays Bank, Hays Allan, Ind Coope, Texaco London, Taylor Hall; private collections in France, Germany, U.S.A., Britain, N.Z., Scandinavia. *Address*: Atelier; Aller, Som., TA10 0QN. *Signs work*: "Ind."

INGHAM, Alan Everard, Lt. Cdr. R.N. retd. (1965), A.R.I.C.S. (1971); painter of landscapes in water-colour; *b* Skipton, 25 Oct., 1932; *s* of Edgar Ingham; *m* Rose; one *d. Educ.*: Ermysteds Grammar School, Skipton; Royal Naval College, Dartmouth. *Exhib.*: R.I., R.B.A., Harrods, Selfridges, etc.; one-man shows: Granby Gallery, Bakewell (1980-90), Halcyon Gallery Birmingham, etc. *Work in permanent collections*: Rolls Royce Motor Co., Rank Hovis McDougall, Ind Coope, etc. *Address*: Farthings, The Cherry Orchard, Staverton Village, Cheltenham GL51 0TR. *Signs work*: "ALAN INGHAM" mid horizontal strokes of letters extended.

INGHAM, George Bryan, A.R.C.A.; artist; *b* Preston, Lancs., 11 June, 1936; *s* of George William Ingham. *Studied art* at St. Martin's School of Art; R.C.A.; British Academy, Rome. *Exhib.*: Francis Graham-Dixon Gallery, London. *Work in permanent collections*: V. & A., Ashmolean, Kunsthalle, Bremen, etc. *Publication*: illustrated catalogue Anthony Gross. *Address*: c/o Francis Graham-Dixon Gallery, 17-18 Gt. Sutton St., London EC1V 0DN. *Club*: Blue Anchor, Helston. *Signs work*: "B. Ingham" on back.

INGLIS, John, R.S.W. (1984), F.S.A. (Scot.) (1983), D.A. (1974), Post. Grad. (1975), Travelling scholar (1976); painter in water-colour, acrylic, lecturer; *b* Glasgow, 27 July, 1953; *s* of Thomas Inglis; *m* Heather Binnie; two *s*, two *d. Educ.*: Hillhead High School, Glasgow; *studied art* at Gray's School of Art, Aberdeen (1970-75, William Littlejohn, Frances Walker, Alexander Fraser). *Exhib.*: R.S.A., R.S.W., R.G.I.F.A., S.S.A., Compass Gallery, Glasgow, Open Eye Gallery, Edinburgh, Park Sq. Gallery, Leeds, Venice, Rome, Canada, Regensberg. *Work in permanent collections*: Aberdeen A.G., Scottish Arts Council, University of Aberdeen, Argyll and Bute Educ. Authority, Scottish Television, Inst. for Cancer Research, Aberdeen Hospitals Collection,

Clackmannan District Council Collection. *Address:* 21 Hillview Rd., Larbert, Stirlingshire FK5 4RL. *Signs work:* "John Inglis" usually on back.

INKERSOLE, Don, Dip.A.D. (1971); artist in oil; *b* Colchester, 8 Apr., 1946. *Studied art* at Maidstone School of Art. *Address:* 17 Fore St., Bampton, Devon EX16 9ND. *Signs work:* "don inkersole."

INNES, William Henry, P.S., U.A.; artist in pastel and oil; President, S.E. London Art Group; *b* London, 23 Feb., 1905; *s* of William John Innes, stereotyper; *m* Violet Gertrude. *Educ.:* L.C.C. School. *Exhib.:* R.A., P.S., U.A., R.S.M.A., N.E.A.C., R.O.I., several one-man shows. *Work in permanent collections:* Southwark and Lambeth Councils, Courbeviou, and many countries worldwide and private collections. *Address:* 38 Ruskin Walk, London SE24 9LZ. *Club:* London Sketch. *Signs work:* "INNES."

INSALL, Donald W., O.B.E., F.S.A., R.W.A., F.R.I.B.A., F.R.T.P.I., S.P.Dip. (Hons); architect; Principal, Donald W. Insall and Assoc. (Architects and Planning Consultants), London SW1; Ex-Commissioner, The Historic Buildings and Monuments Commission for England, Visiting Prof. University of Leuven, Consultant to D.O.E. and City of Chester in National Pilot City Conservation Programme; *b* Clifton, Bristol, 7 Feb., 1926. *Exhib.:* R.A., R.W.A., R.I.B.A., and similar exhbns. *Work in permanent collection:* thirteen Civic Trust Awards/ Commendations. *Publications:* The Care of Old Buildings Today (Architectural Press); Architectural Conservation for Encyclopedia Britannica; Conservation in Action. *Address:* 73 Kew Green, Richmond, Surrey. *Club:* The Athenaeum.

IRENE: see FRÖHLICH-WIENER, Irene.

IRVIN, Albert; painter; *b* London, 21 Aug., 1922; *s* of A. H. J. Irvin; *m* Beatrice Nicolson; two *d. Educ.:* Holloway County; *studied art* at Northampton and Goldsmiths' School of Art; taught at Goldsmiths' College School of Art (1962-82). *Exhib.:* one-man shows: Gimpel Fils, London; New Art Centre, London; Acme, London; 57 Gallery, Edinburgh; Aberdeen A.G.; Third Eye Centre, Glasow; Ikon, Birmingham; Bede, Jarrow; Goldsmiths' College Gallery; Newcastle Polytechnic; Manchester Polytechnic; De Marco, Edinburgh; Exe Gallery, Exeter; Jersey Arts Council; Skulima, Berlin; Lüpke, Frankfurt; Galerie 2, Stuttgart; Städtische Kunstsämmlungen, Ludwigshafen; Berlin Opera House; Galerie im Griechenbeisl, Vienna; Coventry Gallery, Sydney; Kilkenny Castle; Hendriks, Dublin; Carine Campo, Antwerp; Monochrome, Brussels; Gimpel and Weitzenhoffer, N.Y.; Serpentine, London; Talbot Rice, Edinburgh; Oriel and Chapter, Cardiff; Spacex, Exeter, etc. *Official purchases* include: Tate Gallery; Arts Council; British Council; other British and international public collections; Mem. London Group. *Address:* c/o Gimpel Fils, 30 Davies St., London W1. *Signs work:* see appendix.

IRWIN, Flavia; artist in acrylic on canvas, mixed media on paper, tutor; Head of Decorative Arts Dept., City & Guilds of London Art School; *b* London; *d* of Clinton Irwin; *m* Roger de Grey; two *s*, one *d. Educ.:* Hawnes School, Ampthill; *studied art* at Chelsea School of Art (Graham Sutherland, Henry Moore, Robert Medley). *Exhib.:* Zwemmers, London Group, R.A., Ansdell Gallery, Gallery 10 Grosvenor St., Phoenix Gallery, Curwen Gallery, Peoples Theatre, Newcastle, Arts Council Gallery, Bury St. Edmunds, Taranman Gallery. *Work in permanent collections:* Carlyle A.G., D.O.E. *Address:* Camer Street, Meopham, Kent DA13 0XR. *Signs work:* "Flavia Irwin" back of canvas, pencil on drawings. *Dealer:* Redfern Gallery, Cork St., London W1.

IRWIN, Gwyther; painter: oil paint, water-colour and acrylics; *b* Cornwall, 7 May, 1931; *m* Elizabeth; two *s,* one *d. Educ.:* Bryanston; *studied art* at Central School of Art (1952-55). *Exhib.:* Redfern Gallery, London. *Work in permanent collections:* Tate Gallery, British Council, Arts Council, Contemporary Art Soc., Arts Council of N. Ireland, Calouste Gulbenkian, City Art Gallery, Bradford, Albright-Knox, Yale University, Peggy Guggenheim, Peter Stuyvesant. *Address:* 21 Hillbury Rd., London SW17. *Signs work:* "Gwyther Irwin." Studios in London and Cornwall.

ISITT, John, B.A. (1958), I.P.M. (1960), I.P.R. (1961), M.Inst.M. (1970), M.Inst. Ex. (1972), M.B.I.M. (1968); self-employed English teacher, artist in oil, water-colour, prints, writer, actor; mem. Equity and Writer's Guild; Director, Oxbridge Artists and Writers; *b* Newport, Mon., 9 Feb., 1935; *s* of Col. Samuel William Isitt, S.Wales Borderers; formerly *m* Anne Drummond-Leigh; three *s,* one *d. Educ.:* Newport High School; London University; Ashridge Management College; *studied art* at Chelsea (1955-58). *Exhib.:* Chenil Galleries, Thameside Gallery, St.Clement's House, Oxford, Oxford Art Soc., Chester Gallery, Blackfriars, Oxford, St.Aloysius' Church, Oxford (1969), Maison Francaise (Oxford University 1988), University of Oxford (1979), Cardiff, Newport, Bath, etc. *Work in permanent collections:* Australia, S.America, U.S.A., France, Germany, Wales. *Publications:* Sacred and Profane (1980), The Godwalk (1989), Act of Love (1980), The Propitiation (1980); Koestler prize for verse (1980). *Address:* Flat 58, Riverside Ct., Oxford OX1 4NQ. *Clubs:* Royal Overseas, Newport R.F.C., Cardiff R.F.C., London Welsh R.F.C., Oxford and Cambridge, Poetry Soc., Ashmolean and Bodleian 'Friend', etc. *Signs work:* "John Isitt."

ISOM, Graham Michael, N.D.D. (1965), A.A.E.A., S.E.A.; artist in oil; *b* Kent, 5 Mar., 1945; *m*; one *s,* two *d. Educ.:* Dartford; *studied art* at Ravensbourne College of Art (1961-65). *Work in permanent collections:* Kentucky Derby Museum of Racing, Churchill Downs, Louisville. *Address:* 5 Neville Pk., Baltonsborough, Som. BA6 8PY. *Signs work:* see appendix.

IZZARD, Pamela; artist in oil, acrylic and mixed media; *b* London, 1929; *d* of Chas G.Izzard; *m* (1) K.Lucas; two *s,* one *d.;* (2) Jack Millar. *Educ.:* Old Palace School, Croydon, Torquay Grammar School; *studied art* at Beckenham and Bromley Schools of Art. *Exhib.:* R.A., London Group, N.E.A.C., R.B.A., Curwen Gallery, Linton Ct. Gallery, Ashgate Galleries, one-man shows, Ashgate Galleries, Abbot Hall, Kendal, and various provincial galleries. Has taught in art schools in London and the provinces. *Address:* 10 Overhill Rd., Dulwich, London SE22 0PH. *Signs work:* "P. Izzard" on back.

J

JACK, Kenneth William David, A.M. (1987), M.B.E. (1982), R.W.S. (1977), A.W.I. (1955), A.T.D. (1951), A.T.C. (1949); landscape and architectural painter and printmaker in water-colour, acrylic, pastel and most drawing media, lithography, silk-screen; Patron, O.W.S.C. (Australian branch); *b* Melbourne, 5 Oct., 1924; *s* of Harold Jack (decd.), advertising artist for Victorian Railways; *m* Betty Dyer; one *s,* two *d. Educ.:* Melbourne High School; *studied art* at R.M.I.T. (John Rowell, Harold Freedman). *Exhib.:* R.W.S. annually at Bankside Gallery, Leicester Galleries (1975), Fine Art Soc. London, A.W.I.; many one-man shows in Australia. *Work in permanent collections:* National Galleries of all Australian capital cities; 500 works Australian War Memorial, Canberra. *Publications:* many folios and large reproductions of paintings; Kenneth Jack by L. Klepac; Kenneth Jack—World War II Paintings and Drawings (text, K.J.); Kenneth Jack by D. Dundas; The Flinders Ranges (paintings, text by K.J.); The Melbourne Book by C. Turnbull; Charm of Hobart by C. Turnbull. *Address:* P.O.Box 1, Doreen 3754, Victoria, Australia. *Club:* O.W.S.C. *Signs work:* "Kenneth Jack."

JACKLIN, Bill, M.A., R.C.A. (1967), A.R.A. (1989); artist in oil paintings, etching; *b* London, 1 Jan., 1943; *s* of Harold Jacklin, M.C.; *m* Lesley. *Educ.:* Willesden Junior Technical College, Walthamstow Technical College; *studied art* at Walthamstow School of Art (1962-64), R.C.A. (1964-67, Carel Weight). *Exhib.:* one-man shows, London: Nigel Greenwood (1970, 1971, 1975), Hester Van Royen Gallery (1973, 1977), Marlborough Fine Art (1980, 1983, 1988); Marlborough Gallery, N.Y. (1985, 1987, 1990); numerous group shows. *Work in permanent collections:* A.C.G.B., British Council, B.M., Government Arts Coll., Metropolitan Museum, N.Y., Museum of Modern Art, N.Y., Museum Boymans-Van Beuningen, Rotterdam, Tampa Museum, Museum of N.S.W., V. & A., Tate Gallery, Yale Centre for British Art. *Publications:* gallery catalogues and numerous articles and broadcasts. *Addresses:* Apt. 7A, 155 Perry St., N.Y.C., N.Y. 10014; 57 Dovehouse St., London SW3. *Club:* Chelsea Arts. *Signs work:* "Jacklin."

JACKSON, Ashley, F.R.S.A., U.A.; artist in water-colour; lecturer and demonstrator in w/c throughout Britain, U.S.A., Valencia, Milan and Madrid; *b* Penang, Malaysia, 22 Oct., 1940; *s* of Norman Valentine Jackson; *m* Anne; two *d. Educ.:* St. Joseph's, Singapore, Holyrood, Barnsley; *studied art* at Barnsley School of Art (1955-60) under F. Adams, A. Critchley, T. Long. *Exhib.:* R.I., R.B.A., R.W.S., Britain in Water-colour, U.A.; one-man shows: Upper Grosvenor Gallery, Mall Galleries, Christina Foyle Gallery, Huddersfield 1987— opened by H.R.H. Prince of Wales, Huddersfield A.G. (1990), Patchings A.G. Nottingham (1993). *Work in permanent collections:* Royal Navy, Sir Harold Wilson, Sir Yehudi Menuhin, Lord Mason of Barnsley, Rt. Hon. Edward Heath, Yorkshire Bank, Yorkshire Television, N.C.B., Rt. Hon. John Major. *Publications:* autobiography "My Brush with Fortune" (Secker and Warburg, 1982); "An Artists Notebook" (Luddites, 1982), "Painting in the Open Air" (Harper Collins, 1992), "A Brush with Ashley" (Boxtree, 1993). Featured in Y.T.V. documentary "My Own Flesh and Blood" (1981); own series on B.B.C. "Pebble Mill at One"; series of "How to Paint" on Channel 4, titled "Making the Most of" (1982); own series on Y.T.V. "A Brush With Ashley" (1990, 1992, 1993). Founder Member of Yorkshire Watercolour Soc. *Address:* Ashley Jackson Galleries, 13-15 Huddersfield Rd., Holmfirth, Huddersfield HD7 1JR. *Signs work:* see appendix.

JACKSON, H. J., R.E., S.W.E., N.D.D.; works in marketing, printmaker in lino; *b* Kings Lynn, Norfolk, 7 Dec., 1938; *s* of D. S. B. Jackson; *m*; one *d. Educ.:* Melton Constable; *studied art* at Norwich School of Art (1954-58) under G. Wales, R.E. *Exhib.:* Touring Print Exhbns. America and United Kingdom; one-man and group shows throughout East Anglia, print and mixed shows in London. *Official purchases:* various educational authorities. Work included in a number of public collections, and private collections world-wide. *Address:* 12 Whitehall Rd., Norwich NR2 3EW.

JACKSON, William Alexander, A.T.D., P.P.R.B.S.A. (President 1983-87); artist in pastel, oil, acrylic; retd. Principal, Bournville College of Art (1964-81), teacher of drawing and painting since 1947; B/Tec. Art and Design Moderator; *b* B'ham, 11 Sept., 1919; *s* of W.A. Jackson, A.M.I.E.E.; *m* Mary Elizabeth; one *s*, one *d. Educ.:* W. Bromwich Grammar School; *studied art* at Ryland Memorial School of Art (1936-40), B'ham College of Art (1946-47). *Exhib.:* R.B.S.A., Pastel Exhbns. Organising com., B'ham Pastel Exhbn. (1984, 1986, 1988, 1990, 1992). *Work in permanent collection:* Dudley A.G. *Address:* Jubilee Cottage, 19 Avenue Rd., Astwood Bank, Redditch B96 6AU. *Signs work:* "Alex Jackson."

JACOBSON, Ruth Blanche, D.F.A.Lond. (1963); 1st prize, figure drawing at the Slade (1961); painter/printmaker/stained glass artist; *b* London, 1941; *d* of Dr. Henry Taylor, M.R.C.S., L.R.C.P. (decd.); *m* U. Jacobson, F.R.C.S., M.R.C.O.G.; two *s*, one *d. Studied art* at Slade School of Fine Art (1959-63, Peter Brooker, Andrew Forge). *Exhib.:* Agnews, Wildenstein, Royal Festival Hall, Barbican Centre; one-man shows: Camden Arts Centre, Poole Arts Centre, Zionist Confederation House, Jerusalem. *Work in permanent collections:* Panstwowe Muzeum Oswiecim Brzezinka, Poland, Yad Vashem Museum, Israel, Ben Uri Gallery, London. *Commission:* portrait of H.M. Queen Elizabeth the Queen Mother for the Museums Association. *Address:* 25 Holne Chase, London N2 0QL. *Club:* Printmakers Council. *Signs work:* "Ruth B. Jacobson."

JAFFE, Harold, A.S.A. (1973), F.S.V.A. (1978); artist in acrylic and mixed media; interior designer and muralist, teacher and antiquarian; certified fine arts appraiser; President, Louis Comfort Tiffany Soc.; Past President, L.I. Chapter, American Society of Appraiser; Faculty, New York University; *b* New York City, 26 Mar., 1922; *s* of Selig Jaffe; *m* Gisèle Jaffe; one *s. Educ.:* Pratt Institute, Parsons School; *studied art* at Cape Ann, Gloucester under Maxwell Starr. *Work in permanent collections:* Denton Greens Housing Development; *private collections:* Dr. C. MacCormick, Mr. and Mrs. S. Berman, Dr. D. Bernstein, Mr. and Mrs. A. Adler. *Work repro.:* Interiors Magazine, Years Work. *Address:* 5 Devon Rd., Great Neck, New York, U.S.A. *Signs work:* "Harold."

JAFFÉ, Lois; R.D.S. medal (1934); artist in pastel, water-colour, oil; *b* Axminster, 16 Sept., 1918; *d* of Stafford Heal, engineer; *m* Eric Jaffé; one *s. Educ.:* Essex County High School; *studied art:* at St. Martin's School of Art (1939). *Exhib.:* Pastel Soc. (1976-82), Trends, Mall Gallery (1976), Westward TV Plymouth (1975), Civil Service; one-man, Kings Arm Gallery Dorchester, Harbour Gallery, W. Bay, Dorset, V. & A. (1937-39), City of London Guildhall. *Work in permanent collection:* Philpot Museum, Lyme Regis. *Address:* The Old Coach House, Bellair, Charmouth, Dorset. *Signs work:* "LOIS JAFFÉ."

JAGGAR, Margaret Leah, Hon.Retd. R.C.A.; wood engraver, mural painter, commercial artist; *b* 9 July, 1907; *d* of Thomas Webster Blundell, cotton broker; *m* Robert Jaggar (decd.); one *s,* one *d. Educ.:* Cheltenham Ladies' College; Liverpool Art School. *Exhib.:* Soc. of Wood Engravers, etc. *Work repro.:* Murals in Architect, Building News, Architects Journal, Design; W. H. Smith and Sons, Ltd., etc.; murals for Cunard White Star Liner s.s. Caronia, National Trust, etc. *Address:* Croes Efa, Rhydwyn, nr. Holyhead LL65 4EL.

JAGO, Joan E., F.R.S.A. (1989), F.F.P.S. (1992), Wilfred Sirrell Award (City of Westminister Arts Council) 1989, Dip. in Creative Textiles (1985); fibre artist/paper maker; *b* Leeds, 22 Mar., 1930; *d* of Charles E.D. Burrell (decd.). *Educ.:* Aireborough Grammar School, W.Yorks. *Exhib.:* group shows in London and the U.S.A. *Address:* 606 Nelson House, Dolphin Sq., London SW1V 3NZ. *Signs work:* "Joan Jago."

JAKOBER, Ben; sculptor in stone, iron, bronze; *b* Vienna, 31 July, 1930; *s* of Henry Jakober; *m* Yannick Vu; one *s. Educ.:* Mill Hill School; La Sorbonne, Paris. *Exhib.:* 1982: Fundación March, Palma; 1984: Palais des Beaux Arts, Brussels; Louisiana Museum, Humlebaek; Städtische Kunsthalle, Mannheim; Museum Moderner Kunst, Vienna; 1985: Salon de Montrouge; Recklinghausen Museum; Biennale de Sculpture Belfort; Galería Maeght, Barcelona; 1986: Capella de la Misericordia, Palma; Salon de Montrouge; Biennale di Venezia; 1987: Künstlerhaus, Vienna; 1988: Minos Art Symposium, Greece; Olympiad of Art, Seoul; 1990: Galerie Montenay, Paris; Jeune Sculpture, Paris; 1991: MVSEV, Palma; Palacio de Fortea, Zaragoza; Padiglione d'Arte Contemporanea, Ferrara; Musée d'Art Moderne, Pully (VD); Musée de la Poste, Paris; Musée des Jacobins, Morlaix; XV Biennale Internazionale del Bronzetto, Padova; 1992: IMF Center, Washington; Spanish section EXPO 92, Seville; "La Salerniana", Erice; Museo Civico de Gibellina; 1993: Arnolfini, Bristol; Musuem Moderner Kunst Stiftung Ludwig Palais Liechtenstein, Vienna; Sala Bramante, Rome; "MEDIALE", Hamburg; 6 Biennale d'Arte Contemporanea, Marostica; XLV Biennale di Venezia. *Work in permanent collections:* Museo Nacional Centro de Arte Reina Sofía, Madrid; Musée d'Art Moderne, Brussels; Museum of Modern Art, Palais Liechtenstein, Vienna; Museum of Austrian Art of the XIX and XX Centuries, Vienna; Kunsthalle Bremen; Kunsthalle, Hamburg; Musée d'Art Moderne F.A.E., Pully (VD); Colombe d'Or, St Paul de Vence; Fattoria di Celle, Pistoia; E.P.A.D., Paris; Seoul Olympic Park; Fondation Vincent Van Gogh, Arles. *Address:* POB 10, 07400 Alcudia, Mallorca, Spain. *Signs work:* "B.J."

JAMES, Donald; painter, designer; exhibits internationally; P.E., Commonwealth of Massachusetts; M.I.E., Australia; *b* New York, 1932; *s* of Paul Adolph. *Educ.:* M.A. (1960) University of California, B.Sc. (1953) University of New York, San Francisco Art Institute, California School of Fine Arts, San Francisco State College, American University, Corcoran School of Art, Union University, Union College. *Address:* 6 Eccleston St. Belgravia, c/o Eccleston B.O., London SW1W 9LS. *Signs work:* "James."

JAMES, Herbert Norman, Dipl. Ing., F.R.S.A., Assoc. R.Ae.S.; industrial designer, television and film director; *b* Rochford, Essex, 22 Oct., 1918; *s* of Herbert C. James, F.R.I.C.S.; *m* Justine Whateley, painter; one *s,* one *d. Educ.:* Royal Liberty School, University of Bologna; *studied art* at West Ham School of Art, Pratt Inst., Brooklyn, N.Y., Tech. Hochsch., Darmstadt. *Exhib.:* Trienniale, Turin; Museum of Modern Art, N.Y.; Cannes and Venice film festivals, etc. *Work repro.:* current design and scientific periodicals. *Address:* Bourdès, 31480 Puysségur, France. *Signs work:* see appendix.

JAMES, Jeremy, B.A.Hons. (1986), M.A. (1987); ceramist in clay/pen and ink; part time lecturer, Exeter College of Art and Design; *b* Yeovil, Som., 7 Mar., 1964; *s* of Christopher James. *Educ.:* St. Stephen-in-Brannel School, Cornwall, Earlham School, Norwich; *studied art* at Norwich (1983), Exeter (1983-86), Cardiff (1986-87). *Exhib.:* Cinema City, Norwich, Exeter College of Art and Design, Rooksmoor Bath, National Museum of Wales, Mall Galleries, National College of Art and Design Gallery, Dublin, Brighton Polytechnic. *Address:* Rookery Cottage, Hill Rd., Tibenham, Norfolk. *Signs work:* "Jeremy James."

JAMES, Kim, M.A.(R.C.A.), M.Sc., Ph.D., N.D.D., A.T.C.; Consultant to the French National Inst. for training psychiatric personnel, Dijon, France; Director P.S.I. International Ltd.; *b* Wollaston, Northants, 31 July, 1928; *s* of Christopher James; *m;* one *d. Educ.:* Wellingborough Grammar School; *studied* *art* at Borough Polytechnic under David Bomberg and Tom Eckersley; Royal College of Art; Brunel University, School of Applied Biology; and Division of Cybernetics. Special research field psychology of perception. Writings include critical essays and reviews on current theories of Perception and Philosophy (Leonardo, vols. 8, 9, 10, 11, 13, 14). *Exhib.*: R.A., Scottish Arts Council; Middleheim Biennale, Antwerp. *Gallery:* Grosvenor Gallery, London. *Address:* Hickmire, Wollaston, Northants. *Signs work:* "Kim James."

JAMES, Simon, M.A.(R.C.A.) (1989); artist in oil, charcoal and printmaking; *b* 22 Jan., 1965. *Educ.:* Northampton School for Boys; *studied art* at R.A. Schools (1984-87), R.C.A. (1987-89). *Exhib.*: R.A., N.E.A.C., Marks and Spencer Young Artist award (1992), prizewinner in the 10th Cleveland International Drawing Biennale (1991), numerous exhbns. in England, U.S.A., and Berlin. *Work in permanent collections:* Lloyd's of London, Cleveland C.C., The Foreign Office. *Address:* Houseboat Clifton, Blomfield Rd., London W9 2PB. *Signs work:* "SIMON JAMES" or "S.J."

JAMESON, Kenneth Ambrose, R.C.A., R.D.S., F.R.S.A.; artist in oil and drawing; formerly, Art Inspector, I.L.E.A.; formerly Vice-President, Pre-School Playgroups Assoc.; *b* Blackwell, Worcestershire, 21 May, 1913; *s* of Robert B. Jameson, timber merchant; *m* Norma M. Jameson. *Educ.:* King Edward VI Grammar School, Birmingham; *studied art* at Leicester College of Art, Bath Academy of Art. *Work in permanent collections:* Corporation Art Gallery, Birkenhead; colleges and educational establishments. *Publications:* Pre-school and Infant Art, You Can Draw, Flower Painting for Beginners, Starting with Abstract Painting, Junior School Art, Pre-School Play (all Studio Vista), Painting: A Complete Guide (Nelson). *Address:* 111 Hayes Way, Beckenham, Kent BR3 2RR. *Signs work:* see appendix.

JAMESON, Norma Marion, R.B.A., R.O.I., N.D.D., A.T.D., Goldsmiths' Advanced Dip., textiles; painter, lecturer; *b* Burslem, 18 Jan., 1933; *d* of Frank Bertram Salt; *m* Kenneth Ambrose Jameson. *Educ.:* Thistley Hough Grammar School, Stoke-on-Trent; *studied art* at Bath Academy of Art (1951-55); Liverpool University (1955-56); Goldsmiths' College (1978). *Exhib.*: R.A.; various one-man shows in London and the South East. Mem. Royal Society of British Artists and The Royal Inst. of Oil Painters. *Address:* 111 Hayes Way, Beckenham, Kent BR3 2RR. *Signs work:* "Norma Jameson."

JAMILLY, Victor; painter, oil and water-colour; art gallery director; *b* 31 May, 1927; *s* of David Jamilly; *m* Audrey; two *s,* one *d*. *Educ.:* Highgate and Cranleigh Schools; *studied art* at St. Martin's School of Art. *Work in permanent collection:* Euston Gallery, London. *Exhib.*: New English Art Club, R.S.B.A., various group and gallery shows. *Address:* Wendover, 13 Hampstead Way, London NW11. *Signs work:* "V. Jamilly."

JAMISON, Paul, B.A.Hons. (1979), P.G.C.E./A.T.D. (1982); artist in oil and water-colour; *b* Middlesbrough, 16 Sept., 1954; *s* of John Jamison. *Educ.:* St. Mary's College, Middlesbrough; *studied art* at University of Newcastle upon Tyne (1975-79), University of Bristol (1981-82). *Exhib.*: Hatton Gallery, Newcastle (1979), Alpine Gallery, London (1980, 1983). Work in private collections throughout the world. *Address:* 16 Cosway St., London NW1 5NR. *Signs work:* "Jamison" with year, i.e. '92.

JAMMET, Lin; painter in gouache on paper, oil on canvas; *b* 22 May, 1958; *s* of Michel Jammet, architect, and Dame Elizabeth Frink, R.A.; *m* Valerie Jammet; one *s.* *Educ.:* French Lycée, London; C.E.G. d'Anduze, France;

Millfield, Somerset; *studied art* at Chelsea School of Art (sculpture course 1976). *Exhib.:* one-man shows: Beaux Arts Gallery, Bath, St. Jude's Gallery, London, Contemporary Fine Art Gallery, Eton. *Address:* Flat D, 2 Dulwich Rd., London SE24 0PA. *Club:* Chelsea Arts. *Signs work:* "Lin Jammet."

JANÁČEK, Mirice: see MATTAROZZI DI THARASH, Mirella.

JANES, Violeta; portrait painter, still-life, artist in oil, pastel and water-colour; *b* Buenos Aires, Argentina; *d* of A. F. Janes and V. F. M. Coates. *Educ.:* Giffen School, Viña del Mar, Chile; *studied art* at Regent St. Polytechnic School of Art under S. Tresilian, Middleton Todd, E. Osmond. *Exhib.:* R.A., R.O.I., S.W.A., R.S.A., N.E.A.C., R.P., Paris Salon and the provinces; two-man show in the West End, one-man, Broomfield Museum. Member United Society of Artists. Directed art studies at Alma College, Ontario, Canada. *Address:* 2 Salisbury Ave., Harpenden, Herts, 5AL 2QQ. *Signs work:* "Violeta Janes."

JAQUES, Norman Clifford, D.A. (Manc., 1941), M.S.I.A. (retd.); Sen. Lecturer, Manchester Polytechnic (1950-82); *b* 23 Apr., 1922; *s* of John Clifford Jaques; *m* Marjorie Hovell; two *s. Educ.:* Manchester College of Art (J. M. Holmes, P. W. Keen, 1937-42); R. M. I. Heywood Prize; Proctor Travelling Scholarship (1948) Italy, France. Freelance artist. *Agent:* R.P. Gossop, London (1946-89). President, Manchester Academy of Fine Art (1984-90); Visiting Lecturer, Cleveland, U.S.A. (1979). *Exhib.:* London, Manchester, Glasgow, Edinburgh, U.S.A. and Canada, etc. *Official purchases:* V. & A. Museum, M/Cr City A.G., Westminster Bank, Rochdale, Stoke, Manchester, Newcastle Education Committees, etc. *Commissions:* United Steel Co., Post Office, B.B.C., British Transport, Odhams, Macmillan, etc. *Address:* 6 Wardle Rd., Sale, Ches. M33 3BX.

JARAY, Tess, D.F.A. (Lond., 1960); painter in oil and etcher; *b* Vienna, 31 Dec., 1937; *d* of Francis F. Jaray, M.I.Chem.E. *Educ.:* Alice Ottley School, Worcester; *studied art* at St. Martin's School of Art (1954-57), Slade School of Fine Art (1957-60). *Exhib.:* solo exhbns.: Whitworth A.G., Manchester, Ashmolean Museum, Oxford, Serpentine Gallery, London. *Work in permanent collections:* Stadtisches Museum, Leverkusen, Walker Art Gallery, Liverpool, Arts Council of Gt. Britain, Tate Gallery, Graves Art Gallery, Sheffield, Warwick University. *Commissions:* Floor for Victoria Station, London, Centenary Square, Birmingham, Cathedral Precinct pedestrianisation, Wakefield. *Address:* 29 Camden Sq., London NW1. *Signs work:* "Tess Jaray."

JARMAN, Anne Nesta, H.R.M.S. (1981); prize winner for miniature portrait, National Eisteddfod of Wales; artist of miniature portraits in water-colour and pastel; *b* Sutton, Surrey; *d* of the late W. R. Jarman, I.S.O., B.A., F.I.A. *Educ.:* Penarth County School, Bedales School, Petersfield; *studied art* at Cardiff School of Art; Heatherley's, London; privately with the late Alfred Praga in miniature painting. *Exhib.:* R.A., Paris Salon, R.M.S., R.W.A., R.C.A., S. Wales Art Soc., etc. *Work in permanent collection:* Apothecaries Hall, London. *Address:* 4 Ellenborough Ct., 17 Ellenborough Park N., Weston-super-Mare, Avon BS23 1XQ. *Signs work:* "Nesta Jarman."

JARVIS, Gloria, N.D.D.; Médaille d'Argent Paris (1976); Académicien d'Italie, Médaille d'or (1980); artist in oil, water-colour, pastel, ink, gouache; lecturer on historic costume and instructor in costume drawing, Polytechnic, Regent St. (1950-63); *d* of R. V. Jarvis, artist; *m* A. Raymond Smith, B.A. (1964). *Educ.:* Heathfield-Norris School, Harrow; Aylesbury Grammar School; *studied art* at St. Martin's School of Art, London, under James Bateman, R.A.,

A.R.W.S., for drawing, painting and composition; the history of art at Florence University. *Exhib.*: R.A., N.E.A.C., N.S., Leicester Galleries; one-man show, Brussels (1970...). *Work in permanent collections:* Abbot Hall A.G., Kendal; Museum of the Dynasty, Brussels; International Museum of Carnival and Mask, Binche, Belgium; and private collections. *Work repro.*: Macmillan, Brussels Times. Short stories published; broadcast by B.B.C. *Address:* The Bungalow, Tyler Cl., Canterbury, Kent CT2 7BD. *Signs work:* "Gloria Jarvis."

JASINSKI, Alfons B., R.S.W. (1978), Latimer award R.S.A. (1975), D.A. Travelling scholar (1968); artist in acrylic, water-colour, pastel (seashore/landscape); principal teacher of art, St.Andrew's H.S., Kirkcaldy; *b* Falkirk, 1945; *s* of Alfons B. Jasinski; *m* Ann Conlan; one *s*, two *d*. *Studied art* at Edinburgh College of Art (1964-68, Philipson, Houston, Blackadder, Cumming). *Exhib.*: Loomshop Gallery, Lower Largo, Scottish Gallery, Kirkcaldy A.G., Artis: Flying Colours. *Work in permanent collections:* S.A.C., Edinburgh Schools Collection, Aberdeen City A.G., Duke of Devonshire. *Address:* 15 Normand Rd., Dysart, Fife KY1 2XN. *Signs work:* "A. B. Jasinski."

JEFFERSON, Alan, A.R.C.A.; painter; retired from teaching at Dept. of Fine Art, University of Portsmouth (1983); *b* S. Kensington, 7 Apr., 1918; *s* of Arthur Edward Jefferson; *m* Denise Audrey; one *s*, one *d*. *Educ.*: Mitcham County School; *studied art* at Wimbledon School of Art and R.C.A. *Exhib.*: R.A., Redfern, Piccadilly and provincial galleries; one-man exhibitions Bear Lane Gallery, Oxford, Hiscock Gallery, Portsmouth, City A.G., Portsmouth. *Work in private collections:* U.K., South Africa, U.S.A. *Official purchases:* Portsmouth Corp. *Address:* 22 Bell Rd., Cosham, Hants. PO6 3NX. *Signs work:* "ALAN JEFFERSON."

JEFFERSON, Annelise, M.A. (1990), A.R.O.I. (1993); fine art painter in oil on canvas; *b* Pembury, 1965. *Educ.*: Chichester High School; *studied art* at West Surrey College of Art and Design (Stephen Farthing), Royal Academy (Norman Adams). *Exhib.*: R.A. Summer Exhbn. (1988, 1989, 1990, 1991), Bonhams: The New Generation (1990), Royal Overseas League (1990), Rubicorn Gallery, Dublin (1991), The Hunting Art Prizes finalist (U.K. and Paris, 1991), N.E.A.C., Mall Galleries (1991-92). *Work in permanent collections:* South East Arts, Lloyds of London, Leics. C.C.; also private collections in U.K., Eire, Canada. *Address:* Maycotts Lodge, The Green, Matfield, Tonbridge, Kent TN12 7JU. *Signs work:* see appendix.

JELLICOE, Colin; painter in oils and acrylics; art gallery director; *b* 1 Nov., 1942. *Educ.*: Heald Place School; *studied art* at Manchester Regional College of Art. *Exhib.*: one-man shows: Monks Hall Museum (1970), Stockport A.G. (1981), Salford A.G. (1981); group shows: Bulls Eye Gallery, Lichfield (1970), Northern Images Manchester (1974), North West One, Chenil Gallery, London (1976), Five at Salford, Salford A.G. (1979), North West Two, National Theatre, London (1979), Contemporary Arts Fair, Bath (1981, 1982, 1983), Edinburgh Festival Fringe (1983, 1984, 1985), International Contemporary Art Fair, London (1984, 1985, 1986), Royal Exchange Theatre with M. Goddard (1985); open shows: Manchester Academy City A.G. (1972, 1973, 1975, 1976, 1981, 1984, 1985, 1989, 1992), R.A. Summer Exhbn. (1981); many others in Preston, Accrington, Bolton, Southsea, Wimbledon and Manchester. *Address:* 82 Portland St., Manchester M1 4QX. *Signs work:* see appendix.

JELLICOE, Sir Geoffrey Alan, Kt. (1979), C.B.E., F.R.I.B.A., M.T.P.I., P.P.I.L.A.; awarded medal, American Soc. of Landscape Architects (1981); medal, British Landscape Inst. (1985); architect, town-planner, landscape architect; designer of Kennedy Memorial at Runnymede, Sutton Place Landscape, etc.; late trustee, Tate Gallery; *b* London; *s* of George Edward Jellicoe; *m* Ursula Pares. *Educ.:* Cheltenham College; *studied art* at A.A. *Exhib.:* R.A., etc. *Publications:* Italian Gardens of the Renaissance (joint), Studies in Landscape Design, Vols. I, II and III: The Landscape of Man.; The Moody Historical Gardens. *Address:* 14 Highpoint, North Hill, Highgate, London N6 4BA.

JENKINS, Christopher, Slade Dip. (Painting) (1957), A.T.C. (1958); potter in thrown and glazed oxidised stoneware, artist in water-colour; Mem. C.P.A., N.P.A.; *b* B'ham, 1933; *s* of Lincoln and Phyllis Jenkins, both artists; divorced; one *s*, one *d*. *Educ.:* Harrogate Grammar School; *studied art* at Harrogate School of Art (1949-52), Slade School of Fine Art (1952-54 and 1956-57), Central School (ceramics, 1957-59). *Exhib.:* V. & A., Crafts Centre, C.P.A., York, Scarborough, Kendal, Nottingham, Manchester, Liverpool, Tokyo, Copenhagen, Paris. *Work in permanent collections:* North West Arts, L.E.A's: London, Leicester, Bucks., N. Yorks, Kirklees. *Address:* 19 Towngate, Marsden, Huddersfield HD7 6DD. *Signs work:* see appendix.

JENKINS, Heinke, R.B.S.A. (1967), R.B.A. (1977); printmaker in linocut, art teacher; *b* Heilbronn, W.Germany, 2 Jul., 1937; *d* of Dr. Mayer; one *s*. *Educ.:* Heilbronn Grammar School; *studied art:* at Stuttgart Academy of Arts (Prof. Henninger), Stuttgart College of Graphic and Illustration (Prof. Leo Schobinger). *Exhib.:* Germany, U.S.A., England. *Work in permanent collections:* Heilbronn A.G., Stuttgart A.G. *Publications:* illustrated, Arts Review, 'Ambit' poetry magazine, 'Circle' poems, M. Armstrong. *Address:* 26 Allesley Cl., Sutton Coldfield, Birmingham. *Clubs:* R.B.S.A., R.B.A., Heilbronn Kunstler Bund. *Signs work:* "HEINKE."

JENNINGS, Walter Robin; artist in oil; portraits, landscape, and equestrian pictures; *b* Old Hill, Staffs., 11 Mar., 1927; *s* of William Dennis Jennings; *m* Barbara Wilkinson. *Educ.:* Macefields Secondary School; *studied art* at Dudley and Staffordshire Art School, Brierley Hill School of Art, Birmingham School of Art. *Exhib.:* R.B.S.A., R.W.E.A., R.Cam.A., Royal Institute Galleries, Utd. Soc. of Artists, N.E.A.C., etc. *Work in permanent collections:* Allison House, Mr. H. Woodhouse; Enville Hall, Mr. and Mrs. J. Bissel. *Official purchases:* Brierley Hill A.G. *Publications:* Royle, Medici, Solomon and Whitehead, etc. *Address:* Kestrels, Caunsall, Cookley, nr. Kidderminster, Worcs. *Signs work:* see appendix.

JESTY, Ronald, R.B.A. (1982); artist in water-colour and acrylic, part-time lecturer; *b* Weymouth, Dorset, 7 May, 1926; *s* of Benjamin Jesty; *m* Margaret Johnson. *Educ.:* Weymouth Grammar School; no formal art training. *Exhib.:* R.I., R.W.A., R.W.S., R.B.A., R.A.; eight one-man shows. *Work in permanent collection:* Somerset C.C. *Address:* 24B Brunswick St., Yeovil, Som. BA20 1QY. *Club:* Artists 303. *Signs work:* "R. Jesty" and year.

JOBSON, Patrick; landscape and marine painter and draughtsman in oil, water-colour, acrylic and pastel; illustrator in black and white; heraldic artist and designer; demonstrator – oils, water-colour, pastel, charcoal. Signs for many of princ. London brewers. *Work repro.:* illustrations (O.U.P., Blackie, Macmillan), etc. *Address:* 117 Eton Ave., N. Wembley, Middx. *Clubs:* Langham Sketch (Past President), Wapping Group (Past President). *Signs work:* see appendix.

JOHANNESON, Steven Thor; artist in water-colour, gouache, pastel, and some oil; *b* Minneapolis, Minn., 16 June, 1948. *Educ.:* Menominee High School,

Michigan; Bethel College, St. Paul, Minn; *studied art* at Heatherly-Wilson School of Art (1970-73, Clive Duncan, Helen Wilson, David Ufland). *Exhib.:* R.S.M.A., S.WL.A., several mixed and one-man shows in the West Country and London including Arty Facts Padstow, St. Ives Gallery, Mid-Cornwall Galleries, Boscastle Gallery, Gallerie Marin Appledore, Solent Gallery Lymington, White Oak Gallery, Edina, Minneapolis. *Address:* Flat 4, Brentwood Ct., Treyarnon Bay, nr. Padstow, N. Cornwall PL28 8PL. *Signs work:* "S.T. Johanneson."

JOHN, Anthony T.; artist in oil, water-colour, gouache; paints mainly marine subjects; *b* Wales, 1905; *studied art* at Chelsea School under P. H. Jowett, and in Paris. *Exhib.:* Wertheim Gallery, Bloomsbury Gallery, Redfern Gallery; one-man shows in Canada and S. Africa. One time mem., Natal Soc. of Artists, S. African Soc. of Artists, and Artist International Assoc. *Agents:* Piccadilly Gallery, Cork St., W.1. *Address:* Flat 5, Charlwood House, 47 Vauxhall Bridge Rd., London SW1V 2SY. *Signs work:* water-colours and drawings, "Anthony John."

JOHN, Samuel, B.A. (Lond. 1958), M.B.I.M. (1968), I.P.M. (1960), M.Inst.M. (1970), M.Inst.Ex., former Overseas Marketing Manager, Glaxo Group (1972), R.L.S.S.Inst. (1953); artist in oil, pastel, water-colour, writer, former medical student, business entrepreneur; *b* Newport, Mon., 9 Feb., 1935; *s* of Col. Samuel William Isitt, and opera singer Nancy Sully; *m* Anne Drummond-Leigh, actress; three *s*, one *d. Educ.:* Newport High School; London University; Ashridge and Sundridge Management Colleges (Marketing); *studied art* at Chelsea (St. Mark and St. John College) (1955-58, P. G. Roberts, R.A.); qualified as teacher (1957). *Exhib.:* Thames Gallery (1978), Chenil Galleries (1956), The Clement, Oxford (1977-79), Oxford Art Soc. (1977-78), Barclay Gallery, Chester (1980), St. Martin's, London (1983), Royal Overseas League, London (1983). *Work in permanent collections:* St. Helen's Convent, Oxford; Blackfriars, Oxford; Mr. R. Bradon, Australia. *Publications:* The Sacred and The Profane (1980), The Proitiation (1980), The Act of Love (1983); awarded Koestler Prize for Verse (1980). *Films:* (Equity Mem.) Coronation Street, Pardon the Expression, The Jewel in the Crown, The Man in Room 17, etc. *Address:* c/o Browse Darby, 19 Cork St., London W1X 2LP. *Clubs:* Royal Overseas, Oxford and Cambridge. *Literary Agent:* Curtis Brown, London. *Theatrical:* Joan Reddin, London. *Signs work:* "John."

JOHNSON, Annette, S.W.A. (1987); painter-etcher in water-colour and etching; mem. Printmakers Council; *b* London, 24 March., 1943; *m* Alan; one *s,* one *d. Studied art:* etching at Morley College; painting at Sir John Cass College of Art. *Exhib.:* N.S.P.S. (1985), R.S.M.A. (1985), R.I. (1981), R.A. (1985), S.W.A. (1981). *Address:* 3 Ballast Quay, Greenwich, London. *Signs work:* "Annette Johnson."

JOHNSON, Ben; artist in acrylic; *b* Llandudno, 24 Aug., 1946; *m* Sheila Johnson; two *s. Studied art* at R.C.A. (1965-69, Carel Weight, Peter de Francia). *Exhib.:* one-man shows: New York, London, Bradford; group shows: England, Scotland, Ireland, Belgium, U.S.A., Poland, Yugoslavia, Spain, Australia, France, Germany, Switzerland, Portugal, Italy. *Work in public collections:* Boymans-van Beuningen Museum Rotterdam, British Council, Tate Gallery, Contemporary Art Soc., De Beers/CSO Coll., R.I.B.A., Glasgow City A.G., Whitworth Gallery Manchester, Centre Georges Pompidou Paris, V. & A., B.P., Deutsche Bank. *Commissions:* Elemeta Ltd., D.O.E., British Gas, R.I.B.A., Ove Arup & Partners, Société de Vins de France, etc. Numerous publications. *Address:* 16 Wingate Rd., London W6 0UR. *Signs work:* "Ben Johnson."

JOHNSON, Brian Robert, R.I. (1988) Bronze Medal Award (1987), Hon. Citizen, Victoria B.C.; Graduated with distinction from The Art Center College of Design, Los Angeles, Calif. with a Bachelor of Professional Arts (1962); artist in water-colour; *b* Victoria, B.C., Canada, 4 Apr., 1932; *m*; two *s*, one *d. Educ.:* Victoria High School, Victoria College; Art Center College of Design, Los Angeles. *Exhib.:* R.I., R.B.A., A.W.S., F.C.A, C.S.P.W.C., N.W.W.S., C.S.M.A., numerous one-man and group exhbns. in Canada and U.S. *Work in permanent and private collections:* Canada, U.S., Australia, U.K. and Europe. *Address:* 1766 Hauttain St., Victoria, B.C., V8R 2L2, Canada. *Signs work:* "Brian R. Johnson."

JOHNSON, Colin Trever; Mem. Manchester Academy; artist in oils, water-colours, collage, pencil, ink; Artist in Residence: Manchester Music Festival (1980), City of London Festival (1984), Dolton and Dowland Festival, Devon (1986), Wigan International Jazz Festival (1986, 1987), International Nuclear Physics Conference, Harrogate (1986); *b* Blackpool, 11 Apr., 1942; *s* of Richard Johnson. *Educ.:* Worsley Technical College; *studied art* at Salford and Manchester Colleges. *Exhib.:* one-man, N.W.A.'s, Mid-Pennine Arts, Royal Exchange Theatre, Royal Northern College of Music, Theatre Royal York, The Barbican, London, The Guildhall, London, Granada T.V., and the public galleries of: Bolton, Oldham, Derby, Bury, Southport, Salford, Wigan, Worthing, Warrington, Falmouth, Blackpool, Eccles, Scarborough, Harrogate, Buxton, Taunton, Ayr, Bridgewater, Swinton and Blackburn; one-man in private galleries: Salt House, St. Ives; Vernon, Preston; Liberty's, London; Pitcairn, Cheshire; Stables Theatre, Hastings; Roupell, London; Bread St., Penzance; Portico, Manchester, etc.; mixed shows, Tib Lane, Manchester; Park Sq., Leeds; R.A. Business Gallery and Mercury Gallery, London; Manchester Academy; Penwith Soc., St. Ives; New Craftsman, St. Ives and Newlyn Gallery. *Directed:* Swinton Festival (1973), Bolton Festival (1979). *Work in permanent collections:* Accrington, Derby, Salford, Southport, Wigan, Worthing, City of London, City of Manchester, Salford University, Manchester University, B.B.C., Lancs. Libraries and Educ. Com. *Address:* 27 Bedford Rd., St. Ives, Cornwall. *Signs work:* "Colin T. Johnson."

JOHNSON, Joy Alexandra, B.F.A. (Hons.) (1980), Higher Dip. (Lond.); artist in oils, water-colour; *b* Hull, 26 Aug., 1958; *d* of Arnold Johnson. *Educ.:* Hatfield High School, Yorks.; *studied art* at Newcastle upon Tyne Polytechnic (1977-80), Slade School of Fine Art (1982-84, Lawrence Gowing). *Exhib.:* Northern Young Contemporaries (1979), Sainsbury Centre (1980), Mappin Gallery Open Art (1984, 1985), R.A. Summer Exhbn. (1985), several solo exhbns. in London. Received award from Swiss based Vordemberge Gildewart Foundation (1986). *Contact address:* 17 Bempton La., Bridlington, E. Yorks. YO16 5EJ. *Signs work:* "J.A. Johnson."

JOHNSTON, Brenda; painter in oil and scraper board; *b* London, 8 Dec., 1930; *d* of Walter Rumble; *m* David Johnston; two *s*, one *d. Educ.:* Rosebery Grammar School, Epsom; *studied art* at Epsom School of Art (1948-49, 1955-60) under Michael Cadman, Leslie Worth; Reigate School of Art (1961-65) under Eric Waugh. *Exhib.:* R.A., R.B.A., Nimes and Avignon, Arts Council Exhbn. Midlands and East Anglia; nine one-man shows. *Work in permanent collection:* Ryder Memorial Bequest. *Address:* Russells, 36 Oakfield Rd.,

Ashtead, Surrey KT21 2RD. *Clubs:* F.P.S., Thames Valley Art, Leatherhead Art. *Signs work:* "Brenda Johnston" or "BJ."

JOHNSTON, Duncan; sculptor in lignum vitae, bronze, ceramics; *b* Liverpool, 9 Mar., 1924. *Studied* commercial art Liverpool School of Art, self-taught sculptor since demobilisation in 1946, teacher trained 1948, Royal Academy Scholarship 1966, left teaching 1967. Organiser of M-S.S.E. with special reference to blind and partially-sighted visitors. *Work in permanent collections:* Arts Council of Northern Ireland, R.N.I.B., Kingston-upon-Hull Education Committee, Exhall Grange School, The Argory (National Trust), St. George's Church, Museo Michelangelo, Tel Aviv Museum of Modern Art. *Address:* 151 Craddocks Ave., Ashtead, Surrey KT21 1NR. *Signs work:* see appendix.

JOHNSTON, George Bonar, D.A. (Edin.), R.S.W.; artist in oil, gouache and water-colour; adviser in art, Tayside Region Educ. Authority; *b* Edinburgh, 14 June, 1933. *Educ.:* Bathgate Academy; *studied art* at Edinburgh College of Art (1951-56) under William Gillies, P.P.R.S.A., R.S.W., and Robin Philipson, P.P.R.S.A., A.R.A., R.S.W. *Exhib.:* regular exhibitor R.S.A., R.S.W., R.G.I.; one-man shows: Perth, Kirkcaldy, Glasgow, Dundee; mixed shows: Edinburgh, Aberdeen, London, Paris, Toronto, New York. *Work in permanent collections:* Glasgow, Strathclyde, Edinburgh, Dundee, London, Toronto, U.S.A., France, Australia. *Address:* 10 Collingwood Cres., Barnhill, Dundee. *Signs work:* "Johnston."

JOHNSTONE, John, D.A.Edin., A.R.S.A.; painter in oil, lecturer; *b* Falkirk, Stirlingshire, 11 Sept., 1937; *s* of Jack Johnstone; *m* Gwen Rodger; one *s*, two *d*. *Educ.:* Graeme High School, Falkirk; *studied art* at Edinburgh College of Art (1957-61, Sir William Gillies). *Work in permanent collections:* Scottish Arts Council; Arts Council of G.B.; Hamilton A.G., Canada; Olinda Museum, Sao Paulo, Brazil; Aberdeen A.G.; Liverpool University; Watson Trust, Edinburgh; Campden Burgh Council, London; Dunbartonshire Educ. Trust, Dunbarton. *Address:* The Luggie, Lauder, Berwickshire TD2 6QT, Scotland. *Signs work:* "John Johnstone."

JOICEY, Richard Raylton, G.M., V.R.D., R.S.M.A.; painter in oil and water-colour; *b* London, 5 Oct., 1925; *s* of Edward R. Joicey, M.C.; one *d*. *Educ.:* Harrow School; *studied art* at Sir John Cass College of Art (1967). *Publication:* A Mill in a Million, Harbour Sketches, Joicey Minor. *Address:* The Lawn, White Chimney Row, Westbourne, Emsworth, Hants. PO10 8RS. *Signs work:* "Joicey."

JOŃCZYK, Prof. Dr. Leon; painter, graphic artist, art historian, author of publications about theory of art, experimental printing; Memb., National and International Academies for Arts, Sciences and Humanities, Paris, Bordeaux, Naples, Rome; JSAST, San Francisco; University Prof., Academia Polona Artium; Head of Graphic Art Dept., Munich; President, Assoc. of Graphic Artists, W. Germany; *b* Katowice, Poland, 25 July, 1934. *Educ.:* High School, Poland; *studied art* in Poland, Netherlands, Gt. Britain. *Exhib.:* Czechoslovakia, France, Italy, E. and W. Germany, Gt. Britain, Netherlands, Poland, Sweden, Switzerland, Tasmania, Turkey, Yugoslavia, U.S.A. *Work in permanent collections:* more than 30 galleries and museums in Europe, public and private collections in Europe, Australia, U.S.A. *Work repro.:* illustrated monographs in different languages. *Address:* Franz-Joseph-Str. 30/IV, 8080 München, Germany. *Signs work:* "L. Jończyk."

JONES, Allen, N.D.D. (1959), A.T.D. (1960), R.A. (1984); artist in oil, metal, wood, water-colour and lithography; Trustee, British Museum (1990—); *b* Southampton, 1 Sept., 1937; *s* of William Jones; divorced; two *d. Educ.:* Ealing Grammar School; *studied art* at Hornsey College of Art (1955-59), R.C.A. (1960-61). *Exhib.:* since 1961 numerous museum and group shows; now represented by Waddington Galleries, London; James Corcoran, Santa Monica, U.S.A.; Patrice Trigano, Paris; Charles Cowles, N.Y.C. *Work in permanent collections:* public museums and private collection world-wide. *Address:* 41 Charterhouse Sq., London EC1. *Clubs:* Garrick, Chelsea Arts. *Signs work:* "Allen Jones."

JONES, Aneurin M., N.D.D. (1950), A.T.D. (1955); artist in oil, acrylic, mixed media; retd. Head of Art Dept., Preseli Comprehensive School, N. Pembrokeshire; *b* Trecastle, Breconshire, 1930; *m* Julie Jones; one *s*, one *d. Educ.:* Brecon Grammar School; *studied art* at Swansea College of Art (Kenneth Hancock, A.R.C.A., William Price, A.R.C.A.), Prix de Rome Scholar. *Exhib.:* numerous one-man and mixed shows England and Wales. *Work in permanent collection:* National Library of Wales, Aberystwyth. *Address:* Heulwen, Aberystwyth Rd., Cardigan, Dyfed SA43 1LU. *Signs work:* "ANEURIN M. JONES"; 1993 onwards "ANEURIN."

JONES, Edward Scott, R.C.A. (1964); artist in oil, water-colour, gouache; *b* Liverpool, 6 June, 1922; *m* Althea; one *s*, one *d. Educ.:* Anfield Road Elementary School; *studied art* at Liverpool College of Art. *Exhib.:* R.C.A., Williamson A.G., Bluecoat A.G., R.I., R.S.M.A. *Work in permanent collections:* Merseyside Council Libraries, Blackpool Corp. A.G., Salford A.G., Bolton A.G., Williamson A.G., Birkenhead, also works in private collections. *Address:* 18 The Fairway, Knotty Ash, Liverpool L12 3HS. *Signs work:* "E. Scott Jones."

JONES, Ian, B.F.A.(Hons.) (1979), M.F.A. (1982); artist; lecturer in Fine Art; *b* B'ham, 3 July, 1947; *m* Carole A. Jones; two *s. Educ.:* Queensbridge Secondary Modern, Moseley; *studied art* at B'ham Polytechnic School of Fine Art (1975-78, Roy Abel, Trevor Halliday), R.C.A. (1979-82, Peter de Francia). *Exhib.:* regular exhbns. since 1981, group and individual shows. *Work in private and public collections:* Britain, Europe, America. *Address:* Anderson O'Day Gallery, 255 Portobello Rd., London W11 1LR. *Signs work:* "Ian Jones."

JONES, Joan, A.R.B.S.A. (1970); painter in oil and water-colour, also paper collage; painting instructor in still life, portraits, flowers and landscape; *b* Solihull, 16 Apr., 1924; *d* of Leslie Woodhouse Price, M.A., M.D.; *m*; one *s. Educ.:* Malvern Hall, Solihull; *studied art* at Sutton Coldfield, Bourneville, Birmingham (1950-60, Dennis Greenwood, A.T.D., Alex Jackson, A.T.D., R.B.S.A.). *Exhib.:* B'ham, Sutton Coldfield, Worcester, etc. *Address:* Elms Cottage, Grafton Flyford, Worcester WR7 4PG. *Signs work:* "Joan Jones" sloping upwards towards right hand side.

JONES, John Edward, N.D.D. (1951), A.T.D. (1952), Dip.F.A. (Slade 1954), R.W.A.; painter in oil, pen, etc.; University senior lecturer; Regional Director of Open College of the Arts; London University Moderator G.C.E. 'O', 'A' level and G.C.S.E. Art; President, Leeds Fine Art Club; *b* Bristol, 19 Aug., 1926; *s* of Stanley Jones; *m* Gabriela Jones; two *d. Educ.:* Winterbourne Elementary; Colston's School, Stapleton; *studied art* at West of England College of Art (1942-44 (army intervened) 1948-52, George Sweet), Slade School (1952-54, Rogers, Coldstream, Wittkower). *Exhib.:* R.W.A., Leeds Fine Art, and private galleries. *Work in permanent collections:* University of Leeds, R.W.A.

Publications: author, Wonders of the Stereoscope. *Address:* 20 Hollin La., Leeds LS16 5LZ. *Club:* Chelsea Arts. *Signs work:* "J.E. Jones" or "Jones" (and date).

JONES, Joyce Margaret (née Mellor); illustrator, miniature painter of portraits, animals, floral; *b* Bangalore, India. *Studied art* at Regional College of Art, Manchester (1954-57), St. Martin's School of Art (1957-59), Italy (1959-60). *Work purchased by:* Indian Army (portraits), miniature collectors, commercial dealers in U.K., U.S.A., S. Africa, Australia. *Publications:* illustrated books for Longmans, University of Wales Press, Cambridge School Classics, N.W. Arts Assoc., Thames and Hudson, Encyclopedia Britannica, Nature Conservancy. *Address:* 3 Queens Park, Colwyn Bay, Clwyd LL29 7BG.

JONES, Leslie, A.R.E., A.R.C.A., D.A.(Manc.), H.R.Cam.A., Rome Scholar; painter, printmaker, illustrator; taught at Hornsey, Kingston, St. Martin's Schools of Art (1961-67); H.M.I. (1967-83); Bangor (1987-89); *b* Tremadoc, 26 June, 1934. *Studied art* at Regional College of Art, Manchester (1951-55), Royal College of Art (1955-58), British School at Rome (1958-60); visitor at Belgrade Academy (1959). *Exhib.:* London, Rome, U.S.A., Austria. *Work in permanent collections:* V. & A., Arts Council, University of Oregon, University of Wales, National Library Wales, L.E.As. *Publications:* illustrated books for Lion & Unicorn, Longmans, University of Wales Press, Cambridge School Classics Project. *Address:* 3 Queens Park, Colwyn Bay, Clwyd LL29 7BG.

JONES, Nick Harrison, B.A.(Hons.), M.A., Cert.Ed.; artist/designer in pencil, ink, water-colour, mixed media; lecturer in graphic design; *b* Wombourne, Staffs., 2 Aug., 1958; *s* of Cyril James Jones; *m* Claire Miles. *Educ.:* Ounsdale School; *studied art* at Manchester Polytechnic, B'ham Polytechnic. *Exhib.:* Herts. Open Art (1989, 1991), Knapp Gallery, London (1989, 1990). *Work in permanent collection:* Hertford Museum, Herts. *Address:* 380 York Rd., Pin Green, Stevenage, Herts. SG1 4EL. *Club:* S.G.F.A. *Signs work:* "Nick Jones" or "NhJ."

JONES, Olwen, R.A.S. (1968), R.E. (1978), R.W.S. (1989); painter in oil and water-colour, printmaker in relief and etching; *b* London, 1 Mar., 1945; *d* of William Jones; *m* Charles Bartlett. *Educ.:* Harrow School of Art (1960-65); *studied art* at Royal Academy Schools (1965-68), engraving under Gertrude Hermes. *Exhib.:* first one-man: Zaydler Gallery, London (1971). *Work in permanent collections:* National Museum of Wales, Norwich Castle Museum, Reading Museum, Nuffield Foundation. *Address:* St. Andrews, Fingringhoe, nr. Colchester, Essex CO5 7GB. *Signs work:* "Olwen Jones."

JONES, Rosamund, N.D.D. (Painting), R.E.; artist in etching, water-colour; shepherd; *b* Harrogate, 1944; *m*; one *s*, three *d*. *Educ.:* Harrogate; *studied art* at Harrogate College of Art (Mr. Pemsil), Leeds College of Art (1960-64, Mr. Taylor). *Exhib.:* Cartwright Hall Bradford, Oxford Gallery, Zella 9 Gallery, R.A., R.S.A., Bankside Gallery. *Address:* New Bridge Farm, Birstwith, Harrogate. *Signs work:* "Rosamund Jones."

JONES, Royston, Dip. A.D. (1968), M.F.A. (Illinois, 1971); photographer; computer art and design; Head of School, Arts, Media and Design, St. Helens College; *b* Wolverhampton, 15 Jan., 1947; *s* of Percy Jones; *m* Sheila Donoghue. *Studied art* at Birmingham College of Art and Design (1965-68, John Walker, Trevor Halliday), University of Illinois (1969-71, Jerome Savage, Art Sinsebaugh, Bart Parker). *Exhib.:* regularly in Britain and U.S.A. *Address:* School of Arts, Media and Design, St. Helens College, Brook St., St. Helens, Merseyside WA10 1PZ.

JONES, Stanley Robert, A.T.D. (1950), F.S.A.; printmaker and archaeologist; *b* Birmingham, 9 June, 1927; *s* of George Jones, brewery departmental manager. *Educ.:* Elementary School; Yardley Grammar School, Birmingham; *studied art* at Birmingham College of Art under Harold Smith, B. Fleetwood-Walker, A.R.A. (1942-45, 1948-50), R.A. Schools under B. Fleetwood-Walker, A.R.A., Henry Rushbury, R.A. (1950-55). *Exhib.:* R.A., R.B.S.A., Printmakers' Council Venues, South Yorkshire Open. *Work in permanent collection:* Graves Art Gallery, Sheffield. *Address:* 118 Totley Brook Rd., Sheffield S17. *Signs work:* see appendix.

JONES, Steven; Dip. in Illustration (1981); artist/illustrator in oil and watercolour; *b* Chester, 5 Apr., 1959; *s* of Peter Jones; *m* Sian; one *s. Educ.:* Colwyn High School, Colwyn Bay; *studied art* at Wrexham College of Art (1976-81, Keith Bowen). *Exhib.:* Tegfryn A.G., Menai Bridge, Glyn-y-Weddw, Llanbedrog. *Publications:* book covers, magazine illustrations, company reports, film posters and B.P. Calendar. Specialises in figures in landscape scenes particularly beach scenes and golf scenes. Many paintings sold through auctions in Britain including Christies, Bonhams and Chrystals. *Address:* 33 Brynffynnon Rd., Portdinorwic, Gwynedd, N. Wales LL56 4SX. *Signs work:* "Steven Jones."

JONES, Yvonne, B.A.Hons.F.A. (1980); painter; *b* Holywell, N. Wales, 9 Oct., 1946; *d* of Cecil Evans; *m* Peter M. Jones; two *s. Educ.:* Holywell Grammar School; *studied art* at Liverpool College of Art. *Exhib.:* mixed: Welsh Touring Show, Mall Gallery, Liverpool Festival of Arts, Wrexham Arts Centre, Welsh Opens, R.A. Summer Exhbns. (1989, 1990), Portsmouth City Gallery, Doncaster City Gallery; European tour: one-man shows: Theatr Clwyd Mold (supp W.A.C.), Aberystwyth Arts Centre (supp W.A.C.), Bridewell Studios Liverpool (supp Eastern Arts), Quay Arts Centre (supp Southern Arts). *Work in permanent collections:* Welsh Arts Council, Merseyside Arts Trust, New Hall, Cambridge, Contemporary Women Artists; private collections: U.K. and Germany. *Associations:* A.V.A.W., N.A.A., B.P.S. *Address:* Hazelwood, Waters Green, Brockenhurst, Hants. SO42 7RG.

JONES-ROWE, Avril, N.D.D., D.F.A.(Slade), M.F.P.S.; painter in oil and acrylic, sculptor in bronze, landscape gardener, teacher, art historian; *b* New Forest, Hants., 1934. *Studied art* at Southampton Art College (1951-55), Sander Theatre School, Southampton (1952-54), Slade School (1955-57), Perugia University (1959). *Exhib.:* group shows: Young Contemporaries, London Group, Loggia Gallery, Trends, Bloomsbury Gallery, Bougton Aluph Church, Stroud Festival; one-man shows: Bailey House, Canterbury (Artist in Residence, 1965), B'ham University (1967), St. Pancras Hospital (1975), Loggia Gallery (1987). *Address:* 25 Station Rd, Alderholt, Fordingbridge, Hants. *Signs work:* "Jones-Rowe."

JONZEN, Karin, F.R.B.S.; annual award trophy for 'Action Research' and R.A.D.A. (1979); gold medal, Academie Italia delle Arte (1980); gold medal, International Parliament for Safety and Peace, U.S.A. (1983); silver medal, R.B.S. (1983); sculptor (terracotta, bronze, and stone); *b* 1914; *d* of U. Lowenadler. *Studied art* at Slade School, Stockholm Royal Academy. Slade Scholarship and Diploma (1934); Prix de Rome (1939). *Work in permanent collections:* Tate Gallery (1985), Brighton, Bradford, Glasgow, Liverpool, Southend and Melbourne A.G. *Official purchases:* Arts Council; Selwyn College, Cambridge; L.C.C. housing estate at Lewisham (1960); St. Michael's Church, Golder's Green (1961); Guildford Cathedral (1962); World Health Organization Headquarters, New Delhi (1963), World Health Organization Headquarters,

Geneva (1965). Exhibited three works for City of London Festival (1968), one work retained, Madonna and Child, purchased for St. Mary-le-Bow (1969). Exhibited New York, one torso acquired by Andrew White Museum, Cornell University (1969); life size bronze figure commissioned by London Co-operation for site at the Barbican (1970); Over life size group for Guildhall Square. Gift of Lord Blackford to London Co-operation (1972); ¼ life size Pièta for Swedish Church, Marylebone (1975); ¼ life size figure Young Girl purchased for Cadogan Estate erected in Sloane Gdns.; over life size bronze portrait bust of Samuel Pepys purchased for Seething Lane Garden (1983); Madonna and Child purchased for St. Mary and St. Gabriel Church, S. Harting, Hants (1985); Madonna and Child purchased for St. Saviours Church, Maida Vale (1985). Portrait busts include: Malcolm Muggeridge, Sir Alan Herbert, Sir Hugh Casson, Dame Ninette de Valois, Donald Trelford, Sir Monty Finiston, Paul Scofield. *Publication:* Karin Jonzen, Sculptor (Bachman & Turner, 1976). *Address:* 6A Gunter Gr., London SW1 0UJ. *Signs work:* "K. Jonzen."

JOPE, Anne, B.A.Hons. (1970), A.R.E. (1979), R.E. (1984), Central Postgrad. Printmaking Dip. (1981), S.W.E. (1984); painter in oil paint and water-colour, printmaker in wood engraving, woodcut and linocut; *b* Corfe Mullen, Dorset, 31 Jan., 1945; *d* of William John Purrington; *m* John Anthony Jope. *Studied art* at Ealing Art College (1966-67), Central School of Art and Design (1967-70, 1980-81). *Exhib.:* nine one-man shows, R.A., N.E.A.C., R.B.A., Camden Arts Centre, Ferens A.G., Graffiti, Morley Gallery, Royal Western Academy, St. David's Hall, Cardiff. *Work in permanent collections:* Liverpool public libraries, B.M., Malcolmson Collection at Hereford City A.G., Ashmolean Museum, Leics. Educ. Com., N.P.G. *Publications:* The Song of the Reeds and Rushavenn Time. *Address:* Kew Cottage, Lambridge La., Badgemore, Henley-on-Thames, Oxon. *Signs work:* "Anne Jope."

JOSEPH, Jane; painter, draughtsman, printmaker; *b* Surrey, 7 June, 1942; *d* of L. Joseph. *Studied art:* Camberwell School of Art and Crafts (1961-65, Robert Medley, E. Uglow, F. Auerbach, R. Kitaj, R.D. Lee, F. Bowling). *Exhib.:* solo shows: Morley Gallery (1973), Minories, Colechester (1982), Angela Flowers (1987), Flowers East (1989, 1992). *Work in permanent collections:* W.A.C., Government Picture Collection, Castle Museum, Norwich, Unilever House, Imperial College, London, Newcastle Polytechnic. *Address:* c/o Angela Flowers Gallery, 199-205 Richmond Rd., London E8 3NJ. *Club:* Chelsea Arts. *Signs work:* "Jane Joseph."

JOSEPH, Peter; painter; *b* London, 18 Jan., 1929; self-taught. *Work in permanent collections:* Tate Gallery; Stedjelik Museum, Amsterdam; Panza Collection, Varese, Italy; Kunsthaus, Zurich; Kunstmuseum, Basel; Fogg Museum, U.S.A., National Gallery of Australia, Canberra; Manchester City Art Gallery; Museum of Modern Art, Caracas; Contemporary Arts Soc., London; Arts Council of Gt. Britain; British Council; V. & A.; Ind Coope Collection, Southampton City Art Gallery. *Address:* 33 Clevedon Mansions, Lissenden Gdns., London NW5. *Signs work:* see appendix.

JOSSET, Lawrence Leon Louis, A.R.C.A. (1935), R.E. (1951); Mem., Art Workers' Guild; mezzotint engraver and etcher, portrait painter in water-colour and drawing; *b* 2 Aug., 1910; *s* of Leon Antoine Hippolyte Josset. *Educ.:* Bromley County School; Bromley and Beckenham Schools of Art; R.C.A. (Sir W. Rothenstein, Malcolm Osborne, R.A., P.R.E., 1932-35). *Exhib.:* R.A., R.E., etc. *Publications:* Mezzotint engravings, after Fantin Latour, Ben Marshall, Constable, William Shayer, Boucher and Fragonard, Zoffany, etc. *Address:* The

Cottage, Pilgrims' Way, Detling, nr. Maidstone, Kent. *Signs work:* "Lawrence Josset."

JOWITT, John Alan; painter in oil and water-colour; *b* 16 July, 1904; *m*; one *s*, one *d*. *Educ.:* Uppingham School; Yeovil School of Art (G. Mitchell, 1935-39). *Exhib.:* R.A. *Address:* Brook House, Chideock, Dorset. *Signs work:* "JOHN JOWITT."

JUKES, Edith Elizabeth, F.R.B.S., A.R.C.A. (1932), S.R.N. (Bart's, 1945), Mem., Society of Portrait Sculptors; sculptor in clay, wood, stone; teacher of sculpture, Sir John Cass School of Art, City of London Polytechnic (1946-75); *b* Shillong, Assam, 19 Dec., 1910; *d* of the late Capt. Andrew Monro Jukes, M.D., I.M.S. *Educ.:* Norland Pl. School, Kensington; *studied art* at R.C.A. (1928-32) under Profs. Richard Garbe, R.A., Henry Moore, and Herbert Palliser. *Exhib.:* R.A., etc. *Address:* The Studio, 347 Upper Richmond Rd., London SW15 6TL. *Signs work:* see appendix.

K

KALASHNIKOV, Anatolii Ivanovich, R.E.(Hon.), Meritorious Artist of the R.S.F.S.R.; artist/wood engraver in xylography; Chairman, Council of Exlibris and Book Graphics, All-Union Soc. "Kniga"; *b* Moscow, U.S.S.R., 5 Apr., 1930; *s* of Ivan Nikifurovich Kalashnikov; *m* Ludmila Nikolaevna. *Studied art* at Moscow Higher Industrial Art School (formerly Stroganov) under V.V. Golubkin. *Exhib.:* 140 one-man shows in U.S.S.R. and abroad. *Work in permanent collections:* B.M.; National Museum, Prague; Cabinet of Engraving, Bibliotheque Nationale, Paris. *Publications:* Omar Khayam; The Golden Ring; Anglo-Russian Relations; War and Peace. *Address:* 44 Leninskii prospekt, Kv.124, SU-117334 Moscow, U.S.S.R. *Signs work:* see appendix.

KALEDKIEWICZ, Zdzisław Lucjan, M.F.A. (1955); painter and teacher; Lecturer, Technical University, Gdansk, State Schools in Gdansk and Gdynia; *b* Czestochowa, Poland, 31 Aug., 1913; *m* Irena; two *s*, one *d*. *Studied art* at Cracow Academy of Fine Art (1936-39). M.A. in Fine Art, Gdansk (1955). *Exhib.:* representative exhbns. of Polish art abroad (1945-90). *Work in permanent collections:* Gdansk, Oliwa, Cracow. *Publication:* "Muse on Bidet" aphorisms (Gdynia, 1958). *Address:* 80-322 Gdansk-Oliwa, Ul.Lesna 9/2, Poland. *Club:* Freedom and Democracy Union. *Signs work:* "Z. Kaledkiewicz."

KALKHOF, Peter Heinz; painter, lecturer in fine art; *b* Stassfurt, Germany 20 Dec., 1933; *s* of Heinz Kalkhof, company secretary; *m* Jeanne The; one *s*. *Educ.:* Germany; *studied art* at School of Arts and Crafts, Braunschweig; Academy of Fine Art, Stuttgart; Slade School of Fine Art, London; Ecole des Beaux Art, Paris (1954-62). *Exhib.:* Annely Juda Fine Art (1970-79, 1990), Scottish Arts Council, Edinburgh, Glasgow, Juda-Rowan Gallery (1983), Landesmuseum Oldenburg (1988), Camden Arts Centre (1989). *Commission:* 1987 Treaty-Centre: Mural (Taylor Woodrow), Hounslow, London. *Work in permanent collections:* Northern Ireland Trust, Arts Council of Gt. Britain, Leics. Educ. Authority, European Parliament, Landesmuseum Oldenburg. *Address:* c/o Annely Juda Fine Art, 23 Dering St., London W1R 9AA. *Signs work:* "Peter Kalkhof."

KANE, Martin, B.A.(Hons.) (1987); artist in oil on canvas, pastel; *b* Cardiff, 3 June, 1958; *s* of Bernard Kane, B.Ed. *Educ.:* St. Andrew's High School, Clydebank, Glasgow; *studied art* at Glasgow School of Art (1981-82), Edinburgh College of Art (1982-87, David Michie). *Exhib.:* Angela Flowers Gallery (1988), Jill George Gallery (1990), Thumb Gallery, Atlanta, U.S.A. (1990); one-man show: Jill George Gallery (1992, 1993). *Work in permanent collections:* Cleveland, Middlesbrough; Cleveland, Ohio; Glasgow Museums and A.Gs. *Address:* c/o Jill George Gallery, 38 Lexington St., London W1. *Signs work:* "Martin Kane."

KANIDINC, Salahattin; awarded High Moral Prize (1954); artist in pencil, pen, brush, ink, oil, polymer; letterer, calligrapher, designer, expert on historical writing systems (hieroglyphs to Roman alphabet) and modern letter forms; owner-creative director, Kanidinc International; and consultant designer for major corporations; *b* Istanbul, Turkey, 12 Aug., 1927; *s* of Yahya Kanidinc; *m* Seniha Kanidinc; two *s*. *Educ.:* 22nd Elementary School of Uskudar, Uskudar 1st High School, Istanbul, Turkey; *studied art:* Defenbaugh School of Lettering, Minn. (1954), Zanerian College of Penmanship, Ohio (1963), State University of Iowa (1963), University of Minnesota (1964), University of California (1963-64). *Work in permanent collections:* Peabody Inst. Library, Baltimore; W.C.C., N.Y.C.; and in private collections. Listed in 'Who's Who' publications throughout the world. *Publication:* participant designer, Alphabet Thesaurus, Vols. 2-3. *Address:* 33-44 93rd St., Jackson Heights, New York 11372, U.S.A. *Clubs:* S.S.I., W.C.C., International Assoc. of Master Penmen and Teachers of Handwriting, American Inst. of Graphic Arts, International Center for the Typographic Arts, National Advisory Board of the American Security Council. *Signs work:* see appendix.

KAUFFMANN, C. Michael, PhD. (1957), F.B.A. (1987), F.M.A., F.S.A.; Art historian and museum curator (formerly V. & A.); Prof. of the History of Art, and Director; Courtauld Inst., University of London; *b* Frankfurt a/M, 5 Feb., 1931; *s* of Arthur Kauffmann; *m* Dorothea; two *s*. *Educ.:* St. Paul's School; Merton College, Oxford (1950-53); Warburg Inst., London (1953-57). *Publications:* The Baths of Pozzuoli: medieval illuminations of Peter of Eboli's poem (1959); An Altarpiece of the Apocalypse (1968); V. & A. Catalogue of Foreign Paintings; British Romanesque Manuscripts 1066-1190 (1975); Catalogue of Paintings in the Wellington Museum (1982); John Varley (1984). *Address:* Courtauld Institute of Art, Somerset House, Strand, London WC2R 0RN.

KAUR, Permindar, B.A.(Hons.); sculptor in glass, metal, clay, wood, paper; Adviser for Yorkshire Arts; *b* Nottingham, 1965. *Educ.:* Rushcliffe School, Notts.; *studied art* at Sheffield City Polytechnic (1986-87), Glasgow School of Art (1990-92). *Exhib.:* group shows: Midland Arts Group, Nottingham; Cooper Gallery, Barnsley; Herbert A.G., Coventry; Oldknows A.G., Nottingham; R.S.A., Edinburgh; Mappin A.G., Sheffield; Newberry Gallery, Glasgow; Ponypark, Holland; Niort, France. *Address:* 136 Wilton St., Kelvinbridge, Glasgow G20 6DG. *Signs work:* "Permindar Kaur."

KAY, Nora, A.R.C.A., M.C.S.D.; artist in cut paper, lino-cuts, calligraphy, italic writing, studio potter; designer for Yardley's, Jenners Ltd.; teacher at St. Martin's School of Art, Newland Park College, Maltman's Green School. *Educ.:* Wycombe High School, St. Martin's School of Art, R.C.A. *Exhib.:* R.B.A., N.E.A.C. *Work repro.:* General advertising work, London Transport posters, Christmas cards, book jackets. *Publications:* children's books. *Address:* Flat 5, Ethorpe Cres., Gerrards Cross, Bucks SL9 8PW. *Signs work:* "N.K."

KEANE, John, B.F.A. (1976); painter in oil and mixed media on canvas, P.V.A. and mixed media on paper; Official War artist, Gulf (1991); *b* Herts., 12 Sept., 1954. *Studied art* at Camberwell School of Art (1972-76). *Exhib.:* twenty one-man shows in U.K., Europe and U.S.A. since 1980. *Work in permanent collections:* Imperial War Museum, Contemporary Art Soc., Rugby Museum, Cleveland Gallery, The Guardian, Harris Museum, Preston, Glasgow Museum and A.G., Aberdeem A.G., Wolverhampton Museum and A.G., Christies Corporate Collection, British Coal, Financial Times, Unilever PLC, Detroit Art Inst. *Address:* c/o Flowers East, 199-205 Richmond Rd., London E8 3NJ. *Signs work:* "John Keane."

KEANY, Brian James, R.S.W. (1977), D.A. (Edin. 1967); artist in oil, acrylic, water-colour; art teacher; *b* Forfar, Scotland, 16 Jan., 1945; *m* Christina Nicol Herd, D.A.(Edin.); one *s*, two *d. Educ.:* Brechin High School; *studied art* at Edinburgh College of Art (1963-67, Sir William Gillies, Sir Robin Philipson, William J. L. Baillie). *Exhib.:* R.S.A., R.S.W., R.G.I., and several one-man shows and group exhbns. *Address:* 27 Solway Pl., Glenrothes, Fife KY6 2NS. *Signs work:* "BRIAN KEANY."

KEARNEY, Joseph, D.A.Glas. (1961); painter in various media; *b* Glasgow, 14 Sept., 1939; *s* of Joseph Kearney. *Educ.:* St. Aloysius' College, Glasgow; *studied art* at Glasgow School of Art. *Exhib.:* several one-man shows in Glasgow. *Work in permanent collections:* Glasgow A.G. and Museum and in many private collections. *Address:* 97 Elmore Ave., Glasgow G44. *Club:* Glasgow Art. *Signs work:* "Kearney."

KEATES, John Gareth, A.T.D.; artist in oil, gouache and water-colour; Liverpool Council for Educ. (Inc.) Travel Award, 1958; principal lecturer, Liverpool Polytechnic (retd. 1978); *b* Birkenhead, 18 Jan., 1915; *s* of John Willan Keates; *m* (1) Margaret Bishop (decd.); two *d;* (2) Frances Caudell, 1983. *Educ.:* Birkenhead Institute; *studied art* at Liverpool College of Art (1933-38), Central School of Art, London, under Bernard Meninsky (1946-47). *Exhib.:* Arts Council Gallery, F.P.S., London and provincial galleries and abroad; one-man exhibitions, 1964 and 1967. *Work in permanent collections:* Walker Art Gallery, Liverpool, Southport A.G., University of Liverpool; also in private collections. *Address:* 29 Saxon Rd., Birkdale, Southport, Merseyside.

KELL, Lorna Beatrice, S.G.F.A. (President), F.S.B.A., F.R.S.A., F.R.H.S.; artist in drawing, water-colour and gouache; textile designer (studio Lorraine Designs), wood-engraver; botanical flower painter and illustrator; *b* London, 13 Jan., 1914; *d* of the late George and Beatrice Prince. *Educ.:* E. Finchley Grammar School; *studied art* at Hornsey School of Art under J. C. Moody, R.I., R.E., Miss E. Lindquist, Miss S. MacEwan, Norman Janes, R.E., and Frank Winter, R.E. *Exhib.:* R.A., R.E., R.B.A., S.G.F.A., Guildhall, Paris Salon, R.H.S., (Grenfell Medallist), and local exhbns. *Address:* 17 Dinsdale Ct., Great North Rd., Barnet, Herts. EN5 1HD. *Signs work:* "Lorna B. Kell."

KELLY, Deirdre, B.Ed.(Hons.) (1984), M.A. (1987), R.E.; printmaker; *b* London, 1 May, 1962. *Studied art* at Wimbledon School of Art. *Exhib.:* B.P. International. *Work in permanent collections:* Sedgewick Gp. International, Atlantis Paper Co., King's College School. *Address:* c/o Hardware Gallery, 162 Archway Rd., London N6 5BB. *Signs work:* "Deirdre Kelly" or "D.K."

KELLY, Felix; artist in oil; *b* Auckland, N.Z., 1916. *Exhib.:* Lefévre Gallery (1943, 1944, 1946), Leicester Gallery (1950, 1952), Portraits Inc., N.Y. (1947), Charleston, S.C. (1948), Washington, D.C. (1949), Arthur Jeffress Gallery

(1959-62), Arthur Tooth & Sons (1965, 1968, 1971), Kennedy Galleries Inc., N.Y. (1970), Delgado Museum of Art, New Orleans (1970), Partridge Fine Arts, London (1978, 1981). *Work in permanent collections:* Lord Rothermere, Sir Herbert Read, Lord Faringdon, Charles Engelhard, Esq., The Earl of Mountbatten, David Bruce, Esq., Chester Beattie, Esq., The Duke of Buccleuch, Walter Annenberg, Esq., John Hay Whitney, Esq., Lord Aberdare, four murals for Lord Howard at Castle Howard, York. *Publications:* Paintings by Felix Kelly, by Sir Herbert Read; illustrations for Longmans, Macmillans, Hutchinsons, Chatto & Windus. *Theatre sets* for Haymarket, Phoenix, Sadlers Wells, Old Vic. *Address:* 49 Princes Gate, London SW7. *Signs work:* "Felix Kelly."

KELLY, Phil; painter in oil and charcoal; *b* B'ham, 7 Sept., 1950; *m* Ruth. *Educ.:* Rugby School; *studied art* at Bristol University (1970-73). *Exhib.:* U.K., U.S.A., Portugal, Mexico. *Work in permanent collections:* Museum of Contemporary Art, Centro Cultural Arte Contemporaneo Mexico. *Address:* Emscote Lawn, Warwick CV34 5GD. *Signs work:* "Kelly" or "P.K."

KELLY, Victor Charles, R.B.S.A. (1983), A.R.Cam.A. (1991); painter in water-colour, acrylic, pastel, teacher; Hon. Sec. Royal Birmingham Soc. of Artists; *b* B'ham, 6 Sept., 1923; *s* of Charles Alfred Kelly; *m* Sylvia; two *s.* *Educ.:* B'ham Teachers Training College; *studied art* at Liverpool College of Art (1949-50). *Exhib.:* R.B.S.A., R.I., Manchester Academy of Art, Chelsea Art Soc., R.Cam.A., New York, Hong Kong. *Work in permanent collection:* R.B.S.A. *Address:* 90 Sandringham Rd., Perry Barr, B'ham B42 1PH. *Clubs:* Past Pres. B'ham Water-colour Soc., Easel Club, B'ham Art Circle. *Signs work:* "Victor C. Kelly."

KEMPSHALL, Hubert Kim, R.B.S.A. (1985), A.R.C.A. (1960), D.A. (Manc.) (1955); painter/printmaker in oil, acrylic, water-colour, etching, lithography; Course Tutor, B.A. (Hons.) Fine Art, U.C.E. in Birmingham; *b* Manchester, 15 May, 1934; *m* Sylvia; one *s,* one *d.* *Educ.:* Stretford Grammar School; *studied art* at Manchester College of Art (1951-55); Royal College of Art (1957-60). *Exhib.:* R.A., Scottish Royal Academy, Arts Council, several one-man shows. *Work in permanent collections:* Edinburgh City Coll., Scottish Modern A.G., Aberdeen A.G., Dundee A.G., Arts Council, V. & A., Herbert A.G., Whitworth A.G., Birmingham A.G., Wolverhampton A.G., Bradford A.G., City of Lyon, City of Frankfurt, Ecole de Beaux Art, Toulouse. *Address:* Mere House, 49 Henley Ave., Iffley, Oxford OX4 4DJ. *Signs work:* "K.K."

KENDALL, Alice R., D.A. (Edin.), F.R.Z.S. (Scot.), S.W.A., F.R.S.A., P.P.S.W.A. (1977-82); artist in oil, water-colour, pen and ink, writer; *b* N.Y.C.; *d* of James P. Kendall, LL.D., F.R.S., P.R.S.E., Prof. of Chemistry, Edinburgh University. *Educ.:* New York and Edinburgh; *studied art* at Edinburgh under Sir Wm. Gillies, Sir Wm. MacTaggart. *Exhib.:* R.A., Paris Salon, R.B.A., N.E.A.C., R.I., S.W.A., etc. and with the late Alice Kendall (Mother) at Cooling Galleries (1948, 1956) and Chelsea Gallery (1949). *Work in permanent collection:* The Royal Society of Edinburgh: Official portrait of Father (1956). *Publications:* children's book 'Funny Fishes'; articles and poems, many illustrated, in Punch, Poetry Review, The Artist, The Voice of Youth, etc. *Address:* 35 Beaufort Gdns., London SW3 1PW. *Signs work:* "A.R. Kendall."

KENDALL, Kay Thetford, R.M.S., S.W.A.; sculptor and portrait sculptor in bronze, bronze resin, gold, silver and pewter, specialising in cats, miniature sculpture, thimbles and sculptural jewellery; *b* Manchester; *m* D. Wilmer Kendall. *Educ.:* Cheadle Hulme Schools; *studied art* at Malvern College of Art; Hertfordshire College of Art and Design. *Exhib.:* Mall Galleries, London;

S.W.A., S.P.S., R.M.S.; one man shows, Welwyn Garden City, Hatfield, Knebworth, Wembley, Bishop's Stortford. *Awards:* 1st Prize for sculpture, Grolla d'oro, Venice (1981); Bidder & Borne award for sculpture R.M.S. (1986). *Address:* The Studio, 45 Orchard Rd., Tewin, Welwyn, Herts AL6 0HL. *Clubs:* R.M.S., S.W.A. *Signs work:* see appendix.

KENNEDY, Cecil; flower and portrait painter in oils; *b* Leyton, Essex, 4 Feb., 1905; *s* of T. R. Kennedy, artist; *m*; one *s*. *Studied art* in London, Paris, Antwerp, Zürich. *Exhib.:* R.A., R.S.A., R.H.A., Doncaster, Oldham, Bradford, Southport, etc., and many London galleries; also U.S.A. and S. African galleries. Awarded Silver Medal, Paris Salon (1956) and Gold Medal, Paris Salon (1970). *Official purchases:* by H.M. Queen Mary, Merthyr Tydfil Art Gallery, Rochdale Art Gallery. *Work repro.:* Numerous. *Address:* Manor Garden House, 135 Fishpool St., St. Albans, Herts. AL3 4R7. *Signs work:* see appendix.

KENNISH, Jenny, R.M.S. (1985), S.W.A., F.S.B.A.; self taught sculptress in porcelain of wild flowers and animals; school teacher; *b* England, 11 Mar., 1944; *d* of W. J. Otway, teacher; one *s*, one *d*. *Educ.:* Nonsuch County Grammar School for Girls; Whitelands Teacher Training College. *Exhib.:* Westminster Galleries with the R.M.S., S.B.A., S.W.A. and local societies. *Address:* Kinghern, Silchester Rd., Little London, nr. Basingstoke, Hants. RG26 5EX. *Signs work:* "J.K."

KENNY, Michael, R.A., F.R.B.S. (1992), D.F.A.(Lond.); sculptor in plaster, metal, wood, and stone, also painted reliefs; Director of Fine Art Studies, University of London Goldsmiths' College (1983-88); *b* Liverpool, 10 June, 1941; *s* of James Kenny, precision engineer; *m* Angela Smith (marriage dissolved); *re-married* Susan Rowland, 1993; one *s*, two *d*. (by previous marriage to Rosemary Flood). *Educ.:* St. Francis Xavier's College, Liverpool; *studied art:* Liverpool College of Art (1959-61, Phillip Hartas, Arther Ballard), Slade School of Fine Art (1961-64, Reg Butler, Michael Kellaway, F.E. McWilliam). *Exhib.:* retrospective exhbn. (work between 1963-84) Wilhelm Lehmbruck Museum, Duisberg, W. Germany (1984-85); numerous one-man shows and mixed exhbns. in England, Europe, S. America, Australia and Japan. *Work in permanent collections:* V. & A., B.M., Tate Gallery, A.C.G.B., British Council, Staatsgalerie Stuttgart, Lehmbruck Museum, Duisborg, W. Germany, London Borough of Camden, Leics. Educ. Com., Contemporary Art Soc., Hara Museum of Contemporary Art, Tokyo, Leeds City A.G., etc. *Commissioned work at:* Lumsden, Aberdeenshire; Addenbrookes Hospital, Cambridge; Le Parc de la Courneuve, Paris; Yokohama Business Park, Japan; Muraoka-Cho, Japan (1992); Limehouse Link Tunnel (Eastern Entrance) Docklands, London (1993); Prittlewell School, Essex (1993-94). *Publications:* illustrated, I Know the Place by Harold Pinter, Contemporary Artists (1977), Contemporary British Artists (1979, 1989), etc. *Address:* c/o Annely Juda Fine Art, 23 Dering St., London W1R 9AA. *Signs work:* "Michael Kenny," bronze casts sometimes initialled "M.K." and date.

KERN, Doreen; sculptor in bronze; consultant to B.M. Replica Dept.; *b* 9 Aug., 1931; divorced; two *s*. *Educ.:* Hampstead Garden Suburb Institute; studio assistant at the Morris Singer Art Bronze foundry; *studied art* under Howard Bates, R.A. *Exhib.:* Waterloo Fine Arts, Talma Gallery, Tel-Aviv, Ryder Gallery, L.A., Brighton Museum, Galerie Nichido, Tokyo, London University, Bath Festival, National Museum of Archaeology, Valletta, Malta, Design Centre, Bristol Cathedral. *Work in permanent collections:* Dr Kwame Nkrumah, Guyana,

Emperor Haile Selassie (Palace of Addis Ababa). *Studio:* 38 Canons Drive, Edgware, Middx. HA8 7QT. *Signs work:* see appendix.

KERR, Bernadette, B.F.A. Hons. (1981), P.G.C.E. (1982), Slade School Higher Dip. Postgraduate (1984); painter in oil on canvas, lecturer; Winchester School of Art Fellow (in painting) (1987-88), Lecturer in Art, Goldsmiths' College, University of London; *b* Fontainebleau, France, 21 June, 1958; *d* of John Kerr, photographer. *Educ.:* Loreto Grammar School, Nottingham; *studied art* at Mansfield School of Art (1977-78), Trent Polytechnic (1978-81, D. Curruthers), Institute of Education (1981-82), Slade School of Art (1982-84, Lawrence Gowing). *Exhib.:* New Contemporaries I.C.A. (1981, 1983), British Drawing, Hayward Annual (1982), Spirit of London, Royal Festival Hall (1983, 1985), Camden Annual (1983-85), Stowells Trophy, R.A. (1984), London Group, R.C.A. (1984), Contemporary Art Soc. Market (1984-87), Whitechapel Open (1985), two-man Vortex Gallery (1985), Leics. Schools Collection (1986), Monuments in Light, Swiss Cottage Exhbn. Hall (1987), R.A. Summer Show (1987), Pacesetters 7, Peterborough Museum and A.G. (1987). *Official purchases:* London Borough of Camden Arts and Entertainment Dept. *Address:* 31 Belsize Ave., London NW3. *Signs work:* "Bernadette Kerr."

KERSHAW, Walter, B.A. Hons. Fine Art (Dunelm); mural painter and freelance artist in oil, water-colour, mosaic; occasional visiting lecturer in Environmental Art at Universities in the U.K., Brazil and W. Germany; *b* Rochdale, 7 Dec., 1940; *s* of Walter Kershaw. *Educ.:* De la Salle College, Salford; *studied art* at Durham University (1958-62). *Exhib.:* Large scale, public, external murals in Manchester, Trafford Park and N.W. Museum of Science and Industry; Stockton on Tees; Norwich; Brazil, Sao Paulo and Recife. Internal murals for British Aerospace, Manchester United F.C., Ribchester Roman Museum, Salford University, the C.E.G.B., Hollingworth Lake Visitors Centre and Italian Consulate Manchester. Photos of murals at the Serpentine, Whitechapel and Tate galleries. *Work in permanent collections:* V. & A., British Council, Arts Council, Gulbenkian Foundation, 'Cultura Inglesa', Museum of Art, São Paulo, and other public galleries in the U.K. *Recorded:* 'Conversation Piece' with Sue MacGregor, Radio 4 (1983), 'Kaleidoscope' Radio 4 (1986). *Films:* 'Terra Firma' BBC 2 (1976), 'First Graffiti Artist' (1977), 'Nationwide' (1982), '5 x 5' W. Germany (1984), 'Folio' Anglia TV (1987). *Address:* 193 Todmorden Rd., Littleborough, Rochdale OL15 9EG. *Signs work:* "Walter Kershaw."

KETCHER, Jean, B.A.Hons. Fine Art Painting (1976); painter in oil, water-colour, etc.; art teacher, Copleston High School, Ipswich; *b* 6 July, 1955. *Studied art* at Ipswich School of Art (1971-73), Maidstone College of Art (1973-76). *Exhib.:* Halesworth Gallery, Ellingham Mill, Bungay, Corn Exchange, Ipswich. *Address:* 46 Sandown Rd., Ipswich. *Signs work:* "Jean Ketcher."

KEY, Geoffrey, D.A. (1960); painter in oil, sculptor; *b* Manchester, 13 May, 1941; *s* of George Key. *Educ.:* High School of Art, Manchester; *studied art* at Regional College of Art, Manchester (1958-61), under Harry Rutherford, William Bailey. *Exhib.:* Salford A.G., Clermont Ferrand France, London, Nancy France, Germany, Madison Ave., N.Y., Lausanne Switzerland, Dublin, Saint Ouen France, Hong Kong. *Work in permanent collections:* Salford A.G., Manchester City Gallery, Bolton A.G., Granada Television, Wigan Corp., Manchester University, North West Arts. *Address:* 59 Acresfield Rd., Pendleton, Salford M6 7GE. *Club:* Manchester Academy. *Signs work:* see appendix.

KHALIL: see NORLAND (NEUSCHUL), Khalil.

KHAN, Keith Ali, B.A.(Hons.); sculptor in large scale exterior/interior constructions, using fabric and many people; Director, Carnival Designer; *b* Trinidad, 4 Dec., 1963; *s* of Faiz Khan. *Educ.:* King's College, Wimbledon; *studied art:* Wimbledon School of Art, Middlesex Polytechnic (Dante Leonelli), The Street, Port of Spain, Trinidad. *Exhib.:* Houston International Festival, Harris Museum, Preston, Arnolfini, Bristol; one-man shows: Bluecoat Gallery, Liverpool, Greenwich Citizen Gallery; on the streets of Notting Hill, as well as numerous designs on TV and stage. *Address:* 79 Grand Drive, Raynes Pk., London SW20 9DW. *Signs work:* "Khan."

KHANNA, Balraj, M.A. (1962); awarded Winnifred Holtby prize by R.S.L. (1984); painter in acrylic and oil, novelist; *b* 4 Oct., 1940; *s* of Amar Nath; *m* Francine Martine; two *d. Educ.:* Punjab University, Chandigarh. *Exhib.:* forty one-man shows including Ashmolean Museum, Oxford (1968), City A.G., Bristol (1969), Galerie Transposition, Paris (1966, 1968, 1974, 1975), Herbert Benevy Gallery, N.Y. (1971, 1972), Serpentine Gallery (1979), Richard Demarco (1986), Royal Festival Hall (1990), Arnolfini (1991). *Work in permanent collections:* Arts Council; Musee d'Art Moderne, Paris; Ville de Paris; Ashmolean Museum; National Gallery of Modern Art, New Delhi; City A.G., Bristol; City A.G., Bradford; V. & A., etc. *Publications:* Nation of Fools (Michael Joseph and Penguin), Sweet Chillies (Constable), Kalighat, Popular Indian Painting, 1800-1930 (Redstone Press). *Address:* 3A Pindock Mews, London W9 2PY. *Signs work:* "Khanna."

KIDD, Douglas Jessop; founder mem. Medical Artists' Assoc. of Gt. Britain; medical and scientific illustrator in water-colour, monochrome wash and line; artist to the Faculty of Medicine of the University of Liverpool (Retd.); *b* Liverpool, 3 Aug., 1903; *s* of William Beaumont Kidd; *m* Eveline Pover; two *s*, one *d. Educ.:* Holt High School, Liverpool; *studied art* at Liverpool School of Art. *Work in permanent collections:* Human Anatomy Dept., Liverpool University. *Work repro.:* numerous medical, surgical and scientific text-books and journals, etc. *Publications:* Preparing Illustrations for Half-tone Reproduction, Baillière's Atlases of Human Anatomy, etc. *Address:* 60 Almonds Green, Liverpool 12. *Signs work:* "Kidd."

KIDNER, Michael, B.A.(Cantab); painter in oil and cryla; *b* Kettering, 1917; *s* of Norman W. Kidner; *m* Marion Frederick; one *s. Educ.:* Bedales School; *studied art:* self-taught. *Work in permanent collections:* Tate Gallery, Arts Council of G.B., British Council, W.A.G., Huddersfield A.G., Manchester City A.G., Contemporary Art Soc., Sussex University, University of Wales, Gulbenkian Foundation, V. &. A., Museum Sztuki, Lodz, and Poznan Museum, Poland, Museum of Modern Art, N.Y., Southampton City A.G., Anios Anderson Museum, Helsinki, Norrkopings Konstmuseum, Malmo Konsthall. *Publication:* Elastic Membrane. *Address:* 18 Hampstead Hill Gdns., London NW3. *Signs work:* "Michael Kidner."

KILIBARDA, George; artist and draughtsman in oil, acrylic and chalk; *b* Sittingbourne, 10 Aug., 1954; *s* of Michael Kilibarda, electrical engineer; *m* Penelope; two *d. Educ.:* Fort Luton School for Boys; *studied art* at Medway School of Design (technical illustration). *Exhib.:* Manor House Fine Arts, Cardiff; Circle Gallery, Pontypridd; Roy Miles Gallery, London. *Address:* The Oaks, Thornhill Rd., Thornhill, Cardiff DF4 5UA. *Signs work:* "George Kilibarda."

KINAHAN, Lady Coralie; U.S.W.A., U.W.A., R.U.A. (resigned); artist in oil and water-colour; Lady Mayoress of Belfast (1959-62); President, Co. Antrim

Red Cross (1955-67); *b* Surrey, 1924; *d* of Capt. C. de Burgh, D.S.O., R.N.; *m* Sir Robin Kinahan; two *s*, three *d. Educ.:* by 14 governesses and 4 schools; *studied art* at John Hassall, and Chelsea Schools of Art (1943-46); private portrait classes under Sonia Mervyn, A.R.A. (1946-49). *Exhib.:* R.A., R.P., R.O.I., S.WL.A., R.S.A., R.U.A.; solo exhbns. annually, Belfast, Dublin, Wexford, Galway, Bristol and London (1964-85). Opened own gallery (1985) Templepatrick, exhibiting landscapes, wildlife, horses and portraits. *Commissions include:* Lord Bishop of Durham, Rt. Hon. Humphrey and Mrs. Atkins, Rt. Hon. James Prior, General Sir Ian Freeland, and many children's portraits; Army commissions for The Black Watch Regt., The Grenadier Guards, Imperial War Museum and the Ulster Defence Regt.; Sporting pictures for Mr. Victor McCalmont and The Master Beagler, Terence Grainger. *Publications:* historical novels: You can't shoot the English (1982), After the war, came ... Peace? (1987). *Work repro.:* limited edns. 200 prints of Belfast Harbour; and Patrol looking over Belfast. Husband made H.M.'s Lord Lieut. for Belfast (1985). *Address:* Castle Upton, Templepatrick, Co. Antrim, N. Ireland BT39 5BE. *Signs work:* "C. de B.K." oils; "Coralie Kinahan" water-colours.

KINDER, Joan, S.C.F.A. (1965), F.P.S. (1960); painter and printmaker in ink and water-colour of mono prints in abstract expressionism; *b* Yorkshire, 19 June, 1916; *m* K.J. Kinder; two *d. Educ.:* Bridlington High; *studied art* at Scarborough School of Art (1932-36, Edward and Ethel Walker) specialising in textile. *Exhib.:* S.G.F.A., Mall Galleries, C.W.A.C., and solo shows. *Work in private collections:* U.K. and U.S.A. *Address:* 8 Upper Woodcote Village, Purley, Surrey CR8 3HE. *Signs work.* "(Joan) Kinder."

KING, Andrew Norman, B.F.A. (Hons.) (1978), N.S. (1984), R.O.I. (1992); David Murray Scholarship, R.A. Schools (1978); landscape and marine artist in oil and water-colour, interested in light and atmosphere in landscape; *b* Bedford, 1956; *s* of Norman King. *Educ.:* Barnfield College, Luton; *studied at* Hornsey College of Art. *Exhib.:* Britain in Water-colour, R.I., N.E.A.C., N.S., R.S.M.A., R.O.I., R.W.S., Open Exhbn. Bankside; one-man shows, Luton, Hitchin, Linslade, Stowe, London and Aldeburgh. *Work in permanent collections:* Luton Art Council, Beds. C.C., Eagle Star Offices, and in private and royal collections in Britain and abroad. Finalist, Winsor and Newton Young Artists award (1985). *Address:* Pond Cottage, Long Rd., Colby, Norwich NR11 7EF. *Signs work:* "Andrew King."

KING, Mary, A.T.C. (1947), S.W.A. (1979), N.S. (1984), F.R.S.A. (1988); artist in mixed media, water-colour and collage; lecturer, North East Surrey College of Technology (1968-80) and Surbiton Adult Education Centre; *b* London, 17 Oct., 1926; *d* of F.R.C. Dear; *m* Ralph King; one *s*, three *d. Educ.:* Wallington Grammar School; *studied art* at Chelsea College of Art (1946, painting, Ceri Richards; 1948-49, stained glass, Francis Spear), Central School of Arts and Crafts, London, Whitelands College, Putney. *Exhib.:* Fairfield Halls, Croydon, Bourne Hall, Ewell, F.B.A., S.W.A., R.B.A., Mall Galleries, Westminster Gallery (1988-93, annually), R.A. Summer Exhbn. (1981, 1982), Bankside Gallery, London (1985, 1986); solo shows, Farnham Maltings (1983, 1985, 1987), Epsom Playhouse, Ashley Gallery, Epsom, Conway Hall, London (1984), Loggia Gallery (1983, 1984, 1986), many London exhbns. including Heifer Gallery, Islington (1990-93), Hyde Park Gallery, Fine Arts, Bond St. (1991), Bonhams Knightsbridge, Smiths Galleries, Covent Gdn. (1990-93). *Address:* 42 Reigate Rd., Ewell, Epsom, Surrey KT17 1PX. *Signs work:* "Mary King" or "M. King."

KING, Phillip, C.B.E. (1974), R.A.; sculptor in steel, bronze, fibreglass; Prof. of Sculpture, Royal Academy of Art, Prof. Emeritus, Royal College of Art; *b* Tunis, 1934; *m*; one *s* (decd.). *Educ.:* Mill Hill School; Christ College, Cambridge; *studied art* at St. Martin's School of Art. *Exhib.:* Rowan Gallery London, Richard Fergen Gallery N.Y., Venice Biennale, Whitechapel Gallery London, Kunsthalle Mannheim. *Work in permanent collections:* Tate Gallery, M.O.M.A. (N.Y.), National Gallery of Australia, Kroller Muller Museum, New Museum of Contemporary Art Hiroshima, Yorkshire Sculpture Pk., Kunsthalle Mannheim, etc. *Publication:* The Sculpture of Phillip King by Tim Hilton. *Address:* c/o New Rowan Gallery, 25 Dover St., London W1X 3PA. *Signs work:* see appendix.

KING, Robert, R.I. (1970); Mem. Leicester Soc. of Artists (1960); painter in oil, water-colour; etcher and lithographer; *b* Leicester, 28 June, 1936; *s* of Joseph T. King, engineer; *m* Christine James. *Educ.:* Fosse Boys' School, Leicester; *studied art* at Leicester College of Art (1956-58). *Exhib.:* one-man shows, six at Gadsby Gallery, Leicester (1970-80) and Medici Gallery (1980-89); two with Burlington Paintings (1989-91); annually with R.I., R.A., R.O.I., R.S.M.A., Leicester Soc. of Artists. *Work in permanent collections:* Nottingham Educ. Com., Leicester Royal Infirmary, Leicester University. *Publication:* illustrated Denys Brook-Hart's 20th Century British Marine Painting. *Addresses:* 2 Coastguard Cottages, Lepe, Hants; Studio: Whitefield Farm, Lepe Rd., Langley, Hants. *Signs work:* "ROBERT KING."

KINGS, Tarka Huxley, M.A.; painter/printer in oil, silkscreen; *b* London, 24 May, 1961; *d* of John Kings, literary editor, and Ann Huxley, author. *Educ.:* St. Paul's Girls School; *studied art* at City and Guilds, R.A. Schools (1982-87, Peter Greenham, Norman Adams). *Exhib.:* Creative Salvage (1985), R.A., Gallery 24, Phoenix Gallery, Langton Gallery, St. Paul's, Cadogan Contemporary (1988), Bill Thomson Gallery, Rebecca Hossack Gallery (1991, 1993). Asst. to Leonard Rosoman, Lambeth Palace Chapel ceiling. Work in private collections in U.S.A. and England. *Artwork for films:* 'Secrets' (Dir. Phillip Savile), 'The Dream' (Dir. Con Mulgrave). *Address:* 35 Beethoven St., London W10. *Club:* Congress. *Signs work:* "THK."

KINMONT, David Bruce; *b* Kent, 1932. *Educ.:* St. John's College, Cambridge. Senior member of the University of Bristol where, in 1971, he delivered the George Hare Leonard Memorial Lecture. Visiting professorships: George Washington University, Washington D.C. (1974); universities in Beijing, Shanghai (1986), and Hebei (1989), in China; and at the University of Leningrad in 1990. *Exhib.:* one-man shows include, Ferens City A.G., Hull (1963); City A.G., Bangor (1960); St. John's College, Cambridge (1969); Churchill College, Cambridge (1976); University of Durham (1981); University of Exeter (1986); Georges, Bristol (1987). *Address:* The Lent House, Clevedon Rd., Flax Bourton, Bristol BS19 1NQ.

KIRBY, Michael, M.F.P.S.; fine art restorer, artist in oil; *b* Farnham Common, Bucks., 30 Dec., 1949; *s* of H. Kirby, M.I.Nuc.E., L.R.S.H.; *m*; two *s*, two *d*. *Studied art* at High Wycombe School of Art (1967-71) under G. G. Palmer, Romeo Di Gerolamo, R.B.A., Eric Smith, R.B.A., R.W.S., Henry Trivick, R.B.A. *Exhib.:* R.B.A., Open Salon, F.P.S., H.U.A.S. *Address:* 30 Sycamore Rise, Bracknell, Berks. RG12 3BU. *Signs work:* "M. Kirby."

KIRK, Barry, N.D.D. (1954), A.R.C.A. (1959), F.R.S.A. (1989); Travelling scholarship R.C.A. (1959); painter, draughtsman in poly-vinyl acetate, acrylics, etc. to about 1978-79, latterly oil and water-colour; Canterbury College of Art

274

1959-1988 (Vice-Principal 1974-87, Principal 1987-88); thereafter full-time art practice; *b* Deal, Kent, 17 Feb., 1933; *s* of Dudley Kirk, M.B., Ch.B.; *m* Pleasance Kirk, A.R.C.A., M.S.D-C.; two *s. Educ.:* Westminster School; *studied art* at Canterbury College of Art (1950-54), R.C.A. (1956-59, Edwin Ladell, Julian Trevelyan, Alistair Grant, George Haslam). *Exhib.:* R.A.; one-man shows, Alwin Gallery, etc. *Work in permanent collections:* V. & A., Kent C.C., Canterbury C.C., Glasgow C.C. *Address:* 13 High St., Bridge, Canterbury, Kent CT4 5JY. *Signs work:* "Barry Kirk."

KIRK, Douglas William; painter in oil and water-colour; lecturer, City of London Polytechnic (1976-89); *b* Edinburgh, 22 Feb., 1949; *s* of Robert Kirk; *m* Jacqueline Adams; one *s. Educ.:* George Heriot's School, Edinburgh; *studied art* at Duncan of Jordanstone College of Art, Dundee (1967-71), Royal College of Art, London (1971-74). *Exhib.:* S.S.A., Compass Gallery, Glasgow, Fine Art Soc., 57 Gallery, Edinburgh, Fruit Market Gallery, Edinburgh. *Work in permanent collection:* Carlisle Museum and Gallery. *Address:* 146 Darnley Rd., Gravesend, Kent DA11 0SN. *Signs work:* "douglas kirk."

KIRK, Robert Joseph, B.A. (1973), M.Sc. (1978), N.A.P.A. (1988); painter in acrylic and pastel; Executive Council mem., N.A.P.A.; *b* Walsall, 7 Jan., 1932; *m* Sheila M.; two *d. Studied art* at Walsall and Stafford Schools of Art (1955, Angus Macauley, David Bethel). *Exhib.:* N.A.P.A. Annual since 1989. *Address:* West Fortune, Ashford Carbonell, Ludlow, Salop. SY8 4DB. *Clubs:* N.A.P.A., Ludlow Art Soc. *Signs work:* "Robert Kirk."

KIRKWOOD, John Sutherland; artist, mixed media, photography and etching; *b* Edinburgh, 6 Apr., 1947; *s* of J. E. Kirkwood. *Educ.:* George Watson College, Edinburgh; *studied art* at Dundee College of Art. *Exhib.:* one-man shows: 57 Art Gallery, Edinburgh Printmakers Workshop, A.I.R. Gallery, Talbot Rice Art Centre, Demarco Gallery, "Scottish Art Now". *Work in permanent collections:* S.A.C. Loan, Hunterian Museum, University of Glasgow, Scottish Museum of Modern Art. *Address:* 15 Leopold Pl., Edinburgh. *Signs work:* "J. S. Kirkwood."

KITCHIN, Myfanwy, R.Cam.A., N.D.D., A.T.D.; *b* 14 Dec., 1917; *m* 1949; two *s,* one *d. Educ.:* London: St. Aidan's High School, Hornsey School of Art. War years, while nursing and becoming S.R.N., part-time student at Slade School. Post war studied Reading University Dept. of Fine Art (1946-48); studied ceramics Walsall College of Art. *Work in private collections:* paintings and ceramic sculpture: U.K., U.S.A., Canada, N.Z. *Publications:* illustrated books, Phoenix House, Duckworths; many reviews as provincial art critic to the Guardian, Arts News and Review and B'ham Mail during 1960's and 1970's. *Address:* Roslyn, Maes Y Pandy, Dolgellau, Gwynedd LL40 1NE. *Signs work:* see appendix.

KITSON, Linda Frances, B.A. (1967), M.A., R.C.A. (1970); official war artist, Falkland Islands Task Force (1982); artist/tutor; Pres. Army Arts and Crafts Soc. (1983); *b* London, 17 Feb., 1945; *d* of Henry James Buller Kitson. *Educ.:* Tortington Pk., nr. Arundel, Sussex; *studied art* at St. Martin's School of Art (1965-67), R.C.A. (1967-70). *Exhib.:* Workshop Gallery, Illustrators A.G., Imperial War Museum (Falkland's War Exhbn. U.K. tour), National Theatre, R.A. *Work in permanent collections:* Imperial War Museum. *Publications:* Picnic (Jill Norman), The Falklands War, a Visual Diary (Mitchell Beazley), The Plague, Sun, Wind, Sand and Stars (Folio Soc.). *Address:* Flat 3, 25 Onslow Sq., London SW7 3NJ. *Club:* Chelsea Arts. *Signs work:* "Linda Kitson."

KITSON, Prof. Michael, M.A.; art historian; *b* 30 Jan., 1926. *Educ.:* Gresham's School; King's College, Cambridge; *studied history of art* at Courtauld Inst., of Art (1950-52, Anthony Blunt, Johannes Wilde); on staff of Courtauld Inst. (1955-85); Director of Studies, Paul Mellon Centre for Studies in British Art (1986-92). *Exhbns. organized:* 'The Art of Claude Lorrain' (Newcastle and London, Hayward Gallery, 1969); 'La Peinture Romantique Anglaise' (Paris, Petit Palais, 1972); 'Salvator Rosa' (London, Hayward Gallery, 1973); 'Zwei Hunderte Englische Malerie' (Munich, Haus der Kunst, 1979). *Publications:* Turner (1964), The Age of Baroque (1965), Caravaggio (1969), Rembrandt (1969, revised 1992), Claude Lorrain, Liber Veritatis (1978). *Address:* 72 Halton Rd., London N1 2AD.

KITTS, Barry Edward Lyndon, N.D.D. (1964), F.R.S.A. (1972); landscape painter and graphic designer; visiting lecturer, Ravensbourne College of Design and Communication; *b* Bath, 18 Oct., 1943; *s* of George Edward Kitts. *Educ.:* Sutton East County Secondary School (Surrey Special Art Course under George Mackley, M.B.E., R.E.); *studied art* at Kingston School of Art (1959-61) under J. D. Binns, A.R.C.A., D.A. Pavey, A.R.C.A., Wimbledon School of Art (1961-64) under Gerald Cooper, A.R.C.A. *Exhib.:* N.E.A.C., R.B.A., Wessex Artists' Exhbn. *Publication:* Co-author of a Graphic Design Sourcebook (1987). *Address:* 500 Kingston Rd., London SW20 8DT. *Signs work:* "Barry Kitts."

KLEIN, Anita, B.A.Hons. (1983), M.A. (1985), A.R.E. (1991); painter/printmaker in drypoint, woodcut, oil on board; *b* Sydney, Australia, 14 Feb., 1960; *d* of Prof. A.G. Klein; *m* Nigel Swift; two *d. Educ.:* Hampstead School; *studied art* at Chelsea School of Art (1978-79), Slade School of Fine Art (1979-83, Mick Moon, Paula Rego; 1983-85, Barto dos Santos). *Exhib.:* I.C.A., Hayward, R.I., Blond Fine Art; one-man shows: London: Creaser Gallery, Leigh Gallery, Tall House Gallery, Wilson Hale; Print Works, Colchester. *Work in permanent collections:* A.C.G.B., R.E., Ashmolean Museum. *Address:* 57 Chalsey Rd., London SE4 1YN. *Club:* Greenwich Printmakers. *Signs work:* see appendix.

KNAPP-FISHER, John, R.C.A. (1992); painter; *b* London, 2 Aug., 1931; *s* of the late Prof. A.B. Knapp-Fisher, F.R.I.B.A.; *m* Sheila Basset (divorced); one *s,* one *d. Educ.:* Eastbourne College; *studied art* at Maidstone College of Art (1951-53), Designer in Theatre. *Exhib.:* R.A., Business Art Galleries, Oriel, Welsh Arts Council, Upper Grosvenor, Agnews, Fry, Marjorie Parr, Johannesburg, Toronto, N.Y., Pembrokeshire Museums Touring (1984), Beaux Arts, Bath (1986), Henry Thomas Gallery, Faculty of Art and Design, Carmarthan (1989), Martin Tinney Cardiff. *Work in permanent collections:* B.B.C. Cardiff, National Library of Wales, Beecroft A.G., W. Wales Assoc. for the Arts, Swansea University, Haverfordwest Museum, prize winning panel, Withybush Hospital Haverfordwest. *Publications:* illustrated Pembrokeshire Churches (1989); included in: Cymru'r Cynfas by Hywel Harries (Lolfa Press, 1983); *films:* Anglia T.V. The Artist and his Work (1963). *Address:* Trevigan Cottage, Croesgoch, Haverfordwest, Pembrokeshire, SA62 5JP. *Signs work:* "John Knapp-Fisher."

KNEALE, Bryan, R.A. Rome Scholar; sculptor in steel and all metals, wood, etc.; Mem. C.N.A.A. Fine Arts Panel, Royal College of Art, Professor of Sculpture, Royal Academy (1980-83), Head of Sculpture R.C.A. (1985-90), Professor of Drawing (1990—), Chairman A.S.G.; *b* Douglas, I.O.M., 19 June, 1930; *s* of W. T. Kneale, newspaper editor; *m* Doreen Kneale; one *s,* one *d. Educ.:* Douglas High School; *studied art:* Douglas School of Art (1947) under

276

W. H. Whitehead; R.A. Schools (1948-52) under Philip Connard, Henry Rushbury. *Exhib.:* John Moores, Art d'aujourd'hui, Paris, Battersea Park, Whitechapel Retrospective, Cardiff, Leics. Educ. Com., Whitechapel, City of London, Peter Stuyvesant, Southampton, British Sculptors, R.A. Holland Park, Royal Exchange Sculpt., Hayward Gallery, R.A., London Group, Redfern Gallery, New Art Centre. *Work in permanent collections:* Tate, Arts Council, C.A.S., W.A.G., Fitzwilliam Museum, B.M., City Art Galleries of Manchester, Birmingham, Sheffield, Bradford, Wakefield, Leicester, York and Middlesbrough, Sao Paulo, Brazil, Museum of Modern Art, N.Y., National Galleries of N.Z., Queensland and S. Australia, Manx Museum and A.G., Abbot Hall Gallery, Cumberland, Beaverbrook Foundation, Frederickton, Bochum Museum, W. Germany, Bahia Museum, Brazil. *Address:* 10A Muswell Rd., London N10 2BG. *Club:* Chelsea Arts. *Signs work:* "BRYAN KNEALE" (die stamp), "Bryan Kneale" (drawings, etc.).

KNIGHT, Clifford (Edgar Levi), U.A. (1955); painter in water-colour and mixed media, lecturer; *b* Kempston, Beds., 8 Mar., 1930; *s* of the late H.R. Knight; *m* Sheila Gwynn; one *s*, one *d*. *Educ.:* Kempston Secondary Modern School; *studied art* at L.C.C. Central School (1955-57, William Roberts, Merlyn Evans). *Exhib.:* U.A., N.E.A.C.; one-man shows, Upper St. Gallery (1973), Carlton House Terr. (1983), Bedford, Luton, Letchworth, Northampton, Retford, Wellingborough, Welwyn Garden City, Abbotsholme School, Bedford School. *Work in permanent collections:* Luton and Letchworth A.Gs. *Work repro.:* Leisure Painter. *Address:* 104 Bunyan Rd., Kempston, Bedford MK42 8EX. *Signs work:* "Clifford Knight."

KNIGHT, Geoffrey Snowden, F.R.I.B.A.; ret. architect; landscape and marine artist in water-colour of traditional sailing craft; has worked in Africa and Caribbean; *b* Parkstone, Dorset, 1920. *Educ.:* Canford School; *studied painting* at Poole Art School. *Exhib.:* London, Sydney Australia, Chichester. *Address:* 3 The Orchard, Aldwick Bay, Bognor Regis, W. Sussex PO21 4HX.

KNIGHT, Sophie, A.R.W.S. (1990), B.A.(Hons.) Fine Art (1986), Post Grad. Dip. (1989); Ian Tragarthen Jenkins award (1986), Fred Ellwin award (1987), David Murray Scholarship (1988), Erik Kennington award (1989), Hunting Group Student prize (1989), R.W.S. award (1989); painter in water-colour and oil; *b* London, 20 Mar., 1965; *d* of Terence Knight, art director/painter. *Educ.:* The New School, Kings Langley; *studied art* at Herts. School of Art, St.Albans (1982), Camberwell School of Art and Design (1983-86), R.A. Schools (1986-89). *Exhib.:* numerous exhbns. including R.A. Summer Exhbn. (1988), Royal Festival Hall (1988), Mall Galleries (1989), Boundary Gallery (1989), Cadogan Contemporary (1989); one-man show, Cadogan Contemporary (1991). *Work in permanent collection:* B.M. *Address:* 94 Hindmans Rd., E. Dulwich, London SE22 9NG. *Signs work:* "Sophie Knight."

KNOWLER, Ann Patricia, S.W.A. (1993); artist in oil and soft pastels; *b* Pinner, 3 June, 1940; *m* Jonathan Knowler; one *s*, one *d*. *Educ.:* Northwood Secondary Modern School; *studied art* at F.E. classes and privately under Claude Murrills. *Exhib.:* S.W.A. Westminster Gallery, David Curzon Gallery. *Address:* Sundown, 7 Western Rd., Newick, E. Sussex BN8 4LE. *Clubs:* Weald of Sussex Art, The Adventurers Art, Assoc. of Sussex Artists, Guild of Sussex Artists. *Signs work:* "Ann Knowler."

KNOX, Harry Cooke, A.R.U.A. (1953); artist in oil, acrylic, water-colour and pastel, specialty portraits and murals; Pres., Ulster Arts Club (1955), vice-pres. (1951, 1952, 1953); vice-pres., R.U.A. (1950-52); *b* Newtownbutler, Co.

Fermanagh; *s* of Andrew Knox; *m* Lila Mary Knox; two *s*. *Educ.:* Methodist College, Belfast; *studied art* at Belfast College of Art (1924-30). *Exhib.:* R.U.A., R.H.A., R.O.I. *Address:* 109 Marlborough Park South, Belfast 9. *Club:* Ulster Arts. *Signs work:* see appendix.

KNOX, Jack, R.S.A. (1979), R.G.I. (1981), R.S.W. (1987); painter in oil, acrylic, pastel; Head of Painting, Glasgow School of Art (1981-92); *b* Kirkintilloch, 1936; *s* of Alexander Knox, tailor; *m* Margaret; one *s*, one *d*. *Educ.:* Lenzie Academy; *studied art* at Glasgow School of Art (1952-58, William and Mary Armour). *Exhib.:* one-man shows: Scottish Gallery (1966, 1989), Demarco Gallery, Edinburgh (1969), Serpentine, London (1971), Glasgow School of Art (1982), Retrospective (1983), Glasgow A.Gs. (1990). *Work in permanent collections:* Scottish National Gallery of Modern Art, Manchester City A.G., Scottish National Portrait Gallery, Glasgow A.Gs., Arts Council. *Publications:* The Scottish Bestiary by George Mackay Brown (Charles Booth-Olibborn/Paragon Press, 1986), Lapotiniere and Friends by David and Hilary Brown (Century Editions/Random Century Group Ltd., 1990). *Address:* 31 North Erskine Pk., Bearsden, Glasgow G61 4LY. *Signs work:* "Jack Knox."

KOLAKOWSKI, Matthew Edmund, B.A. (1978), M.A. (1979); artist/painter in oil; graphic tutor, Woolwich College, visiting lecturer, Wolverhampton University; *b* Ruislip, Middx., 12 Mar., 1956; *m* Philomena Marmion; one *s*. *Educ.:* Douay Martyrs School, Ickenham; *studied art* at Watford School of Art (Michael Werner, Peter Schmidt, Charles Harrison), Ravensbourne College of Art (Brian Fielding, Victor Kwell, Kit Twyford), Chelsea School of Art (Anthony Wishaw, Ian Stevenson). *Exhib.:* London Group since 1989; one-man show: Duncan Campbell Gallery (1993). *Address:* Brightside Studios, 8-10 Dartford St., London SE17. *Club:* London Group (Hon. Sec.). *Signs work:* "M" in circle or triangle, and see appendix.

KONDRACKI, Henry Andrew; artist in oil on canvas; *b* Edinburgh, 13 Feb., 1953; *m* Sara; two *s*. *Educ.:* Bellevue School, Edinburgh; *studied art* at Slade School of Fine Art (Ron Bowen, Jeffrey Camp, Jock McFadyen, Patrick George). *Exhib.:* Vanessa Deveureux Gallery (1987, 1989), William Jackson Gallery (1991). *Work in permanent collections:* British Council, A.C.G.B., University College London, Manchester A.G. *Publication:* Contemporary Scottish Painting by Bill Hare. *Address:* 20 Marchmont Cres., Edinburgh EH9 1HL. *Signs work:* "H. Kondracki."

KOPEL, Harold, R.O.I. (Hon. Treasurer); painter in oil, acrylic and pastel; art master, lecturer, Further Education I.L.E.A.; *b* Newcastle upon Tyne. *Educ.:* Rutherford Grammar School, Newcastle; University College, London; *studied art:* Central School of Arts, London. *Exhib.:* several one-man shows, numerous mixed shows including R.A., R.B.A., N.E.A.C., R.W.A., Paris Salon (Silver medal), Barcelona biennial, R.G.I., Contemporary Art International, Olympia (1989), many private galleries; Cornelissen prize. *Work in permanent collections:* University College, London, Nuffield Foundation, I.L.E.A. *Address:* 13 Hampstead Gdns., London NW11. *Signs work:* "Kopel."

KORALEK, Paul George, C.B.E., A.R.A. (1986); architect; Senior partner, Ahrends Burton and Koralek; *b* 7 Apr., 1933; *s* of Ernest Koralek (decd.); *m* Jennifer Chadwick; one *s*, two *d*. *Educ.:* Aldenham; *studied architecture:* Architectural Assoc. *Exhib.:* Heinz Gallery, R.I.B.A. (1982), R.A. Summer Show (annually since 1987). *Publication:* Monograph "Ahrends Burton and Koralek". *Address:* c/o Unit 1, 7 Chalcot Rd., London NW1 8LH.

KORDA, Vincent Henry; artist in oil and pastel; *b* London, 4 May, 1957; *s* of Vincent Korda, art director and artist. *Studied art* at City and Guilds, London; R.A. Schools. *Exhib.:* one-man shows: Cylinder Gallery (1984-85), Quinton Green Fine Art (1986). *Address:* 9 Pembroke Studios, Pembroke Gdns., London W8 6HX. *Signs work:* "KORDA."

KOSTER, David, D.F.A. (Lond.), N.D.D., A.T.D., S.WL.A.; printmaker; *b* London, 5 Nov., 1926; *s* of Rowland Koster; *m* Katherine Macrae; one *d. Educ.:* Clayesmore; *studied art* at Slade School. *Work in collections:* Aberdeen City A.G., Royal Ulster Museum, Belfast, Berliner Graphothek, U.C.L., Dept. of Environment, All Soul's College, Oxford, Hokin Gallery, U.S.A., Hamilton Public Library, Canada, University New South Wales, S. London Gallery, Towner A.G., Eastbourne, numerous County Council and Educ. Com. Collections. *Publications:* Wood engraved illustrations 'Down to Earth', drawings 'Fellow Mortals'. *Address:* 5 East Cliff Gdns., Folkestone, Kent CT19 6AR. *Signs work:* "David Koster."

KOWALSKY, Elaine Gloria, Dip. of Art; artist in relief, litho, ceramics; Henry Moore Fellow in Printmaking, Leeds Polytechnic; *b* Winnipeg, Manitoba, 24 Sept., 1948; *d* of Rosemary A. Kowalsky, abstract painter; *m* Elton Bash, painter. *Educ.:* Charleswood Collegiate, Winnipeg; *studied art* at University of Manitoba, St. Martin's School of Art, Brighton Polytechnic. *Exhib.:* R.A., and numerous one-man shows. *Work in permanent collections:* V. & A., Birmingham A.G., Worcester A.G., Leeds A.G., Manchester A.G., Canada Council Art Bank, University of Manitoba, National Gallery of Australia, Smithsonian Inst. *Address:* 27 Aberavon Rd., London E3 5AR. *Signs work:* "Elaine Kowalsky."

KOZARZEWSKA, Magda, L.C.A.D. (1977), S.I.A.D. (1977), B.A.Hons. (1981); artist in oil, charcoal, pencil; *b* Warsaw, 7 Oct., 1952; *d* of Zbigniew Kozarzewski; *m* Jonathan Goldberg; one *s. Educ.:* Grammar School, Warsaw; *studied art* at Chelsea School of Art (1974-77), Slade School of Fine Art (1977-81, Prof. Sir L. Gowing, Patrick George, Euan Uglow). *Exhib.:* solo shows: Polish Cultural Inst. (1975), Sue Rankin Gallery (1988), Thackeray Gallery (1991); major retrospective, Polish Cultural Inst. (1991); group shows: Hayward Gallery (1982), N.P.G. (1986). *Work in private collections:* U.K., Europe, U.S.A., Canada, S. Africa. *Address:* 15 Woodlands Ave., New Malden, Surrey KT3 3UL. *Signs work:* "M.K." or "Kozarzewska."

KRUT, Ansel Jonathan, B.F.A. (1982); painter in oil; awarded Rome prize (1987); *b* Cape Town, 1959; *s* of Dr. Louis Harold Krut. *Educ.:* S. Africa; *studied art* at University of the Witwatersrand (1979-82), R.C.A. (1983-86). *Exhib.:* R.A., John Moores, London Group, Cité des Arts, Paris, 'The Human Touch', Fischer Fine Art (1986); one-man show Fischer Fine Art (1989, 1990). *Address:* Fischer Fine Art, 30 King St., St. James's, London SW1. *Signs work:* "Krut" or "A. Krut."

KUHFELD, Peter, N.E.A.C., R.P., B.A.; artist in oil and pencil; *b* Glos., 4 Mar., 1952; *m* Cathryn Showan, artist; two *d. Educ.:* Gateway School, Leicester; *studied art* at Leicester (1972-76), R.A. Schools (1977-80, Peter Greenham, Jane Dowling, Norman Blamey). *Exhib.:* R.A., N.E.A.C., R.P., R.B.A., R.W.A., N.P.G., Accademia Italiana, New Grafton Gallery, Agnews, W.H. Patterson, Richard Green. *Work in permanent collections:* H.M. The Queen, Baring Bros., Lazards, Cable and Wireless, Hammerson Group, National Trust, Elizabeth Greenshield Foundation, Hambros. *Address:* 42 High St., Wye, nr. Ashford, Kent TN25 5AL. *Club:* Arts. *Signs work:* "Kuhfeld."

KUO, Nancy; author, art critic and painter; gold medallist; *b* Shanghai, China. *Studied art* at Xinhua Art Academy, Shanghai. *Exhib.:* in many countries in Asia, Africa and Europe. *Work in permanent collections:* private collections all over the world, National Museums of Burma and Leyden. *Publications:* author of "Chinese Paper-cut Pictures", "The Sky is Singing" and many other books, essays etc. in Chinese and English. Member of International Assoc. of Art Critics, P.E.N., British Actors' Equity; Adviser, British Assoc. of Writers in Chinese; Founder/Director, Chinese Arts Inst. since 1964. *Address:* Sea-Breeze Studio, 35 Artillery Rd., Ramsgate, Kent CT11 8PT. *Signs work:* "Nancy" in Chinese; see appendix.

L

LACEY, Mary Elliot, A.T.D., S.WL.A.; wildlife painter and illustrator in oils, water-colour and conté chalk; *b* Birmingham, 26 Sept., 1923; *d* of Wilfred Lewis, head teacher; *m* Howard Lacey; one *s*, two *d. Educ.:* Birmingham; *studied art* at Birmingham College of Art (1939-44). *Exhib.:* Tryon Gallery, Birdland Wildlife Gallery, S.WL.A., Mall Galleries. *Work in private collections:* Sultan of Oman, Eric Hosking, Miss Eleanor MacDonald, Rolf Harris. *Publications:* book illustrations for Hamlyn Publishing, South Leigh Press, Balberry Publishing, Royle and Medici. *Address:* Meadowbank, Snape Rd., Sudbourne, Woodbridge, Suffolk IP12 2BA. *Signs work:* "Mary Elliot Lacey."

LACK, Barbara Dacia, A.R.C.A. Lond.; artist in oil, engraving, textile design, draughtswoman; *d* of Charles T. Lack, M.I.Mech.E., A.M.I.E.E. *Educ.:* Perse School, Camb.; *studied art:* Camb. School of Art, R.C.A. *Exhib.:* paintings and engravings, R.C.A. Assoc. Exhbn. at the R.A. (1948) and provinces; painting at Colchester Castle (1950); paintings in Leicester (1963); Norwich (1966); Peterborough (1969-1973); Sudbury (1969-1975); Cambridge, Ely, etc.; textiles, etc., in London, Edinburgh and Copenhagen. *Official purchases:* two purchased by Messrs J. and P. Coats (1945). *Work repro.:* Modern Embroidery, Embroideress, etc. *Address:* Acorn Bank, Temple Sowerby, Penrith, Cumbria. *Signs work:* "B. D. LACK."

LACKNER, Suzanne O., F.I.L., M.F.P.S.; sculptor in marble, onyx, alabaster, soapstone, portland stone, etc. and recently bronze and wood; *b* Berlin, 10 Feb., 1908; *d* of Richard Chotzen, banker; widow; one *d. Educ.:* Berlin Technical University (architecture), in France since 1933; *studied art* at Camden Main Institute. *Exhib.:* Camden Institute (1975), Trends (annually), Camden Arts Centre (1976), City of Westminster Arts Council (1976), Burgh House (1992), etc., Berlin, Paris. *Work in permanent collections:* England, France, Germany, U.S.A., Japan. *Address:* 49 Eton Hall, Eton College Rd., London NW3 2DR. *Signs work:* see appendix.

LA FONTAINE, Thomas Sherwood; painter in oil, water-colour and black and white of portraits and animal subjects; *b* 21 Dec., 1915. *Educ.:* Rottingdean and Tonbridge School; Regent St., Polytechnic (Harry Watson, S. Tresilian, since 1934); City and Guilds, Kennington (Innes Fripp, James Grant, Middleton Todd, since 1936); Spenlove School (Reginald Eves, since 1939). *Address:* East Cottage, Burton Hill, Malmesbury, Wilts. SN16 0EL. *Signs work:* in printed capitals.

LAGO, Darren, B.A. (Fine Art), M.A. (Fine Art); sculptor in installation and object based artworks; Tutor, Kingsway College, London; *b* 22 Sept., 1965. *Educ.:* King Edward VI School, Lichfield; *studied art* at Portsmouth University (Don Hopes), Chelsea School of Art and Design (Shelagh Cluett). *Exhib.:* New Contemporary I.C.A. London, Annely Juda Gallery. *Work in permanent collection:* David Juda, Annely Juda Fine Art, London. *Address:* 23B Lonsdale Rd., London NW6 6RA. *Signs work:* see appendix.

LAING, Gerald Ogilvie-, N.D.D. (1964); artist: figurative (Pop) painting (1962-65), highly finished abstract painting/sculpture (1966-69), abstract 3-dimensional sculpture in the landscape (1970-72), formal figurative sculpture (1973-82), figurative sculpture (1983-to date); Commissioner, Royal Fine Art Commission for Scotland; *b* Newcastle-upon-Tyne, 11 Feb., 1936; *m* Adaline Havemeyer Frelinghuysen; four *s*, one *d*. *Educ.:* Berkhamsted School; R.M.A. Sandhurst; *studied art* at St. Martin's School of Art. *Exhib.:* more than 30 one-man shows worldwide. Major retrospective, Fruitmarket Gallery, Edinburgh (1993). *Work in permanent collections:* Tate Gallery, V. & A., N.P.G., M.O.M.A., N.Y., Whitney Museum, N.Y., and many others; public works: 'Callanish' Glasgow, 'Fountain of Sabrina' Bristol, 'Wise and Foolish Virgins', 'Axis Mundi' and 'Conan Doyle Memorial' Edinburgh. *Publication:* Kinkell — The Reconstruction of a Scottish Castle. *Addresses:* Kinkell Castle, Ross-shire IV7 8AT, Scotland; 139 East 66th St., N.Y. 10021, U.S.A. *Club:* Chelsea Arts. *Signs work:* "Gerald Laing."

LAIRD, Michael Donald, O.B.E., F.R.S.A., F.C.S.D., F.R.I.A.S., (McLaren Fellow 1956-58), R.I.B.A.; R.S.A. Architecture Medal (1968); Awards from Civic Trust, British Steel Corp., Saltire Society, etc.; architect and design consultant; Governor, Edinburgh College of Art; *b* 1928; *s* of G. D. S. Laird; *m* Hon. Kirsty Noel-Paton; two *s*, one *d*. *Educ.:* Loretto School; *studied art* at Edinburgh College of Art and University under Prof. R. Gordon Brown. *Buildings:* include Standard Life Assurance Head Office, Royal Bank Computer Headquarters, Edinburgh University Kings Buildings Centre, Restoration, Maxwelton House and Blairquhan Castle. *Addresses:* 22 Moray Pl., Edinburgh, and Brock, Isle of Tiree, Argyllshire. *Club:* New (Edinburgh).

LAKE, C. Elisabeth Matheson, R.M.S. (1989), F.H.S. (1982); miniature painter in water-colour (interiors); *b* Norwich, 12 Apr., 1939; *d* of James Matheson Fleming, M.R.C.S., L.R.C.P.; *m* Geoffrey N. Lake; one *s*, three *d*. *Educ.:* privately; *studied art* at West of England College of Art (1957-60). *Exhib.:* H.S. (1982-), R.A. Summer Exhbn. (1986), R.M.S. (1984-), many N. American and Canadian exhbns. (1985-89). *Work in private collections:* England, N. America and Europe. *Address:* Hollow End, Hollow Marsh, Farrington Gurney, Somerset BS18 5TX. *Signs work:* see appendix.

LALLY, Richard; painter in oil, pastel and water-colour; *b* London, 2 Oct., 1928; *s* of A. R. Lally. *Educ.:* Brixton College of Building and Architecture (1942-45); *studied art* at Hammersmith School of Art (1955-59, Leon Underwood, Dennis Gilbert). *Exhib.:* one-man shows, Real Club Nautico, Teneriffe (1961), Manolette Gallery, Richmond (1977); R.O.I., N.S., U.A., S.WL.A. *Address:* Strathcroy, Drumbeg, Lairg, Sutherland, Scotland IV27 4NG. *Signs work:* "LALLY."

LAMB, Elspeth, D.A. (Glas.) (1973), H.Dip.A.D. (Manc.) (1974), A.R.S.A. (1990); lecturer/printmaker in printmaking, papermaking, drawing; Lecturer in drawing and painting, Edinburgh College of Art; *b* Glasgow, 28 Mar., 1951; *d* of John Cunningham Lamb, accountant. *Educ.:* Kings Pk. Senior Secondary

School, Glasgow; *studied art* at Glasgow School of Art (Philip Reeves), Manchester Polytechnic, The Tamarind Inst. of Lithography, University of New Mexico, U.S.A. (Lynn Allen). *Exhib.:* Mercury Gallery (1988, 1990), Conservative Management (1990), Marlborough Graphics (1991), Glasgow Print Studio (1990). *Work in permanent collections:* S.A.C., British Council, Japanese Consular Coll., Perth A.G., Glasgow A.G., City Arts. *Address:* Bon a Tirer Editions, 15 E. Campbell St., Glasgow G1 1DG.

LAMBERT, Colin Joseph; sculptor in bronze and stone; *b* Guantanamo Bay, Cuba, 17 Jan., 1948; *s* of Virgil Mangus-Colorado, American Indian poet; *m* Catherine Finn. *Studied art* at Chouinard Art Inst., Los Angeles (1966-68); apprenticed with Karl Gomez in Amsterdam (1980-83). *Work in permanent collections:* Stamford Forum, Stamford, Conn.; London United Bldg., London; Renaissance Vineyard and Winery, Calif.; Warminster Market Centre, Warminster, Wilts. *Address:* Flint Barn Studio, West End, nr. Essendon, Hatfield, Herts. AL9 5RQ. *Signs work:* see appendix

LAMBIRTH, Alan, R.B.A. (1986), R.A. Gold medal (1982), R.A. Schools Advanced Dip. (1983), Higher Surrey Dip. A.D. (1980), De Laszlo medal awarded by R.B.A. (1991); artist in oil, pastel and gouache; *b* Cuckfield, 19 Feb., 1959; *s* of Ivor Edward Lambirth. *Educ.:* Hazelwick School, Crawley; *studied art* at W. Sussex College of Design (1975-77), Epsom School of Art (1977-80, Peter Peterson), R.A. Schools (1980-83, Peter Greenham, R.A.). *Exhib.:* R.A., R.B.A., N.E.A.C., Soc. of Landscape Painters; one-man shows: Odette Gilbert Gallery (1984, 1986), Solomon Gallery (1988), Sheila Harrison Fine Art (1989, 1991); four-man show: Hallam Gallery (1990). *Address:* 22 Brushwood Rd., Roffey, Horsham, W. Sussex RH12 4PE.

LAMONT, Ian James; painter in oil; *b* Carshalton, 16 May, 1964; *s* of John Lamont, scenic artist. *Educ.:* Nork Pk. School; N.E. Surrey College of Technology; Sutton College of Liberal Arts; *studied art* at Kingston Polytechnic School of Art and Design; also portrait painting under Ronald Benham, N.E.A.C., R.B.A. (1982-86). *Exhib.:* R.A., N.E.A.C., R.B.A., R.O.I. (Winsor and Newton Young Artist award finalist 1983-88). *Work in permanent collection:* United Racecourses. *Address:* 25 Woodgavil, Banstead, Surrey SM7 1AA. *Signs work:* "Ian Lamont."

LANCASTER, Brian Christy; artist in water-colour, occasional acrylic, illustrator (mainly architectural); *b* Atherton, nr. Manchester, 3 Aug., 1931; *s* of Harold Lancaster; *m* Pauline Carol Wheler Lancaster. *Educ.:* Lee St. School, Atherton; *studied art* at Bolton College of Art (1946-49, Mr. Gauld), Southport College of Art (1949-52, Mr. Radcliffe). Mem. Bristol Savages (1969) and G.R.A. (1990). *Exhib.:* Atkinson A.G., Southport, Bristol Savages, R.W.A., R.I., R.B.A., R.W.S., G.R.A., R.S.M.A. *Work in permanent collection:* Bristol Savages. *Address:* Galloway, Waterley Bottom, N. Nibley, Glos. GL11 6EF. *Club:* Bristol Savages. *Signs work:* "Brian C. Lancaster."

LANCASTER, John Maurice, N.D.D. (1950), M.Phil., Ph.D. (Lond.) (1984), D.A.E., F.S.A.E., S.H.A. Armiger; painter, calligrapher, heraldic artist; *b* Wigan; *s* of James Lancaster, engineer; *m* Janet Lucy Firth. *Educ.:* King James's School, Huddersfield; *studied art* at Leeds College of Art (1946-51), and advanced painting with Art Foundation (early 1960's, Victor Pasmore). *Exhib.:* one-man shows: Leicester (1965, 1967), Nottingham (1966, 1967), London (1969), Keele (1970, 1974), Bristol (1984), Decatur, Al., U.S.A. (1985), Columbus, Ohio, U.S.A. (1986), Thatcher, Az., U.S.A. (1991), Guild Gallery, Bristol (1993); two-man shows: Rigby Graham and John Lancaster, Compendium, B'ham

(1967), Lancaster and Pickard, B'ham (1968), Davie and Lancaster, Leicester (1970); R.W.A., R.B.A., Hesketh Hubbard, Mod. Art in Yorkshire, W. Riding Artists, John Noott 20th C. Gallery, Broadway, Kenulf Galleries, Winchcombe & London, Guild Gallery, Bristol, Upton Lodge Gallery, Tetbury, and other galleries. *Work in permanent collections:* Europe, Scandinavia and U.S.A. *Publications:* 16 art books published, including Introducing Op Art, Lettering Techniques, Calligraphy Techniques, Painting. Visiting Prof. and Summer School Director, U.S.A.; Gila Valley Arts Council Visiting artist, Az., U.S.A. (1991). *Societies:* N.S.E.A.D., S.S.I., S.H.A., W. Oxon. Arts Assoc. *Address:* 10 Walnut Cl., Cheltenham, Glos. GL52 3AG. *Signs work:* "John Lancaster."

LANG, Wharton, R.S.M.A. (1948), F.R.S.A. (1983); sculptor in wood; Mem. S.WL.A.; *b* Oberammergau, Bavaria, 13 June, 1925; *s* of Faust Lang, wood sculptor; *m* Ingrid. *Educ.:* Newquay Grammar School; *studied art* at Leonard Fuller School of Painting (1946) and privately under Faust Lang (1946-49). *Work in permanent collections:* Ulster Museum, Belfast, R.S.M.A. Diploma Collection, National Maritime Museum, Greenwich, Carving in Relief 'Castle of Mey' presented to H.M. Queen Mother (1967). *Address:* Fauna Studio, Mount Zion, St. Ives, Cornwall. *Signs work:* "W. LANG," "Wharton Lang" and see appendix.

LARGE, George Charles, R.I. (1986), A.T.C.; artist in oil and water-colour; *b* London, 20 Jan., 1936; *m* Pamela Parkinson; three *s*, two *d* (one *s-s,* one *s-d.*). *Educ.:* Downhills Central School, Tottenham; *studied art* at Hornsey College of Art (1958-63, Maurice de Sausmarez, John Titchell, Alfred Daniels). *Exhib.:* R.I., R.B.A., S.W.E.; one-man shows, Mall Galleries, National Gallery Malta, Duncan Campbel Fine Arts. *Work in permanent collections:* British Rail, National Gallery Malta, British Consulate Malta, Cranfield Inst., I.C.I. *Publications:* illustrated, Laughter in the Kitchen, and various magazines. *Address:* 13/14 Market Pl., Woburn, Beds. MK17 9PZ. *Signs work:* "LARGE 90."

LARMONT, Eric, N.D.D., A.T.C.; painter in oil, etcher; part-time art lecturer, *b* South Shields, 27 Sept., 1943. *Studied art* at Sunderland College of Art (1963-65); Goldsmiths' School of Art (1965-66), Post-grad. Belgian Scholarship (1968-69). *Exhib.:* one-man shows, London: 273 Gallery (1969), Scribes Cellar (1978), Holsworthy Gallery (1981), Galerie Blankenese, Hamburg (1983); two-man show, Jonathan Poole Gallery (1986). *Work in permanent collections:* Carlisle Corporation; private collections: various. *Prizes and awards:* Reeves Bi-centenary Premier Award (1966); Second Non-purchase Prize, Northern Painters Exhibition (1966). *Address:* 20 Rainville Rd., London W6 9HA. *Signs work:* see appendix.

LARUSDOTTIR, Karolina, R.E., A.R.W.S., N.E.A.C.; painter in oil and water-colour, etcher and printmaker; *b* Reykjavik, Iceland, 1944. *Studied art:* Ruskin School of Art, Oxford University and Barking College of Art. *Exhib.:* Bankside Gallery, R.E., R.A., R.B.A.; one-man shows: Kjarvalsstadir Reykjavik (1982, 1986), Gallerie Gammelstrand, Kobenhagen, Gallery 10 (1984, 1987, 1991). *Prizes:* The Dicks and Greenbury Award, Bankside Gallery (1989). *Special award:* Premio Internazionale Biella per l'incisione, Italy. *Address:* The Green, High St., Fowlmere, Cambs. *Signs work:* "LARUSDOTTIR."

LASDUN, Sir Denys (Louis), Kt. (1976), C.B.E. (1965); architect. *Principal works* include: housing and schools for Bethnal Green and Paddington; London H.Q., N.S.W. Govt.; Flats 26 St James's Place; Royal College of Physicians; University of East Anglia; London University (SOAS, I. of E., Law Inst.); work for Universities Leicester and Liverpool; Fitzwilliam College, and Christ's

College extension, Cambridge; National Theatre and IBM South Bank; European Investment Bank, Luxembourg; Hurva Synagogue project, Jerusalem; Cannock Community Hospital; Genoa Opera House project; offices Fenchurch Street, EC4 and Milton Court, EC2. *Member Academician:* Paris (1984); San Luca, Rome (1984); Bulgaria (1986). Hon. F. American Institute of Architects (1966), Royal Gold Medal for Architecture, R.I.B.A. (1977); R.A. (1991); Wolf Prize in Arts (Architecture) Wolf Foundation (1992); R.I.B.A. Trustees' Medal (1992). *Publications* include: A Language and a Theme (1976); Architecture in an Age of Scepticism (1984). *Address:* 146 Grosvenor Rd., London SW1V 3JY.

LASUCHIN, Michael, B.F.A., M.F.A.; more than one hundred and forty awards and prizes since 1971; printmaker, teacher and artist in water-colour, acrylics and drawing; Professor, The University of the Arts; *b* Kramatorsk, U.S.S.R., 24 July, 1923. *Educ.:* Philadelphia College of Art; Tyler School of Art, Temple University; *studied art* at Rostow College of Art (1940-41) under Zownir, Tzymbal; Nachwuchsgruppe Bildender Künstler, Regensburg, Germany (1947-49) under Hauser, Wissner; Mahl & Zeichenschule 'Die Form', Munich, Germany (1950) under Konig; Pennsylvania Academy of Fine Art, Philadelphia (1968) under Lueders, Hanlen and Stumpfig. *Work in permanent collections:* Library of Congress; Philadelphia, Museum of Art; Brooklyn Museum of Art; De Cordova Museum of Art; Springville Museum of Art (Mis.); Museum of Modern Art, Barcelona; V. & A.; Museum of Art, Montreal; Museum of Modern Art, New York; Art Museum, Berlin; Art Museum, Stockholm, and more than seventy others. *Address:* 120 E. Cliveden St., Philadelphia, Pa. 19119, U.S.A. *Clubs:* The Print, Boston Printmakers, National Water-colour Soc., American Color Print Soc., Los Angeles Printmaking Soc., Philadelphia Water-color, Audubon Artists. *Signs work:* "Michael Lasuchin."

LAUDER, Kenneth Scott, A.R.C.A. (1939); painter in oil and water-colour; *b* Edinburgh, 1916; *s* of Duncan Fullerton Lauder; *m* (1) Sylvia Morgan (1946); one *s* (*m* dissolved); (2) Marian Mills (1966); two *s*. *Educ.:* King Alfred's Grammar School (Albert Rutherston); *studied art* at Chelsea School of Art (1933-36, H.S. Williamson, G. Sutherland, R. Medley), R.C.A. (1936-39, P.H. Jowett, Gilbert Spencer, Percy Horton). *Exhib.:* R.A., Agnews, Scottish Gallery London and Edinburgh, Liverpool Academy, Newcastle Laing Gallery, Bristol R.W.A., Stratford-on-Avon Ruskin Gallery, Bear Lane Gallery Oxford, William Jackson Gallery London. *Address:* Moreton Lodge, Eye, Leominster, Herefordshire HR6 0DP. *Signs work:* see appendix.

LAW, Enid: see CHAUVIN, Enid.

LAW, Graham Couper, M.A. (Cantab.), A.R.I.B.A. (1951), A.R.S.A. (1980), F.R.I.A.S.; architect; *b* Glasgow, 28 Sept., 1923; *s* of W.R. Law; *m* Isobel E.A. Drysdale; one *s*, three *d. Educ.:* Merchiston Castle School, King's College, Cambridge; *studied art* at Cambridge University School of Architecture (1946-51). *Exhib.:* R.A., R.S.A., etc. *Publication:* Alexander ('Greek') Thomson, illustrated article (Architectural Review, May 1954). *Address:* Easter Soc., Hopetoun, S. Queensferry EH30 9SL. *Club:* New, Edinburgh. *Signs work:* "G.C. Law."

LAWRENCE, Gordon Robert, Dip.A.D. (1951), Teacher's Cert. (1952), 1st Class Hons. Rome Accademia de Belle Arte (1962), M.Ed. Liverpool (1975), Ph.D. (1979); painter/sculptor in acrylic, water-colour, stone; *b* Glasgow, 1930; divorced; three *s. Educ.:* Hillhead High School, Glasgow; *studied art* at Glasgow School of Art, Accademia de Belle Arte, Rome. *Exhib.:* Britain, France,

Germany, Spain, Ireland and U.S.A. *Address:* Camboulit, 46100 Figeac, France. Signs work: see appendix.

LAWRENCE, John; winner, Francis Williams Book Illustration award (twice); freelance illustrator in wood engraving and water-colour; part time lecturer, Camberwell School of Art; external assessor, Exeter College of Art; Duncan of Jordanstone College of Art; Edinburgh College of Art; Kingston School of Art; *b* Hastings, 15 Sept., 1933; *m* Myra; two *d. Educ.:* Salesian College, Oxford; *studied art* at Hastings School of Art and Central School of Art and Design. *Exhib.:* R.E., S.W.E. *Work in permanent collections:* V. & A., Ashmolean Museum, National Museum of Wales and several provincial galleries. *Publications:* over 100 books. *Address:* 22A Castlewood Rd., London N16 6DW. *Clubs:* A.W.G., S.W.E., Double Crown. *Signs work:* "John Lawrence."

LAWRENCE, Mary R.; painter in oil and water-colour; *b* Wimbledon, 17 June, 1922; *d* of Rev. T.R. Harley, M.B.E., M.A.; *m* F.R.M. Lawrence; one *s*, two *d. Educ.:* Downe House, Cold Ash, Newbury; *studied art* at Epsom School of Art and Design (1970-80, John Morley, Alan Dodd, Leslie Worth). *Exhib.:* R.A. Summer Shows (1974-87), N.E.A.C. (1972-76). *Address:* 15 Jackson Cl., Epsom, Surrey KT18 7RA.

LAWSON, Gillian; painter in water-colour and oil, printmaker in etching; *b* 6 May, 1936; *d* of Oliver Massingham, director; *m*; one *s*, two *d. Educ.:* Parliament Hill Grammar School; *studied art* at Camden Institute (silk screen printing, Ingrid Greenfield), Camden Art Centre (1971-75, etching, Dorothea Wight). *Exhib.:* Capetown, S.A., Georgetown, Washington, U.S.A., R.A., Halesworth Gallery, Burgh House, Hampstead, The Ice House, Holland Park, Hinton Gallery, nr. Horley, Ninth British International Print Biennale. *Address:* 7 Oak Hill Way, Hampstead, London NW3 7LR. *Signs work:* "Gillian Lawson."

LAWSON, Simon Nicholas, B.A. Hons. (1985); artist in oil, etching, photography; *b* Waltham, Lincs., 2 Aug., 1964; *s* of David S. Lawson, graphic designer. *Educ.:* Waltham Toll Bar Comprehensive; *studied art* at Grimsby School of Art (1980-82, Peter Todd), Wimbledon School of Art (1982-85, Bernard Cohen), R.A. Schools (1985-88, Norman Adams). *Exhib.:* Symondsbury Gallery, Bridport (1986), Royal Festival Hall (1986), R.A. (1986-87). *Address:* 22 Bursar St., Cleethorpes, S. Humberside. *Signs work:* "S.N. Lawson."

LAWSON, Sonia, R.A., R.W.S., R.C.A., M.A.(1st) (1959); artist in oil, water-colour, etching; Tutor R.A. Schools; *b* Wensleydale, Yorks., 2 June, 1934; *d* of Fred Lawson and Muriel Metcalfe, artists; *m* Charles Congo; one *d. Educ.:* Leyburn School; Southwick Girls' School; *studied art* at Royal College of Art (1956-59, Prof. Carel Weight), Post-graduate year (1959-60), Travelling Scholarship, France. *Exhib.:* retrospective tour, Leicester Polytechnic, Mappin Gallery Sheffield, Ferens Hull, Cartwright Bradford, Central Gallery Milton Keynes (1982-83), Kirklees (1985), Manchester (1987); one-man shows, Wakefield (1988), Bradford (1989), London, Boundary Gallery (1989); mixed shows, New York, Fragments against Ruin tour, China, British Council tour, Arts Council, Tolly Cobbald, John Moores, Edinburgh, R.A. London, Haywards Annual London, Subjective Eye, Midland Group Nottingham. *Work in permanent collections:* Arts Council, Sheffield, Carlisle, Belfast, Bradford, Middlesbrough, Harrogate, Rochdale, Wakefield and Huddersfield A.G.'s, Open University, M. of W., Leeds University, R.C.A., Nuffield, Cranfield, Imperial War Museum and Vatican. *Address:* c/o Royal Academy, Piccadilly, London W1. *Signs work:* "S. Lawson," "Sonia Lawson" or "Lawson."

LAWSON, Thomas, John Christie Prize, life drawing (1953); artist in oil and water-colour; window-dresser; Cert. Fine Art, King's College, Newcastle-upon-Tyne (June, 1958); *b* Newcastle-upon-Tyne, 8 May, 1922. *Educ.:* Elementary school, and College of Art and Industrial Design, Newcastle-upon-Tyne (display); *studied art* at King's College, Newcastle-upon-Tyne, University of Durham, evening classes under Mr. Scott Campbell, drawing, and Mr. Tudor Davies, painting (1951-53). *Exhib.:* Federation of Northern Arts Socs. annual exhbn. (1952, 1953, 1969); Artists of Northern Counties (Laing A.G., Newcastle-upon-Tyne, 1960); Holly House Gallery, Tynemouth (1988, 1989); Newcastle Polytechnic, Laing Collection exhib. (1989, 1990, 1991). *Address:* 13 Tweedmouth Ct., Newcastle-upon-Tyne NE3 1YP. *Club:* Newcastle Society of Artists. *Signs work:* "T. Lawson."

LAWSON-BAKER, Auriol; muralist, sculptor in bronze; Director, L.B.P. Sculpture and Design; owner "Scene Inside" Mural Co.; *b* 7 Sept., 1963; *m* Neil Lawson-Baker; one *s*. *Educ.:* Ditcham Park, Petersfield, Hants. *Exhib.:* R.A., sculpture project managed throughout U.K. and Europe including Houses of Parliament Arts Com., London International Financial Futures Exchange; British Gas plc., etc. *Addresses:* Graingers, West Ashling, W. Sussex; and 16 Wilton Pl., London SW1X 8RL. *Signs work:* "A. Lawson-Baker."

LAWSON-BAKER, Dr. Neil, M.B., B.S. (Lond.), B.D.S., L.D.S. (Lond.), L.D.S., R.C.S. (Eng.); dental surgeon and sculptor in bronze; Director, L.B.P. Sculpture and Design; *b* Watford, 8 Nov., 1938; *m* Auriol Lawson-Baker; one *s*. *Educ.:* Merchant Taylors and London University. *Exhib.:* one-man show: Watermans Gallery, London (1991). *Work in public collections:* Entrance Hall No. 1 Parliament St., Sterling House at Albert Bridge SW11, London International Financial Futures Exchange, Liffe (Stock Exchange Commission), British Gas 'Flame' 7 metres at Reading and Loughborough. *Address:* 31 Wilton Pl., London SW1X 8SH. *Club:* Arts. *Signs work:* "Neil Lawson-Baker."

LAYCOCK, Allan Bracewell, A.T.D. (1951), F.S.A.I. (1975), R.W.A. (1986); landscape painter in acrylic, in situ; lecturer in graphics and illustration; *b* Sutton-in-Craven, 4 June, 1928. *Educ.:* Keighley Grammar School; *studied art* at Keighley School of Art (1945-46, 1948-50), Sheffield College of Art (1950-51), Norwich School of Art (1951). *Exhib.:* one-man and group shows in eastern and S.W. England. Work in private collections in U.K. and overseas. *Address:* Tararua, Broad St., Hartpury, Glos. GL19 3BN. *Signs work:* "Allan Laycock."

LAYZELL, Peter, B.A.(Hons.) Fine Art; artist in oil; part-time lecturer in art at Preston College; *b* Hitchin, Herts., 1962. *Studied art* at Mander College, Bedford and Coventry Polytechnic (1981-84). *Exhib.:* R.A. Summer Exhbn. from 1986-93 (prizewinner, 1990); various group exhbns. *Work in collections:* Morgan Grenfell, St. Martin's College, Lancaster, Warrington Arts Council. *Address:* 72 Vale Rd., Lancaster LA1 2JL. *Dealer:* Houldsworth Fine Art, 46 Bassett Rd., London W10 6JL. *Signs work:* "P. Layzell" on reverse.

LEACH, D.; potter in stoneware and porcelain; *b* Tokyo, 7 May, 1911; *s* of Bernard Leach, C.H., C.B.E., F.R.S.A., potter; *m* Elizabeth Mary; three *s* (all potters). *Educ.:* Dauntsey's School; *studied art* with Bernard Leach. *Exhib.:* numerous in U.K., Germany, Japan, Australia, Turkey, Belgium, U.S.A., Craftsmans Art at V. & A. (1973), British Crafts Centre (1979); one-man, Craftsmen Potters Assoc. (1966, 1981). *Work in permanent collections:* V. & A., Exeter Musuem and A.G., Wakefield Museum, Liverpool Museum and A.G. *Address:* Lowerdown Pottery, Bovey Tracey, Devon TQ13 9LE. *Signs work:* seal in foot of pots, see appendix.

LEAPER, Landreth Francis, A.R.W.A. (1979); self taught artist in water-colour and pencil; *b* Horsham, 22 Dec., 1947. *Exhib.:* numerous in South and S. West England. *Address:* 44 Friezewood Rd., Ashton, Bristol BS3 2AB. *Signs work:* "LEAPER" or "L. LEAPER" or double LL within a circle, sometimes above the year.

LE BAS, Rachel Ann, R.E., N.E.A.C.; Mem. A.W.G., Somerset Guild of Craftsmen; painter, line-engraver, etc.; *b* 9 Apr., 1923; *d* of Capt. R. S. Le Bas, Somerset Light Infantry (retd.). *Educ.:* W. Heath School, Sevenoaks; City and Guilds of London Art School (A. R. Middleton Todd, R.A., R.W.S., R.E.). *Exhib.:* R.A., N.E.A.C., R.B.A., London Group. *Work in permanent collections:* Ashmolean Museum, Exeter Museum, Southampton Civic Centre, R.A. Graphics. *Address:* Winsford, nr. Minehead, Som. TA24 7JE. *Signs work:* "R. A. LE BAS."

LE BROCQUY, Louis, H.R.H.A. (1983), F.C.S.D. (1960), Hon. Litt.D., Dublin (1962), Hon. Ll.D. National University of Ireland (1988), Chevalier de la Légion d'Honneur (1975); *b* Nov., 1916; *s* of Albert le Brocquy. *Studied art:* self-taught. *Exhib.:* Gimpel Fils (London, N.Y.), Galerie Jeanne Bucher (Paris), Taylor (Dublin). *Retrospective exhbns.:* Municipal Gallery of Modern Art, Dublin (1966, 1978), Ulster Museum, Belfast (1967, 1987), Fondation Maeght, St. Paul (1973), Arts Council, Belfast (1975, 1978), Musée d'Art Moderne, Paris (1976), New York State Museum (1981), Palais des Beaux Arts, Charleroi (1982), Festival Centre, Adelaide (1988), Westpac, National Gallery of Victoria, Melbourne (1988), Museum of Contemporary Art, Brisbane (1988), Musée Picasso, Antibes (1989), Museum of Modern Art, Kamakura (1991), Itami Museum of Art, Osaki (1991), City Museum of Contemporary Art, Hiroshima (1991). *Address:* c/o Gimpel Fils, 30 Davies St., London W1Y 1LG.

LEDER, Carolyn, M.A. (1968); Curator, Old Speech Room Gallery, Harrow School (1989–); Trustee, Stanley Spencer Gallery, Cookham (1978-90); formerly Lecturer in History of Art, University of London, Dept. of Extra-Mural Studies (1972-88); *b* Melbourne, 5 Mar., 1945; *d* of Harold Beck, violoncellist; *m* Malcolm Leder; two *s. Educ.:* Courtauld Inst. of Art, University of London. *Publications:* book, Stanley Spencer: The Astor Collection (1976); articles; numerous catalogues. Historical Adviser, BBC 2 Television, 'Stanley', drama-documentary on Stanley Spencer (1988). *Address:* The Steps, Hill Close, Harrow on the Hill, Middx. HA1 3PQ.

LEDGER, Janet; painter in oil and water-colour; *b* Northampton, 22 July, 1931; *d* of William Brown; *m* H.E. Clements, two *d. Educ.:* Northampton School for Girls; *studied art* at Northampton School of Art (1948-52, Tom Wrigley, Henry Bird, A.R.C.A., Lionel Brooks). *Exhib.:* Gt. Room, Somerset House; Edwin Pollard, Wimbledon; Linda Blackstone, Pinner; Medici, London. *Work in permanent collections:* Coal Board, Marks and Spencer, Dallas Texas, Tate Gallery. *Address:* c/o Edwin Pollard, Church Rd., Wimbledon, London SW19. *Club:* S.W.A. *Signs work:* "J. Ledger."

LEE, Joan, B.A., Phi Beta Kappa, M.B.A. (London), Dip. Université de Paris; artist, portraitist in water-colour, oil on canvas, charcoal, etching; designer and editor; *b* Hampton, Va., 23 Dec., 1941; *d* of E.R. Lee, Chief Estimator, Colonial Williamsburg, Va.; two *s. Educ.:* College of William and Mary, U.S.A., University of Bonn, Germany, University of Paris, University of Tunis, City University, London; *studied art* at College of William and Mary, University of Bonn. *Exhib.:* one-man shows: American Cultural Center, Tunis, Loggia Gallery, Latchmere Theatre Gallery, etc.; mixed shows: Williamsburg, Va.,

Foundry Gallery, Washington D.C., and various London shows. U.K. Alumini of the College of William and Mary in Virginia. *Address:* 38 Mallinson Rd., London SW11 1BP. *Clubs:* Amis du Vin, Women Writers Network. *Signs work:* "Joan Lee."

LEE, Rern; painter in oil colour; *b* Jakarta, Indonesia, 19 Sept., 1938; *s* of Lee Man-Fong and Li Mu-Lan; *m* Siew Pui-Sam; two *d. Educ.:* Singapore and Jakarta; *studied art* at Nanyang Academy of Fine Arts, Singapore. Trainee for several years in father's studio, then travelled and worked in England, France, Italy, Holland, Germany and Singapore (1969-72); Australia and New Zealand (1976); U.S.A. and Canada (1981). *Exhib.:* one-man shows: Singapore (1970) and Jakarta (1980), etc. *Work in permanent collections:* Nanyang University Museum, Singapore; Indonesia Palace Museum, Jakarta; The Asia and Pacific Museum, Warsaw, etc. *Honours and Awards:* Academic of Italy with Gold Medal; International Parliament U.S.A. Gold Medal of Merit; conferred Honorary Prize with Memorial Medal of Golden Centaur 1982; Diploma of Honoris Causa "Master of Painting" from the International Seminar of Modern and Contemporary Art and Diploma of Merit from Italian University of Arts. *Address:* Jalan Gedong 11-A, Jakarta Barat, Indonesia. *Signs work:* "R. Lee."

LEE, Rosie, D.F.A. (1957); painter in oil; *b* Rotterdam, 23 Dec., 1935; *d* of James Peters; *m;* four *s. Educ.:* Abbeydale Girls' Grammar School, Sheffield; *studied art* at Sheffield College of Art (1953-55), Slade School (1955-58). *Work in permanent collections:* Walker A.G. (Schools Collection), Hull Educ. Authority, W. Riding of Yorks. Educ. Authority, Surrey Educ. Authority, Dept. of Environment, Coventry City A.G., Sheffield City A.G. *Address:* Cappaghbeg, Mount Kid, Ballydehob, W. Cork, Eire. *Signs work:* see appendix.

LEE, Terry Glyn, D.F.A. (Lond.), 1957; artist in oil and teacher; teaching Sheffield College of Art; *b* Sheffield, 28 Oct., 1932; *s* of G. W. Lee; *m* Rosemary Christina Peters; four *s. Educ.:* King Edward VII School, Sheffield; *studied art* at Sheffield College of Art; Slade School of Fine Art (1955-58); Sir William Coldstream. *Work in permanent collections:* Liverpool Art Gallery, Ferens Art Gallery, Hull, Coventry Art Gallery, Oldham Art Gallery, The Arts Council. *Address:* Calton Houses, Calton Lees, Beeley, nr. Matlock, Derbyshire. *Signs work:* "Terry Lee."

LEECH, Raymond Ian, R.S.M.A. (1986), L.S.I.A.D. (1969); mem. E.Anglian Group of Marine Artists; landscape and seascape painter in oil and water-colour; partner in a design group, Pencil Point Studio; *b* Gt.Yarmouth, 1949; *s* of Gordon William Leech (decd.). *Educ.:* Edward Worledge School, Alderman Leach High School; *studied art* at Gt.Yarmouth College of Art and Design (1965-69). *Exhib.:* R.S.M.A., Hunting Group, Mystic U.S.A., Assembly Rooms Norwich, Ladygate Gallery, and other provincial galleries. *Work in permanent collections:* National Maritime Museum, The Sheik of Oman, Mystic Maritime Gallery U.S.A., etc. *Publication:* represented in Tonal Painting (Quarto). *Address:* 1 The Staithe, Oulton Broad, Lowestoft, Suffolk. *Signs work:* see appendix.

LEES, Stewart Marshall, D.A. (Edin.) (1952), R.O.I. (1987), R.S.W. (1992), A.R.W.S. (1991); *b* Auchtertool, Fife, 15 Jan., 1926. *Educ.:* Edinburgh College of Art (1947-52). *Exhib.:* R.A. Summer Exhbn., Royal Scottish Academy, R.S.W., R.W.S., and privately. *Work in permanent collections:* Glenrothes New Town, Liverpool Educ. Com., Fife Educ. Com., University of Glasgow, University of Nottingham, Nuffield Foundation, Imperial Tobacco Co., Sheffield City A.G., Leverhulme Foundation, Scottish Arts Council, Esso Ltd., Leeds Educ. Com.

Address: Southlands, Arlington Drive, Mapperley Pk., Nottingham NG3 5EN. *Club:* Arts, London. *Signs work:* "Stewart Lees."

LEFTWICH, Peter; painter in oil, tempera, fresco; *b* London, 13 Oct., 1913; *s* of Charles Gerrans Leftwich, C.B.E., I.C.S., retired; *m* Lorraine Ellis; two *s*. *Educ.:* privately; *studied art* at Durban School of Art; Michaelis School of Art, University of Cape Town under Prof. John Wheatley, A.R.A. and Mrs. Grace Wheatley (1932-36). *Exhib.:* R.A., R.P., Paris Salon (1960), Exhbn. of Dominion Art, R.I. Galleries (1936) and at all principal exhbns. in S. Africa; one-man shows in Durban and Johannesburg. *Work in permanent collections:* South African National Gallery, Durban Art Gallery. *Official purchases:* as above. *Address:* Backworth, Eston, Natal. *Club:* Arts, Dover St., London. *Signs work:* "Peter Leftwich."

LEGG, Owen, M.F.P.S.; printmaker and artist in oil on board, lino-cut prints, abstract constructions; *b* London, 1 Aug., 1935. *Educ.:* Alleyns School, Dulwich; *studied art* at Tunbridge Wells Adult Education Centre. *Exhib.:* York University, Tunbridge Wells Library, Loggia Gallery. *Work in permanent collections:* Greenwich Library, Graphotek, Berlin. *Publications:* York Mystery Play—The Armourers Play, Cut in the Chalk, Rubaiyyat of Omar Khayaam; The Garden by V. Sackville West (1989). *Address:* Woodcraft Press, 152 Hadlow Rd., Tonbridge, Kent TN9 1PB. *Signs work:* "Owen Legg."

LEHMANN, Olga, S.G.F.A., N.S., F.R.S.A.; painter; designer; *b* Catemu, Chile, 1912; *d* of A.W. Lehmann; *m* Carl E.R. Huson (decd.); one *s*. *Educ.:* Santiago College, Chile; *studied art* at Slade School of Fine Art (Prof. Schwabe, Alan Gwynne Jones, V. Polunin). In 1941 joined the film industry as scenic artist, later became a designer of sets and costumes. Credits include "Tom Thumb", "Guns of Navarone", "Man in the Iron Mask", "Kidnapped." *Exhib.:* London Group, N.E.A.C., S.G.F.A., N.S., Suffolk Art Soc., Gainsborough House, Thaxted Guildhall, and many others; one-man shows: John Whibley Gallery, A.I.A. Gallery, Rushmore Rooms, and Heffer's Gallery, Cambridge, Guildhall, Finchingfield, County Library, Saffron Walden, Augustine Gallery, Holt, etc. *Work in permanent collections:* Imperial War Museum, R.A.F. Museum. *Addresses:* 1 Artisans Dwellings, Saffron Walden, Essex CB10 1LW; 7 Windsor Mans., Luxborough St., London W1M 3LS. *Signs work:* "Olga Lehmann."

LEHRFREUND, Denise; artist, mainly landscape, in acrylic and charcoal; *b* London, 3 May, 1944; *d* of Lewis Norton; one *s*, two *d*. *Educ.:* N.W. London Grammar School; *studied calligraphy* at Hornsey College of Art (1960). *Exhib.:* London: Loggia Gallery, Barbican Centre (1984), Bloomsbury Gallery (1989), R.A. Summer Exhbn. (1989), Bowmoore Gallery (1989), Waterman Fine Art Ltd. (1989, 1990), Mall Galleries; Usher Gallery, Lincoln, Lauderdale House, Highgate (1992). Re-married 1992; now living in Norfolk. *Address:* Tregony, 71 Lower St., Norwich, Norfolk NR12 8AA. *Club:* F.P.S. *Signs work:* "Denise Lehrfreund" or "DENISE."

LEIGH-PEMBERTON, John, A.F.C.; painter in oil, tempera and gouache; *b* London, 18 Oct., 1911; *s* of Cyril Leigh-Pemberton; *m* Doreen Beatrice Townshend-Webster. *Educ.:* Eton; *studied art* in London, *c* 1928-32. *Exhib.:* R.A., R.O.I., N.S., and all principal London and provincial galleries and in the Commonwealth; past member R.O.I., N.S. *Work in permanent collections:* National Maritime Museum, Imperial War Museum, etc. *Publications:* Many books on Natural History, mostly for children; and many advertising series.

Retired 1982. *Address:* 5 Roehampton Gate, London SW15 5TR. *Signs work:* "Leigh-Pemberton" or see appendix.

LEK, Karel, R.C.A., A.T.D.; artist in oil, water-colour and graphic media; *b* Antwerp, 7 June, 1929; *s* of Hendrick Lek, artist. *Studied art* at Liverpool College of Art; *m;* two children. *Exhib.:* National Museum for Wales, R.A., R.C.A., Cardiff, Woodstock Gallery, W.1, Arts Council, Bangor Gallery, Mostyn Gallery, Llandudno. Beaumaris Festival second prize (1993). *Work in permanent collections:* University Coll. of N. Wales, Contemporary Art Soc. for Wales, National Library of Wales, Aberystwyth, Anglesey C.C. Welsh Collection, Michael Forte Collection, Swansea University, Tunnicliffe Heritage Gallery, Anglesey. *Work repro.:* Football and the Fine Arts, Time Educ. Supp., Studio. *Address:* Studio House, Beaumaris, Gwynedd LL58 8EE.

LEMAN, Martin; artist in oil; former graphic design teacher, Hornsey College of Art (1961-77); *b* London, 25 Apr., 1934; *m* Jill. *Educ.:* Royal Masonic School; *studied art* at Worthing School of Art, and Central School of Arts and Crafts. *Exhib.:* twenty exhbns. *Publications:* twenty-four books, mainly cat paintings. *Address:* 1 Malvern Terr., London N1 1HR. *Signs work:* "Leman."

LENEY, Sheila, S.B.A. (1987); floral artist in water-colour and embroidery; *b* London, 23 Nov., 1930; *d* of William W. Davis, insurance surveyor; *m* Edward W. Leney; two *s,* one *d. Educ.:* St. Helen's School, Streatham; *studied art* at Croydon School of Art (1947-49), Epsom A.E.C. (1982, Jean Canter). *Exhib.:* Mall Galleries; Outwood Gallery, Surrey; Linnean Soc.; Lannards Gallery, Sussex; Westminster Gallery, Knapp Gallery, London; McEwan Gallery, Scotland. Work in private collections. *Work repro.:* greetings cards for Medici Soc. *Address:* Invermene, 107 Newton Wood Rd., Ashtead, Surrey KT21 1NW. *Signs work:* "Sheila Leney."

LENG-SMITH, Barbara; Hon. Mention, Paris Salon, Silver Medal; portrait painter in oil, water-colour and pastel specialising in children; *b* Isle of Man, 7 Mar., 1922; *d* of E. Gibson Teare; *m* Ralph Leng-Smith; one *s,* four *d. Educ.:* Sheffield; *studied art* at Manchester under Harry Rutherford. *Exhib.:* one-man show: Tib Lane Gallery, Manchester; R.P., Paris Salon, R.S.A., Edinburgh. *Address:* Miramar, Arthog Rd., Hale, Altrincham, Cheshire WA15 0LS. *Signs work:* "Leng-Smith."

LEONARD, (Douglas) Michael, painter and illustrator; *b* Bangalore, India, 25 June 1933; *s* of Maj. D. G. R. Leonard, IXth Jat Regt. *Educ.:* Stonyhurst College; *studied art* at St. Martin's School of Art (1954-57). Worked as an illustrator from 1957-72 and subsequently as a painter. *Exhib.:* one-man shows: Fischer Fine Art London (1974, 1977, 1980, 1983, 1988), Harriet Griffin, New York (1977), Gemeentemuseum, Arnhem (1977-78) (retrospective), Artsite, Bath (1989) (retrospective), Stiebel Modern New York (1992), Thomas Gibson Fine Art, London (1993); mixed shows: 'Realismus und Realitat' Darmstadt (1975), John Moores, Liverpool (1976, 1978), "The Craft of Art" Walker A.G. (1979), "Nudes" Angela Flowers, London (1979/80), "The Real British", Fischer Fine Art (1981), "Contemporary British Painters", Museo Municipal, Madrid (1983), "Self Portrait: A Contemporary View", Artsite, Bath (1987), "In Human Terms", Stiebel Modern, New York (1991). Painted H.M. Queen Elizabeth II for Readers Digest (1986). *Work in collections:* The Boymans Van Beuningen Museum Rotterdam, De Beer/C.S.O., N.P.G., V. & A., Fitzwilliam Museum Cambridge, Ferens A.G., Hull. *Address:* 3 Kensington Hall Gdns., Beaumont Ave., London W14 9LS. *Signs work:* "Leonard" or "ML."

LETTS, John Barry; sculptor in clay; *b* Birmingham, 20 Aug., 1930; *s* of Joseph Omer Letts, graphic designer; *m* Patricia Letts; two *s*, one *d. Educ.:* Sharman Cross Senior School, Birmingham; *studied art* at Birmingham College of Art (1945-49) under William Bloye. *Exhib.:* London, Birmingham, Nuneaton, Solihull, Stratford-upon-Avon, Stoke-on-Trent. *Commissioned work:* one and a half times lifesize statue of George Eliot (authoress) for Nuneaton Town Centre (1985). *Work in permanent collection:* Nuneaton and Stratford-upon-Avon galleries. *Address:* The Old School, Church Lane, Astley, nr. Nuneaton, Warwickshire CV10 7QD. *Signs work:* "John Letts."

LEVEE, John, B.A., Grand Prix, Academie Julian (1951), Biennal de Paris (1959); Ford Fellowship (1969); Grand Prix, Wodmark Foundation (1975); painter in oil, gouache, crayon; visiting Professor of Art, University of Illinois (1965), N.Y. University (1967-68), University Southern Calif. (1970-72); *b* Los Angeles, 10 Apr., 1924. *Educ.:* University Calif., New School for Social Research, N.Y.; *studied art* at New School. *Work in permanent collections:* Kunst Museum, Basle; Smith College Museum; Museum of Modern Art, N.Y.; Stedelijk Museum, Amsterdam; Musée du Havre; Towner A.G.; Baltimore Museum; Columbus Gallery of Fine Art, etc. *Work repro.:* 16 Painters of Young, School of Paris, Abstract Art, Dictionary of Abstract Art, Concise History of Modern Art. *Address:* 119 rue Notre Dame des Champs, Paris, 6. *Signs work:* "Levee."

LEVENE, Ben, R.A. (1986); painter (genre) in oils, water-colours; teaches as a visiting Lecturer, Royal Academy Schools; *b* London, 23 Dec., 1938; *m* Susan; one *s*, two *d*. *Studied art* at Slade School of Fine Art (1956-61), Boise Scholarship (1961-62). *Exhib.:* regularly at R.A., and Browse and Darby Gallery, London. Work in many private and public collections. *Address:* c/o The Royal Academy, Burlington House, Piccadilly, London W1V 0DS. *Signs work:* Usually signed on back; since 1975 with monogram "B.L."

LEVI, Edgar: see KNIGHT, Clifford.

LEVY, Mervyn, A.R.C.A. (1935); R.C.A. Continuation Scholarship (1935), Sir Herbert Read drawing prize (1935); artist in all drawing mediums; author; broadcaster (B.B.C. Kaleidoscope, etc.); Visiting lecturer in drawing, R.C.A.; Assoc. Editor, Art News and Review (1956-61); Features Editor, Studio (1958-62); Interviewer, B.B.C. Sound Archives (continuing); *b* Swansea, 11 Feb., 1915; *s* of Louis Levy; *m* Marie Paul (decd.); two *s*, one *d. Educ.:* Swansea Grammar School; R.M.C. Sandhurst (1941); *studied art* at Swansea School of Art (1929-32), R.C.A. (1932-36, Sir William Rothenstein). *Exhib.:* Tate Gallery (1989). *Work in permanent collections:* Tate Gallery, N.P.G., University of Texas. *Publications:* some 26 books; contributor to Royal Academy Magazine, and Dictionary of National Biography (O.U.P.); Biographies of L.S. Lowry and Tristram Hillier, etc. *Address:* c/o Chelsea Arts Club, 143 Old Church St., London SW3. *Club:* Chelsea Arts.

LEWENSTEIN, Eileen, A.T.D., F.S.D-C.; potter (stoneware and porcelain); co-editor, Ceramic Review; council mem., Craft Potters Assoc.; *b* London, 1925; *m* Oscar Lewenstein; two *s. Educ.:* Red Maids School, Bristol; *studied art* at West of England College of Art; University of London Institute of Education. *Exhib.:* Studio Ceramics Today, V. & A. (1983), British Ceramics, Seattle, U.S.A. (1985), Aberystwyth Arts Centre (1992). *Work in permanent collections:* V. & A., Glasgow A.G. and Museum, Museum of Decorative Arts, Prague, etc. *Publication:* New Ceramics (Studio Vista 1974). *Address:* 11 Western Esplanade,

Portslade, Brighton, E. Sussex, BN41 1WE. *Signs work:* "Eileen Lewenstein" and see appendix.

LEWIS, Ann, Royal Cambrian Academician, B.A.; artist/illustrator in gouache, water-colour, mixed media, pencil; *b* St. Asaph, N. Wales, 29 Aug., 1962. *Studied art* at Exeter College of Art and Design (1985-88). *Exhib.:* R.Cam.A., W.A.C., National Library of Wales, Mostyn Gallery, Wales Open, Clwyd Open, Mercier Gallery. *Publications:* books illustrated: six children's books, one collection of poetry, numerous illustrations for published articles. *Address:* 30 Hazelwood Cl., Mochdre, Colwyn Bay, Clwyd. *Society:* R.Cam.A. *Signs work:* "Ann Lewis."

LEWIS, Charles Walter Edward, A.R.C.A., F.R.B.S., A.W.G., Royal Exhibition and Continuation Scholarship (1946); sculptor in stone and wood; Head of Sculpture, Kingston College of Art (1947-78); *b* Southsea, 18 July, 1916; *s* of Charles A. Lewis; *m* Margaret Parkinson; two *s,* one *d. Educ.:* Portsmouth Southern Secondary School; *studied art* at Portsmouth College of Art (1932-36), Royal College of Art, under Prof. Richard Garbe (1936-39). *Exhib.:* retrospective, Weston Press Gallery, New York (1983). *Work in permanent collections:* sculpture commissioned by the Ministry of Public Building and Works, The G.L.C. and several private architects. *Address:* Chemin de Font Fresque, 11120 Bize Minervois, France.

LEWIS, Dennis Reginald, R.W.A. (1979), F.C.S.D. (1986); artist in oil, acrylic, water-colour; Design Group Chairman (retd.); *b* Bristol, 2 Apr., 1928; *s* of Francis George Henry Lewis; *m* Irene Margaret; one *s,* two *d. Educ.:* F.A.S. Bristol; *studied art* at No. 3 Army College (1948, Mervyn Levy), West of England College of Art (1948-52). President, Bristol Savages (1972, 1979, 1989). *Address:* 4 Redcliffe Parade E., Redcliffe, Bristol BS1 6SW. *Signs work:* "Dennis Lewis."

LEWIS, John, A.K.C., B.Sc. (1950), ex F.L.S., M.F.P.S. (1974), Dip.V.A. (Lond.) (1980); phanerogamic taxonomist, poet and amateur artist in oil; International Conifer Registrar (R.H.S.); *b* Chingford, 25 Nov., 1921; *s* of A. H. C. Lewis, bank clerk. *Educ.:* City of London School, Kings College, London; *studied art* at Richmond Adult College and Field Studies Council. *Exhib.:* F.P.S. and privately. *Publications:* numerous scientific papers and one poem. *Address:* Orchard House, Hurst, Martock, Somerset TA12 6JU. *Signs works:* uses ideogram, a rhomboid with two verticals included.

LEWIS, Kit; painter in oil; *b* Lichfield, Staffs., 27 Sept., 1911; *d* of H. G. Fausset-Osborne, civil servant; *m* 1st, Morland Lewis, decd.; 2nd, Sir James Richards, formerly editor of The Architectural Review. *Educ.:* at home; *studied art* at Chelsea School of Art. *Exhib.:* London and provincial galleries and in America, one-man exhbn., Leicester Galleries (1953 and 1971), Holsworthy Gallery (1982), Sally Hunter, Motcomb St. (1988). *Work in permanent collections:* Arts Council, National Museum of Wales, Cambridge and Sussex Schools, Carlisle City A.G., Sir Roland Penrose Collection, Sir Geoffrey Jellicoe Collection. *Address:* 29 Fawcett St., London SW10. *Signs work:* "KIT LEWIS."

LEWIS, Stephen, B.F.A.(Hons.); sculptor in steel; *b* 11 Jan., 1959. *Educ.:* Deyes High School, Maghull, Merseyside; *studied art* at Southport College of Art (1976-77), Manchester Polytechnic (1977-80), Jan van Eyck Academie, Maastricht, The Netherlands. *Exhib.:* New Contemporaries, I.C.I. London (1979), Kunst Europa, Germany (1991); one-man shows: Francis Graham-Dixon

Gallery (1988, 1990, 1993), Holden Gallery, Manchester (1990). *Address:* 76 Royal Hill, Greenwich, London SE10 8RT. *Signs work:* "Stephen Lewis."

LEYDEN, John Michael; hon. mem., S.A. Assoc. of Draughtsmen; cartoonist in black and white; artist in water-colour and etching; staff cartoonist, Daily News, since 1939; S.A. Cartoonist of the Year (1981); awarded Papal Cross, "Pro Pontifice et Ecclesia" (1986); *b* Grangemouth, Scotland, 21 Nov., 1908; *s* of Patrick Joseph Leyden; *m* Annabel Eugenie Wishart; one *s*, three *d*. *Educ.:* St. Aloysius College, Glasgow; *studied art* at Durban School of Art, Heatherley's, Central Schools of Arts and Crafts. *Exhib.:* Natal Soc. of Artists, Durban Art Gallery (one-man shows). *Work in permanent collections:* in Africana Museum, Johannesburg, Durban A.G. and University of Natal (cartoons and caricatures). *Publications:* thirteen books of cartoons. *Address:* 233 Nicholson Rd., Durban, Natal, S.A. *Club:* Patron, Natal Motorcyle and Car Club. *Signs work:* see appendix.

LEYGUE, Louis; Président de l'Académie des Beaux-Arts (1976 and 1982); Membre de l'Institut; sculptor; Prof., head of studio, L'École Nationale Supérieure des Beaux-Arts since 1945; *b* Bourg-en-Bresse, Ain, 25 Aug., 1905; *s* of Albert Leygue; *m* Marianne Cochet, painter; two *s*. *Educ.:* Lycée Charlemagne, Paris; *studied art* at L'École Nationale des Arts décoratifs, Paris, L'Ecole Nationale des Beaux-Arts, Paris, Villa Medicis, Rome. *Work in permanent collections:* Museum of Modern Art, Paris. *Official purchases:* Phenix Université de Caen, Auditorium Maison de la Radio, Paris, French Embassy, Ottawa, Fontaine des Corolles, Paris la Défense, Palais de Justice, d'Abidjan, Piave, Nantua, "Le Soleil" Autoroute Nancy-Dijon (1983). *Address:* 6 rue de Docteur Blanche, Paris XVIe. *Signs work:* "LOUIS LEYGUE."

LEYSHON, Thyrza Anne, S.M., Paris Salon Medaille d'Argent (1968), Medaille d'Or and Prix Rowland Award (1973); *b* Swansea; *d* of Thomas Howell Leyshon. *Studied miniature painting* privately under the late Mrs. Ethol Court, A.R.M.S. *Exhib.:* Circle National Belge d'Art et Esthetique, Brussels (1963), Les Arts en Europe, Brussels (1964, 1967), then Member of Southall School of Miniaturists, Paris Salon (1962, 1965, 1968-74 inclusive), R.A., R.M.S., R.S. Gall. Edinburgh, Glyn Vivian A.G., Swansea, Festival of Wales (Welsh Artists), R.W.S. Gallery London (S.M.) (1969-83), Castle Gallery, Ilkley, Yorks. (S.M.) (1985, 1986), M.A.S. Florida, U.S.A. (1982-83), R.M.S. London (1986). *Address:* Wynn Edge, 25 Goetrefach Rd., Killay, Swansea. *Signs work:* "Thyrza Anne Leyshon."

LIDDELL, John, A.T.D. (1946), D.A.E. (1974); art lecturer, printmaker in relief print, woodcut, lino, wood engraving; part-time lecturer, Bournemouth and Poole College of Art; *b* London, 6 July, 1924; *s* of Rex Liddell; *m* Jo Witchalls; two *s*, one *d*. *Educ.:* Minchenden School, London N14; *studied art* at Hornsey College of Art (1941-46, Russell Reeve, Norman Janes, D.P. Bliss). *Exhib.:* R.A., R.W.A., Scribes, London EC4, Dorset Galleries. *Work in permanent collections:* Print Club, Philadelphia, U.S.A., Poole Art Centre, Dorset (mural). *Work repro.:* for own press, Onzello Press. *Address:* 90 Richmond Pk. Ave., Bournemouth BH8 9DR. *Clubs:* N.S.E.A.D., S.W.E., Printmakers' Council. *Signs work:* "John Liddell" with date.

LILLEY, Geoffrey Ivan; U.A.; painter in oil, author and illustrator in line; experimental work, also seascape and landscape; *b* Cambridge, 1 May, 1930; *s* of Ernest Lilley; *m* Marguerite E.; one *d*. *Educ.:* Cambridge; *studied art* at Cambridge Technical College. *Exhib.:* regularly at major London exhbns., including R.O.I., R.S.M.A., N.S., and U.A., etc., St. Ives, Cornwall, and major galleries in Sussex; one-man shows at London, Oxford, Bourton-on-the-Water. *Work repro.:* Artist, Arts Review, Leisure Painter, etc.; author of several books and over 250 articles on art and craft subjects; over 1,000 drawings published. *Address:* Roosters at Golden Cross, Chiddingly, Lewes, Sussex BN8 6JE. *Signs work:* see appendix.

LIM, Kim, D.F.A.(Slade) (1960); sculptor in stone, printmaker; *b* Singapore, 16 Feb., 1936; *m* William Turnbull; two *s. Studied art* at St. Martin's School of Art (1954-56), Slade School of Fine Art (1956-60). *Exhib.:* Waddington Galleries (1973, 1990), M.O.M.A. (Oxford, 1975), Tate Gallery (1977), National Museum A.G., Singapore (1984) and group exhbns. worldwide. *Work in permanent collections:* Arts Council, Nagaoka Museum of Modern Art, Japan, Tate Gallery, etc. *Address:* c/o Waddington Galleries, 11 Cork St., London W1X 1PD. *Signs work:* "Kim Lim" and see appendix.

LIMBREY, John Nigel Stephens, N.D.D. (1953), M.C.S.D. (1969); Freeman of the Worshipful Company of Goldsmiths, City of London; silversmith and product designer; artist in water-colour and oil; Assistant to Robert Welch, M.B.E., R.D.I., A.R.C.A., F.C.S.D., F.R.S.A.; *b* Hatfield, 2 Feb., 1933. *Educ.:* King Edward's School, B'ham; *studied art* at B'ham College of Art (1949-53). *Exhib.:* R.I., R.W.S., R.S.M.A. *Address:* Silk Mill Cottage, Chipping Campden, Glos. GL55 6DS. *Signs work:* "Limbrey."

LINDGREN, Carl Edwin, M.Ed., Ed.S., Hon.D.Litt., F.R.S.A., F.R.A.S., M.Coll.P. (Essex), A.S.I.I.P.C. (New Delhi); Faulknerian landscape photographer, art historian, antiquarian; *b* 20 Nov., 1949; *s* of Carl and Ruby K. (Corder); *m* Penni Bolton, M.I.Sc.T. (Lond.), Senior Research Technician. *Educ.:* University of Mississippi, College of Preceptors (Essex). *Exhib.:* Center for Faulkner Studies, Center for the Study of Southern Culture, The Cossett Gallery, Northwest College Art Gallery, The University of Mississippi, India Intl. Photographic Council (New Delhi), Manipur University Museum, etc. *Address:* London (occasionally) or P.O.B. 8161, University, MS 38677 U.S.A. *Signs work:* "C.E. Lindgren."

LINFIELD, John Leslie, A.R.W.S. (1988), N.E.A.C. (1982), A.R.C.A. (1953); painter in oil and water-colour; *b* Carshalton Beeches, Surrey, 5 Jan., 1930. *Educ.:* Sutton County School; *studied art* at Wimbledon School of Art, R.C.A. *Exhib.:* R.A., R.B.A., R.P., N.E.A.C.; one-man shows, Trafford Gallery (1961, 1963), Ditchling Gallery (1964, 1965), Halifax House, Oxford (1972). *Work commissioned:* Spink & Sons Ltd., Milton Abbey School, Dorset, Hove Museum and A.G., John Dickinson Ltd., Winsor and Newton Ltd. *Address:* Studio House, 23 Ash Lane, Wells, Somerset BA5 2LR. *Signs work:* "JOHN LINFIELD."

LINLEY-ADAMS, Barbara Mary; sculptor in wood, stone, bone china, pottery; designer, Poole Pottery; *b* 4 Mar., 1923; *d* of Rev. Edward Adams, M.A. (Cantab.). *Educ.:* Châtelard; *studied art* at Slade School under Prof. Schwabe, Central School under Bernard Meninsky. *Exhib.:* R.A., S.WL.A., London and New York galleries. *Work in permanent collection:* Imperial War Museum. *Address:* 57A High St., Budleigh Salterton, Devon EX9 6LE. *Signs work:* see appendix.

LINTON, Robert George, D.A., A.T.D., A.R.U.A., C.E.M.A. Travel Scholarship to Italy (1955); N.I. Arts Council Travel Grant to Holland (1968); artist in oil and sculpture; retd. Head of Art Dept., Limavady Grammar School; *b* Co. Donegal, 4 Feb., 1930; *s* of late Robert G. Linton; *m* Doreen Mary Shaw,

B.A.; two *s. Educ.:* Limavady Technical College and Limavady Grammar School; *studied art* at Belfast College of Art and L.C.C. Central School of Art and Crafts. *Exhib.:* four one-man shows in Belfast and Londonderry; I.L.A. Dublin. *Address:* 100 Glenhead Rd., Limavady, Co. Londonderry BT49 9LZ. *Club:* Royal Ulster Academy. *Signs work:* "Linton" followed by date.

LISTER, Caroline Nicola Josephine, B.A.Hons. (1980), A.R.B.A.; painter and printmaker; printmaking tutor, Guildford College of Art (1980); Director and tutor, Tyger, Tyger Printmaking, Cambridge (Intaglio Printmaking Workshop); Steering Group mem. Cambridgeshire Regional College (1989); *b* Cambridge, 30 Mar., 1958; *d* of Brian Lister, designer of Lister-Jaguar racing car. *Educ.:* Perse School, Cambridge; *studied art* at Cambs. College of Arts and Technology (1976-77), W. Surrey College of Art and Design (1977-80). *Exhib.:* R.B.A., R.E., R.I., P.S., R.W.S., S.W.A., C.D.S. *Addresses:* 79 St. Philips Rd., Cambridge CB1 3DA; studio: Tyger, Tyger Printmaking, Studio One, 37 City Rd., Cambridge CB1 1DP. *Signs work:* "Nicola Lister."

LISTER, Raymond George, P.R.M.S. (1970-80), M.A., Litt.D. (Cantab.); Governor, Federation of British Artists (1972-80); Fellow, Wolfson College, Cambridge; a syndic, Fitzwilliam Museum Cambridge (1981); painter; author; *b* Cambridge, 28 Mar., 1919; *s* of Horace Lister; *m* Pamela Brutnell; one *s,* one *d. Educ.:* Cambs. High School; St. John's College School, Cambridge; *studied art* privately. *Work repro.:* Raymond Lister, by C. R. Cammell and others (1963). *Publications:* Edward Calvert (1962); William Blake (1968); Samuel Palmer and His Etchings (1969); The Letters of Samuel Palmer (1975); George Richmond (1981); The Paintings of Samuel Palmer (1985); Catalogue Raisonné of Samuel Palmer (1988). *Address:* 9 Sylvester Rd., Cambridge CB3 9AF.

LITTLE, Margaret Isabel, M.R.C.S. (Eng.) (1927), L.R.C.P. (Lond.), M.R.C.Psych. (1971), M.F.P.S. (1963); medical practitioner Psycho-analyst, painter in gouache, oil and mosaic; *b* Bedford, 21 May, 1901; *d* of J. T. Little, M.A.; *m* Reginald Sizen, M.C. (decd.). *Educ.:* Bedford H.S.G.; Bedford College; St. Mary's Hospital; Institute of Psycho-Analysis; *studied art* privately under Miss G. Hylton-Hylton (1939-45); Sir John Cass College (1957-65) under John Bowles. *Exhib.:* W.I.A.C., R.B.A., U.A.S., F.P.S., S.W.A., etc.; one-man show at Sevenoaks (1971). *Work repro.:* Revue Moderne des Arts, Paris. *Address:* 1 Mayfield, 72 London Rd., Dunton Green, Sevenoaks, Kent TN13 2UG. *Club:* F.P.S. *Signs work:* "Margaret I. Little" or "ML" joined.

LITTLEJOHN, William Hunter, D.A., R.S.A., R.S.W., R.G.I.; painter in oil and water-colour; former Head of Fine Art Dept., Gray's School of Art, Aberdeen; retd. from teaching 1986; *b* Arbroath, Angus, Scotland, 16 Apr., 1929; *s* of the late William Littlejohn. *Educ.:* Arbroath High School; *studied art* at Dundee College of Art. *Work in permanent collections:* National Gallery of Modern Art, Edinburgh, Arbroath Art Gallery, Aberdeen Art Gallery, Arts Council Collection, Abbot Hall Art Gallery, Kendal, Edinburgh Civic Collection, Edinburgh Education Authority, Paisley Art Gallery, Perth Art Gallery, Towner Art Gallery, Eastbourne. *Address:* 16 Colvill Pl., Arbroath, Angus DD11 1RB, Scotland. *Signs work:* see appendix.

LLOYD, Reginald, R.I.; self taught artist in water-colour, oil, acrylic; *b* Hereford, 21 Dec., 1926; *m* Diana van Klaveren (decd.); three *s,* four *d. Educ.:* Dawlish Boys and County Senior School. *Exhib.:* 'Portrait of the Artist' Tate Gallery, etc. *Work in permanent collections:* Tate Gallery, V. & A., National Maritime Museum, Hatton Gallery Newcastle, Burton Gallery Bideford. *Publications:* illustrated: What is the Truth by Ted Hughes, The Cat and the

Cuckoo by Ted Hughes, The Mermaid's Purse by Ted Hughes. *Address:* Iffield, North Rd., Bideford, Devon EX39 2NW. *Signs work:* "R.J. LLOYD," "R.J.L." or "R.J. Lloyd."

LOBANOI-ROSTOVSKY, Princess Roxane, S.W.A.; water-colourist sculptor in water-colour, alabaster, marble; *b* Athens, 3 Oct., 1932; *d* of Bibica-Rosetti, Greek Ambassador; two *s*, one *d. Educ.:* St. George's Ascot, Pretoria Girls High School; *studied art* at Carlton University, Ottawa; Brighton Polytechnic (Norma Weller, Norman Clarke, R.W.S.). *Exhib.:* numerous exhbns., one-man show: The Grange, Rottingdean (1987), etc. *Address:* Swallowdale, 67 Woodruff Ave., Hove, E. Sussex BN3 6PJ. *Signs work:* "R. Lobanoi-Rostovsky."

LOCHHEAD, Thomas, D.A.; potter; *b* Milngavie, Glasgow, 28 Nov., 1917; *s* of Thomas Lochhead; *m* Anne T. Wilson; three *s,* two *d. Educ.:* Dumfries Academy; *studied art* at Edinburgh College of Art under Princ. Wellington, A.R.C.A., and Alick Wolfenden, A.R.C.A. *Exhib.:* S.S.A. *Official purchases:* Glasgow Art Gallery, Paisley Art Gallery. *Address:* Ashbank, Kirkcudbright. *Signs work:* "Lochhead."

LOCKHART, David, R.S.W. (1969), D.A. (Edin.) (1944); artist in acrylics, oil and water-colour; *b* Leven, Fife, 4 Nov., 1922; *s* of Thomas Lockhart, miner; *m* Jean Lockhart; one *s,* two *d. Educ.:* Beath High School, Cowdenbeath (1934-40); *studied art* at Edinburgh College of Art (1940-46). *Exhib.:* Shed '50 (1974), Carnegie Dunfermline Trust Festival of Arts (1972), Douglas and Fowlis Gallery, Edinburgh (1963) with James Barclay. *Work in permanent collections:* Scottish Committee of the Arts Council, W. Riding of Yorkshire Educ. Authority, Carnegie Dunfermline Trust, Fife County Council, Dunbartonshire Educ. Authority, Harry Cruden Coll. (Pitlochry Festival Theatre), E.I.S. award, R.S.W. (1984). *Address:* 2 Burnside North, Cupar, Fife KY15 4DG. *Signs work:* "David Lockhart" (paintings), and see appendix.

LODGE, Jean, R.E., B.A. (Miami), M.A. (Oxon.); painter/printmaker; Head of Printmaking, Ruskin School, University of Oxford; *b* U.S.A., 1941. *Educ.:* Miami University, Ohio, Oxford University; *studied art* at Beaux Arts de Paris, Atelier 17 with S.W. Hayter. *Exhib.:* solo shows: Europe, Japan, India, Argentina, Venezuela, U.S.A., etc.; numerous international print shows. *Work in permanent collections:* Museums in Europe and N. and S. America. *Address:* Ruskin School of Art, University of Oxford, 74 High St., Oxford OX4 1BG.

LOFTHOUSE, Hermione Thornton, U.A. (1975), N.S.; painter in water-colour, oil and pastel; tutor, Moor Park College (1968-82); Master Classes for Richmond-upon-Thames Arts Council (1982, 1983), Adult Educ., Univ. of Surrey; V.P., Ridley Art Soc.; *d* of Prof. Charles Thornton Lofthouse, musician; *m* F.H. Lockyer; three *s. Educ.:* St. Paul's Girls' School; *studied art* at Heatherleys' (1946-50) under Iain Macnab, Académie Julian and La Grande Chaumière (1950); cert. History of Art, Courtauld Inst. *Exhib.:* Paris, Germany, N.Z. Academy, Wellington Architectural Centre, Bombay Museum, W.A.G., Southport Palette Club, Artists of Chelsea, R.B.A., R.O.I., etc.; eleven solo shows, Royal Hospital, Chelsea, Upper St. Gallery, Mall Galleries, Holland Park, Surrey Univ., Guildford House Museum. *Work in permanent collections:* Richmond Parish Charity Lands, R.A.M., Surrey Univ. etc. *Address:* 48 Compton Way, Farnham, Surrey GU1 01QU. *Club:* C.A.S. *Signs work:* "H. Thornton Lofthouse."

LOGAN, Andrew, Dip.Arch.(Oxon.); sculptor in glass; *b* Witney, 11 Oct., 1945; *s* of William Harold Logan. *Educ.:* Lord Williams' Grammar School;

Burford Grammar School; *studied architecture:* Oxford School of Architecture (1964-70). *Exhib.:* numerous exhbns. including I.C.A. (1970), Whitechapel A.G., Beverly Hills, L.A., Ebury Gallery, Space Gallery, Faerie Fair, Norfolk, Crafts Council, Sandbeck Hall, Yorks., Sculpture Pk., Portland Bill, Commonwealth Inst., German Film Museum, Frankfurt, Hotel Meridian, Singapore, Botanical Gdns., Rome, Angela Flowers (Ireland) Inc., Flowers East (1991), Old Library, Cardiff (1991); first one-man show: New Art Centre, London (1973); retrospective: Museum of Modern Art, Oxford (1991), etc. *Work in permanent collection:* Andrew Logan's Museum of Sculpture, Berriew, Powys. *Address:* The Glasshouse, Melior Pl., London SE1 3QP. *Signs work:* see appendix.

LOIZOU, Renos; painter in oil on canvas, oil on paper and board; *b* Cyprus, 24 Jan., 1948; *s* of Andreas Loizou, tailor; *m* Susan; one *s,* two *d. Educ.:* Shrubbery School, Cambridge; *studied art* at Cambridge School of Art (1963-66, Alec Heath). *Exhib.:* Kettles Yard, Cambridge (1974, 1981), I.C.A. (1975), Orangerie, Cologne (1976), Peterborough Museum of Art (1982), Christopher Hull Gallery, London (1982, 1985, 1987, 1989, 1991), Fine Art Soc. (1990), Fitzwilliam Museum, Cambridge (1990); many mixed shows and overseas exhbns. *Work in permanent collections:* Kettles Yard, Fitzwilliam College, Gonville and Caius College, Magdalene College, Cambridge, M. of E. Cyprus, Arts Council Denmark, University of Surrey, B.P. Coll., Baring Bros., W.H. Smith plc. *Publication:* book cover, Voices of Czechoslovak Socialists. *Address:* Girton Gate, Cambridge CB3 0LH. *Clubs:* Chelsea Arts, National Arts N.Y. *Signs work:* "Renos Loizou."

LOM, Josephine: see LOMNICKA, Azdia Josephine.

LOMNICKA, Azdis Josephine, M.A.; educator, writer, designer, cartoonist and illustrator. Master of Arts, Reading University; Diploma in Education and Teachers' Certificate at London University, Institute of Education; Diploma in Printing and Publishing Studies for Graduates, Certificate in Book Design and Postgraduate Diploma in Design and Media Technology (C.N.A.A.) London College of Printing. *Publications:* Illustrating novels, periodicals, books for children and cartoons. Typographic designing of posters and dust-sleeves for publishers. *Address:* 20 Girdwood Rd., London SW18 5QS. *Signs work:* "Josephine Lom."

LONGBOTHAM, Charles Norman, R.W.S.; painter in water-colour and other media, model maker (specialist in landscape models); Mem. A.W.G.; *b* Carlton, Notts., 6 July, 1917; *s* of George N. Longbotham, mining engineer; *m* Eleanor née Nairn-Allison (died 1972); one *d;* re-married Jeanie Campbell-Taylor née Goodacre, 1979. *Educ.:* Portsmouth Grammar School and H.M.S. Conway, Birkenhead. *Exhib.:* R.A., R.W.S. Galleries, and other London exhbns.; one-man exhbns. London and provinces. *Water-colours in permanent collections:* V. & A., Fitzwilliam, Laing A.G., Norwich Castle Museum, Merseyside Maritime Museum, Southampton City Museum, Nottingham Castle Museum, Abbot Hall A.G., Kendal; models in Imperial War Museum, Commonwealth Inst., etc. *Address:* 35 Owlstone Rd., Cambridge CB3 9JH. *Signs work:* see appendix.

LONGUEVILLE, James, P.S. (1983), R.B.S.A. (1989); landscape painter in oil, pastel and water-colour; lecturer and demonstrator; *b* Waverton, Chester, 22 Sept., 1942; *s* of Charles Longueville Willding-Jones, B.A.; *m* Elizabeth Mary Smith; two *s. Educ.:* Sedbergh School, Cumbria. *Exhib.:* R.O.I., P.S., R.I., R.C.A., R.B.S.A., galleries in U.K. and Eire. *Address:* The Studio, Shocklach, Malpas, Cheshire SY14 7BW. *Club:* R.B.S.A. *Signs work:* "James Longueville."

LOPEZ-REY, Jose, Ph.D. (Madrid, 1935); Doctor of Humane Letters (honorary, Southern Methodist University, 1979); art historian; Prof. Emeritus, New York University; Prize, Elie Faure, Paris, 1981; *b* Madrid, 14 May, 1905; *s* of Leocadio Lopez Arrojo, M.D.; *m* Justa Arroyo López-Rey. *Educ.:* Universities of Madrid, Florence, and Vienna. *Publications:* Antonio del Pollaiuolo y el fin del Quattrocento; Realismo é impresionismo en las artes figurativas españolas del siglo XIX; Goya y el mundo a su alrededor; Goya's Caprichos; Beauty, Reason and Caricature; A Cycle of Cycle of Goya's Drawings: The Expression of Truth and Liberty; Velázquez: A Catalogue Raisonné of his *oeuvre;* Velázquez' Work and World; Velázquez: The artist as a maker. With a catalogue raisonné of his extant works (1979); Vélasquez, artiste et créateur. Avec un catalogue raisonné de son oeuvre intégral (1981); Views and Reflections on Murillo (1987). *Address:* Callejón Sierra, 3, 28120 Ciudad Sto. Domingo (Madrid), Spain.

LORIMER, Hew, O.B.E., R.S.A. (1957), Hon. LL.D., F.R.B.S.; sculptor in stone; *b* Edinburgh, 22 May, 1907; 2nd *s* of the late Sir Robert Lorimer, architect; *m* Mary McLeod Wylie; two *s*, one *d. Educ.:* Loretto; *studied art* at Edinburgh College of Art and under Eric Gill. *Exhib.:* R.S.A., etc. *Address:* Kellie Castle, Pittenweem, Fife KY10 2RF. *Signs work:* unsigned.

LOVELL, Margaret, Dip. F.A. (Slade, 1962), F.R.B.S. (1973), R.W.A. (1972); sculptor in bronze, marble, slate; *b* Bristol, 7 Mar., 1939. *Studied art* at West of England College of Art, Bristol (Ernest Pascoe, 1956-60), Slade School of Fine Art (Professor A. H. Gerrard, 1960-62), Academy of Fine Art, Florence (1962-63), Greek Government Scholarship (1965-66). *Exhib.:* City Art Gall., Bristol, A.C.G.B., Marjorie Parr Gall., (4 one-man shows, 1965, 1968, 1970, 1972), also one-man shows inc. Park Square Gall., Leeds (1968, 1971), Fermoy A.G., King's Lynn (1970), Univ. of Bath (1973), Bruton Gall., Somerset (1973), 1st retrospective Plymouth City A.G., (1972). *Address:* Greenlane Farm, Compton Dando, Bristol BS18 4JU. *Signs work:* "M. Lovell."

LOVETT, Eleanor Selwyn, R.A. Dip.; painter and sculptor in terracotta; mem. Hesketh Hubbard Art Soc. *Educ.:* Goldsmiths' College and R.A. Schools. *Exhib.:* R.A. Summer Exhbn., Arnhem Gallery, Croydon, Carlton House Terrace. *Work in permanent collection:* landscapes and murals, Robert Fleming (Merchant Bankers). Started horse painting in 70's. Now has agent. Sold some terracottas, also large horse picture. *Address:* 12 Elgin Rd., East Croydon. *Signs work:* unsigned.

LOW, Bet, A.R.S.A., R.S.W., R.G.I.; artist in oil and water-colour; *b* Gourock, Renfrewshire, 27 Dec., 1924; *d* of John Low, engineer, tea planter. *Educ.:* Greenock Academy; *studied art* at Glasgow School of Art. *Exhib.:* regularly at Royal Scottish Academy, Water-colour Soc., Royal Glasgow Inst., Fine Art Soc., and widely in U.K. and Europe. Retrospective exhbn. 'Paintings and Drawings 1945-85', Third Eye Centre, Glasgow (1985). *Work in permanent collections:* Scottish Arts Council, Glasgow, Aberdeen, Abbot Hall, Hunterian, Lillie, Perth, Waterford A.G.'s, Fife and Dunbarton Educ. Authorities, Glasgow and Strathclyde Universities, Cruden Collection, Britoil, Clyde Shipping Co., Clydesdale Bank, Flemings, London. *Address:* 53 Kelvinside Gdns., Glasgow G20 6BQ. *Club:* Glasgow Art. *Signs work:* "LOW."

LOW, Jack; artist in oil and water-colours, stone- and wood-carver, carpet designer; L.C.C. art instructor (1945-48); *b* Brondesbury, 17 Oct., 1903; child of Charles Abbot Low and Ethel Low. *Studied art* at City & Guilds School of Art (1941-42), and Goldsmiths' School of Art (1946-50) under Adrian Ryan. *Exhib.:*

R.A., R.B.A., A.I.A., Northbank Artists, Leicester Gallery, Redfern Gallery, London, Neville Gallery, Canterbury; one-man show, Theatre Club, Shaftesbury Avenue, London (1953), etc. *Work in permanent collections:* England, France, Rome, Germany, America. *Address:* Little Stour Cottage, West Stourmouth, nr. Canterbury, Kent CT3 1HS.

LOWE, Adam, M.F.A. (Oxon.), M.A. (R.C.A.); artist in oil, printmaking; *b* Oxford, 18 Feb., 1959; *m* Yuka. *Studied art* at Ruskin School of Drawing, Oxford; R.C.A. (Peter de Francia). *Exhib.:* regularly at Pomeroy Purdy Gallery, also exhbns. in England and America. Commissioned work in Japan. *Work in permanent collections:* Contemporary Art Soc., Atkinson A.G. *Publication:* A Resurgence in Contemporary Painting (Alistair Hicks, Phaidon 1989). *Address:* Reeds Wharf, Mill St., London SE1. *Signs work:*"ADAM LOWE."

LOWE, Ian, M.A., Hon.R.E, (1975); Museum Curator, Ashmolean Museum (1962-87); *b* London, 18 Apr., 1935; *m* Mary Howard; one *s. Educ.:* Oriel College, Oxford. Laurence Binyon prize (1958). *Publication:* author: The Etchings of Wilfred Fairclough (1990). *Address:* Spring Ford, Newton Reigny, Penrith, Cumbria CA11 0AY. *Club:* White's.

LOXTON KNIGHT, Edward, R.B.A.; artist in oil, pastel, water-colour, gouache, woodblock printing; *b* Long Eaton, Notts., 12 July, 1905; *s* of Samuel Knight; *m* Jill Malins (25 Aug., 1952); one *d. Educ.:* Grammar School, Long Eaton; *studied art* at Nottingham School of Art under Joseph Else (1924-29). *Exhib.:* Vancouver, provincial galleries, R.A., R.B.A., R.I., Paris Salon, London, Glasgow, New York, Nottingham, Johannesburg, Derby, Dublin. *Work in permanent collections:* municipal galleries of Nottingham, Derby, Preston, Adelaide, Wanganui (N.Z.). *Work repro.:* in Studio, Artist, Colour, etc. *Address:* 20 Breedon St., Long Eaton, Notts. NG10 4FF. *Signs work:* see appendix.

LOXTON PEACOCK, Clarisse; painter in oil; *b* 7 May, 1926; *m* (1st) G. Loxton Peacock; one *s,* one *d.; m* (2nd) Sir Anthony Grover. *Educ.:* Budapest University; *studied art* at Chelsea School of Art (Dip. course); Central School of Arts and Crafts (Post. Grad. course); St. Martin's School of Art. *Exhib.:* one-man shows, Walker Gallery, London, Grosvenor Gallery, O'Hana Gallery (two), Bodley Gallery, N.Y., Frost and Reed, Gallerie des Artis, Düsseldorf (three), Salisbury Arts Festival, Fox Gallery, London, Wylma Wane Fine Arts, Old Bond St., London (1982), Petöti Museum, Budapest (1988 - sponsored by Hungarian Government), Cadogan Contemporaries, London (1989), Makepiece Art Centre, Dorset (1989). *Work in permanent collections:* U.S.A., Spain, Germany, England, S. Africa (Queen's Gallery), France, Japan. *Address:* 85 Bedford Gdns., London W8. *Signs work:* "C. Loxton Peacock."

LUBELSKI, Jan Stanislaw; Slade Dip. (1949), A.T.D. (1951); sculptor in bronze and stone (clay modelling), specialises in portraiture and animal sculpture; *b* Poznan, Poland, 5 Mar., 1922; *s* of Mieczyslaw Lubelski, sculptor; *m* Josephine G. Enock; two *s;* divorced; *m* 2nd (1964) Christina C. Sheppard; one *s,* one *d. Educ.:* Bonn Grammar School; Polish matriculation; Glasgow; Regent St. Polytechnic School of Art (1945-46); Slade School (Prof. Gerrard, 1946-49); and under Benno Elkan, O.B.E. (1940-41); worked on "New Testament" candelabrum, now in Westminster Abbey; Inst. of Educ. (1950-51). *Exhib.:* Forces Exhbn. at National Gallery; R.A.; Slade School Exhbn., Walker's Galleries; Fine Art Soc.; Royal Copenhagen Gallery, Bond St.; Young Contemporaries at R.B.A., Kingley Galleries, W1; Glasgow Inst. *Work in permanent collections:* St. Gabriel's College, Camberwell; Prof. Paul Glees, Göttingen; the late Leonard Rose, cellist, N.Y.; Jean-Bernard Pommier, concert pianist, Lausanne, and others. *Address:* 61 Claremont Rd., Highgate, London N6. *Signs work:* see appendix.

LUCAS, Suzanne, F.L.S., Médaille de la France Libre, R.H.S. Gold Medal (1975, 1976, 1977, 1978, 1979, 1980, 1982, 1983, 1984, 1985, 1986, 1987, 1988); painter and miniaturist in water-colour; Vice President, Dorset Arts and Crafts Society; President, Royal Society of Miniature Painters; Founder-President, Society of Botanical Artists; *b* Calcutta, 10 Sept., 1915; *d* of S/Ldr. Alfred Craven, B.Sc.Eng. 1st Cl., M.I.Mech.E., M.I.E.E.; *m* Admiral Louis Lucas, C.B.E., Commandeur Legion of Honour. *Educ.:* Roedean School, Edinburgh University; Munich and Grenoble Universities; Berlin School of Art with Professor Schmidt. *Exhib.:* R.A., Paris Salon, R.I.; one-man shows in London: Cooling Galleries (1954), Sladmore Gallery (1973), Mall Galleries (1975, 1979), Liberty's (1977). *Publication:* author and illustrator of large art volume "In Praise of Toadstools" a botanical work. *Address:* Ladymead, Manor Rd., Mere, Wilts. BA12 6HQ. *Signs work:* see appendix.

LUNCH, John, C.B.E. (1975), V.R.D. (1965), F.C.A. (1946), F.R.S.A. (1976); artist in water-colour and oil; retd. Director General, Port of London Authority; Hon. Art Adviser to R.N.L.I.; V.P. and Mem., Committee of Management, R.N.L.I.; *b* Eastbourne, 11 Nov., 1919; *s* of Percy Valentine Lunch; *m* Joyce Barbara Clerke (decd.); two *s. Educ.:* Roborough School, Eastbourne. *Exhib.:* Mall Galleries. *Address:* Martins, East Ashling, Chichester, W. Sussex PO18 9AX. *Club:* Army and Navy. *Signs work:* "John Lunch."

LUPTON, Lewis F.; preacher, writer, historian, painter in oil and water-colour; *b* London, 18 July, 1909. *Studied art* at Sheffield College of Arts (1923-30). Practised commercial art in Strand advertising agency before the war. Freelance since 1940. Exhibition designer during and just after the war. Many paintings in the R.A. at this period. Then turned to the illustration of Christian literature. Numerous exhibitions of own, and wife's work held in recent years. Publisher under the Olive Tree imprint of own History of the Geneva Bible (25 vols.) and other related literature. *Address:* 2 Milnthorpe Rd., London W4 3DX.

LYELL: see ROBINSON, Peter Lyell.

LYNCH, James; Greenshield Foundation Award (1983), Pimms Prize, R.A. (1986); *b* Hitchin, 12 July, 1956; *s* of Ronald Lynch, A.T.D.; *m* Kate Armstrong; two *s*, one *d. Educ.:* Devizes School. *Exhib.:* R.A., R.W.S., Portal, Bath Festival Art Fairs; one-man shows: Linfields, Bradford-on-Avon (1982-83), Nevill, Bath (1984), Odette Gilbert, London (1988), Maas Gallery, London (1991, 1993). *Work in permanent collections:* Longleat House, Chatsworth House, National Trust. *Address:* The Dairy House, North Cadbury, Som. BA22 7DE. *Signs work:* "J. Lynch."

M

MACARA, Andrew, R.B.A. (1983), N.E.A.C. (1984); self taught figurative painter in oil; *b* Ashbourne, Derbyshire, 4 Apr., 1944; *m* Ann; two *s. Educ.:* Derby College of Technology. *Exhib.:* Upstairs Gallery, R.A., Gallery 10, Worthing Museum and A.G., Salisbury Playhouse, New Academy Gallery, London. *Work in permanent collection:* Derby Museum and A.G. *Address:* Aberfoyle, 32 Farley Rd., Derby. *Signs work:* "Andrew Macara."

MACARRÓN, Ricardo, R.P. (1962); 1st prize National Fine Art Exhbn. (1962), Prize Direction of Fine Art (1954); artist in oil of figures, dead nature, landscapes, portraits; *b* Madrid, 9 Apr., 1926; *s* of Juan Macarron, art dealer; *m* Alicia; two *d. Studied art* at Fine Art School of San Fernando, Madrid (1942); scholarship to study in France by French Institute (1950). *Work in permanent collections:* Contemporary Art Museum, Madrid, University of Oslo, National Gallery (Cape Town), Güell Foundation (Barcelona), and several private collections. *Address:* Augustin de Bethencourt 5, Madrid 3, Spain. *Signs work:* see appendix.

MacARTHUR, Ronald Malcolm, R.S.W. (1982), D.A. Painting (1937); painter in water-colour and oil; Principal teacher of Art, Portobello High School, Edinburgh (1952-79); *b* Edinburgh, 1914; *s* of Charles MacArthur; *m* Dorothy Stephenson. *Educ.:* Royal High School of Edinburgh; *studied art* at Edinburgh College of Art (1933-37, William Allison, R.S.A., David Foggie, R.S.A., William MacTaggart, R.S.A.). *Exhib.:* R.S.W. (1948-60 and 1976 onwards). *Work in permanent collections:* Lothian Schools Collection, Strathclyde Schools Collection, and private collections. *Address:* Morden, 1 Duddingston Rd., Edinburgh EH15 1ND. *Signs work:* "Ronald MacArthur, R.S.W."

MACCABE, Gladys, R.O.I., M.A.(Honoris Causa), F.R.S.A., F.I.A.L.; Founder and Past-Pres. Ulster Society of Women Artists; Academician with gold medal Italian Academy; Diploma of Merit, University of Arts, Parma; Hon. Academician, Royal Ulster Academy; Hon. Mem. Ulster Water-colour Soc.; Hon. Mem. Ulster Soc. of Miniaturists; painter in oil and water-colour and various other media; art lecturer, writer and broadcaster; pianoforte soloist; *b* Randalstown, N. Ireland; *d* of George Chalmers, army officer and artist; *m* Max Maccabe; two *s. Educ.:* Brookvale Collegiate School, Ulster College of Art, France and Italy. *Exhib.:* London, Dublin, U.S.A., Canada, Belfast, Scotland, France, etc. *Work in permanent collections:* Irish National Self-portrait Collection, Limerick University (3 works), Imperial War Museum, Ulster Museum, Arts Council of Northern Ireland, The Queen's University, Belfast, Ulster Office, London, Longford County Library, Thomas Haverty Trust, County Dublin Educ. Authority, B.B.C., Cyril Cusack, Esq., Miss Beatrice Lillie, Lady Wakehurst, the late Adlai Stevenson, Esq., Dr. James White, Director, National Gallery of Ireland, etc. *Work repro.:* Many important publications; T.V. programmes at home and abroad. *Address:* 615 Ormeau Rd., Galwally, Belfast, BT7 3JD. *Signs work:* "GLADYS MACCABE."

MACCABE, Max, F.R.S.A., F.I.A.L., W.C.S.I.; Diploma of Merit, University of Arts, Parma; painter in oil and water-colour; art critic and lecturer; orchestral violinist; lecturer, Carnegie U.K. Trust, and Irish School of Landscape Painting; *b* Belfast, 16 Aug., 1917; *s* of Matthew Henry Maccabe; *m* Gladys Chalmers; two *s. Educ.:* Royal Belfast Academical Inst. *Exhib.:* London, U.S.A., Canada, Scotland, Belfast, Dublin. *Work in permanent collections:* The Hon. Mrs. McClintock, The Countess of Antrim, Lady Clark, The Ana M. Berry Memorial Fund, Ernest Milton, Lady Wakehurst, Ulster Museum, Swan Hunter Tyne Shipbuilders, Allied Irish Banks, Dr. James White, Director, National Gallery of Ireland, Limerick University, etc. *Work repro.:* Art News and Review, The Listener, Irish Tatler and Sketch, Sunday Independent, The Studio, International Who's Who in Art and Antiques, etc.; Radio and T.V. programmes on Art matters. *Address:* 615 Ormeau Rd., Galwally, Belfast, BT7 3JD. *Signs work:* "MAX MACCABE."

McCANN, Brian, B.A. Sculpture (1980), M.A. (R.C.A.) (1983), Prix de Rome (1984), Tate Fellow (1989); artist/sculptor in bronze, steel, ceramic, resin; part-time lecturer, Kingston University, R.C.A., and Royal Academy Schools; *b* Glasgow, 2 July, 1959; *s* of William McCann. *Studied art* at Duncan of Jordanstone, Dundee (1977-80), R.C.A. (1980-83). *Exhib.:* Serpentine Gallery Summer Show (1983), Hilderbrandtstrasse, Dusseldorf (1982), Salo Uno, Rome (1988), Tate Gallery, Liverpool (1989), William Jackson Gallery, London (1992), Coexistence Gallery, London (1992). *Work in permanent collections:* Arts Council, Government Collection. *Publications:* 'Sojourn' poetry (1980), 'Plumage of Recognition' catalogue (1991). *Address:* 11 Chandlers House, Fairfield North, Kingston, Surrey. *Signs work:* "Brian McCann."

McCARTER, Keith, D.A.(Edin.) (1960), F.S.I.A. (1968), F.R.S.A. (1969), A.R.B.S. (1991); sculptor in bronze, stainless steel, concrete; *b* Edinburgh, 15 Mar., 1936; *s* of the late Peter McCarter; *m* Brenda Schofield; one *s*, one *d. Educ.:* Royal High School, Edinburgh; *studied art* at Edinburgh College of Art (1956-60, Eric Schilsky, Helen Turner). *Exhib.:* R.A., Monaco, Burleighfield Gallery, Alwin Gallery, Berkeley Sq. Gallery. *Work in private collections:* Numerous countries worldwide. *Commissions:* many public sited sculptures in U.K., U.S.A., Europe, Africa; Moody Gardens, Galveston, U.S.A., with Sir Geoffrey Jellicoe. *Address:* Ottermead, Church Rd., Gt. Plumstead, Norfolk NR13 5AB. *Club:* Farmers, London. *Signs work:* "McCarter"; small works, see appendix.

McCLOY, William Ashby; Henry B. Plant Emeritus Prof., Connecticut College; painter, sculptor, printmaker; *b* Baltimore, Md., 2 Jan., 1913; *s* of Chas. H. McCloy; *m* Patrica C. *Educ.:* Phillips Academy, Andover, Mass., University of Iowa; *studied art* at University of Iowa. *Exhib.:* N.A., Whitney Museum of American Art, Pennsylvania Academy of Fine Arts, Chicago Art Inst., Carnegie Inst., Walker Art Centre, Kansas City Art Inst., Cincinnati Art Museum, Joslyn Mem. Art Museum, Library of Congress, Milwaukee Art Inst. *Address:* 376 Kitemaug Rd., Uncasville, Connecticut. *Signs work:* "WILLIAM A. McCLOY."

McCLURE, David, D.A. (Edin.), R.S.A. (1971), A.R.S.A. (1963), R.S.W. (1965); painter in oils and water-colours; teacher of painting, College of Art, Dundee (1957-85); *b* Lochwinnoch, Scotland, 20 Feb., 1926; *s* of Robert C. McClure, M.M. and Margaret Helena Evans; *m* Joyce Dixon Flanigan; two *s*, one *d. Educ.:* Queen's Park School, Glasgow, Edinburgh Univ.; *studied art* at Edinburgh College of Art (1947-52), Travelling Scholarship (1952-53), Fellow of Edinburgh College of Art (1955-57). *Work in permanent collections:* Arts Council (Scotland), Dundee Art Gallery, Glasgow Art Gallery, Aberdeen Art Gallery, Scottish National Gallery of Modern Art, Towner Art Gallery,

Eastbourne, Edinburgh and St. Andrew's University Staff Clubs, Queen's College, Dundee. *Address:* 16 Strawberry Bank, Dundee. *Signs work:* "D. McClure" or "McClure."

McCOMB, Leonard William, R.A., Slade Dip. (1960); artist-painter, sculptor, printmaker; visiting teacher: R.A. Schools; *b* Glasgow, 3 Aug., 1930; *m* Barbara Elenora. *Studied art* at Manchester School of Art (Harry Suttcliffe), Slade School (Sir William Coldstream, Prof. A.H. Gerrard). *Work in permanent collections:* Tate Gallery Arts Council Collection, V. & A., B'ham, Manchester, Sheffield, Swindon and Worcester city galleries. *Publications:* Arts Council Catalogue (1983), Painting from the South Catalogue (1989), Gillian Jason Gallery; Video Film Arts Council 'Flow of Life' (1983). *Address:* 6 St. Saviours Rd., Brixton Hill, London SW2 5HD. *Signs work:* "McCOMB" and "L.M" within circle and date.

McCOMBS, John, R.O.I., F.R.S.A., N.D.D.; R.A. scholarship award and college prize; Stanley Grimm prize R.O.I. (1990), People's prize Manchester Academy (1991); landscape artist in oil; *b* Manchester, 28 Dec., 1943. *s* of John McCombs. *Educ.:* High School of Art, Manchester; *studied art* at St. Martin's School of Art (1962-67) under F. Gore, Reynolds, Kossoff. *Exhib.:* John McCombs Gallery, Stockport A.G., Manchester and Salford City A.G's, Upper St. Galleries, Chenil Gallery, Tib Lane Gallery, Portland Gallery, Oldham A.G., Mall Galleries. *Work in permanent collections:* Salford A.G., Manchester City A.G., Oldham A.G., Saddleworth Museum. *Address:* 12 King St., Delph, nr. Oldham OL3 5DQ. *Clubs:* R.O.I., Manchester Academy of Fine Art (Council Mem., Selection and Hanging Com. Mem.). *Signs work:* "J. McCombs", sometimes "JMc."

McCRUM, Bridget; sculptor/painter in stone, bronze-mixed media; *b* Yorks., 27 Apr., 1934; *d* of Patrick Bain; *m* Robert S. McCrum; three *d.* *Studied art* at Farnham (1951-55, L. Musjynski; 1980-82 stone carving with John Joekes). *Exhib.:* R.A., R.S.A., Vanessa Deneveux, Eton College, Phoenix, Kingfisher, Fermoy Centre, Louise Hallett, Roche Court, Beaux Arts, Plymouth School of Architecture, Hannah Peschar Gallery. *Address:* Hamblyns, Coombe-Dittisham, Dartmouth, Devon. *Signs work:* "Bridget McCrum" or "McC."

McCULLOCH, Ian, D.A. (1957), S.S.A. (1964), A.R.S.A. (1989); painter in acrylic on canvas; *b* Glasgow, 4 Mar., 1935; *m* Margery Palmer; two *s.* *Educ.:* Glasgow School of Art (1953-57). 1st prize Stirling Smith Biennial (1985), painted murals for Italian Centre, Glasgow (1989), winner Glasgow Concert Hall murals competition (1990). *Exhib.:* recent one-man exhbns.: Aberdeen A.G. (1992), Aberystwyth Arts Centre, Wales (1991), Glasgow Print Studio (1989), Odette Gilbert Gallery, London (1987), Camden Arts Centre London and Richard Demarco Gallery Edinburgh (1986), Artspace Gallery Aberdeen (1984); many group exhbns. including New North, Tate Gallery Liverpool (1990), John Moores, Liverpool (1989).*Work in permanent collections:* Saatchi Collection, Contemporary Arts Soc., S.A.C., Glasgow A.G., Edinburgh City A.G., Universities of Glasgow and Liverpool. *Address:* 51 Victoria Rd., Lenzie, Glasgow G66 5AP. *Signs work:* "Ian McCulloch."

McCULLOUGH, George, M.S.Exc., hons. M. of E. dipl.; artist in oil, water-colour, gouache, pastel; Founder and Tutor, Donegal School of Landscape Painting, Dunfanaghy, Co. Donegal, Rep. of Ireland; *b* Belfast, 2 Oct., 1922; *m*; two *d.* *Educ.:* Belfast College of Technology and Belfast College of Art (1940-47); *studied art* as above. *Exhib.:* R.U.A., United Nations, N.Y., Oriel Gallery, Dublin, Cambridge Gallery, Dublin, Eaton Gallery, Toronto, Flowerfield Art

Centre, Portstewart, Yonge Gallery, Chicago, Bell Gallery, Belfast. *Address:* 20 Joanmount Drive, Carrs Glen, Belfast. *Signs work:* see appendix.

McCUTCHEON, John, D.A. Glas. (1933), R.O.I. (1970), Hon. mention Paris Salon, Assoc.-member Societé des Artistes Français (1970); artist in oil, watercolour and pen and ink; *b* Dalmellington, 1 June, 1910; *s* of Ivie McCutcheon; *m* Christina B. Weir. *Educ.:* Ayr Academy; *studied art* at Glasgow School of Art (1929-1933). *Exhib.:* Paris Salon, R.O.I., R.S.A., R.G.I., R.I. *Work in permanent collection:* Kelvingrove Art Gallery. *Address:* 12 Craigie Ave., Ayr, Scotland. *Club:* Ayr Sketch. *Signs work:* "Jn. McCUTCHEON."

MacDONALD, Alastair James Henderson, R.M.S., F.R.S.A., H.U.A.; Gold Bowl Hon. Men. (1991, 1992); miniature painter; elected Hon. Treas. R.M.S. (1981); *b* Tighnabruaich, Argyll, 5 July, 1934; *s* of Angus Graham MacDonald, licensed master grocer; *m* Juliet Anne Mead; two *s*, three *d*. *Educ.:* Pope Street School, New Eltham; *studied art* at Woolwich Polytechnic School of Art and Crafts under Heber Mathews and Joan Dawson. *Exhib.:* R.M.S., U.A. *Address:* 63 Somers Rd., North Mymms, Herts. *Signs work:* see appendix.

MACDONALD, Frances, A.R.C.A., (1938); artist in oil, water-colour, pencil and ink; *b* Wallasey, Ches., 12 Apr., 1914; *d* of Francis John Macdonald; *m* Leonard Appelbee, A.R.C.A.; one *d*. *Educ.:* Wallasey High School; *studied art* at Wallasey School of Art (Gordon Macpherson), R.C.A. (Barnett Freedman). *Exhib.:* Wildenstein, Brod Gallery. *Work in permanent collections:* Tate Gallery, National Gallery of: Wales, Melbourne and Adelaide, Australia; Newport, Arts Council, Imperial War Museum, War Artist work and Pilgrim Trust drawings in V. & A. and provincial galleries, and work in many private collections. At present, painting landscape, portrait, etc. *Address:* Rosemount, Toll Rd., Kincardine-on-Forth, Fife FK10 4QZ. *Signs work:* "Frances Macdonald."

McDOWELL, Leo, B.A.Hons., C.Ed., R.I.; Winsor and Newton R.I. award Mall Galleries (1990); self-taught artist in water and acrylic colour; Council Mem. R.I.; *b* 19 Jan., 1937. *Educ.:* Keighley Grammar School; Manchester University; Innsbruck University; Cambridge University. *Exhib.:* Shell House Gallery, Ledbury (1987), Blackstone Gallery, Pinner (1991), Phoenix Gallery, London (1991), The Discerning Eye, Mall Galleries, (1990), The British Gallery, Los Gatos, Calif. (1989), La Difference Gallery, Dinslaken, Germany (1987), Lisette Alibert Gallery, Paris (1992). *Work in permanent collection:* H.R.H. The Prince of Wales, Hertfordshire C.C. *Address:* Craigleith, Hanbury La., Essendon, Hatfield, Herts. AL9 6AY. *Signs work:* "Leo McDowell."

MACEY, Leo, C.B.E. (1979), H.S. (1988); picture restorer, painter of miniatures in oil on ivorine and board; Director, Penn Prints Ltd.; *b* Minehead, 23 Feb., 1922; *s* of William Henry Macey (decd.); *m* Isabella; two *s*, one *d*. *Educ.:* English Military School, Cairo; *studied art* at Frobisher School of Painting (1964-66, Lucy Frobisher). *Exhib.:* R.W.A., H.S., Armed Forces Art Soc. *Work in private collections:* Sultan of Negri Sembilan, Malaysia; Officers Mess R.C.M.P.; and others. *Address:* 56 Upper Marsh Rd., Warminster, Wilts. BA12 9PN. *Club:* Professional/Businessmen, Warminster. *Signs work:* see appendix.

McFADYEN, Jock, B.A., M.A.; artist in oil on canvas, plaster, wax and bronze; *b* Paisley, 1950; *s* of James McFadyen; *m* (1) Carol (divorced); one *s.*; (2) Susie; one *d*. *Educ.:* Renfrew High School; *studied art* at Chelsea School of Art (1973-77, Anne Rees Mogg, Ron Bowen, Ian Stephenson). *Exhib.:* 25 one-man shows including Blond Fine Art, Scottish Gallery, Imperial War Museum,

William Jackson Gallery, Camden Arts Centre. *Work in permanent collections:* 20 public collections including British Council, Imperial War Museum, Kunsthalle, Hamburg, National Gallery, V. & A., Tate Gallery. *Address:* 284 Globe Rd., Bethnal Green, London E2. *Club:* Vintage Japanese Motorcycle.

McFALL, David, R.A.; sculptor in stone and bronze; *b* Glasgow, 1919; *s* of David McFall, civil servant; *m* Alexandra Dane, actress; one *s*, one *d. Educ.:* English Martyrs, Spark Hill; *studied art* at Birmingham, R.C.A. and Lambeth. *Work in permanent collections:* Bullcalf (Tate), Churchill (Burlington House), Balfour (House of Commons), Vaughan Williams (Royal Festival Hall), Lord Attlee (Imperial War Museum), bronze study of Prince Charles (Buckingham Palace), Oedipus and Jocasta (W. Norwood Library), Pocahontas, Sir Godfrey Allen (bust) in crypt of St. Paul's Cathedral, 'Son of Man', Canterbury Cathedral. *Address:* 10 Fulham Park Gdns., London SW6 4JX. *Signs work:* see appendix.

MacFARLANE, Sheila Margaret, D.A. (Edin.) 1964; artist, printmaker and engraver; lecturer in printmaking, Duncan of Jordanstone College of Art, Dundee (1970-76); founder and director, Printmakers Workshop at Kirkton of Craig (1976-90); *b* Aberdeen, 2 May, 1943; *d* of Alexander Stewart MacFarlane; *m* Michael Stuart Green, N.D.D., F.R.S.A., interior designer; one *d. Work in permanent collections:* national and private collections in U.K. and private collections Overseas. *Address:* 1 Tangleha', St. Cyrus, Kincardineshire. *Signs work:* "Sheila M. MacFarlane."

McGOWAN, Hilary, M.A., F.M.A., M.B.I.M.; Museums and Heritage Director, Museums and Art Gallery, Bristol. *Address:* City of Bristol Museum and Art Gallery, Queen's Rd., Bristol BS8 1RL.

MacGREGOR, David Roy, M.A. (Cantab). 1948, F.S.A., F.R.Hist.S.; architect, ship draughtsman, author, artist in oil, water-colour and pen; *b* Fulham, 1925; *s* of Lt.-Col. W. W. MacGregor, D.S.O.; *m* Patricia M.A.P. Gilpin. *Educ.:* Eton and Trinity College, Cambridge; *studied art* under Cdr. G. F. Bradshaw, R.N., R.S.M.A. *Exhib.:* R.O.I., N.E.A.C., R.B.A., R.S.M.A.; one-man shows: Woodstock Gallery, London (1974), Princess Elizabeth Gallery, London, (1975, 1976), Digby Gallery, Mercury Theatre, Colchester (1976). *Work repro.:* illustrations to his own books, The Tea Clippers (1952, 1983), Merchant Sailing Ships (3 vols. 1984/85), Fast Sailing Ships 1775-1875 (1973, 1988). *Address:* 99 Lonsdale Rd., London SW13. *Signs work:* "D. R. MacGregor."

MacGREGOR, Robert Neil, M.A., Ll.B.; Director, The National Gallery; *b* 16 June, 1946. *Educ.:* New College, Oxford; Courtauld Institute of Art. *Address:* National Gallery, Trafalgar Sq., London WC2N 5DN. *Signs work:* "Neil MacGregor."

McGUINNESS, Michael, R.W.S. (1993); painter in water-colour and oil; Senior typographic and book designer with Readers Digest and, subsequently, Art Editor of The Independent and The Independent on Sunday (1986-91); *b* Essex, 20 Mar., 1935. *Studied art* at S.E. Essex Technical College (illustration and typography, Harry Eccleston, O.B.E.), Royal Academy Schools (painting, Fleetwood Walker, R.A.), Walthamstow School of Art (Stuart Ray). *Publications:* The Encyclopaedia of Water-colour Techniques (two paintings), Einstein for Beginners (illustration), Jung for Beginners (illustration). *Address:* 4 Denmark Rd., London W13 8RG. *Club:* Wynken de Worde Soc. *Signs work:* "McG."

McINTOSH, Iain, A.R.S.A.; sculptor; *b* Peterhead, 4 Jan., 1945; *s* of James McIntosh, cabinet maker; *m* Freida; two *d. Educ.:* Peterhead Academy; *studied art* at Gray's School of Art (1962-67). *Address:* Powmouth, By Montrose DD10 9LJ. *Signs work:* "I.M." plus year.

McINTYRE, Donald, R.I., R.C.A.; landscape painter in acrylic, oil and water-colour; *b* Yorkshire, 1923; *s* of Dr. Donald McDonald McIntyre; *m* Lauren Lindee. Educ.: Scarborough College, Skipton Grammar School; *studied art* at studio of James Wright, R.S.W. *Work in permanent collections:* H.R.H. Duke of Edinburgh, National Library of Wales, Welsh Arts Council, Robert Fleming Holdings plc, Birkenhead A.G., Newport (Gwent) A.G., Merthyr Tydfil Gallery, Welsh Contemporary Art Soc. *Address:* 3 Waen-y-Pandy, Tregarth, Bangor, Gwynedd LL57 4RB. *Signs work:* see appendix.

MACKAY, Arthur Stewart, R.O.I. (1949); artist in oil; former lecturer, Hammersmith College of Art and Building; *b* Dulwich, London, 25 Feb., 1909. *Educ.:* Wilson's Grammar School, Camberwell, Regent St. Polytechnic School of Art; *studied art* at Regent St. Polytechnic School of Art. *Exhib.:* R.A., R.S.A., Paris Salon and London galleries. *Work in permanent collections:* Imperial War Museum (2 paintings), and many private collections in Britain and Australia. *Publications:* articles on figure painting and outdoor sketching written for the publication, Artist. *Address:* 4 Dog Kennel Hill, East Dulwich, London SE22 8AA. *Signs work:* "A STEWART MACKAY" or "STEWART MACKAY."

MACKAY CLARK, Deirdre, N.D.D. (1959); painter in gouache, mixed media; visiting lecturer; *b* Ilford, 18 Sept., 1937; *d* of the late David Robertson Mackay Edward, carver, gilder, restorer; *m* John Keith Clark; three *s*, one *d. Educ.:* Copthall County Grammar School; *studied art* at Hornsey College of Art (1954-59, Alfred Daniels, Colin Sorensen). *Exhib.:* Minories, Colchester, R.A. Summer Exhbn., R.W.S., Chris Beetles. Work in various private collections. Designing and painting ceramics (1977-82). *Publications:* Artists Cards (1984), R.A. Pubs. (1985), Pimms R.A. Prize for drawing, print (1985), book jackets (1988), range of Fine Art cards and prints (1989). *Address:* Brierley Cottage, Brierley, Leominster, Herefordshire HR6 0NU. *Signs work:* "'D.M.C."

McKEAN, Lorne (Miss), F.R.B.S.; sculptor; silver medal for sculpture combined with architecture; Feodora Gleichen and Leverhulme Scholarships; *m* Edwin Russell, F.R.B.S. *Exhib.:* four one-man shows, London W1. *Portrait sculptures include:* the late Marquess of Salisbury, Hatfield House; H.R.H. Prince Philip on polo pony 'Portano', H.M. The Queen's personal Silver Wedding gift to her husband; the late Prince William of Gloucester, Kensington Palace; Earl of Lichfield for BBC programme 'Portrait'; Prince Charles on 'Pans Folly'. *Public works:* A.A. Milne public memorial of bear cub at London Zoo; Shearwaters, Shearwater House, Richmond Green; Girl and Swan 17' bronze in Reading; 'Galoubet' French show jumping stallion; H.M. The Queen, Drapers Hall. *Address:* Lethendry, Polecat Valley, Hindhead, Surrey. *Signs work:* "Lorne McKean."

McKELLAR, Robert; painter in oil specialising in abstract and still life; *b* Gravesend, 2 July, 1945. *Educ.:* Gravesend Technical School; *studied art* at Medway College of Art, Camberwell School of Art. *Exhib.:* R.A., Hong Kong, London, Los Angeles. Represented by Connaught-Brown Gallery London, Touchstone Gallery, Hong Kong. *Address:* Ringinglow, Staplehurst, Kent TN12 0RW. *Signs work:* "R. McKellar."

McKENNA, Laurence; artist in oil, water-colour, pastel and pencil; postal official; *b* 20 Nov., 1927; *s* of Charles J. McKenna; *m* Carmel Beattie; two *s*, one *d*. *Educ.:* St. Kevin's, Belfast; *studied art:* self-taught. *Exhib.:* Belfast, Dublin, Cork, London, U.S.A. *Work repro.:* Revue Moderne, Paris (drawing, 1947), Sunday Independent, Dublin (drawing, 1956), Irish News (drawing, 1958), Ulster Illustrated (drawing, 1958), Sunday Independent (drawing, 1965). *Address:* 23 Grangeville Gdns., Belfast. *Signs work:* "LAURENCE McKENNA."

MACKENZIE, Phyllis Edith; Slade Dip.; artist in oil, pastel, water-colour, pen and wash, sanguine, pencil, gouache; *b* 3 Aug., 1911; *d* of F. H. Fawkes; *m* K. E. Mackenzie; one *s*. *Educ.:* Cheltenham Ladies' College, Slade School of Art, London, and in Brussels. *Exhib.:* R.A., R.P., N.E.A.C., S.W.A., P.S., etc.; one-man shows: Beaux Arts, Brussels; Iran; Egypt; Singapore; Stockholm; Margery Parr, Chelsea; Bury St. Edmunds; Cheltenham; Berthe Hess Museum, London.; Century Gallery, Henley-on-Thames; Century Gallery, Datchet. *Address:* 11 St. James Cl., Pangbourne, Berks. RG8 7AP. *Club:* East India, *Signs work:* "Phyllis Mackenzie."

McKENZIE, Winifred, D.A. (Glas.); for fourteen years lecturer in Duncan of Jordanstone College of Art, Dundee; artist in oil; wood-engraver; *b* Bombay, 23 Aug., 1905; *d* of George McKenzie, architect. *Educ.:* Prior's Field; *studied art* at Glasgow School of Art and Grosvenor School of Modern Art under Iain MacNab. *Exhib.:* R.S.A., S.S.W.A., etc.; retrospective exhbn. (50 years) English Speaking Union Gallery, Edinburgh (1984). *Work in permanent collections:* Liverpool, Perth, Cork. *Official purchase:* Modern Arts Assoc. *Work repro.:* in Studio, Image and A History of British Wood-engraving. *Address:* 3B Playfair Terr., St. Andrews, Fife KY16 9HX. *Signs work:* "Winifred McKenzie."

McKINNEY, John, N.D.D., A.T.D. (1959), S.G.A.; artist in oil, acrylic, wood-cutting and engraving; Head of Art Dept., St. Peter's School, Bournemouth; *b* Bournemouth, 1 June, 1934; *s* of Patrick Peter McKinney, M.D., B.Ch.; *m* Elizabeth Ann McKinney; two *s*, two *d*. *Studied art* at Bournemouth College of Art (1953-59). *Exhib.:* R.A., R.O.I., S.W.E., Soc. of Painter-Etchers, S.G.A. *Work in permanent collection:* Oxford University. *Address:* 51 Hambledon Rd., Boscombe East, Bournemouth. *Signs work:* "John McKinney."

McLAREN, Sally; Central School of Art Diploma, Etching; French Government Scholarship; painter and printmaker; taught at Goldsmiths' School of Art, etching (1964-65); *b* London, 21 Sept., 1936; *m* David Webster, Q.C.; three *s*. *Studied art* at Central School, London, Atelier 17, Paris. Work in many important international collections. *Exhib.:* R.A., R.E., one-man show of prints, Bear Lane, Oxford, Studio Prints, London; widely in group shows in England and abroad; Llubjana Print Biennale, Seoul Biennale; North-west Printmakers U.S.A.; Cabo Frio Biennial, Brazil; Royal Soc. Painters Etchers; Edinburgh Festival; Atelier 17 Group Show, Paris, La Jeune Gravure Contemporaire, Paris, etc. *Address:* Clouds Cottage, E. Knoyle, Salisbury, Wilts. *Clubs:* Printmakers' Council, Royal Soc. of Painter Printmakers. *Signs work:* "Sally McLaren."

McLEAN, John; self-taught painter in acrylic; *b* Liverpool, 10 Jan., 1939; *m* Janet. *Educ.:* Reform Street School, Kirriemuir, and Arbroath High School. *Exhib.:* over twenty one-man shows worldwide. *Work in permanent collections:* Tate Gallery, Scottish National Museum of Modern Art, Swindon, Southampton and Basildon A.G's. *Address:* c/o Francis Graham Dixon Gallery, 17-18 Gt. Sutton St., London EC1V 0DN. *Signs work:* "John McLean" or "J.M."

McLEAN, Mary, A.R.M.S. (1991), H.S. (1990); miniature painter in water-colour; *b* Farnborough, Kent, 1944; *m* John S. McLean; two *s*, one *d. Educ.:* Marion Vian School, Beckenham; *studied art* privately with Ronald Jesty, A.R.B.A. *Exhib.:* R.A., R.M.S., Llewellyn Alexander (Fine Arts), Old School House Gallery, Woolland Dorset, Japan and U.S.A. Work in private collections. *Publication:* front cover illustration for specialist poultry magazine. *Address:* 24 Plover Rd., Milborne Port, Sherborne, Dorset DT9 5DA. *Signs work:* "Mary McLean."

MACLEAN, W.J., D.A., R.S.A.; lecturer, fine art, Dundee College of Art; *b* Inverness, 12 Oct., 1941; *s* of John Maclean, master mariner; *m* Marian Leven; two *s*, one *d. Educ.:* Inverness Royal Academy, H.M.S. *Conway,* N. Wales; *studied art* at Grays School of Art, Aberdeen (1961-66); British School at Rome (1966). *Exhib.:* one-man shows: Edinburgh, New 57 Gallery, Richard Demarco Gallery, R.H.W. London; group shows: Scottish Arts Council, Leinster Fine Art, 3rd Eye Gallery. *Work in permanent collections:* Aberdeen A.G., Scottish Arts Council, Contemporary Art Society, Scottish National Gallery of Modern Art, Hull A.G., Fitzwilliam Museum, Cambridge, B.M. *Address:* 18 Dougall St., Tayport, Fife, Scotland. *Signs work:* "W. J. Maclean."

MacLENNAN, Alastair MacKay, M.F.A. (1968), D.A. (1965); intermedia artist in mixed media installations, actuations, time-based work, conceptual orientation; Prof. of Fine Art, University of Ulster (1992-); *b* Blairatholl, Scotland, 3 Feb., 1943. *Educ.:* Perth Academy, Scotland; *studied art* at School of the Art Institute of Chicago, U.S.A. (1966-68), Duncan of Jordanstone College of Art, Dundee, Scotland (1960-65). *Exhib.:* national and international festivals of performative and time-based work throughout America, Canada, Britain, E. and W. Europe. *Work in permanent collections:* British Arts Council; private collections in Britain, America, Canada, Germany, Switzerland and Poland. *Publications:* reviews and interviews in art publications and periodicals. *Address:* c/o University of Ulster, Faculty of Art and Design, York St., Belfast BT15 1ED, N. Ireland.

MACLEOD, Duncan, D.A. (1974), R.S.W. (1980); artist in mixed media, water-colour, school teacher; S.A.C. Lecturers Panel; *b* Glasgow, 5 Apr., 1952; *m* Maretta Macleod, artist (divorced); one *s*, one *d. Educ.:* Clydebank High School; *studied art* at Glasgow School of Art (1970-74, David Donaldson). *Exhib.:* R.S.A., R.S.W., R.G.I., and many mixed and one-man shows in Britain. *Work in public and private collections:* U.K., U.S.A., France, Sweden, and the Far East. *Address:* 25 Taylor St., Clydebank, Glasgow. *Signs work:* "Duncan Macleod."

MACLEOD, Flora, B.W.S. (1951-56), S.S.W.A. (1955-67), S.W.A. (1960-78); *b* Forres, 24 Mar., 1907; *d* of Colonel Norman MacLeod. *Educ.:* privately. *Exhib.:* R.B.A. (Open Assembly), R.I., R.S.W., S.S.W.A., S.W.A., R.G.I., R.W.S. Art Club, Ridley Art Club, R.B.S.A., Paisley Art Inst., Aberdeen Artists, Britain in Water-colours. *Address:* Meadowlark Nursing Home, Manachie Rd., Dalvey, Forres, Morayshire IV36 0JT. *Signs work:* "FLORA MACLEOD."

MACLUSKY, Hector John; Slade Dip. (London); painter; illustrator; lecturer, Stevenage College; L.C.C. lecturer (1948-50); art master, Highgate School (1948-50); *b* Glasgow, 20 Jan., 1923; *s* of W. B. McLusky, M.C. *Educ.:* Roundhay and Warwick Schools; *studied art* at Leeds College of Art (1939-40) and Slade School (1945-48). *Exhib.:* R.A., R.B.A., London and provinces. *Work in private collections:* in America and Australia. *Work repro.:* in books and journals; free-lance cartoonist and illustrator for Press and television. *Address:* Hollybush Studio, Baines Lane, Datchworth, Herts. SG3 6RA.

MACMARTIN, John Rayment, D.A., F.R.S.A.; Diploma of Merit, Italy; D.M.D.A.; F.S.A.(Scot.); Industrial Design Consultant and Architectural Designer; Director (Tackle & Guns); artist in oils; inventor; *b* Glasgow, 3 Oct., 1925; Creamola Kid (1936-37); *m* Evelyn Margaret Lindsay Macmartin, embroideress. *Work in collections:* throughout the world. Structural Building MODULE, designed after a visit to Pompeii; invited to Leningrad, Moscow (1985), U.S.A. (1987), China (1988), Florida (1988), France (1989, 1990) and Norway (1991), National Trust for Scotland: V.P., Lanarkshire (1992-93), Probus Mem. (1992-93). Scottish Core of Retired Executives. *Address:* Rosebank, 2 Markethill Rd., East Mains, East Kilbride.

MACMIADHACHÁIN, Pádraig, A.R.W.A.; artist, Travelling Prize to Moscow (1957), Polish Govt. to Poland (1961); *b* Downpatrick, Ireland, 2 Mar., 1929; *s* of Jim McMechan, bank manager; *m* Hazel McCool; two children; divorced; *m* Ann Slacke, one child; divorced; *m* Charlotte Kockelberg (T.A. Charlotte Kienitz); divorced; *m* Bonnie Brown, painter. *Educ.:* Bangor Grammar School; Portora Royal School, Enniskillen; *studied art* at Belfast College of Art (1944-48), National College of Art, Dublin (1948-49), Academy of Art, Krakow, Poland (1960-61). *Exhib.:* one-man: Belfast, Dublin, London, Madrid, Krakow, Seattle, Los Angeles, Vancouver, Las Palmas; group shows: R.A., R.W.A., R.U.A., Gorky Park, Moscow, Irish Exhbn. Living Art. *Work in collections:* Arts Council, Ireland, Ronald Alley, Bob Monkhouse, Sam Wanamaker, Peter Sellers collection, Lord Briggs, King Carlos of Spain, the late President Chernenko of the U.S.S.R., Hertford College, Oxford and Sussex University. *Publications:* three collections of poems. *Address:* MacIntyre Saul Studio, Swanage, Dorset BH19 1DE. *Signs work:* see appendix. Work always in New Academy Gallery, 34 Windmill St., London.

McNEILL, Mary, F.S.D-C.; Mem. Craft Centre, Edinburgh; professional handweaver, consultant; *b* Newcastle-upon-Tyne, 9 May, 1913; *d* of George Nelson Wetherell; *m* Thomas Cragg McNeill; three *s. Educ.:* Lemington Grammar School, Northumberland, School of Art, Mansfield, Notts. (C. & G. 1st class) and later with Dorothy Wilkinson. *Exhib.:* Crafts Council of Gt. Britain Coventry, London, Bristol, Britain Can Make It travel exhbn. early 1950's; Guild: Textiles '68, London, Weaving Today, London, etc.; S.D-C.: London, Oxford, Lincoln, Southampton, Bath; Invited: Ireland House, Dublin; one-man shows: Nat. Museum of Wales, Cardiff, Guildford, Reading and Southsea. 1st Prize (Blue Ribbon) Best Entry State of Idaho State Fair (1962). *Work in permanent collections:* V. & A., Museums at Reading, Winchester, and Berkeley, California; also churches and private. *Publications:* articles in magazines such as Handweaver & Craftsman, U.S.A. *Address:* 32 Parkstone Ave., Southsea, Hants. PO4 0QZ. *Signs work:* "Mary McNeill."

McPAKE, John A., N.D.D., A.T.D., R.E.; painter-etcher working in etching, mixed media prints, gouache, drawings, etc.; Head of Foundation Course, Barnsley College; *b* Burnley, Lancs., 28 June, 1943; *s* of Nicholas McPake; *m* Anne Genner Crawford. *Educ.:* St. Anselm's College, Birkenhead; *studied art* at Wirral College of Art (1961-65), Liverpool Polytechnic (1965-66), Birmingham Polytechnic (1966-67), Leeds Polytechnic (1977-78). *Exhib.:* various group shows including R.E's, R.A. Summer shows, Seoul Print Biennale (1986, 1988), etc. *Work in permanent collections:* Bankside Gallery (R.E's.), various collections in England and abroad. *Address:* 21 Ingbirchworth Rd., Thurlstone, nr. Sheffield S30 6QN. *Signs work:* "John A. McPake."

MACPHAIL, Ian S., F.I.P.R.; artist in typography and print design; European Co-Ordinator, International Fund for Animal Welfare and editor; asst. music controller, E.N.S.A., specializing in publicity; asst. music director, Arts Council of Gt. Britain, responsible for all printing and publicity design; *b* Aberdeen, 11 Mar., 1922; *m* Michal Hambourg; one *s*, one *d*. *Educ.:* Aberdeen Grammar School; *studied art* with Charles W. Hemmingway. *Exhib.:* Exhbns. of posters, Council of Industrial Design. *Work repro.:* British Printer. *Publications:* You and the Orchestra (McDonald & Evans), editor and designer of Dexion News, Good Company and The Griffith Graph, designed literature for the first world conference on gifted children (1975). *Address:* 35 Boundary Rd., St. John's Wood, London NW8. *Club:* Savile. *Signs work:* "Ian Mac. Phail."

MACPHERSON, Hamish, A.R.B.S.; sculptor; teacher, Central School of Arts and Crafts, London (1948-52), Sir John Cass School of Art, London (1948-53); *b* Hartlepool, 20 Feb., 1915. *Educ.:* New Zealand; *studied art* at Elam School of Art, Auckland, N.Z. (1930-32), Central School of Arts and Crafts, London (1934-39). *Exhib.:* one-man exhbns., Picture Hire, Ltd., London (1938), Chelsea Gallery, London (1947), Apollinaire Gallery, London (1950, 1952), Alwin Gallery, London (1968), London Group, N.S., New York, Paris, the Colonies and provinces; work for Festival of Britain (1951). *Address:* Casa Mia, Mitchel Troy Common, Monmouth, Gwent NP5 4JB. *Signs work:* "Hamish Macpherson."

MacSWEENEY, Dale Pring, Dip.A.D.; painter in oil on canvas; *b* London, 1949; *d* of Percy Pring; *m* David MacSweeney, writer, psychiatrist. *Educ.:* Burlington Grammar, W. London; Greycourt Secondary School, Ham, Surrey; *studied art* at Wimbledon School of Art (1966), Waltham Forest College (1967-70). *Exhib.:* R.A., N.E.A.C., Piccadilly Gallery, Cork St., London; Henry Wyndham Fine Art, Jermyn St., London. *Address:* 30 King Edward's Mans., 629 Fulham Rd., London SW6. *Club:* Chelsea Arts. *Signs work:* "Dale Pring MacSweeney" or "Dale MacSweeney."

MADDISON, Robert, S.G.F.A. (1985), M.E.N.S.A. (1987); painter in water-colour, pastel, graphite; *b* Newcastle upon Tyne, 6 May, 1946; *s* of Robert Maddison; *m* Elizabeth Finch; one *s*, one *d*. *Educ.:* Heaton Grammar School; *studied art* at Newcastle College of Art (1962-64, John Crisp), Manchester College of Art (1964-65). *Exhib.:* S.G.F.A., N.S.; numerous one-man shows. *Work in permanent collections:* Durham University; numerous private collections including H.R.H. The Prince of Wales. *Publications:* The Northern Pennines – An Artist's Impressions; articles; television broadcasts. *Address:* Spring Cottage Studio, Dovespool, Allenheads, Northumberland NE47 9HQ. *Signs work:* "R. Maddison."

MADDOX, Ronald, P.R.I., Hon. R.W.S., F.C.S.D., F.S.A.I., F.R.S.A.; illustrator, consultant designer, artist in water-colour, line, gouache, specialising in architecture and landscape; *b* Purley, Surrey, 5 Oct., 1930; *s* of H. G. Maddox; *m* Camilla Farrin, 1958; two *s*. *Studied art* at St Albans School of Art, London College of Printing and Graphic Arts. Design/art direction 1951-61; freelance from 1962. *Exhib.:* R.A., R.I., F.B.A. galleries, national and provincial exhbns., one-man shows. *Work in permanent collections:* Britain, U.S.A., Canada, Germany. Elected President R.I. (1989), Governor F.B.A. (1989). Designer, British Commemorative stamps (1972/78/84/89); Design Council award (1973); Isle of Man Europa stamps, Prix de l'Art Philatelique (1987); Winsor & Newton R.I. Award (1981, 1991); finalist Hunting Group Art Prizes (1980-81-83). *Work* *repro.:* national and international publications. *Address:* Herons, 21 New Rd., Digswell, Welwyn, Herts. AL6 0AQ. *Signs work:* "RONALD MADDOX."

MADERSON, Arthur Karl, N.D.D. (1964); painter in oil, pastel, acrylic and water-colour; *b* London, 27 Dec., 1942. *Educ.:* Battersea County Comprehensive; *studied art* at Camberwell School of Art (1960-64, Robert Medley). *Exhib.:* regularly at R.W.A. (Cornelissen prize winner 1986), R.A., R.H.A., George Gallery, Dublin (1991) (who represent him in Ireland), London and U.S.A. *Work in private and permanent collections:* Europe and abroad. *Work repro.:* contributor to many journals and art publications including The Artist. Mem. Cork Arts Soc. *Address:* Derriheen House, Cappoquin, Waterford, Rep. of Ireland. *Signs work:* "A.K. Maderson," or "A.K.M" on picture and reverse.

MADGWICK, Clive, S.E.A. (1991), R.B.A. (1983), U.A. (1976); self-taught artist in oil, acrylic and water-colour; *b* London, 31 Oct., 1934; *s* of the late Dr. John R. A. Madgwick, M.D.: *m* Joan Patricia; one *s*, one *d. Educ.:* Epsom College and London University. *Exhib.:* 32 one-man shows; R.A., R.B.A., R.O.I., U.A., Royal Soc. of Miniature Artists and Sculptors. Winner Royle Landscape Prize (1978), Higgs & Hill Bursary F.B.A. (1986), Daler Rowney Award Equestrian Soc. (1987), specializing country sports. Works in public and private collections throughout the world. *Address:* Newton House, Newton Rd., Sudbury, Suffolk CO10 6RN. *Signs work:* "C. MADGWICK" and see appendix.

MAER, Stephen, F.S.D-C.; Council Mem. Soc. of Designer-Craftsman, Designer Jewellers Group: Founder-Member and Chairman (1980-83, 1992-), Crafts Council, Index of Craftsmen, Design Council Register of Designers, Soc. of Jewellery Historians, Executive Mem. Crafts Occupational Standards Board; designer jeweller; *b* London, 1933; *s* of Mitchel Maer; *m* Janet Eddington; two *d. Educ.:* Clayesmore School; *studied jewellery design* at R.C.A. under Prof. R. Goodden. *Exhib.:* group shows: British Crafts Centre, R.S.A., Design Centre, Goldsmiths Hall, Barbican Centre. *Address:* 18 Yerbury Rd., London N19. *Signs work:* "SM" (hallmark).

MAGOR, William Laurence, A.R.C.A. (1939), A.T.D. (1940); Principal, Berkshire College of Art (1960-74); artist in water-colour; *b* Mountain Ash, S. Wales, 30 Apr., 1913; *s* of L. L. Magor; *m* Marie Alexander; one *s*, two *d. Educ.:* Crypt Grammar School, Gloucester; *studied art* at Gloucester Art School (1932-36) and R.C.A. (1936-39) under E. Bawden, Paul Nash. *Exhib.:* R.A. *Address:* Gwenville, Sellars Rd., Hardwicke, Glos. *Signs work:* "W. L. Magor."

MAI, Jinyao: see MAK, Kum Siew.

MAK, Kum Siew, (Mai, Jinyao) A.R.C.A. (1967); full-time artist in Chinese and Western media; *b* Singapore, 21 Apr., 1940; two *s. Educ.:* Singapore; *studied art* at St. Martin's School of Art (1961-64) under Frederick Gore, R.C.A. (1964-67) under Carel Weight. *Exhib.:* R.A., I.C.A., R.C.A., Serpentine Gallery, Tate Gallery, Whitechapel Gallery. *Work in permanent collections:* Tate Gallery, London; National Gallery, Singapore; Museum of Modern Art, Hyogo, Japan; Arts Council of G.B. *Address:* Alvernia, The Street, Mortimer, Berks. RG7 3PE.

MAKEPEACE, John, O.B.E. (1988), F.C.S.D., F.I.Mgt., F.R.S.A.; designer and furniture maker since 1961; Founder and Director: The Parnham Trust (1977–); *b* 6 July, 1939; *m* 1983 Jennie Moores. *Study/Consultancy Tours:* Scandinavia; N.America; W.Africa; Australia and Japan. *Furniture commissions* for Nuffield Foundation; Portals plc; Post Office; Royal Society of Arts; Directors' Forum; Boots plc. *Public collections:* Cardiff; Fitzwilliam; Leeds; Frankfurt;

V. & A.; Royal Museum of Scotland; The Art Inst. of Chicago; Lewis College, Richmond, Va. Featured in numerous books, articles and films internationally. *Address:* Parnham House, Beaminster, Dorset DT8 3NA.

MAKINSON, Prof. Trevor Owen; portrait and landscape painter; visiting lecturer, Glasgow School of Art and Glasgow University; *b* Southport, 8 June, 1926; *s* of Owen Makinson. *Educ.:* privately; *studied art* at Hereford Art School, Slade School. *Exhib.:* R.A., R.B.A., R.P., R.S.A., United Soc. of Artists, Soc. of Scottish Artists, R.G.I., Wye Valley Art Soc., Herefordshire Arts and Crafts; one-man shows at Hereford Art Gallery (1944, 1946, 1949, 1955), Buxton (1948), Worcester (1951), Nottingham (1953), Worthing (1954). *Official purchases:* Hereford, Salford, Stoke-on-Trent, Stockholm, Nat. Mus. of Wales, Worthing, Newport A.G., Glasgow A.G., Glasgow University College, Buxton A.G., Worcester A.G., West Bridgford, Notts. A.G. *Address:* c/o Glasgow School of Art (Staff), 167 Renfrew St., Glasgow C3. *Signs work:* "Makinson" or "MAKINSON."

MAKLOUF, Raphael; sculptor in bronze; painter; *b* Jerusalem, 10 Dec., 1937. *Studied art* at Camberwell School of Art (1953-58) under Dr. Karel Vogel. *Official purchases:* Life size bronze bust of H.M. Queen Elizabeth II for Royal Society of Arts, John Adam St., London (1986); life size bronze bust of General Sir John Mogg for Army Benevolent Fund (1987); Tower of London; Carnegie Hall, N.Y., etc. New portrait effigy of H.M. The Queen on all U.K. coinage from 1985. *Address:* 3 St. Helena Terr., Richmond, Surrey. *Signs work:* see appendix.

MALCLES, Jean-Denis; Mem. Salon d'Automne, Salon des Artistes Décorateurs, Salon de l'Imagerie, Officier ordre des Arts et Lettres; Chevalier de la Légion d'honneur; painter in oil, gouache and pastel; lithographer; stage and costume designer; *b* Paris, 15 May, 1912; *s* of Laurent Malcles, sculptor; *m* Janine Malcles. *Educ.:* École Boulle and Académies Peinture; *studied art* under Louis Sognot and Rulhmann. *Work in permanent collections:* Musée d'Art Moderne. *Official purchases:* City of Paris, French Government. *Work repro.:* Vogue, Femina, Plaisir de France, Graphis, Ballets des Champs-Elysées, Art et Style, Style en France. *Theatre decor:* Opéra de Paris, Comedie-Francaise, Scala de Milan, Opéra de Hambourg, Cie Renaud-Barrault, Festival musique d'Aix en Provence, Le Théâtre de Jean Anouilh, Covent Garden. *Publications:* Bel Ami, Lettres de Mon Moulin, La Muse au Cabaret, Affiches, Expositions Galerie des Orfèvres, Paris. *Address:* 152 rue L. M. Nordmann, Paris 13. *Signs work:* see appendix.

MALCOLM, Bronwen A., B.A. (Hons.) (1985); painter in oil on wood; *b* London, 31 July, 1963; *m* S.J. Ackhurst; one *d. Studied art* at Wimbledon School of Art (1981-82), St. Martin's School of Art (1982-85). *Exhib.:* Sue Rankin Gallery, many mixed and solo shows in U.K. *Work in permanent collections:* Merrill Lynch Ltd., Cardinal Beer plc Germany; private: U.S.A., Europe, Canada. *Address:* c/o Sue Rankin Gallery, 40 Ledbury Rd., London W11 2AB. *Club:* Chelsea Arts. *Signs work:* "B.A.M."

MALCOLM, Ellen, R.S.A. (1976), Guthrie Award (1952); artist in oil; teacher; *b* Grangemouth, 28 Sept., 1923; *d* of John Malcolm; *m* Gordon S. Cameron, R.S.A. *Educ.:* Aberdeen Academy; *studied art* at Gray's School of Art, Aberdeen (1940-44) under Robert Sivell, R.S.A., and Dr. D. M. Sutherland, R.S.A. *Work in permanent collections:* Perth City Gallery, Art Gallery, Southend, Lillie Gallery, Milngavie, Edinburgh City Collection, Palace of Holyrood House, Thorburn-Ross and Dr. Arnott Hamilton Collections,

Edinburgh. *Address:* 7 Auburn Terr., Invergowrie, Perthshire. *Signs work:* "E. Malcolm."

MALCOLMSON, Joe; artist in oil and gold leaf, water-colour; *b* Lanarkshire, 28 June, 1932; *m* Joyce Franklin. *Studied art* at Medway College of Art (1959-61). *Exhib.:* R.A., R.W.S., R.I., R.O.I., N.E.A.C., N.S. *Address:* The Cottage, Woodland Way, Kingswood, Surrey KT20 6NU. *Signs work:* "J.L. MALCOLMSOn" capitals except for last letter.

MALENOIR, Mary, R.E. (1984); R.A. Schools Dip. (1964), Rome Scholar in Engraving (1965-67); artist in oil on paper, water-colour, etching, drawing; *b* Surrey, 29 July, 1940; *d* of Walter E. Malenoir; *m* Michael Fairclough, artist; two *d. Studied art* at Kingston School of Art (1957-61), R.A. Schools (1961-64), S.W. Hayter's Atelier 17, Paris (1967). *Exhib.:* Prizewinner in:- P.M.C. National Print Competition (1987), Hunting Group Competition (1987), Humberside Printmaking Competition (1987), Bankside Gallery Open Print Competition (1989), R.A.Summer Exhbns., R.E. and P.M.C. Exhbns. *Work in permanent collections:* Ashmolean Museum, Ipswich Museum and A.G., Graves A.G. Sheffield. *Address:* Tilford Green Cottages, Tilford, Farnham, Surrey GU10 2BU. *Signs work:* "MALENOIR."

MALIN, Suzi; Slade Post. Grad. (1975); painter in tempera; *d* of Michael Malin, textile designer; *m* David Hames. *Educ.:* Badminton, Bristol; *studied art* at Slade School of Art (1969-75, John Aldridge, R.A.). *Exhib.:* one-man shows, J.P.L. Fine Arts, London (1977), Achim Moeller, London (1978), Coe Kerr, N.Y. (1978), Galerie d'Eendt, Amsterdam (1983), Gimpel Fils, London (1982). *Work in permanent collections:* N.P.G.; Raby Castle; Gt. Hall, Christchurch, Oxford; Hull University; East Anglia University; Midland Bank. *Address:* The Meeting Hall, 158A Mill La., London NW6. *Club:* Chelsea Arts. *Signs work:* "S. Malin."

MALINS, Margery Helen, A.T.D., D.A. (Reading), R.C.A., M.F.P.S.; artist in oil, water-colour; *b* Reading; *d* of Dr. E. W. Squire, M.B., B.S. (London); *m* F. M. Malins, A.T.D., D.A. (Reading), R.C.A., M.F.P.S.; four *s. Educ.:* Abbey School, Reading; *studied art* at Reading University under Prof. A. Betts and Walter Bayes, Liverpool College of Art. *Address:* The Mill House, Sandy Cross, Heathfield, E. Sussex TN21 8BS. *Signs work:* "M. Malins."

MALTHOUSE, Eric; painter; *b* Birmingham, 1914; *s* of J. W. Malthouse; *m* Anne Gascoigne (decd.); one *s,* two *d. Educ.:* King Edward's, Birmingham; *studied art* at College of Art, Birmingham (1931-37). Founder of the 56 Group. Mural Paintings: Wales Gas Board, Penylan Hostel and L. G. Harris & Co. Ltd. *Exhib.:* Ten-year Retrospective (1959), Growth of Two Paintings (1963), Paintings, New Vision Gallery (1965), Small Paintings, A.I.A. (1969), Bangor Art Gallery (1970), Oxford Gallery (1971), Exeter Univ. (1975), Oriel, Cardiff (1981). *Work in permanent collections:* National Museum of Wales, Welsh Arts Council, Swansea, Bath, Bristol and Newport Art Galleries, V. & A., Universities of Glasgow, Cardiff and Exeter, etc. *Address:* 56 Porth-Y-Castell, Barry, S. Glam. CF62 6QE.

MANDL, Anita, R.W.A. (1978), R.S.M.A. (1971), F.R.B.S. (1980), Ph.D. (1951), D.Sc. (1960); sculptress, formerly University Reader, Medical School, Birmingham; carvings in wood (mainly tropical timbers) and stone (alabaster, soapstone); also bronzes made from original carvings; *b* Prague, 1926; *m* Dr. Denys Jennings. *Studied art:* part-time at Birmingham College of Art. *Exhib.:* R.A., R.B.A., R.W.A., R.G.I.F.A., R.S.M.A., Llewellyn-Alexander Gallery;

Alresford Gallery, etc. and U.S.A. *Work in permanent collections:* Ulster Museum; Royal West of England Academy. *Address:* 21 Northview Rd., Budleigh Salterton, Devon EX9 6BZ. *Signs work:* Mostly unsigned. (Highly polished carvings are marred by signature).

MANIFOLD, Debra, B.A. (Hons.) Illustration, Advanced Printmaking Postgrad. Dip.; artist in pastel, oil and water-colour, *b* London, 28 Aug., 1961. *Educ.:* Northwood Comprehensive; *studied art* at Harrow School of Art (1978-83), Central School of Art and Design (1983-84, Norman Ackroyd, R.A., David Gluck, R.W.S.). *Exhib.:* Linda Blackstone Gallery, P.S., R.I. Mall Galleries, U.A. Westminster Gallery, Société des Pastellistes de France Paris, Barbican Centre London, National Theatre London, A.O.I. Gallery London, Edward Day Gallery, Kingston, Ontario. *Publications:* Chapter with illustrations in Pastels Masterclass by Judy Martin (Harper Collins); examples of work in The Encyclopedia of Pastel Techniques by Judy Martin (Quarto), Watercolour School by Hazel Harrison (Quarto). *Address:* 8 Spring Gdns., E. Molesey, Surrey KT8 0JA. *Signs work:* "MANIFOLD."

MANLEY, Jim, A.R.U.A.; Patron's prize, E.V.A. Limerick (1984); painter in water-colour, pastel, collage; *b* St. Helen's, 1934; *m* Margaret; three *s. Educ.:* West Park Grammar School, St. Helen's; De La Salle College, Middleton. *Exhib.:* over twenty exhbns. in Ireland and England, including London Gallery, Duncan Campbell Fine Arts, Dublin, Solomon Gallery. *Work in permanent collections:* Abbot Hall Kendal, U.T.V. Belfast, Walker Liverpool, Bank of Ireland Dublin. *Address:* Coastguard Cottages, Killough, Downpatrick, Co. Down. *Club:* United Arts, Dublin. *Signs work:* "J. Manley."

MANN, Alex; painter of 'visual-sound' (music) – portraits, landscapes, castles, homes; *b* Ayr, Scotland, 26 Feb., 1923. *Educ.:* Sidcup School of Art. *Work in public and private collections:* throughout the world. *Address:* Braemar Studio, 3 Chapel Brae, Braemar AB35 5YT. *Signs work:* "Alex Mann."

MANN, Sargy, H.N.D. Mech. (1958), N.D.D. (1964); landscape painter in oil and drawing media; *b* Hythe, Kent, 29 May, 1937; *m* Frances Carey; one *s*, two *d. Educ.:* Dartington; *studied art* at Camberwell School of Arts and Crafts (1960-64, Frank Auerbach, Euan Uglow, Francis Hoyland) (1967, Dick Lee). *Exhib.:* R.A., Hayward Annual (1983), London Group, International Drawing Biennale; one-man shows, Salisbury Festival of Arts, Cadogan Contemporary, Past and Present Arts Council. *Work in permanent collections:* Arts Council of G.B., Contemporary Art Soc., Cleveland C.C. *Publications:* Drawings by Bonnard (Arts Council, 1984), Pierre Bonnard Drawings (J.P.L. Fine Art, 1981), Pierre Bonnard Drawings Vols. 1-2 (J.P.L. Fine Art, 1987), Raoul Dufy (J.P.L. Fine Art, 1987), Pierre Bonnard (Nottingham Castle Museum, 1984), Introduction Past and Present (Arts Council, 1987). *Address:* 58 Lyndhurst Grove, London SE15. *Signs work:* "Sargy Mann" or "Sargy."

MANOUK: see BAGHJIAN, Manouk.

MANSFIELD, Edgar, O.B.E. (1979), F.R.B.S. (1980), M.D.E. (1950), Hon. F.D.B. (1970), F.R.S.A. (1934); sculptor in bronze, graphic artist, designer, formerly also bookbinder; *b* London (N.Z. citizen), 11 Feb., 1907; *m* Gladys. *Educ.:* in New Zealand – Hastings, Napier, Dunedin; *studied art* at Otago School of Art, N.Z. (1926-29), Central, Camberwell and Reimann Schools, London (1934-39). *Exhib.:* most in N.Z. (sculpture), numerous in England and overseas (bookbinding). *Work in permanent collections:* N.Z. (sculpture), mainly in private collections; bookbinding: B.M., V. & A., Ashmolean, Klingspor, Royal

Library The Hague, Stockholm, Spencer Coll., N.Y. Public Library, etc. *Publications:* Modern Design in Bookbinding – The Work of Edgar Mansfield (Peter Owen, 1966); author, 11.2.80 on Creation (Hawk Press, N.Z.); numerous articles, mostly in Europe. *Address:* 5 Nursery Ave., Bearsted, Maidstone, Kent.

MANTLE, Ruth, S.G.F.A. (1984), C.F.A. (Oxon.) (1949); artist in pencil, ink, water-colour of buildings and botanical subjects; illustrator and teacher of drawing; *b* Newbury, Berks., 27 Aug., 1925; *d* of Kenneth Baines; *m* Ian Mantle, M.A.; two *s*, one *d*. *Educ.:* St. Catherine's School, Bramley, Surrey; *studied art* at Ruskin School of Drawing, Oxford (1946-50, Albert Rutherston, Percy Horton; History of Art, Sir Kenneth Clark). *Exhib.:* S.G.F.A. Annual, several provincial exhbns. *Work in permanent collections:* Holdsworth House, Halifax; Heidelberg; mainly private collections. *Publications:* illustrated, The Necklace Villages, Cambridge Itself, My Cambridge (Robson Books). *Address:* 22 Helmeth Rd., Church Stretton, Salop. SY6 7AS. *Clubs:* Ludlow Art Soc., Shropshire Art Soc. *Signs work:* "Ruth Mantle."

MAPP, John Ernest, A.R.C.A. (1948); artist in oil, acrylic, illustrator, etc,; *b* Northampton, 26 Mar., 1926; *s* of E. Mapp; *m* Margaret Trayler; one *s*, one *d*. *Educ.:* Eaglehurst College, Northampton; *studied art* at Northampton School of Art (1941-45), R.C.A. (1945-48) under Barnett Freedman and Gilbert Spencer. *Exhib.:* Various galleries. *Address:* 64A Vineyard Hill Rd., Wimbledon Pk., London SW19 7JJ. *Signs work:* see appendix.

MARA, Pam, M.C.S.D. (1970), N.D.D. (1958); illustrator, designer, painter, printmaker in oil, pastel, acrylic, water-colour, lithography; *b* London, 12 May, 1938; *d* of Harold Faulkner Mara, F.I.B.D. *Educ.:* Henrietta Barnett School, London; *studied art* at Willesden School of Art, Central School of Art. *Exhib.:* mixed shows: Mall Galleries, Barbican, National Theatre, Bloomsbury Gallery, Loggia Gallery, St. Martin's in the Field. *Publications:* illustrated over 50 books, work published in England, America, several European countries, W. Africa, Near and Far East. *Address:* 77B Sutherland St., London SW1V 4JY. *Signs work:* "Pam Mara."

MARAIS, (Mary Rachel Brown); Mem. Visual Artist and Gallery Assoc.; self-taught artist in oil; *b* New York City, 24 Sept., 1921. *Educ.:* New York University. Lived in Paris several years and painted warm, charming nostalgic scenes of Paris completely capturing the ambiance in a very personal style. *Exhib.:* Paris, New York, Switzerland; Centre d'Art Contemporain, Paris (1984), Galerie Chantepierre Auboune, Switzerland; seen on NYC Channel 13 TV (1979, 1980). *Work in permanent collections:* Jean Aberbach, Theodora Settele, Hugo Perls, Dr. M. Reder, Jacques Bellini. *Address:* 33 W. 67th St., New York 10023, N.Y. *Signs work:* "Marais."

MARDEL-FERREIRA, Elizabeth Gilchrist; painter in acrylic, ink and wash, silk-screen printer; *b* Nottingham, 5 May, 1931; *d* of John G. McMeeking, C.B.E., J.P., lace manufacturer; *m* Joseph Charles Mardel-Ferreira; one *s*, two *d*. *Educ.:* Headington School, Oxford; *studied art* at Nottingham College of Art (1949-53). *Exhib.:* Emsworth Group (7), R.A. (1978). Work in private collections. *Address:* 15 Warblington Ave., Havant, Hants. *Club:* Emsworth Group. *Signs work:* "E. Mardel" or "Elizabeth G. Mardel.'

MARDI: see BARRIE, Mardi.

MAREK, Jerzy; self-taught primitive painter in oil; *b* Poland, 1925; *m* Margaret Baird; one *s*. *Exhib.:* Portal and Grosvenor Galleries, London, also in a number of International and Arts Council Exhbns. for primitive painters. *Work* *in permanent collections:* Salford A.G., Bolton A.G., Abbotts Hall Museum, Kendal, Lancaster Museum, Sydney Janis Coll., N.Y. *Publications:* Naive Kunst by Ida Niggli, The Rona Guide to the World of Naive Art, Twentieth Century British Naive and Primitive Artists by E. Lister and S. Williams; postcards by Kirkpatrick Cards, London and Stirling Gallery, Stirling. *Address:* 7 Pittville St., Portobello, Edinburgh EH15 2BZ. *Signs work:* "J. Marek."

MARGRIE, Victor, C.B.E., F.C.S.D.; potter; Visiting Prof. University of Westminster; Director, Crafts Council (1977-84); *b* London, 29 Dec., 1929. *Work in permanent collections:* V. & A., and private collections. External Advisor, School of Fine Art, Cardiff Institute (1993–); Mem. of Board of Studies in Fine Art, University of London (1989–); Mem. UK National Commission for UNESCO (1984-85); Fine Arts Advisory Committee British Council (1983-86). *Publications:* contributed to: Oxford Dictionary of Decorative Arts (1975); Europaischt Keramik Seit (1950, 1979); Lucie Rie (1981); contrib. specialist publications and museum catalogues. *Address:* Bowlders, Doccombe, Moreton-hampstead, Devon TQ13 8SS. *Signs work:* see appendix.

MARINKOV, Saša (Alexandra); artist in printmaking, lecturer; *b* Belgrade, Yugoslavia, 12 Jan., 1949; *d* of Dr. C.B. Marinkov and Mary Lishman; *m* Michael Jones. *Studied art* at Leeds University (1967-71), Central School of Art and Design (1975-76). *Exhib.:* London University, Clare College Cambridge, Woodlands A.G., Bradford Print Biennale, Miniprint Biennale, Korea and Spain, Whitechapel Open, London Group, Riverside Open. *Work in permanent collections:* Leeds University; London University; Brazil; Skopje, Yugoslavia; Clare College, Cambridge; London Hospital. *Awards:* G.L.C. Spirit of London, South Bank Picture Show, R.A. Summer Show, Ministry of Transport. *Address:* Woodcut, Riverside, Twickenham TW1 3DJ. *Signs work:* "S. Marinkov."

MARJ: see BOND, Marj.

MARKS, Laura Anne Celia; Greenshields Foundation award (1982, 1983); artist in oil, water-colour and pencil; *b* Toronto, Canada, 1954; *d* of Benjamin Marks, chemical engineer. *Educ.:* Forest Hill Collegiate, Toronto; *studied art* at Central Technical School, The Three Schools of Art, Art's Sake, and Ontario College of Art (1971-80, Paul Young). *Exhib.:* one-man shows: Evans Gallery, Toronto (1973), Prince Arthur Gallery, Toronto (1980), October Gallery, London (1982), Alberta House, London (1982), Gallery Gabor, Toronto (1984), International Exhbn., Monte-Carlo (1985), John Denham Gallery, London (1991). *Work in permanent collection:* Ontario House, London. *Address:* 26 West End La., London NW6. *Signs work:* "MARKS."

MARKS, Peggie; sculptress; *b* Oldham, Nov., 1914; *d* of Vivian Bethel, physical culturist; *m* Charles Marks; one *s.* *Educ.:* Werneth Grange Convent; *studied art* at Manchester Regional College of Art. *Exhib.:* Oldham A.G., Manchester A.G., Salford A.G., Galerie Vallombreuse Biarritz, Houses of Parliament, N. Regional travelling exhbn., Saddleworth Art Soc. Rooms. *Address:* (studio), 18 Waterloo St., Oldham. *Clubs:* Oldham Artists, Saddleworth Art Soc., Rochdale Sculptors. *Signs work:* "Peggie Marks."

MARKUT, Jan, M.F.A., R.M.S.; portrait painter/miniaturist in oil on ivorine; *b* Ars-sur-Moselle, France, 26 Feb., 1928; *m* Krystyna; two *s.* *Educ.:* Academy of Fine Arts, Poznan, Poland (1949-55, Profs. Taranczewski, Wasilkowski, Polanski, Malina). *Member of:* Z.P.A.P. and M.A.A. Listed in 13th Edn. of Men of Achievement. *Address:* 1208 S. Duncan Ave., Clearwater, Fl. 34616, U.S.A. *Signs work:* "J. MARKUT."

MARR, Leslie, M.A. (1947); painter and draftsman in oil, water-colour, etc.; Secretary, Borough Group (1947-49); *b* Durham, 14 Aug., 1922; *s* of Col. J. Lynn Marr, O.B.E., T.D. *Studied art* at Borough Polytechnic under David Bomberg. *Exhib.:* one-man shows: Everyman Gallery, Drian Galleries, Laing A.G., Newcastle upon Tyne, Woodstock Gallery, Maddermarket Norwich, Fermoy Gallery, Kings Lynn, "Bomberg and the Family" exhbn. Ben Uri Gallery, London, Catto Gallery, London. *Work in permanent collection:* Laing A.G., Newcastle upon Tyne, University of Haifa, Graves A.G., Sheffield. *Publications:* From My Point of View (Acorn Editions 1979). *Address:* Cromes Studio, Wood Norton, Dereham, Norfolk NR20 5BG. *Signs work:* see appendix.

MARRIOTT, Michael, F.R.B.S. (1974), N.D.D. (1960); sculptor in stainless steel, glass, G.R.P., stone, clay, plaster, bronze; *b* London, 3 May, 1940. *Educ.:* Latymer Foundation and Christopher Wren Secondary; *studied art* at St. Martin's School of Art (1956-60, Elizabeth Frink, Anthony Caro, Edward Paolozzi). *Exhib.:* one-man shows: Cockpit Theatre, London (1971), Alwin Gallery, London (1976); two-man show: Europa Gallery, Surrey (1978); group exhbns.: annually all over U.K. since 1960, Margam Park, S. Wales, Barbican Centre, Hannah Peschar Gallery, Surrey; also in U.S.A. and Europe. *Work in permanent collections:* I.B.M. Cosham, Hunting Engineering Bedford, Heron House London, Crown House London. *Address:* 16 Seymour Rd., London SW18 5JA. *Signs work:* see appendix.

MARSHALL, Dunbar: see MARSHALL MALAGOLA, Dunbar.

MARSHALL, John; landscape painter in water-colour; *b* Colchester. *Educ.:* Rugby School; *studied art:* pupil of Cedric John Kennedy (1898-1968). *Exhib.:* British Art Centre, New York, Leicester Galleries, London; one-man exhbns.: Leicester Galleries WC2 (1956-59-62), Anthony Reed's Gallery W1 (1981). *Work in permanent collections:* Wadsworth Atheneum, U.S.A., Columbia Museum of Art, U.S.A., Norwich Castle Museum. *Official purchases:* Hull Education Committee. *Work repro.:* The Studio (July, 1956, Feb., 1960); monographs: Arts Review (June, 1956), The Studio (Feb., 1960). *Publications:* Cedric Kennedy memorial Catalogue and Monograph (1969 and 1972). *Address:* 41 Campden Hill Rd., London W8. *Signs work:* "John (J) Marshall."

MARSHALL, Maria Heléne, B.A.Hons. (1986); sculptor in steel, stone, wood and canvas; *b* India, 14 Feb., 1964; *d* of Samuel Marshall; *m. Educ.:* Millfield School, Somerset, Ardingly College, Sussex; *studied art* at Chelsea Foundation (1982), Wimbledon School of Art (1986, Glyn Williams), Ecole des Beaux Arts, Geneva. *Exhib.:* Gallerie Eric Frank (Geneva, Chicago, Basel); one-man shows: Odette Gilbert Gallery (London and Madrid), Crucral Gallery. Public sculpture 'Goddess' Princes Ct., Brompton Rd. *Address:* The Workshops, 23 Theatre St., London SW11. *Signs work:* "Maria Marshall."

MARSHALL, Richard, P.S. (1983); painter in oil, pastel, gouache, part-time lecturer; *b* Goring, Sussex, 29 Jan., 1943; *s* of Phillip James Marshall; two *d. Educ.:* West Sussex College of Art; *studied art* under William Cartledge, R.I., R.S.M.A. (1969-72), Gyula Sajo (1973-89). *Exhib.:* internationally, mixed shows, London and Sussex; one-man show, Croydon; two-man show, Arundel. *Address:* 27 Warren Cres., East Preston, W. Sussex BN16 1BJ. *Club:* Worthing Atelier Art Group. *Signs work:* "R. Marshall."

MARSHALL MALAGOLA, Dunbar, R.B.A.; painter; mem. Salon d'Automne, Paris (1972); former Sec.-General International Assoc. of Art, UNESCO; *b* Florence, 1918; *m* Daphne Chart. *Studied* at Westminster and Chelsea Schools of Art under Gertler, Meninsky, Robt. Medley, Ceri Richards. *Exhib.:* one-man shows, Grabowski, London (1961, 1964), UNESCO House (1985), Prévôt Gallery, Paris IV (1986, 1989). *Work in permanent collections:* Museums of Contemporary Art: Skoplje and Bihać Yugoslavia; Łodz, Poland; Baghdad, Iraq; Pori, Finland; Academy Savignano, Italy; University of Liverpool; Japan Artists' Centre, Tokyo; Imperial War Museum, Lambeth. *Address:* 14 Cross Hayes, Malmesbury, Wilts. *Signs work:* "DMM" or "Marshall Malagola."

MARTIN, David McLeod, R.S.W., R.G.I., D.A. (Glasgow) (1948), Professional Mem. S.S.A. (1949), Mem. Paisley Inst., Past Vice-Pres. R.S.W.; *b* Glasgow, 30 Dec., 1922; *s* of Allan McLeod Martin; *m* Isobel A.F. Smith; four *s. Educ.:* Glasgow; *studied:* Glasgow School of Art, 1940-42 (R.A.F. 1943-46), 1946-48. *Exhib.:* R.A. (1984), Bath Contemporary Art Fair (1987), numerous group shows; one-man shows in Glasgow, Edinburgh, Perth, Greenock, Stone Gallery, Newcastle and London. Work in numerous public and private collections. Special Award of merit, Robert Coloquhoun memorial art prize exhbn., Kilmarnock (1974); prizewinner, Friends of the Smith Art Gallery, Stirling (1981); May Marshall Brown award, R.S.W. Exhbn. (1984); Mabel McKinlay award, R.G.I. (1990); prizewinner, Laing Exhbn., Mall Gallery, London (1990, 1993). *Address:* The Old Schoolhouse, 53 Gilmour St., Eaglesham, Glasgow G76 0LG. *Signs work:* "DAVID M. MARTIN."

MARTIN, John, R.B.A., B.A.(Hons.), R.A. Post Dip. (1983); painter in oil, gouache and water-colour; *b* London, 25 Jan., 1957; *s* of Robert Albert Martin, gardener. *Educ.:* Houndsfield School, London; *studied art* at Exeter College of Art (Micheal Garton, Alexander MacNeigh), R.A. Schools (Peter Greenham). *Exhib.:* numerous one-man shows in England; mixed shows in France and Canada. *Work in permanent collections:* Norfolk County Collection, Art in Hospital Fund. *Address:* 4 Ship St. Gardens, Brighton, Sussex BN1 1AJ. *Signs work:* "J.M."

MARTIN, Marie-Louise, D.F.A. (1982), B.F.A. (1983); artist printmaker in etching; Director, Black Church Print Studio, Dublin; *b* Dublin, 29 Mar., 1960. *Educ.:* Teresian School, Dublin; *studied art* at National College of Art, Dublin (1978-83). *Exhib.:* R.A. (1987, 1988), R.H.A. (1985-89), R.U.A. (1987, 1988), An T-Oireachtas (1984-88), E.V.A. (1984, 1986, 1988); print exhbns. in Ireland, England, Japan, America, Germany, Spain, Taiwan; exchange print exhbns. to China, Finland, Cuba. Print prizewinner R.H.A. (1989). *Work in permanent collections:* B.P. Oil (Brussels); Kilkenny Castle; Guinness Peat Aviation; National Self portrait Coll.; Contemporary Arts Soc.; Office of Public Works. *Address:* 9 Estate Cottages, Shelbourne Rd., Dublin 4. *Club:* United Arts, Dublin. *Signs work:* see appendix.

MARTIN, Mary Sidonie, N.S. (1986), F.P.S. (1988), C.D.S. (1992); painter in oil on canvas and board, in gouache, pastel, water-colour; retd. solicitor; Chairman, N.Herts Group of Artists; *b* Haslemere, 15 Nov., 1920; *m* John Pearce Martin. *Educ.:* Warren School, Worthing; *studied art* from 1950-88 with Jack Merriott, R.I., Claude Muncaster, R.I., Aubrey Sykes, P.S., Aubrey Phillips, P.S., Christopher Assheton Stones, P.S., with Sylvia Molloy, M.A. (1978-86). *Exhib.:* numerous one-man shows at Stevenage Leisure Centre, Loggia Gallery and Hitchin Museum (1993). *Address:* 42 Benslow Rise, Hitchin, Herts. SG4 9QY. *Clubs:* F.P.S., Hitchin Art, Law Soc. Art, N.Herts. Group of Artists. *Signs work:* "Mary Pearce Martin."

MARTIN, Nicholas Gerard, B.A. (Hons.) (1980); artist in oil-stained acrylics, paper collage and paper mosaics, mural mosaics; educational project artist,

Glyndbourne Touring Opera (1987); *b* Edinburgh, 5 July, 1957; *s* of James Martin; *m* Marion Brandis; two *s*. *Educ.:* Edinburgh Academy; *studied art* at Edinburgh College of Art (1975-80, Ian Davidson). *Exhib.:* R.S.A., Traverse Theatre, Gardner Art Centre, Brighton Polytechnic A.G., Royal Pavilion A.G., Brighton, Dryden St. Gallery, Horsham Arts Centre, Royal Festival Hall A.G., Ramsgate Library Gallery. *Work in permanent collections:* S.E. Arts, Royal Pavilion A.G., Forestry Commission, Edinburgh, Royal Festival Hall, Towner A.G., mosaic mural for Channel Tunnel, Ashford Library (1990), Herne Bay Sea Front Mosaic Fountain (1993), Govan Shipyard Mural, Glasgow (1993). *Educational residencies* with: Glyndebourne Touring Opera, Destafford School, Hextable School, Spinney School. *Address:* 2 College Rd., Brighton BN2 1JA. *Signs work:* "Nicholas Martin."

MARTIN, Pierre Noël; painter calligrapher but now works mainly in wood, metal and perspex creating "Kinetic" illusions on wall-hanging panels, also sculptor of "linear" sculptures; *b* London, 18 Dec., 1920. *Educ.:* a London Technical Inst. (as engineer); R.A.F. (1940-46). *Exhib.:* Hampstead Artists Council, F.P.S., Mall Gallery, Chelsea Artists Gallery, Seen Gallery, Bramptons Gallery, Gallery Petite. *Work in private and public collections:* Gt. Britain, Europe, Israel, the Far East, and U.S.A., British television and universities. *Address:* 17 Princes Ave., London N10 3LS. *Signs work:* "Pierre Noël Martin" and see appendix.

MARTIN, Timothy Stuart, Hon. Major, Alderman, F.R.S.A., A.Coll.H., M.R.S.T., C. and G., Lond.; illustrator; Art and Crafts master, Queen Elizabeth's Grammar School for Boys, Mansfield (1931-73); Hon. Sec., National Soc. for Art Education, E. Midland Area (1937-52); Chairman (1953-56); advisor, C. and G. (1952-73); sometime examiner, N.S.A.M. and U.L.C.I.; *b* Bolsover, 18 Mar., 1908; *s* of John Martin; *m* Ann Johnson; one *s*, one *d*. *Educ.:* University College, Nottingham; *studied art* at Chesterfield and Nottingham. *Work repro.:* Parthenon, Building Times, Illustrated Builder and Carpenter; Editor, Boys' Practical Aid (1937-40). *Address:* Westwood, 323 Chesterfield Rd. South, Mansfield, Notts. NG19 7ES. *Club:* Conservative. *Signs work:* "T. Stuart Martin," v for u.

MARTINA, Toni, B.A. (Hons.) (1978), Prix de Rome scholar (1987), R.E. (elected 1992); many prizes and awards including 1st prize Dept. of Transport National Art Competition (1992), Christie's Contemporary Art award at R.A. (1987), N.Y. National Academy of Design Summer Exhbn. (1986), Lloyds Bank Printmakers award at R.A. (1986); painter/printmaker; *b* London, 7 Mar., 1956; *m* Tessa; one *d*. *Studied art* at Harrow College of Art (1974-75), Kingston Polytechnic (1975-78), Central School of Art (1986). *Exhib.:* Europe and the U.K. including R.A. Summer Show, R.E., Barbican Centre, British School at Rome, Royal Festival Hall, National Academy of Design N.Y., Mall Galleries. *Work in permanent collections:* Cambridge libraries, Plymouth Museum, Rochdale Museum, Oldham Museum, Dept. of Transport. *Address:* 302 Plumstead Common Rd., London SE18 2RT. *Signs work:* "Toni Martina."

MARX, Enid C. D., R.D.I. (1942), F.C.S.D., Hon. F.R.C.A.; designer to the Board of Trade Utility Furniture Design Com.; *b* 20 Oct., 1902; *d* of Robert Marx, consulting engineer. *Educ.:* Roedean School, Central School, Royal College of Art. *Exhib.:* Burlington House, Paris, Leipzig, Boston Museum. *Official purchases:* Arts Council, V. & A., Leipzig, U.S.A., Ontario, Canada. *Works repro.:* in Graphis, International Textiles, etc. *Publications:* Popular and Traditional Art in England (with Margaret Lambert); Victorian Scrapbook (with Margaret Lambert); twelve children's books. Designed the definitive stamps on the accession of H.M. Queen Elizabeth II, Christmas stamps (1976). *Address:* 39 Thornhill Rd., Barnsbury Square, London N1 1JS.

MASCO, Pam; artist in oil and water-colour; *b* Springfield, Mass., 19 Mar., 1953; *m* John Heseltine. *Educ.:* Westfield High School; *studied art* at School of the Boston Museum of Fine Art (1971-76 and 1979, John Burns, Joseph Capacietti, Tim Nichols) (Grad. Dip.). *Exhib.:* Bourne Gallery, Reigate (1983-current), Clarendon Gallery, London (1986), David Messum, London (1990), R.B.A. (1992), R.W.S. (1992), Sunday Times Singer Friedlander Water-colour (1992), Priory Gallery, Cheltenham (1993). *Work in private collections:* Boston, N.Y., Lexington, Kentucky. *Work repro.:* illustrations for all major London publishers (1981-88). *Address:* Keepers, Norwood La., Graffham, W. Sussex GU28 0QQ. *Signs work:* "P. MASCO."

MASON, Cyril Harry, M.C.S.D. (1966), F.C.S.D. (1979), M.S.T.D. (1966), A.R.B.S.A. (1983), R.B.S.A. (1986); landscape and marine painter in water-colour and oil; chartered designer; *b* Halesowen, Worcs., 30 May, 1928; *m* Barbara Hill; one *s*, one *d*. *Educ.:* Halesowen Grammar School. *Exhib.:* R.I., R.W.S., R.S.M.A., R.B.S.A., R.C.A., R.W.A., Clarges Gallery, London and local midland galleries. *Address:* Bank Cottage, Shenstone, nr. Kidderminster, Worcs. DY10 4DP. *Club:* B'ham Water-colour Soc. *Signs work:* until 1986 "Mason"; after 1986 "Cyril H. Mason."

MASON, Michael, A.T.D., D.A. (Manc.) (1956), Fellow in Sculpture B.S. Rome (1976), A.R.B.S. (1992); sculptor in ceramics/bronze; PR/lecturer sculpture, Manchester University; *b* Lancs., 1 June, 1935; *m* Barbara; one *s*, one *d*. *Studied art* at Manchester College of Art, British School, Rome. *Exhib.:* Whitworth A.G., Serpentine Gallery, etc. *Work in permanent collections:* V. & A., A.C.G.B., Zagreb A.G., A.V.A.F. Caracas. *Address:* 89 Park Rd., Hale, Altrincham, Ches. WA15 9LE. *Signs work:* "Michael Mason" or "M.M." in rectangle.

MASON, Richard, M.F.P.S. (1969); sculptor of constructions in metals, wood and perspex, painter in oil and acrylic; *b* Ipswich, 20 June, 1931. *Educ.:* Ipswich Grammar School. *Exhib.:* one-man show: Woodbridge A.G. (1967); regular exhib. with F.P.S. Trends and Ipswich Art Club. *Address:* Upland Gate, 39 Bishops Hill, Ipswich 1P3 8EW. *Clubs:* Ipswich Art, F.P.S., Felixstowe Art Group. *Signs work:* "Richard Mason."

MASTER, Jean, R.O.I. (1987); painter in oil and acrylic; *b* London; *m*; two *s*, one *d*. *Educ.:* St. Joan of Arc Convent, Rickmansworth, Herts.; *studied art* at St. Martin's School of Art (Kenneth Martin), also in Hamburg under Prof. Karl Kluth. *Exhib.:* Royal West of England Academy, Bristol, Mall Galleries, London, Llewellyn Alexander, London, and other mixed exhbns. in London and Bristol. *Address:* Eaton House, Clifton Down, Bristol BS8 3HT. *Signs work:* see appendix.

MATANIA, Franco, U.A., S.G.F.A., S.E.A.; First prize 'Talens' award Mall Galleries (1984), Soc. Equestrian Art prize for drawing (1986, 1988), United Soc. of Artists award (1993); artist in pastels and drawing mediums; *b* Naples, 1922 (British subject 1935); *s* of Mario Matania, business executive; *m* Dona Carmen Rodriguez (Spanish); one *s* Luis, Arch., one *d* Mina, B.A.(Hons). *Educ.:* Salesian College; *studied art* at studio of artist relative, the late Fortunino Matania, R.I. (Chevalier): distinguished artist (Imperial War Museum: Benizet, etc.); student apprentice 1947-55 after military service. *Exhib.:* mixed shows,

R.I., R.O.I., N.S., P.S., U.A., S.G.A., S.E.A.; one-man shows, Campbell and Franks Fine Art, Bajazzo Gallery, Marlborough, Alpine Gallery, Guild Fine Arts; (abroad 1980's), Galleria Maitani, Orvieto, Italy, Galleria Treves, Milan, Italy, Galleria Alandaluz, Granada, Spain, Tanisia Gallery, N.Y. *Work in permanent collections:* Centro Hogar, Granada, Knight Inc. Conference Centre, Boston, Industria Marmo Design of Italy. *Address:* Little Venice Studio, 20 Clarendon Gdns., Maida Vale, London W9 1AZ. *Signs work:* see appendix.

MATCHWICK, Beryl A., Hon. R.M.S.; artist in oil and water-colour; *b* London, 1907; *d* of W. Guildford Matchwick; *m* Anthony M. Tew. *Educ.:* privately; *studied art* at Redhill School of Art under W. Todd-Brown, R.O.I. *Exhib.:* R.A., R.I., R.M.S., R.S.A, Paris Salon, Hull, etc. *Address:* 8 Castle Ct., River Pk., Marlborough, Wilts. SN8 1NH. *Signs work:* "Matchwick."

MATHESON, Andrew Kenneth Mackenzie, D.A., R.B.S.A., Cert. Ed.; artist/ potter and teacher works mainly in stoneware/porcelain — from studio in Lichfield, Staffs.; *s* of Farquhar Mackenzie Matheson, accountant. *Educ.:* Riland Bedford High School, Sutton Coldfield; *studied art* at Madeley College of Education (1968-71), Grays School of Art, Aberdeen (1974-79), Dip. in Art (1978), postgrad. Dip. in Art (1979). *Exhib.:* in Scotland and England. *Address:* 7 Driffold, Sutton Coldfield, W. Midlands. *Clubs:* R.B.S.A., B'ham Art Circle, Midland Potters Assoc. *Signs work:* "Andrew K.M. Matheson" and see appendix.

MATHEWS, Binny; Greenshield Foundation Award (1989); painter in oil, specialising in portraiture, tutor; *b* Dorset, 25 June, 1960. *Studied art* at Bournemouth and Poole College of Art (1977-78), West Surrey College of Art (1978-81), Brighton Polytechnic (1981-82). *Exhib.:* N.E.A.C., Hunting Award, R.P., Mall Galleries, N.P.G. (1981, 1982 1985, 1988, 1990), R.A., etc., numerous one-man shows in the provinces and London. *Work in permanent collections:* La Sainte Union College, Southampton; National Trust, Castle Drogo; Seagrams, British Gas. *Address:* 13 Crescent Pl., Brompton Rd., London SW3 2EA. *Club:* Chelsea Arts. *Signs work:* "Binny Mathews."

MATTAROZZI DI THARASH, Mirella (Mirice Janàcêk); artist-painter, fine arts professor, writer; Diploma, Istituto Belle Arti di Bologna, Accademia di Belle Arti di Bologna; *b* Bologna; *d* of Adelmo. *Exhib.:* Italy, Europe, South America. *Work in permanent collections:* museums, Palazzo Vecchio, Firenze, Castello Sforzesco, Milano, Museo S. Matteo, Pisa, etc. Associate of Incisori d'Italia (I.D.IT.), Ex Libristi d'Italia (E.L.D.IT.). *Publications:* Il Comanducci, Annuario Internazionale di Belle Arti (Berlin), Guida all'arte Italiana, Who's Who in Europe, ed. Feniks, etc., Knight of the Tommaso da Vico Order; Academician of the Accademia dei 500, Rome. Lady-in-waiting of the Corporazione Internazionale della Stella Croce d'Argento (C.I.S.C.A.) dei Cavalieri del Bene. *Address:* via Sigismondo n°33, Cattolica Forlì, Italy.

MATTHEWS, Peter Jeffrey, N.D.D. (1962), R.E. (1983); artist/printmaker in water-colour, etching and lithography; Senior Lecturer in Printmaking, Wimbledon School of Art; *b* London, 29 July, 1942; *s* of Arthur Matthews; *m* Caroline Moore; one *s*, one *d. Studied art* at Ealing School of Art (1958-62). *Exhib.:* numerous mixed shows in G.B. and abroad. *Work in permanent collections:* V. & A., Bibliotheque Royal, Brussels, Albertini Museum, Vienna. *Address:* 1 Manor Rd., London SW20 9AE. *Signs work:* "Peter Matthews."

MATTHEWS, Sharyn Susan, S.W.A.; self taught artist in water-colour, acrylic, gouache, oil; *b* Bristol, 13 Jan., 1951; *d* of Ralph Valentine-Daines, stonemason; *m* Graham Matthews; one *s*, one *d. Educ.:* Howard of Effingham.

Exhib.: numerous one-man shows at home and abroad, including Mall Galleries. Work permanently on show Park Lane Fine Arts, Ashtead, Surrey. *Address:* 19 Longdown La. North, Ewell, Surrey KT17 3HY. *Signs work:* "Sharyn M."

MAYER, Charlotte, A.R.C.A. (1952), F.R.B.S. (1980); sculptor in bronze, steel and wood; *b* Prague, 4 Jan., 1929; *d* of Frederick Mayer; *m* Geoffrey Salmon; one *s*, two *d*. *Studied art* at Goldsmiths' College School of Art (1945-49, Wilson Parker and Roberts Jones), R.C.A. (1949-52, Frank Dobson). *Exhib.:* R.A., V. & A., Iveagh Bequest Kenwood, Bear Lane Gallery, Oxford, Bruton Gallery. *Work in permanent collections:* Wadham College, Oxford; Manchester College, Oxford; City of London; Merseyside C.C.; Basingstoke and N.Hants. Health Authority; Cement and Concrete Assoc.; B.P. *Publications:* illustrated, The Mystery of Creation by Lealman and Robinson; Patronage and Practice, Tate Gallery Liverpool. *Address:* 6 Bloomfield Rd., Highgate, London N6 4ET. *Signs work:* "C.M." or "Mayer."

MAYGER, Chris Henry, R.S.M.A. (1976); marine artist in pencil, gouache and oil; *b* 20 Apr., 1918; *s* of the late Frank Mayger, ornamental plasterer; *m* Matilda Hammond; one *d*. *Studied art* at Camberwell School of Art (1934-38) under Eric Fraser and Cosmo Clark. *Exhib.:* R.S.M.A., Greenwich Village Workshop, U.S.A. *Work in private collections:* in England, Scotland, Canada, Chicago and California; also National Maritime Museum London. *Work repro.:* Marine Art of Chris Mayger (Peacock Press, U.S.A.), book jackets. *Address:* 8 Ashley Rd., Hildenborough, Tonbridge, Kent. TN11 9EB. *Signs work:* "Chris Mayger."

MAZZOLI, Dino (Leopoldo); artist in oil and water-colour; *b* Terni, Italy, 10 May, 1935; *s* of Gino Mazzoli, artist. *Educ.:* Oriani College, Rome; also studied at Villa Massimo, Rome (1953-54, Renato Guttuso), Villa Medici, Rome (1954-56), Eastbourne College of Art (Peter Berrisford) and with Dorothy Swain, R.C.A. *Exhib.:* Don Orione, Farnesina, Rome, Heathfield A.G., E. Grinstead Autumn Show, Towner Museum and A.G., Eastbourne, Brighton Museum and A.G., Star Gallery, Lewes, Blackheath Gallery, etc. *Work in permanent collection:* Premier Gallery, Eastbourne. *Address:* 24-26 South St., Eastbourne, E. Sussex BN21 4XB. Mem. of the Eastbourne Group. *Signs work:* "D. Mazzoli."

MEACHER, Neil, N.D.D. (1955), A.R.C.A. (1960), R.I. (1981); artist/illustrator in ink and water-colour, coloured pencils, teacher; senior lecturer, Ealing C.H.E.; *b* Sandwich, Kent, 20 Dec., 1934; *s* of Reginald John Meacher, architect; *m* Margaret Joyce; one *s*, one *d*. *Educ.:* Sir Roger Manwood's Grammar School; *studied art* at Canterbury College of Art (1951-55), R.C.A. (1957-60, Humphrey Spender, John Drummond, Julian Trevelyan, Edward Ardizzone, Alistair Grant, Geoffrey Ireland). *Exhib.:* Rye Gallery, John Neville Gallery, New Ashgate Gallery, Edwin Pollard Gallery, Mall Galleries. *Address:* 7 Mervyn Rd., Shepperton, Middx. TW17 9HG. *Clubs:* R.I., Assoc. of Illustrators. *Signs work:* "NEIL MEACHER."

MEADOWS, Anthony William, A.R.M.S. (1984); self-taught painter and illustrator in oil, wood engraving; *b* Aldershot, 28 Aug., 1957; *m* Dawn Hardy (jeweller). *Educ.:* Fanshawe School, Ware. *Exhib.:* R.A., R.I., R.M.S. and several one-man shows. *Work in permanent collection:* Hertford Museum. *Address:* 27 Victoria Rd., Oswestry, Salop. SY11 2HT. *Signs work:* "A. W. Meadows".

MEDHURST, Doreen, A.R.M.S. (1987), S.B.A. (1989), S.W.A. (1989); self taught painter in acrylic and oil; *b* London, 5 Aug., 1929; *d* of Sydney Holmes (decd.); *m* Cyril Medhurst; two *s. Educ.:* Sydenham High School. *Exhib.:* R.M.S., S.B.A., S.W.A., Llewellyn Alexander Gallery, Alfriston Gallery, Elan Art Centre, and several one-man shows. *Address:* 45 Blenheim Rd., Orpington, Kent BR6 9BQ. *Signs work:* "D Medhurst."

MEDLEY, Robert, C.B.E., R.A.; painter in oil; *b* London, 19 Dec., 1905. *Educ.:* Gresham's School; *studied art* at Slade School of Fine Art (1923-25). *Exhib.:* Whitechapel A.G. (1963), Oxford Museum of Modern Art (1984). *Work in permanent collections:* Tate Gallery, Birmingham, York, etc. *Publications:* 'Drawn from the Life' a memoir; 'Samson Agonistes' with 26 screen prints. *Address:* 1 Charterhouse, London EC1M 6AN. *Signs work:* "Robt. Medley."

MEESON, Philip, N.D.D. (1951), A.T.D. (1952), Travelling Scholarship (1952-53), F.S.A.E. (1966), F.R.S.A. (1969); artist in oil, pen and wash and art teacher; *b* Liverpool, 14 Feb., 1932; *s* of F. J. Meeson, representative. *Educ.:* Holt High School, Liverpool; *studied art* at Liverpool College of Art under N. M. Bell, A.R.C.A., W. L. Stevenson, O.B.E. *Exhib.:* Walker A. G., Liverpool. *Address:* The University of Brighton, Dept. of Art and Technology in Education, Falmer, Brighton, Sussex. *Signs work:* "P. Meeson."

MELAMED-ADAMS, Alicia, U.A. (1965), Gold medallist, Academie Italia belle arti el Lavore (1981), Art in Edinburgh (1984), Gallery Internationale, Paris (1984); artist in oil; *b* Borystaw, Poland, 26 Sept., 1927; *d* of Jzydre Goldschlag, oil mining engineer; *m*; one *s. Educ.:* St. Martin's School of Art (1960-63); Academie Chaumiere, Paris; Sir John Cass College of Art. *Exhib.:* Foyles A.G., R.B.A., Augustine Gallery, Flower Paintings of Today, Flower Paintings of the World, 100 Years of British Drawing, Galerie Solombo, Paris (1987-89), Crypt Gallery, London, Hunting Group, Mermaid Theatre (1991), Real Art Gallery (1992), Intaglio Gallery, Manchester (1993), Crocodile Gallery (1993), Leicester City Gallery (1993). *Work in private collections:* Brazil, Paris, London. *Address:* 17 Edmunds Walk, London N2 0HU. *Signs work:* "Alicia Melamed."

MELLAND, Sylvia, R.E.; painter-etcher; *b* Altrincham; *d* of Brian Melland, M.D., M.B. (Lond.); *m* Brian Mertian Melland; one *s. Educ.:* Altrincham Grammar School; *studied art* at Manchester College of Art, Byam Shaw, London, Euston Road, Central School (Graphics). *Exhib.:* one-man shows, Wertheim and Jackson's Galleries, Manchester, Zwemmer Gallery, London, Galleria S. Stefano, Venice, Galerie Maurice Bridel, Lausanne, Galerie Bürdeke, Zürich, Agi Katz Fine Art, London. *Work purchased:* Rutherston Collection, S. London A.G., N.Y. Library, Leeds A.G., Brighton Museum, Coventry Educ. Council, Twickenham Educ. Council, Greenwich Library, Ferens A.G., Hull, V. & A., R.A. (Stott Foundation), Talmuseum des Münstertals, Switzerland, New Hall College, Cambridge and in private collections here and abroad. *Address:* 68 Bedford Gdns., London W8. *Signs work:* prints, "Sylvia Melland," oils, "S.M."

MELLOR, Mary, LL.B., A.K.C. (1961), Called to Bar (1962), B.A. Graphics (1984), M.F.P.S.; artist in oil, teacher; *b* Swansea, 1939; *d* of David M. Clement, C.B.E., F.C.A.; *m* His Hon. Judge David Mellor; two *d. Educ.:* Bolton School, Newcastle-on-Tyne Church High School, Sutton High School, G.P.D.S.T., King's College, London, Inner Temple; *studied art* at Norwich School of Art (1979-84). *Exhib.:* Norwich Artists' Group, Norwich Gallery (Norfolk Inst. of Art and Design), Dixon Gallery, London, Loggia Gallery, London, Castle

Museum, Norwich (Norfolk Art Now), Advice Arcade Gallery, Norwich. *Address:* The Old Hall, Mulbarton, Norwich. *Signs work:* "Mary Mellor."

MELLOR, Pamela, F.R.S.A.; painter in oil, writer; Hon. Sec., Chelsea Art Society (1971-1978); Com., Armed Forces Art Society; *b* Sydney, Australia; *d* of Capt. R. C. F. Creer, R.N. retd. and Eulalie Henty; *m* Lt.Col. Gerard Mellor, Royal Signals, retd. *Educ.:* at home and abroad. *Exhib.:* U.A., R.W.S., R.M.S., Artists of Chelsea, Chelsea Art Soc., Leighton House, Ridley Art Soc., Armed Forces Art Soc., Dowmunt Gallery, Qantas Gallery. *Work in permanent collections:* H.R.H. The Prince of Wales, The Agent General of N.S.W., The Agent General of Queensland and other private collections. *Publication:* author, The Mystery of X5 (pub. William Kimber). *Address:* 44 Stanford Rd., Kensington, London W8 5PZ. *Signs work:* "Pam Mellor."

MENDEL, Renée; sculptor and potter; *b* Elmshorn, 22 Sept., 1908; *d* of Oscar Mendel, leather merchant. *Educ.:* Lichtwark School, Hamburg; universities of Berlin, Frankfurt, Paris; *studied art* at Berlin under Ernest de Fiori, Paris under Pablo Gargallo. *Exhib.:* Salon d'automne, Paris, R.A., Hertford House; one-man show at Royal Copenhagen Porcelain Co., 6 Bond St., Heal & Son Exhbn. Sculpture for the Home, Camden Arts Centre, Royal Exchange (1977). *Work repro.:* The Studio, Evening Standard, Semaine à Paris, Artistes d'aujourd'hui, Hampstead and Highgate Express and News, Hornsey Journal. Sculpture of 'Beatles' sold by Sotheby's (21 May 81), Sculpture of James Joyce, N.P.G. (Feb. 1987). Dm. H. Winsley-Stolz, S.P. (bronze portrait 1989). *Address:* 27 Onslow Gdns., London N10 3JT. *Signs work:* "Renée Mendel."

MENDOZA, June, R.P., R.O.I.; portrait painter; *b* Melbourne, Australia; musician parents; *m* Keith Mackrell; one *s*, three *d. Educ.:* Lauriston Girls' School, Australia; *studied art* at St. Martin's School of Art. *Work in permanent collections:* government; H.M. Forces; industry; commerce; medicine; academic and legal professions; theatre; sport, and private collections internationally. *Portraits include:* H.M. The Queen; H.R.H. Prince Charles; H.R.H. Princess of Wales; H.M. Queen Mother; Mrs. Margaret Thatcher; Prime Ministers of Australia and Fiji; Presidents of Philippines and Iceland; series of musicians inc. Sutherland, Solti, Menuhin. *Group portraits include:* House of Commons in Session; Council of Royal College of Surgeons; House of Representatives, Canberra. Hon. D.Litt. Bath University; A.O.(Australia); lectures; T.V. *Address:* 34 Inner Pk. Rd., London SW19 6DD. *Signs work:* "MENDOZA" and see appendix.

MENZIES, Gordon William, D.A.; Josef Sekalski Award for Printmaking; Head of Pottery Dept., Community Centre, Edinburgh; established Iona Pottery, 1982 (Workshop/Gallery) with own ceramics, engravings, landscapes; *b* Motherwell, Scotland, 9 Jan., 1950; *s* of David M. Menzies, storekeeper. *Educ.:* Dalziel High School, Motherwell; *studied art* at Duncan of Jordanstone College of Art, Dundee (1969-73) under Sheila Green, Ron Stenberg; Atelier 17, Paris (1974) under S. W. Hayter. *Exhib.:* Edinburgh, Printmakers Workshop, Compass Gallery, Glasgow, Montpelier Art Institute, France, R.S.A., S.S.A., Edinburgh, many others within Edinburgh and surrounding area. *Publication:* books illustrated mainly within Children's Educational area. *Address:* Lorne Cottage, Isle of Iona, Argyll PA76 6SJ.

MEREDITH, Julian Nelson; artist in woodcut print; *b* Bath, 4 Mar., 1952; *s* of Bernard Nelson Meredith, M.A., A.R.I.B.A.; *m* Jane; three *d. Educ.:* Clifton College; *studied art* at Exeter College of Art (1972, 1974). *Exhib.:* Mall Galleries (1988, 1989), R.A. Summer Exhbn. (1989), Henry Brett Galleries

(1989). *Address:* c/o Jonathan Meredith, 1 Clifton Villas, Balmoral Rd., St. Andrews, Bristol 6. *Signs work:* "J.Meredith."

MEREDITH, Norman, A.R.C.A.; illustrator; tutor University of Aberystwyth (1935) and St. Martin's School of Art; war service M. of A.P. (Farnborough); *s* of Jane Ann Meredith; *m* Violet Mary Brant. *Studied art* at Liverpool College of Art and R.C.A.; travelling scholar. *Exhib.:* frequently at Chris Beetles Gallery, London SW1, since 1984. *Official purchases:* H.R.H. The Duke of Gloucester, etc. Textiles for Moygashel, Crowson Fabrics; designs for Metal Box Co., greetings cards, gift wraps, nursery pictures for Brunott of Holland; nursery china. *Work repro.:* Punch, Tatler, Bystander; books illus. most British publishers, strip cartoonist. *Hobbies:* Recording piano music, photography, travel, (two world tours). *Address:* 35 Gayfere Rd., Stoneleigh, Epsom, Surrey. *Signs work:* "NORMAN MEREDITH."

MERTON, John Ralph, M.B.E. (1942); painter; *b* 7 May, 1913; *s* of late Sir Thomas Merton, K.B.E., F.R.S.; *m* 1939 Viola Penelope von Bernd; two *d* (and one *d* decd.). *Educ.:* Eton; Balliol Coll. Oxford. Served War of 1939-45 (MBE); Air Photo reconnaissance research, Lieut-Col. 1944. *Works include:* Mrs Daphne Wall (1948); The Artist's daughter Sarah (1949); altar piece (1952); The Countess of Dalkeith (1958); A Myth of Delos (1959); Clarissa (1960); Mrs Julian Sheffield (1970); Sir Charles Evans (1973); Iona Duchess of Argyll (1982); Sir David Piper (1985, N.P.G.); H.R.H. The Princess of Wales in Cardiff City hall (1987); Professor James Meade, Nobel Prize Winner (1987); H.M. The Queen (1989) as head of the Order of Merit. Head Master of Eton (1990), Triple portrait of The Duke of Grafton for the National Portrait Gallery (1992), Paul Nitze (1992); Legion of Merit (USA) 1945. *Recreations:* music, making things, underwater photography. *Addresss:* Pound House, Oare, nr. Marlborough, Wilts. SN8 4JA.

MESSELET, Jean; Conservateur honoraire du Musée Nissim de Camondo; *b* Paris, 22 Feb., 1898. *Educ.:* Lycée Louis le Grand; *studied art* at Ecole du Louvre. *Publications:* monographs on French painters; articles in Archives de l'Art Francais, Beaux-Arts, Bulletin Monumental, Bulletin des Musées, etc. *Address:* 2 rue Léonce-Reynaud, Paris XVIe.

METCALFE, Muriel; artist in oil and water-colour; *b* Leyburn, Wensleydale, 1 Oct., 1910; *d* of Ernest Metcalfe, master gilder; *m* Fred Lawson, artist; one *d*. *Studied art* at King's College, Newcastle University (1926, Profs. Dickie and Hatton, Louisa Hodgson). *Exhib.:* one-man and mixed shows 1929-89: Laing, Newcastle, Leeds, Wakefield, Bradford, London, Scarborough, Kendal. *Work in permanent collections:* Temple Newsam Leeds City A.G., Dewsbury, Whitby, Darlington, Wakefield. *Publications:* illustrated, James Kirkup's The Cosmic Shape, and The Creation. *Address:* 'Artists House', Castle Bolton, Leyburn, N. Yorks. DL8 4EX. *Signs work:* "M.M." or "Muriel Metcalfe."

METSON, Peter, M.A. (1975), D.A. (1974), Andrew Grant Award (1975), P.G.C.E. (1976), M.F.P.S. (1986); artist in oil, acrylic, tempera, mixed media, clay (sculptures), teacher; Head of 3D Studies, Woodhouse College, London; *b* Chelmsford, 24 Dec., 1950; *s* of Peter Metson, specialist in radar and electronics; *m* Diane (divorced 1991). *Educ.:* Westlands Secondary Modern; *studied art* at Edinburgh College of Art (1970-74, Elizabeth Blackadder, Sir Robin Philipson, John Houston). *Exhib.:* Barbican Centre (1984), Mall Galleries (1978), Bloomsbury Galleries (1989), F.P.S. Trends, Loggia Gallery (1982, 1989, 1991 one-man shows), R.A. Summer Exhbn. (1991), Pleasance Galleries, Edinburgh Festival (1986), Playhouse Theatre, Harlow (1988-89). *Work in permanent* *collections:* Grant Inst. of Geology, Edinburgh University, Edinburgh College of Art, Cambridgeshire Libraries Picture Loan Collection, Epping Forest District Museum Contemporary Art Collection. *Awards:* Cert. of Excellence for Painting, Art Horizons, New York (1989), Cert. of Excellence for Outstanding Achievement in Painting, Artitudes, New York (international competitions), Daniela Jesson Fine Art prize for landscape study (1990), Most Promising Artist award, Eastern Open (1991). *Address:* 7 Saxon Ct., Bull La., Maldon, Essex CM9 7HS. *Clubs:* Friend of the R.A., F.P.S. *Signs work:* "Graham Peter Metson", recent work "Peter Metson."

MICAH, Lisa, M.F.P.S. (1989), N.A.P.A. prize (1988); artist in acrylic; Council mem. Cambridge Drawing Soc. (1988-91), Consultant, Galeries d'Attente, London (1989-91); *m* M.J. Chapman, A.C.I.Arb.; three *d. Educ.:* in Europe and Africa. *Exhib.:* solo-shows: Lion Yard, Cambridge (1987), Peppin Brown, Whittlesford (1988), Loggia, London (1991), Confluences, Lyon (1993). *Work in permanent collections:* private: Belgium, England, Finland, France and Switzerland; public: Clinique de Montplaisir, France. *Address:* BP19, 69881 Jonage Cédex, France. *Club:* Farmers' London. *Signs work:* "L. Micah."

MICHIE, David Alan Redpath; painter; Prof. Emeritus, Heriot Watt University (1991); Head, School of Drawing and Painting, Edinburgh College of Art (1982-90); *b* St. Raphael, Var, France, 1928; *s* of the late James Michie; *m* Eileen Michie; two *d. Educ.:* Hawick High School; *studied painting* at Edinburgh College of Art (1946-1953), Italy (1953-1954.). *Exhib.:* one-man shows, Mercury Gallery, London (1967, 1969, 1971, 1974, 1980, 1983, 1992), Mercury Gallery, Edinburgh (1986), Lothian Region Chambers (1977), The Scottish Gallery, Edinburgh (1980), Kasteel de Hooge Vuursche, Netherlands (1991). *Work in permanent collection:* Scottish National Gallery of Modern Art. *Address:* 17 Gilmour Rd., Edinburgh EH16 5NS. *Signs work:* "David Michie."

MICKLEWRIGHT, Robert Flavell, D.F.A. (London), R.W.S.; graphic designer, illustrator, painter in oil, water-colour; *b* Staffordshire, 1923. *Studied art* at Croydon School of Art (1939), Wimbledon School of Art (1947-49), Slade School (1949-52). *Work in permanent collections:* regular exhibitor in London, provinces and U.S.A.; pictures in private collections. *Publications:* illustrated numerous books. Work reproduced in the following reference books: Artists of a Certain Line (Bodley Head), Designing a Book Jacket (Studio), Designers in Britain, 5, 6 7 (Andre Deutsch), Drawing for Radio Times (Bodley Head), Illustrators at Work (Studio), Royal Academy Illustrated. *Address:* Mount Hill, Mogador, Tadworth, Surrey 20KT 7HZ.

MIDDLETON, Michael, A.R.E. (1981), R.E. (1986), Dip.A.D. (1971), H.D.A. (1974); lecturer/painter/printmaker in oil, water-colour, etching, woodcut; teaches print-making, art history, Colchester Inst. School of Art and Design; *b* Louth, Lincs., 25 June, 1950; *s* of Roy Middleton. *Educ.:* Heron Wood, Aldershot; *studied art* at West Surrey College of Art and Design (1966-68), Sheffield Polytechnic (1968-71), Chelsea School of Art (1973-74). *Exhib.:* R.A., R.E., and several one-man shows. *Work in permanent collections:* Harlow Town Corp., R.E. *Address:* 104 Maldon Rd., Colchester, Essex CO3 3AP. *Signs work:* "M. Middleton."

MIDDLETON, Michael Humfrey, C.B.E., F.C.S.D., Hon. F.R.I.B.A., Hon. F.L.I.; Assistant Editor/Editor of Picture Post (1949-53); Lilliput (1953-54); House and Garden (1955-57); Deputy Director, the Civic Trust (1957-69), Director (1969-86); art critic, Spectator (1946-56); *b* London, 1 Dec., 1917; *s* of Humfrey Middleton; *m* Julie Harrison; one *s*, two *d. Educ.:* King's School,

Canterbury; Heatherley's. *Publications:* Group Practice in Design; Man Made the Town; Cities in Transition; contributor to many periodicals, etc., on art, design and environment. *Address:* 84 Sirdar Rd., London W11 4EG.

MIDDLETON, Renée, S.G.F.A., S.B.A., S.W.A.; Rexel prize winner (1984); artist in pen and ink specialising in natural forms of stipple and/or line; *b* 19 Mar., 1920. *Educ.:* Old Palace School for Girls, Croydon. *Exhib.:* R.B.A., S.G.A., 'Flowers and Gardens' Mall Galleries and Central Hall, Westminster; three-man show, Fairfield Halls, Croydon. *Address:* Merryhill Corner, Thakeham, W. Sussex RH20 3HB. *Clubs:* S.G.A., S.B.A., S.W.A., local Sussex Socs. *Signs work:* see appendix.

MIDGLEY, Julia, Dip.A.D. (1969); mem.: P.M.C., Manchester Academy of Fine Arts (Vice President); painter and printmaker; senior lecturer, Liverpool John Moores University; *b* 1948; *m*; two *s*. *Studied art* at Northwich School of Art and Design (1965-66), Manchester College of Art and Design (1966-69). *Exhib.* Manchester Academy annually since 1979, R.A. (1983, 1986, 1987), R.E. (1987, 1990), Business A.G's. (1981, 1982, 1983, 1985), New Academy (1987-91), National Print Exhbns. Blackpool (1979, 1981, 1985), Chelsea Arts Club, P.M.C. Exhbns. (1984-93). Represented by New Academy Gallery, London. *Address:* 140 Chester Rd., Northwich, Ches. CW8 4AW. *Club:* Chelsea Arts. *Signs work:* "Julia Midgley."

MIERS, Christopher John Penrose, A.R.B.A. (1985), R.B.A. (1986); artist in oil and water-colour; Hon. Secretary, Armed Forces Art Soc. (1982-87); Secretary, The Arts Club (1986-90); Trustee, The Water-colour Foundation (1988-91); *b* 26 Sept., 1941; *s* of Lt. Col. P.R.P. Miers, R.A.; *m* (1) 1967 Judith Hoare; one *s*, one *d*.; (2) 1993 Liza Thynne. *Educ.:* Wellington College and R.M.A. Sandhurst. *Exhib.:* R.A., R.B.A., N.E.A.C., The Minories, Colchester (1964), Ansdell Gallery, Kensington (1967, 1968), Fortescue Swann, Brompton Rd. (1976), C.D. Soar & Son, Launceston Pl. (1986, 1988), Sally Hunter Fine Art (1990, 1993), Mall galleries (1991). *Work in permanent collection:* Imperial War Museum. *Address:* 114 Bishop's Mans., Bishop's Park Rd., London SW6 6DY. *Clubs:* Arts, Chelsea Arts, Fadeaways. *Signs work:* "C. MIERS" or "C.M."

MILES, June, R.W.A.; painter; Mem. Penwith Society of Artists and Newlyn Society of Artists; *b* London, 4 July, 1924; *d* of William George Hilary Miles, Lt.-Col. Royal Marines (decd.); *m* Paul Mount, sculptor; one *s*, two *d* by previous marriage. *Educ.:* Portsmouth High School; *studied art* at Slade School (1941-43) under Randolph Schwabe. *Work in permanent collections:* Bristol City, A.G., Plymouth City A.G., R.W.A., Nuffield Foundation, Durham University, Sussex Educ. Com. *Address:* Nancherrow Studio, St. Just, Penzance TR19 7LA. *Signs work:* "June Miles" (on back of painting).

MILLAR, Jack Ernest, A.R.C.A. (1950), R.B.A. (1954); artist in oil; former Head of Fine Art, Kingston Polytechnic (retd. 1986); *b* London, 28 Nov., 1922; *s* of Ernest Woodroffe de Cauze Millar, stage designer; *m* Pamela Izzard, artist; one *s*, two *d*. *Educ.:* Sellincourt; *studied art* at Clapham School of Art (1939), St. Martin's School of Art (1941), Royal College of Art (1947-50, 1st Class Dip., awarded Andrew Lloyd Scholarship for landscape painting). *Exhib.:* Odette Gilbert Gallery; one-man shows, Linton Court Gallery, Duncan Campbell Fine Art, Mason-Watts Fine Art. *Work in permanent collections:* Royal Academy (work purchased by President and Council shown at London Group), Leicester Galleries, Piccadilly Gallery, Trafford Gallery, Brighton Art Gallery, Roland,

Browse and Delbanco, David Paul Gallery/Alton Gallery. *Address:* 10 Overhill Rd., East Dulwich, London SE22 0PH. *Club:* Arts. *Signs work:* "J. Millar."

MILLAR, Sir Oliver Nicholas, G.C.V.O., F.B.A., F.S.A.; Director of the Royal Collection and Surveyor of H.M. The Queen's pictures (retd. 1988); Surveyor Emeritus of The Queen's Pictures; *b* Standon, Herts., 26 Apr., 1923; *s* of Gerald Millar; *m* (1954) Delia Dawnay; one *s*, three *d. Educ.:* Rugby, Courtauld Inst. *Publications:* English Art (1625-1714), with Dr. M. D. Whinney; Abraham van der Doort's Catalogue; Tudor, Stuart and early Georgian Pictures in the Collection of H.M. the Queen; Zoffany and His Tribuna; Later Georgian Pictures in the Collection of H.M. the Queen; Inventories and Valuations of the King's Goods; The Queen's Pictures; Victorian Pictures in the Collection of H.M. the Queen; catalogues; articles in various journals. *Address:* The Cottage, Rays Lane, Penn, Bucks.

MILLER, David T., D.A. (Edin.). F.R.B.S., Latimer Award, R.S.A. (1961), Prof. Member S.S.A.; sculptor on wood, stone, bronze, steel, fibreglass resin; lecturer, Moray House College; *b* Bo'ness, 1931; *s* of Robert Miller; *m* Morag Macmurray; one *s*, one *d. Educ.:* Mortlach School, Dufftown; *studied art* at Gray's School of Art, Aberdeen, Edinburgh College of Art (Eric Schilsky), Paris, Vallauris. *Work in permanent collections:* public sculpture in Edinburgh, Selkirk, Dalkeith, Alyth, Linwood, Moray House, Scottish Arts Council. *Address:* Northend House, Pathhead, Ford, Midlothian. *Signs work:* see appendix.

MILLER, Ingrid; printmaker, painter in etching, drypoint, oil, acrylic, watercolour; *b* Copenhagen, 1940; *d* of William Tougaard; *m* R.G. Miller, printmaker. *Educ.:* Copenhagen University; *studied art* at Malmö Printmaking School. *Exhib.:* R.A., R.S.A., Mall Galleries, Leighton House Gallery, Guildhall Gallery, R.A. Copenhagen, National Museum Gdansk, Wainö Aaltonen Museum Finland, Liljevalchs Stockholm, Print Triennales Malmö and Gothenburg, International Print Biennales: Cracow, Ljubljana, Rockford, Horgen, Cadaques, Varna, Maastrich, Biella, Berlin; Museums: Kalmar, Eksjö, Kristianstad, Vetlanda, Växjö. *Work in permanent collections:* Cabo Frio, Brazil; Swedish States Arts Council; Kalmar Museum. *Address:* Bolmen, 34194 Ljungby, Sweden. *Clubs:* Swedish and Danish Federations of Printmakers, G.S., D.G. and K.R.O., S.K., K.K.S., F.S.K., Grant Swedish State. *Signs work:* "Ingrid Miller."

MILLER, Kenneth Alfred; artist in stone, wood, clay, oil, lithography, silk screen; freelance; *b* 19 Oct., 1915; *s* of Thomas Miller; *m* Merrill Miller; two *s. Educ.:* Marylebone Central School; *studied art* at St. Martin's School of Art (1935-39). *Exhib.:* Fermoy Gallery, King's Lynn, Free Artists, Pall Mall Gallery. *Address:* Heathcote, Gt. Massingham, King's Lynn, Norfolk PE32 2HF.

MILLER, Ronald George; printmaker, painter in etching, mezzotint, engraving, acrylic; sculptor in wood; *b* London, 1938; *s* of George Frederick Miller; *m* Ingrid, printmaker. *Educ.:* Haverstock Hill Secondary School; *studied art* at Ingrid Miller's Print Workshop, Ljungby, Sweden. *Exhib.:* R.A., R.S.A. Edinburgh, International Print Biennales in Ljubljana, Krakow, Grenoble, Cadaques, Varna, Biella, Maastrich, Majdanek, Frechen, Berlin; museums in Kristianstad Vetlanda, Kalmar, Växjö, Liljevalchs, 4th National Exhbn. of British Prints, Grundy Gallery, Blackpool. *Work in permanent collections:* Majdanek Museum Poland, Museums in Växjö, Vetlanda, Swedish Arts Council. *Address:* Bolmen, 34194 Ljungby, Sweden. *Clubs:* Federation of Swedish Printmakers, G.S., K.R.O., S.K., Grant Swedish State. *Signs work:* "Ronald Miller."

MILLINGTON, Terence, R.E. (1988); painter/printmaker in oil, water-colour, etching; *b* B'ham, 20 Oct., 1942; *s* of George Millington; *m* Patricia; one *s*. *Educ.:* Moseley Secondary School of Art; *studied painting* at B'ham College of Art (1958-63), and printmaking at Manchester College of Art (1965-66). *Exhib.:* regularly at R.E.; many group and one-man exhbns. throughout Europe and the U.S.A. *Work in permanent collections:* various private and public including Tate Gallery, and V. & A. *Address:* 3 Redworth Terr., Totnes, Devon TQ9 5JN. *Signs work:* "Terence Millington."

MILLIS, Susan M., S.W.A. (1987), A.S.E.A. (1992); pyrographic artist specializing in wildlife and pictorial subjects on hand turned wooden paper-weights, pomanders and plaques; *b* Tidworth, Hants., 14 Nov., 1953; *d* of Major W.G. Lemon, A.R.C.M. psm, R.E. (decd.); *m* Gareth Hughes Millis; one *s*, one *d. Educ.:* Upbury Manor, Gillingham. *Exhib.:* S.W.A., S.E.A. annually, Francis Iles Galleries, Rochester throughout the year. *Publication:* A Burning Art (Popular Crafts, May 1989). *Address:* 30 Buxton Cl., Lordswood, Chatham, Kent ME5 8UP. *Signs work:* "S.M. Millis."

MILLMORE, Mark Alexander, A.R.E. (1989), B.A. (Hons.) Fine Art; artist in etching, painter in oil and water-colour; Council Mem. R.E.; *b* Shanklin, I.O.W., 13 Jan., 1956. *Educ.:* St. Bede's School, Bristol; *studied art* at Falmouth School of Art (1977-80, Prof. Lionel Miskin). *Exhib.:* London, King's Lynn, Bristol, Manchester (1990-91); mixed shows: Japan, U.S.A., Sweden, Taiwan, Australia, Spain, Canada, Kenya and the U.K. since 1987. *Work in permanent collections:* Ashmolean Museum, Victoria A.G. Bath, Kanagawa Prefectural Gallery Japan, Habikino City Hall Japan, Auburn University Contemporary Art Collection U.S.A., International Centre for Wildlife Art Gloucester. *Publications:* author, Etchings I, II and III. *Address:* 4/6 All Saints Rd., Clifton, Bristol BS8 2JH. *Signs work:* "Millmore."

MILLNER ETIENNE, Henry de la Fargue; figurative sculptor in plaster and clay for bronze; *b* Penang, Malaysia, 15 Jan., 1954; *m* Mary Castle; one *s*, one *d. Educ.:* Stowe School; *studied art* at Goldsmiths' College (Michael Kenny, R.A., Ivor Roberts-Jones, C.B.E., R.A.), R.A. Schools. *Exhib.:* R.A. Summer Shows (1979, 1982, 1984, 1985, 1986, 1988), N.P.G. 'New Faces' (1987), 'Art for Sale' Whiteleys (1992), Chelsea Harbour (1993), Cadogan Gallery Summer Show (1993). *Work in permanent collection:* N.P.G. *Address:* Montana Cottage, 7 Priory Gr., London SW8 2PD. *Club:* Chelsea Arts. *Signs work:* see appendix.

MILLS, Clive, B.A.Hons. (1987); painter in oil on canvas; *b* Shoreham, Sussex, 7 Mar., 1964; *s* of G. Mills, builder. *Educ.:* Portslade College; *studied art* at Brighton Polytechnic (1984-87), R.A. Schools (1987-90). *Exhib.:* Mall Galleries (group show 1988; Post Grad. show 1989), R.A. Summer Exhbn. (1989). *Work in permanent collections:* South East Arts and private collections including Switzerland. *Address:* 22 Easthill Drive, Portslade, Brighton E. Sussex BN4 2FO. *Signs work:* "Clive Mills."

MILLS, John W., A.R.C.A., F.R.B.S.; sculptor in bronze; *b* London, 1933; *s* of William Samuel, Mills; *m* Josephine Demarne; one *s*, one *d. Educ.:* Bec School, Tooting; *studied art* at Hammersmith School of Art (1947-54), R.C.A. (1956-60, John Skeaping). *Exhib.:* Arts Council, R.A., Alwin Gallery London, Simsar Gallery Michigan, Beaux Arts Gallery Bath. *Work in permanent collections:* Wellcome Foundation, Chicago Inst. of Fine Art, University of Cambridge, University of Michigan, Orient Express, City of London. *Publications:* 8 books on sculpture techniques, recent - Encyclopedia of Sculpture Technique.

Address: Hinxworth Pl., Hinxworth, Baldock, Herts. SG7 5HB. *Signs work:* "John W. Mills."

MILLWARD, Michael, M.A., A.M.A.; museum curator; Curator and Museum Manager, Blackburn Museum and Art Gallery; *b* Oldham, 9 Nov., 1944; *s* of Alan Millward, solicitor; *m* Dorothy; one *s*, one *d*. *Educ.:* King George V Grammar School, Southport; St. John's College, Cambridge. *Publication:* Victorian Townscape (with Brian Coe) 1974. *Address:* Blackburn Museum and Art Gallery, Museum St., Blackburn, Lancs. BB1 7AJ.

MILNE, Judith Erica, N.D.D. (1965), A.T.D. (1966); painter of botanical, landscape and garden scenes in water-colour; publisher; tutor; *b* Malvern, 30 Oct., 1943; *d* of E.G. Knight, head teacher; *m* J.A.S. Milne; one *s*, one *d*. *Educ.:* St. Mary's Convent, Worcester; *studied art* at B'ham College of Art and Crafts. *Work in permanent collections:* Malvern Hills Art, Malvern, V. & A., Trayne Fine Arts, Berks. *Publications:* Flowers in Water-colour (B.T. Batsford); Wildflowers in Water-colour (B. T. Batsford, 1994); greetings cards and prints. *Address:* 20 Colemans Moor Rd., Woodley, Reading RG5 4DL. *Club:* S.G.F.A. *Signs work:* "Judith Milne."

MILNE, Robert Wilson; artist in pencil and water-colour, pen and ink of historic bldgs., landscape and still life; *b* Hitchin, 4 Mar., 1950; *m*; one *s*, one *d*. *Educ.:* Hitchin Boys' Grammar School; *studied art:* St. Albans College of Art. *Exhib.:* one-man shows: Cheltenham, Hereford, Worcester, R.I.B.A. (1983), Ludlow Festival, Olivia Rumens Gallery (1990). *Work in permanent collection:* Hereford City A.G. *Address:* 2 Pedwardine Cottages, Brampton Bryan, Bucknell, Shropshire SY7 0DW. *Signs work:* "Robert Milne."

MILNER, Donald Ewart, O.B.E., M.A. (Hon., Bristol University), A.R.C.A. (1921), R.W.A. (Hon. Vice-Pres.), elected Vice-Pres. R.W.A. (1970), President (1974-78); artist in oil and water-colour and stained glass; *b* Huddersfield, 19 May, 1898; *s* of J. H. Milner, artist; *m* Mildred Milner, R.W.A.; two *s*. *Educ.:* Royal College of Art. *Work in permanent collections:* Bristol City Art Gallery, City of Gloucester Art Gallery, R.W.A.; stained glass windows at Ivy Hatch, Leicester, Thames Ditton, Courts of Justice, Bristol, and University of Bristol. *Address:* Oakfield House, Ellerncroft Rd., Wotton-under-Edge, Glos. *Signs work:* "D. E. Milner."

MINERS, Neil; artist in oil, water-colour; *b* Redruth, Cornwall, 19 June, 1931; *s* of Charles Arthur Miners; *m* Wendy Noak; two *d*. *Studied art* at Falmouth School of Art under Jack Chalker (1948) drawing only. *Exhib.:* R.I., R.O.I., and Britain in Water-colours; six one-man shows and various in Cornwall. *Work in permanent collections:* R.N.L.I., Trinity House and H.R.H. Prince Charles. *Publication:* Book of Falmouth and Penryn (contributor), Official designs and medals, illustrated book and Flags for Tall Ships start from Falmouth (1966). *Address:* 23 Arwenack St., Falmouth, Cornwall TR11 3JA. *Signs work:* see appendix.

MITCHELL, Brian, R.S.M.A.; painter in oil, water-colour, acrylic; *b* St. Ives, Cornwall, 12 Oct., 1937; *m* Marion; one *s*. *Educ.:* Penzance Grammar School; *studied art* at Penzance (1958-60, Bouverie Hoyton), Falmouth (1960-62), Inst. of Educ. London University (1962-63). *Exhib.:* R.W.E.A., R.W.S., R.I., R.B.A., R.S.M.A. *Address:* Gwaynten, Porthrepta Rd., St. Ives, Cornwall TR26 2NZ. *Signs work:* "MITCHELL."

MITCHELL, Enid G. D., F.R.B.S.; Dip.A.D. (Ceramics), Visual Arts Diploma, London University; Ghilchrist Prize; sculptor of portraits and figures cast in bronze, cement and resin, art ceramics in porcelain and stoneware; *d* of R. J. Mitchell, B.A. Hons., Lond., J.P.; one *s*, two *d. Educ.:* Lady Eleanor Holles School, Hampton, Middx.; *studied art* at Ealing School of Art (sculpture tutors, Tom Bailey and Robert Thomas, A.R.C.A.). *Work in permanent collections:* Leamington Spa, Islip Manor and Drayton Green Primary Schools and private collections: England, Holland, Israel, Denmark, U.S.A., etc. *Address:* 32 Stanier St., Swindon, Wilts. SN1 5QX. *Club:* Royal Society of British Sculptors. *Signs work:* "MITCHELL" or "Enid G. D. Mitchell."

MITCHELL, Gordon Kinlay, Dip.Art (Edin.), awarded Post.Dip. Scholarship and Travelling Scholarship; surrealist artist in water-colour, acrylic, oil; full-time professional artist; *b* Edinburgh, 16 Nov., 1952; *m* Catriona A.C. Mitchell; one *s*, one *d. Studied art* at Edinburgh College of Art (Sir Robin Philipson, David Michie). *Exhib.:* many major exhbns. in the British Isles; one-man shows, Henderson Gallery, Edinburgh (1978, 1981), Open Eye Gallery, Edinburgh (1992), Roger Billcliffe Fine Art, Glasgow (1993). *Work in permanent collections:* Scottish Arts Council, Kansas City Art Inst., Educational Inst. for Scotland, Old City A.G., Jerusalem, Paisley Art Inst., Teachers Whiskey, Scottish Brewers, Alliance & Leicester Bldg. Soc.. *Address:* 10 Argyll Terr., Haymarket, Edinburgh EH11 2BR. *Signs work:* "Gordon K. Mitchell."

MITCHELL, John, R.S.W. (1967); lecturer and teacher; artist in water-colour, silkscreen; Mem. S.S.A.; *b* Glasgow, 21 Dec., 1937. *Educ.:* Glasgow Academy, Royal High School of Edinburgh; *studied art* at Edinburgh College of Art (1956-61). *Work in permanent collections:* Scottish Arts Council, Fife Education Com., British Transport Hotels. *Address:* West Gowanbrae, 4 The Temple, Lower Largo, Fife. *Signs work:* "JOHN MITCHELL."

MITCHELL, S. M., P.P.S.P.S., F.R.B.S., A.R.C.A., N.D.D.; sculptor in clay, wood, stone, fibreglass, resins, concrete, bronze; *d* of Flight Lt. L. J. Mitchell; *m* Charles Bone, artist; two *s. Educ.:* Seager House School, Farnham G.G.S.; *studied art* at Farnham School of Art (1946), under Charles Vyes, Guildford School of Art (1947), under Willi Soukop, R.A., Royal College of Art (1948-51), under Frank Dobson, R.A., John Skeaping, R.A., Edward Folkard, F.R.B.S. *Exhib:* R.A., S.P.S., N.E.A.C., W.I.A., Ashgate Gallery, Furneaux Gallery, Canaletto Gallery, Chenil Gallery; ten one-man exhbns., Medici Gallery, Ashgate Gallery, Gainsborough's House, University of Surrey, Guildford House, Malta, G.C., Tarrystone Gallery. *Portrait commissions* in bronze, terracotta. *Designer* ceramic sculpture, including Royal Worcester Porcelain. Elected first woman president Society of Portrait Sculptors (1977). *Address:* Winters Farm, Puttenham, nr. Guildford, Surrey. *Signs work:* "S. Mitchell." sometimes (B) after signature.

MOCKFORD, Harold; self taught artist in oil; *b* 25 Jan., 1932; *s* of William Mockford; *m* Margaret Beney; three *s*, two *d. Educ.:* St. Mary's C. of E., Eastbourne. *Exhib.:* one-man shows: Towner A.G. (1970, 1987), Hove Museum (1980, 1985), Thackeray Gallery, London (1978); R.A. Summer Exhbns., London Group. *Work in permanent collections:* Tate Gallery, Chantry Bequest, Towner Gallery, Hove Museum of Art, Government Art Collection. *Address:* 31 Milton Rd., Eastbourne BN21 1SH. *Signs work:* "H. Mockford" on back of board.

MOLENKAMP, Nicolaas Ferdinand, Willink van Collem Prize, Amsterdam (1950), Laurens Meeusprize for Painting, Belgium, Silver Medal, Europe, Prize for Painting, Osten (1962); painter; head of department (painting), Academy of Fine Arts, Tilburg; *b* Enschede, Netherlands, 6 Dec., 1920; *s* of Gerrit Jan

Molenkamp; *m* Maria de Mast; one *s*, three *d*. *Studied art* at Academy of Art, Tilburg, and Academy of Fine Art, Antwerp. *Exhib.*: Amsterdam, Schiedam, Tilburg, Gt. Yarmouth, Brussels, Baghdad; van Abbe Museum, Eindhoven, Contour Delft. *Work in permanent collections:* Central Museum, Utrecht; Print Room, Antwerp. *Address:* Koningshoeven 30, Tilburg, Netherlands. *Clubs:* Federated Holland Societies of Artists. *Signs work:* "Molenkamp."

MOLLOY, Sylvia, M.A.; painter in oil and other media; *b* 27 Mar., 1914; *d* of James Leyden, headmaster; *m* Patrick Molloy; two *s*. *Educ.*: Westoe Secondary School, South Shields; *studied art and English* at Armstrong College, Durham University (1932-36), Johannesburg College of Art (1949-52). C.V. in Dictionary of S. African Painters and Sculptors. *Exhib.*: R.A., R.B.A., R.O.I., S.W.A., W.S.; one-man shows, five in London, Letchworth, Hitchin, Lavenham and others. *Work in permanent collections:* S.A.: stained glass in Johannesburg and Pretoria, paintings in East London, Bloemfontein, Johannesburg; U.K.: Letchworth A.G., Sax House, Business Park; Commissioned portrait of Archbishop of Edinburgh. *Address:* 41 Field Lane, Letchworth, Herts. SG6 3LD. *Clubs:* N.S., R.A.S., F.F.P.S. *Signs work:* From 1986 "Sylvia Molloy."

MONGAN, Agnes, A.B. (1927), M.A. (1929), L.H.D. (1941), Litt.D. (1953), Dr.F.A. (1970); art historian, lecturer and writer, former museum director, Fogg Art Museum (1928-71); Timken Gallery, San Diego, California (1971-72); *b* Somerville, Mass., 1905; *d* of Dr. Charles E. Mongan, M.D. *Publications:* author or editor of numerous catalogues of museum collections and exhibitions, articles in periodicals, reviews, etc. *Address:* Drawing Dept., Fogg Art Museum, Harvard University, Cambridge, Mass. 02138. *Clubs:* Harvard Faculty, Cosmopolitan, N.Y.

MONTAGUE, Lucile Christine, L.C.A.D. (1974); painter; *b* London, 1950; *d* of Allan Taylor; *m* (1) Michael Montague (divorced); (2) David Greene; one *s*. *Educ.*: Fyling Hall School, Yorks.; *studied art* at Plymouth College of Art (1967-69), Byam Shaw School of Art (1971-74). *Exhib.*: R.A., Whitechapel Open, London Group, Spirit of London, Leicester Exhbn., South Bank Show, Thumb Gallery; group shows: Ikon Gallery touring, 'Ways of Telling' Mostyn Gallery, Llandudno, 'Subjective City' touring, 'Witnesses and Dreamers' touring; one-man show, Mario Fletcher Gallery, London. *Work in permanent collections:* Bankers Trust, Coopers and Lybrand, Camden Council. *Publication:* Women Artist's Diary (1989). *Address:* 47 Hargrave Pk., London N19 5JW. *Signs work:* "L.C. Montague."

MONTAGUE-GRAINGER, B., A.R.C.A., F.R.S.A., Clerk-in-Minor-Holy Orders, Membre Associaé de la Société des Artistes Français; design consultant and engineer; H.M. Corps R.E., Field Survey and Geodetic Instrument maker, sapper; *b* Paddock Wood, Kent, 16 July, 1907; *s* of William Montague-Grainger; *m* Pattie Revell; two *s*, one *d*. *Educ.*: Ardingly College; *studied art* at Maidstone School of Art, R.C.A. (R.C.A. scholar Post dip.), Central School of Art, Extra Mural under Prof. Freud (Clinical treatment of Insanity School of Tropical Medicine), Bishop Leadbetter (Demonic Possession and Religious Art Theosophy). Hon. Lecturer, Faculty of Architecture, Sheffield University; lecturer, Sheffield College of Art; Past President: Sheffield Soc. of Art, Derbyshire Pennine Club, Craven Pothole Club; Founder mem.: British Spaeological Assoc., Cave Research Group, Peveril Underground Survey Assoc.*Exhib.*: Paris Salon, R.A., Biarritz, Sheffield, Manchester, N.Y. *Work in private collections:* Canada, France, U.S.A., New Zealand, Spain, Sweden, Australia, Iran, British Isles, Goldsmiths' Hall. *Publications:* written work, letters and essays in private circulation:

adolescent development, theology, sexual and sociological studies, military studies, etc. *Address:* Belmont, Terrace Rd., Tideswell, Derbyshire SK17 8NA. *Signs work:* "B.M. Grainger."

MONTANÉ, Roger; painter in oil; Prix Bethouard (1948); President, Groupe 109 (1982); *b* Bordeaux, 21 Feb., 1916; *m*; two *s. Educ.:* Toulouse; *studied art:* self-taught. *Exhib.:* Chicago (1964), New York (1965), Musée de Toulon (1965). *Official purchases:* Musée d'Art Moderne (Paris), Musées de la Ville (Paris), de St. Denis (Paris), de Toulouse, d'Albi, Ishibashi (Tokyo), Groupe International d'Art Figuratif (Japan, 1960), Exposition Particulière la Maison de La Pensée Française, Paris (1961), Aberdeen Museum and Art Gall., Musées de Valence, de Rodez, de Sete, de Bagnols s/Cèze, Wellington Museum (N.Z.), de Grenoble. President, Salon d'Automne (1966-68), Musées de Narbonne, Prague, du Sport (Paris). *Address:* 33 rue Charcot, Paris 13. *Signs work:* see appendix.

MONTGOMERY, Iona Allison Eleanor, B.F.A.(Hons.) (1987), Post.Grad. D.F.A. (1988), R.S.W. (1991); Alexander Graham Munro travel award (1990), Lauder award (1991); artist in painting and printmaking; *b* Glasgow, 14 Apr., 1965; *d* of Hamish Montgomery, artist. *Educ.:* Boclair Academy, Bearsden, Glasgow; *studied art* at Glasgow School of Art (Philip Reeves). *Exhib.:* various one-man and group shows including Ancrum Gallery, Lillie A.G., Solstice Gallery, Glasgow Print Studio, also U.S.A., Europe and U.S.S.R. *Work in permanent collections:* Lillie A.G., Milngavie, B.B.C., etc. *Address:* 171A Maryhill Rd., Flat 2/3, Glasgow G20 7XL. *Clubs:* R.S.W., G.P.S., G.S.W.A. *Signs work:* "Iona A.E. Montgomery."

MONTGOMERY, James Alexander; artist in water-colour, pen and ink, oil; Leader of Complex of Rehabilitation Units, including Art Therapy; *b* Glasgow, 3 Oct., 1928; *s* of James Montgomery; *m* Isabelle, artist; two *s*, one *d. Educ.:* Woodside School, Glasgow; *studied art* at Glasgow School of Art (David Donaldson, Edward Powell), apprenticed to industrial artist. *Exhib.:* Columbus City Museum, U.S.A., Carrollton Nova Lomason A.G., Atlanta. *Address:* 13 Avon Ave., Bearsden, Glasgow G61 2PS. *Club:* Glasgow Art. *Signs work:* "Hamish Montgomery."

MOOD, Kenneth, B.A. (Hons,); artist/writer; *b* Gateshead, 24 Nov., 1950; *m* Margaret; one *s*, one *d. Educ.:* Gateshead; *studied art* at Sunderland Art College. *Exhib.:* Mail Art shows worldwide. *Work in permanent collections:* Arts Council, Whitney Museum (N.Y.). *Address:* 1 Burns Cres., Swalwell, Tyne and Wear NE16 3JE.

MOODIE, Stuart, U.A.; artist-designer in pen and ink, water-colour, acrylic and mixed media; *b* Aberdeen, 7 Apr., 1922; *s* David Moodie; (decd.); *m* Christine Bou; two *d. Educ.:* Robert Gordon's College, Aberdeen; autodidactic in painting but greatly influenced by Robin Philipson. *Exhib.:* Douglas and Foulis Gallery, Edinburgh, Pitlochry Festival Theatre, Craon, La Mayenne, France. *Work in permanent collections:* Britain, America, Canada, Denmark, Spain, France. In the course of a career in architecture has worked on technical illustration, drawings for architectural submissions, reports and competitions. Also book illustration and advertising graphics. With his wife, co-owned and ran two private art galleries in Scotland. Taught art to adults in the artists' town of Altea on Spain's Costa Blanca. *Address:* 4 rue de la Grotte, Bourg de Coesmes, 35134 France. *Signs work:* "Stuart Moodie" and see appendix.

MOODY, Catherine Olive, A.T.D. (1944), P.S. (1960), R.B.S.A. (1965), Exhbn. Scholarship R.C.A. (1941); painter in oil and pastel, writer, designer; Head of School of Art, Malvern Hills College (1962-80); *b* London, 27 Nov., 1920; *d* of Victor Moody, A.R.C.A., Principal, Malvern School of Art. *Educ.:* Stroud High and Thornbank Schools; *studied art* at Malvern School of Art (1935-41, Victor Moody), Royal College Art (1941), Birmingham School of Art (1944, Fleetwood-Walker). *Exhib.:* R.A., P.S., R.P., R.B.S.A., R.I.B.A. *Work in permanent collections:* Worcester City A.G., British Rail Archives. *Publications:* Silhouette of Malvern; Painter's Workshop, and articles. *Address:* 1 Sling La., Malvern, Worcs. *Signs work:* "C.O. MOODY" or "C.M."

MOON, Liz, B.A./M.A. Oxon. (Engineering) 1964, S.W.A. (1987); painter in acrylic, water-colour, airbrush; Adult Tutor in Art; *b* India, 4 Oct., 1941; *d* of Lt.-Col. L. Montague-Jones. *Educ.:* Sherborne Girls' School; St. Hugh's College, Oxford; Redlands College, Bristol; *studied art* at San Francisco Art Inst. *Exhib.:* R.S.M.A., R.W.A., R.B.A., S.W.A., galleries around Cambridge and E. Anglia; Lymington, Solent Gallery; London, Bow House Gallery, Barnet; Heifer Gallery, Highbury; one-man show, Barbican Level 5 West. Large commission for Michael Gerson, International Movers, showing many aspects of their work. *Publication:* article in The Artist (1987). *Address:* 21 Bermuda Terr., Cambridge CB4 3LD.

MOON, Michael; First prize, John Moores Liverpool Exhbn. (1980), print award, Gulbenkian (1984); painter in mixed media; *b* Edinburgh, 9 Nov., 1937; *s* of Donald Moon, Lt.Col.; *m* Anjum Moon; two *s. Educ.:* Shoreham Grammar School, Sussex; *studied art* at Chelsea School of Art (1958-62), R.C.A. (1963). *Exhib.:* one-man shows in U.K., Australia and U.S.A. including Tate Gallery (1976); numerous group exhbns. worldwide. *Work in permanent collections:* Tate Gallery, Arts Council, provincial and overseas. *Address:* 10 Bowood Rd., London SW11. *Signs work:* "Mick Moon."

MOON, Tennant, A.R.C.A., F.S.A.E., F.R.S.A., Principal, Cumbria College of Art and Design (1957-78); Principal, Gravesend School of Art and Crafts (1949-57); Lecturer, Leicester College of Art (1946-49); President, National Society for Art Education (1972-73); Chairman, Association of Art Institutions (1976-77); Chairman, Standing Advisory Committee for Art & Design, Associated Examining Board (1970-86); *b* Penarth, S. Glamorgan; *m* (1) Barbara Ovenden; one *s*, one *d*; *m* (2) Joan Whiting. *Studied art* Cardiff School of Art, Royal College of Art under Sir William Rothenstein. *Exhib.:* R.A., Leicester Galleries, National Museum of Wales, South Wales Group, Newport (Gwent) A.G., Leicester A.G., etc. *Work in permanent collection:* Cumbria Educ. Comm. and private collections. *Address:* 15 Lansdown Parade, Cheltenham, Glos. GL50 2LH.

MOORE, Bridget, R.A.S.Dip., R.B.A., Greenshield Foundation (1985); painter in oil and gouache; *b* Whitstable, 2 Aug., 1960; *d* of Keith Charles Moore; *m* Alistair Milne; one *s. Educ.:* The Sir William Nottidge School, Whitstable; *studied art* at Medway College of Design, Epsom School of Art, R.A. Schools. *Exhib.:* R.A., R.B.A. *Address:* 29E Sylvan Rd., Upper Norwood, London SE19 2RU. *Signs work:* "BRIDGET MOORE" on back.

MOORE, Gerald John, N.D.D. (1958), A.T.C., A.T.D. (Manc.) (1959), B.A.(Hons.Theol.) (1969), F.R.S.A. (1985); traditional painter in water-colour and oil; *b* Ratby, Leics., 1938; *s* of the late Gilbert Moore. *Educ.:* Broom Leys School, Leics; *studied art* at Loughborough (1955-58), Manchester Regional College of Art (1958-59), University of Exeter (Theology 1966-69; History of Art 1974-75). *Exhib.:* Teignmouth, Tiverton, Taunton, Widecombe-in-the-Moor,

Braunton, Bournemouth, Salisbury and Bristol. *Address:* Lower Huntham Farm, Stoke St. Gregory, Taunton, Som. TA3 6EY. *Signs work:* "G.J.M." or "G.J. MOORE."

MOORE, Jean Marigold, A.R.M.S. (1989); painter in oil and water-colour, writer; *b* Valletta, Malta, 24 Nov., 1926; divorced; three *s. Educ.:* privately and Chichester High School for Girls; *studied art* at Lowestoft School of Art. *Exhib.:* Mall Galleries; solo shows in Sussex. *Address:* 17 Garrod House, Charles Rd., St. Leonards, Sussex TN38 0QD. *Signs work:* "J.M. MOORE" (oils), "J.M.M." (water-colours and miniatures).

MOORE, Ken; painter in oil; director, Commonwealth Biennale of Abstract Art London (1963); *b* Melbourne, Australia, 1923; *s* of Albert Moore, teacher of painting Geelong School. *Studied art* at St. Martin's School of Art under Derrick Greaves, Kenneth Martin, Russell Hall. *Work in permanent collections:* New Britten Museum, Connecticut, Phoenix Art Museum Arizona, Cedar Rapids Art Museum, Iowa, Keppe Gallery, Denmark, Lynam Allen Museum, Connecticut, Finch College Museum, N.Y., Tweed Gallery, Minneapolis, Witchita University, Kansas, Bertrand Russell Foundation, The Australian Ballet, University of Sydney, University of Melbourne, University of New England Armidale, H.R.H. Princess Margaret, King George VI and Queen Elizabeth Foundation, Windsor, The American Legation Museum, Tangier. *Address:* 137 Biddulph Mans., London W9 1HU. *Signs work:* "Ken Moore."

MOORE, Leslie Lancelot Hardy, R.I.; artist in water-colour; *b* Norwich, 1907; *m* daughter of Col. J. Plunkett; two *s. Educ.:* City of Norwich School, University of Reading; *studied art* mainly self-taught, otherwise University of Reading and Norwich School of Art. *Exhib.:* R.A., N.E.A.C., Mall Galleries, Edwin Pollard Gallery, Wimbledon, Mandells Gallery, Norwich. *Work repro.:* in colour commercially. *Publications:* illustrated Old Guns and Pistols, Norwich Inns, Call Me at Dawn. *Address:* 26 Suffield Cl., N. Walsham, Norfolk NR28 0HN. *Signs work:* "Leslie L. H. Moore."

MOORE, Richard E. M., D.F.A. (Lond.), Ph.D., F.R.S.A.; research scientist and free-lance medical artist; *b* Poole, 1938; *s* of the late Gwen White, A.R.C.A., (artist and author) and of the late C. Rupert Moore, A.R.C.A., F.M.G.P., Com.R.Ae.S. (aeronautical artist and stained glass designer). *Educ.:* privately, St. Alban's and Royal Holloway College, London University; *studied art* at Regent St. Polytechnic, Medal for Stage Design (1957); Slade School, Anatomy Prize (1958); British School at Rome (1962). *Awards:* Worshipful Company of Goldsmiths (1962); University College London, Provost's (1962, 1963); I.B.M. (1964); Leverhulme (1966-68). *Exhib.:* National Exhbn. Childrens' Art (1948), M. of E. Travelling Exhbn. Best Exam. Work (1957), European Anatomical Congress (1973), Rediscovery of Anatomy, Royal Institution (1974), Caxton, Design Centre (1976), Medical Picture Show, Science Museum (1978), British Council World Travelling Exhbn. British Illustration: from Caxton to Chloe (1985-), etc. *Publications:* Many papers on own research in scientific and archaeological journals. *Work repro.:* illustrations for many medical journals and books; artist to Gray's Anatomy since 1969, Most Beautiful Book Bronze Medal (Leipzig) and Litho-printer Overall Winner Award (1974). *Address:* c/o Dr. Moreton Moore, 32 Whitehall La., Egham, Surrey TW20 9NF. *Signs work:* "REMM" or "RM."

MORESCHI, Maria, A.B.A., F.P.S.; art teacher, portrait artist in oil, pastel and water-colour; art teacher The American School, Cobham; *b* Florence, 18 July, 1949; *d* of Galliano Taddey, Col. in The King's Cavalry; *m*; one *s*, two *d*.

Educ.: SS. Ma. Annunziata; *studied art* at Academia delle Belle Arti; taught portraiture by Annigoni in Florence. *Exhib.:* America, Italy, Holland, England. *Work in permanent collections:* La Loggia, Oxshott, Walton, Epsom, Studio 54 Cobham, The Investment Gallery. *Publication:* in the process of illustrating an animal and wildlife drawing book. *Address:* A.C.S. Middle School, Heywood, Portsmouth Rd., Cobham, Surrey. *Clubs:* Epsom, Oxshott, Walton, Mosley, Cobham, London. *Signs work:* "M. Moreschi."

MORETON, Nicolas, B.A.(Hons.) (1985); fine art sculptor in English stones, plaster, clay, bronze, pencil drawing; *b* Watford, Herts., 22 Oct., 1961; *s* of Cecil Peter Moreton, Ph.F., F.R.I.C.S., F.C.B.S.I.; *m* Julie Rose Bills, *Educ.:* Weston Favell Upper School, Northampton; *studied art* at Nene College, Northampton (1981-82, Frank Cryer), Wolverhampton Polytechnic (1982-85, John Paddison, R.C.A.). *Exhib.:* Leics. Schools and Colleges, Albermarle Gallery, Hobart and Maclean Gallery London, Hannah Peschar Gallery Ockley, Gallerie Samarlande Paris; one-man shows: Northampton Museum (1983), Mall Galleries (1989, 1991), Lamont Gallery (1992). Resident Sculptor, Manorbier Castle, Wales (1988). Anglia Television 'Moving Art' commission (1991). *Address:* 4 West Lodge Cottages, London Rd., Courteenhall, Northampton NN7 2QA. *Signs work:* drawing "Nicolas Moreton"; sculpture see appendix.

MORGAN, Glyn, painter in oil, water-colour, collage; *b* Pontypridd, 16 July, 1926; *s* of Ivor Morgan; *m* Jean Bullworthy. *Educ.:* Pontypridd Grammar School; *studied art* at Cardiff School of Art (1942-44, Ceri Richards), Camberwell School of Art (1947), East Anglian School (1944-82, Cedric Morris). *Exhib.:* one-man shows: Gilbert Parr, London (1978, 1980), Alwin, London (1982, 1983), Richard Demarco Gallery, Edinburgh (1973), Minories, Colchester (1971, 1981), Archway Gallery, Houston, Texas; organised 'The Benton End Circle' exhbn. of work by pupils of Cedric Morris and Lett Haines, Bury St. Edmunds Gallery (1985). *Work in permanent collections:* Auckland and Brisbane A.G's, Derbyshire, Monmouthshire, Oxford and West Riding Educ. Coms., Welsh Arts Council, Contemporary Art Soc. for Wales, Ipswich Borough Museum and A.G. *Address:* 28 Priory Rd., High Wycombe, Bucks. HP13 6SL. *Signs work:* "MORGAN."

MORGAN, Helena Frances, Dip. in Textiles (1985), M.F.P.S. (1991), L.C.G.I. (1992); fibre artist in felt; *b* Mountain Ash, Mid Glam., 11 Feb., 1938; *m* Hugh; one *s*, two *d. Educ.:* Mountain Ash Grammar School; *studied art* at Gloucs. College of Art (1957-61), Regent St. Polytechnic (1963-64), London College of Furniture (1983-85). *Exhib.:* England and France. *Address:* Lansbury, 51A High St., Langford, Beds. SG18 9RU. *Signs work:* "Helena Morgan."

MORGAN, Howard James, M.F.A., R.P.; painter in oil, water-colour, casein; *b* 21 Apr., 1949; *s* of Thomas James Morgan, teacher; *m* Susan Ann; two *s*, one *d. Educ.:* Fairfax High School; *studied art* at Newcastle-upon-Tyne University (Ralph Holland, Charles Leonard Evetts). *Exhib.:* Anthony Mould, Claridges, Agnews, Richmond Gallery. *Work in permanent collection:* N.P.G. *Addresses:* (studio) 401½ Wandsworth Rd., London SW8; (home) 12 Rectory Grove, Clapham, London SW4. *Club:* Chelsea Arts. *Signs work:* roman numerals of month, followed by arabic year and surname, i.e. "MORGAN II 90."

MORGAN, Robert; Ad.Dip.Ed., and Teaching Cert.; painter in oil, water-colour, pastels, etc., designer; was adviser in Special Educ., now full time painter and writer; Mem. Welsh Academy; *b* Glamorgan, 1922; *s* of William H. Morgan, miner; *m*; two *d. Educ.:* Bognor College of Educ.; Southampton University; *studied art* under Charles Woolaston. *Exhib.:* Gosport Museum (1986); fourteen one-man shows: Gosport, Winchester, S. Wales, etc. *Publications:* author, The Night's Prison (Rupert Hart-Davis, 1967); My Lamp Still Burns, autobiography (Gomer Press, 1981); Landmarks (poems) (Indigo Publications, 1989), etc.; many cover designs; work (poetry) translated into Chinese (1985); illustrated Poetry and Broadsheets (1985), Poetry Wales and New Welsh Review (1990). *Address:* 72 Anmore Rd., Denmead, Hants. PO7 6NT. *Signs work:* "R.M." or "R. Morgan."

MORGAN, Ronald, R.B.A. (1984), R.O.I. (1984); draughtsman, painter in water-colour, black and white, oil and pastel, illustrator, linguist, teacher; Mem. Chelsea Art Soc.; *b* Landywood, Staffs., 28 Feb., 1936; *s* of J. Morgan. *Educ.:* Landywood Junior School, Great Wyrley Secondary School, Staffs.; *studied art* at Walsall School of Art (1951-53, George Willott, A.R.C.A.). *Exhib.:* R.A., R.I., R.B.A., N.E.A.C., S.G.A., R.B.S.A., R.S.M.A., R.O.I., Paris Salon, Britain in Water-colours and touring exhbns., etc. *Work in permanent collections:* London Boroughs of Islington, and Tower Hamlets, Graves A.G., Sheffield, Sultan of Oman. *Work repro.:* Leisure Painter, La Revue Moderne (Paris, 1963, 1965), Royal Academy Illustrated. *Address:* 8 Marina Ct., Alfred St., Bow, London E3 2BH. *Signs work:* "R. MORGAN. 1990."

MORREAU, Jacqueline; artist in oil; Prof. of Art, Regent's College, London; *b* Wisconsin, U.S.A.; *m* Patrick Morreau; two *s*, two *d*. *Educ.:* Chouinard Art Inst., L.A.; Jepson Art Inst., L.A., (Rico Lebrun); University of California Medical School, San Franciso. *Exhib.:* one-man shows: Odette Gilbert (1989, 1990), Art Space, London (1986, 1988), retrospective, Ferens A.G., Hull (1988); group shows: Museum of Modern Art, Oxford, 'Women's Images of Men' I.C.A. London and tour. *Work in permanent collections:* A.C.G.B., B.M., V. & A., Open University, Nuffield College Oxford, City Art Galleries, Hull, etc. *Publications:* Women's Images of Men with Sarah Kent (1985, 1989), Bibliography — Jacqueline Morreau, drawings and graphics (1985). *Address:* 40 Church Cres., London N10. *Signs work:* "J. Morreau."

MORRELL, Peter John, N.D.D. (Painting, 1956), A.R.C.A. (Painting, 1959), Rome Scholar in Painting (1959), R.W.S. (1983), Mem. London Group (1990); painter in oil and water-colour, lecturer; part-time lecturer, Central School of Art; *b* Newton Abbot, 28 Feb., 1931; *s* of Arthur Markham, M.A.; *m* Helene Halstuch; one *s,* one *d*. *Educ.:* Worthing High School for Boys; *studied art* at Kingston-upon-Thames College of Art (1952-56), R.C.A. (1956-59, Ruskin Spear, Carel Weight, John Minton, Colin Hayes). *Exhib.:* R.A., John Moores, Grabowski Gallery, New Art Centre, London Group, Beaux Arts Gallery, Arnolfini Gallery, Six Young Painters, Gimpel Fils, R.W.S., Arts Council Touring Exhbns., Gallery Appunto Rome. *Work in permanent collections:* Arts Council, L.C.C., Charterhouse Boys' School, Science Museum. *Address:* Sol del Rey, Carnac-Rouffiac, 46140 Luzech, France. *Signs work:* "MORRELL."

MORRIS, Anthony, R.P., N.D.D. (1958), R.A.S. (1961); painter/illustrator in oil and water-colour; *b* Oxford, 2 Aug., 1938; *s* of Francis Morris; *m* Aileen. *Studied art* at Oxford School of Art, R.A. Schools (Peter Greenham). *Exhib.:* R.A., R.P., Medici Gallery. *Work in permanent collections:* Bodleian Library, Open University, King's College Hospital. *Publications:* B.B.C. and major publishers. *Address:* Drostre House, Talyllyn, Brecon, Powys LD3 7SY. *Signs work:* "MORRIS."

MORRIS, James Shepherd, R.S.A., M.L.A., F.R.I.A.S., A.R.I.B.A.; Mem. Arts Council of Gt. Britain (1973-80), Vice-Chairman, Scottish Arts Council (1976-80), Arts Council Enquiry into Community Arts (1974), Trustee, Nat.

Mus. of Antiquities (1980-86), Past Chairman, Scottish Arts Council Art Com.; Convenor Fellowship Com. R.I.A.S. (1982-87); Mem. Council R.S.A. (1990); Partner, Morris and Steedman, Architects and Landscape Architects, Edinburgh; *b* St. Andrews, Fife, 22 Aug., 1931; *s* of Johanna Sime Morris and Thomas S. Morris, A.R.I.B.A., A.M.T.P.I.; *m* Eleanor Kenner Smith; two *s*, one *d*. *Studied* at Edinburgh College of Art, University of Pennsylvania. R.I.B.A. Award (1974), European Heritage Award (1975), Nine Civic Trust Awards (1962-90). *Address:* Woodcote Pk., Fala, Midlothian, Scotland. *Clubs:* New (Edinburgh), Philadelphia Cricket (Philadelphia), Valderrama (Spain).

MORRIS, John, A.N.S.P.S., Mem., Water-colour Soc. of Wales; painter in water-colour; *b* Deiniolen, N. Wales, 27 Sept., 1922; *s* of Robert Morris; boot and shoe retailer; *m* Eluned Mary; one *s*, one *d*. *Educ.:* Brynrefail County School, Bangor Normal College; *studied art* at Bangor Normal (1955-57, H. Douglas Williams), Press Art School, London (1958-60, Percy V. Bradshaw). *Exhib.:* Williamson A.G. Birkenhead, Oriel Theatre Clwyd Mold, Wrexham Arts Centre, Albany Gallery Cardiff, R.I., N.S., Royal National Eisteddfod of Wales, Water-colour Soc. of Wales. *Work in permanent collections:* Royal Welsh Agricultural Soc., National Libary of Wales, Midland Bank Ltd., Burnley Building Soc., Clwyd C.C. *Publications:* Newid Aelwyd, Newid Bro. *Address:* Elidir, 46 Bryn Awelon, Yr Wyddgrug (Mold), Clwyd CH7 1LU, N. Wales. *Signs work:* "John Morris."

MORRIS, Mali, B.A. (1968), M.F.A. (1970); artist in acrylic on canvas, water-colour etc. on paper; Senior lecturer, Chelsea School of Art. *Studied art* at University of Newcastle upon Tyne (1963-68), University of Reading (1968-70). *Exhib.:* 13 solo shows since 1979, including Francis Graham-Dixon Gallery (1990). *Work in permanent collections:* A.C.G.B., British Council, Contemporary Arts Soc., Eastern Arts Assoc., Lloyds of London, National A.G., Botswana, Northern Arts, W.A.C., etc. *Address:* c/o Francis Graham-Dixon Gallery, 17-18 Gt. Sutton St., London EC1V 0DN. *Signs work:* "Mali Morris."

MORRIS, Stanley William, M.Ed. (1976), A.T.D. (1951), A.R.B.S.A., M.F.P.S.; *b* 1922. *Studied art* at Birmingham College of Art. *Work in permanent collection:* Midlands Arts Centre, wood carving for Prince of Wales Regt., Leeds Permanent Building Soc. *Exhib.:* Paris Salon, R.O.I., N.E.A.C., U.A.S., R.B.S.A. *Address:* Bromley Cottage, Ashbrook La., Abbots Bromley, Staffs. WS15 3DW.

MORRISON, James, A.R.S.A., R.S.W., D.Univ., D.A.; painter in oil and water-colour; *b* Glasgow, 1932; *m*; one *s*, one *d*. *Educ.:* Hillhead High School, Glasgow School of Art. *Work in permanent collections:* Glasgow, Dundee and Aberdeen Art galleries, Arts Council, Argyll, Dundee and Edinburgh Educ. Committees, Glasgow, Edinburgh, Strathclyde and Stirling Universities, H.R.H. the Duke of Edinburgh, Dept. of the Environment, various embassies, Kingsway Technical College, Vaughan College, Leicester, Municipality of the Hague, Earls of Dalhousie, Moray, Airlie, Robert Fleming, Merchant Bankers, BBC, Grampian Television, General Accident, Scottish Amicable, Life Assoc. of Scotland; Banks: Royal, Scotland, Clydesdale, T.S.B. *Publication:* author, Affthe Squerr. *Address:* Craigview House, Usan, Montrose, Angus. *Signs work:* "Morrison" and date.

MORROCCO, Alberto, O.B.E. (1993), D.A. (1937), R.S.A. (1963), R.S.W., R.P., R.G.I., LL.D., Dr.UNIV.; painter in oil and water-colour; *b* Aberdeen, 14 Dec., 1917; *s* of Domenico Antonio Morrocco; *m* Vera Cockburn Mercer; two *s*, one *d*. *Educ.:* Aberdeen; *studied art* at Gray's School of Art, Aberdeen (1932-38) under Robert Sivell, R.S.A., James Cowie, R.S.A. and D. M. Sutherland,

WHO'S WHO IN ART

R.S.A. *Work in permanent collections:* Aberdeen, Dundee, Glasgow, Perth, Paisley and Bristol A.G., Scottish Arts Council, Scottish Modern Arts Assoc., Scottish National Gallery of Modern Art, Edinburgh. Murals at St. Columbas' Church, Glenrothes, and LiffHospital. Portraits include H.M. The Queen Mother; Assgeir Assgeirson, Pres. of Iceland; Lord Boyd Orr; Lord Cameron. *Address:* Binrock, 456 Perth Rd., Dundee DD2 1NG. *Club:* Scottish Arts, Edinburgh. *Signs work:* "Morrocco." *Other interests:* eating.

MORROCCO, Leon, D.A., (Edin.), A.R.S.A.; painter in oil and mixed media; *b* Edinburgh, 4 Apr., 1942; *m* Jean Elizabeth Selby; two *s. Educ.:* Harris Academy, Dundee; *studied art* at Duncan of Jordanstone College of Art, Dundee (1960, Alberto Morrocco, R.S.A.), Slade School of Fine Art (1960-61, Sir William Coldstream), Edinburgh College of Art (1961-65, Sir Robin Philipson, R.S.A.). *Exhib.:* 20 one-man shows since 1966, Scotland, London, Melbourne, Sydney. *Address:* c/o Royal Scottish Academy, The Mound, Edinburgh EH2 2EL. *Signs work:* "Leon Morrocco."

MORSS, Edward James, R.B.A., R.O.I., A.R.C.A. (1930); artist in oil; Principal (retd.) St. Martin's School of Art, 109 Charing Cross Rd., WC2, formerly, Colchester School of Art; and Maidstone College of Art; *b* Exmouth, Devon, 24 Jan., 1906; *s* of Edward Alexander Morss, engineer; *m* Dorothy Cullen; one *d. Educ.:* Orme's School; *studied art* at Sheffield College of Art, R.C.A. (1927-31). *Exhib.:* Various London, Paris and provincial galleries. *Address:* 5 Burnet Cl., Campion Meadow, Woodwater La., Exeter, Devon. *Signs work:* see appendix.

MORTIMER, Martin Christopher Fortescue; Chairman and Managing Director, Delomosne & Son Ltd. Specialist in English Porcelain, English and Irish Glass, particularly English glass lighting fittings, and articles on these subjects in various art journals; *b* London, 4 July, 1928; *s* of George Mortimer (British Aluminium Co.); *m* Sara Ann Proctor. *Educ.:* Shrewsbury School. *Address:* Court Cl., North Wraxall, Chippenham, Wiltshire SN14 7AD.

MORTON, Cavendish, R.I., R.O.I., Hon. S.G.A., Hon. N.S.; painter of landscape, marine, in oil, water-colour, black and white; Vice Pres., Gainsborough's House Society, Vice-Pres., Norfolk Contemporary Arts Society; Past Chairman, Isle of Wight Council for the Arts, Vice-Pres., Isle of Wight Art Society; *b* Edinburgh, 17 Feb., 1911; *s* of Cavendish Morton; *m* Rosemary Britten; one *s,* two *d. Exhib.:* R.A., R.B.A., U.S.A., Canada, Australia, Bermuda; one-man shows: London, York University, Norwich, King's Lynn, Sudbury, Ipswich, Aldeburgh, Henley, Portsmouth. *Work in permanent collections:* B.M., Norwich Castle Museum, Wolverhampton A.G., Contemporary Arts Society, Eastern Arts Assoc., I.O.W. Cultural Services, Glasgow City A.G. *Publications:* illustrations for Dorothy Hammond Innes' Occasions (Michael Joseph, 1972), and What Lands are These (Collins, 1981). *Address:* 6 Fairhaven Cl., Bembridge, I.O.W. PO35 5SX. *Signs work:* "CAVENDISH MORTON."

MOSELEY, Austin Frank, R.B.S.A. (1988), C.A.S. (1987), C.Eng.M.I.-Mech.E. (1958); painter in oil, ink, pastel, charcoal; Council Mem. R.B.S.A.; *b* Tividale, Staffs., 25 Apr., 1930; *s* of Frank Moseley, engineering tool maker; *m* Sylvia; two *s. Educ.:* Dudley Technical College; *studied art* at Dudley School of Art (1946-50, Ivo Shaw). *Exhib.:* R.B.S.A., Chelsea Arts Soc., Dudley Mid. Art, etc. *Work in permanent collections:* Dudley Metropolitan County Borough, R.B.S.A, and many private and commercial collections. *Address:* 24 Raglan Cl., Sedgley, Dudley, W. Midlands DY3 3NH. *Signs work:* "Austin Moseley."

339

MOSELEY, Malcolm, B.A. (1969), M.A. (1973); painter in water-colour and mixed media drawing; *b* Birmingham, 2 Feb., 1947; *m* Christine Chippindale; one *s*. one *d. Educ.:* King Edward, Five Ways Grammar School, B'ham.; *studied art* at Winchester School of Art (1966-69), Central School of Art (1969-70), R.C.A. (1970-73, Alastair Grant). *Exhib.:* R.A., R.S.W., London Group, Mall Galleries, Barbican, Bury St. Edmunds Gallery, A.D. Fine Art London, New Academy Gallery London, John Russell Gallery Ipswich, etc. *Work in permanent collections:* Ipswich Museums, P. & O. *Address:* 133 Norwich Rd., Ipswich, Suffolk IP1 2PP. *Club:* Ipswich Folk. *Signs work:* "M.M" or "Malcolm Moseley."

MOUNT, Paul, A.R.C.A. (1948), R.W.A. (Hon.); sculptor in stainless steel, bronze, G.R.P. concrete; *b* 8 June, 1922; *s* of Ernest Edward Mount, B.Sc.; *m* (1st) Jeanne Martin (div.), (2nd) June Miles; one *s*, one *d. Educ.:* Newton Abbot Grammar School; *studied art* at Paignton School of Art (1937-40), R.C.A. (1940-41, 1946-48). *Exhib.:* one-man shows, A.A. London, Drian Gallery, John Whibley, Marlborough, New Art Centre, Galerie Ruf, Munich, Galerie Contemporaine, Geneva; mixed shows, R.A., R.B.S., London Group. *Work in permanent collections:* Harlow Art Trust, D.O.E., Cornwall Educ. Coll. *Commissions:* Fibreglass Ltd., B.S.C., Government House, Nigeria, Cabinet Offices, Accra, Swiss Embassy, Lagos, C.R.S., York House, Bristol. *Address:* Nancherrow Studio, St. Just, Cornwall TR19 7LA. *Clubs:* Penwith, R.W.A. *Signs work:* "Paul Mount."

MOUNTFORD, Derylie Anne, S.W.A. (1988); artist in pencil, etching, oil and water-colour; *b* London, 17 June, 1943; *d* of Alfred Hobson, F.R.C.S.; *m* Malcolm Mountford, B.A.(Oxon.); two *s. Educ.:* The Study, Wimbledon; *studied art* at Byam Shaw School of Art (1960-62, Peter Greenham, Bernard Dunstan), St. Martin's School of Art (1963). *Exhib.:* R.A., R.B.A., R.M.S., S.W.A., N.S.P.S., C.D.S.; one-man shows: Japan (1986, 1988), Lyric Theatre, Hammersmith (1990), Cambridge (1988); group shows: Cambridge, Ely, Saffron Walden, Salisbury, etc. *Work in permanent collection:* Addenbrookes Hospital Trust. *Address:* 54 Grantchester Meadows, Cambridge CB3 9JL. *Signs work:* "Derylie Mountford" (etchings), "D. Mountford" (paintings).

MOXLEY, Ray, F.R.I.B.A., R.W.A., Hon. F.(W.Eng.), of Moxley Jenner and Partners; architect of Chelsea Harbour and Exhibition Centres; Vice-president R.I.B.A. (1971-74), Chairman A.C.A. (1974-76); *b* 28 June, 1923; *s* of Rev. H.R. Moxley; *m* Jacqueline; one *s*, two *d. Educ.:* Caterham; *studied architecture* at Oxford (1940-42 and 1946-49). *Exhib.:* R.W.A. annual 1960 onwards, A.C.A. Salons at the Royal Academy (1982, 1984, 1986). *Publications:* Building Construction (Batsford), Fee Negotiations (A.P.), Architects Eye (G.P.C.), Building Management by Professionals (Butterworth). *Address:* 1 Hobhouse Ct., Suffolk St., London SW1Y 4HH. *Signs work:* "Ray Moxley."

MOYSE, Arthur; artist in collage, water-colour, pen and ink; art critic for Freedom Press, London Correspondent for Chicago Industrial Worker; *b* London, 21 June, 1914; *s* of Arthur Moyse, able seaman. *Educ.:* Addison Gardens L.C.C. Primary School. *Exhib.:* Angela Flowers Gallery, Woodstock and others. *Work in permanent collection:* Transport Museum. *Publications:* More in Sorrow, Zero One, Revolutionary Manifesto, Peterloo. *Address:* 39 Minford Gdns., W. Kensington, London W14 0AP. *Club:* Hon. Mem. Chelsea Arts. *Signs work:* "Arthur Moyse."

MUIR, Jane, artist, designer in mosaic and natural stone, charcoal and water-colour; *b* 1929; *d* of H. Pinches, M.D.; *m* A. W. E. Muir; two *s. Educ.:* Rye St. Antony School, Oxford University, Teesside College of Art under Joan Haswell.

M.A. Oxon (1950), Dip. Architectural Decoration (1969), F.C.S.D. (1974). *Main commissions:* St. Anne's College Oxford, Open University, Princes Sq., Glasgow, Rycote Development, Becket's Well, Northampton. Oxon County Museum, Buckinghamshire Educ. Authority, Canterbury Longmarket. *Private commissions:* in U.K., Arabian Gulf, Kenya, Australia. Represented U.K. at International Study Days in Modern Mosaic, Ravenna, Italy, 1980; International Contemporary Mosaic Symposium, Trier, W. Germany (1984), Louvain, Belgium (1986). *Address:* Butcher's Orchard, Weston Turville, Aylesbury, Bucks. *Signs work:* "Muir."

MULLEN GLOVER, Sybil, R.I. (1962), R.S.M.A. (1964), R.W.A. (1965); artist in water-colour; *b* Cheshire; *d* of W. T. C. W. Jeffery, step-daughter of Capt. A. J. C. Moore, O.B.E., R.N.; *m* Dr. W. E. Glover, Colonial Medical Service, Retd. *Educ.:* privately; *studied art* at St. Martin's School of Art and private tutors, including Vivian Pitchforth, R.A. *Exhib.:* R.A., N.E.A.C., R.O.I. and most leading galleries, including U.S.A. and Sweden. *Work in permanent collections:* Plymouth Museum A.G., R.W.A., Brighton A.G., National Maritime Museum, Sweyne School and Walsall. Gold and silver medals, Paris Salon. *Address:* Park Place, 108 Molesworth Rd., Stoke, Plymouth. *Signs work:* "Sybil Mullen Glover."

MULLETT, Vivien, A.R.M.S. (1992), H.S. (1990), B.A. Fine Art (1974); artist in water-colour, graphic designer; *b* Oxford, 1952; *m* Bill Bradford. *Educ.:* Milham Ford School, Oxford; *studied art* at Reading University (1970-74, Keith Critchlow). *Exhib.:* R.A. Summer Show, R.M.S., H.S., M.A.S.-F. *Publication:* illustrated The Night Watchman - collection of stories. *Address:* 111 Penwith Rd., Earlsfield, London SW18 4PY. *Signs work:* "V.M."

MULLINS, Edwin Brandt, M.A. (Hons.) Oxford University (1957); writer and film-maker, mainly on art subjects; *b* London, 1933; *s* of Claud Mullins, Metropolitan Magistrate; *m* Gillian Brydone (d. 1982); one *s*, two *d; m* Anne Kelleher (1984). Educ.: Midhurst Grammar School and Oxford University. *Publications:* numerous books and over 200 television films. *Address:* c/o Curtis Brown Ltd., 162 Regent St., London W1.

MULLINS, Gwen, O.B.E.; weaver in wool and linen with natural dyes; co-director of Graffham Weavers; *b* London, 10 Apr., 1904; *d* of Augustus Phillip Brandt, merchant banker; *m* Claud Mullins; one *s*, two *d. Exhib.:* Tea Centre (1965), Craft Centre, Red Rose Guild; Designer—Craftsmen yearly exhbn. in Graffham. *Work in permanent collection:* Royal Scottish Museum, Crafts Council, Textile Study Centre, V. & A. *Address:* Shuttles, Graffham, Petworth, Sussex. *Clubs:* British Crafts Centre, S.D.-C., Red Rose Guild, London Guild of Weavers, Spinners & Dyers. *Signs work:* "Gwen Mullins."

MUMBERSON, Stephen Leonard, A.R.E. (1991), M.A. (1981), B.A. (Hons.) (1977); Associate senior lecturer/printmaker in print/paint/mixed media; *b* Beaconsfield, 16 Feb., 1955. *Educ.:* Secondary Modern School, Bucks.; *studied art* at Brighton Polytechnic (1977-78), R.C.A. (1978-81, Prof. Grant, Chris. Orr), Cité des Arts, Paris (1980). *Exhib.:* R.E., Bankside London, Art Now London. *Work in permanent collections:* V. & A., U.S.A., Japan, S.America, Europe, Canada, Zambia, Zimbabwe. *Address:* c/o Fine Art Dept., Faculty of Performance, Art and Design, Middlesex University, Quicksilver Pl., Western Rd., London N22 6XH. *Signs work:* "Stephen Mumberson" or "S. Mumberson."

MUNDY, William Percy, R.M.S., F.S.C.D., M.A.A.; self-taught artist in water-colour and oil, miniaturist, portrait and Trompe l'oeil painter; *b*

Wokingham, 30 Oct., 1936; *s* of P. W. Mundy. *Educ.:* Forest School, Berks. *Exhib.:* R.A., R.M.S., R.P. Awarded "Exhibit of the Year" at 1980 and 1982 R.A. Summer Exhbns; Silver medal, Paris Salon (1982); Gold Memorial Bowl, R.M.S. (1986); Bell Award (1987). *Work in permanent collections:* H.R.H. The Duke of Edinburgh; H.M. King Bhumipol Aduladej of Thailand; The Yang di Pertuan Agong of Malaysia; H.R.H. The Sultan of Johore; Quaboos Bin Said, The Sultan of Oman; V. & A., London; Cincinatti Museum of Art, U.S.A. *Address:* 2 Marsh Mills, Wargrave Rd., Henley-on-Thames, Oxon. *Club:* Tanglin, Singapore; Phyllis Court, Henley. *Signs work:* "W. P. Mundy."

MURGATROYD, Keith, P.P.S.T.D., F.C.S.D., M.Inst.Pkg., (Hon.) M.R.N.C.M., F.R.S.A.; Managing director of Royle Murgatroyd Design Associates Ltd.; *m* Wendy Jean Nancy; two *d.* Chairman S.I.A.D., N.W. Region (1967-68); Treasurer and Vice-President of I.C.O.GRA.D.A. (1968-74); President Soc. of Typographic Designers (1969-73); Secretary-General of I.C.O.GRA.D.A. (1979-81); Mem. of New York Art Directors' Club and Type Directors' Club of New York. Visiting Prof. of Design at San Fernando State College; lecturer and author. *Work repro.:* Design Magazine, Print, Graphic Annual, Modern Publicity, etc. *Exhib.:* one-man shows: Monotype House, British Embassy, Washington, D.C., and numerous national and international colleges. *Address:* 41 Muswell Rd., Muswell Hill, London N10.

MURISON, Neil, A.T.D. (1951), R.W.A. (1979); painter in oil and acrylic; Co-ordinator, Dept. of Foundation Studies, Bristol Polytechnic (1961-87); previously art master, Queen Elizabeth's Hospital, Bristol (1952-61); *b* Bath, 10 Oct., 1930; *s* of William Murison, M.P.S., Ph.C.; *m* (1) Valerie Elizabeth John; one *s*, one *d;* (2) Sheila May Tilling (1985). *Educ.:* Bristol Grammar School; *studied art* at West of England College of Art (1946-51). *Work in permanent collections:* Nuffield, Wills Tobacco Co., Bank of America, Skopje Modern Art Museum, Yugoslavia, Trumans Breweries, Bridgwater Public Library, Bristol, Devon, Leeds, Herts., Hull, Leics., Liverpool, Surrey and West Riding of Yorks, Educ. Authorities. *Address:* 110 Redland Rd., Redland, Bristol 6. *Signs work:* "Murison."

MURRAY, Dawson Robertson, D.A. (1965), B.A.Hons. (1982), R.S.W. (1988); painter in water-colour, acrylic, etching; Head of Art and Design Dept., Boclair Academy, Bearsden; President, Glasgow Group of Artists; *b* Glasgow, 29 June, 1944; *s* of Dawson Murray, engineer and gardener; *m* Liz Murray; two *d. Educ.:* Albert Senior Secondary, Glasgow; *studied art* at Glasgow School of Art (1961-66, William Armour, Geoffrey Squire), L'Accademia delle Belle Arti, Venice (1966, Giuseppe Santomasso). *Exhib.:* one-man show: Richard Demarco Gallery (1990); Sarajevo (1986), Gallerio del Cavallino Venice (1982), R.S.A., S.S.A., R.S.W. *Work in permanent collections:* S.A.C., B.B.C. Scotland. *Address:* 7 Glencart Grove, Kilbarchan PA10 2DH. *Signs work:* "Dawson Murray."

MURRAY, Donald, B.A., D.A.; artist and designer in calligraphy, water-colour and pastel; Head of Art, Robert Gordon's College, Aberdeen; *b* Edinburgh, 1940; *s* of James Murray; *m* Mary F. Low; two *s. Educ.:* George Heriot's School, Edinburgh; *studied art* at Edinburgh College of Art (1958-63). *Exhib.:* R.S.W., S.S.A., Pitlochry Festival Theatre, Aberdeen Artists' Society. *Work in permanent collections:* Edinburgh District Council, Heriot-Watt University, Moray House College of Education, Edinburgh Merchant Company. *Publications:* illustrated Growing up in the Church, Christian Symbols, Ancient and Modern. *Address:* Manorlea, Commerce St., Insch, Aberdeenshire AB52 6JB. *Signs work:* "Donald Murray."

MUSGRAVE, Barbara, N.D.D.; sculptress specialising in portraiture and animals; painter in oil; *b* London 1937; *d* of Reginald Taylor, solicitor; *m* Peter Musgrave; one *s*, two *d*. *Educ.:* Maltman's Green, Gerrards Cross; *studied art* at Regent St. Polytechnic (1955-59) under Mr. Deeley. *Exhib.:* Harrow Art Soc., Mall Galleries, Compass Theatre, Ickenham, Smiths Covent Garden, Cow Byre Ruislip. *Address:* 25 Bury St., Ruislip, Middx. HA4 7SX. *Club:* N.S. *Signs work:* "B. Musgrave" or "B.M."

MUSZYNSKI, Leszek Tadeusz, D.A. (Edin.); artist in oil, pastel, watercolour, drawing, lithograph; Retd. Head of Painting School, West Surrey College of Art and Design; *b* Poland, 19 Apr., 1923; *s* of Alexander Muszynski; *m* Patricia; one *s*. *Educ.:* in Poland; *studied art* at Edinburgh College of Art (W. Gillies, J. Maxwell, W. MacTaggart); Travelling Scholarship to Paris, Florence, Arezzo, Assisi. *Work in permanent collections:* V. & A., N.P.G., L.C.C., National Museum, Poland, Museum of Art, Dallas, Texas, Museum, Durban, S. Africa. *Exhib.:* R.S.A. Edinburgh; one-man shows: London, Edinburgh, Copenhagen, Basle, Dallas, Texas, Warsaw, Cracow, Poznan. *Address:* West Wing, Bramshott Ct., Liphook GU30 7RG. *Signs work:* see appendix.

MYERS, Bernard, N.D.D. (1951), A.R.C.A. (1954), Hon. F.R.C.A., Hon. Prof. R.C.A.; painter in oil, water-colour, oil pastel, printmaker; taught at various London art schools and R.C.A.; Visiting Prof., Indian Inst. of Technology, New Delhi (1968-72), Prof., Brunel University (1980-85); *b* London, 22 Apr., 1925; *s* of D.N. Myers; *m* Pamela Blanche Fildes. *Studied art* at St. Martin's (1947-49), Camberwell School of Art (1949-51), R.C.A. (1951-54). *Address:* 5 St. Peter's Wharf, Hammersmith Terr., London W6 9UD. *Signs work:* "B. Myers" or "B.M."

MYERS, Mark Richard, B.A.(Hons.), R.S.M.A. (1975), A.S.M.A. (1978), C.S.M.A. (1985); marine artist in acrylic on canvas and water-colour; *b* San Mateo, Calif., U.S.A., 19 Nov., 1945; *s* of Jackson Sandine Myers, airline pilot; *m* Peternella Bouquet; one *s*, two *d*. *Educ.:* Pomona College, Calif. *Exhib.:* R.S.M.A., A.S.M.A., New York, London, Seattle. *Work in permanent collections:* National Maritime Museum, Greenwich, San Francisco Maritime Museum, N. Devon Maritime Museum. *Work repro.:* various maritime books illustrated. *Address:* The Old Forge, Woolley, Bude, Cornwall EX23 9PP. *Signs work:* "Mark Myers," "Mark Richard Myers" or "Myers."

MYNOTT, Derek George, N.E.A.C., D.F.A. (Lond.); painter in oil and water-colour, printmaker; *b* London, 27 Nov., 1926; *m* Patricia Barton, artist; two *s*, one *d*. *Studied art* at Slade School of Fine Art (1946-50). *Exhib.:* R.A., N.E.A.C., R.B.A.; one-man shows: R.B.A. Galleries (1953), Trafford Gallery (1959), Gstaad (1968), Jasper Galleries, Houston (1972-73) and New York (1974), Mall Galleries (1975), B.A.G. Royal Academy (1983, 1985). *Awards:* Medaille d'argent, Paris Salon (1974); Worshipful Co. of Painters Stainers (1987). *Work in permanent collections:* Tate Gallery (Curwen Archive), galleries, embassies, ministries and private collections in Europe, America, Japan. *Address:* 23 Mount Park Rd., London W5. *Signs work:* see appendix.

MYNOTT, Gerald P., S.S.I.; topographical artist, printmaker and calligrapher; *b* London, 1957; *s* of Derek Mynott, N.E.A.C., and Patricia Mynott, artist. *Studied art* at Reigate College of Art; College of Arms, London; Vienna Kunstlerhaus, Austria. *Exhib.:* Francis Kyle Gallery, London, continuously from

1980, New York (1984), Bath Festival (1983), Arts Club, London (1987). *Work repro.:* The Times, The Observer, Tatler, Radio Times, Weidenfeld and Nicolson, Penguin Books, V. & A. Publications, The Field, B.B.C. *Work in private and permanent collections:* V. & A., Tate Gallery (Curwen Archive), The Savoy Group, Chevening Estate, U.S.A., Tokyo. Lloyds Printmakers Award (1981). *Address:* 3 Belgrave House, 157 Marine Parade, Brighton, Sussex. *Club:* Arts.

MYNOTT, Katherine S., B.A.; illustrator/printmaker in gouache, line and lino; *b* London, 1962; *d* of Derek Mynott, N.E.A.C., and Patricia Mynott, artist; one *s. Studied art* at Heatherley School of Art, Central School of Art and St. Martin's School of Art. *Work repro.:* Vogue, Radio Times, Daily Telegraph, Tatler, Harpers and Queen, B.B.C., Palace Pictures, Cosmopolitan, Time Out, Over 21, 19, The Observer, The Listener, I.P.C., New Society, Economist, etc. *Address:* 23 Mount Park Rd., London W5. *Signs work:* "K. Mynott."

MYNOTT, Lawrence, M.A. (R.C.A.), A.O.I.; portrait painter, illustrator in water-colour, oil, line and gouache; lecturer and art writer; *b* London, 1954; *s* of Derek Mynott, N.E.A.C., and Patricia Mynott, artist. *Studied art* at Chelsea School of Art (1972-76), Royal College of Art (1976-79). *Exhib.:* R.A., European Illustrators, Folio Soc., Thames Television; two one-man shows of portraits at Cale Art, Chelsea. *Work in permanent collections:* N.P.G., National Gallery of Wales, Hull A.G., Arts Council. Awarded D. & A.D. silver award (1985). Lecturer at V. & A., 'The Sitwells as Patrons', Neo-Romanticism, The Rococo Revival. *Work repro.:* Radio Times, Vogue, Tatler, Harpers and Queen, The Observer, Penguin Books, Macmillans, Hamish Hamilton, etc. *Address:* c/o "The Organisation", 69 Caledonian Rd., London N1. (Agent). *Club:* Chelsea Arts. *Signs work:* "Lawrence Mynott", "Mynott" or monogram "L.M."

MYNOTT, Patricia; film designer, illustrator and natural history artist working in water-colour, line and gouache; *b* London, 1927; *m* Derek Mynott, N.E.A.C.; two *s*, one *d. Educ.:* Dominican Convent, Chingford; *studied art* at S.W. Essex School of Art. *Films:* National Screen Service, National Savings, Film Producers Guild. *Publications:* illustrated, Marine Life of the Caribbean, Guide to the Seashore, Beaches and Beachcombing, Folklore of Fossils, The Curious Lore of Malta's Fossil Sharks Teeth, Edible Seaweeds; children's books: Encyclopedias, Educational Teaching Alphabet. *Publishers:* Blackies, Readers Digest, Paul Hamlyn, Michael Joseph, Macdonalds, Pitmans, Sacketts. *Address:* 23 Mount Park Rd., London W5. *Signs work:* "Patricia Mynott" or "Barton."

N

NALECZ, Halima, F.F.P.S.; Dip. U.S.B. (Wilno), Dame Chevalier d'Honneur (18 May, 1957); Bronze Medal, Europe prize for painting, Kursaal, Ostend,Belgium (1969, 1971); painter in oils and mixed media; Founder and Director of Drian Galleries, London; *b* Wilno, Poland, 2 Feb., 1917; *d* of Antoni Kzrywicz-Nowohonski, landowner; *m* Zygmunt Nalecz, writer. *Educ.:* Lycée, Wilno; *studied art* under Professor Roube, Professor Szyszko-Bohusz, Professor Zahorska, and in Paris under H. J. Closon. *Exhib.:* most municipal and public galleries in England, and W.I.A.C., A.I.A., Free Painters and Sculptors, London Group, Salon de Réalités Nouvelle, Galerie Collette Allendy, Salon des

Divergences, Galerie Creuze (Paris); one-man exhbns. at Walker Galleries, London (1956), New Vision Centre, London (1957, 1959), Ewan Phillips, London (1967), County Town Gallery, Lewes (1967), Drian Galleries, London (1968-69), R.A. Summer Exhbn. (1967, 1968, 1969), S.S.W.A., Edinburgh. *Work in permanent collections:* Britain, France, Spain, Italy, Germany, Australia, U.S.A., Sweden, Nuffield Foundation, London, National Gallery of Israel, Bezalel, Jerusalem, National Museum in Warsaw, Gdansk, Poznan. *Work repro:* Quadrum, Apollo, Arts Review, Art and Artists, Wiadomosci, Art International, etc.; prefaces to catalogues by Denis Bowen and Pierre Rouve. Paintings featured in film, The Millionairess. *Address:* 7 Porchester Pl., Marble Arch, London W2 2BT. *Clubs:* A.I.A., W.I.A.C., Hampstead Artists Association, Free Painters and Sculptors, Polish Hearth. *Signs work:* see appendix.

NAPP, David, Dip. C.S.D., Elizabeth Greenshields Foundation award (1986, 1990); artist in chalk, pastel, oil and water-colour; sessional lecturer, Kent Inst. of Art and Design; *b* London, 5 Mar., 1964. *Educ.:* Queen Elizabeth's School, Faversham; *studied art* at Canterbury College of Art (1981-85). *Exhib.:* Bourne Gallery, Reigate (1987-), Art London (1989, 1990, 1991), Walker Galleries, R.W.S., R.B.A., P.S., Napier Gallery Jersey. *Publication:* illustrations: Encyclopaedia of Pastel Techniques (Headline). *Address:* Windmill Cottage, Mill La., Barham, Canterbury, Kent CT4 6HH. *Signs work:* "David Napp" and date.

NAPPER, Helen, B.A. (1980), M.F.A. (1983), P.G.C.E. (1985); painter in oil on board; *b* Wivenhoe, 29 Mar., 1958; *d* of Peter Napper. *Educ.:* Friends School, Saffron Walden; Colchester County High School for Girls; *studied art* at Colchester Art School, Wimbledon Art School (Maggi Hambling, Colin Cina), Reading University (Adrian Heath, Terry Frost), London University Central School of Art (Norman Ackroyd, Bernard Cheese). *Exhib.:* Sue Rankin Gallery (1989-91), L.A. Contemporary Art Fair (1989, 1990), Olympia Art, London (1990, 1991) with Sue Rankin Gallery, Tatistcheff and Co., N.Y. and L.A. (1992, 1993). *Work in permanent collection:* Citicorp Bank, London. *Address:* 5 Castle Hill, Orford, Suffolk. *Signs work:* "Helen Napper."

NASH, Tom, A.T.D., R.C.A.; artist in oil, P.V.A., gouache, collage, murals in retroreflective plastics, etc.; awarded the Geoffrey Crawshay Memorial Travelling Scholarship; West Wales Association for the Arts, Research Award; *b* Ammanford, 1931; *s* of William Nash; *m* Enid Williams; two *d. Educ.:* Llandeilo; *studied art* at Swansea, Paris, Provence; associated with Paul Jenkins in Paris. *Exhib.:* one-man and mixed exhibitions in London, provinces, Washington, D.C., Argentine, Toronto. *Work in permanent collections:* National Museum of Wales, Nuffield Foundation, Arts Council, Clare, Churchill, Pembroke Colleges, Cambridge, various county collections, Caerleon College of Education, Glynn Vivian Art Gallery, Swansea, Steel Company of Wales, C.A.S., Caiman Museum, Argentina, Wadham College, Oxford, University of Wales, India Rubber Co., Macco Corp., California, Brasenose College, Oxford, Trinity College of Education, 3M United Kingdom Limited, University of Bradford, Church of Wales Collection; private collections in Britain, France, Germany, U.S.A., Canada, New Zealand. *Address:* Clydfan, Llandeilo, Dyfed, Wales. *Signs work:* "Tom Nash."

NEAGU, Paul; sculptor, painter, Anglo-romanian; lecturer (1972-91); *b* Bucharest, 1938; *s* of Tudor Neagu. *Educ.:* Inst. 'N. Grigorescu' Bucharest (1959-65). *Major works:* 'Palpable and tactile objects' (1965-90), 'Anthropo-cosmos' (1968-81), 'Performance' (1969-77), 'Hyphen' (1974-93), 'Nine Catalytic

Stations' (1975-87), 'Unnamed' (1983-92), 'Newhyphen' (1991-93). *Permanent collections:* U.K., U.S.A., Japan, Germany, Romania, France, Ireland. *Outdoor sculpture;* Middlesbrough, London, Bucharest, Timisoara. *Publications:* 'Palpable Art' (1969), 'Generative Arts' (1977), 'Hyphen' (1985), 'Deep Space and Solid Time' (1988). *Address:* 31C Jackson Rd., London N7 6ES. *Signs work:* "Paul Neagu" or "P. Neagu."

NEAL, Arthur Richard, Dip.A.D.; painter/printmaker in oil, water-colour and etching; *b* Chatham, 15 Mar., 1951; *m* Jane; one *s,* one *d. Educ.:* Reeds School; *studied art* at Camberwell School of Art. *Exhib.:* R.A. Summer Shows, Cadogan Contemporary. *Publication:* Illustrated Poems of Edward Thomas. *Address:* 32 Duke St., Deal, Kent CT14 6DT. *Club:* N.E.A.C. *Signs work:* "ARN" or "ARNEAL" or not at all.

NEAL, Charles William, B.Sc. Hons. (1980); landscape painter in oil; *b* Carshalton, 27 Nov., 1951; *m* Susan Ann; one *s. Educ.:* Highview High School/ City of London University; *studied art:* initially private tuition with Malcolm Domingo and Francis Lane-Mason; later self taught to perfect style and technique. *Exhib.:* Omell Gallery (1982); R.B.A.: Omell Gallery (1983), Godalming Gallery (1984), Harrods Picture Gallery (1985); annual exhbns. at John Campbell Gallery. *Work in permanent collections:* one royal and many private and commercial collections both national and international. *Address:* Woodmancote, Glos. *Gallery affiliation:* John Campbell Gallery, 164 Walton St., London SW3 2JL. *Signs work:* C. Neal."

NEAL, James, A.R.C.A. (1939); artist; *b* Islington, 18 Jan., 1918; *s* of James Abram Neal; *m* Doreen Barnes; two *s,* one *d. Educ:* St. John Evangelist; *studied art* at St. Martin's School of Art; R.C.A. *Exhib.:* R.A., R.S.A., N.E.A.C., London Group, Redfern Galleries; one-man shows Trafford Gallery, Wildensteins, etc. *Official purchases:* Nottingham A.G., Wakefield A.G., Ferens A.G., Hull, Beverley A.G., Graves A.G., Sheffield, London County Council, Hull Educ. Com., W. Riding Educ. Com., East Riding Educ. Com., Derbyshire Educ. Com., Durham Educ. Com., etc. *Address:* 205 Victoria Ave., Hull, N. Humberside HU5 3EF. *Signs work:* "James Neal."

NEAL, Trevor; self-taught artist in oil; *b* York, 1947; *m* Sharon; one *d. Exhib.:* Graves A.G. (1972-75, 1977), White Rose Gallery Bradford (1974), R.A. (1975, 1980, 1981, 1992), Art Centre St. Petersburg, U.S.A. (1980, 1982), Anderson Marsh Galleries St. Petersburg (1983), Ginnel Gallery Manchester (1988), Evander Preston Gallery St. Petersburg (1988, 1989, 1991), S. Yorks. Open Cooper A.G. Barnsley (1989). *Work in public and private collections:* U.K., U.S.A., France, Germany, Israel. *Commissioned work:* U.K., U.S.A., Germany. *Address:* Fossdale Towers, 23 Fossdale Rd., Sheffield S7 2DA. *Signs work:* see appendix.

NEALE, John; self taught landscape and seascape painter in oil and water-colour; *b* 13 Sept., 1944; divorced; two *s,* one *d. Studied art:* self taught, but privately helped by Edward Seago. *Exhib.:* Omell Galleries, Quantas Galleries, Frost and Reed, Bristol, John Noott, Broadway, Chime Gallery, N.J., etc. *Work in private collections* in Europe and U.S.A. *Address:* Maple Leaf House, 59 Maidenhead Rd., Stratford-on-Avon. *Signs work:* "John Neale."

NEASOM, Norman, R.W.S. (1978), R.B.S.A. (1947), Hon.S.A.S. (1976); artist in water-colour and gouache; retd. art master; *b* Tardebigge, 7 Nov., 1915; *s* of Arthur Neasom, farmer; *m* Jessie Mary; two *d. Educ.:* Redditch County High; *studied art* at Birmingham College of Art (1931-35, Harold H. Holden,

Michael Fletcher, Fleetwood Walker, R.A., W.F. Colley, H. Sands). *Exhib.:* R.A. (1970, 1974, 1976), R.W.S., R.B.S.A., Stratford Art Soc., Mall Galleries. *Work in permanent collections:* West Midland Arts Council and various private collections. *Work repro.:* articles for Leisure Painter, covers for Readers' Digest. *Address:* 95 Bromfield Rd., Redditch, Worcs. B97 4PN. *Club:* Redditch Sailing (founder). *Signs work:* "N. NEASOM" and date.

NEILAND, Brendan, R.A. (1992), Dip.A.D. (1966), M.A. (1969), Silver Medal R.C.A. (1969); painter in acrylic on canvas, printmaker in silkscreen, lithography; *b* Lichfield, 23 Oct., 1941; *m* Hilary; two *d. Educ.:* St. Philip's G.S., B'ham; St. Augustine's Seminary, Ireland; *studied art* at B'ham College of Art (1962-66, William Gear, John Walker, Ivor Abrahams), R.C.A. (1966-69, Carel Weight, Roger de Grey). *Exhib.:* Angela Flowers Gallery, Fischer Fine Art, Redfern Gallery. *Work in permanent collections:* Tate Gallery, V. & A., British Council, Arts Council. *Addresses:* 24 The Chase, London SW4 0NH; Crepe, La Greve sur Mignon, Courcon 17170, France. *Club:* Chelsea Arts. *Signs work:* "Brendan Neiland" on all prints and paper work; "NEILAND" stencilled onto back of canvas on stretcher.

NEILL, Errol James, LL.B. (Lond.), Paris Salon: Silver Medallist (1980), Gold Medallist (1981); solicitor; artist in oil and pastel; *b* Doune, Perthshire, 15 Aug., 1941; *s* of James Francis Neill; *m* Audrey Bradbury; one *s*, two *d. Educ.:* Christ Church, Preston. *Exhib.:* R.B.A., R.O.I., R.S.M.A., N.E.A.C., U.A., S.E.A., Lancashire Art, Société des Artistes Francais, Paris, Deauville, N.Y., Melbourne, Australia. *Work in private collections:* Britain, France, Eire, U.S.A., S. America. *Work repro.:* Travelling the Turf 1987 to 1992. *Address:* Bridge House, 217 Chapel La., New Longton, Preston, Lancs. PR4 4AD. *Clubs:* Law Soc. Art Group, New Longton Artists. *Signs work:* "ERROL NEILL."

NELLENS, Roger; painter in oil on canvas; *b* Liege, Belgium, 11 May, 1937; *s* of Gustave Nellens; one *s*, two *d. Educ.;* College St. Michel et St. Louis, Brussels, and London Academy; autodidact. *Work in permanent collections:* Collection de l'Etat Belge; Musée d'Ostende; Collection de la Flandre Occidentale, Bruges; Museum Boymans-van Beuningen, Rotterdam; Musée d'Art et d'Industrie, St. Etienne France; CNAC, Paris; McCrory Corp., N.Y.; Tate Gallery, London; Musée d'Art Moderne, Brussels. *Address:* Fort St. Pol, Zoutelaan, 280, 8300 Knokke-Heist, Belgium. *Signs work:* on the back; see appendix.

NELSON, Kathleen, A.R.M.S. (1984), H.S.F. (1982); Hon. Men. Gold Memorial Bowl award R.M.S. (1985), Drummond award R.M.S. (1984); wildlife, equestrian and natural history artist in water-colour and oil; *b* Durham City, 12 Mar., 1956. *Educ.:* Whinney Hill Secondary School, Durham, and Durham Wearside. *Exhib.:* R.M.S., H.S., Medici Gallery, Llewellyn Alexander Gallery; solo shows: Darlington A.G., Durham A.G. *Work in permanent collection:* Durham A.G. *Publication:* chapter with illustrations, The Techniques of Painting Miniatures by S. Burton (B.T. Batsford Ltd., 1994). *Address:* 18 Beverley Gdns., Chester-le-Street, Co. Durham DH3 3NB. *Signs work:* "Kathleen Nelson."

NESSLER, Walter H.; Gold and Silver Medal, Academy Campanella, Rome; landscape painter in oil, polyester resin, reliefs; teacher; *b* Leipzig, 19 Jan., 1912; *m*; one *s. Studied art* at Castelli, Italian Art School at Dresden (1933-35), and self-taught. *Exhib.:* R.A., R.B.A., Leger Galleries, Redfern Gallery, Arcade Gallery, Twenty Brook St. Gallery, Galerie des Beaux-Arts (Paris), Bradford City Art Gallery, New Vision Gallery, Gallery One, Obelisk Gallery, John

Whibley Gallery, O'Hana Gallery, Molton Gallery, Hendon Group, New End Gallery, Madden Galleries, Harlow Festival, Alwin Gallery, Gallery Petit, Rotunda Gallery, Erica Bourne Gallery, German Embassy, M. Fisher Gallery, London, Galerie Grigerson, Hamburg, Centaur Gallery, Pentonville Gallery, John Denham Gallery, Art in Exile Berlin-London. *Work in permanent collections:* C.A.S., Municipal Museum, Leicester, R.A.F. Museum, Hendon, Ein Harod Museum (Israel); and private collections in America, S. Africa, England, Norway. *Address:* 16 Somali Rd., London NW2 3RJ. *Club:* C.A.S. *Signs work:* "Nessler."

NEUENSCHWANDER, James Brody, Ph.D., M.Phil., A.B.; calligrapher, lettering artist, graphic designer, textile designer in ink and paint on paper, cloth, vellum, glass engraving; *b* Houston, Texas, 8 Sept., 1958. *Educ.:* Princeton University, Courtauld Inst.; *studied art* at Roehampton Inst. under Ann Camp. *Exhib.:* Princeton University Library, Museum of Fine Arts, Houston, Warwick University, Sheffield City A.G. *Work in permanent collections:* Princeton University, Westminster Cathedral. *Publications:* Modern German Calligraphy - Special issue of Letter Exchange Magazine; Letterwork - Creative Letterforms for Graphic Design (Phaidon, London 1993). *Address:* Spinolarei 2, 8000 Bruges, Belgium. *Signs work:* "Brody Neuenschwander."

NEVETZ: see COX, Stephen B.

NEVIA: see ROGERS, Joseph Shepperd.

NEW, Vincent Arthur; Elected M.A.W.G. (1938); topographical illustrator, water-colour painter; handprinter, etcher, line engraver, black and white; Naval Intelligence Division Illustrator (1943-67); *b* Bromley, 27 Apr., 1906; *s* of Frederick New, produce surveyor (cargo); *m* Dorothy Keeler; one *s*, five *d*. *Educ.:* Bromley County School; *studied art* at Bromley and Beckenham Art Schools (1925-29) under Mr. Schofield, H. A. Budd, Baylis Allen, Roland Gill; Camberwell School of Art (1931) lithography. *Work in permanent collections:* Napier, N.Z. Prints, Bromley and Sevenoaks Libraries, N.B.L. *Publication:* 75 Villages of Kent for the Kentish Times, etc. (1931-33). *Address:* Stanholm, Mill Hill, Edenbridge, Kent TN8 5DB. *See Obituary.*

NEWBERRY, John Coverdale, A.R.W.S. (1990), O.A.S. (1987), B.A. Dunelm (1960), M.A.Oxon. (1989); Water-colour Foundation prize R.W.S. Open (1990); painter of landscapes in water-colour and figure compositions in oil; tutor, Ruskin School of Drawing, Oxford (1963-89); *b* Horsham, 8 May, 1934; *s* of G.W. Newberry, M.A. *Educ.:* Kingswood School, Bath; School of Architecture, Cambridge; *studied art* at King's College, Newcastle upon Tyne (1957-60, Lawrence Gowing, Victor Pasmore). *Exhib.:* R.W.S., O.A.S., R.A., R.I., N.E.A.C., numerous one-man shows mostly in Oxford: Ashmolean (1978), Chris Beetles (1990, 1991), Duncan Campbell (1993). *Address:* Barn Cottage, Old Boars Hill, Oxford OX1 5JQ. *Signs work:* "Newberry."

NEWBURY, Brian James, F.R.S.A., Mem. B.A.D.A.; specialist in marine, military, sporting and topographical prints, paintings and water-colours, ship models, etc.; Chairman and Managing Director of the Parker Gallery; *b* London, 24 Dec., 1941; *s* of Bertram Newbury; *m* Barbara Mary Williams; one *s*. *Educ.:* Bembridge School, I.O.W. *Address:* 49 Peplins Way, Brookmans Park, Herts. AL9 7UR. *Clubs:* Naval, Sloane.

NEWCOMB, Mary, painter; B.Sc. Natural Sciences; *b* Harrow-on-the-Hill, 25 Jan., 1922; *m* Godfrey Newcomb; two *d*. *Address:* Rushmeadow, Newton Flotman, Norwich, Norfolk NR15 1QX. *Signs work:* "Mary Newcomb."

NEWICK, John; lecturer in education, University of London Institute of Education (1968-86); lecturer in art education, Birmingham College of Art and Design (1952-62, 1964-65); lecturer then reader in art education, University of Science and Technology, Ghana (1962-64); lecturer, Faculty of Education, Makerere University College, Uganda (1965-66); staff exchange, School of Education, University of California, Berkeley (1969); visiting lecturer, University of British Columbia (summer 1970, 1975-76) and Stanford University (summer 1973); *b* Bristol, 30 Nov., 1919. *Educ.:* The Grammar School, Bristol; *studied art* at West of England College of Art. *Address:* Beechwood Lodge, Bannerdown Rd., Bath BA1 7NE.

NEWLAND, Anne; Edwin Abbey Major Scholarship (1938); *b* Wilts., 11 Jan., 1913. *Educ.:* Byam Shaw Art School (1934-38). *Address:* 4 Vaughan Rd., London SE5 9NZ.

NEWMAN, Colin Ralph; artist in water-colour and pen and ink; (retd.); 30 years litho-artist Mardon Son & Hall; *b* Chipping Sodbury, 1923; *m* Hylda; one *d. Educ.:* St. John's Chipping Sodbury; *studied art:* Academy of Art, Florence and West of England Academy; printing at Merchant Venturers, Bristol. *Exhib.:* R.W.A., R.W.S., S.B.A., and many west country galleries. *Work in permanent collections:* Barclays Bank Head Office, D.R.G. Head Office; private collections in Europe, America, S. Africa and U.K. *Publications:* greetings cards and calendars. *Address:* 28 Field View Drive, Downend, Bristol BS16 2TT. *Signs work:* "Colin Newman."

NEWTON, Irene Margaret, N.R.D. (1940), F.R.S.A. (1940), F.I.A.L. (1958); woven textile designer (handweaving and machine), artist in oils, black and white, water-colour; senior lecturer in art and crafts at Elizabeth Gaskell College of Education, Manchester; asst. at Stourbridge School of Art (1949-59); asst. at Hereford School of Art (1946-49); *b* 23 Dec., 1915. *Educ.:* High School for Girls, Truro, Cornwall; *studied art* at Truro School of Art. *Exhib.:* Hereford, Wolverhampton, R.B.S.A., Worcester, Paris Salon, R.B.A. and United Soc. *Work repro.:* in La Revue Moderne. *Address:* 119 Garstang Rd., Southport. *Signs work:* "I. M. Newton", or see appendix.

NEWTON, Joanna Dawson; Dip. in Art (1982); artist in oil on canvas, charcoal drawing; *b* Oxford, 24 Apr., 1958; *d* of Dr. G. F. Newton. *Educ.:* Headington School, Oxford; *studied art* at Byam Shaw School of Art (1979-82, P. Gopal-Chowdhuny, N. Volley). *Exhib.:* Whitechapel Open, N.P.G., John Player award, R.A. Summer Exhbn., Picture Brokers Exhbn. *Address:* 60 St. Dionis Rd., Fulham, London SW6. *Club:* Chelsea Arts. *Signs work:* "Joanna D. Newton."

NEWTON-DAVIES, Diana Elizabeth: see WHITESIDE, Diana Elizabeth Hamilton.

NG, Kiow Ngor, Dip.F.A. (1989); artist in painting and printmaking; *b* Singapore, 6 Apr., 1963. *Studied art* at Nan Yang Academy of Fine Arts (1986-89), Slade School of Fine Art (1991-93). *Exhib.:* London Group (1992), R.A. Summer Show (1992, 1993). *Address:* 9A Kang Choo Bin Rd., Singapore 1954. *Signs work:* see appendix.

NGUYEN, Tân-Phuoc; Mem. Confédération Internationale des Associations des Experts et de Conseils auprès de Conseil Economique et Social de l'Onu; Director, Galerie Arts Anciens de Chine et Extrême-Orient; Président de la Chambre International de Commerce Vietnam-Suisse; art expert on Asiatic archaeology, specialised in the founding of Fine Art Collections and Muséums, historian, writer; *b* 10 Nov., 1932; *s* of Van-Phùng Nguyen, mandarin; *m* Hélène Gerber; two *s. Educ.*: Saigon, S. Vietnam, and Paris; *studied art* at l'Institut Hautes, Etudes Indochinoises, and Ecole du Louvre. *Publications*: Archéologie asiatique, Netzuke, La Culture de Ban-Chiang (Siam) 7.000-5.000 ans, Fouilles archéologiques à Ban-Chiang. Conférencier invité à Davos Symposium (from 1985) by E.M.F. *Address*: 30 Grand Rue, Genève 1204. *Clubs*: Club Alpin Suisse, Musée d'Ethnographie, Musée des Collections Baur-Duret, Union Internationale des Experts, Croix Rouge Suisse, Intérêt de Genève, Kiwanis International, Président, Asia Africa Museum (GVA) (1993), Chevalier du Tastevin.

NICHOLAS, Peter, N.D.D. (1956), A.R.C.A. (1962), F.R.B.S. (1993); sculptor in stone, bronze, G.R.P.; *b* Ebbw Vale, S. Wales, 1934; *m* Marjorie (decd.); one *s*, two *d. Educ.*: Ebbw Vale County Grammar School; *studied art* at Cardiff College of Art (1951-56, Frank Roper, Geof Milsom), R.C.A. (1958-61, John Skeaping). *Exhib.*: Jonathan Poole Fine Art. *Work in private and public collections*: U.K., Europe, U.S.A. *Publications*: Art in Architecture an Architects Choice (Eugene Rosenberg), The Encyclopedia of Sculpture Techniques (John Mills). *Address*: Craig-y-Don, Horton, Gower, W. Glam. SA3 1LB. *Signs work*: "P.W. NICHOLAS."

NICHOLLS, Howard John, B.A. (Hons.) (1975), R.B.A. (1983); painter in oils, drawings mixed media, lecturer; Lecturer in Fine Art, Epsom School of Art and Design (1979-84); *b* 14 Jan., 1950; *s* of E. J. Nicholls. *Educ.*: Selhurst Grammar School; *studied art* at Camberwell School of Art (1972-75), R.A. Schools (1975-78). *Exhib.*: R.A., R.B.A. *Official purchase*: S.I.U. Cooke Fund (1979). *Work repro.*: Home Artist. *Address*: 19 Drakefield Rd., London SW17. *Signs work*: "H. Nicholls."

NICHOLS, Patricia Mary, R.M.S., S.W.A.; portrait painter in miniature and full size portrait drawings in sanguine, chalk; Mem. Royal Society of Miniature Painters; and Soc. of Women Artists; *d* of the late W/Cdr. E. T. Carpenter, A.F.C., R.A.F.; *m* John Trevor Nichols, M.C.I.T.; one *s*, one *d. Educ.*: innumerable private schools; *studied art* at Central School of Arts and Crafts London. *Exhib.*: R.I., Mall Galleries, Westminster Gallery and several others, and has undertaken many important, including royal, commissions. *Work repro.*: The Artist, Illustrated county magazines and newspapers. *Address*: Sealand, Wodehouse Rd., Old Hunstanton, Norfolk PE36 6JD. *Signs work*: "Patricia Nichols."

NIVEN, Margaret Graeme, R.O.I. (1936), N.S. (1932); painter of landscapes, still life and portraits; *b* 1906; *d* of William Niven, F.S.A., J.P., A.R.E. *Educ.*: Prior's Field, Godalming; Heatherley School of Fine Art, and under Bernard Adams, R.P., R.O.I. *Exhib.*: R.A., R.P., R.O.I., National Soc., Leicester Galleries, Wildenstein's, etc; three one-man shows. *Official purchases*: Bradford City Art Gallery; Homerton College, Cambridge; Ministry of Works for embassies abroad, Bedford College, London. *Work repro.*: flower pieces. *Address*: Broomhill, Sandhills, Godalming, Surrey, GU8 5UF. *Signs work*: "Niven."

NOAKES, Michael, P.P.R.O.I., R.P., C.P.S., Hon. N.S., Hon. U.A., Cert. R.A.S., N.D.D.; landscape and portrait painter (subjects include H.M. the Queen, other members royal family, etc.); Chairman (1971) Contemporary Portrait Society; Pres. Royal Institute of Oil Painters (1972-78); art critic (1964-68), B.B.C. Television; *b* Brighton, 28 Oct., 1933; *m;* two *s*, one *d. Educ.*: Downside; *studied art* at R.A. Schools. *Exhib.*: R.A., R.O.I., R.P., R.B.A., N.S., etc. *Work in permanent collections*: H.M. the Queen, H.R.H. the Prince of

Wales, B.M., National Portrait Gallery, etc. *Work repro.:* widely. *Publication:* A Professional Approach to Oil Painting (Pitmans, 1968). *Address:* 146 Hamilton Terr., London NW8 9UX. *Signs work:* "Michael Noakes," with date underneath.

NOELLE: see SIMPSON, Noelle.

NOOTT, Edward John, B.A.; painter in oil; *b* W. Midlands, 4 Oct., 1965; *s* of John Noott, Fine Art Dealer; *m* Denise Cardone; one *s. Educ.:* Cheltenham College; *studied art* at Gloucestershire College of Art, Cheltenham, Trent Polytechnic College, Nottingham, State University of N.Y. *Exhib.:* John Noott Galleries. *Address:* c/o 14 Cotswold Ct., Broadway, Worcs. WR12 7AA. *Signs work:* "Edward Noott."

NORBURY, Ian, B.A. (1979); sculptor in wood, metal, semi precious stones; *b* Sheffield, 21 Aug., 1948; *s* of Kenneth Peter Norbury; *m* Betty Ann; two *s*, one *d. Educ.:* Andover Grammar; St. Paul's College, Cheltenham; *studied art* at St. Paul's College, Cheltenham (Harold Sayer, R.E., R.W.A., A.R.C.A.). *Exhib.:* annual one-man. *Work in permanent collections:* Tower of London, Fine Art Museum of the South of Mobile, U.S.A., many private collections. *Publications:* Techniques of Creative Woodcarving, Projects for Creative Woodcarving, Relief Woodcarving and Lettering, Fundamentals of Figure Carving (1993). *Address:* White Knight Gallery, 28 Painswick Rd., Cheltenham, Glos. GL50 2HA. *Signs work:* "IAN NORBURY," "I. NORBURY" or "I.N."

NORDEN, Gerald, A.R.C.A. (1937); still-life painter in oil; *b* Hampstead, London, 28 June, 1912; *s* of Alfred van Noorden, merchant; *m* Lilian Moorhead; one *s*, two *d. Educ.:* Arnold House, NW8; *studied art* at Thanet School of Art (J. Moody, B. Willis), R.C.A. (Gilbert Spencer, Percy Horton). *Exhib.:* Trafford Gallery (1969-75), King St. Gallery (1976-86), Catto Gallery (1991-93). *Publication:* A Practical Guide to Perspective (Longman). *Address:* 11 Julian Rd., Folkestone, Kent CT19 5HP. *Signs work:* "NORDEN."

NORLAND (NEUSCHUL), Khalil, M.A. Physics (Oxon.); artist-painter in mixed media; *b* Aussig (Usti), Czechoslovakia, 25 Mar., 1934; *s* of Ernest Neuschul-Norland, artist-painter; *m* Layla Shamash; three *s. Educ.:* Merton College, Oxford; *studied art* at Ruskin College of Art, Oxford (1953-57), Slade School of Art London University (1959-60). *Exhib.:* Artist House, Jerusalem (1959), Woodstock Gallery, London (1961), Gallerie Lambert, Paris (1964), Camden Arts Centre, London (1987), Queen Elizabeth House, Oxford (1987), Loggia Gallery, London (1988), Haus am Lützowplatz, Berlin (1991). *Address:* 25 Southmoor Rd., Oxford OX2 6RF. *Signs work:* see appendix.

NORMAN, Barbara; Paris Salon bronze medal (1975), silver medal (1976); glass engraver in diamond point, flexible drive drill; *b* London; *d* of Augustus Arthur Norman. *Studied art* at Stanhope Institute and glass engraving at Morley College under Mary Stevens. *Exhib.:* Bourne Hall, Ewell, New Ashgate Gallery, Farnham, Florida Gulf Coast Art Center, Clearwater, Florida, Tampa Bay Art Center, Florida. *Publications:* Engraving and Decorating Glass (David and Charles 1972, McGraw Hill, U.S.A. 1972); Glass Engraving (David and Charles 1981, ARCO, U.S.A. 1981, A. H. & A. W. Reed, Australia 1981). *Address:* 9 Downs Lodge Court, Church St., Epsom, Surrey. KT17 4QG. *Signs work:* "Barbara Norman."

NORMAN, Michael Radford, R.S.M.A. (1975); artist/model maker, in pen and water-colour, often of river and coastal scenes; *b* Ipswich, 20 Aug., 1933; *s* of Frank Norman, builder; two *d. Educ.:* Woodbridge School; *studied art* at Bournemouth School of Art. *Exhib.:* R.I., R.S.M.A.; one-man shows, Colchester,

Ipswich, Norwich, etc. *Work in permanent collection:* water-colour at D.O.E. *Publication:* illustrated, The Suffolk Essex Border by John Salmon. *Address:* The Studio, Woolverstone, Ipswich, Suffolk. *Signs work:* "Michael Norman" usually in black ink.

NORRIS, David, Cert. R.A.S., F.R.B.S.: sculptor in bronze; Vice-Pres. Royal Soc. of British Sculptors; *b* São Paulo, Brazil, 26 Sept., 1940; *s* of Sir Alfred Norris, K.B.E.; *m* Carol; three *d. Educ.:* Millfield; *studied art* at Guildford School of Art and R.A. Schools. *Exhib.:* R.A., Mall Galleries, Royal Mint. *Work in permanent collections:* 'Women and Doves' Stevenage Town Park; 'Britannia' for the Falklands Monument; 'Mother and Child' Portland Hospital; Sir Barnes Wallis, R.A.F. Museum Hendon; 'Spindrift' 3.5m. high stainless steel spiral with bronze seagulls for P. & O. liner Royal Princess. Awarded the Sir Otto Beit medal. *Address:* The Orchard House, Cranleigh, Surrey GU6 8LR. *Signs work:* "David Norris."

NORRIS, Katharine, B.A.(Hons.) graphic design and illustration; decorative mural artist and stenciller and fine artist of figurative work, landscape, life, decorative still life in acrylic, oil, pastel, coloured pencil, charcoal; *b* Worthing. *Educ.:* Trinity School, Carlisle; *studied art* at Cumbria College of Art and Design (1977-78), Norwich School of Art (1978-81). *Address:* 30 Esk Bank, Longtown, Carlisle, Cumbria CA6 5PT. *Club:* Life Drawing, Penrith. *Signs work:* "Kate Norris."

NORTON, Maureen Joan, R.S.M. (1982), S.M. (1981); marine and landscape artist in oil on canvas and oil on ivorine; *b* Norwich, 1928; *d* of B. Wright; *m* Denis Norton; one *d. Exhib.:* three one-man shows at Ancient House, Holkham, also soc. exhbns. at Mall Galleries, The Westminster Gallery. *Work in private collections* in America, Germany, Australia and Mexico. *Address:* 179 Wroxham Rd., Sprowston, Norwich NR7 8AG. *Signs work:* "M.J. Norton."

NOSWORTHY, Ann Louise, N.D.D. (1952), A.T.D. (1953); painter in oil, gouache, pastel and charcoal; *b* Stonehaven, Scotland, 24 Aug., 1929; *d* of Col. J. M. Savege, R.A.M.C.; *m* T. L. Nosworthy; one *s. Educ.:* Beacon School, Bridge-of-Allan, Scotland. *Exhib.:* one-man shows: Redcar, Yorks. (1968), Castle de Vide, Portugal (1966). *Work in permanent collection:* Municipal Art Gallery, Port Allegre, Portugal. *Address:* Brackengarth, Lealholm, Whitby, Yorks. YO21 2AE. *Signs work:* "A. L. Nosworthy."

NOWELL, Stanley, M.B., F.R.C.R., A.R.Cam.A.; artist in oil; consultant radiologist (retd.); *b* 10 May, 1903; *s* of Herbert Nowell; widower. *Educ.:* Cheltenham College; *studied art* at Wrexham College of Art (part time). *Exhib.:* R.Cam.A. (9 yrs.), Lancashire Artists, International Amateur Exhbn. (twice). *Address:* 28 Grosvenor Rd., Wrexham, Clwyd LL11 1BU, N. Wales. *Signs work:* "S. Nowell" or "S.N."

NOYES, Margot, N.D.D. (1960); painter in oil; *b* London, 17 Aug., 1939; *d* of Frederick Henry Noyes and Margaret Jane Noyes; divorced; one *s*, one *d. Educ.:* Fulham County Grammar School; *studied art* at Camberwell School of Arts and Crafts (1956-60, Robert Medley, Anthony Eyton, Richard Lee, Michael Salaman, Richard Eurich, Henry Inlander). *Exhib.:* Many one-man shows and mixed shows nationwide. *Address:* Marsh Cottage, Wenhaston, Halesworth, Suffolk. *Signs work:* "M. Noyes," very small works initials only.

O

OATES, Bennett; painter in oils, specialising in flowers; *b* London, 1 Jan., 1928; *s* of Joseph Bennett Oates, F.P.E.; *m* Phyllis Mary, senior lecturer in Art History and Designer A.R.C.A.; two *d*. *Educ.:* Raynes Park Grammar School; *studied art* at Wimbledon School of Art (1943-46, Gerald Cooper), R.C.A. (1948-51, Robin Darwin and Ruskin Spear). *Work in permanent collection:* Stacy-Marks Gallery. Founder Mem. Guild of Norwich Painters. *Address:* Studio and principal address: The Grange, Little Plumstead, Norwich NR13 5DJ. *Signs work:* "Bennett Oates."

OATES, Christine Tate, A.R.C.A., A.T.D.; artist in oil and water-colour; teacher at Ely High School (1939-43), Lancaster Girls' Grammar School (1943-45), Truro High School (1945-70); *b* Bradford, 13 Jan., 1913; *d* of Herbert Johnson Oates. *Educ.:* Bradford Girls' Grammar School; Bradford Regional College of Art under H. Butler (1930-35); Royal College of Art (1935-39). *Official purchases:* V. & A. (textiles) and other material for circulation to schools. *Publications:* illustrated, Pydar Street and High Cross, Truro; Princes Street and Quay Area, Truro; Boscawen Street Area, Truro; River Street and its Neighbourhood; written and illustrated, Truro City Trail (1983). *Address:* 6 The Parade, Truro, Cornwall. *Clubs:* Soc. for Educ. through Art, National Soc. for Art Educ., R.C.A. Old Students' Assoc. *Signs work:* "C. T. Oates."

O'BRIEN, Brigid: see GANLY, Rosaleen Brigid.

O CEALLACHAIN, Diarmuid, A.N.C.A. (1940); Bronze Medal, Paris Salon; Diploma di Merito, Universita delle Arti, Italy; artist, teacher; *b* Cork, 1915; *s* of Ellen and Patrick Callaghan, R.N.; *m* Joan O Sullivan: one *s*, one *d*. *Educ.:* St. Patrick's and North Monastery; *studied art* under John Power and John Keating. *Exhib.:* Salon. R.H.A., Oireactas, Europe, U.S.A.; holds one-man shows. Painted in Athens and Holy Land (1971). *Address:* Gartan, Farranlea Pk., Model Farm Rd., Cork, Eire. *Signs work:* see appendix.

OCEAN, Humphrey; winner Imperial Tobacco Award (1982); artist; *b* Pulborough, 22 June, 1951; *s* of Capt. M.E. Butler-Bowdon, O.B.E., R.N.; *m* Miranda Argyle; two *d*. *Educ.:* Ampleforth; *studied art* at Tunbridge Wells Art School (1967-69), Brighton College of Art (1969-70), Canterbury College of Art (1970-73). *Exhib.:* R.A., Whitechapel Open, Haus der Kunst Munich, British Council; one-man shows: N.P.G. (1984), Ferens A.G. Hull (1987), Dulwich P.G., Whitworth A.G. and Tate Gallery, Liverpool (1991). *Work in permanent collections:* N.P.G., Imperial War Museum, Ferens A.G., Scottish N.P.G., R.A.F. Museum, Royal Collection, Hertford College, Oxford. *Publications:* The Ocean View (Plexus 1982), Big Mouth (Fourth Estate 1990). *Address:* 22 Marmora Rd., London SE22 0RX.

OCKENDEN, John Richard, B.Ed. (Hons.) (1978); artist in water-colour and acrylic; Vice Chairman, Deeside Art Group; *b* Cheltenham, 6 Aug., 1946; one *d*. *Educ.:* Alsager C.H.E., Chester C.H.E. *Exhib.:* one-man shows: Theatr Clwyd Gallery since 1988; many mixed shows in England and Wales, including International Spring Fair, N.E.C. B'ham. *Work repro.:* limited editions. *Address:* 29 Marksway, Pensby, Wirral L61 9PB. *Signs work:* "John R. Ockenden."

O'CONNOR, John, R.W.S., A.R.C.A.; painter, illustrator and wood engraver; *b* Leicester, 11 Aug., 1913; *s* of Vernon Feargus O'Connor; *m* Jenny Tennant; one *s* (Michael Feargus). *Educ.:* Wyggeston School; *studied art* at Leicester

353

College of Art; Royal College of Art. *Exhib.:* one-man shows, Zwemmer Gallery (1955-68), Clare College (1965), New Grafton Gallery (1970-80), Broughton Gallery, Borders (1978 onwards); mixed shows, R.A., Bankside Gallery, London SE1 (R.W.S.). *Work in permanent collections:* N.Y. Public Library, Columbia University; public galleries, Oxford, Cambridge, and other Universities and Colleges. *Publications:* written and illustrated: Canals, Barges and People (Shenval Press), A Pattern of People (Hutchinson); books illustrated for Golden Cockerel Press, Dropmore Press, Boston Imprint, Limited Editions Club, N.Y., Florin Press, Whittington Press. Technical, several books on Graphic Arts. *Address:* Craigmore, Parton, Castle Douglas DG7 3NL, Scotland. *Club:* Double Crown. *Signs work:* "John O'Connor."

O'CONNOR, Marcel, B.A. (Hons.) Fine Art (1981); artist/teacher in oil and wax encaustic painting; *b* Lurgan, Co. Armagh, 19 Nov., 1958. *Educ.:* St. Michael's High School, Lurgan; *studied art* at Liverpool Polytechnic (1977-78), Brighton Polytechnic (1978-81, Jack Smith, Stephen Cox), Cyprus College of Art (Stass Paraskos). *Exhib.:* Scotland, Ireland, England, Cyprus, Hungary. *Publications:* catalogues: 'Boundaries' in Edinburgh and Belfast; 4 Artists in Hungary; 'Europe 24' in Hungary. *Address:* W.A.S.P.S. Studios (115), Patriothall, Stockbridge, Edinburgh. *Signs work:* "Marcel O'Connor."

ODDY, Mercy; seascape painter in water-colour, miniaturist; Council Mem. Soc. of Women Artists, Mem. Hilliard Soc. of Miniaturists, Sec. Christchurch Arts Guild; *b* Southsea; *d* of William Kingston; *m* David Oddy; two *d. Exhib.:* solo show: Red House Museum and A.G., Christchurch, Dorset (Mar./Apr. 1994). Address: 1 Lyme Cres., Highcliffe, Dorset BH23 5BJ. *Signs work:* "Mercy Oddy" larger works; "M.O." miniatures.

O'DONOGHUE, Declan, M.C.S.D. (1986), F.S.C-D. (1991), M.Inst.P.I. (1991), M.S.D.I. (1991); chartered designer and furniture maker in wood, metal, stone, glass; Director, Wikogold Ltd. (1985), Adviser, Connemara West plc. (1992), Partner, S.F. Furniture (1980), Principal visiting tutor, Furn. Coll. Letterfrock (1988); *b* Cork, 18 Oct., 1960; *m* Fiona Mary Curry; two *d. Educ.:* St. Vincent's College, Castleknock, Dublin; *studied* at Parnham College (1978-80, R. Ingham). *Exhib.:* National Theatre, Barbican, Camden Arts Centre, Mall Galleries, Bath Festival, Kilkenny Design Dublin, British Crafts Centre, British Crafts, Cheltenham. *Publications:* numerous exhbn. catalogues, articles, book features, B.B.C. (1981), H.T.V. (1992-93). *Address:* Street Farm, Acton Turville, Badminton, Avon GL9 1HH. *Club:* Royal Cork Yacht.

O'FARRELL, Bartholomew Patrick, B.Ed.Hons. (Wales), Dip.A.D.; landscape painter in acrylic, pastel, water-colour and oil; Lecturer in Illustration, Faculty of Art, W.G.I.H.E., Swansea (1981-85); *b* Ogilvie, mid-Glamorgan, 11 Aug., 1941. *Educ.:* Caerphilly Grammar-Technical School; *studied art* at Cardiff College of Art (1959-62), Polytechnic of Wales, Barry (1974-78). *Exhib.:* Cornwall and S. Wales; annual one-man shows in Cornwall from 1986 onwards at Trelowarren, Helston Folk Museum, Camborne School of Mines Museum and Gallery, St. Austell Arts Centre. *Work in permanent collection:* National Library of Wales. *Address:* Treleague Farm, St. Keverne, Helston, Cornwall TR12 6PQ. *Signs work:* "Bart O'Farrell."

OFFEN, John, B.A.(Hons.); designer and author; partner Ken Moore Design Associates; *b* 15 Mar., 1951; *s* of Raymond Offen. *Educ.:* University of Exeter. *Positions held:* British Council, UNESCO, Asst. Cultural Attache, British Embassy, Tunis. *Publications:* A History of Irish Lace, Thoroughbred Style. *Address:* 137 Biddulph Mans., London W9 1HU.

OGDEN, Catherine, A.R.B.S.A. (1992), A.R.M.S. (1990), S.W.A. (1988); miniature seascape painter and flower pastelist; *b* London, 10 Apr., 1951. *Educ.:* Plashet Secondary Modern, Kingsway College. *Exhib.:* R.M.S., S.W.A., R.I., R.B.S.A., R.W.S., Mid 'Art' 86 Dudley, Laing Art collection competition, John Noott Gallery, Llewellyn Alexander Gallery. *Address:* Forge House, Brimfield, Ludlow, Shropshire SY8 4NG. *Signs work:* "C. Ogden."

O'HARA, D. Patrick; botanical sculptor (original works in porcelain, engraving and enamelling on crystal); *b* Windsor, 17 June, 1936; *m* Anna Greenwood, landscape painter; one *s*, one *d*. *Educ.:* Haileybury and Reading University; *studied art* at Malvern Art School (1969-71). *Exhib.:* Cartier, N.Y. (1972), Tryon and Moorland Gallery (1973), Chicago Flower Show (1975), Wexford Festival (1976), Victor Zelli (1978), R.H.S. (1979), Bank of Ireland (1980), Meister Gallery, Zurich (1980, 1981), Chester Beatty Library, Dublin (1984), Palais des Nations (1984), EXPO 90, Osaka (1990). *Work in permanent collections:* Lewis Ginter Botanical Gdn., Richmond, Va.; Flagler Museum, Florida; Jones Museum, Maine; International Museum of Wildlife Art, Gloucester; Chicago Horticultural Soc.; Gloucester City Museum; Adachi Inst., Tokyo; Smithkline Beecham Corp., Sumitomo Group. *Address:* Manor House, Currabinny, Carrigaline, Co. Cork, Ireland. *Signs work:* "Patrick O'Hara."

OHL, Gabrielle; painter in oil, inks, stained glass; *b* Diego-Suarez, Madagascar; *d* of René Ohl (decd.); *m* Serge Pesquès. *Studied art* at Paris Academie Julian (1949-50), Madrid Beaux Arts (1950-51), Melbourne Technical College of Arts (1951-53), Paris. *Exhib.:* Paris salons: Independents, Marine, Automne, Femmes Peintres; Maison de l'Alsace Germany, U.S.A. One-man shows, Paris, Belgium, London, Italy, Malaya, Korea, Koweit, Luxemburg, Sardinia, La Coupole, Paris, Stasburg, Rosheim. *Awards:* Medaglia "Nuova Critica Europea" Italy (1969); Gold Medal, Paternoster Academy, London (1971), Palmes d'or, Paris-Critique (1977), Gold Medal, Baden Baden (1981), Bronze Medal, New York (1983), Gold Medal, Milan (1989). *Address:* 10 Rue des Halles, Paris. *Signs work:* see appendix.

OLDFIELD, Joy M., A.T.D. (1943); painter, sculptor and potter in oil, pastel, charcoal, clay and stone; *b* Hampstead, 1920; *d* of Reginald Royston Course, F.D.S., R.C.S.; *m* John Oldfield; one *s*, two *d*. *Educ.:* Camden School for Girls; *studied art* at Westminster and Central Schools of Art (1938-40, K. Jamieson, R. Millard), Regent St. Polytechnic Art School (1940-42, S. Tresillian), Hornsey School of Art (1943). *Exhib.:* R.P., S.W.A.; one-man show, Watatu Gallery, Nairobi (1980). *Work in private collections:* England, Scotland, Ireland and Kenya. *Address:* White Lodge, West Rd., Weaverham, Ches. CW8 3HL. *Signs work:* "Joy M. Oldfield."

OLIVER, Charles William, A.R.C.A. (1933), Liverpool Academy (1938); artist in oil; Vice-Principal, Laird School of Art, Birkenhead (retd.); *b* Youngstown, Ohio, U.S.A., 21 Apr., 1911; *s* of Charles Oliver; *m* Ena Landon Davies; two *s*. *Educ.:* Wade Deacon Grammar School, Widnes, Lancs.; *studied art* at City School of Art, Liverpool, and at R.C.A. under Sir W. Rothenstein (1930-34). *Exhib.:* R.P.S., R.B.A., R.Scot.A., Liverpool Academy of Arts, Southport, R.Cam.A., Wirral Soc. of Arts. *Work in permanent collections:* Liverpool, Birkenhead A.G.; Portraits: Liverpool University, Birkenhead School, Society of Anaesthetists, Chester Cathedral Library, etc. *Publications:* Anatomy and Perspective (Studio Vista, 1972). *Address:* 1 South Bank, Oxton, Birkenhead. *Signs work:* "C. W. OLIVER" and date.

OLIVER, Kenneth Herbert, R.W.S., R.E., A.R.C.A., R.W.A.; etcher, lithographer, artist in water-colour; taught at Gloucestershire College of Arts and Technology, Cheltenham; *b* Norwich, 7 Feb., 1923; *s* of Herbert B. Oliver; *m* Joyce Margaret Beaumont, A.R.C.A.; three *d*. *Educ.:* King Edward VI Grammar School, Norwich; *studied art* at Norwich School of Art and R.C.A. *Exhib.:* R.W.S., R.W.A., Bristol, R.A., R.E., Cheltenham Group of Artists, etc., and abroad. *Work in permanent collections:* Royal West of England Academy, Bristol, Cheltenham A.G. *Address:* Vyners, Halfway Pitch, Pitchcombe, nr. Stroud, Glos. GL6 6LJ. *Signs work:* "KENNETH H. OLIVER."

O'MALLEY, Mrs. Peter Diarmiud: see WARBURTON, Joan.

OMAN, Julia Trevelyan, C.B.E. (1986), Hon. D.Litt. (1987), R.D.I., F.C.S.D., Des.R.C.A. Royal Scholar, R.C.A.; 1st Class; Silver Medal R.C.A.; Designer of the Year Award (1967); designer for films, theatre, television, books; Director, Oman Productions Ltd.; *b* 11 July, 1930; *m* Sir Roy Strong, former Director, V. & A. *Educ.:* R.C.A., London. *Exhib.:* design of productions for: National Theatre, Royal Opera Covent Garden, Royal Ballet, Royal Shakespeare Co., Hamburg Opera, West End Theatres, Burg Theater Vienna, Boston Ballet, Stockholm Opera, Kassel Opera, Glyndebourne, B.B.C. Television, films. *Work in permanent collection:* V. & A. *Publications:* Street Children (photographs); Elizabeth R. (design); Mary Queen of Scots (design); Merchant of Venice (Folio Society). *Address:* The Laskett, Much Birch, Hereford HR2 8HZ. *Signs work:* "Julia Trevelyan Oman."

ONIANS, Richard (Dick) Lathbury, M.A.(Cantab.), A.R.B.S. (1989); City and Guilds Art School Cert. of Merit (1968); sculptor in wood and stone, lecturer; Head of Carving, City and Guilds of London Art School; *b* Chalfont St. Giles, 19 May, 1940; *s* of Prof. R.B. Onians, M.A., Ph.D.; *m* Frances Clare Critchley. *Educ.:* Merchant Taylors' School, Northwood; Trinity College, Cambridge; *studied art* at City and Guilds of London Art School (1966-68). *Exhib.:* Mall Galleries, Marjorie Parr Gallery, Century Galleries, Henley-on-Thames, Galleria Kenata, Chicago, Clementi House Gallery, Edith Grove Gallery, Bow House Gallery, London. *Address:* Woodside, Commonwood, King's Langley, Herts. WD4 9BA. *Signs work:* "R.L.O."

ORAM, Ann, B.A.(Hons.) 1980, Post Grad. Dip. in Fine Art (1981), R.S.W. (1986); painter in water-colour, gouache, ink, oil; *b* London, 3 May, 1956; *d* of Thomas Alexander Oram. *Educ.:* Grantown Grammar School, Inverness Royal Academy; *studied art* at Edinburgh College of Art/Heriot Watt University (1976-82). *Exhib.:* one-man shows: Thackeray Gallery, Scottish Gallery, University of Edinburgh Staff Club, Macauley Gallery; group shows: R.S.A., R.S.W., R.A., R.G.I., Stowell's Trophy, Royal Overseas League (Edinburgh), Compass - New Generation, Scottish Gallery, Macauley Gallery, S.T.V. Student Show, Thackeray Gallery, Bath Air Fair. *Work in permanent collections:* Britain and abroad. *Address:* 39 Barony St. Edinburgh EH3 6NX. *Club:* Scottish Arts. *Signs work:* "Ann Oram."

O'REILLY, Faith, N.D.D., Dip. R.A., A.T.C.; semi-figurative painter and portraitist, lecturer in Art; *b* Boston, Mass., U.S.A., 6 Aug., 1938; *d* of Eileen O'Reilly. *Studied art* at Berkshire College of Art, Royal Academy Schools, and Hornsey. Helped to found Stanley Spencer Gallery. *Exhib.:* group and one-man shows: Midland Group Gallery; 273 Gallery, London; shows in Universities. *Address:* 13 Walpole Terr., Kemptown, Brighton, Sussex BN2 2EB. *Signs work:* "F.O.R." and "Faith O'Reilly." Returned to "O'Reilly" from adoptive name "Gibbon" in 1975. Studio in S. France; Le Vernet, 34240 Combes.

O'REILLY, Richard, F.P.S.; artist in oil, water-colour, ink, wood; *b* London, 11 May, 1932; *m* P. Turner; two *s,* one *d. Educ.:* Avondale School, Cheadle Heath, Ches.; *studied art* under William Redgrave, sculptor-draughtsman – 'One to One'. *Exhib.:* Guildhall London, Ragley Hall, Foyles's King's College, Vienna 9th International, P.S., Tattershall Castle, Cambridge Union, University of Essex, House of Commons. *Work in permanent collections:* Loggia Gallery, The Investment Gallery, Paris, Berlin, Vienna. *Address:* 12 Acanthus Rd., Battersea, London SW11 5TY. *Signs work:* "O'Reilly."

ORGAN, Robert, D.F.A. (Lond.), R.W.A.; painter in oil, water-colour, sometimes tempera, architectural designer; Artist in Residence, Royal Albert Museum, Exeter (1987); *b* Hutton, Som., 27 Jan., 1933; *s* of Edward Organ, architect; *m* Val Buston; one *s,* three *d. Studied art* at West of England College of Art, Slade School (George Sweet, Claude Rogers). *Exhib.:* Beaux Arts, Bath (1983-91), Browse & Darby (1981-93). *Work in permanent collections:* Plymouth City A.G., Brighton and Hove A.G., Exeter Royal Albert Museum, Devon Educ. Com., Cornwall Educ. Com., R.W.A. Collection, S.W.A. Collection. *Publications:* various articles, art and architectural journals. *Address:* Lower Ridge, Wambrook, Chard, Som. *Signs work:* "Robert Organ" usually on back.

ORR, Chris, M.A. (1967); artist in painting, etching, lithography; tutor in printmaking, Royal College of Art; *b* London, 1943; *m* Catherine Terris; one *s,* one *d. Educ.:* Penge Academy; *studied art* at R.C.A. (1964-67). *Exhib.:* R.A. Summer Exhbn.; one-man shows: London, America, Australia, France. *Work in permanent collection:* V. & A. *Publications:* John Ruskin (1976), Arthur (1977), Many Mansions (1990). *Address:* 7 Bristle Hill, Buckingham MK18 1EZ. *Signs work:* "Chris Orr."

OSBORNE, Stuart John, A.R.C.A., A.T.D., M.F.P.S.; sculptor, models portraits, figures and animals; stone and wood carver; *b* Weston-s-Mare, Som.; *s* of H. T. Osborne; *m* Margaret Cole, A.T.D., portrait and animal painter; one *d. Educ.:* Kingsholme School, Weston-s-Mare; *studied art* at Bristol College of Art, and Royal College of Art, London. *Exhib.:* societies: F.P.S., Galerie Salammbo, Paris, Vallombreuse, Biarritz, International, New York, Geneva, Mall, London. *Address:* 64 Burton Manor Rd., Stafford ST17 9PR. *Signs work:* "Osborne."

OSMOND, Edward, A.T.D., M.S.I.A., Carnegie Award; artist in oils, wash, line, illustrations, commercial drawing and book design; *m* C. M. ("Laurie") Osmond, sc. and painter. *Address:* Downland Cottage, Lullington Cl., Seaford, E. Sussex BN25 4JH. *Signs work:* in full, block caps.

OSTLE, Roy John, N.D.D. (Painting 1950), A.T.D. (Liverpool 1951), council member R.Cam.A.; art lecturer and antique dealer, artist in oil, acrylic and mixed media (graphic work); former senior lecturer in art, St. Mary's College, Bangor, N. Wales; lecturer in art appreciation, Extra Mural Dept., University College of North Wales, Bangor; *b* Chester, 3 July, 1930; *s* of Harry Ostle; *m* Margery; one *s,* two *d. Educ.:* Chester Grammar School; *studied art* at Chester School of Art (A. J. Mayson, A.R.C.A.), Liverpool College of Art (A. Tankard, A.T.D.). *Exhib.:* Welsh Arts Council, Tegfryn Gallery (Menai Bridge), Peterloo Gallery, Manchester, Ashbarn Gallery, Petersfield, New Art Centre, London, Albany Gallery, Cardiff, Gorstage Gallery (Weaverham, Cheshire), Edinburgh Festival, Rozengalerie, Amsterdam. *Address:* Plas Penisarnant, Nant Ffrancon, nr. Bethesda, Gwynedd, N. Wales. *Clubs:* R.Cam.A., Conwy. *Signs work:* "Roy Ostle."

OTLEY, Barbara Kathleen, B.A. (1936), M.F.P.S. (1964); portrait and landscape painter in oil and pastel; *b* 26 Dec., 1918; *d* of Edward Foster, textile merchant; *m* Kenneth P. Otley; one *s*, one *d. Educ.:* Leytonstone County High School and finishing school Holland; *studied art* under Kristin Berge, pupil of Oskar Kokoschka (1960). *Exhib.:* Arts Council, Chenil Galleries, Mall Galleries, Little Bookshop Gallery, Arundel. *Work in permanent collections:* A. King, Esq., England, Mrs. Ron Greenwood, H. Robinson, Toronto, Dr. Gewalt of La Jolla, California. *Address:* Monkmead, 61A Sea Ave., Rustington, W. Sussex BN16 2DN. *Clubs:* F.P.S., Chigwell Art Soc., Chichester Art Soc., Downland Art Soc., The Atelier Group, West Sussex Art. *Signs work:* "Fiennes-Foster."

OTTEY, Piers Ronald Edward Campbell, B.A.(Hons.); painter in oil on canvas and panel, teacher/lecturer; *b* London, 27 Sept., 1955; *s* of Ronald Harry Ottey, F.S.C.A.; *m* Annelise; one *s*, one *d. Educ.:* King's College School, Wimbledon; *studied art* at Chelsea School of Art (1974-78, Patrick Symons, Myles Murphy). *Exhib.:* R.A., Bath Contemporary Arts Fair, London, Sussex, Paris; one-man shows: Brighton (1988), Midhurst (1991). *Work in private collections:* England, France, Denmark. *Address:* Bishop's Hill Cottage, Graffham, nr. Petworth, W. Sussex GU28 0QA. *Signs work:* "Piers Ottey" on reverse of work only.

OWEN, Glynis, B.F.A. (1966), A.T.C. (1967), F.R.B.S. (1990); sculptor in stone and bronze; *b* Gravesend, 22 May, 1945; *d* of Henry Joseph Collins Jones, company director; *m*; two *s*, one *d. Educ.:* Portsmouth High School, G.P.D.S.T.; *studied art* at Portsmouth College of Art (1962-66), University of London, Goldsmiths' College (1966-67). *Exhib.:* Barbican Centre (1990), R.I.B.A. (1991). *Work in permanent collections:* Alton College, Hants. commissioned by Hants. Architects Dept.; Stevenage Town Centre, life size family group, commissioned by Stevenage Development Corp. *Publications:* Carving Techniques by Glynis Beecroft (Batsford 1976), Casting Techniques by Glynis Beecroft (Batsford 1979). *Address:* Pilgrim's Studio, 52 Pilgrim's La., Hampstead, London NW3 1SN. *Signs work:* "Glynis Owen."

OWEN, Muriel Sylvia, N.D.D., A.T.D., S.W.A., U.A., F.R.S.A.; painter in water-colour, lecturer; Head of Art and Deputy Principal, Dixon and Wolfe, Tutors, London SW1 (1969-82); Vice-Pres., Soc. of Women Artists; *b* Welwyn Garden City; *d* of Arthur Tremlett Cuss; *m* Edward Eardley Owen, M.A.; three *s* by previous marriage. *Educ.:* Welwyn Garden City Grammar School; *studied art* at St. Albans School of Art (1946-50 under Gwen White and Christopher Sanders, R.P., R.A.), London University (1951). *Exhib.:* R.I., S.W.A., U.A., Llewellyn Alexander Gallery, London; ten one-man shows, London, Fairfield Halls, Croydon, Yarmouth Castle, I.O.W. official galleries. *Work in permanent collections:* 38 paintings English Heritage, I.O.W. Arts Council. *Official purchases:* Bank of England, Queen Elizabeth Military Hospital, Woolwich, Atomic Energy Commission, London, 12 paintings Dodecanese Co. *Work repro.:* St.Paul's, Westminster, floral, (Henry Ling), calendars 1988, 1989 and 1991 (I.O.W. County Press), series of 4 art teaching videos (1992). *Address:* Briarwood House, Church Hill, Totland, I.O.W. PO39 0EU. *Signs work:* "Muriel Owen."

OXENBURY, Helen Gillian; illustrator/writer in water-colour; Kate Greenaway medal (1969), Smarties award (1989), Boston Globe award, Kurt Maschler award (1985); *b* 2 June, 1938; *m* John M. Burningham; one *s*, two *d. Studied art* at Ipswich School of Art and Central School of Arts and Crafts, London. *Publications:* illustrated: The Three Little Wolves and the Big Bad Pig (1993), Farmer Duck (1991), We're Going on a Bear Hunt (1989). *Address:* c/o Walker Books, 87 Vauxhall Walk, London SE11 5HJ. *Signs work:* "Helen Oxenbury."

OXENBURY, Thomas Bernard, C.Eng., F.I.C.E. (1944), F.R.T.P.I. (1943), R.I.B.A., distinction in town planning; town-planning consultant; artist in water-colour and woods (marquetry); *b* Totnes, 5 Mar., 1904; *s* of Thomas Henry Oxenbury, business director; *m* Muriel Helen Oxenbury; one *s*, one *d. Educ.:* King Edward VI Grammar School, Totnes; *studied art* at school. *Exhib.:* Ipswich Art Club exhbns. *Publications:* in Architects' Journal, Planning Survey of Suffolk, T.P.I. Journal. *Address:* 4 East Heath Rd., Hampstead, London NW3. *Club:* Ipswich Art. *Signs work:* "TBO."

OXLADE, Roy; painter in oil; *b* 13 Jan., 1929; *s* of William Oxlade, engineer; *m* Rose Forrest Wylie; one *s*, two *d. Studied art* with David Bomberg (1950-53). *Exhib.:* Young Contemporaries (1952-54), Borough Bottega Group, Heffer's Gallery, Cambridge (1954), Walker's Gallery, London (1955), Winnipeg Biennial (1st prize drawing, 1960), John Moores, Liverpool (1964, 1991), Midland Group, Nottingham (1966-68), Hayward Annual, London (1982), Odette Gilbert Gallery (1984-91); one-man shows, Vancouver A.G. (1963), New Metropole, Folkestone (1983), Air Gallery (1983), Odette Gilbert Gallery (1985, 1987, 1988). *Publication:* David Bomberg (R.C.A. Papers 3 1981). *Address:* Forge Cottage, Newnham, Sittingbourne, Kent ME9 0LQ. *Club:* Arts. *Signs work:* "R. Oxlade" on reverse.

OXLEY, Ursula; Board of Educ. drawing exam. (1937); artist in black and white, crayon, conte, pastel and water-colour; specialist in child portraiture; *b* Ealing, 4 May, 1918; *d* of Lawrence Deller, portrait painter; *m* Laurence Oxley; one *s*, one *d. Educ.;* privately; *studied art* at Winchester School of Art under E. E. Anderson, A.R.C.A. (1935-39). *Exhib.:* P.S., S.W.A., S.G.A., R.I., Guildford Art Soc., Woking Art Soc., N.S., Winchester Art Club, Alresford Art Soc. *Publications:* illustrated 1971 and subsequent editions of History of Alresford, and Sketches of My Cat. *Address:* The Studio Bookshop, Alresford, Hants. SO24 9AW. *Clubs:* Winchester Art, Alresford Art Soc. *Signs work:* "Ursula Oxley."

OXTOBY, David Jowett Greaves, D.A., B.F.D., R.A.S.C.; artist in drawing, painting and prints; *b* Horsforth, nr. Leeds, 23 Jan., 1938; *s* of John Henry Oxtoby, managing rep. for carpet factors. *Educ.:* Horsforth Council School; *studied art* at Bradford College of Art (1950-57) under John Fleming; R.A. Schools (1960-64) under Sir Henry Rushbury. *Exhib.:* over 25 international one-man exhbns., various mixed exhbns. *Work in permanent collections:* V. & A., Tate Gallery, B.M., Museum of Modern Art, N.Y., Minneapolis Institute of Art, Leeds City A.G., Cartwright Hall Bradford, Sheffield City, Fundacao des Museum Regionais Da Bahia, Wakefield City, Towner Gallery Eastbourne, Contemporary Arts Society, Manchester City, L.A. County Museum. *Publication:* Oxtoby's Rockers, written by David Sandison (Phaidon Press, 1978). *Address:* James Associates, 110 Westbourne Grove, London W2 5RU. *Clubs:* Bag O'Nails, etc. *Signs work:* "David J. G. Oxtoby."

P

PACE, Shirley; sculptor and artist in bronze, charcoal, pen and ink, conté, monochrome, the Ashling Collection representational, equestrian sculptor to

Susse Fondeur, Paris; *b* Worthing, Sussex, 16 Feb., 1933; *d* of Arthur Blasdale, musician, writer, artist; *m* Roy Pace; two *d. Educ.:* Worthing Convent; *studied art* at Worthing School of Art (1948-51). *Exhib.:* Mall Galleries, Alwin Gallery, many provincial and overseas galleries. *Work in permanent collections:* Life and a quarter dray-horse, London; private collections: England, U.S.A., Bermuda, New Zealand, Australia, Hong Kong. *Address:* Field House, Newells La., West Ashling, Chichester, W. Sussex PO18 8DD. *Clubs:* S.E.A., Chichester Art Soc. *Signs work:* "Shirley Pace."

PACKARD, Gilian E., Des.R.C.A. (1962), F.S.D-C. (1963), F.R.S.A. (1975), F.C.S.D. (1977); first woman freeman of Goldsmiths' Company by special grant (1971); designer of jewellery in gold, platinum, silver and stones; *b* Newcastle upon Tyne, 16 Mar., 1938; *d* of John L. Packard. *Educ.:* Claremont School, Esher; *studied art* at Kingston-upon-Thames School of Art (1955-58), Central School of Arts and Crafts (1959), Royal College of Art (1959-62). *Work in permanent collections:* Goldsmiths Hall, De Beers, V. & A. *Address:* 8.2 Stirling Ct., 3 Marshall St., London W1V 1LQ. *Signs work:* "G.E.P." within oval, (Hallmark).

PACKER, William John, N.D.D. (Painting) (1963), A.T.D. (1964), Hon. F.R.C.A. (1988); painter in oil and water-colour; Art Critic, The Financial Times (since 1974); *b* Birmingham, 19 Aug., 1940; *s* of Rex Packer; *m* Clare Winn; three *d. Educ.:* Windsor Grammar School; Wimbledon School of Art (1959-63), Brighton College of Art (1963-64). *Exhib.:* R.A.; group exhbns.: Angela Flowers, Cadogan Contemporary and many other galleries. *Publications:* The Art of Vogue Covers (Octopus, 1980), Fashion Drawing in Vogue (Thames & Hudson, 1983), Henry Moore (with Gemma Levine) (Weidenfeld & Nicolson, 1985). *Address:* 39 Elms Rd., Clapham, London SW4 9EP. *Clubs:* Brooks's, Chelsea Arts. *Signs work:* "W.P." or "W. PACKER."

PADDEN, Daphne, R.M.S. (1984); artist and graphic designer in water-colour and gouache; *b* London, 21 May, 1927; *d* of Percy Padden, A.R.C.A. *Educ.:* Rosebery County School; *studied art* at Epsom and Ewell School of Art (1944-49, David Birch, R.O.I., R.O. Dunlop, R.A., Leslie Worth, A.R.C.A., Ronald Benham). *Exhib.:* R.M.S., Medici Gallery, Bourne Gallery, Reigate, Edwin Pollard Gallery, Wimbledon. *Work in private collections:* U.K. and overseas. *Address:* 30 Marshalls Cl., Epsom, Surrey KT19 8HZ. *Signs work:* see appendix.

PAGE, Charles, R.I. (1988), M.S.I.A. (1955); painter, illustrator and graphic designer in water-colour, acrylic, mixed media, collage; *b* Leighton Buzzard, 17 Apr., 1910; *m* (1) Jessie Stevens (decd.); (2) Beryl Sheaves; one *s. Educ.:* Luton Grammar School; *studied art* at Central School of Art and Crafts (1928-29). *Exhib.:* R.I., R.W.S., R.S.A., R.B.S.A. and several provincial galleries. *Work in permanent collections:* Luton A.G., Letchworth A.G. *Address:* 13 Carisbrooke Rd., Harpenden, Herts. AL5 5QS. *Signs work:* "Charles Page."

PAGE-ROBERTS, James; painter in oil, sculptor, and artist in black and white; *b* Silchester, 5 Feb., 1925; *s* of Frederick William Page-Roberts; *m* Margaretha Klees. *Educ.:* Wellington College, and Taft, U.S.A.; *studied art* at Central School of Arts and Crafts and Old Vic School of Theatre Design. *Exhib.:* one-man shows at Galerie de Seine, Reid Gallery, Kintetsu Gallery, Osaka, Qantas Gallery, Cambridge, Loft Gallery. Work reproduced widely. *Publications:* author, Vines in your Garden (Argus); wine writer/illustrator first four editions of The Best Wine Buys in the High Street (Foulsham); The Oldie Cookbook (Carbery Press). *Address:* 37 St. Peter's Grove, London W6 9AY. *Signs work:* "P R" and "PAGE-ROBERTS."

PAINE, Ken, P.S., V.P.S.P.F.; portrait artist in pastel, oil, water-colour; *b* London, 2 Nov., 1926. *Studied art:* worked with R.O. Dunlop, R.A., also studied at Twickenham College of Art. *Exhib.:* Llewellyn Alexander Gallery, Linda Blackstone Gallery, P.S., R.P., R.I. Mall Galleries, U.A. Westminster Galleries; many solo and mixed exhbns. in and around London, U.S.A., France, Germany, Edward Day Gallery, Kingston, Ontario, Société des Pastellistes de France, Paris. *Publications:* Chapter in Pastels Masterclass by Judy Martin (Harper Collins), The Complete Portrait Painting Course by Angela Gair (Mitchell Beazley), The Encyclopedia of Pastel Techniques by Judy Martin (Quarto); plus numerous articles on painting techniques. *Address:* 8 Spring Gdns., E. Molesey, Surrey KT8 0JA. *Signs work:* "PAINE."

PAINE, Ula; R.D.S. teacher-artist cert. (1931); painter in oil and water-colour; *b* Surbiton, 26 Sept., 1909; *d* of Charles Albert Paine, solicitor. *Educ.:* St. Winifred's, Eastbourne; Oak Dene, Beaconsfield; *studied art* at Queen Anne's Studio, Chelsea (1929-31, Lettuce MacMunn), Chelsea Polytechnic (H.S. Williamson, O.B.E.), and later under Vivian Pitchforth, R.A. *Exhib.:* R.A., R.B.A., R.O.I., W.I.A.C., Britain in Water-colours, Mall Galleries, U.A., Phoenix Gallery, Lavenham, Paris Salon, South Bank Picture Show; one-man show: Gallery 10, London W1. *Work repro.:* The Artist. *Address:* 32 Astell St., Chelsea, London SW3 3RU. *Signs work:* "Ula Paine."

PAINTER, Tom, F.R.B.S., R.B.A., A.R.C.A. (Sculpture, 1949) Travelling Scholar; sculptor in bronze, concrete, resin/fibre glass, wood, stone; *b* 29 Nov., 1918; *s* of the late Tom Painter; *m* Muriel Jeffery, A.R.C.A.; one *d. Educ.:* Wolverhampton; *studied art* at Wolverhampton School of Art (R.J. Emerson). *Exhib.:* R.B.S., R.B.A., R.A. *Work in private collections:* U.K., U.S.A., Canada, Italy. *Address:* 5 Garlies Rd., Forest Hill, London SE23 2RU. *Signs work:* "Tom Painter."

PALMER, Eugene Oliver, B.A. (Hons.), M.A.; artist in oil; lecturer in painting, Wolverhampton University; *b* Kingston, Jamaica; *m;* two *d. Studied art* at Wimbledon School of Art; Goldsmiths' College. *Exhib.:* Duncan Campbell Gallery. *Work in permanent collection:* Arts Council. *Address:* 25A Gautrey Rd., London SE15 2JE. *Signs work:* see appendix.

PALMER, Herbert Ralph, awarded Scholarship of Art, Johannesburg, S. Africa (1932-36); F.R.B.S.; sculptor in all known media and painter in oil and water-colour; working in the Art Dept., V. & A.; art teacher, Tower Bridge Institute, London (1950-51), Senior Professional Officer and Curator of Art, McGregor Museum, Kimberley, Cape Province (1974-76), Curator, Zululand Historical Museum, Eshowe, Natal (1980-); *b* Richmond Surrey, 13 Dec., 1916; *s* of Herbert Jesse Palmer, Professor of Music, and the late Marie Menges, the well-known violinist and 'cellist. *Educ.:* Christian Brothers College, Pretoria, S. Africa; *studied art* at Johannesburg Art School, and one-time pupil of Anton Van Wouw and P. H. Jowett. *Exhib.:* in twenty leading galleries in London, New York, South Africa, Portugal. *Work in permanent collections:* (1947) worked with Sir William Reid Dick, K.C.V.O., R.A., on the Roosevelt Monument. *Work repro.:* numerous commissions, including two ecclesiastical figures, St. James Church, Fulham, London; bronze Mother and child, South Africa House, London; Dr. Basil Merriman Bronze, Carter Foundation, London, etc. *Hobby:* Violin-making. *Address:* 91 Vausedale Rd., Queensburgh 4093, Natal, S. Africa. *Club:* Chelsea Arts. *Signs work:* "R. Palmer."

PALMER, Jean, B.A. (Hons.) Fine Art; painter in oil; *b* Southport, 1961; *m* Peter Layzell. *Studied art* at Southport College of Art (1977-79), Preston

Polytechnic (1979-82). *Exhib.:* R.A. Summer Show (1992, 1993), Houldsworth Fine Art, Gillian Jason Gallery. *Work in permanent collections:* Manchester City A.G., NatWest Coll., Warrington Arts Council. *Address:* 72 Vale Rd., Lancaster LA1 2JL. *Signs work:* "J. Palmer" on reverse.

PALMER, John Frederick, R.W.A. (1991); Cornelissen prize R.W.A. annual exhbn. (1985); graphic designer; artist in oil, water-colour, gouache; P.P., Bristol Savages; *b* Bristol, 11 Aug., 1939; *s* of Robert Palmer. *Educ.:* Carlton Park, Bristol; *studied art* at West of England College of Art (1955-56, J. Arnold). *Exhib.;* Bristol Artists, Arnolfini. *Work in permanent collection:* Bristol Savages, Leeds Bldg. Soc., NatWest Assurance, British Aerospace, Atomic Energy Authority. *Publication:* Drawing & Sketching (1993). *Address:* 18 Haverstock Rd., Knowle, Bristol BS4 2BZ. *Club:* Bristol Savages. *Signs work:* "J.F. Palmer."

PALMER, Juliette, N.D.D. (1950), A.T.D. (1951); painter in water-colour, illustrator, author; *b* Romford, 18 May, 1930; *d* of Sidney Bernard Woolley; *m* Dennis Palmer; one *d. Educ.:* Brentwood County High School; *studied art* at S.E. Essex School of Art (1946-50, Alan Wellings, William Stobbs, Bernard Carolan). *Exhib.:* R.A., R.I., N.E.A.C., R.O.I., R.W.A.; group gallery shows, Philadelphia, U.S.A., Sheffield, Windsor, Henley, Barnes, Bloomsbury; one-man shows, S. Australia, Tokyo, Cambridge, Chipping Norton, Cookham. Finalist in Hunting, Laing, Singer & Friedlander/Sunday Times National Art Competitions. *Work in permanent collections:* Barking Library, Leicestershire Educ. Com. *Publications:* 60 children's books illustrated; author/illustrator, 6 children's picture/information books (Macmillan). *Address:* Melmott Lodge, The Pound, Cookham, Maidenhead, Berks. SL6 9QD. *Signs work:* "Juliette Palmer."

PALMER, Margaret, A.T.D., P.S., N.S.; portrait painter in oil and pastel, animal and genre painter, book illustrator; *b* London, 10 Sept., 1922; *d* of R. E. A. Palmer; *m* R. G. W. Garrett; two *d. Studied art* at Hornsey School of Art (1938-39), Salisbury School of Art (1939-41), Bournemouth College of Art (1941-42). *Exhib.:* R.P., R.O.I., etc.; one-man shows in London, Guildford, Farnham, Leatherhead, works in worldwide collections. *Publications:* written and illustrated, Honeypot and Buzz; also illustrated books published by Harrap, Heinemann, etc. *Address:* Robins Oak, Wonersh, nr. Guildford, Surrey. *Signs work:* "Margaret Palmer."

PALMER, Robert Derrick, R.O.I. (1978), R.B.A. (1983); painter in oil; *b* Cambridge, 13 June, 1927; *s* of Herbert Palmer; *m* Jean Parker; one *s,* one *d. Educ.:* Central School, Cambridge; *studied art* at Cambridge School of Art (part-time 1951-58). *Exhib.:* one-man shows, Richard Bradley Atelier, Norwich (1968), Fermoy Gallery, Kings Lynn (1980). Awarded De Laszlo Medal at R.B.A. exhbn. (1990). *Address:* 19 Court Rd., Bournemouth, Dorset. *Signs work:* "R. PALMER" or "R.P."

PALTENGHI, Julian Celeste, B.F.A.; Winner 1993 Hunting/Observer art prizes: Travel award – Australia; painter in oil, sculptor in plaster and bronze; *b* London, 28 Aug., 1955; *s* of David Celeste, ballet dancer/film director; *m* Katy; one *d. Educ.:* Stowe, Bucks; *studied art* at Cambridge (1976-77), Loughborough College of Art (1978-81). *Exhib.:* 'Critic's Choice' Clare Henry: Cooling Gallery, Beaux Arts Galleries, Bath, Swiss Artists in Britain: October Galleries, William Marler Gallery, Shropshire, Stephen Bartley, Chelsea, Camden Annual, G.L.C. Spirit of London Festival Hall, Centre Georges Pompidou, Paris, Royal West of England Academy, Hunting Group, Albany Gallery, Gallery 10 London W1. *Address:* 143 Old Church St., London SW3. *Club:* Chelsea Arts. *Signs work:* "PALTENGHI."

PANCHERI, Robert, A.R.B.S., Dip. (1977); sculptor in wood and stone; *b* Bromsgrove, 22 June, 1916; *s* of Celestino Pancheri, wood carver; *m* Bridget Milligan; two *s*, two *d*. *Educ.:* Bromsgrove School; *studied art* at Birmingham School of Art (1934-39, William Bloye). *Work in permanent collections:* statues at: Winwick Lancs; Great Malvern Priory; Franciscan Friary, Chester; St. Peter's Church, Swinton, Manchester; sculpture panel, Sheldon Fire Station. *Address:* 12 Finstall Rd., Bromsgrove B60 2DZ. *Signs work:* "R. Pancheri" lower case letters.

PANNETT, Juliet, M.B.E. (1992), F.R.S.A.; portrait painter; *b* Hove, Sussex; *m* Major M. R. D. Pannett (died 1980); one *s*, one *d*. *Work in permanent collections:* 22 portraits in National Portrait Gallery, Hove Art Gallery. *Portraits include:* H.M. The Queen; H.R.H. Prince Andrew and H.R.H. Prince Edward for H.M. The Queen; Lord Goodman; Lord Tonypandy; Lavinia Duchess of Norfolk for Arundel Castle; Oxford and Cambridge colleges. Special artist to the Illustrated London News from 1958-64. *Work repro.:* Illustrated London News, The Times, Daily Telegraph, Radio Times, Birmingham Mail. *Address:* Pound House, Angmering Village, Sussex BN16 4AL. Awarded freedom of Worshipful Company of Painter Stainers; Freeman of City of London (1960). *Signs work:* "Juliet Pannett."

PAOLOZZI, Sir Eduardo Luigi, Kt. (1989), C.B.E. (1968), R.A. (1979), Hon. Dr. (R.C.A.), D.Litt. (Glas.); sculptor; Visiting Professor, Royal College of Art; *b* Leith, Scotland, 7 Mar., 1924. *Studied art* at Edinburgh College of Art, Slade School. *Exhib.:* one-man shows, Mayor Gallery (1947), 30th Venice Biennale (1960), M.O.M.A New York (1964), Rijksmuseum, Otterlo (1967), Stadtische Kunsthalle Dusseldorf, Tate Gallery (1971), V. & A. (1973, 1977), Nationalgalerie Berlin (1975), Kolnischer Kunstverein (1979), Royal Scottish Academy (1984), Museum Ludwig (1985). *Publication:* Eduardo Paolozzi by Winfried Konnertz (Dumont Verlag, 1984). *Address:* 107 Dovehouse St., London SW3 6JZ. *Signs work:* "Eduardo Paolozzi."

PARFITT, Margaret, C.B.E. (1980), S.R.N., S.W.A., C.A.S., S.E.L.A.S.; sculptor in wood and metal; *b* Romford, 23 Oct., 1920; *d* of Ion Victor Cummings, F.C.A.; *m* Ronald Parfitt; two *d*. *Educ.:* Brentwood County High School; *studied art* at Evening Classes (Don Smith). *Exhib.:* Sun Lounge, Fairfield (1991), Outwood Gallery (1988-90). *Address:* The White House, 165 Shirley Church Rd., Shirley, Croydon CR0 5AJ. *Signs work:* "Margaret Parfitt' or "M.P." joined.

PARK, Alistair, D.A. (Edin.), Post-Graduate (1952); artist; Senior Lecturer, Newcastle upon Tyne Polytechnic, Fine Art Dept.; *b* Edinburgh, 22 Apr., 1930; *s* of William Park; two *s*, one *d*. *Educ.:* Kirkcaldy High School; *studied art* at Edinburgh College of Art (1947-52). *Exhib.:* Rowan Gallery, Demarco Gallery, Scottish Gallery, '57 Gallery, Stone Gallery, Hayes Gallery, York, Gallery House, London, Ceolfrith, Sunderland. *Work in permanent collections:* National Gallery of Modern Art, Edinburgh, Abbot Hall Art Gallery, Kendal and Collection of Arts Council, Scotland, Tate Gallery, Tyne Wear Galleries. *Address:* 55 Woodbine Rd., Gosforth, Newcastle upon Tyne. *Signs work:* "A. Park" or "Alistair Park."

PARKER, Constance-Anne, A.T.D., F.R.B.S.; Lecturer, Archivist and Travelling Exhbns. Organiser, Royal Academy (1986-), Librarian, Royal Academy of Arts (1974-86), Assistant Librarian (1958-74); Landseer Scholar, Sir David Murray Scholarship, Leverhulme Scholarship; painter in oil, sculptor in wood and clay; *b* London, 19 Oct., 1921. *Educ.:* privately; *studied art:*

Polytechnic School of Art and Royal Academy Schools (four silver and three bronze medals). *Exhib.:* R.A., London galleries and provinces. *Publication:* Mr. Stubbs the Horse Painter (1971), Royal Academy Cookbook (1981), Stubbs Art Animals, Anatomy (1984). *Address:* 1 Melrose Rd., Barnes, London SW13 9LG. *Club:* Reynolds (Chairman).

PARKER, Herbert, F.R.S.A.; for 19 years deputy headmaster, Colomendy Hall Boarding School and Environmental Study Centre; one time tutor for Educational Development Assoc. at summer vacation courses held at Aberystwyth University and Normal College, Bangor; tutor under 'Quality of Life' experiment (1975) courses in art; *b* Buckley, N. Wales, 22 Mar., 1908; *s* of Richard Henry Parker; *m* Marjorie; one *d. Studied art* at Normal College, Bangor and short courses at Liverpool and Chester Schools of Art, etc. *Exhib.:* R.Cam.A. Conway, Old Water-colour Soc. Club, London, Summer Salon R.I., Paris Salon, Britain in Water-colour Exbhn. Mall Gallery, London and various one-man shows. *Address:* Bryn Eithin Two, Forestry Rd., Llanferres, Mold, Clwyd CH7 5SJ, N. Wales. *Club:* Clwydian Art Soc. President and founder mem. *Signs work:* "H. Parker."

PARKER, Walter F., A.R.C.A., M.S.I.A.D., A.T.D., F.R.S.A.; Principal, Hartlepool College of Art (1953-78); War Service in Middle East as F/Lieut. in R.A.F.; senior posts held at Preston and Hastings Schools of Art; since retirement in 1978 takes a number of regular painting schools in Britain specialising in water-colours and printmaking; *b* Carlisle, 11 May, 1914; *m* Joy E. Turk, contralto, Guildhall School of Music. *Educ.:* Carlisle Grammar School (1922-30), Carlisle Art School (1930-35), R.C.A. (1935-38), Courtauld Inst. (1938-39). *Address:* 19 The Cliff, Seaton Carew, Hartlepool TS25 1AP. *Club:* Pres., Lake Artists' Soc. *Signs work:* "Walter F. Parker."

PARKIN, Ann; artist in oil and pastel of impressionist paintings; *b* Bristol, 11 Aug., 1939; two *s. Exhib.:* solo shows each year at the Rooksmoor Gallery Bath; R.I. Mall Galleries (1988). *Work in permanent collection:* Lord Bath. *Address:* 10 Priston Village, Bath, Avon BA2 9EB. *Signs work:* "Ann Parkin" or "A.P."

PARKIN, Michael Robert; art dealer; chairman/managing director, Michael Parkin Fine Art Ltd.; *b* London, 1 Dec., 1931; *s* of Frank Robert Parkin; three *d. Educ.:* Mill Hill and St. George's Schools; Magdalen College, Oxford. *Exhbns.:* at Michael Parkin Gallery, 11 Motcomb St., SW1. Cover British Art 1850-1950, have included The Cafe Royalists, Four for Whistler, The Fitzrovians, Claude Flight, A Salute to Marcel Boulestin and J. E. Láboureur, Jean Cocteau, Cecil Beaton Memorial Exhbn., Artists of the Yellow Book, Nina Hamnett, Walter Sickert, Walter Greaves, Rex Whistler and Stephen Tennant, Walter Bayes, Jaques Emile Blanche, Artists of Corsham - a Celebration, Sylvia Gosse, Therese Lessore, the 7 & 5 Society, Paul Stevenson and John Pawle. *Publications:* Old Chelsea (Newson, London 1975), Louis Wain's Cats (Thames & Hudson, London 1983), Louis Wain's Edwardian Cats (Thames & Hudson, New York 1983); in preparation: Modern British Art 1860-1960; Walter Greaves. *Address:* Gunton Hall, Hanworth, Norfolk. *Clubs:* Beefsteak, Bucks, B.A.F.T.A., Chelsea Arts.

PARKINSON, Gerald; painter in oil, gouache and water-colour; *b* Shipley, Yorks., 5 Nov., 1926; *s* of Edward Parkinson; *m* Sylvia Mary; one *s,* one *d. Educ.:* Woodhouse Grove School, nr. Leeds; *studied art* at Bradford College of Art (1951-54). *Exhib.:* R.A., West of England Academy, John Moores, Sussex Artists, Yorks. Artists, S.E.A.; one-man shows: London, Bologna, Stockholm, Brighton, York, Bristol, Monte Carlo, Lewes, Bradford, Hove, Tunbridge Wells.

Work in permanent collections: Glasgow, Brighton, Leicestershire C.C., L.C.C., Surrey C.C., West Riding C.C., Mural for National Westminster Bank. *Address:* The Gate House, Wootton Manor, Polegate, Sussex BN26 5RY. *Club:* A.I.A. *Signs work:* "Gerald Parkinson."

PARKINSON, Richard Henry, Dip. A/D (1967); painter in oil on canvas/board, restorer, critic, designer, frame maker; Prop./M.D. Wye Art Gallery, tutor for Pitman's Correspondence Courses since 1967, judge at Royal College for Ensign Prize since 1988; *b* Epsom, 23 Mar., 1947; *s* of Freddy Parkinson (decd.) art director and publisher, Principal, Heatherleys Art School; *m* Susan Sanders; one *s*, one *d. Educ.:* Ewell Castle, Epsom; *studied art:* Folkestone School of Art (1963-67), Heatherleys School of Art (1968-71). *Exhib.:* R.A. since 1967, Wye, Henley, Wimbledon, R.W.E.A., Mall Galleries, R.B.A., Stockbridge, etc. *Work in permanent collections:* Woolworth Holdings, various Boardrooms. *Publications:* Introductory Art (Pitman), Mounting Water-colours (The Artist). *Address:* Gallery House, Bridge St., Wye, Kent TN25 5EA. *Club:* Chelsea Arts. *Signs work:* "R.H.P." or "Richard Parkinson."

PARROTT, Denis William, N.D.D.(Painting) (1953), A.T.C. (1958), Ph.D. (1993), Fulbright Scholar, U.S.A. (1970-71), F.R.S.A. (1977), F.S.A.E. (1980); painter, printmaker; lecturer, Nene College, Northampton; *b* Dewsbury, Yorks., 22 Mar., 1931; *s* of Ernest and Edith Parrott; *m* Kathleen Hendry; one *s. Educ.:* Dewsbury Technical College; *studied art* at Dewsbury and Batley School of Art (1948-51), Camberwell School of Art (1951-53), Leeds College of Art (1957-58). *Exhib.:* R.A., Mall Gallery, U.S.A., Centre International d'Art Contemporain de Paris and Galerie Salammbo, Paris. *Work in collections:* England, Europe and U.S.A. *Work repro.:* author for Schools Council. *Address:* 37 Bowling Green Rd., Kettering, Northants. NN15 7QN. *Signs work:* "Denis W. Parrott."

PARRY, David, S.WL.A.; wildlife artist in water-colour; *b* Liverpool, 23 June, 1942. *Educ.:* in Tunbridge Wells; *studied art* at Tunbridge Wells School of Art, Central School of Art, London. *Exhib.:* one-man shows, Brasted, Kent, Lanhydrock House, Cornwall PL22 0JN. *Address:* Castle Cottage, Lostwithiel, Cornwall. *Signs work:* "David Parry."

PARRY, Leigh, M.A. (1946), P.S. (1966), P.P.S. (1983-88), A.R.B.A. (1988), P.S. (Canada) (1987), S.E.A. (1983); painter in pastel and water-colour of equestrian subjects, landscapes, buildings, etc.; *b* London, 12 Apr., 1919; forebear, Walter Parry Hodges, sporting artist. *Educ.:* Uppingham; Pembroke College, Cambridge, *studied art* at St. Martin's School of Art (1945). *Exhib.:* R.A., Paris Salon, New Grafton, Linda Blackstone, Pinner, R.B.A., N.E.A.C., P.S.; one-man shows, Canada and London. *Work in permanent collections:* Kesteven C.C., Essex C.C., Lincolnshire museums, Midland Bank. *Publications:* illustrated Climbing and equestrian publications. *Address:* 6 Wharf Rd., Stamford, Lincs. PE9 2DU. *Signs work:* "Leigh Parry."

PARRY, Sheila Harwood, R.M.S. (1971), F.R.S.A. (1971), Dip. M.H. Societé des Artistes Français, Paris Salon (1971), Mem. S.M. (1969), Mem. American Soc. of Miniaturists, Florida; artist in gouache on vellum, oils on canvas; artist member of Fine Arts Trade Guild; *b* Salford, 5 Mar., 1924; *d* of William Harwood, engineer; *m* Alan Parry, Eng. Director; one *s*, three *d. Educ.:* Salford Technical College (1937-39); *studied art* at Salford College of Art (1940-42), under Leslie F. N. Reid, D.A. Edin. *Exhib.:* group exhbns.: Moreton Gallery, Australia, Suffolk St. Galleries, S.M.; flower exhbns.: R.W.S., Royal Society of Miniaturists, Royal Academy, Washington and Florida, U.S.A., Societé des Artistes Français (Paris Salon). *Work in permanent collections:* Southport

Municipal (Atkinson) Gallery, mainly held in private collections of art dealers and art publishers including W. H. Patterson (Albemarle); also in private collections in Canada, Holland, Belgium, Lebanon, Spain and Australia. Works published by Royles. *Address:* 19 Pilkington Rd., Southport, Lancs. *Signs work:* "S. Harwood Parry" and see appendix.

PARSONS, Denis Alva, M.B.E. (1993), A.R.B.S. (1992); sculptor in wood and stone; Sculptor/Carver, Linford-Bridgeman; *b* Polesworth, Warwickshire, 14 Nov., 1934; one *s*, one *d*. *Educ.:* Tamworth Secondary Modern; *studied art:* apprenticeship to R. Bridgemen Ltd. (1950-55); Birmingham College of Art (1953-55, part-time). Work in various churches and public buildings. *Address:* Alderways, Fosseway La., Pipe Hill, Lichfield, Staffs. WS13 8JX. *Signs work:* see appendix.

PARTINGTON, Peter Norman, N.D.D., A.T.C., S.WL.A.; painter in water-colour, oil, drypoint etching, art lecturer; Com. mem. S.WL.A.; *b* Cambridge, 29 Sept., 1941; *m* Josephine; two *s*, one *d*. *Educ.:* Poole Grammar School; *studied art* at Bournemouth College of Art and Design (1960-66), Middlesex Polytechnic (1967-68). *Exhib.:* various galleries in London including Tryon Gallery, Glos., Wilts. *Work in permanent collection:* Nature in Art Museum. *Publications:* illustrations, 'Down the River' H.E. Bates (Gollancz 1987), 'Painting Birds in Watercolour' (Collins 1989), 'A Floating World' own poetry and illustration. *Address:* 15 Primrose Terr., Gravesend, Kent DA12 1JN. *Signs work:* "Peter Partington."

PARTRIDGE, John Arthur; antique dealer; Chairman, Partridge Fine Arts PLC; Chairman, Fine Art and Antiques Export Com.; Hon. Treasurer, Society of London Art Dealers; *b* London, 6 July, 1929; *s* of the late Claude A. Partridge; *m*; two *s*, one *d*. *Educ.:* Elstree and Harrow. *Address:* 144-146 New Bond St., London W1.

PASCOE, Ernest, D.F.A. (London Univ.), F.R.B.S., R.W.A.; sculptor and painter; Former Head of Fine Art, Bristol Polytechnic and Executive Vice-Pres., Royal West of England Academy (retd. 1987); *m* Jean Denwood; four *d*. *Studied art* at Carlisle (1938-41), R.A.F. 1941-45, Slade School (1945-48) awarded Wilson Steer Medal, Tonks drawing Prize, Robert Ross Scholarship. *Exhib.:* Arts Council, R.A., London Group, R.B.A, R.W.A., provincial galleries. etc. *Work in permanent collections:* Chantrey Bequest, Oxford University, Royal College of Surgeons, City Art Gallery Bristol, R.W.A. and many private collections. *Address:* The Old Rectory, Weston-in-Gordano, Bristol BS20 8PZ. *Signs work:* "E. Pascoe" or "Ernest Pascoe."

PASCOE, Jane, B.A.(Hons.) Fine Art (1977), A.T.C. (1978), R.W.A. (1988); painter/sculptor/printmaker, teacher (Head of Art Dept.); *b* Bristol, 9 May, 1955; *d* of Ernest Pascoe, D.F.A. (Lond.), F.R.B.S., R.W.A.; *m* Patrick John; one *s*. *Educ.:* The Redmaids School, Bristol (Bristol Foundation Scholarship 1966-73); *studied art* at Bristol Polytechnic Faculty of Art and Design, Dept. of Fine Art (1974-77). *Exhib.:* R.W.A., Eye Gallery, Bristol, Parkin Fine Art, Mall Galleries, London, Salisbury Arts Centre, Swindon Museum and A.G., Victoria Gallery, Beaux Arts Gallery Bath. *Work in permanent collections:* R.W.A., Avon County Art Collection, Cheltenham and Gloucester Bldg. Soc. Art Collection. *Address:* 42 Shaftesbury Rd., Wilton, Salisbury, Wilts. SP2 0DR. *Signs work:* "Jane Pascoe."

PASMORE, Victor, C.H. (1981), C.B.E. (1959), R.A. (1983); painter; Director of Painting, Durham University (1954-61); Director of urban design, S.

W. Area, Peterlee (1954-77); *b* 3 Dec., 1908; *s* of E. S. Pasmore, M.D.; *m* Wendy; one *s*, one *d. Educ.:* Harrow; *studied art* privately. Carnegie prize, Pittsburgh International (1964); Grand Prix d'Honneur, international biennale, Llubljana (1977); Wollaston Prize, R.A. (1983). *Work in public collections:* Tate Gallery; Liverpool; Manchester; Edinburgh; Belfast; Museum of Modern Art, New York; Chicago; Dallas; Museo d'Arte Moderna, Rome; Boymans Museum, Rotterdam; Rijksmuseum Kroller-Muller, Otterlo; Bordeaux, Calais, Melbourne, Sydney, Adelaide, Ottawa, Montreal, Wellington. *Addresses:* Dar Gamri, Gudja 2TN, Malta; and Marlborough Fine Art, 6 Albemarle St., London W1. *Club:* Arts. *Signs work:* see appendix.

PASMORE, Wendy; painter; teacher of painting at Sunderland College of Art, (1955-58), and at Leeds College of Art (1958-67); *b* Dublin, 1915; *d* of J. Lloyd Blood; *m* Victor Pasmore; one *s*, one *d. Educ.:* privately; *studied art:* privately, Mem. London Group. *Work in permanent collections:* Tate Gallery, Arts Council, Leeds Education Committee. *Addresses:* Dar Gamri, Gudja 2TN, Malta, and 12 St. Germans Pl., Blackheath, London SE3 0NN. *Club:* Arts.

PASS, Derek Percy; artist in ceramic enamels, water-colour; ceramic artist, Royal Doulton Tableware, Ltd.; *b* Newcastle, Staffs., 19 Apr., 1929; *s* of Frank Pass; *m* Doreen Odell; two *d. Educ.:* Knutton Elementary School; Burslem School of Art; *studied art* at Stoke-on-Trent College of Art (1942) under Gordon Forsyth, R.I. and Reginald Haggar, R.I. *Exhib.:* Trends, Britain in Water-colours, N.S. *Work in permanent collections:* Newcastle-u-Lyme Post House. *Address:* 12 Thirlmere Pl., Clayton, Newcastle, Staffs. ST5 3QJ. *Signs work:* "Derek Pass," "D. Pass" (ceramic).

PASS, Donald James, N.D.D.; portrait and landscape painter in oil, pastel and water-colour; noted for large works of a visionary nature; *b* Congleton, Ches., 9 Sept., 1930; *s* of Arthur James Pass, master builder; *m* Anne Jacqueline Whitelegge; two *s*, three *d. Studied art* at Macclesfield School of Art, Stoke-on-Trent Regional College of Art, R.A. Schools. *Work in permanent collections:* Gdansk National Museum, Poland, Stoke-on-Trent A.G., Yorkshire Educ. Com., Gallery of Contemporary Art Skopje, Yugoslavia, Gallery of Art Lissone, Milan, University of Keele, Church of St. Mary the Virgin, Elmley Castle, Worcs., Graves A.G., Sheffield, Sir John Rothenstein. *Publications:* Apollo Magazine article by Sir John Rothenstein, Quarto Press, work included in Encyclopedia of Water-colour Techniques. *Address:* 2 Green Lane Lodge, Old Rd., Wheatley, Oxford OX9 1NY. *Signs work:* "D. Pass" or "DONALD PASS."

PATERSON, Donald M., D.A.; artist in water-colour, teacher; elected Mem. Royal Scottish Soc. of Painters in Water-colour; *b* Kyleakin, Isle of Skye, 28 Nov., 1950; *m* Alexandra; two *s. Educ.:* Portree High School; *studied art* at Glasgow School of Art (1969-73). *Exhib.:* one-man show: Fair Maids Gallery, Perth; mixed shows: 'Artists under 30' Third Eye Centre, Glasgow, Glasgow Herald Exhbn. Collins Gallery, Strathclyde University, R.S.A. Annual, G.I. Annual. *Address:* Blaven, Torr Rd., Bridge of Weir, Renfrewshire PA11 3BE. *Signs work:* "D.M. Paterson."

PATERSON, Michael Hugh Orr, B.A., F.R.S.A.; Hon. Curator, Thomas Coram Foundation for Children; art restorer; freelance lecturer and archivist; trainee, City A.G., Birmingham (1953-54); asst., City A.G., Hereford (1954-55); asst.-in-charge, Municipal A.G., Oldham (1956); asst. keeper, City A.G., Leicester (1957-58); Curator, Russell-Cotes A.G. and Museums, Bournemouth (1958-66); Curator of Art, London Borough of Enfield (1966-81); *b* London, 7 Dec., 1927; *s* of G. E. Paterson; *m* Maureen Robinson. *Educ.:* Kirkcudbright

Academy; Cranleigh School; Manchester and Edinburgh Universities; *studied art* at various art colleges (part-time). *Address:* 24 Adamsrill Cl., Enfield, Middx., EN1 2BP.

PATERSON WALLACE, A., N.D.D. Chelsea (1949), M.F.P.S., B.W.S.; artist in water-colour, oil, pastel; *b* Montrose, Scotland, 17 Aug., 1923; *d* of A. F. Paterson; *g-d* of James Paterson, R.S.A., P.R.S.W., R.W.S.; *m* Alan Duncan Wallace; three *s*, one *d*. *Educ.:* Perth Academy, Scotland; Chelsea School of Art (1946-49). *Exhib.:* one-man shows: throughout East Anglia, Broughton, Scotland and London galleries. *Publications:* illustrated, East Anglia from the Sea by D. & J. Hay. *Address:* Ferry Farm, Butley, Woodbridge, Suffolk IP12 3NJ. *Clubs:* Ipswich Art Soc., Founder Mem. Group 'Eight Plus One' (1985), Founder Mem. British Water-colour Soc., Yorkshire (1985). *Signs work:* "Paterson Wallace."

PATRICK, J. McIntosh, R.S.A., R.O.I., A.R.E., LL.D.; oil and water-colour painter and etcher; *b* 1907; *s* of A. G. Patrick, architect; *m* Janet Watterston; one *s*, one *d*. *Educ.:* Dundee, Morgan Academy; Glasgow School of Art. *Exhib.:* R.A., R.S.A., Pittsburgh. *Official purchases:* Chantrey Bequest; Manchester; Glasgow; Aberdeen; National Gallery of S. Africa; British Museum; Carnegie Inst., Pittsburgh; National Gallery, S. Australia; W.A.G.; Lady Lever Gallery; Dundee; Scottish Modern Arts Assoc.; Pilgrim Trust, etc. *Work repro.:* Many paintings reproduced as large-scale prints. *Address:* c/o Fine Art Soc., Plc., 148 New Bond St., London W1. *Signs work:* "McINTOSH PATRICK."

PATRICK, Marion, N.D.D.; painter in oil on hardboard; *b* Liverpool, 30 July, 1940; *d* of John Philip Ridehalgh, cotton manufacturer; *m* Roger Lamprill Patrick. *Educ.:* Penrhos College; *studied art* at Burnley Municipal School of Art. *Exhib.:* Manchester, Bolton, Chatham, London, Mall Galleries, Basildon, Kent. *Work in permanent collections:* Institute of Psychiatry, Maudsley Hospital, Bristol University. *Address:* 'Pendle', 86 Downs Rd., Istead Rise, Gravesend, Kent DA13 9HQ. *Signs work:* "M.P." joined.

PAVEY, Don, F.R.S.A., A.R.C.A.; director, Micro Academy producing art education videos and computer art software; author; lecturer in design and colour; a founder of the National Art Education Archive (Leeds Univ.), the Junior Arts and Science Centres. Freedom of the City of London, (July, 1987). *Publications:* The Artist Colourmen's Story (Winsor & Newton's Museum of Colour Guide, 1985), Color (Architectural Digest of America, 1980), Art-based Games (Methuen, 1979), Methuen Handbook of Colour and Colour Dictionary (Methuen, 1961, 1967, 1978). *Societies:* Mem., R.C.A. Colour Reference Collection Advisory Com. *Address:* Studio House, 30 Wayside, Sheen, London SW14.

PAYNE, David, N.D.D., A.T.C. (1954); painter in oil and water-colour (triptychs); formerly senior lecturer in painting, Bedford College of Educ.; *b* Dover, 29 July, 1928; *m* Iris; one *s*, one *d*. *Studied art* at Canterbury, Farnham and Brighton Colleges of Art until 1954, R.A. Schools (1980-81). *Exhib.:* R.A. (1976, 1978-89, 1991, 1992), Singer Friedlander/Sunday Times (1991, 1992, 1993), N.E.A.C. (1992), R.W.S. (1992, 1993), London galleries, Ellingham Mill (1979, 1982), Ash Barn Gallery, Sotheby's (1981); one-man show, The Gallery, Wellingborough (1983-85), Reynolds Club, New Ashgate Gallery, Farnham (1987). *Work in permanent collections:* Beds. Educ. Loan Service and private collections. *Work repro.:* reviews, I.T.V. (1982), B.B.C.2 (1983), Academy Illustrated (1983, 1984, 1991). *Address:* 25 Willmers Cl., Bedford MK41 8DX. *Signs work:* "David Payne."

PAYNE, Margaret A., N.D.D. (1959), A.T.C. (1960), B.A.(Hons.) History of Art (1981), M.A. (Art Educ.) (1983), R.E. (1975); graphic artist including computer graphics, painter in oil, etcher; Lecturer at Digby Stuart College, Roehampton Inst. London; *b* Southampton, 14 Apr., 1937; *d* of G. E. B. Payne, M.D., D.P.H. *Educ.:* St. Helen's School, Northwood, Middx.; *studied art* at Harrow School of Art (1955-59), Goldsmiths' College (1959-60). *Exhib.:* R.A., R.E., Paris Salon, Society of Women Artists, Young Contemporaries, R.I. *Work in permanent collections:* Sheffield and Nottinghamshire C.C., Pictures for Schools circulation. Currently researching children's learning in N.C. Art at KS1 & 2. *Address:* 11A Wallorton Gdns., London SW14 8DX.

PAYNTER, Hilary, N.D.D. (1964), A.T.C. (1965), M.A. (Psych.Ed., 1982), A.R.E. (1984), F.R.S.A. (1986); wood engraver; educational psychologist; Hon. Sec. S.W.E., Council Mem. R.E.; *b* Dunfermline, 16 June, 1943; *d* of Comdr. E.V.K. Paynter, R.N.; *m* Gerry Bradley; one *s*, one *d*. *Studied art* at Portsmouth College of Art (Gerry Tucker). *Exhib.:* S.W.E., R.E., Xylon, Switzerland; major engraving exhbns.: Durham (1982), Medici (1980), Hereford (1982), Sydney, Australia (1986-87), Ex Libris Internationals; one-man: Buckden (1976) and Kew (1985), R.A., etc. *Work in permanent collections:* Hereford City A.G., Ashmolean Museum. *Publications:* contributions to: The Imprisoned Heart (Gryphon, 1979), Hilary Paynter's Picture Book (Carr, 1985). *Address:* P.O. Box 355, Richmond, Surrey TW10 6LE. *Signs work:* "Hilary Paynter."

PAYNTON, Colin Frank, R.C.A. (1993), R.E. (1986), S.WL.A. (1986), S.W.E. (1984), A.R.E. (1983); painter, etcher and engraver in water-colour, etching and wood engraving; *b* 1946; *s* of Frederick Paynton; *m* Susie See. *Educ.:* Bedford; *studied art* at Northampton School of Art (1963-65, Henry Bird). *Exhib.:* R.A., R.E., R.W.S., S.W.E., S.WL.A. *Work in permanent collections:* Ashmolean Museum Oxford, Beecroft A.G., Southend, Bedford C.C., Freemantle Museum, Australia, National Museum of Wales, S.W.A.N., and many others. *Publications:* illustrations in many private press and commercial publications. *Address:* Oerle Hall, Berriew, Powys, Wales, SY21 8QX. *Signs work:* see appendix.

PEACE, Dr. David, M.B.E., D.Sc.Tech., F.S.A., A.R.I.B.A., F.R.T.P.I.; glass engraver, lettering and heraldic designer; Master, A.W.G. (1973); first Chairman, Guild of Glass Engravers (1975), President (1980-86); Liveryman, Glaziers Co. (1977); *b* Sheffield, 13 Mar., 1915; *m* Jean Margaret Lawson, A.R.C.A.; two *d*. *Educ.;* Mill Hill; University of Sheffield, Hon.D.Sc.Tech. (1991); *studied art* under Clarence Whaite. *Exhib.:* 12 one-man shows; Retrospective (1990). *Work in permanent collections:* V. & A., Fitzwilliam, Kettle's Yard, Brierley Hill Glass Museum, Corning Museum, N.Y., etc.; much presentation glass; windows in many churches; also engraved screens and doors - e.g. St. Nicholas, Liverpool, St. Albans Abbey, Westminster Abbey; memorial to G.M. Hopkins, Poets Corner. *Address:* Abbots End, Hemingford Abbots, Huntingdon, Cambs. PE18 9AA. *Club:* Arts. *Signs work:* see appendix.

PEACOCK, Brian; A.R.C.A. Silver medal (1960), Prix de Rome, painting (1960); painter in oil on board; Head of Painting and Printmaking, Sheffield Polytechnic until 1988; *b* London, 1934. *Educ.:* Sir Joseph Williamsons Mathematical School, Rochester; *studied art* at R.C.A. (1957-60, Carol Weight, Roger de Grey). *Exhib.:* R.A., John Moores, Bristol Art Show; one-man shows include Piccadilly Gallery, John Davies Fine Art, Stow, Mistral Galleries, Dover St. *Work in permanent collections:* Contemporary Arts Soc., Government Collection, D.O.E., M. of W., Nuffield Foundation, Free University Amsterdam,

Pembroke College Oxford, many provincial and overseas galleries. *Address:* 107 Meersbrook Pk. Rd., Sheffield. *Signs work:* "B. Peacock."

PEACOCK, Carlos (Charles Hanbury), B.A.(Cantab.); writer and art critic; *s* of W. E. Peacock, M.D. *Educ.:* Uppingham and Cambridge. *Publications:* Painters and Writers (Tate Gallery), co-author (with John Rothenstein) of essay on Tate Gallery in The Nations Pictures (Chatto and Windus, 1951), John Constable (John Baker Ltd.), Samuel Palmer (John Baker Ltd.), Richard Parkes Bonington (Barrie & Jenkins). *Arranged:* Constable Exhbn. at Aldeburgh Festival (1948), Pre-Raphaelite Exhbn. at Bournemouth (1951). *Address:* 26 Brompton Sq., London SW3.

PEARCE, Antony, B.A. (Exeter) (1963), F.R.S.A. (1990), A.N.S. (1991); teacher/full time artist in water-colour and acrylic since 1980; *b* Leigh, Essex, 21 July, 1933. *Educ.:* Mayfield College, Sussex; *studied art:* self taught, but inspired principally by Rowland Hilder and Edward Seago. *Exhib.:* Edwin Pollard Gallery, Wimbledon (annually), numerous one-man shows. *Work repro.:* by Sharpe's, Castlebar Graphics, Kingsmead Publications. *Address:* Studio Flat, 35 Seymour Rd., E. Molesey, Surrey KT8 0AD. *Club:* R.S.A. *Signs work:* "Antony Pearce."

PEARCE, John Allan; Vice-Pres., Turner Society; painter in oils; retd. solicitor; *b* Sidcup, Kent, 1912; *s* of J.W.E. Pearce, M.A.; *m* Raffaella Baione; two *s.* *Educ.:* Charterhouse and B.N.C. Oxon.; *studied art* with Giorgio de Chirico and privately. *Exhib.:* R.A., N.E.A.C., R.B.A., R.O.I., Chelsea Art Soc., etc. *Address:* 32 Brompton Sq., London SW3. *Club:* Travellers. *Signs work:* "A.P."

PEARCEY, Eilean, B.A. Melb. (1922), M. Univ. Surrey (1987); figure and landscape painter in oil, water-colour, etching, Indian ink, conté, writer; specialized in drawing dancers in action (classical – Pavlova, Dolin, Ulanova, Kirov and Bolshoi; African, Indian and Far East); figure painter *b* Melbourne, Australia, 28 May, 1901; *m* A. Ramsay Moon, B.A., B.Sc. (Melb.), M.I. Struct.E.; one *s* (decd.). *Educ.:* P.L.C. Melbourne; Melbourne University (1919-21); *studied art* at National Gallery School, Melbourne (1922-25, L. Bernard Hall); Académie LHote, Paris (1932); Iain Macnab London School of Modern Art. *Exhib.:* Melbourne and Sydney, Australia (1938, 1955), Paris Salon, London, Galerie Apollinaire (1952, 1953), R.A., U.A., India House (1974, 1980), 'The Place' L.C.D.T. (2), University of Surrey, Guildford (3); various mixed shows. *Work in permanent collections:* University of Surrey Dance Centre, Marcel Marceau Museum; Robin Howard, C.B.E. (Martha Graham drawings), Ram Gopal (ten drawings of himself). *Publications:* drawings published in U.S.A. 'The Christian Science Monitor' and 'Dance Observer', N.Y.; 'Marg' Bombay; 'Sangeet Natak Academi Journal' Delhi; David Bolland's 'Guide to Kathakali'; Massey's Dances of India' (1989); The Times, Sunday Telegraph, Ballet Annual, Soviet Weekly, and wrote for seven years on Indian dance for Dance and Dancers. *Address:* 6A Shaftesbury Villas, Allen St., London W8 6UZ. *Clubs:* F.P.S., V. & A. *Signs work:* "Eilean Pearcey," before 1952 "EILEEN PEARCEY."

PEARSON, James E.; artist in oil, clay, bronze; William Boyd Andrews, Best of Show, 1961; Gold Keys, 1951, 1954, 1956; Scholastic Art Awards, Carnegie Institute; art instructor, Woodstock, Comm. High School, Woodstock, Illinois, U.S.A.; Bachelor of Science in Education (1961), Master of Science in Education (1962), Master of Fine Art (1964); *b* Woodstock, Illinois, U.S.A., 12 Dec., 1939; *s* of John C. Pearson. *Educ.:* McHenry Community High School, McHenry, Illinois; Northern Illinois University, Dekalb, Illinois; *studied art* at Northern Illinois University, Dekalb, Illinois. *Work in permanent collections:* Northern

Illinois University; over 100 private collections (company and individual). *Publications:* McHenry County, 1832-1968. *Address:* 5117 Barnard Mill Rd., Ringwood, Illinois, 60072, U.S.A. *Signs work:* see appendix.

PEART, Tony, B.A. (Hons.) (1983), M.A. (1986); painter in oil; associate lecturer, Cumbria College of Art and Design; *b* Darlington, 23 June, 1961; *m* Sharyn Brown. *Educ.:* Eastbourne School; *studied art* at Cheltenham College of Art, Leeds Polytechnic, Newcastle Polytechnic. *Exhib.:* Piccadilly Gallery (1988-). *Work in permanent collections:* Carlisle A.G., Darlington A.G., Government Painting Coll., Rank Xerox, Newcastle University, Northern Arts. *Address:* 4 Beanley Ave., Lemington, Newcastle upon Tyne NE15 8SP. *Signs work:* "Tony Peart" always on reverse.

PECKHAM, Barry Arthur, S.E.A. (1984); landscape, marine and equestrian artist in oil, water-colour, pastel, etching; *b* New Forest, Hants., 30 Dec., 1945; *m* Georgina Babey; three *d*. *Educ.:* Bartley School; *studied art* at Southampton College of Art. *Exhib.:* R.A., R.I., R.O.I., P.S., R.S.M.A., S.E.A., N.E.A.C., Royal West of England Academy. *Work in permanent collection:* Royal Marines, Poole. *Awards:* Royle prize (1984), Cuneo medal (1989), Crossgate Gallery award (1989), Pastel award (1990), Champagne Mumm Marine Artist (1990). *Address:* Fletchwood Cottage, Busketts Way, Ashurst, Southampton, Hants. SO4 2AE. *Signs work:* "B.A. PECKHAM."

PEDLEY, Nada Marija, A.R.M.S. (1991); sculptor in clay and terracotta; freelance sculptor, Royal Doulton; *b* 1 Aug., 1944; *m* John Pedley; two *s*, one *d*. *Studied art* at Slovenija Ljubljana Commercial Art (1964-67), Horsham Art School (1974-78, ceramics: John Green). *Exhib.:* R.M.S. (1987-), Doulton Gallery, Stoke-on-Trent. *Work in permanent collection:* Doulton Gallery, Stoke-on-Trent. *Address:* 9 Garrick Rd., Worthing, Sussex BN14 8BB. *Signs work:* "Nada M. Pedley," "Nada" or "N.M. Pedley."

PELL, Robert Leslie, N.D.D. (Painting) (1948), R.B.A. (1958), F.R.S.A. (1968); painter in oil and polymer and lecturer; *b* Northampton, 24 Nov., 1928; *s* of Harry Pell; *m* Pamela Crake; one *s*, one *d*. *Educ.:* Technical High School, Northampton; *studied art* at Northampton School of Art and Camberwell School of Art and Crafts. *Exhib.:* R.C.A. Galleries, R.B.A., Foyle's Gallery, Canaletto Gallery, Leicester Gallery (Artists of Fame and Promise), Piccadilly Gallery, Bear Lane Gallery, Oxford. *Work in permanent collections:* University College and Balliol College, Oxford, Leicestershire, Reading, Surrey and Northumberland Education Committees, The John Lewis Organisation, Northampton Art Gallery, Coventry City Art Gallery, private collections in England, America and Finland. *Work repro.:* La Revue Moderne, Art Review, The Artist, The Oxford Magazine, The Studio. *Address:* The Studio House, 141 High St., Brackley, Northants. NN13 5BN. *Club:* Royal Society of Arts. *Signs work:* "Pell" (written in italic script).

PELLING, John Arthur, A.R.C.A.; painter in oil on canvas; clergyman, Church of England; *b* Hove, 9 Aug., 1930; *s* of Arthur Robert Pelling; divorced; four *s*. *Educ.:* Brighton, Hove and Sussex Grammar School; *studied art* at Brighton College of Art (1946-49) and Royal College of Art (1951-55). *Exhib.:* eight one-man shows, London, Sussex University, Manchester. *Work in permanent collections:* National Gallery Poland, Nuffield Foundation, Vittorio 'de Sica private collection, Italy. At present full time painter in Monte Carlo. Member of Comite Monégasque des Arts Plastiques, A.I.A.P., UNESCO. *Address:* Villa Riviera, 6 Av. de Grande-Bretagne, Monte-Carlo. M.C. 98000. *Signs work:* "PELLING" (on paintings), "John Pelling" (on drawings).

PELLY, Frances, R.S.A., D.A.; sculptor in wood, stone, clay, paper; *b* Edinburgh, 1947; *d* of Russell Steele Pelly, forester. *Educ.:* Morrisons Academy, Crieff; *studied art* at Duncan of Jordanstone, Dundee (1965-71, Scott Sutherland, Alistair Smart). *Exhib.:* R.S.A., S.S.A., R.G.I.; solo shows, Collective Gallery, Edinburgh (1986), Crawford Art Centre, St.Andrews (1987), 'Nousts', travelling exhbn. in Highland Region and Norway (1992-93). *Work in permanent collections and public places:* Fine Art Soc., Scottish Arts Council, Dundee, BBC Glasgow, Perth, Dumfries, Orkney, Aberdeen, Royal Concerthall Glasgow and Banff. *Address.:* Costa Schoolhouse, Evie, Orkney KW17 2NJ. Rarely signs work.

PELZ, Peter, M.A. (Cantab.) (1968); artist in oil, tempera, water-colour, drawing; *b* Oxford, 18 Sept., 1945. *Educ.:* King's College, Cambridge; *studied art:* Wigan, Lancs. (1957-63, Theodore Major). *Exhib.:* Rebecca Hossack Gallery, London. *Work in permanent collections:* on commission (chief works): triptychs at Huyton, Liverpool, and St. James's, Piccadilly; mural at St. Peter's, Morden. *Publication:* Prayer for the Day (Cairns). *Address:* 1 The Green, Ascott-under-Wychwood, Chipping Norton, Oxfordshire OX7 6AB. *Signs work:* "Peter Pelz" and date.

PEMBERTON, Christopher Henry, M.A. (1948); landscape, portrait and still life painter in oil, pencil and pen; Head of Foundation Studies, Camberwell School of Art (1982-85; taught at Camberwell 1958-85); *b* London, 14 Mar., 1923; *s* of Richard Pemberton, H.M.I.; *m* Hester Riddell; four *s,* one *d. Educ.:* Eton College, Christ Church Oxford; *studied art* at Camberwell School of Art (1948-50, Claude Rogers). *Exhib.:* Woodlands, Blackheath (1977), Wells Centre, Norfolk (1987); one-man shows: Gainborough's House, Sudbury, Cadogan Contemporary (1989). *Work in permanent collection:* Newnham College, Cambridge. *Publication:* translation of Gasquet's memoir on Cézanne (Thames & Hudson, 1991). *Address:* Place Farmhouse, Bardwell, Bury St.Edmunds, Suffolk. *Signs work:* "C. Pemberton."

PEMBERTON, Muriel Alice, A.R.C.A., R.W.S., C.S.D., Senior F.R.C.A.; artist in water-colour, oil, chalk, pencil, etc., designer; ex Head of Fashion/ Textile Faculty, St. Martin's School of Art; fashion artist, News Chronicle (1945-52); *b* 8 Sept., 1909; *m* John Hadley Rowe, A.R.C.A. *Educ.:* Brown Hills High School, Stoke-on-Trent; *studied art* at Burslem School of Art (1925-28, Gordon Forsyth), Royal College of Art (1928-32, Prof. Tristram and Sir William Rothenstein). *Exhib.:* one-man shows, Leicester Gallery (1952), Lewes County Town Gallery, Worthing Museum and A.G. (1973), Hanley Museum, Stoke-on-Trent, Grand Parade Gallery, Brighton (1980); R.A., Beaux Arts Gallery, Ledger Gallery. *Work in permanent collections:* Arts Council of Gt. Britain, Worthing Museum and A.G., Rochdale Hanley Museum and A.G., and private collections in London and abroad. *Work repro.:* Vogue and Vogue Export, Connoisseur, Unicef, Arts Council of Gt. Britain, Arts Review. *Address:* Hurst-Dene, Stonestyle La., Hastings, E. Sussex. *Signs work:* "Muriel Pemberton" or "M.P."

PENDERED, Susan Marjorie Anne, M.C.S.P., R.I. (1983); painter in water based medium; Winner of the Winsor & Newton R.I. Award (1988); *b* London, 15 June, 1925; *d* of the late Robert Kenrick Cornish-Bowden; *m* John H. Pendered, G.P., M.B.E., M.B., B.S.; one *s,* two *d. Educ.:* Lillesden School for Girls, Hawkhurst, Kent; *studied art* part-time at Brighton Polytechnic (1975-82, Norma Weller). *Exhib.:* Mall Galleries, R.I., R.A. Summer Exhbn., R.W.A., Bristol, participated in travelling exhbn. to Vancouver, Canada and Seattle,

U.S.A. (1986), Salammbo Galerie, Paris (1987). *Address:* Littleway, West Furlong La., Hurstpierpoint, W. Sussex BN6 9RH. *Clubs:* Sussex Painters, Assoc. of Sussex Artists, Phoenix Group. *Signs work:* "S. Pendered."

PENNEY, Victor E.; painter in oils and water-colour, both representational and abstract, also portraiture in chalk and pastel; *b* Dublin, 8 July, 1909; *m* Eileen C. Penney; one *s*, one *d. Educ.:* High School, Dublin; *studied art* at College of Art, Dublin. *Exhib.:* Royal Hibernian Academy, the United Artists and the Watercolour Society of Ireland. *Address:* Studio, Correston, Carrickbrack Rd., Baily, Dublin 13. *Signs work:* "Victor E. Penney."

PEPYS, Rhoda Gertrude, N.A.T.C. (South Africa); artist, portrait painter, tutor; *b* Port Elizabeth, 12 Mar., 1914 (née Kussel); *m* Prof. Jack Pepys (1938); two children. *Educ.:* Collegiate, School of Arts and Crafts, Port Elizabeth; Silver Medal (1934). *Exhib.:* one-man shows: S.A.; Italy; Paris (1962); London: Hampstead Art Cellar (1963), Barbican (1982), Studio 36 (1967-89); U.S.A.: Washington (1985); group shows in London: R.A. Summer Exhbn. (1966, 1989), Images of Italy (1987-89), Israel Paintings (1988). *Awards:* Academie International de Lutèce, Paris, Silver Medal, (1978); Accademia Italia, Gold Medal (1980); Centauro D'Oro (1982). *Commissions:* Univ. of London, Portrait of (1) Prof. G. Scadding (1974); (2) Prof. Jack Pepys (1979). *Address:* 34 Ferncroft Ave., London NW3 7PE. *Club:* Accademia Italia. *Signs work:* "Pepys" and "Rhoda Pepys."

PEPYS, Sandra Lynn, B.A. (Hons.), London; artist, art historian, journalist, illustrator, art teacher and lecturer; *b* Cape Town, 27 Jan., 1942; *m* A. Heidecker (1969). *Educ.:* South Hampstead and S.O.A.A.S., Univ. of London; awarded 1st Prize, Univ. of London Exhbn. (1966). *Exhib.:* one-man shows: London: Hampstead Art Cellar (1962); Everyman (1963); Mermaid Theatre (1966); Studio 36 (annually from 1966-1976); Oxford: Halifax House (1963); Paris: Galerie Tedesco (1962); Italy: Sperlonga (1962, 1965); Rome: Galleria Coppella (1965); Artists House, Jerusalem (1979-1982); group shows: H.A.C., W.A.C. Univ. of London, Guildhall, R.A. Summer Exhbn. (1973, 1977, 1978). *Commissions:* mural paintings, London University (1966) and Brit. Railways (1967). *Address:* 34 Ferncroft Ave., London NW3. *Clubs:* Florentine Assoc., Italy, Jerusalem Artists Assoc. *Signs work:* "Sandra Pepys."

PERKINS, Stuart M.G., R.M.S. (1991), M.A.A. (1990), A.T.D., N.D.D. (1956), M.P.S.G., M.A.S.-F., M.A.S.-N.J.; miniaturist in water-colour and gouache; *b* Leicester, 4 July, 1935; *m* Joan Chatterley, A.T.D.; three *d. Educ.:* Alderman Newton Boys G.S., Leicester; *studied art* at Leicester College of Art (1952-56, Albert Pountney). *Exhib.:* R.M.S., R.W.A., R.W.S. Summer Show, W.A.C.; many mixed exhbns. in England and Wales, miniature exhbns. in U.K., Canada, U.S.A. *Work in permanent collections:* M.A.S.-F., G.M.A.S. *Address:* The Old School, Scowles, Coleford, Glos. GL16 8QT. *Signs work:* "S. PERKINS, R.M.S., M.A.A." (dated), "Stuart Perkins."

PERRE, Hugo A. J. van de; author, critic and broadcaster; mem. of P.E.N., Critics' Circle and F.P.A.; Hon. Member F.P.S.; *b* Antwerp, 24 Jan., 1914; *s* of Dr. A. van de Perre; *m* Selma; two *s. Educ.:* Antwerp and Louvain. *Publications:* books in English, French and Dutch on art, literature and history, e.g., Présences belges à Londres: Petit discours sur la contribution belge à l'histoire de la Capitale anglaise (Brussels-Aldington, 1954); Dutch Guide Book for London; Contemporary Flemish Literature (India); John Osborne, boze jonge man (Tielt/ The Hague); Five Belgian Painters from London (publ. in English, French and Dutch, 1961); Vier Belgische Schilders uit Londen, Bruges (1968), co-editor

Focus on English III (1972) and IV (1973), poems and fiction. *Address:* 95 Black Lion La., London W6 9BG.

PERRIN, Brian, A.R.C.A., Rome Scholar (1954); painter/etcher; Head of Printmaking Dept., Wimbledon School of Art; Mem. C.N.A.A. Fine Art Board; *b* 19 Aug., 1932; *s* of Charles Perrin; *m* Jane Lisle; two *s. Educ.:* Whitgift Middle School; *studied art* at Croydon School of Art (1948-51), R.C.A. (1951-54). *Exhib.:* extensively in Europe and U.S.A., including international print Biennales. *Work in permanent collections:* Library of Congress, Washington, V. & A., Arts Council, British Council; Museums of Art: Metropolitan N.Y., Perth, Jerusalem, Boston, Cincinatti, Glasgow. *Address:* 293 Kings Rd., Kingston-upon-Thames, Surrey. *Signs work:* "Brian Perrin."

PERRY, Roy, R.I. (1978); painter in oil, water-colour and acrylic; awarded R.I. Medal (1978), R.I. Council (1979); *b* Liverpool, 1935; *s* of Sydney Perry, chartered accountant; *m* Sallie Charlton; one *s*, one *d. Educ.:* John Lyon School, Harrow and Southampton University. *Exhib.:* R.A., R.I., R.B.A., R.S.M.A., etc.; one-man shows, Oxford, Guildford, London, Henley and Cambridge. *Work in permanent collections:* many large business corporations; The Fleet Air Arm Museum; H.R.H. The Duke of Edinburgh and other private collections throughout the world. *Work repro.:* Lithographs, New York, Industrial Reviews and Laings Calendar. *Address:* The Mill House, Donhead St. Mary, Shaftesbury, Dorset SP7 9DS. *Signs work:* "Roy Perry."

PESKETT, Eric Harry, A.T.D. (1934), A.R.C.A. (1938), R.C.A. travelling scholar (1939), F.R.B.S. (retd); sculptor; *b* Guildford, 31 Jan., 1914; *s* of Charles John Peskett; *m* Marjorie Ayling; one *s. Educ.:* Brighton, Hove and Sussex Grammar School; *studied art* at Brighton College of Art (1929-35), R.C.A. (1935-39). *Official purchases:* (drawings) V. & A.; (brick reliefs) Congress Theatre, Eastbourne; Church of Holy Cross, Patricroft, Lancs.; Veterinary Bldg., Liverpool University; (altar Crucifixes) St. Mary's Church Denton, Lancs.; Church of the Holy Cross, Patricroft; (fountain pool) Tower Block, Borough Polytechnic, London. *Address:* 12 Court Bushes Rd., Whyteleafe, Surrey CR3 0BG. *Club:* Architectural Association. *Signs work:* "Peskett."

PESKETT, Tessa, B.A. (Hons.) Fine Art (1979), P.G.C.E. (1982), H.Postgrad.Dip.Painting (1992); Chadwick Healey prize for painting (1992); artist in oil, water-colour, charcoal; *b* Three Bridges, Sussex, 25 Apr., 1957. *Educ.:* Beaumont School, St. Albans; *studied art* at Reading University (1975-79), City & Guilds of London Art School (1992). *Exhib.:* R.A. Summer Shows, R.B.A., R.O.I., Linda Blackstone Gallery, Mall Galleries. *Address:* 63 Swanmore Rd., Boscombe, Bournemouth, Dorset BH7 6PD. *Signs work:* "Tessa D. Peskett."

PETERSON, Peter Charles, N.D.D., V.P.R.B.A. (1988), R.B.A. (1978); mem. Turner Landscape Soc. (1989), Vice Chairman, Soc. of Landscape Painters; Daler Rowney Prize (1983), First Prize (1988); artist in oil, water-colour and gouache; lecturer, Visual Research Dept. Chesterfield College of Art; senior lecturer, Fine Art Dept. Epsom College of Art; visiting lecturer, Falmouth College of Art (1986); *b* 4 Apr., 1934. *Studied art* at Hornsey College of Art. *Exhib.:* R.A. Summer Exhbn. since 1968, R.B.A. since 1978, Falmouth A.G., Hallam Gallery, N.E.A.C., Crossgate Gallery, U.S.A.; one-man shows, Portal Gallery, Highgate, Southwell-Brown Gallery, Richmond, Gt.Yarmouth Museum; group shows, Odette Gilbert Gallery (1983-84), Southwell-Brown Gallery, Richmond, Alexander Gallery London. *Address:* 101 Selhurst Rd., S. Norwood, London SE25. *Signs work:* "Peter Peterson."

PETO, Michael James, B.A. (Arch.) (Lond.), M.I.A.Z., Donaldson Medal (1950), Dip. T.P. (1952); architect; artist in water-colour, ink; *b* Jaffna, Ceylon, 9 Feb., 1928; *s* of the Rev. Henry Peto. *Educ.:* St. John's, Leatherhead; *studied art* at Canterbury School of Art under Robert W. Paine and Gerald Norden (1944-45); Bartlett School of Architecture, London University, under Prof. H. O. Corfiato (1945-51). *Exhib.:* Canterbury, St. John's Wood, Zimbabwe. *Work repro.:* Christmas cards, etc. *Address:* P.O. Box 270, Harare, Zimbabwe. *Signs work:* "James Peto."

PETTERSON, Melvyn Lawrence, R.E. (1991), B.A. (1986); painter/printmaker in oil, etching, water-colour; partner, Artichoke Print Workshop; *b* Cleethorpes, 7 July, 1947; *m* Glynis; one *d. Educ.:* Cleethorpes-Beacon Hill Sec. Modern; *studied art* at Grimsby Art School (Peter Todd, Alf Ludlam, Nev Tipper), Camberwell School of Art (Graham Giles, Francis Hoyland, Anthony Eyton, R.A., Ben Levene, R.A.). *Exhib.:* R.A., N.E.A.C., R.O.I., Bankside Gallery, museums and galleries in U.S.A., France, Russia, China, Spain, Sweden, Finland, Mont Carlo. *Work in permanent collections:* Oxford, Leicester, galleries in U.S.A. *Publication:* British Painters/Sculptors. *Address:* The Vicarage, 81 Camberwell Church St., London SE5 8RB. *Club:* R.E. *Signs work:* "M.L. Petterson" or "M.L.P."

PETTY, Anthony, A.A. (Hons.) Dip. (1948), S.P. Dip. (1949); architect and painter in water-colour, gouache and mixed media; *b* Southampton, 1918; *s* of Clive Petty; *m* Christine Durell; two *d. Studied art* at Southern College of Art (1934-38, William Dring), Architectural Assoc. School (1946-48, Gordon Brown). *Exhib.:* R.A., and many provincial galleries. *Address:* Curtle, Blackhill, Lindfield, Sussex. *Signs work:* "Anthony Petty."

PETZSCH, Helmut Franz Günther, D.A. (Edin.) 1951; F.S.A. Scot.; painter in oil and water-colour; *b* Berlin, 13 Dec., 1920; *s* of Max Leberecht Petzsch; *m* Catherine Oag Craigie; one *s*, two *d. Educ.:* Hamburg and London; *studied* at Edinburgh College of Art (1947-51). *Exhib.:* R.S.A., S.S.A., '57 Gallery, Edinburgh. *Publication:* author of Architecture in Scotland (Longman). *Address:* 32 Canaan Lane, Edinburgh EH10 4SU. *Signs work:* "Helmut Petzsch."

PHILLIPS, Aubrey, R.W.A., P.S.; Gold Medal, Paris Salon (1966); artist in pastel, water-colour and oil, teacher; *b* Astley, Worcs., 18 June, 1920; *m* Doris Kirk; three *s. Studied art* at Stourbridge School of Art (E. M. Dinkel), Kidderminster School of Art (W. E. Daly, C. J. Lavenstein). *Exhib.:* F.B.A. Galleries, National Library of Wales, City A.G.'s of Worcester, Hereford and Gloucester. *Work in permanent collections:* Worcester A.G., Worcester County Museum. *Publications:* Two works on pastel and one on water-colour publ. by Search Press. *Work repro.:* Leisure Painter and Artist. *Address:* 16 Carlton Rd., Malvern, Worcs. WR14 1MH. *Signs work:* "Aubrey R. Phillips."

PHILLIPS, Ewan Godfrey, M.A. (Lond.), History of Art (1938); art consultant, art historian and dealer in nineteenth- and twentieth-century paintings and sculpture, Mem. International Association of Art Critics, Association of Art Historians, I.C.A.; *b* London, 16 Mar., 1914; *s* of Godfrey Phillips, late of Godfrey Phillips Galleries. *Educ.:* Epsom College and Courtauld Institute of Art (Univ. of London); *studied art* at Goldsmiths' College of Art, Courtauld Institute of Art under Prof. Anthony Blunt, Professor W. G. Constable, Professor T. S. R. Boase, etc. *Publications:* Thesis, English Expressionist and Artists in the Nineteenth Century (see note in "William Blake.", by Dr. Bronowski). *Address:* Marsh Farm, Thorington, Saxmundham IP17 3RD. *Club:* The Savile.

WHO'S WHO IN ART

PHILLIPS, Francis Douglas; painter and illustrator in water-colour, oil, acrylic, pastel, ink; *d* Dundee, 19 Dec., 1926; *s* of James Phillips, engineer; *m* Margaret Parkinson; one *d. Educ.:* Dundee; *studied art* at Dundee College of Art (J. Milne Purvis). *Exhib.:* R.S.A., R.S.W., R.G.I.; two 'Grampian' T.V. appearances (Feb. and July 1987) 'Tayside Artist'. *Work in permanent collections:* National Trust for Scotland, English Speaking Union, Northern College of Educ.; private collections worldwide. *Work repro.:* Limited Edn. Prints. *Publications:* illustrated over 100 books; covers on British and French Reader's Digest. *Address:* 278 Strathmore Ave., Dundee DD3 6SJ. *Signs work:* "Phillips."

PHILLIPS, John Edward, N.D.D. (Sculpture) 1958, A.T.C. (Lond.) 1961; full-time sculptor and Artist in Residence; *b* Ealing, London, 28 June, 1937; *s* of William Francis Phillips; *m* Valerie Maughan; one *s,* one *d. Educ.:* Ealing College; *studied art* at Ealing School of Art (1953-58), Hornsey College of Art (1960-61). *Exhbns. and residencies:* various galleries, art centres, libraries, schools in London, Southern England and France. *Work in permanent collections:* Hillingdon Civic Centre, Uxbridge Library and various schools in the London area, Bucks., Herts. and Oxford. *Address:* Lanhael, Hedgerley Hill, Hedgerley, nr. Slough SL2 3RW. *Signs work:* "John Phillips."

PHILLIPS, John Henry, A.T.D., M.C.C.Ed. (1947), F.R.S.A.; finalist, City and Guilds (handicrafts), Lond. (1948); artist in oil, water-colour; lately, Administrator, School Examinations Dept., University of London, responsible for art, technical subjects (retd. 1980); Head of Art, Handicraft, Harold Hill Gram. Sch., Romford (1957-65), Chatham House Gram. Sch., Ramsgate (1952-57), Luton Gram. School (1947-52); *b* Horsham, Sussex, 26 May, 1920; *s* of E. H. E. Phillips, M.Coll. H.; *m* Gladys Phillips, S.R.N.; one *s,* one *d. Educ.:* Gram. Sch., Cowbridge, Glam.; *studied art:* College of Art, Cardiff, from 1936, under Evan Charlton, William Pickles. *Exhib.:* New Herts. Art Soc., Ramsgate Art Soc. *Address:* 3 Priory Rd., Harold Hill, Romford, Essex. *Signs work:* "J. Phillips."

PHILLIPS, Karen Erica, D.A.T.E.C. (1982), B.A.Hons. (1985), M.F.A. (1987); painter in oil, ink, charcoal, acrylic; *b* Kidderminster, 1 Nov., 1962; *d* of Alan Neville Phillips, N.D.D., S.D.A.S. *Educ.:* Franche Middle School, Kidderminster; Ilfracombe Comprehensive; *studied art* at North Devon College (1979-82, Robin Wiggins), Bristol Polytechnic (1982-85, Ernest Pascoe), Newcastle University (1985-87, Norman Adams). *Exhib.:* New Theatre Gallery, Barnstaple (shared exhbn. with father), Zetland Studios, Bristol, Burton A.G., Bideford, Jigsaw, Barnstaple, Long Gallery, Newcastle, R.W.A., R.A., Vicarage Cottage Gallery, North Shields. *Address:* 10 Shafto St., Scotswood, Newcastle-upon-Tyne NE15 6AX. *Signs work:* "K. Phillips."

PHILLIPS, Patrick Laurence: specialist in 19th and 20th century art; Joint Managing Director, Ernest Brown and Phillips Ltd., Proprietors of the Leicester Galleries, c/o 3 Elystan St., SW3, and responsible for a great number of first exhibitions in England including Epstein, Matisse, Van Gogh, Camille Pissarro, Picasso, Degas, Gauguin, Redon, Cézanne, Renoir, Kokoschka, Burra, Pryde, Ensor, Soutine, Drysdale. Organiser of the 1964 Festival exhbn., Henry Moore at King's Lynn, held in the open air throughout the town. Has also concentrated on original prints and is associated with Leicester Art Books (Fine Art Reference Books), 60 Oxford St. (P.O. Box 4YT), London W1; *b* London, 1 July, 1912; *s* of Cecil Laurence Phillips, co-founder of the Leicester Galleries, Leicester Sq., in 1902; *m* Margaret Elinor Chapman; two *s. Educ.:* Stonyhurst College; *studied*

376

art in the museums of Europe. *Addresses:* 164 Coleherne Ct., London SW5, and Brandon House, Horn Hill, Dartmouth.

PHILLIPS, Rex, Cdr.R.N. (retd.); marine and landscape artist in oil and water-colour; *b* March, Cambs., 19 July, 1931; *m* Shirley Chadwick; one *s*, two *d*. *Educ.:* Nautical College, Pangbourne. *Exhib.:* R.S.M.A., A.F.A.S., and various one-man shows. *Work in permanent collections:* Royal Naval, Royal Marines and Fleet Air Arm Museums, London and provincial galleries; private collections in U.K. and abroad, naval ships and establishments, R.N.L.I. and other institutions. *Address:* 15 Westbourne Ave., Emsworth, Hants. PO10 7QT. *Signs work:* "Rex Phillips."

PHILLIPS, Tom, R.A. (1988), R.E., M.A. (Oxon.), N.D.D.; artist in oil, water-colour, book productions, television director (A TV Dante, etc.); *b* London, 25 May, 1937; *m* Jill (divorced); one *s*, one *d*. *Educ.:* St. Catherine's, Oxford; *studied art* at Camberwell School of Art (Frank Auerbach). *Work in permanent collections:* Tate Gallery, B.M., V. & A., Moma, N.Y., etc. *Address:* 57 Talfourd Rd., London SE15. *Clubs:* S.C.C.C., Groucho. *Signs work:* "Tom Phillips."

PHIPPS, Howard, B.A.(Hons.), R.W.A., S.W.E.; wood engraver, painter and illustrator; *b* Colwyn Bay, 1954. *Studied:* Fine Art, Cheltenham Art College (1971-75). *Exhib.:* R.W.A., S.W.E., also at R.A. Summer Exhbns. where in 1985 awarded Christies Contemporary Print prize; one-man exhbns. include five in Salisbury and a major show at Dorset County Museum (1993). *Work in permanent collections:* Cheltenham A.G., Salisbury Museum, Fremantle A.G. (Australia), R.W.A. *Publications:* illustrated books for: Bloomsbury, Century, Perdix, Folio Soc. (Shakespeare, Bronte, Tennyson) and Whittington Press who published the artist's own books Interiors (1985) and Further Interiors (1991). Contributor to Country Life. *Address:* 53 Ravenscroft, Salisbury SP2 8DL.

PICHÉ, Roland, 1st Class N.D.D., A.R.C.A., Medal for Work of Distinction, R.C.A.; sculptor in resin, fibreglass, stainless steel, stone and bronze; lecturer in sculpture; Principal Lecturer, Canterbury College of Art; *b* London, 21 Nov., 1938; two *d*. *Educ.:* Romsey College, Embley Park, Hants.; *studied art* at Hornsey College of Art (Mr. C. Anderson, A.R.C.A., 1956-60), Royal College of Art (Mr. B. Meadows, A.R.C.A., 1960-64). *Work in permanent collections:* The Arts Council of Great Britain and Wales, São Paulo Museum, Gothenburg Museum, Sweden, National Gallery of Western Australia. *Publications:* Private View (B. Robertson and T. Armstrong-Jones), Dada, Surrealism (W. S. Rubin). *Address:* Victoria Studios, Tollesbury, Essex. *Signs work:* see appendix.

PICKARD JENKINS, Percy, F.S.I.A., F.I.A.L.; designer, painter and teacher, package design, advertising and stained glass; designer, Metal Box Co. Ltd. (1936-40); draughtsman, Metal Box Co. Ltd. (1940-45); art director, J. Walter Thompson Co. Ltd. (1945-50); freelance since 1950; lecturer, London School of Printing and Graphic Arts (1951-54); consultant designer, Metal Box Co. Ltd. (1954-58); head of Department of Graphic Design, Croydon College of Art (1961-71); *b* Swansea, 1 Sept., 1908; *m* (1) Elsa Lewis; (2) Winifred Jervis. *Studied art* at Swansea College of Art. Designer of Pickard Tuscan Type-Face for W. S. Cowell. *Exhib.:* paintings, Le Salon des Nations, Paris (1983). *Work repro.:* International Design Publications. *Address:* 2 St. Rhidian Drive, Killay, Swansea, W. Glam. SA2 7EL. *Signs work:* "P. Pickard Jenkins" or "P.P.J."

PICKEN, Mollie, N.D.D. (1963), A.T.C. (1964); freelance artist in illustration, embroidery and fabric collage; *b* 13 Oct., 1940. *Studied art* at Goldsmiths' College School of Art (1959-64) under Constance Howard and Betty Swanwick.

Work in private collections: Education Authorities. *Publications:* Illustrated books by Constance Howard. Recently collaborated with Christine Bloxham to produce Love and Marriage (Pub. date: Feb. 1990). Art work for Oxfordshire Museum Services, Embroiderers Guild. *Address:* The Old Post Office, Sibford Gower, Banbury, Oxon. *Clubs:* S.D-C.; Embroiderers' Guild Practical Study Group; Assoc. of Illustrators.

PICKING, John, N.D.D. (1960), D.A. Edin. (1962), A.T.D. (1966); painter and lecturer; Mem. Manchester Academy; Senior Lecturer in Fine Art, Manchester Polytechnic. *Studied art* at Wigan School of Art, 1956-60 (Governors Medal); Edinburgh College of Art, 1960-63 (Postgrad. Scholarship); Goldsmiths' College, London, 1965-66. *Exhib.:* regularly with Scottish Gallery, Edinburgh, Colin Jellicoe Gallery, Manchester, Mercury Gallery, London, Galleria Robinia, Palermo. *Work in permanent collections:* Salford University, Edinburgh Corp., private collections in many parts of the world. Often living and painting in Sicily; interested in peasant-type communities, Sicily to Lapland to Armenia; gives illustrated talks to societies, etc. *Address:* c/o Colin Jellicoe Gallery, 82 Portland St., Manchester 1.

PIDOUX, Janet Anne, S.W.A. (1992); painter in pastel; *b* High Wycombe, Bucks., 2 Sept., 1950; *m* Derek; one *s*, one *d*. *Educ.:* Wellesbourne. *Exhib.:* S.W.A., S.WL.A., P.S. *Address:* c/o Penn Barn Gallery, By the Pond, Elm Rd., Penn, Bucks. HP10 8LB. *Signs work:* "JANET PIDOUX."

PIERCE, Norman F., F.R.B.S., A.R.C.A.; sculptor; *b* Lewisham, 1915; *s* of Edith and Charles F. Pierce; *studied art* at Reading University under Prof. A. W. Seaby (1931-35); under Prof. Garbe, R.A., at R.C.A. (1935-38). *Exhib.:* R.A., Paris Salon, Mall Galleries and provincial galleries. *Public works:* eight heraldic coats of arms New County Offices, Winchester; Figure of Christ in Benediction, carved in Portland Stone Grammar School, Highcliffe; Madonna and Child St. Stephen's Church, Winchester; Portrait figures Madame Tussaud's; 9ft. bronze figure of late Sir Seretse Khama, Botswana; bust of Lord Lister for Wimpole St., London. *Address:* 4 Wessex Drive, Winchester Hants. SO22 6DQ. *Signs work:* "Norman Pierce" and see appendix.

PIERSON, Rosalind, R.M.S., H.S., M.M.A.S., U.S.M.; Paris Salon silver medal (1978), gold medal (1981); artist in water-colour; *b* Tavistock, Devon, 14 Sept., 1954; *d* of L.G. Pierson, M.A. *Educ.:* St. Audries School, West Quantoxhead, Som., *studied art* at Ruskin School of Drawing and Fine Art (John Newberry). *Exhib.:* R.A., Paris Salon, Bilan de l'Art Contemporain, Paris, Quebec, New York, Florida, W. Virginia, Montana, Tavistock, Bath, Wells, Monaco, Ulster. *Work in permanent collection:* Miniature Art Soc., Florida. *Address:* Brangwyn House, Kilworthy Hill, Tavistock, Devon. *Societies:* Royal Soc. Miniature Painters, Sculptors and Gravers, Hilliard Soc. (Co-founder), Montana Miniature Art Soc., Ulster Soc. of Miniaturists, W.W.F., R.S.P.B., I.F.A.W. *Signs work:* "R. Pierson."

PIKE, Septimus: see WATTS, Michael Gorse.

PIKESLEY, Richard Leslie, N.E.A.C., Dip. A.D. (1973), A.T.C. (1974); finalist, Hunting Group Prize (1981 and 1989), winner, E.F. Hutton Prize (1987), W.H. Patterson Prize (1988); painter in oil and water-colour; *b* London, 8 Jan., 1951; *s* of Leonard Leslie Pikesley; *m* Susan Margaret Stone. *Studied art* at Harrow School of Art (1969-70), Canterbury College of Art (1970-73). *Exhib.:* R.A., R.O.I., R.W.A., R.I.; one-man shows include New Grafton Gallery London (1990), Linfield Gallery, Bradford-on-Avon (1986), St. James's

Gallery, Bath Festival (1986). *Address:* Middlehill Farm, Marrowbone Lane, Bothenhampton, Bridport, Dorset. *Club:* N.E.A.C. *Signs work:* "Richard Pikesley."

PILCHER, Terence John, A.R.C.A. (1952); landscape and portrait painter in oil and water-colour; *b* Barnehurst, Kent, 1926; *m* Mary; four *s*, two *d*. *Studied art* at Sidcup School of Art (1940-44, 1947-49), R.C.A. (1951-54, Ruskin Spear, John Minton). *Exhib.:* R.A., R.W.A. *Work in permanent collections:* Mermaid Inn, Rye, Sussex; private collections in Australia and Britain. *Address:* 2 White Horse Cottages, Washford, Watchet, Som. TA23 0JZ. *Signs work:* "Terry Pilcher."

PILKINGTON, Richard Godfrey, M.A. (Cantab.); art dealer and publisher; Partner (Co-founder) Piccadilly Gallery, 16A Cork St., W1, since 1953; Chairman of Society of London Art Dealers (1974-77); editor The Art Bulletin (1951-60); *b* Stafford, 8 Nov., 1918; *s* of Guy R. Pilkington; *m* Evelyn (Eve) Vincent; two *s*, two *d*. *Educ.:* Clifton and Trinity College, Cambridge. *Address:* 45 Barons Court Rd., London W14 9DZ.

PILKINGTON, Ruth Jane, R.O.I. (1976), S.W.A. (1985); painter in oil; *b* Manchester, 2 May, 1924; *d* of the late Sir Leonard Behrens; *m* Eric W. L. Pilkington (decd.); one *s,* one *d*. *Educ.:* Ladybarn House School, Manchester and Maltman's Green, Gerrard's Cross; *studied art* at Johannesburg Technical College (1947-48), Macclesfield C.F.E. (1962-65). *Exhib.:* R.B.A., R.O.I., Paris Salon, Manchester Academy, etc., other group exhbns., one-man show in Channel Islands (1976). *Work in permanent collections:* Barreau A.G., Société Jersiaise, Jersey. *Address:* Sondela, La Rue à Don, Grouville, Jersey, JE3 9DA, C.I. *Signs work:* "Ruth J. Pilkington."

PILLOW, Lorna Mary Carol, A.R.C.A.; Sir Frank Warner Memorial Medal; freelance textile, exhibition and graphic designer; taught, Croydon and Berkshire Colleges of Art; senior lecturer, West Surrey College of Art and Design (retd.); *d* of W. Farquhar Pillow; *widow* of Peter John Palmer; one *s*. *Educ.:* Wolverhampton and Leeds; *studied art* at Leeds, Hull and the Royal Colleges of Art. *Exhib.:* Beverley Art Gallery, Ferens Art Gallery, Guildhall, R.W.S. Galleries, Mall Galleries, London, W.S.C.A.D. Gallery, Farnham, R.S.A. Travelling Exhibition, Design Centre, London. *Work repro.:* International Textiles; illustrated Geography of Flowering Plants. *Address:* 33 Havelock Rd., Maidenhead, Berks. SL6 5BJ. *Signs work:* "Lorna Pillow."

PINCUS, Helen Frances, B.A. Hons. (1982), M.F.P.S. (1984), Adult Educ. Dip. (1979); fibre and textile artist, designer, embroiderer in fibres, yarns, aluminium mesh, wood, piano wire and pure silk; freelance lecturer, writer and musician; *b* Acton, London, 22 Oct., 1938. *Educ.:* Haberdashers' Aske's Acton Girls' School; The Arts Educational Schools; *studied art* at Nottingham University; Loughborough College of Art and Design. *Exhib.:* numerous one-man shows and mixed exhbns. both in the U.K. and abroad including Commonwealth Inst. A.G., Cork St. Fine Arts, Leighton House, Savaria Muzeum (Hungary), Westminster Abbey, Galeria Bellas Artes (Spain), Smith's Gallery, University of Surrey, Loggia Gallery, Contemporary Arts (Hong Kong), Hampton Court Palace, Guild Gallery, Heifer Gallery, Bloomsbury Gallery, Vincent A.G. (Australia), Southwark Cathedral, Cecilia Colman Gallery, Metro Toronto Convention Centre (Canada), Del Bello A.G. (Canada). The Fourth Annual International Exhbn. of Miniature Arts in Toronto, Canada, awarded a special distinction (1989). *Work in permanent collection:* Savaria Muzeum, Hungary. *Address:* Lower Studio, 14 West Lodge Ave., London W3 9SF. *Clubs:*

F.P.S., Embroiderers' Guild, New Embroidery Group, Contemporary Applied Arts, London Symphony Chorus, St. Endellion Festival Chorus, Film Artistes' Assoc., The Colour Group (G.B.), Registered with the Crafts Council.

PINE, Diana, Assoc. Sussex Artists (1974, Hon. Sec. 1978-83); artist in water-colour, pastel and oil; documentary film director, Crown Film Unit, Wessex, etc. B.B.C.; part-time teacher, Mole Valley A.E.C. and Day Centre; *b* London; *d* of Charles F. R. and E. M. Gubbins. *Educ.:* Jersey, France, London, P.N.E.U.; *studied art* at Regent St. Polytechnic (1936-37) under Clifford Ellis, Chelsea Art School under H. S. Williamson, Central School; apprentice Edward Carrick for Art Direction, Films (-1940), Ernest Savage, Aubrey Sykes (1968-75). *Exhib.:* R.I., P.S., S.W.A. (1976-86), Assoc. Sussex Artists, Horsham, Augustine Gallery, Holt, Barns Green, Dorking Group. *Address:* 2 Lodge Close, North Holmwood, Dorking, Surrey RH5 4JU. *Signs work:* "D. Pine."

PINKNEY, Richard, N.D.D., A.T.D. (1960); painter, sculptor, printmaker; teacher, Ipswich (1960-66), Colchester (1966-74), St. Martin's (1966-75) Schools of Art, currently teaching, Kingsway College, London; *b* Ipswich, 22 July, 1938; *m* Judith Foster; two *s*. *Educ.:* Ipswich School; *studied art* at Ipswich School of Art (1955-59, Phillip Fortin, Colin Moss), West of England College of Art (1959-60). *Exhib.:* one-man shows: London, Edinburgh, Leicester, Peterborough, Ipswich, Colchester. *Work in permanent collections:* Tate Gallery, V. & A., B.M., and libraries in the U.K. and abroad. *Work repro.:* Trivia, Circle and Tetrad Presses. *Address:* 10 The Street, Bramford, Ipswich, Suffolk IP8 4EA. *Signs work:* "R. Pinkney" and date; occasionally "R.P." and date.

PINSKY, Michael, B.A. (Hons.) Fine Art (1991); artist in photography, sculpture, site-specific installation; *b* Scotland, 24 Nov., 1967. *Educ.:* James Gillespies High School; *studied art* at Manchester Polytechnic (1987-88), Brighton Polytechnic (1988-91, Bill Beach), R.C.A. (1993-). *Exhib.:* one-man shows: Collective Gallery Edinburgh, Traverse Theatre Edinburgh, The Warehouse Amsterdam, The Gantry Southampton, Open Eye Gallery Liverpool, Viewpoint Gallery Manchester, Stockport A.G., Cranford Arts Centre St. Andrews, Russell-Cotes A.G. Bournemouth; group shows: U.K. and Europe. *Address:* 42 Dalkeith Rd., Edinburgh EH16 5BS.

PIOTTI, Vittorio; Dip. of Artistic Maturity, Art-Liceum, Carrara (1967), Knighthood of Italian Republic (Cav.) (1978), R.W.A. (1983); Major Alpini Parachutists; sculptor in iron; *b* Brescia, Italy, 5 Mar., 1935; *s* of Mario Piotti, bookkeeper, bank director; *m* Andreina; one *s*, one *d*. *Studied art* at Art Liceum of Venezia; Art-Liceum of Carrara. *Exhib.:* (1967-93): Brescia, Trento, Padova, Vicenza, Mantova, Cremona, Bari, Pavia, Biarritz and Parigi (France), Venezia, Pompeii, Cassino, Bolzano, Verona, Bergamo, Torino, Bristol (England), Genova, Monaco and Mainz (Germany). *Work in permanent collections:* in Italy, Libya, France, England, Germany. *Public monuments:* in Italy and Germany, etc. *Address:* via Columbaia 17, 25050 Rodengo, Saiano, Brescia, Italy. *Signs work:* "V. PIOTTI" or "Vittopiotti."

PITFIELD, Thomas Baron, N.R.D., Hon. F.R.M.C.M.; artist in water-colour, reed-pen, lino-cut, lettering; composer; art master; *b* Bolton, Lancs., 5 Apr., 1903; *s* of Thomas Baron Pitfield; *m* Alice Maud Astbury. *Educ.:* Bolton and Manchester; *studied art:* Municipal School of Art, Bolton (apprenticed in Engineer's drawing-office). *Exhib.:* R.A., Northern Academy of Fine Arts, and various one-man exhbns. *Work repro.:* Artist, Countryman, and other periodicals, calendars, etc. *Publications:* Junior Course in Art Teaching, Senior Course in Art Teaching, The Poetry of Trees, Bowdon and "Limusicks" (40 limericks), (texts, script, illustrations), Recording a Region (drawings and hand-lettered script), and a large number of musical compositions; autobiographies: A Cotton Town Boyhood, No Song, No Supper, A Song after Supper. *Address:* Lesser Thorns, 21 East Downs Rd., Bowdon, Ches. *Signs work:* see appendix.

PITMAN, Primrose Vera, S.G.A. (1953), L.R.A.M., Gold Medal for Design; painter in water-colour, commercial artist in pencil; etcher; *d* of James L. Pitman. *Educ.:* St. Hilda's School; *studied art* at Royal Albert Memorial School of Art under Burman Morrall and James Sparks. *Exhib.:* R.W.A. and provincial galleries. *Work in permanent collection:* Royal Albert Memorial Museum. *Official purchases:* City of Exeter. *Publications:* Etchings and pencil drawings in This Jewel Remains (1942). *Work repro.:* repro. of pencil drawing of Exeter Cathedral for Preservation Fund organized by Mayor of Exeter. *Address:* Marlands, 4 Victoria Park Rd., Exeter. *Clubs:* Exeter Art Soc., Kenn Group. *Signs work:* "Primrose V. Pitman."

PLATT, Eric Warhurst, A.R.C.A., Silver Medallist (1940); artist in line and wash, water-colour, etching, graphic design, and creative cut card relief; Head of Design, Doncaster M.Inst. of H.E. (retd. July 1980); *b* Cudworth, Yorks., 2 May, 1915; *s* of John R. Platt, A.V.C.M.; *m* Mary Elizabeth; one *s*, one *d*. *Educ.:* Wakefield and Doncaster School of Art; *studied art* at R.C.A. under Malcolm Osborne, R.A., and Robert Austin, R.A. (1937-40). *Exhib.:* R.A., Brighton, West Riding Artists exhbn., Yorkshire Artists exhbn., Doncaster A.G., Feren's Gallery, Hull, Graves Gallery, Sheffield, etc. *Address:* 11 Alston Rd., Bessacarr, Doncaster. *Signs work:* "Eric Platt."

PLATT, Michael, A.R.C.A.; painter and designer; taught painting at Southampton College of Art (1945-53); Birmingham College of Art (1953-55); head of art dept., Mayfield School, Putney (1960-63); Senior lecturer in art, N.W. Polytechnic, NW5 (1967-69); *b* 29 Sept., 1914; *m* 1939, Joan Dickson, A.R.C.A.; one *s*, two *d*. *Exhib.:* London Group, Arts Council. *Special interests:* Space and colour. *Official purchases:* paintings by L.C.C. *Address:* "Thirty One", Cowleys Rd., Burton, Christchurch, Dorset BH23 7NB. *Signs work:* "Michael Platt."

PLINCKE, J. Richard, R.I. (1984), R.I.B.A., A.A.Dip. (1951); painter in water-colour and mixed media; work includes designs for tapestries, and stained glass windows at St. Mark's Church, Kempshot; *b* Woldingham, Surrey, 29 Oct., 1928; *s* of John Plincke; *m* Rosemary D. Ball; two *d*. *Educ.:* Stowe, Bucks.; *studied architecture* at the Architectural Assoc. School of Architecture, London; *studied art* at Southampton Inst. of Higher Educ., gaining Higher Cert. (Distinction). *Exhib.:* R.A., R.W.A., R.I., R.S.M.A., Manor House Gallery, Chipping Norton, Linda Blackstone Gallery, Pinner, Shell House Gallery, Ledbury. Work included in a number of private collections. *Address:* P.L.& B., 5 The Square, Winchester SO23 9ES. *Signs work:* "R.P." followed by the date.

PLUMMER, Brian, R.A.S.; painter in acrylic and water-colour relief; Director of Foundation Studies, University of Westminster; *b* London, 1934. *Studied art* at Hornsey College of Art, R.A. Schools. *Exhib.:* R.A., Expo Montreal, Barcelona Bienal (prize winner), Toronto, Abbot Hall, Kendal, Lucy Milton, Galerie van Hulsen, Amsterdam, Rex Irwin Sydney, Sloane St. Gallery, Audun Gallery. Represented by The Macquarie Galleries, Sydney. *Work in permanent collections:* D.O.E., St. Thomas' Hospital, Power Collection Sydney, Ministero Cultura Madrid, Mobil Oil Co., Lancaster University, Abbot Hall, Kendal. *Address:* 89 Palmerston Rd., London N22 4QS. *Signs work:* "BRIAN PLUMMER" on acrylics, hand written on water-colours.

POLLARD, Malcolm; sculptor, draughtsman, teacher; *b* Raunds, Northants, 14 Mar., 1941; *s* of John William Pollard; *m* Elke Kairies Addis; two *s. Address:* 42 East Park Parade, Northampton NN1 4LA. *Signs work:* "MALCOLM POLLARD" – christian name above surname.

POLLOCK, (Sir) George F., Bt., M.A. (Cantab.), Hon. F.R.P.S., F.R.S.A., F.B.I.P.P., A.F.I.A.P.; artist-photographer, a-v producer; past President, Royal Photographic Society; *b* 13 Aug., 1928; *s* of Sir John Pollock, Bt., Officer Legion of Honour (etc.); *Educ.:* Eton College and Trinity College, Cambridge. *Exhib:* numerous. *Work in permanent collections:* British Council, R.P.S., National Gallery of Victoria, Musée de Photographie, Bièvres, Towner A.G., Eastbourne, Texas University, University of Surrey. *Address:* 83 Minster Way, Bathwick, Bath, Avon BA2 6RL. *Signs work:* "George F. Pollock."

POLLOCK, Helen, D.A. (Edin.); painter in acrylic; creative embroiderer; theme of work includes abstract and semi abstractions based on natural and man made objects; *b* Limavady, Co. Derry, 23 Mar., 1945; *d* of the late Samuel Pollock, poet and teacher; *m* Laurence Roche, D.A. (Edin.). *Studied art* at Edinburgh College of Art (1963-67). *Exhib.:* R.S.A., R.W.A., S.S.A., R.S.W., S.S.W.A., and numerous other exhbns. Work in many private collections in Britain and abroad. *Address:* 16 Belmont Rd., Stroud, Glos. GL5 1HH. *Signs work:* "Helen Pollock."

POMERANCE, Fay; painter; *b* 1912; *d* of Sol Levy; *m* Ben Pomerance. *Educ.:* King Edward's High School; Art School, Birmingham. *Exhib.:* one-man: "Lucifer Theme – The Sphere of Redemption" and other works 1949-1983, Archer and Ben Uri Galleries, St. James's and St. Botolph's Churches, London; Liverpool, Wakefield, Batley, Derby, Middlesbrough, Newcastle, Gateshead municipal galleries, R.B.S.A., Birmingham, Theatre and University Centres, Oxford, Sheffield, Leicester, Nottingham, Cambridge, Durham, Solihull. Represented London exhbns.: Leicester, Redfern, Molton. *Permanent collections:* Trevelyan and Grey College, Durham, Hull, Staffordshire Educ. Committees, Batley, Gateshead Picture Lending, Ben Uri, Israel; reproduced work in books by Fred Gettings, Douglas Baker, Francis X. King. Designed stained glass window Birmingham Synagogue. *Address:* 92A Ranmoor Rd., Sheffield SIO 3HJ.

POOLE, David James, R.P. (1969), A.R.C.A.; artist; President, Royal Soc. of Portrait Painters (1983-91); Senior lecturer in Painting and Drawing, Wimbledon School of Art (1962-77); *b* 5 June, 1931; *s* of Thomas Herbert Poole; *m* Iris Mary Toomer; three *s. Educ.:* Stoneleigh Secondary School; *studied art* at Wimbledon School of Art, R.C.A. *Exhib.:* one-man shows: Zurich and London. *Portraits include:* H.M. The Queen, H.R.H. The Duke of Edinburgh, H.M. The Queen Mother, H.R.H. Prince Charles, H.R.H. Princess Anne, H.R.H. Princess Margaret, Earl Mountbatten of Burma and The Duke of Kent; also distinguished members of govt., industry, commerce, medicine, the academic and legal professions. *Work in private collections:* H.M. The Queen and H.R.H. The Duke of Edinburgh; and in Australia, S. Africa, Bermuda, France, W. Germany, Switzerland, Saudi Arabia, U.S.A. *Addresses:* The Granary, Oxton Barns, Kenton, Exeter, Devon EX6 8EX; Studio 6, Burlington Lodge, Rigault Rd., Fulham, London SW6 4JJ.

POOLE, Monica, A.R.E. (1967), R.E. (1975); Central School Diploma (1949); Member of the Art Workers' Guild; wood engraver; *b* Canterbury, 20 May, 1921; *d* of C. Reginald Poole; *m* Cmdr. A. G. M. Small, R.N., F.I.H.V.E. *Educ.:* Abbotsford, Broadstairs; *studied art* at Central School of Arts and Crafts (1945-49). *Exhib.:* R.A., R.E., etc. *Work in permanent collections:* Fitzwilliam

Museum, B.M., S.N.G.M.A., V. & A., Ashmolean Museum, Museum Boymans van Beunegen, Rotterdam, Hunt Botanical Museum, Pittsburgh, U.S.A., Pistoia A.G., South London A.G. *Publication:* The Wood Engravings of John Farleigh (1985). *Address:* 67 Hadlow Rd., Tonbridge, Kent. *Signs work:* "MONICA POOLE."

POPE, Perpetua, D.A. (Edin.) 1947; painter in oil; lecturer in visual arts, Moray House College of Education (1968-73); *b* Solihull, Warwicks., 29 May, 1916; *d* of John Robert Pope. *Educ.:* Albyn School, Aberdeen; *studied art* at Edinburgh College of Art under W. G. Gillies, John Maxwell, Leonard Rosoman. *Exhib.:* one-man shows: Scottish Gallery, Edinburgh; mixed shows: R.A., R.S.A., S.S.A., S.S.W.A., Aberdeen Artists, Stirling Gallery. *Work in permanent collections:* H.R.H. The Duke of Edinburgh, Scottish Arts Council, Nuffield Trust, Argyll County Council. *Address:* 27 Dean St., Edinburgh EH4 1LN. *Signs work:* "Perpetua Pope."

PORTEOUS WOOD, James, R.S.W. (1945); landscape, mural and portrait artist in oils, water-colour, black and white; specialist in architectural subjects; art director and chief designer Asprey, Bond St. (1956-1980); designer of important gold and silver and objets d'art – works in many of the premier world contemporary collections; murals and paintings in royal and presidential palaces in Near, Middle and Far East; *b* Edinburgh, 1919; *m*; one *s. Educ.:* George Heriot's School; *studied* at Edinburgh College of Art (1935-40) (Travelling Scholarship), and under Sir D. Y. Cameron, R.A., R.S.A. *Exhib.:* R.A., R.S.A., R.S.W., G.I., and several one-man shows. *Publications:* private editions with miniatures and calligraphy mainly on vellum, Midland Riches (Hancock), Yorkshire Sketchbook. *Work repro.:* many editorial drawings mainly architectural, industrial, and portrait in national Press, top magazines and prestige books. *Address:* Caimbe Bridge, Arisaig, Inverness-shire PH39 4NT. *Signs work:* "PORTEOUS WOOD."

PORTMAN, Joanne Merle; landscape painter in water-colour and water soluble pens; *b* Worcester, 21 Feb., 1965; *d* of David George Portman, glass engraver. *Studied ceramic art* at Boehm of Malvern. *Exhib.:* Malvern Arts (1989, 1991, 1993). *Work in permanent collections:* Malvern Galleries, Worcester Antiques Centre; private collections in Europe and U.S.A. *Address:* Flat 1, Scarsdale, 22 Priory Rd., Malvern, Worcs. WR14 3DR. *Club:* Malvern Art. *Signs work:* "J.M. Portman."

PORTSMOUTH, Delia; painter of landscapes, portraits, flowers, birds, wildlife in oils; *b* Mottram, Ches., 6 Aug., 1939; *d* of Edward Ford, farmer; *m* A. C. Portsmouth; four *d. Educ.:* Hyde and Bala Grammar Schools; *studied art:* self taught. *Exhib.:* R.O.I., Hesketh Hubbard, Flower Painters' Summer Salon; one-man shows: Chester, Lampeter, Bala, Brantwood, St. Davids, Usher Gallery, Lincoln, Public Gallery, Oldham. *Work in permanent collections:* National Library of Wales, National Museum of Wales, Liverpool Corp. and numerous private collections worldwide. *Address:* Charlton, 57 Embankment Rd., Kingsbridge, Devon TQ7 1LA. *Club:* founder member, Modern Millais Association. *Signs work:* "Delia Portsmouth."

PORTWAY, Douglas Owen; European painting prize (Belgium) Bronze Medal (1969), Gold Medal (1971); taught at Witwatersrand School of Art and Witwatersrand University (1941-46); delegate to Ford and Rockefeller Foundations International Art Programme (1952); painter in oil on canvas and paper; *b* Johannesburg, 1922, (British Citizenship, 1960); *m* Caroline Shackell (1966); two *s*, one *d. Educ.:* mainly self-educated; *studied art* at Witwatersrand

School of Art, S.A. (1940-41). *Exhib.:* one-man shows: Spain, Germany, Paris, Africa,England and Switzerland; retrospective: Pretoria Art Museum (1967); mixed: Venice Biennale (1956), John Moores (1961), Musée d'Art Moderne, Paris (1965). *Work in permanent collections:* Tate Gallery, V. & A., Scottish National A.G., Stuyvesant Foundation, Musée des Beaux Arts, Belgium, School Art Loans, Leeds, Manchester City A.G., Nuffield Foundation, Tatham A.G., Durban A.G., Schlesinger Organization, S. African National Gallery, King George VI A.G., Sandton A.G., Johannesburg A.G., University of Witwatersrand, Anglo-American Corp., William Humphries Museum, Kimberly, National Galleries of Poland, Warsaw, and Gdansk; Winterthur Collection, Zurich. *Work repro.:* in Contemporary British Art by Herbert Read (Pelican); biography Douglas Portway – A Painters Life by Dr. Paul Hodin (Springwood Books); monograph Douglas Portway by George Butcher (20th Century Masters Publishing Co.); The Story of S. African Painting, and Art and Artists of S. Africa (both by Esme Berman and published by A. A. Balkema); Contemporary Artists (St. James Press); Contemporary British Artists (Bergstrom & Boyle); Douglas Portway, Selected Graphic Works (Zelena One Gallery, Hampstead, London, and Olivero Masi, Milan, Italy). *Addresses:* 11 Christchurch Rd., Clifton, Bristol BS8 4EE; and "Le Sage", Razac d'Eymet, 24500 Dordogne, France.

POSNETT, David Wilson, M.A.; art dealer; Managing Director, The Leger Galleries; Chairman, The Society of London Art Dealers (1990-93); *b* 6 May, 1942. *Educ.:* The Leys, and Trinity, Cambridge. *Address:* 13 Old Bond St., London W1X 3DB.

POTTER, Donald, F.R.B.S.; sculptor in stone, wood and ivory; *b* Newington, Kent, 21 Apr., 1902; *m* Mary Potter; one *s*, one *d*. Studied art: pupil of Eric Gill. *Official purchases:* Sculptures in St. George's Chapel, Windsor, St. Paul's Cathedral, Zomba Cathedral (Nyasaland), The Baden-Powell Statue (Queens Gate), St. Sebastian, Winchester College. *Address:* Bryanston, Blandford, Dorset. *Signs work:* see appendix.

POTTINGER, Frank, D.A. Sculpture (1963), R.S.A. (1991); sculptor in bronze, stone, wood, clay; *b* Edinburgh, 1 Oct., 1932; *s* of William Pottinger, stone mason; *m* Norah Smith, 1991. *Educ.:* Boroughmuir School; *studied art* at Edinburgh College of Art (1958-63). *Exhib.:* Richard Demarco Gallery, Yorkshire Sculpture Park, Landmark Scottish Sculpture Trust, Camden Arts Centre, Pier Arts Centre Orkney, Kildrummy Castle, S.S.W. Open. *Work in permanent collections:* Heriot Watt University, Hunterian Museum, I.B.M., Scottish Development Agency, Leeds Educ. Authority, Scottish Arts Council, L.A.S.M.O., The Woodland Trust. *Address:* 30/5 Elbe St., Leith EH6 7HW.

POTTS, Kenneth Arthur, A.R.B.S. (1988), Dip.A.D., B.A. (1972), C.I.C. (1969); sculptor in bronze, stoneware, terracotta and fine porcelain; *b* Macclesfield, 16 Mar., 1949; *s* of Reginald Potts; *m* Anne; one *s*, one *d*. *Educ.:* Stockport C.F.E. (1966); *studied art* at Stafford College of Art (1969), Stoke-on-Trent College of Art (1972). *Exhib.:* R.A. Summer Show, Festival Hall, Sladmore Gallery, Art Expo N.Y., R.B.S. West of England Academy, Tokyo, etc. *Work in permanent collections:* Dyson Perrins Museum, Raphael Djanogly Trust. Principal works: bronze statue, national monument to Edward Elgar; bronze statue of A.E. Houseman (poet). *Address:* Clater Pk., Bringsty, Worcester WR6 5TP. *Signs work:* "Kenneth Potts."

POUNTNEY, Monica (née Brailey); cup for oils S.E.I.F.A.S. (1976); free-lance artist in oil, water-colour, acrylic, pastel, etc.; *b* London; *m* D. H. Pountney;

one *s. Studied art* at Hammersmith School of Arts and Crafts (Carel Weight and Ruskin Spear), Central School (John Farleigh). *Exhib.:* Federation of British Artists, U.A., S.W.A., R.I., N.S., and various mixed exhbns. *Work in permanent collections:* landscapes in London, Moscow and U.S.A. *Work repro.:* books illustrated for Heinemann, Blackie and others. *Address:* 3 Thickwood House, Bedford Rd., S. Woodford, London E18 2AH. *Clubs:* U.A., L.A.G. *Signs work:* "M.P." or full name.

POWELL, Christopher Alan, LL.B. (1957); former journalist; painter mainly in oil with occasional water-colour and tempera of landscapes, seascapes, city scenes, still life and flower studies; sub-editor on The Times (1968-92); *b* Newcastle upon Tyne, 11 July, 1935; *s* of Alan Powell, counsulting engineer. *Educ.:* Queen Elizabeth Grammar, Hexham; *studied law* at King's College, Newcastle upon Tyne; *studied art* part time at City Literary Inst., London (Cecil Collins). *Exhib.:* Mall Galleries, Leighton House, various art societies in London. *Work in private collections:* U.K., U.S.A., Japan. *Address:* Flat A7, Sloane Ave. Mans., Chelsea, London SW3 3JF. *Signs work:* "C.A. POWELL."

POWELL, John, A.R.C.A.; painter; *b* Nottingham, 27 Aug., 1911; *s* of William Powell; *m* Freda Heathcote; one *d. Studied painting* at R.C.A. under Gilbert Spencer (1935-39) and Nottingham College of Art (1932-35). *Exhib.:* R.A., R.B.A., R.O.I., N.E.A.C., London Group, S.M.A., N.S., United Artists, also mixed and travelling exhbns. in London galleries, museums and provincial galleries. Main exhbns.: New Ashgate Gallery, Farnham (1981), Bosham Walk Gallery, W. Sussex (1990). *Official purchases:* Bristol Educ. Com. (The Harbour, Tenby), Manchester Educ. Com., (Child at Breakfast, A Fair at Twilight). Work in private collections. *Address:* Fishbourne Farmhouse, Fishbourne, Chichester, W. Sussex PO18 8AW. *Signs work:* "John Powell" usually on back.

POWELL, Sir Philip, C.H., O.B.E., R.A., F.R.I.B.A., A.A. Dip. (Hons.), R.I.B.A. Gold Medallist (1974); Member, Royal Fine Art Commission; architect (Powell, Moya, 1946-91); *b* Bedford, 15 Mar., 1921; *s* of Rev. Canon A. C. Powell, M.A.; *m* Philippa (*née* Eccles). *Educ.:* Epsom College. *Works include* Churchill Gdns., Pimlico; South Bank Skylon; British Pavilion, Expo. '70, Osaka; Hospitals at Swindon, Slough, High Wycombe, Maidstone, Great Ormond Street; Wolfson College, Oxford; new buildings at Brasenose, Christ Church and Corpus Christi, Oxford, and St. John's and Queens' Colleges, Cambridge; Chichester Festival Theatre; Museum of London; Queen Elizabeth II Conference Centre, Westminster. *Address:* 16 The Little Boltons, London SW10 9LP.

POWELL, Roy Owen, N.D.D. (1956), A.T.D. (1959); landscape and still life artist in oil on canvas, charcoal and pencil drawings; retd. art teacher; *b* Chepstow, 3 Dec., 1934; *s* of Ivor Powell, primitive painter (decd.). *Educ.:* Monmouth School and West Mon School, Pontypool; *studied art* at Cardiff College of Art (1952-56, Eric Malthouse, J.C. Tarr). *Exhib.:* regularly at National Eisteddfod; various group shows in England, Wales and Scotland including 'Celtic Vision'. *Publications:* articles for 'Link' magazine. *Address:* 10 Mill St., Brecon, Powys LD3 9BD. *Club:* The Welsh Group. *Signs work:* "R.O. Powell."

POWER, Philip Ian, B.A.(Hons.) (1980), M.F.A. (1983); artist in light, glass, perspex, copper, sound; lecturer, University of Edinburgh Architecture Dept.; *b* Swansea, 26 Apr., 1955; *m* Maggie Bolt; one *s. Educ.:* King Edward's School, Witley; *studied art* at Maidstone College of Art (1977-80, Mike Upton, Kerry Trengove), University of Reading (1981-83, Bill Culbert, Ron Harewen, Marc Chatmowicz). *Exhib.:* New Contemporaries (1982, 1983), R.S.A. Edinburgh,

Fruit Market Edinburgh, Third Eye Centre Glasgow, etc. *Commission:* collaboration with Phoenix Dance Co. (1987). *Address:* 20A Rankeillor St., Edinburgh EH8 9HY. *Signs work:* "Power," "Philip Power" or "P.P."

PRATT, David Ellis, S.WL.A., Federation of British Artists; artist in oil, gouache, black and white; *b* Kobe, Japan, 21 June, 1911; *m* Pamela Margaret; two *s*, one *d*. Exhib.: Mall Galleries, Federation of British Artists. *Publications:* many, natural history, anatomical and biology. *Address:* Penselwood, 7 Tremena Rd., St. Austell, Cornwall PL25 5QC. *Signs work:* "David E. Pratt."

PRENDERGAST, Peter, D.F.A. (1967), M.A. (1970); painter draughtsman/ landscape painter in water-colour, oil, charcoal, pencil and ink on paper, canvas, board; *b* 27 Oct., 1946; *s* of Martin Prendergast, coal miner; *m* Lesley; two *s*, two *d*. *Educ.:* Cardiff; *studied art* at Slade School of Fine Art (William Coldstream, Frank Auerbach, Jeffery Camp), Reading University. *Exhib.:* Mostyn Gallery touring to Swansea, Durham, London, Tate Gallery, Norwich A.G., A.C.G.B. touring show, National Parks Exhbn., V. & A., also toured U.S.A., Land and Sea exhbn. with Len Tabner, Scarborough (1992), National Museum of Wales (1993-94), Agnews, London. *Work in permanent collections:* Tate Gallery, B.M., A.C.G.B., W.A.C., Contemporary Art Soc., etc. *Address:* 6 Gordon Terr., Garth Rd., Bangor, N. Wales LL57 2RU. *Agents:* Thomas Agnew, 43 Old Bond St., London. *Signs work:* "Peter Prendergast."

PRENTICE, David; painter in oil, pastel, water-colour; Fellow in Fine Art, Nottingham University (1986-87); co-founder/director, Ikon Gallery, B'ham; (1964-71); lecturer, School of Fine Art, B'ham (1968-86); *b* Solihull, 4 July, 1936; *s* of H.G. Prentice (decd.); *m* Dinah White; four *d*. *Educ.:* Moseley School of Art, B'ham; *studied art* at B'ham College of Art and Design. *Exhib.:* Serpentine, M.O.M.A., N.Y., Betty Parsons, N.Y., Albright Knox. Winner of the £15,000 Singer & Friedlander/Sunday Times water-colour prize (1990). *Address:* Ashdown Villa, 9 Hanley Terr., Malvern, Worcs. WR14 4PF. *Signs work:* "David Prentice." Represented by Cowleigh Gallery, Malvern and M.C.A. Ltd., B'ham.

PRESTON GODDARD; painter and designer; *b* Liverpool, 5 May, 1928; *m* Kathleen Fleming, picture restorer/business manager. *Studied art* under R.A. Wilson, A.R.C.A., at Croydon. *Exhib.:* foremost London and provincial galleries; one-man shows at Beaux Arts Gallery, Leicester Galleries, Somerville College, Oxford; British Art in Moscow. *Work in permanent collections:* Leicestershire Education Committee, Surrey Education Committee, Oxford University; *private collections:* U.S.A., Europe, and Australia. *Work repro.:* in leading art journals. Director, Chelsea Arts Trust Ltd.; Chairman, Artists' Com. Chelsea Open Air Art Exhbn., Royal Ave., Chelsea, SW3. *Address:* Studio Hse., 46 Selborne Rd., Croydon. *Signs work:* "PRESTON GODDARD."

PRETSELL, Peter, D.A. (Edin.); artist in printmaking, painting; lecturer in printmaking, Nene College, Northampton; lecturer, Edinburgh College of Art (1985); *b* Edinburgh, 1942; *s* of William Pretsell; *m* Philomena Pretsell; three *s*. *Educ.:* George Heriots School, Edinburgh; *studied art* at Edinburgh College of Art (1960-65). *Exhib.:* New 57 Gallery, Printmakers Workshop, S.S.A. and Fruitmarket Gallery (Edinburgh), Northampton, Birmingham, Newcastle, Kettering, Bedford, Thumb Gallery, London, Bradford Print Biennale Prizewinner. *Work in permanent collections:* V. & A., Scottish Arts Council, Edinburgh Corp., Hull, Northampton A.G. *Address:* c/o Edinburgh College of Art, Edinburgh. *Signs work:* "Pretsell."

PRICE, E. Jessop, H.R.S.W.A. (1987), S.W.A. (1951), Mem. of Council (1956); painter in oils; *b* Ashby-de-la-Zouch; *d* of J. N. Moxon; *m* Rev. A. Jessop Price; four *s. Educ.:* Ashby and Versailles. *Studied art* at St. Ives School of Art (Leonard Fuller), St. Martin's School of Art (Archibald Zeigler), Heatherley's (Iain Macnab). *Exhib.:* one-man show at R.W.S. Gallery (1949), S.W.A., R.O.I., Bradford Art Gallery, City of London Guildhall, etc.; awarded Freedom of the Worshipful Company of Painter Stainers in 1957. *Official purchases:* St. Paul's Cathedral, Chase National Bank, N.Y., Newton Chambers, etc. *Work repro.:* The Soho Gallery, Daily Telegraph, etc. *Address:* Sefton, Stade St., Hythe, Kent CT21 6DY. *Signs work:* "E. Jessop Price."

PRIESTNER, Stephen Miles; artist in acrylic paint, collages; *b* Altrincham, Ches., 1 May, 1954; *s* of Arthur Priestner. *Educ.:* Ellesmere College, Salop. (1967-70), Blackpool College of Art (1971-72), Manchester Polytechnic (1972-74); *studied art* at École des Beaux Arts, Paris (1978, B. Neiland). *Exhib.:* Olympian Arts, London (1993), Salford Museum (1988). *Work in permanent collections:* Whitworth A.G.; drawings: Ghent Museum, Belgium; M.O.M.A., New York (prints); Musée d'Art Moderne, Paris; paintings in private collections worldwide. *Work repro.:* The Artist, Apollo Magazine, etc. *Address:* 17 Stamford Park Rd., Hale, Ches. WA15 9EH. *Signs work:* with monogram "S.P." or "Stephen M. Priestner."

PRIMON, Gastone; painter, sculptor, ceramist; Prof., Istituto Statale d'Arte, Rome; *b* Este, Padova; *m* Adriana; one *s. Studied ceramics* at Accademia di Belle Arte, Rome; graduate, Istituto Statale d'Arte, Rome. *Exhib.:* Monaco di Bavaria, Cervia, Este, Faenza, Caltagirone, Gualdo Tadino, Tunis, Valauris, Biennale di Pietra a San Marino, Rome, Quadrienale d'Arte, Rome. *Work in permanent collections:* churches, public places, museums, and private collections. *Addresses:* (studio): Este (PD), Piazza Trento 22; (home): Via Coll di Lana 158, Ciampino, Rome. *Signs work:* "Gastone Primon."

PRITCHARD, Marion Ruth, S.W.A. (1987); painter and illustrator in oil and water-colour; *b* London, 10 Nov., 1934; *d* of Albert Henry Latter; *m* Ronald Pritchard; two *s,* one *d. Educ.:* Minchenden Grammar School; *studied art* at Hornsey College of Art and Crafts (1951-56, graphic design). *Exhib.:* R.A., R.B.A., R.I., R.O.I., S.W.A., S.WL.A., S.G.A., S.B.A., R.S.M.; mixed exhbns. at several London galleries. *Address:* 50 Arnos Grove, Southgate, Londn N14 7AR. *Signs work:* "Marion Pritchard."

PROCKTOR, Patrick; painter; *b* Dublin, 12 Mar., 1936; *m* Kirsten Benson, *née* Bo-Andersen (decd.); one *s. Studied art* at Slade School (1958-62). *Exhib.:* since 1963 fourteen one-man shows at Redfern Gallery, London, and other one-man shows abroad. Works represented in numerous public collections. *Publications:* author of One Window in Venice, publ. 1974 (16 water-colour views, published by Galleria Cavallino, Venice); new edition of The Rime of the Ancient Mariner by S. T. Coleridge with twelve etching illustrations, publ. 1976 by Editions Alecto, London; A Chinese Journey, suite of acquatint landscapes of China, publ. 1980 by Editions Alecto; Patrick Procktor, monographs by Patrick Kinmonth publ. by Cavallino 1986. *Address:* 26 Manchester St., London W1.

PROCTER (née PALMER), Marjorie, A.T.D. (1940); artist in water-colour, pencil and wash; art teacher, Ealing School of Art (1943-74); art teacher, Liverpool Inst. for Boys (1941-43); *b* Birmingham, 17 Feb., 1918; *d* of the late W. H. Palmer, B.A. (Cantab.), M.I.Chem.E., F.R.I.C.; *m* Kenneth Procter, painter (1964). *Educ.:* Wade Deacon Grammar School, Widnes; *studied art* at Liverpool City School of Art (1935-40). *Exhib.:* R.A., R.I., R.B.A., Nat. Soc.,

United Soc. of Artists, S.M.A., S.W.A., R.I. Summer Salon, Britain in Water-colour. *Address:* Spring Cottage, Woonton, Almeley, Herefordshire HR3 6QL. *Signs work:* "Marjorie Procter," either written or in block capitals.

PRYSE: see SPENCER PRYSE, Tessa.

PUHN, Franklin; sculptor in stone, wood, plastic, metal, objects in paper; *b* Erfurt, Germany, 20 May, 1925; *m* Regina-Maria Kittel; two *d. Educ.:* Elementary and High School, Erfurt; Schiffbaupraktikant, Hamburg; *studied art* at Holzbildhauerei, Erfurt (1948-52) and at Akademie d.b. Kunste, Stuttgart under Prof. Otto Baum, sculptor. *Exhib.:* Stuttgart (1952), Berlin (1952), London (1953), Dusseldorf (1953), Ulm (1968), Aalen (1969), Göppingen (1970), Paris u. Biarritz (1971). *Official purchases:* various commemorative medals, many fountains and industry-sculptures, Wurttemberg (1952-53). *Address:* 792 Heidenheim. Teckstr. 15, Germany. *Clubs:* Wurttemberg, Verband d. bild., Kunstler Stuttgart. *Signs work:* see appendix.

PULLAN, Margaret Ida Elizabeth; Paris Salon: Gold Medal (1972), Silver Medal (1967); artist in oil; *b* Saharanpur, U.P., India, 6 Nov., 1907; *d* of Ayrton George Popplewell Pullan, M.A. (Oxon), late I.C.S. *Educ.:* Highfield, Oxhey Lane, Watford, Herts; *studied art:* privately. *Exhib.:* Paris Salon (1957-58, 1963 (hon. mention), 1965-71), R.P., R.B.A., Leicester Galleries, Bournemouth, Bradford, Cartwright Memorial Hall, United Soc. of Artists. *Work in permanent collections:* Rugby A.G. *Address:* The Dene, Forest Way, Tunbridge Wells, Kent. *Signs work:* see appendix.

PULLEE, Edward, C.B.E. (1967), A.R.C.A. (1929), F.S.A.E. (1945), N.E.A.C.; artist in oil and water-colour; retd. Chief Officer, N.C.D.A.D. (1967-74); *b* London, 19 Feb., 1907; *s* of Ernest Pullee; *m* Margaret, A.R.C.A., N.E.A.C.; one *s. Educ.:* St. Martin's School, Dover; *studied art* at Dover School of Art (1922-26), R.C.A. (1926-30, Profs. William Rothenstein, Randolph Schwabe, Malcolm Osbourne). *Exhib.:* R.A., N.E.A.C., London and provincial galleries. *Work in permanent collections:* Leeds City A.G., Leicester City A.G. *Address:* 3 March Sq., The Drive, Summersdale, Chichester, W. Sussex PO19 4AN. *Signs work:* "Pullee."

PULLÉE, Michael Edward, Des.R.C.A., F.C.S.D., N.E.A.C., F.R.S.A.; artist in oil, designer and educational consultant; former H.M. Inspector of Schools; *b* London, 8 Sept., 1936; *m* Sheila Mary Threadgill; two *d. Educ.:* Bootham School, York; *studied art* at Leeds College of Art, R.C.A. *Exhib.:* New English Annual, Pattersons. *Address:* White Gables, 48 Wray Common Rd., Reigate, Surrey RH2 0NB. *Club:* N.E.A.C. *Signs work:* "Michael E. Pullée."

PURNELL, John; painter, printmaker, photographer; M.Ph.E., A.R.P.S., A.B.P.A.; *b* Birmingham, 8 Jan., 1954; *s* of the late Prof. A. H. Whitehead. *Educ.:* Boldmere High School for Boys, Sutton Coldfield College of F.E.; *studied art and photography* at West Bromwich College, Hall Green College, Bournville College of Art. Photography tutor, Midlands Arts Centre (1979-82). *Address:* 18 Beresford Rd., Splott, Cardiff CF2 1RA. *Clubs:* I.A.A., N.A.A., Mensa. *Signs work:* "John Purnell" and see appendix.

PYE, William, A.R.C.A., F.R.B.S., Hon.F.R.I.B.A.; sculptor, film; *b* 16 July, 1938; *s* of Sir David Pye, M.A., Sc.D., F.R.S., C.B.; *m* Susan; one *s*, two *d. Educ.:* Charterhouse; *studied art* at Wimbledon School of Art (1958-61) under Freda Skinner, R.C.A. Sculpture School (1961) under Prof. B. Meadows. *Work in permanent collections:* Arts Council, Museum of Modern Art, N.Y., Contemporary Art Soc., G.L.C., University of Warwick, Leicester Educ.

Authority, Royal Albert Memorial Museum, Exeter, Graves City A.G., Sheffield, Middlesbrough City A.G., Birmingham City A.G., Szépmúvészeti Muzeum, Budapest, National Museum of Wales, Wakefield A.G. *Address:* 43 Hambalt Rd., Clapham, London SW4. *Signs work:* see appendix.

PYNE, Doris Grace, A.T.D. (1934), oil painting cert., Slade School; freelance artist in water-colour, art teacher; *b* Wealdstone, 8 Oct., 1910; *d* of John Herman Binder, O.B.E., A.R.C.S. *Studied art* at Hornsey School of Art (1930-34, Norman Janes, A.R.C.A., R.E., Douglas Percy Bliss, M.A.), Slade School (Randolph Schwabe). *Exhib.:* one-man show, Salon des Nations, Paris (1984), Mall Gallery, London (1982); Norwich (1967, 1969, 1972, 1978), Park Gallery, Chislehurst (1973), Aldeburgh (1974), International Art Centre, London (1975), frequent exhib. R.I., Graphic Artists, Mall Galleries. *Address:* 32 Clarendon Way, Marlings Pk., Chislehurst, Kent BR7 6RF. *Clubs:* F.B.A., Bromley Art Soc. *Signs work:* "PYNE."

PYTEL, Walenty, N.D.D. (1961), A.R.B.S.; sculptor in bronze, mild steel and bone china; *b* Sarny, Poland, 10 Feb., 1941; *m* Janet Mary; one *s*, one *d*. *Studied art* at Hereford College of Art (1956-61, Kenneth Craddock, John Wright). *Exhib.:* Mitukoshi Gallery, Tokyo (1988), Don Carlos, Marbella (1985), U.S.A., Jersey, W. Germany, S.WL.A. Mall Galleries (1988 award winner, 1989, 1991, 1992). *Work in permanent collections:* Hereford Museum and A.G., Worcester Library and A.G., Stockport Library and A.G., New Palace Yard Westminster, B'ham International Airport, Lord Montague Beaulieu, Berkeley Hotel London, J.C.B. Uttoxeter. *Publications:* London Art and Antiques Guide (1991), Debrett's Distinguished People of Today (1988-92). *Addresses:* Hartleton, Linton, Ross on Wye; Wyebridge Interiors, Bridge St., Hereford HR4 9DG. *Signs work:* "W. Pytel," "WALENTY PYTEL" (brass plaque), "W.P." or not at all.

Q

QUINN, Mary P. (née McLAUGHGLIN), Hons. sculpture (1986); sculptor in bronze portrait busts; *b* Co. Down, N.I., 26 May, 1943; *m* Jerry Quinn, 1976; three *d*; (*m* dissolved). *Educ.:* St. Dominic's High School, Belfast; *studied art* at Richmond Adult College (1982-89). *Exhib.:* many group shows since 1985. *Work in permanent collections:* Archbishop Cranmer (bronze bust) at St. James Garlickhythe, London EC4; John Wesley (bronze bust) editions at Wesley's Chapel, City Rd., London, Leeds, Peterborough, Methodist museums in N. Carolina, New Jersey, Nashville, Georgia, Texas, California and Germany; George Whitefield in Billy Graham's Seminary in Boston and Savannah, Georgia; Cardinal John Henry Newman (bust) in St. Mary's College, Twickenham and Oratory School, Reading; Mother Teresa (bust) in Westminster Cathedral, London; Sir Edward Appleton (bust) in Bradford University; Our Lady of Walsingham (statue) in St. Mary's Church, Teddington; Lord Learie Constantine (bust) at Willesden Green, London; private collections in Ireland and England. *Address:* 1 Exeter Rd., Hanworth, Feltham, Middx. TW13 5PE. *Clubs:* F.P.S., S.C.A. *Signs work:* "Mary Quinn."

R

RACZKO, Julian Henryk, Dip. Eng. (Warsaw, 1963); artist; *b* Warsaw, 2 Jan., 1936; *s* of Waclaw Raczko; *m* Malena Raczko, architect; two *d. Educ.:* Warsaw Technical University; *studied art* at Warsaw Academy of Fine Art (1963-65, Prof. Alexander Kobzdej). *Exhib.:* one-man shows: Poland, Denmark, Norway, Sweden, France, (C.K. Norwid art critics award 1980). *Work in permanent collections:* National Museums of Warsaw, Wroclaw, Poznan, Arts Museum Lodz, galleries of Chelm, Bydogoszcz, Vostell Museum of Malpartida de Caceres, Arts Museum Norrköping, Museum of Modern Art, Hünfeld, Van Reekum Museum of Apeldoorn, Fyns Kunstmuseum, Odense. *Address:* J. Bruna 34 m 35, 02-594 Warsaw, Poland. *Signs work:* "Julian H. Raczko."

RADLOFF, Celeste Pauline; artist in oil; *b* Pretoria, S. Africa, 1 Nov., 1930; *d* of George Radloff, teacher; *m* Edward Bishop, artist; one *s. Educ.:* matriculated Pretoria; *studied art:* no formal training, first paintings hung in R.A. *Exhib.:* R.A. annually, Grosvenor Gallery ("The Spontaineous Eye"—featured on BBC 2), Roland, Browse & Delbanco, Cork St. Gallery. *Work in permanent collections:* W.A.G., and private collections all over the world. *Address:* 6 East Heath Rd., Hampstead, London NW3 1BN. *Signs work:* "C.R."

RAE, John; works in mixed media, often in combination with PVA, and also makes screen prints and etchings, and draws in conté and pencil. Subjects include landscape, plants and trees, buildings, people, and life paintings. Formerly a lecturer in Architecture at University College London, the Architectural Association, and at Hornsey College of Art. He has travelled and painted in Australasia, Africa, and the New World; *b* Exeter, 1931. *Address:* 14 Orchard St., St. Albans, Herts. AL3 4HL. *Signs work:* "John Rae."

RAEBURN, Kenneth Alexander, D.A.(Edin.) (1966); Post Grad. Scholarship (1966-67); sculptor in bronze, resins and wood, of free-standing figures, portraits and relief murals; principal teacher of art, Comprehensive School; *b* Haddington, E. Lothian, 9 June, 1942; *s* of Francis James Raeburn; *m* Helen Raeburn; one *s,* one *d. Educ.:* Trinity Academy, Edinburgh; *studied art* at School of Sculpture, Edinburgh College of Art under Eric Schilsky. *Exhib.:* R.S.A., S.S.A., various group exhbns. in Scotland, Salon des Nations Exhbn., Paris (1983); one-man show, Metropolis Galerie d'Art, Geneva (1985). *Work in permanent collections:* commissioned panel depicting Baptism of Christ by St. John, in St. John the Baptist Primary School, W. Lothian (awarded Saltire Society Commendation, 1972); commissioned woodcarving of St. Columba in St. Columba's Church, Boghall, West Lothian; commissioned life-sized seal, with her pup, (concrete), South Queensferry; work in numerous private collections in U.K. *Address:* 46 Belsyde Ct., Linlithgow, W. Lothian EH49 7RW. *Signs work:* "Raeburn."

RAINE, Sarah Lamar (Woodie); portrait artist, illustrator, graphic designer in chalk, conté, charcoal, pastel, pencil; Publicity Designer, Methuen General Books; *b* Atlanta, Georgia, U.S.A., 30 June, 1940; *d* of John Miller Raine, V.P. of Marsh and McLennan Insurance, and American football sportsman. *Educ. and studied art* at The Lovett School, Atlanta (Jan Savage), University of Georgia (Lamar Dodd), Stratford College, Va. (David Clarke), Atlantic College of Art (Mr. Grecco). *Exhib.:* Sesame Club (1982), Saville Club (1983). *Address:* 61 Stanlake Rd., London W12. *Club:* Friend of Federation of British Artist. *Signs work:* see appendix.

RAMBISSOON, Sonnylal, A.C.P. (1958), N.D.D. (1964), A.T.C. (1965), Hon. Retd. A.R.E. (1991), Silver Medal of Merit T. & T. (1972); printmaker, sculptor, painter; Past Principal, Ste. Madeleine J.S. School (1977-82), past adviser, Trinidad and Tobago Stamp Com. (1969-72), past lecturer, Fine Art Extra Mural Dept. U.W.T. (1966-72); *b* 1926; *s* of Kalap Rambissoon; *m* Sheila Atwarie; one *s. Educ.:* Government Training College for Teachers (1945-47); *studied art* at Brighton College of Art (1959-64), Goldsmiths' College, University of London (1964-65); numerous summer workshops (1963-87). *Exhib.:* over 100 exhbns. including R.A. (1970), Sao Paulo Biennale (1969, 1971, 1973), A.G.P.A. Travelling (1977), Printmakers of the Americas Travelling (1977-78), Contemporary Open British Watercolourists (1984, 1987, 1993). *Work in permanent collections:* President of T. & T.; Museums of Modern Art: New York, Mexico City, Caracas, Bogota, San Juan and Port of Spain, A.R.E. Collection Ashmolean Oxford (1993). *Address:* 284 Mt. Stewart Village, Naparima Mayaro Rd., Princes Town P.O., Republic of Trinidad and Tobago. *Signs work:* see appendix.

RAMSDEN, Eric, N.D.D. (1950), A.R.E. (1960), Fellow, Society of Wood Engravers; artist in gouache, oil, wood engraving; *b* Cheshire, 22 June, 1927; *s* of William Ramsden; *m* Anna Maria; one *s. Studied art* at Liverpool College of Art (1943-45, 1948-50). Studio Manager and Chief Designer, Portals Ltd., papermakers to The Bank of England (retd. 1992). *Exhib.:* R.A., R.W.S. Galleries, South London Gallery, provincial galleries, Liverpool Walker Art Gallery. *Work in private collections* in America and England. *Address:* The Priory, Freefolk, Whitchurch, Hants. *Signs work:* "Eric Ramsden."

RANDALL, Edward Mark; graphic designer, painter in oil, pastel, water-colour; *b* Coventry, 24 Feb., 1921; *s* of A.G.E. Randall; *m* Marjory; two *s*, one *d. Educ.:* Coventry Technical College; *studied art* at Coventry Art School, Hornsey and Central Schools. *Work in permanent collections:* Marks and Spencer, Plessey Co. private collection, R.C.M. Printing Group. *Address:* 35 Trenance Gdns., Goodmayes, Ilford, Essex IG3 9NQ. *Signs work:* "Mark Randall."

RANDLE, Susan Ann, Dip.H.E.; painter, muralist and graphic artist in oil, water-colour, gouache, pen and ink; *b* Portsmouth, 16 June, 1936; *d* of Harry Wilson, director; *m* Dave Randle, writer; one *s*, one *d. Educ.:* Dominican Convent, Salisbury, Zimbabwe; *studied art* at Dartington College of Art, Totnes (1978-80, Chris Crickmay, John Gridley). *Exhib.:* Carlos Gallery, London, Arnolfini, Bristol; one-man show: Bruyas Gallery, Torquay. *Address:* 2A Granville Rd., Sidcup, Kent DA14 4BN. *Signs work:* "Sue Randle."

RANK-BROADLEY, Ian, H.D.F.A. (Lond.) (1976), A.R.B.S. (1989), F.S.N.A.D. (1990); Boise scholar (1976); sculptor in bronze; Council mem. R.B.S.; *b* Walton-on-Thames, 4 Sept., 1952; *s* of John Kenneth Broadley; *m* Hazel Rank; one *s*, one *d. Studied art* at Epsom School of Art (1970-74, Bruce McLean), Slade School of Fine Art (1974-76, Reg Butler). *Work in permanent collections:* B.M., University of Surrey, Fitzwilliam Museum, Cambridge, States Museum, Berlin, Rijksmuseum, Leiden, National Collection of Finland, Helsinki, Royal Swedish Coin Cabinet, Royal Mint, Goldsmiths' Hall, London, H.M. The Queen, H.M. The Queen Mother. *Address:* Stanfields, Kingscourt La., Rodborough, Stroud, Glos. GL5 3QR. *Signs work:* see appendix.

RASMUSSEN, Roy, F.F.P.S. (1961); sculptor in hand beaten and welded aluminium; Director, Loggia Gallery, London (1984-); *b* London, 29 Apr., 1919. *Exhib.:* John Whibley Gallery London (1968-77), F.P.S. (1957-93), and many other London galleries. *Work in permanent collections:* Towner Gallery and Museum Eastbourne, Paris, Berlin and U.S.A. *Publication:* author: The Free Painters and Sculptors 1952-1992. *Address:* 123 Canterbury Rd., N. Harrow, Middx. HA1 4PA. *Signs work:* "RASMUSSEN."

RATCLIFF, John, O.B.E. (1952), F.R.I.B.A. (1955), F.R.T.P.I. (1972), F.F.P.S. (1959); architect and painter in oil on canvas; President, F.P.S.; *b* Mirfield, Yorks., 22 Jan., 1914; *s* of Claud Francis Ratcliff. *Educ.:* Shrewsbury School, Dijon and Göttingen; *studied architecture* at Architectural Assoc., London (1932-37). *Exhib.:* British Pavilion, Brussels International Exhbn. (1958), R.A., John Moores, F.P.S. *Work in permanent collections:* City and Guilds H.Q., London W1, British Council H.Q., London SW1, 82 Lombard St., London EC3, etc. *Address:* 97 High St., Swanage, Dorset BH19 2LZ. *Signs work:* see appendix.

RAVERA, John, P.P.R.B.S., F.R.S.A.; President, R.B.S. (1988-90); sculptor in clay; *b* Surrey, 27 Feb., 1941; *m* Daphne. *Studied art* at Camberwell School of Art (1954-62). *Exhib.:* York Open Air Show (July, 1971), Rye (July, 1971), Hounslow Festival Sculpture (June 1972), R.A. (1975, 1976), Alwin Gallery (1977), Woodlands (1977), Bexleyheath (1985), Haywards Heath (1985). *Major commissioned works:* Academy of Arts Hong Kong (1982), Morgan's Walk London (1983), London Dockland Development, bronze bust (1986), Bayswater London, bronze group of children (1987), Barbican London, bronze group dolphins (1989), Elstree London, stainless steel abstract (1989). *Address:* Studio, 82 Latham Rd., Bexleyheath, Kent. *Signs work:* "John E. Ravera."

RAWLINS, Janet, N.D.D. (Illustration), A.T.D., book illustration, fabric collage, gouache, water-colour; *b* Horsforth, Leeds, 3 May, 1931; *d* of E. J. Rawlins; *m* John G. Leyland, F.C.A.; one *s. Educ.:* Gt. Moreton Hall, Ches.; *studied art:* Leeds College of Art. *Exhib.:* R.A., northern galleries. *Official purchases:* Bradford, Harrogate and Batley Art Galleries, Leeds, Huddersfield, West Riding, Leicester and Essex Education Committees, Leeds Permanent Building Society, I.W.S., N.C.B., I.C.I. *Work repro.:* children's books by William Mayne and Jane Gardam; compiled and illustrated A Dales Countryside Cookbook (1993). *Address:* West End House, Askrigg, Wensleydale, N. Yorks. DL8 3HN. *Signs work:* "Janet Rawlins."

RAWLINSON, William Thomas, A.T.D., Médaille d'or Paris Salon (1960), S.W.E. (1971), F.R.S.A.; painter, engraver, art teacher; R.A.F. (1941-46); official war artist (1943-46); *b* Liverpool, 12 Jan., 1912; *s* of Thomas Rawlinson, schoolmaster; *m* F. E. Patricia Martin. *Educ.:* Quarry Bank High School; *studied art* at Liverpool College of Art (1929-35). Senior City Art Travelling Scholarship (1932) studied abroad in France, Italy, Czechoslovakia, Austria and Germany. *Exhib.:* R.E., Paris Salon, R.A., R.C.A., R.S.A., Salon des Nations, Paris (1983). *Work in permanent collections:* Imperial War Museum, R.A.F. Museum, Hendon, Ashmolean Museum Oxford (Dept. of Western Art), Liverpool Walker A.G., Appleton Gall., N.Y., Brighton A.G., Letchworth A.G. *Work repro.:* four engravings in A History of British Wood Engraving by Albert Garrett (1978). *Address:* Scargill, Myatt's Field, Harvington, Evesham WR11 2NG. *Signs work:* "William T. Rawlinson."

RAY: see HOWARD-JONES, Ray.

RAY, Karen; painter in oil, water-colour, pencil, coloured pencil, lecturer; *b* Queensland, Australia, 8 Dec., 1931; *m* Stuart Ray (decd.); three *s. Studied art* at Walthamstow School of Art (Stuart Ray, John Tichell, Fred Cuming); R.A.

Schools (Peter Greenham). *Exhib.:* many times in the R.A. Summer Exhbn. *Address:* 91 Mountview Rd., London N4 4JA. *Signs work:* "K. Ray."

RAYMENT, Brenda, A.R.M.S. (1991); artist in oil on ivorine; *b* Paddock Wood, Kent, 5 May, 1951; *m* Laurence Rayment; one *s*, one *d*. *Educ.:* Kidbrooke School; *studied art* at Bexley A.E.C. (1980-90, Barry Shiraishi, R.M.S.). *Exhib.:* S.W.A., R.M.S. *Address:* Heather Cottage, 5 Gwel-an-Garrek, Mullion. Cornwall TR12 7RW.

RAYNER, Desmond, L.G.S.M., F.R.S.A.; self taught artist in gouache, charcoal, pencil, oil, literary agent, writer, actor; *b* London, 31 Oct., 1928; *m* Claire Rayner; two *s*, one *d*. *Educ.:* theatre: Guildhall School of Music and Drama. *Exhib.:* Heals, London; Embankment Gallery, Tattershall Castle, London; Grays, Mayfair; Talent Store, Belgravia; October Gallery, U.S.A.; Mall Galleries, London; Seven Dials Gallery, London; Barbican Centre, London; Wylma Wayne Fine Art, London; Building Centre, London, etc. *Work in private collections:* U.S.A., Canada, Australia, U.K. *Publications:* The Dawlish Season, The Husband. *Address:* Holly Wood House, Roxborough Ave., Harrow-on-the-Hill, Middx. HA1 3BU. *Club:* Savage. *Signs work:* "RAYNER."

RAYNOR, Trevor Samuel; Mem. Associé, Société des Artistes Français (1977); textile designer, artist in oil and water-colour and floral subjects in gouache; *b* Oldham, 13 May, 1929; *s* of the late William Ernest Raynor, produce merchant; *m* Margaret Joyce Marwood; one *s*. *Educ.:* Werneth Council School; *studied art* at Oldham School of Art (1942-45), Manchester School of Art (1945-49). *Exhib.:* Paris Salon (1975, 1976, 1977); one-man shows, Salford City A.G., Swinton Memorial A.G. Work in private collections. *Work repro.:* prints of floral work. *Address:* 1 Hollin Cres., Greenfield, Oldham OL3 7LW. *Signs work:* "RAYNOR" or "T.S. RAYNOR."

READ, Sue, R.I. (1985), N.D.D. (1963), A.T.D. (1964); artist in water-colour; *b* Slough, 1941; *d* of John Melia (decd.); *m* Robert Read (divorced); three *s*. *Educ.:* Aylesbury Grammar School; *studied art* at High Wycombe School of Art (1959-63), Royal West of England College of Art (1963-64). *Exhib.:* Mall Galleries, R.A. Summer Exhbn., Shell House Gallery, Ledbury. *Address:* Horsefair House, West St., Buckingham MK18 1HP. *Signs work:* "S.R."

REAL, Jacqueline, F.F.P.S. (1992); contemporary painter in acrylic, collage and mixed media; *b* Zürich, 5 Oct., 1931; *d* of Fred Berger, architect; *m* Christopher Butler; one *s*, one *d*. *Studied art* in Zürich (1975-78), Academy of Modern Art, Masterclass, Salzburg (1979), Painting Course in Meran (1980). *Exhib.:* solo and group shows: Switzerland, London, U.S.A. and Germany. *Work in permanent collections:* Switzerland, England, U.S.A., Germany, including Mark Rich Switzerland, Union Bank of Switzerland Zürich and London, VITA Insurance Zürich, Credit Swiss Bank Zürich, British Government, Johnson & Johnson. *Represented by:* "Art for Offices", London and Tokyo; and Wills Lane Gallery, St. Ives. *Address:* 92 Woodland Drive, Hove BN3 6DE. *Clubs:* F.P.S., Soc. of Swiss Painters, Sculptors and Architects, Eastbourne Group of Artists. *Signs work:* "J. Real."

RECKITT, Rachel; Hon. mem. S.W.E. and Somerset Guild of Craftsmen; semi-retd. sculptor and wood engraver, painter in wood engraving, iron and oil paint; *b* St. Albans, 21 Nov., 1908. *Studied art* at Grosvenor School of Modern Art, London (1934-38, Iain MacNab). *Exhib.:* Duncan Campbell Gallery London, Bridgewater Art Centre. *Work in permanent collections:* Salford A.G., Bridgewater Arts Centre (relief collage). *Publications:* illustrated: East London

(Myers), People with Six Legs, English Short Stories (Anthology), Seven Psalms, etc. *Address:* Golsoncott House, Rodhuish, Minehead, W. Som. TA24 6QU. *Signs work:* "Rachel Reckitt."

REDDICK, Peter, D.F.A. (Slade, 1951), R.E., R.W.A.; printmaker and wood-engraver, freelance illustrator; *b* Essex, 1924. *Studied art* at Slade School of Fine Art (1948-51); Gregynog Arts Fellow (1970-80). Chairman, Bristol Printmakers Workshop. *Address:* 18 Hartington Park, Bristol BS6 7ES. *Signs work:* "Peter Reddick."

REDFERN, June, D.A. (1972); prizewinner, Scottish Young Contemporaries; Artist in Residence, National Gallery (1985); painter in oil and water-colour; *b* St. Andrews, Fife, 16 June, 1951. *Educ.:* Dunfermline High School, Fife; *studied art* at Edinburgh College of Art (1968-73, Robin Philipson, David Michie, Elizabeth Blackadder, John Houston). *Exhib.:* many throughout Britain and U.S.A. including National Gallery, London (1985). *Work in permanent collections:* S.N.G.M.A., National Gallery London, B.B.C. Television, Robert Fleming plc, Arthur Andersen, Texaco, Hiscox Holdings. *Address:* 12 Lawley St., London E5 0RJ. *Signs work:* "June Redfern" on reverse of oils only.

REDINGTON, Simon, B.A. (Fine Art), Postgrad.Dip. in Art Therapy, Cert. of Advanced Printmaking; artist/printmaker in etching, woodcuts, letterpress, painting, mixed media; Council mem. R.E.; *b* London, 28 Sept., 1958. *Educ.:* Pimlico School; *studied art* at Goldsmiths' College, Hertfordshire College of Art, Central St. Martin's College of Art. *Exhib.:* N.P.G., R.A. Summer Show, Slaughterhouse Gallery. *Work in permanent collections:* V. & A., Theatre Museum, Ashmolean Museum. *Publications:* 'Hangman' Edn. 20-boxed set of 20 prints (woodcut/letterpress). *Address:* 149 Archway Rd., London N6 5BL. *Club:* R.E. *Signs work:* "S. Redington."

REDPATH, Barbara, D.A. (Edin.); works in oils and water-colour; *b* London 1924. Educ.: Streatham; *studied* at Edinburgh College of Art under W. G. Gillies, P.R.S.W. *Exhib.:* R.S.A., S.S.A., S.S.W.A., R.G.I., Edinburgh, Glasgow, London, Cannes, Paris. *Work in permanent collections:* Dept. of Fine Art, University of Glasgow, University of Strathclyde. *Address:* 32 Glasgow St., Glasgow, G12. *Signs work:* "Babs Redpath."

REDVERS, John Stephen (formerly PIGGINS, John Redvers Stephen, changed 1979), Slade Dip. (1948), P.S. (1984); portrait painter in pastel, oil; *b* Birmingham, 18 July, 1928; *s* of Major Charles Redvers Piggins, R.A.O.C.; *m* Mary Pennel; one *s*, two *d*. *Educ.:* Solihull School, Warwickshire; *studied art* at Slade School of Art (1945-48, Prof. Randolph Schwabe), Ruskin School of Art, Oxford (1950, Prof. Albert Rutherston). *Exhib.:* R.P., P.S., Hopetoun House, W. Lothian (1977); one-man show, Chakrabongse Palace, Bangkok (1962). *Address:* Tweenhills, Hartpury, Gloucester GL19 3BG. *Signs work:* "JOHN REDVERS" or "REDVERS" ("J.R.S. Piggins" or "John Piggins" pre 1979).

REES JONES, Stephen, M.Sc., F.Inst.P., F.S.A., F.I.I.C.; physicist specializing in the technology of art and conservation; Emeritus Prof., University of London; Prof. of Chemistry, Royal Academy of Arts (retd.); formerly head of the Technology Dept., Courtauld Inst. of Art; Hon. Fellow, International Institute for Conservation of Historic and Artistic Works; *b* Holywell, Clwyd, 1 Sept., 1909; *s* of William Rees Jones, schoolmaster; *m* Margaret Lafineur; two *s*. *Educ.:* Holywell Grammar School; *studied science* at University of Wales, Bangor. *Publications:* Papers in various professional periodicals on art conservation, scientific examination of paintings, colour. *Address:* 29 Gundreda Rd., Lewes BN7 1PT. *Club:* Athenaeum.

REEVE, Marion José, N.D.D. (1953), M.F.P.S. (1968); landscape painter in acrylic and gouache; retd. civil servant, Building Research Establishment; life mem. International Assoc. of Art; *b* Watford, 26 Sept., 1926; *d* of Richard John Reeve; *m* Albert Edward Butcher (decd.). *Educ.:* St. Joan of Arc Convent, Rickmansworth; *studied art* at Watford College of Technology, School of Art (1947-53) under Alexander Sutherland, M.A. *Exhib.:* one-man show: Loggia Gallery (1974), Young Contemporaries (1954), F.P.S. Annual and Travelling exhbns. at Kings Lynn Festival, South of France, etc. *Work in permanent collection:* St. Michael and All Angels Church, Watford (Stations of the Cross), also design for Christ in Majesty. *Address:* 10 Kelmscott Cres., Watford, Herts. WD1 8NG. *Club:* Watford and Bushey Art Soc. *Signs work:* "M. Reeve" and date.

REEVES, Philip Thomas Langford, A.R.C.A. (1954), R.E. (1963), R.S.W. (1959), A.R.S.A. (1971), R.S.A. (1976), R.G.I. (1981); painter-etcher; *b* Cheltenham, 7 July, 1931; *s* of Herbert John Reeves, printer; *m* Christine MacLaren; one *d*. *Educ.:* Naunton Park Senior Secondary School, Cheltenham; *studied art* at Cheltenham School of Art (1945-49), Royal College of Art (1951-54). *Work in permanent collections:* Arts Council of Gt. Britain, V. & A., Contemporary Art Soc., Gallery of Modern Art, Edinburgh, Glasgow A.G., Glasgow University Print Collection, Aberdeen A.G., Paisley A.G., Milngavie A.G., Dundee A.G., Edinburgh University, Stirling University, Dept. of the Environment. *Address:* 13 Hamilton Drive, Glasgow G12. *Signs work:* "Philip Reeves."

REID, Elspeth Margaret Georgina, A.R.B.S. (1979), L.C.A.D. (1976), City and Guilds Cert. of Merit (1961); sculptor in wood, stone and cast clay; Sculpture tutor, London Borough of Hillingdon; *b* Blackheath, Kent, 9 Apr., 1930; *d* of Duncan George Reid, Comdr. R.N. *Educ.:* Northwood College, and privately; *studied art* at City and Guilds of London Art School (1956-62, Sydney Harpley, David McFall, James Butler), Hammersmith College of Art. *Exhib.:* R.A., R.B.A., S.P.S., R.B.S., S.W.A.; five one-man shows. *Address:* Weathervane Cottage, 39 Wieland Rd., Northwood, Middx. HA6 3QX. *Signs work:* "E.M.R." or since 1981 see appendix.

REID, John, Dip. Arch. (Distinction), R.I.B.A., P.P.C.S.D.; architect and general consultant designer; *b* 1 Dec., 1925; *m* Sylvia Reid, Dip. Arch., A.R.I.B.A., F.C.S.D. *Educ.:* Wellingborough Grammar School; *studied architecture* at Polytechnic School of Architecture, W1. Partner, John & Sylvia Reid since 1951; Pageantmaster to the Lord Mayors of London since 1972; Dean of Art and Design, Middlesex Polytechnic (1975-78). Four Design Council awards, Silver medallist 12th and 13th Milan International Triennales. President, International Council of Societies of Industrial Design (1969-71). Unido Consultant on industrial design in India, Pakistan, Egypt and Turkey (1977-79). Trustee, The Geffrye Museum (1990—). *Address:* 5 The Green, Southgate, London N14 7EG.

REID, Sir Norman Robert, Kt. (1970), D.A. (Edin., 1937), D.Litt., F.M.A., F.I.I.C., joined Tate Gallery, 1946; appointed Director, 1964; Chairman, British Council Fine Arts Committee; Fellow and Vice-Chairman, International Institute for Conservation of Historic and Artistic Works; Member, British National Cttee. of I.C.O.M.; Mem. Culture Adv. Cttee.; President, Council of the Rome Centre; *b* London, 27 Dec., 1915; *s* of Edward Reid; *m* Jean Bertram; one *s*, one *d. Educ.:* Wilson's Grammar School; *studied art* at Goldsmiths' College, Edinburgh College of Art (1933-38) and Edinburgh University. *Work in permanent collections:* paintings in Tate Gallery and S.N.G.M.A. *Address:* The Tate Gallery, Millbank, London SW1.

REITER, Laura, B.A. (Hons.) (1986), M.A. (1989), A.R.E. (1989); painter in oil, acrylic and water-colour, printmaker mainly in silkscreen/linocut; teacher/lecturer; *b* London, 25 Aug., 1950; three *d. Educ.:* Brondesbury and Kilburn High School; *studied art* at Kingston School of Art (1983-86), Wimbledon School of Art (1986-89). Numerous group exhbns. *Address:* 52 Gatehill Rd., Northwood, Middx. HA6 3QP. *Signs work:* "Laura Reiter."

REMFRY, David, R.W.S.; painter, Mercury Gallery, London; oil, water-colour; *b* Sussex, 30 July, 1942. *Studied:* Hull College of Art (1959-64). *Exhib.:* one-man shows: Mercury, London (1978/80/82/84/86/88/90/92), Edinburgh (1983), New Grafton Gallery (1973), Editions Graphiques (1974), Old Fire Engine House, Ely (1975/77/79/81/83/86/90/92), Ferens A.G., Hull (1975), New Art Centre, Folkestone (1976), Ankrum Gallery, Los Angeles (1980/81/ 83/85/87), Bohun Gallery, Henley (1978/81/83/85/87/89/91/93), Galerie de Beerenburght, Holland (1979/80/83/86), Middlesbrough A.G. (1981), Zack Shuster Gallery, Florida (1986/88/90), Margaret Lipworth Fine Art, Florida (1992), N.P.G. (1992). *Work in public collections:* N.P.G., V. & A., Middlesbrough A.G., Minnesota Museum of Art, U.S.A., Swarthmore College, Pennsylvania, U.S.A., Museo Rayo, Columbia. *Address:* 19 Palace Gate, London W8. *Clubs:* Chelsea Arts, Groucho. *Signs work:* "David Remfry."

REMINGTON, Mary, A.R.C.A. (Lond., 1933), N.E.A.C. (1954), R.O.I. (1962); painter in oil; *b* Reigate, Surrey, 1910. *Educ.:* privately; *studied art* at Redhill School of Art; awarded scholarship to Royal College of Art (1930) under Sir William Rothenstein; later at Académie de la Grande Chaumière, Paris. *Exhib.:* R.A., N.E.A.C., R.O.I., R.B.A., Arts Council and principal provincial galleries. *Work in permanent collections:* Grundy Gallery, Blackpool; Brighton Municipal Gallery; Kensington Public Library; Tower Hamlets Public Library. *Work in private collections:* Italy, Germany, Belgium, Persia, Switzerland, Canada and Gt. Britain. *Address:* White Post Studio, 13 Stanley Rd., Sutton, Surrey. *Signs work:* "Mary Remington."

RENNIE, Neil, M.C. (1945), B.Sc.(Econ.), M.F.P.S. (1988); expressionist artist in pastel, water-colour, acrylic and collage; Treasurer, F.P.S.; *b* Wandsworth, London of Scottish lineage, 25 Apr., 1921; *s* of Robert Rennie and Eva Mushett (decd.). *Educ.:* Rutlish, Merton Park and London School of Economics; *studied art* privately since 1980 with Elyn Carleton, founder of Creators. *Exhib.:* frequent two-man shows. *Work in private collections:* Australia, England and France. *Address:* Flat E, 10 King's Rd., London SW19 8QN. *Signs work:* "Neil Rennie," "N.R.R." or "N.R."

RENTON, Joan, D.A., R.S.W.; painter and teacher in oil, water-colour and mixed media; *b* 1935; *née* Biggins; *m* R. S. Renton, D.A.; two *s*, one *d. Educ.:* Dumfries Academy and Hawick High School; *studied art* at Edinburgh College of Art, Post.Dip. Travelling Scholarship. *Work in permanent collections:* H.R.H. the Duke of Edinburgh, Yorkshire Educ. Dept., Scottish Hospitals, Lothian Region Collection, Royal College of Physicians, paintings in hospitals and Jean Watson Trust; private collections in Europe, U.K., U.S.A. and N.Z. *Address:* Holmcroft, 4 Tweeddale Ave., Gifford, E. Lothian EH41 4QN. *Signs work:* "Joan Renton."

REYNOLDS, Bernard Robert, F.R.B.S., retired lecturer in sculpture, Suffolk College; *b* 2 June, 1915; *s* of Edward Bernard Reynolds; *m* Gwynneth Jane Griffiths; one *s*, three *d*. *Educ.*: City of Norwich School; *studied art* at Norwich School of Art (1932-37), L.C.C. Westminster School of Art. *Exhib.*: regularly at Norwich, Aldeburgh, Ipswich and Colchester (sculpture). Founder-mem. Norwich 20-Group (1944). *Commissions* include pair 20-ft. pylons in aluminium for Suffolk College, 25-ft window for St. Matthew's School, and fountain sculpture for Ipswich Civic Centre which won the Sir Otto Beit Award given by the R.B.S. (1972). *Address:* Old Schoolhouse, Barham, Ipswich IP6 0PG.

REYNOLDS, Daphne; Chairman, Women's International Art Club (1964-67); Fellow, Printmaker's Council (1973); Founder, Gainsborough's House Printworkshop (Chairman 1978-79); painter and engraver in oil, gouache, mezzotint; *b* Huddersfield, 12 Jan., 1918; *d* of Thomas Dent, photographer; *m* Graham Reynolds (*q.v.*). *Educ.*: Wentworth School, Huddersfield; *studied art* at Huddersfield School of Art (1934-36). *Exhib.*: Galerie Creuze, Paris (1959), Drian Galleries (1961, 1964), City of Oldham A.G. (1969, 1975), Angela Flowers (1975), Gainsborough's House, Sudbury, Suffolk (1976, 1989), Ipswich City A.G. (1977), Bill Thomson, Albany Gallery, London (1991, 1993), etc. *Work in permanent collections:* Arts Council, V. & A., B.M., D.O.E., Bibliotheque Nationale, Paris, I.C.I., National Galleries in Australia and N.Z., Minneapolis Inst. of Fine Art, New Orleans Museum, Library of Congress, Washington D.C., etc. *Address:* The Old Manse, Bradfield St. George, Bury St. Edmunds, Suffolk IP30 0AZ. *Signs work:* "Daphne Reynolds."

REYNOLDS, Graham, O.B.E. (1984), B.A. (1935), F.B.A. (1993); keeper, Dept. of Prints and Drawings, and Paintings, V. & A. (1959-74); *b* 10 Jan, 1914; *s* of Arthur T. Reynolds; *m* Daphne Reynolds, *née* Dent (*q.v.*). *Educ.*: Highgate School and Queens' College, Cambridge. *Publications:* Twentieth-century Drawings (1946), Nicholas Hilliard and Isaac Oliver (1947) 2nd edition (1971), English Portrait Miniatures (1952) 2nd edition (1988), Painters of the Victorian Scene (1953), The Constable Collection, Victoria and Albert Museum (1960) 2nd edition (1973), Constable, the Natural Painter (1965), Victorian Painting (1966), 2nd edition (1987), Turner (1969), A Concise History of Water-colours (1971), Portrait Miniatures, Wallace Collection (1980), Constable's England (1983), The Later Paintings and Drawings of John Constable (1984), awarded Mitchell Prize (1984), English Watercolours (1988). *Address:* The Old Manse, Bradfield St. George, Suffolk IP30 0AZ.

REYNOLDS, Ruth Evelyn Millicent, F.R.S.A.; sculptor and artist in oil and water-colour; *b* India, 4 Oct., 1915; *d* of Lt.-Col. C. E. W. S. Fawcett, R.A.M.C.; *m* Lt.-Col. D. L. C. Reynolds, O.B.E.; one *s*, two *d*. *Educ.*: abroad and Conamur, Sandgate, Kent; *studied art* at Guildford School of Art under Victor Burnand, A.R.C.A.; Prof. Arthur Pan of Academie Authentique, Budapest; Wycombe School of Art. *Exhib.*: one-man shows: Halifax House, Oxford University Graduate Centre (1965), English-Speaking Union (1967), County Museum, Aylesbury, sponsored by Bucks C.C. (1976), Loggia Gallery (1982), Century Galleries, Henley-on-Thames (1987); group show: Amnesty International Sculpture Exhbn. *Work in permanent collections:* Anne, Duchess of Westminster's Arkle Coll.; Rev. J. Studd, M.A.; Guinness (Park Royal) Ltd.; Mrs Jenny Hopkinson, Palo Alto, California; Mr Fuad Mulla Hussein, Kuwait Planning Board; R.A.F. Halton, Bucks; St. Dunstan's Church, Monks Risborough, Aylesbury; Welch Regiment Museum, Cardiff Castle; BBONT, Oxford; Stoke Mandeville Hospital, Aylesbury; Lambeth Palace Garden, SE1.; Mrs. Charlotte

Steel. *Address:* 30 The Retreat, Princes Risborough, Bucks. HP17 9NG. *Signs work:* "RUTH REYNOLDS" or "R.R."

REYNOLDS, Vicki, B.A.(Hons.) (1976), Dip.R.A.S. (1979); British Inst. award (1978), Richard Ford scholarship (1980), S.J. Solomon silver medal for painting (1979); prizewinner, The Spirit of London; painter in oil, water-colour, charcoal, sculptress in clay; part-time assistant, Royal Academy; *b* Portsmouth, 8 June, 1946; *d* of Cyril William Mitchell; divorced. *Educ.:* Paulsgrove and Southsea Schools, Portsmouth; *studied art* at Goldsmiths' College (1972-76, John Thompson), R.A. Schools (1976-79, Peter Greenham). *Exhib.:* Stowells Trophy, New Contemporaries, Three College Show, R.A. Summer Exhbn., Vortex Gallery; group shows, R.A., The London Group, Gallery 10. *Address:* 4 Whidborne Cl., St. John's Vale, London SE8. *Signs work:* "V.R."

RHOADES, Peter G., C.F.A.Oxon. (1958), N.D.D. Painting (1959), M.A. Cardiff (1992), R.E. (1989); artist/lecturer in printmaking, drawing, photography; Tutor in Art, Christ Church College, Oxford, Visiting Tutor in Drawing, Ruskin School of Drawing, University of Oxford; *b* Watford, 6 May, 1938; *partner* Jane Harrison; one *s*, three *d. Educ.:* Bryanston School; *studied art* at Ruskin School of Drawing (1955-59, Percy Horton), Central School of Art and Crafts (1960-61, William Turnbull, Alan Davie), Cardiff Inst. of Higher Educ. (1990-92, John Gingell). *Exhib.:* periodic one-man shows, numerous selected exhbns. in Britain, Europe and U.S.A. *Work in permanent collections:* Ashmolean Museum Oxford, John Radcliffe Hospital Oxford, Art in Hospitals. *Address:* Seven Stars, Spurt St., Cuddington, Aylesbury, Bucks. HP18 0BB. *Signs work:* "PETER RHOADES" or "P.G.R."

RHODES, Marion, R.E., F.R.S.A., S.G.A., Paris Salon, Hon. Mention, bronze, silver and gold medals, Silver Medal and Diploma, Rome (1970), Associate Artistes Français (1971-81); artist in black and white, water-colour, oil; *b* Huddersfield, 1907; *d* of Samuel Rhodes, woollen manufacturer. *Educ.:* Greenhead High School, Huddersfield Art School, Leeds College of Art, Central School of Arts, London. *Exhib.:* R.A., Paris Salon, R.S.A., W.A.G. and provincial galleries, S. Africa and U.S.A. *Work in permanent collections:* British Museum and V. & A. print room, Bradford, South London, Brighouse, Huddersfield. *Address:* 2 Goodwyn Ave., Mill Hill, London NW7 3RG. *Signs work:* "Marion Rhodes."

RICE, Bernard; painter in oil, fresco, portrait sculptor, wood-engraver; *b* Innsbruck, Austria, 28 June, 1900; *s* of Bernard Rice, stained-glass painter. *Studied art* in Innsbruck, at R.C.A. and R.A. schools. *Work in permanent collections:* B.M. (Print Room), V. & A. (Print Room), Cairo Modern Art Gallery. *Work repro.:* A History of British Wood engraving by Albert Garrett. *Address:* c/o Midland Bank Ltd., 337 Kings Rd., Chelsea, London SW3. *Signs work:* see appendix.

RICE, Elizabeth Helen, S.WL.A., S.B.A., R.H.S. Gold Medal; botanical painter in water-colour; illustrator; *b* Canterbury, 4 Apr., 1947; *d* of Patrick Arthur Rice, F.R.S.A., farmer retd. *Educ.:* Ashford School, Kent; *studied art* at Exeter College of Art (1963-65), bursary to study wallpaper design with Arthur Sanderson & Sons (1965-70). *Exhib.:* Mall Galleries, Medici Gallery, Pawsey & Payne, St. James's, Jersey Wildlife Preservation Trust, C.I., McEwan Gallery, Scotland, etc. *Work in permanent collections:* H.R.H. The Princess of Wales, Sultan of Oman, Sissinghurst Castle, Kent. *Work repro.:* contributor to Collins Fieldguide to Crops of Britain and Europe, Reader's Digest Fieldguide to

Butterflies, Collins Gem Guide to Herbs, etc. *Address:* Little Langdale, Marsh Rd., Seaton, Devon EX12 2LQ. *Signs work:* "Elizabeth H. Rice."

RICE, Seán, Prix de Rome (1953-55); sculptor/painter in bronze, mixed media, oil and water-colour; *b* London, 5 Nov., 1931; *m* Janet Teniers; two *s*, one *d. Educ.:* Brighton and Hove County Grammar School; *studied art* at Brighton College of Art (1947-51, James Woodford, R.A.), R.A. Schools (1951-53, Maurice Lambert, R.A.), British School at Rome (1953-55). Winner of Constance Fund Sculpture competition (1970). *Exhib.:* R.A.; one-man shows: 15 in G.B. and Italy including eight at Alwin Gallery London; Art Scene London. *Major public commissions:* Noah Fountain, Chester Zoo; Poseidon Fountain, Gravesend; Atlantic Tower Sculptures, Liverpool; Stations of the Cross, Metropolitan Cathedral of Christ the King, Liverpool. *Address:* studio: 72 Mandeville St., Walton, Liverpool L4 5TL. *Signs work:* "Rice" or not at all.

RICHARDS, E. Margaret (*née* TURNER); exhbn. scholarship R.C.A. (1940), Drawing prize (1943), A.R.C.A. (Painting) (1943), M.F.P.S. (1976); artist in oil and water-colour; *b* Kingston, Surrey, 29 Dec., 1918; *m* E. M. Richards, LL.B.; three *s*, one *d. Educ.:* St. Paul's Convent, Teddington; *studied art* at Kingston School of Art (1935) under Reginald Brill, R.C.A. (1939-40) under Gilbert Spencer. *Exhib.:* R.A., R.O.I., London Group, R.B.A., N.E.A.C., Trends. *Address:* 3 Cheapside, Horsell, Woking GU21 4JG. *Club:* F.P.S. *Signs work:* "E. Margaret Richards" on back, sometimes "Peggy E. M. Turner."

RICHARDS, Patricia, N.D.D.; freelance display artist, art tutor with Adult Educ. including art for the handicapped, pre-school toddlers and paper sculpture for primary school children; diversional therapist for the elderly, Clare House Nursing Home, Walton, Surrey; artist in oil, water-colour, pencil and pen work; *b* New Malden, Surrey, 9 Nov., 1935; *d* of Harold Richards; divorced; one *s*, one *d. Educ.:* Wimbledon County Grammar School; *studied art* at Kingston Art School (1950-55, Reginald Brill). *Exhib.:* Graphic Artists (1984), Heritage '84 (National Trust), R.A. (1984), Mall Galleries, Festival Hall, London, Guildford House, Blaydon Gallery, Parkshot Gallery, Richmond, Garden Gallery, Kew, Boathouse Gallery, Walton; one-man show, Trends (F.P.S.) and Esher. Work in private collections. *Address:* 39 Woodlands, Meadowlands Pk., Weybridge Rd., Addlestone, Surrey KT15 2RQ. *Signs work:* "P. Richards" or "P.RICHARDS."

RICHARDSON, Geoffrey Philip; landscape artist in oil, water-colour, etching, drypoint; *b* Woodbridge, 15 Apr., 1928; *s* of Philip John Richardson, cabinet maker. *Educ.:* Woodbridge Elementary School; *studied art* at Ipswich School of Art (1940-44) under A. Ward, A.R.C.A., A. W. Bellis, A.R.C.A., Miss E. Wood, A.R.C.A. *Exhib.:* R.I., N.S. Summer Salon; one-man shows, Haste Gallery, Ipswich, Deben Gallery, Woodbridge; and various group shows. *Work in private collections:* England, America, Germany, Turkey, New Zealand. *Address:* 21 Old Barrack Rd., Woodbridge, Suffolk IP12 4ET. *Club:* Ipswich Art. *Signs work:* "G. Richardson", followed by date and monogram, paintings, and "G" engraved in etchings and drypoint.

RICHARDSON, Ilana, Dip. A.D. (1968); painter in water-colour and screen printer; *b* Haifa, Israel, 1946. *Studied art* at Betzalel Academy of Art, Jerusalem (1963-67), Hornsey College of Art (1967-68). *Exhib.:* C.C.A. Galleries London, Oxford, Bath, Amalgam Gallery London, Window Gallery Brighton, R.A. *Publications:* participated as artist in The New Guide to Screen Printing by Brad Faine. Prints published by C.C.A. since 1982 printed at the artist's studio and Coriander Studio London. *Address:* 12 Dalebury Rd., London SW17 7HH. *Signs work:* "Ilana Richardson."

RICHARDSON, John Frederick, A.T.D., Dip. Art History (London), F.S.A.I.I., S.B.A., S.G.A., F.R.S.A.; artist in water-colour, pastels, oil and drawing media; Head of Art Dept., Emanuel School, London (1951-74), Hove Grammar School (1938-50), East Sheen (1937-38), University College School (1934-37); *b* London, 23 Apr., 1912; *s* of E. F. Richardson. *Educ.:* Wilson's Grammar School; *studied art* at Camberwell School of Art (1928-31); London Day Training College (1931-32). *Exhib.:* R.A., R.P., R.S.M.A., R.S.A., R.H.A., P.S., N.E.A.C., R.W.S. Galleries, South London Group; one-man show: Ickworth (1971, 1973). *Address:* 33 Downsway, Sanderstead, Surrey. *Clubs:* Langham, London Sketch. *Signs work:* "John F. Richardson."

RICHMOND, Donald Edward, N.D.D., painting (1952), A.T.C., London (1953); painter and theatrical designer; hon. treas. (1952), hon. adviser (1953), Young Contemporaries; senior lecturer in stage design, West Midlands College (since 1966); *b* Ilford, Essex, 13 Aug., 1929; *s* of H. J. Richmond. *Educ.:* Ilford County High School; *studied art* at S.W. Essex Technical College and School of Art (1946-48 and 1950-52), Brighton College of Art (1952-53). *Exhib.:* Young Contemporaries, R.B.A. galleries (1952-53). *Designer:* Tower Theatre, N.1 (1956-61); English première Goyescas (Granados), Morley College (1965-66). *Address:* Portsea House, 3 Sea Lane Cl., E. Preston, W. Sussex BN16 1NQ. *Signs work:* "DON RICHMOND."

RICHMOND, Robin, B.A., M.A.; artist in water-colour, pastel, mixed media, oil; writer and broadcaster; *b* Philadelphia, U.S.A., 7 Nov., 1951; *d* of Patricia Cooper Richmond, M.A.; *m* Dr. James Hampton; one *s*, one *d*. *Educ.:* St. George's English School, Rome; *studied art* at Chelsea School of Art (1969-74). *Exhib.:* (selected) Mercury Gallery (1989, 1990, 1992), Barbican Centre (1992); group shows: (selected) Cleveland Biennale (1990), Southwestern Arts, Dallas (1993), etc. *Work in permanent collections:* San Francisco Fine Art Museum, Middlesbrough A.G., M.O.M.A. (N.Y.). *Publications:* (selected) illustrated: The Magic Flute (Faber); author: Michelangelo and the Creation of the Sistine Chapel (Barrie and Jenkins, 1992), Introducing Michelangelo (Little Brown, 1992), Story in a Picture, Vols. I, II (Ideals, 1992, 1993), Frida Kahlo in Mexico (Pomegranate, 1993). *Address:* c/o Rebecca Hossack Gallery, 35 Windmill St., London W1. *Signs work:* "Robin Richmond."

RIDGEWELL, John, A.R.C.A. (1961); artist in oil, printmaking; *b* Halstead, Essex, 26 Dec., 1937; *s* of Herbert Charles Ridgewell. *Educ.:* Earls Colne Grammar School; *studied art* at Colchester Art School (1954-58), R.C.A. (1958-61). *Exhib.:* one-man shows: Austen Hayes Galleries, York (12 exhbns. between 1963 and 1985), Mansard Gallery, Ogilvy and Mather (1970), Upper Grosvenor Gallery, London (1970), Fischer Fine Art, London (1974, 1976, 1979, 1981), Gallery 69, Gothenburg (1976, 1979, 1984), Galleria Academia, Salzburg (1977), Albert White Gallery, Toronto (1978), Solomon Gallery, Dublin (1981), Phoenix Gallery, Lavenham (1986), Art Gallery, Luxembourg (1987, 1988). *Address:* Campion Hill, Wissington, Nayland, Colchester, Essex. *Signs work:* "J. RIDGEWELL."

RIDLEY, Philip, B.A.(Hons.); artist in oil and charcoal; *b* London, 29 Dec., 1962. *Educ.:* St. Martin's School of Art. *Exhib.:* The Vinegar Blossoms. *Address:* c/o Lamont Gallery, 65 Roman Rd., Bethnal Green, London E2 0GN. *Signs work:* "Philip Ridley."

RIGDEN, Geoffrey, N.D.D. (1963), A.R.C.A. (1966); painter/sculptor in acrylic, oil, canvas, wood; visiting artist, Cyprus College of Art; *b* Cheltenham, 22 July, 1943; *s* of John S. Rigden. *Educ.:* King's School, Gloucester, Grammar

School, Weston-super-Mare; *studied art:* Somerset College of Art, Taunton (1960-63, Terence Murphy), R.C.A. (1963-66). *Exhib.:* John Moores Liverpool (prize, 1965), Tolly Cobbold (prize, 1977), Hayward Annual (1980-82); one-man shows: Francis Graham-Dixon Gallery (1988-93). *Work in permanent collections:* Arts Council, Contemporary Art Soc., Eastern Arts Assoc. *Address:* c/o Francis Graham-Dixon Gallery, 17 Gt. Sutton St., London EC1V 0DN. *Signs work:* "Rigden."

RILEY, Bridget, C.B.E. (1972), A.R.C.A.; 1st English painter to win the major Painting Prize at Venice Biennale (1968); painter; *b* London, 1931; *studied art* at Goldsmiths' College of Art; Royal College of Art. *Permanent collections include:* Arts Council, Tate Gallery, V. & A., British Council, Museum of Modern Art, New York, Albright Knox Gallery, Buffalo, Gulbenkian Foundation, Art Gallery of Victoria, Melbourne, Stuyvesant Foundation, Chicago Institute, Whitworth A.G., Manchester, Power Gallery of Contemporary Art, Sydney, Walker A.G., Liverpool, Dept. of the Environment, Fitzwilliam Museum, Cambridge, Scottish National Gallery of Modern Art, Edinburgh, Ulster Museum, Belfast, Museum Boymans van Beuningen, Rotterdam, Stedilijk Museum, Amsterdam, Ohara Museum, Okayama-Ken, National Gallery of Australia, Canberra. *Address:* Karsten Schubert Ltd., 41-42 Foley St., London W1.

RISOE, Paul Schjelderup, Dip. A.D. (Painting) (1968), A.T.C. (1972); landscape painter in acrylic collage on board; Head of Art History Dept., Downe House; *b* Calcutta, 19 Mar., 1945; *s* of V.S. Risoe, M.B.E., B.Sc., C.Eng.F.I.E.E.; *m* Clare Perry; two *s*, one *d*. *Educ.:* Christ College, Brecon; *studied art* at Epsom (1963-65, Leslie Worth), Chelsea (1965-68, Brian Young, Jeremy Moon). *Exhib.:* Young Contemporaries, R.A.; one-man shows, London, Middlesbrough, Newbury; various mixed exhbns. *Work in permanent collection:* B.P. International, Leicester Educ. Authority etc. *Address:* Fencewood House, Slanting Hill, Hermitage, Berks. RG16 9QQ. *Signs work:* "Paul Risoe."

RITCHIE, Paul Stephen, Dip.A.D. (1972); etcher and intaglio printmaker; established and runs, Manchester Etching Workshop; formerly ran, Two Rivers Paper Co. (1984-88); *b* Chatham, 29 Oct., 1948. *Educ.:* Taunton School; *studied art* at Somerset College of Art, Manchester College of Art and Design (Norman Adams, Brendan Neiland), Croydon College of Art. *Exhib.:* R.A., R.S.A., S.A.C., M.A.F.A., Whitworth A.G. *Work in permanent collections:* Arts Council, S.A.C., Johnsonian, S.N.G.M.A., Hunterian, Aberdeen A.G., Salford A.G., Bradford A.G.; Oldham A.G., Rochdale A.G. *Publication:* in conjunction with V. & A. and B.M.: facsimile edition of William Blake's Songs of Innocence and of Experience (1983). *Address:* 91 Northern Gr., West Didsbury, Manchester M20 8NN. *Signs work:* "Paul Ritchie."

RIZVI, Jacqueline Lesley, R.B.A. (1992), R.W.S. (1986), A.R.W.S. (1983), N.E.A.C. (1982), Dip.A.D. (1966); painter; *b* Dewsbury, Yorks., 25 June, 1944; *d* of Fred Haigh Sterry, F.C.A., A.A.C.C.A.; *m* Syed Muzaffar Rizvi; one *d*. *Educ.:* Whitley Bay Grammar School; *studied art* at The Polytechnic, Regent St. (1962-63), Chelsea School of Art (1963-66, Patrick Symons, R.A., Norman Blamey, R.A.). *Exhib.:* R.A., R.I., R.S.M.A., N.E.A.C., R.W.S., City of London Exhbn., Barbican Centre, Exhbn. of Contemporary Art, B.P., Britannic House, I.C.A.F., Bath Festival, London Chamber of Commerce, Sothebys, World of Watercolours, Park Lane, Lineart, Ghent, 20th Century British Art Fair, Minton Fine Art Toronto, Ruthven Gallery, Ohio, Glyndebourne, The Upstairs Gallery, R.A., New Grafton Gallery, The New Academy Gallery, Agnews, National

Trust Foundation for Art, Fosse Gallery, Patterson Gallery, Milne and Moller, Tokyo, St. James' Art Group, The Arts Club, The Hague, Castle Museum, Norwich, Catto Gallery, Waterman Fine Art, Exchange Quay, Manchester, Visions of Venice; S.A.V.E., The Heart of the City, Enchanted Gardens; Duncan Miller; King St. Galleries; Albany Gallery, Cardiff; Driffold Gallery, Sutton Coldfield; Wherry Key Gallery, Ipswich; Malcolm Innes, Edinburgh; Bilbao; Seville; Barcelona; six one-man shows, The Sallyport Tower, Newcastle-upon-Tyne, Cale Art, Chelsea, New Grafton Gallery, The Upstairs Gallery, R.A., The New Academy Gallery. *Work in permanent collections:* mural for The Medical School, St. Mary's Hospital, Paddington; London Underground Ltd., London Clubs Ltd. *Address:* 24 Sunny Gardens Rd., Hendon, London NW4 1RX. *Signs work:* "J.L.R." and year.

RIZZELLO, Michael Gaspard, O.B.E. (1977), Prix de Rome (1951), P.P.S.P.S. (1968-73), P.P.R.B.S. (1976-86), F.C.S.D. (1977); sculptor and chartered designer; *b* London, 2 Apr., 1926; *s* of Arthur Marius Rizzello; *m* Sheila Semple Maguire; one *d. Educ.:* Oratory Boys School; *studied art:* R.C.A. (1947-50), British School in Rome (1951-53). *Work in permanent collections:* London, Cardiff, Dublin and Saudi Arabia, etc.; Welsh National Memorial: David Lloyd George; busts: Sir Thomas Beecham: Royal Opera House, Royal Festival Hall and St. Helens, Lancs.; Nelson Mandela: Dublin, Tanzania and London. *Address:* Melrose Studio, 7 Melrose Rd., London SW18 1ND. *Club:* Reform. *Signs work:* "Rizzello."

ROBARDS, Audrey; R.D.S.Hons.; freelance artist in water-colour, oil, collage; *b* B'ham, 1924; *d* of W.R. Peck, publisher; *m* Jack Robards; two *s*, one *d. Educ.:* Park House School, Malvern; *studied art:* B'ham College of Art (Alex Jackson), Sutton Coldfield College of Art (Dennis Greenwood), Bournville College of Art (Alex Jackson). *Exhib.:* numerous one-man shows in the Midlands. *Work in permanent collections:* hotels, boardrooms, theatres in G.B. and various European venues. *Address:* Ivy Cottage, Main St., Wick Pershore, Worcs. *Clubs:* Stratford on Avon Art Soc., Sutton Coldfield Soc. of Arts, Worcs. Soc. of Arts. *Signs work:* "Audrey Robards."

ROBERT, Mary, M.A. (1985), B.A. (1973; photographer and graphpic artist in photographic and mixed media; Senior lecturer and Lens Media Programme Co-ordinator at Richmond International University, London; Tutor in Photography, Royal College of Art; *b* Atlanta, Georgia, 11 Dec., 1951; *d* of R.R. Robert, engineers. *Educ.:* Miami University, Oxford, Ohio; University of Akron, Akron, Ohio; R.C.A., London. *Work in permanent collections:* Biblioteque Nationale, Paris, N.P.G. London, and private collections in U.S.A., Britain, Europe, Asia. *Address:* 47 Creffield Rd., London W5 3RR. *Signs work:* "Mary Robert."

ROBERTS, Gladys Gregory, R.C.A.; artist in oil and acrylic; *b* Rhyl; *d* of C. Wesley Haslam, surveyor; *m* Prof. E. J. Roberts, M.A., M.Sc. (decd.); one *d. Educ.:* Pendre Private School, Prestatyn; *studied art* at Bangor Technical College (1959-63). *Exhib.:* Royal Cambrian Academy of Art, Tegfryn Gall., Menai Bridge, Anglesey. *Address:* "Bryn Llinos", Victoria Drive, Bangor LL57 2EY. *Signs work:* "G. Roberts."

ROBERTS, John Vivian, R.W.S., R.E., A.R.C.A., R.C.A.; artist in acrylic, mixed intaglio media, water-colour; *b* Tredegar, Mon., 26 Jan., 1923; *s* of Goronwy Roberts; *m* Gwendoline Thomas; one *s*, one *d. Educ.:* Cathays High School, Cardiff; *studied art* at Cardiff School of Art (1939-42), Royal College of Art (1947-51), Engraving School under Prof. Robert Austin. *Work in* *permanent collections:* Arts Council, Nat. Mus. of Wales. *Publications:* books illustrated for a variety of publishers. *Address:* Ty Meini 16 Cross Sq., St. Davids, Dyfed. *Signs work:* "John Roberts."

ROBERTS, Marguerite Hazel: see HARRISON, Marguerite Hazel.

ROBERTS, Phyllis Kathleen, R.O.I. (1961); Paris Salon Silver Medal (1959) and Gold Medal (1964); portrait and landscape painter in oil, and sculptor; *b* London, 11 June, 1916; *d* of Ernest Hart Aspden; *m* A. Gwynne Roberts, F.C.I.I. *Educ.:* Clifton College, London; *studied art* at Hornsey College of Art. *Exhib.:* R.A., Paris Salon, R.O.I., N.E.A.C., R.B.A., R.P., Contemporary Portrait Society, and principal provincial municipal art galleries, etc. *Work in private collections:* British Isles, France, Portugal, Spain, etc. *Publications:* articles in Leisure Painter. *Address:* Wisteria Cottage, 23 Westingway, Aldwick, Bognor Regis, W. Sussex PO21 2XU. *Signs work:* see appendix.

ROBERTS, Walter James, F.R.S.A.; artist in water-colour, oil, polymer and black and white; retired civil servant; Agricola Art Club (1956–), Soc. of Staffordshire Artists (1961–), chairman, Crewe Music and Arts Soc. (1964-75) (President 1987); *b* Doncaster, 10 Dec., 1907; *s* of J. H. A. Roberts; *m* Edith Wareing; two *s. Educ.:* Doncaster Grammar School; *studied art* at Doncaster School of Art under F. J. Glass. *Exhib.:* London and provincial galleries, SS. Queen Mary, Laguna Beach, London Gallery, L.A., Art Collectibles, Ventura, California. *Work in permanent collections:* Stoke-on-Trent, Santa Paula, California; National Trust, Cheshire C.C., Crewe and Nantwich Borough Council. *Address:* 591 Crewe Rd., Wistaston, Crewe CW2 6PU. *Signs work:* see appendix.

ROBERTS, Will, R.C.A.; Bynge-Stamper Prize (awarded by Lord Clark, 1962); Welsh expressionist painter; draws and paints figures in landscape, religious themes, flowers; born and lives in Wales; *m*; one *d. Studied art* at Swansea School of Art (1930's); began painting after war service in R.A.F. *Exhib.:* first one-man shows, London (1954); Arts Council tour (1962-63); London Group, John Moores; retrospective exhbn. Llandaff Festival (1973), N.E.A.C., R.A. *Work in permanent collections:* National Museum of Wales, City of Coventry, City of Hereford, Contemporary Art Soc., Arts Council, Steel Corp., B.P. Llandarcy, B.P. Chemicals, and private collections; film feature B.B.C. *Address:* 10 Bilton Rd., Neath SA11 1YU. *Signs work:* "Will R."

ROBERTS-JONES, Ivor, C.B.E. (1975), R.A.; sculptor; *b* 2 Nov., 1913; *s* of William Roberts-Jones, solicitor and Welsh International footballer. *Educ.:* Worksop College; *studied art* at Goldsmiths' College and Royal Academy Schools. *Exhib.:* R.A., R.B.S., John Moore, Battersea Park, Margham Sculpture Park, etc. *Work in permanent collections:* Tate Gallery, N.P.G., Beaverbrook Foundation, New Brunswick, Arts Council, Welsh Arts Council; National Museum, Cardiff. *Public commissions* include Augustus John Memorial (Fordingbridge), Sir Winston Churchill (Parliament Sq., and also in Oslo and New Orleans), The Attlee Memorial, Houses of Parliament, "Janus Rider" group, Harlech Castle, Rupert Brooke Memorial, Rugby (1987), Field Marshal Slim (1990), Lord Alanbrooke (1993). *Portrait commissions* include H.R.H. The Duke of Edinburgh, H.R.H. The Prince of Wales, Yehudi Menuhin, Somerset Maugham, Speaker George Thomas, Geraint Evans, etc. *Work repro.:* British Art since 1900 (John Rothenstein), British Sculptors (Tiranti), Architectural Review, etc. *Address:* The Bridles, Hall La., Shimpling, nr. Diss, Norfolk IP21 4UH. *Signs work:* see appendix.

ROBERTSON, Anderson Bain, D.A. (1955), A.T.C. (1956), B.A.Hons. (1982); painter in oil and water-colour; formerly Principal Art Master, Prestwick Academy; *b* Bristol, 22 Oct., 1929; *s* of Mungo Robertson; *m* Mary M.M. Christie; two *s. Educ.:* Ardrossan Academy, Ayrshire; *studied art* at Gray's School of Art, Aberdeen (1951-52, Robert Sivell), Glasgow School of Art (1952-55, 1981-82, David A. Donaldson, William Armour, Jack Knox). *Exhib.:* R.S.A., R.S.W., R.G.I., S.S.A., R.P. Work in many private collections. *Address:* "Window Rock", Sandy Beach, Innellan, Argyll PA23 7TR. *Club:* Glasgow Art. *Signs work:* "Anderson B. Robertson."

ROBERTSON, Barbara Janette, D.A. (1970), S.S.A. (1974), Lily MacDougall, S.S.W.A. (1975); printmaker in linoprint, part-time lecturer; *b* Broughty Ferry, Dundee, 16 Aug., 1945; *d* of James Fleming Robertson, inn-keeper. *Educ.:* Blairgowrie High School; *studied art* at Duncan of Jordanstone College of Art, Dundee (1965-71) under Ron Stenberg, Josef Sekalski. *Exhib.:* Aberdeen Art Centre, Print Exchange, Galerie Tendenz; Contributor R.S.A. (1973-75), Prints in Folios of Compass Gallery, Glasgow, Glasgow Print Workshop, Molesey Gallery, Kingston on Thames. *Work in permanent collections:* Leeds, Aberdeen, Glasgow, Stirling, Angus. *Publications:* illustrated The Cuckoo's Nest by Carl McDougall; The Oath Takers, Sea Green Ribbons, by Naomi Mitchison. *Address:* 10 The Row, Douglastown, Forfar DD8 1TL, Scotland. *Signs work:* "Barbara Robertson."

ROBERTSON, Richard Ross, F.R.B.S. (1963), R.S.A. (1977); sculptor in clay, wood, stone; retd. lecturer, Aberdeen Art College; *b* Aberdeen, 1914; *s* of Rev. R.R. Robertson, M.A., B.D.; *m* Kathleen Hatts; two *d. Studied art:* Glasgow and Aberdeen Schools of Art (1934-38, Benno Schotz, T.B. Huxley Jones). *Exhib.:* R.S.A. Edinburgh, Glasgow Inst., Open Eye Gallery, Kingfisher Gallery Edinburgh. *Work in permanent collections:* Aberdeen A.G., Peterhead A.G., Metropolitan Gallery, N.Y., Boston University. *Address:* Creaguir, Rosemount, Woodlands Rd., Blairgowrie. *Signs work:* "R.R. Robertson."

ROBERTSON, Seonaid Mairi, Dip. in Design and Crafts, Edinburgh (1935), A.T.D., Postgrad. Dip. in Psychology, London University (1947); educator, lecturer, craftswoman; fellow of Edinburgh College of Art (1944-47), and senior lecturer, Bretton Hall (1948-54), Senior Research Fellow in Educ., Leeds University (1954-57), Deputy Head A.T.C. Goldsmiths' College, London (retd.); *b* Perth, Scotland; *d* of Theodore Robertson. *Educ.:* Edinburgh University and College of Art. Visiting Prof. or Lecturer in six U.S.A. Universities, and in Brazil. Founder/Mem. W.C.C., I.N.S.E.A., British Soc. of Aesthetics. *Exhib.:* London, Manchester, Edinburgh and the U.S.A. *Publications:* Creative Crafts in Education, Rosegarden and Labyrinth, Dyes from Plants, Using Natural Materials, articles in Craftsman Potter, Studio Potter, Parabola, etc. *Address:* 3 Seaview Ct., Selsey PO20 0JS. *Signs work:* "S.M.R."

ROBERTSON, Sheila Macleod, R.S.M.A., S.W.A., Mem. St. Ives Society of Artists; artist in oil, water-colour and animal studies in wire sculpture; *b* London, 1927; *d* of A. L. Robertson, chartered accountant. *Educ.:* St. Michael's School, Leigh-on-Sea; *studied art* at Watford Art School, Central School of Arts and Crafts. *Exhib.:* R.O.I., R.S.M.A., S.W.A. and St. Ives. *Work in permanent collection:* National Maritime Museum. *Address:* 18 Clarkfield, Mill End, Rickmansworth, Herts. *Signs work:* "S. M. ROBERTSON" and see appendix.

ROBINSON, Basil William, F.B.A., F.S.A., M.A., B.Litt. (1938); museum curator (retd. 1976); deputy keeper, Victoria and Albert Museum (1954), keeper (1966), Keeper Emeritus (1972); President, Royal Asiatic Society (1970-73); *b*

London, 20 June, 1912; *s* of William Robinson, Life Assurance sec.; *m* 1st., Ailsa Mary Stewart (decd. 1954); 2nd, 1958, Oriel Hermione Steel; one *s*, one *d*. *Educ.:* Winchester, Corpus Christi (Oxford). *Publications:* A Primer of Japanese Sword Blades (1955), Descriptive Catalogue of the Persian Paintings in the Bodleian Library (1958) and other books, booklets, articles and reviews on Persian and Japanese Art. *Address:* 41 Redcliffe Gdns., London SW10.

ROBINSON, Hilary, B.A.(Hons.) (1979), M.A. (1987); lecturer, writer, artist; lecturer, History and Theory of Art, University of Ulster; *b* U.K., 25 June, 1956. *Educ.:* John Mason School, Abingdon; *studied art* at University of Newcastle upon Tyne (1975-79, Prof. Kenneth Rowntree), R.C.A. (1985-87, Prof. Christopher Frayling). *Exhib.:* U.K., Italy, Hungary. *Publications:* author: Visibly Female: Feminism and Art Today (Camden Press 1987, Universe (N.Y.) 1988), The Rough Guide to Venice (1989, 1993); many catalogue essays including: Mothers, Ikon Gallery, Birmingham (1990), Sounding the Depths, I.M.M.A., Dublin (1992); Editor, Alba (1990-92). *Address:* Dept. of Fine Art, University of Ulster, Belfast BT15 1ED.

ROBINSON, Ivor, M.B.E., Hon. Fellow, Oxford Brookes University; artist, bookbinder; President, Designer Bookbinders (1968-73); *b* 28 Oct., 1924; *m*; one *s*, one *d*. *Studied:* Bournemouth College of Art (1939-42). Royal Navy (1942-45). Lecturer: Salisbury College of Art (1946-52), London School of Printing and Graphic Arts (1953-58), Oxford Polytechnic (1959-89). *Exhib.:* one-man shows: Hantverket, Stockholm (1963), Galleria del Bel Libro, Ascona (1969). *Work in permanent collections:* B.M., V. & A., Swedish Royal Library, Danish Royal Library, Royal Library, The Hague; Röhsska Museum, Gothenburg; Bodleian Library, Oxford; Crafts Council Collection, London. *Publication:* Introducing Bookbinding (Oxford Polytechnic Press 1984). *Address:* Trindles, Holton, Oxford OX33 1PZ. *Signs work:* "IR" and date.

ROBINSON, John Edward; self taught sculptor in bronze and tapestry; *b* London, 4 May, 1935; *s* of L. B. Robinson; *m* Margaret; three *s*. *Educ.:* Melbourne Grammar, Sandroyd, Rugby. *Permanent exhib.:* Freeland Gallery, London, and Beaver Galleries, Canberra, Australia. *Work in permanent collections:* Canberra, Melbourne, Sydney, Seattle, London, Portsmouth, Glyndebourne, Harrogate, Canada, Hawaii. *Commissions 1985:* 33 ft. high Pole Vaulter for Canberra, Australia; 50 ft. high sculpture of The Acrobats for Melbourne, Australia. *Address:* Freeland Gallery, 18 Albemarle St., London W1. *Club:* Atheneum, Melbourne. *Signs work:* see appendix.

ROBINSON, Oliver J.; Art Editor, National Magazine Co. (1930-46); Editor-in-Chief, Good Housekeeping (1947-67); Production Director, National Magazine Co. (1968-78); *b* 7 Apr., 1908; *s* of Heath Robinson, artist; *m*. *Educ.:* Cranleigh School. *Address:* 92 Charlbert Ct., London NW8. *Clubs:* Savage, London Sketch.

ROBINSON, Peter Lyell, B.A.(Hons.) (Geog. Geol.); sculptor in clay, plaster, bronze, stone; *b* Melbourne, Australia, 12 Apr., 1962; *m* Kate MacNab; one *s*. *Educ.:* King's School, Bruton; *studied art* at Durham University. Apprenticed to sculptor John Robinson (1987-90). *Exhib.:* Art Scene London, Arlesford Gallery Hants., Beaver Galleries, Australia. *Address:* Bralorne, Charlton Horethorne, Sherborne, Dorset DT9 4PQ. *Signs work:* "LYELL."

ROBINSON, Sonia, R.S.M.A. (1979), S.W.A. (1990), N.S.A. (1977); paints in oil, gouache and water-colour; Chairman, St. Ives Soc. of Artists; *b* Stockport, 24 May, 1927; *d* of Philip Robinson, C.B.E., company director. *Educ.:* Glasgow

High School; Manchester High School; Copthall School, Mill Hill, London; *studied art:* Manchester School of Art (1943-45, Principal John Holmes), Hornsey School of Art (1945-47, Russell Reeve). *Exhib.:* London: R.S.M.A., R.I., Singer and Friedlander (F.B.A. Galleries), S.W.A. (Westminster Galleries), Orangery, Holland Park, Heals, Thackeray Gallery and St. Katherine's Dock; shared R.S.M.A. exhbns. at Guildford House Gallery and Century Gallery, Datchet; solo show at Coach House Gallery, Guernsey (1990); exhbns. abroad: Mystic, Connecticut, U.S.A., Prouds, Sydney, Australia, and Pont Aven, France; Cornwall: St. Ives Soc. of Artists, Newlyn Soc. of Artists, Trellisick and Horizon Galleries. *Address:* 3 Paul La., Mousehole, Penzance, Cornwall TR19 6TR. *Signs work:* "SR" on oils; "Sonia Robinson" on gouaches and water-colours.

ROBINSON, Virginia Susanne Douglas; artist in pastel, oil, acrylic; *b* London, 27 July, 1933; *d* of the late Douglas Stannus Gray, R.P.; *m* Lowther. *Educ.:* privately; *studied art* at Brighton College of Art, R.A.S. *Exhib.:* R.A., Bradford, York, Cheltenham, Gottingen, Annecy. *Address:* 49 The Green, Southwick, Brighton BN42 4FY. *Club:* Cheltenham Group of Artists. *Signs work:* "Virginia S.D. Robinson."

ROBOZ, Zsuzsi; painter in oils, acrylics, pencil and charcoal, sculptor in clay; *b* Budapest; *m.* Studied art at Regent St. Polytechnic, R.A. under Peter Greenham, and in Florence under Annigoni. *Work in permanent collections:* Museum of Fine Arts, Budapest, National Portrait Gallery, Tate Gallery, V. & A., Royal Festival Hall, London, Bradford Museum, Graves A.G., Sheffield. *Publications:* Eux et Elles, Dix ans d'Arts Graphiques, La Femme dans l'art contemporain, Les Arts en Europe, Women and Men's Daughters, Chichester 10—Portrait of a Decade, British Ballet To-day, British Art Now with E. Lucie-Smith (1993). *Address:* The Studio, 76 Eccleston Sq. Mews, London SW1. *Signs work:* "Roboz."

ROBSON, Hugh Mather; artist in oil, gouache, pen and ink; *b* Hinckley, Leics., 28 June, 1929; *m* Barbara Ann Mills; four *d. Educ.:* Hinckley Grammar School; *studied fine art* at St. Martin's School of Art (1945-49, William Craig, Russell Hall); Slade School of Art (1949-53, Lucien Freud, Sam Carter, tutor). *Exhib.:* Arthur Jeffress, Trafford Gallery, Windsor Fine Arts, King St. Gallery, Mallets at Bourdon House, Colefax and Fowler, Nina Campbell's and Stephanie Hoppens Gallery. *Murals* include Crockfords, Park Lane Hotel, Belfry Club, Capital Hotel, 45 Park Lane, Croix des Gardes and many private houses. Visuals of gardens for Peter Coats; visuals of interiors for Interior decorators including John Siddley, Nina Campbell and Colefax and Fowler. Fabric designs for Nina Campbell. Bookplates, letterheads and tile designs. A series of Genre Singerie water-colours (96 to date), also a series of 20 military pansy figures (signed EWL). *Publications:* articles in House and Garden, Country Life, Connaissance des Arts, World of Interiors, Harpers, Southern Accents, etc. *Address:* 47 Loraine Rd., London N7 6HB. *Signs work:* "Hugh Robson." or "H. M. Robson."

ROCHE, Laurence, N.D.D., D.A.(Edin.), G.R.A.; marine, landscape and industrial painter; Company Artist to A.S.W. (Holdings) plc.; *b* Goodwick, Pembs., 1 May, 1944; *m* Helen Pollock, D.A.(Edin.). *Educ.:* Fishguard County Secondary School; Swansea College of Art (1961-65); Edinburgh College of Art (1965-68); Postgrad. scholarship; Moray House College of Educ., Edinburgh (1969-79). Many group and one-man exhbns. *Work in private and corporate collections:* in U.K. and abroad. *Address:* 16 Belmont Rd., Stroud, Glos. GL5 1HH. *Signs work:* "Laurence Roche."

RÖDER, Endre Zoltán Eugene; painter in oil on canvas and board; formerly art teacher in secondary schools, art gallery educ. officer, senior lecturer (Art History); *b* Budapest, 17 Aug., 1933; *s* of Pál Röder, journalist (decd.); *m* Carole; two *s*. *Educ.*: St. John's College, Southsea; *studied art:* Sheffield College of Art (1956-60, W.S. Taylor, Eric Jones). *Exhib.*: R.O.I., various Open Shows (provinces), but generally in private galleries in England, Scotland and U.S.A. *Work in permanent collections:* Sheffield City A.Gs., Sheffield University, etc. *Address:* 50 Clifford Rd., Sheffield S11 9AQ. *Signs work:* "RÖDER."

RODGER, Willie, A.R.S.A. (1989); artist in lino and wood cuts; *b* Kirkintilloch, 3 Mar., 1930; *s* of Robert Gilmour Rodger, pawnbroker (decd.); *m* Anne Henry, illustrator; two *s*, two *d. Educ.*: Lenzie Academy; *studied art* at Glasgow School of Art (1948-53, Lennox Paterson). *Exhib.*: many one-man since 1964, also group in U.K. and abroad, including R.S.A., R.A., S.S.A., R.G.I.F.A., Glasgow Group, 'In Between the Lines' retrospective, Collins Gallery, Glasgow (1986). *Work in permanent collections:* V. & A., S.A.C., numerous public collections in U.K. *Publications:* Scottish Historical Playing Cards (1975); illustrated, The Field of Thistles (1983). *Address:* Stenton, Bellevue Rd., Kirkintilloch G66 1AP. *Signs work:* "Willie Rodger."

RODGERS, Harry Stewart; painter in acrylic, pastel; *b* Stamford, 18 July, 1920; *s* of Charles E. Rodgers, C.M.B.H.I.; *m* Pamela. *Educ.*: Stamford School; *studied art* with Ian Macnab (1951-52). *Exhib.*: Boston, Stamford, London, Dublin. *Work in permanent collection:* Lincolnshire Arts. *Address:* 1 Tinwell Rd., Stamford, Lincs. PE9 2QQ. *Club:* R.A.F.A. *Signs work:* "H.S. Rodgers" or "Roger."

RODWELL, Jenny, B.A. Fine Art (1967), R.A.Dip. (1970); painter in oil, water-colour, acrylic; *b* Zimbabwe, 1946. *Studied art* at St. Martin's School of Art and R.A. Schools. *Exhib.*: Young Contemporaries, R.A. Summer Show. *Publications:* author: Paintings with Acrylics; Painting Portraits; Flower Painting; Complete Guide to Water-colour Painting; illustrated several children's books. *Address:* The Warren, Edale, nr. Sheffield S30 2ZD. *Signs work:* "J.R."

ROGERS, John Rowland; painter, mainly landscapes, in water-colour and oil; Art Com., W.A.C.; *b* Cardiff, 28 May, 1939; *s* of Ronald Edwin Rogers; *m*; three *s*. *Studied art:* Cardiff (John Roberts, Phil Jennings, David Tinker). *Exhib.*: R.S.M.A., I.C.A., W.A.C. (touring), Mostyn Gallery, Wales, Edwin Pollard Gallery, London, John Rogers' retrospective touring (1991). *Work in permanent collections:* Haverfordwest County Museum, West Wales Arts, W.A.C., Museum and A.G., Newport, Gwent, National Library of Wales, Aberystwyth. *Address:* Peter's La., St. Davids SA62 6SD, Wales. *Signs work:* "John Rogers."

ROGERS, Joseph Shepperd (Nevia), B.A. (1967), M.F.A. (1969), Instructor, Corcoran School of Art, Columbia Inst. of Art (1970-72), M.P.S.G.S (Jamieson Award, 1982); artist in oil and collage; V.P., American Art League Admission Com., Arts Club of Washington; *b* Washington, D.C., 10 Mar., 1943; *s* of the late James Webb Rogers, LL.B., developer. *Educ.*: Longfellow School for Boys, Bethesda, Md.; *studied art* at Corcoran School of Art, D.C., Greensboro College, N.C., (Irene Cullis, U.N.C.G., M.F.A., Gilbert Carpenter, Peter Agostini, Stephen Antonakos), American University (Dr. Turak). *Exhib.*: "Five American Artists" Galerie Geilsdorfer, Köln, W. Germany (1982), "Art on Paper" Weatherspoon Gallery, U.N.C.G. (1970-80), "New Members" Spectrum Gallery, Georgetown, D.C.: seven one-man shows, etc. *Work in permanent collections:* University of Maryland, "Maryland Collection", main altar collage, Chapel,

Bishop Dennis J. O'Connell School, Arlington, Va. *Address:* Bealls Pleasure, P.O. Box 1268, Landover, Md., U.S.A. *Clubs:* Soc. of Architectural Historians, Arts Club of Washington, N. Va. Fine Arts Assoc., American Assoc. of Museums. *Signs work:* see appendix.

ROGERS, Richard George, M.Arch., R.I.B.A.; Richard Rogers Partnership, Rogers P.A. Technical and Science Centre; Piano and Rogers, France; *b* 23 July, 1933; *m*; three *s*; *m* Ruth Elias (1973); two *s*. *Educ.:* Architectural Assoc. (graduate, Dip.); Yale Univ. (Fulbright, Edward D. Stone, and Yale Scholar, M.Arch), R.I.B.A.; Chairman, Tate Gallery (1984); Royal Gold Medal for Architecture (1985); Royal Academician; Hon. Fellow Royal Academy of the Hague; Hon. Fellow American Institute of Architects; Saarinen Professor Yale University (1985); Mem. United Nations Architects Committee; IBM Fellow; Mem. R.I.B.A. Council; Visiting Lecturer/Professor: U.C.L.A., Princeton, Harvard, Berkeley, Cornell U.S.A., McGill Canada, Hong Kong University, Aachen Germany, Cambridge University England. Winner of internat. competition from 680 entries for Centre Pompidou (1 million sq. ft. in Paris for Min. of Culture) (1977); winner of Lloyd's internat. competition for 600,000 sq. ft. Headquarters in City of London (1978). *Projects* include: Music res. centre for Pierre Boulez and Min. of Cultural Affairs, Paris (1977); B. & B. Factory, Como, Italy (1972); P.A. Science Lab. Princeton, U.S.A. (1984); Urban Conservation, Florence Italy (1984); HQ Wellcome Pharmaceuticals Esher U.K. (1984); Cummins/Fleetguard factory, Quimper, France (1980); Electronics Factory for Reliance Controls Ltd., Swindon U.K. (1967); P.A. Technology Centre, Phases 1, 2 and 3, near Cambridge U.K. (1975); Inmos semi-conductor manufg. facilit, Newport, S. Wales (1982). *Prizes* include: Fin. Times Indust. Arch. Award for Most Outstanding Indust. Bldg. 1967, (Reliance Controls, Swindon), and 1976 (Patscentre) and 1983 (Inmos); Auguste Perret Prize, Internat. Union of Architects (1978), Premier Europeo Umberto Biancamano (1979), Royal Institute of British Architects Research Award (1970), Royal Institute of British Architects Commendations (1976), British Steel Structural Design Award (1975, 1982), Eurostructpress Award (1983), Architectural Design Awards (1964, 1965, 1968). Subject of BBC documentary, Building for Change (1980). *Publications* incl. contribs. to Architectural Design, Global Arch. and Arch. and Urbanism. Monograph. G.A. Beaubourg. *Offices and studios* at Thames Wharf, Rainville Rd., London. *Address:* 18 Belsize Grove, London NW3 4UM.

ROMER, Caroline Eve; Byam Shaw Dip. (Painting); painter in oil, water-colour, etching; *b* Braughing, Herts., 25 Sept., 1955; *d* of Mark L.R. Romer, barrister-at-law; *m* David Marzo; three *d*. *Educ.:* Ware Grammar School for Girls; *studied art* at Cambridge Polytechnic (1972-73), Byam Shaw School of Art (1974-76). *Exhib.:* R.A., R.B.A., N.E.A.C.; one-man shows, Brotherton Gallery (2), Prades Festival, Thackeray Gallery (1989, 1991). *Addresses:* Casa Rectoral, Gabas, Esterri-de-Aneu, Prov. de Lerida, Spain; The Old Vicarage, Braughing, Ware, Herts. *Signs work:* "C.E. Romer."

ROMER, Philippa Maynard; portrait painter in oil; *b* Hitchin, Herts; *d* of Maynard Tomson, M.C., F.R.I.C.S. *Studied art* at Cambridge School of Art and R.A. Schools. *Exhib.:* R.A., R.P., R.B.A., N.E.A.C., S.W.A. *Address:* The Old Vicarage, Braughing, nr. Ware, Herts. SG11 2QR.

RONN: see HILL, Ronald James.

ROONEY, Michael John, N.D.D. (1964), A.R.C.A., M.A. (1967), A.R.A. (1990); painter in gouache, water-colour, tempera, oil; Lecturer in painting,

Royal Academy Schools; *b* Epsom, 1944; *s* of John Rooney, steel fixer (decd.); *m* (1) Patricia Anne (divorced); one *s*, one *d*; (2) Alexandra; one *s*. *Studied art:* Sutton School of Art (1959-62, E. Bulley, C. Clairmonte), Wimbledon School of Art (G. Cooper, N. Stokoe), R.C.A. (Prof. C. Weight, C.B.E., Ruskin Spear, Roger de Grey, Peter Blake). *Exhib.:* R.A. Summer Shows (1978-90), Mercury Gallery, Arts Council touring, Hunting Group annual, Tolly Cobbold, also Amsterdam, The Hague, etc. *Work in permanent collections:* Hove Museum, Towner Museum, S.E. Arts, Rye A.G., University of Aston, Museo Ralli, Uraguay. *Address:* The Old Sorting House, 19 Alder Rd., Mortlake, London SW14 8ER. *Clubs:* Chelsea Arts, Dover St. Arts. *Signs work:* "Rooney."

ROPER, Geoffrey John; painter in oil and water-colour; *b* Nottingham, 30 July, 1942; *s* of Tom Roper, O.B.E., political agent. *Educ.:* Manvers School, Nottingham Sec. Art School; *studied art* at Nottingham College of Art (1958-60); Edinburgh College of Art (1960-65) under Sir Robin Philipson, P.R.S.A. *Exhib.:* Fine Art Society (1972, 1974, 1975, 1977, 1980, 1988), Teesside A.G. (1972), Great King St. Gallery, Edinburgh (1970, 1971, 1972), Middlesbrough Civic A.G. (1968), King St. Gallery, Dublin (1968), David Letham, Edinburgh (1968, 1969), Douglas Foulis Gallery, Edinburgh (1967), William St. Gallery, Edinburgh (1964, 1965, 1966), Silver Coin Gallery, Harrogate (1965, 1966). *Work in permanent collections:* Middlesbrough Civic Art Galleries, Edinburgh New Town Conservation Com., New University of N. Ireland. *Address:* Whinstane Cottage, Midcalder, W. Lothian EH53 0HR. *Signs work:* see appendix.

ROSCINI, Count M., F.R.S.A. (1967), M.F.P.S. (1985), B.A. (1960); sculptor in bronze; *b* Rome, 22 Dec., 1933; divorced; one *d*. *Educ.:* Rome and Cambridge University; *studied art* at Accademia dell'Art Rome. *Exhib.:* Hamilton Gallery, Drian Gallery, Loggia Gallery, Salon de Provence, Grenoble, Tevere Expo Rome. *Work in permanent collections:* Morristown N.J., Manilla, Lambeth Palace. *Work repro.:* Sounds of the Cross by David Owen. *Address:* 19A Annandale Rd., Greenwich, London SE10 0DD. *Signs work:* "Roscini."

ROSE, Diana Cecilia, M.F.P.S. (1976); artist in oil; *b* Chiswick, 12 June, 1921; *d* of H. V. Base; *m* Donald Rose. *Educ.:* Lourdes Mount Convent, Ealing and Westcliff High School for Girls, Westcliff-on-Sea; *studied art* at Southend-on-Sea Art School (1948-60 part-time) under Leo Hardy; St. Martin's Art School (1946-47) under A. Ziegler. *Exhib.:* Whitechapel A.G., Mall Galleries, Trends, Barbican A.G., Beecroft A.G., Southend-on-Sea. *Work in private collections* in Britain, U.S.A. and Sweden. *Address:* 19B Cliff Parade, Leigh-on-Sea, Essex SS9 1AS.

ROSE, Muriel (Miss), R.O.I. (1966), R.B.A. (1968), W.I.A.C. (1967), F.F.P.S., N.S.; painter in oils, designer, printmaker, ceramic sculptor, potter; Lecturer in ceramics and painting in Adult Education; *b* London, 1923; *d* of H. C. Rose, F.C.A. *Educ.:* Richmond Grammar School; *studied art* at Richmond School of Art, pottery at Hammersmith College of Art. *Exhib.:* R.A., R.B.A., R.O.I., Royal Scottish Academy, R.W.A., Paris Salon, Gallery Creuze, Paris, U.S.A., South Africa, National Museum of Wales, Glasgow Institute of the Fine Arts. *Work in permanent collections:* Oxford, Nottingham E.C., Herts E.C., Welsh E.C., Univ. of Texas A.G., Danish Court of Justice, Lady Docker, Mrs. Michael Foot, etc. *Address:* 9 Temple Sheen, London SW14. *Signs work:* "Muriel Rose."

ROSEMAN, Stanley, B.F.A. (1967), M.F.A. (1972); painter, engraver, draughtsman and sculptor in oil, drypoint, engraving, chalk, pen and ink, bronze;

b Boston, Mass., 4 Sept., 1945; *s* of Bernard Roseman. *Studied art:* Cooper Union College of Art and Architecture, N.Y.C. (1965-67), Pratt Inst., N.Y.C. (1970-72). *Exhib.:* one-man shows, N.Y.C., Zurich, Vienna, Oxford, Dublin, London, Bordeaux, Haarlem, Brussels, Washington. *Work in permanent collections:* (among others) V. & A.; Ashmolean; National Gallery of Art, Washington D.C.; Los Angeles County Museum of Art; Dallas Museum of Art; Denver Art Museum; New Orleans Museum of Art; Bibliothèque Nationale, Paris; Musée des Beaux-Arts, Rouen; Cabinet des Dessins, Strasbourg; Musée des Beaux-Arts, Bordeaux; Musée Ingres, Montauban; Museum of Modern Art, Brussels; Bibliothèque Royale, Brussels; Teylers Museum, Haarlem; Prentenkabinet der Rijksuniversiteit, Leyden; Museum of Modern Art, Rio de Janeiro; National Museum of Wales, Cardiff; National Gallery of Ireland, Dublin; Vatican Museum, Rome; Staatliche Graphische Sammlung, Munich; Museum of Fine Art, Budapest; Israel Museum, Jerusalem; Albertina, Vienna; China Museum of Fine Arts, Beijing; H.M. The Queen. *Addresses:* Irne Davioud, 75016 Paris; and Postfach 66, 3780 Gstaad, Switzerland. *Signs work:* see appendix.

ROSEN, Ismond, M.B., B.Ch. (1946), D.P.M. (1951), Witwatersrand M.D. (1954), Associate Mem. British Institute of Psycho-analysis (1959), (Member, 1971), F.R.C.Psych. (1971); psychiatrist, sculptor, painter, photographer; *b* Johannesburg, S. Africa, 2 Aug., 1924; *s* of Harry Rosen. *Educ.:* Witwatersrand University; *studied art:* mainly self-taught and at Academie Julien and Ecole des Beaux Arts, Paris (1952), Regent St. Polytechnic. *Exhib.:* S. African Academy; private shows, Johannesburg (1949); Pretoria (1951); one-man shows: John Whibley Gallery, Cork St., London (1972), "Genesis" Borough of Camden, Camden Arts Centre, (1974), "Sinai as Inspiration" Camden Arts Centre, Royal Free Hospital, Nikon Gallery, London (1982), R.A. *Work in permanent collections:* in many London medical insts. especially Royal Society of Medicine, Royal College of Psychiatrists; full-size bronze figure – "The Revelation" presented by CCJ to Pope John-Paul II and is in The Vatican; "Holocaust Sculptures" exhbn., St. Paul's Cathedral, London (Oct. 1992-May 1993). *Address:* Charlecote, 3 Hampstead Hill Gdns., London NW3 2PH. *Club:* Fellow Soc. of Portrait Sculptors. *Signs work:* "Ismond Rosen."

ROSMAR: see BOOTH, Rosa-Maria.

ROSOMAN, Leonard, O.B.E. (1981), A.R.A. (1960), R.A. (1970); artist and teacher; teacher of illustration, Camberwell School of Art; teacher of mural decoration, Edinburgh College of Art; tutor at the Royal College of Art, London; *b* Hampstead, London, 27 Oct., 1913; *s* of Henry Rosoman. *Educ.:* Deacons School, Peterborough; *studied art* at King Edward VII School of Art, Durham University; Central School of Arts and Crafts; R.A. School. *Exhib.:* Fine Art Society, Roland, Browse & Delbanco, Leicester Galleries, Leger Gallery, St. George's Gallery, Sheffield, Bradford, Edinburgh, Dublin, and provincial galleries, and Lincoln Center, N.Y., State University of New York at Albany. *Address:* 7 Pembroke Studios, Pembroke Gdns., London W8 6HX. *Signs work:* "Leonard Rosoman."

ROSS, Alastair Robertson, O.St.J., F.R.B.S., A.R.S.A.; sculptor; Lecturer in Fine Art, Duncan of Jordanstone College of Art, Dundee; D.A. (1965), Postgrad. (1966), F.R.S.A. (1966), F.S.A.Scot. (1971), A.R.B.S. (1968), F.R.B.S. (1975), A.R.S.A. (1980), Mem. of Council, S.S.A. (1972-75), Scottish Mem. of Council, R.B.S. (1972-), Vice Pres., R.B.S. (1988-90); *b* Perth, Scotland, 1941; *s* of Alastair J. Ross, F.S.A. Scot.; *m* Kathryn Wilson; one *d. Educ.:* St. Mary's

Episcopal School, Dunblane, McLaren High School, Callander; Duncan of Jordanstone College of Art, Dundee. *Awards:* Dickson Prize (1962), Holokrome Award (1962), S.E.D. Travelling Scholarship (1963), R.S.A. Chalmers Bursary (1964), R.S.A. Carnegie Travelling Scholarship (1965), Duncan of Drumfork Scholarship (1965), S.E.D. Post-grad. Scholarship (1965-66), bronze and silver medallist Paris Salon, Sir William Gillies award of R.S.A. (1989), Sir Otto Beit Medal of R.B.S. (1989), Freeman of the City of London (1989). Work in numerous collections in this country and abroad. *Address:* Ravenscourt, 28 Albany Terr., Dundee DD3 6HS. *Signs work:* see appendix.

ROSS-CRAIG, Stella, F.L.S.; artist in water-colour, pencil, and pen and ink; *b* Aldershot, Hants, 19 Mar., 1906; *d* of John Ross-Craig, M.P.S.; *m* J. Robert Sealy, B.Sc., F.L.S. *Educ.:* privately; *studied art* at Thanet Schools of Art, and botany at Chelsea Polytechnic. *Work in permanent collections:* Reference Collection, Herbarium of Royal Botanic Gdns., Kew (approx. 500 water-colours, several hundred pen-and-ink and pencil drawings); Hunt Botanical Library, Pittsburgh, Penn., U.S.A. *Work repro.:* in Hooker's Icones Plantarum, Botanical Magazine, and many other scientific publications. *Publications:* Drawings of British Plants. *Address:* c/o The Herbarium, Royal Botanic Gdns., Kew, Surrey. *Signs work:* "SR-C" or "Stella Ross-Craig."

ROSSER, John, R.O.I. (1978), N.D.D. (1952); painter; *b* London, 8 June, 1931; *s* of Edward John Rosser; *m* Margaret Barnett. *Studied art* at Regent St. Polytechnic and Watford School of Art (1947-52) under A. J. B. Sutherland. *Exhib.:* R.O.I., R.A., R.B.A., N.E.A.C., R.I., Young Contemporaries, Medici Gallery, Compton Gallery, Windsor, Blackheath Gallery, Neville Gallery, Bath, Sandford Gallery, Paris Salon; one-man shows: Brian Sinfield Gallery, Burford (1987), Hallam Gallery, SW14 (1989); finalist in the Hunting Group art prizes (1981). *Work repro.:* Elgin Court, Foyles Books, Rosenstiels, Medici. *Address:* 4 Beachview, 91 Banks Rd., Poole, Dorset BH13 7QQ. *Signs work:* capital R.

ROSSIE, Kay, Dip.F.A. (1986), A.Dip. (1987), M.F.P.S. (1988); abstract painter/sculptor in acrylic, oil, wood, metal constructions; *b* Porthcawl, 1940. *Studied art* at Croydon College (1983-86), one year advanced sculpture (1986-87). *Exhib.:* one-man show, Loggia Gallery, London; many mixed exhbns. of painting and sculpture, including Trends. *Work in permanent collections:* Croydon College, Price Waterhouse, Exhbn. Business Design Centre. *Address:* 12 Brokes Cres., Reigate, Surrey RH2 9PS. *Clubs:* F.P.S., Reigate Soc. of Artists. *Signs work:* "Kay Rossie."

ROSSITER, Anthony, M.C.S.D. (1963), R.W.A. (1964), Arts Council awards, Literature (1967, 1970), T.V. James Mossman's Review (1970); painter in oil and water-colour, writer, lecturer; Lecturer, Bristol Polytechnic (early retirement 1983); started Dalesford Studio, teaching small groups painting within own studio (1983); *b* London, 29 Mar., 1926; *s* of Leonard Rossiter; *m* Anneke; one *s*, one *d*. *Educ.:* Eton; *studied art* at Chelsea Polytechnic (1947-51). *Exhib.:* Artists in National Parks (1988-90). *Work in permanent collections:* V. & A., Bristol City Art Gallery, Reading City Art Gallery, London Transport, John F. Kennedy Centre, Smithsonian Institute, U.S.A., Ministry of Works, etc. *Publications:* The Pendulum (Gollancz, 1966), The Golden Chain (Hutchinson, 1970), The Pendulum, A Round Trip to Revelation (Garrett Publications, U.S.A.; Foreword W. H. Auden); illustrated Elizabeth Jennings's Poems A Dream of Spring (Celandine Press, 1980). B.B.C. TV documentary, Work as Painter, Lecturer, Writer (1981). Represented British Landscape and Figure

Painting 1930-1985 Irma Stern Museum, Cape Town, S. Africa (1987). *Address:* Dalesford House, Litton, nr. Bath, Somerset. *Signs work:* "A.R."

ROWAN, David Paul, R.B.A. (1979), R.A. Schools Post. Grad. Cert. (1972-75), Dip.A.D. (Painting, 1969-72); artist in acrylic; *b* Colne, Lancs., 28 Apr., 1950; *s* of William Rowan, careers officer. *Studied art* at Maidstone College of Art (1969-72, D. Winfield, R.B.A., W. Bowyer, R.A.), R.A. Schools (1972-75, P. Greenham, C.B.E., R.A., Margaret Green, John Holden). *Exhib.:* R.B.A., Mid-Pennine Arts, Colne. *Work in private collections:* F. Kobler, London; A. Whalley, Windsor. *Address:* 1 Sandown Rd., London SE25 4XD. *Signs work:* "DAVID ROWAN" or "D.P. Rowan."

ROWAN, Evadné Harris, M.C.S.D. (1952), A.I.A. (1949); free-lance artist in pen and ink, water-colour, oil, lithography; *b* Warsash, Hants; *d* of Capt. F. H. Rowan; *m* F. H. Paul. *Studied art:* Gloucester School of Arts and Crafts and Central School of Arts and Crafts, Southampton Row. *Exhib.:* Senefelder Club and Artists International Assoc. *Work repro.:* Heinemann, Macmillan, Penguin Books, Methuen, Harvill Press, Rupert Hart-Davis, Odhams, Collins, Putnams, G.P.O., Dents, O.U.P., Michael Joseph, Ward Lock, Longmans, B.B.C. *Publications:* work in Radio Times, Sunday Times. *Address:* Flat 7, 35 Elm Pk. Gdns., London SW10 9QF. *Signs work:* "Evadné Rowan."

ROWBOTHAM, Mark A., Dip.A.D., P.S. (1992); painter in oil and pastels; *b* Sarawak, Borneo, 1959; *m* Sherree E. Valentine-Daines; one *s*, one *d*. *Studied art* at Epsom School of Art (1977-81). *Exhib.:* R.B.A., R.O.I., R.W.S., R.P., N.E.A.C., P.S. *Address:* Misty Ridge, 126 The Street, Ashtead, Surrey KT21 1AB. *Signs work:* "M.A.R."

ROWE-EVANS, Prue, B.A. (Lond.), Dips. in Painting and Printmaking (mid-Warwickshire C.F.E.), M.F.P.S.; painter; *b* London, 30 July, 1921; *d* of David Low, political cartoonist; *m* Adrian; one *s*. *Educ.:* Frognal School, Hampstead; University College, London; *studied art* at Slade, and mid-Warwickshire C.F.E. *Exhib.:* numerous mixed exhbns. in London, The Midlands; one-man shows: Uganda (1964), University of Warwick (1978, 1986), Ibis Gallery, Leamington (1979), Phoenix, Leamington (1987), Loggia Gallery, London (1989), Pump Room, Leamington (1992, 1993). *Address:* 48 New St., Kenilworth CV8 2EZ. *Clubs:* Leamington Soc. of Artists, Westgate Painters, Coventry and Warwickshire Soc. of Artists. *Signs work:* "P. ROWE-EVANS" or "Prue Rowe-Evans."

ROWLAND, Dawn, A.R.B.S.; sculptor in stone and bronze; Council mem. R.B.S.; *b* London, 24 Sept., 1944; *m* Prof. Malcolm Rowland; two *d. Educ.:* Orange Hill Girls' Grammar School. *Exhib.:* Chelsea Harbour Sculpture (1993), Konishi Gallery Kyoto, R.A. Summer Show, Salford A.G. *Address:* The Pines, 39 Bramhall Park Rd., Bramhall, Stockport, Ches. SC7 3NN. *Signs work:* "DAWN" in semicircle with date under.

ROWLETT, George Goldie; painter of land, town and seascapes, portrait and figure in oil, water-colour and charcoal; *b* Troon, Ayrshire, 29 June, 1941; *m* Marion Sneller; two *s. Educ.:* De Aston Grammar, Market Rasen; *studied art* at Grimsby School of Art (1960-62), Camberwell School of Art (1962-65), R.A. Schools (1965-68). *Exhib.:* one-man shows: Grimsby Museum (1962), Greenwich Theatre Gallery (1975), Woodlands Gallery (1982), Zur Torkel Zehn, Konstanz (1985, 1986, 1987), D.M. Gallery (1987), Everard Read Gallery, Johannesburg (1987, 1988, 1990), Smith-Jariwala Gallery (1989), Cleveland Bridge Gallery, Bath (1989), Albemarle Gallery (1990); mixed shows: approx. 90 including R.A., Whitechapel Open, Cleveland Drawing Biennale, N.P.G., Hayward Annual 'A

Singular Vision', Hunting Group, Spirit of London, South Bank Picture Show, London Group, Druce-Constable, Zur Torkel Zehn, Konstanz, Read Stremmel San Antonio, Everard Read Johannesburg, Architectural Arts Co. Dallas, Elizabeth Gordon Durban, Cleveland Bridge, Bath, Albemarle. *Work in permanent collections:* Grimsby Museum and A.G., Northern Arts, Cleveland Museum Service, Nuffield Foundation, Baring Bros., Manny Davidson Discretionary Trust, Equitable Real Estate Investment, M.N. & M.N.T., Atlanta, Ga., Kelmac Group, Price Forbes Ltd., Auto & General Ltd., Innovative Marketing Ltd., Ken Solomon (Pty) Ltd., African Salt Works (Pty) Ltd., Weedon Minerals, Anglo American Ltd., A.G. Diamond Cutters, Mesquite Investments, Philip Loot's Assoc., Sumrie of London, Stephen Fauke Interiors, Altron Ltd., Charles Glass Soc., Rose Gardens (Pty) Ltd., Nedfin Bank Ltd., Head Interiors, Momentum Components, Grinrod Unicorn Group Ltd. *Address:* 23 Farrins Rents, Rotherhithe, London SE16. *Signs work:* "George Rowlett."

ROWSELL, Joyce, B.A. (1988), H.S. (1982), H.S.F. (1992); painter, miniaturist and illustrator in oil and water-colour; *b* S. Wales, 20 Nov., 1928; *m* Geoff N. Rowsell; two *s. Educ.:* Coborn School, Bishop Fox's School, Taunton; *studied art* privately and at Courtauld Inst. (History of Art). *Exhib.:* R.M.S., H.S. *Publications:* children's stories, illustrations, book jackets. *Address:* Spring Grove Farm, Spring Gr., Milverton, Som. TA4 1NW. *Signs work:* "Joyce Rowsell."

ROWSON, Hugh Thomas, B.A., R.S.W.; artist in water-colour, acrylic, printmaking, educationalist; former Educ. Officer, Aberdeen A.G.; former V.P., Aberdeen Artists Soc.; *b* Aberdeen, 4 Aug., 1946; *m* Lesley (divorced); two *s. Studied art* at Grays School of Art, The Robert Gordon University (1965-70, Alexander Fraser, Ian Fleming), Open University (1972-76). *Exhib.:* Aberdeen University, Aberdeen Arts Centre. *Work in permanent collection:* Aberdeen Royal Infirmary. *Publication:* Childrens' Guide to Aberdeen Art Gallery. *Address:* Peacock Printmakers, Castle St., Aberdeen. *Club:* R.S.W. *Signs work:* "Hugh T. Rowson" or "H.T.R."

ROXBY, Brian, A.R.O.I. (1988); painter in oil, acrylic and water-colour; *b* 25 Oct., 1934; *s* of Thomas Roxby (decd.); *m* Christina Mary; one *s,* two *d. Educ.:* St. Cuthbert's Grammar School, Newcastle upon Tyne; *studied art* at Sunderland College of Art (1951-55, Harry Thubron), R.C.A. (1955-58, Leonard Rosoman, Robert Buhler). *Exhib.:* R.B.A., N.E.A.C., R.I., R.O.I., Contemporary British Painters, Wildenstein (1958); one-man shows: Queen's Hall Gallery, Hexham (1988), Trevelyan College, Durham (1989). *Work in permanent collection:* National Gallery of Wales. *Address:* South House, Eppleton Hall, Hetton-le-Hole, Houghton-le-Spring, Tyne and Wear DH5 0QZ. *Signs work:* "B. Roxby."

ROY, Michael (Michael Roy Pressley-Roy), A.T.C. (1970), Dip. Art Educ. (1976); artist (mixed media) landscapes, marinescapes, figurations, flower-pieces and fun-fantasy themes; retd. art teacher; *b* London, 20 Apr., 1928. *Educ.:* Upton Grammar, Berks.; *studied art* at Newland Park College (1967-70) and later at Hornsey College of Art (Eric Sonntag). *Exhib.:* London and Provinces. *Work in permanent collections:* various private and public, U.K. and abroad. *Books written:* "The rôle of the Art Teacher" (1976); "The Art Lark" (1992). *Address:* 53 Lyon St., Southampton SO2 0LW. *Signs work:* "Michael Roy" with symbol of small spider and date, see appendix.

RUBINSTEIN, Gerda; sculptor in clay and wax; teacher "Open Sculpture Studio" under I.L.E.A. Greenwich. *Studied* at Ryksakademie, Amsterdam; Grand Chaumiere, Paris (Zadkine). *Exhib.:* one-man shows: Martinus Lienur,

The Hague, Rotterdamse Kunstkring, Gallery 66 Blackheath, Woodlands Gallery Greenwich, Gallery Petit Amsterdam, Playhouse Gallery Harlow. *Work in permanent collections:* Ooster Park Amsterdam, "City" Bishopsfield, Harlow, thirty eight birds at Merry Hill Centre, Dudley, Birmingham. *Address:* 15 Quentin Rd., London SE13 5DQ. *Signs work:* see appendix.

RUFFING, A. E.; professional artist in water-colour; *b* Brooklyn, N.Y.; *d* of J. P. Frampton, architectural engineer; *m* George Ruffing; one *d. Educ.:* Cornell University, Drexel Institute of Technology; *studied art* under John Pike (1964). *Work in permanent collections:* Metropolitan Museum of Art, Smithsonian Institute, Library of Congress, Brooklyn Museum, Harvard University, Institute of Early American History and Culture, Albany Institute of History and Art, Atwater Kent Museum, Johnston Historical Museum, N.Y. Historical Society. *Address:* P.O. Box 125, Bloomington, N.Y. 12411. *Signs work:* "A. E. Ruffing."

RUNSWICK, Eddie; Director of Community and Leisure Services, Borough of Blackburn. *Address:* Town Hall, Blackburn BB1 7DY.

RUSHMER, Gordon, S.D.A.D.Hons. (1976); landscape painter in water-colour, designer; *b* Petersfield, 12 July, 1946; *s* of George Benjamin Walter Rushmer; *m* Shirley Ann Holland; one *s,* one *d. Educ.:* Petersfield School; *studied art* at Farnham School of Art (1962-67, Victor Ambrus, Brian Ingham). *Exhib.:* Furneaux Gallery, Edwin Pollard Gallery, Ceri Richards Gallery, Swansea, R.I., Ashbarn Gallery, Petersfield, New Ashgate Gallery, Farnham, Peter Hedley Gallery, Wareham, Gallery East, N.Y. *Work in permanent collections:* National Library of Wales, I.C.I., Leach Group. *Address:* 2 Sherwood Cl., Liss, Hants. GU33 7BT. *Signs work:* "Gordon Rushmer."

RUSSELL, Edwin John Cumming, F.R.B.S., Cert. R.A.S., R.A. Gold Medal for sculpture; Sir Otto Beit Medal for sculpture (1991); sculptor in bronze, stone, wood; *b* Heathfield, 4 May, 1939; *m* Lorne McKean, sculptor; two *d. Studied art* at Brighton College of Art and Crafts (1955-59), Royal Academy Schools (1959-63). *Work in permanent collections:* Crucifix, and St. Michael, St. Paul's Cathedral; Bishop, Wells Cathedral; Dolphin Sundial, Greenwich; Sundials for Oman University and Dubai Parliament Sq.; Mad Hatters Tea Party, Warrington; Lion and Lamb, best shopping centre (1987); Alice and White Rabbit, Guildford; Panda, W.W.F., H.Q.; Forecourt Sculpture, Rank Xerox U.K., H.Q. *Address:* Lethendry, Hindhead, Surrey. *Signs work:* "E.R."

RUSSELL, Ena, R.O.I. (1972); painter in oils, water-colour, inks, freelance journalist; joint winner, Stanley Grimm Prize, R.O.I. (1987); *b* Cleveland, Yorks.; *d* of the late A. Forrester, F.R.I.B.A.; *m* the late Sir Ronald Russell, M.P., and author; one *s,* one *d. Educ.:* Acton Reynald Shrewsbury; *studied art* at St. Albans, Chelsea, and Sir John Cass College of Art. *Exhib.:* R.A., R.P., R.B.A., R.I., N.E.A.C., R.O.I. Centenary (1988), Pictures for Schools, Royal Welsh Academy, Paris Salon, Herts. and Wembley galleries; one-man shows, St. John's Wood, House of Commons (1974), Qantas (1980); tour exhbn. Contemporay Art in Kyoto and Osaka, Japan (1988). *Work repro:* The Lady, Daily Telegraph, Artist, Leisure Painter, provincial papers, etc., writes and illustrates articles on travel, and arts and crafts subjects. *Address:* 29 Acacia Rd., St. John's Wood, London NW8. *Signs work:* "Ena Russell."

RUSSELL, Kathleen Barbara, D.A.Edin. (1962); Membre Associé Société des Artistes Français; artist in oil, pastel and water-colour; *b* Edinburgh, 1940; *d* of John Sandilands Russell; *m* John Caskey. *Educ.:* The Mary Erskine School for Girls; *studied art* at Edinburgh College of Art (1958-63) under Sir Wm. Gillies,

R.A., R.S.A. and Sir Robin Philipson, P.R.S.A. *Exhib.:* one-man shows since 1965. *Work in permanent collections:* Watson Coll., Edinburgh Corp. Schools Coll., Nuffield Collection, Durham University, Kings College, London, Royal Botanic Gardens, Kew. *Publication:* illustrated Magnus the Orkney Cat. *Address:* 113 Laleham Rd., Catford, London SE6. *Signs work:* "Kathleen Russell" or "K. Russell" or "K."

RUSSELL, Pat, F.S.S.I., M.A.W.G.; textile artist in fabric collage, lettering artist, calligrapher; *b* Wembley, 17 Aug., 1919; *d* of Herbert Cooch; *m* Birrell Russell; one *s*, one *d*. *Educ.:* Farnborough Hill; *studied art* at Chelsea College of Art under M. C. Oliver. *Exhib.:* Oxford Gallery and various group exhbns. *Work in permanent collections:* V. & A., Oxford City and County Museum, Reading Museum. *Publications:* Lettering for Embroidery (Batsford); Decorative Alphabets Throughout the Ages (Bestseller Publications). *Address:* 48 East Saint Helen's St., Abingdon OX14 5EB. *Signs work:* "Pat Russell."

RUSSON, Bobbie Jane, B.A.Hons. (1987), M.A. (1990); Brian Robb Venice Scholarship (1989); artist in acrylic, mixed media, photography; *b* Birmingham, 27 Jan., 1966; *d* of Mary Russon. *Educ.:* Selly Park Girls School; *studied art* at Bourneville School of Art (1982-84), St. Martin's School of Art (1984-87, Chris Corr, Liz Pyle, Chris Brown), R.C.A. (1988-90, Quentin Blake, Andre Klimousky, Danfern, Jake Tilson, David Blamey). *Exhib.:* Whitworth Young Contemporaries (1987), Benson and Hedges (prize) Illustration Exhbn. (1987), Folio Soc. (1989, prize). *Work repro.:* Pandora, book jacket (Kindergarten) by Ettinger, also cards, packaging, murals, etc. *Address:* 27 Evelyn Rd., Richmond, Surrey.

RUSSON, Mary Georgina, N.D.D. (1963), A.T.D. (1971); artist in ink, gouache, acrylic; art teacher, B'ham (1971-79); *b* Hockley, B'ham, 1937; *d* of Norman Russon, electrical contractor; one *d*. *Educ.:* Holly Lodge Grammar School, Smethwick; *studied art* at B'ham College of Art and Crafts (1960-63, Glyn Griffiths). *Exhib.:* Central Hall, Westminster (1960's). *Publications:* illustrated many children's books, some magazine and other work. *Address:* 4 The Hawthorns, Woodbridge Rd., Moseley, Birmingham B13 9DY.

RYAN, Adrian; painter in oil, water-colour; teacher, Goldsmiths' School of Art (1948-83); Cambridge School of Art (1969-85); *b* Hampstead, 3 Oct., 1920; *s* of Vivian D. Ryan, painter; *m* 1st. Peggy Rose, one *d*; 2nd. Barbara Pitt, two *d*; 3rd. Susan Curnow. *Educ.:* Eton; *studied art* at Slade School. *Exhib.:* R.A., London Group, Tate, etc. *Work in permanent collections:* Tate Gallery, V. & A., Belfast Art Gallery, Manchester Art Gallery, National Gallery of New Zealand, Plymouth Art Gallery, etc. *Official purchases:* Gulbenkian Foundation, Chantrey Bequest, Arts Council of G.B., Contemp. Art Soc., etc. *Publication:* author, Still Life Painting Techniques. *Address:* 8 Camden Studios, Camden St., London NW1 0LG. *Signs work:* "Ryan."

RYAN, John Gerald Christopher; freelance artist, illustrator, writer and cartoon film-maker; *b* Edinburgh, 4 Mar., 1921; *s* of Sir Andrew Ryan, diplomat; *m*; three children. *Educ.:* Ampleforth College; *studied art* at Regent St. Polytechnic. *Exhib.:* R.A. Creator "Captain Pugwash" "Sir Prancelot" and various other children's cartoon characters. *Work repro.:* internationally in various magazines and picture-books. Cartoonist 'Catholic Herald' since 1967. *Address:* Gungarden Lodge, The Gungardens, Rye, E. Sussex TN31 7HH. *Signs work:* "RYAN."

RYAN, Thomas, P.P.R.H.A., D.Litt., A.N.C.A.D., Hon.R.A., Hon.R.S.A.; painter in oil, water-colour, pastel, red chalk; President, United Arts Club,

Dublin, and Limerick Art Soc.; Council mem. Stamp Design Com.; *b* Limerick, Ireland, 16 Sept., 1929; *m* Mary Joyce; four *s,* two *d. Educ.:* Christian Brothers School, Limerick; *studied art* at Limerick School of Art (Richard Butcher, A.R.C.A.), National College of Art, Dublin (Seän Keating, Maurice McGonigle). *Exhib.:* many one-man and mixed shows in Ireland, G.B., Ukraine, U.S.A., Latvia. *Work in permanent collections:* National Gallery of Ireland, President of Ireland, Cardinal's residence Armagh, European Court, E.E.C. Brussels, St. Patrick's College, Maynooth. *Address:* Robertstown Lodge, Robertstown, Ashbourne, Co. Meath, Ireland. *Clubs:* Arts Dublin, Friendly Brothers of St. Patrick, Dublin. *Signs work:* "Thomas Ryan."

RYDER, Betty Pamela Dorothy; landscape painter in oil on canvas and board; *b* London, 5 Jan., 1924; *d* of .D.S.R. Ryder, OBE.; *m* P.B.H. Furlong, D.F.C., F.R.I.C.S.; two *s,* one *d. Educ.:* L.M.S., Parsons Green; *studied art* at Epsom School of Art – mature student (1969-75, John Morley). *Exhib.:* N.E.A.C., R.B.A., R.A., Edwin Pollard Gallery, David Curzon, Thames Ditton, etc. *Address:* 22 Lansdowne Rd., Wimbledon, London SW20 8AW. *Signs work:* "B. Ryder."

RYDER, Margaret Elaine, V.P.R.M.S., S.W.A., S.M., F.S.B.A., Member of the Royal Society of Miniature Painters, Sculptors and Gravers (1963); portrait, flower and landscape painter in oil, pastel, and water-colour, and miniaturist on ivory; for 20 years a freelance commercial artist; *b* Sheffield, 1908; *m* Norman Vint. *Educ.:* Sheffield High School; *studied art* at Sheffield College of Art; numerous scholarships. *Exhib.:* R.A., Paris Salon, Pastel Society, Royal Institute, Exhbn. of Flowers and Gardens, Manchester Academy, Aberdeen Society of Arts, Sheffield Society of Artists, Australia, U.S.A.; five one-man shows in Sheffield. *Address:* 26 Bents Dr., Sheffield S11 9RP. *Signs work:* see appendix.

RYDER, Susan, R.P. (1992), N.E.A.C. (1980), N.D.D. (1964), David Murray Travel scholarship (1964); N.E.A.C. Critics prize (1990, 1993), Barney Wilkinson prize (1990), Alexon Portrait Competition (1991); painter in oil and water-colour; *b* Windsor, 1944; *d* of Capt. Robert Ryder, R.N., V.C.; *m* Martin Bates; one *s,* one *d. Studied art:* Byam Shaw School of Painting (1960-64, Maurice de Sausmarez, A.R.A., Bernard Dunstan, R.A.). *Exhib.:* R.A., Portrait Painters, N.E.A.C.; one-man shows, Haste Gallery, Ipswich (2), W.H. Patterson, Albemarle St., W1. (1989). *Work in permanent collection:* "Miss Pears 1984" Pears Collection. *Address:* 2 Pembroke Rd., London W8 6NT. *Signs work:* "Ryder."

S

SADDINGTON, Donald William; painter in oil, pastel, water-colour, specialising in landscape and marine; artist in typography and print design; *b* Dartford, 31 Aug., 1935; *s* of William S. Saddington; *m* Vivienne Crouch (decd.); one *s,* one *d. Educ.:* Wordsworth Secondary; *studied art* at London College of Printing and Graphic Arts (1950-55), Cricklade College, Andover. *Exhib.:* City A.G., Southampton, Guildhall Gallery, Winchester, Winchester Street Gallery, Salisbury, Wykeham Galleries, Stockbridge, Mall Galleries, P.S., R.I., Edwin Pollard, Linda Blackstone Gallery. *Work in permanent collection:*

National Graphical Assoc., Salisbury. *Address:* 85 Highlands Rd., Andover, Hants. SP10 2PZ. *Club:* S.G.A. *Signs work;* "D. Saddington."

SAHAI, Virendra, O.B.E., Dip.T.P., A.R.I.B.A.; painter; *b* Shahjehanpur, India, 25 June, 1933; *s* of Girwar Sahai. *Educ.:* trained as an architect and townplanner, Polytechnic, Regent St., London; *studied art* at Central School of Art. *Exhib.:* one-man shows: New Vision Centre and Biggins Gallery, London (1961), Commonwealth Institute, London (1966), Galerie Suzanne de Coninck, Paris (1967), Bear Lane Gallery, Oxford (1967); group and mixed exhbns.: Redfern Gallery, London, Commonwealth Biennale of Abstract Art (1961-67), Reading Museum, Bradford Museum, Brighton Museum, Beaune Gallery, Paris, and several others. *Work in permanent collections:* Bradford Museum, Councils for Art Education, Leicester and Oxford. *Private collections:* in England, Nigeria, U.S.A., Canada, Germany, Hong Kong and Spain. *Work repro.:* Guardian, Art International. *Address:* 39 New Rd., Barton, Cambs. CB3 7AY. *Signs work:* see appendix.

SAILO, Nina; sculptor and designer; *b* St. Petersburg, 26 July, 1906; *d* of Albert Stunkel, architect; *m* Alpo Sailo, sculptor (*died* 6 Oct., 1955); three *s*, one *d.* *Studied art* at Drawing School, Viipuri (1921-24), Technical school in Harrow-on-the-Hill (1930-31), pupil of Alpo Sailo from 1932. *Exhib.:* Kalevalatalo, Helsinki. *Work in permanent collections:* Kalevala Ladies' Soc., Helsinki, in museums (Finland) and in Sweden; memorial medals in Finland, Sweden and Norway. *Official purchases:* public monuments at Helsinki, Lappeenranta, Seinäjoki, Tornio, Rauma, Ämmansaari, Vierumäki and Imatra and Porvoo, Svulrya, Norway, Borås, Sweden. *Address:* Kotikuja 02420 Jorvas, Finland. *Clubs:* Charter mem. of Kalevalatalo Foundation, mem. of Kalevala Ladies' Soc. *Signs work:* "Nina Sailo."

SALAMAN, Christopher; artist in oil, bronze and resin bronze; *b* Dorking, 4 Nov., 1939; *s* of Easton Salaman, A.R.I.B.A.; *m*; one *s.* *Educ.:* Bedales School; *studied art* at Camberwell School of Art and Crafts under Karel Vogel. *Exhib.:* Woodstock Gallery, Upper Street Gallery, Mall Galleries, Margaret Fisher Gallery. *Address:* West Park Lodge, High Ongar, Essex. *Signs work:* "Christopher Salaman."

SALMON, James Marchbank, D.A. (Edin.) (1937), M.O.I. Artist (1939-42), F.I.A.D. (1942), F.R.S.A. (1948), M.C.S.D. (1957), F.S.A.E. (1968), Hon. Mem. Tamagowa University, Tokyo (1978) Dean Emeritus (1981), Prof. and Dean, University of Calgary (1973-81), Principal: Croydon (1960-73) and Lincoln (1947-60) Colleges of Art, Lecturer, St. Paul's T.T. College/Cheltenham School of Art (1938-47); artist in oil, water-colour, lithography, pottery; *b* Edinburgh, 1 Apr., 1916; *s* of George Salmon, S.S.C.; *m* Margaret Hodges; one *s*, one *d.* *Educ.:* Edinburgh; *studied art* at Edinburgh College of Art (1933-37), Kunst Akademie, Berlin (1936). *Exhib.:* R.A., R.S.A., S.S.A., R.W.S., etc. *Work in collections:* Usher Gallery, Lincoln; many private collections. *Work repro.:* Radio Times, Country Life, Batsford, Medici, etc. *Address:* Crofters, Wych Cross, E. Sussex RH18 5JN. *Signs work:* "J. Marchbank Salmon," "J. MARCHBANK SALMON" or "SALMON."

SALMON, Martin; artist in water-colour and gouache; designer (Advertising); *b* Barnehurst, Kent, 19 Apr., 1950; *m* Janice. *Educ.:* Dartford Technical School. *Exhib.:* Edwin Pollard Gallery. *Work in permanent collections:* Hong Kong, N.Z., Italy, N. America, etc. *Address:* 17 Dome Hill, Caterham, Surrey CR3 6EE. *Signs work:* "Martin Salmon."

SALMOND, Ronald, A.T.D. (1938), S.G.A. (1967); wood engraver, etcher, painter, etc.; Head of Art Dept., Preston Manor High School, Wembley (retd.); *b* Hornsey, 30 Dec., 1912; *s* of Ralph M. Salmond; *m* Mary; one *s. Educ.:* Tollington Grammar School; *studied art* at Hornsey College of Art (print-making under Norman Janes). *Exhib.:* R.A., R.E., R.B.A. *Work in permanent collection:* South London A.G., Ashmolean Museum. *Address:* 13 Treve Ave., Harrow, Middx. HA1 4AL. *Signs work:* "Ronald Salmond."

SALTER, Anthony, Dip.A.D. (1969); graphic designer and printmaker in etching; graphic designer, University of Greenwich; *b* London, 2 Mar., 1949. *Studied art* at Goldsmiths' College of Art (1966-69). *Exhib.:* R.A., R.S.P.E.E., P.M.C. *Work in permanent collections:* Rank Zerox, London Borough of Greenwich. *Address:* 34 Lizban St., London SE3 8SS. *Signs work:* "ANTHONY SALTER."

SALTZMAN, William, B.S. Education, University of Minnesota (1940); easel and mural painter, designer, teacher; Prof. Emeritus, Macalester College (since 1984); Director-resident artist, Rochester Art Centre, Rochester, Minn. (1948-63), Freelance Studio, Minneapolis, Minn. (since 1963); Prof. of Art, Macalester College, St. Paul, Minn. (since 1966); currently painting and designing stained glass and sheet copper sculpture reliefs for many architectural commissions; exhibiting paintings widely coast to coast; (3) I.F.R.A.A. National awards; Regional/National awards; *b* Mpls., Minn., 9 July, 1916; *s* of Jacob Saltzman; *m* Muriel; one *s*, two *d. Educ.:* University of Minnesota; Art Students League, N.Y.C.; *studied art* as above. *Address:* Studio: 210 North 2nd St., Suite 060, Minneapolis, Minn. 55401. *Signs work:* see appendix.

SAMPE, Prof. Astrid, Hon. Doctor (1989), Hon. R.D.I., London (1949), S.I.D., Dame of the Order of Vasa (1961); Member of A.I.D., New York (1963); designer; director, A.B. Nordiska Kompaniet's design studio since 1937; designer for contract interiors, textile designer for industries making carpets, curtains, upholstery; *b* Stockholm; *d* of Otto Sampe, textile manufacturer, decd.; *m*, divorced; one *s*, one *d. Educ.:* Konstfackskolan, Stockholm; R.C.A., London; *studied art* at Atelier Vignal, Paris (1933), and on scholarship to Germany (1934), Italy (1936). *Exhib.:* one-man show, Nationalmuseum, Stockholm (1984); other exhbns. Sweden, Tokyo, New York, etc. *Publication:* Textile Bilderbok, with Vera Djurson (1948). *Address:* Consult Interior and Industrial Design, Karlaplan 4, Stockholm, Sweden. *Club:* Faculty of Royal Designers in Royal Society of Arts, London. *Signs work:* "Astrid Sampe, Professor."

SANCHA, Carlos, R.P.; portrait painter in oil; *b* London, 27 Apr., 1920; *s* of Luis Sancha y Lengo, B.A.; *m* Sheila Neal Green; two *s*, one *d. Educ.:* Lindisfarne College; *studied art* at Central School of Arts & Crafts under Rodrigo Moyniham, A.R.A., J. Grant; Byam Shaw School under Patrick Philips, R.P. *Exhib.:* R.A., R.P. *Address:* 8 Melbury Rd., London W14.

SANDERS, Rosanne Diana, S.B.A.; R.H.S. gold medal (1981, 1984, 1985, 1988), R.H.S. silver gilt medal (1977, 1980), R.A. miniature award (1985); botanical artist; *b* Stoke Poges, Bucks., 21 June, 1944; *d* of Robert Burnet; one *s. Educ.:* Roedean; *studied art* at High Wycombe College of Art for one year, otherwise self taught. *Exhib.:* 'Flowers and Gardens' exhbn. Westminster Gallery annually. *Publications:* Portrait of a Country Garden (Aurum Press, 1980), The Art of Making Wine (Aurum Press, 1982), Painting the Secret World of Nature (Search Press, 1987), The English Apple (Phaidon Press, 1988). *Address:* Mattiscombe Cottage, Stokenham, Kingsbridge, Devon TQ7 2SR. *Signs work:* "R.D.S."

SANDERS, Susan Mary, D.F.A. (1968), R.A. Schools Post Grad. Cert. (1971); painter in oil, water-colour, pencil, chalk and gouache; Partner, Wye Art Gallery; *b* Haslemere, 11 Aug., 1946; *d* of Air Commodore P.J. Sanders, D.F.C.; *m* Richard Henry Parkinson; one *s*, one *d. Educ.:* St. Mary's School, Baldslow Hastings; *studied art:* Byam Shaw School (1964-68), R.A. Schools (1968-71). *Exhib.:* R.A. Summer Exhbn. (1971-89), R.W.E.A., (1983-88), Mall Galleries (1986-89), Bath, Bristol, Stockbridge, etc. *Work in permanent collections:* Merchant Navy Pensions London, B.& Q. Southampton, and various boardrooms and offices. *Work repro.:* Whatmans Ltd. Calendar (1989), advertising of B.& Q. Southampton. *Address:* Gallery House, Bridge St., Wye, Kent TN25 5EA. *Clubs:* Reynolds, R.A. Schools. *Signs work:* "S. Sanders," "Susan Sanders," or "S.S."

SANDERSON, C. J.; 1st prize Corfu Landscapes (1967); Dip. d'Honneur Salon International Biarritz (1974); artist in oil, acrylic, water-colour, pastel, gouache, pencil, etching, Indian ink, stone, clay and wood; *b* London, 18 Aug., 1949; *s* of James Comber Sanderson, printer. *Educ.:* Millfield; *studied art* at Byam Shaw School of Art (1967-71) under Maurice de Sausmarez and Ruskin Spear, R.A. *Exhib.:* one-man shows: Woodstock Gallery (1974), Gallery Vallombreuse (1974), Gallery Mouffe (1974); Drian Gallery (1979); mixed shows: John Neville (1974), Ashgate Gallery (1973, 1974), Paris Salon (1974), R.A. (1970, 1972, 1973, 1983, 1984, 1985), Wylma Wayne Gallery (1983), and other mixed shows London and abroad. *Work in permanent collections:* D. J. Redwood White, London, and Paris. *Address:* 7 Gordon Pl., London W8 4JD. *Club:* The Organ. *Signs work:* "C.J. Sanderson."

SANDERSON, Roger, N.D.D. (1951), S.G.F.A. (1985), A.O.I. (1980); painter in water-colour, illustrator, designer (landscapes, figurative, humorous); Senior tutor, Linguaphone Institute's Paris School of Art since 1982; *b* London, 23 Nov., 1923; *s* of Herbert Arthur Sanderson, banker; *m* Hilde Kokorz; one *s*, three *d. Educ.:* Dulwich College; *studied art:* Croydon and Epsom Art Schools (Barbara Jones, Michael Cadman, Leslie Worth, Ray Evans). *Exhib.:* R.I., R.W.S. Open, R.B.A., P.S., U.A., etc. H.W. Peel prizewinner—drawing S.G.F.A. (1992). Work in private and corporate collections. *Publications:* illustrations for leading publishers. *Address:* Bucklers Lodge, St. Ives, Ringwood, Hants. BH24 2NY. *Signs work:* "ROGER SANDERSON."

SANDLE, Michael Leonard, A.R.A., D.F.A. (Lond.); artist in water-colour and ink, sculptor in bronze; Prof. at The Academy for Visual Arts, Karlsruhe, W. Germany; *b* Weymouth, 18 May, 1936; *s* of Charles Edward Sandle, C.P.O., R.N.; divorced; one *s; m* Demelza Spargo, 1988. *Educ.:* Douglas High School; *studied art* at Douglas School of Art, I.O.M. (1951-54), Slade School of Fine Art (1956-59). *Exhib.:* group: Young Contemporaries (1957-59), Grabowski Gallery, London (1964, 1966), British Sculptors '72, R.A. (1972), Hayward Annual (1978), Träume vom Frieden, Recklinghausen (1982), etc.; one-man: Drian Gallery (1963), Haus am Lützowplatz, Berlin (1975), Allen Gallery, Vancouver (1975), Fischer Fine Art (1981, 1985), Wilhelm Lehmbruck Museum (1984), Whitechapel (1988), Württembergischer Kunstverein, Stuttgart (1989), Ernst Museum, Budapest (1990), etc. *Work in permanent collections:* Arts Council, British Council, B.M., Imperial War Museum, Leics. A.G., Leics. Educ. Authority, Metropolitan Museum, N.Y., Museum des 20. Jahrhunderts, Vienna, Neuberger Museum of Modern Art, U.S.A., Neue Sammlung, Munich, National-Galerie, Warsaw, Preston Art Museum, Tate Gallery, V. & A., W. German

WHO'S WHO IN ART

Government, etc. *Address:* Schloss Scheibenhardt, D 7500 Karlsruhe, W. Germany. *Signs work:* "Michael Sandle."

SANDWITH, Noelle; artist in egg tempera, water-colour, line, etching, oil, acrylic; *d* of Francis Sandwith. *Educ.:* Carshalton House, Surrey; *studied art* at Kingston-on-Thames, Croydon and Heatherley's. *Exhib.:* R.A., R.B.A., S.W.A., Brighton A.G., Waldorf Astoria, New York; one-man show: Foyle's Art Gallery. *Work repro.:* The Times, Sydney Morning Herald, R.A. Illustrated, Revue Moderne, Frost & Reed, etc. *Work in permanent collections:* Royal Naval College, Greenwich, Starr Commonwealth, Albion, Michigan, U.S.A., Royal Free Hospital, London, Auckland Inst. and Museum, N.Z., National Museum of Australia. *Address:* 17 Addison Rd., Wanstead, London E11 2RG. *Signs work:* "Noelle Sandwith."

SANFORD, Sheila, R.I., R.M.S.; artist in water-colour, miniaturist; *b* Singapore, 1922; *d* of A. E. Thornley Jones, shipping agent; *m* Roy Sanford; three *s. Educ.:* Brentwood School, Southport; *studied art* at St. Martin's School of Art. *Exhib.:* Edwin Pollard Gallery, Wimbledon; Llewellyn Alexander Fine Art Ltd.; M.A.S.-F.; R.I.; R.M.S.; H.S.; R.A. Summer Exhbn. (1992, 1993). *Work in permanent collections:* M.A.S.-F., Llewellyn Alexander Fine Art Ltd. *Address:* Sheepwash Cottage, Uploders, Bridport, Dorset DT6 4PH. *Signs work:* "Sheila Sanford."

SANZ-PASTOR Fz. de PIÉROLA, Consuelo, Doctor of History; Chairman of I.C.O.M. National Committee (1981-84); Mem. of I.C.A.M.T. (1977); Mem. Hispanic Society of America (1959); Directora Museo Cerralbo (1942-86); Inspectora Museos Bellas Artes (1963-69); Mem. of Sup. Council of Culture and Fine Arts (1976-78); Chairman of Sup. Council of Museums (1980-82); Mem., Trustees the Prado Museum (1980-85); Directora Honoraria Museo Cerralbo (since 1986); Presidenta Academia de San Damaso; *b* Madrid. *Publications:* Guia Museo Cerralbo (4th ed. 1981), Catálogos Exposiciones A. Berruguete (1960), San Pablo en el Arte (1963), Francisco de Zurbarán (1964), Museos y Colecciones de España (15th ed. 1990). Guia Museo Casas Reales (Rep. Dominicana 1976), Museo Cerralbo: Catálogo de Dibujos (1976). *Address:* Juan Hurtado de Mendoza 9-28036 Madrid.

SAPIEHA, Christine, S.W.A., A.P.A.; painter in acrylic, portraits, sculpture; therapist; *b* Vienna, 5 May, 1934; *d* of Prince Paul Sapieha, (Lt. Col. U.S. Army) (decd.); *m* Adam Fremantle; two *s. Educ.:* The Brearley, N.Y.C., Georgetown University, Washington D.C.; *studied art* at Abbott School of Art, Washington D.C. (1951-52), Parsons School of Design, N.Y.C. (1952-56). *Exhib.:* Mall Galleries, Spirit of London, R.A. Summer Show, Francis Kyle, Stable Gallery, Ice House, Bush House, Beach Thomas Gallery, Burford, Gallery East, N.Y., Westminster Gallery. *Work in permanent collections:* Sheldon Weisfeld, Brownsville, Tex., W.A.S.L. *Publications:* illustrated science and fiction for children. *Address:* 20 Macduff Rd., Battersea, London SW11 4DA. *Signs work:* see appendix.

SAUNDERS, Jutta Gabrielle, Slade Dip. (1951); painter in oil and water-colour, sculptor in clay; tutor; *b* 10 July, 1929; *d* of Felix Callman, L.D.S., R.C.S.; *m* Vernon Saunders; one *s*, one *d. Educ.:* The Hall School, Somerset, St. Maurs, Weybridge; *studied art* at Kingston School of Art (1945-48), Slade School of Fine Art (1948-51) under William Coldstream, John Piper; sculpture under F.E. McWilliam. *Exhib.:* R.A., R.W.A., Leicester, London and provincial galleries; sculpture in London. *Work in collections* in England, U.S.A., Brazil,

420

Germany and France. *Address:* Flint House, Oatlands Mere, Weybridge, Surrey KT13 9PD. *Signs work:* "Jutta Saunders" or "J.G.S."

SAVAGE, Judith, L.D.A.D.; artist in oil on canvas; *b* Sydney, Australia; one *s. Educ.:* Australia; *studied* Interior Design and Decoration and Mural Design, Chelsea College of Art (1977-80). *Exhib.:* London: Loggia Gallery, Leighton House, C.W.A.C., etc. Specialises in colour: therapeutic, psychological, symbolic aspects. Studies in art therapy, psychology, sociology (1991-92). Guest Lecturer Chelsea College of Art. Currently working St. Bernards Psychiatric Hospital, Ealing. *Address:* 32 Mansell Rd., The Vale, London W3 7QH. *Signs work:* "J. Savage."

SAVEGE, Roma; painter in oil, gouache, tempera, sculptor in welded steel and glass: sand, blasting, gilding, colouring and engraving; Hon. mem. N.S.; *b* Christchurch, N.Z., 17 July, 1907; *m* R.M. Savege, O.B.E., M.C., F.R.C.S.; six *s. Educ.:* Queenwood, Eastbourne; *studied art* at Canterbury College of Art, N.Z., and Richmond and Hounslow Colleges, England. *Exhib.:* one-man shows, Richmond Hill Gallery, R.A.G., Contemporary Portrait Soc., Circuit Painters, N.E.A.C., Guildhall, etc. *Address:* Pembroke House, The Green, Richmond, Surrey. *Clubs:* N.S., F.P.S., I.P.I., R.A.S. *Signs work:* "Roma Savege."

SAWYERS, David Robert, A.T.C. (1964), A.R.E. (1964), M.A. (1983); topographical draughtsman in pen and ink with water-colour washes; *b* Brighton, 29 Apr., 1941; *m. Educ.:* Varndean Grammar School, Brighton; *studied art* at Brighton College of Arts and Crafts (1959-64), University of Sussex (1982-83). *Exhib.:* Gardner Centre, Bankside Gallery, Pig and Fig Gallery Brighton. *Address:* 19 Foundry St., Brighton BN1 4AT. *Signs work:* "D.R. Sawyers."

SAYCE, Harry H., F.I.A.L., N.D.D.; painter; Head of the Art Department, Paddington School; *m* Oonagh McCarthy; one *s*, three *d. Educ.:* Trent Park College; *studied art* at Hammersmith School of Art; lithographic artist with the R.E. Field Survey (Reproduction Unit) in North Africa and Italy, Colchester School of Art (1942), Harrow School of Art (1938), Instituta Delle Arte, Florence (1945). *Exhib.:* R.A., R.B.A., New Burlington Galleries, Square and Mirror, A.I.A., Football and the Fine Arts, Arts Council Tours, Portsmouth, Worthing, Graves Gallery, Sheffield, Brighton, Piccadilly Gallery. *Address:* 9 Brackley Rd., Chiswick, London W4. *Club:* Chelsea Arts. *Signs work:* "Sayce."

SAYERS, Brian, B.A. (1978); painter in oil on canvas; *b* Bromley, Kent, 3 Oct., 1954. *Educ.:* St Olave's Grammar School, Kent; *studied art* at Slade School of Fine Art (1974-78, Jeffery Camp, Patrick George). *Exhib.:* R.A., N.P.G., Royal Overseas League, Riverside Open, Long & Ryle. *Address:* 22C Walterton Rd., London W9 3PN. *Signs work:* "Brian Sayers" on reverse.

SCAMPTON, Ann, R.W.A., F.R.I.B.A.; artist in pencil, ink, water-colour, etching; architect and director, Moxley, Jenner & Partners, London & Bristol; *b* Shanghai, China, 2 Feb., 1933; *d* of J. E. March, M.C., A.R.I.B.A.; *m* Peter Scampton; three *d. Educ.:* Clifton High School, Bristol; *studied art* at Royal West of England Academy School of Architecture. *Exhib.:* one-man shows, R.W.A. Annual Exhbns. *Address:* 1 Hobhouse Ct., Suffolk St., London SW1. *Club:* Cruising Assoc. *Signs work:* "A.S."

SCARFE, Laurence, A.R.C.A.; painter, graphic artist, writer. *Murals* for the Festival of Britain; *s.s. Orcades* and *Oriana; Jamestown Museum, Virginia; Royal Garden Hotel, London; penthouse mural, New York, etc. *Publications:* Rome (1950), Venice (1952), Alphabets (1954), Italian Baroque (Motif, 1961). Sometime art editor and contributor for The Saturday Book. Ceramic design for

Carters, Wedgwood, K. Clark. *Exhib.*: West End and provincial galleries, U.S.A., Italy; prints for Curwen Gallery. Work in V & A., Tate Gallery, R.I.B.A. Library, Imperial War Museum, Science Museum, Brighton A.G. Lecturer, London Central School of Art & Design (1945-70) and Faculty of Art, Brighton Polytechnic. *Address:* (studio) 4 Jeffreys St., London NW1.

SCHAEFER, Carl Fellman, R.C.A. (Canada, 1964), F.I.A.L. (1958), C.S.G.A. (1932), C.S.P.W.C. (1933), C.G.P. (1936); Head of Drawing and Painting Dept., Ontario College of Art (1956); Chairman Emeritus (1968-69); Canada Centennial Medal (1967); Queen Elizabeth II Coronation Medal (1953); Canada Silver Jubilee Medal Elizabeth II (1977); Member Order of Canada (1978); awarded J. S. Guggenheim memorial fellowship for creative painting (1940); painter in oil, water-colour and oil-tempera, printmaker, engraver and lithographer; *b* Hanover, Ontario, 30 Apr., 1903; *s* of John D. Schaefer; *m* Lillien Marie Evers; two *s. Educ.:* Hanover, Ontario and Toronto; *studied art* at Ontario College of Art. *Address:* 157 St. Clement's Ave., Toronto, Ontario M4R 1H1. *Signs work:* "C. Schaefer."

SCHIFFNER, Fritz; painter and draughtsman; mem. of The Art Soc., Aschaffenburg; *b* Graslitz (Czechoslovakia), 26 Aug., 1910; *s* of Franz Schiffner, headmaster. *Educ.:* two schools of art in Czechoslovakia; *studied art* at Academy of Art, Prague (1937-41) under Nechleba and Honich. *Exhib.:* Prague, Berlin, Stuttgart, R.A., Wuerzburg, Aschaffenburg, Darmstadt, Regensburg (Ostdeutsche Galerie), provinces. *Work in permanent collections:* wall paintings, mosaics on big buildings, in schools, hospitals, swimming pools, and churches in Germany. *Official purchases:* Minister of Public Worship and Instruction, Prague; City Hall Aschaffenburg, Museum Aschaffenburg. *Address:* Stockstadt/ Main, nr. Aschaffenburg, Germany.

SCHILSKY, Mrs. Eric: see FOOT, Victorine Anne.

SCHLEE, Anne H., P.P.N.S.; artist in water-colour, acrylic, ink; Cert. Fine Art (1972); Hon. Officer, National Soc. Painters, Sculptors and Printmakers since 1989; *b* Shanghai, China, 1931; *d* of the late Anker B. Henningsen; *m* Charles A. Schlee; three *d. Educ.:* Katharine Branson School, California; *studied art* at International School (1962-65, Chinese art: Chow Chian-Chui), Famous Artists' School (1970-72, Charles Reid, John Pellew, Joseph Laskar, Ray Peese). *Exhib.:* Hong Kong, N.S., Chelsea Art Soc., Ridley Art Soc., etc. *Work repro.:* House and Garden. *Work in permanent collections:* Guildford House Museum and Gallery; private collections in U.S.A., Canada, Australia, U.K., etc. *Address:* Brackenbrook, Smithwood Common, Cranleigh, Surrey GU6 8QX. *Signs work:* "Anschlee."

SCHOFIELD, Arlette Marie Elvire Julie; painter in oil on canvas and gesso panel, mixed media, woodcut, linocut, etching; art teacher, examiner, art critic, book illustrator (1944-52), broadcaster of talks on B.B.C. Overseas Service (1950-51); *b* Stanleyville, Zaire, 11 Sept., 1926; *d* of Francois van Calck, Chevalier de l'Ordre de Léopold, colonial civil servant; *m* John McM. Schofield, F.R.C.S.; two *s*, one *d. Educ.:* Couvent des Dames de Marie, Brussels; *studied art* at Ecole Nationale Supérieure d'Architecture et des Arts Decoratifs, Brussels (1944-48, Joris Minne, L.Hasaerts); Warwickshire C.F.E. (Simon Lewty, Barry Burman) (part time Dip.). *Exhib.:* Musée de la Gravure, Brussels, Galerie Portenaert, Brussels, Museum of Religious Art, Ostend, R.A., R.W.E.A., Westminster Cathedral, London, Warwick, Leamington Spa, B'ham, Coventry, Cirencester, Ribérac (France). *Address:* Brookhampton Farm, Kineton, Warwick CV35 0NR. *Club:* Anglo-Belgian. *Signs work:* "A. Schofield" or "A.S."

SCHWARZ, Hans, R.B.A. (1981), R.W.S. (1982), N.E.A.C (1982), R.P. (1990), Hunting Group Prize (1981); painter in water-colour and oil; *b* Vienna, 29 Dec., 1922; *s* of Victor Schwarz; *m* Lena; two *s. Educ.:* Vienna; *studied art* at Vienna Kunstgewerbeschule (1937-38), Birmingham College of Art (1941-43). *Exhib.:* R.W.S., R.A., R.B.A., N.E.A.C., R.P.; eighteen one-man shows since 1960: A.I.A., Camden Arts Centre, Cambridge, Thackeray Gallery. *Work in permanent collections:* Glasgow A.G., National Maritime Museum, Newport A.G., Halifax N.Z. A.G., Oxford University, N.P.G. *Publications:* Studio Vista: Figure Painting; Colour for the Artist; Painting in towns; four for Pitmans, etc. *Address:* c/o R.W.S., Bankside Gallery, 48 Hopton St., London SE1 9JH. *Signs work:* see appendix.

SCOTT, David Henry George Montagu Douglas; landscape painter and illustrator in oil and water-colour; *b* Edinburgh, 29 Jan., 1945; *s* of Molly Bishop, portrait artist; *m* Laura Harmsworth; two *d. Educ.:* Eton; *studied art* at Byam Shaw School of Art (1963-66, Maurice de Sausmarez), R.A. Schools (1966-67, Peter Greenham). *Exhib.:* R.A., R.B.A., R.P., Rutland Gallery, Thomas Gibson Fine Art, Maclean Gallery, The Scottish Gallery, French Embassy, Wildenstein 'Venice Observed', etc. *Work in permanent collections:* Dublin Art Museum, Thameside Council. *Publications:* illustrated five children's books for Walker Books and Methuen; contributed to 'The Children's Book' (Walker Books), 'Open Door' Series (Thomas Nelson). *Address:* 19 Petworth St., London SW11. *Signs work:* "D.S." and date on back of picture.

SCOTT, George, Dip. Art (1962), Dip. Graphic Design Technician (1977); graphic design technician in alkyd, oil, gouache, pen and ink and biro; part-time lecturer, Sidney Stringer College A.E.C.; *b* Glasgow, 25 Sept., 1938; *s* of William Scott; *m* Margaret Scott; two *s-d. Educ.:* St. Gerards Senior Secondary, Glasgow; *studied art* at Glasgow School of Art (1958-62) under Philip Reeves. *Exhib.:* Rugby, Leamington, Farnborough; one-man shows: Glasgow, Barnet, Coventry, Nuneaton, Kenilworth. *Address:* 107 School St., Wolston, Coventry. *Clubs:* Coventry & Warwickshire Soc., Group 74, Coventry Art Guild. *Signs work:* "George Scott."

SCOTT, Irene Mary, D.A. (Edin.) (1965), B.A.(Hons.) (1990), R.S.W. (1989); artist in water-colour, oil, etching; Com. mem. R.S.W.; *b* Penicuik, Midlothian, 31 Dec., 1942; *d* of Andrew H. Scott; *m* Brian S. Duffield; four *s*, one *d. Educ.:* Lasswade High School; *studied art* at Edinburgh College of Art (1961-65). *Exhib.:* R.S.A., R.S.W., S.S.A., various group exhbns., etc. *Work in private collections:* Britain, Norway, Poland and U.S.A. *Address:* 26 Elbe St., Leith, Edinburgh EX6 7HW. *Signs work:* "Irene M. Scott."

SCOTT, John Edward, A.T.D., R.C.A.; Senior lecturer, College of Art, N. Wales; artist in acrylic and mixed media; *b* Beckenham, Kent, 21 Apr., 1934. *Educ.:* Windsor Grammar School; *studied art* at Reading University School of Fine Art (1954-57) under Prof. J. Antony Betts. Work owned privately in Europe, esp. London. *Address:* 8 Halkyn Rd., Chester CH2 3QE. *Signs work:* "John Scott."

SCOTT, Judy, N.D.D. (1961), C.S.D. (1962); painter in gouache; part-time teacher adult educ. and summer schools; *b* Herts., 7 Nov., 1939. *Studied art* at Maidstone College of Art (1956-58, Dick Lee), Central School of Arts and Crafts (1958-62). *Exhib.:* solo shows: Cadogan Gallery London, Wells Art Centre Norfolk, Bacons Gallery Aysham; mixed shows: New Grafton, Abbott & Holder London, N.E.A.C., R.P., R.W.S., R.I., Bircham Gallery nr. Kings Lynn;

R.W.S. Abbott & Holder Travel award (1993). *Address:* 4 Church Cottage, Bale, Fakenham, Norfolk NR21 0QZ. *Signs work:* "J. Scott."

SCOTT, Marian D., R.C.A.; mem. Conseil des Artistes Peintre du Québec and C.A.R., former mem. Canadian Group of Painters; painter in acrylic polymer; teacher; *b* Montreal, 26 June, 1906; *d* of R. J. Dale; *m* Frank R. Scott (decd.); one *s.* Studied art at Art Assoc. of Montreal, Ecole des Beaux-Arts (Montreal), Slade School. *Exhib.:* N.Y. World's Fair (1939), Canadian National Exhbn., O.S.A., Canadian Group, and in U.S.A., Brazil, Australia, S. Africa, London. *Work in permanent collections:* Montreal Museum of Fine Arts, Quebec Provincial Museum, Toronto A.G., National Gallery of Canada, Vancouver A.G., Bezalel Museum (Jerusalem), Beaverbrook Museum (Fredrickton, N.B.), Thomas Moore Inst., etc. *Address:* 451 Clarke Ave., Montreal, Qué., Canada, H3Y 3C5. *Signs work:* "M. Scott."

SCOTT-KESTIN, Colin, A.R.M.S. (1992), H.S. (1989); painter in oil, water-colour and gouache of landscapes, equestrian and other animal subjects, especially miniatures; *b* 14 Jan., 1921; *m* Mary Widdows. *Educ.:* St. Giles School, St. Leonard-on-Sea; *studied art* at Beckenham School of Art (1938-39, Henry Carr, R.P.). *Exhib.:* R.M.S., H.S., S.Eq.A., Llewellyn Alexander (Fine Art). *Work in permanent collections:* war sketches, Royal Signals Museum, Blandford. *Address:* Strapp Cottage, Skillgate La., Chiselborough, Som. TA14 6TP. *Signs work:* "C. SCOTT-KESTIN."

SCOTT-MOORE, Elizabeth, R.W.S., N.E.A.C.; portrait and landscape painter and illustrator; *b* Dartford, Kent; *d* of Henry Brier, M.I.M.E.; *m* John Scott-Moore, F.S.S., F.S.A.A. *Educ.:* Dartford, Kent; *studied art* at Goldsmiths' School of Art, Central School of Art. *Exhib.:* R.A., R.W.S., R.P., N.E.A.C. *Awards:* Gold Medal for Painting, Paris Salon (1962), 1st Prize for water-colour, Glastonbury, Conn., U.S.A., Queen Elizabeth Dip. for Water-colour painting. *Work in many private and permanent collections* including R.W.S. Dip Coll., the Royal Coll., and in America, Italy, Norway and British Isles. *Work repro.:* illustrated numerous children's books for Oxford University Press, Nelson, Blackies, Cassells, etc. *Official purchases:* Min. of Works; Hull Corp. *Address:* Merlewood, Callow Hill, Virginia Water, Surrey GU25 4LR. *Signs work:* "Elizabeth Scott-Moore."

SCOTT-TAGGART, Elizabeth Mary Josephine, N.D.D.; sculptor working in bronze, aluminium, ceramics; mainly stone- and wood-carver; *b* nr. Croydon, 10 Oct., 1927. *Educ.:* Old Palace School, Croydon; *studied art* at Central School of Arts and Crafts, and St. Martin's, London (1945-49). *Exhib.:* R.A.; group shows: R.B.A., Trends at Mall Galleries, Loggia Gallery, Wooburn and Cookham Festivals, Burleighfields International Art Centre, nr. High Wycombe, Bucks, Century Galleries, Henley-on-Thames, Barton A.G., Tenterden; two-man show: Threehouseholds Gallery, Chalfont St. Giles. Full mem. F.P.S. *Address:* 96 Gregories Rd., Beaconsfield, Bucks. *Signs work:* "est."

SCROPE-HOWE, Pat, Sociétaire of Société des Artistes Indépendants Paris (1973); Sociétaire of Artistes Français Le Salon Paris (1975); painter in oil, pastel, acrylic, water-colour; sculptor in cire perdue and GRP/bronze; *b* London, 27 Jan., 1926; *m*; two *s.* Studied art at Torbay Art School (1958-59), Saskatchewan Art Council (1959-60), Bourneville Art School (1961-62), Manchester Fine Arts (1963-69), Florence, Rome and Venice. Also travelled and painted in France, U.S.A., Spain, Egypt, Far East, South America and the Caribbean. Studied under Harry Rutherford (pupil of Sickert) for portraiture and studies in pastel and oils, Terry McGlynn for abstract and experimental art,

Ian McDonald Grant for History of Art, life and composition. *Exhib.*: Paris: Salon des Nations (1984), Grand Palais (Indépendants and Artistes Français) since 1973; provinces: Salford Open (1964), Withington, Liverpool Open (bi-annual), Colin Jellicoe Gallery, Manchester College; London: R.S.M.A. Boat Show and National Tour (1969-73). Painting rented via R.S.M.A. for a Polaris Submarine which went under North and South Poles (1973); London International Open, S.W.A. and their National Tour (1972), Laing Competition (1975), Hesketh Hubbard Soc., U.A., Long Gallery, Isleworth (solo show), Royal Horticultural Art Exhbn., Festival of Paintings and Graphic Art (1972); Ireland: Kilkenny (solo show), Dunmore East, Waterford (Studio, permanent solo show). *Work in private collections:* Canada, Australia, Gt. Britain, Ireland and the continent. Has appeared on CKBI TV (Canada) to talk on art. *Address:* Chandos, 185 Spring Grove Rd., Isleworth, Middx. TW7 4AL. *Signs work:* "Pat Scrope-Howe."

SCRYMGEOUR WEDDERBURN, Janet, F.R.B.S. (1980), R.S.A. Ottillie Helen Wallace Scholarship (1972), R.S.A. Benno Schotz Prize (1973), Paris Salon bronze medal, silver medal; sculptor in clay and bronze, stained glass window designer; *b* Winchester, 14 Aug., 1941; *d* of Lt. Col. the Hon. David Scrymgeour Wedderburn, D.S.O.; *m* Mervyn Fox-Pitt; one *s,* two *d. Educ.:* Kilgraston, Convent of the Sacred Heart, Bridge of Earn, Perthshire; *studied art* with Alastair Ross, F.R.B.S. (1970-71). *Exhib.:* R.S.A. (1971-76, sculpture); Paris Salon (1972, 1973, sculpture). *Work in permanent collection:* East Window of the Episcopal Church of St. James the Great, Cupar, Fife; West Window the Chapel Royal, Falkland Palace; Meditation Window Bedale Church, Yorks.; Victory and Freedom Windows, R.A.F. Leuchars, St. Paul's Church (1993). *Address:* Grange Scrymgeour, Cupar, Fife. KY15 4QH. *Signs work:* "J.S.W."

SCULL, Paul Harvey, B.F.A.Hons. (1975), H.D.F.A.Lond. (1978), R.E. (1986), M.Ed. (1988); graphic artist; lecturer in charge of printmaking, Herefordshire College of Art and Design; *b* London, 1953. *Educ.:* Kimbolton School, Cambs.; *studied art* at Northampton School of Art (1971-72), Maidstone College of Art (1972-75, Stuart Brisley, William Bowyer, Joan Williams), Slade School of Fine Art (1976-78, David Leverett). *Exhib.:* R.A. Summer Exhbns., R.E., National Exhbn. of Prints, Blackpool, Humberside Printmaking Competition. *Work in permanent collections:* Rank Xerox, Sheffield Metropolitan Borough, Bedfordshire, Kent, Hereford and Worcester C.C's. *Address:* Fair View, Brockhampton, Hereford HR1 4SQ. *Signs work:* "Paul Scull."

SEAGER, Harry Abram, A.T.D. (Birm., 1955); sculptor in glass and mixed media, cast and constructed metals; Senior Lecturer, College of Art, Stourbridge, W.Midlands; *b* Birmingham, 9 May, 1931; *s* of Maurice Seager; *m*; two children. *Educ.:* Holly Lodge Grammar School, Smethwick, Warley, W.Midlands; *studied art* at College of Art, Birmingham. *Work in permanent collections:* City Art Gallery, Leeds, C.A.S., London, Joseph H. Hirshorne Coll., U.S.A., D.O.E. London, V. & A., W.Midlands Arts; private collections in Canada, U.K., U.S.A., Holland, Italy. *Address:* 1 Baylie St., Stourbridge, W.Midlands DY8 1AZ.

SEAL, Norman; painter in oil, ink, water-colour, calligrapher; *b* Warsop, Notts., 26 Feb., 1921; *s* of George Seal; one *s,* one *d. Educ.:* Mansfield Technical College; *studied art* at Mansfield College of Art (1963). *Exhib.:* Nottingham Castle (1965), Fermoy, Kings Lynn (1978), Hudson Gallery, Wisbech (1978), Assembly House, Norwich (1978, 1990), Municipal Gallery, Mansfield (1981), Angles Theatre, Wisbech (1988), Central Library, Cambridge (1988). *Address:*

15 Westfield Rd., Wisbech, Cambs. PE13 3EU. *Club:* Cambridge Arts Forum. *Signs work:* "N. Seal" and see appendix.

SEARLE, Ronald; *b* Cambridge, 3 Mar., 1920; *studied* Cambridge School of Art (1936-39). *Exhib.:* Leicester Galleries (1948, 1950, 1954 and 1957); Kraushaar Galleries, New York (1959); Bianchini Gallery, New York (1963); Kunsthalle, Bremen (1965); Wilhelm-Busch Museum, Hanover (1965, 1976); Wolfgang Gurlitt Museum, Linz, Austria (1966); Galerie La Pochade, Paris (1966, 1967, 1968, 1969, 1971, 1976); Galerie Carmen Cassé, Paris (1975, 1977), Galerie Gurlitt, Munich (1967, 1969, 1970, 1971 and 1973); retrospectives: Bibliothèque Nationale, Paris (1973), Prussian National Gallery (1976), etc. *Address:* c/o Tessa Sayle, 11 Jubilee Pl., London SW3 3TE. *Club:* Garrick. *Signs work:* see appendix.

SEDDON, Richard Harding, R.W.S., A.R.C.A., Ph.D.; painter in oil and water-colour, and writer on art. *Educ.:* King Edward VII School and Reading University; *art training:* Sheffield College of Art (1932-36); Royal College of Art (1936-39). *Exhib.:* R.A., R.W.S. *Official acquisitions:* H.M. The Queen, V. & A., Imperial War Museum, Sheffield, Leeds, Derby, Southport, Reading, Philadelphia (U.S.A), Neufchatel (France). *Publications:* The Academic Technique of Oil Painting (1960), A Hand Uplifted (War Artist Memoirs) (1963), Art Collecting for Amateurs (1965), A Dictionary of Art Terms (1982) (with K. Reynolds), The Artist's Studio Book (1983); art criticism in The Guardian and most art journals; London art critic of Birmingham Post (1961-70); of Yorkshire Post since 1974. *Address:* 6 Arlesey Cl., London SW15 2EX.

SEDLECKA, Irena, F.R.B.S., S.P.S.; Laureat of State Prize, Czechoslovakia (1953), Prize of City, Prague (1953); sculptor; *b* Pilsen, Czechoslovakia, 1928. *Educ.:* Academy of Fine Arts, Prague. *Work in permanent collections:* Monument for Victims of Fascism, Velke Mezirici, Moravia; Monument of Julius Fucik, Pilsen; National Gallery, Prague; work in private collections in Britain, U.S.A, and Czechoslovakia. *Address:* 1A Quarry Rd., London SW18. *Signs work:* "SEDLECKA/90."

SEGAL, Hyman, R.B.A.; artist in charcoal and all mediums; founder mem. Penwith Soc.; *b* London, 26 May, 1914; *s* of Fredel Segal; *m* Diane Christie. *Educ.:* Elementary and J.F.S., London; *studied art* at St. Martin's (Leon Underwood, Vivian Pitchforth). *Exhib.:* one-man shows: Bankfield Museum, Halifax, Batley, Nairobi, E. Africa, International Club, Manchester, Downings Bookshop, Heffer Gallery, Castle Gallery, St. Ives, The Crypt, St. Ives, Penwith Soc., St. Ives Soc. of Artists. *Work in permanent collections:* 'Bernard Leach' National Museum of Wales, 'Study of a Footballer' Manchester City A.G., The Sloop Inn, St. Ives permanent exhbn. since 1948. *Publications:* "Familiar Faces of St. Ives"; Art Colony"; "As I was Going to St. Ives." *Address:* 10 Porthmeor Studios. *Club:* Chelsea Arts. *Signs work:* "H. Segal."

SELBIE, Rosy; artist in oil, water-colour, pastel; *b* Wales, 1 Oct., 1930; *m* Robert, civil engineer; one *s*, one *d*. *Educ.:* Birtwhistles, London SW1; *studied art* at Sir John Cass Foundation (Roy Marsden). *Exhib.:* solo shows: Knapp Gallery, Burghclere Manor; numerous mixed shows including Mall Galleries. *Work in permanent collection:* Regents College. *Address:* Fellowes Cottage, Hurstbourne Priors, Whitchurch, Hants. RG28 7SE. *Club:* Sloane. *Signs work:* "Selbie."

SELBY, William, A.R.B.A. (1988), A.R.W.S. (1987), R.O.I. (1982); painter; *b* Fitzwilliam, nr. Pontefract, Yorks., 25 Dec., 1933; *s* of Henry Selby, miner; *m*

Mary. *Educ.:* Fitzwilliam Secondary Modern. *Prizes:* Christina Leger award R.O.I. (1985, 1987), Chris Beetle award (1986), L. Cornelissen & Son award R.O.I. (1988). *Work in private collection:* Mapin Gallery, Sheffield. *Address:* 22 Sandringham Rd., Byrom, Knottingley, Yorks. WF11 9NS. *Club:* Leeds Fine Art. *Signs work:* "SELBY" or "WILLIAM SELBY."

SELL, Richard, A.T.D. (1949); artist in lithography, water-colour, drawing; Vice Pres. Cambridge Drawing Soc., Soc. of Graphic Fine Art; *b* Berkhamsted, 26 Jan., 1922; *s* of F.R. Sell, Prof. of English, Mysore Educ. Service; *m* Jean Bryant; one *s*, one *d. Educ.:* Berkhamsted School; *studied art* at Chelsea School of Art (Brian Robb, Morland Lewis, Harold Jones, Ceri Richards, Ella Griffin). *Exhib.:* one-man shows: Old Fire Engine House Ely, Heffer Gallery Cambridge, Trumpington Gallery Cambridge; R.A. Summer Shows, National Exhbn. Prints and Drawings R.I. Gallery (1964), E. Anglian Art Today R.I. Gallery (1969), Mall Prints (1971, 1972, 1973), Art in Business, Arthur Young, Cambridge (1987, 1988). *Address:* 22 Station Rd., Fulbourn, Cambridge CB1 5ES. *Signs work:* "Richard Sell 1992."

SEMMENCE, John Oswald, D.A. Travelling Scholarship Award (1953), U.A.; retd. teacher of art, artist in oil, gouache and pencil; Former Head of Art Dept., St. John's Comprehensive School, Newham; *b* Kincardine-o-Neil, Aberdeenshire, 14 Feb., 1930; *s* of Adrian G. Semmence, M.A., headmaster; *m* Vivienne Semmence. *Educ.:* Robert Gordon's College, Aberdeen; *studied art* at Gray's School of Art (1947-52) under Robert Sivell, R.S.A. *Exhib.:* R.S.A., R.S.P.P., R.B.A., N.E.A.C., U.A., Societé des Independants, Paris; one-man shows: 6½ Suffolk St. (1965-71), Edinburgh Festival (1972), Gallery Paton (1974), Mall Galleries (1976), Commonwealth Institute, Edinburgh (1978, 1984), F.B.A., Bradshaw Room (1981, 1983). *Work in permanent collections:* Cruden Coll., Pitlochry, Edinburgh City Coll., Edinburgh Hospitals, Nuffield Foundation, Fields Gallery, Oklahoma and Simonow Collection. *Address:* 32 Church Ave., Beckenham, Kent. *Club:* Scottish Arts. *Signs work:* "J. SEMMENCE" (oils), "J. Semmence" (gouache and drawings).

SEMPLE, Patricia Frances, S.S.A. (1980), R.S.W. (1987); painter of expressionist landscape in water-colour, ink, oil, charcoal; tutor, Open College of the Arts; *b* Kintyre, Argyll, 3 July, 1939; *d* of Neil Thompson Semple, merchant naval officer. *Educ.:* Lasswade Grammar; *studied art* at Edinburgh College of Art (1958-63), post. grad. (1963-64). *Exhib.:* Stirling Gallery, Art Space Aberdeen, Edinburgh University, Aberdeen University, Dundee College of Art, Open Eye Gallery Edinburgh, regularly with R.S.A., S.S.A., R.S.W.; group shows: Glasgow Group, Scottish Gallery, Compass Gallery, Arts Council Travelling Exhbn. Scotland and Yugoslavia. *Work in permanent collections:* S.A.C., Aberdeen A.G., B.B.C., Globus, Gateway Inc. N.Y., Educ. Inst. of Scotland, Grampian TV, Aberdeen Hospitals, Shell U.K. *Address:* Tigh-Nan-Uiseagan, By Drumnadrochit, Inverness-shire. *Signs work:* "Pat Semple."

SENFT, Nadin, A.R.B.S. (1980), City and Guilds D.F.A. (1968); sculptor in bronze, stone, wood, perspex; *b* London, 8 Mar., 1932; *d* of Basil Andreanoff, B.Sc.; *m* Dr. Paul Senft (decd.). *Educ.:* St. Mary's Abbey, London; Eversley, Lymington, Hants.; *studied art* at Leicester College of Art; City and Guilds of London College of Art, Kennington. *Exhib.:* R.A., Alwin Gallery, Royal Exchange, Jordan Gallery, Annely Juda Fine A.G., Hertford Museum, Sutton College of Art, Natalie Stern Gallery, Richard Demarco Gallery, Edinburgh, Scone Palace, Perth, Shakespeare Centre, Stratford-on-Avon. *Public commissions:* 'St. George and the Dragon', St. George's Centre, Preston; 'Seated Bronze

Figures' Guildhall Sq., Portsmouth. *Publication:* Sixteen Stories as they Happend by Michael Bullock. *Address:* Willowbrook, Cotswold Cl., Tredington, Warwicks. *Signs work:* "Nadin Senft" and see appendix.

SENIOR, Bryan; painter of figures, landscape, still-life; *b* Bolton, 1935. *Exhib.:* one-man shows: Crane Kalman Gallery, London (1965, 1968, 1971), Demarco, Edinburgh (1970, 1973), Vaccarino, Florence (1968, 1970, 1975), Pucker-Safrai, Boston, U.S.A. (1968), Bolton A.G. (1961), Fieldborne Galleries, London (1972), Ashgate Gallery, Farnham (1973), Exeter Museum (1974), Exeter University (1975), Galleria Acropoli, Milan (1976), Lad Lane Gallery, Dublin (1977), Architectural Assoc., London (1982), Hampstead Museum (1983), Manor House, Finchley (1989), Tricycle Gallery (1990), Hooper Gallery, London (1991). *Prizes:* G.L.C. 'Spirit of London'; Druce Competition. *Address:* 80 Hay La., Kingsbury, London NW9 0LG.

SEROTA, Nicholas Andrew; Director, Tate Gallery (since 1988); *b* 27 Apr., 1946; *s* of Stanley Serota and Beatrice Serota; *m* Angela Mary Beveridge; two *d. Educ.:* Haberdashers' Askes School, Hampstead and Elstree; Christ's College, Cambridge (B.A.); Courtauld Inst. of Art, London (M.A.). Regional Art Officer and Exhbn. Organiser, Arts Council of G.B. (1970-73); Director, Museum of Modern Art, Oxford (1973-76); Director, Whitechapel A.G. (1976-88). Mem., Fine Art Advisory Com., British Council (1976-), Chairman 1992; Trustee, Public Art Development Trust (1983-87); Trustee, Architecture Foundation (1992-). Selector 'A New Spirit in Painting', R.A. (1981), Carnegie International, Carnegie Museum of Art, Pittsburgh (1985, 1988). *Address:* Tate Gallery, London SW1P 4RG.

SERRA-BADUE, Daniel F.; Guggenheim Foundation Fellowships, N.Y. (1938, 1939); Walter Lippincott Prize, Penn. Acad. of Fine Arts, Philadelphia (1941); Purchase Prizes: II Bienal Hispano Americana, VII Salon Nacional, Havana (1954); Cintas Foundation Fellowships, N.Y. (1963, 1964); painter, graphic artist in oil and lithograph and art teacher; Instructor of Painting, Professor of Art History, St. Peter's College, Jersey City, N.J.; *b* Santiago de Cuba, 8 Sept., 1914; *s* of Daniel Serra y Navas, lawyer and educator, and Eloisa Badue y de las Cuevas; *m* Aida Betancourt Zabala; one *d. Educ.:* Universities of Barcelona and Havana; *studied art* at Escuela de Bellas Artes, Santiago de Cuba (1924-26), Studios of Borrell-Nicolau and Muntane, Escuela de Bellas Artes, Barcelona (1932-36), The Art Students League, The National Academy of Design, Columbia University, N.Y. (1938-40). *Work in permanent collections:* Museo Municipal, Santiago de Cuba, Museo Nacional, Havana, Metropolitan Museum, N.Y., Public Library, N.Y., Museum of Modern Art, N.Y., Instituto de Cultura Hispanica, Madrid, Museum of Contemporary Latin American Art, Washington, D.C., The Brooklyn Museum, N.Y., University of North Dakota, U.S.A. *Publications:* The Visual Arts in Santiago de Cuba during the Colonial Period. *Address:* 15 West 72nd St., New York, N.Y., 10023. *Signs work:* see appendix.

SETCH, Terry, D.F.A. (Lond., 1959); painter; Senior Lecturer in Fine Art, Cardiff College of Art (1964—); *b* London, 11 Mar., 1936; *s* of Frank Arthur Setch, welder; *m* Dianne Shaw; one *d. Educ.:* Sutton and Cheam School; *studied art* at Sutton School of Art (1950-54), Slade School of Fine Art (1956-60). *Work in permanent collections:* Tate Gallery, Arts Council of G.B., Welsh Arts Council, Aberystwyth University, Contemporary Arts Soc. of Wales, V. & A., University College, London, Gallery of Modern Art, Lodz, Poland, Swansea University, British Council, National Museum of Wales, Contemporary Arts Soc., Coleg Harlech, Wakefield City A.G., Glynn Vivian Museum and A.G.,

Northampton A.G. *Address:* 111 Plymouth Rd., Penarth, Glamorgan CF64 5DF, S. Wales. *Signs work:* "Terry Setch."

SEUPHOR, Michel; writer, painter (in Chinese ink, and coloured paper collage), art historian, poet; *b* Antwerp, 10 Mar., 1901; *m* Suzanne Plasse; one *s. Educ.:* Antwerp and University of Louvain. *Exhib.:* Galerie Berggruen, Paris; Galerie Denise Renée, Paris; Rose Fried Gallery, New York; Galleria Lorenzelli, Milan; Moderne Galerie, Basel; Galerie der Spiegel, Cologne; Documenta II, Kassel; Galerie St. Stephen, Wien; Galerie Saint Laurent, Brussels; Galerie Ziegler, Zürich; Robles Galleries, Los Angeles; Galerie Martano, Turin; Musée National d'Art Moderne, Paris; Musée de le Boverie, Liége. *Publications:* Seuphor, Centre Pompidou, Paris. Tapestries, mosaics and ceramics (Sèvres). *Address:* 83 avenue Emile Zola, F. 75015 Paris, XV. *Signs work:* see appendix.

SEWARD, P., A.R.C.A., Hon. Retd. A.R.E., R.W.S., Rome Scholar, Dip. in Paper Conservation; artist in pen and ink, water-colour, gesso; *b* London, 1926. *Studied art* at Royal College of Art, Camberwell School of Art and Crafts (Conservation of Prints and Drawings). *Exhib.:* R.A., Bankside Gallery, Barbican, London. *Publications:* children's books, cookery books. *Address:* 30 Sekforde St., London EC1R 0HH. *Signs work:* "P. Seward."

SEWELL, Peggy Joan Kearton, M.F.P.S. (1986); painter of landscapes and flowers in oil on canvas and hardboard; *b* London, 18 Dec., 1920; *d* of Albert E. Chandler, Director; *m* Robert H. Sewell, Ch.M., F.R.C.S.; two *d. Educ.:* Manchester High School, and Merchant Venturers College, Bristol; *studied art* at Croydon Art College and privately with Richard Walker, N.D.D., A.T.D. *Exhib.:* Guildhall London, Royal Exchange, Fairfield Halls Croydon. *Address:* 4 Bayards, Warlingham, Surrey CR6 9BP. *Clubs:* Croydon Art Soc., Purley Art Group, F.P.S., Tandridge Art Soc. *Signs work:* "Joan Sewell."

SEWTER, Albert Charles, B.Sc.(Econ.), M.A., F.M.A., F.R.S.A.; art historian; Reader, University of Manchester (1966); *b* 29 Nov., 1912; *m* 1st, Annie Beatrice Dibdin (d. 1941); 2nd Margarita Masters (div. 1964); two *s. Publications:* Glyn Philpot (Batsford, 1951), On the Relationship between Painting and Architecture (Tiranti, 1952), The Art of Fresco Painting (Tiranti, 1952), Modern British Woodcuts and Wood-engravings in the Whitworth Art Gallery (1962), I Disegni di G. B. Piazzetta, Rome (1969), Baroque and Rococo Art (Thames & Hudson, 1971), The Stained Glass of William Morris and his Circle (Yale U.P., 1974-75), etc. *Address:* c/o 31 Ernest Grove, Beckenham, Kent BR3 3HY.

SEYMOUR, Helen, S.W.A. (1982), Mem. Printmakers Council (1985); teacher, artist in water-colour, oil, etching, lino-printing, sculpture; *b* Dorset, 9 Mar., 1929; one *s,* one *d. Educ.:* S. Dorset Technical College; *studied art* at Bournemouth and Poole College of Art (1980-85). *Exhib.:* R.A., R.W.A., R.B.A., S.W.A.; one-man shows: The Hambledon Gallery, Blandford, The Red House, Christchurch, Havant Museum and A.G. *Publication:* article in The Artist (1983). *Address:* Coombe House, 63 Coombe Ave., Weymouth, Dorset. *Signs work:* "Helen Seymour."

SEYMOUR, Jack, N.D.D. (1954), Ad.Cert.Ed. (1962); painter of landscapes, interiors and portraits in oil, pencil and water-colour; part time lecturer; *b* London, 23 Apr., 1928; *s* of Clive Seymour (decd.); one *s,* two *d. Educ.:* Southall Technical School; *studied art* at Harrow School of Art (1948-52, C. Sanders, T. Ward), Gloucester College of Art (1952-54, R.S.G. Dent), St. Paul's College, Cheltenham (1960-62, H.W. Sayer). *Exhib:* R.B.A., R.P., R.A., R.W.A.; one-man show, Stroud, Gloucs.; provincial galleries and travelling exhbns. *Work in* *private collections:* Britain and abroad. *Address:* 3 Holeground, School Hill, Wookey Hole, Som. BA5 1BU. *Signs work:* "SEYMOUR" and year.

SHACKLETON, Keith Hope, R.S.M.A., S.WL.A., Hon.Doctor of Laws; oil painter, writer, naturalist, T.V.; *b* Weybridge, 16 Jan., 1923; *m* Jacqueline; two *s*, one *d*. *Educ.:* Melbourne, Australia, Oundle. *Work in permanent collections:* R.S.M.A. Maritime Museum, Greenwich, Birkenhead, Belfast A.G., LYW Art Museum Wisconsin, U.S.A. *Publications:* Wake, Tidelines, Wild Animals in Britain, Ship in the Wilderness, Wildlife and Wilderness. *Address:* Woodley Wood Farm, Woodleigh, Kingsbridge, Devon TQ7 4DR. *Signs work:* see appendix.

SHANKS, Duncan Faichney, D.A., A.R.S.A. (1972), R.G.I. (1983), R.S.W. (1987), R.S.A. (1990); artist in oil; *b* Airdrie, 30 Aug., 1937; *s* of Duncan Faichney, D.A.; *m* Una Brown Gordon. *Studied art* at Glasgow School of Art. *Exhib.:* Art Spectrum, Contemporary Art from Scotland (1981-82), Five Glasgow Painters, Scottish Painting—Toulouse, About Landscape—Edinburgh Festival, Scottish Painting—Rio de Janeiro, Ten Scottish Painters—London, Scottish Painting—Wales, Bath, Basle, London Art Fairs; one-man shows: Stirling University, Scottish Gallery, Fine Art Soc.—Glasgow and Edinburgh, Talbot Rice Gallery, Edinburgh (cat.), Crawford Centre, St. Andrews, Maclaurin Gallery, Ayr, Glasgow A.G. (1990), Touring Exhbn. Wales (1991-92) (Cat.), Billcliffe Fine Art (1992). *Work in permanent collections:* A.C.G.B., Scottish Art Council, Glasgow, Dundee and Swansea A.Gs., Hunterian Museum, Edinburgh University, City Art Centre, Edinburgh, Lillie A.G., Government Art Collection, Scottish TV., 'Talking Pictures', STV film. *Address:* Davingill House, Crossford By Carluke, Clyde Valley. *Signs work:* "SHANKS."

SHANKS, Una Brown, D.A. (Textiles) (1962), R.S.W. (1988); artist in watercolour, pen and ink; *b* Hartwood, 9 June, 1940; *d* of Lawrence Gordon; *m* D.F. Shanks. *Educ.:* Wishaw High School; *studied art* at Glasgow School of Art (1958-62). *Exhib.:* Scottish Artists Shop (1987), Fine Art Soc. (1988, 1989). *Awards:* Alexander Stone R.G.I. (1990, 1991), Betty Davies R.S.W. (1993). *Address:* Davingill House, Crossford By Carluke, Clyde Valley. *Signs work:* "Una B. Shanks."

SHARP, Elizabeth, S.Eq.A. (1988), A.S.E.A. (1984), S.W.A. (1986), B.H.S.A.I. (1969); artist in oil, pastel, acrylic and sculptor specializing in animal and equestrian subjects; breeds American Morgan horses; *b* 7 Jan., 1947; *d* of H.S. Sharp (decd.). *Educ.:* Kesteven and Grantham Girls' High School; *studied art* at Leicester College of Art and Design (1965-66), Stoke Rochford College (1966-70). *Exhib.:* regularly with S.E.A. and S.W.A. in London; occasionally one-man shows. *Work in permanent collections:* sculpture in Victoria Centre, Sydney, Australia; Flying Horse Centre, Nottingham; Reindeer Court, Worcester.*Address:* The Old Rectory, Denton, Grantham, Lincs. NG32 1JT. *Club:* British Horse Soc. *Signs work:* "Elizabeth Sharp."

SHAVE, Terry, B.A.(Hons.), H.D.F.A. (Slade); artist in oil, acrylic on canvas, etching; lecturer; Head of Painting, Staffordshire Polytechnic; *b* 8 June, 1952. *Studied art:* Loughborough College of Art (1972-75), Slade School of Fine Art (1975-77). *Exhib.:* Anderson O'Day Gallery. *Work in permanent collections:* A.C.G.B., Unilever, B'ham City Museum and A.G., Stoke Museum and A.G. *Address:* c/o Anderson O'Day, 255 Portobello Rd., London W11 1LR. *Signs work:* Terry Shave."

SHAW, Geoff, N.D.D.; artist in oil of naval scenes, steam locos, aircraft, cars, harbour views, etc.; *b* Mossley, Lancs., 17 Dec., 1924. *Educ.:* Ashton Grammar School; *studied art* at Falmouth. *Work in private collections* in seventeen countries. *Work repro.:* prints and various book covers. *Address:* 31B Church St., Falmouth, Cornwall. *Signs work:* "GeoffShaw."

SHAW, Sax Roland, D.A. (Edin.), F.M.G.P.; former Head of Stained Glass Dept., Edinburgh College of Art (retd. 1984); works in tapestry, stained glass, mural decoration, water-colour paintings; *b* Huddersfield, 5 Dec., 1916; *s* of Roland Wilfred Shaw; *m* Mary; two *s*. *Educ.:* Almondbury Grammar School; *studied art* at Huddersfield, Edinburgh, Paris. *Work in permanent collections:* private and public buildings in Edinburgh, London, New York, San Francisco, Iceland. At present working on windows and tapestries for the Marquis of Bute. *Address:* 25 Howe St., Edinburgh EH3 6TF. *Signs work:* "Shaw."

SHEARS, Marcelle Dorothy, R.M.S., S.M., S.W.A., F.H.S.; silhouette artist and miniature painter in water-colour on vellum, ivory, plaster, glass and card; Hunting Group finalist (1981), U.S.A., M.A.S.F. 1st (1981), 2nd (1983), G.M.A.S. 2nd (1992), H.S., Lucas award (1985), R.M.S. Hon. Mention gold memorial bowl (1986); *b* Croydon, 16 May, 1926; *d* of the late George H. Tozer, artist and signwriter; *m* Arthur D. Shears; two *d*. *Educ.:* Chipstead Valley School, Surrey; *studied art* with George H. Tozer. *Exhib.:* R.A., Mall Galleries, Westminster Gallery, Southampton A.G., Medici A.G., M.A.S.F., U.S.A., Portsmouth A.G., Llewellyn Alexander A.G. *Work in permanent collections:* Royal Soc. of Miniature Painters, Sculptors and Gravers, Fareham Museum, Hants., Picture Gallery, Linslade. *Address:* Trout Cottage, Two Bridges, nr. Princetown, Yelverton, Devon PL20 6SW. *Signs work:* see appendix.

SHEPHARD, Rupert, Hon. A. L'Accademia Fiorentina; R.P., N.E.A.C.; painter, graphic artist; Slade Dipl.; lecturer, Central School, St. Martin's School of Art (1945-48); Professor of Art, University of Cape Town (1948-63); *b* 12 Feb., 1909; *m* 1st, Lorna Wilmott (decd., 1962); one *s*, two *d*; 2nd, Nicolette Devas (1965). *Exhib.:* one-man: Calmann Gall. (1939), Agnews (1962, 1980), Upper Grosvenor Gall. (1966, 1970), Kunsthalle, Bielefeld, Germany (1973), Collectors Gall., Johannesburg (1975), Patrick Seale Gall. (1975, 1979), Sally Hunter Gall. (1985, 1987, 1989, 1991), National Museum of Wales, Parkin Gallery (1977), Cape Town (seven) and Johannesburg (three) (1949-63); general: London: R.A., R.P., etc.; Venice Biennale (1958), São Paulo Bienal (1957), Ljubljana Biennale (1955, 1957, 1959, 1961). *Work purchased:* C.E.M.A. British Museum, War Artists, National Portrait Gall., National Museum of Wales, South African National Gall., Johannesburg Municipal Gall. *Illustrated books:* Capescapes (1954), Passing Scene (1966). *Address:* 68 Limerston St., London SW10 0HJ.

SHEPHEARD, Sir Peter (Faulkner), Kt. (1980), C.B.E. (1972), B.Arch., Liverpool (1936), P.P.R.I.B.A., M.R.T.P.I., P.P.I.L.A.; architect, town planner, landscape architect, draughtsman and illustrator. In private practice (Shepheard, Epstein & Hunter) (1948-1989); Prof. of Environmental Design (and Dean 1971-76) of the Graduate School of Fine Arts, University of Pennsylvania, Philadelphia (1971-); mem. National Parks Commission (1966-68), Countryside Commission (1968-71), Royal Fine Art Commission (1968-71), Artistic advisor, Commonwealth War Graves Commision (1977-); *b* Birkenhead, 1913; *s* of Thomas Faulkner Shepheard F.R.I.B.A.; *m* Mary Bailey; one *s*, one *d*. *Educ.:* Birkenhead School; *studied* at Liverpool School of Architecture and Dept. of Civic Design. *Exhib.:* R.A., etc. *Publications:* Modern Gardens (Arch. Press,

1953), Gardens (C.O.I.D., 1969); illustr.: A Book of Ducks and Woodland Birds. *Address:* 21 Well Rd., London NW3 1LH. *Signs work:* "Peter Shepheard."

SHEPHERD, David, O.B.E. (1979), F.R.S.A. (1986), F.R.G.S. (1988); artist; *b* 25 Apr., 1931; *s* of Raymond Oxley Shepherd; *m* Avril Gaywood; four *d.* *Educ.:* Stowe; *studied art* under Robin Goodwin (1950-1953); started career as aviation artist, founder member of Guild of Aviation Artists; many worldwide trips for aviation and military paintings for Services; began specializing in African wildlife subjects (1960). *Exhib.:* R.A., R.P.; one man exhbns. London (1962, 1965, 1971, 1978), Johannesburg (1966, 1969), New York (1967). *Work in permanent collections:* 15ft reredos of Christ for Army Garrison Church, Bordon, Hants (1964). *Portraits:* H.E. Dr Kenneth Kaunda, President of Zambia (1967), H.M. The Queen Mother (1969), H.E. Sheikh Zaid of Abu Dhabi (1970). Life story subject of BBC TV documentary "The Man Who Loves Giants" (1971), Harlech TV documentary, "Elephants and Engines", etc. Auctioned five wildlife paintings in U.S.A. in 1971 and raised funds for Bell Jet Ranger Helicopter for anti-poaching work in Zambia, in return President Kaunda presented an 1896 steam locomotive, it's return to Britain subject of BBC TV documentary "Last Train to Mulobezi" (1974); painted "Tiger Fire" 1973, raised £127,500 for Operation Tiger (1973). Purchased two mainline steam locomotives 92203 Black Prince, and 75029 The Green Knight (1967) and founded The East Somerset Steama Railwy, Cranmore, Somerset, a registered charity and fully operational steam railway. *Awards:* Order of Golden Ark by H.R.H. Prince Bernhard of The Netherlands (1973), Hon.D.F.A.Pratt Inst. N.Y. (1971), Hon. Doctor of Science, Hatfield Polytechnic (1990), Member of Honour, World Wildlife Fund (1979), Order of British Empire (1979). *Publications:* Artist in Africa (1967), The Man who Loves Giants (1975), Paintings of Africa and India (1978), A Brush with Steam (1983), David Shepherd: The Man and his Paintings (1985), An Artist in Conservation (1992). *Videos:* The Man who Loves Giants: The Most Dangerous Animal; Behind the Scenes, In Search of Wildlife I and II. In 1986 set up The David Shepherd Conservation Foundation, a registered charity in both the U.K. and the U.S.A., to raise funds for the conservation of wildlife and the habitat. *Ambition:* to drive Black Prince into Waterloo. *Recreations:* driving steam locomotives and raising money for wildlife. *Address:* Winkworth Farm, Hascombe, Godalming, Surrey GU8 4JW.

SHEPHERD, Gerald, M.F.P.S. (1990); painter and graphic artist in oil, acrylic, ink and pencils; currently co-ordinating the 'Artists for Animals' project; Director, Ionist Art Group; *b* 1955. *Exhib.:* solo and group exhbns. in London and south of England, including Loggia Gallery, London. *Work in permanent collection:* Surrey University. *Publication:* edited, Ion Exchange Magazine. *Address:* 18 Ham Cl., Aughton, Collingbourne Kingston, nr. Marlborough, Wilts. SN8 3SB. *Clubs:* Founded: Ionist Art Group, Process Art, Artists for Animals; F.P.S., Marlborough Artists. *Signs work:* usually "G.S." occasionally "GERALD SHEPHERD"; signature often incorporated into composition.

SHEPHERD, S. Horne, D.A.(Glas.); painter in oil and water-colour, printmaker and sculptor; *b* Dundee, 30 Dec., 1909; *s* of Thomas Shepherd; *m* Helen Margaret Hale. *Educ.:* Harris Academy; *studied art* at Glasgow School of Art. *Work in permanent collection:* V. & A. *Exhib.:* N.S., F.P.S., Rome, Washington, Boston and New York. *Address:* Atheldene, Loxwood Road, Rudgwick, Horsham, West Sussex RH12 3DW.

SHEPHERD, Valerie Mary, S.W.A. (1987), Cert.A.D.; graphic artist and printmaker in monotype with gouache, water-colour, oil, linocuts, etching; *b* Orpington, Kent, 5 Feb., 1941; *d* of John Freed, consulting electrical engineer; *m* Norman Shepherd, dental surgeon; one *s*, two *d. Educ.:* St. Philomena's Convent; *studied art* at Gyula Sajo Atelier; Brighton Polytechnic. *Address:* Bacon Hall, Poling, nr. Arundel, Sussex BN18 9PO. *Clubs:* S.W.A., Soc. of Sussex Painters, W. Sussex Art, Arun Art Soc., Atelier Art, Assoc. of Sussex Artist. *Signs work:* "Valerie Shepherd."

SHEPPARD, Faith Tresidder; landscape and marine painter; Médailles d'Or (1978) and d'Argent Paris Salon (1975), Men.Hon. (1970), Diplôme d'Honneur, Cannes (1974), First Prize Herts. Countryside (1975); Welwyn Trophy (1982, 1989), Prize water-colour Bury A.G. (Granada TV); *b* London; *d* of Capt. Robert L. Sheppard, O.B.E.; niece of former Provost of King's, Cambridge. *Studied art:* under Mother, Nancy Huntly (R.A. Schools 1910-1914 frequent exhibitor R.A. two Silver Medals Nat.Comp.); R.A. Schools; Byam Shaw, Chelsea. *Exhib.:* R.A., Harrods, B.B.C., Mall Galleries, home and abroad. *Work in permanent collections:* Buckingham Palace, Prime Minister Thatcher, Barbara Cartland, Sir Derrick Holden-Brown, Home Counties Newspapers. *Work repro.:* "Bruges"; "Caernarfon", "20th Century British Marine Painting" (Brook-Hart); Laing's Calendar "Chartres." *Clubs:* Reynolds, Chelsea Art, W.G.C., Hertford, St. Alban's (Vice-President). *Address:* Studio, 29 Digswell Rd., Welwyn Garden City, Herts. *Signs work:* "Faith Sheppard."

SHEPPARD, Liz; Intermediate in Arts Crafts (1953), N.D.D. Painting (1955), A.T.D. (Lond. 1956), Scholarship Pratt bequest (1956, to Italy); painter, printmaker in etching; *b* Tonbridge, 20 Dec., 1933; *d* of D. O. Pearce; *m* Clive Sheppard, sculptor (decd.); two *s*, one *d. Educ.:* St. Albans Girls Grammar School; *studied art* at St. Albans School of Art (1950-52); St. Martin's College of Art (1952-55) under Frederick Gore, Derrick Greaves; London University Institute (1955-56). *Exhib.:* Digswell House, Bear Lane Gallery, Oxford, City Gallery, Milton Keynes, R.A. Summer Exhbn. (1977, 1978), Cartoon (1978), Wavendon Festival (1979), Margaret Fischer (1980), Bedford School (1990), Leighton Buzzard Arts Centre (1990), Milton Keynes Exhbn. Gallery (1991), Bromham Mill Gallery, Bedford (1992), S.W.A. (1993), Art in Milton Keynes (1993). *Work in permanent collection:* H.R.H. The Princess Margaret; John Dankworth and Cleo Laine; The Open University; Milton Keynes Development Corp.; M.K. Hospital; Anglian Water, Huntingdon; Bedford Art Loan Collection; Bedfordshire Library; Leicester Royal Infirmary; Ernst and Young, etc. *Address:* 6 Leighton St., Woburn, Milton Keynes, MK17 9PJ. *Club:* Friends of Royal Academy. *Signs work:* "Liz Sheppard."

SHEPPARD, Maurice, P.P.R.W.S., M.A. (R.C.A.), Dip.A.D.; professional painter in oil and water-colour; *b* Llangwm, Pembrokeshire, 25 Feb., 1947; *s* of the late W. E. Sheppard. *Educ.:* Haverfordwest Grammar School; *studied art* at Loughborough College of Art; Kingston College of Art under Alfred Heyworth; R.C.A. under Hamilton-Fraser, Buhler, Spear, Weight. *Exhib.:* London and abroad. *Work in permanent collections:* V. & A., National Museum of Wales, Cardiff, B'ham Museum and A.G., B.M. *Publication:* Old Water-colour Soc. Club Annual Vol. 59. *Addresses:* 33 St. Martin's Pk., Crow Hill, Haverfordwest, Pembrokeshire SA61 2HP, Wales; and 14 Apsley St., Rusthall Common, Tunbridge Wells, Kent TN4 8NU. *Signs work:* "Maurice Sheppard."

SHEPPERSON, Patricia Ann; artist in pastel, wildlife, still life and landscape; *b* London, 1929; *m* Desmond Vereker; one *s*, one *d. Educ.:* Holy Trinity Convent,

Bromley; *studied drama* at Guildhall School of Music and Drama (1946-49); *studied art* at Heatherly School of Art (1959-62, Patrick Larking, R.O.I.), Sir John Cass School of Art (1963-67). *Exhib.:* one-man shows, London and The Hague, mixed exhbns., R.A., Mall Galleries. *Work in private collections:* U.K. and abroad. *Address:* 2 Grange Rd., Norwich, Norfolk NR2 3NH. *Signs work:* "Patricia Shepperson."

SHERLOCK, Siriol Ann, B.A.Hons. (1977), S.B.A. (1988); R.H.S. Gold Medal (1993); textile designer, water-colour painter, botanical artist; *b* Nantwich, 28 Aug., 1954; *d* of Dr. Alexander Cattanach; *m* Stephen Paul Sherlock; two *d. Educ.:* Fernhill Manor School; Brockenhurst College; *studied art* at Winchester School of Art (1973-77). *Exhib.:* many galleries in south of England, The Hillier Gdns. and Arboretum (1990), Kew Gdns. Gallery (1992). *Work in permanent collection:* The Hillier Gdns. and Arboretum, Romsey. *Work repro.:* in The Kew Magazine. *Address:* Elizabethan Cottage, Michelmersh, nr. Romsey, Hants. SO51 0NW. *Signs work:* "Siriol Sherlock."

SHETLAND, Ilric (alias), Hornsey Dip., S.I.A.D. (1969); artist in pencil, ink, sprayed pictorial sculpture, mixed media; *b* London, 24 Oct., 1946; *s* of John Preston; *m* Naurika Lenner. *Educ.:* Forest Hill Comprehensive School; *studied art* at Hornsey College of Art (1966-69). *Exhib.:* International Cultural Centre, Antwerp, Gamstyl, Brussels, Basle '75, Serpentine Gallery, London, Treadwell Gallery, London, Patrick Seale Gallery, London. *Address:* 38 Chalcot Rd., London NW1. *Clubs:* A.I.R., A.M.P. *Signs work:* "Ilric Shetland."

SHIELD, George William, B.Sc., Lond.; sculptor, particularly in wood and concrete, terra-cotta, metal, plaster, little stone; head, Mexborough G.S.; *b* Leicester, 7 July, 1919; *s* of William Henry Shield; *m* Jean; one *s,* two *d. Educ.:* Gateway School; University College, Leicester; *studied art* at College of Art, Leicester, under A. Pountney and A. T. White (1948-52). *Exhib.:* R.A., R.S.A., R.B.A., R.I., Glasgow, S.S.A., Contemp. Artists, Bradford. *Work in permanent exhbns.:* Joan Farrier bust in Paisley A.G., portrait head, Warden Harrison, Merton College, Oxford. *Address:* 30 Lewes Rd., Conisborough, S. Yorks. *Clubs:* Midland Group, Leicester Soc. of Artists. *Signs work:* "SHIELD" inscribed with modelling tool.

SHIELDS, Christopher Ronald, Dip.A.D. (1973), B.W.S. (1985); wildlife artist in water-colour, gouache and acrylic; *b* Sale, Ches., 7 June, 1954; *s* of Ronald Brian Shields, A.M.I.P.; divorced; one *d. Educ.:* Sale Moor Secondary School; *studied art* at Northwich College of Art and Design (1970-73). *Exhib.:* Warrington Museum and A.G. (1983, 1986, 1989, 1992), Wildfowl Trust Martin Mere (1985), Towneley Hall A.G. and Museum, Burnley (1988), Stockport A.G. (1991), plus several other one-man shows in private art galleries throughout the country. *Work in permanent collections:* Trafford Borough Council's Art Archives, City of Wakefield Educ. Resource Service Collection. *Publications:* illustrated over 50 books including Collins New Generation Guide — Wild Flowers, Collins Gem Guide — Pond Life, Tracks and Signs of the Birds of Britain and Europe (Helm Publishing); plus commissions for the R.S.P.B. and the Worldwide Fund for Nature. *Address:* 2 Bramble Walk, Sale, Ches. M33 5LL. *Signs work:* "Chris Shields" — always includes moth or butterfly in every work.

SHIELS, Anthony Nicol; painter in oil and gouache; *b* Salford, 24 May, 1938; *s* of Thomas Daniel Shiels; *m* Mary Christine Price; two *s,* three *d. Educ.:* King Edward VII School, Lytham; *studied art* at Heatherley School of Art, London, under Gilmore Roberts (1954-56). *Exhib.:* one-man shows: Gallery Mingus and

Rawinsky Gallery, London; group shows: London, Bristol, St. Ives, Colchester, Newlyn, Oxford, Bath, Amsterdam, Dublin, etc. *Publications:* 'Nnidnid', Surrealist Review; three books on magic. *Work repro.:* Arts Review, Apollo, Link, International Times, etc. *Address:* 3 Vale View, Ponsanooth, Truro, Cornwall. *Clubs:* A.I.A. (London) and Penwith Society (St. Ives). *Signs work:* see appendix.

SHINN, Michael Lawrence, D.F.A. (Slade), A.R.W.A.; landscape and portrait painter in oil; artist and teacher; head of Dept. of Art and Design Studies, Gloucestershire College of Arts and Technology; R.W.A. Council Member; *b* London, 5 Mar., 1934; *s* of F. E. Shinn; *m* Jennifer Margaret; one *s*, two *d*. *Studied art* at Wimbledon School of Art (1951-55), Slade School of Fine Art (1957-59) under Sir William Coldstream. *Work in permanent collections:* Royal West of England Academy, City Museum and Art Gallery, Plymouth, City Museum and Art Gallery, Gloucester, Cheltenham Art Gallery and Museum, Bristol Education Authority. *Address:* Old Gable House, Southam, nr. Cheltenham, Gloucs. *Signs work:* "Michael L. Shinn."

SHIPSIDES, Frank, M.A.; painter in oil and water-colour, specialising in marine painting; President, Bristol Savages (1974-75); *b* Mansfield, Notts., 1908; *m* Phyllis; one *s*, one *d*. *Educ.:* King Edward School, Mansfield; *studied art* at Mansfield College of Art (1923) under Buxton; Nottingham College of Art (1925) under Else. *Exhib.:* Alexander Gallery, Bristol (5). *Work in permanent collections:* Bristol Maritime Heritage Centre "Visit of H.M. The Queen", Bristol Council House, H.M.S. Bristol paintings 1653-1983. *Publications:* Frank Shipsides Bristol; Somerset Harbours; Bristol Impressions; Original Graphic—Days of Steam & Sail; Bristol—Portrait of a City; Bristol—Maritime City. *Address:* 5 Florence Pk., Bristol BS6 7LS. *Club:* Bristol Savages (Pres. 1983-84). *Signs work:* see appendix.

SHIRLEY, Rachel, B.A.Hons. (1986); animal and landscape artist in oil; *b* Nuneaton, 26 May, 1965; *d* of Sidney Raymond Shirley. *Studied art:* N. Warwickshire College of Art, Nuneaton (1981-83), Kingston Polytechnic School of Fine Art (1983-86). *Exhib.:* one-man shows: Museum and A.G., Nuneaton (1987), Hinckley Municipal A.G., Leics. (1988), Whitmoors Fine A.G., Leics. (1989); group shows: Hurlingham Gallery, London, Warwick University, Twycross Zoo Gallery, Leics. Work in Midland private collections. *Address:* c/o Croft Cottage Studio, 31 Weston La., Bulkington, Nuneaton, Warwickshire CV12 9RS. *Signs work:* "Rachel Shirley."

SHIRLEY, Sidney Raymond; Médaille d'Argent (Paris Salon, 1981); still-life artist in oil; *b* Coventry, 27 Nov., 1930; *s* of the late Horace James Shirley; *m* Sylvia Denise Elizabeth; six *d*. *Studied art* privately. *Exhib.:* one-man shows, Museum and A.G., Nuneaton (1968, 1974, 1982); group shows, R.A., N.E.A.C., R.B.A., R.O.I., R.B.S.A., New King's Rd., and 20th Century Galleries, London. *Work in private collections:* Australia, N.Z., France, Austria, U.K. *Work repro.:* R.A. Illustrated, La Revue Moderne, Le Monde, etc. *Address:* Croft Cottage Studio, 31 Weston Lane, Bulkington, Nuneaton, Warwickshire CV12 9RS. *Clubs:* Membre Associé, Société des Artistes Français, Founder mem, Bedworth Civic and Arts Soc. (1969). *Signs work:* "R. SHIRLEY" or "R.S".

SHOA, Nahem, B.A.(Hons); artist in oil; *b* 4 Oct., 1968. *Educ.:* Holland Park Comprehensive; *studied art* at London College of Printing (1987-88), Manchester School of Art (1988-91). *Exhib.:* R.A. Summer Show (1992, 1993), Discerning Eye Mall Galleries (1992), winner Carol Foundation award R.P., Mall Galleries

(1992), B.P. National Portrait award N.P.G. (1993). *Address:* 263 Portobello Rd., London W11 1LR. *Signs work:* "N. Shoa."

SHORE, Jack, A.T.D. (1943); artist in collage, drawing in various media; President, Royal Cambrian Academy of Art (1976-82); *b* Ramsbottom, Lancs., 17 July, 1922; *s* of Frank Shore; *m* Olive Brenda Shore; one *s*, one *d*. *Educ.:* Haslingden Grammar School; *studied art* at Accrington and Manchester Schools of Art (1938-43, S. V. Lindoe, John M. Holmes). *Exhib.:* R.Cam.A.; one-man shows, Theatre Clwyd, N. Wales (1979), R.Cam.A., Conwy (1980), Oriel Gallery, Bangor (1984). *Work in permanent collections:* Bury A.G., and University College, N. Wales. *Address:* 11 St. George's Cres., Queen's Pk., Chester. *Signs work:* "J. Shore." or "J.S."

SHORES, Margot; painter in oil and acrylic; lecturer in painting, University of Newcastle upon Tyne (1985-90); visiting lecturer, R.A. Schools (1987-88); *b* 1961. *Exhib.:* 'Young Masters' Solomon Gallery (1985), R.A. Summer Show (1986-87), Cleveland Drawing Biennale (1989). *Address:* 70 On the Hill, Old Whittington, Chesterfield, Derbyshire S41 9HA. *Signs work:* "Margot Shores."

SHORTHOUSE, G. Sydney, V.P.R.M.S., M.A.A., H.S., F.I.D. (1969-83); retd. Company Director; artist in water-colour, mainly miniature portraiture; Display and Advertising Manager, Leicester Corp., Area Design Manager, E. Midlands Gas Board, Design Director, City Design and City Leather Companies; *b* Whitwick, Leics., 1925; *s* of Alfred John Murby-Shorthouse, general manager; *m*; one *s*, one *d*. *Educ.:* Hugglescote School. *Exhib.:* R.M.S., Hilliard Soc., Florida and Washington D.C. *Awards:* Hon. men. (1988, 1989) R.M.S. Gold Bowl award; 1st International Portrait award Washington D.C. (1989); 2nd International Portrait award Florida (1990); Best In Exhbn. (1987), Bell award (1989) Hilliard Soc.; Suzanne Lucas award (1985). *Address:* The Barn, Main St., Wilson, Derbyshire DE7 1AF. *Signs work:* see appendix.

SHUKMAN, Barbara Benita; Jacox Students Painting Prize, Edmonton, Canada (1968), John Radcliffe Purchase Prize, Oxford (1983); painter in acrylic on paper and canvas, and inks on silk, and printmaker, etchings, etc.; *b* London, 25 Nov., 1934; *d* of Denys King-Farlow, M.B.E.; *m* (1) Harold Jacobs; one *s*, two *d;* (2) Harold Shukman. *Educ.:* U.S.A. primary schools; Queen's College, London; *studied art* at University Saskatchewan, Regina, Canada (1963-65), University Alberta, Edmonton, Canada (1966-70). *Exhib.:* group shows: Canada, U.K., Spain; solo shows: U.K., U.S.A. *Work in permanent collections:* U.S.A.: Solomon Guggenheim Museum, N.Y.; Georgia Museum of Art; New Orleans Museum. Turkey: Sheraton Voyager, Antalya. U.K.: Sedgwick Group; British and Commonwealth; Sarm Film Studios; Bain and Co.; Jardine and Co.; Strutt and Parker; Chartwell Land: Christiana Bank, (all London). John Radcliffe Hospital Oxford. *Address:* 11 Cunliffe Cl., Oxford OX2 7BJ. *Signs work:* "Barbara Shukman."

SHURROCK, Christopher, A.T.D.; painting, sculpture, print; *b* Bristol, 1939. *Educ.:* Bristol Cathedral School; *studied:* West of England College of Art, postgraduate, A.T.D.(Dist.) (1960). Art adviser, University Settlement, Bristol (1961), Cardiff College of Art, Foundation Dept. 1962-91 (Senior Lecturer/ Director). *Work in permanent collections:* National Gallery of Slovakia, Bratislava, National Museum of Wales, University College of Wales, W.A.C., C.A.S.W., John Caroll University, Ohio, etc. *Work repro.:* Studio International (June, 1966) D'Ars Agency N36-37 (1967), Art and Artists (Jan. 1969), Art in Britain, 1969-70 (Dent), Studio International 991/2 (1981), Art in Wales 1850-1980 (U.W.P.). *Address:* 9 Min-y-Nant, Rhiwbina, Cardiff CF4 6JR.

SIDERY, Vera Ethel; painter in pastel and oil; *b* 3 Aug., 1916; *d* of Charles Chapman; *m* Albert Sidery (decd.); two *s*, two *d*. *Educ.:* Tottenham High School; *studied art* with Leonard and Margaret Boden. *Exhib.:* P.S., Mall Galleries, Enfield; one-man show, Broomfield Museum, Southgate. *Address:* 8 Roedean Cl., Enfield, EN3 5QR. *Clubs:* P.S., Enfield Art Soc. *Signs work:* "V.E. Sidery."

SIDOLI, Dawn Frances, N.E.A.C. (1990), R.W.A. (1987), Teacher's Cert. (1956); painter, screen printer; *b* Gosport, Hants., 24 Nov., 1933; *d* of Patrick A. Thompson, accountant; *m* Frank P. Sidoli; two *s*, one *d*. *Educ.:* Wigton High School, Cumbria; Notre Dame Convent, Northampton; *studied art* at Northampton Art School (1949-52). *Exhib:* R.A. from 1977, R.W.A., N.E.A.C., Cardiff, etc. Finalist, Laing '85, '86, Hunting Group '86, '87, '89, Inveresk w/ col, Singer and Friedlander w/col. competition '89. Laing National First Prize '88. *Work in permanent collections:* R.W.A., Mid-Glamorgan C.C., Cardiff School of Economics (Schools Art Avon, Cardiff, Salisbury). *Address:* 10 Elgin Pk., Redland, Bristol BS6 6RU. *Clubs:* Bath Soc. of Artists, Clifton Arts. *Signs work:* "Dawn Sidoli" or "SIDOLI."

SILBER, Evelyn Ann, Ph.D.(Cantab.), M.A.(Cantab.), M.A. (University of Pennsylvania); art historian and museum curator; Asst. Director, Birmingham Museums and Art Gallery; *b* Welwyn Garden City, 22 May, 1949; *d* of Martin Silber, M.Sc. *Educ.:* Hatfield Girls' Grammar School; *studied history of art* at New Hall, Cambridge (1968-72), University of Pennsylvania (Thouron Fellowship, 1972-73), Clare Hall, Cambridge (Leverhulme Fellowship, 1975-78). *Exhib.:* organised: Jacob Epstein, Sculpture and Drawings, Leeds City A.G., and Whitechapel A.G. (1987). *Publications:* The Sculpture of Jacob Epstein (Phaidon, 1986); catalogues, articles, lectures. *Address:* 6 Regent Rd., Harborne, Birmingham B17 9JU.

SILLMAN, Norman H., A.R.C.A., F.R.B.S.; sculptor, coin and medal designer, Royal Mint; Fine Art Dept. (retd.), Nottingham Polytechnic; *b* May, 1921; *m* Gillian M.; one *d*. Studied art at Blackheath School of Art, Royal College of Art. *Exhib.:* R.A., R.B.A., London Group, Midland Group, Arts Council "Sculpture in the Home" Exhbn., R.C.A. Open Air Exhbn.; medals exhib. in Europe and U.S.A. *Work in permanent collections:* B.M., Derby Educ. Com. (two), Kelham Hall, Notts, (three). Designed R.I.B.A. Awards (1990), £2 British coin (1986). *Publications:* articles in Saeculum (1981), Tubingen, Jour. Indian Anthrop. Soc. (1983). *Address:* 33 Church St., Eye, Suffolk. *Signs work:* "N. Sillman."

SIMCOCK, Jack; painter; *b* Biddulph, Staffs., 6 June, 1929; *m* Beryl Shallcross; one *s*, one *d*. *Educ.:* Stoke-on-Trent. *Exhib.:* 50 one-man shows, England and abroad, c/o Piccadilly Gallery, London; mixed shows, Britain, France, Italy, U.S.A., etc. *Official purchases:* Contemporary Art Society, and many public art galleries and education authorities in England; universities and colleges in England and U.S.A.; also many private collectors at home and abroad. *Work repro.:* Arts Review, Time and Tide, The Listener, Das Kuntswerk, The Guardian, The Northern Echo, Birmingham Post, Woman's Journal Supplement, Country Life, Studio International, Cheshire Life, Apollo, The Daily Telegraph. *Publications:* Simcock, Mow Cop, an autobiography (1975), Midnight Till Three, a volume of poems (1975). *Address:* 13 Primitive St., Mow Cop, Stoke-on-Trent ST7 3NH. *Signs work:* "Simcock."

SIMEON, Margaret, A.R.C.A. (1933), R.C.A. Travelling Scholar (1934), M.S.I.A. (1945); textile and wallpaper designer; teacher of Textile Design and Printing, R.C.A. (1936-40); teacher of textile design and history of art at

437

Wimbledon School of Art (1934-84); *b* 1910; *d* of Harry Simeon, ceramic designer. *Educ.:* Chelsea School of Art, R.C.A. *Exhib.:* International Exhbn. at Paris, Stockholm, New York, Arts and Crafts Exhbn. Soc. (1935-54), Britain Can Make It Exhbn. (1946), Festival of Britain (1951). *Work repro.:* in International Textiles, Architectural Review, Studio, Designers in Britain, Decorative Art. *Publications:* The History of Lace; How to Draw Garden Flowers. *Address:* Springfield House, 6 Stoke Rd., Cobham, Surrey KT11 3AS.

SIMMONDS, Jackie, H.N.D.; artist in pastel and water-colour; *b* Oxford, 27 Dec., 1944; *m* Geoffrey Simmonds; two *d. Educ.:* Preston Manor Grammar; *studied art* at Harrow School of Art (1978-82). *Exhib.:* Linda Blackstone Gallery, Pinner, P.S., R.I., Britain's Painters (1992). *Address:* 23 Unksway, Northwood, Middx. HA6 2XA. *Signs work:* "Jackie Simmonds."

SIMMONS, Fay, N.D.D. (1959), Cert.R.A. (1963), Leverhulme Scholarship (1963), A.R.B.S. (1976); sculptor in bronze or gesso composition with mixed media; V.S.O. Business/Social Development, Uganda; *b* New Zealand, 1938; *d* of Eric Simmons, M.R.C.V.S.: *m* Sean Mullaney. *Educ.:* Stella Maris Convent, Bideford; *studied art* at Bideford School of Art; Hammersmith College of Art; R.A. Schools. *Exhib.:* R.A., Nicholas Treadwell Gallery, A.I.A., Alec Mann Birmingham, XVIII Gallery Knightsbridge, Jersey, Guernsey, Gallery Oste Hamburg, New York, Washington. *Address:* 54 Coburg Cl., Greencoat Pl., London SW1P 1DP. *Club:* R.B.S. *Signs work:* "F.S."

SIMMONS, Rosemary, N.D.D. (1953), Hon. R.E. (1990); artist in relief printmaking, water-colour; writer; Editor, Printmaking Today; *b* Brighton, 19 Oct., 1932; *d* of Donald Simmons, B.Sc.; *m* Anthony Christie, M.A., F.S.A. *Studied art* at Chelsea School of Art (1949-53). *Exhib.:* International Gdn. Festival (1984), Museum of Gdn. History (1985), St. John's, Smith Sq. (1987). *Work in permanent collection:* Tate Gallery print collection. *Publications:* Collecting Original Prints (1980), Complete Manual of Relief Printmaking with Katie Clemson (1988). *Address:* 14B Elsworthy Terr., London NW3 3DR. *Signs work:* "Simmons."

SIMPSON, Alan John, R.S.M.A.; marine and landscape artist in oil, water-colour, pastel; *b* Basingstoke, 22 July, 1941; *s* of Arthur James Simpson; *m* Denise; two *s. Studied art:* informal training at College of Art, Bournemouth. *Exhib.:* R.S.M.A., R.O.I., R.I., Britain in Water-colour, Mystic, Seaport, U.S.A., Richard Beard Gallery, Vancouver, Harrison Galleries, Vancouver. *Address:* 24 Waltham Rd., Boscombe East, Bournemouth, Dorset BH7 6PE. *Signs work:* "Alan Simpson."

SIMPSON, Cathy, B.A.(Hons.), A.R.B.S.A., R.M.S., H.S.; freelance illustrator in water-colour and gouache; *b* Kingston on Hull, 15 Nov., 1959. *Educ.:* Christ's Hospital Girls' School, Hertford; Leicester University; *studied art* at Central St. Martin's School of Art. *Exhib.:* R.I., S.WL.A., S.W.A., S.B.A., R.M.S., H.S., R.B.S.A., M.A.S.-F. *Address:* 20 Bilberry Rd., Kings Heath, Birmingham B14 6RJ. *Signs work:* see appendix.

SIMPSON, Ian, A.R.C.A. (1958); Abbey Travelling Scholar (1958); freelance artist-writer in oil, acrylic and drawing media; Principal, St. Martin's School of Art (1972); Assistant Rector, The London Institute, Head of School, St. Martin's School of Art (1986-88); *b* Loughborough, Leics., 12 Nov., 1933. *Educ.:* Bede Grammar School, Sunderland; *studied art* at Sunderland College of Art (1950-53); Royal College of Art (1955-58). *Work in permanent collections:* Glasgow City A.G., Nuffield Foundation, Hull Education Authority, Northumberland

Education Authority. *Publications:* Eyeline (B.B.C.), Picture Making (B.B.C.) Drawing: Seeing and Observation (Van Nostrand Reinhold) 3rd Revised Edn. (A. & C. Black 1992), Ian Simpson's Guide to Painting and Composition (Warnes), Painters Progress (Allen Lane), The Encyclopedia of Drawing Techniques (Headline), The Challenge of Landscape Painting (Collins 1990), The New Guide to Illustration (Chartwell Books 1990), Anatomy of Humans (Studio Editions 1991), Collins Complete Painting Course (Harper Collins 1993), Collins Complete Drawing Course (Harper Collins 1994). T.V. Programmes written and presented: Eyeline (B.B.C. 1968), Picture Making (B.B.C. 1972), Reading the Signs (B.B.C. 1976). *Address:* Motts Farm House, Chilton St., Clare, Sudbury, Suffolk CO10 8QS. *Signs work:* "Simpson."

SIMPSON, Leslie, F.R.S.A. (1985); portrait artist in oil and water-colour working to commission on all subjects; Director, Soc. of Miniaturists, British Water-colour Soc., British Soc. of Painters; Founder, Yorkshire Artists Exhbn. (1981); Principal, International Guild of Artists; *b* Horsforth, 28 May, 1930; *s* of Sidney Arthur Simpson (decd.); *m* Margaret; one *s. Educ.:* Bridlington School; *studied art* at Hull College of Art. *Work in permanent collections:* portrait of the full Wakefield City Council (1974); portraits of the Lady Lord Mayors of Leeds, Bradford, Sheffield and London; 'The Winning Throw' portrait of Tessa Sanderson, Los Angeles Olympics (1984). Descendant of James Simpson (1791-1864) leading non-conformist architect in the North, and John Simpson official portrait artist to Queen Donna Marie II of Portugal (1837). *Address:* Ralston, 41 Lister St., Riverside Gdns., Ilkley, W.Yorks. LS29 9ET. *Signs work:* "Leslie Simpson."

SIMPSON, Noelle; painter, colourist of joyous landscapes, nudes, interiors and portraits in oil on canvas and acrylic; *b* Auckland, N.Z., 10 Aug., 1950; *d* of Noel Simpson, racehorse breeder; one *d. Educ.:* Chatelard, Switzerland; Moreton Hall, Shropshire; *studied art* under Philip Sutton, R.A., and Frederick Deane, R.P. (1985), Van Wieringen, Bali (1986-90). *Exhib.:* J. Weston Gallery, London (1985), Symon Gallery, Bali (1987), Bowmoore Gallery, London (1991), Hilton International, Bali (1992), Gagliardi Gallery, London (1992), Pacific Rim Gallery, San Diego (1993). *Work in permanent collection:* Agung Rai Museum, Bali. *Publication:* Then Till Now — Noelle Simpson. *Address:* 18 Cottesmore Gdns., London W8 5PR. *Signs work:* see appendix.

SIMS-WILLIAMS, Dorothy Audrey Constance, F.R.S.A., Hon. Mention, Paris Salon, R.A.S. Cert., Leverhulme Leaving Scholar Silver and Bronze medal; artist in oil and pastel, teacher, lecturer; *b* Disley, Ches., 26 May, 1909; *d* of R. S. O. Mais, registrar, High Court of Justice; *m* Rev. L. T. Sims-Williams; three *s,* one *d. Educ.:* privately; *studied art* at Stockport Art School (1926-28), R.A. Schools (1928-33) under W. W. Russell, R.A. and F. E. Jackson, A.R.A. *Exhib.:* R.P and various London exhbns. *Work in permanent collections:* St. Matthew's Church, Stockport; St. John's Church, Hopwood, Lancs.; St. Andrew's Church, Dearnley, Lancs. *Address:* Stonehays, Westcliff Rd., Charmouth, Dorset DT6 6BG. *Signs work:* "D. Sims-Williams."

SINCLAIR, Elizabeth, N.D.D. (1950), A.T.D. (1958), M.F.P.S. (1986), Visual Arts Dip. (1969), Dip. in History of Art (1972); painter in oil, pastel, acrylic, teacher; *b* Glasgow, 18 Jan., 1933; *d* of Surgeon Captain, A.D. Sinclair, M.B., Ch.B., F.F.A., R.C.S. *Educ.:* 'Wings', Charlton Pk., Wilts; *studied art* at Plymouth School of Art, Bath Academy of Art, London University. *Exhib.:* one-man shows: Hong Kong, Italy; group shows: Hong Kong, Germany, Plymouth, London, Reigate, etc. *Work in permanent collection:* Plymouth A.G. *Address:*

10 Cockshot Hill, Reigate, Surrey RH2 8AE. *Clubs:* Reigate Soc. of Artists, North Weald Group, F.P.S. *Signs work:* "Elizabeth Sinclair."

SINCLAIR, Frances; painter in oil; *d* of Major Annesley St. George Knox-Gore; *m* Rear Admiral Sinclair, C.B., D.S.C.; two *s*. *Educ.:* privately; *studied art* under John Tichell, A.R.A. *Exhib.:* R.A. for many years, also at Easton Rooms, Rye, Wykeham Galleries at Stockbridge and Barnes and others in the South West. *Work repro.:* paintings by Medici Soc. *Address:* Island Cottage, Wittersham, Kent. *Signs work:* "F. Sinclair."

SINCLAIR, Helen, B.F.A.(Hons.) (1976); sculptor in cast stone and metal; *b* S. Wales, 27 Feb., 1954; *d* of Noël Sinclair, electrical engineer; *m* Terry Ryall, sculptor. *Educ.:* Llanelli Girls' Grammar School; *studied art* at Dyfed School of Art, Wimbledon School of Art (1973-76, Peter Startup, Jim Turner). *Exhib.:* Edwin Pollard Gallery, Heifer Gallery, Highbury, Holland Gallery, Holland Pk., Hann Gallery, Bath. *Work in permanent collections:* Bultarbo Estate, Sweden, Grand Theatre, Swansea. *Address:* Rhossili Farmhouse, Rhossili, Gower, W. Glamorgan SA3 1PL. *Signs work:* "Helen Sinclair" or "H.S."

SINCLAIR, N. T., M.A., F.M.A.; curator, Museum and Art Gallery, Borough Rd., Sunderland, SR1 1PP.

SINNOTT, Kevin; artist in oil on canvas; part-time lecturer, St. Martin's School of Art; *b* Wales, 1947; *m* Susan; three *s*, one *d*. *Studied art:* Cardiff College of Art (1967-68), Gloucester College of Art (1968-71), R.C.A. (1971-74). *Exhib.:* one-man shows: Ikon Gallery (1980), Blond Fine Art (1982, 1984), Chapter Arts Centre, Cardiff (1984), Bernard Jacobson Gallery (1986, 1987, 1988, 1990). *Work in permanent collections:* British Council, B.M., A.C.G.B., R.C.A., Whitworth Manchester, Wolverhampton City Gallery. *Address:* c/o Flowers East, 199 Richmond Rd., London E8 3NJ. *Club:* Chelsea Arts. *Signs work:* initials right hand corner.

SITWELL, Pauline, S.W.E., R.A. Dip. (1937), L.I.S.T.D., F.R.G.S.; painter, printer, poet and lecturer; *b* Malta, 5 Oct., 1916; *d* of Group Captain William George Sitwell. *Educ.:* full stage training and young career; *studied art* at St. John's Wood School of Art (1930), Royal Academy Schools of Art (1933-37). *Exhib.:* S.W.E., R.S.M.A., and Mall Prints tour of G.B., etc.; Laureat Paris Salon de Printemps, Auribeau s/Siagne, France (1988); one-man show sponsored by Westminster City Council, many others. *Work in seven countries. Publications:* Green Song; Train Journey to Deal and other Poems (Outposts, 1981). *Address:* 46 Porchester Rd., London W2. *Clubs:* Royal Academy, Reynolds (Hon. Treasurer), S.I.A.C. *Signs work:* "Pauline Sitwell" and see appendix.

SKEA, Janet, S.W.A. (1987), B.F.A. (1968); painter in water-colour and tempera; *b* Johannesburg, S.Africa, 15 Sept., 1947. *Educ.:* Parktown Girls' High, Johannesburg; *studied art:* Stellenbosch University (1965-68, Prof. Otto Schröder). *Exhib.:* widely in the U.K., mainly London, and at the Bankside, Mall and Westminster Galleries. Mem. St. Ives Soc. of Artists. *Address:* 30 Queen St., Penzance, Cornwall TR18 4BH. *Signs work:* "Janet Skea" dated on reverse.

SKELTON, John, M.B.E.; sculptor, letter cutter; *b* 1923; *m*; one *s*, two *d*. *Educ.:* Norwich Cathedral Choir School; Bablake, Coventry; School of Art and Architecture, Coventry; apprenticed Eric Gill; army, Far East; own Workshop-Studio (1950), mediums: stone, wood, all metals. Many Royal lettering commissions. *Work* in Norwich, Lincoln, Hereford, Chichester, Portsmouth and St. Paul's Cathedrals; museums: Toledo, U.S.A., Chichester and Coventry.

Exhib.: R.A. regularly; Herbert (Coventry), Battersea Park, Sussex University, Hamburg, Washington, Paris Salon, Brighton Festival, U.N. Pavilion and International Sculpture Symposium, Yugoslavia, representing Gt. Britain (1964). Served Arts Council, Scotland; Royal Soc. of British Sculptors; R.S.A. *Address:* Blabers Mead, Streat, Hassocks, Sussex BN6 8RR.

SKILLINGTON, Nancy: see TALBOT, Nancy Wilfreda Hewitt.

SKINNER, Freda, A.R.C.A. (1932), R.B.S. (1972); sculptor in bronze, wood, stone, terracotta; Head of Dept. Sculpture, Wimbledon School of Art (retd. 1971); *b* Upper Warlingham, Surrey, 31 Jan., 1911; *d* of Norman Skinner, farmer. *Educ.:* Warlingham Grammar School; *studied art:* R.C.A. (Henry Moore, Gilbert Ledward). *Exhib.:* R.A., London Group, Portrait Soc. *Work in permanent collections:* public works: 14 Stations of the Cross, St. John's Church, Richmond-on-Thames; statue St. Peter, St. Peter's Church, Walworth, London; The Risen Christ, St. Paul's Church, London SE17; Christ on the Cross, St. Francis Church, Isleworth; bronze figure, Edward VII Park, Brent; Madonna and Child, St. Elpheges Church, Wallington; carved inscription, Barbican Art Centre. *Publication:* Wood Carving (Bonanza Books, Crown Publishers, N.Y.). *Address:* The Old Dairy, W. Amesbury, Salisbury, Wilts. SP4 7BH. *Signs work:* "Freda Skinner."

SLADE, Roy, N.D.D., A.T.D., G.S.M. (British Army); Kt. First Class of the Order of the White Rose of Finland (1985); artist in acrylics; Chairman, Commission on Art in Public Places for the State of Michigan (1984-85); President, Cranbrook Academy of Art; Director, Corcoran Gallery of Art (1972-77); Dean, Corcoran School of Art (1970-77); *b* Cardiff, Wales, 1933; American citizen (Oct. 1975); *s* of David Trevor Slade. *Educ.:* University of Wales (1953-54), Cardiff College of Art (1949-54), Royal Army School of Education (1954). *Work in permanent collections:* Arts Council of Great Britain, Contemporary Art Society, Westinghouse Corp., Cadbury Bros. Ltd., Nuffield Foundation. *Work repro.:* articles published: Studio International, "American Art Education" (Nov., 1972); Art Journal, "Atlantic Storm" (Spring, 1972); Studio International, "Up the American Vanishing Point" (Nov., 1968); Detroid News, "Speaking of Art — In the Future Tense" (Mar., 1985); N.A.S.A.D. and A.A.M.D., "Toward Understanding and Collaboration" (1982); N.C.A.A., "The Temple Flourishes" (1980); Lewis and Clark College, "The Gallery Symposium" (1978); "Art Gallery" (Jan. 1975). *Address:* 1221 N. Woodward, Box 801, Bloomfield Hills, Michigan 48303-0801.

SLANEY, Noël, R.S.W.; artist in Batik oils and water-colour; *b* Glasgow, 26 Dec., 1915; *d* of George Wilson Slaney (George Woden, novelist); *m* George Frederick Moules, painter; four *d*. *Educ.:* Girls' High School, Glasgow; *studied art* at Glasgow School of Art under the late Hugh Adam Crawford, R.S.A., D.A. (1937), Post Dip. with distinction (1939). *Work in permanent collections:* water-colours in Aberdeen and Dundee; oils in Arts Council, Glasgow A.G., Lillie A.G. Milngavie, Hunterian Museum Glasgow. *Address:* 6 Southpark Terr., Glasgow G12 8LG. *Signs work:* "Slaney."

SLICER, Sheila Mary, A.R.M.S. (1978); first prize M.A.S.-F. (1983, 1986, 1992); freelance miniature portraitist in water-colour; *b* Yorks., 26 Sept., 1930; *m* Robert Slicer; two *d*. *Educ.:* Bradford Girls Grammar School; *studied art* at Bradford Regional College of Art (1946-49). *Exhib.:* R.M.S., M.A.S.-F., Andorra, Yorks. Water-colour Soc., Brighouse and Bradford Art Clubs, Victoria and Queensland, Australia. *Work in permanent collections:* England, Bermuda, Florida, Australia, Hong Kong, Andorra. *Addresses:* Edifici La Solana, Escala

A. Plantas 2. La Massana, Principai d'Andorra; Faraway, Lot 2E Don Rd., Launching Pl., Victoria 3139, Australia. *Clubs:* R.M.S., M.A.S.-F., Victoria and Queensland Miniature Societies, Australia. *Signs work:* "Sheila M. Slicer."

SLOWE, Vikki, R.E., P.M.C.; printmaker in etching; *b* London, 24 May, 1947; *d* of David Ross; *m* Martin Slowe; two *d. Educ.:* Camden School for Girls; *studied art* at London College of Fashion; Camden Arts Centre. *Exhib.:* R.A., R.E., Bradford Biennale. *Work in permanent collections:* Smithsonian Inst., Washington, Tel Aviv Museum, Israel. *Address:* 35 Ornan Rd., London NW3 4QD. *Signs work:* "Vikki Slowe."

SMART, Jeffrey: painter in oil, pen and ink; *b* Adelaide, S. Aus., 26 July, 1921; *s* of Francis I. Smart. *Educ.:* Pulteney Grammar School, Adelaide; *studied art* at S.A. School of Arts, Adelaide (1940), Grand Chaumiere (1948) under McEvoy, Academie Montmartre (1949) under Fernand Leger. *Exhib.:* Whitechapel (1962), Tate Gallery (1963); one-man shows: Redfern Gallery (1967, 1979, 1982), Galleria 88 Rome (1968), Leicester Galleries (1970). *Work in permanent collections:* National Galleries of Sydney, Melbourne, Adelaide and Perth, Mertz Coll., Corcoran Gallery, Washington, Yale University, Von Thyssen Coll., Lugano, De Beers Coll., 20th Century Art, London. *Work repro.:* Art International (May, 1968), Present Day Australian Art (Ure Smith), Masterpieces of Australian Art (1970), 200 Years of Australian Art (1971), The Moderns (Phaidon Press, 1976), Jeffrey Smart (S. McGrath, Art International Vol. XXI/I, 1977), Jeffrey Smart (David Malouf, Art International, Nov. 1982); Jeffrey Smart by Peter Quartermaine (Gryphon Press, 1983). Documentary film BBC "Omnibus" (1984). *Address:* c/o Redfern Gallery, Cork St., London. *Signs work:* "Jeffrey Smart."

SMITH, Barry Edward Jervis, B.A.; artist/illustrator in ink and water-colour; *b* Sydney, Australia, 27 Apr., 1943; *s* of A.J.W. Smith, musician. *Educ.:* Coburg High School; *studied art:* University of Melbourne (1969-73, lithography Peter Baer, etching Mary Louise Coulouris). *Exhib.:* various group shows in London; one-man shows: Nantes, Edinburgh, Sweden and Australia. *Publications:* written and illustrated several children's books. *Address:* P.O. Box 846, London E8 1ER *Signs work:* "B. Smith" or "Barry Smith".

SMITH, Colin Hilton, B.A.(Hons.), M.A.(R.C.A.); Harkness Fellow (Yale University), Royal Overseas League joint first prize winner; painter in oil on canvas, acrylic etc. on paper; part-time lecturer, Canterbury School of Art; *b* Harpenden, Herts., 21 Feb., 1953; *s* of Reginald Walter Smith, headmaster; *m* Rosemary Victoria; one *s. Educ.:* Hitchin Boys Grammar School; *studied art:* St. Albans School of Art (1971-72, Arnold Van Praag), Falmouth School of Art (1972-75, Karl Weschke), R.C.A. (1975-79, John Walker), Yale (1983-85, Andrew Forge). *Exhib.:* Nicola Jacobs Gallery (1982, 1984, 1987, 1989), Ruth Siegal, N.Y. (1986), Anderson O'Day (1991), Kunst Europa (1991), Gallery 30, N.Y. (1993), Barbican Concourse Gallery, London (1993), Art Itinera 83 Italy, 14th International Festival of Painting, France (1982), etc. *Work in permanent collections:* R.C.A., Unilever, A.C.G.B., Contemporary Art Soc., Prudential, Pepsi Cola, Arthur Anderson, B.A., etc. Obituary for Richard Diebenkorn, Artscribe (1991). *Address:* c/o Anderson O'Day Fine Art, 255 Portobello Rd., London W11 1LR. *Club:* Chelsea Arts. *Signs work:* "Colin Smith."

SMITH, David Henry, M.Art, R.C.A. (1971), Hugh Dunn Plaque (1971); artist in oil and water-colour; *b* Cleethorpes, 29 Oct., 1947; *s* of Henry Smith; *m* Irena Ewa Flynn. *Educ.:* Elliston Secondary Modern School, Cleethorpes; *studied art* at Grimsby School of Art (1965-68); R.C.A. (1968-71). *Exhib.:* one-man shows, New Art Centre, London (1970-72), Fischer Fine Art, London (1974, 1976, 1978, 1981), Vienna (1976), W. Germany (1976), Sweden (1979). *Work in permanent collection:* Arts Council, Contemporary Art Soc. *Address:* Hall Lodge, Holton-cum-Beckering, Wragby, Lincoln. *Signs work:* "D. H. Smith."

SMITH, Edward John Milton, A.T.D. (1952), N.D.D. 2nd Cl. Hons. (1951), F.S.A.E., F.R.S.A.; artist in lettering, writing and illumination; Principal Lecturer, Subject Leader (Art) P.G.C.E. Course, Leeds Polytechnic 1963-85 (now retd.); art teacher, West Monmouth School, Pontypool (1952-62); visiting lecturer, Newport College of Art (1954-62); President N.S.A.E. (1972); *b* Stonehouse, Glos., 3 May, 1922; *s* of Edward Milton Smith; *m* Doreen; one *s,* two *d. Educ.:* Central School, Stroud, Glos.; *studied art* at Stroud School of Art (1936-38), Gloucester College of Art (1939-40), Leeds College of Art (1946-52). *Address:* Glevum, 30 Burnham Rd., Garforth, Leeds, Yorks. LS25 1LA. *Signs work:* see appendix.

SMITH, Gregor, R.S.W., D.A. (1966), Post-grad. scholarship (1967); artist in oil and water-colour, teacher; *b* Renton, Dunbartonshire, 15 July, 1944; *s* of Rev. Henry Smith, M.A. (decd.); *m* Elizabeth. *Educ.:* Wishaw High School; *studied art* at Edinburgh College of Art (1962-67). *Exhib.:* R.S.A., R.S.W., Compass Gallery, Glasgow, numerous group and one-man shows. *Work in permanent collections:* H.R.H. The Duke of Edinburgh, S.A.C., numerous educ. authorities and district councils. *Address:* 14 Muirside Ave., Mount Vernon, Glasgow G23 9LD. *Signs work:* "Gregor W. Smith."

SMITH, Ian McKenzie, O.B.E., D.A., R.S.A., P.R.S.W., LL.D. (Aberdeen University, 1991), F.R.S.A., F.S.S., F.M.A., F.S.A. Scot; City Arts and Recreation Officer, City of Aberdeen; artist in oil and gouache; *b* Montrose, 3 Aug., 1935; *s* of James McKenzie Smith; *m* Mary Rodger Fotheringham; two *s,* one *d. Educ.:* Robert Gordon's College, Aberdeen; *studied art* at Gray's School of Art (1953-59) under Ian Fleming and R. Henderson Blyth; Hospitalfield College of Art, Arbroath (1958 and 1959). *Work in permanent collections:* Scottish National Gallery of Modern Art, Scottish Arts Council, Abbot Hall Gallery, Kendal, Aberdeen A.G., Glasgow A.G., City Arts Centre, Edinburgh, Perth A.G., Royal Scottish Academy, Arts Council of Northern Ireland, Contemporary Art Soc. *Address:* 70 Hamilton Pl., Aberdeen. *Signs work:* normally unsigned, labelled on reverse.

SMITH, Ivor Stanley, M.A., LL.D., R.I.B.A., A.A. Dip.; consultant architect; visiting professor, The Caribbean School of Architecture, Kingston, Jamaica; *b* Leigh-on-Sea, Essex; *s* of H.S. Smith, M.A.; *m* Audrey; one *s,* three *d. Educ.:* Bartlett, Cambridge; A.A. Schools of Architecture, Southend School of Art. *Address:* The Station Officer's House, Prawle Point, Kingsbridge, Devon TQ7 2BX. *Signs work:* "Ivor Smith."

SMITH, Jack; artist in oil; *b* Sheffield, 18 June, 1928; *s* of John Edward Smith; *m* Susan. *Educ.:* Nether Edge Grammar School; *studied art:* R.C.A. (1949-52). *Exhib.:* twenty one-man shows in England. *Work in permanent collections:* Tate Gallery, Arts Council, Berlin Internatioal Gallery, Guggenheim Museum, Gottenburg Museum. *Address:* 29 Seafield Rd., Hove, Sussex. *Signs work:* "Jack Smith" or "Jacksmith."

SMITH, Joan, M.A. (Hons.) (1987), Postgrad. Dip. in Painting (1988), M.F.A. (1989); artist in acrylic and mixed media on canvas and paper, printmaking principally lithography; Council mem. Edinburgh Printmakers'

Workshop; Management com. The Collective Gallery, Edinburgh; *b* Dundee, 28 June, 1964. *Educ.:* Monifieth High School, Dundee; *studied art* at Edinburgh University (1982-87, Prof. Fernie), Edinburgh College of Art (1982-89, Prof. David Michie). *Exhib.:* solo shows: Collective Gallery, Edinburgh (1992), Crawford Art Centre, St. Andrews (1993); many group shows. *Work in permanent collections:* R.S.A., Edinburgh College of Art, Edinburgh City Art Centre, Heriot Watt University, Glasgow Museums and Art Galleries. *Address:* 14 Coillesdene Gdns., Edinburgh EH15 2JS. *Signs work:* "Joan Smith."

SMITH, Muriel Constance; portrait painter, drawings, miniatures; R.M.S., silver medal, Paris Salon (1935); hon. mention (1934); *b* Gunthorpe, Notts.; *d* of W. Stanley Smith, accountant. *Educ.:* Hollygirt, Nottingham; *studied art* at Nottingham College of Art and under Alyn Williams, P.R.M.S. *Exhib.:* R.A., R.M.S., U.S.A., one-woman show, Walker's Galleries, Bond St. *Address:* 16 Forest Rd. East, Nottingham, NG1 4HH. *Signs work:* "Muriel C. Smith, R.M.S."

SMITH, Norman, N.E.A.C. (1970); painter of still-life and landscape; former visiting teacher of drawing and painting; *b* Walsall, 8 Dec., 1910. *Educ.:* Blue Coat School, Walsall; *studied art* part-time at schools in Lancashire, and later in London. *Exhib.:* R.A., R.S.A., R.W.A., N.E.A.C.; one-man shows, Woodlands Gallery, Blackheath (1980), Thellusson Gallery, Ashbourne, Derbys (1980), Honor Oak Gallery, SE23 (1987). *Work in permanent collection:* City A.G., Salford. *Official purchases:* Borough of St. Marylebone, Borough of St. Pancras. *Work in private collections* in Britain and America. *Address:* 7 Baird Gdns., Dulwich Wood Park, London SE19 1HJ. *Signs work:* "Norman Smith."

SMITH, Peter William, D.F.C.; artist in oils and water-colour; *b* New Malden, Surrey, 3 July, 1920; *s* of A. W. Smith. *Educ.:* Whitgift, Croydon: *studied art* at Reigate Art School. *Exhib.:* East Sussex Art Club, Hastings (1947 and 1948), International Amateur Art (1969). *Address:* Dean Cottage, Blanks Lane, Newdigate, Surrey RH5 5ED. *Signs work:* "Peter Smith."

SMITH, Richard Michael, B.A. (Hons.) (1993); winner, Carroll Foundation award (R.P.); painter in oil on canvas, pastel, pencil; *b* Warlingham, Surrey, 15 June, 1957; two *s,* one *d. Educ.:* Caterham School; *studied art* at Coventry Art School (1977-80, Colin Saxton, Harry Weinberger), and in studio of John Ward, R.A. *Exhib.:* R.A. Summer Exhbns., R.P., Brian Sinfield Gallery, Burford. *Work in permanent collection:* G.L.C. *Address:* 191 Hillbury Rd., Warlingham, Surrey CR6 9TJ. *Signs work:* "Richard Smith," "R.S." or "R.M.S."

SMITH, Rita, B.A. (Hons.) (1978), H.D.F.A. (Lond.) (1980), Boise Travelling Scholarship (1980); artist in water-colour; *b* London, 9 Mar., 1946; two *s. Educ.:* Collingwood Secondary Girls' School, Peckham; *studied art* at Camberwell School of Art (1974-78), Slade School of Fine Art (1978-80). *Exhib.:* many mixed shows in U.K.; winner, The Guinness award at R.A. *Address:* 1 Gnaton Terr., Albaston, nr. Gunnislake, Cornwall PL18 9AG. *Signs work:* "RITA SMITH."

SMITH, Stan, R.W.S., M.A. (Oxon.), M.A. (R.C.A.); painter/draughtsman; Hon. Life President, London Group; former Head of Fine Art, Ruskin School, University of Oxford; Fellow, Linacre College, Oxford (1981); *b* Hull, 1929. *Exhib.:* widely in U.K. and abroad. Work in national, corporate and private collections worldwide. Prizewinner: R.A. and Hunting Group. *Publications:* include books and articles on art and art theory. Consultant on magazines, TV and radio programmes. *Address:* 1 Brunswick Cl., Twickenham, Middx. TW2 5ND. *Clubs:* The Arts Club, Chelsea Arts.

SMITH, William Branston; painter in acrylic, working in Norway; *b* Blackhill, 2 Mar., 1930. *Educ.:* Dunston Hill School, West Boldon School and The Gordon School; *studied art* at Sunderland College of Art, King's College of Art, Newcastle upon Tyne. *Exhib.:* group shows in Scandinavia and Europe; one-man shows: Slott Zeist, Nederland, U.K. and Scandinavian galleries. *Official purchases:* Norwegian Arts Council, Telemark, Ostford, West Agder Counties Cultural Authority, Bede Gallery, Jarrow (U.K.), I.C.A., Australia. *Address:* Løkkeveien 14, 3915: Porsgrunn, Norway. *Artists organisations:* M.F.P.S. (London), N.B.K. (Oslo), U.K.S., L.M.N., B.I.T., T.K.S. *Signs work:* "BILL SMITH."

SNELLING, John, F.R.S.A. (1966); landscape and marine artist in water-colour and oils; *b* Greenwich, 15 Nov., 1914; *s* of William Snelling; *m* Margaret Snelling; three *s*, one *d. Educ.:* Camberwell School of Art; *studied art* under Horace Brodzky. *Exhib.:* Mall Galleries, Guildhall Gallery and numerous one-man shows. *Work in permanent and private collections:* Great Britain, U.S.A., S.A., Finland, Norway, Germany, Italy, etc. *Publications:* written and illustrated: Painting Defects (Spon), Painters Book of Facts (Technical Press). *Address:* 306 Wennington Rd., Rainham, Essex. *Signs work:* see appendix.

SNOW, Graham, Dip.A.D. (1968), H.Dip. (1972); Mombusho scholar, Japan (1974-77), Artist in Residence, Cambridge University (1977-81); artist in oil and water-colour; *b* Exeter, 28 Oct., 1948. *Educ.:* Colfox School, Dorset; *studied art* at Bournemouth College of Art (1966-68), Hornsey College of Art (1968-70), Slade School of Fine Art (1970-72). *Exhib.:* one-man shows in London, New York and Tokyo. *Work in permanent collections:* Arts Council, Chase Manhattan Bank, Texaco, etc. *Address:* c/o Grob Gallery, 20 Dering St., London W1R 9AA. *Signs work:* "G. SNOW."

SNOWDEN, Hilda Mary, B.A. (Hons.) Open University, F.I.A.L.; artist in pastels, oils, water-colour, embroidery, sculpture; *b* Bradford, 13 Apr., 1910; *d* of James Snowden, textile manager. *Educ.:* Grange Upper School, Hillcroft College, Surbiton; *studied art* at Regional College of Art, Bradford, Positano Art Workshop, Italy. *Exhib.:* London, Bradford, Harrogate, Ilkley. *Publications:* author and illustrator, Dalesman (Nov. 1985); Under Stag's Fell—A History of Simonstone-Wensleydale (1989); author, Bradford Antiquary. *Address:* Flat, Victoria Mans., Dawson St., Thackley, Bradford BD10 8LH. *Signs work:* see appendix.

SNOWDON, Brian Robert; private Fine Art Dealer and adviser specialising in modernist, post-war and contemporary paintings and sculpture; Quality stock holdings: enquiries and commissions by institutions and private clients for major works welcomed and undertaken; *b* Darlington, 27 June, 1942. *Educ.:* Darlington C.F.E. *Address:* Nepenthe Cottage, 7 Park St., Stow-on-the-Wold, Glos. GL54 1AQ.

SOAR, John Richardson, M.A. (1966), B.Sc. (1952), U.A. (1989), H.S. (1989); landscape painter in pastel (from miniature to large size pastel paintings); Principal, Swindon Technical College and School of Art (retd. 1984); Inspector of Further Education for Essex C.C. (1965-70); *b* London, 30 May, 1927; *s* of John C. Soar (decd.); *m* Miriam Theresa; one *s*, one *d. Educ.:* West Ham Municipal College; King's College, London. *Exhib.:* U.A. (annually), Westminster Gallery; Hilliard Soc. of Miniaturists (annually), Bishop's Palace, Wells; R.M.S.

Westminster Gallery; Britain's Painters '89, Mall Galleries; Chelsea Art Soc. Open; Wantage Museum Gallery (1987, 1988, 1989); regular contributor to galleries at Bath, Lechlade, Marlborough, Medici Gallery and Llewellyn Alexander Gallery, London. *Work in private collections:* mostly in West of England, U.S.A., and Canada. *Address:* 81 Chestnut Springs, Lydiard Millicent, Swindon, Wilts. SN5 9NB. *Clubs:* Guild of Wiltshire Artists, Fossenay Artists. *Signs work:* "JOHN SOAR."

SOBIEN, Inka; Grand Prix Humanitaire de France avec Medaille d'Argent (1977), La Palme D'or, Belgo-Hispanique (1977); artist; lecturer, Hornsey College of Art and Central Academy of Film, Art and Drama, London (1963-66), St. Martin's School of Art (1963-67); *b* 25 Feb., 1939; *d* of Prof. Sobieniewski Zdzislaw; *m* Stewart Steven; one *s* (Jack-Kuba Steven). *Studied art* at St. Martin's School of Art (1959-63). *Exhib.:* one-man shows: Upper St. Gallery, London (1974), Gallerie Raymond Duncan, Paris (1975), New Jersey (1975), Ligoa Duncan, N.Y. (1975), Philadelphia (1975), Florida (1976), Festival International de Peinture et d'Art Graphico-Plastique de St. Germain-des-Pres, Paris (1976), Scribes Writers' Club, London (1978), Little Palace, Warsaw (1979), B.W.A. Gallery, Cracow (1979), Avant Garde Gallery, Wroclaw (1979), Barbican Centre (1985), Budapest (1985), Camden Arts Centre (1989); mixed shows: Grande Palais Paris; London: Marjorie Parr Gallery, Gallery XVIII, Annely Juda Fine Art, Leinster Fine Art, Salomon Gallery. *Work in permanent collections:* National Museum, Warsaw and Cracow, Museum of Modern Art, Budapest. *Address:* 29 Priory Ave., London W4. *Signs work:* "Inka Sobien."

SOFRONIOU, Michael John, B.A. (Oxon.) (1978), B.A. Illustration and Graphic Design (1982); artist in oil, pastel and water-colour, teacher, illustrator; Artist in Residence, Royal Shakespeare Co. Stratford (1991); *b* London, 20 Mar., 1957; *s* of Nicholas Sofroniou; *m* Rachel; one *s*, two *d*. *Educ.:* Colfes Grammar School, Keble College, Oxford; *studied art:* Wimbledon School of Art, Camberwell School of Art. *Exhib.:* Burgh House Hampstead (1985), Stables Gallery, Oxford (1987), Westgate Library, Oxford (1987), R.I. (1988-90), Medici Soc., John Noott, Broadway, Newcastle Central Library (1992), Barbican Centre (1992). *Work in permanent collections:* Cheltenham City Art, R.S.C. Collection, Stratford. *Address:* The Post Office, Little Barrington, Oxon. OX18 4TE. *Signs work:* "Michael Sofroniou."

SOKOLOV, Kirill Konstantinovich; painter, printmaker, illustrator, sculptor, engraver; co-editor, "Leonardo"; *b* Moscow, 27 Sept., 1930; *s* of Konstantin Mikhailovich Sokolov, constructivist architect, and Irina Konstantinovna Sokolova-Kirschbaum; *m* Avril Pyman; one *d*. *Educ.:* Special Art School, Moscow (1942-49); *studied art* at Surikov Institute, Moscow (1949-56). *Exhib.:* Gulbenkian Gallery, Newcastle, Durham University, St. Helier, C.I., London University, Bishopsgate Foundation, Academy of Art, Riga, House of Artists, Krymskaia Naberezhnaia, Moscow, Art Gallery, Perm, Hatton Gallery Newcastle, and various venues in U.S.S.R., China, U.S.A., Norway, Germany. *Work in public collections:* Pushkin Museum, Trediakov Gallery, Latvian State Museum of Arts, Graphic Archive, Munich, Perm Gallery, Optyno-Pustyn, Taras Shevchenko, Dostoevsky and Aleksandr Blok Memorial Museums, Shakespeare Memorial Museum, Stratford-on-Avon, V. & A., Faust Soc., Knittlingen, Lyric Theatre, Hammersmith, Theatre Royal, Newcastle, Hatton Gallery, Newcastle. *Publications:* over 60 titles in Russian and English. *Address:*

213 Gilesgate, Durham DH1 1QN. *Signs work:* "Kirill Sokolov," also "K.S." and "K.C." (until 1974 in cyrillic).

SONNIS, Alexander, A.R.C.A., lithographer R.C.A.; painter in various mediums; part-time instructor, St. Martin's School of Art (1946-73); also periods at other art schools; *b* 1904; *s* of Samuel Sonnis, furniture maker. *Educ.:* L.C.C., part-time student of Bernard Meninsky, Central School of Arts and Crafts (1924-27); textile designer B.C.P.A. (1927-29); Royal College of Art award (1929-32). *Exhib.:* N.E.A.C. (London Group), R.A., miscellaneous galleries. *Official purchases:* War Advisory Committee (1942). *Address:* 51 Cresswell Rd., Twickenham, Middx. TW1 2EA. *Signs work:* "Alex Sonnis" or "A. SONNIS."

SOREL, Agatha, R.E., Churchill Fellow (1967), Fellow, Printmakers Council; printmaker, sculptor, lecturer; *b* Budapest, 1935; *m* G. Sitkey; one *s*. *Studied art* at Academy of Fine Art, and Academy of Applied Art, Budapest; Camberwell School of Art and Crafts (Michael Rothenstein, S.W. Hayter); Atelier 17, Paris. *Exhib.:* one-man shows: Curwen Gallery, London, Arleigh Gallery, San Francisco, Philadelphia Print Club, Ben Uri Gallery, London, Old Jaffa Gallery, Tel Aviv, Oxford Gallery, Camden Arts Centre, O.U.P., Robertson Gallery, Ottawa, Mälargalleriet, Stockholm, Sculpture at Paul Kövesdy Gallery, N.Y., Intaglio Printmaker, London, watercolours at Trumpington Gallery, Cambridge; retrospective exhbn. Herbert Read Gallery, Canterbury. *Work in permanent collections:* in 33 major museums including B.M., Tate Gallery, Los Angeles Museum of Art, Philadelphia Museum of Art, Chicago Art Inst., National Gallery, Washington. *Publication:* illustrated: Jean Genet, Le Balcon. *Address:* 34 Wilton Row, London SW1X 7NS. *Clubs:* R.E., Printmakers Council. *Signs work:* "Agatha Sorel."

SORRELL, Adrian; sculptor in wax and clay cast in bronze, painter; lecturer, Bolton College of Art (1961-75); *b* Salford, 1932. *Studied art* at Salford School of Art (1949-54). *Exhib.:* Sladmore Gallery, London (1972-78), Les Animaliers, 150 Years of Animal Sculpture, Sladmore Gallery (1976), Morris Singer Exhbn., Dubai (1977), Sportsmans Edge Gallery, N.Y. (1978), Moorland Gallery, London (1979), Dominion Gallery, Montreal (1980), R.A. Summer Exhbn. (1980-89), Tryon Moorland Gallery, London (1983, 1987), Liverpool Museum (1985), Church St. Gallery, Stow (1987), Reid Stremmel Gallery, Texas (1986-87). *Address:* 74 Ringley Rd., Whitefield, Lancs. M25 7LN. *Signs work:* "SORRELL."

SORRELL, Richard, Dip.A.D. (1969), R.A. Schools Post. Grad. Cert. (1972), R.W.S. (1978), R.B.A. (1989); artist in oil, water-colour and acrylic; *b* Thundersley, Essex, 24 Sept., 1948; *s* of Alan and Elizabeth Sorrell, artists; *m* Doreen Burke; two *s*. *Educ.:* Eton House School, Thorpe Bay, Essex; *studied art* at Walthamstow Art School (1965-66), Kingston College of Art (1966-69), R.A. Schools (1969-72). *Exhib.:* R.A., R.W.S., R.B.A., The Lane Studio, New Grafton Gallery, Agnews, Cadogan Gallery. *Work in permanent collection:* V. & A., Museum of London, Beecroft A.G., Southend-on-Sea. *Work repro.:* The Artist, Country Life. *Address:* East Side, Syers Rd., Beeston, King's Lynn, Norfolk PE32 2NJ. *Signs work:* "Richard Sorrell."

SOUKOP, Willi, R.A. (1969); sculptor; Chelsea School of Art since 1947 and Master of the Sculpture School of the Royal Academy (1969-82); *b* Vienna, 5 Jan., 1907; *s* of Karl Soukop, craftsman; *m* Simone Michelle, dancer; one *s*, one *d*. *Studied art* at Vienna Academy of Fine Art. *Exhib.:* R.A., R.B.A., Edinburgh Festival, Battersea Park, Arts Council, Antwerp Bienale. *Work in permanent collections:* Cheltenham A.G., Cordova Museum (U.S.A.), Tate Gallery. *Official*

WHO'S WHO IN ART

purchases: Herts. C.C.; Leicester Educ. Com.; L.C.C.; Kidbrooke Comprehensive School; Camberwell housing estate. *Work repro.:* The Studio, Listener, British Artist Craftsmen, etc. *Address:* 26 Greville Rd., London NW6 5JA. *Signs work:* see appendix.

SOULAGES, Pierre; painter; *b* Rodez, France, 24 Dec., 1919; *s* of Amans Soulages; *m* Colette Llaurens. *Exhib.:* one-man shows in Museums of Hannover, Zurich, Essen, De Hagen (1960-61), Copenhagen (1963), Houston (1966), National d'art moderne, Paris (1967), Buffalo, Pittsburgh, Montréal (1968), Mexico, Caracas, Rio de Janeiro, Sao Paulo, Maracaibo (1975-76), Centre G. Pompidou, Paris (1979), Liège et Salzburg (1980), Tokyo (1984), Kassel, Valencia, Nantes (1989). *Official purchases:* Centre G. Pompidou, Paris, Museum of Modern Art, Guggenheim Museum, N.Y., National Gallery, Washington, National Gallery of Australia, Canberra, Museo de Arte Moderna, Sao-Paulo, Tate Gallery, London, etc. *Address:* 18 rue des Trois-Portes, 75005 Paris, 5. *Signs work:* see appendix.

SOUZA, F. N.; painter; founder of Progressive Artists Group, Bombay (1948); *b* Goa, 12 Apr., 1924; *s* of Newton J. Souza, schoolmaster; *m* (1) Maria Figuereido (divorced); one *d*; (2) Liselotte Kristian (in common law); three *d*; (3) Barbara Zinkant (divorced); one *s*. *Educ.:* St. Xavier's College; Sir J. J. School of Art; Central School of Art; Ecole des Beaux Arts. *Exhib.:* one-man shows, London, Paris, Stockholm, Copenhagen, Johannesburg, Germany, U.A.E., U.S.A., etc.; retrospective exhbns., London, New Delhi, Leicester, Detroit; Minneapolis Int. Art (1972); Expo '67, Montreal; Commonwealth Inst., London (1977); Contemporary Indian Artists (N.Y., 1978); Festival of India, R.A. and Oxford (1982), etc. *Work in permanent collections:* New Delhi, Tate, Haifa, Melbourne, etc. *Publications:* Words and Lines (autobiography); The White Flag Revolution (1982); New Poems (1985). *Address:* 148 West 67 St., New York, N.Y. 10023. *Signs work:* see appendix.

SOWERBY, Brian Holgate, R.E.; etcher; part-time lecturer, Norfolk Inst. of Art and Design; *b* Grimsby, 2 July, 1920; *s* of Herbert Edward Sowerby, soldier; *m* Ellen Bromley; two *s*. *Educ.:* St. James and Nunsthorpe, Grimsby. *Exhib.:* regularly with Royal Soc. of Painter-Printmakers, several one-man shows in Norwich. *Work in permanent collection:* Wilts. C.C. *Address:* 7 Norvic Drive, Eaton, Norwich, Norfolk NR4 7NL. *Signs work:* "Brian Sowerby."

SPAFFORD, George, M.A., B.C.L., R.C.A. (1990); artist in acrylic; *b* Manchester, 1 Sept., 1921; *s* of Christopher Spafford; *m* Iola; one *s*, one *d*. *Educ.:* Rugby, Oxford. *Address:* 57 Hawthorn La., Wilmslow, Ches. SK9 5DQ. *Signs work:* "G.S."

SPAFFORD, Iola Margaret, D.F.A. (1953), R.C.A. (1984), mem. M.A.F.A.; artist in oil, pen and ink, water-colour, etching; *b* Cambridge, 24 Aug., 1930; *d* of B.L. Hallward, M.A.; *m* George Spafford; one *s*, one *d*. *Educ.:* Queen Anne's, Caversham; *studied art* at Bristol Art School (1947), Nottingham Art School (1948-50), Slade School of Fine Art (1950-54). *Exhib.:* one-man shows, Tib Lane Gallery, Manchester (4). *Work in permanent collections:* Manchester A.G. (Rutherston Collection), Salford A.G., and many private collections. *Address:* 57 Hawthorn La., Wilmslow, Ches. SK9 5DQ. *Signs work:* "Iola Spafford."

SPALDING, Julian, F.M.A. (1983); Director, Glasgow Museum and Art Galleries; *b* London, 15 June, 1947; *m* (1) Frances Crabtree (divorced); one *s*; (2) Gillian Tait. *Educ.:* Chislehurst and Sidcup Grammar School for Boys;

studied art at University of Nottingham (B.A.Hons. Fine Art). *Address:* Glasgow Art Gallery and Museum, Kelvingrove, Glasgow G3 8AG.

SPENCE, T. Everard; portrait and landscape artist in oil; linen manufacturer. *Educ.:* Bootham School, York. *Exhib.:* R.A., R.B.A., R.H.A., R.U.A., several one-man shows; collection of portrait miniatures. *Address:* 45 Deramore Park, Belfast, N. Ireland. *Signs work:* see appendix.

SPENCER, Charles Samuel; lecturer and art critic; *b* London, 26 Aug., 1920. Former editor, Art and Artists; Former editor, Editions Alecto Collectors Club; Lecturer, Theatre and Art. *Publications:* author: Erté (1970); A Decade of Print Making (1973); Leon Bakst (1973); Cecil Beaton (1975); The World of Serge Diaghilev (1974); editor: The Aesthetic Movement (1973); Alecto Monographs on Kenneth Armitage, Colin Lanceley, Tom Phillips, Achilles Droungas, Ed Meneely, Harald Becker, Igino Legnaghi. *Address:* 24A Ashworth Rd., London W9 1JY.

SPENCER, Claire, N.D.D. (1958), A.R.C.A. (1963), A.T.D. (1973), R.B.S.A. (1980), P.S. (1985); painter in oil, pastel, water-colour; *b* Kingsbury, Middx., 17 May, 1937; *m* Christopher Postins; one *s. Educ.:* Harrow County School for Girls; *studied art* at Hornsey College of Art (1954-58), R.C.A. (1960-63), Accademia di Belle Arti, Perugia (1966). Numerous individual and group exhbns. *Work in permanent collections:* Nuffield Collection, West Midlands Arts Collection. *Address:* Rotherwood, 17 Summerfield Rd., Clent, Stourbridge, Worcs. DY9 9RG. *Signs work:* "Claire Spencer."

SPENCER, Gwen, N.S.; painter in oil, pastel and gouache; Hon. sec., National Soc. of Painters, Sculptors and Printmakers; *b* Argentine, 2 Oct., 1927; *d* of Edwin Arthur Conran, mechanical engineer; *m* Christopher Spencer, F.C.A.; two *s*, one *d. Educ.:* St. Hilda's College, Buenos Aires; *studied art* at Atelier Josse, Buenos Aires, and Putney School of Art. *Exhib.:* N.S., R.O.I., P.S., Ridley Soc. *Work repro.:* Medici Soc. *Work in public and private collections:* U.K., N. and S. America, Italy, Holland, Denmark. *Address:* 122 Copse Hill, Wimbledon, London SW20 0NL. *Signs work:* "Gwen Spencer" or "G. Spencer."

SPENCER, Pamela Mary; artist in oil, water-colour, pencil; *b* Manchester, 11 Jan., 1924; *d* of Percy Julius Spencer, M.A. (Cantab). *Educ.:* P.N.E.U. Schools, Queen's College, Radbrook College of Domestic Science (Shrewsbury); *studied art* at St. Martin's School of Art under J. Bateman, Barry Craig, J. L. Wheatley, H. A. Freeth, K. Martin (1945-51). *Exhib.:* R.A., N.E.A.C., S.W.A., N.S., R.B.A., R.O.I., P.S., Russell-Cotes Museum, and other provincial galleries. *Address:* 33 Damer Gdns., Henley-on-Thames, Oxon. RG9 1HX. *Signs work:* "Pamela M. Spencer" or "P. M. Spencer."

SPENCER, Sarah, B.A. (Hons.) (1988), Post. Dip. R.A. Schools (1991); painter in oil, charcoal, pastel; part-time lecturer, Canterbury College; *b* Sevenoaks, 26 Sept., 1965. *Educ.:* Tonbridge Grammar School, West Kent College of F.E.; *studied art* at Camberwell School of Art and Crafts (1985-88), R.A. Schools (1988-91). *Exhib.:* solo shows: New Grafton Gallery, Waterman's Fine Art; many mixed shows. *Work in permanent collection:* West Wales Arts Council. *Address:* 7 Marine Terr., Whitstable, Kent CT5 1EJ. *Signs work:* full signature on reverse of works, sometimes "S.S." on front.

SPENCER PRYSE, Tessa, R.B.A. (1986); painter of portraits, landscapes and interiors in oil, water-colour, lithography; *b* Highcliff on Sea, 28 Sept., 1939; *d* of Capt. Gerald Spencer Pryse, artist and lithographer; *m* E.D.A. Cameron; one *s*, one *d. Educ.:* France and Switzerland; *studied art* at Byam Shaw School of

Art (1960-64, Peter Greenham, Bernard Dunstan). *Exhib.:* R.A., R.P., R.B.A., N.E.A.C., R.S.A., R.W.S.; one-man shows: Edencourt, Inverness, Phoenix Gallery, Lavenham, Hayletts Gallery, Colchester, Alpine Gallery, London, Digby Gallery, Colchester, John Russell, Ipswich, Arthur Andersen, London. *Work in permanent collection:* Essex Museum. *Address:* 9 Anchor Hill, Wivenhoe, Colchester, Essex CO7 9BL. *Signs work:* "PRYSE."

SPENDER, Humphrey, Hon. Des. R.C.A.; painter, photographer; designer, textiles, wallpapers, carpets; four C.O.I.D. Awards; *b* London, 19 Apr., 1910; *m* Pauline Wynn, actress; two *s. Studied:* Architectural Assoc. *Exhib.:* one-man: Redfern, Leicester Galleries, New Art Centre, Windsor, Farnham, Colchester, Bristol; group: C.A.S., Arts Council, John Moores, Bradford, Aldeburgh, R.A. *Work in permanent collections:* V. & A., N.P.G., M. of W., Southampton, Wolverhampton, Brighton, Manchester, Johannesburg. *Murals:* Festival of Britain, P. & O. Liners Orcades, Orsova, Oriana, Canberra, Shell Centre, Pilkingtons. *Publications:* Worktown People (Falling Wall Press, 1982), Lensman (Chatto & Windus, 1987). *Address:* The Studio, Ulting, Maldon, Essex CM9 6QX.

SPENDLOVE, Gerald Hugh, A.T.D. (Dist.) (1954), F.S.D-C. (1972); designer-craftsman in calligraphy, lettering, illumination and ceramics; formerly Head of Ceramics, Herts. College of Art, St. Albans; *b* Derby, 1929; *s* of Horace Albert Spendlove; *m* Valerie Spendlove; one *s,* three *d. Educ.:* Salisbury School of Art (1949-51), L.C.C. Central School of Art (1951-53), N.D.D. Pottery and Calligraphy. *Exhib.:* Nottingham, Southampton, Bath, York, St. Albans, London. *Work in permanent collections:* H.M. the Queen, Herts. C.C., Nevers (France); private collections in U.S.A., France, Norway, Germany, Nigeria, U.K. *Address:* The Sycamores, New Rd., Swanmore, Hants. SO3 2PE. *Signs work:* "G. H. Spendlove", stamp GHS in square.

SPOWART, Robert Henry Donald, N.D.D. (Painting, Special Level, 1962), A.T.D./A.T.C. (Manc. 1965); artist in collage and assemblage; art teacher; Head of Arts and Crafts Dept., The John Masefield High School, Ledbury; *b* Farnborough, Hants., 30 Apr., 1939; *s* of Harry Théophile Spowart; *m* Julie Ann; two *s. Educ.:* Luton Grammar School; *studied art* at St. Albans School of Art (1959, Norman Adams), St. Martins School of Art (1959-62, Frederick Gore, Joe Tilson, Anthony Caro, Derrick Greaves). *Exhib.:* Ashbarn Gallery, nr. Petersfield (1970), Great Malvern Library (1973), Worcester Arts Workshop (1975). Work in private collections. *Address:* 7 Layton Ave., Malvern, Worcs. WR14 2ND. *Club:* Hornby Railway Collectors Assoc. *Signs work:* see appendix.

SPRAKES, John, R.O.I., R.B.A., F.R.S.A.; Andrew Grant scholarship, D.A. (Edin.) post grad.; prizewinner Singer Friedlander/Sunday Times water-colour (1992); artist in tempera, oil, acrylic; *b* 17 Oct., 1936; *s* of T.B. Sprakes; *m* Barbara Ann; three *s. Studied art* at Doncaster College of Art, Edinburgh College of Art (1954-57). *Exhib.:* R.A., Mem. of The Manchester Academy; Manchester Academy (prize 85), Barclays Bank award (1986, 1991), P/P award (1989), group and one-man shows. Work in public and private collections. Agent in London, J. Corless, Blackheath Gallery. *Address:* 39 Douglas Rd., Long Eaton, Nottingham NG10 4BH. *Signs work:* "John Sprakes" or "J. Sprakes."

SPURRIER, Raymond, R.I., A.R.W.A.; writer, illustrator, painter, printmaker; Hon. Secretary R.I.; *b* Wellingborough, 1920. *Educ.:* Wellingborough Grammar School; *studied art* part-time at St. Martin's and Central School. Practising town planner until 1980 and part-time freelance illustrator and writer. *Exhib.:* R.A., R.W.A., R.I., etc.; finalist Hunting Group prize competition (1980, 1982);

Winsor & Newton R.I. Award (1984). *Work in permanent collections:* Dept. of the Environment and private. *Work repro:* R.A. illustrated and calendar, contributor, The Artist Magazine and instructional art books; author: Sketching with Raymond Spurrier. *Address:* Halstead Cottage, Halstead, Sevenoaks, Kent. *Signs work:* "Raymond Spurrier."

SQUIRE, Geoffrey, D.F.A. (Lond.) 1948, A.R.S.A. (1977), R.G.I. (1980), R.S.W. (1983); painter in oil, acrylic, water-colour, pastel; retd. senior lecturer, Glasgow School of Art (1988); *b* Yorks., 21 Feb., 1923; *s* of Norman Squire (decd.); *m* Jeanmarie; one *s*, one *d*. *Studied art* at Leeds College of Art (1939-41); Slade School of Art, Oxford (1941-42), London (1946-48, Randolph Schwabe). *Exhib.:* Yorks., Glasgow, Fife, Edinburgh. *Work in permanent collections:* Glasgow A.G., Greenock A.G., Paisley A.G., Dunkeld A.G., Jordanhill College of Educ., Royal Scottish Academy. *Address:* The Studio, Links Pl., Elie, Fife. *Club:* Lagonda. *Signs work:* "SQUIRE."

STABELL, Waldemar Christian; painter in oil, wax drawings; *b* Hillsboro, N.B., Canada, 1913; *s* of Lorentz Stabell, shipowner (1865-1933), and Laura Edna (*b* Forbes Edgett, 1890-1968); *m* Margit Baugstö; one *s*, one *d*. *Educ.:* Canada, Norway; *studied art:* Scandinavia, Anglo-French Art Centre, London, Brighton College of Art (etching). *Exhib.:* first one-man show in London (1947), St. George's Gallery; several one-man shows and mixed exhibitions. *Work repro.:* Studio, Canada's Weekly, Contact Book, Arts Review, London. Founder of the Voss School of Fine Arts (1964) Voss, Norway. *Publications:* Edvard Munch and Eva Mudocci; Bernt Tunold 1877-1977; Phillip King – En Engelsk Billedhugger (1969); British Artists at the Voss Summer School of Fine Arts. *Address:* Sydneskleven 31, Bergen, Norway. *Signs work:* "Stabell."

STAFFORD, C. Carolyn, C.P.S. (1988), S.G.F.A. (1986), P.M.C. (1987), N.D.D., D.A. (Manc.) (1955), Dip. Fine Art (1957); painter in oil and water-colour printmaker in etching, woodcut, litho; tutor; *b* Bolton, 1935; *d* of Stanley and Elizabeth Stafford; *m* Gordon Clough, broadcaster; one *s*, three *d*. *Educ.:* Bolton School; *studied art:* Bolton School of Art, Manchester College of Art (Ralph Downing, Ian Grant), Slade School of Fine Art (William Coldstream, Claude Rogers, Anthony Gross), Esmond Scholar British Inst. in Paris, etching with S.W. Hayter (1957-58). *Exhib.:* John Moores, Liverpool. R.A., Bankside Open Prints, London Group, Arts Council tours, R.I., R.B.A., Printmakers Council, Malta, U.S./U.K., Art Olympia (1990-93), Pump House (1993), Contemporary Portrait Soc., S.G.F.A., Northern School (Pelter-Sands and touring exhbn.), Lvov (1991), New Academy Gallery (1991), Universities of Bristol, Cambridge, Durham, London, Oxford and Surrey (1980-90). *Work in permanent collections:* Slade School, D.O.E., Bolton School (Girls Div.), Bolton A.G., Lvov A.G. *Address:* 52 Ellerton Rd., London SW18 3NN. *Signs work:* "Carolyn Stafford," "Carolyn Stafford Clough" or "C. STAFFORD."

STAINTON, Frances: see EASTON, Frances.

STANDEN, Peter, D.A. (Edin.); works in oil, acrylic, etching, lithography: subjects allegorical, imaginary future ruins, and cats; Mem. Edinburgh Printmakers Workshop (Council 1974-87; Chairman 1979-82); Mem. Soc. of Scottish Artists (Council 1990-93); Scottish Art Council Awards incl. 'Artist in Industry' Ferranti plc (1987); *b* Carshalton, 3 Apr., 1936; *s* of Charles Standen and Isabel (née) Ogier; *m* Helen; one *s*, one *d*. *Educ.:* Epping Secondary; *studied art* at Nottingham College of Art (1954-56), Edinburgh College of Art (1956-59). *Exhib.:* one-man shows: 'Up the Nile' Commonwealth Inst., Edinburgh (1965), 'Paintings' New 57 Gallery, Edinburgh (1977), 'Mr. Cat' Traverse

Theatre Club, Edinburgh (1985), 'Looking Back to the Future' P.M.W. Edinburgh (1988); group shows: 'Art into Landscape' I and III Serpentine Gallery, London (1974, 1979), '5 Scottish Printmakers' selected by Peter Fuller, P.M.W. Edinburgh Festival (1983), 'Ljubljana Biennial' Yugoslavia (1987), 'Festive City' Fine Art Soc., Edinburgh Festival (1988). *Work in permanent collections:* Hamilton A.G., Ontario, Scottish Arts Council, City of Edinburgh, International Club London, Moray House College Edinburgh, Eastern General Hospital Edinburgh, The University of Edinburgh, Royal Bank of Scotland. *Address:* 5 Lee Cres., Portobello, Edinburgh EH15 1LW. *Signs work:* prints: "P. Standen" (pencil signature); paintings: "P. STANDEN."

STARK, Marjorie Jean, R.S.W. (1974); artist in oil and water-colour; *b* Edinburgh, 1914; *d* of William Thow Munro, C.B.E., woollen manufacturer; *m* Alan F. Stark, M.B.E., W.S. *Educ.:* Edinburgh; *studied art* at Edinburgh College of Art (1949-55). *Work in permanent collections:* H.R.H. the Duke of Edinburgh, Nottingham Educ. Authority, Scottish Arts Council, Edinburgh Educ. Authority, etc. *Address:* Wellgate, Morebattle, Kelso, Roxburghshire TD5 8QN. *Signs work:* "Marjorie Stark."

STARR, Marion; artist in oil; *b* Hitchin, Herts., 19 Apr., 1937; *d* of Walter Starr; *m* Christopher Fielder; two *d. Educ.:* various Grammar Schools in U.K. and abroad; studied art under Frederick Cuming, Charles Hardaker. *Exhib.:* R.A., N.E.A.C., R.O.I., Spirit of London, Lang, Easton Rooms, Rye. *Address:* 23 Military Rd., Rye, E. Sussex TN31 7NX. *Signs work:* "M.S." or "Marion Starr."

STAUVERS, Feliks, R.V.D.S. Arts Academy School (Riga, Latvia); Diploma of Merit, University of Art, Italy; artist in oil, pen, ink, water-colour, dry pigments, restorer, art historian, freelance lecturer in Art and Old Master Paintings; *b* Riga, Latvia, 22 Apr., 1926; *s* of C. Stauvers, farmer; *m* M. E. Stauvers; two *s. Educ.:* Latvia; *studied art* at Riga Government Arts Academy School (1939-44) under, Prof. Brumel, Dr. V. Luans, Daluns Paks, R.V.D.S. *Exhib.:* Nuneaton, Coventry, London. *Works in permanent collection:* Nuneaton Museum A.G. *Address:* 83 Windmill Rd., Exhall, Coventry CV7 9GP. *Club:* Former Associate of I.I.C. London. *Signs work:* "Feliks Stauvers."

STEADMAN, Alfred T., M.F.P.S. (1972), C.Eng. (1971), F.Inst.F. (1975), F.R.S.A. (1987); artist in oil, water-colour, pastel; retd. Fuel Engineer; *b* Derby, 1912; *s* of Alfred G.H. Steadman, coal cleaning plant manager; *m* Esther; one *d. Educ.:* schools in Derbyshire, and Sheffield University; *studied art* at Nottingham (Dame Laura Knight), Birmingham (Gilbert Mason). *Exhib.:* London, Lichfield, Leamington Spa, B'ham, and an annual one-man show Solihull. *Address:* 5 Melplash Ave., Solihull, W. Midlands B91 1LP. *Signs work:* "Alfred Steadman."

STEPHENS, Ian, N.D.D. (1961), R.E. (1984), S.W.E. (1984), P.M.C. (1990); artist in wood engraving, water-colours; *b* Gt. Linford, Bucks., 19 May, 1940; *s* of the late A.B. Stephens; *m* Valerie; two *s. Educ.:* Wolverton Technical School; *studied art* at Northampton School of Art (1956-61). *Exhib.:* R.E. (1975 onwards), Fremantle, Jeune Gravure Contemporaine, Paris, Humberside (1985); one-man show Daventry (1989, 1993), British Miniature Print International, Bristol (1989), Cadaqués (1991). *Work in permanent collections:* Northants C.C., Notts. C.C., Surrey C.C., Warwicks. Museums, Kettering B.C., Daventry D.C., Fremantle Arts Centre. *Address:* 46 Yardley Drive, Northampton NN2 8PE. *Signs work:* "I. Stephens" or "Ian Stephens."

STEPHENS, Nicholas Anthony, N.D.D. (1960), A.R.C.A. (1963), Harkness Fellowship, U.S.A. (1963-65), Arts Council Major award (1977), A.R.B.S. (1981); sculptor in bronze; Principal Lecturer in Fine Art, Glos. College of Art and Technology; visiting teaching: U.C. Davis, California (1971), Victoria College, Prahran, Australia (1983); *b* Nottingham, 6 June, 1939; *s* of R.S. Stephens; *m* Jenifer Beesley (divorced 1984); two *s. Educ.:* Nottingham High School; *studied art* at Central School (Wm. Turnbull), R.C.A. (1960-63, Lord Queensbury), Pratt Inst., N.Y. (1964), San Francisco Art Inst. (1965, James Melchert). *Exhib.:* Davis Cal. (1971), S.W. Arts (1978), The State of Clay (1978-80), R.A. (1980, 1981, 1983, 1984), R.B.S. Scone Palace (1983), Park Gallery Cheltenham (1982, 1985), St. Donat's Castle, Wales (1983), Nicholas Tredwell Gallery (1985), Air Gallery, Harkness Arts (1985), St. David's Hall, Cardiff (1988). *Address:* The Red House, Bredon, Tewkesbury, Glos. GL20 7LM. *Signs work:* "N.A. STEPHENS."

STEPHENSON, Prof. Ian, B.A.Hons.(Dunelm), R.A.; painter; former Studio Demonstrator (pioneered 1st foundn. course in U.K. dedicated to new creativity in art) and Dir. of Foundn. Studies (introd. 1st alternating approach between perceptual and conceptual studies to an academic syllabus), Fine Art, Ncle. Univ.; former Dir. of Postgrad. Painting (created 1st M.A. fine art course in London), Chelsea School of Art; taught many distinguished British artists; *b* nr. Meadowfield, Co. Durham, 11 Jan., 1934; *s* of Jas. Stephenson; *m* Kate Brown; one *s,* one *d. Educ.:* Blyth Grammar School, Northld.; *studied art* at King Edw. VII School of Art, King's College, Durham Univ., Ncle. *Exhib.:* (Retrospectives) Laing A.G., Ncle. (1970); Hayward Gallery (1977); City A.G., Birmingham (1978); often repr. U.K. abroad. *Work in permanent collections:* worldwide. *Work repro.:* in numerous publications; Cubism & After, B.B.C. Michael Gill film; Blow-up, M.G.M. Antonioni film. *Address:* c/o Royal Academy of Arts, Piccadilly, London W1V 0DS.

STETTLER, Michael, D.Sc.; art historian; architect; Director of Bernese Historical Museum from 1948 to 1961; Director Abegg Foundation (1961-77); P. Helvetia Foundation (1965-71); *b* Berne, 1 Jan., 1913; *s* of Wilhelm Stettler de Graffenried, architect; *m* Barbara von Albertini; four *d. Educ.:* Berne; *studied art* at Zürich Inst. of Technology and University under J. Zemp and H. Wölfflin, and at Rome. *Publications:* Das Rathaus zu Bern (1942), Inventory of Historical Monuments of Canton Aargau (Vol. I, 1948, Vol. II, 1953); Swiss Stained Glass of the 14th Century (English Edition, 1949); Of Old Berne (1957); Rat der Alten (1962); Bernerlob (1964), Neues Bernerlob (1967); Aare, Bär und Sterne (1972); Machs na (1981); Ortbühler Skizzenbuch (1982); A la Rencontre de Berne (1984); Sulgenbach (1992). *Address:* Ortbühl, CH-3612 Steffisburg, Switzerland.

STEVENS, Chris, B.F.A. (Hons.); artist in oil; *b* Basingstoke, 1956. *Studied art:* University of Reading (1974-78). *Exhib.:* one-man shows: U.K., London and Holland; group shows: London, Germany and U.S.A; shows with Sue Williams, London. *Work in permanent collections:* National Gallery of Wales. *Address:* Space Studios, Deborah House, Retreat Pl., London E9.

STEVENSON, David John; painter in egg tempera and oil; *b* Leicester, 26 Nov., 1956; *s* of Samuel Stevenson; *m* Alison Wilkins; two *s. Educ.:* Guthlaxton College, Leicester. *Exhib.:* Leicester Museum, Loseby Gallery, Leicester, Tettenhall Gallery, R.A. *Address:* 15 Wartnaby St., Market Harborough, Leics. *Club:* Leicester Soc. of Artists. *Signs work:* "D. Stevenson."

STEWART, Charles William; taught at Byam Shaw School (1950-58); artist and illustrator in water-colour, pen and ink; *b* Ilo-Ilo, Panay, Philippine Islands, 18 Nov., 1915. *Educ.:* Radley College: *studied art* at The Byam Shaw School of Drawing and Painting (1932-38) under Ernest Jackson. *Publications:* illustrated: Pendennis (Thackeray), Limited Editions Club, N.Y.; Vathek (Beckford), Bodley Head; The Lady of the Linden Tree (Barbara Leonie Picard), O.U.P.; Grimbold's Other World (Nicholas Stuart Gray), Faber; The Visiting Moon (Celia Furse), Faber; Uncle Silas (Sheridan Lefanu) Folio Soc.; Mistress Masham's Repose (T.H. White) Folio Soc., etc. *Address:* Flat 1, Ritchie Court, 380 Banbury Rd., Oxford OX2 7PW. *Signs work:* "Charles W. Stewart."

STEWART, John Dunlop, M.S.I.A. (1947-70), N.R.D. (1945), probationer, R.I.B.A. (1944); industrial designer and product design consultant; founder and hon. sec., Paisley Rocketeers' Society (1936-39 and from 1968); designer and producer of multiple originals — numbered and initialled rocket mail flown in experimental models; draughtsman-designer, Universal Pulp Containers Ltd. (1941-48); designer-photographer, H. Morris & Co. Ltd., Glasgow (1948); designer, Design Industries, Beckenham (1949-52); Burndept-Vidor Ltd., Erith (1952-56); Scottish Aviation Ltd (1956-59); *b* Paisley, 3 Sept., 1921; *s* of Peter Stewart, R.P. *Educ.:* John Neilson Inst., Paisley; *studied art* at Glasgow School of Art, Glasgow School of Architecture and Royal Technical College, Glasgow, and Govt. Training Centre, Thornliebank. *Address:* Greystone, 15 Bushes Ave., Paisley PA2 6JR.

STEWART-JONES, Elizabeth; painter, mainly of portraits, in oil and gouache; *b* Lewes, 10 Nov., 1910; *d* of Thorold Stewart-Jones; *m* Major F.H.D. Pulford; two *d*. *Studied art* at Chelsea School of Art. *Exhib.:* pre-war open: S.W.A. (1932, 1934, 1936, 1938), R.A. (1935), R.O.I. (1937, 1938), N.E.A.C., London Group, Artists International (1938), Paris (1939); post-war open: R.B.A., R.A., R.W.E.A., N.S., F.P.S., etc. Current paintings mostly abstract portraits based on the colour of sound. *Address:* Penlanole, nr. Llandrindod-Wells, Powys LD1 6NN. *Signs work:* "E.S-J." or "E. Stewart-Jones."

STIEGER, Jacqueline; sculptor/jewellery/medals – lost wax technique, casting, bronze and precious metals; *b* London, 26 Jan., 1936; *d* of H. J. Stieger, F.R.Ae.S.; 2 *s-s. Educ.:* Bedales, Hants; The Mount School, York; *studied art* at Edinburgh College of Art (1952-58) under W. Gillies. *Work in permanent collections:* Eidgenosische Kunstkommission, Bern Ch; Museum of Medallic Art, Cracow, Poland; Goldsmiths' Hall Collection; B.M. *Address:* Welton Garth, Welton, N. Humberside. *Signs work:* "J. Stieger."

STIRLING, James, Dipl.Arch. (1950), Alvar Aalto award (1977), R.I.B.A. Gold Medal (1980), Pritzker Prize (1981), A.R.A. (1985), Thomas Jefferson award (1986); architect; Prof. Kunstacademie Dusseldorf (1977-); *b* Glasgow, 1926; *m* Mary Shand; one *s*, two *d. Educ.:* Liverpool School of Architecture (1945-50). *Exhib.:* Museum of Modern Art, N.Y. (1969), Heinz Gallery, London (1974), Venice Biennale (1976), R.A. (1986), Tate Gallery (1987), etc. *Publications:* James Stirling, Buildings and Projects, James Stirling and Michael Wilford (Rizzoli, N.Y. 1984), The Clore Gallery for the Turner Collection, Tate Gallery (opening catalogue, 1987), etc. *Address:* 8 Fitzroy Sq., London W1. *Signs work:* "James Stirling."

STIVEN, Frederic William Binning, D.A. (1950), M.C.S.D. (1964), A.R.S.A. (1984); artist in wood and mixed media, constructivist; Head of Design, Grays School of Art, Aberdeen (retd. 1987); *b* Cowdenbeath, Fife, 25 Apr., 1929; *s* of William Downie Stiven; *m* Janet Isabella; two *s*, two *d. Educ.* E. Thurrock

School, Grays, Essex; Beath High School, Cowdenbeath; *studied art* at Edinburgh College of Art (1946-50, Leonard Rosoman, John Kingsley Cook). Post. Grad. Scholar (1950-51). *Exhib.:* Edinburgh, Glasgow, Aberdeen, London, Leeds, Burnley, Middelburg, Weert, Bergen, Helsinki, Venice, New York. *Work in permanent collections:* Scottish National Gallery of Modern Art, S.A.C., Aberdeen City A.G., Dundee City A.G., Leeds Educ. Authority, Strathclyde Regional Council, Temple Newsam House, Ulster Museum. *Address:* Sheallagan, Golf Course Rd., Rosemount, Blairgowrie PH10 6LJ. *Signs work:* "Fred Stiven."

STOBART, Jane, R.E. (1986); artist in etching and relief printmaking methods; part-time teacher at various colleges of art; Fellow, Royal Soc. Painter-Printmakers; *b* S. Shields, Tyne and Wear, 10 Nov., 1949; *d* of Robert William Stobart; *m* Mustafa Sidki. *Educ.:* S.E. Essex Technical School, Dagenham; *studied art* Central School of Art and Design. *Exhib.:* Fremantle Print Exhbn., W. Australia (1988), An Exhbn. of Modern English Graphics, Moscow (1989), Bradford Print Biennale (1986), Whitechapel Open (1986), R.A. Summer Show (1976-77, 1980-82, 1984-86, 1993). *Address:* 138 Windsor Rd., London E7 0RB.

STOCK, Andrew Nicholas, S.WL.A.; Richard Richardson award for bird illustration (1980); P.J.C. award for individual merit (1990), prizewinner in Natural World fine art awards (1989, 1990), runner-up in BBC World Magazine's Wildlife Artist of the Year (1991); Council mem. S.WL.A. (1992-); self taught painter in water-colour, etching, oil, pen and ink; *b* Rinteln, W. Germany, 25 Mar., 1960; *s* of Lt. Col. Peter William Stock, M.B.E., M.A.; *m* Melanie Vass; one *d*. *Educ.:* Sherborne School, Dorset. *Exhib.:* S.WL.A., etc.; one-man shows, Malcolm Innes Gallery, London (4), Alpine Club Gallery, London (2), Edinburgh and Cerne Abbas, Dorset (2). *Publication:* illustrated Driven Game Shooting by D. Bingham (Unwin Hyman, 1989). *Address:* The Studio Gallery, White Hart Yard, Beaminster, Dorset DT8 3AE. *Signs work:* "Andrew Stock."

STOCKHAUS, Eva H. M.; artist in wood-engraving; Mem. Swedish Printmakers' Assoc.; R.E.; Mem. British Soc. of Wood Engravers; *b* Gothenburg, Sweden, 4 Apr., 1919; *d* of Hugo Lindegrén, engineer; *m* Bengt Stockhaus; one *d*, one *s*. *Educ.:* Stockholm University; art studies Stockholm and London. *Work in permanent collections:* National Museum, Stockholm; Nasjonalgalleriet, Oslo; New York Public Library; Graphische Sammlung Albertina, Vienna; various museums Scandinavia etc. Recipient artist's grant of the Swedish State (1975, 1976). *Address:* Appelbovagen 10, 161 40 Bromma, Sweden. *Signs work:* "Eva Stockhaus."

STOKES, Vincent, B.A. (Hons.) Photography and Semiotics; designer/ photographer; art director; *b* 9 Jan., 1964; *s* of Vincent Stokes. *Studied art:* London College of Printing (1986-89, Ann Williams, Peter Osborn). *Exhib.:* Camera Work U.K., Camera Work San Francisco, Photographers Gallery, Arnolfini Bristol, New Orleans, Buffalo, Vancouver, N.Y. *Address:* 14 Beckley House, Hamlets Way, London E3 4SZ. *Signs work:* see appendix.

STOKOE, Michael Arthur, N.D.D. (1957); painter; mem. Printmakers Council; senior lecturer, Ravensbourne College of Design; *b* London, 1933; *s* of Dr. Neville Stokoe, M.A.; *m* Gillian Stacey. *Educ.:* King's School, Bruton; *studied art* at St. Martin's School of Art (1953-57). *Exhib.:* R.A., R.B.A., R.O.I., R.S.O.P.P., Young Contemporaries, Arts Council, Belfast, Piccadilly Gallery, Arnolfini Gallery, Hamilton Gallery, John Moores, New Gallery, Belfast etc.; one-man shows: Temple Gallery, Drian Galleries, Bear Lane Gallery, Nottingham City A.G., Oxford Gallery, Anna Mei Chadwick Gallery, London SW6. *Work* *in permanent collections:* Arts Council of N. Ireland, V. & A., W.A.G., Ferens A.G., Hull, Leeds City A.G., etc., and 20 educational authorities. *Address:* 11 Bowerdean St., London SW6 3TN. *Signs work:* "STOKOE."

STONES, Angela (Mrs.); painter and art teacher in oil, water-colour, pastel; member Chelsea Art Soc., and National Soc.; *b* London, 26 May, 1914; *m;* one *s. Educ.:* Sherborne School for Girls, Dorset; *studied art* at Heatherley's Art School and Sir John Cass School of Art, London (1956-57) (Jack Merriott, R.I., R.O.I., Patrick Larking, R.P., R.O.I., Harold Workman, R.O.I., R.B.A.). *Exhib.:* one-man show: Gallery 19. *Work in permanent collection:* H.R.H. Prince Michael of Kent. *Address:* The Studios, 6 Chelsea Embankment, London SW3. *Club:* Chelsea Arts. *Signs work:* "A. Stones" or "Angela Stones."

STONES, Anthony, F.R.B.S. (1992); sculptor in clay for bronze; *b* Glossop, Derby., 8 Feb., 1934; *s* of Arnold Stones, dyer. *Educ.:* St. Bede's College, Manchester; *studied art:* Manchester Regional College of Art (1950-51). *Work in permanent collections:* bronze portrait heads: John Piper in Reading Civic Centre; Prof. Dorothy Hodgkin, O.M., Somerville College, Oxford; Sir Ronald Syme, O.M. and Sir Isaiah Berlin, O.M., Wolfson College, Oxford; Liam Ó Flaherty, National Gallery of Ireland; commemorative bronze figures: The Hon. Peter Fraser, Wellington, N.Z.; Lord Freyburg, V.C., Auckland, N.Z.: Jean Batten, Auckland International Airport; Victorian Navvy (1992), Gerrards Cross Railway Station; Seven Pacific Explorers for New Zealand Pavilion Expo 92 Seville. *Publications:* edited: Celebration (Penguin Books, 1984); wrote and illustrated: Bill and the Ghost of Grimley Grange (Wolfhound Press, 1988), Bill and the Maze at Grimley Grange (Wolfhound Press, 1990). *Address:* 42 Beauchamp Pl., Oxford OX4 3NE. *Signs work:* "Anthony Stones."

STONES, Christopher John Assheton-, L.S.I.A. (1970), P.S.; painter in pastel, designer, lecturer; Council mem. Pastel Soc.; *b* Ceylon, 19 Apr., 1947; *s* of Angela Stones, artist; *m* Penelope Barlow. *Educ.:* Shrewsbury School; *studied art* at Exeter College of Art, Bournemouth and Poole College of Art. *Exhib.:* Paris Salon, R.W.A., R.O.I., R.S.M.A., P.S., etc. *Publications:* author of Working with Pastel, and Towns and Buildings in Pastel (published in G.B., U.S.A. and Australia); Video publication: Discovering Pastel. *Address:* The Lane Hall, Weasdale, nr. Kirkby Stephen, Cumbria CA17 4LY. *Signs work:* "CJA-STONES" and date.

STONES, Thomas Fiendley, O.B.E. (1981), B.A. (Admin.), F.M.A.; *b* Astley, Lancs., 25 July 1920; *s* of Thomas Stones and Agnes Fiendley Stones; *m* Elizabeth Mackie; one *d. Educ.:* Leigh Grammar School and Manchester University. Served R.A.F. (1941-46); Keeper of the Rutherston Collection, Manchester City Art Galleries (1946-52); Keeper of Modern European Dept. and Print Dept., Royal Ontario Museum of Archæology, Toronto; special lecturer in art and archæology, University of Toronto (1953-54); British Council, Fine Arts Dept., Fine Arts Officer, Paris; Cultural Attaché, British Embassy, Budapest; etc. *Address:* c/o National Westminster Bank, 101 New Oxford St., London WC1A 1DX.

STOREY, Terence; President, R.S.M.A., (Council Member 1979-80-81-82-83); marine, landscape and industrial artist in oils and water-colour; *b* Sunderland, 17 Apr., 1923. *Educ.:* Sunderland Art School and Derby College of Art under Alfred Bladen. *Exhib.:* N.S., R.B.A., R.S.M.A., R.O.I., N.E.A.C. and S.WL.A.*Work in permanent collections:* H.R.H. the Prince of Wales, R.S.M.A. Diploma Collection, The Picture collection of the Port of London Authority, The Royal Eagles Club, The Royal Burnham Yacht Club, and private collections in

U.S.A., Canada, Australia, New Zealand, Germany and the U.K. Works published by Winsor and Newtons, Rolls-Royce Limited, 20th Century British Marine Painting, and numerous Shipping lines. *Address:* Merlewood, 6 Queensway, Derby DE22 3BE. *Signs work:* see appendix.

STOREY, Warren, V.P.R.W.A. (1988-Mar.93), R.W.A. (1976), A.T.D. (1950), Brit. Inst. Scholarship (1948); painter, general and ecclesiastical designer, mural artist; Head of Weston-super-Mare School of Art (1958-84); extra mural art history lecturer, Bristol University; *b* S. Shields, 19 Aug., 1924; *s* of Joseph Storey; *m* Lilian Evans; five *d. Educ.:* S. Shields High School; *studied art* at S. Shields School of Art under Ernest Gill, A.R.C.A. (1941-44), and Regent St. Polytechnic School under Wm. Matthews and Norman Blamey (1947-50). *Exhib.:* R.A., R.B.A., R.W.A., etc. *Publication:* contributor to Leisure Painter since 1987. *Address:* 14 Leighton Cres., Weston-super-Mare, BS24 9JL.

STOWASSER, Friedrich: see HUNDERTWASSER.

STRACHAN, Walter John, M.A. (Cantab.); created Chevalier des Arts et Lettres (1968) and Commandeur des Palmes Académiques (1970); NADFAS lecturer, Modern French Tapestry, Henry Moore and Modern Sculpture. *Publications:* translator Pop Art (Eyre Methuen 1977), The Prodigy by Hermann Hesse (Penguin), Demian (Granada), Peter Camenzind by Hesse (Penguin Modern Classics, 1982); author of The Artist and the Book in France (Peter Owen Ltd., 1969), Towards Sculpture (Thames & Hudson, 1975), Henry Moore Animal Sculpture (Aurum Press, 1983), The Living Curve (Letters to W.J. Strachan) (Taranman Gallery, 1983), Open Air Sculpture in Britain (Tate Gallery, Zwemmer, 1984), A Relationship with Henry Moore (1942-86, 1988). *Address:* 10 Pleasant Rd., Bishop's Stortford, Herts.

STRAIN, Robert William Magill, Commander, Order of St. John, B.Sc., M.D., Ph.D., F.R.C.P.I.; physician; artist in oil and water-colour; *b* Belfast, 1907; *s* of David Strain; *m* Eileen Mary Clapham. *Educ.:* Royal Belfast Academical Inst.; The Queen's University of Belfast. *Exhib.:* R.U.A., Walker's Gallery, London (Medical Art Soc.). *Work in permanent collections:* decorated maps, Ulster Museum. *Work repro.:* End Papers, Book of Belfast by Robert Marshall (1937). *Publications:* The Heraldry of Medicine (Ulster Medical Journal), Belfast and Its Charitable Society (O.U.P.). *Address:* Flat 3, 5 Royal Parade, Bayshill Rd., Cheltenham GL50 3AY. *Signs work:* "R.W.M. Strain."

STREVENS ROMER, Bridget Julia, M.A. (Cantab., 1979); artist and illustrator in oil, water-colour, line, art historian and specialist translator; *b* Ongar, Essex, 24 Sept., 1956; *d* of John Strevens, painter; *m* Stephen Romer; one *s. Educ.:* King's College, Cambridge University; *studied art* at Ecole Nationale Superieure des Beaux Arts, Paris. *Publications:* 'Toto's Travels' (Little, Brown & Co.), Matisse by Pierre Schneider (Thames & Hudson), Claude Monet's Letters (Macdonald). *Address:* 59 Rue de Meaux, 60300 Senlis, France. *Signs work:* "B. Strevens Romer" or "Biddy Strevens."

STRONG, Sir Roy, Ph.D. Fellow Ferens (1976), Prof. of Fine Art (1972), Hon.D.Litt. (Leeds) (1983), Hon.D.Litt. (Leele) (1984); writer and historian; Director, Victoria and Albert Museum (till Dec. 1987); *b* London, 23 Aug., 1935; *s* of G.E.C. Strong; *m* Dr. Julia Trevelyan Oman. *Educ.:* Edmonton County Grammar School; Queen Mary College, London; Warburg Inst., London. *Publications:* author: Portraits of Queen Elizabeth I (1963), Holbein – Henry VIII (1967), Tudor – Jacobean Portraits (1969), The English Icon: English – Jacobean Portraiture (1969), Van Dyck: Charles on Horseback (1972), Splendour at Court: Renaissance Spectacle – the Theatre of Power (1973), Nicholas Hilliard (1975), The Cult of Elizabeth: Elizabethan Portraiture – Pageantry (1977), And When Did You Last See Your Father? (1978), The Renaissance Garden in England (1979), Britannia Triumphans: Inigo Jones, Rubens and Whitehall Palace (1980), The English Renaissance Miniature (1983), Art – Power (1984), Strong Points (1985), Henry, Prince of Wales – England's Lost Renaissance (1986), Creating Small Gardens (1986), Gloriana, Portraits of Queen Elizabeth I (1987), A Small Garden Designer's Handbook (1987), Cecil Beaton, The Royal Portraits (1988), Creating Small Formal Gardens (1989), Small Period Gardens (1992), A Celebration of Gardens (1992); other books jointly with Julia Trevelyan Oman, J.A. van Dorsten, Stephen Orgel, Colin Ford and J. Murrell; contributor to numerous books and learned journals. *Address:* 3cc Morpeth Terr., London SW1P 1EW. *Clubs:* Garrick, Grillions.

STUART, Kiel, A.P.S.; artist in papier mache, mixed media and fibre, writer; Editor, Keystrokes; *b* N.Y.C., 1951; *m* Howard Austerlitz. *Educ. and studied art* at Suny New Paltz, Suny Stony Brook. *Exhib.:* Lynn Kottler Galleries, N.Y.C.; Gallery II RSVP, Virginia; Artforum, Mills Pond House, N.Y.; Myths, Music and Magic, East End Arts Council, N.Y.; Gallery North, Setauket, N.Y. *Work in permanent collection:* National Museum of Women's Art, Washington DC. *Publication:* cover, Island Women Anthology (N.S.W.W.A. Press). *Address:* 12 Skylark Ln., Stony Brook, N.Y. 11790, U.S.A. *Signs work:* see appendix.

STUBBS, Constance, A.R.C.A.; painter and etcher in collage and acrylic; *b* Cheltenham, 6 Aug., 1927; *m* Harold Yates; two *s,* one *d. Studied art at* Cheltenham School of Art, Royal College of Art (1949-51, Carel Weight, Ruskin Spear, John Minton, Barnett Freedman). *Exhib.:* mixed shows: R.A., Hayward, Mall Galleries, C.P.S., S.C.A., Print Biennale-Berlin, Cracow and Rijeka; solo shows: Anglo Hellenic League Athens, John Russell Ipswich, Chappel Essex, Market Cross and St. Johns St., Bury St. Edmunds, Oxford Gallery. *Work in permanent collections:* the late Princess Marina, Christchurch Mansions Ipswich, Unilever, Prudential, etc. *Address:* The Old School, Church Hill, Pakenham, Bury St. Edmunds, Suffolk IP31 2LN. *Signs work:* "C. STUBBS."

STUBLEY, Trevor Hugh, D.A. (Edin.) (1951), R.P. (1974), A.R.B.A. (1986); landscape and portrait painter; *b* Leeds, 27 Mar., 1932; *s* of Frank Stubley; *m* Valerie Churm; four *s. Studied art* at Leeds College of Art (1947-49); Edinburgh College of Art (1949-53). *Exhib.:* Bologna, Bratislava, Wichita Falls, U.S.A., Edinburgh, London, etc. *Work in permanent collections:* Doncaster A.G., Huddersfield A.G., Leeds City A.G., Lincoln, Usher A.G., The Royal Institution, N.P.G., Oxford: Green College, St. Catherine's College, St. John's College, Worcester College; Sheffield, Graves A.G., Wakefield City A.G., British Library, Inst. of Electrical Engineers, Westminster Hospital. *Work repro.:* illustrated over 400 children's books. *Address:* Trevor Stubley Gallery, Greenfield Rd., Holmfirth, nr. Huddersfield HD7 2XQ. *Signs work:* "Stubley."

STULTIENS, Jeff, Dip.A.D. (1966), R.P. (1990); First Prize – The Portrait Award, National Portrait Gallery (1985); Hon. Sec. R.S.P.P.; Senior Lecturer at Hertfordshire College of Art and Design, (1974-1987); painter in oil; *b* Blackpool, 12 Sept., 1944; *s* of Thomas Stultiens; *m* Catherine Knowelden. *Educ.:* Hutton and Tiffin Schools; *studied art* at Kingston School of Art under Alfred Heyworth and Camberwell School of Art under Robert Medley R.A. (1961-1966). *Exhib.:* John Player Portrait Award – N.P.G., British Portraiture 1980-85, Drawings for All, R.S.P.P., Hunting/Observer, Nikkei Exhbn. – Tokyo, The Portrait Award 1980-89. *Work in permanent collections:* N.P.G., Merton

458

and Oriel Colleges – Oxford, National Heart and Lung Inst., R.N.L.I., Royal Medical Foundation, R.A.M. Many other public and private commissions. *Address:* 26 St. George's Cl., Toddington, Beds. LU5 6AT. *Signs work:* "Stultiens."

SULLIVAN, Jason, B.A. (1979); painter in oil; *b* Poole, Dorset, 31 Mar., 1958; *s* of Michael Sullivan; *m* Una; one *s*. *Educ.:* Queen Elizabeth Grammar School, Horncastle, Lincolnshire; *studied art* at Grimsby College of Art (1974-76, Mr. Todd), Sheffield College of Art (1976-79, Mr. Peacock). Numerous exhbns. *Address:* 19 Meersbrook Pk. Rd., Sheffield, S. Yorks. *Signs work:* see appendix.

SULLIVAN, Wendy Lilian Verdin; poet, painter, visionary; artist in oil, water-colour, pastel, charcoal, ink and conte; *b* London, 18 May, 1938. *Educ.:* Notre Dame High School, Battersea; largely self-taught in art but attended Sir John Cass and Goldsmiths' Colleges; life drawing with Leonard McComb, A.R.A. anatomy with Prof. Pegington, F.R.S. (U.C.H.). *Exhib.:* R.A. Summer Shows, Galerie Dagmar, Portobello Opens, South Bank Show (R.F.H.), Tamsins, Brixton Gallery; slides at W.A.S.L. *Work in permanent collections:* U.C.H. (anatomy slides), St, John's Church, Angell Town. *Address:* 127 Crescent La., London SW4 8EA. *Signs work:* "Wendy Sullivan" and see appendix.

SUMMERS, Leslie John, F.F.P.S. (1968); sculptor in bronze, perspex (acrylic); *b* London, 2 Nov., 1919; *s* of John Summers; *m* Prof. Janet Margaret Bately. *Educ.:* Dulwich College and London University; *studied art* at Chelsea School of Art. *Exhib.:* R.A., R.B.A., Walker A.G., Cork St. Gallery, Alwin Gallery, Richmond Gallery London, Brussels Exhbn., Vth International Bienal Barcelona (Prizewinner). *Work in permanent collections:* National Museum of Wales (purchased by Contemporary Art Soc. of Wales); Hull University, U.S. Atomic Energy Commission, Nat. Exhbn. Centre, Birmingham, Brighton Centre, Rochester Museum of Western Art, N.Y., G.L.C., British Tourist Authority, etc. *Work repro.:* Studio International, Exploring Sculpture, Creative Plastics. *Address:* 86 Cawdor Cres., London W7. *Signs work:* see appendix.

SUMSION, Peter Whitton, A.R.C.A. (1955); painter and printmaker in oil, relief and mono prints, drawing, lecturer; Lecturer, Glasgow School of Art; *b* Gloucester, 23 Aug., 1930; *s* of Dr. H. W. Sumsion, C.B.E., composer and cathedral organist; *m* Sarah Noble; two *s*, two *d*. *Educ.:* St. George's Choir School, Windsor, St. Thomas' Choir School, New York City, Rendcomb College, Glos.; *studied art* at Cheltenham School of Art (1949), Chelsea School of Art (1950-52), R.C.A. (1952-55, Carel Weight, John Minton, Robert Buhler). *Exhib.:* one-man, Drawing Schools Gallery, Eton College (1960, 1978), Bury St. Edmunds Gallery; group shows, R.P., R.G.I. *Work in permanent collection:* Brewhouse Gallery, Eton College, *Address:* Bachie Bhan House, Cairndow, Argyll. *Signs work:* "Peter Sumsion."

SUNAR, Mina, A.R.B.S; sculptor in bronze and stone; *b* Tokat. *Studied art:* Paris, and Sir John Cass and Ealing Schools of Art. *Exhib.:* R.I.B.A. exhbn. Cardiff and London, also various parts of Britain, the U.S.A., Austria and Germany. *Work in permanent collections:* United Nations Bldg., Vienna; Queen Elizabeth Hall, London; 1½ × life bronze of The Pope at Castel Gandolfo, Rome; 2½ × life of President Inonu in Ankara. *Address:* The Studio, Queen Anne's Gdns., London W3 0TG. *Clubs:* The Hurlingham, Les Ambassadeurs, Institute of Directors.

SUNLIGHT, Benjamin Clement; professional artist; painter in oils and printmaker; *b* Brighton, 7 Apr., 1935; *s* of the late Joseph Sunlight, L.R.I.B.A.; *m* Vivien Baskin. *Educ.:* Clifton and Magdalene College, Cambridge; *studied art* at London Central School of Art and Design (Mural Diploma, 1962) under Alan Davie, Hans Tisdall, Harold Cohen and Tony Harrison. Part-time teacher, Hornsey College of Art (1964-65), Cranfield Institute of Technology (1973-74); Fellow and Vice-Chairman, Free Painters and Sculptors (1965-68); Mem., International Arts Guild; Gold medallist, International Academy, Rome, and Italian Academy, Parma. *Address:* 227 Kingston Rd., Teddington, Middx. TW11 9JJ. *Signs work:* "Ben Sunlight."

SURREY, Kit, Dip.A.D. Theatre design (1968); theatre designer and artist in several media, mainly pastel and charcoal drawing; *b* B'ham, 23 June, 1946; *m* Meg Grealey; one *s,* one *d. Educ.:* Tauntons Grammar School, Southampton; *studied art* at Southampton College of Art (1963-65), Wimbledon School of Art (1965-68). *Exhib.:* R.A., International Drawing Biennale Cleveland (1991). *Work in permanent collection:* R.S.C. Coll., Stratford. *Publication:* included in British Theatre Design – The Modern Age. *Address:* 77 Queens Rd., St. Thomas, Exeter, Devon EX2 9EW. *Signs work:* "KIT SURREY" or not at all.

SUTHERLAND, Carol Ann, B.A.Hons. (1973); artist in water based mixed media; *b* Greenock, Scotland, 16 Mar., 1952; *d* of James Sutherland; three *s. Educ.:* St. Columba School for Girls, Kilmacolm, Renfrewshire; *studied art:* Glasgow School of Art (1969-73, Donaldson, Goudie, Grant, Robertson). *Exhib.:* Mercury Gallery. *Work in permanent collections:* McNay Museum, San Antonio, Tex., Middlesbrough A.G., paintings in hospitals. *Publication:* Leafy and Adam at the Seaside (handmade artist's book). *Address:* c/o Mercury Gallery, 26 Cork St., London W1X 1HB. *Signs work:* "Carol Ann Sutherland" or "C.A.S."

SUTTON, Linda Olive, M.A. (R.C.A.) (1974); painter in oil on canvas, etching, water-colour; *b* Southend-on-Sea, 14 Dec., 1947. *Educ.:* Southend College of Technology; *studied art* at Winchester School of Art (1967-70), R.C.A. (1971-74). *Exhib.:* one-man shows, Galerij de Zwarte Panter, Antwerp; Bedford House Gallery, London; L'Agrifoglio, Milan; World's End Gallery, London; Ikon Gallery, Birmingham; Chenil Gallery, London; Royal Festival Hall, London; Stephen Bartley Gallery, London (1986); Christopher Hull Gallery (1988); Jersey Arts Centre (1988); Beaux Arts, Bath (1988); Austin/Desmond, Bloomsbury (1989); Isis Gallery, Essex (1993); Lamont Gallery, London (1993). *Address:* 192 Battersea Bridge Rd., London SW11 3AE. *Signs work:* "Linda Sutton."

SUTTON, Philip, R.A. (1989); artist in oil and water-colour; *b* Poole, Dorset, 20 Oct., 1928; *m* Heather; one *s,* three *d. Studied art* at The Slade School of Fine Art. *Exhib.:* Roland, Browse & Delbanco (1954-79), Australia, S. Africa and U.S.A. *Work in permanent collection:* Tate Gallery, etc. *Address:* 3 Morfa Terr., Manorbier, Tenby, Dyfed SA70 7TH, Wales. *Signs work:* "Philip Sutton."

SWAIN, Dorothy Louisa; artist in oil; private art teacher; *b* Wimbledon, 21 July, 1922; *d* of Robert May, journalist; *m* A.C. Swain; two *s,* two *d. Educ.:* Wimbledon College of Art; *studied art* at Royal College of Art (Charles Mahony, Gilbert and Stanley Spencer, Paul and John Nash). *Exhib.:* R.A., R.C.A., Russell Cotes Gallery. *Work in permanent collection:* Premier Gallery, Eastbourne. *Address:* Hawthorn, West St., Mayfield, E. Sussex TN20 6DR. *Signs work:* "D.L. Swain."

SWAN, Ann, S.B.A., S.G.F.A.; R.H.S. Silver-gilt medal (1990), Gold medal (1991); botanical artist in pencil, coloured pencil, oil pastel, water-colour; *b* England, 7 Apr., 1949. *Educ.:* Gravesend Grammar School for Girls; *studied art* at Manchester College of Art and Design. *Exhib.:* Hampton Ct. International Flower Show (1990, 1991), S.B.A. (1991, 1992), R.H.S. (1990, 1991), Century Gallery Henley (1991), Lyric Theatre Hammersmith (1992). *Work repro.:* limited edns. prints, and greetings cards. *Address:* 33 St. Winifred's Rd., Teddingon, Middx. TW11 9JS. *Signs work:* "Ann Swan."

SWANN, Marilyn, F.F.P.S.; painter; Women Artists, Slide Library; *b* Kent, 1932; *d* of H.H. Whiddett and C.W. Swann. *Studied art* at Woolwich Poly. (1945-50), Central, Chelsea and Sidcup (evenings). *Exhib.:* Trends (Mall, Wieghouse, Barbican, Bloomsbury Galleries, etc.), F.P.S. shows since 1973; solo shows, Brangwyn Studio (1976/7), Univ. of Surrey, Old Bull, Barnet (1978), Loggia Gallery (1984), Holland Park Orangery (1987), Hall Place Libraries, Bexley Borough, Multi-Venues in Bexley (1990). *Work in permanent collections:* Univ. of Surrey, Wilfred Sirrel Collection, Westminster Arts Council, Queen Mary's Hospital, Sidcup. *Address:* 6 Garrard Cl., Bexleyheath, Kent. DA7 4LX. *Club:* A.C.S.A.C. *Signs work:* "SWANN."

SWANN, Peter C., M.A. (Oxon.), LL.D. (Brock, Queens, Waterloo and Wilfred Laurier); keeper, Department of Eastern Art, Ashmolean Museum, Oxford; Director Royal Ontario Museum, Toronto, Canada (1966-72); Director East Asian Studies, Waterloo, Ontario, Canada; *b* London, 1921; *m* Elizabeth Hayden; three *s*, two *d*; div.; *m* Susan MacPhee. *Educ.:* Tottenham Grammar School, Oxford University, London University, Leiden University. *Publications:* Introduction to the Arts of Japan (1958), Chinese Painting (1958), Hokusai (1959), Two Thousand Years of Japanese Art (with Y. Yashiro, 1959), The Monumental Art of China (1963), The Arts of China, Korea and Japan (1963); editor of Oriental Art (1955-68). *Address:* 133 Claremont Ave., Kitchener, Ont. N2M 2P9, Canada. *Signs work:* "Peter C. Swann."

SWEET, George; painter; *b* London, 20 Nov., 1909; *m* Audrey Hannam (decd.); one *d*. *Studied art* at Slade School of Fine Art (1929-33, Orpen Bursary 1932), Paris, Barcelona and Madrid. *Exhib.:* London Group, R.A., etc., retrospective: Browse and Darby (1987). *Address:* 30 Cornwallis Cres., Clifton, Bristol BS8 4PH. *Signs work:* "G.S."

SWERLING, Anthony, M.A. (Cantab.); painter in oil and acrylic; graphic artist in line and half-tone; writer; *b* Manchester, 31 July, 1944; *s* of Morris Swerling. *Educ.:* Sorbonne and Cambridge; *studied art:* self-taught. *Exhib.:* London, Cambridge, Barcelona, Paris, Madrid, Stockholm. *Work in permanent collections:* various graphics in private collections in England, France, Spain, Sweden, U.S.A. *Publications:* Concerning the Art of Translation; La Poinçonneuse Apocalyptique and Le Timbre-Poste Concentrationnaire; The Rape of Czechoslovakia; A Madman's Manifesto (transl. from Strindberg's French); The Cambridge Plague; Sex and Mr. X; Strindberg's Impact in France 1920-60; In Quest of Strindberg; The Truth About Strindberg, various short stories, poems, plays in U.S.A. and Sweden. *Address:* 26 Shaftesbury Rd., Manchester 8. *Signs work:* see appendix.

SWETCHARNIK, Sara Morris, Fulbright Fellow (1987-88, 1988-89); painter, sculptor; *b* Shelby, N. Carolina, 1955; *d* of William Morris; *m* William Swetcharnik. *Studied art* at Art Students League, N.Y.; Schuler School of Fine Art, Baltimore, Maryland. *Address:* 7044 Woodville Rd., Mt. Airy, Maryland 21771, U.S.A. *Signs work:* "Sara Morris Swetcharnik."

SWETCHARNIK, William Norton, P.S.A., Fulbright Fellow (1987-89), Yaddo Foundation (1987), Cintas Foundation (1985), Millay Colony for the Arts Fellowship (1983), Stacey Foundation (1983); painter in oil, pastel, tempera, encaustic; *b* Philadelphia, Pennsylvania, 1951; *s* Charles Jacob Swet; *m* Sara Morris. *Educ.:* Sandy Spring Friends School, Maryland; *studied art* at Rhode Island School of Design, University of California, New York Art Students League. *Exhib.:* Springville (Utah) Museum of Art, Butler Inst. of American Art, Youngstown, Ohio, Washington County (Maryland) Museum of Art, National Arts Club, N.Y.C., Hermitage Museum, Norfolk, Virginia. *Address:* 7044 Woodville Rd., Mt. Airy, Maryland 21771 U.S.A. *Signs work:* "Wm. Swetcharnik."

SWINGLER, Brian Victor, N.D.D., A.T.D., R.B.S.A. (1986); artist in watercolour and acrylics; part time teacher at Birmingham, Hereford and Worcester; *b* Birmingham, 8 July, 1939; *s* of Ernest Swingler; divorced; two *s*. *Educ.:* Yardley Grammar School; *studied art* at Birmingham Art School (1962-65, Gilbert Mason, Roy Abell). *Exhib.:* mainly at Cowleigh Gallery, Malvern, also at Compendium Gallery, Ombersley Gallery, R.B.S.A., Timaeus Gallery, Helios Gallery, Cedric Chivers Gallery, Pictures, Henry-Brett Gallery, Richard Hagen Gallery, New Gallery, Moseley Gallery, Bankside, Frames. *Address:* 17 Beverley Rd., Rubery, Birmingham B45 9JG. *Clubs:* R.B.S.A., Art Circle, Cofton Hackett Art Soc., Birmingham Water-colour Soc. *Signs work:* "B.V. Swingler."

SYKES, Sandy (Ms.), B.A.Hons. (1966), R.E. (1987), M.A. (1987); printmaker in wood, lino, etching and silkscreen, painter and lecturer in art; *b* Wakefield, 13 Mar., 1944. *Studied art* at Leeds College of Art (1962-66), Middlesex Polytechnic (1966-67), Wimbledon College of Art (1984-87). *Exhib.:* recent solo shows: Pentonville Gallery (1988), Creaser Gallery (1988), Hardware Gallery (1988), Wakefield A.G. (1988-89); many mixed shows in Britain, America, Russia and Europe. *Work in permanent collections:* V. & A., Wakefield A.G., Rank Xerox, Petro-Diamond, U.K., National Art Collections Fund, Mappin A.G. *Publication:* Lament for Ignacio Sanchez Mejias by Federico Garcia Lorca. *Address:* 12 Kirkley Rd., London SW19 3AY. *Signs work:* "Sandy Sykes."

SYKES, Steven, R.C.A.; designer and sculptor; *b* Formby, Lancs., 30 Aug., 1914; *s* of Dr. A. B. Sykes (decd.); *m* Jean Judd; two *s*, one *d*. *Educ.:* Oratory, Caversham; *studied:* R.C.A. *Exhib.:* Galerie Apollinaire, Hanover Gallery; one-man shows Guillaume Gallozzi, N.Y., Redfern Gallery. *Work in permanent collections:* V. & A., Walker Gallery, Liverpool; Ashmolean, Oxford; Ceramic Museum, Faenza. *Sculpture:* Coventry Cathedral, U.S. National War Memorial, Washington Cathedral; water sculpture, British Pavilion, Expo 67; tapestry, Hammersmith and W. London Coll. Library (1980); decorative relief panels J. Sainsbury, Braintree (1982). *Work repro.:* Drawings of Normandy Invasion (pub. Sunday Times Magazine, June 1984); garden sculpture featured Crafts Magazine (Nov./Dec. 1990); "Deceivers Ever" (Spellmount) 1990 written and illustrated war memoirs. *Address:* Studio, Hopkiln Bepton, Midhurst, Sussex. *Signs work:* "Steven Sykes."

SYLVESTER, Diana, R.W.A. (1986), A.R.O.I.; artist in oil; Wilts. County Council part-time lecturer; Sec. Bath Soc. of Artists; *b* Bath, Som., 16 Mar., 1924; *d* of Edgar King, solicitor; *m* Robin Sylvester; three *s*, one *d*. *Educ.:* Bath High School; *studied art* at Chippenham Technical College, Corsham and Bristol Polytechnic. *Exhib.:* R.A., R.W.A., R.O.I., etc. *Work in permanent collections:* R.W.A., Bristol Schools Art Service. *Address:* Upper Farm, South Wraxall, nr.

Bradford-on-Avon, Wilts. BA15 2RJ. *Club:* Bath Soc. of Artists. *Signs work:* "DIANA SYLVESTER."

SYMONS, Patrick S., R.A.; artist in oil, charcoal and pencil; *b* Bromley, Kent, 24 Oct., 1925; *s* of N. H. Symons, Insurance broker (decd.). *Educ.:* Bryanston School, Blandford, Dorset; *studied art* at Camberwell School of Arts and Crafts under W. Coldstream, C. Rogers, J. Dodgson. *Work in permanent collections:* Tate Gallery, Doncaster Museum. *Agent:* Browse and Darby, 19 Cork St., London W1. *Address:* 20 Grove Hill Rd., Camberwell, London SE5 8DG. *Signs work:* "Symons."

SYNGE, Pamela: see de MEO, P.

SZOMANSKI, Wladyslaw, F.R.S.A., M.C.S.D., Dip. Academy of Fine Arts, Warsaw; commercial designer; Display World's International Display Contest, U.S.A., bronze medal (1950), bronze medal (1952), gold medal and silver medal (1955); *b* Baturyn, Poland, 3 Oct., 1911; *s* of Jan Szomanski, director, Health Insurance; *m* Krystyna Lipinska. *Educ.:* Secondary School, Rowno, Polytechnicum (architecture), Lwow; *studied art and graduated* at Academy of Fine Arts, Warsaw, under Prof. Skoczylas, Bartlomiejczyk, Wyczolkowski (1932-39). *Exhib.:* Warsaw, Berlin, Paris, Bucharest, Edinburgh, Rome (all poster exhbns.). *Address:* 20 Sinclair Gdns., London W14 0AT. *Signs work:* "Szomanski."

T

TACHON, Miriam M., M.B.E.; silver and gold medallist Paris Salon (1977, 1980); painter in water-colour and oil; retd. nurse; tutor, Dover Soc. of Miniature Painters; *b* Guernsey, C.I., 1909; *d* of Francis Tachon, farmer. *Educ.:* in Guernsey; *studied art* at Dover Art School (H. Busby, T. Greville). *Exhib.:* R.M.S., Mall Galleries, Société des Artistes Français, Paris Salon. *Work in permanent collections:* S.M., R.W.S. Galleries. *Address:* 56 Rokesley Rd., Dover, Kent CT16 2EH. *Club:* Dover Art. *Signs work:* "M.M. Tachon."

TAIT, Wendy Ann; water-colour artist and demonstrator; *b* Derby, 19 Apr., 1939; *d* of W.G. Kirk; *m* H.D.L. Tait; two *s*, two *d*. *Studied art* at Joseph Wright School of Art, Derby (1952-55), Adult Educ. (1974-78, Roy Berry). *Exhib.:* numerous Derbyshire galleries; demonstrations regularly given to local clubs and societies and for 'Maimeri' artists materials at N.E.C. and Business Design Centre, London. *Address:* Harwen, 1 Chevin Rd., Duffield, Derbys. DE6 4DS. *Clubs:* Derby Sketching, Derby Womens Art. *Signs work:* "W.A. Tait."

TAJIRI, Shinkichi, William and Noma Copley Award for sculpture (1959); John Hay Whithey Found. Opp. Fellowship (1960); Mainichi Shibum Prize, Tokyo Biennale (1963); sculptor in bronze and brass; Prof. of Sculpture, Hochschule für Bildende Kunste, W. Berlin (retd. 1989); *b* Los Angeles, 7 Dec., 1923; *m* Ferdi (decd.); two *d*; *m* Suzanne Van Der Kapellen (1976). *Educ.:* Los Angeles; *studied art* under Donald Hord, San Diego (1948-51); O. Zadkine and F. Leger, Paris. *Work in permanent collections:* Stedelijk Museum, Amsterdam, Gemeente Museum, Den Haag, Modern Museum, Stockholm, Town of Arnhem, Holland, Museum of Modern Art, N.Y., etc. *Address:* Kasteel Scheres, 5991 NC Baarlo, Limburg, Holland. *Signs work:* see appendix.

TALBOT, Nancy Wilfreda Hewitt, D.A. (Lond.) (1948); painter in oil and stage designer; consultant, Talbot Film Productions; teacher of painting for Hampshire (1950-66); *b* Coventry, 31 Aug., 1925; *d* of Wilfred John Skillington, lawyer; *m* Major Leon Talbot. *Educ.:* Leamington High School, Leamington Spa; *studied art* at Ruskin Drawing School, Oxford (1945) (Albert Rutherston), Slade School, London (1945-48) (Randolph Schwabe, Vladimir Polunin). *Exhib.:* first one-man show, Alfred Herbert Gallery, Coventry (1965); current work, Kaleidoscope Gallery. *Work in permanent collections:* mural and portrait commissions, privately owned. *Address:* Greensleeves, Avon Castle, Ringwood, Hants. BH24 2BE. *Signs work:* "Nancy Talbot" or "Nancy Skillington."

TALBOT KELLY, Chloë Elizabeth, M.C.S.D. (1968), S.WL.A. (1964), M.B.O.U. (1960); freelance bird artist/illustrator in water-colour and gouache; *b* Hampstead, 15 July, 1927; *d* of the late Major R. B. Talbot Kelly (Richard Barrett), M.B.E., M.C., S.WL.A.; *m* Jeffrey Smith; one *s. Educ.:* St. George's School for Girls, Convent of the Sacred Heart; advisor, father and Bird Room, B.M.N.H. *Exhib.:* S.WL.A. and provincial galleries in U.K. and Australia. *Work repro.:* Field Guides to Birds N.Z. and Seychelles; contributor to New Dictionary of Birds, African Handbook of Birds etc. *Address:* 22 St. Philip's Rd., Leicester LE5 5TQ. *Club:* British Ornithologists. *Signs work:* "C.E. Talbot Kelly" semi printed in paint or written, or initials only.

TAMBLYN-WATTS, Harold, F.Z.S.; artist and illustrator in water-colour and line; *b* Settle, Yorks, 1900; *s* of T. M. F. Tamblyn-Watts, A.M.I.E.E., F.R.S.A.; *m;* two *s. Educ.:* Stanstead School; *studied art* at Southend School of Art; Emmett Group Studio Manager (1935-48). *Exhib.:* Fleet St. Artists, Croydon Art Soc., Private Art Exhbn., Bouverie St. (1948), Fairfield Halls Croydon (1974). *Work repro.:* in Modern Publicity in War, Aeroplane, Flight; books illustrated, The Young Naturalist, Wonderful Plants, and children's books; book jackets, etc. *Address:* 25 Bennett's Way, Shirley, Surrey CR0 8AE. *Signs work:* see appendix.

TAMBURRINI, Mosé; sculptor, direct carver in marble, stone and wood - bronze casts from these; *b* Buenos Aires, 29 Nov., 1905. *Educ.:* St. Martin's School of Art. *Exhib.:* recent one-man shows: John Hunt Galleries, E. Sussex, Bexhill Museum. *Work in permanent collections:* John Hunt Galleries; private collections in U.K., Europe and U.S.A. *Address:* 21 Glenleigh Pk. Rd., Bexhill, E. Sussex TN39 4EE. *Signs work:* "M. TAMBURRINI" carved on marble, stone pieces; engraved on bronzes.

TAMPLIN, Heather, M.F.P.S. (1984); artist in oil and water-colour; *b* Caterham, 4 Aug., 1950; one *s,* one *d. Studied art* at Wimbledon College of Art (1967). *Exhib.:* Loggia Gallery and Barbican with F.P.S., Mall Galleries, Fermoy Centre, King's Lynn; one-man shows locally. *Address:* Orchard House, The Green, Aldborough, Norfolk NR11 7AA. *Signs work:* "H. TAMPLIN."

TANATO, Agus Dermawan; painter and art critic; *b* Rogojampi, Java, 29 Apr., 1952; *m* Iliana; one *s. Educ.:* Surabaya High School; *studied art* at Academy of Fine Arts, Yogayakarta (1971-76). *Exhib.:* Jakarta, Yogayakarta, Solo, Pontianak, etc. Since 1977 free-lance art critic with Kompas Daily and layout designer for youth magazine 'Gadio.' Layout designer, Indonesian Publishers Assoc. (1982-84). *Publications:* author and layout designer: R. Basoeki Abdullah, Ambassador of Indonesian Painting (P.T. Gramedia, Jakarta); Bric-a-brac of Fine Arts (P.T. Grafiti Press, Jakarta); edited: Zaini, Manusia, Lukisan dan Kabut, Apresiasi Seni, etc. *Address:* Jalan Kempul 9, (Complex Kelapa Gading), Jakarta Utara 14240, Indonesia.

TANDY, Michael Roy, A.R.B.S.; sculptor and artist; and a leading impressionism painter; *b* Malvern, Worcs., 8 Mar., 1942; *s* of the late Herbert Charles; *m* the late Beatrice Maud; two *s*, one *d. Educ.:* Chase High School, Malvern; *studied art* at Malvern Hills College of Art. *Work in permanent collections:* Buckingham Palace, Worcester City Museum, Howarth A.G. Lancs., Butler Museum of American Art, Cleveland, Ohio, Metropolitan Museum, N.Y., plus many private collections. *Address:* Ivy Cottage, Upper Colwall, nr. Malvern, Worcs. *Signs work:* paintings "TANDY," porcelain see appendix.

TARR, James C., A.R.C.A., A.T.D. (1929); artist in oil and water-colour; princ., Cardiff College of Art, 1946-70 (retired); princ., Lydney School of Art (1936-38); High Wycombe School of Art (1938-46); *b* Oystermouth, Swansea, 27 May, 1905; *s* of J. M. Tarr, master mariner; *m* K. M. Tydeman, A.R.C.A.; one *s. Educ.:* Swansea; *studied art* at Cheltenham School of Art (1922-25), and R.C.A. (1925-29). *Exhib.:* R.A., A.C.E.S., National Museum of Wales, various London and provincial galleries. *Address:* 21 Oakfield St., Cardiff CF2 3RD.

TARRANT, Olwen, R.O.I., N.S.; oil painter, sculptor, lecturer, art teacher; Hon. Sec. and Council R.O.I.; President, Brentwood Arts Council; *b* Newport, Gwent, 1927; *d* of Thomas Lewes, Merchant Navy officer; *m* John Tarrant, BBC and Fleet St. journalist and author. *Educ.:* Newport High School, Gwent; *studied* at Sir John Cass School of Art. *Exhib.:* R.O.I. (winner, Cornelissen Prize, 1987), R.B.A., N.S., Medici Gallery, and others. *Work in permanent collections:* London Polytechnic, and the late Sir Charles Wheeler, P.P.R.A. *Work repro.:* in art books, calendars, greetings cards. *Addresses:* Studio: Puerto Pollensa, Mallorca; Henleaze House, 156 Hanging Hill La., Hutton, Brentwood, Essex CM13 2HE. *Signs work:* "Olwen Tarrant."

TARRANT, Peter, F.N.D.D.; artist in oil; *b* Shropshire, 1943. *Educ.:* Morville School; *studied art* at Shrewsbury Art School. *Work in permanent collection:* Birmingham City Museum and A.G. *Address:* 10 Lower Bromdon, Wheathill, Burwarton, nr. Bridgnorth, Salop. WV16 6QT.

TARRANT, Terence Richard, F.M.A.A.; medical artist; ophthalmic artist at Theodore Hamblin Ltd. (1945-48); ophthalmic artist at Queen Alexandra's Military Hospital, Millbank (1948-50); medical artist at Inst. of Ophthalmology, London (1950-84); *b* London, 7 Jan., 1930; *s* of R. J. Tarrant; *m*; one *s*, two *d. Educ.:* London; *studied art* at Camberwell School of Arts and Crafts. *Work in permanent collections:* Moorfields Eye Hospital. *Work repro.:* Stallard's Eye Surgery, Roper-Hall; Clinical Ophthalmology, J.J. Kanski; System of Ophthalmology, Duke-Elder; Operative Surgery, Rob & Smith. *Address:* 11 Portman Drive, Child Okeford, Blandford Forum, Dorset DT11 8HU. *Signs work:* "TARRANT" with tops of the Ts joined.

TATE, Barbara, P.S.W.A., R.M.S., F.R.S.A., I.A.A., Ass. Société des Artistes Français; Silver Medal, Paris Salon (1968); Gold Medal, Paris Salon (1969); Prix Marie Puisoye (1971); Special Mention Palme d'or des Beaux-Arts, Monte Carlo (1972); Laureat Grand Prix de la Côte d'Azur (1972); painter in oil; President, Society of Women Artists; Hon. Prof. Thames Valley University; *b* Uxbridge, Middlesex; *m* James Tate, also a painter; one *d. Educ.:* Dormers Wells School, Southall; *studied art* at Ealing School of Art (1940-45, under T. E. Lightfoot, A.R.C.A., T. Bayley, A.R.C.A., J. E. Nicholls, A.R.C.A.) and Wigan Art School (1945-46). 1957-58, under Peter Coker, R.A., A.R.C.A. *Exhib.:* BBC2 Television, Royal Academy, Royal Society of Portrait Painters, Royal Institute of Oil Painters, Royal Society of British Artists, New English Art Club, National Society, Royal Society of Miniature Painters, Sculptors and Gravers,

United Society of Artists, Society of Women Artists, Hesketh Hubbard Art Society, Royal Institute, Free Painters and Sculptors, R.W.S. Galleries' Flower Painting Exhbn., Chenil Galleries, Chelsea, Paris Salon, Salon Terres Latines, Salon du Comparaisons, Ville Eternal, Rome, Nice, Monte Carlo, Royal Festival Hall. *Work repro.:* The Green Shawl, Clematis, Nasturtiums, Golden Girl, Marigolds, King's Pawn, Moon Goddess, Josephine, as prints for hanging, published by Solomon & Whitehead, London, and Marigold published by Felix Rosenstiel's widow and son. *Address:* Willow House, Ealing Green, London W5 5EN. *Signs work:* see appendix. Some work done in collaboration with husband (see appendix).

TAULBUT, John Maurice, A.R.W.A.; Jack Goldhill award for sculpture R.A. (1987); sculptor in stone and wood, teacher; *b* Gosport, 19 Jan., 1934; *s* of Patrick John Taulbut (decd.); *m* Janet Marian Rickards; three *s*. *Educ.:* Portsmouth College of Art, Highbury Technical College; *studied art* at Eaton Hall College of Educ., Retford. *Exhib.:* R.A., R.B.A., R.W.A., S.WL.A., R.S.M.A., Sotheby's, Southampton A.G., Swindon A.G., Oxford Soc., Cheltenham Soc., 3D Gallery, Bristol, Rooksmoor Gallery, Bath, Ceri Richards Gallery, Swansea, Ash Barn, Petersfield, Swansea Arts Workshop. Work in private collections. *Address:* Cambria House, Llanstephan, Carmarthen, Dyfed SA33 5JQ. *Signs work:* "John Taulbut."

TAVENER, Robert, R.E., A.T.D., N.D.D.; illustrator and printmaker; formerly Deputy Principal, Eastbourne College of Art and Design; *b* London, 1920; *m*; one *d*. *Studied art* at Hornsey College of Art (1946-50). *Exhib.:* 30 one-man exhibitions; work selected for eight Arts Council exhibitions. *Work in permanent collections:* over 2000 prints purchased for national collections in U.K. and abroad by galleries, museums, local educational authorities. *Publications:* illustrated series of children's books for Longmans Green and Oxford University Press; and commissioned work for B.B.C., London Transport, G.P.O., Shell, I.C.I., Nuffield Foundation, etc. *Address:* Tussocks, Link Rd., Meads, Eastbourne BN20 7TA. *Signs work:* see appendix.

TAYLOR, Alan, N.D.D. (1954), A.R.C.A. (1957); artist in water-colour, gouache, ink, chalks; T.V. Designer/Art Director; retd. from T.V., painting full time; *b* India, 5 June, 1930; *s-s* of Vladimir Shibayev, Prof. of Languages, Delhi University; *m* Rachel Taylor. *Studied art* at R.C.A. (Prof. John Skeaping, Leon Underwood). *Exhib.:* one-man shows: three in Wales, one in Holland; mixed shows: Wales, England, France, Holland and U.S.A. *Work in permanent collections:* University of Wales, Bangor, University of Wales, Cardiff, B.B.C. *Publications:* illustrated Song of the Harp (Christopher Davies); illustrations for B.B.C. T.V. and H.T.V. *Address:* 75 Preston Ave., Newport, Gwent NP9 4JD. *Signs work:* see appendix.

TAYLOR, Alan, B.A.(Hons.) (1973), A.T.C. (1974); painter in acrylic; *b* Wembley, Middx., 1942; *s* of John and Constance Taylor; *m* Josephine; one *d*, Sophia. *Educ.:* Hornchurch Grammar School; *studied art* at Colchester School of Art (1963-65, drawing: John Nash), Stourbridge College of Art (1965-68 and 1972-73), University of Sussex Art Teachers' Certificate (1973-74). *Exhib.:* Midland Young Contemporaries (1966-67), London, Trends in Modern Art (1966), Corning Museum, N.Y. (1968), numerous mixed and one-man shows Birmingham, London, Colchester, Wivenhoe, Exeter, Chudleigh, Sidmouth. *Represented in private collections:* U.K., Europe, Middle East, Australia, U.S.A. Works mainly to commission, runs La Chapelle Painting & Drawing Holidays

(June-Sept). *Address:* La Chapelle, Foulognes, 14240 Caumont L'Evente, Calvados, Normandie, France. *Signs work:* "ALAN TAYLOR."

TAYLOR, Eric, R.E., A.R.C.A. (1934); painter, sculptor and printmaker; teacher of art at Camberwell School of Art (1936-39), Willesden School of Art (1936-39 and 1945-49), Central School of Arts (1946-48); Head of Design School, Leeds (1949-56); Principal, Leeds College of Art (1956-69); Assistant Director, Leeds Polytechnic (1969-71); *b* 6 Aug., 1909; *s* of Thomas John Taylor; *m*; one *s*, one *d*. *Educ.:* William Ellis School, Hampstead; R.C.A. (1932-35). *Exhib.:* R.A., London Group, N.E.A.C. *Work in permanent collections:* Washington A.G., Art Institute Chicago, Imperial War Museum, B.M. and V. & A. Print Rooms, Leeds A.G., Ashmolean Museum. *Address:* Linton Springs Farm, Sicklinghall, Wetherby. *Signs work:* "Eric Taylor."

TAYLOR, James Spencer, A.R.C.A., B.Sc.(Econ.) (Hons.), F.R.S.A., M.M.A.F.A.; painter; lecturer, Bolton College of Art (1948-79); *b* Burnley, 7 May, 1921; *s* of Harry Taylor; *m* Joyce B. Haffner; one *s*, one *d*. *Studied art* at Burnley School of Art, Slade School of Fine Art, Royal College of Art (1945-48). *Exhib.:* Red Rose Guild of Craftsmen, Crafts Centre of Gt. Britain, Society of Designer Craftsmen, Arts Council Touring, R.A., R.W.S., R.B.A., R.I., V. & A., C. of I.D., and many provincial galleries. *Work in permanent collections:* Towneley Hall A.G., Burnley; Bolton A.G. Executed many commissions in Great Britain and abroad. *Address:* 7 Leaverholme Cl., Cliviger, Burnley, Lancs. *Signs work:* "JT" (books, 1948-70), "J. S. Taylor" or "JST" (paintings).

TAYLOR, Jane Winifred, A.R.C.A. (1946), R.W.S. (1988), R.B.A. (1988); artist in gouache, private tutor; *b* Sheffield, 20 June, 1925; *d* of Wilmot Taylor; *m* Leslie Worth; one *s*, three *d*. *Educ.:* Sheffield High School G.P.D.S.T.; *studied art* at Sheffield College of Art (1941-43, Eric Jones), R.C.A. (1943-46, Gilbert Spencer). *Exhib.:* R.B.A., R.W.S., R.A., Linfield Gallery, Jon Leigh Gallery, and others. *Work in permanent collections:* Graves A.G. Sheffield, and various Educ. authorities. *Publications:* magazine articles on drawing and painting. *Address:* 11 Burgh Heath Rd., Epsom, Surrey KT17 4LW. *Signs work:* "Jane Taylor."

TAYLOR, Joan D., A.T.D. (1946); textile designer and printer and painter; instructor in printed textiles, Laird School of Art, Birkenhead (1946-67); *d* of George H. Taylor, company director. *Educ.:* St. Edmund's College, Liverpool; *studied art* at Liverpool College of Art. *Exhib.:* R.A., N.E.A.C., Liverpool Academy of Arts, Bluecoat Display Centre, Liverpool. *Address:* 79 Grosvenor Rd., Birkenhead L43 1UD. *Signs paintings:* "J. D. Taylor."

TAYLOR, John Russell, B.A.(Cantab.1956), M.A.(Cantab.1959); writer; Art Critic, The Times since 1978; *b* Dover, 19 June, 1935; *s* of Arthur Russell Taylor. *Educ.:* Jesus College, Cambridge; Courtauld Inst., London. *Publications:* The Art Nouveau Book in Britain; The Art Dealers; Impressionism; Edward Wolfe; Bernard Meninsky; Impressionist Dreams; Ricardo Cinalli; Monet: Artist in Context, etc. *Address:* The Times, 1 Virginia St., London E1 9BD.

TAYLOR, Joyce Barbara, Oxford Delegacy, A.T.D., C.G.L.I. (Embroidery); lecturer, Bolton College of Adult Education; artist in embroidery and water-colour; *b* Burnley, 6 Aug., 1921; *d* of J.H. Haffner; *m* James S. Taylor; one *s*, one *d*. *Educ.:* Burnley High School; *studied art* at Burnley School of Art, Manchester College of Art. *Exhib.:* Red Rose Guild of Craftsmen, Embroiderers Guild, Whitworth A.G., R.W.S. Galleries, London, Manchester and Hereford Cathedrals. *Work in permanent collections:* Altar Frontals etc. for Bolton and

Walmsley Parish Churches, and other churches; Banners and other work in private collections in England and U.S.A. *Address:* 7 Leaverholme Cl., Cliviger, Burnley BB10 4TT. *Signs work:* "J.B.T." and "Joyce B. Taylor."

TAYLOR, Mrs. M.: see BRIDGE, Muriel Elisabeth.

TAYLOR, Martin, B.A.(Hons.) (1975), A.T.D. (1976); artist in water-colour, etching; *b* Hayes, Middx., 10 May, 1954; *m* Marianne Read; one *s*, one *d*. *Studied art* at Ealing School of Art, Wimbledon School of Art, Goldsmiths' College. *Exhib.:* Bankside Gallery (1986-93), Contemporary British Water-colours (1983-93), Mercury Gallery, Cork St., Edwin Pollard Gallery, Wimbledon, Linda Blackstone Gallery Pinner, Savage Fine Art, Northampton. Main dealer Chris Beetles Gallery, Ryder St., St. James', London; R.A. Summer Exhbns. (1982, 1985), Singer & Friedlander/Sunday Times water-colour exhbns. (1987-92). *Work in collections:* The Prudential. *Publications:* contributor to: Encyclopedia of Water-colours (Quarto), Buildings (Quarto); articles in The Artist magazine. *Address:* 13 St. Georges Ave., Northampton NN2 6JA. *Signs work:* "Martin Taylor."

TAYLOR, Michael John, Dip.Arch. (1953), A.R.I.B.A. (1955), S.G.F.A., M.S.A.I.; architect and illustrator in water-colour, gouache, linocuts; Hon. Treasurer, S.G.F.A.; *b* Scarborough, 22 Sept., 1930; *s* of H.S.P. Taylor, artist; *m* Molly Crowther; one *s*, one *d. Educ.:* Scarborough Boys High School; *studied art* at Leeds College of Art, School of Architecture (1948-53). *Exhib.:* R.A., R.I., R.S.M.A., S.G.F.A., "Not the RA" Llewellyn Alexander Gallery, Laing and Singer and Friedlander competitions; one-man shows: Bath, Canterbury, Harrogate. *Publications:* book jackets for Foyle, Hodder and Stoughton. *Address:* 4 Sewell Ave., Wokingham, Berks. RG11 1NS. *Signs work:* "Michael J. Taylor" and see appendix.

TAYLOR, Michael Ryan, B.A.Hons.(Lond.); artist in oil; *b* Worthing, 17 Feb., 1952; *s* of Patrick Taylor; *m* Caroline; one *s*, one *d. Educ.:* Worthing High School for Boys; *studied art* at Goldsmiths' School of Art (1970-73). *Exhib.:* Morley Gallery, N.P.G. John Player Award (winner 1983), Millfield Open (winner 1989), Hunting Group Art Prize (1989), R.A., Worthing A.G., Quay Arts Centre, I.O.W., Beaux Arts, Bath. *Work in permanent collections:* N.P.G., Christchurch Hall, Oxford. *Address:* 1 Upper St., Child Okeford, Blandford Forum, Dorset DT11 8EF. *Club:* Shaston Snooker.

TAYLOR, Newton: see TAYLOR, William Henry.

TAYLOR, Pamela, A.R.B.S. (1980), S.P.S. (1975); sculptor in bronze, resin bronze; *b* Pontypridd, 13 May, 1929; *d* of the late W.G. Archer; *m* Peter William Taylor; two *s. Educ.:* South Shields and Wick High Schools; *studied art* at Sir John Cass College School of Art (1947-50, Bainbridge Copnall, M.B.E., P.R.B.S., and Beth Jukes, F.R.B.S.). *Exhib.:* Mall Galleries, Guildhall, Royal Exchange. *Principle public works:* R.A.F. and Allied Air Forces WW2 Monument, Plymouth Hoe; R.A.F. and Battle of Britain Museums, Hendon; Shakespeareplatz, Berlin; Chalmers Bequest Coll.; Colgate-Palmolive Head Office; Bancrofts School; Tobacco Dock London; Georgetown Guyana. *Address:* Merrydown, 88 Haltwhistle Rd., S. Woodham Ferrers, Chelmsford, Essex CM3 5ZF. *Signs work:* see appendix.

TAYLOR, Sean, Hons.D.F.A. (1982), M.A.F.A. (1983), F.F.A. (1989); sculptor in mixed media; Director, Glasgow Sculpture Studios; *b* Cork, 16 Aug., 1959. *Educ.:* Presentation Brothers College, Cork; *studied art* at Crawford College of Art and Design, Cork (1979-82), University of Ulster, Belfast, N.I.

(1982-83), Kunstenacademie, Rotterdam (1988-89). *Exhib.:* 13 one-man shows since 1983 worldwide. *Work in permanent collections:* museums in Poland, Mexico; commissions in Glasgow. *Address:* Flat T/L, 6 Firpark Terr., Dennistoun, Glasgow G31 2JU. *Signs work:* "Sean Taylor."

TAYLOR, Wendy Ann, C.B.E. (1988); sculptor; Mem. Royal Fine Art Commission since 1981; Specialist Adviser, Com. for Arts Design since 1988; Mem. Advisory Group P.C.F.C. (1989-90); F.Z.S. (1989-); Mem. Design Advisory Panel, London Docklands Development Corp. (1989-); *b* 29 July, 1945; *d* of Edward Philip Taylor and Lilian Maude Wright; *m* 1982, Bruce Robertson; one *s. Educ.:* St. Martin's School of Art, L.D.A.D. (Hons.). *Exhib.:* one-man shows: (1970-86): London, Norfolk, Oxford, Dublin; over 100 group exhbns. (1964-82). *Work in permanent collections:* G.B., U.S.A., Eire, N.Z., Germany, Sweden, Qatar, Switzerland, Seychelles. *Major commissions:* throughout the U.K. including Phoenix 1989-90 E. Kilbride; Armillary Sundial 1989 The New Towns, Essex; Globe Sundial, London Zoological Gdns., 1990; Continuum 1990 Guildford, Surrey. *Address:* 73 Bow Rd., London E3 2AN. *Signs work:* see appendix.

TAYLOR, William Henry (Newton Taylor), A.R.C.A. (1934), A.R.E. (1957), Free Studentship (1932), Prix-de-Rome Finalist in Engraving (1935); artist in oil (portrait and landscape), water-colours, etching and engraving on metal and wood; Head (retd.) School of Art, Amersham; lecturer, demonstrator, critic; *b* Normanton, Yorks., 31 Aug., 1911; *s* of James Taylor; *m* Elsie May Newton; three *s. Educ.:* Normanton Boys' Grammar School, Yorks; *studied art* at Wakefield School of Art; Leeds School of Art; R.C.A. *Exhib.:* Yorks. Artists Soc., Bucks. Art Soc., R.P.E., R.B.A., R.A. *Address:* Newstone Bungalow, Bovingdon Green, Marlow, Bucks. *Signs work:* "NEWTON TAYLOR" in two lines.

TAYLOR, W. S., A.R.C.A., M.Phil.; painter, art historian and film maker; editor of Manuals Series for Thames and Hudson Ltd.; Dean of Faculty, Sheffield Polytechnic (1972-75); *b* 26 Sept., 1920; *s* of W. Taylor; *m* Audrey Wallis; one *d. Educ.:* City Grammar School, Sheffield; *studied art* at Sheffield College of Art and R.C.A. *Exhib.:* R.A., etc. and provincial galleries. *Publications:* Catalogue of Burne-Jones Exhbn., Sheffield City Art Galleries (1971); King Cophetua and the Beggar Maid, Apollo Magazine (Feb. 1973); King Cophetua and the Beggar Maid (film), Arts Council of Great Britain and the Tate Gallery; Portrait of Beardsley (1976), (film), Yorks. Arts Assoc. *Address:* Lower Manaton, South Hill, Callington, Cornwall PL17 7LW.

TAYLOR WILSON, Joanne, M.A. Fine Art (Edin. 1977), A.T.C. Goldsmiths' College (1978), R.A. Schools Post. Grad. Cert. (1981), Elizabeth Greenshields Scholarship (1981-82); still life, landscape and portrait painter in oil and water-colour; *b* Bolton, Lancs., 12 Sept., 1953; *d* of James Spencer Taylor, A.R.C.A.; *m* Ivan Wilson, R.I.B.A.; one *s*, one *d. Educ.:* Canon Slade Grammar School, Bolton; *studied art* at Edinburgh College of Art (1972-77), R.A. Schools (1978-81, Peter Greenham, R.A.). *Exhib.:* Royal Scottish Academy (1975, 1987), R.A. (1979, 1980, 1982, 1983, 1986, 1987), R.B.A. (1980), Manchester Academy (1979-83, 1985-91), Manchester; one-man show, Bolton A.G. (1979). *Work in permanent collections:* Bolton A.G., West Midlands College of Education. *Address:* 4 Beechwood Ave., Clitheroe, Lancs. BB7 1EZ. Mem. of Manchester Academy of Arts (1985). *Signs work:* "J. TAYLOR WILSON" or "J.T.W."

TEASDILL, Graham, F.R.S.A., F.R.N.S., F.Z.S., F.M.A.; curator, Museum of the Bournemouth Natural Science Soc. since 1989; *b* Horsforth, 5 Oct., 1935;

s of late Clifford Humphrey Teasdill, bank official, of Guiseley; *m* Nova Ann Pickersgill of Horsforth, 22 July, 1960; one *s* (Michael Graham, *b* at Dewsbury, 5 Dec., 1962), two *d* (*see* Workman, Caroline Nova; Andrews, Pauline Ann). *Educ.:* Ilkley Grammar School. Assistant at Ilkley (1950-55), Leeds (1955-56) and Huddersfield (1956-60); assistant curator, Cheltenham (1960-62). Curator, Batley (1962-66); curator Russell-Cotes A.G. and Museum, Bournemouth (1966-88). President, Yorkshire Federation of Museums (1966-67); South-Eastern Federation (1969-70). *Address:* 99 Carbery Ave., Southbourne, Bournemouth BH6 3LP.

TEED, John; actor, antique dealer, landscape painter in water-colour, portrait artist in pastel; *b* London, 18 Jan., 1911; *s* of Harry Williamson Teed, inventor. *Educ.:* Westminster School; *studied art* at L.C.C. School of Art, Westminster. *Exhib.:* R.A., P.S., R.I., Blackpool. *Work in permanent collections:* National Gallery, N.S.W. *Publication:* illustrated, Owens Second Story Book. *Address:* The Old Manor House, Bradford-on-Avon, Wilts. BA15 1JU. *Signs work:* "John Teed."

TEMPEST, Victor, A.R.C.A. (1935); artist in oil and tempera; *b* Swaffham, Norfolk, 23 Mar., 1913; *s* of Loftus Tempest. *Studied art* at Woolwich Polytechnic School of Art (1927-32), R.C.A. (1932-36, Sir William Rothenstein). *Exhib.:* R.A., R.B.A., N.E.A.C., and provincial galleries. *Work in permanent collections:* City of Leicester A.G., Wolverhampton Municipal A.G., R.A., New York, Tokyo. *Address:* 12 Forest Ridge, Keston Pk., Keston, Kent BR2 6EQ. *Signs work:* "Tempest."

TEMPLE, Nigel Hal Longdale, Ph.D., M.Litt. in Architecture, N.D.D., A.T.D., F.S.A.E., R.W.A.; painter, lecturer; architectural and garden historian; Council Mem. Garden History Soc., Companion of the Guild of St. George; Visiting lecturer, A.A. School of Architecture; *b* Lowestoft, 1926; *m* Judith Tattersill; one *s*, one *d*. *Studied art* at Farnham, Sheffield. *Exhib.:* R.W.A.; Cheltenham Group; Städtisches Museum, Göttingen; Musée du Château d'Annecy; Cheltenham Festivals; University of Reading; University of Bristol; New Ashgate. *Publications:* author: Farnham Inheritance (1956, 1965), Farnham Buildings and People (1963, 1973), Looking at Things (1968), Seen and Not Heard (1970), John Nash and the Village Picturesque (1979), George Repton's Pavilion Notebook: a catalogue raisonné (1993). *Address:* 4 Wendover Gdns., Christchurch Rd., Cheltenham GL50 2PA. *Signs work:* "Nigel Temple" and date.

TENGBERG, Violet, City of Gothenburg award for cultural achievement (1966), Bronze Medal, Europe Prize for painting (1971), Ostende, Belgium; Accademico Tiberino, Rome, Il Premio Adelaide Ristori, Rome (1984); City of Gothenburg Hon. Award (1987); Swedish State Award (1989); artist in oil and graphic work, and enamels *on iron*; *b* Munktorp, Sweden, 21 Feb., 1920; *d* of A. Englund, master builder; *m* J. G. A. Tengberg, D.H.S.; one *s*, one *d*. *Educ.:* Dipl. Academy of Fine Arts, Gothenburg (1958-63) "Valand". *Exhib.:* 19 one-man shows, Stockholm, Helsinki, London, Brussels, Paris, Rome, Viterbo, etc.; nearly 200 group shows all over Europe; Riksutställningar travelling exhbn. *Work in permanent collections:* Museums and official collections in Sweden; Institut Tessin, Paris; Musée de Pau and Musée de Caen, France; Bibliothèque Nationale, Paris; Musée Vatican, Italy; Tate Gallery, London; Museo Nationale, Gdansk, Poland; Galleria Nationale, Varsavia, Poland; Museo di Viterbo, Italy. *Publications:* Swedish Art Lexicon, part V, Allhem; Enciclopedia Universale "SEDA" della Pittura Moderna, Milano, etc. (colour ill.); "Violet Tengberg –

Paintings, drawings, graphics and poems" (1982) in three languages and with 45 colour reproductions; Creative Mysticism—a Psychological Study of Violet Tengberg's religious visions and artistic creations by Prof. Antoon Geels (University of Lund, 1989). Essays by (Prof.) J.P. Hodin, Teddy Brunius (Prof. art History, University of Copenhagen) and Benkt-Erik Benktson (Prof. University of Gothenburg). *Address:* Götabergsgatan 22, 41134 Gothenburg, Sweden. *Clubs:* A.I.A., W.I.A.C., F.P.S., K.R.O. *Signs work:* "VT," "Violet Tengberg."

TENNENT, John Richard Moncrieff, S.WL.A.; artist in silk-screen and water-colour specializing in birds and landscapes; *b* Singapore, 5 Nov., 1926; *s* of Roy Stanhope Tennent; *m* (1) Margaret Evelyn Rose (decd.); one *s,* one *d.* (2) Dianne Scott. Educ.: Bryanston School, Pembroke College, Oxford; *studied art* at St. Martin's College of Art (part-time). *Exhib.:* S.WL.A., Mall Gallery (1970-93), Clarges Gallery (1972-83), Dorset County Museum (1973-90), Mignon Gallery, Bath (1975), Palais des Congrès, Paris (1976, 1977), Cornell University (1979), Patricia Wells Gallery, Bristol (1984), Medici Gallery, London (1989), etc. Commissioned to paint wildlife in Zambia (1973 and 1985), Zimbabwe and Okarango (1988-90). Works to Sultan of Oman (1992). *Address:* Bucknowle Hanger, Wareham, Dorset. *Signs work:* "John Tennent."

TERRY, John Quinlan, F.R.I.B.A. (1962); architect, artist in pen and ink, water-colour, linocut; *b* London, 24 July, 1937; *s* of the late Philip Terry, solicitor; *m* Christine; one *s,* four *d. Educ.:* Bryanston School; *studied architecture* at Architectural Assoc., London. *Exhib.:* R.A. Summer Show since 1962, Biennale in Venice (1980), San Francisco (1982), Paris (1981), Real Architecture Building Centre (1987); one-man shows: Rye A.G. (1980), Architectural Design (1981), Anthony Mould Gallery (1986), Judd St. Gallery (1987), Vision of Europe, Bologna (1992). *Address:* Old Exchange, Dedham, Colchester, Essex.

THELWELL, Norman, A.T.D. (1950); cartoonist and freelance illustrator in pen, line and wash, water-colour and gouache; teacher of design and illustration, College of Art, Wolverhampton (1950-56); now freelance; *b* Birkenhead, Ches., 3 May, 1923; *s* of Christopher Thelwell, machinist; *m* Rhona E. Ladbury; one *s,* one *d. Educ.:* Rock Ferry High School, Birkenhead; *studied art* at Liverpool College of Art under H. P. Huggill, A.R.C.A., M.A., A.R.E., principal, and G. H. Wedgwood, A.R.C.A., teacher of graphic design (1947-50). *Address:* Herons Mead, Timsbury, Romsey, Hants. SO51 0NE. *Signs work:* see appendix.

THEXTON, Ronald; painter in oil; retd. oral surgeon; *b* Burton, Westmoreland, 21 Feb., 1916; *s* of Benjamin Salkeld Thexton; *m* Barbara J. Stevens; one *s,* one *d. Educ.:* Solihull School, Birmingham and Edinburgh Universities; *studied art:* Edinburgh (evenings); private assistance from James Cowie, R.S.A., Hayward Veal, Allen Gwynne-Jones, R.A. *Exhib.:* R.A., R.B.A., R.W.A., S.S.A. *Work in permanent collections:* Newport (Gwent) Corp., Thamesdown Corp. *Address:* Tallett Steps, Barnsley, Cirencester, Glos. GL7 5EF. *Club:* Centre Art. *Signs work:* "Thexton."

THICKE, Thelma Gwendoline, N.D.D., A.T.D., Dip. H.E., M.F.P.S.; dealer in fine art, restorer and painter in oil and water-colour; principal: Thicke Gallery, and Swansea Antique Club; *b* 20 Aug., 1921. *Educ.:* St. Leonards-on-Sea; *studied art* at Hastings School of Art (Vincent Lines), West of England College of Art, Bristol University, B'ham University (1966-67). *Exhib.:* R.A., R.B.A., N.E.A.C., F.P.S., R.W.S. *Address:* 8 Coed Mor, Derwen Fawr, Swansea SA2 8BQ, S. Wales. *Clubs:* I.O.D., Royal Overseas League, L.A.P.A.D.A. *Signs work:* "T.G. Thicke."

THISTLETHWAITE, Ann, N.D.D. painting; artist, landscape painter in oil, pastel and charcoal; *b* Birmingham, 22 Oct., 1944; *d* of C. E. D. Thistlethwaite, dental surgeon. *Educ.:* Edgbaston Church of England College; *studied art* at Birmingham College of Art and Design (1961-66) under Gilbert Mason and Mr. Francis. *Exhib.:* one-man shows: London, Birmingham, Worcester, Tunbridge Wells, Malvern, R.B.A., R.O.I., R.S.M.A., P.S., Contemporary Art. (Royal Overseas Commonwealth Art 1st Prize (1969) presented to H.M. the Queen). *Address:* 4 King George Ave., Droitwich, Worcs. *Signs work:* "Ann Thistlethwaite."

THOMAS, David Arthur, B.A. (1972), P.G.C.E. (1982); artist in oil and acrylic; retd. teacher; *b* Croydon, 30 Apr., 1928; *s* of Arthur Thomas, M.I.M.E. *Educ.:* Wallington County Grammar School; *studied art* at Croydon Polytechnic (1949-53), Farnborough Technical College (1962), Roehampton Adult Inst. (1982). *Exhib.:* Compass Theatre Co., Sheffield; several one-man shows. *Address:* 21 Baileys Rd., Southsea, Hants. PO5 1EA. *Club:* F.P.S. *Signs work:* "D. THOMAS."

THOMAS, Margaret, R.W.A., R.B.A., N.E.A.C.; painter; *b* 26 Sept., 1916; *d* of the late F. S. Thomas. *Educ.:* privately; *studied art* at Slade School (1936-38), R.A. Schools (1938-39). *Exhib.:* R.A., L.G., S.E.A., R.S.A. and S.S.A. Edinburgh, etc.; one-man exhbns. include Leicester Galleries (1949 and 1950); Aitkin Dott's Edinburgh (1952, 1955 and 1966); Canaletto Gallery (1961); Edinburgh Festival (1962); Howard Roberts, Cardiff (1963); Minories, Colchester (1964); Queen's University, Belfast (1967); Mall Galleries (1972); Octagon, Belfast (1973); Court Lodge, Kent (1974); Paton Gallery, Edinburgh (1976); Scottish Gallery, Edinburgh (1982), Sally Hunter Gallery, London (1988, 1991). *Official purchases:* H.R.H. Duke of Edinburgh; Chantrey Bequest; Arts Council; Exeter College, Oxford; Min. of Educ.; Min. of Works (Coronation painting for British Embassy at Santiago); Paisley, Hull and Carlisle Art Galleries; G.L.C. and numerous county Educ. Coms.; Edinburgh City Corporation; Welsh Schools Service; Steel Company of Wales; Financial Times; Nuffield Foundation Trust; Scottish National Orchestra; Robert Fleming Morgan Guaranty Trust, Sock Shops International, Lloyds of London, and the Warburg Group. *Addresses:* Ellingham Mill, nr. Bungay, Suffolk NR35 2EP; 8 North Bank St., Edinburgh. *Signs work:* see appendix.

THOMAS, Norma Marion; B.A. (1980); artist in oil; *b* Hawarden, Ches., 9 Jan., 1922; *d* of Alfred Robinson, chief marine engineer; *m* Leslie Gurwin Thomas, A.T.D. (decd.); three *s. Educ.:* Hawarden Grammar School; Normal College, Bangor; *studied art,* pottery at Liverpool School of Art, Goldsmiths' and Hornsey College of Art. Art mistress in Liverpool, Wisbech and Wirral Grammar School. Own studio and exhbn. gallery. Paintings in Gt. Britain and abroad. *Address:* Old School Studio, Blaenporth, Cardigan SA43 2AP. *Signs work:* "Norma M. Thomas."

THOMAS, Robert, A.R.C.A. (1952), Otto Beit Medal R.B.S. (1963), R.B.S. Silver Medal (1966); sculptor in bronze, stone; Past-President, Society Portrait Sculptors; Past V.P.R.B.S.; *b* Cwmparc, Treorchy, Rhondda, Glam., 1 Aug., 1926; *m* Mary Gardiner, Des. R.C.A.; two *s,* one *d. Educ.:* Pentre Grammar School, Rhondda; *studied art* at Cardiff College of Art (1947-49), R.C.A. (1949-52). *Work in permanent collections:* Sculptures at Coalville, Leics., Birmingham City Centre, Blackburn Town Centre, Ealing Broadway Centre, London, Cardiff, Swansea; portraits include, H.R.H. Princess Diana, Viscount Tonypandy, Lord Parry, Lord Chalfont, Aneurin Bevan, Cliff Morgan, Sir Geraint Evans, Sir

Julian Hodge, Dame Gwyneth Jones, Gwyn Thomas, Ryan, Carwyn James. *Address:* Villa Seren, 23 Park Rd., Barry, S. Glam. *Signs work:* "Robert Thomas sculptor."

THOMAS, Shanti; artist in oil, pastel and charcoal, teacher; Artist in Residence, Gatwick Airport (1993); *b* London, 3 Dec., 1949. *Studied art* at School of Signa Simi (1965), Academy of Fine Arts, Florence (1965-67), Camberwell School of Art and Crafts (1971-73, Sargy Mann). *Exhib.:* Commonwealth Inst. (1987), Ikon touring (1984, 1989), Whitechapel Open (1987, 1989), Athena Arts Award Open, Barbican (1987), 'Critical Realism' Nottingham, Camden Arts Centre (1988), 'Black Art, Plotting the Course' Oldham (1988), 'The Artist Abroad' Usher Gallery, Lincoln (1989). *Work in permanent collections:* A.C.G.B., Leicester Schools, and private collections. *Publications:* Birthday Book, Women's Artist Diary (1988), catalogues, Critical Realism, Black Art, The Artist Abroad, etc. *Address:* 18 Cornwall Rd., London N4 4PH. *Signs work:* "Shanti Thomas."

THOMPSON, Kevin Barry; self-taught artist in oil, acrylic, water-colour; *b* Dorking, Surrey, 11 Mar., 1950; *s* of B.P. Thompson; *m* Vanessa Jane; one *s*, one *d*. *Educ.:* Roman Hill School, Lowestoft; studied general design at Lowestoft College (1985-87). *Exhib.:* R.O.I., R.S.M.A.; one-man shows: Norwich (1982), Aldeburgh (1986), Southwold (1989), Gt. Yarmouth (1991). *Address:* 24 Pound Farm Drive, Lowestoft, Suffolk NR32 4RQ. *Signs work:* "KEVIN.B. THOMPSON."

THOMSON, Diana, B.A., F.R.B.S.; sculptor in bronze, terracotta, wood, resin; *b* Manchester, 1939. *Studied art* at Kingston Polytechnic Sculpture Dept. *Exhib.:* R.A., R.W.A., New College, Oxford, Margam Park, S. Wales, and various group shows. *Commissions:* 'Woking Market' bronze plaque 7'3" x 4'6" at Network House, Bradfield Cl., Woking; 'Father and Child' bronze over life-size at Central House, off New St., Basingstoke; 'The Swanmaster' bronze 7' at Fairfield Ave., Staines; 'The Hurdler' bronze life-size, at APC International, The Lodge, Harmondsworth, Middx.; 'The Inheritors' bronze life-size group; 'Portrait of Yvonne de Galais and her daughter' life-size group; 'The Bargemaster' bronze 7' at Data-General Tower, Brentford, Middx.; 'Portrait of D.H. Lawrence' bronze life-size, at Nottingham University. *Address:* The Summerhouse, 64 Mincing La., Chobham, Surrey GU24 8RT. *Signs work:* "D.C. Thomson" or "D.C.T."

THOMSON, George L., D.A. (Edin.), S.S.A., F.S.S.I.; calligrapher; principal art teacher (retd.); *b* Edinburgh, 15 Dec., 1916. *Studied art* at Edinburgh College of Art (1932-37). *Publications:* Better Handwriting (Puffin, 1954), Traditional Scottish Recipes (1976), New Better Handwriting (1977), Scribe (1978), Christmas Recipes (1980), Rubber Stamps (1982), Traditional Irish Recipes (1983), (Canongate), Dear Sir, (1984), The Calligraphy Work Book (1985), The Calligrapher's Book of Letters (1990) (Thorsons), The Art of Calligraphy (1987, Treasure Press), My Life as a Scribe (Canongate, 1988), others in preparation. *Address:* The White Cottage, Balgrie Bank, Bonnybank, by Leven. *Signs work:* "George L. Thomson."

THORN, Mary Elizabeth, N.S. (1980), mem. Bucks. Art Soc. (1975); painter in oil, water-colour, sculptor in stone, bronze; *b* Egypt, 25 Jan., 1928; *d* of George Wadley, M.B.E.; *m* Royston Thorn; two *s*, one *d*. *Educ.:* Sacre Coeur (Egypt), Notre Dame, Grey Coat Hospital, Barrett St. Technical College; *studied art* at Amersham C.F.E. and art oils with D. Berryman; sculpture, A. Southwell. *Exhib.:* in mixed exhbns., also one-man shows. *Address:* Morten

House, First Avenue, Amersham, Bucks. *Signs work:* "Mary Thorn" or "M.E.T."

THORNBERY, Mary; painter in oil; *b* Bredhurst, Kent, 23 May, 1921; *m* Michael Dobson, F.R.A.M.; one *s. Studied painting:* London, Florence, Rome. *Exhib.:* R.A., London Group, W.I.A.C., New English Art Club, Royal West of England Academy, Bristol (permanent collection). *Address:* Rose Hill, Brechfa, Carmarthen, Dyfed SA32 7RA. *Signs work:* "MARY THORNBERY."

THORNE, Angela Rosemary, (pre-1945 Angela Deane), mem. Academia Italia (gold medal, 1979); Hon. N.S., Hon. Mention Soc. des Artistes Français, Paris Salon (1969); painter, sculptress, illustrator; *b* London, 1911; *d* late Gerald Deane of Tattersalls; *m* Major C. B. Thorne, M.C. (died 1981). *Studied art:* Winchester School of Art (1921-23), Academie Julien, Paris (1928-29) under Stanley Grimm. *Exhib.:* Paris Salon, R.S.A., R.P., P.S., R.S.M.A., R.O.I., N.S. Major works incl: 34 portrait illustrations presentation book H.R.H. Prince of Wales, Duchy of Cornwall (1933); oil portraits incl: H.M. the Queen and H.R.H. Prince Philip, commd: 1976; H.M. Queen Elizabeth, The Queen Mother, commd: 1980; altarpiece Pilgrim Crusader, Prestbury Church, Cheshire (1977). *Private collections* in U.K., Europe, U.S.A., Canada, S. Africa. *Address:* Fullerton Manor, Andover SP11 7LA. *Signs work:* "Angela Thorne" (paintings and illustrations), "A. Thorne" (sculpture).

THORNTON, Leslie, A.R.C.A. (1951); *b* Skipton, 1925. *Studied art* at Leeds College of Art (1945-48), R.C.A. (1948-51). *Exhib.:* One-man shows, Gimpels Fils (1957, 1960, 1969); I.C.A. (1955); Berne (1955); British Council Young Sculptors Exhbn. (Germany, 1955-56), Sweden (1956-57); São Paolo Biennal (1957); Holland Park (1957); C.A.S. Religious Theme Exhbn., Tate Gallery; British Embassy, Brussels (1958); Middelheim Biennial, Antwerp (1959). *Official purchases:* Museum of Modern Art, New York; Arts Council of Gt. Britain; Leeds Art Gallery; Felton Bequest, Australia; Albright Museum; Fogg Art Gallery; National Gallery of Scotland. *Private collections* in U.K., Europe, U.S.A. and S. America. *Address:* Stable Cottage, Chatsworth Pl., Harrogate.

THURSBY, Peter, A.T.D., F.R.B.S., R.W.A.; sculptor; *b* Salisbury, 1930; *s* of the late Major and Mrs. L. A. Thursby; *m* Maureen Suzanne Aspden. *Educ.:* Bishop Wordsworth's School, Salisbury; *studied art* at West of England College of Art, Bristol; Exeter College of Art. *Exhib.:* 50 Years of Sculpture, Grosvenor Gallery (1965); one-man shows: Arnolfini Gallery; A.I.A. Gallery; Plymouth City A. G. (2); Marjorie Parr Gallery (3) (1964, 1965, 1971); Westward TV Studios, Plymouth; Northampton Museum and A. G.; Sheviock Gallery; Royal Albert Memorial Museum and A.G., Exeter; University of Sheffield; Haymarket Theatre; Leicester; Nottingham Playhouse; University of Exeter; Alwin Gallery; R.W.A. Bristol. Water sculpture at the Paul Temple Interior Garden, International Garden Festival, Liverpool (1984); 1st prize winner Laurence Olivier Awards Open Sculpture Competition (1984); Designer of 1986 'Art and Work' award; awarded R.B.S. Silver medal (1987). *Public commissions:* Harrow, Croydon, Exeter, Las Colinas, Dallas, Texas, U.S.A., Mazda Cars (U.K.), Tunbridge Wells, Rowan House, Greycoat St., Westminster, London, Coca-Cola Schweppes Beverages Ltd., Uxbridge, McDonald's Head Office, London. *Public collections:* A.T.E.I. Collection, London; Gloucestershire Regt.; Arnolfini Gallery, Bristol; Westminster College of Education, Oxford; Plymouth City A. G.; Royal West of England Academy; University of Exeter; National Guard of Saudi Arabia; Wates Built Homes Ltd.; Soc. of West End Theatres; Newcastle College of Arts and Technology. *Address:* Oakley House, Pinhoe, Exeter EX1 3SB.

Club: Chelsea Arts. *Signs work:* "P.T." and date (sculpture), or "PETER THURSBY" and date (graphic work).

THYNN, Alexander (7th Marquess of Bath), B.A., M.A.(Oxon.); painter in oil, novelist; *b* London, 6 May, 1932; *s* of Henry Thynn (6th Marquess of Bath); *m* Anna Gael; one *s*, one *d. Educ.:* Eton and Christchurch, Oxford; *studied art* in Paris: Grande Chaumiere (Henri Goetz), Academie Julian (Andre Planson), Academie Ranson (Roger Chastel). *Work in permanent collection:* murals at Longleat House. *Publication:* Lord Weymouth's Murals by Alexander Thynn; novels, The Carry-Cot (W. H. Allen 1972), The King is Dead (Longleat Press 1976), Pillars of the Establishment (Hutchinson 1981). *Address:* Longleat House, Warminster, Wilts.

TIDMARSH, Roy John Eric; painter in oil (mainly interiors); *b* Birmingham, 15 Feb., 1944; *s* of Leslie John Cleaver-Tidmarsh, wood carver; *m* Joan Patricia Lakin; one *s*, one *d. Educ.:* Moseley School of Art (1956-59); *studied art* at College of Art, Birmingham (1960-63). *Exhib.:* N.E.A.C., R.B.A., R.A., Royal Inst. of Oil Painters, and provincial galleries. *Work in collections* throughout the U.K. and U.S.A. *Address:* 4 Dockers Cl., Balsall Common, Warwickshire. *Signs work:* "Roy Tidmarsh" (always bottom left).

TIDNAM, Nicholas Rye, N.D.D. (1961); painter, illustrator, lecturer; visiting lecturer, Medway College of Design; *b* Oadby, Leics., 13 May, 1941; *s* of Albert Arthur Tidnam; *m* Ruth Murray; one *s*, one *d. Educ.:* Kings Park, Eltham; *studied art* at Camberwell School of Art (1957-61, Michael Rothenstein, Frank Martin, Henry Inlander, Richard Lee, Bernard Dunstan). *Exhib.:* Mercury Gallery, London and Edinburgh, R.A., N.E.A.C., R.B.A., Drew Gallery, Canterbury, The Peter Hedley Gallery, Wareham. *Work in permanent collections:* Unilever, Leics., Notts. and W. Riding Educ. authorities and numerous private collections. *Work repro.:* magazine illustrations. *Address:* 16 Roebuck Rd., Rochester, Kent ME1 1UD. *Signs work:* "Nicholas Tidnam" or "N.T."

TIERNEY, James Richard Patrick, Dip.A.D.(1966), Postgrad. Dip. in Printmaking (1967); artist in all painting and printmaking media; principal lecturer; *b* Newcastle upon Tyne, 23 May, 1945; *m* Janet Rosemary; one *d. Educ.:* The Royal Grammar School, Newcastle; *studied art* at Sunderland Polytechnic (1961-66, David Gormley), Brighton Polytechnic (1966-67, Jennifer Dickson). *Address:* Laburnum Cottage, 29 Mill La., Lindford, Hants. GU35 0PE.

TIERNEY, Robert, D.A.Dip. (1956); International artist, Cos.; textile designer/graphics, etc.; artist in water-colour, oil, design colours; début U.K. and Paris (1958); since 1958 annually engaged by numerous companies throughout three continents; *b* Plymouth, 9 Aug., 1936; *s* of Hilda Tierney. *Studied art* at Plymouth College of Art (Joan Lee, A.T.D.), Central School, London (1956-58, Alan Reynolds). *Exhib.:* from 1959, London Design Centre, Paris, Vienna, Italy, Australia, Sweden, Denmark, U.S.A., Canada, Munchen, Switzerland; five tours of Japan (1977-81), U.S.A. tour (1981), exhbns. in European, U.S.A., Far East cities (1982, 1983, 1984, 1985). *Work in permanent collections:* Boston Museum of Fine Arts (1981), honoured by five works accepted by V. & A. Museum (1986), etc., and private collections. *Address:* Chub Cottage, 31 Church St., Modbury PL21 0QR. *Signs work:* "Tierney" or "Robert Tierney."

TILL, Michael John, S.G.F.A.; artist in graphic, engraving, etching, pastel; Insurance Broker; *b* Sri Lanka, 23 Mar., 1939; *m* Kathleen Margaret; two *d. Educ.:* St. George's College, Weybridge; *studied art* at City and Guilds (1970-

72 part-time). *Exhib.:* S.G.F.A. *Address:* 57 Southway, Carshalton Beeches, Surrey SM5 4HP. *Club:* Bosham S.C. *Signs work:* see appendix.

TILLING, Robert, R.I. (1985); painter in water-colours and acrylic; lectures include Tate Gallery and Exeter University; awarded R.I. Medal (1985); prizewinner, International Drawing Biennale (1989); *b* Bristol, 1944; *m* Thelma, N.D.D.; two *d. Educ.:* Bristol; studied art, architecture and education Bristol and Exeter. *Exhib.:* one-man exhbns. include London, Bristol, Exeter, Southampton, Guernsey, and Jersey; various mixed exhbns. include the R.A., R.W.S., Barbican Centre (1988). *Work in permanent collections* include Lodz Museum, Poland and the States of Jersey. *Publications:* illustrations to 'Twenty One Poems', by Charles Causley C.B.E., (Cellandine Press); various reviews/ criticism on jazz and blues in many magazines. *Address:* Paul Mill, La Rosiere, St. Saviour, Jersey, C.I. *Signs work:* "Robert Tilling."

TILLYER, William; artist in acrylic on canvas and panel, water-colour, print; French Government Scholarship (1962); Artist in Residence, Melbourne University (1981-82); *b* Middlesbrough, 1938; *m* Judith; one *s*, one *d. Studied art* at Slade School of Fine Art (1960-62, William Coldstream, Anthony Gross), Atelier 17, Paris (1962, gravure under William Hayter). *Exhib.:* one-man shows: Bernard Jacobson Gallery (1978-80, 1983, 1984, 1987, 1989, 1991), Wildenstein & Co. (1991). *Work in permanent collections:* V. & A., A.C.G.B., Tate Gallery, M.O.M.A. (N.Y.). *Publication:* illustrations for A Rebours by J.K. Huysmans. *Address:* c/o Bernard Jacobson Gallery, 14A Clifford St., London W1. *Signs work:* surname on back.

TILMOUTH, Sheila, Dip.A.D. (Hons.), A.T.C.; artist in oil on gesso panel; *b* London, 25 Sept., 1949; *m* Mick Exall; two *s*, one *d. Educ.:* Latymer Grammar School, London; *studied art* at Hornsey College of Art (1969-72, Jack Smith, Nigel Hall, Norman Stevens), Byam Shaw School (1974-75, Bill Jacklin). *Exhib.:* R.A. Summer Exhbn. (1978 to present day), Portland Gallery London, Hart Gallery Nottingham, Alresford Gallery, Leeds, Harrogate, etc. *Work in permanent collection:* Calder Museums. *Publications:* Limited Edn. prints (Buckingham Fine Arts, and Contemporary Arts Group). Founder mem. Calder Rural Arts Group (C.R.A.G.). *Address:* Hillside House East, Church Rd., Todmorden, Lancs. OL14 8HP. *Signs work:* "S.T.'90."

TILSON, Joe; painter, sculptor; *b* London, 24 Aug., 1928; *s* of Frederick A.E. Tilson; *m* Joslyn; one *s*, two *d. Studied art* at St. Martin's School of Art (1949-52), R.C.A. (1952-55). *Exhib.:* Venice Biennale (1964), Marlborough Gallery (1960-77), since 1977 Waddington Galleries, internationally since 1961. *Work in permanent collections:* major museums in Gt. Britain, U.S.A., Italy, S. America, Australia, Germany, Holland, Denmark, Belgium, N.Z., etc. *Address:* The Old Rectory, Christian Malford, Wilts. SN15 4BW. *Signs work:* "Joe Tilson."

TINDLE, David, R.A. (1979), Hon. F.R.C.A. (1984), M.A. (Oxon.) (1985); painter in egg tempera; Ruskin Master of Drawing, University of Oxford (1985-87), Hon. Fellow at St. Edmund Hall, Oxford; Hon. mem. R.B.S.A.; *b* Huddersfield, 29 Apr., 1932. *Studied art* at Coventry School of Art (1945-47). *Exhib.:* Fischer Fine Art since 1985, Piccadilly Gallery (1954-83), Galerie XX, Hamburg (1974, 1977, 1980). *Work in permanent collections:* Tate Gallery, Manchester City A.G., Wakefield, Coventry, Whitworth, A.G.'s., Bradford, Huddersfield, R.A., N.P.G. *Address:* c/o 4 Rue Naude, 56160 Guémené sur Scorff, Morbihan, France. *Signs work:* "David Tindle" or "D.T."

476

TIPPETT, Jane, freelance artist in water-colour, tempera, also lithography, and teacher; *b* London, 25 Feb., 1949; *d* of George Thomas Tippett. *Studied art* at Gloucestershire College of Art and Design, R.A. Schools (1977-80). Artist in Residence, Oundle School (1980-82). *Exhib.:* R.A. Summer Exhbn. (1978-90), Agnew's Albermarle St. Gallery (1982), Church St. Gallery, Saffron Walden (1983, 1984, 1986); 14 lithographs made at the Curwen Studio. *Address:* 56 Searle St., Cambridge CB4 3DB. *Signs work:* "Jt."

TISDALL, Hans; painter and designer; *b* 1910. *Exhib.:* in London, Paris, Rome, Brussels, Germany, Spain, Switzerland. *Commissions:* murals, tapestries. *Address:* 7 Brunel House, 105 Cheyne Walk, London SW10 0DF. *Signs work:* see appendix.

TITCHELL, John, R.A. (1993), A.R.C.A. (1951), A.R.A. (1986); artist in oil and water-colour; *b* Crayford, Kent, 6 Aug., 1926; *m* Audrey Ward; one *s*, one *d*. *Educ.:* Crayford Elementary School; *studied art* at Sidcup School of Art (1940-44), R.C.A. (1947-51). *Address:* Frith Farm, Pluckley, Kent TN27 0SY.

TITCOMBE, Cedric Anthony N.D.D. (1962); painter and screen-printer in charcoal, oil, screenprints; maker of carding tools trading as "Hedgehog Equipment"; *b* Gloucester, 11 Dec., 1940; divorced; two *s*, two *d*. *Educ.:* Crypt Grammar School, Gloucester; *studied art* at Gloucester College of Art (1959-63, James Tucker, John Whiskerd, Gordon Ward). *Exhib.:* R.A., R.W.A., and numerous mixed shows. *Work in private collections:* Trevor Barnes, etc. *Address:* Prescott House, Old Hill, Longhope, Gloucester GL17 0PF. *Signs work:* "TITCOMBE."

TITHERLEY, Hazel M., R.C.A. (1985), A.T.C., A.T.D.(Manc.); painter; *b* Little Singleton, Lancs., 4 Mar., 1935; *d* of Tom C. Burgoyne; *m* Philip Titherley, F.R.I.B.A., M.R.T.P.I.; one *s*. *Educ.:* Queen Mary School, Lytham, Blackpool School of Art (1953-58), Manchester Regional College of Art (1958-59). *Exhib.:* 28 solo, many open and groups shows, incl. International Art Symposium, W. Germany. *Work in permanent collections:* Salford A.G. and private collections in Europe, U.S.A., and Far East. Teaches drawing, painting and calligraphy. *Address:* Woodside, Woodside Ave., New Longton, Preston, Lancs. PR4 4YD. *Club:* Founded New Longton Artists (1969). *Signs work:* "Hazel Titherley."

TODD, Daphne Jane, R.P. (1985), N.E.A.C. (1985), H.D.F.A.(Lond.) (1971); awards: 2nd prize John Player award (1983), G.L.C. prize (1984), 1st prize Hunting Group (1984); painter in oil on panel; Hon. Sec. R.P. (1990-), Director of Studies, Heatherley School of Art, Chelsea (1980-86); *b* York, 27 Mar., 1947; *d* of Frank Todd; *m* Lt.Col. P.R.T. Driscoll; one *d*. *Educ.:* Simon Langton Grammar School, Canterbury; *studied art* at Slade School (1965-71). *Exhib.:* R.A., R.P., N.E.A.C., Patterson Gallery, retrospective Morley Gallery (1989). *Work in permanent collections:* Chantrey Bequest; University College, London; Royal Hollaway and Bedford A. G.; H.Q. Irish Guards; Pembroke College, Cambridge; Lady Margaret Hall, Oxford; St. David's University; N.P.G; St. Catharine's College, Cambridge; Science Museum. *Address:* Salters Green Farm, Mayfield, E. Sussex TN20 6NP. *Club:* Chelsea Arts. *Signs work:* "D. Todd."

TODD, Peter William, A.R.C.A. (1949); artist in oil; Head of Grimsby School of Art (retd.); *b* Sheffield, 13 May, 1921; *s* of William James Todd, physicist. *Studied art* at Sheffield College of Art, Royal College of Art (1946-49). *Exhib.:* R.A., London Group, R.B.A., N.E.A.C., New Grafton Gallery. *Address:* School House, Walesby, nr. Market Rasen, Lincs. LN8 3UW. *Club:* Caterpillar. *Signs work:* "Peter Todd."

TODD WARMOTH, Pip, B.A.(Hons.), M.A.; artist in oil and pastel; *b* Brigg, Lincolnshire, 5 Oct., 1962. *Educ.:* Caistor Grammar School; *studied art* at Grimsby School of Fine Art (1981-82, Peter Todd), Camberwell School of Fine Art (1982-85, Noel Forster), R.A. Schools (1985-88, Edward Middleditch). *Exhib.:* Catto Gallery, New Grafton Gallery, C.A.C.; group shows: R.A., Thompson Gallery, Mall Galleries (R.O.I. and N.E.A.C.), Bonhams, Cadogan. *Work in permanent collections:* Franklin Trust, Kingston Lacey – National Trust, Montecute – National Trust. *Address:* 396 Brixton Rd., London SW9 7AW. *Clubs:* Dover St. Arts, Chelsea Arts. *Signs work:* "Pip T.W."

TOLLEY, Sheila, A.R.W.A. (1985); artist in oil and water-colour; *b* Birmingham, 28 June, 1939; *d* of Ernest Saville Atkins; *m* Bryan William Tolley. *Educ.:* Richard C. Thomas School for Girls, Staffs.; *studied art* at Bournemouth and Poole College of Art (1972-74, Edward Darcy Lister, A.R.C.A.). *Exhib.:* R.A. Summer Exhbns. (1978-81, 1983-89), R.W.A. (1976-77, 1980-87). *Address:* 39 New Rd., Northbourne, Bournemouth BH10 7DW. *Signs work:* "sheila tolley."

TOLSON, Roger Nicholas, B.A.; painter in oil; Gallery Manager, Whitechapel Art Gallery; *b* Sheffield, 2 Dec., 1958; *s* of James Eric Tolson, M.A. (decd.). *Educ.:* King Edward VII School, Sheffield; Oriel College, Oxford; *studied art* at Camden Arts Centre (1983-89), Sir John Cass College of Art (1986-90). *Exhib.:* R.A. Summer Show (1986-87), Hunting Group (1987), Whitechapel Open (1988, 1989, 1992), N.E.A.C. (1988); one-man show: Cadogan Contemporary (1990). *Address:* 4 Kelross Rd., London N5 2QS.

TOMALIN, Peter John, R.I.B.A. Dip.Arch. (Leics. 1964), F.S.A.I. (1978), U.A. (1978); first prize in B.B.C. Christmas painting competition (1977); self employed architectural illustrator and water-colour artist; *b* Kettering, 18 Oct., 1937; *s* of Sidney Tomalin; *m* Marjorie Elizabeth; two *s. Educ.:* Kettering Technical College, Leicester School of Architecture; *studied art* at Northampton School of Art (1976-79, Peter Atkin, Frank Cryer). *Exhib.:* Mall Galleries, U.A., R.I., Grosvenor Gallery, Hitchin, Northampton A.G. *Address:* 170 Sywell Rd., Overstone, Northampton. *Clubs:* Northampton Town and County Art Soc., S.A.I. *Signs work:* "Peter Tomalin."

TOMLINSON, Ernest, M.A., Dip.A.G.M.S.; Curator, Grundy Art Gallery, Blackpool; *b* Crosby, nr. Liverpool, 27 July, 1939; *s* of Ernest Tomlinson. *Educ.:* Merchant Taylors School, University of Edinburgh, and Manchester University. *Addresses:* 60 Bold St., Fleetwood; Grundy Art Gallery, Queen St., Blackpool FY1 1PX.

TOMS, Peter Edward, A.R.M.S. (1991); marine and landscape painter in water-colour; principal designer, British Aerospace, to 1982; full time painter since then; *b* Hayes, Middx., 28 May, 1940; *s* of Edward James Toms, athlete; three *s. Educ.:* Mellow Lane School, Hayes; *studied engineering and design:* Southall Technical College (1956-63). *Exhib.:* R.S.M.A., R.I., R.M.S., R.B.A., N.S., U.A., numerous London and provincial one-man and other exhbns. including Alpine Club, Century, Edwin Pollard, Oliver Swann, Omell, Skipwith, Solent and Wykeham Galleries. *Work in permanent collections:* P. & O. "SS Canberra", Royal Hampshire Regt., Royal Navy (H.M.S. "Osprey"), NV Amev Group (Utrecht), H.M. Land Registry, Astrid Trust and many other corporate and private collections. *Address:* Stoneways, Springfield Rd., Broadway, Weymouth, Dorset DT3 5DX. *Club:* Dorchester (President). *Signs work:* "Peter Toms."

TONKS, John, A.T.D., F.R.B.S., V.P.R.B.S.; freelance sculptor in stone, wood, terracotta, bronze; part-time lecturer, Birmingham University; V.P., Royal Soc. of British Sculptors (1990-91); *b* Dudley, Worcs., 14 Aug., 1927; *s* of John Henry Tonks; *m* Sylvia Irene; one *s*, one *d*. *Educ.:* Dudley Grammar School; *studied art* at Wolverhampton and B'ham Colleges of Art specialising in sculpture (William Bloy, Albert Willetts, Tom Wright). *Exhib.:* one-man shows: University of B'ham (1974, 1984), Ombersley Gallery, Worcs. (1983), Helios Gallery, B'ham (1984); V.B. Gallery, St. Louis, U.S.A. (1981), Poole Willis Gallery, N.Y. (1983), Liverpool International Gdn. Festival (1984), Gardens of New College, Oxford (1988), Garden Festival, Wales (1992). *Address:* Downshill Cottage, Comhampton, Stourport-on-Severn, Worcs. DY13 9ST. *Signs work:* "J.T." joined.

TOOKEY, John Michael, P.S. (1982); commercial artist in oil, water-colour and pastel; *b* Ilford; *s* of C. J. Tookey. *Educ.:* Gearies Secondary Modern School; *studied art* at Sir John Cass School of Art. *Exhib.:* R.I., R.B.A., R.O.I., R.W.S. Art Club. *Work in permanent collections:* Bowes Museum Educ. Service, Gateshead County Library, Hackney Borough Council. *Works repro.:* illustrations for 'The Countryman', 'East Anglia', 'The Yorkshire Ridings', 'Kent, Surrey & Sussex', 'The Cotswolds'. *Address:* 1A Calne Ave., Clayhall, Ilford, Essex. *Signs work:* "John Tookey."

TOOP, Bill, R.I. (1979), M.C.S.D. (1971); artist and illustrator in water-colour, line and wash, line, with own gallery in Salisbury; *b* Bere Regis, Dorset, 27 May, 1943; *m* Elizabeth Thurstans; one *s*, one *d*. *Educ.:* Weymouth Grammar School, Blandford Grammar School; *studied art* at Bath Academy of Art (1961-63, Robyn Denny, Howard Hodgkin), Southampton College of Art (1964-66, Peter Folkes), Bristol Polytechnic Art Faculty (1967-68, Derek Crowe). *Exhib.:* R.I., R.W.A., numerous one-man shows. *Work in permanent collections:* The Sultan of Oman, Northern Telecom, British Gas, Whitbread Inns, Coutts & Co., The Sedgwick Group, N.F.U. Mutual and Avon Insurance, Royal School of Signals, Atomic Energy Authority, Inst. of Directors, etc. *Work repro.:* illustrated Portrait of Wiltshire (Pamela Street), National Gardens Scheme Handbook, etc. *Address:* Bill Toop Gallery, 5 St. John's St., Salisbury, Wilts. SP1 2SB. *Signs work:* "Bill Toop."

TOPLIS, Valma Maud, M.F.P.S.; artist in etching and aquatint, teacher; *b* Maidenhead, 18 June, 1946; *d* of Thomas Oldfield Jones Toplis, retd. businessman. *Educ.:* Clark's College, Ilford; Beal Grammar School for Girls; *studied art* at St. Osyth's Training College (1964-67, Graham Eccles, Michael Kaye), Barking Technical College (1967-80, Harry Eccleston, O.B.E.). *Exhib.:* Loggia Gallery, Bankside Gallery, R.E., The Barbican. *Work in private collections:* Britain and America. *Address:* 62 Chadville Gdns., Chadwell Heath, Romford, Essex RM6 5UA. *Clubs:* Ilford Art Soc., Essex Art. *Signs work:* "VALMA TOPLIS."

TOTTY, Vivienne Helen Bland, B.A.Hons. Fine Art (1984), A.M.A. (Art) (1990); curator/fine art; Fine Arts Officer, Middlesbrough Art Gallery (1985-88), Exhbns. Officer, Scunthorpe Museum (1989-); *b* Edinburgh, 16 Feb., 1962; *d* of Alan Bland Totty, M.B.E., B.A. *Educ.:* The Rudolf Steiner School, Edinburgh; *studied history of art and architecture* at University of E. Anglia, Norwich (1981-84), Sainsbury Centre for Visual Arts. *Exhib.:* initiated and mounted numerous exhbns. at Middlesbrough A.G. and Scunthorpe Museums, local, national, international art and artists. *Publications:* gallery leaflets and

WHO'S WHO IN ART

catalogues. *Address:* Scunthorpe Museum and Art Gallery, Oswald Rd., Scunthorpe, S. Humberside DN15 7BD.

TOVEY, Robert Lawton, A.T.D. (1947); painter in oil; *b* Birmingham, 3 Apr., 1924; *s* of Edward Francis Tovey; *m* Annette Suzanne Hubler. *Educ.:* The George Dixon Grammar School, Birmingham; *studied art* at Birmingham College of Art under B. Fleetwood-Walker (1939-43, 1946-47). *Exhib.:* R.B.S.A., R.B.A., A.I.A., N.E.A.C., R.O.I., R.W.A., one-man shows, Geneva (1957, 1962, 1964, 1980, 1981, 1982, 1983, 1984, 1985), Baden (1973, 1976). *Work in permanent collections:* Musée d'Art et d'Histoire, Geneva; Dudley A.G. *Official purchases:* oil painting, The Red Scarf, for above (1953). *Address:* 2 Place de L'Octroi, 1227 Carouge, Geneva, Switzerland. *Signs work:* "R. L. TOVEY."

TOWER, Meriel Theresa, F.S.D-C.; freelance textile designer, painter, teacher; on technical staff, Campbell Fabrics (1936-39); teacher, Upton House School, Windsor (1948-72), St. George's School, Windsor Castle (1953-70), from 1974 part-time teacher, Bucks. County Council Adult Educ.; *b* Windsor, 1911; *d* of Canon Henry Tower, C.V.O. *Educ.:* St. Paul's Girls' School; *studied art* at Westminster School of Art (1929-31) and Chelsea School of Art under Boris Heroys (1931-34). *Exhib.:* one-man show, Museum of Oxford (1978), R.A. (1984). *Publications:* British Textile Designers Today (Lewis), British Designers: Their Work, Series I (Lewis), Designers in Britain, 1947 (published for S.I.A.), Decorative Art, 1950-51 (The Studio Publications), Design for Applied Decoration in the Crafts, by John Farleigh (Bell). *Address:* The Thatch, Aston Rowant, Oxford.

TOWNSEND, Storm Diana, N.D.D. (Sculpture) (1960), A.T.C. (1962), Siswa Lokantara Foundation Resident Fellowship Award, Indonesia (1960-61), Huntington Hartford Foundation Resident Fellowship Award, Calif. (1963); sculpture in bronze, cements; sculpture instructor, University of Albuquerque, New Mexico; *b* London, 31 Aug., 1937. *Studied art* at London University, Goldsmiths' College (1955-60) under Harold S. Parker, Ivor Roberts-Jones. *Exhib.:* throughout U.S.A. *Work in permanent collection:* Museum of New Mexico, many private collections. *Commissions:* over life-size bronze "To Serve and Protect" commissioned by the City of Albuquerque and others, New Mexico (1984). *Address:* P.O. Box 1165, Corrales, New Mexico, 87048, U.S.A. *Signs work:* "STORM."

TOWSEY, Mary, T.D.; artist in oil and mixed media; *b* Epsom, 24 July, 1936; *d* of G.T.N. Prideaux; *m* Robin Towsey; three *d*. *Educ.:* Clare Park, Farnham; *studied art* at Goldsmiths' College (1955-57), part-time, Epsom College of Art (1960-67, Leslie Worth, Peter Oliver). *Exhib.:* Fairfield Halls Croydon, Lizard Gallery Farnham, Wintershall Gallery Bramley, Hallam Gallery London, Edwin Pollard Gallery, Ebury Gallery London, Wykeham Gallery London, Jonleigh Gallery Wonersh, Galerie de Vétheuil, France, R.B.A., R.O.I., N.E.A.C., R.W.S., S.W.A., S.B.A. B.B.C.2 television series 'Painters'. *Address:* Ambelor, Lands End La., Lindford, Bordon, Hants. GU35 0SS. *Signs work:* "Mary Towsey."

TOYNBEE, Lawrence; painter; Past Director of the Morley Gallery and Art Centre, Morley College; *b* London, 1922; *s* of Arnold Toynbee, C.H.; *m* Jean Asquith; six *d*. *Educ.:* Ampleforth and New College, Oxford; *studied art* at Ruskin School of Drawing (Albert Rutherson, Percy Horton). Work in many public and private collections in Britain and U.S.A. *Address:* Ganthorpe, Terrington, York. *Club:* M.C.C. *Signs work:* "L.L.T." and year.

480

TRANT, Carolyn, D.F.A.(Lond.) (1973); artist in egg tempera, drawings, etchings and lithographs; *b* Middx., 29 Oct., 1950; *d* of Brian Trant, musician; two *s*, one *d. Educ.:* North London Collegiate School; *studied art* at Slade School of Fine Art (1969-73). *Exhib.:* New Grafton Gallery, Business Arts Gallery, Brighton Festival and throughout S. East. *Work in permanent collection:* R.A., E.S.C.C./S.E. Arts commission: 'Rituals and Relics' - Earthworks on the Downs. *Address:* 17 St. Anne's Cres., Lewes, E. Sussex BN7 1SB. *Signs work:* "Carolyn Trant" on back of work.

TRAPPE, Paul; sculptor in stone; *b* Göttingen, Germany; *s* of Heinrich Trappe; *m* G. Schaeffter; one *s. Educ.:* Göttingen, Northeim Düsseldorf. *Exhib.:* Canberra, Adelaide, Bonn, London, Milwaukee. *Work in permanent collections:* Düsseldorf, Canberra, Adelaide, Tanunda, Milwaukee, Sydney, Dubuque, Baden-Baden, Northeim, West Bend, Saskatoon. *Publications:* Vantage, Adelaide; Kunstreport, Berlin; Art Works of Canberra, Düsseldorf Creativ; Wondabyne, Paul Trappe-Sculpture 1969-1989; Living Stone. *Addresses:* Box 302 P.O. Tanunda, S. Australia 5352; and Wildenbruchstr. 15, 40545 Dusseldorf. *Signs work:* "tr."

TRATT, Richard, S.WL.A. (1981), S.B.A. (1987); painter in oil, acrylic; *b* Enfield, 19 Oct., 1953; *s* of Robert Tratt; *m* Hilary Wastnage. *Educ.:* Crewe Grammar School; *studied art* at Northwich College of Art (1970-72), Dartington College of Arts (1972-74). *Exhib.:* R.A., Mall Galleries, Blake Gallery, Alresford Gallery, Peter Hedley Gallery, British Artists Show, Spirit of London, etc.; sixteen one-man shows. *Work in permanent collections:* S.W.A.N., Royal Palace of Oman. *Work repro.:* Reynard Fine Art, Royles, McDonald, Rosenstiel's. *Address:* 10 Sharpley Cl., Fordingbridge, Hants. SP6 1LG. *Signs work:* "Tratt."

TRAVERS-SMITH, Dorothea; painter in oil, water-colour, of portraits, flowers, trees, cats. *Educ.:* at private schools at Eastbourne, Cuckfield and Paris; Regent St. Polytechnic, etc., but studied almost entirely with the late Arthur Lindsey, pres. of R.M.S. *Exhib.:* R.A., Paris Salon, R.B.A., R.I., W.I.A.C., London Group, London Portrait Soc., etc. *Address:* 40 St. George's Ct., Gloucester Rd., London SW7 4RA. *Signs work:* "Travers-Smith" or "T-S."

TRAYHORNE, Rex, R.M.S. (1988); artist in water-colour and gouache; art teacher, demonstrator and writer; exhbns. organiser, Wessex Artists Exhbns.; *b* 13 Oct., 1931; *m* Geraldine; two *s* (one *s-s*), two *d* (one *s-d*). *Educ.:* Newbury Grammar School; *studied art* at Reading College (1958). *Exhib.:* R.I., R.M.S., R.W.S., local art societies, Wessex Artists Exhbns., etc. *Publication:* Adventure into Water-colour. *Address:* Stable House Studio, Newton Lane, Romsey, Hants. SO51 8GY. *Clubs:* Romsey Art, Ringwood Art Soc. *Signs work:* "Rex Trayhorne."

TREANOR, Frances, P.S. (1978), A.T.C. (1967), N.D.D. (1966); L'Artiste Assoifee awards winner (1975), Diplome d'Honneur, Salon d'Antony, France (1975), George Rowney award (1982), Frank Herring award (merit) (1984), Conté (U.K.) award (1986), Government Print Purchase (1987); *b* Penzance, Cornwall, 1944; *d* of George Treanor, musician; *m* (1) Frank Elliott, (2) Anthony Taylor (divorced); one *d. Educ.:* Assumption Convent, Kensington; Sacred Heart Convent, Hammersmith; *studied art:* Goldsmiths' College (1962-66) Hornsey College of Art (1966-67). *Exhib.:* London, Paris, Yugoslavia, Berlin. Stage set design commission 'As You Like It' O.U.D.S. Summer Tour (Japan, U.S.A., U.K.) 1988. *Publication:* Pastel Masterclass (Harper Collins). *Address:* 121 Royal Hill, London SE10 8SS. *Signs work:* "Treanor" or "F.T."

TREE, Michael Lambert; etcher, draughtsman and illustrator; *b* New York; *m* Lady Anne Tree. *Educ.:* Eton. *Exhib.:* Hochmann Gallery, N.Y. (1982), Fine Arts, London (1984), St. Jame's Gallery (1989). *Publications:* illustrations to Summoned by Bells by John Betjeman (1960). *Address:* 29 Radnor Walk, London SW3. *Club:* White's. *Signs work:* "M. Tree."

TRELEAVEN, Richard Barrie, S.WL.A. (founder member), M.B.O.U.; artist in oil on canvas, alkyd, gouache, specialises in painting birds of prey; company director of family business; *b* London, 16 July, 1920; *s* of G. L. Treleaven; *m* Margery (decd.). *Educ.:* Dulwich College (1932-36); *studied art* under G. E. Lodge. *Exhib.:* S.WL.A. Art Exhbns. Bureau, Moorland Gallery, etc.; one-man show, Bude (1953), Launceston (1973, 1980). *Work in permanent collections:* Batley and many private collections. *Publications:* Peregrine (1977); and ornithological journals. *Address:* Blue Wings, South Petherwin, Launceston, Cornwall. *Club:* British Falconers. *Signs work:* "R. B. Treleaven."

TRESS, David; painter in water-colour based mixed media, including gouache, ink and oil crayon, charcoal, oil; *b* London, 11 Apr., 1955. *Educ.:* Latymer Upper School, Hammersmith; *studied art* at Harrow College of Art (1972-73), Trent Polytechnic, Nottingham (1973-76). *Exhib.:* regularly in Wales, England, Holland and France, recently 'Five Leading Welsh Artists' San Francisco. *Work in permanent collections:* National Library of Wales, C.A.S.W. *Address:* 17 Castle St., Haverfordwest, Pembrokeshire SA61 2ED. *Signs work:* "David Tress."

TRIBE, Barbara, F.R.B.S.; *b* Sydney, Australia. *Studied art:* Trained in sculpture, student of G. Rayner Hoff, East Sydney Technical College; graduated with honours, awarded Diploma and Bronze Medal for sculpture. Won the New South Wales travelling art scholarship for sculpture to the Royal Academy Schools, London. Fellow of the Royal Society of British Sculptors, Member of the Society of Portrait Sculptors. *Works represented:* Anzac War Memorial, Sydney, Australia; National Gallery of Australia, Canberra; Australian War Memorial, Canberra; Art Gallery of New South Wales, Sydney, Australia; Art Gallery of South Australia, Adelaide; Bathurst Regional Art Gallery, New South Wales; Stoke-on-Trent City Museum and Art Gallery; Spode Potteries Museum, Stoke-on-Trent; Doncaster Museum and Art Gallery, Yorkshire; R.A.F. Museum, Hendon, London; in many private collections in U.K., U.S.A., Canada, Australia, Far East – Japan and Thailand. Exhibited widely and worked abroad. *Exhib.:* Royal Academy; Royal West of England Academy; Royal Scottish Academy; Cambrian Academy of Art; Paris Salon; Royal Society of British Sculptors; Society of Portrait Sculptors; London Group; Fieldborne Galleries, London; Newlyn and St. Ives Society of Artists; Penwith Society of Artists, St. Ives; Beaver Gallery, Canberra, Australia; Barry Stern Gallery, Sydney, Australia; MacQuarie Galleries, Sydney, Australia; Blaxland Galleries, Sydney, Australia. *Major retrospective exhbns.:* Stoke-on-Trent City Museum and Art Gallery; Guildford House Galleries, Guildford; Mall Galleries, London. *Publications:* 'British Sculpture' by Eric Newton; 'On View' – acquisitions in Britain; 'Art and Australia' – Sam Ure Smith; 'A Matter of Taste' – investing in Australian art by Terry Ingram; 'Australian Sculptors' by Ken Scarlett; Encyclopaedia 'British Pottery and Porcelain Marks' by Geoffrey A. Godden. *Disciplines:* sculpture, painting, drawing and ceramics. *Instructor* of modelling and sculpture, Penzance School of Art (1948-88). *Address:* The Studio, Sheffield, Paul, Penzance, Cornwall TR19 6UW, England. *Signs work:* "Barbara Tribe" see appendix.

TROITZKY, Nina, A.R.O.I.; painter in oil; *d* of the Rev. Nicanor Troitzky, Archimanderite, Russian Orthodox Church in Exile. *Studied art* at Leeds College of Art (part time) Icon painting, Chelsea School of Art (part time). *Exhib.:* R.O.I., Mall Galleries, London Contemporary Art Fair, British Painters, Discerning Eye, Mall Galleries, Anna Mei, Clifford St. Fine Arts, Halkin Arcade Galleries 'Women and Art', Abbot & Holder, Llewellyn Alexander, Wykham, Chelsea Arts Club, Century Windsor, Hann Bath, Example Art London, River Gallery Arundel, and many provincial and European galleries. *Work repro.:* Medici card. *Address:* 91 Tarrant St., Arundel, W. Sussex BN18 9DN. *Club:* Chelsea Arts. *Signs work:* "N.T."

TROTH, Miriam Deborah, B.A. Hons. (1983); artist in mixed media; *b* Edgbaston, 1 Oct., 1951. *Educ.:* Avonbourne; *studied art* at Bournemouth and Poole College of Art; W. Surrey College of Art and Design (1980-83). *Exhib.:* Barbican, British Commonwealth Inst., Swansea A.G., Bradford House Glass Museum, Coleridge Gallery, Bristol A.G., Seven Dials, R.A., Bankside Gallery, Salisbury Arts Centre, Poole Arts Centre, Russell Cotes Museum, Smiths Gallery, Royal Soc. of Artists Gallery, Salisbury Museum, Windsor Arts Centre, Peterborough A.G. *Work in private collections:* London, Sydney, Detroit, Frankfurt; *public collections:* Wiltshire C.C. *Address:* 125 Seafield Rd., Bournemouth, Dorset BH6 3JL.

TROWELL, Jonathan Ernest Laverick, N.D.D. (1959), R.A.S.Dip. (1962), F.R.S.A. (1983), N.E.A.C. (1986); painter in oil, pastel and water-colour; *b* Easington Village, Co. Durham, 1938; *m* Dorothea May Howard. *Educ.:* Robert Richardson School; *studied art* at Sunderland College of Art, R.A. Schools. *Exhib.:* New Bauhaus Cologne, Young Contemporaries, John Moores, R.A., Lee Nordnes N.Y., Bilan de Contemporain Paris, R.B.A., N.E.A.C.; one-man shows, Brod Gallery London, Century Gallery, Culham College Oxford, Richard Stone-Reeves New York, Osborne Gallery London, Stern Galleries Australia. *Work in permanent collections:* Bank of Japan; Culham College, Oxford; de Beers (Diamond Co.); Oriental Diamond Co.; Ciba-Geigy; Imperial College of Science; R.C.A.; B.P. *Address:* Blenheim House, Litcham, Norfolk PE32 2NS. *Club:* Chelsea Arts. *Signs work:* "TROWELL."

TRUZZI-FRANCONI, Jane, B.A. (1977); Angeloni prize (1979), Discerning Eye prize (1990); sculptor in bronze; Supervisor, Fiorini Fine Art Foundry; *b* London, 26 July, 1955; one *d. Educ.:* Sydenham School; *studied art* at Goldsmiths' College of Art (1973-74), Ravensbourne College of Art (1974-77), R.C.A. (1978-79). *Exhib.:* R.A., Mall Galleries, many mixed shows in London, E. Anglia, Kent and Surrey. *Address:* 4 Wolsey Cottages, Strickland Manor Hill, Yoxford, Suffolk IP17 3JE. *Signs work:* "J.E.T.F."

TUCKER, Loraine Read, F.C.S.D. (1985), M.C.I.B.S. (1979); industrial designer specializing in lighting fittings and metalwork; *b* St. John's Wood, 21 Dec., 1910; *s* of Claude Loraine Tucker; *m* Frances Maude Phillipps; one *s. Educ.:* Colston's School, Stapleton, Bristol; *studied art* at Regent St. Polytechnic and received architectural training with Herbert L. Smith, L.R.I.B.A., A.M.I.Struct.E. (1927-31). *Address:* Little Paddock, Penn, Bucks. *Signs work:* "L. Read-Tucker."

TUCKER, Patricia Rosa, N.D.D. (1950), A.T.D. (1951); artist in oil and water-colour specializing in architectural landscapes, art teacher; Chairman, Bromley Art Soc.; Visual Arts Officer, Bromley Arts Council (1970-87); Sec. Chelsea Open Air Art Exhbn. (1967-87); *b* London, 2 Jan., 1927; *d* of Michael Madden; *m* Leslie J. Tucker; two *s*, one *d. Educ.:* Mayfield School, Putney; St.

Catherine's School, Swindon; *studied art* at Swindon School of Art (Harold Dearden), West of England College of Art (Donald Milner). *Exhib.:* R.A., A.U.A. Bankside, Guildhall London; one-man shows, London, Swindon, Denmark, Bromley, Chelsea, Gloucester, Greenwich. *Work in permanent collections:* Bromley Pictures for Schools; Gloucester Training College; Kensington and Chelsea Library; Swindon; stained glass for Church of Scotland. *Publication:* illustrated, Parenting Plus. *Address:* 5 Bromley Ave., Bromley, Kent BR1 4BG. *Club:* B.A.S. *Signs work:* "Patricia Tucker."

TUCKWELL, George Arthur, D.F.M. (1942), A.T.D. (1952), N.D.D. (1951); painter in oil and water-colour, sculptor in wood, metals and ivory, illustrator, teacher; mem. National Soc.; *b* Burwell, Cambs., 4 Mar., 1919; *s* of Arthur Tuckwell; *m* Joyce; three *d. Educ.:* Sir George Monoux Grammar School; *studied art* at Sir John Cass (1947-51, Kenneth Martin, Bainbridge Copnall), Goldsmiths' College (1951-52). *Exhib.:* R.B.A., R.I., R.O.I., London Group, R.W.S., N.S., Arts Council, U.S., Piccadilly Gallery, Gimpel Fils, Stone Gallery, Newcastle, John Hunt Gallery, Lewes Gallery. *Work in permanent collections:* Ashmolean Museum — War Artists Collection, Oxford, Cambridge, Surrey and London Universities; public and private collections in U.K., U.S.A., Australia, N.Z., S. Africa, S. America. *Publications:* illustrated numerous books principally on transport. *Address:* Kintail, 38 Geers Wood, Ghyll Rd., Heathfield, E. Sussex TN21 0AR. *Signs work:* see appendix.

TULLY, Joyce Mary, U.A. (1978), A.M.N.S. (1974); artist in oil and water-colour, teacher; speaker at local societies; teaches calligraphy and exhibits examples of work; *b* Wooler, Northumberland; *d* of Walter Tully. *Educ.:* Duchess Grammar School, Alnwick; *studied art* at Hammersmith Art College (part-time) and private tuition with Mr. Harold Workman, R.O.I., R.B.A., R.S.M.A. *Exhib.:* Paris Salon, R.O.I., R.B.A., Chelsea Artists, N.S., U.A., Ridley Soc. and in Australia, British Painting in 1979. *Work in permanent collections:* Copeland Castle, and private collections in England, Europe and America. *Address:* Kia-or, 26 Tenter Hill, Wooler, Northumberland NE71 6DG. *Signs work:* "J. M. Tully."

TURNBULL, William; sculptor and painter; *b* Dundee, 11 Jan., 1922; *m* Kim Lim; two *s. Studied art* at Slade School of Fine Art (1946-48). *Exhib.:* I.C.A. (1957), Waddington Galleries (1967, 1969, 1970, 1976, 1978, 1981, 1985, 1987, 1991), Tate Gallery (1973); one-man and major group shows worldwide. *Work in permanent collections:* Arts Council, Tate Gallery, Scottish National Gallery of Modern Art; numerous provincial and overseas collections. *Address:* c/o Waddington Galleries, 11 Cork St., London W1X 1PD. *Signs work:* see appendix.

TURNER, Cyril B., M.A.A. (1988), M.P.S.G. (1985), I.G.M.A. Fine Art (1991); Fine Art master miniaturist in most categories including illuminated miniatures; inventor of Lumitex, an acid free, ultra-violet proof substitute for ivory as a miniature base; introduced cold enamel as a medium for miniature paintings; artist in oils, cold enamel, soft pastel, gouache, acrylic; *b* Aldeby, Norfolk, 10 Sept., 1929. *Educ.:* Beccles Area School. *Exhib.:* since 1983 annual one-man exhib. 100-150 original fine art miniature paintings Museum Galleries Gt. Yarmouth. Many other U.K. one-man miniature shows, R.A., Salon des Nations Paris, annually International Miniature Shows Washington D.C., New York, Colorado, New Jersey, Nevada, Montana, Wyoming, Georgia, Florida, New Mexico, Ulster, Tasmania, New South Wales; others W. Virginia, S. Carolina, Ohio, Pennsylvania, Arizona, Kentucky, Canada, France. *Work in* *permanent collections:* State Theatre New Jersey, Picturecraft Holt Norfolk, M.A.S.-F. *Awards:* over 50 miniatures have won awards, of which 20 are Best of Show, Highest Merit or 1st Place awards. *Publications:* author: Painting Miniatures in Acrylics (1990), miniature section of painting in Acrylics (English and French edns. 1991). Currently engaged in writing and publishing a 21 pocket book Informative Series 'Painting Original Fine Art Miniatures' 1 Bases (Lumitex) and 2 Bases Various (1993). *Address:* 5 Stone Rd., Cobholm, Gt. Yarmouth, Norfolk NR31 0AQ. *Signs work:* "C.B. Turner."

TURNER, Jacquie, B.A.; painting in mixed media and collage on paper; *b* 27 Mar., 1959; *m* Nigel Wheeler; one *s. Educ.:* Rickmansworth School, Herts.; *studied art* at Winchester School of Art (1979-81, Gillian Ayres, Graham Crawley, Leonard McComb). *Exhib.:* Linda Blackstone Gallery Pinner, Conservation Management London, Charlotte Lampard Gallery London. *Work in permanent collections:* Leics. Coll. for schools and colleges, Norsk Hydro Oslo, Adam Bank London, Shangri La Hong Kong. *Address:* 46 Park Rd., Chiswick, London W4 3HH. *Signs work:* "Jacquie Turner."

TURNER, Lynette, Hons.B.Sc. (Zoology, 1968), H.N.D.D. (Graphic design, 1970); printmaker in coloured etchings using zinc; *b* London, 28 May, 1945; *d* of Engineer Rear-Admiral A. Turner. *Educ.:* Hall School, Wincanton, Som., Manchester University; *studied art* at Brighton Art School (1963), City and Guilds Art School (1969, etching Henry Wilkinson, Tim Edmunds), Manchester Art School. *Exhib.:* Century Gallery, Henley (1976), Margaret Fisher Gallery (1976), R.A. (1977), S.E. London Art Group, Y.M.C.A., Gt. Russell St., WC1, (1983), R.A. Summer Show (1987), December 1989 exhbn. in Crypt of St. Martin's-in-the-Fields. (etchings and water-colours) urban ecology influence. *Address:* 54 Hanover Gdns., London SE11. *Signs work:* "Lynette Turner."

TURNER, Martin William, N.D.D. (1961), R.O.I. (1974), N.S. (1975); painter in oil, acrylic and water-colour, printmaker; *b* Reading, 3 Oct., 1940; *s* of William Alexander Turner. *Educ.:* Gravesend Technical School; *studied art* at Medway College of Art under David Graham, C. Stanley Hayes. *Exhib.:* R.A., R.O.I., R.B.A., N.S., R.S.M.A., R.E. *Work in permanent collections:* Abbot Hall Gallery, Swansea University, Cardiff Museum, Glamorgan Educ. Com., Liverpool A.G. *Work repro.:* articles for Leisure Painter. *Address:* 24 Marshall Rd., Rainham, Kent ME8 0AP. *Clubs:* R.I., N.S.P.S., Hampstead Artists' Council. *Signs work:* "Martin Turner."

TURNER, Peggy E. M.: see RICHARDS, E. Margaret.

TURNER, Prudence, freelance artist in oil on canvas; *b* 15 Mar., 1930; *d* of Brigadier Charles Ernest Windle, O.B.E., M.C.. *Studied art* in India, Egypt, France and England, learning from artists already famous. Fine Art Publication copyrights purchased from 1967 onwards and given international circulation, including limited editions of signed prints. Scottish landscape painter specifically since 1966; plus portraiture, etc. *Work in private collections:* in U.K., and Overseas. *Address:* 49 Romulus Ct., Justin Cl., Brentford Dock Marina, Brentford, Middx. TW8 8QW. *Signs work:* "Prudence Turner."

TURNER, William Ralph, R.C.A., F.R.S.A.; artist in oil and water-colour; *b* Chorlton-on-Medlock, 30 Apr., 1920; *s* of the late Ralph Matthew Turner; *m* Anne Grant (decd.); one *d. Studied art* at Derby College of Art (1945). *Exhib.:* R.B.A., R.I., R.C.A., O'Mell Galleries London, Christopher Cole Galleries, Henley-on-Thames, Pitcairn Galleries, Knutsford, Boundary Gallery, London. *Work in permanent collections:* Manchester Educ. Com., Stockport A.G., Saab

(Manchester) Ltd.; private collections in New York, Los Angeles, Kenya, Portugal, Switzerland, Zaire. *Work repro.:* Cheshire Life Magazine. *Address:* (studio) Renrut, 23 Gill Bent Rd., Cheadle Hulme, Cheadle, Ches. *Signs work:* "William Turner" and see appendix.

TURPIN, Louis, Dip.Ad.(Hons.) Fine Art (1971); painter in oil on canvas; *b* 25 Apr., 1947; *s* of Digby Denis Turpin, film director; *m* Davida Smith; two *s*. *Educ.:* Alleyns, Dulwich; Sunbury Grammar School, Sunbury-on-Thames; *studied art* at Guildford School of Art (1967-68), Falmouth Art School (1968-71). *Exhib.:* Odette Gilbert, London, Beaux Arts, Bath, N.P.G., Bohun Gallery, Henley-on-Thames, Rye A.G. *Work in permanent collections:* Rye A.G., South East Arts, Towner A.G., Bath University, John Radcliffe Hospital, Oxford. *Address:* 19 Udimore Rd., Rye, E. Sussex TN31 7DS. *Club:* Rye Soc. of Artists. *Signs work:* "Louis Turpin."

TUTE, George William, N.D.D. Illustration, N.D.D. Painting, R.A.Cert., M.A. (R.C.A.), R.E., R.W.A., S.W.E.; artist in oil, water-colour, printmaking; freelance graphic designer; *b* Hull, 23 Mar., 1933; *s* of G. W. Tute; *m* Iris Tute; two *s. Educ.:* Bainse Grammar School, Lancs.; *studied art* at Blackpool School of Art (1951-54); Royal Academy Schools (1954-59); Royal College of Art (1981-82). *Exhib.:* R.A., R.W.A., R.E.; private and public galleries. Exhibits prints and paintings, book illustration and general illustration for commissions. *Address:* 46 Eastfield, Westbury-on-Trym, Bristol BS9 4BE. *Signs work:* "G. W. Tute."

TWEED, Jill, F.R.B.S., F.R.S.A., Slade Dip. (1954); sculptor in bronze; *b* U.K., 7 Dec., 1931; *m* Philip Hicks; one *s*, one *d. Studied art* at Slade School of Art (1954, F. E. McWilliam). *Exhib.:* Marjorie Parr Gallery, London, Ladlane Gallery, Dublin, Embankment Gallery, London, Bruton St. Gallery, London, Flowers East Gallery, London, Poole-Wills Gallery, N.Y. *Work in permanent collections:* H.M. The Queen; Corps of the Royal Military Police, Chichester; Royal Engineers, Mill Hill, London; Struthers Ltd., Glasgow; Austin Reed Ltd., London; Picker Collection, Kingston-upon-Thames; Hampshire C.C.; Amec U.K. Ltd., London. *Address:* Radcot House, Buckland Rd., Bampton, Oxon. OX18 2AA. *Signs work:* "Jill Tweed."

TYSOE, Peter, N.D.D., A.T.C. (Lond.), F.S.D.-C., F.M.G.P., Churchill Fellow; full-time designer-craftsman/sculptor in glass, metals, resins; Head of Glass Dept., Jam Factory Workshops; Past Chairman, Federation of British Craft Societies and Devon Guild of Craftsmen; *b* Bedford, 22 June, 1935; *s* of Harold L. Tysoe; *m* Patricia; three *s. Educ.:* Oxford Technical School; *studied art* at Oxford School of Art (1952-56), Goldsmiths' College School of Art (1956-57). *Work in permanent collections:* Plymouth A.G., commissioned works in London, Birmingham and in public and private buildings in Britain and Europe. *Publications:* Glass, Resin and Metal Construction (Mills & Boon). *Address:* c/o Jam Factory Workshops Inc., P.O. Box 145, St. Peters, S. Australia 5069. *Signs work:* see appendix.

TYSON, Rowell, A.R.C.A., R.B.A.; painter in oil and water-colour; *b* London, 5 Jan., 1926; *s* of Rowell Tyson, engineer; *m* Monica Lyon. *Studied art* at Tunbridge Wells School of Art, Beckenham School of Art, Royal College of Art (1946-1950), fourth year scholarship (1949-1950). Senior Mem of Royal Soc. of British Artists. *Exhib.:* R.A., R.S.A., R.B.A., R.O.I., R.S.M.A., provincial galleries and touring exhbns. *Work in public and private collections* include Leo-Burnett, Miles Laboratories, Shell, Lopex, Leicester Educ. Com., Carlisle City A.G., K.C.C., Paxus, Sumicorp Finance Ltd., Merrill Lynch, Arthur Andersen

& Co., Qatar National Bank, Inst. of Directors. *Address:* 29 Fisher St., Sandwich, Kent CT13 9EJ. *Signs work:* "ROWELL TYSON."

TYSON EDWARDS, Marian, D.F.A.; sculptor in bronze, cement fondu, terracotta; *b* Manchester, 2 Oct., 1937; *d* of Henry Tyson Edwards, civil servant; *m* John T. Sharples; one *s,* one *d. Studied art* at Liverpool College of Art and High Wycombe College of Art. *Exhib.:* Mall Galleries, galleries in Henley, Birmingham, Chalfont, etc. *Work in permanent collections:* Windsor and Eton Fine Art. *Address:* Wispington House, Worster Rd., Cookham, Berks. SL6 9JC. *Signs work:* "M. Tyson Edwards."

U

UDEN, E. Boye; painter in oil, water-colour, draughtsman, commercial artist, teacher; official artist, N.F.S. (1941-45); Head of Graphic Design Department, Reigate School of Art; *b* London, 8 July, 1911; *s* of Ernest Uden, artist; *m* Frances Hilder; two *d. Educ.:* Aske's, Hatcham; *studied art* at Camberwell School of Art and Goldsmiths' School of Art. *Exhib.:* R.A., N.E.A.C., R.I., U.S.A., etc. *Work in permanent collections:* Oxford and Canterbury. *Official purchases:* many for National War Records. *Work repro.:* in War Pictures by British Artists, and other official publications. *Address:* Kingsbury Cottage, Upper Rd., Sudbury, Suffolk. *Signs work:* "BOYE UDEN."

UGLOW, Euan; painter in oil; First Prize John Moores (1972); awarded Austin Abbey Premiere Scholarship; artist Trustee, National Gallery, London; teacher at Slade School of Art; *b* London, 10 Mar., 1932; *s* of E. W. Uglow, company accountant. *Educ.:* Strand Grammar School for Boys; *studied art* at Camberwell School of Art and Slade School. *Work in permanent collections:* Tate Gallery, Arts Council, Glasgow Art Gallery, Southampton Art Gallery, South Australia National Gallery, Liverpool University, Ferens A.G., Hull. *Gallery & Agent:* Browse & Darby, Cork St., W1. *Address:* 11 Turnchapel Mews, Cedars Rd., London SW4. *Signs work:* "Euan Uglow."

UHT, John, R.I. (1976); painter in oil and water-colour, sculptor in bronze, marble, wood, lead sheet; *b* Dayton, Ohio, 30 Aug., 1924; *s* of E. J. Uht, occupational therapist; *m* Jill Gould; two *s,* one *d. Educ.:* Danville High School, Illinois; *studied art* at University of Illinois Fine and Applied Arts College (1943-47, Marvin Martin, John Kennedy) and Ishmu Naguchi (1948). *Exhib.:* Art, U.S.A. (1958), Reading Museum (1970), Edwin Pollard Gallery, Barry M. Keene Gallery, R.A., R.I. *Work in permanent and private collections:* R.A. (bronze), Nelson Rockefeller (bronze). *Address:* 44 Dorchester Rd., Weymouth, Dorset. *Clubs:* R.I., Sherborne Arts. *Signs work:* painting, "JOHN UHT," sculpture, "UHT."

UNDERWOOD, Keith Alfred; Leverhulme Research Award in Fine Art (France, 1957-58); realist painter in oil and water-colour; sculptor; restorer; *b* Portsmouth, 21 June, 1934; *s* of the late A. T. Underwood, B.E.M., late R.E. *Educ.:* Monmouth School (1946-53); *studied art* at Newport College of Art (1953-57) under the late Tom Rathmell, A.R.C.A, and the late Hubert Dalwood; West of England College of Art (1960-61). *Exhib.:* Welsh Arts Council, Pictures for Schools, British Art for Moscow, Young Contemporaries, Mall Galleries, Chepstow locale. *Work in permanent collections:* Margaret Cleyton Memorial restoration (St. Mary's, Chepstow 1984), Onitsha Cathedral, Nigeria (portrait bronze 1985), Earl of Worcester armorial sculpture (Chepstow Town Gate 1988); large historical mural, Drill Hall, Chepstow, and town map (1991); paintings in private collections: U.K., U.S.A., Australia, S. Africa and Netherlands. *Address:* 1 Madocke Rd., Sedbury, nr. Chepstow, Gwent NP6 7AY. *Signs work:* "KAU" until *c*1974, "K. Underwood" and "Keith Underwood" thereafter, see appendix.

UPTON, Michael; Cert. R.A.S. (1962), Abbey Scholar (Rome Scholarships); artist in mixed media, lecturer; lecturer, Royal Academy Schools (1980—); visiting lecturer various art colleges; *b* 5 Feb., 1938; *s* of E. J. Upton; *m* Susan E. Young; one *s,* one *d. Educ.:* King Edward VI School, Birmingham; *studied art* at Birmingham College of Art (1954-58) under Gilbert Mason; R.A. Schools (1958-62) under Peter Greenham. *Exhib.:* Various London and touring exhbns. *Work in collections:* include Arts Council, British Council and private collections. *Work repro.:* Studio International, Artscribe, Flash Art, etc. *Address:* c/o Anne Berthoud Gallery, 10 Clifford St., Bond St., London W1. *Club:* Chelsea Arts. *Signs work:* "Michael Upton."

UTERMOHLEN, William C.; painter; *b* Philadelphia, Pa., 1933. *Studied art* at Pennsylvania Academy of Fine Art, Philadelphia; Ruskin School of Drawing, Oxford. *Exhib.:* one-man shows: Traverse Theatre Gallery, Edinburgh Festival (1963), Bonfiglioli Gallery, Oxford (1965, 1967), Nordness Gallery, N.Y. (1967), Marlborough New London Gallery (1969), Galerie d'Eendt, Amsterdam (1970, 1971), Mead Art Museum, Amherst College, Amherst, Massachusetts (1974). Visiting artist, Amherst College (1972-74). Mural, Liberal Jewish Synagogue, St. Johns Wood, London (1981); mural, Royal Free Hospital, Hampstead (1985). *Address:* 35 Blomfield Rd., London W9 2PF. *Signs work:* "Utermohlen."

V

VAIZEY, Marina (Lady Vaizey), B.A. Radcliffe, M.A. (Cantab.); Art Critic, Sunday Times (1974-91); Editor, National Art Collections Fund (1991-); Art Critic, Financial Times (1970-74); Trustee, National Galleries and Museums on Merseyside; *b* New York City, 16 Jan., 1938; *m* Lord Vaizey (decd. 1984); two *s,* one *d. Exhib.:* Painter as Photographer, Arts Council (1982-85). *Publications:* 100 Masterpieces of Art (1979); Andrew Wyeth (1980); Artist as Photographer (1982); Peter Blake (1985); Christo (1990); Christiane Kubrick (1990); organised Critic's Choice, Tooth's (1974). *Address:* 24 Heathfield Terr., London W4 4JE.

VALENTINE-DAINES, Sherree E., Dip. A.D., U.A. (1983), S.W.A.; painter in oil; *b* Effingham, 1956; *d* of Rose and Ralph Valentine-Daines, master builder and stone mason; *m* Mark Alun Rowbotham; one *s,* one *d. Studied art* at Epsom School of Art and Design (1976-80, Leslie Worth, Peter Petersen). *Exhib.:* R.B.A., R.A., Tate Gallery, R.O.I., R.W.S., R.P., Royal Overseas League, N.E.A.C., U.A., P.S., Olympic Games Exhbn., Royal Festival Hall, Barbican, Laing Landscape, N.S.P.S. *Commissions* include Test Cricket, 5 Nations Rugby, Royal Ascot, Henley Royal Regatta. *Address:* Misty Ridge, 126 The Street, Ashtead, Surrey KT21 1AB. *Signs work:* "S.E.V.D."

VANGO, David, M.F.P.S.; self taught artist in oils and mixed media; *b* London, Feb., 1950. *Studied art:* private studies at the Courtauld Inst. and Witt

Gallery, and galleries and museums here and abroad. *Exhib.:* one-man shows: Vidal Gallery, Barcelona (1977), Picture Workshop (1979), Gallery Three (1983, 1984), Loggia Gallery (1989); more than twenty group shows including: Bloomsbury Gallery (June 1989), Brighton Polytechnic A.G. (Aug. 1989). Selected works for the Arts Centre, Hemel Hempstead (Nov. 1989), and for St. Martin's A.G., Trafalgar Sq. (Feb. 1990), Stevenage, Lauderdale House, Fairfield Halls Croydon, Usher Gallery Lincoln, Scunthorpe Museum and A.G., Gagliardi Dynamic Structure and Form (1992), etc. *Contributor:* British Contemporary Art (1993). *Work in private collections:* Japan, France, Spain, Germany, Italy, Australia, America etc. *Address:* 68 Alexander Terr., Lincoln LN1 1JE. *Signs work:* see appendix.

VAN NIEKERK, Christo Barrie, R.E. (1990); printmaker in woodcut, designer; *b* 22 Jan., 1931; *m* Sarah; one *s,* two *d. Studied art* at Heatherleys School of Art (1951, Iain Macnab), Central School of Art (1954, Jesse Collins). *Exhib.:* Bankside Gallery, R.A., R.W.A., S.W.E., Geffrye Museum, Holburne Museum, Festival Hall, Art in Action, etc. *Address:* Priding House, Saul, Glos. *Clubs:* R.E., P.M.C. *Signs work:* "Chris van Niekerk."

VAN NIEKERK, Sarah Compton, R.E. (1976), S.W.E. (1974), A.R.W.A. (1992); wood engraver; Tutor, City and Guilds of London Art School since 1978, R.A. Schools (1976-86); *b* London, 16 Jan., 1934; *d* of D.J. Hall, writer; *m* Chris Van Niekerk; one *s,* two *d. Educ.:* Bedales; *studied art* at Central School of Art, Slade School of Fine Art. *Exhib.:* R.A., Bankside Gallery, Duncan Campbell, U.S.A., 23 one and two-man exhbns. *Work in permanent collections:* V. & A., Fitzwilliam, Ashmolean, National Museum of Wales, National Library of Wales, U.C.L.A., Wood Engravers Soc. U.S.S.R., Fremantle Arts Centre, Graves, Hereford Museum. *Publications:* illustrations for Folio Soc., Gregynog, O.U.P., Readers Digest, Pavilion, Virago, Silent Books, Rider. *Address:* Priding House, Saul, Glos. GL2 7LG. *Clubs:* R.E., S.W.E., P.M.C., A.W.A. *Signs work:* "Sarah van Niekerk" in pencil.

VAN ROSSEM, Ru, Hon. Mem., Academy of Fine Arts, Florence; Premio Milano (1988); Euro-medal in gold, Bonn; Gold Medal Biennale, Perugia; M.A.I. International Graphic Prize, Biennales Gorizia, Italy, Malbork, Poland; Head of Graphic Department, Tilburg Academy of Fine Art, Holland; *b* Amsterdam, 19 Mar., 1924; *s* of Karl van Rossem; *m* 1st Miriam Pollock (decd.); two *s,* one *d; m* 2nd Marianne van Dieren; one *s. Educ.:* Rijksmuseumschool of Fine Art; Grammar School, Zaandam. *Exhib.:* most European countries and U.S.A. *Work in permanent collections:* Rijksmuseum and Municipal Museum, Amsterdam, Boymans Museum, Rotterdam, Bibliothèque Nationale, Paris, Museum of Modern Art, New York, National Museum, Cracow, Cincinnati Museum, etc. *Work repro.:* biography written by Frans Duister (1977). *Address:* Burg, Vonk de Bothstr. 54, Tilburg, Holland. *Signs work:* "Ru Van Rossem."

VEALE, Anthony McKenzie; self taught painter in oil and acrylic, sculptor (surrealist and figurative work) in bronze and wood, also abstract painting and minimalist work; *b* Tonbridge, 20 Oct., 1941; *m* Susan; one *s,* two *d. Educ.:* Sevenoaks School. *Exhib.:* Tryon Gallery (1979), 20th Century Gallery (1985), Mall Galleries (1992). *Publications:* cartoon illustrations: 'Hippo, Potta and Muss' (Chatto, Boyd & Oliver U.K., 1969), 'A Lemon Yellow Elephant called Trunk' (Harvey House Inc. U.S.A., 1970). *Address:* Buckstone House, Upton Hellions, nr. Crediton, Devon EX17 4AE. *Signs work:* "Tony Veale," "Anthony Veale" or "A.V."

VENNING, Virginia, S.W.A.; sculptor in stone, wood, clay for bronze, terracotta, including portrails; painter in water-colour; *b* London, 1913; *d* of John Venning, M.C.; *m* Capt. E. D. T. Churcher, C.B.E., R.N. (decd.). *Educ.:* privately; *studied art* in Paris and Florence; Regent St. Polytechnic (1931), R.A. Schools (1934-39). *Exhib.:* R.A. Summer Exhbn. (from 1933), S.W.A. Annual. *Work in permanent collections:* wood and stone carvings for churches, (mostly in Somerset) and other buildings, portraits. Bronze panels in Buckingham St., London. *Address:* 26 Bimport, Shaftesbury, Dorset SP7 8AZ. *Signs work:* "V.M. Venning."

VERDIJK, Gerald, Silver Medal, Prix Europe (1966), Maris Prize (1964, 1967); painter; *b* Boxmeer, Holland, 1934. *Exhib.:* one-man shows: Galerie Gunar, Düsseldorf, Galerie Orez, The Hague (1961, 1962, 1964, 1965, 1967, 1971, 1979), Galerie Potsdammer, Berlin, Casino Ostende, Museum Municipal, The Hague (1967), Von der Heidt Museum, Wuppertal (1968), Galerie Palette, Zürich Galerie Lock St. Gallen (1984), Groninger Museum (1970), Gemeente Museum, The Hague (1972), Galerie Peccolo Livorno (1978), Galerie La Citta, Verona, Galerie La Polena, Geneva, Galerie Jeanneret, Geneva (1979), Galerie Artline Den. Haag, Galerie E. München (1981); Abbemuseum Eindhoven (1985), Stedelijk Museum, Amsterdam 1993 (retrospective); group shows: Amsterdam, Delft, The Hague, Berlin, Wuppertal, Brussels, Belfast, Dublin, Cork; Bienale de Paris (1961), World Fair, Montreal (1967), London, Liverpool, Paris, Stockholm, Los Angeles, Frankfurt, Tokyo, Copenhagen. *Work in permanent collections:* Museums of The Hague, Schiedam, Brussels, Wuppertal, London, Ostend, Rotterdam. *Address:* "Les Places" Marcillac-St. Quentin, par 24200 Sarlat, Dordogne, France. *Signs work:* see appendix.

VERGE, Norman Welby, B.A. (1970); painter in oil and acrylic; lecturer, Eastbourne C.F.E.; *b* Whitefish, Montana, U.S.A., 22 May, 1931; *s* of Norman Harold Verge; *m* Daphne Elizabeth Rogers. *Educ.:* Marist Brothers High School, Port Elizabeth, S.A.; *studied art* at Queen's College, City University of N.Y., Arizona State University, Arizona School of Art, Art Students' League. *Exhib.:* Tempe Civic Centre, Mountain Shadows, Scottsdale, U.S.A., Harrow Library, Upper Street Gallery, Eastbourne Library, Brighton Museum and A.G. *Address:* 5 Mayfair Ct., Wish Hill, Willingdon, E. Sussex BN20 9HE. *Signs work:* "VERGE" or "NORMAN WELBY VERGE" or "N. WELBY VERGE."

VERITY, Colin, A.R.I.B.A. (1965), R.S.M.A. (1975); architect, artist in oil, water-colour and gouache; retd. principal architect, Humberside C.C., Pres., Hornsea Art Soc., Mem. Fylingdales Group of Artists (N. Yorks.), Guild of Aviation Artists; *b* Darwen, Lancs., 7 Mar., 1924; *s* of Thomas Verity; *m* Stella Elizabeth Smale; one *s,* three *d. Educ.:* Malet Lambert High School, Hull and privately; *studied art* at Hull School of Architecture. *Exhib.:* R.S.M.A., Mystic Maritime Gallery, Connecticut, U.S.A., Francis Iles Gallery, Rochester, Ferens Gallery, Hull. *Work in permanent collections:* National Maritime Museum, Greenwich, Sultanate of Oman, Ben Line, Harrison Line, P. & O. Line, Town Docks Museum, Hull, — 16 countries. *Address:* Melsa, Meaux, Beverley, E. Yorks. HU17 9SS. *Signs work:* "Colin Verity."

VERNON-CRYER, Joan, A.R.C.A., R.W.S. (1970); painter in water-colour; *b* Blackburn, 21 Mar., 1911; *d* of Harold Cryer; *m* W. Fairclough; one *s,* one *d. Educ.:* Blackburn High School and Blackburn Technical College; *studied art* at Royal College of Art (Painting School). *Exhib.:* Hunting Group Competition, Mall Galleries (1990), Sunday Times Water-colour Exhbn., Mall Galleries, Glasgow Cultural Year (1990). *Work repro.:* in Old Water-colour Society's volumes, Visions of Venice (Michael Spender, 1990); Water-colour Drawings and Artists Magazine (1991). *Address:* 12 Manorgate Rd., Kingston-upon-Thames, Surrey. *Signs work:* "Joan Vernon-Cryer."

VERRALL, Nicholas Andrew, N.D.D. (1965); artist in oil, pastel, water-colour, etching and litho; *b* Northampton, 4 Jan., 1945; *s* of R.E. Verrall, civil servant; *m* Alayne Page; one *s*, one *d*. *Studied art* at Northampton College of Art (1960-65). Full-time artist since 1970. *Prizes:* R.W.S. Barcham Green Prize for Water-colour, Royal Horticultural Grenfell Medal, R.A. Committee Prize from B.A.T. *Exhib.:* R.A., R.W.S., R.E., R.B.A. and N.E.A.C.; mixed shows: Tryon Gallery, R.A. Upstairs Gallery, Abbott & Holder, Gallery 10; one-man shows: Upper Grosvenor, Langton Gallery Chelsea, Railings Gallery, Scene Gallery and Catto Gallery. *Work in permanent collections:* City of London, B.A.T. Coll., Crown Life, Painshill Park Trust, Coys of Kensington. Private collections in Britain, France, America and Japan. *Address:* The Orchard, Ivy La., Woking, Surrey GU22 7BY. *Signs work:* "N Verrall."

VICARY, Richard Henry, R.E., R.W.A.; printmaker, (woodcuts etc.), painting, typography; late Head Printmaking Dept., Shrewsbury School of Art; *b* Sutton, Surrey, 1918; *s* of Simon Jesty, author; *m* Deirdre Vicary; one *s*, one *d*. *Educ.:* Judd School, Tonbridge; Medway School of Art (1936-39); Brighton College of Art (1946); Camberwell School of Art and Crafts; Central School of Art. *Exhib.:* A.I.A., Whitechapel, R.W.S., R.W.A. (Bristol) and many private galleries. *Work in permanent collections* of various Universities and Education Authorities. *Publications:* Manual of Lithography and Manual of Advanced Lithography, (Thames & Hudson, 1976, 1977). *Address:* The Holding, Dunns Heath, Berwick, Shrewsbury, SY4 3HY. *Signs work:* "Richard Vicary."

VICARY, Stephen, B.A. (Hons.) Fine Art; artist in acrylic, mixed media, 'mail art'; co Founder/Director 'Two-Part-Art'; *b* Birkenhead, 26 June, 1957; *s* of Francis Edward Vicary. *Educ.:* Pershore House School, Wirral; *studied art* at Wirral College of Art and Design (1981-82), Stourbridge College of Art (1982-85). *Exhib.:* 1981-91: Gt. Britain, Belgium, Italy, Germany, Poland, U.S.S.R., Japan, U.S.A., Canada, France, Spain, Yugoslavia. *Work in permanent collections:* Williamson Museum and A.G., Birkenhead, and private collections nationally and internationally. *Address:* Grange Cottage, Grafton Walk, West Kirby, Wirral L48 7EF. *Signs work:* "S.V." on reverse of works.

VIEIRA DA SILVA, Marie-Hélène; artist in oil, water-colour, gouache and tempera; *b* Lisbon, 1908; *d* of Marcos; *m* Arpad Szenes. *Studied art* under Bourdelle, Despiau, Dufresne, Friesz F. Léger, Bissière and Hayter. *Work in permanent collections:* Paris, Grenoble, Lyon, Rouen, Nantes, Marseille (8), London, New York, Amsterdam, Rotterdam, Bâle, Lausanne, São Paulo, Rio de Janeiro, Essen, Mannheim, Düsseldorf, Washington, Helsinki, Oslo, Aalborg, Turin, Venice. *Work repro.:* Kô et Kô (1933); Editions Jeanne Bucher; L'Inclémence Lointaine; Poemes de R. Char. Commandeur de l'Ordre des Arts et des Lettres. Grand Croix de l'Ordre de Sant Iago a Espada. Prix National des Arts, Paris (1963). Prix International de Peinture Biennale de São Paulo (1961). Grand Prix Florence Gould (1986). Naturalisée Française (1956). *Address:* c/o Guy Weelen, 8 Ave. Frochot, Paris 9°. *Signs work:* "Vieira da Silva."

VOLLER, Peter Robert; painter in oils, acrylic polymer and painted paper collage; *b* Fleet, Hants., 26 Sept., 1943; *m* Tessa Philpot; two *s*, one *d*. *Studied art* at Farnham School of Art. *Exhib.:* R.A., London and provinces. *Address:* 53 The Street, Wrecclesham, Farnham, Surrey GU10 4QS. *Signs work:* "Voller" or "Peter Voller."

von HARTMANN, Sylvia, D.A. (Edin.) (1965), Post. Dip. (1966), R.S.W. (1983); artist in wax; *b* Hamburg, Germany, 8 Dec., 1942; *d* of Wolf von Hartmann, merchant; *m* Hamish Dewar; one *s*, one *d*. *Educ.:* Walddoerfer Schule, Hamburg-Volksdorf; *studied art* at Werkkunstschule, Hamburg (1961-63), Edinburgh College of Art (1963-66). *Exhib.:* R.A., R.S.A. Edinburgh, R.S.W., R.G.I.F.A., The Scottish Gallery, Edinburgh, National Trust of Scotland, Grosvenor Gallery, London, Open Eye Gallery, Edinburgh, etc. *Work in permanent collections:* Scottish Arts Council, Scottish National Gallery of Modern Art, City of Edinburgh Art Collection, Dundee Museum and Art Galleries, National Westminster Bank, Edinburgh, The Royal Infirmary, Edinburgh. *Publications:* Living Light, Books II and III (Holmes McDougall), The Scots Magazine (June, 1984), The Green Book Press Ltd., Bath. *Address:* Rhododendron House, 5 Whitehorse Cl., Canongate, Edinburgh EH8 8BU. *Signs work:* "Sylvia von Hartmann."

W

WADDELL, Heather, M.A. St. Andrews (1972), D.F.A. (1976); author, photographer, art critic; *b* Scotland, 1950. *Exhib.:* Battersea Arts Centre (1979), N.S.W. House A.G., (1980), ACME Studio (1977-80). International Visual Artists Exchange Programme (1978). *Articles on art:* Artline, Artnews, Art and Australia, The Artist, Art Monthly, Glasgow Herald (1978-84), London correspondent, Vie des Arts (1979-89), The Independent, The European. *Publications:* author/photographer: London Art and Artists Guide (6th ed. 1993); co-author, The Artists Directory (3rd edn. 1988); photographer: Glasgow Arts Guide, N.P.G. 20th c. Archives; contributor: Encyclopaedia of London (Macmillan), Henri Goetz Catalogue (1986), Time Out Publications (1990). *Address:* 27 Holland Park Ave., London W11 3RW.

WADSWORTH, Freda Muriel, M.B.E. (1979), F.M.A.A. (1968), F.F.P.S. (1984); painter of geometrical abstracts, using unique technique in gouache; lecturer in medical art, University of London (1956-79); Hon. Newsletter Editor, F.P.S.; *b* London, 31 Jan., 1918; *d* of Sydney Herbert Wadsworth. *Educ.:* Vardean School, Brighton; *studied art* at Brighton School of Art (1935-39, Charles Knight, R.W.S.). *Exhib.:* one-man shows: Loggia Gallery (1979, 1982, 1985, 1988); numerous London group shows including Mall Galleries and the Barbican. *Address:* 11 Burnham Ct., Moscow Rd., London W2 4SW. *Signs work:* "Freda Wadsworth."

WADSWORTH, Hilda Marjorie, F.F.P.S. (1988); painter in gouache of 17th and 18th c. architectural and sculptural features in historic parks and gardens; design and display executive, British Cellophane Ltd. (1949-71), free-lance design (1972-80), Hon. sec. F.P.S. (1981-87); Hon. pro. F.P.S.; *b* London, 5 July, 1911; *d* of Sydney Herbert Wadsworth. *Educ.:* Brighton Polytechnic (1927-29); *studied art* at Brighton School of Art (1929-34, Charles Knight, R.W.S.). *Exhib.:* solo shows: Loggia Gallery (1988, 1992); group shows in London at Mall Galleries, Barbican, Loggia Gallery. *Address:* 11 Burnham Ct., Moscow Rd., London W2 4SW. *Signs work:* "M. Wadsworth."

WALBOURN, Peter, U.A. (1982); portrait painter in oil and water-colour; *b* Chingford, 22 Aug., 1910; *s* of Ernest Walbourn, R.B.A.; *m* Gweneth; one *d*. *Educ.:* Bishop's Stortford; *studied art* Heatherleys, R.A. Schools (1928-32, Gerald Kelly, Walter Russel, Gerald Brockhurst, Fredrick Whiting). *Exhib.:* R.P.. R.O.I., U.A., P.S. *Work in permanent collections:* Old Bailey, Middle Temple, University of Coleraine, American, Arab and Iranian banks. *Commissions:* portraits: H.M. Queen Elizabeth the Queen Mother for Middle Temple; Lord Denning, Master of the Rolls; Sir Hugh Wontner, Lord Mayor of London; The Duke of Abercorn and Sir Wilfred Cockcroft, Chancellors of universities; Sir James Steel and Col. Ingleton-Webber, High Sheriffs of counties; etc. *Address:* 1 Fair Green, Sawbridgeworth, Herts. CM21 9AG. *Signs work:* "Peter Walbourn."

WALDRON, Dylan Thomas, B.A.Hons.; artist in egg tempera, pencil and water-colour; *b* Newcastle-under-Lyme, 21 Aug., 1953; *s* of Jack L. Waldron, sculptor and lecturer in fine art. *Educ.:* King Edward VI Grammar School, Stourbridge; *studied art* at Stourbridge College of Art (1971-72), Wolverhampton Polytechnic, Faculty of Art and Design (1972-76). *Exhib.:* R.A. Summer Exhbn. (1983 to 1993), regular exhibitor at Piccadilly Gallery, Cork St., London. *Work in permanent collection:* West Midlands Arts. *Address;* 2 Hallaton Rd., Slawston, nr. Market Harborough, Leics. LE16 7UA. *Signs work:* "Dylan Waldron" paintings initialled "D.W."

WALKER, Edward Donald; marine artist in oil, publisher; owner, Sumar Publications; *b* 2 Aug., 1937; *s* of A.E. Walker, ship constructor; *m* Susan; one *s,* one *d. Educ.:* Warbreck School, Liverpool; *studied art* at Liverpool College of Art (1950-56). *Exhib.:* R.S.M.A., Paris Salon, Talbot Gallery, Ethos Gallery, Lancs., Harrods London, Fulmar Gallery, N. Wales, and galleries throughout U.S.A. *Work in permanent collections:* Liverpool Museum and private collections world-wide. *Address:* 1 Richmond Grove, Lydiate, Merseyside L31 0BL. *Clubs:* Liverpool Nautical Research Soc., Fine Art Trade Guild. *Signs work:* "E.D. Walker."

WALKER, Jeffery, Dip. (1982), B.A.Hons. (1985), S.D-C. (1985), F.P.S. (1989), I.S.A.S.T. (1991); painter in oil, charcoal and computer; P/T lecturer, Farnham, Worthing, Bournemouth and Winchester; *b* Scunthorpe, 11 May, 1962. *Educ.:* Brumby Comprehensive, N. Lindsey Technical College, Lincoln College; *studied art* at Grimsby College (1982), Brighton Polytechnic (1985). *Exhib.:* De Richter Gelder, Arnhem (1989), Diamond Valley, Australia (1989), Barbican (1991), Erte, Czechoslovakia, Wroclaw, Poland, Leningrad, U.S.S.R. *Address:* 41 Waldegrave Rd., Brighton, E. Sussex BN1 6GR. *Signs work:* "J.W." and usually signed and dated on back.

WALKER, Richard Ian Bentham, N.D.D. (1947), A.T.D. (1949); Mem. United Soc. of Artists, Armed Forces Art Soc., Soc. of Graphic Fine Arts; portrait and landscape painter; teacher of oil painting, Croydon Art School (1948-53); *b* Croydon, 18 Mar., 1925; *s* of Norman Walker, I.C.S., deceased. *Educ.:* Canford School, Dorset; Queen's College, Oxford; *studied art* at Croydon School of Art (1945-48), London University (1949), Slade School. *Exhib.:* R.A., R.P., R.B.A., R.O.I., Paris Salon, Imperial Institute, etc.; one-man shows, Oxford, Croydon, Mall Galleries (1978), Alpine Galleries (1981). *Work in permanent collections:* Portraits of: Dr. Herbert Howells for Royal College of Music (1972); A. K. Chesterton (1973); Sir Reginald Wilson for the Brompton Hospital; Sir Thomas Holmes Sellors for the Middlesex Hospital; C.B. Canning (1989), John Hardie (1990), Ian Wallace (1991), all for Canford School. *Official* *purchase:* London panorama, Museum of London (1978). *Publications:* drawings of Stokowski, Havergal Brian, etc., published Triad Press, London (1971-73); illustrations to C. Palmer's biography of Herbert Howells (1993). *Address:* Lisvane, 72 Coombe Rd., Croydon CR0 5SH. *Signs work:* "RICHARD WALKER" and see appendix.

WALKER, Roy, A.R.E. (1975); painter/etcher; Director, Print Workshop, Penwith Society of Arts, St. Ives, Cornwall; *b* Welling, Kent, 25 Aug., 1936; *s* of Edwin James Walker; *m* Margaret Anne Walker; two *s*, one *d. Studied art* at Gravesend School of Art (1951-52), Regent St. Polytechnic (1952-54); Central School of Art (1957-60). *Exhib.:* one-man shows: Camel Gallery, Wadebridge, Orion Gallery, Penzance, Plymouth Art Centre; three-man show: Marlborough Graphics; joint shows: Penwith Society of Arts, Wills Lane Gallery, St. Ives, Newlyn Gallery. *Work in permanent collection:* Print Room, V. & A. *Addresses:* Warwick House, Sea View Terr., St. Ives; Studio: 6 Porthmeor Studios, Back Rd. West, St. Ives. *Signs work:* "Roy Walker."

WALKLIN, Carol, A.R.C.A. (1953), F.R.E. (1986); graphic artist and relief printmaker; *m* Colin Walklin, A.R.C.A., M.C.S.D. Freelance illustrator and tutor-lecturer in printmaking, general art subjects. *Studied art* at Beckenham School of Art and Royal College of Art. *Exhib.:* widely in U.K. including Bankside Gallery and R.A. Summer Exhbns. *Work in private collections:* U.K., U.S.A., Europe and the Far East. *Commissions:* British Council, BBC T.V. 'Jackanory', Post Office U.K. (stamp designs and air letters). *Address:* 2 Thornton Dene, Beckenham, Kent BR3 3ND. *Signs work:* "Walklin."

WALLER, Jonathan Neil, B.F.A. (Hons.), M.A. (Painting); artist in oil and charcoal; *b* Stratford upon Avon, 16 Apr., 1956; *s* of Douglas Waller. *Educ.:* Cherry Orchard High, Northampton, Northampton Grammar School; *studied art* at Nene College, Northampton (1979-80), Coventry (Lanchester) Polytechnic (1980-83), Chelsea School of Art (1984-85). *Exhib.:* one-man shows: Paton Gallery, London (1986, 1988), Flowers East, London (1990); group shows: 1984: New Contemporaries, I.C.A. London, Midland View 3 (major prizewinner), 1988: London, Glasgow, N.Y., Metropolitan Museum, N.Y., New British Painting, Cincinnati (touring), 1989: The Thatcher Years, Flowers East, 1991: Kunst Europa, Karlsruhe, Germany. *Publication:* Jonathan Waller (Flowers East, 1990). *Address:* Basement Flat, 166 Amhurst Rd., London E8 2AZ. *Signs work:* "J.W.92."

WALLER, Margaret Mary, F.I.A.L. (1958, mem. of Council), A.T.D., Mem. Liverpool Academy (1953); painter in oils, portrait, landscape, and decorative church work in gold leaf, also water-colour and egg tempera; *b* Yorks., 13 Nov., 1916; *d* of Arthur Basset Waller; *m* Stephen Bryant, 1989. *Educ.:* Friary Convent School (Venice), Belvedere School (Liverpool); *studied art* at Liverpool College of Art (1934-37) and R.A. schools (1937-39). *Exhib.:* R.A., S.W.A., R.P., Paris Salon, Funchal, Madeira (1992); executed Altar-piece for the Chapel of St. John, Guernsey (1960); also large decorative panels for St. Stephen's Church (1964). Invited to U.S.A. (1986) to give exhbn. of water-colours. Commissioned to paint in St. Malo, France (1993). *Addresses:* Les Sauterelles, St. Jacques, Guernsey; Mayfield Studio, Sark. *Clubs:* Sandon Studios Soc. (Liverpool), Reynolds (London). *Signs work:* "MARGARET WALLER."

WALPOLE, Josephine Ailsa; artist specialising in flower painting and botanical illustration; *b* Cockfield, Suffolk, 27 Apr., 1927; *d* of Joseph James Horn; *m* Derek Walpole; one *s. Educ.:* East Anglian School for Girls, Bury St. Edmunds; Notre Dame High School, Norwich; *studied art* privately under Stuart

Somerville. *Exhib.:* London and East Anglia. *Publications:* 'Anna' Memorial, Biography of Anna Zinkeisen; Biography of Leonard Squirrell, R.W.S., R.E.; Leonard Squirrell, Etchings and Engravings; Life and Work of Martin Kidner; Vernon Ward (Biography); 'Roses in a Suffolk Garden'. *Address:* The Green House, 15 Cooper's Rd., Martlesham Heath, Ipswich, Suffolk. *Signs work:* "J. Walpole."

WALTON, Barbara Louise, M.F.A. (Hons.) (1981), Post.Grad. Dip. Painting and Drawing (1982); painter in oil and acrylic paint on canvas and paper; *b* Bishop Auckland, 30 Dec., 1955; *d* of Martin and Mavis Walton, teachers; *m* Dursun Cilingir, doctor. *Educ.:* Queen Anne Grammar School; *studied art* at Edinburgh University/College of Art (Elizabeth Blackadder, David Michie). *Exhib.:* York University (1982), Gloucester College of Art (1983), Paisley Art Inst. drawing competition (1987), N.P.G. portrait competition (1987, 1989), Mall Galleries Open (1989); solo shows: Mercury Gallery (1988, 1993), Grape Lane Gallery, York (1989); regular exhib. with Mercury Gallery since 1986. *Address:* 31 St. John's Rd., Exeter EX1 2HR. *Signs work:* "B.L. Walton"

WALTON, John, D.F.A. (Lond. 1949), R.P. (1976); portrait painter in oil and tempera; Principal, Heatherley School of Fine Art, London; Governor, Federation of British Artists, Mem., Royal Soc of Portrait Painters; *b* Birkenhead, 5 Dec., 1925; *s* of Eric Walton; divorced; two *s*, one *d*. *Educ.:* Birkenhead School, Edge Grove School, Aldenham School; *studied art* at Ruskin School of Fine Art (1944-45, Albert Rutherston), Slade School of Fine Art (1945-49, Randolph Schwabe). *Exhib.:* R.A., R.P., Paris Salon (Hon. mention), Academie des Beaux Arts, Institut de France. *Address:* 30 Park Rd., Radlett, Herts. *Club:* Chelsea Arts. *Signs work:* "John Walton."

WARBURTON, Joan; artist in oils, of landscape and still-life, wash drawings, gouache and pastels; *b* 17 Apr., 1920, in Edinburgh; *m* Peter O'Malley, Des.R.C.A., potter; one *s*. *Studied art* with Oswald Poreau in Brussels (1936-37); East Anglian School of Painting, Dedham, Essex, under Cedric Morris (1937-39). *Exhib.:* R.A., S.E.A., W.I.A.C.; one-man shows, Foyles (1959), Ansdell Gallery (1968), Chateau du Tremblay (1975), Hintlesham Hall (1976), Parkin Fine Arts (1978), Falcon House Gallery (1980), Tradescant Trust (1982), Quay Theatre (1983), Parkin Fine Arts (1984), The Minories (1987), Sally Hunter Fine Art (1992). *Official purchases:* Rugby Art Gallery (1947), Hull Educ. Com. (1953), Derby Educ. Com. (1952), Lancashire Educ. Com. (1968), Herts. Educ. Com. *Work repro.:* Studio, Sphere, Field, Vogue, Arts Review and Country Life. *Address:* The White House, Stoke-by-Nayland, nr. Colchester. *Signs work:* "J.W."

WARBURTON, Stanley, A.M.C.T. (1944); artist in water-colour and oil, retd. lecturer in engineering; Chairman, Turner Society; *b* 19 Mar., 1919; *s* of Harry Warburton, draughtsman; *m* Sheila Lomas; one *s*. *Educ.:* Central School, Heywood, and College of Technology, Manchester; *studied art* at School of Art, Bury. *Exhib.:* R.B.A., Manchester Academy of Fine Arts; ten one-man shows; exhib. in over fifty provincial galleries. *Work in permanent collections:* Bury, Rochdale, Royal Leamington Spa and Blackburn A.G's., Bankfield Museum, Halifax, Towneley Hall A.G., Burnley. *Work repro.:* illustrated, The Dalesman Magazine. *Address:* 46 Meadway, Rochdale. *Clubs:* P.P., Rochdale Art Soc., V.P., Bury Art Soc. *Signs work:* "S. Warburton."

WARD, Gordon, D.F.A. Lond., R.W.A.; artist in all mediums; formerly Head of Painting, Gloucestershire College of Arts and Technology; *b* N. Walsham, Norfolk, 1932; *s* of William Ward; *m* Maureen Liddell; one *s*, two *d*. *Educ.:*

Paston Grammar School, N. Walsham, Norfolk; *studied art* at Norwich School of Art (1949-53), Slade School of U.C.L. (1955-57). *Work in permanent collections:* Royal West of England Academy, Robert Fleming Holdings, The Royal Bank of Scotland, Prudential Assurance and various private collections in Europe, America and Australia. *Address:* 131 Hales Rd., Cheltenham, Glos. GL52 6ST. *Signs work:* "GORDON WARD" and date.

WARD, Joan, A.R.C.A. (1949), N.S. (1979); sculptor in resins, wood, stone, etc.; *b* London, 10 Jan., 1925; *d* of F. N. Palmer, L.D.S., R.C.S.Eng.; *m* T. W. Ward; one *s*,one *d. Educ.:* Croydon High School for Girls; *studied art* at Bromley Art School, Royal College of Art (1945-48, Willi Soukop, Frank Dobson). *Exhib.:* R.B.A, N.E.A.C., N.S., Coach House Gallery, C.I. (1987); group exhbns. in London Parks and Questers, Ealing. *Address:* Hollydene, Ipswich Rd., Holbrook, nr. Ipswich, Suffolk. *Club:* N.S. *Signs work:* "Joan Ward."

WARD, J. S., A.R.C.A., V.P.R.P., R.A.; painter in oil and water-colour; *b* Hereford, 1917; *s* of Russel Stanton Ward; *m* Alison Ward; four *s*, two *d. Educ.:* St. Owens School, Hereford; *studied art* at R.C.A. under Gilbert Spencer. *Work in permanent collections:* H.M. the Queen, N.P.G., R.A., Preston A.G., Maas Gallery, Hereford. *Publications:* Alphonse by George Ward; Cider with Rosie by Laurie Lee; Little Kingdom by Richard Church; Autobiography of H. E. Bates. *Address:* Bilting Ct., Bilting, nr. Ashford, Kent. *Club:* Athenæum. *Signs work:* "John Ward."

WARD, Margaret Hester; miniaturist in water-colour; Council mem. Hilliard Soc.; *b* Bampford, Derbyshire, 6 Aug., 1920; *m* Thomas Geoffrey Camden; three *s. Studied art* at Heatherley School of Art under the late Helen Wilson. *Exhib.:* R.A., H.S., Limners, S.M. *Address:* Higher Westways, Uplonman Rd., Tiverton, Devon EX16 4LU. *Signs work:* see appendix.

WARD, Nicholas, Dip.A.D. (1971), R.A. Schools (1974), R.E. (1992); artist and printmaker in etching and pencil; *b* Gt. Yarmouth, 10 Jan., 1950; *m* Elizabeth Somerville; one *s. Educ.:* Lowestoft County Grammar School; *studied art* at Lowestoft School of Art (1967-68), St. Martin's School of Art (1968-71, Alan Cooper, James Stroudley), R.A. Schools (1971-74, Denis Lucas, Peter Greenham). *Exhib.:* R.A. Summer Shows (1982, 1984-87, 1990), East Open (1991), R.E. Annual (1988-93), British Miniature Print (1989), Bradford Print Biennale (1990); one-man shows 1974-92. *Work in permanent collections:* Norfolk Museums, Ipswich Museum. *Address:* 38 Bulmer La., Winterton-on-Sea, Gt. Yarmouth, Norfolk NR29 4AF. *Signs work:* "N. Ward."

WARD, Thomas William, A.R.C.A. (1949), R.E. (1953), R.W.S. (1957); water-colour painter, draughtsman, etcher, illustrator of maritime subjects; one time Director of Studies (Illustration) Harrow C.H.E.; *b* Sheffield, 8 Nov., 1918; *s* of John B. Ward, master stationer; *m* Joan; one *s*, one *d. Educ.:* Nether Edge Grammar School, Sheffield; Sea Service 1936-37; *studied art* part time, Sheffield (1937-39, Eric Jones, A.R.C.A.); Military Service (1939-46); R.C.A. (1946-50, (Silver Medal 1949), R.S. Austin, R.A., Malcolm Osborne, R.A.). *Exhib:* Walker Gallery (1957-60), Wakefield City A.G. (1962), Shipley A.G. (1962), Middlesbrough A.G. (1963), St. John's College, York (1965), Bohun Gallery (1974, 1982), Digby Gallery (1981), Coach House Gallery, C.I. (1987), Bankside Gallery (1987). *Work in permanent collections:* National Gallery of New Zealand, V. & A., Oxford University Junior Common Room, S. London A.G. *Publications:* illustrated, Fast Sailing Ships, Merchant Sailing Ships 1775-1815, Merchant Sailing Ships 1815-1850, Merchant Sailing Ships 1850-1875, Schooners in Four Centuries (all by D.R. MacGregor), Country Life Book of Nautical

Terms under Sail. *Address:* Hollydene, Ipswich Rd., Holbrook, Ipswich IP9 2QT. *Signs work:* see appendix.

WARDEN, Peter Campbell, A.R.B.A. (1982), D.A. (1976), Post. Dip. (1977), award, Robert Colquhoun (1976); 1st prize Devon and Cornwall figurative art competition (1992); painter in oil, water-colour, pen, pencil; *b* Vancouver, Canada, 19 Mar., 1950; *s* of John Gordon Warden, B.A., B.Sc.; *m* Lorna Hawes; one *d. Educ.:* Windlesham House, Lancing College; *studied art* at Glasgow School of Art (1972-77, David Donaldson, Michael Roschlau). *Exhib.:* R.A., R.S.A., R.B.A., R.G.I., R.S.W., R.B.S.A.; one-man shows: Malaga, Marbella, Dumfries, Moffat. *Work in permanent collections:* Kilmarnock and Loudon D.C.; Sociedad Economica, Malaga. *Address:* 57 Sunrising Estate, E. Looe, Cornwall. *Signs work:* "Peter C. Warden."

WARDLE, Piers; artist in paint or other materials on canvas or wall; *b* Beckenham, 1960. *Studied art* at Exeter Art College (1976-77), Ruskin School of Drawing, Oxford (1977-80). *Exhib.:* one-man shows: Northcott Theatre, Exeter (1979), Acme Gallery, London (1981), Pomeroy Purdy Gallery, London (1989, 1990), Eastbourne Clark Gallery, Florida (1990), Bernard Baron Gallery, London (with Tim Long) (1990); group shows: Museum of Modern Art, Oxford (1982), London Group (1985), The Crypt, London (1987, 1988), Pomeroy Purdy Gallery (1988, 1990). *Work in permanent collection:* Courtauld Inst. Loan. *Media:* The Late Show B.B.C. TV (1990). *Publication:* Longinus and Stephaton: Limited Edn. book with Tim Long (1990). *Address:* c/o Pomeroy Purdy Gallery, At Jacob St. Film Studios, Mill St., London SE1 2BA. *Signs work:* "Piers Wardle" on back.

WARMAN, Oliver Byrne, R.B.A., R.O.I.; painter in oil of landscapes, houses, gardens, boats, cattle; Chief Executive, Federation of British Artists; Director, Arts News Agency (1983-92); *b* London, 10 June, 1932. Former regular officer Welsh Guards. *Educ.:* Stowe, Exeter University, Royal Military College of Science, Balliol College, Oxford; *studied art* at Exeter University. *Exhib.:* R.A., R.B.A., R.W.A., N.E.A.C., R.S.M.A., R.O.I. *Work in permanent collections:* Lancaster House, all major Banks, Sultan of Oman, Emir of Kuwait, American Embassy. *Address:* Le Moulin de la Roque, 50210 Montpinchon, France. *Clubs:* Cavalry and Guards, Chelsea Arts, Royal Cornwall Yacht, Arts. *Signs work:* "O.B.W." or "Oliver Warman."

WARMAN, Sylvia (Mrs.), Ass. des A. Francais; portrait sculptor and painter; Wells Prize in Fine Art Reading University (1952); Owen Ridley Prize in Fine Art Reading University (1954); Bronze Medal (Sculpture) Paris Salon (1969); Silver Medal (Sculpture) Paris Salon (1973); Gold Medal Accademia Italia (1981); Hon. Sec. National Society Painters, Sculptors Printmakers (1978-83) Vice-President (1984/5); *b* St. Leonards on Sea, Sussex; *m* J. Royce Warman; three *d. Studied art:* Reading University (1947-54). *Exhib.:* various including R.A., West of England R.A., five times Paris Salon. *Address:* 1 Chester St., Caversham, Reading RG4 8JH.

WARNER, Robert; artist in oil and water-colour; *b* Colchester, 14 Sept., 1947. *Studied art* at Colchester School of Art (1964-71, John Nash, Peter Coker). *Exhib.:* R.O.I., N.E.A.C., R.I., R.A. (1974-84, 1986, 1988, 1991, 1992, 1993), Athena Art Awards (1987), Hunting Group (1988), Sunday Times Exhbns. (1988, 1990, 1992), Laing Art Competition (1990, 1991, 1992), Mall Galleries, prizewinner 32nd Essex Open and 35th best water-colour; one-man shows: The Minories, Colchester (1973), Mercury Theatre (1972, 1980, 1985). *Work in permanent collection:* Epping Museum, private collections in Britain and

America. *Address:* St. Elmer, Queens Rd., W. Bergholt, Colchester, Essex CO6 3HE. *Club:* Colchester Art. Soc. *Signs work:* "R. Warner."

WARNES, Robin, B.A.(Hons), R.A. Schools Cert. (Postgrad.); painter in oil, charcoal, pastel, acrylic, pencil; David Murray Studentship, Turner Gold medal for Landscape Painting (1980), regional prize winner, Laing Landscape Exhbn. (1990); Artist in Residence, Ipswich Museums and Galleries (1989-90); *b* Ipswich, 13 Mar., 1952; *m* Vanessa; two *s*, one *d. Studied art* at Ipswich School of Art (1972-74, Colin Moss), Canterbury College of Art (1974-77, Tom Watt), R.A. Schools (Peter Greenham, C.B.E., R.A.). *Exhib.:* R.A., Federation of British Artists, Laing Landscape, John Russell Gallery Ipswich, Cadogan Gallery London, Chappel Gallery Colchester. *Work in permanent collections:* Ipswich Borough Council, Suffolk C.C. *Address:* 77 Rosehill Rd., Ipswich, Suffolk IP3 8ET. *Signs work:* "R. Warnes" or "R.W."

WARREN, Charles Wyatt, D.L., J.P., D.P.A.; artist in oil; former Mem. N. Wales Assocn. for the Arts; Arts Society of Paddington; Caernarvon Art Group; founder sec., Caernarvon Art Club; former Chairman, North Wales Art Group; *b* Caernarvon, 15 Aug., 1908; *s* of Charles Wyatt Warren, artist and engraver; *m;* two *d. Educ.:* Caernarvon Grammar School; *studied art* self-taught. *Exhib.:* R.Cam.A., Royal National Eisteddfod of Wales, North Wales Group and several provincial exhbns.; 50 one-man exhbns., incl. New York and Toronto. *Address:* Lady Jane Residential Home, Bulls Cross, Slad, Glos. GL6 7HU. *Signs work:* see appendix.

WARREN, Michael John, N.D.D. (1958), S.WL.A. (1971); artist in acrylic; *b* Wolverhampton, 26 Oct., 1938; *s* of Herbert Leslie Warren; *m* Kathryne; one *s,* one *d. Educ.:* Wolverhampton Grammar School; *studied art* at Wolverhampton College of Art (1954-58). *Exhib.:* one-man shows, Moorland Gallery (1972, 1974, 1977, 1979), Carl Battaglia Galleries, N.Y. (1978), Barbican Art Centre (1984), Jane Neville Gallery (1988). Designed 1980 issue British Post Office stamps 'Birds'; designed Audubon U.S.A. stamps 1985-93. Designed 1990/1 issue Republic of Marshall Islands postage stamps. *Publication:* Shorelines. *Work in permanent collection:* S.W.A.N. *Bibliography;* 20th Century Wildlife Artists. *Address:* The Laurels, The Green, Winthorpe, Notts. NG24 2NR. *Signs work:* "warren" (paintings), "Michael Warren" (prints).

WASIM, L.; painter in oil and water-colours; nominated as an "Academic of Italy with Gold Medal" and Gold Plaque "Premio d'Italia 1986"; awarded Golden Centaur 1982 Prize with Gold Medal; and International Parliament U.S.A. Gold Medal of Merit; conferred Honoris Causa diploma "Master of Painting" from Salsomaggiore International Seminar of Modern and Contemporary Art, and Diploma of Merit from Italian University of Arts; Institute of Art Contemporer at Milano conferred the Great Gold Medal with the Institute's emblem in 24 carat gold on brass with box and relative certificate of merit for "Premio Milano 1988"; *b* Bandung, Java, 9 May, 1929. Graduated from The Central Academy of Arts, Beijing (1956). Instructor of Shanxi Provincial College of Fine Arts, Xian (1956-59). Court painter in Indonesian Presidential Palaces, Jakarta and Bogor (1961-67). Study tour in Asia and Europe (1975-80); participated several art exhbns. in Indonesia and Europe. *Work in permanent collections:* Indonesian Palaces Museums, Jakarta and Bogor; The Asia and Pacific Museum, Warsaw, etc. *Address:* Jalan Tavip V/6, Tanah Sereal Barat, Jakarta 11210, Indonesia. *Signs work:* "L. Wasim" and see appendix.

WATERFIELD, Ken, S.WL.A. (1972); landscape and wildlife artist in oil; *b* Watford, 7 Nov., 1927; *s* of George Waterfield; *m* Enid; two *s*, two *d. Studied* *art* at Watford School of Art (1940-43). *Exhib.:* Mall Galleries, Medici, Guildhall London, Southern Regional Galleries; major one-man show, Winchester City Gallery (1979). *Work in permanent collections:* Oxford C.C., King Alfred's College, Winchester. *Work repro.:* illus. profiles, R.S.P.B. Magazine 'Birds' (Autumn, 1978); Oxford Mail (28 Oct., 1976). Winner, Natural World Art Award (1988). *Address:* Plaintiles, Uploders, Bridport, Dorset DT6 4NR. *Signs work:* "Waterfield."

WATERS, Linda Mercedes, B.A.Hons. (1977); painter, illustrator and designer in water-colour, pen and ink, wood engraving; *b* Monmouthshire, 10 Nov., 1955; *d* of H. Ivor Waters, local historian and writer. *Educ.:* Chepstow School; *studied art* at Gwent C.H.E. Faculty of Art and Design, Newport (1974-77). *Exhib.:* Royal West of England Academy, Medici Gallery, Oriel Cardiff, etc. *Work in permanent collections:* historic reconstruction of Chepstow in Chepstow Museum; many private collections. *Publications:* several books illustrated. *Address:* 41 Hardwick Ave., Chepstow, Gwent NP6 5DS. *Signs work:* "Linda Waters" or "L. Waters."

WATKINS, Frances Jane Grierson (Peggy); oil, water-colour, pencil artist; jewellery; instructor silverwork and jewellery Hereford College of Art (1957-72); *b* 24 July, 1919; *d* of Thomas Vaughan Milligan, A.R.C.A.; *m* Rev. Alfred Felix Macironi Watkins; one *s,* one *d. Educ.:* Elms Private School, Herefordshire School of Art, Birmingham School of Jewellery. *Exhib.:* R.A., R.S.A., R.B.A., R.W.A., R.B.S.A., National Eisteddfod, Herefordshire Arts and Crafts. *Official purchases:* Lady Hawkins Grammar School; Agric. Exec. Com.; Hereford City Art Gallery; Hereford RDC (badge of office). *Address:* Leylines, 26 Southbank Rd., Hereford HR1 2TJ. *Signs work:* "PEGGY WATKINS."

WATSON, Arthur James, D.A., A.R.S.A.; sculptor/printmaker; Director, Peacock Printmakers, Aberdeen; Chairman, Richard Demarco Gallery; *b* Aberdeen, 6 June, 1951. *Educ.:* Aberdeen Grammar School; *studied art* at Grays School of Art, Aberdeen (1969-74). *Exhib.:* Venice Biennale (1990), New Directions, Sarajevo (1988). *Work in permanent collections:* Aberdeen A.G. and Museum, Aberdeen University, North of Scotland Hydroelectric Board. *Address:* 16 Pilot Sq., Footdee, Aberdeen AB2 1DS. *Signs work:* see appendix.

WATSON, Heather, A.R.M.S. (1992); miniaturist painter in water-colour on vellum; *b* Coventry, 10 Mar., 1939; *m* William James Egerton Smith. *Educ.:* Stoke Park School, Coventry. *Exhib.:* R.A., R.M.S., Llewellyn Alexander Gallery; solo shows: Dorset and N. Yorks. *Address:* Dale Cottage, Dale End, Kirkbymoorside, N. Yorks. YO6 6EQ. *Signs work:* see appendix.

WATSON-GANDY, Basia, B.A.Hons., S.W.A., I.P.A., Grollo d'Ora Silver Medal (1980), Gold Medal (1981); painter on china, porcelain and ceramics using glazes, lustres, goldwork; lecturer and researcher in the Industry; lecturer, Missenden Abbey; Founder Com. mem. and past president, B.C.P.A.A. Commissioned work in private collections throughout the world. *Publications:* many magazine articles; appearances on TV and radio. *Address:* Squirrel Court Studio, Hare La., Little Kingshill, Gt. Missenden, Bucks. HP16 0EF. *Clubs:* S.W.A., Confraternity of Polish Artists, Virginia Water Art Soc., Visual Images Group. *Signs work:* see appendix.

WATSON STEWART, (Lady) Avril Veronica, F.R.S.A. (1969), Hon.F.B.I.D. (1979), Hon.M.Aust.S.C. (1983); artist/calligrapher/lettering designer on vellum, glass, metals, stone; world wide lecturer; *b* Glasgow; *m* Sir James Watson Stewart, Bt. (decd. 1988). *Educ.:* Glasgow High School for Girls,

Glasgow and West of Scotland College of Commerce (now University of Strathclyde); *studied art* at Glasgow School of Art (1950, Prof. Colin Horsmann). *Exhib.:* California, Norfolk, Va., St. Andrews, Dunfermline, Greenock A.G., National Library of Scotland, Australia. *Work in permanent collections:* V. & A., and private collections. *Address:* Undercliff Court, Wemyss Bay. PA18 6AL, Scotland. *Signs work:* owl followed by maiden name – see appendix.

WATT, Gilbert, D.A. (1946), A.R.B.S. (1982), Landseer bronze medal; Cert. of Merit (R.A. 1952), Prix de Rome (1952); sculptor in clay, stone, steel, wood; *b* Aberdeen, 19 Sept., 1918; *s* of James Watt, master blacksmith; *m* Irene Mae. *Studied art:* Gray's School of Art, Aberdeen, under T.B. Huxley-Jones; R.A. Schools under Maurice Lambert; British School at Rome. *Exhib.:* R.A.; R.S.A.; Rome; Leicester Galleries; Royal Festival Hall; Arts Council Travelling Exhbn.; G.I.; Aberdeen A.G.; Scone Palace; Shakespeare Birthplace Trust Exhbn.; Taliesin Art Centre, Swansea University; one-man show, Inverurie, Aberdeenshire. *Work in permanent collections:* Britain, America, W. Germany, *Address:* Riverside, 4 Ellon Rd., Bridge of Don, Aberdeen AB2 8EA. *Signs work:* "Gilbert Watt."

WATTS, Mrs. Dorothy, S.W.A. (1952), Mem. Federation of British Artists; artist in water-colour; early years, fashion designer for London and Northern papers; *b* London, 3 Apr., 1905; *d* of S. C. Ravenshoe; *m* A. Gordon Watts, LL.B., solicitor. *Studied art* at Brighton College of Arts under J. Morgan Rendle, R.I., R.B.A. *Exhib.:* R.A., R.I., R.B.A., S.W.A., Britain in Water-colours and provincial galleries. *Work in permanent collection:* Hove Art Collection. *Work repro.:* in Londoner's England, various Christmas cards and in newspapers, London and provincial. *Address:* Southwoods, 65 Surrenden Rd., Brighton, Sussex BN1 6PQ. *Club:* S.W.A. *Signs work:* see appendix.

WATTS, Joan Alwyn, A.R.M.S.; portrait miniatures and water-colour landscapes; *b* Birmingham, 19 Dec., 1921; *d* of J. Lineker, sales manager; *m* Ronald O. Watts; one *s*, one *d*. *Educ.:* Birmingham College of Art. *Exhib.:* Birmingham Soc. of Artists, Royal Miniature Soc., Paris Salon, various exhbns. in America and Australia; permanent exhbn. Art Bureau, London. *Address:* Dial Cottage, Bannut Tree La., Bridstow, nr. Ross-on-Wye, Herefords.

WATTS, Meryl; colour woodcut artist; painter in oil and water-colour; modeller; *b* 1910; *d* of Charles I. Watts; *m* Prof. J. S. Allen, D.Litt., P.P.R.T.P.I. *Educ.:* Blackheath High School; Blackheath Art School (John Platt, James Woodford, R.A., Charles Paine, William Clause, Reginald Brill). *Exhib.:* R.A., New York World's Fair; Exhbn. of British Art 1735 to 1935, Vienna, Prague, etc.; British Council in most of the world's capitals; London Societies, etc. *Official purchases:* Contemporary Art Soc.; British Council; M. of E.; Prague; Baghdad, etc. *Work repro.:* in the Art Review. *Addresses:* 1 Bron-Avon, Borth-y-Gest, Porthmadog, Gwynedd, and Bleach Green Farm, Ovingham, Northumberland. *Signs work:* see appendix.

WATTS, Michael Gorse (otherwise PIKE, Septimus—cartoonist), A.R.I.B.A. (1965), M.F.P.S. (1989); artist, cartoonist, illustrator, in ink, acrylic, water-colour; *b* Stepney, London, 3 Dec., 1934; *s* of the late George Watts, O.B.E.; *m* Meg Wattson Dean; three *s*, one *d* by first marriage. *Educ.:* St. Edward's School; *studied art* at Oxford School of Technology and Art (1951-54), S.W. Essex School of Art (1960-62). *Exhib.:* Group, solo, etc., in London, the home counties and the provinces. Work in private collections at home and abroad. *Work repro.:* numerous articles, cartoons and illustrations. *Address:* 27 Sutherland St., London

SW1V 4JU. *Clubs:* Free Painters and Sculptors, Chichester, Lewisham, Selsey. *Signs work:* see appendix.

WATTS, Peter, F.R.B.S. (1970); sculptor in wood and stone; *b* Chilcompton, Bath, 12 Oct., 1916; *s* of Nevile Hunter Watts B.A., schoolmaster at Downside and author; *m* Anne Mary Coulson; two *s*, one *d*. *Educ.:* Downside School; *studied art* at Bath School of Art (1937) under Clifford Ellis, apprenticed (1938) to Lindsey Clark, F.R.B.S., in London; also at City and Guilds School of Art, Kennington (1938-39). *Principal commissioned works in U.K.:* Oban Cathedral (1951), St. Mary and St. Joseph's Church, Poplar, (1952), St. Mary's Church, Highfield St., Liverpool (1953), Bath Abbey, (West Front) (1959-60), Prinknash Abbey (1971), Downside Abbey (1974); in U.S.A.: Gethsemani Abbey, Kentucky (1955-64), St. John's Abbey, Collegeville, Minn. (1962), Sun of Justice Church, Benson, Vermont (1962-65), private collection of Mr. Chauncey Stillman, Amenia, N.Y. (1965-1970). *Address:* The Maltings, Wellow, Bath, Avon. BA2 8QJ. *Signs work:* carved monogram, see appendix.

WATTSON DEAN, Meg; specialist in miniatures and glass engraving; artist/ sculptor; *b* Luton, 11 Nov., 1929; *m* Michael Watts; one *s*, one *d*. *Educ.:* Bedford High School; *studied art:* Rolle College, Exmouth (1968-70). *Exhib.:* with R.M.S. (1989-92), Hilliard Soc., 'A Million Brushstrokes' at Llewellyn Alexander Gallery, Florida and Georgia Miniature Art Socs. (1991-93), Guild of Glass Engravers, Westminster Arts Council; two-person exhbns. with Michael Watts. *Work in permanent collections:* Chelsea and Westminster Hospital, private collections U.K. and U.S.A. *Address:* 27 Sutherland St., London SW1V 4JU. *Clubs:* Hilliard Soc., Guild of Glass Engravers, Chichester and Lewisham Art Socs. *Signs work:* "Meg Wattson Dean" and see appendix.

WAUGH, Eric, A.R.C.A. (1953), R.I. (1990); artist in water-colour; *b* London, 15 Dec., 1929. *Studied art* at Croydon School of Art (1946-50), R.C.A. (1950-53). *Exhib.:* Ashgate Gallery, Farnham (1965-67), Geffrye Museum (1968), Roland, Browse & Delbanco (1971), Arte Benimarco, Spain (1980), Galeria de Arte Denia, Spain (1981), Galeria de Arte Javea, Spain (1982), R.A., R.I., R.B.A., London Group, Sport in the Fine Arts, Madrid. *Work in private collections:* Mexico, U.S.A., Australia, Spain, U.K. *Publications:* articles written for various magazines; Painting in Acrylics — A Correspondence Course (Pitmans). *Address:* 9 Mead Rd., Edenbridge, Kent TN8 5DD. *Signs work:* "Eric Waugh."

WAUTERS, Jef; artist (painter); *b* B9910 Mariakerke, 26 Feb., 1927; *m* Denise D'hooge; one *s*, one *d*. Sup. Inst. St. Lucas and Academy of Fine Arts, Ghent. *Exhib.:* numerous one-man and group exhbns. *Private art collections:* New York, Chicago, San Francisco, Los Angeles, Paris, München, Brussels, Rome, Bern, The Haegue e.o. Diff. museums. *Publications:* Palet (300 numb. ex.), "Paris-Roma" sketch-book, (500 numbered ex.), Jef Wauters by J. Murez, Jef Wauters (Ed. Aro, Roma) by G. Selvaggi, Jef Wauters (ed. Arben Press Switzerland). *Addresses:* 7 Rode Beukendreef, 9831 St. Martens Latem, Belgium; 3 rue Chérubini, Paris 2. *Signs work:* see appendix.

WEBB, Elizabeth, A.R.C.M., (1953), G.R.S.M. (London) (1955); artist in oil on canvas or board; music teacher; *b* Fakenham, 7 Sept., 1931; *m* (1) Frank Rayer (decd.), (2) Graham Webb (decd.); two *s*. *Educ.:* The Park School, Yeovil; Royal College of Music, London; *studied art* at Evening Classes with Mary Bairds (1989-93). *Address:* La Guelle, Guelles Rd., St. Peter Port, Guernsey, C.I. GY1 2DE. *Signs work:* "Elizabeth Webb."

WEBB, Kenneth, N.D.D. (1952), A.T.D.Dist. (1953), N.S., F.R.S.A., A.R.U.A., A.R.W.A.; artist in oil and acrylic; head of Painting School, Ulster College of Art (1953-59); *b* London, 21 Jan., 1927; *s* of William George Webb; *m* Joan Burch; two *s*, two *d. Educ.:* Bristol Grammar School; Lydney Grammar School and School of Art; *studied art* at Gloucester College of Art (1948-52); University College, Swansea (1953). *Exhib.:* London and Dublin, Verhoff, Washington; one-man shows 1954 to 1987; group shows in Canada, U.S.A., Gt. Britain, Ireland, Holland, France, Spain and Italy. *Work in permanent collections:* Arts Councils of England, Wales, N. Ireland, Republic of Ireland, Courtauld, Carreras & Rothman, Haverty Trust, Ministry of Commerce, etc. *Publication:* Webb - Profile of an Artist by Thomas Kenny (Pub. 1990). *Address:* Portland House, Chagford, Devon TQ13 8AR. *Signs work:* "Webb."

WEBBER, Angela Mary, S.C.A.; painter and maker of religious images, writer on and tutor of animal painting; founder and secretary, S.S.S.A.; *b* London, 4 Jan., 1931; *d* of Ambrose Webber, shipping merchant; *m* Russell Arlen Bedingfield, art and antiques collector. *Studied art* at Hull College of Art (1949-52). *Exhib.:* O'Mell Gallery (1976), Solange de la Bruyere Gallery, Saratoga Springs, U.S.A. (1976-77), S.E.A. (1981), N.S. (1980), N.E.A.C. (1983). *Work in permanent collections:* Martin S. Vickers, Stella A. Walker, Miss Wiesenthall, U.S.A. *Work repro.:* The Webber Prints, Quartilles International, etc. *Address:* 2 Marina Cottage, Willingdon Lane, Jevington, Polegate, Sussex BN26 5QH. *Signs work:* "A. M. WEBBER."

WEBBER, Michael H., A.T.D.; Music Adviser, English Heritage; mem. Ben Uri Gallery; mem. International Assoc. of Art Critics; Concert promoter (Louis Armstrong and Duke Ellington Anniversary Concerts, etc); Chairman, London Lyric Orchestra; freelance writer, critic, journalist; Catalogues: East Anglian Art Today (1969), Artists in Camera (1972), Ipswich Arts Club Centenary Ex. (1975), "Critics Choice" (1983), Anna Airy Exhbn. (1985); *b* London, 30 June, 1926; *s* of Joseph E. Webber; *m* Miriam Broughton; two *d. Educ.:* Kilburn Grammar School (1937-43); *studied art* at Northampton School of Art; Chelsea School of Art; Central School of Arts. *Address:* 19 Netherhall Gardens, London NW3 5RL.

WEBSTER, John Robert, A.T.C., D.A.E.; W.A.C. travel grant to Ireland (1991); artist in etching, printmaking, gouache; senior lecturer, St. Mary's College, Bangor, N. Wales (1968-75); Dip. in Art Educ., Leeds University Inst. (1975-76); Lecturer in Art Educ., U.C.N.W. Bangor (1977-89); part-time Curator, U.C.N.W. Art Gallery (1982-); *b* Bridlington, E. Yorks., 22 May, 1934; *s* of Joe Webster, commercial traveller; *m* Dorothy Lloyd Webster; one *s*, four *d. Educ.:* Leeds G.S.; *studied art:* Leeds College of Art (1951-55-57). *Exhib.:* Mold, Conway (1969-), National Eisteddfod Llangefni (1983), Cardiff, Aberystwyth Open (from 1986), Birkenhead (1986), Anglesey Eisteddfod (1986), etc. *Work in permanent collection:* Schools Museum, Cardiff, D.O.E., National Library, Aberystwyth. *Address:* Tyfi' Cae, Paradwys, Bodorgan, Anglesey, Gwynedd LL62 5PF.

WEBSTER, Norman, R.W.S., R.E., A.R.C.A.; painter etcher; *b* Southend-on-Sea, 6 May, 1924; *s* of George W. Webster; *m* Joan W. Simpson, A.R.C.A.; three *s. Educ.:* Dover Grammar School; Tunbridge Wells School of Art (1940-43, E. Owen Jennings, R.W.S.); Royal Navy (1943-46); R.C.A. School of Engraving (1946-49, Malcolm Osborne, C.B.E., R.A., Robert Austin, R.A.). *Exhib.:* Painter Etchers, R.W.S., R.A., Yorkshire Artists at Leeds, Bradford, Wakefield and Hull City A.G.'s, with Yorkshire Printmakers in Britain, U.S.A.,

Israel and Canada. *Work in permanent collections:* Ashmolean Museum; Salford University; Leeds City A.G. and Arts Council of G.B. *Address:* 48 The Drive, Cross Gates, Leeds, LS15 8EP. *Signs work:* "Norman Webster."

WEEKS, John Lawrence Macdonald, L.R.M.S. (1984), A.R.M.S. (1987), F.N.C.M. (1984); artist in oil and water-colour; private music teacher and organist; *b* Chelmsford, 28 Apr., 1954. *Educ.:* Moulsham High School, Chelmsford; *studied art* at Colchester Inst. of H.E. (1973-74, John Buler). *Exhib.:* R.M.S. annual and one-man shows. *Address:* 47 Prescott, Hanworth, Bracknell, Berks. RG12 7RE. *Signs work:* name followed by date and device (see appendix).

WEGNER, Fritz, M.C.S.D., Mem. Art Workers' Guild; freelance artist, retired lecturer, St. Martin's School of Art; *b* Vienna, 15 Sept., 1924; *m* Janet Wegner; two *s*, one *d*. *Studied art* at St. Martin's School of Art. *Work repro.:* bookjackets and illustrations for British, American and Continental publishers; cover designs and illustrations for magazines; educational publications; G.P.O. Christmas and Anniversaries sets of stamps. Examples of work reproduced in several manuals on illustration. *Address:* 14 Swains Lane, London N6 6QS. *Club:* Chelsea Arts. *Signs work:* "Wegner."

WEIGHT, Carel, C.B.E. (1962), A.R.A. (elect., 1955), R.A. (1965), Hon. A.R.C.A. (1956), R.B.A., Mem. R.W.A. (1954), London Group (1950); painter in oil; Official War Artist (1945-46); Prof. Emeritus, Royal College of Art (1972); Trustee, Royal Academy (1975); *b* London, 10 Sept., 1908; *s* of Sidney L. Weight. *Educ.:* Sloane School, Chelsea; Hammersmith School of Art; Goldsmiths' College. *Exhib.:* one-man shows: retrospective at R.A. (1982), New Grafton Gallery (1974, 1976, 1981), Arts Centre, Folkestone (1975). *Work in permanent collections:* A.C.G.B., Imperial War Museum, R.A., Tate Gallery. *Publication:* illustrations for Oxford Illustrated Old Testament (1968). *Address:* c/o Bernard Jacobson Gallery, 14A Clifford St., London W1. *Signs work:* "Carel Weight."

WEIL, Hanna, N.T.D. (1943); painter in oil, water-colour, gouache; tutor, Hammersmith School of Arts and Crafts (1945-48); St. Martin's School of Art (1945-87); *b* Munich, 19 May, 1921; *d* of Ernest Weil, Ph.D.; *m* R. S. Strauss, F.I.M.; one *d*. *Educ.:* North London Collegiate School; *studied art* at St. Martin's School of Art (1940-43). *Exhib.:* R.A., Leicester Galleries, Liverpool, Brighton, London Transport (posters), Pro Arte Kasper Gallery, Switzerland, Arthur Jeffress (Pictures) Ltd., 4 galleries Munich, Portal Gallery, Elaine Benson Gallery, U.S.A. *Work repro.:* Amalgamated Press, The Queen, Art News and Review, The Studio, The Artist; postcards, calendars, prints of paintings. *Address:* 34 Christchurch Hill, London NW3 1JL. *Signs work:* "H. Weil."

WEINBERGER, Harry; artist in oil and all kinds of drawing; *b* Berlin, 7 Apr., 1924; *m*; one *d*. *Educ.:* Continent and England; *studied art* at Chelsea School of Art under Ceri Richards, and privately with Martin Bloch. *Exhib.:* 28 one-man shows, including twelve in London, one in Berlin and two in Stuttgart. *Present gallery:* Duncan Campbell Fine Art, 15 Thackeray St., Kensington Sq., London. *Address:* 28 Church Hill, Leamington Spa, Warks. CV32 5AY. *Signs work:* "HW."

WELCH, Robert Joseph, B.A. (1979), M.A. (1981); painter in oil and acrylic on canvas; *b* 22 Feb., 1956; *s* of V.R. Welch. *Educ.:* Regis Comprehensive, Wolverhampton; *studied art* at Hull C.H.E. (1976-79, John Clarke), Manchester Polytechnic (1980-81, David Sweet). *Exhib.:* Castlefield Gallery, Manchester,

Showroom Gallery, London, Winchester School of Art, Mall Galleries; one-man shows: Patricia Brown, Dulwich, Smith-Sariwala, London. *Address:* 4A Husbourne House, Chilton Grove, London SE8 5DZ. *Signs work:* "Welch, R.J.W."

WELLER, Antony, F.P.S.; sculptor in fibreglass, marble, bronze; *b* London, 4 May, 1927; *m* Julia Heseltine; one *s. Educ.:* Sutton County Grammar; *studied art* at Wimbledon under Freda Skinner, R.A. Schools under Maurice Lambert, R.A. *Work in permanent collections:* U.S.A., U.K., S. Africa, Japan, and private collections. *Publications:* Patron, Sculpture in Plastics. *Address:* 4 Stamford Bridge Studios, London SW6. *Signs work:* "Antony Weller" and see appendix.

WELLINGS, Tricia; self taught artist in gouache, charcoal and ink and gouache; *b* Guildford, 20 Mar., 1959. *Educ.:* Horsham High School. *Exhib.:* Painters Hall, London EC2, Mall Galleries, London SW1, Edith Grove Gallery, London SW10, Wattis Fine Art, Hong Kong, Ramsay Galleries, Honolulu, Hawaii. *Work in private collections:* U.S.A., Australia, Mexico, U.K., Hong Kong. *Address:* New House Farm, Ford La., Ford, nr. Arundel, W. Sussex BN18 0DE. *Club:* The Nine Elms Group of Artists. *Signs work:* "T. Wellings."

WELLS, Peter, Dip.Soc. (Lond.) (1970), M.F.P.S. (1987); painter in oil, poet; *b* London, 12 Jan., 1919; *s* of Herbert Percy Wells (decd.); *m* (1) Elisabeth Van der Meulen (decd.); (2) Gillian Anne Hayes-Newington; one *d. Educ.:* privately, and Universities of London and Manchester; *studied art* at Hornsey School of Art—part time (1952-54, J.D. Cast). *Exhib.:* Hornsey Artists (1953), Ellingham Mill Art Soc. (1981), The Crest Gallery, London (1982), Minsky's Gallery, London (1982), Wells Arts Centre, Norfolk (1982), Loggia Gallery (1988), Fermoy Gallery, King's Lynn (Eastern Open Competition 1992). *Publication:* Poems (Badelesmere Press). *Address:* Model Farm, Linstead Magna, Halesworth, Suffolk IP19 0DT. *Club:* P.E.N. *Signs work:* "P.W." or "Peter Wells."

WELTMAN, Boris; Nature miniaturist, cartographer, illustrator in water-colour, pen and ink; *b* London, 29 Nov., 1921; *m* Phyllis Joyce. *Educ.:* Chatham House, Ramsgate; Folkestone College; art and light craft. Work in collections world wide. *Publications:* educational, historical, heritage, scientific, technical, military, architectural, religious, travel and cultural books. *Address:* Temptye Farmhouse, Worth, Deal, Kent, CT14 0DJ. *Signs work:* on back of miniature paintings, see appendix.

WERGE-HARTLEY, Alan, N.D.D. (Leeds) 1952, A.T.D.; painter in oil, pen and wash of marine landscapes, lecturer; senior lecturer Dept. of Education, Portsmouth Polytechnic (1962-90); *b* Leeds, 1931; *m* Jeanne Werge-Hartley; two *d. Studied art* at Leeds College of Art (1947-53) under Maurice de Sausmarez and E. E. Pullée; Hornsey College of Art (1972-73) (sabbatical). *Exhib.:* in group exhbns. and one-man shows in Hampshire from 1962. *Work in permanent collections:* Portsmouth City Gallery and numerous private collections in England and abroad. *Address:* 5 Maisemore Gdns., Emsworth, Hants. *Signs work:* see appendix.

WERGE-HARTLEY, Jeanne, N.D.D., F.SD-C., F.R.S.A.; designer/jeweller/goldsmith; Vice-Chairman and Founder Mem., Designer Jewellers Group; Vice-President and past Chairman, Soc. of Designer-craftsmen; *b* Leeds, 1931; *d* of Edgar Vauvelle; *m* Alan Werge-Hartley; two *d. Educ.:* Leeds Girls' High School; *studied* at Leeds College of Art (1948-52) under Eric Taylor, A.R.C.A. *Exhib.:* nationally and internationally. *Commissioned work:* U.K., U.S.A., Europe, New Zealand, Japan. Freeman of the Worshipful Company of Goldsmiths and the City of London (1986). Included on Craft Council Index and represented on the BBC Domesday Project. *Address:* 5 Maisemore Gdns., Emsworth, Hants. *Signs work:* see appendix.

WESSELMAN, Frans, R.E. (1986); painter-printmaker in water-colour and etching; *b* The Hague, Holland, 1953; *m* Susan Hallett. *Studied* printmaking and photography at Groningen College of Art (1976-78). Work based on studies from nature which through composition studies are arranged until the pattern of textures, shapes and colours is to my liking. Then transferred to 'good' water-colour paper or plate, although right until the end new ideas may give rise to changes. *Exhib.:* R.E., R.A., R.W.S., R.W.A., Catto Gallery, London, Ombersley Gallery, Ombersley, Manor House Gallery, Chipping Norton. *Address:* 119 Watling St. South, Church Stretton SY6 7BJ.

WESSELOW, Eric, M.A., M.F.A., Prix de Rome, R.C.A., S.C.A., F.R.S.A.; past Pres. Independent Art Assoc. and Quebec Soc. for Educ. through Art; painter, artist in water-colour, acrylic, chalk and glass (patented system of coloured glass lamination), of portraits, landscapes, abstracts; teacher, linguist; *b* Marienburg, Germany, 12 Sept., 1911. *Studies:* Philology, University Koenigsberg; *art and art educ.:* Academy of Fine Arts, Koenigsberg. *Exhib.:* one-man shows: Montreal Museum of Fine Arts; Waddington Gallery, Montreal; N.Y. State University, Plattsburgh; Inaugural Exhbn. Eaton A.G., Montreal; Robertson Galleries, Ottawa; Toronto Dominion Centre; Ontario Assoc. of Architects, Toronto, etc. Represented in numerous national and international art exhbns. *Work in permanent collections:* architectural laminated coloured glass relief windows and screens: Montreal Airport Dorval; Hospital Dortmund, W. Germany; Sanctuaries Congregation Beth-El, Montreal; Temple Emanu-El-Beth Sholom, Montreal; Temple Sinai, Toronto; Humbervalley United Church, Toronto; St. Dunstan of Canterbury Anglican Church, West Hill, Ontario; Baptistery Church of the Resurrection, Valois, Quebec. *Publications:* Sparks, illustrated own aphorisms (1980); New Sparks (1985 and 1992). *Address:* 5032 Victoria Ave., Montreal, Quebec, Canada H3W 2N3. *Signs work:* "Wesselow" or "W" followed by date or year.

WEST, Steve, Dip.A.D. (1969), R.A.S. Higher Cert. (1972), Prix de Rome (1972), A.R.B.S. (1992); sculptor in bronze, glass fibre, wood; *b* Warrington, 6 Apr., 1948; *m* Jenny; one *s,* one *d. Educ.:* Penketh and Sankey Secondary Modern; *studied art* at Liverpool College of Art and Design (1965-69), R.A. Schools (1969-72, Willi Soukop). *Exhib.:* Crescent Gallery Scarborough, Oldknows Gallery Nottingham, Lanchester Gallery Coventry, Tabor Gallery Canterbury, Woodlands Gallery Blackheath, Marcus & Marcus Gallery Amsterdam. Undertakes ecclesiastical commissions. *Address:* 17 Swift St., Barnsley, S. Yorks. S75 2SN. *Signs work:* "Steve West."

WESTLEY, Ann; artist, sculptor and printmaker in etching, relief printing, mixed media; part-time lecturer in printmaking, Colchester School of Art and Design; *b* Kettering, 5 Mar., 1948. *Educ.:* Bedford High School; *studied art* at Northampton School of Art (1965-67), Bristol Polytechnic (1967-70, Ernest Pascoe, Ralph Brown, Bob Clatworthy), Gulbenkian Rome Scholarship in Sculpture (1970-71). *Exhib.:* Serpentine Gallery (1976), Out of Print, South Hill Arts Centre, Bracknell (1983), British Miniature Print Biennale (1990), A New Generation of British Printmakers, Xylon Museum, Germany (1992). *Work in permanent collections:* Gulbenkian Foundation, Ashmolean Museum, Fredrikstaad Museum Norway. *Address:* Gore Cottage, 4 Gore La., Rayne, Braintree, Essex CM7 8TU. *Club:* R.E. *Signs work:* "Ann Westley."

WESTON, David J., A.R.M.S., B.W.S., S.M., U.A., F.R.S.A.; seascape and landscape painter in water-colour and other media; miniaturist; *b* 21 Sept., 1936. *Exhib.:* one-man shows: Clare Hall Cambridge, Hemel Hempstead Art Centre, Old Fire Engine House Ely; two-man shows: Mall Galleries and Newport Gallery; frequent exhibitor, B.W.S., U.A., R.M.S., Mall and Westminster Galleries with R.S.M.A., R.B.A., R.I., N.E.A.C., R.M.S., U.A. Work in archives of National Westminster Bank PLC and Barclays Bank PLC. *Address:* Little Glebe, 11 Longcroft Ave., Harpenden, Herts. AL5 2RD. *Signs work:* "DAVID J. WESTON" or "D.J.W." (miniatures and small works).

WESTWOOD, John, A.R.C.A. (1948); designer for book production; Head of Typographic Design, later Director of Graphic Design, at Her Majesty's Stationery Office, London (1960-1978); *b* Bromley, 26 Sept., 1919; *s* of W. H. Westwood; *m* Margaret Wadsworth; two *s. Educ.:* Bromley County Grammar School; *studied art* at Bromley College of Art (1936-39) and R.C.A. (1940 and 1947-48). *Exhib.:* South Bank (1951). *Publications:* articles on graphic design, International Meccanoman, etc. *Address:* The Malt House, Church La., Streatley, Reading RG8 9HT.

WHALLEY, Ann Penelope, N.D.D., A.T.D., A.T.C., S.W.A.; artist in water-colour and pastel; tutor and organiser for painting holidays abroad; *b* Yorks., 1 Apr., 1935; *d* of Dr G.M. Mayhall, M.D., F.R.C.S.; *m* Theo Whalley; four *s. Educ.:* Pontefract Girls' High School; *studied art* at Leeds College of Art (1950-55, Mr. Pullé). *Exhib.:* one-man shows: Albany Gallery, Cardiff, Fountain Gallery Llandeilo, Library Hall, Haverfordwest annually since 1981, Workshop, Wales (1983), Bloomfield Hall (1986), Coachhouse (1987), Henry Thomas Gallery, Carmarthen, Patricia Wells Gallery (1987); group shows: St. Ives Gallery (1984), Beacon Gallery, Painswick (1985), B.W.S. (1986), Laing Comp. (1987), S.W.A. (1987), R.I. (1986), Albany Gallery, Cardiff, Century Gallery, Henley-on-Thames, Bromley Gallery, Kent. *Publication:* illustrated, About Pembrokeshire; author, Painting under a Blue Sky; author, Painting Water in Water-colour (Batsfords); articles for Artist and Illustrator, and Leisure Painter. *Address:* Haroldston House, Haverfordwest, Pembs. SA61 1UH. *Signs work:* "Ann Whalley."

WHEELER, Colin, S.G.F.A. (1986); graphic artist, illustrator and cartographer in ink, pencil and pastel; *b* Amersham, Bucks., 4 July, 1946; *s* of Arthur Wheeler, retd. industrial engineer. *Educ.:* Alleyne's Grammar School, Stevenage; *studied art:* privately. *Exhib.:* S.G.F.A., various one-man shows including Fermoy Gallery, King's Lynn, Lion Yard, Cambridge, Theatre Royal, Norwich, Denington Gallery, Stevenage. *Work in permanent collections:* B.Ae., Stevenage and N. Herts. Museum. *Publications:* travel and tourist brochures. *Address:* 39 Plash Drive, Stevenage SG1 1LN. *Signs work:* "Colin Wheeler."

WHEELER, Sir H. Anthony, Kt. (1988), O.B.E. (1973), P.P.R.S.A., A.R.S.A. (1963), R.S.A. (1975), P.R.S.A. (1983-90), B.Arch. (Strath), F.R.I.B.A., P.R.I.A.S. (1973-75); architect and planner, Consultant, Wheeler & Sproson, Edinburgh and Kirkcaldy since 1986 when ceased to be senior partner; mem. of the Royal Fine Art Commission for Scotland, (1967-85); trustee of the Scottish Civic Trust (1970-83); *b* Stranraer, Scotland, 7 Nov., 1919; *m* Dorothy Jean Wheeler. *Studied architecture:* Glasgow School of Architecture under Prof. W. J. Smith, and Glasgow School of Art; graduated 1948; John Keppie Scholar, Rowand Anderson Studentship R.I.A.S. (1948); R.I.B.A. Grissell Gold Medallist (1948); R.I.B.A. Neale Bursar (1949); 22 Saltire Awards and Commendations for Housing and Reconstruction; 12 Civic Trust Awards and Commendations.

Address: Hawthornbank House, Dean Village, Edinburgh EH4 3BH. *Clubs:* Scottish Arts, New Club. *Signs work:* "H. A. Wheeler."

WHEELER, Zona Lorraine, B.F.A., F.I.A.L., N.S.M.P.; advertising designer, painter, sculptor, white sheet-vinyl; proprietor, 3-D Studio; senior Art Director, McCormick-Armstrong Co. (1970-79); *b* Lindsborg, Kansas, 15 Feb., 1913; *d* of agriculturist, originator of U.S. Govt.-recognized species, Wheeler Sudan Grass. *Studied art* under Dr. Birger Sandzen, Bethany Coll., Lindsborg, American Academy of Art, Chicago, Wichita Art Assoc. School. *Exhib.:* Rugby, Boston, England, San Francisco Art Assoc.; solo shows in white sheet-vinyl, Sandzen Memorial Gallery, Lindsborg, Kansas, Fort Hays Kansas State University, Wichita Art Assoc. (retrospective 1987). *Address:* 230 South Belmont, Wichita, Kansas 67218. *Clubs:* Nat. League American Pen Women, Nat. Soc. Mural Painters.

WHEELER-HOPKINSON, John Samuel, S.G.A. (1983); graphic artist in pen and ink, pencil and colour wash; *b* Prestatyn, N. Wales, 1 Mar., 1941; *m* Claire Follett; two *d*. *Educ.:* Grammar School, Colne, and King's College, London. *Address:* Le Champ Peron, Bayet 03500, St. Pourçain sur Sioule, France. *Signs work:* "J.W-H." and date as ideogram.

WHIDBORNE, Timothy Charles Plunket; artist in oil, tempera, sanguine, crayon, sculptor; Director, Pheasantry Studios Ltd.; *b* Hughenden, Bucks., 25 July, 1927; *s* of Charles Whidborne; *m* Wendy. *Educ.:* Stowe School; *studied art* at St. Martin's Art School (1944), La Grande Chaumiere, Paris (1948), with Mervyn Peake, Chelsea (1945) and Pietro Annigoni, Florence (1949). *Exhib.:* R.A., R.P. (1986), S.P.S., etc.; one-man show: Upper Grosvenor Galleries (1969). *Official purchases:* portrait of H.M. The Queen, H.Q. Irish Guards, London; St. Katherine of Alexandria, Worshipful Company of Haberdashers, London. *Address:* The Studio, 30 Albert Rd., Deal, Kent CT14 9RE. *Club:* Chelsea Arts. *Signs work:* "T. Whidborne" or "T.W."

WHISHAW, Anthony, A.R.A., A.R.C.A. (1955), Travelling Scholarship, R.C.A., Abbey Premier Scholarship (1982), Lorne Scholarship (1982-83), John Moores minor prize; *b* 22 May, 1930. *Exhib.:* one-man shows: Madrid (1956), Roland, Browse and Delbanco (1960, 1961, 1963, 1965, 1968), I.C.A. (1971), New Art Centre (1972), Hoya (1974), Hayward Annual (1980), Nicola Jacobs (1981, 1983, 1984), Mappin A.G. (1985). *Work in permanent collections:* National Gallery, Melbourne, Australia, Seattle Museum, Arts Council, Coventry Museum, Leicester Museum, Chantrey Bequest, Bolton A.G., Bayer Pharm., Western Australia A.G., Museo de Bahia, Brazil, Power A.G., European Parliament, Ferens A.G., Tate Gallery, Graves A.G. Sheffield. *Address:* 7A Albert Pl., Victoria Rd., London W8.

WHISKERD, Jennifer, B.A. Hons. Fine Art (Chelt.); painter; *b* Gloucester, 23 Mar., 1962; *d* of John Whiskerd, artist. *Exhib.:* international and national. Work in public and private collections. Fine Art tutor. *Address:* Springfield Cottage, Kilcot, Newent, Gloucs. GL18 1NS. *Signs works:* "J.H. Whiskerd."

WHISTLER, Laurence, C.B.E.; *b* 1912. *Educ.:* Stowe and Balliol. *Work in permanent collections:* V. & A.; Ashmolean, Oxford; Fitzwilliam, Cambridge; Brighton A.G.; Cecil Higgins, Bedford; Corning Museum, N.Y., etc. *Engraved church windows:* Moreton, Dorset; Hannington and Wootton St. Lawrence, Hants.; Salisbury Cathedral; Eastbury and Radley College, Berks.; Thornham Parva, Suffolk, etc. *Publications:* The Engraved Glass of Laurence Whistler (1952), Engraved Glass 1952-58 (1959), The Initials in the Heart (1964),

Pictures on Glass (1972), The Image on the Glass (1975), Scenes and Signs on Glass (1985), The Laughter and the Urn: The Life of Rex Whistler (1985). *Address:* Windmill Farm House, Watlington, Oxford OX9 5PZ. *Signs work:* "LW" with year date.

WHITAKER, Rita Elizabeth, R.M.S., S.M.; professional artist specialising in stoving enamel on copper, and with her husband owns a gallery in Newport, Dyfed; *b* 3 Sept., 1936; two *s. Educ.:* Sion Convent, Worthing; *studied art* at Regent St. Polytechnic under Stuart Tresilian. *Exhib.:* Mall Galleries, R.A., Medici's, Welsh Arts Council, Assoc. of Sussex Artists, Miniature Soc. Ilkley, Georgia, Oregon, Florida and various galleries throughout England and Wales. *Work in permanent collections:* Royal Exchange, London and Carningli Centre, Newport, Dyfed; private collections throughout the world. *Address:* Carningli, East St., Newport, Dyfed SA42 0SY Wales. *Signs work:* "R. E. Whitaker."

WHITCOMBE, Susan Anne Clare, S.E.A. (1979); painter in oil and water-colour of equestrian portraits; *b* London, 17 June, 1957; *d* of Philip Whitcombe; *m* Robin Marriott; two *s. Educ.:* N. Foreland Lodge, Hants.; *studied art* at Heatherley School of Fine Art (John Walton, Bernard Hailstone). *Exhib.:* S.E.A.; one-man shows: London (1981, 1988), Tokyo (1985, 1987), Melbourne (1982). *Address:* Gardener's Hill, Churt, Farnham, Surrey GU10 2ND. *Signs work:* "Susie Whitcombe."

WHITE, Charles, D.F.A. (Lond.), F.R.S.A.; Pres. European Group; former Head of Art Department, United World College; *b* London, 11 Feb., 1928; *m* Mary White, calligrapher, potter. *Educ.:* Stoneleigh; *studied art* at Sutton School of Art, Newport, Kingston-upon-Thames, Slade, London University (1948-50). *Exhib.:* one-man shows in England, Wales, France and Germany. *Work in permanent collections:* Her Majesty Queen Elizabeth II, H.R.H. Prince Charles, Secretary of State for Wales, Mayor of Zürich, Contemporary Art Society, National Museum of Wales, England, America, Canada, Germany, Belgium, France, Sweden, Holland and Luxembourg. *Address:* Zimmerplatzweg 6, 55599 Wonsheim, Germany. *Signs work:* "Charles White."

WHITE, David, Des.R.C.A. (1959); potter, producing individual porcelain pots for sale in most of the leading galleries throughout the country; Joint Winner of the Duke of Edinburgh's Prize for Elegant Design (1960); *b* Margate, Kent, 27 June, 1934; *s* of C. H. P. White (decd.); *m* (1962) Diana Groves; one *s,* one *d. Studied art* at Thanet School of Art (1950-54) and Royal College of Art (1956-59). Accepted as Full mem. Craftsmen Potters' Assoc. (Apr. 1991). *Address:* 4 Callis Court Rd., Broadstairs, Kent CT10 3AE.

WHITE, James; LL.D. (N.U.I.); Chairman, Irish Arts Council (1978-84); Director, National Gallery of Ireland (1964-80), Curator, Municipal Gallery of Modern Art, Dublin (1960-64); lecturer, Dublin and National Universities; *b* Dublin, 16 June, 1913; *s* of Thomas John White; *m* Agnes Bowe; three *s,* two *d. Educ.:* Belvedere College, Dublin. *Publications:* The National Gallery of Ireland (Thames & Hudson); Irish Stained Glass (Gill & Co.); Jack B. Yeats (Martin Secker & Warburg); John Butler Yeats and the Irish Renaissance (Dolmen Press); Masterpieces of the National Gallery of Ireland (Jarrolds, Norwich); Pauline Bewick, Painting a Life (Wolfhound Press); Gerard Dillon, Painting a Life (Wolfhound Press). *Address:* 15 Herbert Pk., Dublin 4.

WHITE, John Norman, N.D.D. (1951); painter, illustrator, oil, gouache, and water-colour; *b* Chipperfield, Herts., 27 Mar., 1932; *s* of John Eugene White. *Educ.:* Belmont Senior Modern School; *studied art* at Harrow School of Art

(1945-51). *Exhib.:* R.A., Young Contemporaries. *Address:* Northwood Lodge, Bullockstone Rd., Herne, Herne Bay, Kent. *Signs work:* "JOHN—WHITE."

WHITE, Laura, B.A.(Hons.); sculptor in stone, wood and bronze; *b* Worcester, 10 Mar., 1968. *Educ.:* Alice Ottley School, Worcester; *studied art* at Worcester Art College, Loughborough College of Art and Design. *Exhib.:* various mixed and solo shows in U.K. *Work in permanent collections:* Art Scene London, Gallery Shurini London. *Address:* Flat B, 4 Corporation Oaks, Woodborough Rd., Nottingham NG3 4JY. *Signs work:* "LAURA WHITE" or not at all.

WHITE, Mary; ceramic artist and calligrapher; awarded Rheinland-Pfalz Staatspreis (1982); *b* Croesyceiliog, Wales, 1926; *née* Rollinson; *m* Charles White, artist. *Educ. and studied art* at St. Julian's High School; Newport College of Art; Hammersmith College of Art; London University Goldsmiths' College of Art. *Work in permanent collections:* British Museums: V.&.A., Fitzwilliam Cambridge, Newport, Cardiff, Winchester, Bristol, Norwich Castle, Swindon; Collections: Bath Study Centre, Leicester Educ. Authority, Aberystwyth Univ., Welsh Arts Council; U.S.A.: Pennsylvania State Museum; Museums in Germany: Kunstgewerbemuseum Köln, Veste Coburg, Westerwald Keramion, Deidesheim, Stuttgart, Mainz, Darmstadt. Many private collections. *Work repro.:* Ceramic Review, Ceramic Monthly, German Keramik Magazines; work included in many books in G.B., Germany, France, Belgium and U.S.A. *Address:* Zimmerplatzweg 6, 55599 Wonsheim, Germany. *Societies:* C.P.A., Fellow S.S.I, Deutscher Handwerkskammer. *Signs work:* see appendix.

WHITE-OAKES, Sue, M.C.S.D.; metal sculptor in copper and bronze; *b* 26 May, 1939; *m* Roger Oakes; two *s. Educ.:* St. Martin's High School, London; *studied art* at Central School of Art. *Exhib.:* Edinburgh, Glasgow, St. Andrews, London. *Publications:* articles: Craftsman Magazine and The Scotsman colour supplement. *Address:* Tarfhauga Farmhouse, W. Linton, Peeblesshire EH46 7BS. *Club:* C.S.D. *Signs work:* "Sue White-Oakes."

WHITEFORD, Joan, N.D.D. (1963), A.T.D. (1964); artist in etching and wood engraving; *b* St. John, Cornwall, 5 May, 1942; *d* of Francis Kinsmund Doidge; *m* David Whiteford. *Educ.:* Grammar School, Tavistock, Devon; *studied art* at Plymouth College of Art (1958-63, William Mann, Jeff. Clements), Bournemouth College of Art (1963-64). *Exhib.:* R.A., R.E., N.S., S.W.A., N.E.A.C., R.I., Mall Print. *Address:* Meadowside, Cockwells, Penzance, Cornwall TR20 8BD. *Signs work:* "J. Whiteford."

WHITEFORD, Kate, Dip.A.D. (1973), Dip.F.A. (1976) History of Art; Sargant Fellow, British School at Rome (1993-94); artist in oil on gesso, also land drawings; *b* Glasgow, 9 Mar., 1952; *m* Alex Graham. *Educ.:* Glasgow High School; *studied art* at Glasgow School of Art (1969-73), Glasgow University (1974-76, History of Art, Prof. Martin Kemp). *Exhib.:* Institute of Contemporary Art (1983), Riverside Studios (1986), Whitechapel A.G. (1988), Glasgow Museum and A.G. (1990). *Work in permanent collections:* Tate Gallery, British Council, C.A.S., A.C.G.B., National Gallery of Modern Art Edinburgh, S.A.C., Glasgow Museum and A.G. *Publications:* artists books published by Whitechapel A.G. (1988), Tetra Press and Advanced Graphics (1992), Cairn Gallery (1992), Sitelines (1992), Graeme Murray Gallery (1992). *Address:* c/o Frith St. Gallery, 60 Frith St., London W1V 5TA. *Signs work:* "Whiteford" or "Kate Whiteford."

WHITELEY, Alfred, A.R.C.A. (1952); Arts Council major award (1977); painter in oil; *b* Chesterfield, 18 Nov., 1928; *s* of Alfred Whiteley, butcher; *m* Ottoline Reynolds; one *s*, one *d. Educ.:* Tapton House, Chesterfield; *studied art* at Chesterfield School of Art (1945-47), R.C.A. (1949-52). *Exhib.:* R.A., Odette Gilbert Gallery; one-man shows Odette Gilbert, Vorpal Gallery, N.Y. and Pride Gallery. *Work in private collections:* U.K., U.S.A., Germany. *Work repro.:* The Times, Sunday Times, Art Line, etc. *Address:* Fairfield, Mogador Rd., Tadworth, Surrey KT20 7EW. *Signs work:* "Alfred Whiteley."

WHITESIDE (formerly Newton-Davies), Diana Elizabeth Hamilton; miniature painter in water-colour; *b* London, 13 Jan., 1942; *d* of the late Borras Noel Hamilton Whiteside, M.P.; *m* John Newton Davies (1964-87); two *d. Educ.:* Lycée Français de Londres, Glendower School, Sydenham House, Devon; *studied art* at Simi's and L'Accademia delle Belle Arti, Florence (1959-60), Camberwell School of Art (1961-62). *Exhib.:* R.A., R.M.S., R.H.S., Tate Gallery, Mall Galleries, Anna-Mei Chadwick's, Westminster Gallery, Medici Gallery. *Address:* Chapel Lands, Chailey, nr. Lewes, Sussex. *Signs work:* "19 D.E.N.D. 85" (or relevant year); "D.E. 1993 H.W." (or relevant year).

WHITFORD, Christopher; artist in water-colour and acrylic; *b* Malvern, Worcs., 18 Feb., 1952; *m* Filippa; two *d. Studied art* at Malvern. *Exhib.:* R.M.S., John Noott, Broadway. *Address:* c/o John Noott Twentieth Century, 14 Cotswold Ct., Broadway, Worcs. WR12 7DP. *Signs work:* "C. Whitford" or "C.W."

WHITFORD, Filippa; artist in water-colour; *b* Italy, 22 Jan., 1951; *m* Christopher Whitford; two *d. Exhib.:* R.M.S, R.W.S., John Noott, Broadway. *Address:* c/o John Noott Twentieth Century, 14 Cotswold Ct., Broadway, Worcs. WR12 7DP. *Signs work:* "Filippa Whitford."

WHITTEN, Jonathan Philip, B.A. Hons. (1977), P.G.C.E. (1978); teacher and potter in ceramic; Head of Art, Sir James Smith's School, Camelford; *b* Eastbourne, 23 Sept., 1954; *s* of Philip Whitten, A.R.C.A.; *m* Sally Bowler; two *s. Educ.:* Eastbourne Grammar School; *studied art* at Eastbourne College of Art and Design (1972-73, Geoffrey Flint, A.R.C.A.), University of E. Anglia (1974-77, Prof. Andrew Martindale), University of London (1977-78, William Newland); apprentice potter to Michael Leach (1978-79) and Roger Cockram (1980-81). *Exhib.:* Brewhouse Gallery, Taunton (1979), Devon Guild of Craftsmen (1981), Leics. Guild of Craftsmen (1983-87), etc. *Address:* Cocks Cottage, St. Teath, Bodmin, N. Cornwall PL30 3LH.

WHITTEN, Philip John, A.R.C.A. (1949), F.R.S.A. (1952); painter in oil, pastel; teacher, London University Inst. of Educ. (1968); senior lecturer; examiner, Cambridge and London University Insts. of Educ. (retd.); *b* Leyton, Essex, 19 June, 1922; *s* of Albert Edward Whitten, engineer; four *s*, one *d. Educ.:* Bishopshalt, Hillingdon; *studied art* at Hornsey College of Art (1937-40), R.C.A. (1946-49). *Exhib.:* R.B.A., Dowmunt Gallery, Bond St., Towner Gallery, Cecil Higgins, Bedford, Shoreditch and Bedford Colleges, private galleries in Weybridge, Walton and Eastbourne areas. *Work in permanent collections:* Towner Gallery, Brunel University. Work sold by Christie's and Sotheby's. *Address:* 10 Beechwood Cres., Eastbourne BN20 8AE. *Signs work:* "Philip Whitten."

WHITTINGHAM, Dr. Selby, B.A. (1964), M.A., Ph.D. (1975); art historian; founded Turner Soc. 1975 (Hon. Sec. 1975-76, 1980-84; Vice Chairman 1984-85); and Watteau Soc. 1984 (Sec. General and Editor); and J.M.W. Turner, R.A. (Co-Editor), 1988; *b* Batu Gajah, Malaya, 8 Aug., 1941; *s* of H.R. Oppenheim, F.C.A.; *m* Joanna Dodds. *Educ.:* Shrewsbury School; Universities of Oxford and Manchester. *Publications:* An Historical Account of the Will of

J.M.W. Turner, R.A. (1989); The Fallacy of Mediocrity: The Need for a Proper Turner Gallery (1992); World Directory of Artists' Museums (1993). *Address:* Turner House, 153 Cromwell Rd., London SW5 0TQ.

WHITTLESEA, Michael, R.W.S. (1985); painter, book illustrator; *b* London, 6 June, 1938; *s* of Sydney Charles Whittlesea; *m* Jill. *Studied art* at Harrow School of Art. *Exhib.:* prize winner, Spirit of the Sea Exhbn. (1981), World of Newspapers Exhbn. (1982) in assoc. with R.A., Daily Mirror, and Sotheby's, N.E.A.C. *Address:* Richmond Cottage, High St., Hurley, Berks. SL6 5LT. *Club:* Chelsea Arts. *Signs work:* "Michael Whittlesea."

WIELICZKO, Jan; painter, sculptor and designer; Director, Centaur Gallery, London; lecturer and demonstrator, Slade School (1949); *b* Wilno, Poland, 1921; *s* of Boleslaw Wieliczko; *m* Dinah Wieliczko; two *s. Educ.:* Wilno, Poland; *studied art* at Slade School, London (1945-48) (1st prize Decorative Painting). *Exhib.:* Irving Gallery (1953), Redfern Gallery (1954), Centaur Gallery; all the principal mixed exhbns. in London. *Address:* 82 Highgate High St., London N6. *Signs work:* "J. Wieliczko."

WIGGLESWORTH, Kathleen Lindsay, N.E.A.C.; landscape painter in oil and water-colour; *b* London, 5 Nov., 1900; *d* of Alfred Wigglesworth. *Educ.:* West Heath School, Sevenoaks; *studied art* at Byam Shaw School (1948-57, B.D.L. Thomas, Patrick Phillips, Peter Greenham). *Exhib.:* R.A., R.B.A., N.E.A.C., Mall Galleries, R.W.E.A., Alpine Gallery, and in Lewes and Suffolk; three-man show in Patricia Wells Gallery, Thornbury, Bristol (Nov. 1986). *Address:* 4 Loudwater House, Loudwater Drive, Rickmansworth, Herts. WD3 4HN. *Clubs:* University Women's, N.E.A.C. *Signs work:* "K.W."

WILD, David Paul, D.F.A. Slade (1955), Abbey Major Scholarship to Rome (1955); artist in oil and water-colour; Founder, Friends of the Weavers Triangle; *b* Burnley, 14 Apr., 1931; *s* of Benjamin Wild. *Educ.:* Burnley Grammar School; *studied art* at Burnley School of Art, Slade School of Fine Art. *Exhib.:* extensively in the north of England since 1957; Woodstock Gallery (1965), John Moores (1965, 1970), R.A. (1972-74), Arts Council 'Drawings of People' Serpentine Gallery. *Work in permanent collections:* W.A.G., Manchester City A.G., Rutherston Coll., Granada TV, Arts Council of G.B., Salford A.G., Bolton, Blackburn and Burnley Municipal galleries. *Address:* 66 Rosehill Rd., Burnley. *Signs work:* "D. Wild."

WILES, Gillian, A.R.B.S., I.B.H.S.; sculptor/painter/illustrator; *b* Johannesburg, 1942; *d* of Dr. G.G. Wiles; *m* Dr. Robin Catchpole. *Educ.:* Royal Veterinary College, London (dissection and anatomy); *studied art* at Cape Town University, and Heatherley, London. *Exhib.:* one-man shows: Sladmore, London, John Pence, San Francisco, The Collector, Johannesburg; exhib. at Tryon, London, R.B.S., Denis Hotz, London, Sportsmen's Edge, N.Y., Collector's Covey, Dallas. *Work in permanent collections:* bronze sculptures: Genesee Museum, N.Y.S., Toyota S.A., Nikon S.A. *Work repro.:* illustrations for advertising. *Address:* c/o R.B.S., 108 Old Brompton Rd., London SW7 3RA. *Signs work:* "Gill Wiles."

WILKINS, William Powell, R.C.A., A.R.C.A.; artist in oil, lecturer and consultant; Chairman, Welsh Historic Gardens Trust; *b* Kersey, Suffolk, 4 Apr., 1938; *m* Lynne Brantly; two *d. Educ.:* Malvern College; *studied art* at Swansea and Royal College of Art. *Exhib.:* London, New York, San Francisco, Swansea. *Work in permanent collections:* National Museum of Wales, Glynn Vivian

Museum Swansea, Hirshorn Museum Washington D.C. *Address:* c/o Piccadilly Gallery, 16A Cork St., London W1X 1PF.

WILKINSON, Ronald Scotthorn, M.A., B.M., B.Ch. (Oxon.); physician, playwright, novelist, artist in oil, water-colour; *b* Melton Mowbray; *s* of T. G. Wilkinson, B.Sc.; two *d. Educ.:* Shrewsbury School, Merton College, Oxford; *studied art* under H. B. Hewlett. *Exhib.:* Public Schools Exhbn., Leicester Soc. of Artists' Exhbn., R.A. Summer Exhbn. (1977); one-man show, Fine Art Trade Guild (1986). *Address:* 50 Hanover Steps, St. George's Fields, Albion St., London W2 2YG.

WILKINSON-CLEMENTSON, William Henry, R.E., A.R.C.A., F.I.A.L. (1946), Ph.D. (1980); line engraver and painter; Head of Dept. Engraving, City and Guilds of London Art School; *b* Bath, 1921; *s* of H. R. Wilkinson, A.R.C.A., Head, Bath School of Art; *m* Lady Margaret Ewer; one *d. Educ.:* Winchester; *studied art* at Royal College of Art under Malcolm Osborne and Robert Austin, Heidelberg and Lindau, Germany, Fiorenza, Italy. *Work in permanent collections:* Holland, Switzerland, Italy and America. *Address:* Crane Cottage, Tatsfield, Westerham, Kent TN16 2JT. *Clubs:* Chelsea Arts, Aviemore, Scotland, Swiss Alpine. *Signs work:* "HENRY WILKINSON."

WILLIAM-ELLIS, David Hugo Martyn, R.C.A. (1993), A.R.B.S. (1992); sculptor in clay for bronze and terracotta; *b* Ireland, 6 Apr., 1959; *m* Serena Stapleton; one *s,* one *d* (decd.). *Educ.:* Headfort School, Ireland; Stowe School; *studied art* in Florence (1977-78, Signorina Nerina Simi), Carrara (1979-80), Sir John Cass (1981-83). *Exhib.:* London, Belfast, Paris, U.S.A., Japan. *Commissions:* C. Hoare and Co., National Trust, R.C.N., Duchess of Westminster, Sir Richard Baker-Wilbraham, Lord Mansfield, Hon. Simon and Mrs. Laura Weinstock, etc., and more than seventy commissions in Europe and the U.S.A. *Address:* The Atlas Works, 287 Upper Richmond Rd., London SW15 6SP. *Club:* Arts. *Signs work:* "D.W.E." dated with signet ring eagle on larger pieces.

WILLIAM-POWLETT, Katherine, S.W.A. (1966); artist in water-colour; Hon. Sec., Chelsea Art Soc. (1978-85); *b* Fareham, Hants., 24 Oct., 1911; *d* of the late Admiral of the Fleet Baron Keyes, G.C.B., C.M.G., D.S.O.; *m* Peter William-Powlett; one *s,* one *d. Educ.:* privately; *studied art* with Edward Wesson, R.I., R.B.A., R.S.M.A. *Exhib.:* Clarges Gallery (1970, 1979, 1981), R.I. (1977-80), Newbury Festival (1980). *Address:* 22 St. Leonard's Terr., London SW3 4QG. *Signs work:* "K.W-P."

WILLIAMS, Alex, N.D.D., A.T.D.; artist in oil on canvas; *b* Reading, 1942; *s* of Sqn. Ldr. Albert George Williams; *m* Valmai; one *s,* one *d. Educ.:* St. Peter's School, Huntingdon; *studied art* at St. Martin's School of Art (1962-66, Peter Blake, Peter de Francia, David Tindle). *Exhib.:* Helen Greenberg Gallery, Los Angeles (1978, 1980), Henry Brett Galleries (1984, 1987), Hereford City Museum (1982), John Noott, Broadway (1991). *Work in permanent collections:* National Library of Wales, Hereford and Worcester City Museums; public and private collections in U.S.A. *Publication:* illustrated The Bird who Couldn't Fly (Hodder & Stoughton, 1988). *Address:* Bronllys Castle, Bronllys, Powys LD3 0HL. *Signs work:* "Alex Williams '92."

WILLIAMS, Glynn; Rome Scholarship in sculpture; sculptor in stone; Prof. of Sculpture, R.C.A.; *b* Shrewsbury, 1939; *m* Heather; two *d. Studied art* at Wolverhampton College of Art (1955-60, 1960-61 Post Dip.). *Exhib.:* one-man shows: Blond Fine A.G. (1982), Bernard Jacobson Gallery (1985, 1986, 1988,

1991), Artsite Gallery, Bath (1987), Retrospective exhbn. at Margam Park, S. Wales (1992). *Work in permanent collections:* A.C.G.B., Hakone Open Air Museum, Japan, V. & A., Tate Gallery. *Address:* c/o Bernard Jacobson Gallery, 14A Clifford St., London W1X 1RF. *Signs work:* "G.W."

WILLIAMS, Guy R. O., A.T.D., Saxon Barton Prize (1950); artist in oil; wood-engraver; taught at Parmiter's School; *b* Mold, Flint, 23 Aug., 1920; *s* of Dr. Owen E. Williams. *Educ.:* St. Edward's School, Oxford; *studied art* at Manchester College of Art (1937-40) and Hornsey School of Art (1946-50). *Exhib.:* R.A., R.B.A., S.E.A., A.I.A., London and provincial galleries. *Official purchases:* L.C.C. *Publications:* author of the "Use Your" books (Chapman & Hall); Pencil Drawing (Pitman); Enjoy Painting in Oils (Gollancz); Woodworking Step by Step and Drawing and Sketching Step by Step (Museum Press); Collecting Pictures and Making Mobiles (Arco); Augustus Pugin versus Decimus Burton: A Victorian Architectural Duel (Cassell). *Address:* 1A Earl Rd., London SW14 7JH.

WILLIAMS, Idris Elgina (Idris Aeron); *b* Erdington, Birmingham 1918; residing Walmley, Sutton Coldfield, Warwicks to 1970. *Educ.:* St. Agnes' Convent, Erdington; Royal Drawing Society, Honours Standard; *studied art* at Birmingham College of Art; Union of Educational Institutions, First Place with Distinction; major Ryland Scholarship; Board of Education Exams. in Drawing and Painting. Former art journalist Birmingham Evening Despatch. Commissions Stud Advertisement Photography and Drawing. *Exhib.:* Midland Federation of Photography; Alderman Cobb Trophy; Soc. of Equestrian Artists, London; one-woman exhbns. supported by Welsh Arts Council, Haverfordwest and Carmarthen (1977). W.A.C. Grant (1976). *Publications:* Welsh Pony and Cob Society Stud book, Arabian Horse Society News, Catalogue Ponies of Britain, etc.; illustrated biographical articles in Pony World 1978, American Year Book 1980. Present subject of work: Illustrated lifetime research into woodland wildlife; avian language recordings, medical research, individual avian biographies. Mem. Friends of the Earth, W.W.F. etc. *Address:* Bramble Cottage, New Quay, Dyfed SA45 9RF. *Signs work:* "IDRIS AERON."

WILLIAMS, Joan Barbara Price, A.R.C.A., R.E., R.W.S.; printmaker and painter; *b* Pontypridd, S. Wales. *Educ.:* High Wycombe High School; *studied art* at High Wycombe School of Art, Royal College of Art. *Exhib.:* R.A., Bankside Gallery, International Biennales of Graphic Art, Ljubljana, Frechen, Germany, Biella, Italy. *Work in public collections:* Arts Council, Welsh Arts Council, Sheffield, Oldham, Newcastle, Norwich, Glasgow and Hull Art Galleries and many university collections. *Address:* 42 Rochester Rd., Aylesford, Kent. *Signs work:* "Joan Williams."

WILLIAMS, Kyffin, O.B.E. (1982), A.R.A. (1970), R.A. (1974), Hon.M.A. (Wales), D.L.; artist in oil and water-colour, printing; Winston Churchill Fellow (1968); Hon. Fellow, Univ. College of Bangor, Swansea and Aberystwyth; Cymmrodorion Medal (1991); *b* Llangefni, Anglesey, 1918; *s* of Henry Inglis Wynne Williams. *Educ.:* Shrewsbury School; *studied art* at Slade School of Fine Art (1941-44). *Exhib.:* Colnaghi (1947, 1949, 1970), Leicester Galleries (1951, 1954, 1957, 1967, 1970), Thackeray Gallery (1977, 1979, 1981, 1983, 1985, 1987, 1989, 1991, 1993) and in the provinces; retrospective exhbn. National Museum of Wales (1987). *Work in permanent collections:* National Museum of Wales, Arts Council, Chantrey Bequest. *Publications:* autobiography, Across the Straits (Duckworth, 1973), A Wider Sky (Gwasg Gomer, 1991); illustrated,

513

Gregynog, Kate Roberts (1981). *Address:* Pwllfanogl. Llanfairpwll, Gwynedd LL61 6PD. *Signs work:* "K.W."

WILLIAMS, Mary, R.W.A., S.W.A.; painter of landscape, marine and architectural subjects, also of flowers in water-colour and oil; *b* Ottery St. Mary, Devon; *d* of Fred Williams. *Studied art* at Exeter. *Exhib.:* R.A., R.S.A., Paris Salon, R.I., R.B.A., etc., and in many municipal galleries; one-man show: R.A.M. Museum, Exeter (1974). *Work in permanent collections:* Exeter Art Gallery, Sunderland Art Gallery, R.W.A. Bristol. *Address:* Dormers, Orchard Close, Manor Rd., Sidmouth, Devon. *Signs work:* "Mary Williams."

WILLIAMS, Peter Ernest, N.D.D., A.T.D., F.R.S.A.; artist in oils, water-colour, plaster, wood, metal, terra-cotta, ceramics; formerly Head of Art Department, Oldershaw School (now retd.); muralist and designer for exhbn. and shop-window display; *b* Bebington, 25 Jan., 1925; *s* of John Henry Williams; *m* 1st, Muriel E. Hammer, B.Sc. (*d* 25 June, 1964); 2nd, Patrica D. Wilson (*d* 9 Nov., 1988); two *s,* one *d. Educ.:* Wirral Grammar School; *studied art* at Liverpool College of Art. *Exhib.:* Liverpool Academy of Arts, etc. *Work in permanent collections:* Liverpool University and mural decorations in several churches. *Address:* Hedge-Lea, 43 Higher Bebington Rd., Bebington, Wirral, Merseyside L63 2PH. *Signs work:* "Peter E. Williams."

WILLIAMS, Stephen Lionel, B.A. (1977); artist in pen and ink, water-colour, pencil, printmaker (relief and silk screen); art teacher, Speke Comprehensive School, Liverpool; Director, Bridge Arts Centre, Widnes, Ches.; *s* of Rev. N. F. L. Williams. *Educ.:* Tower College, Rainhill; *studied art* at Liverpool College of Art (1966-68), Harris College School of Art (1968-70), St. Katharine's College of Education, Liverpool (1970-73) under Duncan Glenn, E. Scott Jones, Tony Daffern. *Exhib.:* R.S.A., Mall Galleries, Bridge Arts Centre, Widnes; one-man show, Pentagon Gallery, Stoke-on-Trent. *Work in permanent collections:* St. Katharine's College and private collections; many works on loan. *Address:* 10 Daffodil Cl., Widnes, Ches. *Signs work:* "S. L. Williams."

WILLIAMS, Susan, R.A. Schools Dip.; artist in oil and water-colour; *b* Lichfield, Staffs., 23 July, 1944; *m* Ben Levene; one *s. Educ.:* Lichfield Central School; *studied art* at Byam Shaw School, R.A. Schools. *Exhib.:* regularly at R.A. Summer Exhbn., Spirit of London (prize winner 1984), Ogle Gallery, Cheltenham, Duncan Campbell Gallery, Waterman Gallery, London. *Address:* 26 Netherby Rd., London SE23. *Signs work:* "S.W."

WILLIAMS, Vivian Claud Craddock, M.A. (Oxon.); sculptor and illustrator; Kensington and Chelsea Arts Council (1968); Council of Industrial Design (1959); Trustee, Arts Centre Foundation of Zambia (1975); artist in oil, pen and wash; *b* Hampstead, 3 Mar., 1936; *s* of the late M. S. A. Williams. *Educ.:* Stouts Hill, Uley, Glos.; Repton School, Derbyshire; *studied art* at Repton School under Arthur Norris and Dennis Hawkins; Ruskin School of Drawing, Oxford. *Exhib.:* Wye Valley Art Soc. Exhbn., Coleford Art Exhbn., Chelsea Pottery Exhbn., Lusaka A.C.F. Exhbn., Yemen Arts Assoc., San'a (1982-85), Solecki Arts Foundation L.A., U.S.A (1986). *Addresses:* P.O. Box 7184, Kampala, Uganda; 18 Linver Rd., London SW6; Brasted House, Monmouth. *Signs work:* "V.C.C.W."

WILLIAMSON-BELL, James, R.M.S., S.WL.A.; gold and silver medals, Paris Salon, mem. S.A.F., life mem. Bilan d'l'art Contemporain, silver and gold medals, Art Expo. N.Y.; artist in water-colour, all print forms, sculpture; *b* Willington Quay, 25 Sept., 1938; *m* Lorraine Anne. *Exhib.:* annually R.M.S.,

S.WL.A., R.S.M.A., R.E., Paris Salon, Art Expo, N.Y., and many private and municipal galleries in the U.K., U.S.A., Norway, Switzerland, France. *Work in permanent collections:* Fyldes National Print Collection, Pushkin Museum of Fine Art, Moscow. *Address:* 2 Pauline Gdns., Newcastle-on-Tyne NE15 7TD. *Signs work:* "Williamson-Bell" and see appendix.

WILLIES, Joan, R.M.S. (1976) (Eng.), Hon. Mem. M.A.S.-F., F.I.G.M.A. (U.S.A.), Hon. Mem. Dayton Miniature Soc., Mem. Washington, and New Jersey Miniature Socs., U.S.A.; painter in oils and alkyds, specialising in miniatures; *b* Bristol, England, 23 Dec., 1929; *d* of the late B. Cornish, Royal Marines; *m* Mark Willies; three *s. Educ.:* Bristol Commercial College, additional art studies under private tutors. *Exhib.:* R.M.S., R.I., S.W.A., U.A.(Eng.), M.A.S.-F., Washington, N.J., Zaragoza, Spain, Frankfurt, Germany, Dalhousie University A.G., Canada, Tiffanys, Atlanta, U.S.A., Tokyo, Japan; permanent exhbn. Bilmar Hotel, Treasure Island, Florida. *Publications:* The Artists Work-Book on Miniature Painting; illustrated childrens' books, prints worldwide, St. Francis of Assisi, U.S.A. Ltd. Edn. Cincinnati, Ohio, teaching articles, artist magazines. Finalist Hunting Group award, England. *Address:* Apt. 303, 1001 Pearce Drive, Clearwater, Florida, U.S.A. 34624. *Signs work:* "Joan Willies, R.M.S." and see appendix.

WILLOUGHBY, Trevor John, R.P. (1970); painter in oil, chalk, pastel; illustrator, teacher; visiting lecturer at St. Martin's College of Art, Sir John Cass College of Art, Middlesex Polytechnic; *b* Hull, Yorks., 1926; *s* of F. T. Willoughby; four *s. Educ.:* Hymers College, Hull; Belfast Technical College; *studied art* at Kingston upon Hull College of Art; London School of Printing. *Exhib.:* R.A., R.P., Compendium Gallery, Arts Unlimited, Rye Gallery, Ogilby, Benson & Mather, Quangle Prints, Queen's Elm Gallery, Chenil Gallery, R.B.A. *Work repro.:* illustrations in Queen magazine; Homes and Gardens; Fashions and Fabrics; leading advertisers. *Address:* 4 Offerton Rd., Clapham Common, London SW4 0DH. *Club:* Chelsea Arts. *Signs work:* "Willoughby."

WILLS, Joan, P.V.P.S.W.A., U.A., A.S.A.F., F.R.S.A.; mention hon. (Paris Salon); oil painter; past Vice-Pres., Soc. of Women Artists, Ass. Société des Artistes Français; Council Mem. United Soc. of Artists; *b* Shrewsbury; *d* of the late Keith Abercromby; *m* Major-Gen. J. A. R. Robertson, C.B., C.B.E., D.S.O., D.L.; one *d. Educ.:* Albyn School, Aberdeen; *studied art* at Sir John Cass College, City and Guilds, London, and privately with the late Kenneth Green and the late Stanley Grimm. *Exhib.:* R.O.I., R.B.A., S.W.A., U.A., R.M.S., N.S., Artists of Chelsea, Paris Salon. *Address:* 36 Marlborough Pl., London NW8 0PD. *Signs work:* "Wills."

WILLS, Richard Allin, N.D.D., A.U.A.; painter in oil and water-colour, etc.; art tutor; visiting lecturer; *b* Monmouth, 11 Sept., 1939; *s* of W.L.J. Wills; *m* Vera Elizabeth; one *s*, two *d. Educ.:* King Henry VIII Grammar, Abergavenny; *studied art* at Newport College of Art (1956-61, Thomas Rathmell). *Exhib.:* R.A., R.W.A., Welsh Young Contemporaries, R.S.P.P., U.A., W.C.S.W. *Work in permanent collections:* British Steel Corp., Welsh Div. British Steel, Rank Xerox. *Work commissioned and hung:* Welsh Office, Whitehall; Guildhall School of Music, London; Polytechnic of Wales; Yamazaki Mazak Europe; Royal Monmouthshire Royal Engineers. *Work purchased:* Contemporary Art Society. *Address:* The Studio, Mansard House, Vine Acre, Monmouth, Gwent. *Signs work:* "Richard A. Wills."

WILSON, Arnold, M.A., F.S.A., F.M.A.; Art Consultant; Council Mem. Royal West of England Academy; Chairman of Trustees, Holburne of Menstrie

Museum, Bath, and serves on numerous other Coms.; formerly Director, City Art Gallery, Bristol; *b* Dulwich, 1932; *s* of Robert Arthur Wilson, artist; twice married, two *d* by first marriage. *Educ.:* Selwyn College, Cambridge, and Courtauld Inst. of Art. *Publications:* author: Dictionary of British Marine Painters (3 eds.); Dictionary of British Military Painters; Exploring Museums: South West England; numerous articles for Burlington Magazine, Apollo, Connoisseur, Country Life, etc. *Address:* 4 George St., Bathwick Hill, Bath BA2 6BW. *Club:* Bristol Savages.

WILSON, Chris, B.A.(Hons.) (1982), M.A. (1985); artist in oil and collage; *b* Belfast, 27 Dec., 1959; *m* Cindy Friers; one *s. Educ.:* Belfast Royal Academy; *studied art* at Brighton College of Art (1979-82), University of Ulster (1984-85). *Exhib.:* 'Shocks to the System' A.C.G.B. (1991), 'On the Balcony of the Nation' touring U.S.A. (1991-92), 'Shadows of Light' one-man touring Romania (1992), Bulgaria (1993). *Work in permanent collections:* A.C.G.B., Arts Council of Ireland, Aer Rianta Dublin, Queens University Belfast; private collections in Ireland, England, Germany, U.S.A. *Address:* 44 Victoria Rd., Bangor, Co. Down BT20 5EX. *Signs work:* "CHRIS WILSON" or "C. WILSON" with date.

WILSON, David; painter in oil, acrylic, water-colour, etching; *b* Gillingham, Kent, 23 May, 1936; *s* of Jack Wilson, R.N. (decd.); *m* Sheila; two *s*, two *d. Educ.:* Sir Joseph Williamson's Mathematical School, Rochester; Joint Services School of Linguists; *studied art* at Heatherley's (Evening classes 1976-77, Terry Shave). *Exhib.:* R.A., R.B.A., Royal National Eisteddfod, N.E.A.C., S.G.A.; one-man shows: numerous including Riverside Gallery, London. *Work in permanent collection:* National Library of Wales, Aberystwyth. *Addresses:* Treleddyn Isaf, Bridell, Cardigan, Dyfed SA43 3DQ; The Studio, 3 Cambrian Quay, Cardigan, Dyfed SA43 1EZ. *Signs work:* "David Wilson, Bridell."

WILSON, Douglas, R.C.A., D.F.A., F.R.S.A.; painter in oil and water-colour; *b* 1936; *s* of George William Wilson; *m* Heather Hildersley Brown; one *s. Studied art* at Oxford University (1959-62, Percy Horton, Richard Naish, Geoffrey Rhodes). *Exhib.:* R.A., R.B.A., R.O.I., R.Cam.A., Vis Art I (prizewinner), Edinburgh Festival, National Library of Wales, New Grafton Gallery, Piccadilly Gallery, Thackeray Gallery, Jablonski Gallery, London; one-man shows: Bluecoat Gallery, Williamson A.G. (1981, 1983), King St. Galleries, St. James' (1983, 1986, 1991), Metropolis International Galerie d'Art Geneva (1985), Phoenix Gallery, Lavenham (1987, 1989), Phoenix Gallery, Kingston upon Thames (1987), Anthony Dawson Artists at the Barbican (1987, 1990), Outwood Gallery (1987), Newburgh St. Gallery (1988). *Publication:* author, Wirral Visions. *Address:* 123 Masons Pl., Newport, Salop. *Signs works:* "Douglas Wilson."

WILSON, Eleanor Mavis: see GRÜNEWALD, Eleanor Mavis.

WILSON, Peter Reid, D.A.; artist in oil paint on canvas, lecturer; Head of Painting, Loughborough College of Art and Design; *b* Glasgow, 4 Sept., 1940. *Studied art* at Glasgow School of Art (1960-64). *Exhib.:* Lamont Gallery. *Work in permanent collections:* Contemporary Arts Soc., A.C.G.B., S.A.C., Sheffield City A.G., Ferens A.G. Hull, Nottingham Castle Museum and A.G., Leicester Museum and A.G., Glasgow A.G., Kelvingrove, Stoke-on-Trent Museum and A.G., Kettles Yard, Cambridge, etc. *Publications:* Peter Wilson — Paintings 1979-1985 (Third Eye, Glasgow, 1985), Dacapo — Drawings (Arc Publications, 1989). *Address:* 1 The Square, South Luffenham, Oakham, Leics. LE15 8NS. *Signs work:* c within a circle "Peter Wilson" and date.

WILSON, Susan Ahipara, B.F.A., Dip.R.A. Schools; Abbey Award to British School at Rome; painter in oil on canvas and hardboard; Fellow of Painting, Glos. College of Art and Technology; *b* Dunedin, N.Z., 22 May, 1951; *d* of Rev. C.R. Wilson, B.A. *Educ.:* Westlake Girls High School, N.Z.; *studied art* at Camberwell School of Art (1978-82, Arnold van Praag, Tony Eyton, Dick Lee), R.A. Schools (1982-85, John Le Soeur). *Exhib.:* R.A., Hayward Annual, Northern Young Contemporaries, John Player Portrait award, N.Z. House Gallery, G.L.C. Spirit of London, Richard Ford scholarship to Spain. *Address:* 51 Faraday Rd., Ladbroke Gr., London W10.

WILSON, Timothy Hugh, M.A., M.Phil., F.S.A. (1989), Hon.R.E, (1991), Fellow of Balliol (1990); Keeper of Western Art, Ashmolean Museum, Oxford; *b* Godalming, 8 Apr., 1950; *m* Jane Lott; two *s,* one *d. Educ.:* Winchester College; Corpus Christi College, Oxford; Warburg Inst. (London University); Dept. of Museum Studies (University of Leicester). *Publications:* books and articles on Italian maiolica and Renaissance applied arts. *Address:* Balliol College, Oxford OX1 3BJ.

WILSON, Vincent John, A.T.D., Mem. Newlyn Soc. of Artists, Plymouth Soc. of Artists, Penwith Soc. of Arts; painter and etcher; *b* Mold, Flintshire, 24 Nov., 1933; *s* of J. Wilson; *m* Sheila Richards; one *d. Educ.:* Alun Grammar School, Mold; *studied art* at Chester School of Art (1950-54), Liverpool College of Art (1954-55). *Exhib.:* R.A., R.W.A., R.C.A., Piccadilly, Thackeray, Penwith Galleries, Celle, W. Germany, Welsh Arts Council (1958, 1974, 1981), Cornwall Now (Sussex 1986), Cornwall in the Eighties (Chichester 1987); one-man shows: Exeter University (1966), Newlyn (1971, 1972, 1980), Penzance, Dartmouth (1974), Mold (1976), Plymouth (1979), Taunton (1981). *Work in permanent collection:* Plymouth A.G., Devon C.C., Surrey Educ. Com., Royal Cambrian Academy, Celle. *Address:* 3 Drakefield Drive, Saltash, Cornwall. *Signs work:* "V. Wilson."

WILTON, Andrew, M.A., F.R.S.A., Hon.R.W.S.; museum curator; Keeper of British Art, Tate Gallery (1989—); Curator, Turner Collection, Clore Gallery (1985-89), Curator of Prints and Drawings, Yale Center for British Art (1976-80), Asst. Keeper, Dept. of Prints and Drawings, British Museum (1967-76, 1981-84); *b* Farnham, Surrey, 7 Feb., 1942. *Educ.:* Dulwich College; Trinity College, Cambridge. *Publications:* British Watercolours 1750-1850 (1977); The Life and Work of J.M.W. Turner (1979); Turner and the Sublime (1980); Turner in his Time (1987) and numerous exhbn. catalogues, articles and reviews. *Address:* Tate Gallery, London SW1P 4RG. *Club:* Athenaeum.

WINDSOR, Alan, B.A. (Lond.), Dip.F.A. (Lond.), N.D.D., D.A.(Manc.); artist and writer; art historian; Senior Lecturer, Reading University; *b* Fleetwood, Lancs., 10 July, 1931; *s* of Major G. V. Windsor, M.C., M.B.E.; *m* Elfriede Windsor; one *s,* two *d. Educ.:* Audenshaw Grammar School; *studied art* at Regional College of Art, Manchester (1949-54); Slade School, University College (1954-56); Universities of Paris and Aix (1956-57); Courtauld Institute, London University (1967-69). *Exhib.:* Young Contemporaries, London Group, Gimpel Fils, Roland, Browse & Delbanco, Pollock, Toronto, New Ashgate, Farnham. *Publications:* Peter Behrens, 1868-1940, Architect and Designer (Architectural Press, 1981); Handbook of Modern British Painting, 1900-1980 (Scolar Press, 1992). *Address:* 2 Wykeham Rd., Farnham, Surrey GU9 7JR. *Club:* Architectural Association. *Signs work:* "A. Windsor."

WINER, Zalmon, A.R.B.A. (1984); painter in oil, pastel, acrylic, water-colour; designer, etcher and lithographer; *b* Gateshead, Co. Durham, 21 Nov., 1934; *s* of Louis Winer; *m*; one *s*, two *d*. *Educ.*: Gateshead Grammar School; *studied art and architecture* at Durham University; etching at Central School of Art and Design. *Exhib.*: R.A., R.B.A., P.S., U.A., N.S., Ben Uri Gallery, C.P.S., Safrai Gallery, Jerusalem, Discerning Eye Exhbn. at Mall Galleries (1990), etc. *Work in permanent collections:* Shipley A.G., Oundle Public School Gallery. *Publication:* illustrated Haggadah for the Exilarchs Foundation. *Address:* 11 Gloucester Drive, London NW11 6BH. *Signs work:* see appendix.

WINGATE, Robert Bray, F.R.S.A., Affiliate, Royal Soc. of Medicine; freelance heraldic and medical illustrator; *b* 21 Sept., 1925. *Educ.*: A.B., Lebanon Valley (1948); M.A., Johns Hopkins (1951); M.S., Drexel (1960); Sc.D., Clayton (1982); *studied art* at Pa. Academy of Fine Arts, Phila. (1948); Dept. Art as Applied to Medicine, Johns Hopkins Univ. Medical School, Balto. (1948-51). *Work repro.:* illustrator of Berens and King (1961), King and Wadsworth (1970), An Atlas of Ophthalmic Surgery; Fasanella, Modern Advances in Cataract Surgery (1963); Fasanella, Management of Complications in Eye Surgery (1965); von Noorden and Maumenee, Atlas of Strabismus (1967, 1973); author-illustrator, Perceptions: Glimpses of Our World and Ourselves (1984). *Address:* 136 Shell St., Harrisburg, Pa. 17109, U.S.A. *Signs work:* see appendix.

WINKELMAN, Joseph William, B.A. (1964), C.F.A. (1971), R.E. (1982), R.W.A. (1989); artist and printmaker; President, Royal Soc. of Painter-Printmakers; *b* Keokuk, Iowa, U.S.A., 20 Sept., 1941; *s* of George Winkelman, B.A.; *m* Lowell Belin; two *d*. *Educ.*: University of the South, University of Pennsylvania; *studied art* at University of Oxford, Ruskin School of Drawing (1968-71). *Exhib.:* New Grafton Gallery, R.A., Bohun Gallery, Lumley Cazalet Gallery, Graffiti Gallery, Anthony Dawson, Oxford Gallery. *Work in permanent collections:* Ashmolean Museum, Hereford Museum, Usher Gallery, Victoria A.G., National Museum of Wales. *Address:* The Hermitage, 69 Old High St., Headington, Oxford OX3 9HT. *Signs work:* "J. W. Winkelman."

WINTER, Faith, F.R.B.S., Feodora Gleichen Sculpture Award; sculptor in stone, wood, and bronze; *b* Richmond, Surrey, 1927; *d* of J. F. Ashe, architect; *m* Col. F. M. S. Winter, M.B.E., F.R.S.A.; two *s*, one *d*. *Educ.*: Oak Hall; *studied art* at Guildford and Chelsea Schools of Art. *Exhib.:* R.A., R.B.A., R.W.S., Glasgow Academy of Fine Art, Covent Garden and elsewhere in the U.K.; International Centre of Contemporary Art, Paris; Malaysia and Singapore. *Commissions* include: "The Soldiers" Catterick Camp; "Compassion" Hambro Foundation; The Falklands Islands Memorial relief; The Mysteries of the Rosary, Church of Our Lady Queen of Peace, East Sheen; John Ray statue, Braintree; Air Chief Marshal Lord Dowding and Marshal of the Royal Air Force Sir Arthur "Bomber" Harris statues, The Strand, London; Lennard standing figure 'The Spirit of Youth', Ontario, Canada; Salters' Hall Coat-of-arms, London; Archbishop George Abbot, Guildford; H.R.H. The Princess Royal, The President of Kenya, Jeffrey Archer, Maria Callas and the late Kamal Jumblatt. *Address:* Venzers Studio, Venzers Yard, The Street, Puttenham, Guildford, Surrey GU3 1AU. *Signs work:* "Faith Winter" (formerly "Faith Ashe.")

WINTER, Francis John, R.E., A.T.D. (Lond.), P.P.S.G.A.; senior lecturer (retd.), Hornsey College of Art; artist in water-colour, wood engraver; *b* London, 29 Oct., 1901; *s* of John Ernest Winter; *m* Freda Margaret Lindsay; one *s*, two *d*. *Educ.*: Latymer School, Edmonton; *studied art* at Hornsey School of Art (1915-26) under F. H. Swinstead, R.B.A., J. C. Moody, R.I., R.E., J. H. Willis, R.B.A., A.R.C.A.; London Day Training College under Prof. Nunn, Prof. Burt,

Marion Richardson. *Address:* Ash House, Aspenden, Buntingford, Herts. SG9 9PE.

WINTERINGHAM, Claude Richard Graham, Dip. Arch., F.R.I.B.A., R.B.S.A.; architect; chairman, Sir Barry Jackson Trust (1982-); R.N.V.R. Fleet Air Arm Lt. (1941-46), chairman, Solihull Round Table (1956-57), founder mem. and vice chairman, Solihull Civic Soc. (1958-62), president, B'ham Architecture Assoc. (1971-72); *b* Louth, Lincs., 2 Mar., 1923; *s* of Francis Winteringham, M.B.E. (decd.); *m* Lesley Patricia; two *s*, one *d*. *Awards:* Mason Court Civic Trust (1969), Lichfield City Hall, Civic Soc. Commendation (1976), Lench's Close, Moseley, D.O.E. Housing Design (1983), B'ham Repertory Theatre Architecture (1972). *Address:* 7 Sir Harry's Rd., Edgbaston, Birmingham B15 2UY. *Clubs:* R.I.B.A. Sailing, B'ham Chamber of Industry and Commerce.

WISE, Gillian; artist, architectonic reliefs and paintings; *b* London, 1936. *Educ.:* Wimbledon School of Art (1954-57). *Awards:* Unesco Fellowship, Prague (1968); post-graduate, Repin Institute, Leningrad (1969-70); Research Grant, International Communication Agency (1981); Graham Foundation for the Fine Arts, Chicago (1983-86). *Exhib.:* I.C.A. with Anthony Hill (1963), Tokyo Biennale (1965), "British Sculpture in The Sixties," C.A.S. (1965), "Relief/ Construction/Relief," Museum of Contemporary Art Chicago (1968), Nuremburg Biennale (1969), Systems (1972), Hayward Annual (1978), R.A. Summer Shows (1981-83, 1986-87), Blom and Dorn Gallery, N.Y.C. (1984-85). *Work in permanent collections:* Tate Gallery, British Council, Arts Council, Contemporary Arts Society, V. & A., Gulbenkian, Lisbon. *Architectural commissions:* Foyer wall in stainless steel and acrylic, Nottingham University Hospital; murals in mirror-glass and aluminium, Barbican Centre Cinema. *Address:* 3 passage Rauch, 75011 Paris. *Signs work:* "G. WISE" or "Gillian Wise."

WISHART, Michael; painter, writer; Knight of St. Lazarus; nominated Academician of Italy with gold medal (1980); *b* London, 12 June, 1928; *s* of E. E. Wishart; *m* 1950, Anne, *d* of Sir James Dunn, Bt.; one *s*. *Studied art,* Academie Julian, Paris (1948). *Exhib.:* one-man shows: Archer Gallery (1944), Redfern Gallery (1956, 1958, 1960), Leicester Galleries (1963, 1967, 1969, 1973), portrait of Rudolf Nureyev, Royal Academy (1968), Arts Council "Six Young Painters" (1957), Contemporary Art Society "Recent Acquisitions" Whitechapel Gallery (1968), Morley Gallery (1969); retrospective exhbn., "Paintings 1964-76" David Paul Gallery, Chichester (1976); Parkin Gallery (1985); R.A. Summer Exbhn. (1980, 1985, 1988, 1989, 1990). *Work in permanent collections:* Arts Council, C.A.S., Garman Ryan Collection, Walsall. *Work repro:* Apollo, Burlington Magazine, Studio International, The Book of Joy, The Observer, Arts Review, Dance and Dancers, La Revue Moderne, Art and Literature, "High Diver" (autobiography), 1977. *Address:* 34 Brunswick Sq., Hove, E. Sussex BN3 1ED. *Clubs:* Travellers', Chelsea Arts. *Signs work:* "Michael Wishart."

WITHINGTON, Roger, Dip.A.D. (Graphics) (1966), A.T.D. (1967), A.R.E. (hon. retd.); artist/designer in pencil and water-colour; artist at Bank of England (1986-93), designed new series of banknotes known as Series E; *b* Prestwich, 4 Oct., 1943; *m* Rose-Marie Edna Cobley; one *s*, one *d*. *Educ.:* Barry Grammar/ Technical School, S. Glam.; *studied art* at Cardiff College of Art (1962-63, etching: Philip Jennings, A.R.E.), Newport (Gwent) College of Art (1963-66, illustration: John Wright). *Exhib.:* R.E. Galleries, Bankside Galleries. *Publications:* designed/part author series of booklets to accompany new banknotes. *Address:* 86 Thorley Hill, Bishops Stortford, Herts. CM23 3NB. *Signs work:* "R. Withington" or "R.W."

WITHROW, William John, Honour B.A., Art and Archaeology (1950), Art Specialist, O.C.E. (1951), B.Ed. (1955), M.Ed. (1958), M.A. (1965); Director Emeritus, Art Gallery of Ontario; Member: Order of Canada (1980), Fellow, Canadian Museums Assoc. (1985), Canadian Art Museums Directors Organisation, American Assoc. of Museums, Assoc. of Art Museum Directors, Canadian National Com. for I.C.O.M., Art Advisory Com., University Club of Toronto; *b* Toronto, 30 Sept., 1926; *s* of W. F. Withrow; *m* Jure Roselea Van Ostrom; three *s*, one *d*. *Educ.:* University of Toronto; *studied art* at University of Toronto (1946-65, Professor Peter Brieger, Professor Stephen Vickers). *Publications:* Sorel Etrog Sculpture, Contemporary Canadian Painting. *Address:* 7 Malabar Pl., Don Mills, Ontario. *Club:* University Club of Toronto.

WOLKERS-RANSOME, Joan Elizabeth Margaret, N.D.D. (Painting, 1948), Abbey Scholarship (1949), R.A. Silver Medals (1951, 52, 53); retd. teacher; *b* Tunbridge Wells, 28 Aug., 1928; *d* of M. E. Ransome; *m* G.L. Wolkers; one *s*. *Educ.:* Lawnside, Malvern; *studied art* at Malvern School of Art under Victor Hume Moody (1945-50) and R.A. Schools under Henry Rushbury, Fleetwood Walker and William Dring (1950-54); Royal Academy, Amsterdam (1954-58). *Exhib.:* R.A., R.B.S.A., R.P., N.E.A.C., Brighton A.G., Worcester A.G., Malvern Art Club, Kenn Group, Exeter. Specialises in portraiture. *Address:* 37 Powderham Cres., Exeter EX4 6BZ. *Signs work:* "J.E.M. Wolkers-Ransome."

WOLSTENHOLME, Jonathan; artist/illustrator in water-colour, oil, pen and ink; *b* London, 22 Nov., 1950; *m* Margaret; one *s*. *Educ.:* Purley Grammar School; *studied art* at Croydon College of Art (1969-72). *Exhib.:* two one-man shows in London, others in Paris and Brussels. *Work in permanent collection:* John Campbell Gallery London. *Address:* 32 Faraday Rd., Wimbledon, London SW19 8PD. *Signs work:* "Jonathan Wolstenholme."

WOLVERSON, Margaret Elizabeth, N.D.D., A.T.D., elected A.R.M.S. (1977); painter of equestrian scenes, portraits etc.; formerly taught at Hornsea Inst. of Further Education and Stourbridge College of Art; *b* 1937; *d* of Charles Lloynes Smith, F.I.M.T.A., A.C.C.A.; *m* 1961; one *s;* (div. 1985); *m* 1987, S. Jones-Robinson. *Studied art* at Dudley School of Art, Wolverhampton College of Art, Leicester College of Art. *Exhib.:* R.M.S., Mall Galleries, Cheltenham Group, Britain's Painters; one-man show Dean Heritage Centre (1993). *Work in permanent collections:* East Riding Collection for Schools, Ferens A.G.; private collections in U.K., U.S.A. *Address:* Sunny Bank, Pope's Hill, Newnham-on-Severn, Glos. GL14 1JS. *Signs work:* see appendix.

WOLVERSON, Martin, F.R.B.S. (1971), F.R.S.A. (1976); R.B.S. Silver medal (1971), Trident Television Fine Art Fellow (1977-78), Fulbright Prof. Kansas City Art Inst. (1985); sculptor in wood, stone, metal, lecturer; *b* Wolverhampton, 26 May, 1939; *s* of Cyril Wolverson, accountant; *m* (1) Margaret Smith; one *s*; (2) Sandra Tipper. *Educ.:* Wednesbury Boys High School; *studied art* at Wolverhampton School of Art (1956-60, Tom Wright, John Paddison), Goldsmiths' College (1960-61). *Exhib.:* widely in the North, London and Kansas. *Work in permanent collections:* Ferens A.G., Hull, Usher A.G., Lincoln, Yorkshire Television, N.C.B., Ecclesiastic Insurance Co. Ltd., Lincolnshire and Humberside Arts, Humberside C.C., Leeds City A.G., and private collections. *Address:* The Holbrooks, Mount Pleasant East, Robin Hoods Bay, Whitby, N. Yorks. YO22 4RF. *Signs work:* "M. Wolverson."

WONG, Ying; artist-paintress in Canadian Chinese water-colour; b Guangzhou, China; 21 Feb., 1936; graduated from The Cantonese Academy of Arts, Guangzhou (1962). *Exhib.:* one-man shows, Hongkong and Singapore (1976); participated in Chinese Cultural Week in Fort Erie, Ontario; and Chinese Cultural Centre in Toronto (1978); agency: Studio Colleen, 459 Sussex Drive, Ottawa, Canada. *Publications:* How to paint flowers and birds, and How to paint traditional Chinese characters (Hongkong 1970). *Address:* 104 Margaret Ave., Willowdale M2J-4C5, Canada. *Signs work:* "Wong Ying" and see appendix.

WONNACOTT, John Henry, Slade Dip. (1962); painter in oil; b London, 1940; s of John Alfred Wonnacott, A.R.I.B.A.; m Anne Rozalie Wesolowska, B.Sc.; two d. *Educ.:* University College School; *studied art* at Slade School (1958-63). *Exhib.:* Hayward (1974), R.A. Jubilee (1952-77), Marlborough (1981), Marlborough, N.Y. (1983), Tate Gallery (1984), The Foudation Veranneman (1986-87), The Pursuit of the Real, Barbican (1990); one-man shows, Minories, Colchester (1972), Rochdale (1978); touring, Marlborough (1980-81, 1985, 1988), Scottish National Portrait Gallery (1986-87). *Work in permanent collections:* M. of W., Arts Council, Rochdale A.G., Norwich Castle Museum, Tate Gallery, Scottish National Portrait Gallery. *Address:* 5 Cliff Gdns., Leigh-on-Sea, Essex.

WOOD, Andy, Dip.A.D. (1970), A.R.B.A. (1980), R.I. (1981); painter in acrylic, oil and water-colour; b Porlock, Som., 1947; s of H.E. Wood. *Educ.:* schools in Walton-on-Thames, Hersham and Dorking; *studied art* at Croydon and Newport Colleges of Art (1965-70). *Exhib.:* R.I., R.B.A., Thackeray Gallery, etc. *Address:* Charm Cottage, The Street, Charmouth, Dorset DT6 6NX. *Signs work:* "Andy Wood" or "A. Wood."

WOOD, Annette (Mrs.): see GARDNER, Annette.

WOOD, Christopher Paul, B.A.Hons. (1984), M.A. (1986); painter in oil on canvas and printmaking mediums; A/L lecturer in Art and Design, York College of Art/Leeds Polytechnic (part-time); b Leeds, 10 June, 1961; s of Peter Liddle Wood; m Simone Abel; two d. *Educ.:* St. Matthew's C. of E. School, Allerton Grange High School, Leeds; *studied art* at Jacob Kramer School of Art (1980-81), Leeds Polytechnic (1981-84), Chelsea School of Art (1985-86). *Exhib.:* one-man shows: Oldham City A.G. (1986), Sue Williams Gallery, London (1989, 1990, 1992, 1994); mixed shows: Festival Hall (1986), I.C.A. Young Contemporaries (1986), Art London (1989, 1990, 1991), Oldham City A.G. (1989), New Generation, London (1990), Bonhams, Knightsbridge (1991), etc. *Publication:* From the Land to the Seas — Limited Edn. (Artist Books, 1984). *Address:* 1 Norfok Pl., Chapel Allerton, Leeds LS7 4PT. *Signs work:* full signature on back of canvas; initialled on front of paintings — "C.P.W." and date.

WOOD, Duncan, N.E.A.C. (1991), B.A. (Hons.) (1984); artist in oil, pastel, pencil, water-colour; b London, 14 Nov., 1960. *Educ.:* Kingham Hill School, Oxfordshire; *studied art* at Gloucester College of Art (1980-81), Sheffield College of Art (1980-84, Brian Peacock, Terry Lee). *Exhib.:* R.A., N.E.A.C., R.O.I., Cardiff, Birkenhead, Edinburgh, Fosse Gallery, Waterman Fine Art, Discerning Eye (1991, 1992), W.H. Patterson Fine Art. *Work in permanent collections:* Sheffield University and private collections in London and throughout the country, also N.Y., and Japan. *Address:* Flat 1, 1 Church St., Baslow, Derbyshire DE45 1RY. *Club:* N.E.A.C. *Signs work:* "Duncan Wood."

WOOD, Gerald Stanley Kent, M.B.I.A.T. (1968), M.S.A.I. (1977), F.E.T.C. (1978); artist and architectural illustrator in pencil, ink, water-colour, gouache and tempera, perspectivist, architectural technician, tutor, lecturer; *b* Cambridge, 29 Oct., 1923; *s* of Harry Stanley Wood. *Educ.:* Perse Preparatory School, Cambridge, Elmers Grammar School, Old Bletchley, Bucks.; *studied art* under H. Sylvester Stannard, R.B.A. (1934-39). *Exhib.:* R.A., R.B.A., R.I., R.M.S., N.E.A.C., U.A., N.S., S.B.A., S.G.A., P.S., Contemporary British Watercolours, Pictures for Schools, Britain in Water-colours, Britain's Painters, Lord Mayor's Art Award, Hesketh Hubbard Art Soc., Chelsea Art Soc., Open Salon, Luton Museum. *Official purchase:* Theatre Museum. *Work in permanent collections:* Theatre Royal, Haymarket, National Westerminser Bank; *private collections:* England, Wales, Australia, Canada, Germany, Saudi Arabia. *Address:* 21 Salisbury Rd., Luton, Beds. LU1 5AP. *Signs work:* see appendix.

WOODFORD, David, N.D.D., A.T.C. with distinction, Cert. R.A.S.; painter in oil and water-colour; *b* Rawmarsh, Yorks., 1 May, 1938; *m* June; two *s*. *Educ.:* Lancing College; *studied art* at West Sussex College of Art (1955-59), Leeds College of Art (1959-60), Royal Academy Schools (1965-68). He lives by his painting. Cambrian Academician. *Address:* Ffrancon House, Ty'n-Y-Maes, Bethesda, Bangor, Gwynedd LL57 3LX. *Signs work:* "David Woodford."

WOODIE: see RAINE, Sarah Lamar.

WOODINGTON, Walter, R.P., R.B.A., N.E.A.C.; painter in oil and water-colour; part-time teacher, Woolwich Polytechnic Art School (1946-60); appointed Curator, Royal Academy Schools (1961-84); *b* London, June, 1916; *s* of Frederick Woodington; *m* Jacqueline Murray. *Studied art* at Woolwich Polytechnic Art School and City and Guilds Art School under A. R. Middleton-Todd, R.A. *Exhib.:* R.A., R.P., R.B.A., N.E.A.C., etc. *Work repro.:* for Hutchinson's and Odhams Press. *Address:* 5 Kenver Ave., Finchley, London N12 0PG. *Signs work:* "WOODINGTON."

WOODS, Grace Mary, A.R.C.A.; artist in black and white and pastel, and weaving; *b* Ilford, Essex, 25 Feb., 1909; *d* of Charles J. Kaye; *m* Sidney W. Woods, A.R.C.A. (decd.); two *s*, three *d*. *Educ.:* Ursuline Convent, Forest Gate, E7; *studied art* at West Ham Art School and Royal College of Art in Design and Engraving Schools. *Exhib.:* R.A. and other London galleries. *Work purchased:* by private collectors. *Address:* 157 Warren Rd., Chelsfield, Orpington, Kent BR6 6ES. *Signs work:* "Mary Woods."

WOOLF-NELLIST, Meg, B.A., A.T.D., F.S.D.-C; awarded Exhibition, R.C.A. (1949); formerly lecturer in art, Rachel McMillan College of Educ., Director, Bermuda Art Assoc. School (1950-52); artist in stone, wood, calligrapher; *b* Isle of Thanet, 10 Dec., 1923; *d* of Dr. E. A. Woolf, D.Litt.; *m* Anthony Nellist; one *s*, three *d*. *Educ.:* Couvent des Oiseaux; *studied art* at Ravensbourne College of Art, Brighton College of Art (1939-42). *Exhib.:* Roland, Browse and Delbanco, A.I.A., R.B.A., R.A., V. & A., Russell Cotes, Hove A.G. (one-man, 1948); with Designer Craftsmen (1968-69), Hornchurch A.G. (1986, 1987, 1989, 1991). *Work repro.:* Studio. *Work in private collections:* Canada, U.S.A., Germany, Australia. *Address:* 84 Front Lane, Cranham, Upminster, Essex. *Signs work:* see appendix.

WOOLFORD, Harry Russell Halkerston, O.B.E. (1970), M.A.(Hon.) Dundee University (1976); until 1970 specialist in picture restoration; chief restorer, National Gallery of Scotland; Hon. Mem. Assoc. of British Picture Restorers; *b* Edinburgh, 23 May, 1905; *s* of H. Woolford, engineer; *m* Nancy Philip; one *d*.

Educ.: Edinburgh; *studied art* at Edinburgh College of Art (painting and drawing) and R.S.A. Life School (Carnegie Travelling Scholarship and Chalmers Bursary, London, Paris and Italy). Fellow, Museums Association and International Institute for Conservation of Historic and Artistic Works. *Address:* 7A Barntongate Ave., Edinburgh EH4 8BD. *Club:* Scottish Arts.

WOOLLASTON, Mountford Tosswill; artist in oil, water-colour, pen, pencil; *b* Toko, N.Z., 1910; *s* of J. R. Woollaston, farmer; *m* Edith Alexander; three *s*, one *d. Educ.:* Stratford Technical High School, N.Z.; *studied art* at Nelson under Hugh Scott (1930), Christchurch under Len Booth (1931), Dunedin under R. N. Field (1932), and particularly under Flora Scales from Hans Hoffman's School in Munich (1935). *Exhib.:* many one-man shows in N.Z., Melbourne and Sydney (1958). *Official purchases:* National Gallery of Victoria, Melbourne, Art Gallery of N.S.W., Sydney, all main N.Z. galleries and universities. *Address:* Upper Moutere, Nelson 7152, N.Z. *Signs work:* "Woollaston."

WOOTTON, Frank, A.A.; President, Guild of Aviation Artists; artist in oil and water-colour, gold medallist, travelling scholarship (1930), official artist R.A.F. (1944-46); *b* Milford, 30 July, 1914; *s* of F. Wootton, R.N.; *m* Virginia Cawthorne; two *s*, one *d. Educ.:* Eastbourne; *studied art* under Reeve-Fowkes, Eric Ravillious, Eastbourne School of Art. *Exhib.:* R.A., Towner Art Gallery, Eastbourne, R.O.I., Imperial War Museum, Paris, Rangoon, New York. *Work in permanent collections:* Sussex Collection, Eastbourne; Command Stations, R.A.F.; Imperial War Museum; Smithsonian Inst. National Air and Space Museum; Australian War Memorial, Canberra. *Publications:* How to Draw Aircraft, How to Draw Cars, Wie Zeichne Ich Autos. The Aviation Art of Frank Wootton, At Home in the Sky, The Landscape Paintings of Frank Wootton (1959), Frank Wootton 50 Years of Aviation Art. *Address:* Mayflower House, Alfriston, Sussex. *Signs work:* "Wootton."

WORKMAN, Mrs. Caroline Nova; dress designer; *b* Dewsbury, 31 Oct., 1965; *d* of Graham Teasdill, museum and art gallery curator; *m* Andrew Paul Workman. *Educ.:* Stourfield and Beaufort Schools, Bournemouth, and the School of Fashion, Bournemouth and Poole College of Art and Design. Practices as Caroline Nova Fashions. *Address:* 99 Carbery Ave., Southbourne, Bournemouth BH6 3LP.

WORSLEY, John Godfrey Bernard; portrait painter, marine artist, sculptor, illustrator, glass engraver, oil, water-colour, charcoal, ink; Past Pres. (1983-88) R.S.M.A.; Lieut. R.N.V.R. (1939-45), Official Naval War Artist (1943-45); creator of 'Albert R.N.', the dummy P.O.W. escape device (1944); *b* 16 Feb., 1919. *Studied art* at Goldsmiths' College (1935-38). *Exhib.:* R.S.M.A. annually, R.A., R.P.; one-man shows: Mall Galleries. *Work in permanent collections:* Imperial War Museum, National Maritime Museum, provincial galleries and Exxon Collection N.Y. *Publications:* Drawing Ships, and many children's book and television programme illustrations. *Address:* Park Studio, Putney Park La., London SW15 5HD. *Clubs:* Savage, Naval. *Signs work:* "John Worsley."

WORTH, Leslie Charles, A.R.C.A. (Lond.) (1946), R.B.A. (1951), R.W.S. (1959), F.R.S.A. (1992); prize-winner Hallmark International Art Award, New York (1955); painter in water-colour and oil; President, R.W.S., R.B.A.; *b* Bideford, Devon, 6 June 1923; *m* Jane Taylor; one *s*, three *d. Educ.:* St. Budeaux School, Plymouth; *studied art* at Plymouth School of Art (1938-39, 1942-43), Bideford School of Art (1940-42), Royal College of Art (1943-46). *Exhib.:* Agnews, Mercury Gallery, Wildenstein. Several mural commissions. *Work in permanent collections:* R.A., National Gallery of New Zealand, Aberdeen,

Birmingham, Brighton, Burton (Bideford), Rochdale, Southport and Wakefield Art Galleries, Eton College, West Riding of Yorks. Educ. Authority, G.L.C., Admiralty; private collections: H.M. Queen Elizabeth, Queen Mother and several private collections. *Publications:* The Practice of Watercolour Painting (Pitmans and Watson Guptil, 1977, Search Press 1980); magazine articles. *Address:* 11 Burgh Heath Rd., Epsom, Surrey KT17 4LW. *Club:* Arts. *Signs work:* "Leslie Worth."

WORTH, Philip, M.A., LL.B., Hon. Sec. F.P.S.; self taught artist in acrylic; *b* Gillingham, 23 June, 1933; *s* of Lloyd Worth, Major (R.E.); *m* Jennifer Louise; two *d*. *Educ.:* Royal High School, Edinburgh, Edinburgh University. *Exhib.:* many one-man and group shows throughout U.K. since 1984. *Address:* The White House, 282 St. John's Rd., Boxmoor, Hemel Hempstead, Herts. HP1 1QG. *Signs work:* "P. WORTH."

WRAY, Peter, R.E. (1991), M.A. (1992), P.G.Dip.A.D. (1984), Cert.Ed. (1972); artist in printmaking/painting; Senior lecturer in Printmaking, University College of Ripon and York St. John; *b* Sedgefield, Co. Durham, 27 Oct., 1950; *m* Cecilia; two *d*. *Educ.:* St. Mary's School, Darlington; *studied art* at St. Mary's College, Strawberry Hill, Twickenham (1969-72), Goldsmiths' College (1983-84, John Rogers, Peter Mackarrell), Leeds Polytechnic (1990-92, Geoff Teasdale). *Exhib.:* R.E., International Print Biennale, New Academy Gallery, Tesser Gallery, etc. *Address:* 53 South Parade, Northallerton, N. Yorkshire DL7 8SL. *Signs work:* "P. Wray."

WRIGHT, Austin Andrew; Ricardo da Silvera Acquisition Prize, São Paulo Biennale (1957); Gregory Fellowship in Sculpture, Leeds University (1961-64); Hon. Doctorate, York University (1977); Hon. Fellow Humberside College (1986); sculptor in wood, lead, aluminium and bronze; *b* Chester, 1911. *Work in permanent collections:* Art Galleries of Bradford, Wakefield, Leeds, York, Fitzwilliam, Swansea, V. & A., Whitworth, Sheffield, Huddersfield, Arts Council, Arts Council for Wales, Contemporary Art Soc., National Museum of Wales, Abbott Hall, Kendal, Preston, Leeds Univ., York Univ., G.L.C., Museum of Modern Art, São Paulo, public collections in Sweden, Venezuela and U.S.A. *Address:* The Green, Upper Poppleton, York YO2 6DP.

WRIGHT, Bert, R.S.M.A., F.R.S.A.; Council mem., Royal Soc. of Marine Artists, mem., Wapping Group of Artists who specialise in paintings of the River Thames; marine painter, but also includes architectural subjects and landscapes. *Studied art* at Nottingham College of Art. *Exhib.:* R.A., and regularly at major galleries in the London area and in the U.S.A. *Work in private collections:* U.K., U.S.A., and the Far East. *Commissions:* New York Yacht Club, Sultan of Oman, Daily Express, Standard Chartered Bank, British American Tobacco, Mullard Electronics, Beecham Group, Lloyds, Allied Dunbar. *Address:* 19 Carew Rd., Ealing, London W13 9QL.

WRIGHT, Gordon Butler, F.B.S. Comm., F.Inst.C., Mem. International Association of Artists; professional artist in oils; *b* Darlington, Co. Durham, 2 Apr., 1925; *s* of Reginald Wright; *m* Joan. *Educ.:* Gladstone School, Darlington and Kings College, Newcastle; *studied art* at Chichester College of Art (1943-44) followed by two periods of study in Amsterdam and The Hague. Influenced by the Dutch Romantic School. *Exhib.:* Galerie Montmartre, Paris, Grosvenor Gallery and Portal Gallery, London, Trinity Art Gallery, Wareham, Whitgift Galleries, London, Recorded in the National Maritime Museum, Greenwich. *Publications:* The Collector's Guide to Paintings as an Investment. *Address:* 123 Wetherby Rd., Harrogate, Yorks. *Signs work:* "G. B. Wright."

WRIGHT, H. W.; painter in oil and water-colour of genre, landscapes, architecture and nudes in representational style; *b* Walsall, 9 Aug., 1912. *Educ.:* Queen Mary's School; *studied* at Dudley Training College and Bournemouth College of Art. *Exhib.:* since 1945 exclusively in London; since 1952 worked intensively in Avignon. *Official purchasers:* City of London, municipal galleries of Kensington and Chelsea, Bournemouth, Bury and Walsall. Livery mem. of Painter-Stainers, City Freeman and mem. of City Livery Club and Guild of Freeman. A.G.B.I. steward for City (1977). Mem. Chelsea Art Soc. *Address:* 44G Holland Park, London W11. *Signs work:* "H.W. WRIGHT."

WRIGHT, Valerie Margaret, B.Ed.Hons. (1977), S.W.A. (1986), S.B.A. (1987); landscape, botanical and wildlife painter in water-colour; *b* Manchester, 6 Jan., 1934; *d* of Sydney Wainwright Musgrove; *m* Norman Wright; one *s*, two *d. Educ.:* Peterborough High School, Hendon Polytechnic; *studied art* at Coloma College (Constance Stubbs, Norma Jameson). *Exhib.:* R.I., S.W.A., S.B.A., Portico Gallery, Manchester, Manchester Academy, B.W.S., Gorstella Gallery; one-man shows: Chester, Warrington, Bolton Octagon Theatre, Frodsham Arts Centre, Norton Priory. *Address:* Appletree Cottage, 55 Rushgreen Rd., Lymm, Ches. WA13 9PS. *Signs work:* "Valerie Wright."

WROUGHTON, Julia, N.D.D. (1957), A.R.C.A. (1960), A.R.W.A. (1963); painter in oil and water-colour; Principal, Inniemore School of Painting since 1967; *b* Bridge of Allan, Stirlingshire, 24 Oct., 1934; *d* of Robert Lewis Wroughton, Controller of Customs, Zanzibar; *m* Alastair Macdonald; one *s,* three *d. Educ.:* Beacon School, Bridge of Allan; *studied art* at Colchester School of Art (1953-57) under John O'Connor, Hugh Cronyn, Royal College of Art (1957-60) under Carel Weight, R.A., Colin Hayes, R.A. *Exhib.:* R.A., one-man show: Torrance Gallery, Edinburgh. *Work in permanent collections:* Royal West of England Academy, Nuffield Foundation. *Address:* Inniemore Lodge, Pennyghael, Isle of Mull. *Signs work:* "Julia Wroughton," "J. W."

WU, Ching-Hsia; artist; paintress in water-colour and poetess; Prof. Shanghai Academy of Fine Arts, Prof. Shanghai Normal University; Vancouver Golden Jubilee Chinese Carnival Honorary Prize, Canada (1936); *b* Changchow, China, 11 Feb., 1910. *Educ.:* at home and studied art under father. *Exhib.:* Shanghai, Nanking, Peking, Rome, Jakarta, Surabaya, Singapore, Helsinki, Tokyo, Hong Kong, Osaka, Paris, Stockholm, Canton, etc. *Work in permanent collections:* Shanghai Art Gallery; Katesan House, Jakarta; etc. *Publication:* Select Work of Wu Qing-Xia. *Address:* 301/3, Lane 785, Ju Lu Road, Shanghai (China). *Clubs:* China Art Society, Shanghai, Accademico d'Europa. *Signs work:* "WU Ching-Hsia," (Wu Qing-Xia).

WUNDERLICH, Paul; painter in oil, gouache, lithography; sculptor; *b* Eberswalde, 10 Mar., 1927; *s* of Horst Wunderlich, pilot; *m* Karin Székessy; two *d. Educ.:* Berlin High School; *studied art* at Hochschule für Bildende Künste, Hamburg, under Prof. W. Titze. *Exhib.:* all over Europe, United States, Japan, S. Africa and Australia. *Work in permanent collections:* in museums in Europe, U.S.A. and Japan. *Publications:* Paul Wunderlich (Denoel, Paris 1972), Lithografien 1959-73 (Office du Livre, Fribourg Suisse), Monographie 1978 (Filipacchi Paris), Monographie (1955-80), Huber, Offenbach, Homo Sum 1978 (Piper, Munich), Bilder zu Manet (Cotta, Germany 1978). *Address:* Haynstr. 2. D-20249 Hamburg 20. *Signs work:* "Paul Wunderlich."

WYATT, Arthur Leonard, T.D. (art pottery), F.F.P.S.; artist in acrylics, mixed media; art teacher (1950-82); *b* London, 6 Dec., 1922; *s* of A.A. Wyatt; *m* Margaret Sybil Lucy; two *s. Educ.:* West Ham Grammar School; *studied art* at

Hornsey School of Art (1950's). *Exhib.:* 19 one-man shows in U.K., America, Germany, Norway, S. Africa; numerous group shows with F.P.S.; invited exhibitor (11 works) 49th World Sci-Fi Convention, Brighton (1987). *Work in permanent collections:* Pennsylvania Museum of Modern Art, City A.G. Lichfield, Gateshead Municipal Collection. *Publications:* Illustrated five rambling books (Essex, Herts.). *Address:* 1 Kenwood Gdns., Gants Hill, Ilford, Essex. *Signs work:* "WYATT."

WYATT, Joyce Eileen (Mrs Derek Wraith), R.M.S., U.A.S., S.W.A., P.S.; Prix Rowland and Mention Honorable (Paris Salon, 1963); Médaille D'Argent (Paris Salon, 1965); Médaille D'Or (Paris Salon, 1969); Member of La Société des Artistes Français (1969); portrait painter in oil, water-colour; *b* London; *d* of Francis W. Wyatt, company director; *m* Dr. Derek Greenway Wraith; one *s,* one *d. Educ.:* Copthall School, Mill Hill; *studied art* at Hornsey College of Art, and under Francis Hodge and W. Durac Barnett. *Exhib.:* R.A., R.P., R.M.S., R.B.A., Société des Artistes Français, U.A., S.W.A., etc.; one-man shows: Federation British Artists, Edinburgh Festival Exhbn., Rutland Sq., Edinburgh, La Galerie Mouffe, Paris. *Address:* Archgate, North Stoke, nr. Wallingford, OX9 6BL. *Signs work:* "WYATT."

WYE, Charles; painter in oil and pastel; *b* London, 5 June, 1925; *s* of the late Yngve Stromberg. *Educ.:* Alpine College, Arveyes, Switzerland and King's College, London; *studied art* privately under E. Parnell-Bailey, A.R.Cam.A., F.Ph.S., U.A. (1947-53). *Exhib.:* R.O.I., U.A., N.S., etc. *Work in permanent collection:* Sun Life of Canada Building, London. *Publication:* Concept of Progress. *Address:* 33 Mall Chambers, Kensington Mall, London W8. *Signs work:* "WYE."

WYER, Annraoi, B.A. Hons. Fine Art (1986), Dip. Design Hons. (1985); Greenshield Foundation award, Montreal (1988), President's Gold medal (1987); Prof. of Art, Blackrock College; painter, printmaker, illustrator; *b* Dublin, 7 Sept., 1963; *d* of Henry A. Wyer. *Educ.:* Blackrock College; *studied art* at National College of Art and Design, Dublin, Dublin Inst. of Technology (1981-84, Alice Hanratty, Patrick Graham). *Exhib.:* Ljubljana (1987, 1989), Varna (1989, 1991), Taipei (1988), various national exhbns. Work in corporate and private collections. *Address:* 146 Upper Glenageary Rd., Dun Laoire, Co. Dublin, Eire. *Clubs:* Assoc. of Artists in Ireland, Black Church Print Studio. *Signs work:* "Annraoi Wyer."

WYLES, June, B.A. (Hons.) Fine Art, M.A. Printmaking; painter/printmaker in oil, charcoal—landscape and the human form; lecturer of art, Berkshire College of Art and Design; *b* Berks., 1955. *Studied art* at St. Martin's School of Art. *Exhib.:* one-man shows: Dusseldörf, London. *Address:* 14A Eldon Rd., Reading, Berks. RG1 4DL. *Signs work:* "June Wyles."

WYLIE, Rose Forrest, N.D.D., M.A., R.C.A.; painter in oil; *b* Hythe, Kent, 1934; *d* of Alexander Forrest Wylie, O.B.E., Director of Ordnance, India; *m* Roy Oxlade; one *s*, two *d*. *Studied art* at Folkestone and Dover School of Art, Goldsmiths' College, R.C.A. *Exhib.:* Hayward Annual (1982), Cleveland International Drawing Biennale (1985), Metropole Gallery Winter Show (1985), S.E. Arts Exhbn. Open View (1986-87), Scottish Drawing Competition (1988), Odette Gilbert Gallery 'Women and Water' (1988), John Moores (1991); one-man show: Trinity Arts Centre, Tunbridge Wells (1985); two-man show: Odette Gilbert Gallery (1988); group shows: Pomeroy Purdy Gallery (1988), Towner Gallery (1991), R.A. Summer Exhbn. (1992, 1993). *Address:* Forge Cottage, Newnham, Sittingbourne, Kent ME9 0LQ. *Signs work:* "Rose Wylie."

WYLLIE, George Ralston, A.R.S.A., R.G.I., D.Litt.; Fellow, Hand Hollow, N.Y.; sculptor; writer; performer; *b* Glasgow, 1921; *s* of Andrew and Harriet Wyllie; *m* Daphne Winifred Watts; two *d. Educ.*: Allan Glen's and Bellahouston, Glasgow. *Exhib.:* (selected): Demarco Gallery, Third Eye, Serpentine, Watermans, Worcester Art Museum, U.S.A., World Finance Center, N.Y. *Events:* 'A Day Down A Goldmine', Edinburgh Festival, I.C.A., London; 'Tramway', Glasgow; 'Straw Locomotive, Glasgow'; 'Paper Boat', Glasgow, London, New York, Antwerp. *Collections:* (selected): A.C.G.B.; S.A.C.; Glasgow, Whitworth Manchester, Worcester (U.S.A.) museums; U.F.A. Fabrik, Berlin; Getty Foundation. *Address:* 9 McPherson Drive, Gourock, Renfrewshire PA19 1LJ. *Signs work:* "G.R.W."

WYLLIE, Gordon Hope, D.A. (Glas. 1953), R.S.W. (1967); artist in water-colour, acrylic and oil; *b* Greenock, 12 Feb., 1930; *s* of James Wyllie; *m* Helen Wyllie; two *s. Educ.*: Greenock High School; *studied art* at Glasgow School of Art (1949-53) under Wm. Armour, R.S.A., R.S.W.; Hospitalfield College of Art (1953) under Ian Fleming, R.S.A., R.S.W. and Mary Armour, R.S.A., R.S.W. *Exhib.:* R.S.A., R.G.I., R.S.W., Compass Gallery, Glasgow; one-man shows in Gateway, Edinburgh, Douglas & Foulis, Edinburgh, Citizens Theatre, Glasgow, Blythswood Gallery, 208 Gallery, Glasgow, Strathclyde University Staff Club, Lillie A.G., Compass Gallery, regular exhibitor Open Eye Gallery, Edinburgh. *Work in permanent collections* of Argyll, Fife, Renfrewshire, Ross and Cromarty Authorities, Paisley A.G., Lillie A.G., Milngavie and many private collections in U.K., U.S.A., Israel, Germany, etc. *Work repro.:* at one time part-time illustrator for the Glasgow Bulletin. *Address:* 17 Fox St., Greenock. *Signs work:* "Wyllie."

WYNNE, Althea, A.R.C.A. (1960), A.R.B.S. (1990); sculptor in clay and plaster; *b* Bedford, 6 Oct., 1936; *d* of Group Capt. F.R. Wynne, M.B.E.; *m* Antony Barrington-Brown; one *s*, two *d. Educ.*: North Foreland Lodge School; *studied art* at Farnham Art School, Hammersmith College, R.C.A. (John Skeaping). *Exhib.:* Salisbury Festival (1991), Margam Sculpture Pk. (1991). *Work in public collections:* 3 horses 1½ × L/size, bronze, Mincing Lane EC1; Family of goats L/size bronze, Barnard's Wharf Rotherhithe; Trilithon, 2.5 m stone, Salisbury District Hospital. *Address:* Turner's Chapel, Weaveland Rd., Tisbury, Wilts. SP3 6HJ.

Y

YALLUP, Pat, Dip.Ad.S.A. (1956), S.I.A.D., A.T.D. (1963); artist in water-colour (landscapes and abstracts), oil (portraits); graphic designer, Academy Wales, and Pat Yallup Studio/Gallery, Llandogo, Gwent, (teacher Academy Wales own School); *b* Johannesburg, S. Africa, 29 Sept., 1929; *d* of Hugh Astley Treadwell, accountant; *m* R. W. Yallup; three *s. Studied art* at Witwatersrand, Johannesburg under Major Gardiner, Todd Davis and Braham; Byam Shaw School (portraiture). *Exhib.:* 25 one-man shows, six in London (1984-91). *Work in permanent collections:* S. Africa, Canada, Germany, America, Australia and New Zealand. *Work repro.:* Calendars, Limited Prints. *Addresses:* Mill Cottage, Llandogo, nr. Monmouth, Gwent; The Yallup Gallery, Llandogo, Gwent. *Signs work:* "Pat Yallup" (water-colours and abstracts), see appendix.

YARDLEY, John Keith, R.I.(1990); painter, particularly interior and street subjects, in oil and water-colour; *b* Beverley, Yorks., 11 Mar., 1933; *s* of R.E. Yardley; *m* Brenda; two *s*, one *d. Educ.:* Hastings Grammar School. *Exhib.:* R.I., R.W.S., N.E.A.C., numerous one-man shows; awarded Water-colour Foundation prize R.I. (1990). *Work in permanent collections:* Merrill Lynch, C.T. Bowring, A.P.V., and private collections. *Publications:* The Art of John Yardley by R. Ranson; Water-colour Impressionists by R. Ranson. *Address:* 5 Evesham Rd., Reigate, Surrey RH2 9DF. *Signs work:* "John Yardley" in script.

YATES, Alan, A.R.B.S. (1976), M.S.D-C. (1973), Cert.Ed. (1969), F.R.S.A. (1973); sculptor in cast bronze and aluminium, art teacher; *b* Bishop Auckland, 30 Nov., 1947. *Educ.:* Leeholme School; Bishop Auckland Grammar School; *studied art* at Bede College, Durham University (1966-69). *Exhib.:* R.A., R.S.A., R.W.A., Paris, Durham University, York, Grantham, Darlington, Perth, Newcastle Polytechnic, Edinburgh, S. Shields, Swansea University, Stratford, Northern Open Touring Exhbn., Chelsea Harbour. *Work in public places:* St. James' Youth Centre, Coundon; Grey College, Durham University. *Address:* 53 Bankwell Drive, High Etherley, Bishop Auckland, Co. Durham DL14 0HG. *Signs work:* "A. YATES."

YATES, Eric, N.S. (1981), M.F.P.S. (1978); sculptor in wood, stone, bronze, painter of seascapes and landscapes; *b* Horsham, Sussex, 1919; *m* Dorothy Beezley; one *s*, one *d. Educ.:* Elmhurst Grammar School, Street; St. Luke's, Exeter; Southampton University; *studied art* part-time Newton Abbot, Douglas and St. Albans Art Colleges. *Exhib.:* regularly at R.B.A., R.S.M.A., R.M.S., N.S., F.P.S. *Address:* Woodlands Studio, 109 Woodlands Ave., Emsworth PO10 7QD. *Signs work:* "E.Y." or "Eric Yates."

YATES, Marie, B.A.Hons (1971); artist; *b* Lancashire, 9 Aug., 1940. *Studied art* at Manchester and Hornsey. *Exhib.:* Arts Council, British Council, Arnolfini. *Work in permanent collection:* Arts Council, Arnolfini Trust, Cornwall Educ. Com., Plymouth City A.G. *Publication:* A Re-Evaluation of a Proposed Publication (1978). *Address:* 17 Victoria Rd., London N22. *Signs work:* "Marie Yates."

YATES JONES, Hazel May, N.D.D., A.T.D., Cert.Ed., B.A.; designer/ illustrator/calligrapher, water-colour painter; *b* Hastings; *m* B. H. Jones. *Educ.:* Northampton School of Art (1957-61); West of England College of Art, Bristol University Faculty of Educ. (1964). *Exhib.:* Mall Galleries, Liberty & Co., Hitchin Museum, Bedford Central Library. *Work in permanent collections:* Bedford Central Library, County Hall, Bedford, Bingen, W. Germany; Commissioned by N. Herts. District Council, Twinning Documents Letchworth with Wissen and Hitchin with Bingen Am Rhein; by Great Wymondley Parish Council for scroll 'History of Great Wymondley' presented to H.M. Queen Elizabeth II. *Address:* Chestnut Cottage, Chard Rd., Drimpton, Beaminster, Dorset DT8 3RF. *Signs work:* "Hazel Yates Jones."

YEOMAN, Andrew John Metcalfe, R.I.B.A., B.Arch.Hons. (1981), Dip. Arch. (1985), Dip.A.A. U.S.S.R. (1991); architect, artist in ink, plastic and plaster; lecturer in architecture, University of Greenwich and U.C.L.; *b* 28 Dec., 1958; *s* of Prof. Philip Metcalfe Yeoman, orthopaedic surgeon. *Educ.:* Stowe; *studied architecture* at Polytechnic of Central London (1979-81, 1984-85). *Exhib.:* Venice Biennale (1985), nationally in Gt. Britain, London (Architecture Foundation, R.I.B.A.), R.A. (1986, 1987, 1991, 1993), France, Spain, Greece, Italy, Slovenia, Croatia, Moscow U.S.S.R., Chicago U.S.A. *Publications:* Architects Journal, Architectural Review, A + U (Japan), Architectural Design.

Address: Tower 151 Architects, Gate 27 First Floor, London Central Markets, London EC1A 9NA. *Signs work:* "Andrew Yeoman."

YEOMAN, Martin, R.P., N.E.A.C.; artist in oil, pencil, pen and ink, silver point; *b* Egham Hythe, 21 July, 1953; *s* of Arthur John Yeoman. *Studied art* at R.A. Schools (Peter Greenham). *Exhib.:* Agnews, New Grafton Gallery, R.A., N.P.G. *Address:* 2A Turquand St., London SE17 1LT. *Clubs:* R.P., N.E.A.C. *Signs work:* "Yeoman."

YHAP, Laetitia, D.F.A.(Lond.) (1965); artist; *b* St. Albans, 1 May, 1941; *d* of Dr. L.N. Yhap; one *s*. *Educ.:* Fulham County Grammar School; *studied art* at Camberwell School of Art (1958-62, Euan Uglow, Frank Auerbach), Slade School of Fine Art (1963-65, Harold Cohen, Anthony Green). *Exhib.:* solo shows, Piccadilly Gallery (1968-73), Serpentine Gallery (1979), Air Gallery (1984), 'Life at the Edge' Charleston Farmhouse (1993); 'The Business of the Beach' 1988-89 Touring show organised by Laing A.G., Newcastle-upon-Tyne. *Work in permanent collections:* Tate Gallery, Unilever House, Hove A.G., Hastings Museum, Rugby Museum. *Address:* 12 The Croft, Hastings, Sussex TN34 3HH. *Signs work:* "Laetitia Yhap."

YOUNG, Florence, R.M.S., S.W.A., Associe, Société des Artistes Français; Hon. Mention, Paris Salon (1968), Prix Marie Louise Jules Richard, Paris Salon (1971), Diplôme d'honneur, Biarritz (1971), silver medal, Paris Salon (1981); self taught artist in oil, pastel and water-colour, miniaturist; *b* Preston, Lancs., 19 Nov., 1919; *d* of George Laraway, textile ind. (Bolton); *m* Kenneth Young; one *s*, one *d*. *Educ.:* Farnworth Grammar School, Lancs. *Exhib.:* P.S., R.I., S.W.A., R.W.S. Flower Painting, R.I. Galleries Summer and Winter Salons, Paris Salon, S.M., U.A. *Work in permanent collections:* Hillingdon Borough Council, Swedish Tool Mfrs., Kingston, Diaform Ltd. Uxbridge, Public Address Engineers Assoc., Harrow, Barclays Bank, Uxbridge. *Address:* 1A Maylands Drive, Uxbridge, Middx. UB8 1BH. *Signs work:* "F. Young."

YOUNG, Helen Jean, R.B.A., N.E.A.C.; de Laszlo medal (1975); painter in oil, black and white artist; *b* 1914. *Educ.:* Grove School, Hindhead; Farnham (1931); R.A. Schools; medallist; Belle Arti, Florence (1938). *Exhib.:* R.A., R.B.A., N.E.A.C., London Group, Leicester Galleries, Leger Gallery; one-man shows, London, Canterbury, Bath. *Official purchases:* B.E.A., Denbigh, Derby, Leics, and Mon. Educ. Cttees.; U.S.A., Germany, Canada. *Work repro.:* Print, Chanticleer, by Solomon and Whitehead; The Nativity, The Watercress Gatherers. *Publications:* illustrations and decorations in The Poetry of Easter, The Poetry of Christmas, The Hound of Heaven (Mowbrays, Ltd.), various illustrations for Black. *Address:* 6 Gatehill, Northwood, Middx. *Signs work:* "Jean Young" (in block letters).

YOUNG, Dr. Joseph L., F.I.A.L.; pioneer of reintegration of art in architecture; creator of over 50 cultural landmarks for civic, educational and religious structures throughout America, including works in mosaic, metal, wood, stained glass, concrete, granite, etc.; author of 2 books on mosaics published by Reinhold, N.Y. (1957-63); guest lecturer and artist-in-residence at numerous institutions of higher learning in U.S.A. and Europe; *b* Pittsburgh, Pa., 27 Nov., 1919; *m* Millicent E. Young; two children. *Educ.:* Westminster College, New Wilmington, Pa.; *studied art* at Boston Museum School of Fine Arts; American Academy of Art, Rome. *Address:* Art in Architecture, 7917½ W. Norton Ave., Los Angeles, Ca. 90046, U.S.A. *Signs work:* "J. Young."

YOUNGER, Alan Christopher Wyrill, F.M.G.P.; stained glass designer and maker; part-time lecturer, Richmond University; *b* London, 13 Mar., 1933; *m* Zoë Birchmore; two *d. Educ.*: Alleyn's School; *studied art* at Central School of Art (1954-57), and in the Studios of Carl Edwards and Lawrence Lee. First prize Worshipful Company of Glaziers (1960), Sir Arthur Evans travelling scholarship (1961). *Exhib.*: Centre International du Vitrau, Chartres (1982). *Work in permanent collections:* Durham, St. Alban's, Southwark and Chester Cathedrals, numerous parish churches in Britain including Luton, Tamworth, Boldre, Haselbech and Monea. *Publication:* The Laporte Rose Window (1989). *Address:* 44 Belvedere Rd., London SE19 2HW. *Signs work:* overlapping A and Y — see appendix.

YOUNGER, Elspeth Chalmers, D.A. (1957), Post Dip. (1958); embroiderer, painter in inks, water-colour, gouache; *b* Paisley; *d* of William Younger; *m* John Gardiner Crawford; one *s*, one *d. Educ.*: Camphill Secondary School, Paisley; *studied art* at Glasgow School of Art (1953-58, Kathleen Whyte); National Wool Textile Award (1957), Travelling Scholarship, Paris (1958). *Exhib.*: one-man shows: 57 Gallery, Edinburgh (1965), Lane Gallery, Bradford (1965), Civic Arts Centre, Aberdeen (1969, 1971), University of Aberdeen (1971), Cornerstone Gallery, Dunblane (1983, 1984, 1988, 1989), Haddo House, Aberdeen (1988), McEwan & Ritchie Fine Art, Dundee (1990), Tolquhon Gallery, Tarves (1992), Cottage Gallery, Newtyle (1993); group shows include Glasgow School of Art, S.A.C., S.S.A., Scottish Gallery, R.S.W., etc. *Work in permanent collections:* Aberdeenshire Educ. Authority, Tayside Educ. Authority, North British Hotel, Dundee A.G., and private collections throughout Britain, and Norway, Holland, Germany, France, Australia, Canada, U.S.A. *Work repro.:* in various publications, and in "20th Century Embroidery in Gt. Britain", Vols. 2, 3, 4, by Constance Howard. *Address:* 34 Strachan St., Arbroath, Angus DD11 1UA, Scotland. *Signs work:* "ELSPETH YOUNGER" and date, embroidery unsigned, label on reverse.

YOUNGMAN, Nan, O.B.E. (1987), Slade Dip. (1927), A.T.D. (1929); painter; art adviser Cambs. Educ. Com. (1944-54); Founder of annual Pictures for Schools Exhbns. in London and Wales. *Exhib.*: London Group, W.I.A.C., A.I.A., R.A.; one-man shows: Leicester and Zwemmer Galleries, London; retrospectives: The Minories, Colchester (1971), Kettle's Yard, Cambridge (1986). *Work in permanent collections:* many educ. authorities in England and Wales, Manchester and Salford City A.G., Min. of Works, Welsh C.A.S. and Arts Council for Wales, Whipple Museum, Cambridge. *Address:* The Hawks, Waterbeach, Cambridge CB5 9NN. *Signs work:* "Nan Youngman."

YULE, (Duncan) Ainslie, D.A. (1963); sculptor/teacher; Head of Sculpture, Kingston University 1982- (Reader 1987-); *b* North Berwick, 1941; *s* of Edward Campbell Yule and Elizabeth Morgan Yule; *m* (1) Patricia Carlos (*m* dissolved); one *d;* (2) 1982, Mary Johnson. *Educ.*: Edinburgh College of Art. *Exhib.*: regular solo and group exhbns. including Whitechapel A.G. (1973), Gubbio Biennale (1973), Silver Jubilee Exhbn. Battersea Park (1977), Fruitmarket Gallery and travelling (1977-79), Angela Flowers (1986), Scottish Gallery (1989-91). *Work in private and public collections:* include Aberdeen A.G., A.C.G.B., Dundee A.G., Leeds City A.G., S.A.C. University of Leeds, Gregory Fellow (1974-75). *Address:* 218 Sheen La., London SW14 8LB. *Club:* Chelsea Arts. *Signs work:* "Ainslie Yule."

YUNUS (Ghulam Haider), A.R.B.S. (1981); sculptor in bronze, brass, copper and mild-steel; *b* Pakistan, 1943; *m* Elizabeth Haider; one *s*, one *d*. Studied art at St.Martin's School of Art (1963, Philip King), Hammersmith College of Building. *Exhib.:* one-man shows, Commonwealth Inst., London, Bear Lane Gallery, Oxford, Primavera Gallery, Cambridge, etc.; R. A. Summer Exhbn., Alwin Gallery, Drian Gallery, etc. *Work in private collections:* U.K., Switzerland, Italy, Germany, Netherlands and America. *Address:* 21 Portmore Park Rd., Weybridge, Surrey KT13 8ET. *Signs work:* "Yunus."

Z

ZALMON: see WINER, Zalmon.

ZAO, Wou Ki; Officier de la Légion d'Honneur; Commandeur de Mérite National; painter; *b* Pekin, 13 Feb., 1921; *m* Francoise Marquet. *Studied art:* Ecole Nationale de Beaux Arts at Hang Tcheou (1935-41). Professor of Drawing at Hang Tcheou (1941-47). *Work in permanent collections:* in Germany, England, Austria, Belgium, Brazil, Canada, Switzerland, U.S.A., France, Hong Kong, Israel, Italy, Japan, Luxembourg, etc. *Address:* 19 bis, Rue Jonquoy, 75014, Paris, France.

ZEVI, Bruno B., Hon. Doctor in Architecture; Academician of San Luca; critic and architect; Prof. of History of Architecture, Rome University; President, International Committee of Architectural Critics; Hon. Mem. of the Italian Parliament; *b* Rome, 22 Jan., 1918; *s* of Guido Zevi, engineer; *m* Tullia Calabi; one *s,* one *d. Educ.:* Rome and Harvard University; *studied architecture* at Cambridge, Mass., U.S.A. *Publications:* Towards an Organic Architecture, Architecture as Space, Storia dell'Architettura Moderna, Biagio Rossetti, Architectura in nuce, Michelangiolo Architetto, Erich Mendelsohn, Cronache di architettura, Saper vedere l'urbanistica, Spazi dell'architettura moderna, The modern language of architecture; author of the Voice "Architecture" in Universal Encyclopedia of the Arts; editor of L'architettura-cronache e storia (Rome and Milan), architectural columnist of the weekly L'Espresso. *Address:* Via Nomentana 150, Rome.

ZIAR, Elizabeth Rosemary; painter (water-colour preferred); *b* St. Ives, Cornwall; *d* of Charles and Grace Rowe; *m* Ian Ziar, L.D.S., R.C.S.; one *s. Educ.:* West Cornwall School for Girls (art mistress Miss M.E. Parkins of "Newlyn School"); Penzance School of Art (1936-41 James Lias); Leonard Fuller (1945). *Exhib.:* over 30 solo shows in Britain, France and Italy with usual complement of mixed international expositions, e.g. Paris Salon, Monaco, Biarritz (Dip. d'Honneur 1973), Juan-les-Pins (premier award Coupe d'Antibes 1979), R.I., R.B.S.A., S.W.A., U.A., Hesketh Hubbard, etc. *Publication:* 'Good Morrow, Brother.' *Address:* Trevidren, Penzance, TR18 2AY. *Signs work:* "ZIAR" or with monogram (see appendix); occasionally: "E. R. ZIAR" or "E.R.Z."

ZWEMMER, A. Ltd.; specialist dealers in books on fine art, decorative arts and architecture; out-of-print; mail order service. Catalogue available. *Addresses:* 24 Litchfield St., London WC2H 9NJ; St. George's Gallery, 8 Duke St., London SW1Y 6BN; 80 Charing Cross Rd., London WC2H 0BB (film, photography, design); Courtauld Gallery, Somerset House, Strand, London WC2R 0RN; Whitechapel Gallery, 80 Whitechapel High St., London E1 7QZ.

ZYW, Aleksander; painter; *b* Lida, Poland, 29 Aug., 1905; *s* of J. S. Zyw; *m* Leslie Goddard; two *s*. *Studied art* in Warsaw, Athens, Rome and Paris. *Exhib.:* Warsaw, Paris, Basle, Milan, London, Edinburgh. *Work in permanent collections:* State Collection of Poland, National Gallery of Poland, Union of Polish Painters, Tate Gallery, Glasgow Art Gallery, Arts Council of Scotland, University of Edinburgh, Scottish National Gallery of Modern Art, Rhodes National Gallery, Salisbury, Carnegie Trust. *Addresses:* Bell's Brae House, Dean Village, Edinburgh 4, and Poggio Lamentano, Castagneto-Carducci (Livorno), Italy. *Signs work:* "Zyw."

APPENDIX I

MONOGRAMS AND SIGNATURES

Ackroyd, Norman

Adam-Tessier,
Maxime

Adams,
(Dorothea Christina) Margaret

Arnold, Phyllis
Anne

Asscher, Sofy

Atkin, Ann

Auld,
J. L. M.

Aynscomb-Harris,
Martin John

Backhouse,
David John

Baczkowska, Pam   SCULPTURE

533

Baines, Richard
John Manwaring

Baker, Hilary Jayne

Balfour, Maria

Baynes, Pauline
Diana

Beauvais,
Walter John

Beilby,
Pauline Margaret

Beltrán, Félix

Benenson,
Leslie Charlotte

(wood engraving & sculpture)

(drawings etc.)

Benjamin,
Anthony

534

Bennett, William

Bensusan-Butt,
John Gordon

Benton, Graham

Berlin,
Sven   or

Bicât, André

Bill, John Gordon

Bill, M.

Bishop, Edward

535

Blaker, Michael *Blaker*

Blik, Maurice *Maurice Blik*

Bohusz-Szyszko, Marian *MB*

Bond, Jane *Bond - or B.*

Bowen, T. A. E. *Bowen 1949 or*

Bradley, Frank *Frank Bradley.*

Bransbury, Allan Harry *Allan Bransbury*

Brazier, Connie

CMB (water-colours)

CMB (engraved glass)

Brent, Isabelle

Isabelle Brent.

Brent, R. R. A.

or

Angus Brent

Bridgeman, John

Brindley, Donald

Brody, F. J.

Broughton, Aya

Brown, Neil
Dallas

Brown, Ralph

Ralph Brown. Bronges–

(Drawings)   (Stamped)

Browne, C. R.

CLIVE BROWNE.

Bruce, George J. D.

George J.D. Bruce

or

G

Budd,
Kenneth George

Budd, Rachel

R Budd

Bumphrey, Nigel

(N B)

Burrough, Thomas
Hedley Bruce

    or   *Burrough*

Butler,
Alice Caroline

Alice C. Butler

538

Butler, Vincent

Vincent Butler or **V.B.**

Butt, Anna Theresa

AA

Caine, O.

Osmund Caine a Florint

Camp, Jeffery

Jeffery Camp

Carrick, Desmond

CARRAIS

CARRAIS (Up to and including 1979)

CARRICK (After 1979)

Carter, Joan
Patricia

Chang,
Chien-Ying

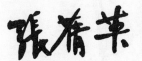

539

Chao, Shao-An

Chatterton,
George Edward

Chauvin, E.

Chesser, Sheila

Clark,
Kenneth Inman Carr

Clyne, Henry Horne

HHC '76

Cochran, Margi

Collins, Michael

Conner, Angela

Conway, Jennifer
Anne

(miniatures)

Cook, David Albert

(Paintings)

(Pen & Ink)

Cooke, S.

Cooper, Emmanuel

Coote, Michael
Arnold

Corbett, Peter George

Cornwell,
Arthur Bruce

Coutu, Jack

Inset silver plate.

Carvings

Couve de Murville-
Desenne,
Lucie-Renée

Cox, Stephen B.  or

(on designs/interiors etc.)

(on art work)

Cramp,
Jonathan David   on oils   on some drawings

J. CRAMP   or   J.C.   J. Cramp.

Crawshaw, June

(ceramic signature)

Creber, Frank

FC 91
FC reber 91

Crossley, Gordon   GTC

Crow, Kathleen Mary   (KM)

Crowther, Hugh M.

Crowther, Stephen

Cuneo, Terence Tenison

Curtis,
Anthony Ewart

Czimbalmos,
Magdolna Paal

Czimbalmos,
Szabo Kalman

Dakeyne, Gabriel

Dalby, Claire

Danvers, Joan

d'Arbeloff, Natalie

543

Das, Jatin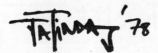

Davidson Davis,
Philomena

Davidson-Houston,
A. C.

**ACDH
1.9 49.**

de Francia, Peter

Demel, Richard

De Vasconcellos,
Josephina

Dickens, Alison Margaret

Dickson,
Evangeline Mary Lambart

Di Girolamo, Megan Ann

Dowling, Jane

Dring, L. M.

Duffy, Stephen
James

Duffy, Terry

Dufty, A. R.

Dunlop, Jim

Dunne, Berthold

Durrant, Roy
Turner

or

Dyke, John C. A.

Eastop, Geoffrey
Frank

Edwards, Benjamin Ralph

Elstein, Cecile

Emery, Edwina

Emmerich,
Anita Jane

Evans, Margaret Fleming

Evans, Ray

Fakhoury, Bushra

Farrell,
Alan Richard

and dated on
reverse of painting

Faulds, James
Alexander

Faur, Aurel-Sebastian

Feeny, P. A.

Fei, Cheng-Wu

Fellows, Elaine Helen

Finch, Michael

Fisher, Don Mulready

Flanders, D.

Fleming,
James Hugh

on illustrations
and prints

Folland, Ronald Norman

Forward,
Hubert W. F.

'**H**' monogram (prints & ceramics)

Foster, Sir Norman Robert

547

Francyn
(Dehn Fuller)

Frankenthaler,
Helen

Fraser, D. H.

Frenkiel,
Stanislaw

Friers, R. B.

Gamlen, Mary

Gay, Barbara

on all glazed, coloured
stoneware pottery figures.
Every piece numbered.

Gear, William

548

Giardelli, Arthur

Gilley, Leonard
Christopher

Goaman, Michael

Goodwin, Leslie Albert

Gow, Neil

Gray, Jane Campbell

Guevara, Jose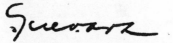

Gunn, James
Thomson

Haccuria, Maurice

Hackney, Arthur

Hampton, Michael

('M' x 'H' WITH GREBES HEAD)

Harden, Gerald A. C.

Harris, Alfred

Harvey, Jake

Haughton,
Wilfred James

Hawthorn,
Raymond
Humphrey Millis

Herman, Josef

550

Heron,
Susanna

Herriott,
Alan B.

illustrations

and dated

Hill, Anthony

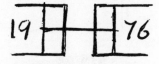

Hinchcliffe, Michael

ᔑHINCHCLIFFE

Hitchcock,
Harold Raymond

19 ⊞⊞ 76

Hoare, Diana C.

Hoflehner, Rudolf   GRAPHIKEN: *R. Hoflehner.*   PLASTIKEN HR

Homes, R. T. J.

Hooke, Robert Lowe, Jr.

Hooper, G.

Horsnell, Walter
Cecil

House,
Ceri Charles

Hoyland, John

Huckvale, Iris

Hudson, Thomas
Roger Jackson

Hughes, Jim

552

Hundertwasser,
Friedrich

or

Hurn, J. Bruce

(oils and acrylic paintings)

(drawings and gouache paintings)

Huston, John I.

Irvin, Albert

Isom,
Graham Michael

Jackson, Ashley

James, H. N.

Jameson,
Kenneth Ambrose

Jefferson,
Annelise

Jellicoe, Colin

Jenkins, Christopher   (potters stamp)

Jennings, Walter
Robin

Jobson, Patrick

Johnston, Duncan   or

Jones, Stanley
Robert

Joseph, Peter

Jukes, E. E.

Kalashnikov, Anatolii Ivanovich

Kanidinç, Salahattin

Kendall, Kay Thetford

Kennedy, C.

Kern, Doreen

Key, Geoffrey

King, Phillip

Kitchin, Myfanwy

Klein, Anita

Knox, Harry
Cooke

Kolakowski,
Matthew Edmund

Kuo, Nancy

Lackner, Suzanne O.

Lago, Darren

Lake, C. Elizabeth Matheson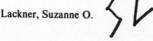

Lambert, Colin
Joseph

Lang, Wharton

Larmont, Eric

Lauder, Kenneth Scott

Lawrence,
Gordon Robert

Leach, D.

  or   seal in foot of pots.

Lee, Rosie

 or B

Leech,
Raymond

557

Leigh-Pemberton, John

 or LEIGH-PEMBERTON
. 65

Lewenstein, Eileen

Leyden, J. M.

Lilley, Geoffrey
Ivan

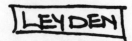

Lim, Kim

Linley-Adams,
Barbara Mary

Littlejohn,
William Hunter

558

Lockhart, David

Logan, Andrew

Longbotham,
Charles Norman

Loxton Knight,
Edward

Lubelski, J. S.

Lucas, Suzanne

Macarrón, Ricardo

McCarter, Keith (on small works)

McCullough, George

MacDonald,
Alastair James
Henderson or

Macey, Leo

McFall, David

McIntyre, Donald

Macmiadhachain,
Padraig

560

Madgwick, Clive

Maklouf, Raphael

Malcles,
Jean-Denis

Mapp, John Ernest

Margrie, Victor

Marr, Leslie

Marriott, Michael

Martin, Marie-Louise

Martin, Pierre Noël   *Pierre Noël Martin*   (with the year on centre right)

Master, Jean

Matania,
Franco

Matheson, Andrew
Kenneth Mackenzie

Mendoza, June

Middleton, Renée   19 RM·85   (or appropriate date)

562

Miller,
David T.

Millner Etienne,
Henry de la Fargue

Miners, Neil

Montané, Roger

Moodie, Stuart

Moreton, Nicolas   (sculpture)

Morss,
Edward James

Muszynski,
Leszek Tadeusz

Mynott, Derek G.

Nalecz, Halima

Neal, Trevor

Nellens, Roger

Newton, I. M.

Ng, Kiow Ngor

Norland (Neuschul),
Khalil

O'Ceallachain,
Diarmuid

Ohl, Gabrielle

Padden, Daphne

Palmer,
Eugene Oliver

Parry,
Sheila Harwood

Parsons,
Denis Alva

Initials
Banker mark based on
hobby of unicycling

Pasmore, Victor

Paynton, Colin
Frank

Peace, David

Pearson, James E.

Piché, Roland

Pierce, Norman F.

Pitfield,
Thomas Baron

Potter, Donald

Puhn, Franklin

Pullan, Margaret
Ida Elizabeth

Purnell, John

stamped on sculpture

Pye, William  or

Raine, Sarah Lamar
(Woodie)

Rambissoon,
Sonnylal

Rank-Broadley, Ian

Ratcliff, John

566

Reid, Elspeth
Margaret Georgina

Rice, Bernard

Bernard RICE

or

Roberts,
Marguerite Hazel

MR.

Roberts,
Phyllis Kathleen

P. K. ROBERTS

Roberts,
Walter James

Walter J. Roberts

Roberts-Jones,
Ivor

Robertson,
Sheila Macleod   (on still life and flower paintings)

Robinson, John
Edward

Realistic   Symbolic   Tapestry

Rogers, Joseph
Shepperd (Nevia)

Roper, Geoffrey John

Roseman, Stanley

Ross, Alastair
Robertson

Roy, Michael

Rubinstein, Gerda

568

Ryder, Margaret Elaine	*M E Ryder.*
Sahai, Viréndra	*viren sahai*
Saltzman, William	*W. Saltzman*
Sapieha, Christine	Ⓢ SAPIEHA
Schwarz, Hans	*H Schwarz*
Seal, Norman	*(monogram)*
Searle, Ronald	*Ronald · Searle* ; OR RS. OR *Searle*
Senft, Nadin	(signature on bronzes etc.)
Serra-Badue, Daniel F.	*Daniel Serra Badue*
Seuphor, Michel	*Seuphor*

Shackleton,
Keith Hope

Shears,
Marcelle Dorothy

OR

Shiels, Anthony
Nicol

Shipsides, Frank

Shorthouse, G. Sydney

Simpson, Cathy

Simpson, Noelle

Sitwell, Pauline

Smith, Edward
John Milton

Snelling, John

Snowden,
Hilda Mary

Soukop, Willi

Soulages, Pierre

Souza, F. N.

Spence, T. Everard

Spowart, Robert
Henry Donald

Stokes, Vincent

Storey, Terence

Stuart, Kiel

Sullivan, Jason

Sullivan, Wendy Lilian Verdin

Summers,
Leslie John

Swerling, Anthony

Tajiri, Shinkichi

Tamblyn-Watts,
Harold

Tandy, Michael Roy   (porcelain)   (paintings)

Tate, Barbara

Tate,
Barbara and James

Tavener, Robert

Taylor, Alan

Taylor, Michael John

93

red

Taylor, Pamela

or

Taylor, Wendy Ann

(prints and work)

Thelwell, Norman

Thomas, M.

Till, Michael John

Tisdall, H.

Tribe, Barbara

Tuckwell, George Arthur

Turnbull, William

Turner, William Ralph

Tysoe, Peter

Underwood,
Keith Alfred

Vango, David

Verdijk, Gerard

Walker, Richard
Ian Bentham

Ward,
Margaret Hester

Ward,
Thomas William

Warren,
Charles Wyatt

Wasim, L.

Watson,
Arthur James

Watson, Heather

Watson-Gandy, Basia (Butterfly hidden in design)

Watson Stewart,
Avril Veronica (Owl followed by maiden name, Avril V. Gibb)

Watts, Dorothy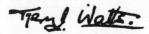

Watts, M.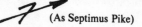

Watts, Michael
Gorse (Generally)   (As Septimus Pike)

Watts, Peter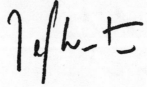

Wattson Dean, Meg 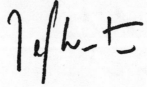 (miniatures)

Wauters, Jef

Weeks, John
Lawrence Macdonald

Weller, Antony

Weltman, Boris

Werge-Hartley,
Alan

Werge-Hartley,
Jeanne

White, Mary

Williamson-Bell, James

Willies, Joan

Winer, Zalmon

Wingate, Robert Bray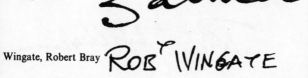

577

Wolverson,
Margaret
Elizabeth

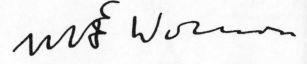

Wong, Ying

Wood,
Gerald Stanley Kent 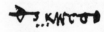 Monogram Stamp

Woolf-Nellist,
Meg

Yallup, Pat

Younger, Alan
Christopher Wyrill

Ziar, Elizabeth
Rosemary

OBITUARY

AGAR, Eileen
ALLOWAY, Lawrence
AMBROSE, Raymond Frank
AYLING, Joan, Hon.Mem.R.M.S., F.R.S.A.
BACON, Cecil Walter, M.C.S.D.
BALLANTYNE, David, A.T.D., F.S.D-C.
BANHAM, Shirley Mary, S.G.A.
BATTEN, Mark, A.S.A.F., P.P.R.B.S., F.R.B.S., R.B.A., F.R.S.A.
BENHAM, Ronald, R.B.A., N.E.A.C.
BOURNE, John Frye
BRATBY, John Randall, R.A., A.R.C.A., F.I.A.L., R.B.A.
BRAY, Phyllis
CARSTENSEN, Thelma (Mrs. Phillips), W.I.A.C.
CATTERMOLE, Lance, R.O.I.
CHAMOT, Mary
CHARMAN, Clifford, R.O.I., N.D.D.
COOPER, John Hubert, B.A., F.R.S.A.
CUNDY, Clifford Benjamin, N.S.
DALE, Antony, B.Litt., M.A., F.S.A.
DASI SUTTON, Pamela Ann, F.R.S.A., S.G.F.A.
DAVID, Illtyd, R.Cam.A.
DOBBS, Honor, F.P.S.
EURICH, Richard, Ernest, O.B.E., R.A., N.E.A.C.
FEDARB, Daphne, R.B.A.
FISHER, Roger Ronald Sutton, C.B.E., D.S.C., R.S.M.A., F.R.S.A.
FLETCHER, Rosamund M. B., F.R.B.S., M.G.L.C.
FRINK, Elizabeth, D.B.E., R.A.
GEER, Sheila
GILLESPIE, Stirling, F.R.G.S.
GILMOUR, Elaine
GOLDEN, Grace, A.R.C.A.
GORDON, (Alexander) Esmé, R.S.A., F.R.I.B.A., F.R.I.A.S.
GOURLEY, Alan Stenhouse, P.R.O.I., D.A.
GREENHAM, Peter, C.B.E., R.A., R.B.A., N.E.A.C., R.P., B.A.
HALL, Patrick
HALLSEY-WINN, Leonard
HSÜ, Chung-Ming
HULTON, John, M.A., Dip.L.A.
HURUM, Per
INGLEFIELD, Sir Gilbert Samuel, G.B.E., T.D., M.A., D.Sc., A.R.I.B.A., A.A.Dip., F.R.S.A., Hon.G.S.M., Hon.R.B.A., Hon.F.L.C.M.
JONES, Harold, A.R.C.A.
JONES, Harold Harris, B.Sc., F.R.S.A., D.P.A.

JONES, Thomas DEMPSTER
KENNEDY, Richard
KENYON, Ley, D.F.C., F.R.G.S.
KOENIG, Ghisha
LEA, Sheila
LEE-JOHNSON, Eric
LOBB, Howard Leslie Vicars, C.B.E., F.R.I.B.A., F.R.S.A.
McARTHUR, Thomas William Herbert, D.F.Astrol.S., N.S.
McGUIRE, Edward Augustine, F.R.S.A.I.
MACKERTICH, Robin, D.F.A., R.B.A., N.E.A.C., A.R.W.A.
McWILLIAM, F. E., C.B.E., R.A.
MANESSIER, Alfred
MAY, William Edward
MAYES, Reginald Harry Duncan, M.S.I.A.
MAYES, W. Philip, F.M.A.
MILLS, John FitzMaurice, P.R.D.S., F.S.A., F.I.I.C., F.R.S.A.I., F.R.S.A.
MUNRO, James Burnet, D.A., A.R.B.S.
NEW, Vincent Arthur, M.A.W.G.
NOBLE, James
PEPLOE, Denis Frederic Neil, R.S.A.
PETTS, John
PHILIPSON, Sir Robin, Kt., P.R.S.A., R.A., R.G.I., LL.D., F.R.S.A., R.S.W.
PHILLIPS, Doris
PIPER, John, C.H.
PRINET, Jean
PRITCHARD, Arthur, A.R.I.C.S., A.R.Cam.A.
PROCTER, Anthony, M.B.E.
REIACH, Alan, O.B.E., R.S.A., R.S.W., F.R.I.B.A.
ROBERTSON, Alexander, D.A.(Edin.)
ROTHENSTEIN, Sir John Knewstub Maurice, C.B.E., K.C.St.G., Ph.D., Hon.LL.D.
ROTHENSTEIN, Michael, R.A.
RUSZKOWSKI, Zdzislaw
SALMON, Thomas Graham, M.A., LL.B., J.P., S.S.C., F.R.I.A.S.(Hon.)
SANDS, Frederick, R.I.
SCHÖFFER, Nicolas
SEABY, Wilfred A., F.S.A., F.M.A., Hon.M.A.
SMART, Professor Alastair, M.A., D.A., F.S.A., F.R.S.A.
SMITH, Mary W., W.I.A.C.
SPEIGHT, Sadie, B.A., M.A., A.R.I.B.A., F.C.S.D., F.R.S.A.
STREVENS, John
SUMMERSON, Sir John Newenham, C.H., C.B.E., F.B.A., F.S.A., A.R.I.B.A.
THORNTON, Valerie (Mrs. Michael Chase), N.D.D., R.E.
THORP, William Eric, P.S., R.S.M.A.
VARLEY, Mabel Illingworth, A.T.D.
WICKHAM, Mabel Frances, R.I., S.W.A.
WILLIAMS, Aubrey Sendall, C.C.H.
WILLIAMS, Norah Marguerite
WOLLASTON, Charles, S.G.A., D.F.A., A.T.D., F.R.S.A.

APPENDIX III

QUALIFICATIONS AND GENERAL ABBREVIATIONS

In using this list of abbreviations care should be taken to split up any compound abbreviation into its constituent parts, e.g., "F.R.S." should be broken into "F." and "R.S.," the equivalents of these letters being found under "F." and "R.S." respectively.

A.	Associate; Associate-Engraver (of Royal Academy).
A.A.	Architectural Association; Automobile Association.
A.A.A.	Allied Artists of America; Australian Academy of Art.
A.A.D.W.	Association of Artists/Designers in Wales (disbanded).
A.A.H.	Association of Art Historians.
A.A.I.	Association of Art Institutions.
A.A.L.	Academy of Art and Literature.
A.A.P.L.	American Artists Professional League.
A.A.S.	Aberdeen Art Society.
A.B.	Art's Bachelor (American).
A.B.I.R.A.	American Biographical Institute Research Association.
A.B.P.R.	Association of British Picture Restorers.
A.C.A.	Association of Consultant Architects; Atlanta College of Art.
A.C.G.B.	Arts Council of Great Britain.
A.C.T.C.	Art Class Teacher's Certificate.
A.D.	Anno Domini.
A.D.A.E.	Advanced Diploma in Art Education.
A.D.B.	Associate of the Drama Board.
A.D.C.	Aide-de-camp.
A.D.G.	Architect Diplôme par le Gouvernement.
A.D.M.S.	Assistant Director of Medical Services.
A.E.C.	Adult Education Centre.
A.F.I.A.P.	Artiste, Fédération Internationale de l'Art Photographique.
A.G.	Art Gallery.
A.G.B.I.	Artists' General Benevolent Institution.
A.G.I.	Artistes Graphiques Internationales.

A.G.M.S.	Art Gallery and Museum Services.
A.G.P.A.	Artes Graficas de Pan America.
A.G.P.P.	Academia Gentium Pro Pace.
A.I.	Auctioneers' Institute.
A.I.A.	Academy of Irish Art; American Institute of Architecture.
A.I.A.L.	Association of International Institute of Art and Letters.
A.I. Archts.(Scot.).	Association of the Incorporation of Architects in Scotland.
A.I.C.A.	Association Internationale des Critiques d'Art.
A.I.D.	American Institute of Decorators.
A.I.I.D.	American Institute of Interior Design.
A.K.C.	Associate, King's College.
A.M.	Air Ministry; Member of Order of Australia.
A.M.A.	Associate of the Museums Association.
A.M.C.	Art Masters' Certificate.
A.M.I.P.	Associate Member, Institute of Plumbing.
A.M.T.C.	Art Masters' Teaching Certificate.
A.N.A.	American National Academy.
A.O.C.	Artists of Chelsea.
A.O.I.	Association of Illustrators.
A.P.A.	Association of Polish Artists.
A.P.S.	American Portrait Society.
A.R.C.A.	Associate of the Royal College of Art.
Ariz.	Arizona.
A.R.W.A.	Associate of the Royal West of England Academy.
A.S.A.	American Society of Artists Inc.
A.S.G.	Art Services Grants.
A.S.L.A.	American Society of Landscape Architects.
A.S.M.A.(Q).	Australian Society for Miniature Art (Queensland).
Assoc.	Association.
Asst.	Assistant.
A.S.T.M.S.	Association of Scientific, Technical and Managerial Staff.
A.T.C.	Art Teachers' Certificate.
A.T.D.	Art Teachers' Diploma.
A.U.C.	Anno Urbis Conditæ (from the foundation of the city).
A.V.A.W.	Association of Visual Artists in Wales.
Ave.	Avenue.
A.W.G.	Art Workers' Guild.
A.W.I.	Australian Water-colour Institute.
b.	born.

B.A.	Bachelor of Arts; British Airways.
B.A.A.T.	British Association of Art Therapists.
B.A.C.	British Aircraft Corporation.
B.A.D.A.	British Antique Dealers' Association.
B.Ae.	British Aerospace.
B-A.S.	Britain-Australia Society.
Batt.	Battalion.
B.B.C.	British Broadcasting Corporation.
B.C.	Before Christ.
B.C.C.	British Craft Centre.
B.Chrom.	Bachelor of Chromatics.
B.C.L.	Bachelor of Civil Law.
B.D.	Bachelor of Divinity.
B.E.A.	British European Airways.
B.Ed.	Bachelor of Education; Board of Education.
B.E.D.A.	Bureau of European Designers' Association.
Beds.	Bedfordshire.
B.E.F.	British Expeditionary Force.
B.E.N.A.	British Empire Naturalist Association.
Berks.	Berkshire.
B.F.A.	Bachelor of Fine Arts.
B'ham.	Birmingham.
B.H.P.	Broken Hill Priority Ltd.
B.H.S.A.I.	British Horse Society Assistant Instructor.
B.I.A.T.	British Institute of Architectural Technicians.
B.I.F.	British Industries Fair.
B.I.I.A.	British Institute of Industrial Art.
B.I.I.D	British Institute of Interior Design.
B.I.M.	(see I.Mgt.).
B.I.P.P.	British Institute of Professional Photography.
B.I.S.	British Interplanetary Society.
B.L.	Barrister-at-Law.
Bldg.	Building.
B.Litt.	Bachelor of Letters.
Blvd.	Boulevard.
B.M.	British Museum.
B.O.A.C.	British Overseas Airways Corporation.
B.of E.	Board of Education.
B.O.U.	British Ornithologists' Union.
B.P.D.	British Society of Posters Designers.
B.P.S.	British Psychological Society.
B.R.C.	British Refugee Council.
Bros.	Brothers.
B.S.C.	British Society of Cinematographers.
B.Sc.	Bachelor of Science.
B.S.I.	British Standards Institution.
B.S.M.G.P.	British Society of Master Glass Painters.

B.Soc.Sc.	Bachelor of Social Science.
Bt.	Baronet.
B.T.A.	British Travel Association.
Bucks.	Buckinghamshire.
B.W.S.	British Water-colour Society.
C.	Central.
c.	century.
C.A.C.	Chertsey Art Club.
Caerns.	Caernarvonshire.
Calif.	California.
Cambs.	Cambridge; Cambridgeshire.
Capt.	Captain.
C.A.S.	Cathcart Art Society.
C.A.S.T.	Centre for Art, Science and Technology.
C.A.S.W.	Contemporary Art Society for Wales.
Cav.	Cavalière (Knight).
C.B.	Companion of the Bath.
C.B.E.	Commander Order of the British Empire.
C.C.	County Council; County Councillor.
C.C.H.	Cacique Crown of Honour.
C.D.S.	Cambridge Drawing Society.
C.E.R.N.	Centre for European Nuclear Research.
Cert.	Certificate.
Cert. A.D.	Certificate in Art and Design.
Cert. F.A.	Certificate in Fine Art.
Certs.	Certificates.
C.F.E.	College of Further Education.
Chas.	Chambers.
Ch.B.	Bachelor of Surgery.
C.H.E.	College of Higher Education.
C.I.	Channel Isles.
C.I.A.D.	Central Institute for Art and Design.
C.I.E.	Companion of the Order of the Indian Empire.
C.I.H.A.	Comité Internationale de l'Histoire de l'Art.
C.I.S.	Institute of Chartered Secretaries and Administrators.
Cl.	Close.
C.M.	Master of Surgery.
C.M.G.	Companion of St. Michael and St. George.
C.N.A.A.	Council for National Academic Awards (disbanded).
Co.	Company; County.
c/o	care of.
C.O.I.D.	Council of Industrial Design.
Col.	Colonel.
Com.	Committee; Common.

Comdr.	Commander.
Conn.	Connecticut.
Corp.	Corporation.
Cos.	Companies.
C.P.	College of Preceptors.
C.P.A.	Craft Potters Association.
C.P.R.	Canadian Pacific Railway.
C.P.S.	Contemporary Portrait Society.
Cres.	Crescent.
C.S.	Chemical Society; Conchological Society of Great Britain and Ireland.
C.S.D.	The Chartered Society of Designers (formerly Society of Industrial Artists and Designers).
C.S.I.	Companion of the Order of the Star of India.
C.S.M.A.	Cornish Society of Marine Artists.
C.S.P.	Chartered Society of Physiotherapists.
C.T.	Connecticut.
Ct.	Court.
Cttee.	Committee.
C.U.P.	Cambridge University Press.
C.V.O.	Commander of the Royal Victorian Order.
C.W.A.C.	City of Westminster Arts Council.
d.	daughter.
D.A.	Diploma of Art; Diploma of Edinburgh College of Art; Doctor of Arts.
D.A.E.	Diploma in Art Education.
D.B.E.	Dame Grand Cross Order of the British Empire.
D.C.	District of Columbia.
D.C.L.	Doctor of Civil Law.
D.C.M.	Distinguished Conduct Medal.
D.D.	Doctor of Divinity.
decd.	deceased.
Dept.	Department.
Des. R.C.A.	Designer of the Royal College of Art.
D.F.A.	Diploma of Fine Art.
D.F.Astrol.S.	Diploma of the Faculty of Astrological Studies.
D.I.A.	Design and Industries Association.
Dip.A.D.	Diploma in Art and Design.
Dip.F.A.	Diploma in Fine Art.
Dip.H.E.	Diploma in Higher Education.
D.L.	Deputy Lieutenant.
D.Litt.	Doctor of Letters.
D.N.B.	Dictionary of National Biography.
D.O.E.	Department of the Environment.
Dr.	Doctor.

D.S.	Dental Surgery; Dental Surgeon.
D.Sc.	Doctory of Science.
D.S.L.U.	Association of the Slovene plastic artists.
D.S.O.	Companion of the Distinguished Service Order.
E.	East.
E.A.G.M.A.	East Anglian Group of Marine Artists.
E.C.I.A.	European Committee of Interior Architects.
Educ.	Educated; Education.
E.E.C.	European Economic Community.
E.I.S.	Educational Institute of Scotland.
E.M.F.	European Management Foundation.
E.S.	Entomological Society.
Esq.	Esquire.
etc.	etcetera.
Exam.	Examination.
Exhbn.	Exhibition.
Exhib.	Exhibited.
F.	Fellow; Foreign Member.
F.B.A.	Fellow of the British Academy.
F.B.S.Comm.	Fellow of the British Society of Commerce.
F.C.A.	Federation of Canadian Artists.
F.C.B.S.I.	Fellow of the Chartered Building Societies Institute.
F.E.T.C.	Further Education Teacher's Certificate.
F.F.S.	Fellow of the Franklin Society.
F.G.A.	Fellow of the Gemmological Association.
F.G.E.	Fellow of the Guild of Glass Engravers.
F.I.A.L.	Fellow of the International Institute of Arts and Letters.
F.Inst.C.	Fellow of the Institute of Commerce.
F.I.S.A.	International Federation of Works of Art.
F.N.C.F.	Federation Nationale de la Culture Française.
F.P.E.	Fellow, Philosophical Enquiry.
F.P.S.	Free Painters and Sculptors.
F.S.I.	Fellow of the Surveyors' Institute.
F.S.P.	Fellow of Sheffield Polytechnic.
F.S.S.	Federation of Scottish Sculptors.
Ft.	Feet; Foot.
F.T.D.A.	Fellow of the Theatrical Designers and Craftsmen's Association.
G.B.E.	Knight Grand Cross Order of the British Empire.
G.C.B.	Knight Grand Cross of the Bath.
G.C.M.G.	Knight Grand Cross of St. Michael and St. George.

G.C.S.I.	Knight Grand Commander of the Star of India.
g-d.	grand-daughter.
Gdn.	Garden.
Gdns.	Gardens.
G.E.S.M.	Group for Educational Services in Museums.
G.I.	Royal Glasgow Institute of Fine Arts.
G.L.C.	Guild of Lettering Craftsmen; Greater London Council.
Glos.	Gloucestershire.
G.M.A.S.	Miniature Art Society of Georgia.
G.M.C.	Guild of Memorial Craftsmen.
Govt.	Government.
G.P.D.S.T.	Girls' Public Day School Trust.
G.P.Fire E.	Graduate Institution of Fire Engineers.
G.P.O.	General Post Office.
G.P.S.	Glasgow Printmaking Society.
Gr.	Grove.
G.R.A.	Guild of Railway Artsts.
g-s.	grandson.
G.S.	Geological Society.
G.S.A.	Glasgow School of Art.
G.S.W.A.	Glasgow Society of Women Artists.
Gt.	Great.
H.	Hon. Member.
H.A.C.	Hampstead Artists Council.
Hants.	Hampshire.
H.D.F.A.	Higher Diploma in Fine Art.
H.Dip.A.D.	Higher Diploma in Art and Design.
Herts.	Hertfordshire.
H.F.R.A.	Hon. Foreign Academician.
H.L.I.	Highland Light Infantry.
H.M.	His Majesty; Her Majesty.
H.M.I.	H.M. Inspector of Schools.
H.M.S.O.	Her Majesty's Stationery Office.
H.R.H.	His Royal Highness; Her Royal Highness.
H.S.	Hilliard Society.
H.S.A.	Hampstead Society of Artists.
H.S.S.	History of Science Society (American).
Hunts.	Huntingdonshire.
I.A.A.	International Association of Art.
I.A.A.S.	Incorporated Association of Architects and Surveyors.
I.Ae.E.	Institute of Aeronautical Engineers.
I.A.L.	International Institute of Arts and Letters.

I.Arb.	Institute of Arbitrators.
I.A.S.	Incorporated Association of Surveyors; Irish Art Society.
I.B.A.	International Biographical Association.
I.B.D.	Institute of British Decorators and Interior Designers.
I.B.I.A.	Institute of British Industrial Art.
I.C.	Institute of Chemistry.
I.C.A.	Institute of Contemporary Arts.
I.C.E.	Institute of Civil Engineers.
I.C.O.GRA.D.A.	International Council of Graphic Design Association.
I.C.O.M.	International Council of Museums.
I.C.O.M.O.S.	International Council of Monuments and Sites.
I.C.S.	Indian Civil Service.
I.C.S.I.D.	International Council of Societies of Industrial Design.
I.D.	Institute of Directors; Institute of Decorators.
I.E.E.	Institute of Electrical Engineers.
I.E.L.A.	Irish Exhibition of Living Art.
I.F.A.	Incorporated Faculty of Arts.
I.F.A.W.	International Fund for Animal Welfare.
I.F.I.	International Federation of Interior Architects/ Designers.
I.F.S.	Irish Free State.
I.G.B.	Brazilian Institute of Genealogy.
I.I.C.	International Institute for Conservation of Paintings.
I.L.E.A.	Inner London Education Authority.
I.L.G.A.	Institute of Local Government Administration.
Ill.	Illinois.
I.M.B.I.	Institute of Medical and Biological Illustration.
I.M.C.E.	Institute of Mechanical and Civil Engineers.
I.M.E.	Institute of Mechanical Engineers; Institute of Engineers.
I.Mgt.	Institute of Management (formerly British Institute of Management).
I.M.M.	Institute of Mining and Metallurgy.
Imp.	Printer (Imprimerie, Imp).
I.N.A.	Institute of Naval Architects.
Inst.	Institute; Institution.
I.O.M.	Isle of Man.
I.O.W.	Isle of Wight.
I.P.A.	Portuguese Institute of Archaeology.
I.P.A.T.	International Porcelain Artist Teachers.
I.P.D.	Institute of Professional Designers.

590

I.P.G.	Independent Painters Group; Industrial Painters Group.
I.P.I.	Institute of Patentees and Inventors.
I.P.M.	Institute of Personnel Management.
I.S.	International Society of Sculptors, Painters and Gravers.
I.S.C.A.	International Society of Catholic Artists.
I.S.L.F.D.	Incorporated Society of London Fashion Designers.
I.S.O.	Imperial Service Order.
I.S.T.D.	Imperial Society of Teachers of Dancing.
I.T.A.C.	Imperial Three Arts Club.
I.T.D.	Institute of Training and Development.
I.W.S.	International Wool Secretariat.
I.W.S.P.	Institute of Work Study Practitioners.
J.H.A.M.I.	Johns Hopkins University Association of Medical Illustrations.
J.I.	Institute of Journalists.
J.P.	Justice of the Peace.
Junr.	Junior.
K.A.A.G.	Kirkles Art Action Group.
K.B.E.	Knight Commander Order of the British Empire.
K.C.	King's Counsel.
K.C.B.	Knight Commander of the Bath.
K.C.C.	Kent County Council.
K.C.M.G.	Knight Commander of St. Michael and St. George.
K.C.S.G.	Knight Commander of St. Gregory the Great.
K.C.S.I.	Knight Commander of the Star of India.
K.C.V.O.	Knight Commander of the Royal Victorian Order.
K.G.	Knight of the Order of the Garter.
Kt.	Knight.
L.	Licentiate.
La.	Louisiana; Lane.
L.A.	Library Association; Los Angeles.
L.A.A.	Liverpool Academy of Arts.
L.A.M.D.A.	London Academy of Music and Dramatic Art.
Lancs.	Lancashire.
L.A.W.	Liverpool Artists Workshop.
L.C.	Legislative Council.
L.C.A.D.	London Certificate in Art and Design.
L.C.C.	London County Council.

L.D.A.D.	London Diploma of Art and Design.
L.D.S.	Licentiate in Dental Surgery.
Leics.	Leicestershire.
L.G.	Life Guards.
L.G.S.M.	Licentiate, Guildhall School of Music and Drama.
L.I.	Landscape Institute.
Lieut.	Lieutenant.
L.I.F.A.	Licentiate of International Faculty of Arts.
Lincs.	Lincolnshire.
L.I.S.T.D.	Licentiate of the Imperial Society of Teachers of Dancing.
L.L.A.	Lady Literate in Arts.
LL.B.	Bachelor of Laws.
LL.D.	Doctor of Laws.
LL.M.	Master of Laws.
L.P.T.B.	London Passenger Transport Board.
L.S.	Linnean Society.
L.S.A.	Licentiate of the Society of Apothecaries.
L.S.I.A.	Licentiate of the Society of Industrial Artists.
L.S.U.	Louisiana State University.
Ltd.	Limited.
M.	Member; Ministry; Monsieur.
m.	married.
M.A.	Master of Arts.
M.A.A.	Medical Artists' Association; Miniature Artists of America.
M.A.F.A.	Manchester Academy of Fine Arts.
M.A.I.	Master of Fine Arts International.
Mans.	Mansions.
M.A.S.-F.	Miniature Art Society/Florida.
M.A.S.-N.J.	Miniature Art Society/New Jersey.
M.A.S.-W.	Miniature Art Society/Washington.
Mass.	Massachusetts.
M.B.	Bachelor of Medicine.
M.B.E.	Member of the Order of the British Empire.
M.C.	Military Cross.
M.Chrom.	Master of Chromatics.
M.D.	Doctor of Medicine; Managing Director.
M.D.E.	Mitglieder—Meister der Einbandkunst.
Mem.	Member.
men.	mention.
Messrs.	Messieurs.
M.F.A.	Master of Fine Art.
M.G.P.	Master Glass Painters.

592

Mich.	Michigan.
Middx.	Middlesex.
Minn.	Minnesota.
M.Inst.M.	Member, Institute of Marketing.
M.Inst.Pkg.	Member, Institute of Packaging.
M.L.	Licentiate in Medicine.
M.Litt.	Master of Letters.
Mme.	Madame.
Mo.	Missouri.
M.of D.	Ministry of Defence.
M.of E.	Ministry of Education.
M.of H.	Ministry of Health.
M.O.I.	Ministry of Information.
M.of S.	Ministry of Supply.
M.of W.	Ministry of Works.
M.O.M.A.	Museum of Modern Art.
Mon.	Monmouthshire.
M.P.S.G.	Miniature Painters, Sculptors and Gravers Society of Washington D.C.
M.S.	Society of Miniaturists; Motor Ship.
MS.	Manuscript.
M.S.M.	Meritorious Service Medal.
M.Soc.Sc.	Master of Social Science.
MSS.	Manuscripts.
M-S.S.E.	Multi-Sensory Sculpture Exhibitions.
M.V.O.	Member of the Royal Victorian Order.
N.	North.
N.A.	National Academy of Design (New York).
N.A.A.	National Artists Association.
N.A.D.F.A.S.	National Association of Decorative and Fine Arts Societies.
N.A.M.M.	National Association of Master Masons.
N.A.P.A.	National Acrylic Painters' Association.
N.B.	North Britain.
N.B.A.	North British Academy.
N.B.L.	National Book League.
N.C.	North Carolina.
N.C.B.	National Coal Board.
N.C.D.A.D.	National Council for Diplomas in Art and Design.
N.C.R.	National Cash Register.
N.D.D.	National Diploma in Design.
N.E.A.C.	New English Art Club.
N.E.C.	National Executive Committee.
N.E.C.A.	National Exhibition of Children's Art.

N.F.T.	National Film Theatre.
N.F.U.	National Froebel Union.
N.I.	Northern Ireland.
N.J.	New Jersey.
No.	Number.
Notts.	Nottinghamshire.
Notts. S.A.	Nottingham Society of Artists.
N.P.	Notary Public.
N.P.G.	National Portrait Gallery.
N.P.S.	National Portrait Society.
nr.	near.
N.R.D.	National Registered Designer.
N.S.	National Society.
N.S.A.	New Society of Artists; Natal Society of Artists; Newlyn Society of Artists.
N.S.A.E.	National Society for Art Education.
N.S.M.P.	National Society of Mural Painters.
N.S.P.S.	National Society of Painters, Sculptors and Printmakers.
N.S.W.	New South Wales.
N.U.M.	National Union of Mineworkers.
N.U.T.	National Union of Teachers.
N.Y.	New York.
N.Y.S.	New York State.
N.Z.	New Zealand.
O.	Ohio.
O.A.S.	Oxford Society of Artists.
O.B.E.	Officer Order of the British Empire.
O.C.	Order of Canada (Officer).
O.C.R.	Officer of the Crown of Roumania.
O.C.S.	Oriental Ceramic Society.
O.D.A.C.A.	Original Doll Artist Council of America.
O.H.M.S.	On Her Majesty's Service.
Okla.	Oklahoma.
O.L.J.	Officer Companion of Order of St. Lazarus of Jerusalem.
O.S.	Optical Society.
O.S.A.	Ontario Society of Arts.
O.S.B.	Order of St. Benedict.
O.St.J.	Officer of the Most Venerable Order of the Hospital of St. John of Jerusalem.
O.U.D.S.	Oxford University Dramatic Society.
O.U.P.	Oxford University Press.
O.W.S.	Old Water-colour Society.
Oxon.	Oxford.

594

P.	President.
P.A.I.	Paisley Art Institute.
P.A.S.I.	Professor Associate of the Surveyor's Institution.
P.C.	Privy Councillor.
P.C.F.C.	Polytechnics and Colleges Funding Council.
P.E.N.	Poets, Playwrights, Editors, Essayists, Novelists Club.
Penn.	Pennsylvania.
P.G.C.E.	Post Graduate Certificate of Education.
Ph.B.	Bachelor of Philosophy.
Ph.D.	Doctor of Philosophy.
Phil.	Philosophy.
P.I.	Portrait Institute.
Pk.	Park.
Pl.	Place.
P.M.C.	Personnel Management Centre.
P.& O.	Peninsular and Oriental Steam Navigation Co., Ltd.
Pres.	President.
Princ.	Principal; Principle.
Prof.	Professor.
P.S.	Pastel Society.
Q.C.	Queen's Counsel.
Q.E.H.	Queen Elizabeth's Hospital School.
R.A.	Royal Academician; Royal Academy.
R.A.A.	Runnymede Association of Arts.
R.A.A.S.	Royal Amateur Art Society.
R.A.C.	Royal Automobile Club.
R.A.E.	Royal Aircraft Establishment.
R.A.F.	Royal Air Force.
R.A.I.	Royal Anthropological Institute.
R.A.M.	Royal Academy of Music.
R.A.M.C.	Royal Army Medical Corps.
R.A.S.	Royal Astronomical Society; Royal Asiatic Society; Richmond Art Society; Ridley Art Society.
R.B.A.	Royal Society of British Artists.
R.B.C.	Royal British Colonial Society of Artists.
R.B.S.	Royal Society of British Sculptors.
R.B.S.A.	Royal Birmingham Society of Artists.
R.C.A.	Royal College of Art; Royal Canadian Academy; Royal Cambrian Academician.
R.Cam.A.	Royal Cambrian Academy.
R.C.I.	Royal Colonial Institute.

R.C.M.	Royal College of Music.
R.C.N.	Royal College of Nursing.
R.C.O.	Royal College of Organists.
R.C.O.G.	Royal College of Obstetricians and Gynaecologists.
R.C.P.	Royal College of Physicians.
R.C.S.	Royal College of Surgeons.
R.C.S.E.	Royal College of Surgeons, Edinburgh.
Rd.	Road.
R.D.I.	Royal Designer of Industry.
R.D.S.	Royal Drawing Society.
R.E.	Royal Society of Painter-Printmakers (formerly Royal Society of Painter-Etchers and Engravers); Royal Engineers.
Regt.	Regiment.
Retd.	Retired.
Rev.	Reverend.
R.F.A.	Royal Field Artillery.
R.G.A.	Royal Garrison Artillery.
R.G.I.	Royal Glasgow Institute.
R.G.I.F.A.	Royal Glasgow Institute of Fine Art.
R.G.S.	Royal Geographical Society; Royal Graphic Society.
R.H.A.	Royal Hibernian Academy.
R.H.S.	Royal Horticultural Society.
R.Hist.S.	Royal Historical Society.
R.I.	Royal Institute of Painters in Water-colours.
R.I.A.	Royal Irish Academy.
R.I.A.I.	Royal Institute of the Architects of Ireland.
R.I.A.S.	Royal Incorporation of Architects in Scotland.
R.I.B.A.	Royal Institute of British Architects.
R.I.C.S.	Royal Institution of Chartered Surveyors.
Rly.	Railway.
Rlys.	Railways.
R.M.	Royal Marines.
R.M.A.	Royal Military Academy.
R.M.I.T.	Royal Melbourne Institute of Technology.
R.M.S.	Royal Society of Miniature Painters.
R.N.	Royal Navy.
R.N.C.M.	Royal Northern College of Music.
R.N.I.B.	Royal National Institute for the Blind.
R.N.L.I.	Royal National Lifeboat Institution.
R.N.R.	Royal Naval Reserve.
R.N.V.R.	Royal Naval Volunteer Reserve.
R.O.I.	Royal Institute of Oil Painters.
R.P.	Royal Society of Portrait Painters and Member.

R.P.S.	Royal Photographic Society.
R.S.	Royal Society.
R.S.A.	Royal Scottish Academy; Royal Society of Arts.
R.S.A.I.	Royal Society of Antiquaries of Ireland.
R.S.E.	Royal Society of Edinburgh.
R.S.F.S.R.	Russian Soviet Federative Socialist Republic.
R.S.G.S.	Royal Scottish Geographical Society.
R.S.L.	Royal Society of Literature.
R.S.M.A.	Royal Society of Marine Arts.
R.S.P.A.	Royal Society for Prevention of Accidents.
R.S.P.B.	Royal Society for the Protection of Birds.
R.S.T.	Royal Society of Teachers.
R.S.W.	Royal Scottish Water-colour Society or Royal Scottish Society of Painters in Water-colours.
Rt.	Right.
R.T.P.I.	Royal Town Planning Institute.
R.T.Y.C.	Royal Thames Yachting Club.
R.U.A.	Royal Ulster Academy of Painting, Sculpture and Architecture; Royal Ulster Academician.
R.W.A. (R.W.E.A.)	Royal West of England Academician; Royal West of England Academy.
R.W.S.	Royal Water-Colour Society (formerly Royal Society of Painters in Water-colours).
S.	South.
s.	son; sons.
S.A.	Society of Antiquaries; Society of Apothecaries.
S.A.A.	Society of Aviation Artists.
S.A.A.C.	Society of Scottish Artists and Artist Craftsmen.
S.A.B.A.	Scottish Artists' Benevolent Association.
S.A.C.	Scottish Arts Council.
S.A.E.	Society of American Etchers; Society of Automobile Engineers (American).
S.A.F.	Société des Artistes Français.
S.A.G.A.	Society of American Graphic Artists.
S.A.I.	Scottish Arts Institute; Society of Architectural Illustrators.
S.A.I.I.	Society of Architectural and Industrial Illustrators.
Salop.	Shropshire.
S.A.M.	National Society of Art Masters.
S.A.P.	Society of Artist Printmakers.
S.B.A.	Society of Botanical Artists.
S.B.St.J.	Serving Brothers of the Order of St. John of Jerusalem.

S.C.	Senefelder Club; South Carolina.
Sc.	Sculptor.
S.C.A.	Society of Catholic Artists.
S.C.F.	Solidarité de la Culture Française.
S.C.O.R.E.	Scottish Core of Retired Executives.
Sculpt.	Sculpture.
s-d.	step daughter.
S.D.-C.	Society of Designer Craftsmen and Craft Centre (formerly Arts and Crafts Exhibition Society).
S.E.A.	Society for Education in Art; Society of Equestrian Artists (see S.Eq.A.).
Sec.	Secretary.
S.E.F.A.S.	South Eastern Federation of Art Societies.
S.Eq.A.	Society of Equestrian Artists (formerly S.E.A.).
S.G.A.	Society of Graphic Art.
S.G.E.	Society of Glass Engravers.
S.G.F.A.	Society of Graphic Fine Art (formerly Society of Graphic Art).
S.G.P.	Society of Graver Printers.
S.G.T.	Society of Glass Technology.
S.I.	Surveyors' Institute.
S.I.A.C.	Société Internationale des Artistes Chretiens.
S.I.A.D.	(see C.S.D.).
S.I.D.	Society of Industrial Designers of U.S.A.; Mem. Swedish Industrial Designers.
S.I.P.E.	Société Internationale de Psychopathologie de l'Expression, Paris.
S.K.M.	South Kensington Museum.
S.M.	Society of Miniaturists.
S.M.O.M.	Knight of Magistral Grace of the Sovereign Military Order of Malta.
S.M.P.	Society of Mural Painters.
S.N.G.M.A.	Scottish National Gallery of Modern Art.
S.N.P.G.	Scottish National Portrait Gallery.
Soc.	Société; Society.
Socs.	Societies.
Som.	Somerset.
South. S.A.	Southern Society of Artists.
S.P.	Société Internationale de Philogie, Sciences et Beaux Arts.
S.P.A.B.	Society for the Protection of Ancient Buildings.
S.P.C.K.	Society for the Promotion of Christian Knowledge.
S.P.D.A.	Society of Present-Day Artists.
S.P.E.	International Society of Philosophical Enquiry.

S.P.S.	Society of Portrait Sculptors.
S.P.S.A.S.	Swiss Society of Painters, Sculptors and Architects.
Sq.	Square.
s-s.	step son.
S.S.	Royal Statistical Society.
S.S.A.	Society of Scottish Artists.
S.S.C.	Solicitor to the Supreme Court (in Scotland).
S.S.I.	Society of Scribes and Illuminators.
S.S.N.	Sociétaire de la Société Nationale des Beaux Arts.
S.S.S.A.	Society of Sussex Sporting Artists.
S.S.W.A.	Scottish Society of Women Artists.
St.	Saint; Street.
Staffs.	Staffordshire.
S.T.C.	Sydney Technical College.
S.T.D.	Society of Typographical Designers.
S.W.A.	Society of Women Artists.
S.W.A.N.	Society for Wildlife Art of the Nations.
S.W.A.S.	Society of Women Artists of Scotland.
S.W.E.	Society of Wood Engravers.
S.WL.A.	Society of Wildlife Artists.
T. &. T.	Trinidad and Tobago.
T.C.D.	Trinity College, Dublin.
T.C.M.	Trinity College of Music.
T.C.T.A.	Teaching Certificate for Teachers of Art.
T.D.	Territorial Decoration; Teacher's Diploma.
Terr.	Terrace.
T.E.S.	Times Educational Supplement.
Tex.	Texas.
T.G.C.	Teacher's General Certificate.
T.L.S.	Times Literary Supplement.
T.P.I.	Town Planning Institute.
T.R.H.	Their Royal Highnesses.
T.S.B.	Trustee Savings Bank.
U.	Unionist.
U.A.	United Society of Artists.
U.A.E.	United Arab Emirates.
U.C.H.	University College Hospital.
U.C.L.	University College, London.
U.L.U.J.	Union of the plastic artists of Yugoslavia.
U.S.A.	United States of America.
U.S.M.	Ulster Society of Miniaturists.
U.S.S.R.	Union of Soviet Socialist Republics.

U.S.W.A.	Ulster Society of Women Artists.
U.W.A.	Ulster Women Artists.
U.W.P.	University of Wales Press.
U.W.S.	Ulster Water-colour Society.
V.	Vice.
v.	versus.
V. & A.	Victoria and Albert Museum.
Va.	Virginia.
V.A.D.	Voluntary Aid Detachment.
V.C.	Victoria Cross.
V.D.	Volunteer Officers' Decoration; Victorian Decoration.
Vol.	Volume.
V.P.	Vice-President.
V.R.D.	Volunteer Reserve Decoration.
W.	West.
W.A.	Western Australia.
W.A.C.	Welsh Arts Council.
W.A.G.	Walker Art Gallery.
W.A.S.C.E.	World Art Science and Cultural Exchanges.
W.C.C.	World Crafts Council.
W.C.S.I.	Water-colour Society of Ireland.
W.C.S.W.	Water-colour Society of Wales.
W.E.A.	Workers' Educational Association.
W.E.R.P.	Wood Engravers and Relief Printers.
W.G.I.H.E.	West Glamorgan Institute of Higher Education.
W.I.A.C.	Women's International Art Club.
W.I.A.S.	Women's International Art Society.
Wilts.	Wiltshire.
Wis.	Wisconsin.
Worcs.	Worcestershire.
W.W.F.	World Wildlife Fund.
Xmas	Christmas.
Y.A.E.	Yorkshire Artists' Exhibition.
Y.M.(W.)C.A.	Young Men's (Women's) Christian Association.
Yorks.	Yorkshire.
Y.W.D.A.	Yiewsley and West Drayton Arts Council.
Z.S.	Zoological Society.